MODERN Criticism

THEORY and PRACTICE

MODERN
Criticism
THEORY and PRACTICE

Edited by WALTER SUTTON
SYRACUSE UNIVERSITY

and RICHARD FOSTER
UNIVERSITY OF MINNESOTA

NEW YORK

THE ODYSSEY PRESS•INC•

Foreword

As teachers of criticism we have tried to prepare an anthology that would lend itself handily, from the point of view of both selection and organization, to a wide variety of courses in modern literary theory and criticism, from historical surveys to courses in critical composition. We have concentrated upon material of intrinsic value and representative importance, and we have attempted to provide a workable balance between the two major concerns of criticism—theory and practice. We believe that we have succeeded in avoiding the temptations of partisanship and that the selection represents fairly the range and catholicity of modern criticism in English, especially that written since World War II.

Although we are in agreement that we do not like textbooks with too much "machinery," we have wanted the plan of this book to reflect the organization and major emphases of the usual courses in modern criticism. These often trace the historical beginnings of modern criticism, usually provide an opportunity for the analysis of examples of both critical theory and practice, and sometimes require that students write criticism along lines suggested by course reading. While Part One of the anthology presents examples of theoretical critical writing in historical sequence, Part Two is divided into three interrelated categories representing the broadest functional emphases of critical practice (Origins, Ideas and Values, Form), with the selections arranged chronologically in the order of subject within each category. This functional arrangement should be more convenient, for cross-referencing and comparative study, than the usual historical arrangement—especially since Part One provides a historical perspective for the book as a whole and a basis for the analysis of the techniques of the individual critics represented in Part Two.

Both the theory and practice sections contain examples, not only of the familiar New Critical "ontological" concerns, but also of numerous other interests—political, sociological, anthropological, mythographic, psychological, typological—representative of the great variety of contemporary critical approaches. In addition, distinguished modern literary scholarship is represented by Arthur O. Lovejoy, C. S. Lewis, Austin Warren, M. H. Abrams, and C. L. Barber, all authors of notable "classics" of scholarly criticism.

The anthology has several other distinctive features. We have chosen, as far as possible, the criticism of major literature by major writers, since to be pedagogically useful in the most complete way a piece of criticism must deal with material known to the student. Part Two presents practical criticism of works with which most college students can be assumed to have some familiarity: *Hamlet, Huckleberry Finn, The Ambassadors, The Scarlet Letter,* and the poetry of Donne, Keats, Poe, and Yeats. It is our belief that success in the criticism course is to a large extent dependent upon a considerable use of comparison and contrast, and upon an opportunity for real intensiveness. We have accordingly included selections with differing viewpoints on the same writer or the same critical problem. Beyond this the material provides an extensive basis for cross-reference and continuity among many of the selections. It will be possible for a teacher to develop, if he so wishes, "units" of comparative work on the criticism of certain major works and writers (*Hamlet,* metaphysical poetry, Coleridge, Hawthorne, James, Twain, Yeats), or on certain speculative topics (romanticism, realism and naturalism, the nature of tragedy or of comedy, the function of literature, the use of psychoanalysis and myth in criticism), or on certain dialectical controversies (science and poetry, innovation and tradition, image and symbol, form and content). It has been our editorial aim, in short, to make this collection representative, intrinsically excellent and interesting, and, above all, useful.

For helpful suggestions and criticisms, and various other kindnesses, we wish to express our thanks to M. H. Abrams, Frank Piskor, Leonard Unger, and John Dennis Hurrell.

W. S.
R. F.

Contents

PART TWO Practice

Origins

Ideas and Values

Form

Introduction

In the present century, literary criticism has become a major intellectual discipline. Its growth and flourishing condition are largely the result of the revolutionary developments in the modern arts, the rising prestige of the physical sciences, and the emergence of the social sciences. While the efficiency of the sciences pointed up the need for improved critical theory and methods, the contributions of psychology, anthropology, and sociology revealed the possibilities of new critical approaches. An active and continuing exploration of both literary and extra-literary sources of knowledge has provided modern criticism with a multiplicity of viewpoints and traditions of greater or lesser continuity.

During the past fifty years or so, literary critics have been especially conscious of the interaction between past and present, between the principles of continuity and change or innovation. Although their interests have ranged from the poetics of Plato and Aristotle, through the theory and criticism of the Renaissance, and into the eighteenth and nineteenth centuries, they have been most deeply indebted to the nineteenth century. Of all earlier literary movements, romanticism is most important for modern criticism, which shares its preoccupation with the creative imagination and many of its rebellious attitudes. It is possible, in fact, to see most of the important developments in critical theory over the past century and a half as a continuing revolution of taste forwarded by successive insurrections—each demanding a re-examination of principles and a re-formulation of terms and objectives. Just as romanticism reacted against an outworn neoclassicism, in the later nineteenth century realism repudiated a romanticism grown decadent, and in the early twentieth century the modernist revolt cast off oppressive Victorian aesthetic and social conventions.

This chain of reactions, in which the critical thought of the past was transformed rather than completely rejected, did not, of course, begin with the romantics. Even earlier, in the eighteenth century, Dr. Samuel Johnson, whose criticism has been too much neglected in recent years, bluntly attacked the prescriptive rules and terminology of neoclassical genre criticism and anticipated Wordsworth's interest in the language of common life and in the experience of the common reader as a test of aesthetic value. Like many later critics, Johnson was a close reader whose critical judgments were based upon an examination of literary texts. Although his analysis of the techniques of the metaphysical poets in his "Life of Cowley" was not entirely sympathetic, it was drawn upon by the twentieth century critics who helped to revive the seventeenth century tradition. One of Johnson's enduring con-

3

cerns, which is valuable for our own time, was his belief in the moral function of literature and the social responsibility of the critic.

Of the two principal leaders of the English romantic movement, William Wordsworth and Samuel Taylor Coleridge, Wordsworth has had more impact upon subsequent poetic practice and Coleridge upon criticism and theory. This is not to deny the importance of Wordsworth's theory of poetry for later critical thought. His attacks upon eighteenth century poetic diction and verse form in successive prefaces to his works foreshadowed the revolt of twentieth century poets and critics against Victorian conventions in language and metrics. His insistence on a language derived from a life close to nature anticipated the emphasis upon sensuousness and concreteness in the theory of the twentieth century Imagists and later New Critics.

Coleridge, who disagreed with Wordsworth's theory of poetic language, has enjoyed the greater prestige among modern critics. His conception of the poem as a union and balance of opposing elements, set forth in *Biographia Literaria* (1817), was adopted by I. A. Richards and the American New Critics. His psychological and metaphysical preoccupations and his discussion of the creative imagination and of the poem as the utterance of the "whole soul of man" have proved especially congenial to critics interested in literature as a possible source of suprarational (and supra-scientific) knowledge and values. Coleridge's "revelation doctrines," as Richards called them, reinforced by the psychological theory of C. G. Jung, supplied the foundation for much twentieth century myth criticism.

Primarily through Coleridge, English romantic thought affected nineteenth century American theory and practice, notably that of Emerson and Poe. Of the American romantics, Ralph Waldo Emerson has most importance for modern criticism—as has been increasingly recognized during the past twenty years or so. His theory of literature from the time of *Nature* (1836) emphasized the symbolic power of a concrete and sensuous poetic language. His conception of the poet as a seer and a bard was taken over by Walt Whitman, who democratized it by introducing equalitarian ideals—thus inaugurating a tradition of liberal democratic and radical criticism that was to burgeon in a later day. Both Emerson in "The Poet" (1844) and Whitman in his preface to *Leaves of Grass* (1855), and in the poems themselves, promoted the romantic theory of organic form, which was not to receive its fullest development until the twentieth century. The importance of both Emerson and Whitman for the later study of literature through symbol and myth has been demonstrated by such works as F. O. Matthiessen's *American Renaissance* (1941).

Although Emerson's contemporary, Edgar Allan Poe, has often been dismissed as an exotic and hence unrepresentative American literary figure, he is closely related to both his own time and ours. His essay "The Poetic Principle" (1850) has many affinities with Emerson's transcendental theory, with the significant difference that Poe stressed the suggestive and musical qualities of poetry as an art concerned with beauty and feeling rather than with conceptual thought or morality. This purist attitude, which explains his invention of such terms of censure as *epic mania* and *heresy of the didactic*, was adopted by Baudelaire and other French symbolists, who in turn influenced twentieth century ideas of pure poetry. Because of his interest in technique, Poe has been identified as a forerunner of the New Critics. As a culturally alienated poet he has also appealed to writers like Allen Tate, in "Our Cousin, Mr. Poe" (1949), who have seen in him the prototypical representative of the divided consciousness of the modern intellectual and artist.

The romantics tended to magnify the self-sufficiency of the individual and his creative imagination. Critics of the later nineteenth century became increasingly sensitive to the pressures of industrialization and urbanization and to the implications of evolutionary and other scientific thought. In a time of widespread confusion and doubt, many of them stressed the social responsibility of the writer and critic and the importance of literature as a source of values. In England, Matthew Arnold struck the keynote of the new age with his idea of the poet as the critic of culture rather than as the romantic prophet and seer. Although Arnold shared many of the attitudes of the romantics and although he thought of literature as a substitute for religion, his work was typical of a period in which the mystical and transcendental impulse of the earlier age gave way to a humanism that has remained a continuing tradition, although subject to modification and to varying, sometimes conflicting. interpretations. It has, however, tended to preserve the earlier romantic identification of the writer with an elite—now cultural rather than temperamental or religious—opposed to the forces of Philistinism.

Among American writers of the post Civil War period, a growing sense of social pressures can be seen in the work of the realists. The American expatriate Henry James explored in great detail the fictional milieus of the morally perplexed characters of his novels. His dramatic method, which he analyzed in his prefaces, provided a bridge to later twentieth century dramatic and impersonal theories and encouraged the modern preoccupation with technique. In "The Art of Fiction" (1884; 1888), he refined the organic theory of form, firmly grounding it in the social experience of the writer and the reader. James insisted that the novel, like history, is a representation of social reality—that it *is*, in fact, "history."

For William Dean Howells, who like James thought of the novel as the successor to the poem as the dominant art form, the American novelist was to assume the role of Whitman's democratic bard. In *Criticism and Fiction* (1891) Howells was frankly didactic and moralistic in asserting the responsibility of the writer and critic to maintain the standards of an equalitarian democratic tradition. His belief in the social importance of literature was confirmed by the early twentieth century New Realists and given its greatest emphasis in the liberal and radical criticism of the 1930's.

With the growing interaction between American and English critics in the twentieth century, modern criticism became internationalized. By the first World War both Ezra Pound and T. S. Eliot had settled in London and found a place in its literary life. At a somewhat later date the British critic I. A. Richards took up residence in America, thereby reinforcing and extending his considerable influence on American criticism. During the same period critics in both countries drew upon European sources of theory, including the work of the French symbolist poets and critics and the expressionist aesthetic of Benedetto Croce.

Twentieth century criticism in English received its greatest single impetus, perhaps, from the literary avant-garde led by T. E. Hulme and Ezra Pound in London

in the years before the first World War, a group which not only fostered the international Imagist movement, inaugurating a poetic renaissance, but also developed
a theory to support it. Pound's importance as a crusader in breaking the mold of
old forms, pioneering in new ones, and advocating a rigorous discipline for both
the critic and the poet cannot easily be overemphasized. His efforts in criticism
were supported and extended by T. S. Eliot, whose first prose collection, *The Sacred
Wood, Essays on Poetry and Criticism,* appeared in 1920, when writers and critics
were in general rebellion against prevailing standards in art and taste. Reacting
against both impressionism and moralism, Eliot and other "classicists" focused
upon problems of technique and structure. Their criticism was formalist and aesthetic in that it was largely concerned with the nature of the literary work, rather
than with the work in relation to its author, its audience, or the circumstances of
its composition. Although aesthetic in emphasis, it reflected a competitive awareness of the commanding position of the sciences in the critics' preoccupation with
impersonality, "objectivity," and precision of method.

As a leader of the newer "technical" criticism, Eliot helped to establish the
postwar vogue of seventeenth century metaphysical poetry and the poetic criteria
of intellectuality, wit, and detachment. His "impersonal theory" of poetry and
his definitions of the "objective correlative" and "dissociation of sensibility" also
became guiding principles of the later New Criticism.

At the same time, criticism was being affected by developments in history and
the social sciences, particularly anthropology, psychology, and sociology. In psychology, the most important development of the early century was the psycho-
analytical theory of Sigmund Freud. Freud's influence, a pervasive one in both
theory and practical criticism, encouraged in its first phase, during the 1920's, an
interest in dream symbolism, the stream of consciousness, and psychobiography.

These new developments in literary study inspired a counterrevolution against
the forces of science and modernism. The New Humanists, led by Irving Babbitt,
the "warring Buddha" of Harvard, and Paul Elmer More, his chief lieutenant,
attacked the twin evils of romanticism and naturalism. Opposing the monism of
these traditions, they stressed the dualism of man and nature. Rejecting determinism, they asserted man's moral responsibility and his need of discipline by the
"inner check" (which their modernist opponents identified with the Puritan conscience). Like Matthew Arnold, whom they admired, the Humanists considered
themselves leaders of a select group, an elite guard entrusted with the defense of
traditional moral and cultural values in an age of confusion. Their moralism, their
distrust of democracy, and their hostility to the literature of their own time won
them many enemies with whom they engaged in an extended controversy. The
polemical battle of modernist and anti-modernist forces culminated in the publication, in 1930, of rival symposia defending and attacking the New Humanist position. These were *Humanism and America,* edited by Norman Foerster, and *The
Critique of Humanism,* edited by C. Hartley Grattan. Although the New Humanists
tended to be more interested in moral and cultural questions than in critical theory,
Norman Foerster outlined a methodology for Humanist criticism in the conclusion
to *American Criticism, A Study in Literary Theory from Poe to the Present* (1928).

In the midst of the general deprivation of the 1930's, when the advocacy of a cultural elite became increasingly repugnant, the New Humanists ceased to function as a distinct critical group, although many of their attitudes persisted. During these years, which saw a growing concern for the social, economic, and political implications of literature, the liberal and radical criticism of an earlier day was at first supported and then largely supplanted by Marxist criticism, which in both England and America viewed literature as a weapon and an instrument of propaganda in the cause of revolution. Marxism contributed to literary and critical theory in such works as Christopher Caudwell's *Illusion and Reality, A Study of the Sources of Poetry* (1937) and Bernard Smith's *Forces in American Criticism* (1939). By the mid-Thirties, when Marxism assumed the status of an orthodoxy and critics and writers were being scrutinized for their adherence to the Party "line," many leading critics were reacting against the rigidity and over-simplifications of proletarian theory. Men like Edmund Wilson and Kenneth Burke, in sympathy with the general objectives of the revolutionary movement, considered the problem of the relation of Marxism and literature and attempted to integrate Marxist theory within a larger progressive view which could also accommodate psychology and other systems of thought.

The simplifications and the revolutionary optimism of much Marxist criticism produced an inevitable reaction during the period of the Soviet-German pact and the second World War: a growing emphasis upon complexity in literature and upon the irresolvable ironies of the "tragic vision." Reflecting a general disillusionment among liberal and radical critics, this stress was supported by new (or renewed) theories of poetic language and of the relation between literature and myth. I. A. Richards, who had begun his career in the 1920's, continued to psychologize romantic poetic theory, which he adapted to modern interests in *Coleridge on Imagination* (1935) and other books. He helped to give irony and complexity a new importance as criteria of literary value and encouraged further studies assuming the identity of poetry and myth. Together with T. S. Eliot, Richards was the leading forebear of the New Criticism that emerged in the late 1930's.

The nucleus of this movement, which was already well established when John Crowe Ransom's *The New Criticism* appeared in 1941, consisted of Cleanth Brooks, Allen Tate, R. P. Warren, and others associated with Ransom at Vanderbilt University in the 1920's and early Thirties. The group, which came to include Yvor Winters and R. P. Blackmur, attracted many followers and achieved a position of strength, particularly in the universities, where a curricular revolution was accomplished and criticism won acceptance as a discipline rivalling and sometimes displacing the older historical scholarship. Unlike the socially oriented criticism of the Thirties, the more formalistic New Criticism was devoted to problems of language and structure. The emphasis on wit and paradox and irony, already introduced by Eliot and Richards, became programmatic in works like Cleanth Brooks's *Modern Poetry and the Tradition* (1939) and *The Well Wrought Urn, Studies in the Structure of Poetry* (1947). Taking their cue from I. A. Richards' distinction between the language of poetry and the language of science, most of the New Critics accepted and promoted Ransom's idea of an "ontological" critical theory that would give poetry status as a unique source of knowledge. They also attempted to maintain a distinction between formal or aesthetic criticism and criticism which is in some sense social or historical. This distinction was reinforced by René Wellek and Austin Warren's *Theory of Literature* (1949), which assumed a dichotomy between "intrinsic" and "extrinsic" modes of literary study.

Although the theory deriving from Coleridge and Richards implied the identity of literature and myth, most of the leading New Critics occupied themselves with rhetorical and linguistic analysis rather than myth study. Many of their followers, however, inspired by works like Maud Bodkin's *Archetypal Patterns in Poetry* (1934), drew upon Jungian psychology to develop a flourishing myth and archetype criticism which enjoyed its greatest vogue during the 1940's and early Fifties. Finding further support for their views in anthropology and Ernst Cassirer's philosophy of symbolic forms, many myth critics modified and extended Jung's theory in speculating upon the nature and function of the literary archetype. One such was Northrop Frye, who in *Anatomy of Criticism* (1957) made use of many sources, but especially Jung and Aristotle, to develop a systematic critical theory based on the concept of the archetype.

Like every dominant critical school, the formalist New Criticism provoked reactions and counterrevolutionary movements. The first organized opposition came from Ronald S. Crane and the Chicago neo-Aristotelian critics, who attempted to supplant New Critical theory and practice by a methodology derived largely from the *Poetics* of Aristotle. The neo-Aristotelian movement, which had its beginnings in the 1930's as a reaction against the historical and philological tradition, became prominent in the late 1940's and early Fifties. Its theory and practice are most fully represented by the symposium *Critics and Criticism* (ed. R. S. Crane, 1952) and by Crane's *The Languages of Criticism and the Structure of Poetry* (1953). To counteract the New Critical emphasis on poetic language, the Aristotelians attempted to establish a revised theory of imitation and saw individual works as artistic wholes to be classified and discussed in relation to a system of historical genres and types. One result of their program was to call attention to a neglected critical tradition and to demonstrate the value of scholarship to criticism.

In the years following the second World War, other critics also reacted against the narrowness of the New Criticism, especially its minimizing of environmental factors and its unwillingness to draw upon extra-literary sources of knowledge. During the ignominious McCarthy era F. O. Matthiessen and other liberal critics protested the neglect, in literary criticism, of pressing social and political issues. Some, rejecting the progressive liberalism of the 1930's, turned to an older cultural and political tradition. Richard Chase in *Herman Melville* (1949) and Lionel Trilling in *The Liberal Imagination* (1950) asserted the social and political relevance of literature from a position identified as a "New Liberalism."

In more recent years, there has been a trend in both practical criticism and theory toward a greater recognition of the social and historical aspects of literature. During the 1950's a number of younger critics skilled in analytic techniques turned to broader studies concerned with the political, social, and cultural contexts of literary works. In theory there has been an increasing tendency to re-examine the assumptions of modern formalist criticism and to broaden its base to admit environmental considerations. In "Dissociation of Sensibility" (1957), Frank Kermode reconsiders the influential term and concept that T. S. Eliot had earlier introduced into modern criticism. In "The Necessary Stylist: A New Critical Revision" (1960-61), Mark Spilka summarizes recent developments in critical theory and discusses the idea of style as a necessary bridge between the individual literary work and its larger literary and social environment.

Although contemporary theory, like the practical criticism with which it continuously interacts, represents a seemingly infinite variety of interests, its most conspicuous and important present phase is that which recognizes the contributions of the New Criticism and other critical movements and accommodates them to a larger view, in which literary form is conceived as open and relative and organically involved in its linguistic, cultural, and social environment. While literature may be discussed from any point of view, present criticism increasingly tends to regard it in its social setting and to make use of all pertinent literary or extra-literary sources of knowledge in interpreting its form. This broadening of the contexts of literature is accompanied by a renewed emphasis on the social nature of criticism itself—a theme stressed by Alfred Kazin in "The Function of Criticism Today" (1960).

The social emphasis and the reliance upon various sources of knowledge indicate a growing awareness of the need of relating literature to an increasingly complex environment. The movement toward a broader role for criticism—one in which the critic's moral and social responsibilities are stressed—is a recognition that in a nuclear age writers and critics, like all intellectuals, contribute to the formulation of the values by which men live in a world that must, if it is to survive, be viewed as one world.

W. S.

SAMUEL JOHNSON
(1709-1784)

Lexicographer, poet, novelist, playwright, editor of Shakespeare, and critical biographer of the English poets, Johnson was the greatest critic and man of letters of the eighteenth century. A late defender of neoclassical literary theory, he derives his defense from a fresh recognition of the moral bases of the classicist view. In Johnson's work the criteria of "general nature" and "reason" signify ideals of historical continuity and personal self-control which supply a basis for the idea of freedom, and even "progress," in thought and the arts. Thus Johnson's objections to Thomas Gray's experiments are protests against a willed artistic libertinism, while his acceptance of some of the radical effects of the metaphysical poets is his recognition that they are confronting new possibilities for responsibility. Johnson's classicism, then, as represented by his rejection of criticism by a priori rule and his corresponding respect for the strengths of Shakespeare's anarchic creativity, is a classicism renewed by his personal reaffirmation of the moral bases of literary judgment. The imperative always to qualify the received wisdom of classical principles by testing their moral relevance to life is a feature of Johnson's criticism that makes him a prophetic figure, a figure interesting in many ways to modern criticism. His most important work in literary theory and criticism is contained in *The Rambler* (1750-52), *The History of Rasselas* (1759), the preface to his edition of *Shakespeare* (1765), and *The Lives of the Poets* (1779, 1781). Boswell's *Life of Johnson* (1791) is also an important source book of Johnsonian critical thought and judgment.

From *The History of Rasselas* (1759)

Chapter X. Imlac's History Continued. A Dissertation on Poetry.

"Wherever I went, I found that poetry was considered as the highest learning, and regarded with a veneration somewhat approaching to that which man would pay to the Angelic Nature. And yet it fills me with wonder, that, in almost all countries, the most ancient poets are considered as the best; whether it be that every other kind of knowledge is an acquisition gradually attained, and poetry is a gift conferred at once; or that the first poetry of every nation surprised them as a novelty, and retained the credit by consent, which it received by accident at first; or whether, as the province of poetry is to describe nature and passion, which are always the same, the first writers took possession of the most striking objects for description, and the most probable occurrences for fiction, and left nothing to those that followed them, but transcription of the same events, and new combinations of the same images. Whatever be the reason, it is commonly observed that the early writers are in possession of nature, and their followers of art; that the first excel in strength and invention, and the latter in elegance and refinement.

"I was desirous to add my name to this illustrious fraternity. I read all the poets of Persia and Arabia, and was able to repeat by memory the volumes that are suspended in the mosque of Mecca. But I soon found that no man was great by imitation. My desire of excellence impelled me to transfer my attention to nature and to life. Nature was to be my

10

subject, and men to be my auditors: I could never describe what I had not seen: I could not hope to move those with delight or terror, whose interests and opinions I did not understand.

"Being now resolved to be a poet, I saw everything with a new purpose; my sphere of attention was suddenly magnified: no kind of knowledge was to be overlooked. I ranged mountains and deserts for images and resemblances, and pictured upon my mind every tree of the forest and flower of the valley. I observed with equal care the crags of the rock and the pinnacles of the palace. Sometimes I wandered along the mazes of the rivulet, and sometimes watched the changes of the summer clouds. To a poet nothing can be useless. Whatever is beautiful and whatever is dreadful must be familiar to his imagination: he must be conversant with all that is awfully vast or elegantly little. The plants of the garden, the animals of the wood, the minerals of the earth, and meteors of the sky, must all concur to store his mind with inexhaustible variety: for every idea is useful for the enforcement or decoration of moral or religious truth; and he who knows most will have most power of diversifying his scenes, and of gratifying his reader with remote allusions and unexpected instruction.

"All the appearances of nature I was therefore careful to study; and every country which I have surveyed has contributed something to my poetical powers."

"In so wide a survey," said the prince, "you must surely have left much unobserved. I have lived, till now, within the circuit of these mountains, and yet cannot walk abroad without the sight of something which I had never beheld before or never heeded."

"The business of a poet," said Imlac, "is to examine, not the individual, but the species; to remark general properties and large appearances; he does not number the streaks of the tulip, or describe the different shades in the verdure of the forest. He is to exhibit in his portraits of nature such prominent and striking features as recall the original to every mind; and must neglect the minuter discriminations, which one may have remarked, and another have neglected, for those characteristics which are alike obvious to vigilance and carelessness.

"But the knowledge of nature is only half the task of a poet; he must be acquainted likewise with all the modes of life. His character requires that he estimate the happiness and misery of every condition; observe the power of all the passions in all their combinations, and trace the changes of the human mind as they are modified by various institutions and accidental influences of climate or custom, from the sprightliness of infancy to the despondence of decrepitude. He must divest himself of the prejudices of his age or country; he must consider right and wrong in their abstracted and invariable state; he must disregard present laws and opinions, and rise to general and transcendental truths, which will always be the same; he must therefore content himself with the slow progress of his name; contemn the applause of his own time, and commit his claims to the justice of posterity. He must write as the interpreter of nature, and the legislator of mankind, and consider himself as presiding over the thoughts and manners of future generations; as a being superior to time and place.

"His labor is not yet at an end; he must know many languages and many sciences: and, that his style may be worthy of his thoughts, must, by incessant practice, familiarize to himself every delicacy of speech and grace of harmony."

Lives of the Poets (1779, 1781)

From Abraham Cowley

. . . Wit, like all other things subject by their nature to the choice of man, has its changes and fashions, and at different times takes different forms. About the beginning of the seventeenth century appeared a race of writers that may be termed the *metaphysical poets,* of whom in a criticism on the works of Cowley it is not improper to give some account.

The metaphysical poets were men of learning, and to shew their learning was their whole endeavour; but, unluckily resolving to shew it in rhyme, instead of writing poetry they only wrote verses, and very often such verses as stood the trial of the finger better than of the ear, for the modulation was so imperfect that they were only found to be verses by counting the syllables.

If the father of criticism has rightly denominated poetry τέχνη μιμητική, *an imitative art,* these writers will without great wrong lose their right to the name of poets, for they cannot be said to have imitated any thing: they neither copied nature nor life; neither painted the forms of matter nor represented the operations of intellect.

Those however who deny them to be poets allow them to be wits. Dryden confesses of himself and his contemporaries that they fall below Donne in wit, but maintains that they surpass him in poetry.

If Wit be well described by Pope as being 'that which has been often thought, but was never before so well expressed,' they certainly never attained nor ever sought it, for they endeavoured to be singular in their thoughts, and were careless of their diction. But Pope's account of wit is undoubtedly erroneous; he depresses it below its natural dignity, and reduces it from strength of thought to happiness of language.

If by a more noble and more adequate conception that be considered as Wit which is at once natural and new, that which though not obvious is, upon its first production, acknowledged to be just; if it be that, which he that never found it, wonders how he missed; to wit of this kind the metaphysical poets have seldom risen. Their thoughts are often new, but seldom natural; they are not obvious, but neither are they just; and the reader, far from wondering that he missed them, wonders more frequently by what perverseness of industry they were ever found.

But Wit, abstracted from its effects upon the hearer, may be more rigorously and philosophically considered as a kind of *discordia concors*; a combination of dissimilar images, or discovery of occult resemblances in things apparently unlike. Of wit, thus defined, they have more than enough. The most heterogeneous ideas are yoked by violence together; nature and art are ransacked for illustrations, comparisons, and allusions; their learning instructs, and their subtlety surprises; but the reader commonly thinks his improvement dearly bought, and, though he sometimes admires, is seldom pleased.

From this account of their compositions it will be readily inferred that they were not successful in representing or moving the affections. As they were wholly employed on something unexpected and surprising they had no regard to that uniformity of sentiment, which enables us to conceive and to excite the pains and the pleasure of other minds; they never inquired what on any occasion they should have said or done, but wrote rather as beholders than partakers of human nature; as beings looking upon good and evil, impassive and at leisure; as Epicurean deities making remarks on the actions of men and the vicissitudes of life, without interest and without emotion. Their courtship was void of fondness and their lamentation of sorrow. Their wish was only to say what they hoped had been never said before.

Nor was the sublime more within their reach than the pathetic; for they never attempted that comprehension and expanse of thought which at once fills the whole mind, and of which the first effect is sudden astonishment, and the second rational admiration. Sublimity is produced by aggregation, and littleness by dispersion. Great thoughts are always general, and consist in positions not limited by exceptions, and in descriptions not descending to minuteness. It is with great propriety that subtlety, which in its original import means exility of particles, is taken in its metaphorical meaning for nicety of distinction. Those writers who lay on the watch for novelty could have little hope of greatness; for great things cannot have escaped former observation. Their attempts were always analytick: they broke every image into fragments, and could no more represent by their slender conceits and laboured particularities the prospects of nature or the scenes of life, than he who dissects a sun-beam with a prism can exhibit the wide effulgence of a summer noon.

What they wanted however of the sublime they endeavoured to supply by hyperbole; their amplification had no limits: they left not only reason but fancy behind them, and produced combinations of confused magnificence that not only could not be credited, but could not be imagined.

Yet great labour directed by great abilities is never wholly lost: if they frequently threw away their wit upon false conceits, they likewise sometimes struck out unexpected truth: if their conceits were far-fetched, they were often worth the carriage. To write on their plan it was at least necessary to read and think.

No man could be born a metaphysical poet, nor assume the dignity of a writer by descriptions copied from descriptions, by imitations borrowed from imitations, by traditional imagery and hereditary similes, by readiness of rhyme and volubility of syllables.

In perusing the works of this race of authors the mind is exercised either by recollection or inquiry; either something already learned is to be retrieved, or something new is to be examined. If their greatness seldom elevates their acuteness often surprises; if the imagination is not always gratified, at least the powers of reflection and comparison are employed; and in the mass of materials, which ingenious absurdity has thrown together, genuine wit and useful knowledge may be sometimes found, buried perhaps in grossness of expression, but useful to those who know their value, and such as, when they are expanded to perspicuity and polished to elegance, may give lustre to works which have more propriety though less copiousness of sentiment. . . .

WILLIAM WORDSWORTH

(1770-1850)

Wordsworth collaborated with Samuel Taylor Coleridge to inaugurate the English romantic movement with the publication of the *Lyrical Ballads* (1798). His ideas about the nature of poetry and the function of the poet are expressed through both his poems and a series of prefaces beginning with the "Observations" included in the second edition of the *Lyrical Ballads* (1800) and continuing through the prefaces to the editions of 1802 and 1805 and to the *Poems, Including Lyrical Ballads* (1815). The prefaces constitute a revolutionary romantic manifesto in which Wordsworth sets forth the idea of the poet as a "man speaking to men" in words that are a "selection of the real language of men in a state of vivid excitement." His rejection of the "adulterated phraseology" and corrupt diction of eighteenth century verse in favor of the common language of a life close to nature has been one of the most influential features of his theory. Unlike Coleridge and most of the later New Critics, Wordsworth denied that there could be any essential difference between the language of poetry and that of prose, or science. His own prose remains important, not only for his discussions of the creative imagination and for his famous definition of poetry as "the spontaneous overflow of powerful feelings" taking its origin from "emotion recollected in tranquillity" but also for his emphasis on the social function of poetry. Despite his revolutionary role, Wordsworth is very close to his great eighteenth century forebear, Dr. Johnson, in his concern for the relation of literature to its social environment and his affirmation of the involvement of imaginative literature in the deepest moral and spiritual needs of man. Sources of Wordsworth's critical prose include his *Prose Works* (ed. William Knight, 2 vols., 1896) and his *Literary Criticism* (ed. N. C. Smith, 1905).

Preface to *Lyrical Ballads* (1802)

The first Volume of these Poems has already been submitted to general perusal. It was published, as an experiment, which, I hoped, might be of some use to ascertain, how far, by fitting to metrical arrangement a selection of the real language of men in a state of vivid sensation, that sort of pleasure and that quantity of pleasure may be imparted, which a Poet may rationally endeavour to impart.

I had formed no very inaccurate estimate of the probable effect of those Poems: I flattered myself that they who should be pleased with them would read them with more than common pleasure: and, on the other hand, I was well aware, that by those who should dislike them they would be read with more than common dislike. The result has differed from my expectation in this only, that I have pleased a greater number, than I ventured to hope I should please.

For the sake of variety, and from a consciousness of my own weakness, I was induced to request the assistance of a Friend, who furnished me with the Poems of *The Ancient Mariner*, "The Foster-Mother's Tale," "The Nightingale," and the Poem entitled "Love." I should not, however, have requested this assistance, had I not believed that the Poems of my Friend would in a great measure have the same tendency as my own, and that, though there would be found a dif-

ference, there would be found no discordance in the colours of our style; as our opinions on the subject of poetry do almost entirely coincide.

Several of my Friends are anxious for the success of these Poems from a belief, that, if the views with which they were composed were indeed realized, a class of Poetry would be produced, well adapted to interest mankind permanently, and not unimportant in the multiplicity, and in the quality of its moral relations: and on this account they have advised me to prefix a systematic defence of the theory, upon which the Poems were written. But I was unwilling to undertake the task, because I knew that on this occasion the Reader would look coldly upon my arguments, since I might be suspected of having been principally influenced by the selfish and foolish hope of *reasoning* him into an approbation of these particular Poems: and I was still more unwilling to undertake the task, because, adequately to display my opinions, and fully to enforce my arguments, would require a space wholly disproportionate to the nature of a preface. For to treat the subject with the clearness and coherence, of which I believe it susceptible, it would be necessary to give a full account of the present state of the public taste in this country, and to determine how far this taste is healthy or depraved; which, again, could not be determined, without pointing out, in what manner language and the human mind act and re-act on each other, and without retracing the revolutions, not of literature

The Preface, which first appeared in 1801 under the date 1800, is here presented in the fuller text of the 1802 edition of *Lyrical Ballads*.

alone, but likewise of society itself. I have therefore altogether declined to enter regularly upon this defence; yet I am sensible, that there would be some impropriety in abruptly obtruding upon the Public, without a few words of introduction, Poems so materially different from those, upon which general approbation is at present bestowed.

It is supposed, that by the act of writing in verse an Author makes a formal engagement that he will gratify certain known habits of association; that he not only thus apprizes the Reader that certain classes of ideas and expressions will be found in his book, but that others will be carefully excluded. This exponent or symbol held forth by metrical language must in different aeras of literature have excited very different expectations: for example, in the age of Catullus, Terence, and Lucretius and that of Statius or Claudian; and in our own country, in the age of Shakespeare and Beaumont and Fletcher, and that of Donne and Cowley, or Dryden, or Pope. I will not take upon me to determine the exact import of the promise which by the act of writing in verse an Author, in the present day, makes to his Reader; but I am certain, it will appear to many persons that I have not fulfilled the terms of an engagement thus voluntarily contracted. They who have been accustomed to the gaudiness and inane phraseology of many modern writers, if they persist in reading this book to its conclusion, will, no doubt, frequently have to struggle with feelings of strangeness and awkwardness: they will look round for poetry, and will be induced to inquire by what species of courtesy these attempts can be permitted to assume that title. I hope therefore the Reader will not censure me, if I attempt to state what I have proposed to myself to perform; and also, (as far as the limits of a preface will permit) to explain some of the chief reasons which have determined me in the choice of my purpose: that at least he may be spared any unpleasant feeling of disappointment, and that I myself may be protected from the most dishonourable accusation which can be brought against an Author, namely, that of an indolence which prevents him from endeavouring to ascertain what is his duty, or, when his duty is ascertained, prevents him from performing it.

The principal object, then, which I proposed to myself in these Poems was to choose incidents and situations from common life, and to relate or describe them, throughout, as far as was possible, in a selection of language really used by men; and, at the same time, to throw over them a certain colouring of imagination, whereby ordinary things should be presented to the mind in an unusual way; and, further, and above all, to make these incidents and situations interesting by tracing in them, truly though not ostentatiously, the primary laws of our nature: chiefly, as far as regards the manner in which we associate ideas in a state of excitement. Low and rustic life was generally chosen, because in that condition, the essential passions of the heart find a better soil in which they can attain their maturity, are less under restraint, and speak a plainer and more emphatic language; because in that condition of life our elementary feelings coexist in a state of greater simplicity, and, consequently, may be more accurately contemplated, and more forcibly communicated; because the manners of rural life germinate from those elementary feelings; and, from the necessary character of rural occupations, are more easily comprehended; and are more durable; and lastly, because in that condition the passions of men are incorporated with the beautiful and permanent forms of nature. The language, too, of these men is adopted (purified indeed from what appear to be its real defects, from all lasting and rational causes of dislike or disgust) because such men hourly communicate with the best objects from which the best part of language is originally derived; and because, from their rank in society and the sameness and narrow circle of their intercourse, being less under the influence of social vanity they convey their feelings and notions in simple and unelaborated expressions. Accordingly, such a language, arising out of repeated experience and regular feelings, is a more permanent, and a far more philosophical language, than that which is frequently substituted for it by Poets, who think that they are conferring honour upon themselves and their art, in proportion as they separate themselves from the sympathies of men, and indulge in arbitrary and capricious habits of expression, in order to furnish food for fickle tastes, and fickle appetites, of their own creation.[1]

I cannot, however, be insensible of the present outcry against the triviality and meanness both of thought and language, which some of my contemporaries have occasionally introduced into their metrical compositions; and I acknowledge, that this defect, where it exists, is more dishonourable to the Writer's own character than false refinement or arbitrary innovation, though I should contend at the same time that it is far less pernicious in the sum of its consequences. From such verses the Poems in these volumes will be found distinguished at least by one mark of difference, that each of them has a worthy *purpose*. Not that I mean to say, that I always began to write with a distinct purpose formally conceived; but I believe that my habits of meditation have so formed my feelings, as that my descriptions of such objects as strongly excite those feelings, will be found to carry along with them a *purpose*. If in this opinion I am mistaken, I can have little right to the name of a Poet. For all good poetry is the spontaneous overflow of powerful feelings: but though this be true, Poems to which any value can be attached, were never produced on any variety of subjects but by a man, who being possessed of more than usual organic sensibility, had also thought long and deeply. For our continued influxes of feeling are modified and directed by our thoughts, which are indeed the representatives of all our past feelings; and, as by contemplating the relation of these general representatives

to each other we discover what is really important to men, so, by the repetition and continuance of this act, our feelings will be connected with important subjects, till at length, if we be originally possessed of much sensibility, such habits of mind will be produced, that, by obeying blindly and mechanically the impulses of those habits, we shall describe objects, and utter sentiments, of such a nature and in such connection with each other, that the understanding of the being to whom we address ourselves, if he be in a healthful state of association, must necessarily be in some degree enlightened, and his affections ameliorated.

I have said that each of these poems has a purpose. I have also informed my Reader what this purpose will be found principally to be: namely to illustrate the manner in which our feelings and ideas are associated in a state of excitement. But, speaking in language somewhat more appropriate, it is to follow the fluxes and refluxes of the mind when agitated by the great and simple affections of our nature. This object I have endeavoured in these short essays to attain by various means; by tracing the maternal passion through many of its more subtle windings, as in the poems of "The Idiot Boy" and "The Mad Mother"; by accompanying the last struggles of a human being, at the approach of death, cleaving in solitude to life and society, as in the Poem of "The Forsaken Indian"; by shewing, as in the Stanzas entitled "We Are Seven," the perplexity and obscurity which in childhood attend our notion of death, or rather our utter inability to admit that notion; or by displaying the strength of fraternal, or to speak more philosophically, of moral attachment when early associated with the great and beautiful objects of nature, as in *The Brothers*; or, as in the incident of "Simon Lee," by placing my Reader in the way of receiving from ordinary moral sensations another and more salutary impression than we are accustomed to receive from them. It has also been part of my general purpose to attempt to sketch characters under the influence of less impassioned

---

[1] It is worth while here to observe that the affecting parts of Chaucer are almost always expressed in language pure and universally intelligible even to this day. [W. W.]

feelings, as in "The Two April Mornings," "The Fountain," "The Old Man Travelling," "The Two Thieves," &c. characters of which the elements are simple, belonging rather to nature than to manners, such as exist now, and will probably always exist, and which from their constitution may be distinctly and profitably contemplated. I will not abuse the indulgence of my Reader by dwelling longer upon this subject; but it is proper that I should mention one other circumstance which distinguishes these Poems from the popular Poetry of the day; it is this, that the feeling therein developed gives importance to the action and situation, and not the action and situation to the feeling. My meaning will be rendered perfectly intelligible by referring my Reader to the Poems entitled "Poor Susan" and "The Childless Father," particularly to the last Stanza of the latter Poem.

I will not suffer a sense of false modesty to prevent me from asserting, that I point my Reader's attention to this mark of distinction, far less for the sake of these particular Poems than from the general importance of the subject. The subject is indeed important! For the human mind is capable of being excited without the application of gross and violent stimulants; and he must have a very faint perception of its beauty and dignity who does not know this, and who does not further know, that one being is elevated above another, in proportion as he possesses this capability. It has therefore appeared to me, that to endeavour to produce or enlarge this capability is one of the best services in which, at any period, a Writer can be engaged; but this service, excellent at all times, is especially so at the present day. For a multitude of causes, unknown to former times, are now acting with a combined force to blunt the discriminating powers of the mind, and unfitting it for all voluntary exertion to reduce it to a state of almost savage torpor. The most effective of these causes are the great national events which are daily taking place, and the increasing accumulation of men in cities, where the uniformity of their occupations produces a craving for extraordinary incident, which the rapid communication of intelligence hourly gratifies. To this tendency of life and manners the literature and theatrical exhibitions of the country have conformed themselves. The invaluable works of our elder writers, I had almost said the works of Shakspeare and Milton, are driven into neglect by frantic novels, sickly and stupid German Tragedies, and deluges of idle and extravagant stories in verse.—When I think upon this degrading thirst after outrageous stimulation, I am almost ashamed to have spoken of the feeble effort with which I have endeavoured to counteract it; and, reflecting upon the magnitude of the general evil, I should be oppressed with no dishonourable melancholy, had I not a deep impression of certain inherent and indestructible qualities of the human mind, and likewise of certain powers in the great and permanent objects that act upon it which are equally inherent and indestructible; and did I not further add to this impression a belief, that the time is approaching when the evil will be systematically opposed, by men of greater powers, and with far more distinguished success.

Having dwelt thus long on the subjects and aim of these Poems, I shall request the Reader's permission to apprize him of a few circumstances relating to their *style*, in order, among other reasons, that I may not be censured for not having performed what I never attempted. The Reader will find that personifications of abstract ideas rarely occur in these volumes; and, I hope, are utterly rejected as an ordinary device to elevate the style, and raise it above prose. I have proposed to myself to imitate, and, as far as is possible, to adopt the very language of men; and assuredly such personifications do not make any natural or regular part of that language. They are, indeed, a figure of speech occasionally prompted by passion, and I have made use of them as such; but I have endeavoured utterly to reject them as a mechanical device of style, or as a family language which Writers in metre seem to lay claim to by prescription. I have wished to keep my

Reader in the company of flesh and blood, persuaded that by so doing I shall interest him. I am, however, well aware that others who pursue a different track may interest him likewise; I do not interfere with their claim, I only wish to prefer a different claim of my own. There will also be found in these volumes little of what is usually called poetic diction; I have taken as much pains to avoid it as others ordinarily take to produce it; this I have done for the reason already alleged, to bring my language near to the language of men, and further, because the pleasure which I have proposed to myself to impart is of a kind very different from that which is supposed by many persons to be the proper object of poetry. I do not know how without being culpably particular I can give my Reader a more exact notion of the style in which I wished these poems to be written than by informing him that I have at all times endeavoured to look steadily at my subject, consequently, I hope that there is in these Poems little falsehood of description, and that my ideas are expressed in language fitted to their respective importance. Something I must have gained by this practice, as it is friendly to one property of all good poetry, namely, good sense; but it has necessarily cut me off from a large portion of phrases and figures of speech which from father to son have long been regarded as the common inheritance of Poets. I have also thought it expedient to restrict myself still further, having abstained from the use of many expressions, in themselves proper and beautiful, but which have been foolishly repeated by bad Poets, till such feelings of disgust are connected with them as it is scarcely possible by any art of association to overpower.

If in a Poem there should be found a series of lines, or even a single line, in which the language, though naturally arranged and according to the strict laws of metre, does not differ from that of prose, there is a numerous class of critics, who, when they stumble upon these prosaisms as they call them, imagine that they have made a notable discovery, and exult over the Poet as over a man ignorant of his own profession. Now these men would establish a canon of criticism which the Reader will conclude he must utterly reject, if he wishes to be pleased with these volumes. And it would be a most easy task to prove to him, that not only the language of a large portion of every good poem, even of the most elevated character, must necessarily, except with reference to the metre, in no respect differ from that of good prose, but likewise that some of the most interesting parts of the best poems will be found to be strictly the language of prose, when prose is well written. The truth of this assertion might be demonstrated by innumerable passages from almost all the poetical writings, even of Milton himself. I have not space for much quotation; but, to illustrate the subject in a general manner, I will here adduce a short composition of Gray, who was at the head of those who by their reasonings have attempted to widen the space of separation betwixt Prose and Metrical composition, and was more than any other man curiously elaborate in the structure of his own poetic diction.

In vain to me the smiling mornings shine,
And reddening Phoebus lifts his golden fire:
The birds in vain their amorous descant join,
Or chearful fields resume their green attire:
These ears alas! for other notes repine;
A different object do these eyes require;
My lonely anguish melts no heart but mine;
And in my breast the imperfect joys expire;
Yet Morning smiles the busy race to cheer,
And new-born pleasure brings to happier men;
The fields to all their wonted tribute bear;
To warm their little loves the birds complain.
I fruitless mourn to him that cannot hear
And weep the more because I weep in vain.

It will easily be perceived that the only part of this Sonnet which is of any value is the lines printed in Italics: it is equally obvious, that, except in the rhyme, and in the use of the single word "fruitless" for fruitlessly, which is so far a defect, the language of these lines does in no respect differ from that of prose.

By the foregoing quotation I have shewn that the language of Prose may yet be well adapted to Poetry; and I have previously asserted that a large portion of the language of every good poem can in no respect differ from that of good Prose. I will go further. I do not doubt that it may be safely affirmed, that there neither is, nor can be, any essential difference between the language of prose and metrical composition. We are fond of tracing the resemblance between Poetry and Painting, and, accordingly, we call them Sisters: but where shall we find bonds of connection sufficiently strict to typify the affinity betwixt metrical and prose composition? They both speak by and to the same organs; the bodies in which both of them are clothed may be said to be of the same substance, their affections are kindred and almost identical, not necessarily differing even in degree; Poetry[2] sheds no tears "such as Angels weep," but natural and human tears; she can boast of no celestial Ichor that distinguishes her vital juices from those of prose; the same human blood circulates through the veins of them both.

If it be affirmed that rhyme and metrical arrangement of themselves constitute a distinction which overturns what I have been saying on the strict affinity of metrical language with that of prose, and paves the way for other artificial distinctions which the mind voluntarily admits, I answer that the language of such Poetry as I am recommending is, as far as is possible, a selection of the language really spoken by men; that this selection, wherever it is made with true taste and feeling, will of itself form a distinction far greater than would at first be imagined, and will entirely separate the composition from the vulgarity and meanness of ordinary life; and, if metre be superadded thereto, I believe that a dissimilitude will be produced altogether sufficient for the gratification of a rational mind. What other distinction

would we have? Whence is it to come? And where is it to exist? Not, surely, where the Poet speaks through the mouths of his characters: it cannot be necessary here, either for elevation of style, or any of its supposed ornaments: for, if the Poet's subject be judiciously chosen, it will naturally, and upon fit occasion, lead him to passions the language of which, if selected truly and judiciously, must necessarily be dignified and variegated, and alive with metaphors and figures. I forbear to speak of an incongruity which would shock the intelligent Reader, should the Poet interweave any foreign splendour of his own with that which the passion naturally suggests: it is sufficient to say that such addition is unnecessary. And, surely, it is more probable that those passages, which with propriety abound with metaphors and figures, will have their due effect, if, upon other occasions where the passions are of a milder character, the style also be subdued and temperate.

But, as the pleasure which I hope to give by the Poems I now present to the Reader must depend entirely on just notions upon this subject, and, as it is in itself of the highest importance to our taste and moral feelings, I cannot content myself with these detached remarks. And if, in what I am about to say, it shall appear to some that my labour is unnecessary, and that I am like a man fighting a battle without enemies, I would remind such persons, that, whatever may be the language outwardly holden by men, a practical faith in the opinions which I am wishing to establish is almost unknown. If my conclusions are admitted, and carried as far as they must be carried if admitted at all, our judgments concerning the works of the greatest Poets both ancient and modern will be far different from what they are at present, both when we praise, and when we censure: and our moral feelings influencing, and influenced by these judgments will, I believe, be corrected and purified.

Taking up the subject, then, upon general grounds, I ask what is meant by the word Poet? What is a Poet? To whom does he address himself? And what lan-

[2] I here use the word "Poetry" (though against my own judgment) as opposed to the word Prose, and synonymous with metrical composition. But much confusion has been introduced into criticism by this contradistinction of Poetry and Prose, instead of the more philosophical one of Poetry and Matter of Fact, or Science. The only strict antithesis to Prose is Metre; nor is this, in truth, a *strict* antithesis; because lines and passages of metre so naturally occur in writing prose, that it would be scarcely possible to avoid them, even were it desirable. [W. W.]

guage is to be expected from him? He is a man speaking to men: a man, it is true, endued with more lively sensibility, more enthusiasm and tenderness, who has a greater knowledge of human nature, and a more comprehensive soul, than are supposed to be common among mankind; a man pleased with his own passions and volitions, and who rejoices more than other men in the spirit of life that is in him; delighting to contemplate similar volitions and passions as manifested in the goings-on of the Universe, and habitually impelled to create them where he does not find them. To these qualities he has added a disposition to be affected more than other men by absent things as if they were present; an ability of conjuring up in himself passions, which are indeed far from being the same as those produced by real events, yet (especially in those parts of the general sympathy which are pleasing and delightful) do more nearly resemble the passions produced by real events, than any thing which, from the motions of their own minds merely, other men are accustomed to feel in themselves; whence, and from practice, he has acquired a greater readiness and power in expressing what he thinks and feels, and especially those thoughts and feelings which, by his own choice, or from the structure of his own mind, arise in him without immediate external excitement.

But, whatever portion of this faculty we may suppose even the greatest Poet to possess, there cannot be a doubt but that the language which it will suggest to him, must, in liveliness and truth, fall far short of that which is uttered by men in real life, under the actual pressure of those passions, certain shadows of which the Poet thus produces, or feels to be produced, in himself. However exalted a notion we would wish to cherish of the character of a Poet, it is obvious, that, while he describes and imitates passions, his situation is altogether slavish and mechanical, compared with the freedom and power of real and substantial action and suffering. So that it will be the wish of the Poet to bring his feelings near to those of the persons whose feelings he describes, nay, for short spaces of time perhaps, to let himself slip into an entire delusion, and even confound and identify his own feelings with theirs; modifying only the language which is thus suggested to him, by a consideration that he describes for a particular purpose, that of giving pleasure. Here, then, he will apply the principle on which I have so much insisted, namely, that of selection; on this he will depend for removing what would otherwise be painful or disgusting in the passion; he will feel that there is no necessity to trick out or to elevate nature: and, the more industriously he applies this principle, the deeper will be his faith that no words, which his fancy or imagination can suggest, will be to be compared with those which are the emanations of reality and truth.

But it may be said by those who do not object to the general spirit of these remarks, that, as it is impossible for the Poet to produce upon all occasions language as exquisitely fitted for the passion as that which the real passion itself suggests, it is proper that he should consider himself as in the situation of a translator, who deems himself justified when he substitutes excellences of another kind for those which are unattainable by him; and endeavours occasionally to surpass his original, in order to make some amends for the general inferiority to which he feels that he must submit. But this would be to encourage idleness and unmanly despair. Further, it is the language of men who speak of what they do not understand; who talk of Poetry as of a matter of amusement and idle pleasure; who will converse with us as gravely about a *taste* for Poetry, as they express it, as if it were a thing as indifferent as a taste for Rope-dancing, or Frontiniac or Sherry. Aristotle, I have been told, hath said, that Poetry is the most philosophic of all writing: it is so: its object is truth, not individual and local, but general, and operative; not standing upon external testimony, but carried alive into the heart by passion; truth which is its own testimony, which gives strength and divinity to the tribunal to which it appeals, and receives them from the same tribunal. Poetry is the image of man and nature. The obstacles which stand in the way of the fidelity of the Biographer and Historian, and of their consequent utility, are incalculably greater than those which are to be encountered by the Poet who has an adequate notion of the dignity of his art. The Poet writes under one restriction only, namely, that of the necessity of giving immediate pleasure to a human Being possessed of that information which may be expected from him, not as a lawyer, a physician, a mariner, an astronomer or a natural philosopher, but as a Man. Except this one restriction, there is no object standing between the Poet and the image of things; between this, and the Biographer and Historian there are a thousand.

Nor let this necessity of producing immediate pleasure be considered as a degradation of the Poet's art. It is far otherwise. It is an acknowledgment of the beauty of the universe, an acknowledgment the more sincere because it is not formal, but indirect; it is a task light and easy to him who looks at the world in the spirit of love: further, it is a homage paid to the native and naked dignity of man, to the grand elementary principle of pleasure, by which he knows, and feels, and lives, and moves. We have no sympathy but what is propagated by pleasure: I would not be misunderstood; but wherever we sympathize with pain it will be found that the sympathy is produced and carried on by subtle combinations with pleasure. We have no knowledge, that is, no general principles drawn from the contemplation of particular facts, but what has been built up by pleasure, and exists in us by pleasure alone. The Man of Science, the Chemist and Mathematician, whatever difficulties and disgusts they may have had to struggle with, know and feel this. However painful may be the objects with which the Anatomist's knowledge is connected, he feels that his knowledge is pleasure; and where he has no pleasure he has no knowledge. What then does the Poet? He considers man and the objects that surround him as acting and re-acting upon each other, so as

to produce an infinite complexity of pain and pleasure; he considers man in his own nature and in his ordinary life as contemplating this with a certain quantity of immediate knowledge, with certain convictions, intuitions, and deductions which by habit become of the nature of intuitions; he considers him as looking upon this complex scene of ideas and sensations, and finding every where objects that immediately excite in him sympathies which, from the necessities of his nature, are accompanied by an overbalance of enjoyment.

To this knowledge which all men carry about with them, and to these sympathies in which without any other discipline than that of our daily life we are fitted to take delight, the Poet principally directs his attention. He considers man and nature as essentially adapted to each other, and the mind of man as naturally the mirror of the fairest and most interesting qualities of nature. And thus the Poet, prompted by this feeling of pleasure which accompanies him through the whole course of his studies, converses with general nature with affections akin to those, which, through labour and length of time, the Man of Science has raised up in himself, by conversing with those particular parts of nature which are the objects of his studies. The knowledge both of the Poet and the Man of Science is pleasure; but the knowledge of the one cleaves to us as a necessary part of our existence, our natural and unalienable inheritance; the other is a personal and individual acquisition, slow to come to us, and by no habitual and direct sympathy connecting us with our fellow-beings. The Man of Science seeks truth as a remote and unknown benefactor; he cherishes and loves it in his solitude: the Poet, singing a song in which all human beings join with him, rejoices in the presence of truth as our visible friend and hourly companion. Poetry is the breath and finer spirit of all knowledge; it is the impassioned expression which is in the countenance of all Science. Emphatically may it be said of the Poet, as Shakspeare hath said of man, "that he looks before and after." He is the rock of defence of human nature; an upholder and preserver, carrying every where with him relationship and love. In spite of difference of soil and climate, of language and manners, of laws and customs, in spite of things silently gone out of mind and things violently destroyed, the Poet binds together by passion and knowledge the vast empire of human society, as it is spread over the whole earth, and over all time. The objects of the Poet's thoughts are every where; though the eyes and senses of man are, it is true, his favorite guides, yet he will follow wheresoever he can find an atmosphere of sensation in which to move his wings. Poetry is the first and last of all knowledge—it is as immortal as the heart of man. If the labours of men of Science should ever create any material revolution, direct or indirect, in our condition, and in the impressions which we habitually receive, the Poet will sleep then no more than at present, but he will be ready to follow the steps of the man of Science, not only in those general indirect effects, but he will be at his side, carrying sensation into the midst of the objects of the Science itself. The remotest discoveries of the Chemist, the Botanist, or Mineralogist, will be as proper objects of the Poet's art as any upon which it can be employed, if the time should ever come when these things shall be familiar to us, and the relations under which they are contemplated by the followers of these respective Sciences shall be manifestly and palpably material to us as enjoying and suffering beings. If the time should ever come when what is now called Science, thus familiarized to men, shall be ready to put on, as it were, a form of flesh and blood, the Poet will lend his divine spirit to aid the transfiguration, and will welcome the Being thus produced, as a dear and genuine inmate of the household of man.—It is not, then, to be supposed that any one, who holds that sublime notion of Poetry which I have attempted to convey, will break in upon the sanctity and truth of his pictures by transitory and accidental ornaments, and endeavour to excite admiration of himself by arts, the necessity of which must manifestly depend upon the assumed meanness of his subject.

What I have thus far said applies to Poetry in general; but especially to those parts of composition where the Poet speaks through the mouths of his characters; and upon this point it appears to have such weight that I will conclude, there are few persons, of good sense, who would not allow that the dramatic parts of composition are defective, in proportion as they deviate from the real language of nature, and are coloured by a diction of the Poet's own, either peculiar to him as an individual Poet, or belonging simply to Poets in general, to a body of men who, from the circumstance of their compositions being in metre, it is expected will employ a particular language.

It is not, then, in the dramatic parts of composition that we look for this distinction of language; but still it may be proper and necessary where the Poet speaks to us in his own person and character. To this I answer by referring my Reader to the description which I have before given of a Poet. Among the qualities which I have enumerated as principally conducting to form a Poet, is implied nothing differing in kind from other men, but only in degree. The sum of what I have there said is, that the Poet is chiefly distinguished from other men by a greater promptness to think and feel without immediate external excitement, and a greater power in expressing such thoughts and feelings as are produced in him in that manner. But these passions and thoughts and feelings are the general passions and thoughts and feelings of men. And with what are they connected? Undoubtedly with our moral sentiments and animal sensations, and with the causes which excite these; with the operations of the elements and the appearances of the visible universe; with storm and sun-shine, with the revolutions of the seasons, with cold and heat, with loss of friends and kindred, with injuries and resentments, gratitude and hope, with fear and sorrow. These, and the like, are the sensations and objects which the Poet describes, as they are the sensations of other men, and the objects which interest them. The Poet thinks and feels in the spirit of the passions of men. How, then, can his language differ in any material degree from that of all other men who feel vividly and see clearly? It might be *proved* that it is impossible. But supposing that this were not the case, the Poet might then be allowed to use a peculiar language, when expressing his feelings for his own gratification, or that of men like himself. But Poets do not write for Poets alone, but for men. Unless therefore we are advocates for that admiration which depends upon ignorance, and that pleasure which arises from hearing what we do not understand, the Poet must descend from this supposed height, and, in order to excite rational sympathy, he must express himself as other men express themselves. To this it may be added, that while he is only selecting from the real language of men, or, which amounts to the same thing, composing accurately in the spirit of such selection, he is treading upon safe ground, and we know what we are to expect from him. Our feelings are the same with respect to metre; for, as it may be proper to remind the Reader, the distinction of metre is regular and uniform, and not like that which is produced by what is usually called poetic diction, arbitrary, and subject to infinite caprices upon which no calculation whatever can be made. In the one case, the Reader is utterly at the mercy of the Poet respecting what imagery or diction he may choose to connect with the passion, whereas, in the other, the metre obeys certain laws, to which the Poet and Reader both willingly submit because they are certain, and because no interference is made by them with the passion but such as the concurring testimony of ages has shewn to heighten and improve the pleasure which co-exists with it.

It will now be proper to answer an obvious question, namely, why, professing these opinions, have I written in verse? To this, in addition to such answer as is included in what I have already said, I reply in the first place, because, however I may have restricted myself, there is still left open to me what confessedly constitutes the most valuable object of all writing whether in prose or verse, the great and universal passions of men, the most general and interesting of their occupations, and the entire world of nature, from which I am at liberty to supply myself with endless combinations of forms and imagery. Now, supposing for a moment that whatever is interesting in these objects may be as vividly described in prose, why am I to be condemned, if to such description I have endeavoured to superadd the charm which, by the consent of all nations, is acknowledged to exist in metrical language? To this, by such as are unconvinced by what I have already said, it may be answered, that a very small part of the pleasure given by Poetry depends upon the metre, and that it is injudicious to write in metre, unless it be accompanied with the other artificial distinctions of style with which metre is usually accompanied, and that by such deviation more will be lost from the shock which will be thereby given to the Reader's associations, than will be counterbalanced by any pleasure which he can derive from the general power of numbers. In answer to those who still contend for the necessity of accompanying metre with certain appropriate colours of style in order to the accomplishment of its appropriate end, and who also, in my opinion, greatly under-rate the power of metre in itself, it might perhaps, as far as relates to these Poems, have been almost sufficient to observe, that poems are extant, written upon more humble subjects, and in a more naked and simple style than I have aimed at, which poems have continued to give pleasure from generation to generation. Now, if nakedness and simplicity be a defect, the fact here mentioned affords a strong presumption that poems somewhat less naked and simple are capable of affording pleasure at the present day; and, what I wished *chiefly* to attempt, at present, was to justify myself for having written under the impression of this belief.

But I might point out various causes why, when the style is manly, and the subject of some importance, words metrically arranged will long continue to impart such a pleasure to mankind as he who is sensible of the extent of that pleasure will be desirous to impart. The end of Poetry is to produce excitement in co-existence with an overbalance of pleasure. Now, by the supposition, excitement is an unusual and irregular state of the mind; ideas and feelings do not in that state succeed each other in accustomed order. But, if the words by which this excitement is produced are in themselves powerful, or the images and feelings have an undue proportion of pain connected with them, there is some danger that the excitement may be carried beyond its proper bounds. Now the copresence of something regular, something to which the mind has been accustomed in various moods and in a less excited state, cannot but have great efficacy in tempering and restraining the passion by an intertexture of ordinary feeling, and of feeling not strictly and necessarily connected with the passion. This is unquestionably true, and hence, though the opinion will at first appear paradoxical, from the tendency of metre to divest language in a certain degree of its reality, and thus to throw a sort of half consciousness of unsubstantial existence over the whole composition, there can be little doubt but that more pathetic situations and sentiments, that is, those which have a greater proportion of pain connected with them, may be endured in metrical composition, especially in rhyme, than in prose. The metre of the old Ballads is very artless; yet they contain many passages which would illustrate this opinion, and, I hope, if the following Poems be attentively perused, similar instances will be found in them. This opinion may be further illustrated by appealing to the Reader's own experience of the reluctance with which he comes to the reperusal of the distressful parts of *Clarissa Harlowe*, or *The Gamester*. While Shakspeare's writings, in the most pathetic scenes, never act upon us as pathetic beyond the bounds of pleasure —an effect which, in a much greater degree than might at first be imagined, is to be ascribed to small, but continual and regular impulses of pleasurable surprise from the metrical arrangement.—On the other hand (what it must be allowed will much more frequently happen) if the Poet's words should be incommensurate with the passion, and inadequate to raise the Reader to a height of desirable excitement, then, (unless the Poet's choice of his metre has been grossly injudicious) in the feelings of pleasure which the Reader has been accustomed to connect with metre in general, and in the feeling, whether chearful or melancholy, which he has been accustomed to connect with that particular movement of metre, there will be found something which will greatly contribute to impart passion to the words, and to effect the complex end which the Poet proposes to himself.

If I had undertaken a systematic defence of the theory upon which these poems are written, it would have been my duty to develope the various causes upon which the pleasure received from metrical language depends. Among the chief of these causes is to be reckoned a principle which must be well known to those who have made any of the Arts the object of accurate reflection; I mean the pleasure which the mind derives from the perception of similitude in dissimilitude. This principle is the great spring of the activity of our minds, and their chief feeder. From this principle the direction of the sexual appetite, and all the passions connected with it take their origin: It is the life of our ordinary conversation; and upon the accuracy with which similitude in dissimilitude, and dissimilitude in similitude are perceived, depend our taste and our moral feelings. It would not have been a useless employment to have applied this principle to the consideration of metre, and to have shewn that metre is hence enabled to afford much pleasure, and to have pointed out in what manner that pleasure is produced. But my limits will not permit me to enter upon this subject, and I must content myself with a general summary.

I have said that poetry is the spontaneous overflow of powerful feelings: it takes its origin from emotion recollected in tranquillity: the emotion is contemplated till by a species of reaction the tranquillity gradually disappears, and an emotion, kindred to that which was before the subject of contemplation, is gradually produced, and does itself actually exist in the mind. In this mood successful composition generally begins, and in a mood similar to this it is carried on; but the emotion, of whatever kind and in whatever degree, from various causes is qualified by various pleasures, so that in describing any passions whatsoever, which are voluntarily described, the mind will upon the whole be in a state of enjoyment. Now, if Nature be thus cautious in preserving in a state of enjoyment a being thus employed, the Poet ought to profit by the lesson thus held forth to him, and ought especially to take care, that whatever passions he communicates to his Reader, those passions, if his Reader's mind be sound and vigorous, should always be accompanied with an overbalance of pleasure. Now the music of harmonious metrical language, the sense of difficulty overcome, and the blind association of pleasure which has been previously received from works of rhyme or metre of the same or similar construction, an indistinct perception perpetually renewed of language closely resembling that of real life, and yet, in the circumstance of metre, differing from it so widely, all these imperceptibly make up a complex feeling of delight, which is of the most important use in tempering the painful feeling which will always be found intermingled with powerful descriptions of the deeper passions. This effect is always produced in pathetic and impassioned poetry; while, in lighter compositions, the ease and gracefulness with which the Poet manages his numbers are themselves confessedly a principal source of the gratification of the Reader. I might perhaps include all which it is *necessary* to say upon this subject by affirming, what few persons will deny, that, of two descriptions, either of passions, manners, or characters, each of them equally well executed, the one in prose and the other in verse, the verse will be read a hundred times where the prose is read once. We see that Pope by

the power of verse alone, has contrived to render the plainest common sense interesting, and even frequently to invest it with the appearance of passion. In consequence of these convictions I related in metre the tale of "Goody Blake and Harry Gill," which is one of the rudest of this collection. I wished to draw attention to the truth that the power of the human imagination is sufficient to produce such changes even in our physical nature as might almost appear miraculous. The truth is an important one; the fact (for it is a *fact*) is a valuable illustration of it. And I have the satisfaction of knowing that it has been communicated to many hundreds of people who would never have heard of it, had it not been narrated as a Ballad, and in a more impressive metre than is usual in Ballads.

Having thus explained a few of the reasons why I have written in verse, and why I have chosen subjects from common life, and endeavoured to bring my language near to the real language of men, if I have been too minute in pleading my own cause, I have at the same time been treating a subject of general interest; and it is for this reason that I request the Reader's permission to add a few words with reference solely to these particular poems, and to some defects which will probably be found in them. I am sensible that my associations must have sometimes been particular instead of general, and that, consequently, giving to things a false importance, sometimes from diseased impulses I may have written upon unworthy subjects; but I am less apprehensive on this account, than that my language may frequently have suffered from those arbitrary connections of feelings and ideas with particular words and phrases, from which no man can altogether protect himself. Hence I have no doubt, that, in some instances, feelings even of the ludicrous may be given to my Readers by expressions which appeared to me tender and pathetic. Such faulty expressions, were I convinced they were faulty at present, and that they must necessarily continue to be so, I would willingly take all reasonable pains to correct. But it is dangerous to make these alterations on the simple authority of a few individuals, or even of certain classes of men; for where the understanding of an Author is not convinced, or his feelings altered, this cannot be done without great injury to himself: for his own feelings are his stay and support, and, if he sets them aside in one instance, he may be induced to repeat this act till his mind loses all confidence in itself, and becomes utterly debilitated. To this it may be added, that the Reader ought never to forget that he is himself exposed to the same errors as the Poet, and perhaps in a much greater degree: for there can be no presumption in saying, that it is not probable he will be so well acquainted with the various stages of meaning through which words have passed, or with the fickleness or stability of the relations of particular ideas to each other; and above all, since he is so much less interested in the subject, he may decide lightly and carelessly.

Long as I have detained my Reader, I hope he will permit me to caution him against a mode of false criticism which has been applied to Poetry in which the language closely resembles that of life and nature. Such verses have been triumphed over in parodies of which Dr. Johnson's stanza is a fair specimen.

"I put my hat upon my head,
And walk'd into the Strand,
And there I met another man
Whose hat was in his hand."

Immediately under these lines I will place one of the most justly admired stanzas of the "Babes in the Wood."

"These pretty Babes with hand in hand
Went wandering up and down;
But never more they saw the Man
Approaching from the Town."

In both these stanzas the words, and the order of the words, in no respect differ from the most unimpassioned conversation. There are words in both, for example, "the Strand," and "the Town," connected with none but the most familiar ideas; yet the one stanza we admit as admirable, and the other as a fair example of the superlatively contemptible. Whence arises this difference? Not from the metre, not from the language, not from the order of the words; but the *matter* expressed in Dr. Johnson's stanza is contemptible. The proper method of treating trivial and simple verses to which Dr. Johnson's stanza would be a fair parallelism is not to say, this is a bad kind of poetry, or this is not poetry; but this wants sense; it is neither interesting in itself, nor can *lead* to any thing interesting; the images neither originate in that same state of feeling which arises out of thought, nor can excite thought or feeling in the Reader. This is the only sensible manner of dealing with such verses: Why trouble yourself about the species till you have previously decided upon the genus? Why take pains to prove that an ape is not a Newton when it is self-evident that he is not a man?

I have one request to make of my Reader, which is, that in judging these Poems he would decide by his own feelings genuinely, and not by reflection upon what will probably be the judgment of others. How common is it to hear a person say, "I myself do not object to this style of composition or this or that expression, but to such and such classes of people it will appear mean or ludicrous." This mode of criticism, so destructive of all sound unadulterated judgment, is almost universal: I have therefore to request, that the Reader would abide independently by his own feelings, and that if he finds himself affected he would not suffer such conjectures to interfere with his pleasure.

If an Author by any single composition has impressed us with respect for his talents, it is useful to consider this as affording a presumption, that, on other occasions where we have been displeased, he nevertheless may not have written ill or absurdly; and, further, to give him so much credit for this one composition as may induce us to review what has displeased us with more care than we should otherwise have bestowed upon it. This is not only an act of justice, but in our decisions upon poetry especially, may conduce in a high degree to the improvement of our own taste: for an *accurate* taste in poetry, and in all the other arts, as Sir Joshua Reynolds has observed, is an *acquired* talent, which can only be produced by thought and a long continued intercourse with the best models of composition. This is mentioned, not with so ridiculous a purpose as to prevent the most inexperienced Reader from judging for himself, (I have already said that I wish him to judge for himself;) but merely to temper the rashness of decision, and to suggest, that, if Poetry be a subject on which much time has not been bestowed, the judgment may be erroneous; and that in many cases it necessarily will be so.

I know that nothing would have so effectually contributed to further the end which I have in view as to have shewn of what kind the pleasure is, and how that pleasure is produced, which is confessedly produced by metrical composition essentially different from that which I have here endeavoured to recommend: for the Reader will say that he has been pleased by such composition; and what can I do more for him? The power of any art is limited; and he will suspect, that, if I propose to furnish him with new friends, it is only upon condition of his abandoning his old friends. Besides, as I have said, the Reader is himself conscious of the pleasure which he has received from such composition, composition to which he has peculiarly attached the endearing name of Poetry; and all men feel an habitual gratitude, and something of an honourable bigotry for the objects which have long continued to please them: we not only wish to be pleased, but to be pleased in that particular way in which we have been accustomed to be pleased. There is a host of arguments in these feelings; and I should be the less able to combat them successfully, as I am willing to allow, that, in order entirely to enjoy the Poetry which I am recommending, it would be necessary to give up much of what is ordinarily enjoyed. But, would my limits have permitted me to point out how this pleasure is produced, I might have removed many obstacles, and assisted my Reader in perceiving that the powers of language are not so limited as he may suppose; and that it is possible that poetry may give other enjoyments, of a purer, more lasting, and more exquisite nature. This part of my subject I have not altogether neglected; but it has been less my present aim to prove, that the interest excited by some other kinds of poetry is less vivid, and less worthy of the nobler powers of the mind, than to offer reasons for presuming, that, if the object which I have proposed to myself were adequately attained, a species of poetry would be produced, which is genuine poetry; in its nature well adapted to interest mankind permanently, and likewise important in the multiplicity and quality of its moral relations.

From what has been said, and from a perusal of the Poems, the Reader will be able clearly to perceive the object which I have proposed to myself: he will determine how far I have attained this object; and, what is a much more important question, whether it be worth attaining; and upon the decision of these two questions will rest my claim to the approbation of the public.

SAMUEL TAYLOR COLERIDGE

(1772-1834)

Samuel Taylor Coleridge is the most important and influential critic of the romantic movement. His general position as a romantic can usefully be defined by comparing his criticism with that of his great neoclassicist forebear, Samuel Johnson. One notices first that where Johnson was primarily a "practical" critic, Coleridge was primarily a "theorist." Johnson, with his working acceptance of certain traditional metaphysical, psychological, and moral assumptions, goes straight to the artist and his work of art with the question, "Does this poem satisfy our common sense for emotional and moral truth and validity?" But Coleridge, initially certain only of the mysterious existence, in a continuum, of nature and the mind, asks the question, "What is the structure of reality?" Coleridge sees works of art as data of the mind's structure and organic operation, which reflect, in turn, nature's structure and operation. So literary criticism is for Coleridge intimately bound up with, and finally perhaps subordinated to, a quest for metaphysical knowledge. Coleridge may also be distinguished from his friend Wordsworth in much the same way. Though a romantic in general conviction and feeling, Wordsworth as a critic is much closer to Johnson than to Coleridge in his insistence on judging poetry directly by the standard of the emotional and moral integrity of its language. And so, Wordsworth and Coleridge's well-known disagreement on the nature of poetic language may be explained by a difference in their ideas of its function. When Wordsworth claimed that there was no essential difference between the languages of poetry and prose, he was thinking of language as a kind of matter or medium to be "used"—vocabulary and grammatical conventions. When Coleridge countered that there *was* an essential difference, he was thinking of language as an action of the mind capable of directing itself to "essentially" different ends—in his terminology, those of the "understanding" or those of the "reason." The chief compendium of Coleridge's critical thought is the *Biographia Literaria* (1817). Other posthumously published, shorter, or fragmentary works appear in *Specimens of the Table-Talk* (ed. H. N. Coleridge, 1835), *Literary Remains* (ed. H. N. Coleridge, 1836-1839), *Anima Poetae* (ed. H. N. Coleridge, 1895), *Shakespearian Criticism* (ed. T. M. Raysor, 1930), and *Miscellaneous Criticism* (ed. T. M. Raysor, 1936).

Biographia Literaria (1817)

From Chapter IV. . . . On Fancy and Imagination—The Investigation of the Distinction Important to the Fine Arts

. . . During the last year of my residence at Cambridge, I became acquainted with Mr. Wordsworth's first publication entitled "Descriptive Sketches"; and seldom, if ever, was the emergence of an original poetic genius above the literary horizon more evidently announced. In the form, style, and manner of the whole poem, and in the structure of the particular lines and periods, there is an harshness and acerbity connected and combined with words and images all a-glow, which might recall those products of the vegetable world, where gorgeous blossoms rise out of the hard and thorny rind and shell, within which the rich fruit was elaborating. The language was not only peculiar and strong, but at times knotty and contorted, as by its own impatient strength; while the novelty and struggling crowd of images, acting in conjunction with the difficulties of the style, demanded always a greater closeness of attention, than poetry, (at all events, than descriptive poetry) has a right to claim. It not seldom therefore justified the complaint of obscurity. In the following extract I have sometimes fancied, that I saw an emblem of the poem itself, and of the author's genius as it was then displayed.

" 'Tis storm; and hid in mist from hour to
  hour,
All day the floods a deepening murmur pour;
The sky is veiled, and every cheerful sight:
Dark is the region as with coming night;
And yet what frequent bursts of
  overpowering light!
Triumphant on the bosom of the storm,
Glances the fire-clad eagle's wheeling form;
Eastward, in long perspective glittering, shine
The wood-crowned cliffs that o'er the lake
  recline;
Wide o'er the Alps a hundred streams unfold,
At once to pillars turn'd that flame with
  gold;
Behind his sail the peasant strives to shun
The West, that burns like one dilated sun,
Where in a mighty crucible expire
The mountains, glowing hot, like coals of
  fire."

The poetic PSYCHE, in its process to full developement, undergoes as many changes as its Greek namesake, the butterfly.[1] And it is remarkable how soon genius clears and purifies itself from the faults and errors of its earliest products; faults which, in its earliest compositions, are the more obstrusive and confluent, because as heterogeneous elements, which had only a temporary use, they constitute the very *ferment*, by which themselves are carried off. Or we may compare them to some diseases, which must work on the humours, and be thrown out on the surface, in order to secure the patient from their future re-currence. I was in my twenty-fourth year, when I had the happiness of know-ing Mr. Wordsworth personally, and while memory lasts, I shall hardly forget the sudden effect produced on my mind, by his recitation of a manuscript poem, which still remains unpublished, but of which the stanza, and tone of style, were the same as those of the "Female Va-grant," as originally printed in the first volume of the "Lyrical Ballads." There was here no mark of strained thought, or forced diction, no crowd or turbulence of imagery; and, as the poet hath himself well described in his lines "on re-visiting the Wye," manly reflection, and human associations had given both variety, and an additional interest to natural objects, which in the passion and appetite of the first love they had seemed to him neither to need or permit. The occasional ob-scurities, which had risen from an imper-fect controul over the resources of his native language, had almost wholly dis-appeared, together with that worse de-fect of arbitrary and illogical phrases, at once hackneyed, and fantastic, which hold so distinguished a place in the *tech-nique* of ordinary poetry, and will, more or less, alloy the earlier poems of the truest genius, unless the attention has been specifically directed to their worth-lessness and incongruity. I did not per-ceive anything particular in the mere style of the poem alluded to during its recitation, except indeed such difference as was not separable from the thought and manner; and the Spenserian stanza, which always, more or less, recalls to the reader's mind Spenser's own style, would doubtless have authorized, in my then opinion, a more frequent descent to the phrases of ordinary life, than could with-out an ill effect have been hazarded in the heroic couplet. It was not however the freedom from false taste, whether as to common defects, or to those more properly his own, which made so unusual an impression on my feelings immediate-ly, and subsequently on my judgement. It was the union of deep feeling with pro-found thought; the fine balance of truth in observing, with the imaginative faculty in modifying the objects deserved; and above all the original gift of spreading the tone, the *atmosphere*, and with it the depth and height of the ideal world around forms, incidents, and situa-tions, of which, for the common view, custom had bedimmed all the lustre, had dried up the sparkle and the dew drops.

---

[1] The fact, that in Greek Psyche is the common name for the soul, and the butterfly, is thus alluded to in the following stanzas from an unpublished poem of the author:
"The butterfly the ancient Grecians made
The soul's fair emblem, and its only name—
But of the soul, escaped the slavish trade
Of mortal life! For in this earthly frame
Our's is the reptile's lot, much toil, much blame,
Manifold motions making little speed,
And to deform and kill the things, whereon we feed."
[S. T. C.]

"To find no contradiction in the union of old and new; to contemplate the ANCIENT of days and all his works with feelings as fresh, as if all had then sprang forth at the first creative fiat; characterizes the mind that feels the riddle of the world, and may help to unravel it. To carry on the feelings of childhood into the powers of manhood; to combine the child's sense of wonder and novelty with the appearances, which every day for perhaps forty years had rendered familiar;

'With sun and moon and stars throughout the year,
And man and woman;'

this is the character and privilege of genius, and one of the marks which distinguish genius from talents. And therefore is it the prime merit of genius and its most unequivocal mode of manifestation, so to represent familiar objects as to awaken in the minds of others a kindred feeling concerning them and that freshness of sensation which is the constant accompaniment of mental, no less than of bodily, convalescence. Who has not a thousand times seen snow fall on water? Who has not watched it with a new feeling, from the time that he has read Burns' comparison of sensual pleasure

'To snow that falls upon a river
A moment white—then gone for ever!'

In poems, equally as in philosophic disquisitions, genius produces the strongest impressions of novelty, while it rescues the most admitted truths from the impotence caused by the very circumstance of their universal admission. Truths of all others the most awful and mysterious, yet being at the same time of universal interest, are too often considered as *so* true, that they lose all the life and efficiency of truth, and lie bedridden in the dormitory of the soul, side by side with the most despised and exploded errors."
—THE FRIEND, p. 76, No. 5.

This excellence, which in all Mr. Wordsworth's writings is more or less predominant, and which constitutes the character of his mind, I no sooner felt, than I sought to understand. Repeated meditations led me first to suspect, (and a more intimate analysis of the human faculties, their appropriate marks, functions, and effects matured my conjecture into full conviction,) that fancy and imagination were two distinct and widely different faculties, instead of being, according to the general belief, either two names with one meaning, or, at furthest, the lower and higher degree of one and the same power. It is not, I own, easy to conceive a more opposite translation of the Greek *Phantasia* than the Latin *Imaginatio*; but it is equally true that in all societies there exists an instinct of growth, a certain collective, unconscious good sense working progressively to desynonymize[2] those words originally of the same meaning, which the conflux of dialects had supplied to the more homogeneous languages, as the Greek and German: and which the same cause, joined with accidents of translation from original works of different countries, occasion in mixt languages like our own. The first and most important point to be proved is, that two conceptions perfectly distinct are confused under one and the

[2] This is effected either by giving to the one word a general, and to the other an exclusive use; as "to put on the back" and "to indorse;" or by an actual distinction of meanings, as "naturalist," and "physician;" or by difference of relation, as "I" and "Me" (each of which the rustics of our different provinces still use in all the cases singular of the first personal pronoun). Even the mere difference, or corruption, in the *pronunciation* of the same word, if it have become general, will produce a new word with a distinct signification; thus "property" and "propriety;" the latter of which, even to the time of Charles II. was the *written* word for all the senses of both. Thus too "mister" and "master," both hasty pronunciations of the same word "magister," "mistress," and "miss," "if" and "give," &c., &c. There is a sort of *minim immortal* among the animalcula infusoria which has not naturally either birth, or death, absolute beginning, or absolute end: for at a certain period a small point appears on its back, which deepens and lengthens till the creature divides into two, and the same process recommences in each of the halves now become integral. This may be a fanciful, but it is by no means a bad emblem of the formation of words, and may facilitate the conception, how immense a nomenclature may be organized from a few simple sounds by rational beings in a social state. For each new application, or excitement of the same sound, will call forth a different sensation, which cannot but affect the pronunciation. The after recollection of the sound, without the same vivid sensation, will modify it still further, till at length all trace of the original likeness is worn away.   [S. T. C.]

same word, and (this done) to appro-priate that word exclusively to one mean-ing, and the synonyme (should there be one) to the other. But if (as will be often the case in the arts and sciences) no syn-onyme exists, we must either invent or borrow a word. In the present instance the appropriation has already begun, and been legitimated in the derivative ad-jective: Milton had a highly *imaginative*, Cowley a very *fanciful* mind. If therefore I should succeed in establishing the actual existences of two faculties gen-erally different, the nomenclature would be at once determined. To the faculty by which I had characterized Milton, we should confine the term *imagination*; while the other would be contradistin-guished as *fancy*. Now were it once fully ascertained, that this division is no less grounded in nature, than that of delir-ium from mania, or Otway's

"Lutes, lobsters, seas of milk, and ships of amber,"

from Shakespeare's

"What! have his daughters brought him to this pass?"

or from the preceding apostrophe to the elements; the theory of the fine arts, and of poetry in particular, could not, I thought, but derive some additional and important light. It would in its immedi-ate effects furnish a torch of guidance to the philosophical critic; and ultimately to the poet himself. In energetic minds truth soon changes by domestication into power; and from directing in the dis-crimination and appraisal of the prod-uct, becomes influencive in the produc-tion. To admire on principle, is the only way to imitate without loss of originality.

It has been already hinted, that meta-physics and psychology have long been my hobby-horse. But to have a hobby-horse, and to be vain of it, are so com-monly found together, that they pass almost for the same. I trust therefore, that there will be more good humour than contempt, in the smile with which the reader chastises my self-complacency, if I confess myself uncertain, whether the satisfaction from the perception of a

truth new to myself may not have been rendered more poignant by the conceit, that it would be equally so to the public. There was a time, certainly, in which I took some little credit to myself, in the belief that I had been the first of my countrymen, who had pointed out the diverse meaning of which the two terms were capable, and analyzed the faculties to which they should be appropriated. Mr. W. Taylor's recent volume of syn-onymes I have not yet seen; but his specification of the terms in question has been clearly shown to be both insufficient and erroneous by Mr. Wordsworth in the Preface added to the late collection of his "Lyrical Ballads and other poems." The explanation which Mr. Wordsworth has himself given will be found to differ from mine, chiefly perhaps, as our ob-jects are different. It could scarcely in-deed happen otherwise, from the ad-vantage I have enjoyed of frequent conversation with him on a subject to which a poem of his own first directed my attention, and my conclusions con-cerning which, he had made more lucid to myself by many happy instances drawn from the operation of natural ob-jects on the mind. But it was Mr. Words-worth's purpose to consider the influ-ences of fancy and imagination as they are manifested in poetry, and from the different effects to conclude their diver-sity in kind; while it is my object to in-vestigate the seminal principle, and then from the kind to deduce the degree. My friend has drawn a masterly sketch of the branches with their *poetic* fruitage. I wish to add the trunk, and even the roots as far as they lift themselves above ground, and are visible to the naked eye of our common consciousness.

Yet even in this attempt I am aware, that I shall be obliged to draw more largely on the reader's attention, than so immethodical a miscellany can author-ize; when in such a work (the *Eccle-siastical Polity*) of such a mind as Hooker's, the judicious author, though no less admirable for the perspicuity than for the port and dignity of his lan-guage; and though he wrote for men of learning in a learned age; saw nevertheless occasion to anticipate and guard against "complaints of obscurity," as often as he was about to trace his subject "to the highest well-spring and fountain." Which, (continues he) "because men are not accustomed to, the pains we take are more needful a great deal, than acceptable; and the matters we handle, seem by reason of newness (till the mind grow better acquainted with them) dark and intricate." I would gladly therefore spare both myself and others this labor, if I knew how without it to present an intelligible statement of my poetic creed; not as my *opinions*, which weigh for nothing, but as deductions from established premises conveyed in such a form, as is calculated either to effect a fundamental conviction, or to receive a fundamental confutation. If I may dare once more adopt the words of Hooker, "they, unto whom we shall seem tedious, are in no wise injured by us, because it is in their own hands to spare that labor, which they are not willing to endure." Those at least, let me be permitted to add, who have taken so much pains to render me ridiculous for a perversion of taste, and have supported the charge by attributing strange notions to me on no other authority than their own conjectures, owe it to themselves as well as to me not to refuse their attention to my own statement of the theory, which I *do* acknowledge; or shrink from the trouble of examining the grounds on which I rest it, or the arguments which I offer in its justification.

From Chapter XIII. On the Imagination, or Esemplastic Power

. . The IMAGINATION then, I consider either as primary, or secondary. The primary IMAGINATION I hold to be the living Power and prime Agent of all human Perception, and as a repetition in the finite mind of the eternal act of creation in the infinite I AM. The secondary Imagination I consider as an echo of the former, co-existing with the conscious will, yet still as identical with the primary in the *kind* of its agency, and differing only in *degree*, and in the *mode* of its operation. It dissolves, diffuses, dissipates, in order to recreate; or where this process is rendered impossible, yet still at all events it struggles to idealize and to unify. It is essentially *vital*, even as all objects (*as* objects) are essentially fixed and dead.

FANCY, on the contrary, has no other counters to play with, but fixities and definites. The Fancy is indeed no other than a mode of Memory emancipated from the order of time and space; while it is blended with, and modified by that empirical phenomenon of the will, which we express by the word CHOICE. But equally with the ordinary memory the Fancy must receive all its materials ready made from the law of association.

Whatever more than this, I shall think it fit to declare concerning the powers and privileges of the imagination in the present work, will be found in the critical essay on the uses of the Supernatural in poetry, and the principles that regulate its introduction: which the reader will find prefixed to the poem of *The Ancient Mariner*.

Chapter XIV. Occasion of the *Lyrical Ballads* . . . , Philosophic Definitions of a Poem and Poetry with Scholia

During the first year that Mr. Wordsworth and I were neighbors, our conversations turned frequently on the two cardinal points of poetry, the power of exciting the sympathy of the reader by a faithful adherence to the truth of nature, and the power of giving the interest of novelty by the modifying colors of imagination. The sudden charm, which accidents of light and shade, which moon-light or sun-set diffused over a known and familiar landscape, appeared to represent the practicability of combining both. These are the poetry of nature. The thought suggested itself (to which of us I do not recollect) that a series of poems might be composed of two sorts. In the one, the incidents and agents were to be, in part at least, supernatural; and the excellence aimed at was to consist in the interesting of the affections by the dramatic truth of such emotions, as would naturally accompany such situations, supposing them real. And real in *this* sense they have been to every human being who, from whatever source of delusion, has at any time believed himself under supernatural agency. For the second class, subjects were to be chosen from ordinary life; the characters and incidents were to be such, as will be found in every village and its vicinity, where there is a meditative and feeling mind to seek after them, or to notice them, when they present themselves.

In this idea originated the plan of the "Lyrical Ballads"; in which it was agreed, that my endeavours should be directed to persons and characters supernatural, or at least romantic; yet so as to transfer from our inward nature a human interest and a semblance of truth sufficient to procure for these shadows of imagination that willing suspension of disbelief for the moment, which constitutes poetic faith. Mr. Wordsworth, on the other hand, was to propose to himself as his object, to give the charm of novelty to things of every day, and to excite a feeling analogous to the supernatural, by awakening the mind's attention from the lethargy of custom, and directing it to the loveliness and the wonders of the world before us; an inexhaustible treasure, but for which, in consequence of the film of familiarity and selfish solicitude we have eyes, yet see not, ears that hear not, and hearts that neither feel nor understand.

With this view I wrote "The Ancient Mariner," and was preparing among other poems, "The Dark Ladie," and the "Christabel," in which I should have more nearly realized my ideal, than I had done in my first attempt. But Mr. Wordsworth's industry had proved so much more successful, and the number of his poems so much greater, that my compositions, instead of forming a balance, appeared rather an interpolation of heterogeneous matter. Mr. Wordsworth added two or three poems written in his own character, in the impassioned, lofty, and sustained diction, which is characteristic of his genius. In this form the "Lyrical Ballads" were published; and were presented by him, as an *experiment*, whether subjects, which from their nature rejected the usual ornaments and extra-colloquial style of poems in general, might not be so managed in the language of ordinary life as to produce the pleasureable interest, which it is the peculiar business of poetry to impart. To the second edition he added a preface of considerable length; in which, notwithstanding some passages of apparently a contrary import, he was understood to contend for the extension of this style to poetry of all kinds, and to reject as vicious and indefensible all phrases and forms of style that were not included in what he (unfortunately, I think, adopting an equivocal expression) called the language of *real* life. From this preface, prefixed to poems in which it was impossible to deny the presence of original genius, however mistaken its direction might be deemed, arose the whole long-continued controversy.[1] For from the conjunction of perceived power with supposed heresy I explain the inveteracy and in some instances, I grieve to say, the acrimonious passions, with which the controversy has been conducted by the assailants.

Had Mr. Wordsworth's poems been the silly, the childish things, which they were for a long time described as being; had they been really distinguished from the compositions of other poets merely by

---

[1] Coleridge is referring to the controversy over Wordsworth's poetic theory.

meanness of language and inanity of thought; had they indeed contained nothing more than what is found in the parodies and pretended imitations of them; they must have sunk at once, a dead weight, into the slough of oblivion, and have dragged the preface along with them. But year after year increased the number of Mr. Wordsworth's admirers. They were found too not in the lower classes of the reading public, but chiefly among young men of strong sensibility and meditative minds; and their admiration (inflamed perhaps in some degree by opposition) was distinguished by its intensity. I might almost say, by its *religious* fervor. These facts, and the intellectual energy of the author, which was more or less consciously felt, where it was outwardly and even boisterously denied, meeting with sentiments of aversion to his opinions, and of alarm at their consequences, produced an eddy of criticism, which would of itself have borne up the poems by the violence, with which it whirled them round and round. With many parts of this preface, in the sense attributed to them, and which the words undoubtedly seem to authorize, I never concurred; but on the contrary objected to them as erroneous in principle, and as contradictory (in appearance at least) both to other parts of the same preface, and to the author's own practice in the greater number of the poems themselves. Mr. Wordsworth in his recent collection has, I find, degraded this prefatory disquisition to the end of his second volume, to be read or not at the reader's choice. But he has not, as far as I can discover, announced any change in his poetic creed. At all events, considering it as the source of a controversy, in which I have been honored more than I deserve by the frequent conjunction of my name with his, I think it expedient to declare once for all, in what points I coincide with his opinions, and in what points I altogether differ. But in order to render myself intelligible I must previously, in as few words as possible, explain my ideas, first, of a POEM; and secondly, of POETRY itself, in *kind*, and in *essence*.

The office of philosophical *disquisition* consists in just *distinction*; while it is the priviledge of the philosopher to preserve himself constantly aware, that distinction is not division. In order to obtain adequate notions of any truth, we must intellectually separate its distinguishable parts; and this is the technical *process* of philosophy. But having so done, we must then restore them in our conceptions to the unity, in which they actually co-exist; and this is the *result* of philosophy. A poem contains the same elements as a prose composition; the difference therefore must consist in a different combination of them, in consequence of a different object being proposed. According to the difference of the object will be the difference of the combination. It is possible, that the object may be merely to facilitate the recollection of any given facts or observations by artificial arrangement; and the composition will be a poem, merely because it is distinguished from prose by metre, or by rhyme, or by both conjointly. In this, the lowest sense, a man might attribute the name of a poem to the well-known enumeration of the days in the several months;

Thirty days hath September,
April, June, and November, &c.

and others of the same class and purpose. And as a particular pleasure is found in anticipating the recurrence of sounds and quantities, all compositions that have this charm super-added, whatever be their contents, *may* be entitled poems.

So much for the superficial *form*. A difference of object and contents supplies an additional ground of distinction. The immediate purpose may be the communication of truths; either of truth absolute and demonstrable, as in works of science; or of facts experienced and recorded, as in history. Pleasure, and that of the highest and most permanent kind, may *result* from the *attainment* of the end; but it is not itself the immediate end. In other works the communication of pleasure may be the immediate purpose; and though truth, either moral or intellectual, ought to be the *ultimate* end, yet this will distinguish the character of the author, not the class to which the work belongs. Blest indeed is that state of society, in which the immediate purpose would be baffled by the perversion of the proper ultimate end; in which no charm of diction or imagery could exempt the Bathyllus even of an Anacreon, or the Alexis of Virgil, from disgust and aversion!

But the communication of pleasure may be the immediate object of a work not metrically composed; and that object may have been in a high degree attained, as in novels and romances. Would then the mere superaddition of metre, with or without rhyme, entitle *these* to the name of poems? The answer is, that nothing can permanently please, which does not contain in itself the reason why it is so, and not otherwise. If metre be superadded, all other parts must be made consonant with it. They must be such, as to justify the perpetual and distinct attention to each part, which an exact correspondent recurrence of accent and sound are calculated to excite. The final definition then, so deduced, may be thus worded. A poem is that species of composition, which is opposed to works of science, by proposing for its *immediate* object pleasure, not truth; and from all other species (having *this* object in common with it) it is discriminated by proposing to itself such delight from the *whole*, as is compatible with a distinct gratification from each component *part*.

Controversy is not seldom excited in consequence of the disputants attaching each a different meaning to the same word; and in few instances has this been more striking, than in disputes concerning the present subject. If a man chooses to call every composition a poem, which is rhyme, or measure, or both, I must leave his opinion uncontroverted. The distinction is at least competent to characterize the writer's intention. If it were subjoined, that the whole is likewise entertaining or affecting, as a tale, or as a series of interesting reflections, I of course admit this as another fit ingredient of a poem, and an additional merit. But if the definition sought for be that of

a *legitimate* poem, I answer, it must be one, the parts of which mutually support and explain each other; all in their proportion harmonizing with, and supporting the purpose and known influences of metrical arrangement. The philosophic critics of all ages coincide with the ultimate judgement of all countries, in equally denying the praises of a just poem, on the one hand, to a series of striking lines or distiches, each of which, absorbing the whole attention of the reader to itself, disjoins it from its context, and makes it a separate whole, instead of an harmonizing part; and on the other hand, to an unsustained composition, from which the reader collects rapidly the general result, unattracted by the component parts. The reader should be carried forward, not merely or chiefly by the mechanical impulse of curiosity, or by a restless desire to arrive at the final solution; but by the pleasureable activity of mind excited by the attractions of the journey itself. Like the motion of a serpent, which the Egyptians made the emblem of intellectual power; or like the path of sound through the air; at every step he pauses and half recedes, and from the retrogressive movement collects the force which again carries him onward. "Praecipitandus est *liber* spiritus," says Petronius Arbiter most happily. The epithet, *liber*, here balances the preceding verb; and it is not easy to conceive more meaning condensed in fewer words.

But if this should be admitted as a satisfactory character of a poem, we have still to seek for a definition of poetry. The writings of Plato, and Bishop Taylor, and the "Theoria Sacra" of Burnet, furnish undeniable proofs that poetry of the highest kind may exist without metre, and even without the contra-distinguishing objects of a poem. The first chapter of Isaiah (indeed a very large portion of the whole book) is poetry in the most emphatic sense; yet it would be not less irrational than strange to assert, that pleasure, and not truth, was the immediate object of the prophet. In short, whatever *specific* import we attach to the word, poetry, there will be found involved in it, as a necessary consequence, that a poem of any length neither can be, or ought to be, all poetry. Yet if an harmonious whole is to be produced, the remaining parts must be preserved *in keeping* with the poetry; and this can be no otherwise effected than by such a studied selection and artificial arrangement, as will partake of *one*, though not a *peculiar* property of poetry. And this again can be no other than the property of exciting a more continuous and equal attention than the language of prose aims at, whether colloquial or written.

My own conclusions on the nature of poetry, in the strictest use of the word, have been in part anticipated in the preceding disquisition on the fancy and imagination. What is poetry? is so nearly the same question with, what is a poet? that the answer to the one is involved in the solution of the other. For it is a distinction resulting from the poetic genius itself, which sustains and modifies the images, thoughts, and emotions of the poet's own mind.

The poet, described in *ideal* perfection, brings the whole soul of man into activity, with the subordination of its faculties to each other, according to their relative worth and dignity. He diffuses a tone and spirit of unity, that blends, and (as it were) *fuses*, each into each, by that synthetic and magical power, to which we have exclusively appropriated the name of imagination. This power, first put in action by the will and understanding, and retained under their irremissive, though gentle and unnoticed, controul (*laxis effertur habenis*)[2] reveals

2 "Is carried along with loose reins."

itself in the balance or reconciliation of opposite or discordant qualities: of sameness, with difference; of the general, with the concrete; the idea, with the image; the individual, with the representative; the sense of novelty and freshness, with old and familiar objects; a more than usual state of emotion, with more than usual order; judgement ever awake and steady self-possession, with enthusiasm and feeling profound or vehement; and while it blends and harmonizes the natural and the artificial, still subordinates art to nature: the manner to the matter; and our admiration of the poet to our sympathy with the poetry. "Doubtless," as Sir John Davies observes of the soul (and his words may with slight alteration be applied, and even more appropriately, to the poetic IMAGINATION)

Doubtless this could not be, but that she turns
  Bodies to spirit by sublimation strange,
As fire converts to fire the things it burns,
  As we our food into our nature change.

From their gross matter she abstracts their
    forms,
  And draws a kind of quintessence from
    things;
Which to her proper nature she transforms,
  To bear them light on her celestial wings.

Thus does she, when from individual states
  She doth abstract the universal kinds;
Which then re-clothed in divers names and
    fates
  Steal access through our senses to our minds.

Finally, GOOD SENSE is the BODY of poetic genius, FANCY its DRAPERY, MOTION its LIFE, and IMAGINATION the SOUL that is everywhere, and in each; and forms all into one graceful and intelligent whole.

On Poesy or Art (1818)

Man communicates by articulation of sounds, and paramountly by the memory

This essay, first published after Coleridge's death in his *Literary Remains*, is in actuality the notes for a lecture given by Coleridge in 1818. It contains certain parallels (probably outright borrowings) to the work of Friedrich Wilhelm von Schelling, one of the German philosophers in whom the mature Coleridge found so many congenial likenesses to his own aesthetic and philosophical thought.

in the ear; nature by the impression of bounds and surfaces on the eye, and through the eye it gives significance and appropriation, and thus the conditions of memory, or the capability of being remembered, to sounds, smells, &c. Now Art, used collectively for painting, sculpture, architecture and music, is the mediatress between, and reconciler of, nature and man. It is, therefore, the power of humanizing nature, of infusing the thoughts and passions of man into everything which is the object of his contemplation; color, form, motion, and sound, are the elements which it combines, and it stamps them into unity in the mould of a moral idea.

The primary art is writing;—primary, if we regard the purpose abstracted from the different modes of realizing it, those steps of progression of which the instances are still visible in the lower degrees of civilization. First, there is mere gesticulation; then rosaries or *wampum*; then picture-language; then, hieroglyphics, and finally alphabetic letters. These all consist of a translation of man into nature, of a substitution of the visible for the audible.

The so called music of savage tribes as little deserves the name of art for the understanding, as the ear warrants it for music. Its lowest state is a mere expression of passion by the sounds which the passion itself necessitates;—the highest amounts to no more than a voluntary reproduction of these sounds in the absence of the occasioning causes, so as to give the pleasure of contrast,—for example, by the various outcries of battle in the song of security and triumph. Poetry also is purely human; for all its materials are from the mind, and all its products are for the mind. But it is the apotheosis of the former state, in which by excitement of the associative power passion itself imitates order, and the order resulting produces a pleasureable passion, and thus it elevates the mind by making its feelings the object of its reflexion. So likewise, whilst it recalls the sights and sounds that had accompanied the occasions of the original passions, poetry impregnates them with an interest not their own by means of the passions, and yet tempers the passion by the calming power which all distinct images exert on the human soul. In this way poetry is the preparation for art, inasmuch as it avails itself of the forms of nature to recall, to express, and to modify the thoughts and feelings of the mind. Still, however, poetry can only act through the intervention of articulate speech, which is so peculiarly human, that in all languages it constitutes the ordinary phrase by which man and nature are contradistinguished. It is the original force of the word "brute," and even "mute" and "dumb" do not convey the absence of sound, but the absence of articulated sounds.

As soon as the human mind is intelligibly addressed by an outward image exclusively of articulate speech, so soon does art commence. But please to observe that I have laid particular stress on the words "human mind,"—meaning to exclude thereby all results common to man and all other sentient creatures, and consequently confining myself to the effect produced by the congruity of the animal impression with the reflective powers of the mind; so that not the thing presented, but that which is re-presented by the thing, shall be the source of the pleasure. In this sense nature itself is to a religious observer the art of God; and for the same cause art itself might be defined as of a middle quality between a thought and a thing, or, as I said before, the union and reconciliation of that which is nature with that which is exclusively human. It is the figured language of thought, and is distinguished from nature by the unity of all the parts in one thought or idea. Hence nature itself would give us the impression of a work of art, if we could see the thought which is present at once in the whole and every part; and a work of art will be just in proportion as it adequately conveys the thought, and rich in proportion to the variety of parts which it holds in unity.

If, therefore, the term "mute" be taken as opposed not to sound but to articulate speech, the old definition of painting will in fact be the true and best definition of the Fine Arts in general, that is, *muta poesis*, mute poesy, and so of course poesy. And, as all languages perfect themselves by a gradual process of desynonymizing words originally equivalent, I have cherished the wish to use the word "poesy" as the generic or common term, and to distinguish that species of poesy which is not *muta poesis* by its usual name "poetry"; while of all the other species which collectively form the Fine Arts, there would remain this as the common definition,—that they all, like poetry, are to express intellectual purposes, thoughts, conceptions, and sentiments which have their origin in the human mind,—not, however, as poetry does, by means of articulate speech, but as nature or the divine art does, by form, color, magnitude, proportion, or by sound, that is, silently or musically.

Well! it may be said—but who has ever thought otherwise? We all know that art is the imitatress of nature. And, doubtless, the truths which I hope to convey would be barren truisms, if all men meant the same by the words "imitate" and "nature." But it would be flattering mankind at large, to presume that such is the fact. First, to imitate. The impression on the wax is not an imitation, but a copy, of the seal; the seal itself is an imitation. But, further, in order to form a philosophic conception, we must seek for the kind, as the heat in ice, invisible light, &c., whilst, for practical purposes, we must have reference to the degree. It is sufficient that philosophically we understand that in all imitation two elements must coexist, and not only coexist, but must be perceived as coexisting. These two constituent elements are likeness and unlikeness, or sameness and difference, and in all genuine creations of art there must be a union of these disparates. The artist may take his point of view where he pleases, provided that the desired effect be perceptibly produced,—that there be likeness in the difference, difference in the likeness, and a reconcilement of both in one. If there be likeness to nature without any check of difference, the result is disgusting, and the more complete the delusion, the more loathsome the effect. Why are such simulations of nature, as wax-work figures of men and women, so disagreeable? Because, not finding the motion and the life which we expected, we are shocked as by a falsehood, every circumstance of detail, which before induced us to be interested, making the distance from truth more palpable. You

set out with a supposed reality and are disappointed and disgusted with the deception; whilst, in respect to a work of genuine imitation, you begin with an acknowledged total difference, and then every touch of nature gives you the pleasure of an approximation to truth. The fundamental principle of all this is undoubtedly the horror of falsehood and the love of truth inherent in the human breast. The Greek tragic dance rested on these principles, and I can deeply sympathize in imagination with the Greeks in this favorite part of their theatrical exhibitions, when I call to mind the pleasure I felt in beholding the combat of the Horatii and Curiatii most exquisitely danced in Italy to the music of Cimarosa.

Secondly, as to nature. We must imitate nature! yes, but what in nature,— all and every thing? No, the beautiful in nature. And what then is the beautiful? What is beauty? It is, in the abstract, the unity of the manifold, the coalescence of the diverse; in the concrete, it is the union of the shapely (*formosum*) with the vital. In the dead organic it depends on regularity of form, the first and lowest species of which is the triangle with all its modifications, as in crystals, architecture, &c.; in the living organic it is not mere regularity of form, which would produce a sense of formality; neither is it subservient to any thing beside itself. It may be present in a disagreeable object, in which the proportion of the parts constitutes a whole; it does not arise from association, as the agreeable does, but sometimes lies in the rupture of association; it is not different to different individuals and nations, as has been said, nor is it connected with the ideas of the good, or the fit, or the useful. The sense of beauty is intuitive, and beauty itself is all that inspires pleasure without, and aloof from, and even contrarily to, interest.

If the artist copies the mere nature, the *natura naturata*, what idle rivalry! If he proceeds only from a given form, which is supposed to answer to the notion of beauty, what an emptiness, what an unreality there always is in his productions, as in Cipriani's pictures! Believe me, you must master the essence, the *natura naturans*, which presupposes a bond between nature in the higher sense and the soul of man.

The wisdom in nature is distinguished from that in man by the co-instantaneity of the plan and the execution; the thought and the product are one, or are given at once; but there is no reflex act, and hence there is no moral responsibility. In man there is reflexion, freedom, and choice; he is, therefore, the head of the visible creation. In the objects of nature are presented, as in a mirror, all the possible elements, steps, and processes of intellect antecedent to consciousness, and therefore to the full development of the intelligential act; and man's mind is the very focus of all the rays of intellect which are scattered throughout the images of nature. Now so to place these images, totalized, and fitted to the limits of the human mind, as to elicit from, and to superinduce upon, the forms themselves the moral reflexions to which they approximate, to make the external internal, the internal external, to make nature thought, and thought nature,—this is the mystery of genius in the Fine Arts. Dare I add that the genius must act on the feeling, that body is but a striving to become mind,—that it is mind in its essence!

In every work of art there is a reconcilement of the external with the internal; the conscious is so impressed on the unconscious as to appear in it; as compare mere letters inscribed on a tomb with figures themselves constituting the tomb. He who combines the two is the man of genius; and for that reason he must partake of both. Hence there is in genius itself an unconscious activity; nay, that is the genius in the man of genius. And this is the true exposition of the rule that the artist must first eloign himself from nature in order to return to her with full effect. Why this? Because if he were to begin by mere painful copying, he would produce masks only, not forms breathing life. He must out of his own mind create forms according to the severe laws of the intellect, in order to

generate in himself that co-ordination of freedom and law, that involution of obedience in the prescript, and of the prescript in the impulse to obey, which assimilates him to nature, and enables him to understand her. He merely absents himself for a season from her, that his own spirit, which has the same ground with nature, may learn her unspoken language in its main radicals, before he approaches to her endless compositions of them. Yes, not to acquire cold notions—lifeless technical rules—but living and life-producing ideas, which shall contain their own evidence, the certainty that they are essentially one with the germinal causes in nature,—his consciousness being the focus and mirror of both,—for this does the artist for a time abandon the external real in order to return to it with a complete sympathy with its internal and actual. For of all we see, hear, feel and touch the substance is and must be in ourselves; and therefore there is no alternative in reason between the dreary (and thank heaven! almost impossible) belief that every thing around us is but a phantom, or that the life which is in us is in them likewise; and that to know is to resemble, when we speak of objects out of ourselves, even as within ourselves to learn is, according to Plato, only to recollect;—the only effective answer to which, that I have been fortunate to meet with, is that which Pope has consecrated for future use in the line—

And coxcombs vanquish Berkeley with a grin! [1]

The artist must imitate that which is within the thing, that which is active through form and figure, and discourses to us by symbols—the *Natur-geist*, or spirit of nature, as we unconsciously imitate those whom we love; for so only can he hope to produce any work truly natural in the object and truly human in the effect. The idea which puts the form together cannot itself be the form. It is above form, and is its essence, the universal in the individual, or the individu-

[1] John Brown, "Essay on Satire, Occasioned by the Death of Mr. Pope," II, 224.

ality itself,—the glance and the exponent of the indwelling power.

Each thing that lives has its moment of self-exposition, and so has each period of each thing, if we remove the disturbing forces of accident. To do this is the business of ideal art, whether in images of childhood, youth, or age, in man or in woman. Hence a good portrait is the abstract of the personal; it is not the likeness for actual comparison, but for recollection. This explains why the likeness of a very good portrait is not always recognized; because some persons never abstract, and amongst these are especially to be numbered the near relations and friends of the subject, in consequence of the constant pressure and check exercised on their minds by the actual presence of the original. And each thing that only appears to live has also its possible position of relation to life, as nature herself testifies, who where she cannot be, prophesies her being in the crystallized metal, or the inhaling plant.

The charm, the indispensable requisite, of sculpture is the unity of effect. But painting rests in a material remoter from nature, and its compass is therefore greater. Light and shade give external, as well as internal, being even with all its accidents, whilst sculpture is confined to the latter. And here I may observe that the subjects chosen for works of art, whether in sculpture or painting, should be such as really are capable of being expressed and conveyed within the limits of those arts. Moreover they ought to be such as will affect the spectator by their truth, their beauty, or their sublimity, and therefore they may be addressed to the judgement, the senses, or the reason. The peculiarity of the impression which they may make, may be derived either from color and form, or from proportion and fitness, or from the excitement of the moral feelings; or all these may be combined. Such works as do combine these sources of effect must have the preference in dignity.

Imitation of the antique may be too exclusive, and may produce an injurious effect on modern sculpture;—1st, generally, because such an imitation cannot fail to have a tendency to keep the attention fixed on externals rather than on the thought within;—2ndly, because, accordingly, it leads the artist to rest satisfied with that which is always imperfect, namely, bodily form, and circumscribes his views of mental expression to the ideas of power and grandeur only;—3rdly, because it induces an effort to combine together two incongruous things, that is to say, modern feelings in antique forms;—4thly, because it speaks in a language, as it were, learned and dead, the tones of which, being unfamiliar, leave the common spectator cold and unimpressed;—and lastly, because it necessarily causes a neglect of thoughts, emotions and images of profounder interest and more exalted dignity, as motherly, sisterly, and brotherly love, piety, devotion, the divine become human,—the Virgin, the Apostle, the Christ. The artist's principle in the statue of a great man should be the illustration of departed merit; and I cannot but think that a skilful adoption of modern habiliments would, in many instances, give a variety and force of effect which a bigoted adherence to Greek or Roman costume precludes. It is, I believe, from artists finding Greek models unfit for several important modern purposes, that we see so many allegorical figures on monuments and elsewhere. Painting was, as it were, a new art, and being unshackled by old models it chose its own subjects, and took an eagle's flight. And a new field seems opened for modern sculpture in the symbolical expression of the ends of life, as in Guy's monument, Chantrey's children in Worcester Cathedral, &c.

Architecture exhibits the greatest extent of the difference from nature which may exist in works of art. It involves all the powers of design, and is sculpture and painting inclusively. It shews the greatness of man, and should at the same time teach him humility.

Music is the most entirely human of the fine arts, and has the fewest *analoga* in nature. Its first delightfulness is simple accordance with the ear; but it is an associated thing, and recalls the deep emotions of the past with an intellectual sense of proportion. Every human feeling is greater and larger than the exciting cause,—a proof, I think, that man is designed for a higher state of existence; and this is deeply implied in music, in which there is always something more and beyond the immediate impression.

With regard to works in all the branches of the fine arts, I may remark that the pleasure arising from novelty must of course be allowed its due place and weight. This pleasure consists in the identity of two opposite elements, that is to say—sameness and variety. If in the midst of the variety there be not some fixed object for the attention, the unceasing succession of the variety will prevent the mind from observing the difference of the individual objects; and the only thing remaining will be the succession, which will then produce precisely the same effect as sameness. This we experience when we let the trees or hedges pass before the fixed eye during a rapid movement in a carriage, or, on the other hand, when we suffer a file of soldiers or ranks of men in procession to go on before us without resting the eye on any one in particular. In order to derive pleasure from the occupation of the mind, the principle of unity must always be present, so that in the midst of the multeity the centripetal force be never suspended, nor the sense be fatigued by the predominance of the centrifugal force. This unity in multeity I have elsewhere stated as the principle of beauty. It is equally the source of pleasure in variety, and in fact a higher term including both. What is the seclusive or distinguishing term between them?

Remember that there is a difference between form as proceeding, and shape as superinduced;—the latter is either the death or the imprisonment of the thing; —the former is its self-witnessing and self-effected sphere of agency. Art would or should be the abridgment of nature. Now the fulness of nature is without character, as water is purest when without taste, smell, or color; but this is the highest, the apex only,—it is not the whole. The object of art is to give the whole *ad hominem*; hence each step of nature hath its ideal, and hence the possibility of a climax up to the perfect form of a harmonized chaos.

To the idea of life victory or strife is necessary; as virtue consists not simply in the absence of vices, but in the overcoming of them. So it is in beauty. The sight of what is subordinated and conquered heightens the strength and the pleasure; and this should be exhibited by the artist either inclusively in his figure, or else out of it, and beside it to act by way of supplement and contrast. And with a view to this, remark the seeming identity of body and mind in infants, and thence the loveliness of the former; the commencing separation in boyhood, and the struggle of equilibrium in youth: thence onward the body is first simply indifferent; then demanding the translucency of the mind not to be worse than indifferent; and finally all that presents the body as body becoming almost of an excremental nature.

RALPH WALDO EMERSON

(1803-1882)

The prophet of American transcendentalism, Emerson first formulated his optimistic idealistic philosophy in *Nature* (1836), and his later collections of essays—First and Second series (1841, 1844), *Representative Men* (1850), and subsequent volumes— present further extensions and applications of his established point of view, with but slight modification. Emerson's symbolic theory of expression, based on his romantic idealism, is sketched forth in the brief chapters on "Beauty" and "Language" in *Nature*. The most concentrated and detailed statement of his literary theory is given in the essay "The Poet" (1844), to which Walt Whitman owed an obvious debt. Emerson's conception of the creative imagination and his ideas of organic form are, like those of the English romantics, Coleridge and Wordsworth, extremely relevant to modern critical theory.

From *Nature* (1836)

III. BEAUTY

A nobler want of man is served by nature, namely, the love of Beauty.

The ancient Greeks called the world κόσμος, beauty. Such is the constitution of all things, or such the plastic power of the human eye, that the primary forms, as the sky, the mountain, the tree, the animal, give us a delight *in and for themselves*; a pleasure arising from outline, color, motion, and grouping. This seems partly owing to the eye itself. The eye is the best of artists. By the mutual action of its structure and of the laws of light, perspective is produced, which integrates every mass of objects, of what character soever, into a well colored and shaded globe, so that where the particular objects are mean and unaffecting, the landscape which they compose is round and symmetrical. And as the eye is the best composer, so light is the first of painters. There is no object so foul that intense light will not make beautiful. And the stimulus it affords to the sense, and a sort of infinitude which it hath, like space and time, make all matter gay. Even the corpse has its own beauty. But besides this general grace diffused over nature, almost all the individual forms are agreeable to the eye, as is proved by our endless imitations of some of them, as the acorn, the grape, the pine-cone, the wheat-ear, the egg, the wings and forms of most birds, the lion's claw, the serpent, the butterfly, sea-shells, flames, clouds, buds, leaves, and the forms of many trees, as the palm.

For better consideration, we may distribute the aspects of Beauty in a threefold manner.

1. First, the simple perception of natural forms is a delight. The influence of the forms and actions in nature is so needful to man, that, in its lowest functions, it seems to lie on the confines of commodity and beauty. To the body and mind which have been cramped by noxious work or company, nature is medicinal and restores their tone. The tradesman, the attorney comes out of the din and craft of the street and sees the sky and the woods, and is a man again. In their eternal calm, he finds himself. The health of the eye seems to demand a horizon. We are never tired, so long as we can see far enough.

But in other hours, Nature satisfies by its loveliness, and without any mixture of corporeal benefit. I see the spectacle of morning from the hilltop over against my house, from daybreak to sunrise, with emotions which an angel might share. The long slender bars of cloud float like fishes in the sea of crimson light. From the earth, as a shore, I look out into that silent sea. I seem to partake its rapid transformations; the active enchantment reaches my dust, and I dilate and conspire with the morning wind. How does Nature deify us with a few and cheap elements! Give me health and a day, and I will make the pomp of emperors ridiculous. The dawn is my Assyria; the sunset and moonrise my Paphos, and unimaginable realms of faerie; broad noon shall be my England of the senses and the understanding; the night shall be my Germany of mystic philosophy and dreams.

Not less excellent, except for our less susceptibility in the afternoon, was the charm, last evening, of a January sunset.

The western clouds divided and subdivided themselves into pink flakes modulated with tints of unspeakable softness, and the air had so much life and sweetness that it was a pain to come within doors. What was it that nature would say? Was there no meaning in the live repose of the valley behind the mill, and which Homer or Shakspeare could not re-form for me in words? The leafless trees become spires of flame in the sunset, with the blue east for their background, and the stars of the dead calices of flowers, and every withered stem and stubble rimed with frost, contribute something to the mute music.

The inhabitants of cities suppose that the country landscape is pleasant only half the year. I please myself with the graces of the winter scenery, and believe that we are as much touched by it as by the genial influences of summer. To the attentive eye, each moment of the year has its own beauty, and in the same field, it beholds, every hour, a picture which was never seen before, and which shall never be seen again. The heavens change every moment, and reflect their glory or gloom on the plains beneath. The state of the crop in the surrounding farms alters the expression of the earth from week to week. The succession of native plants in the pastures and roadsides, which makes the silent clock by which time tells the summer hours, will make even the divisions of the day sensible to a keen observer. The tribes of birds and insects, like the plants punctual to their time, follow each other, and the year has room for all. By watercourses, the variety is greater. In July, the blue pontederia or pickerel-weed blooms in large beds in the shallow parts of our pleasant river, and swarms with yellow butterflies in continual motion. Art cannot rival this pomp of purple and gold. Indeed the river is a perpetual gala, and boasts each month a new ornament.

But this beauty of Nature which is seen and felt as beauty, is the least part. The shows of day, the dewy morning, the rainbow, mountains, orchards in blossom, stars, moonlight, shadows in still water, and the like, if too eagerly hunted, become shows merely, and mock us with their unreality. Go out of the house to see the moon, and 'tis mere tinsel; it will not please as when its light shines upon your necessary journey. The beauty that shimmers in the yellow afternoons of October, who ever could clutch it? Go forth to find it, and it is gone; 'tis only a mirage as you look from the windows of diligence.

2. The presence of a higher, namely, of the spiritual element is essential to its perfection. The high and divine beauty which can be loved without effeminacy, is that which is found in combination with the human will. Beauty is the mark God sets upon virtue. Every natural action is graceful. Every heroic act is also decent, and causes the place and the bystanders to shine. We are taught by great actions that the universe is the property of every individual in it. Every rational creature has all nature for his dowry and estate. It is his, if he will. He may divest himself of it; he may creep into a corner, and abdicate his kingdom, as most men do, but he is entitled to the world by his constitution. In proportion to the energy of his thought and will, he takes up the world into himself. "All those things for which men plough, build, or sail, obey virtue;" said Sallust. "The winds and waves," said Gibbon, "are always on the side of the ablest navigators." So are the sun and moon and all the stars of heaven. When a noble act is done,—perchance in a scene of great natural beauty; when Leonidas and his three hundred martyrs consume one day in dying, and the sun and moon come each and look at them once in the steep defile of Thermopylae; when Arnold Winkelried, in the high Alps, under the shadow of the avalanche, gathers in his side a sheaf of Austrian spears to break the line for his comrades; are not these heroes entitled to add the beauty of the scene to the beauty of the deed? When the bark of Columbus nears the shore of America;—before it the beach lined with savages, fleeing out of all their huts of cane; the sea behind; and the purple mountains of the Indian Archipelago around, can we separate the man from the living picture? Does not the New World clothe his form with her

Theory

palm-groves and savannahs as fit drapery? Ever does natural beauty steal in like air, and envelope great actions. When Sir Harry Vane was dragged up the Tower-hill, sitting on a sled, to suffer death as the champion of the English laws, one of the multitude cried out to him, "You never sate on so glorious a seat!" Charles II., to intimidate the citizens of London, caused the patriot Lord Russell to be drawn in an open coach through the principal streets of the city on his way to the scaffold. "But," his biographer says, "the multitude imagined they saw liberty and virtue sitting by his side." In private places, among sordid objects, an act of truth or heroism seems at once to draw to itself the sky as its temple, the sun as its candle. Nature stretches out her arms to embrace man, only let his thoughts be of equal greatness. Willingly does she follow his steps with the rose and the violet, and bend her lines of grandeur and grace to the decoration of her darling child. Only let his thoughts be of equal scope, and the frame will suit the picture. A virtuous man is in unison with her works, and makes the central figure of the visible sphere. Homer, Pindar, Socrates, Phocion, associate themselves fitly in our memory with the geography and climate of Greece. The visible heavens and earth sympathize with Jesus. And in common life whosoever has seen a person of powerful character and happy genius, will have remarked how easily he took all things along with him,—the persons, the opinions, and the day, and nature became ancillary to a man.

3. There is still another aspect under which the beauty of the world may be viewed, namely, as it becomes an object of the intellect. Beside the relation of things to virtue, they have a relation to thought. The intellect searches out the absolute order of things as they stand in the mind of God, and without the colors of affection. The intellectual and the active powers seem to succeed each other, and the exclusive activity of the one generates the exclusive activity of the other. There is something unfriendly in each to the other, but they are like the alternate periods of feeding and working in animals; each prepares and will be followed by the other. Therefore does beauty, which, in relation to actions, as we have seen, comes unsought, and comes because it is unsought, remain for the apprehension and pursuit of the intellect; and then again, in its turn, of the active power. Nothing divine dies. All good is eternally reproductive. The beauty of nature re-forms itself in the mind, and not for barren contemplation, but for new creation.

All men are in some degree impressed by the face of the world; some men even to delight. This love of beauty is Taste. Others have the same love in such excess, that, not content with admiring, they seek to embody it in new forms. The creation of beauty is Art.

The production of a work of art throws a light upon the mystery of humanity. A work of art is an abstract or epitome of the world. It is the result or expression of nature, in miniature. For although the works of nature are innumerable and all different, the result or the expression of them all is similar and single. Nature is a sea of forms radically alike and even unique. A leaf, a sunbeam, a landscape, the ocean, make an analogous impression on the mind. What is common to them all,—that perfectness and harmony, is beauty. The standard of beauty is the entire circuit of natural forms,—the totality of nature; which the Italians expressed by defining beauty "il più nell' uno." Nothing is quite beautiful alone; nothing but is beautiful in the whole. A single object is only so far beautiful as it suggests this universal grace. The poet, the painter, the sculptor, the musician, the architect, seek each to concentrate this radiance of the world on one point, and each in his several work to satisfy the love of beauty which stimulates him to produce. Thus is Art a nature passed through the alembic of man. Thus in art does Nature work through the will of a man filled with the beauty of her first works.

The world thus exists to the soul to satisfy the desire of beauty. This element I call an ultimate end. No reason can be asked or given why the soul seeks beauty. Beauty, in its largest and profoundest sense, is one expression for the universe. God is the all-fair. Truth, and goodness, and beauty, are but different faces of the same All. But beauty in nature is not ultimate. It is the herald of inward and eternal beauty, and is not alone a solid and satisfactory good. It must stand as a part, and not as yet the last or highest expression of the final cause of Nature.

IV. LANGUAGE

Language is a third use which Nature subserves to man. Nature is the vehicle of thought, and in a simple, double, and threefold degree.

1. Words are signs of natural facts.
2. Particular natural facts are symbols of particular spiritual facts.
3. Nature is the symbol of spirit.

1. Words are signs of natural facts. The use of natural history is to give us aid in supernatural history; the use of the outer creation, to give us language for the beings and changes of the inward creation. Every word which is used to express a moral or intellectual fact, if traced to its root, is found to be borrowed from some material appearance. *Right* means *straight*; *wrong* means *twisted*. *Spirit* primarily means *wind*; *transgression*, the crossing of a *line*; *supercilious*, the *raising of the eyebrow*. We say the *heart* to express emotion, the *head* to denote thought; and *thought* and *emotion* are words borrowed from sensible things, and now appropriated to spiritual nature. Most of the process by which this transformation is made, is hidden from us in the remote time when language was framed; but the same tendency may be daily observed in children. Children and savages use only nouns or names of things, which they convert into verbs, and apply to analogous mental acts.

2. But this origin of all words that convey a spiritual import,—so conspicuous a fact in the history of language, —is our least debt to nature. It is not words only that are emblematic; it is things which are emblematic. Every natural fact is a symbol of some spiritual fact. Every appearance in nature corresponds to some state of the mind, and that state of the mind can only be described by presenting that natural appearance as its picture. An enraged man is a lion, a cunning man is a fox, a firm man is a rock, a learned man is a torch. A lamb is innocence; a snake is subtle spite; flowers express to us the delicate affections. Light and darkness are our familar expression for knowledge and ignorance; and heat for love. Visible distance behind and before us, is respectively our image of memory and hope.

Who looks upon a river in a meditative hour and is not reminded of the flux of all things? Throw a stone into the stream, and the circles that propagate themselves are the beautiful type of all influence. Man is conscious of a universal soul within or behind his individual life, wherein, as in a firmament, the natures of Justice, Truth, Love, Freedom, arise and shine. This universal soul he calls Reason: it is not mine, or thine, or his, but we are its; we are its property and men. And the blue sky in which the private earth is buried, the sky with its eternal calm, and full of everlasting orbs, is the type of Reason. That which intellectually considered we call Reason, considered in relation to nature, we call Spirit. Spirit is the Creator. Spirit hath life in itself. And man in all ages and countries embodies it in his language as the FATHER.

It is easily seen that there is nothing lucky or capricious in these analogies, but that they are constant, and pervade nature. These are not the dreams of a few poets, here and there, but man is an analogist, and studies relations in all objects. He is placed in the centre of beings, and a ray of relation passes from every other being to him. And neither can man be understood without these objects, nor these objects without man. All the facts in natural history taken by themselves, have no value, but are barren, like a single sex. But marry it to human history, and it is full of life. Whole floras, all Linnaeus' and Buffon's volumes, are dry catalogues of facts; but the most trivial of these facts, the habit of a plant, the organs, or work, or noise of an insect, applied to the illustration of a fact in intellectual philosophy, or in any way associated to human nature, affects us in the most lively and agreeable manner. The seed of a plant,—to what affecting analogies in the nature of man is that little fruit made use of, in all discourse, up to the voice of Paul, who calls the human corpse a seed,—"It is sown a natural body; it is raised a spiritual body." The motion of the earth round its axis and round the sun, makes the day and the year. These are certain amounts of brute light and heat. But is there no intent of an analogy between man's life and the seasons? And do the seasons gain no grandeur or pathos from that analogy? The instincts of the ant are very unimportant considered as the ant's; but the moment a ray of relation is seen to extend from it to man, and the little drudge is seen to be a monitor, a little body with a mighty heart, then all its habits, even that said to be recently observed, that it never sleeps, become sublime.

Because of this radical correspondence between visible things and human thoughts, savages, who have only what is necessary, converse in figures. As we go back in history, language becomes more picturesque, until its infancy, when it is all poetry; or all spiritual facts are represented by natural symbols. The same symbols are found to make the original elements of all languages. It has moreover been observed, that the idioms of all languages approach each other in passages of the greatest eloquence and power. And as this is the first language, so is it the last. This immediate dependence of language upon nature, this conversion of an outward phenomenon into a type of somewhat in human life, never loses its power to affect us. It is this which gives that piquancy to the conversation of a strong-natured farmer or backwoodsman, which all men relish.

A man's power to connect his thought with its proper symbol, and so to utter it, depends on the simplicity of his character, that is, upon his love of truth and his desire to communicate it without loss. The corruption of man is followed by the corruption of language. When simplicity of character and the sovereignty of ideas is broken up by the prevalence of secondary desires,—the desire of riches, of pleasure, of power, and of praise,—and duplicity and falsehood take place of simplicity and truth, the power over nature as an interpreter of the will is in a degree lost; new imagery ceases to be created, and old words are perverted to stand for things which are not; a paper currency is employed, when there is no bullion in the vaults. In due time the fraud is manifest, and words lose all power to stimulate the understanding or the affections. Hundreds of writers may be found in every long-civilized nation who for a short time believe and make others believe that they see and utter truths, who do not of themselves clothe one thought in its natural garment, but who feed unconsciously on the language created by the primary writers of the country, those, namely, who hold primarily on nature.

But wise men pierce this rotten diction and fasten words again to visible things; so that picturesque language is at once a commanding certificate that he who employs it is a man in alliance with truth and God. The moment our discourse rises above the ground line of familiar facts and is inflamed with passion or exalted by thought, it clothes itself in images. A man conversing in earnest, if he watch his intellectual processes, will find that a material image more or less luminous arises in his mind, contemporaneous with every thought, which furnishes the vestment of the thought. Hence, good writing and brilliant discourse are perpetual allegories. This imagery is spontaneous. It is the blending of experience with the present action of the mind. It is proper creation. It is the working of the Original Cause through the instruments he has already made.

These facts may suggest the advantage which the country-life possesses, for a powerful mind, over the artificial and curtailed life of cities. We know more from nature than we can at will communicate. Its light flows into the mind evermore, and we forget its presence. The poet, the orator, bred in the woods, whose senses have been nourished by their fair and appeasing changes, year after year, without design and without heed,—shall not lose their lesson altogether, in the roar of cities or the broil of politics. Long hereafter, amidst agitation and terror in national councils,—in the hour of revolution,—these solemn images shall reappear in their morning lustre, as fit symbols and words of the thoughts which the passing events shall awaken. At the call of a noble sentiment, again the woods wave, the pines murmur, the river rolls and shines, and the cattle low upon the mountains, as he saw and heard them in his infancy. And with these forms, the spells of persuasion, the keys of power are put into his hands.

3. We are thus assisted by natural objects in the expression of particular meanings. But how great a language to convey such pepper-corn informations! Did it need such noble races of creatures, this profusion of forms, this host of orbs in heaven, to furnish man with the dictionary and grammar of his municipal speech? Whilst we use this grand cipher to expedite the affairs of our pot and kettle, we feel that we have not yet put it to its use, neither are able. We are like travellers using the cinders of a volcano to roast their eggs. Whilst we see that it always stands ready to clothe what we would say, we cannot avoid the question whether the characters are not significant of themselves. Have mountains, and waves, and skies, no significance but what we consciously give them when we employ them as emblems of our thoughts? The world is emblematic. Parts of speech are metaphors, because the whole of nature is a metaphor of the human mind. The laws of moral nature answer to those of matter as face to face in a glass. "The visible world and the relation of its parts, is the dial plate of the invisible." The axioms of physics translate the laws of ethics. Thus, "the whole is greater than its parts;" "reaction is equal to action;" "the smallest weight may be made to lift the greatest, the difference of weight being compensated by time;" and many the like propositions, which have an ethical as well as physical sense. These propositions have a much more extensive and universal sense when applied to human life, than when confined to technical use.

In like manner, the memorable words of history and the proverbs of nations consist usually of a natural fact, selected as a picture or parable of a moral truth. Thus; A rolling stone gathers no moss; A bird in the hand is worth two in the bush; A cripple in the right way will beat a racer in the wrong; Make hay while the sun shines; 'Tis hard to carry a full cup even; Vinegar is the son of wine; The last ounce broke the camel's back; Long-lived trees make roots first; —and the like. In their primary sense these are trivial facts, but we repeat them for the value of their analogical import. What is true of proverbs, is true of all fables, parables, and allegories.

This relation between the mind and matter is not fancied by some poet, but stands in the will of God, and so is free to be known by all men. It appears to men, or it does not appear. When in fortunate hours we ponder this miracle, the wise man doubts if at all other times he is not blind and deaf;

> "Can such things be,
> And overcome us like a summer's cloud,
> Without our special wonder?"

for the universe becomes transparent, and the light of higher laws than its own shines through it. It is the standing problem which has exercised the wonder and the study of every fine genius since the world began; from the era of the Egyptians and the Brahmins to that of Pythagoras, of Plato, of Bacon, of Leibnitz, of Swedenborg. There sits the Sphinx at the road-side, and from age to age, as each prophet comes by, he tries his fortune at reading her riddle. There seems to be a necessity in spirit to manifest itself in material forms; and day and night, river and storm, beast and bird, acid and alkali, preëxist in necessary Ideas in the mind of God, and are what they are by virtue of preceding affections in the world of spirit. A Fact is the end or last issue of spirit. The visible creation is the terminus or the circumference of the invisible world. "Material objects," said a French philosopher, "are necessarily kinds of *scoriae* of the substantial thoughts of the Creator, which must always preserve an exact relation to their first origin; in other words, visible nature must have a spiritual and moral side."

This doctrine is abstruse, and though the images of "garment," "scoriae," "mirror," etc., may stimulate the fancy, we must summon the aid of subtler and more vital expositors to make it plain. "Every scripture is to be interpreted by the same spirit which gave it forth,"—is the fundamental law of criticism. A life

in harmony with nature, the love of truth and of virtue, will purge the eyes to understand her text. By degrees we may come to know the primitive sense of the permanent objects of nature, so that the world shall be to us an open book, and every form significant of its hidden life and final cause.

A new interest surprises us, whilst, under the view now suggested, we contemplate the fearful extent and multitude of objects; since "every object rightly seen, unlocks a new faculty of the soul." That which was unconscious truth, becomes, when interpreted and defined in an object, a part of the domain of knowledge,—a new weapon in the magazine of power.

The Poet (1844)

Those who are esteemed umpires of taste are often persons who have acquired some knowledge of admired pictures or sculptures, and have an inclination for whatever is elegant; but if you inquire whether they are beautiful souls, and whether their own acts are like fair pictures, you learn that they are selfish and sensual. Their cultivation is local, as if you should rub a log of dry wood in one spot to produce fire, all the rest remaining cold. Their knowledge of the fine arts is some study of rules and particulars, or some limited judgment of color or form, which is exercised for amusement or for show. It is a proof of the shallowness of the doctrine of beauty as it lies in the minds of our amateurs, that men seem to have lost the perception of the instant dependence of form upon soul. There is no doctrine of forms in our philosophy. We were put into our bodies, as fire is put into a pan to be carried about; but there is no accurate adjustment between the spirit and the organ, much less is the latter the germination of the former. So in regard to other forms, the intellectual men do not believe in any essential dependence of the material world on thought and volition. Theologians think

it a pretty air-castle to talk of the spiritual meaning of a ship or a cloud, of a city or a contract, but they prefer to come again to the solid ground of historical evidence; and even the poets are contented with a civil and conformed manner of living, and to write poems from the fancy, at a safe distance from their own experience. But the highest minds of the world have never ceased to explore the double meaning, or shall I say the quadruple or the centuple or much more manifold meaning, of every sensuous fact; Orpheus, Empedocles, Heraclitus, Plato, Plutarch, Dante, Swedenborg, and the masters of sculpture, picture, and poetry. For we are not pans and barrows, nor even porters of the fire and torch-bearers, but children of the fire, made of it, and only the same divinity transmuted and at two or three removes, when we know least about it. And this hidden truth, that the fountains whence all this river of Time and its creatures floweth are intrinsically ideal and beautiful, draws us to the consideration of the nature and functions of the Poet, or the man of Beauty; to the means and materials he uses, and to the general aspect of the art in the present time.

The breadth of the problem is great, for the poet is representative. He stands among partial men for the complete man, and apprises us not of his wealth, but of the common wealth. The young man reveres men of genius, because, to speak truly, they are more himself than he is. They receive of the soul as he also receives, but they more. Nature enhances her beauty, to the eye of loving men, from their belief that the poet is beholding her shows at the same time. He is isolated among his contemporaries by truth and by his art, but with this consolation in his pursuits, that they will draw all men sooner or later. For all men live by truth and stand in need of expression. In love, in art, in avarice, in politics, in labor, in games, we study to utter our painful secret. The man is only half himself, the other half is his expression.

Notwithstanding this necessity to be published, adequate expression is rare. I know not how it is that we need an interpreter, but the great majority of men seem to be minors, who have not yet come into possession of their own, or mutes, who cannot report the conversation they have had with nature. There is no man who does not anticipate a supersensual utility in the sun and stars, earth and water. These stand and wait to render him a peculiar service. But there is some obstruction or some excess of phlegm in our constitution, which does not suffer them to yield the due effect. Too feeble fall the impressions of nature on us to make us artists. Every touch should thrill. Every man should be so much an artist that he could report in conversation what had befallen him. Yet, in our experience, the rays or appulses have sufficient force to arrive at the senses, but not enough to reach the quick and compel the reproduction of themselves in speech. The poet is the person in whom these powers are in balance, the man without impediment, who sees and handles that which others dream of, traverses the whole scale of experience, and is representative of man, in virtue of being the largest power to receive and to impart.

For the Universe has three children, born at one time, which reappear under different names in every system of thought, whether they be called cause, operation, and effect; or, more poetically, Jove, Pluto, Neptune; or, theologically, the Father, the Spirit, and the Son; but which we will call here the Knower, the Doer, and the Sayer. These stand respectively for the love of truth, for the love of good, and for the love of beauty. These three are equal. Each is that which he is, essentially, so that he cannot be surmounted or analyzed, and each of these three has the power of the others latent in him, and his own, patent.

The poet is the sayer, the namer, and represents beauty. He is a sovereign, and stands on the centre. For the world is not painted or adorned, but is from the beginning beautiful; and God has not made some beautiful things, but Beauty is the creator of the universe. Therefore the poet is not any permissive potentate, but is emperor in his own right. Criticism is infested with a cant of materialism, which assumes that manual skill and activity is the first merit of all men, and disparages such as say and do not, overlooking the fact that some men, namely poets, are natural sayers, sent into the world to the end of expression, and confounds them with those whose province is action but who quit it to imitate the sayers. But Homer's words are as costly and admirable to Homer as Agamemnon's victories are to Agamemnon. The poet does not wait for the hero or the sage, but, as they act and think primarily, so he writes primarily what will and must be spoken, reckoning the others, though primaries also, yet, in respect to him, secondaries and servants; as sitters or models in the studio of a painter, or as assistants who bring building-materials to an architect.

For poetry was all written before time was, and whenever we are so finely organized that we can penetrate into that region where the air is music, we hear those primal warblings and attempt to write them down, but we lose ever and anon a word or a verse and substitute something of our own, and thus miswrite the poem. The men of more delicate ear write down these cadences more faithfully, and these transcripts, though imperfect, become the songs of the nations. For nature is as truly beautiful as it is good, or as it is reasonable, and must as much appear as it must be done, or be known. Words and deeds are quite indifferent modes of the divine energy. Words are also actions, and actions are a kind of words.

The sign and credentials of the poet are that he announces that which no man foretold. He is the true and only doctor; he knows and tells; he is the only teller of news, for he was present and privy to the appearance which he describes. He is a beholder of ideas and an utterer of the necessary and causal. For we do not speak now of men of poetical talents, or of industry and skill in metre, but of the true poet. I took part in a conversation the other day concerning a recent writer of lyrics, a man of subtle mind, whose head appeared to be a music-box of delicate tunes and rhythms, and whose skill and command of language we could not sufficiently praise. But when the question arose whether he was not only a lyrist but a poet, we were obliged to confess that he is plainly a contemporary, not an eternal man. He does not stand out of our low limitations, like a Chimborazo under the line, running up from a torrid base through all the climates of the globe, with belts of the herbage of every latitude on its high and mottled sides; but this genius is the landscape-garden of a modern house, adorned with fountains and statues, with well-bred men and women standing and sitting in the walks and terraces. We hear, through all the varied music, the ground-tone of conventional life. Our poets are men of talents who sing, and not the children of music. The argument is secondary, the finish of the verses is primary.

For it is not metres, but a metre-making argument that makes a poem,— a thought so passionate and alive that like the spirit of a plant or an animal it has an architecture of its own, and adorns nature with a new thing. The thought and the form are equal in the order of time, but in the order of genesis the thought is prior to the form. The poet has a new thought; he has a whole new experience to unfold; he will tell us how it was with him, and all men will be the richer in his fortune. For the experience of each new age requires a new confession, and the world seems always waiting for its poet. I remember when I was young how much I was moved one morning by tidings that genius had appeared in a youth who sat near me at table. He had left his work and gone rambling none knew whither, and had written hundreds of lines, but could not tell whether that which was in him was therein told; he could tell nothing but that all was changed,—man, beast, heaven, earth and sea. How gladly we listened! how credulous! Society seemed to be compromised. We sat in the aurora of a sunrise which was to put out all the stars. Boston seemed to be at twice the distance it had the night before, or was much farther than that. Rome,—what was Rome? Plutarch and Shakspeare were in the yellow leaf, and Homer no more should be heard of. It is much to know that poetry has been written this very day, under this very roof, by your side. What! that wonderful spirit has not expired! These stony moments are still sparkling and animated! I had fancied that the oracles were all silent, and nature had spent her fires; and behold! all night, from every pore, these fine auroras have been streaming. Everyone has some interest in the advent of the poet, and no one knows how much it may concern him. We know that the secret of the world is profound, but who or what shall be our interpreter, we know not. A mountain ramble, a new style of face, a new person, may put the key into our hands. Of course the value of genius to us is in the veracity of its report. Talent may frolic and juggle; genius realizes and adds. Mankind in good earnest have availed so far in understanding themselves and their work, that the foremost watchman on the peak announces his news. It is the truest word ever spoken, and the phrase will be the fittest, most musical, and the unerring voice of the world for that time.

All that we call sacred history attests that the birth of a poet is the principal event in chronology. Man, never so often deceived, still watches for the arrival of a brother who can hold him steady to a truth until he has made it his own. With what joy I begin to read a poem which I confide in as an inspiration! And now my chains are to be broken; I shall mount above these clouds and opaque airs in which I live,—opaque, though they seem transparent,—and from the heaven of truth I shall see and comprehend my relations. That will reconcile me to life and renovate nature, to see trifles animated by a tendency, and to know what I am doing. Life will no more be a noise; now I shall see men and women, and know the signs by which they may be discerned from fools and satans. This day shall be better than my birthday: then I became an animal; now I am invited into the science of the real. Such is the hope, but the fruition is postponed. Oftener it falls that this winged man, who will carry me into the heaven, whirls me into mists, then leaps and frisks about with me as it were from cloud to cloud, still affirming that he is bound heavenward: and I, being myself a novice, am slow in perceiving that he does not know the way into the heavens, and is merely bent that I should admire his skill to rise like a fowl or a flying fish, a little way from the ground or the water; but the all-piercing, all-feeding, and ocular air of heaven that man shall never inhabit. I tumble down again soon into my old nooks, and lead the life of exaggerations as before, and have lost my faith in the possibility of any guide who can lead me thither where I would be.

But, leaving these victims of vanity, let us, with new hope, observe how nature, by worthier impulses, has insured the poet's fidelity to his office of announcement and affirming, namely by the beauty of things, which becomes a new and higher beauty when expressed. Nature offers all her creatures to him as a picture-language. Being used as a type, a second wonderful value appears in the object, far better than its old value; as the carpenter's stretched cord, if you hold your ear close enough, is musical in the breeze. "Things more excellent than every image," says Jamblichus, "are expressed through images." Things admit of being used as symbols because nature is a symbol, in the whole, and in every part. Every line we can draw in the sand has expression; and there is no body without its spirit or genius. All form is an effect of character; all conditions, of the quality of the life; all harmony, of health; and for this reason a perception of beauty should be sympathetic, or proper only to the good. The beautiful rests on the foundations of the necessary. The soul makes the body, as the wise Spenser teaches:—

"So every spirit, as it is more pure,
And hath in it the more of heavenly light,
So it the fairer body doth procure
To habit in, and it more fairly dight,
With cheerful grace and amiable sight.
For, of the soul, the body form doth take,
For soul is form, and doth the body make."

Here we find ourselves suddenly not in a critical speculation but in a holy place, and should go very warily and reverently. We stand before the secret of the world, there where Being passes into Appearance and Unity into Variety.

The Universe is the externization of the soul. Wherever the life is, that bursts into appearance around it. Our science is sensual, and therefore superficial. The earth and the heavenly bodies, physics, and chemistry, we sensually treat, as if they were self-existent; but these are the retinue of that Being we have. "The mighty heaven," said Proclus, "exhibits, in its transfigurations, clear images of the splendor of intellectual perceptions; being moved in conjunction with the unapparent periods of intellectual natures." Therefore science always goes abreast with the just elevation of the man, keeping step with religion and metaphysics; or the state of science is an index of our self-knowledge. Since every thing in nature answers to a moral power, if any phenomenon remains brute and dark it is because the corresponding faculty in the observer is not yet active.

No wonder then, if these waters be so deep, that we hover over them with a religious regard. The beauty of the fable proves the importance of the sense; to the poet, and to all others; or, if you please, every man is so far a poet as to be susceptible of these enchantments of nature; for all men have the thoughts whereof the universe is the celebration. I find that the fascination resides in the symbol. Who loves nature? Who does not? Is it only poets, and men of leisure and cultivation, who live with her? No; but also hunters, farmers, grooms, and butchers, though they express their affection in their choice of life and not in their choice of words. The writer wonders what the coachman or the hunter values in riding, in horses and dogs. It is not superficial qualities. When you talk with him he holds these at as slight a rate as you. His worship is sympathetic; he has no definitions, but he is commanded in nature by the living power which he feels to be there present. No imitation or playing of these things would content him; he loves the earnest of the north wind, of rain, of stone, and wood, and iron. A beauty not explicable is dearer than a beauty which we can see to the end of. It is nature the symbol, nature certifying the supernatural, body overflowed by life which he worships with coarse but sincere rites.

The inwardness and mystery of this attachment drive men of every class to the use of emblems. The schools of poets and philosophers are not more intoxicated with their symbols than the populace with theirs. In our political parties, compute the power of badges and emblems. See the great ball which they roll from Baltimore to Bunker Hill! In the political processions, Lowell goes in a loom, and Lynn in a shoe, and Salem in a ship. Witness the cider-barrel, the log-cabin, the hickory-stick, the palmetto, and all the cognizances of party. See the power of national emblems. Some stars, lilies, leopards, a crescent, a lion, an eagle, or other figure which came into credit God knows how, on an old rag of bunting, blowing in the wind on a fort at the ends of the earth, shall make the blood tingle under the rudest or the most conventional exterior. The people fancy they hate poetry, and they are all poets and mystics!

Beyond this universality of the symbolic language, we are apprised of the divineness of this superior use of things, whereby the world is a temple whose walls are covered with emblems, pictures, and commandments of the Deity,—in this, that there is no fact in nature which does not carry the whole sense of nature; and the distinctions which we make in events and in affairs, of low and high, honest and base, disappear when nature is used as a symbol. Thought makes everything fit for use. The vocabulary of an omniscient man would embrace words and images excluded from polite conversation. What would be base, or even obscene, to the obscene, becomes illustrious, spoken in a new connection of thought. The piety of the Hebrew prophets purges their grossness. The circumcision is an example of the power of poetry to raise the low and offensive. Small and mean things serve as well as great symbols. The meaner the type by which a law is expressed, the more pungent it is, and the more lasting in the memories of men; just as we choose the smallest box or case in which any needful utensil can be carried. Bare lists of words are found suggestive to an imaginative and excited mind; as it is related of Lord Chatham that he was accustomed to read in Bailey's Dictionary when he was preparing to speak in Parliament. The poorest experience is rich enough for all the purposes of expressing thought. Why covet a knowledge of new facts? Day and night, house and garden, a few books, a few actions, serve us as well as would all trades and all spectacles. We are far from having exhausted the significance of the few symbols we use. We can come to use them yet with a terrible simplicity. It does not need that a poem should be long. Every word was once a poem. Every new relation is a new word. Also we use defects and deformities to a sacred purpose, so expressing our sense that the evils of the world are such only to the evil eye. In the old mythology, mythologists observe, defects are ascribed to divine natures, as lameness to Vulcan, blindness to Cupid, and the like,—to signify exuberances.

For as it is dislocation and detachment from the life of God that makes things ugly, the poet, who re-attaches things to nature and the Whole,—re-attaching even artificial things and violations of nature, to nature, by a deeper insight,—disposes very easily of the most disagreeable facts. Readers of poetry see the factory village and the railway, and fancy that the poetry of the landscape is broken up by these; for these works of art are not yet consecrated in their reading; but the poet sees them fall within the great Order not less than the beehive or the spider's geometrical web. Nature adopts them very fast into her vital circles, and the gliding train of cars she loves like her own. Besides, in a centred mind, it signifies nothing how many mechanical inventions you exhibit. Though you add millions, and never so surprising, the fact of mechanics has not gained a grain's weight. The spiritual fact remains unalterable, by many or by few particulars; as no mountain is of any appreciable height to break the curve of the sphere. A shrewd country-boy goes to the city for the first time, and the complacent citizen is not satisfied with his little wonder. It is not that he does not see all the fine houses and know that he never saw such before, but he disposes of them as easily as the poet finds place for the railway. The chief value of the new fact is to enhance the great and constant fact of Life, which can dwarf any and every circumstance, and to which the belt of wampum and the commerce of America are alike.

The world being thus put under the mind for verb and noun, the poet is he who can articulate it. For though life is great, and fascinates and absorbs; and though all men are intelligent of the symbols through which it is named; yet they cannot originally use them. We are symbols and inhabit symbols; workmen, work, and tools, words and things, birth and death, all are emblems; but we sympathize with the symbols, and being infatuated with the economical uses of things, we do not know that they are thoughts. The poet, by an ulterior intellectual perception, gives them a power which makes their old use forgotten, and puts eyes and a tongue into every dumb and inanimate object. He perceives the independence of the thought on the symbol, the stability of the thought, the accidency and fugacity of the symbol. As the eyes of Lynceus were said to see through the earth, so the poet turns the world to glass, and shows us all things in their right series and procession. For through that better perception he stands one step nearer to things, and sees the flowing or metamorphosis; perceives that thought is multiform; that within the form of every creature is a force impelling it to ascend into a higher form; and following with his eyes the life, uses the forms which express that life, and so his speech flows with the flowing of nature. All the facts of the animal economy, sex, nutriment, gestation, birth, growth, are symbols of the passage of the world into the soul of man, to suffer there a change and reappear a new and higher fact. He uses forms according to the life, and not according to the form. This is true science. The poet alone knows astronomy, chemistry, vegetation and animation, for he does not stop at these facts, but employs them as signs. He knows why the plain or meadow of space was strown with these flowers we call suns and moons and stars; why the great deep is adorned with animals, with men, and gods; for in every word he speaks he rides on them as the horses of thought.

By virtue of this science the poet is the Namer or Language-maker, naming things sometimes after their appearance, sometimes after their essence, and giving to every one its own name and not another's, thereby rejoicing the intellect, which delights in detachment or boundary. The poets made all the words, and therefore language is the archives of history, and, if we must say it, a sort of tomb of the muses. For though the origin of most of our words is forgotten, each word was at first a stroke of genius, and obtained currency because for the moment it symbolized the world to the first speaker and to the hearer. The etymologist finds the deadest word to have been once a brilliant picture. Language is fossil poetry. As the limestone of the continent consists of infinite masses of the shells of animalcules, so language is made up of images or tropes, which now, in their secondary use, have long ceased to remind us of their poetic origin. But the poet names the thing because he sees it, or comes one step nearer to it than any other. This expression or naming is not art, but a second nature, grown out of the first, as a leaf out of a tree. What we call nature is a certain self-regulated motion or change; and nature does all things by her own hands, and does not leave another to baptize her but baptizes herself; and this through the metamorphosis again. I remember that a certain poet described it to me thus:—

Genius is the activity which repairs the decay of things, whether wholly or partly of a material and finite kind. Nature, through all her kingdoms, insures herself. Nobody cares for planting the poor fungus; so she shakes down from the gills of one agaric countless spores, any one of which, being preserved, transmits new billions of spores to-morrow or next day. The new agaric of this hour has a chance which the old one had not. This atom of seed is thrown into a new place, not subject to the accidents which destroyed its parent two rods off. She makes a man; and having brought him to ripe age, she will no longer run the risk of losing this wonder at a blow, but she detaches from him a new self, that the kind may be safe from accidents to which the individual is exposed. So when the soul of the poet has come to ripeness of thought, she detaches and sends away from it its poems or songs,—a fearless, sleepless, deathless progeny, which is not exposed to the accidents of the weary kingdom of time; a fearless, vivacious offspring, clad with wings (such was the virtue of the soul out of which they came) which carry them fast and far, and infix them irrecoverably into the hearts of men. These wings are the beauty of the poet's soul. The songs, thus flying immortal from their mortal parent, are pursued by clamorous flights of censures, which swarm in far greater numbers and threaten to devour them; but these last are not winged. At the end of a very short leap they fall plump down and rot, having received from the souls out of which they came no beautiful wings. But the melodies of the poet ascend and leap and pierce into the deeps of infinite time.

So far the bard taught me, using his freer speech. But nature has a higher end, in the production of new individuals, than security, namely *ascension*, or the passage of the soul into higher forms. I knew in my younger days the sculptor who made the statue of the youth which stands in the public garden. He was, as I remember, unable to tell directly what made him happy or unhappy, but by wonderful indirections he could tell. He rose one day, according to his habit, before the dawn, and saw the morning break, grand as the eternity out of which it came, and for many days after, he strove to express this tranquillity, and lo! his chisel had fashioned out of marble the form of a beautiful youth, Phosphorus, whose aspect is such that it is said all persons who look on it become silent. The poet also resigns himself to his mood, and that thought which agitated him is expressed, but *alter idem*, in a manner totally new. The expression is organic, or the new type which things themselves take when liberated. As, in the sun, objects paint their images on the retina of the eye, so they, sharing the aspiration of the whole universe, tend to paint a far more delicate copy of their essence in his mind. Like the metamorphosis of things into higher organic forms is their change into melodies. Over everything stands its daemon or soul, and, as the form of the thing is reflected by the eye, so the soul of the thing is reflected by a melody. The sea, the mountain-ridge, Niagara, and every flower-bed, pre-exist, or super-exist, in pre-cantations, which sail like odors in the air, and when any man goes by with an ear sufficiently fine, he overhears them and endeavors to write down the notes without diluting or depraving them. And herein is the legitimation of criticism, in the mind's faith that the poems are a corrupt version of some text in nature with which they ought to be made to tally. A rhyme in one of our sonnets should not be less pleasing than the iterated nodes of a seashell, or the resembling difference of a group of flowers. The pairing of the birds is an idyl, not tedious as our idyls are; a tempest is a rough ode, without falsehood or rant; a summer, with its harvest sown, reaped, and stored, is an epic song, subordinating how many admirably executed parts. Why should not the symmetry and truth that modulate these, glide into our spirits, and we participate the invention of nature?

This insight, which expresses itself by what is called Imagination, is a very high sort of seeing, which does not come by study, but by the intellect being where and what it sees; by sharing the path or circuit of things through forms, and so making them translucid to others. The path of things is silent. Will they suffer a speaker to go with them? A spy they will not suffer; a lover, a poet, is the transcendency of their own nature,—him they will suffer. The condition of true naming, on the poet's part, is his resigning himself to the divine *aura* which breathes through forms, and accompanying that.

It is a secret which every intellectual man quickly learns, that beyond the energy of his possessed and conscious intellect he is capable of a new energy (as of an intellect doubled on itself), by abandonment to the nature of things; that beside his privacy of power as an individual man, there is a great public power on which he can draw, by unlocking, at all risks, his human doors, and suffering the ethereal tides to roll and circulate through him; then he is caught up into the life of the Universe, his speech is thunder, his thought is law, and his words are universally intelligible as the plants and animals. The poet knows that he speaks adequately then only when he speaks somewhat wildly,

or "with the flower of the mind;" not with the intellect used as an organ, but with the intellect released from all service and suffered to take its direction from its celestial life; or as the ancients were wont to express themselves, not with intellect alone but with the intellect inebriated by nectar. As the traveller who has lost his way throws his reins on his horse's neck and trusts to the instinct of the animal to find his road, so must we do with the divine animal who carries us through this world. For if in any manner we can stimulate this instinct, new passages are opened for us into nature; the mind flows into and through things hardest and highest, and the metamorphosis is possible.

This is the reason why bards love wine, mead, narcotics, coffee, tea, opium, the fumes of sandalwood and tobacco, or whatever other procurers of animal exhilaration. All men avail themselves of such means as they can, to add this extraordinary power to their normal powers; and to this end they prize conversation, music, pictures, sculpture, dancing, theatres, travelling, war, mobs, fires, gaming, politics, or love, or science, or animal intoxication,—which are several coarser or finer *quasi*-mechanical substitutes for the true nectar, which is the ravishment of the intellect by coming nearer to the fact. These are auxiliaries to the centrifugal tendency of a man, to his passage out into free space, and they help him to escape the custody of that body in which he is pent up, and of that jail-yard of individual relations in which he is enclosed. Hence a great number of such as were professionally expressers of Beauty, as painters, poets, musicians, and actors, have been more than others wont to lead a life of pleasure and indulgence; all but the few who received the true nectar; and, as it was a spurious mode of attaining freedom, as it was an emancipation not into the heavens but into the freedom of baser places, they were punished for that advantage they won, by a dissipation and deterioration. But never can any advantage be taken of nature by a trick. The spirit of the world, the great calm presence of the Creator, comes not forth to the sorceries of opium or of wine. The sublime vision comes to the pure and simple soul in a clean and chaste body. That is not an inspiration, which we owe to narcotics, but some counterfeit excitement and fury. Milton says that the lyric poet may drink wine and live generously, but the epic poet, he who shall sing of the gods and their descent unto men, must drink water out of a wooden bowl. For poetry is not 'Devil's wine,' but God's wine. It is with this as it is with toys. We fill the hands and nurseries of our children with all manner of dolls, drums, and horses; withdrawing their eyes from the plain face and sufficing objects of nature, the sun, and moon, the animals, the water, and stones, which should be their toys. So the poet's habit of living should be set on a key so low that the common influences should delight him. His cheerfulness should be the gift of the sunlight; the air should suffice for his inspiration, and he should be tipsy with water. That spirit which suffices quiet hearts, which seems to come forth to such from every dry knoll of sere grass, from every pine-stump and half-imbedded stone on which the dull March sun shines, comes forth to the poor and hungry, and such as are of simple taste. If thou fill thy brain with Boston and New York, with fashion and covetousness, and wilt stimulate thy jaded senses with wine and French coffee, thou shalt find no radiance of wisdom in the lonely waste of the pinewoods.

If the imagination intoxicates the poet, it is not inactive in other men. The metamorphosis excites in the beholder an emotion of joy. The use of symbols has a certain power of emancipation and exhilaration for all men. We seem to be touched by a wand which makes us dance and run about happily, like children. We are like persons who come out of a cave or cellar into the open air. This is the effect on us of tropes, fables, oracles, and all poetic forms. Poets are thus liberating gods. Men have really got a new sense, and found within their world another world, or nest of worlds; for, the metamorphosis once seen, we

divine that it does not stop. I will not now consider how much this makes the charm of algebra and the mathematics, which also have their tropes, but it is felt in every definition; as when Aristotle defines *space* to be an immovable vessel in which things are contained;—or when Plato defines a *line* to be a flowing point; or *figure* to be a bound of solid; and many the like. What a joyful sense of freedom we have when Vitruvius announces the old opinion of artists that no architect can build any house well who does not know something of anatomy. When Socrates, in Charmides, tells us that the soul is cured of its maladies by certain incantations, and that these incantations are beautiful reasons, from which temperance is generated in souls; when Plato calls the world an animal, and Timaeus affirms that the plants also are animals; or affirms a man to be a heavenly tree, growing with his root, which is his head, upward; and, as George Chapman, following him, writes,—

"So in our tree of man, whose nervie root Springs in his top;"—

when Orpheus speaks of hoariness as "that white flower which marks extreme old age"; when Proclus calls the universe the statue of the intellect; when Chaucer, in his praise of 'Gentilesse,' compares good blood in mean condition to fire, which, though carried to the darkest house betwixt this and the mount of Caucasus, will yet hold its natural office and burn as bright as if twenty thousand men did it behold; when John saw, in the Apocalypse, the ruin of the world through evil, and the stars fall from heaven as the figtree casteth her untimely fruit; when Aesop reports the whole catalogue of common daily relations through the masquerade of birds and beasts;—we take the cheerful hint of the immortality of our essence and its versatile habit and escapes, as when the gypsies say of themselves "it is in vain to hang them, they cannot die."

The poets are thus liberating gods. The ancient British bards had for the title of their order, "Those who are free throughout the world." They are free, and they make free. An imaginative book renders us much more service at first, by stimulating us through its tropes, than afterward when we arrive at the precise sense of the author. I think nothing is of any value in books excepting the transcendental and extraordinary. If a man is inflamed and carried away by his thought, to that degree that he forgets the authors and the public and heeds only this one dream which holds him like an insanity, let me read his paper, and you may have all the arguments and histories and criticism. All the value which attaches to Pythagoras, Paracelsus, Cornelius Agrippa, Cardan, Kepler, Swedenborg, Schelling, Oken, or any other who introduces questionable facts into his cosmogony, as angels, devils, magic, astrology, palmistry, mesmerism, and so on, is the certificate we have of departure from routine, and that here is a new witness. That also is the best success in conversation, the magic of liberty, which puts the world like a ball in our hands. How cheap even the liberty then seems; how mean to study, when an emotion communicates to the intellect the power to sap and upheave nature; how great the perspective! nations, times, systems, enter and disappear like threads in tapestry of large figure and many colors; dream delivers us to dream, and while the drunkenness lasts we will sell our bed, our philosophy, our religion, in our opulence.

There is good reason why we should prize this liberation. The fate of the poor shepherd, who, blinded and lost in the snow-storm, perishes in a drift within a few feet of his cottage door, is an emblem of the state of man. On the brink of the waters of life and truth, we are miserably dying. The inaccessibleness of every thought but that we are in, is wonderful. What if you come near to it; you are as remote when you are nearest as when you are farthest. Every thought is also a prison; every heaven is also a prison. Therefore we love the poet, the inventor, who in any form, whether in an ode or in an action or in looks and behavior has

yielded us a new thought. He unlocks our chains and admits us to a new scene.

This emancipation is dear to all men, and the power to impart it, as it must come from greater depth and scope of thought, is a measure of intellect. Therefore all books of the imagination endure, all which ascend to that truth that the writer sees nature beneath him, and uses it as his exponent. Every verse or sentence possessing this virtue will take care of its own immortality. The religions of the world are the ejaculations of a few imaginative men.

But the quality of the imagination is to flow, and not to freeze. The poet did not stop at the color or the form, but read their meaning; neither may he rest in this meaning, but he makes the same objects exponents of his new thought. Here is the difference betwixt the poet and the mystic, that the last nails a symbol to one sense, which was a true sense for a moment, but soon becomes old and false. For all symbols are fluxional; all language is vehicular and transitive, and is good, as ferries and horses are, for conveyance, not as farms and houses are, for homestead. Mysticism consists in the mistake of an accidental and individual symbol for an universal one. The morning-redness happens to be the favorite meteor to the eyes of Jacob Behmen, and comes to stand to him for truth and faith; and, he believes, should stand for the same realities to every reader. But the first reader prefers as naturally the symbol of a mother and child, or a gardener and his bulb, or a jeweller polishing a gem. Either of these, or of a myriad more, are equally good to the person to whom they are significant. Only they must be held lightly, and be very willingly translated into the equivalent terms which others use. And the mystic must be steadily told,—All that you say is just as true without the tedious use of that symbol as with it. Let us have a little algebra, instead of this trite rhetoric,— universal signs, instead of these village symbols,— and we shall both be gainers. The history of hierarchies seems to show that all religious error consisted in making the symbol too stark and solid, and was at last nothing but an excess of the organ of language.

Swedenborg, of all men in the recent ages, stands eminently for the translator of nature into thought. I do not know the man in history to whom things stood so uniformly for words. Before him the metamorphosis continually plays. Everything on which his eye rests, obeys the impulses of moral nature. The figs become grapes whilst he eats them. When some of his angels affirmed a truth, the laurel twig which they held blossomed in their hands. The noise which at a distance appeared like gnashing and thumping, on coming nearer was found to be the voice of disputants. The men in one of his visions, seen in heavenly light, appeared like dragons, and seemed in darkness; but to each other they appeared as men, and when the light from heaven shone into their cabin, they complained of the darkness, and were compelled to shut the window that they might see.

There was this perception in him which makes the poet or seer an object of awe and terror, namely that the same man or society of men may wear one aspect to themselves and their companions, and a different aspect to higher intelligences. Certain priests, whom he describes as conversing very learnedly together, appeared to the children who were at some distance, like dead horses; and many the like misappearances. And instantly the mind inquires whether these fishes under the bridge, yonder oxen in the pasture, those dogs in the yard, are immutably fishes, oxen, and dogs, or only so appear to me, and perchance to themselves appear upright men; and whether I appear as a man to all eyes. The Bramins and Pythagoras propounded the same question, and if any poet has witnessed the transformation he doubtless found it in harmony with various experiences. We have all seen changes as considerable in wheat and caterpillars. He is the poet and shall draw us with love and terror, who sees through the flowing vest the firm nature, and can declare it.

I look in vain for the poet whom I describe. We do not with sufficient plainness or sufficient profoundness address ourselves to life, nor dare we chaunt our own times and social circumstance. If we filled the day with bravery, we should not shrink from celebrating it. Time and nature yield us many gifts, but not yet the timely man, the new religion, the reconciler, whom all things await. Dante's praise is that he dared to write his autobiography in colossal cipher, or into universality. We have yet had no genius in America, with tyrannous eye, which knew the value of our incomparable materials, and saw, in the barbarism and materialism of the times, another carnival of the same gods whose picture he so much admires in Homer; then in the Middle Age; then in Calvinism. Banks and tariffs, the newspaper and caucus, Methodism and Unitarianism, are flat and dull to dull people, but rest on the same foundations of wonder as the town of Troy and the temple of Delphi, and are as swiftly passing away. Our logrolling, our stumps and their politics, our fisheries, our Negroes and Indians, our boats and our repudiations, the wrath of rogues and the pusillanimity of honest men, the northern trade, the southern planting, the western clearing, Oregon and Texas, are yet unsung. Yet America is a poem in our eyes; its ample geography dazzles the imagination, and it will not wait long for metres. If I have not found that excellent combination of gifts in my countrymen which I seek, neither could I aid myself to fix the idea of the poet by reading now and then in Chalmers's collection of five centuries of English poets. These are wits more than poets, though there have been poets among them. But when we adhere to the ideal of the poet, we have our difficulties even with Milton and Homer. Milton is too literary, and Homer too literal and historical.

But I am not wise enough for a national criticism, and must use the old largeness a little longer, to discharge my errand from the muse to the poet concerning his art.

Art is the path of the creator to his work. The paths or methods are ideal and eternal, though few men ever see them; not the artist himself for years, or for a lifetime, unless he come into the conditions. The painter, the sculptor, the composer, the epic rhapsodist, the orator, all partake one desire, namely to express themselves symmetrically and abundantly, not dwarfishly and fragmentarily. They found or put themselves in certain conditions, as, the painter and sculptor before some impressive human figures; the orator, into the asssembly of the people; and the others in such scenes as each has found exciting to his intellect; and each presently feels the new desire. He hears a voice, he sees a beckoning. Then he is apprised, with wonder, what herds of daemons hem him in. He can no more rest; he says, with the old painter, "By God it is in me and must go forth of me." He pursues a beauty, half seen, which flies before him. The poet pours out verses in every solitude. Most of the things he says are conventional, no doubt; but by and by he says something which is original and beautiful. That charms him. He would say nothing else but such things. In our way of talking we say 'That is yours, this is mine;' but the poet knows well that it is not his; that it is as strange and beautiful to him as to you; he would fain hear the like eloquence at length. Once having tasted this immortal ichor, he cannot have enough of it, and as an admirable creative power exists in these intellections, it is of the last importance that these things get spoken. What a little of all we know is said! What drops of all the sea of our science are baled up! and by what accident it is that these are exposed, when so many secrets sleep in nature! Hence the necessity of speech and song; hence these throbs and heart-beatings in the orator, at the door of the assembly, to the end namely that thought may be ejaculated as Logos, or Word.

Doubt not, O poet, but persist. Say 'It is in me, and shall out.' Stand there, balked and dumb, stuttering and stammering, hissed and hooted, stand and strive, until at last rage draw out of thee that *dream*-power which every night shows thee is thine own; a power transcending all limit and privacy, and by virtue of which a man is the conductor of the whole river of electricity. Nothing walks, or creeps, or grows, or exists, which must not in turn arise and walk before him as exponent of his meaning. Comes he to that power, his genius is no longer exhaustible. All the creatures by pairs and by tribes pour into his mind as into a Noah's ark, to come forth again to people a new world. This is like the stock of air for our respiration or for the combustion of our fireplace; not a measure of gallons, but the entire atmosphere if wanted. And therefore the rich poets, as Homer, Chaucer, Shakspeare, and Raphael, have obviously no limits to their works except the limits of their lifetime, and resemble a mirror carried through the street, ready to render an image of every created thing.

O poet! a new nobility is conferred in groves and pastures, and not in castles or by the swordblade any longer. The conditions are hard, but equal. Thou shalt leave the world, and know the muse only. Thou shalt not know any longer the times, customs, graces, politics, or opinions of men, but shalt take all from the muse. For the time of towns is tolled from the world by funereal chimes, but in nature the universal hours are counted by succeeding tribes of animals and plants, and by growth of joy on joy. God wills also that thou abdicate a manifold and duplex life, and that thou be content that others speak for thee. Others shall be thy gentlemen and shall represent all courtesy and worldly life for thee; others shall do the great and resounding actions also. Thou shalt lie close hid with nature, and canst not be afforded to the Capitol or the Exchange. The world is full of renunciations and apprenticeships, and this is thine; thou must pass for a fool and a churl for a long season. This is the screen and sheath in which Pan has protected his well-beloved flower, and thou shalt be known only to thine own, and they shall console thee with tenderest love. And thou shalt not be able to rehearse the names of thy friends in thy verse, for an old shame before the holy ideal. And this is the reward; that the ideal shall be real to thee, and the impressions of the actual world shall fall like summer rain, copious, but not troublesome to thy invulnerable essence. Thou shalt have the whole land for thy park and manor, the sea for thy bath and navigation, without tax and without envy; the woods and the rivers thou shalt own, and thou shalt possess that wherein others are only tenants and boarders. Thou true land-lord! sea-lord! air-lord! Wherever snow falls or water flows or birds fly, wherever day and night meet in twilight, wherever the blue heaven is hung by clouds or sown with stars, wherever are forms with transparent boundaries, wherever are outlets into celestial space, wherever is danger, and awe, and love,—there is Beauty, plenteous as rain, shed for thee, and though thou shouldst walk the world over, thou shalt not be able to find a condition inopportune or ignoble.

EDGAR ALLAN POE

(1809-1849)

A close contemporary of Emerson, Poe was the first major American literary critic and theorist. He differed from the transcendentalists, however, in his neoclassical emphasis—in "The Philosophy of Composition" (1846)—on the artist's need of a rational, self-conscious discipline and in his preference for elaborate traditional metrical forms. He also rejected the moral and didactic interests of his New England contemporaries in favor of a theory of poetry as the rhythmical expression of pure beauty. Poe's most succinct statement of this theory appears in "The Poetic Principle" (1850), an essay which also reveals a deep affinity with romantic transcendentalism in his identification of the creative principle with the "elevating excitement of the soul" in its struggle to apprehend a "supernal beauty." Many of Poe's ideas were adopted by Baudelaire and other French symbolist poets who contributed to modern theories of pure poetry. His concern for "unity" and "design," derived in part from Coleridge, and his interest in theory and in problems of technique—seen in an essay like "The Rationale of Verse" (1848)—have sometimes caused him to be regarded as a nineteenth century forerunner of the New Critics. Poe's critical writings have been gathered in *The Complete Works of Edgar Allan Poe* (ed. J. A. Harrison, 1902), in *Literary Criticism*, Vols. 8-14, and *Marginalia*, Vol. 16. A needed new edition of his works is being prepared by T. O. Mabbott.

From The Poetic Principle (1850)

In speaking of the Poetic Principle, I have no design to be either thorough or profound. While discussing, very much at random, the essentiality of what we call poetry, my principal purpose will be to cite for consideration, some few of those minor English or American poems which best suit my own taste, or which, upon my own fancy, have left the most definite impression. By "minor poems" I mean, of course, poems of little length. And here, in the beginning, permit me to

Originally prepared as a lecture in 1848, "The Poetic Principle" was first published in *Sartain's Union Magazine*, VII (1850), 231-239. Most of the poems included by Poe as elocutionary readings have been omitted from the version presented here.

say a few words in regard to a somewhat peculiar principle which, whether rightfully or wrongfully, has always had its influence in my own critical estimate of the poem. I hold that a long poem does not exist. I maintain that the phrase, "a long poem," is simply a flat contradiction in terms.

I need scarcely observe that a poem deserves its title only inasmuch as it excites, by elevating the soul. The value of the poem is in the ratio of this elevating excitement. But all excitements are, through a psychal necessity, transient. That degree of excitement which would entitle a poem to be so called at all, cannot be sustained throughout a composition of any great length. After the lapse of half an hour, at the very utmost, it flags—fails—a revulsion ensues—and then the poem is, in effect, and in fact, no longer such.

There are, no doubt, many who have found difficulty in reconciling the critical dictum that the *Paradise Lost* is to be devoutly admired throughout, with the absolute impossibility of maintaining for it, during perusal, the amount of enthusiasm which that critical dictum would demand. This great work, in fact, is to be regarded as poetical, only when, losing sight of that vital requisite in all works of art, unity, we view it merely as a series of minor poems. If, to preserve its unity—its totality of effect or impression—we read it (as would be necessary) at a single sitting, the result is but a constant alternation of excitement and depression. After a passage of what we feel to be true poetry, there follows, inevitably, a passage of platitude which no critical pre-judgment can force us to admire; but if, upon completing the work, we read it again; omitting the first book—that is to say, commencing with the second—we shall be surprised at now finding that admirable which we before condemned—that damnable which we had previously so much admired. It follows from all this that the ultimate, aggregate, or absolute effect of even the best epic under the sun is a nullity:— and this is precisely the fact.

In regard to the *Iliad*, we have, if not positive proof, at least very good reason, for believing it intended as a series of lyrics; but, granting the epic intention, I can say only that the work is based in an imperfect sense of art. The modern epic is, of the supposititious ancient model, but an inconsiderate and blindfold imitation. But the day of these artistic anomalies is over. If, at any time, any very long poem *were* popular in reality, which I doubt, it is at least clear that no very long poem will ever be popular again.

That the extent of a poetical work is, *ceteris paribus*, the measure of its merit seems undoubtedly, when we thus state it, a proposition sufficiently absurd—yet we are indebted for it to the Quarterly Reviews. Surely there can be nothing in mere *size*, abstractly considered—there can be nothing in mere *bulk*, so far as a volume is concerned, which has so continuously elicited admiration from these saturnine pamphlets! A mountain, to be sure, by the mere sentiment of physical magnitude which it conveys *does* impress us with a sense of the sublime—but no man is impressed after *this* fashion by the material grandeur of even the *Columbiad*. Even the Quarterlies have not instructed us to be so impressed by it. *As yet*, they have not *insisted* on our estimating Lamartine by the cubic foot, or Pollok by the pound—but what else are we to *infer* from their continual prating about "sustained effort"? If, by "sustained effort," any little gentleman has accomplished an epic, let us frankly commend him for the effort—if this indeed be a thing commendable—but let us forbear praising the epic on the effort's account. It is to be hoped that common sense, in the time to come, will prefer deciding upon a work of art, rather by the impression it makes, by the effect it produces, than by the time it took to impress the effect or by the amount of "sustained effort" which had been found necessary in effecting the impression. The fact is, that perseverance is one thing, and genius quite another—nor can all the Quarterlies in Christendom confound them. By-and-by, this proposition, with many which I have been just urging, will be received as self-evident. In the meantime, by being generally condemned as falsities, they will not be essentially damaged as truths.

On the other hand, it is clear that a poem may be improperly brief. Undue brevity degenerates into mere epigrammatism. A *very* short poem, while now and then producing a brilliant or vivid, never produces a profound or enduring effect. There must be the steady pressing down of the stamp upon the wax. De Béranger has wrought innumerable things, pungent and spirit-stirring; but, in general, they have been too imponderous to stamp themselves deeply into the public attention; and thus, as so many feathers of fancy, have been blown aloft only to be whistled down the wind.

A remarkable instance of the effect of undue brevity in depressing a poem—in keeping it out of the popular view—is afforded by the following exquisite little serenade:

I arise from dreams of thee
　In the first sweet sleep of night,
When the winds are breathing low,
　And the stars are shining bright;
I arise from dreams of thee,
　And a spirit in my feet
Has led me—who knows how?—
　To thy chamber window, sweet!

The wandering airs, they faint
　On the dark, the silent stream—
The champak odors fail
　Like sweet thoughts in a dream;
The nightingale's complaint,
　It dies upon her heart,
As I must die on thine,
　O, beloved as thou art!

O, lift me from the grass!
　I die, I faint, I fail!
Let thy love in kisses rain
　On my lips and eyelids pale.
My cheek is cold and white, alas!
　My heart beats loud and fast:
Oh! press it close to thine again,
　Where it will break at last!

Very few, perhaps, are familiar with these lines—yet no less a poet than Shelley is their author. Their warm, yet delicate and ethereal imagination will be appreciated by all—but by none so thoroughly as by him who has himself arisen from sweet dreams of one beloved to bathe in the aromatic air of a southern midsummer night.

. . . .

While the epic mania—while the idea that, to merit in poetry, prolixity is indispensable—has for some years past been gradually dying out of the public mind, by mere dint of its own absurdity—we find it succeeded by a heresy too palpably false to be long tolerated, but one which, in the brief period it has already endured, may be said to have accomplished more in the corruption of our poetical literature than all its other enemies combined. I allude to the heresy of the *didactic*. It has been assumed, tacitly and avowedly, directly and indirectly, that the ultimate object of all poetry is truth. Every poem, it is said, should inculcate a moral; and by this moral is the poetical merit of the work to be adjudged. We Americans especially have patronized this happy idea; and we Bostonians, very especially, have developed it in full. We have taken it into our heads that to write a poem simply for the poem's sake, and to acknowledge such to have been our design, would be to confess ourselves radically wanting in the true poetic dignity and force;—but the simple fact is that, would we but permit ourselves to look into our own souls, we should immediately there discover that under the sun there neither exists nor *can* exist any work more thoroughly dignified—more supremely noble than this very poem—this poem *per se* —this poem which is a poem and nothing more—this poem written solely for the poem's sake.

With as deep a reverence for the true as ever inspired the bosom of man, I would, nevertheless, limit in some measure its modes of inculcation. I would limit to enforce them. I would not enfeeble them by dissipation. The demands of truth are severe. She has no sympathy with the myrtles. All *that* which is so indispensable in song, is precisely all *that* with which *she* has nothing whatever to do. It is but making her a flaunting paradox to wreathe her in gems and flowers. In enforcing a truth, we need severity rather than efflorescence of language. We must be simple, precise, terse. We must be cool, calm, unimpassioned. In a word, we must be in that mood which, as nearly as possible, is the exact converse of the poetical. *He* must be blind, indeed, who does not perceive the radical and chasmal differences between the truthful and the poetical modes of inculcation. He must be theory-mad beyond redemption who, in spite of these differences, shall still persist in attempting to reconcile the obstinate oils and waters of poetry and truth.

Dividing the world of mind into its three most obvious distinctions, we have the pure intellect, taste, and the moral sense. I place taste in the middle, because it is just this position which, in the mind, it occupies. It holds intimate relations with either extreme; but from the moral sense is separated by so faint a difference that Aristotle has not hesitated to place some of its operations among the virtues themselves. Nevertheless, we find the *offices* of the trio marked with a sufficient distinction. Just as the intellect concerns itself with truth, so taste informs us of the beautiful while the moral sense is regardful of duty. Of this latter, while conscience teaches the obligation, and reason the expediency, taste contents herself with displaying the charms: —waging war upon vice solely on the ground of her deformity—her disproportion, her animosity to the fitting, to the appropriate, to the harmonious—in a word, to beauty.

An immortal instinct, deep within the spirit of man, is thus, plainly, a sense of the beautiful. This it is which administers to his delight in the manifold forms, and sounds, and odors, and sentiments amid which he exists. And just as the lily is repeated in the lake, or the eyes of Amaryllis in the mirror, so is the mere oral or written repetition of these forms, and sounds, and colors, and odors, and sentiments a duplicate source of delight. But this mere repetition is not poetry. He who shall simply sing, with however glowing enthusiasm, or with

however vivid a truth of description, of the sights, and sounds, and odors, and colors, and sentiments which greet *him* in common with all mankind—he, I say, has yet failed to prove his divine title. There is still a something in the distance which he has been unable to attain. We have still a thirst unquenchable, to allay which he has not shown us the crystal springs. This thirst belongs to the immortality of man. It is at once a consequence and an indication of his perennial existence. It is the desire of the moth for the star. It is no mere appreciation of the beauty before us—but a wild effort to reach the beauty above. Inspired by an ecstatic prescience of the glories beyond the grave, we struggle, by multiform combinations among the things and thoughts of time, to attain a portion of that loveliness whose very elements, perhaps, appertain to eternity alone. And thus when by poetry—or when by music, the most entrancing of the poetic moods—we find ourselves melted into tears—we weep then—not as the Abbate Gravina supposes—through excess of pleasure, but through a certain, petulant, impatient sorrow at our inability to grasp *now*, wholly, here on earth, at once and forever, those divine and rapturous joys, of which *through* the poem, or *through* the music, we attain to but brief and indeterminate glimpses.

The struggle to apprehend the supernal loveliness—this struggle, on the part of souls fittingly constituted—has given to the world all *that* which it (the world) has ever been enabled at once to understand and *to feel* as poetic.

The poetic sentiment, of course, may develop itself in various modes—in painting, in sculpture, in architecture, in the dance—very especially in music—and very peculiarly, and with a wide field, in the composition of the landscape garden. Our present theme, however, has regard only to its manifestation in words. And here let me speak briefly on the topic of rhythm. Contenting myself with the certainty that music in its various modes of meter, rhythm, and rhyme is of so vast a moment in poetry as never to be wisely rejected—is so vitally important an adjunct, that he is simply silly who declines its assistance—I will not now pause to maintain its absolute essentiality. It is in music, perhaps, that the soul most nearly attains the great end for which, when inspired by the poetic sentiment, it struggles—the creation of supernal beauty. It *may* be, indeed, that here this sublime end is, now and then, attained *in fact*. We are often made to feel, with a shivering delight, that from an earthly harp are stricken notes which *cannot* have been unfamilar to the angels. And thus there can be little doubt that in the union of poetry with music in its popular sense we shall find the widest field for the poetic development. The old bards and minnesingers had advantages which we do not possess—and Thomas Moore, singing his own songs, was, in the most legitimate manner, perfecting them as poems.

To recapitulate, then:—I would define, in brief, the poetry of words as *the rhythmical creation of beauty*. Its sole arbiter is taste. With the intellect or with the conscience, it has only collateral relations. Unless incidentally, it has no concern whatever either with duty or with truth.

A few words, however, in explanation. *That* pleasure which is at once the most pure, the most elevating, and the most intense is derived, I maintain, from the contemplation of the beautiful. In the contemplation of beauty we alone find it possible to attain that pleasurable elevation or excitement *of the soul* which we recognize as the poetic sentiment, and which is so easily distinguished from truth, which is the satisfaction of the reason, or from passion, which is the excitement of the heart. I make beauty, therefore—using the word as inclusive of the sublime—I make beauty the province of the poem, simply because it is an obvious rule of art that effects should be made to spring as directly as possible from their causes:—no one as yet having been weak enough to deny that the peculiar elevation in question is at least *most readily* attainable in the poem. It by no means follows, however, that the incitements of passion, or the precepts of duty, or even the lessons of truth may not be introduced into a poem, and with advantage; for they may subserve, incidentally, in various ways, the general purposes of the work:—but the true artist will always contrive to tone them down in proper subjection to that *beauty* which is the atmosphere and the real essence of the poem.

. . . .

From Alfred Tennyson—although in perfect sincerity I regard him as the noblest poet that ever lived—I have left myself time to cite only a very brief specimen. I call him, and *think* him the noblest of poets—*not* because the impressions he produces are, at *all* times, the most profound—*not* because the poetical excitement which he induces is, at *all* times, the most intense—but because it *is*, at all times, the most ethereal—in other words, the most elevating and the most pure. No poet is so little of the earth, earthy. What I am about to read is from his last long poem, *The Princess*:

Tears, idle tears, I know not what they
     mean,
Tears from the depth of some divine despair
Rise in the heart, and gather to the eyes,
In looking on the happy autumn-fields,
And thinking of the days that are no more.

Fresh as the first beam glittering on a sail
That brings our friends up from the under-
     world,
Sad as the last which reddens over one
That sinks with all we love below the verge;
So sad, so fresh, the days that are no more.

Ah, sad and strange as in dark summer
     dawns
The earliest pipe of half-awakened birds
To dying ears, when unto dying eyes
The casement slowly grows a glimmering
     square;
So sad, so strange, the days that are no more.

Dear as remembered kisses after death,
And sweet as those by hopeless fancy feigned
On lips that are for others; deep as love,
Deep as first love, and wild with all regret;
O Death in Life, the days that are no more!

Thus, although in a very cursory and imperfect manner, I have endeavored to convey to you my conception of the

Poetic Principle. It has been my purpose to suggest that, while this principle itself is strictly and simply the human aspiration for supernal beauty, the manifestation of the principle is always found in *an elevating excitement of the soul*—quite independent of that passion which is the intoxication of the heart—or of that truth which is the satisfaction of the reason. For, in regard to passion, alas! its tendency is to degrade, rather than to elevate the soul. Love, on the contrary —love—the true, the divine Eros—the Uranian, as distinguished from the Dionaean Venus—is unquestionably the purest and truest of all poetical themes. And in regard to truth—if, to be sure, through the attainment of a truth, we are led to perceive a harmony where none was apparent before, we experience, at once, the true poetical effect—but this effect is referable to the harmony alone, and not in the least degree to the truth which merely served to render the harmony manifest.

We shall reach, however, more immediately a distinct conception of what the true poetry is, by mere reference to a few of the simple elements which induce in the poet himself the true poetical effect. He recognizes the ambrosia which nourishes his soul, in the bright orbs that shine in heaven—in the volutes of the flower—in the clustering of low shrubberies—in the waving of the grain-fields —in the slanting of tall, eastern trees— in the blue distance of mountains—in the grouping of clouds—in the twinkling of half-hidden brooks—in the gleaming of silver rivers—in the repose of sequestered lakes—in the star-mirroring depths of lonely wells. He perceives it in the songs of birds—in the harp of Aeolus— in the sighing of the night wind—in the repining voice of the forest—in the surf that complains to the shore—in the fresh breath of the woods—in the scent of the violet—in the voluptuous perfume of the hyacinth—in the suggestive odor that comes to him, at eventide, from far-distant, undiscovered islands, over dim oceans, illimitable and unexplored. He owns it in all noble thoughts—in all unworldly motives—in all holy impulses— in all chivalrous, generous, and self-sacrificing deeds. He feels it in the beauty of woman—in the grace of her step—in the luster of her eye—in the melody of her voice—in her soft laughter—in her sigh—in the harmony of the rustling of her robes. He deeply feels it in her winning endearments—in her burning enthusiasms—in her gentle charities—in her meek and devotional endurances—but above all—ah, far above all—he kneels to it—he worships it in the faith, in the purity, in the strength, in the altogether divine majesty—of her *love*.

Let me conclude—by the recitation of yet another brief poem—one very different in character from any that I have before quoted. It is by Motherwell, and is called "The Song of the Cavalier." With our modern and altogether rational ideas of the absurdity and impiety of warfare, we are not precisely in that frame of mind best adapted to sympathize with the sentiments, and thus to appreciate the real excellence of the poem. To do this fully, we must identify ourselves, in fancy, with the soul of the old cavalier.

Then mounte! then mounte, brave gallants, all,
  And don your helmes amaine:
Death's couriers, Fame and Honor, call
  Us to the field againe.
No shrewish teares shall fill our eye
  When the sword-hilt's in our hand,—
Heart-whole we'll part, and no whit sighe
  For the fayrest of the land;
Let piping swaine, and craven wight,
  Thus weepe and puling crye,
Our business is like men to fight,
  And hero-like to die!

WALT WHITMAN

(1819-1892)

The preface to the first edition of *Leaves of Grass* (1855), which inaugurated the modern free verse movement, contains numerous echoes of Emerson's essay "The Poet" (1844). Like the transcendentalist, Whitman thinks of the poet as both a "representative man" and a seer, and his idea of poetic form follows the organic theory of Emerson. But Whitman's statement is important in its own right for certain distinctive qualities—a magnanimity and expansiveness and a commitment to eighteenth century revolutionary ideals. It was Whitman's conviction—reaffirmed in *Democratic Vistas* (1871)—that America's greatest literature would reflect the values of an ideal democracy. In this respect his position anticipates that of many later twentieth century liberal and radical critics.

Preface to *Leaves of Grass* (1855)

America does not repel the past or what it has produced under its forms or amid other politics or the idea of castes or the old religions . . . accepts the lesson with calmness . . . is not so impatient as has been supposed that the slough still sticks to opinions and manners and literature while the life which served its requirements has passed into the new life of the new forms . . . perceives that the corpse is slowly borne from the eating and sleeping rooms of the house . . . perceives that it waits a little while in the door . . . that it was fittest for its days . . . that its action has descended to the stalwart and wellshaped heir who approaches . . . and that he shall be fittest for his days.

The Americans of all nations at any time upon the earth have probably the fullest poetical nature. The United States themselves are essentially the greatest poem. In the history of the earth hitherto the largest and most stirring appear tame and orderly to their ampler largeness and stir. Here at last is something in the doings of man that corresponds with the broadcast doings of the day and night. Here is not merely a nation but a teeming nation of nations. Here is action untied from strings necessarily blind to particulars and details magnificently moving in vast masses. Here is the hospitality which forever indicates heroes.

The text presented here is that of the first edition (1855) of *Leaves of Grass* by Walt Whitman.

. . . Here are the roughs and beards and space and ruggedness and nonchalance that the soul loves. Here the performance disdaining the trivial unapproached in the tremendous audacity of its crowds and groupings and the push of its perspective spreads with crampless and flowing breadth and showers its prolific and splendid extravagance. One sees it must indeed own the riches of the summer and winter, and need never be bankrupt while corn grows from the ground or the orchards drop apples or the bays contain fish or men beget children upon women.

Other states indicate themselves in their deputies . . . but the genius of the United States is not best or most in its executives or legislatures, nor in its ambassadors or authors or colleges or churches or parlors, nor even in its newspapers or inventors . . . but always most in the common people. Their manners speech dress friendships—the freshness and candor of their physiognomy—the picturesque looseness of their carriage . . . their deathless attachment to freedom—their aversion to anything indecorous or soft or mean—the practical acknowledgment of the citizens of one state by the citizens of all other states—the fierceness of their roused resentment—their curiosity and welcome of novelty—their self-esteem and wonderful sympathy—their susceptibility to a slight—the air they have of persons who never knew how it felt to stand in the presence of superiors—the fluency of their speech —their delight in music, the sure symptom of manly tenderness and native elegance of soul . . . their good temper and openhandedness—the terrible significance of their elections—the President's taking off his hat to them not they to him—these too are unrhymed poetry. It awaits the gigantic and generous treatment worthy of it.

The largeness of nature or the nation were monstrous without a corresponding largeness and generosity of the spirit of the citizen. Not nature nor swarming states nor streets and steamships nor prosperous business nor farms nor capital nor learning may suffice for the ideal of man . . . nor suffice the poet. No reminiscences may suffice either. A live nation can always cut a deep mark and can have the best authority the cheapest . . . namely from its own soul. This is the sum of the profitable uses of individuals or states and of present action and grandeur and of the subjects of poets.— As if it were necessary to trot back generation after generation to the eastern records! As if the beauty and sacredness of the demonstrable must fall behind that of the mythical! As if men do not make their mark out of any times! As if the opening of the western continent by discovery and what has transpired since in North and South America were less than the small theatre of the antique or the aimless sleepwalking of the middle ages! The pride of the United States leaves the wealth and finesse of the cities and all returns of commerce and agriculture and all the magnitude of geography or shows of exterior victory to enjoy the breed of fullsized men or one fullsized man unconquerable and simple.

The American poets are to enclose old and new for America is the race of races. Of them a bard is to be commensurate with a people. To him the other continents arrive as contributions . . . he gives them reception for their sake and his own sake. His spirit responds to his country's spirit . . . he incarnates its geography and natural life and rivers and lakes. Mississippi with annual freshets and changing chutes, Missouri and Columbia and Ohio and Saint Lawrence with the falls and beautiful masculine Hudson, do not embouchure where they spend themselves more than they embouchure into him. The blue breadth over the inland sea of Virginia and Maryland and the sea off Massachusetts and Maine and over Manhattan bay and over Champlain and Erie and over Ontario and Huron and Michigan and Superior, and over the Texan and Mexican and Floridian and Cuban seas and over the seas off California and Oregon, is not tallied by the blue breadth of the waters below more than the breadth of above and below is tallied by him. When the long Atlantic coast stretches longer and the Pacific coast stretches longer he easily stretches with them north or south. He spans between them also from east to west and reflects what is between them. On him rise solid growths that offset the growths of pine and cedar and hemlock and liveoak and locust and chestnut and cypress and hickory and limetree and cottonwood and tuliptree and cactus and wildvine and tamarind and persimmon . . . and tangles as tangled as any canebreak or swamp . . . and forests coated with transparent ice and icicles hanging from the boughs and crackling in the wind . . . and sides and peaks of mountains . . . and pasturage sweet and free as savannah or upland or prairie . . . with flights and songs and screams that answer those of the wildpigeon and highhold and orchard-oriole and coot and surf-duck and redshouldered-hawk and fish-hawk and white-ibis and indian-hen and cat-owl and waterpheasant and qua-bird and pied-sheldrake and blackbird and mockingbird and buzzard and condor and night-heron and eagle. To him the hereditary countenance descends both mother's and father's. To him enter the essences of the real things and past and present events—of the enormous diversity of temperature and agriculture and mines—the tribes of red aborigines—the weather-beaten vessels entering new ports or making landings on rocky coasts—the first settlements north or south—the rapid stature and muscle—the haughty defiance of '76, and the war and peace and formation of the constitution . . . the union always surrounded by blatherers and always calm and impregnable—the perpetual coming of immigrants—the wharffhem'd cities and superior marine—the unsurveyed interior—the loghouses and clearings and wild animals and hunters and trappers . . . the free commerce—the fisheries and whaling and gold-digging—the endless gestation of new states—the convening of Congress every December, the members duly coming up from all climates and the uttermost parts . . . the noble character of the young mechanics and of all free American workmen and workwomen . . . the general ardor and friendliness and enterprise—the perfect equality of the female with the male . . . the large amativeness—the fluid movement of the population—the factories and mercantile life and laborsaving machinery—the Yankee swap—the New-York firemen and the target excursion—the southern plantation life—the character of the northeast and of the northwest and southwest—slavery and the tremulous spreading of hands to protect it, and the stern opposition to it which shall never cease till it ceases or the speaking of tongues and the moving of lips cease. For such the expression of the American poet is to be transcendant and new. It is to be indirect and not direct or descriptive or epic. Its quality goes through these to much more. Let the age and wars of other nations be chanted and their eras and characters be illustrated and that finish the verse. Not so the great psalm of the republic. Here the theme is creative and has vista. Here comes one among the wellbeloved stonecutters and plans with decision and science and sees the solid and beautiful forms of the future where there are now no solid forms.

Of all nations the United States with veins full of poetical stuff most need poets and will doubtless have the greatest and use them the greatest. Their Presidents shall not be their common referee so much as their poets shall. Of all mankind the great poet is the equable man. Not in him but off from him things are grotesque or eccentric or fail of their

sanity. Nothing out of its place is good and nothing in its place is bad. He bestows on every object or quality its fit proportions neither more nor less. He is the arbiter of the diverse and he is the key. He is the equalizer of his age and land . . . he supplies what wants supplying and checks what wants checking. If peace is the routine out of him speaks the spirit of peace, large, rich, thrifty, building vast and populous cities, encouraging agriculture and the arts and commerce—lighting the study of man, the soul, immortality—federal, state or municipal government, marriage, health, freetrade, intertravel by land and sea . . . nothing too close, nothing too far off . . . the stars not too far off. In war he is the most deadly force of the war. Who recruits him recruits horse and foot . . . he fetches parks of artillery the best that engineer ever knew. If the time becomes slothful and heavy he knows how to arouse it . . . he can make every word he speaks draw blood. Whatever stagnates in the flat of custom or obedience or legislation he never stagnates. Obedience does not master him, he masters it. High up out of reach he stands turning a concentrated light . . . he turns the pivot with his finger . . . he baffles the swiftest runners as he stands and easily overtakes and envelops them. The time straying toward infidelity and confections and persiflage he withholds by his steady faith . . . he spreads out his dishes . . . he offers the sweet firmfibred meat that grows men and women. His brain is the ultimate brain. He is no arguer . . . he is judgment. He judges not as the judge judges but as the sun falling around a helpless thing. As he sees the farthest he has the most faith. His thoughts are the hymns of the praise of things. In the talk on the soul and eternity and God off of his equal plane he is silent. He sees eternity less like a play with a prologue and denouement . . . he sees eternity in men and women . . . he does not see men and women as dreams or dots. Faith is the antiseptic of the soul . . . it pervades the common people and preserves them . . . they never give up believing and expecting and trusting. There is that indescribable freshness and unconsciousness about an illiterate person that humbles and mocks the power of the noblest expressive genius. The poet sees for a certainty how one not a great artist may be just as sacred as the greatest artist. . . . The power to destroy or remould is freely used by him but never the power of attack. What is past is past. If he does not expose superior models and prove himself by every step he takes he is not what is wanted. The presence of the greatest poet conquers . . . not parleying or struggling or any prepared attempts. Now he has passed that way see after him! there is not left any vestige of despair or misanthropy or cunning or exclusiveness or the ignominy of a nativity or color or delusion of hell or the necessity of hell . . . and no man thenceforward shall be degraded for ignorance or weakness or sin.

The greatest poet hardly knows pettiness or triviality. If he breathes into any thing that was before thought small it dilates with the grandeur and life of the universe. He is a seer . . . he is individual . . . he is complete in himself . . . the others are as good as he, only he sees it and they do not. He is not one of the chorus . . . he does not stop for any regulations . . . he is the president of regulation. What the eyesight does to the rest he does to the rest. Who knows the curious mystery of the eyesight? The other senses corroborate themselves, but this is removed from any proof but its own and foreruns the identities of the spiritual world. A single glance of it mocks all the investigations of man and all the instruments and books of the earth and all reasoning. What is marvelous? what is unlikely? what is impossible or baseless or vague? after you have once just opened the space of a peachpit and given audience to far and near and to the sunset and had all things enter with electric swiftness softly and duly without confusion or jostling or jam.

The land and sea, the animals, fishes and birds, the sky of heaven and the orbs, the forests mountains and rivers, are not small themes . . . but folks expect of the poet to indicate more than the beauty and dignity which always attach to dumb real objects . . . they expect him

to indicate the path between reality and their souls. Men and women perceive the beauty well enough . . . probably as well as he. The passionate tenacity of hunters, woodmen, early risers, cultivators of gardens and orchards and fields, the love of healthy women for the manly form, seafaring persons, drivers of horses, the passion for light and the open air, all is an old varied sign of the unfailing perception of beauty and of a residence of the poetic in outdoor people. They can never be assisted by poets to perceive . . . some may but they never can. The poetic quality is not marshalled in rhyme or uniformity or abstract addresses to things nor in melancholy complaints or good precepts, but is the life of these and much else and is in the soul. The profit of rhyme is that it drops seeds of a sweeter and more luxuriant rhyme, and of uniformity that it conveys itself into its own roots in the ground out of sight. The rhyme and uniformity of perfect poems show the free growth of metrical laws and bud from them as unerringly and loosely as lilacs or roses on a bush, and take shapes as compact as the shapes of chestnuts and oranges and melons and pears, and shed the perfume impalpable to form. The fluency and ornaments of the finest poems or music or orations or recitations are not independent but dependent. All beauty comes from beautiful blood and a beautiful brain. If the greatnesses are in conjunction in a man or woman it is enough . . . the fact will prevail through the universe . . . but the gaggery and gilt of a million years will not prevail. Who troubles himself about his ornaments or fluency is lost. This is what you shall do: Love the earth and sun and the animals, despise riches, give alms to every one that asks, stand up for the stupid and crazy, devote your income and labor to others, hate tyrants, argue not concerning God, have patience and indulgence toward the people, take off your hat to nothing known or unknown or to any man or number of men, go freely with powerful uneducated persons and with the young and with the mothers of families, read these leaves in the open air every season of every year of your life, re-examine all you have been told at school or church or in any book, dismiss whatever insults your own soul, and your very flesh shall be a great poem and have the richest fluency not only in its words but in the silent lines of its lips and face and between the lashes of your eyes and in every motion and joint of your body. . . . The poet shall not spend his time in unneeded work. He shall know that the ground is always ready plowed and manured . . . others may not know it but he shall. He shall go directly to the creation. His trust shall master the trust of everything he touches . . . and shall master all attachment.

The known universe has one complete lover and that is the greatest poet. He consumes an eternal passion and is indifferent which chance happens and which possible contingency of fortune or misfortune and persuades daily and hourly his delicious pay. What balks or breaks others is fuel for his burning progress to contact and amorous joy. Other proportions of the reception of pleasure dwindle to nothing to his proportions. All expected from heaven or from the highest he is rapport with in the sight of the daybreak or a scene of the winterwoods or the presence of children playing or with his arm round the neck of a man or woman. His love above all love has leisure and expanse . . . he leaves room ahead of himself. He is no irresolute or suspicious lover . . . he is sure . . . he scorns intervals. His experience and the showers and thrills are not for nothing. Nothing can jar him . . . suffering and darkness cannot—death and fear cannot. To him complaint and jealousy and envy are corpses buried and rotten in the earth . . . he saw them buried. The sea is not surer of the shore or the shore of the sea than he is of the fruition of his love and of all perfection and beauty.

The fruition of beauty is no chance of hit or miss . . . it is inevitable as life . . . it is exact and plumb as gravitation. From the eyesight proceeds another eyesight and from the hearing proceeds another hearing and from the voice proceeds another voice eternally curious of the harmony of things with man. To these respond perfections not only in the committees that were supposed to stand for the rest but in the rest themselves just the same. These understand the law of perfection in masses and floods . . . that its finish is to each for itself and onward from itself . . . that it is profuse and impartial . . . that there is not a minute of the light or dark nor an acre of the earth or sea without it—nor any direction of the sky nor any trade or employment nor any turn of events. This is the reason that about the proper expression of beauty there is precision and balance . . . one part does not need to be thrust above another. The best singer is not the one who has the most lithe and powerful organ . . . the pleasure of poems is not in them that take the handsomest measure and similes and sound.

Without effort and without exposing in the least how it is done the greatest poet brings the spirit of any or all events and passions and scenes and persons some more and some less to bear on your individual character as you hear or read. To do this well is to compete with the laws that pursue and follow time. What is the purpose must surely be there and the clue of it must be there . . . and the faintest indication is the indication of the best and then becomes the clearest indication. Past and present and future are not disjoined but joined. The greatest poet forms the consistence of what is to be from what has been and is. He drags the dead out of their coffins and stands them again on their feet . . . he says to the past, Rise and walk before me that I may realize you. He learns the lesson . . . he places himself where the future becomes present. The greatest poet does not only dazzle his rays over character and scenes and passions . . . he finally ascends and finishes all . . . he exhibits the pinnacles that no man can tell what they are for or what is beyond . . . he glows a moment on the extremest verge. He is most wonderful in his last half-hidden smile or frown . . . by that flash of the moment of parting the one that sees it shall be encouraged or terrified afterwards for many years. The greatest poet does not moralize or make applications of morals . . . he knows the soul. The soul has that measureless pride which consists in never acknowledging any lessons but its own. But it has sympathy as measureless as its pride and the one balances the other and neither can stretch too far while it stretches in company with the other. The inmost secrets of art sleep with the twain. The greatest poet has lain close betwixt both and they are vital in his style and thoughts.

The art of art, the glory of expression and the sunshine of the light of letters is simplicity. Nothing is better than simplicity . . . nothing can make up for excess or for the lack of definiteness. To carry on the heave of impulse and pierce intellectual depths and give all subjects their articulations are powers neither common nor very uncommon. But to speak in literature with the perfect rectitude and insouciance of the movements of animals and the unimpeachableness of the sentiment of trees in the woods and grass by the roadside is the flawless triumph of art. If you have looked on him who has achieved it you have looked on one of the masters of the artists of all nations and times. You shall not contemplate the flight of the graygull over the bay or the mettlesome action of the blood horse or the tall leaning of sunflowers on their stalk or the appearance of the sun journeying through heaven or the appearance of the moon afterward with any more satisfaction than you shall contemplate him. The greatest poet has less a marked style and is more the channel of thoughts and things without increase or diminution, and is the free channel of himself. He swears to his art, I will not be meddlesome, I will not have in my writing any elegance or effect or originality to hang in the way between me and the rest like curtains. I will have nothing hang in the way, not the richest curtains. What I tell I tell for precisely what it is. Let who may exalt or startle or fascinate or sooth I will have purposes as health or heat or snow has and be as regardless of observation. What I experience or portray shall go from my composition without a shred of my composi-

tion. You shall stand by my side and look in the mirror with me.

The old red blood and stainless gentility of great poets will be proved by their unconstraint. A heroic person walks at his ease through and out of that custom or precedent or authority that suits him not. Of the traits of the brotherhood of writers savans musicians inventors and artists nothing is finer than silent defiance advancing from new free forms. In the need of poems philosophy politics mechanism science behaviour, the craft of art, an appropriate native grand-opera, shipcraft, or any craft, he is greatest forever and forever who contributes the greatest original practical example. The cleanest expression is that which finds no sphere worthy of itself and makes one.

The messages of great poets to each man and woman are, Come to us on equal terms, Only then can you understand us, We are no better than you, What we enclose you enclose, What we enjoy you may enjoy. Did you suppose there could be only one Supreme? We affirm there can be unnumbered Supremes, and that one does not countervail another any more than one eyesight countervails another . . . and that men can be good or grand only of the consciousness of their supremacy within them. What do you think is the grandeur of storms and dismemberments and the deadliest battles and wrecks and the wildest fury of the elements and the power of the sea and the motion of nature and of the throes of human desires and dignity and hate and love? It is that something in the soul which says, Rage on, Whirl on, I tread master here and everywhere, Master of the spasms of the sky and of the shatter of the sea, Master of nature and passion and death, And of all terror and all pain.

The American bards shall be marked for generosity and affection and for encouraging competitors. . . . They shall be kosmos . . . without monopoly or secresy . . . glad to pass any thing to any one . . . hungry for equals night and day. They shall not be careful of riches and privilege . . . they shall be riches and privilege . . . they shall perceive who the most affluent man is. The most affluent man is he that confronts all the shows he sees by equivalents out of the stronger wealth of himself. The American bard shall delineate no class of persons nor one or two out of the strata of interests nor love most nor truth most nor the soul most nor the body most . . . and not be for the eastern states more than the western or the northern states more than the southern.

Exact science and its practical movements are no checks on the greatest poet but always his encouragement and support. The outset and remembrance are there . . . there are the arms that lifted him first and brace him best . . . there he returns after all his goings and comings. The sailor and traveler . . . the atomist chemist astronomer geologist phrenologist spiritualist mathematician historian and lexicographer are not poets, but they are the lawgivers of poets and their construction underlies the structure of every perfect poem. No matter what rises or is uttered they sent the seed of the conception of it . . . of them and by them stand the visible proofs of souls . . . always of their fatherstuff must be begotten the sinewy races of bards. If there shall be love and content between the father and the son and if the greatness of the son is the exuding of the greatness of the father there shall be love between the poet and the man of demonstrable science. In the beauty of poems are the tuft and final applause of science.

Great is the faith of the flush of knowledge and of the investigation of the depths of qualities and things. Cleaving and circling here swells the soul of the poet yet is president of itself always. The depths are fathomless and therefore calm. The innocence and nakedness are resumed . . . they are neither modest nor immodest. The whole theory of the special and supernatural and all that was twined with it or educed out of it departs as a dream. What has ever happened . . . what happens and whatever may or shall happen, the vital laws enclose all . . . they are sufficient for any case and for all cases . . . none to be hurried or retarded . . . any miracle of affairs or persons in-

admissible in the vast clear scheme where every motion and every spear of grass and the frames and spirits of men and women and all that concerns them are unspeakably perfect miracles all referring to all and each distinct and in its place. It is also not consistent with the reality of the soul to admit that there is anything in the known universe more divine than men and women.

Men and women and the earth and all upon it are simply to be taken as they are, and the investigation of their past and present and future shall be unintermitted and shall be done with perfect candor. Upon this basis philosophy speculates ever looking toward the poet, ever regarding the eternal tendencies of all toward happiness never inconsistent with what is clear to the senses and to the soul. For the eternal tendencies of all toward happiness make the only point of sane philosophy. Whatever comprehends less than that . . . whatever is less than the laws of light and of astronomical motion . . . or less than the laws that follow the thief the liar the glutton and the drunkard through this life and doubtless afterward . . . or less than vast stretches of time or the slow formation of density or the patient upheaving of strata—is of no account. Whatever would put God in a poem or system of philosophy as contending against some being or influence, is also of no account. Sanity and ensemble characterise the great master . . . spoilt in one principle all is spoilt. The great master has nothing to do with miracles. He sees health for himself in being one of the mass . . . he sees the hiatus in singular eminence. To the perfect shape comes common ground. To be under the general law is great for that is to correspond with it. The master knows that he is unspeakably great and that all are unspeakably great . . . that nothing for instance is greater than to conceive children and bring them up well . . . that to be is just as great as to perceive or tell.

In the make of the great masters the idea of political liberty is indispensable. Liberty takes the adherence of heroes wherever men and women exist . . . but never takes any adherence or welcome from the rest more than from poets. They are the voice and exposition of liberty. They out of ages are worthy the grand idea . . . to them it is confided and they must sustain it. Nothing has precedence of it and nothing can warp or degrade it. The attitude of great poets is to cheer up slaves and horrify despots. The turn of their necks, the sound of their feet, the motions of their wrists, are full of hazard to the one and hope to the other. Come nigh them awhile and though they neither speak or advise you shall learn the faithful American lesson. Liberty is poorly served by men whose good intent is quelled from one failure or two failures or any number of failures, or from the casual indifference or ingratitude of the people, or from the sharp show of the tushes of power, or the bringing to bear soldiers and cannon or any penal statutes. Liberty relies upon itself, invites no one, promises nothing, sits in calmness and light, is positive and composed, and knows no discouragement. The battle rages with many a loud alarm and frequent advance and retreat . . . the enemy triumphs . . . the prison, the handcuffs, the iron necklace and anklet, the scaffold, garrote and leadballs do their work . . . the cause is asleep . . . the strong throats are choked with their own blood . . . the young men drop their eyelashes toward the ground when they pass each other . . . and is liberty gone out of that place? No never. When liberty goes it is not the first to go nor the second nor third to go . . . it waits for all the rest to go . . . it is the last. . . . When the memories of the old martyrs are faded utterly away . . . when the large names of patriots are laughed at in the public halls from the lips of the orators . . . when the boys are no more christened after the same but christened after tyrants and traitors instead . . . when the laws of the free are grudgingly permitted and laws for informers and bloodmoney are sweet to the taste of the people . . . when I and you walk abroad upon the earth stung with compassion at the sight of numberless brothers answering our equal friendship and calling no

man master—and when we are elated with noble joy at the sight of slaves . . . when the soul retires in the cool communion of the night and surveys its experience and has much extasy over the word and deed that put back a helpless innocent person into the gripe of the gripers or into any cruel inferiority . . . when those in all parts of these states who could easier realize the true American character but do not yet—when the swarms of cringers, suckers, doughfaces, lice of politics, planners of sly involutions for their own preferment to city offices or state legislatures or the judiciary or congress or the presidency, obtain a response of love and natural deference from the people whether they get the offices or no . . . when it is better to be a bound booby and rogue in office at a high salary than the poorest free mechanic or farmer with his hat unmoved from his head and firm eyes and a candid and generous heart . . . and when servility by town or state or the federal government or any oppression on a large scale or small scale can be tried on without its own punishment following duly after in exact proportion against the smallest chance of escape . . . or rather when all life and all the souls of men and women are discharged from any part of the earth—then only shall the instinct of liberty be discharged from that part of the earth.

As the attributes of the poets of the kosmos concentre in the real body and soul and in the pleasure of things they possess the superiority of genuineness over all fiction and romance. As they emit themselves facts are showered over with light . . . the daylight is lit with more volatile light . . . also the deep between the setting and rising sun goes deeper many fold. Each precise object or condition or combination or process exhibits a beauty . . . the multiplication table its—old age its—the carpenter's trade its—the grand-opera its . . . the hugehulled cleanshaped New-York clipper at sea under steam or full sail gleams with unmatched beauty . . . the American circles and large harmonies of government gleam with theirs . . . and the commonest definite intentions and actions with theirs. The poets of the kosmos advance through all interpositions and coverings and turmoils and stratagems to first principles. They are of use . . . they dissolve poverty from its need and riches from its conceit. You large proprietor they say shall not realize or perceive more than any one else. The owner of the library is not he who holds a legal title to it having bought and paid for it. Any one and every one is owner of the library who can read the same through all the varieties of tongues and subjects and styles, and in whom they enter with ease and take residence and force toward paternity and maternity, and make supple and powerful and rich and large. . . . These American states strong and healthy and accomplished shall receive no pleasure from violations of natural models and must not permit them. In paintings or mouldings or carvings in mineral or wood, or in the illustrations of books or newspapers, or in any comic or tragic prints, or in the patterns of woven stuffs or anything to beautify rooms or furniture or costumes, or to put upon cornices or monuments or on the prows or sterns of ships, or to put anywhere before the human eye indoors or out, that which distorts honest shapes or which creates unearthly beings or places or contingencies is a nuisance and revolt. Of the human form especially it is so great it must never be made ridiculous. Of ornaments to a work nothing outre can be allowed . . . but those ornaments can be allowed that conform to the perfect facts of the open air and that flow out of the nature of the work and come irrepressibly from it and are necessary to the completion of the work. Most works are most beautiful without ornament. . . . Exaggerations will be revenged in human physiology. Clean and vigorous children are jetted and conceived only in those communities where the models of natural forms are public every day. . . . Great genius and the people of these states must never be demeaned to romances. As soon as histories are properly told there is no more need of romances.

The great poets are also to be known by the absence in them of tricks and by the justification of perfect personal candor. Then folks echo a new cheap joy and a divine voice leaping from their brains: How beautiful is candor! All faults may be forgiven of him who has perfect candor. Henceforth let no man of us lie, for we have seen that openness wins the inner and outer world and that there is no single exception, and that never since our earth gathered itself in a mass have deceit or subterfuge or prevarication attracted its smallest particle or the faintest tinge of a shade—and that through the enveloping wealth and rank of a state or the whole republic of states a sneak or sly person shall be discovered and despised . . . and that the soul has never been once fooled and never can be fooled . . . and thrift without the loving nod of the soul is only a foetid puff . . . and there never grew up in any of the continents of the globe nor upon any planet or satellite or star, nor upon the asteroids, nor in any part of ethereal space, nor in the midst of density, nor under the fluid wet of the sea, nor in that condition which precedes the birth of babes, nor at any time during the changes of life, nor in that condition that follows what we term death, nor in any stretch of abeyance or action afterward of vitality, nor in any process of formation or reformation anywhere, a being whose instinct hated the truth.

Extreme caution or prudence, the soundest organic health, large hope and comparison and fondness for women and children, large alimentiveness and destructiveness and causality, with a perfect sense of the oneness of nature and the propriety of the same spirit applied to human affairs . . . these are called up of the float of the brain of the world to be parts of the greatest poet from his birth out of his mother's womb and from her birth out of her mother's. Caution seldom goes far enough. It has been thought that the prudent citizen was the citizen who applied himself to solid gains and did well for himself and his family and completed a lawful life without debt or crime. The greatest poet sees and admits these economies as he sees the economies of food and sleep, but has higher notions of prudence than to think he gives much when he gives a few slight attentions at the latch of the gate. The premises of the prudence of life are not the hospitality of it or the ripeness and harvest of it. Beyond the independence of a little sum laid aside for burial-money, and of a few clapboards around and shingles overhead on a lot of American soil owned, and the easy dollars that supply the year's plain clothing and meals, the melancholy prudence of the abandonment of such a great being as a man is to the toss and pallor of years of moneymaking with all their scorching days and icy nights and all their stifling deceits and underhanded dodgings, or infinitesimals of parlors, or shameless stuffing while others starve . . . and all the loss of the bloom and odor of the earth and of the flowers and atmosphere and of the sea and of the true taste of the women and men you pass or have to do with in youth or middle age, and the issuing sickness and desperate revolt at the close of a life without elevation or naivete, and the ghastly chatter of a death without serenity or majesty, is the great fraud upon modern civilization and forethought, blotching the surface and system which civilization undeniably drafts, and moistening with tears the immense features it spreads and spreads with such velocity before the reached kisses of the soul. . . . Still the right explanation remains to be made about prudence. The prudence of the mere wealth and respectability of the most esteemed life appears too faint for the eye to observe at all when little and large alike drop quietly aside at the thought of the prudence suitable for immortality. What is wisdom that fills the thinness of a year or seventy or eighty years to wisdom spaced out by ages and coming back at a certain time with strong reinforcements and rich presents and the clear faces of wedding-guests as far as you can look in every direction running gaily toward you? Only the soul is of itself . . . all else has reference to what ensues. All that a person does or thinks is of consequence. Not a move can a man or woman make that affects him

or her in a day or a month or any part of the direct lifetime or the hour of death but the same affects him or her onward afterward through the indirect lifetime. The indirect is always as great and real as the direct. The spirit receives from the body just as much as it gives to the body. Not one name of word or deed . . . not of venereal sores or discolorations . . . not the privacy of the onanist . . . not of the putrid veins of gluttons or rum-drinkers . . . not peculation or cunning or betrayal or murder . . . no serpentine poison of those that seduce women . . . not the foolish yielding of women . . . not prostitution . . . not of any depravity of young men . . . not of the attainment of gain by discreditable means . . . not any nastiness of appetite . . . not any harshness of officers to men or judges to prisoners or fathers to sons or sons to fathers or of husbands to wives or bosses to their boys . . . not of greedy looks or malignant wishes . . . nor any of the wiles practised by people upon themselves . . . ever is or ever can be stamped on the programme but it is duly realized and returned, and that returned in further performances . . . and they returned again. Nor can the push of charity or personal force ever be any thing else than the profoundest reason, whether it bring arguments to hand or no. No specification is necessary . . . to add or subtract or divide is in vain. Little or big, learned or unlearned, white or black, legal or illegal, sick or well, from the first inspiration down the windpipe to the last expiration out of it, all that a male or female does that is vigorous and benevolent and clean is so much sure profit to him or her in the unshakable order of the universe and through the whole scope of it forever. If the savage or felon is wise it is well . . . if the greatest poet or savan is wise it is simply the same . . . if the President or chief justice is wise it is the same . . . if the young mechanic or farmer is wise it is no more or less . . . if the prostitute is wise it is no more nor less. The interest will come round . . . all will come round. All the best actions of war and peace . . . all help given to relatives and strangers and the poor and old and sorrowful and young children and widows and the sick, and to all shunned persons . . . all furtherance of fugitives and of the escape of slaves . . . all the self-denial that stood steady and aloof on wrecks and saw others take the seats of the boats . . . all offering of substance or life for the good old cause, or for a friend's sake or opinion's sake . . . all pains of enthusiasts scoffed at by their neighbors . . . all the vast sweet love and precious suffiering of mothers . . . all honest men baffled in strifes recorded or unrecorded . . . all the grandeur and good of the few ancient nations whose fragments of annals we inherit . . . and all the good of the hundreds of far mightier and more ancient nations unknown to us by name or date or location . . . all that was ever manfully begun, whether it succeeded or not . . . all that has at any time been well suggested out of the divine heart of man or by the divinity of his mouth or by the shaping of his great hands . . . and all that is well thought or done this day on any part of the surface of the globe . . . or on any of the wandering stars or fixed stars by those there as we are here . . . or that is henceforth to be well thought or done by you whoever you are, or by any one— these singly and wholly inured at their time and inure now and will inure always to the identities from which they sprung or shall spring. . . . Did you guess any of them lived only its moment? The world does not so exist . . . no parts palpable or impalpable so exist . . . no result exists now without being from its long antecedent result, and that from its antecedent, and so backward without the farthest mentionable spot coming a bit nearer to the beginning than any other spot. . . . Whatever satisfies the soul is truth. The prudence of the greatest poet answers at least the craving and glut of the soul, is not contemptuous of less ways of prudence if they conform to its ways, puts off nothing, permits no let-up for its own case or any case, has no particular sabbath or judgment-day, divides not the living from the dead or the righteous from the unrighteous, is satisfied with the present, matches every

thought or act by its correlative, knows no possible forgiveness or deputed atonement . . . knows that the young man who composedly periled his life and lost it has done exceeding well for himself, while the man who has not periled his life and retains it to old age in riches and ease has perhaps achieved nothing for himself worth mentioning . . . and that only that person has no great prudence to learn who has learnt to prefer real longlived things, and favors body and soul the same, and perceives the indirect assuredly following the direct, and what evil or good he does leaping onward and waiting to meet him again—and who in his spirit in any emergency whatever neither hurries or avoids death.

The direct trial of him who would be the greatest poet is today. If he does not flood himself with the immediate age as with vast oceanic tides . . . and if he does not attract his own land body and soul to himself and hang on its neck with incomparable love and plunge his semitic muscle into its merits and demerits . . . and if he be not himself the age transfigured . . . and if to him is not opened the eternity which gives similitude to all periods and locations and processes and animate and inanimate forms, and which is the bond of time, and rises up from its inconceivable vagueness and infiniteness in the swimming shape of today, and is held by the ductile anchors of life, and makes the present spot the passage from what was to what shall be, and commits itself to the representation of this wave of an hour and this one of the sixty beautiful children of the wave—let him merge in the general run and wait his development. . . . Still the final test of poems or any character or work remains. The prescient poet projects himself centuries ahead and judges performer or performance after the changes of time. Does it live through them? Does it still hold on untired? Will the same style and the direction of genius to similar points be satisfactory now? Has no new discovery in science or arrival at superior planes of thought and judgment and behaviour fixed him or his so that either can be looked down upon? Have the marches of tens and hundreds and thousands of years made willing detours to the right hand and the left hand for his sake? Is he beloved long and long after he is buried? Does the young man think often of him? and the young woman think often of him? and do the middle-aged and the old think of him?

A great poem is for ages and ages in common and for all degrees and complexions and all departments and sects and for a woman as much as a man and a man as much as a woman. A great poem is no finish to a man or woman but rather a beginning. Has any one fancied he could sit at last under some due authority and rest satisfied with explanations and realize and be content and full? To no such terminus does the greatest poet bring . . . he brings neither cessation nor sheltered fatness and ease. The touch of him tells in action. Whom he takes he takes with firm sure grasp into live regions previously unattained . . . thenceforward is no rest . . . they see the space and ineffable sheen that turn the old spots and lights into dead vacuums. The companion of him beholds the birth and progress of stars and learns one of the meanings. Now there shall be a man cohered out of tumult and chaos . . . the elder encourages the younger and shows him how . . . they too shall launch off fearlessly together till the new world fits an orbit for itself and looks unabashed on the lesser orbits of the stars and sweeps through the ceaseless rings and shall never be quiet again.

There will soon be no more priests. Their work is done. They may wait awhile . . . perhaps a generation or two . . . dropping off by degrees. A superior breed shall take their place . . . the gangs of kosmos and prophets en masse shall take their place. A new order shall arise and they shall be the priests of man, and every man shall be his own priest. The churches built under their umbrage shall be the churches of men and women. Through the divinity of themselves shall the kosmos and the new breed of poets be interpreters of men and women and of all events and things. They shall find their inspiration in real objects today,

symptoms of the past and future. . . . They shall not deign to defend immortality or God or the perfection of things or liberty or the exquisite beauty and reality of the soul. They shall arise in America and be responded to from the remainder of the earth.

The English language befriends the grand American expression . . . it is brawny enough and limber and full enough. On the tough stock of a race who through all change of circumstances was never without the idea of political liberty, which is the animus of all liberty, it has attracted the terms of daintier and gayer and subtler and more elegant tongues. It is the powerful language of resistance . . . it is the dialect of common sense. It is the speech of the proud and melancholy races and of all who aspire. It is the chosen tongue to express growth faith self-esteem freedom justice equality friendliness amplitude prudence decision and courage. It is the medium that shall well nigh express the inexpressible.

No great literature nor any like style of behaviour or oratory or social intercourse or household arrangements or public institutions or the treatment by bosses of employed people, nor executive detail or detail of the army or navy, nor spirit of legislation or courts or police or tuition or architecture or songs or amusements or the costumes of young men, can long elude the jealous and passionate instinct of American standards. Whether or no the sign appears from the mouths of the people, it throbs a live interrogation in every freeman's and freewoman's heart after that which passes by or this built to remain. Is it uniform with my country? Are its disposals without ignominious distinctions? Is it for the evergrowing communes of brothers and lovers, large, well-united, proud beyond the old models, generous beyond all models? Is it something grown fresh out of the fields or drawn from the sea for use to me today here? I know that what answers for me an American must answer for any individual or nation that serves for a part of my materials. Does this answer? or is it without reference to universal needs? or sprung of the needs of the less developed society of special ranks? or old needs of pleasure overlaid by modern science and forms? Does this acknowledge liberty with audible and absolute acknowledgment, and set slavery at naught for life and death? Will it help breed one goodshaped and wellhung man, and a woman to be his perfect and independent mate? Does it improve manners? Is it for the nursing of the young of the republic? Does it solve readily with the sweet milk of the nipples of the breasts of the mother of many children? Has it too the old ever-fresh forbearance and impartiality? Does it look with the same love on the last born and those hardening toward stature, and on the errant, and on those who disdain all strength of assault outside of their own?

The poems distilled from other poems will probably pass away. The coward will surely pass away. The expectation of the vital and great can only be satisfied by the demeanor of the vital and great. The swarms of the polished deprecating and reflectors and the polite float off and leave no remembrance. America prepares with composure and goodwill for the visitors that have sent word. It is not intellect that is to be their warrant and welcome. The talented, the artist, the ingenious, the editor, the statesman, the erudite . . . they are not unappreciated . . . they fall in their place and do their work. The soul of the nation also does its work. No disguise can pass on it . . . no disguise can conceal from it. It rejects none, it permits all. Only toward as good as itself and toward the like of itself will it advance half-way. An individual is as superb as a nation when he has the qualities which make a superb nation. The soul of the largest and wealthiest and proudest nation may well go half-way to meet that of its poets. The signs are effectual. There is no fear of mistake. If the one is true the other is true. The proof of a poet is that his country absorbs him as affectionately as he has absorbed it.

MATTHEW ARNOLD

(1822-1888)

The greatest English critic of the nineteenth century after Coleridge, Matthew Arnold has been charged by certain twentieth century neo-orthodox critics with the heresy of making poetry a substitute for religion. The charge has interest as an insight into Arnold's mind and temperament, and as an especially revealing contemporary response to his criticism. He regretted, with the nostalgia characteristic of the Victorian agnostic intellectual, the passing of the old forms and faiths, and he feared their replacement by the modern chaos of secular interests and values. Arnold's criticism, supported by his prose on social and religious matters, is an attempt to extemporize something very like a corrective religion. He sees the history of western thought and the arts as a repository of "wisdom," with literature as the chief source of the feelings by which the mind's creative discernment and absorption of that wisdom is made possible. His conception of literature as the medium in which the moral and spiritual life can be lived most fully in a religionless world makes him in some degree vulnerable to the charge that he tried to turn literature into a "religion." Concerned with the relationship of the literary work to the reader, Arnold views literature as the seed bed of the all-necessary life of the feelings; and "ideas," the accumulated thought of the past, he views as the constant critic and judge of feeling, and of the validity of its expression in words. As a practical critic, then, notably in his essays on the English, German, and French romantics, Arnold judges literary worth ultimately in terms of a classicist-like moral utility, though the norms of his classicism remain, by design, indefinite, undefined. Arnold, though a principled anti-dogmatist, is surely the great moralist of latter day English romantic criticism, as Coleridge is its earlier great metaphysician and epistemologist. The three series of Arnold's *Essays in Criticism* have been republished many times. The most comprehensive body of his criticism is contained in his *Works* (15 vols., 1903-1904) and *The Complete Prose of Matthew Arnold*, (ed. R. H. Super, 1960—) now being published.

The Function of Criticism at the Present Time (1864)

Many objections have been made to a proposition which, in some remarks of mine on translating Homer, I ventured to put forth; a proposition about criticism, and its importance at the present day. I said: "Of the literature of France and Germany, as of the intellect of Europe in general, the main effort, for now many years, has been a critical effort; the endeavor, in all branches of knowledge, theology, philosophy, history, art, science, to see the object as in itself it really is." I added, that owing to the operation in English literature of certain causes, "almost the last thing for which one would come to English literature is just that very thing which now Europe most desires,—criticism;" and that the power and value of English literature was thereby impaired. More than one rejoinder declared that the importance I here assigned to criticism was excessive, and asserted the inherent superiority of the creative effort of the human spirit over its critical effort. And the other day, having been led by a Mr. Shairp's excellent notice of Wordsworth[1] to turn

again to his biography, I found, in the words of this great man, whom I, for one, must always listen to with the profoundest respect, a sentence passed on the critic's business, which seems to justify every possible disparagement of it. Wordsworth says in one of his letters:—

"The writers in these publications" (the Reviews), "while they prosecute their inglorious employment, cannot be supposed to be in a state of mind very favorable for being effected by the finer influences of a thing so pure as genuine poetry."

And a trustworthy reporter of his conversation quotes a more elaborate judgment to the some effect:—

"Wordsworth holds the critical power very low, infinitely lower than the inventive; and he said to-day that if the quantity of time consumed in writing critiques on the works of others were given to original composition, of whatever kind it might be, it would be much better employed; it would make a man find out sooner his own level, and it would do infinitely less mischief. A false or malicious criticism may be much injury to the minds of others, a stupid invention, either in prose or verse, is quite harmless."

It is almost too much to expect of poor human nature, that a man capable of producing some effect in one line of literature, should, for the greater good of society, voluntarily doom himself to impotence and obscurity in another. Still

[1] I cannot help thinking that a practice, common in England during the last century, and still followed in France, of printing a notice of this kind,—a notice by a competent critic,—to serve as an introduction to an eminent author's works, might be revived among us with advantage. To introduce all succeeding editions of Wordsworth, Mr. Shairp's notice might, it seems to me, excellently serve; it is written from the point of view of an admirer, nay, of a disciple, and that is right; but then the disciple must be also, as in this case he is, a critic, a man of letters, not, as too often happens, some relation or friend with no qualification for his task except affection for his author.

less is this to be expected from men addicted to the composition of the "false or malicious criticism" of which Wordsworth speaks. However, everybody would admit that a false or malicious criticism had better never have been written. Everybody, too, would be willing to admit, as a general proposition, that the critical faculty is lower than the inventive. But is it true that criticism is really, in itself, a baneful and injurious employment; is it true that all time given to writing critiques on the works of others would be much better employed if it were given to original composition, of whatever kind this may be? Is it true that Johnson had better have gone on producing more *Irenes* instead of writing his *Lives of the Poets*; nay, is it certain that Wordsworth himself was better employed in making his Ecclesiastical Sonnets than when he made his celebrated Preface, so full of criticism, and criticism of the works of others? Wordsworth was himself a great critic, and it is to be sincerely regretted that he has not left us more criticism; Goethe was one of the greatest of critics, and we may sincerely congratulate ourselves that he has left us so much criticism. Without wasting time over the exaggeration which Wordsworth's judgment on criticism clearly contains, or over an attempt to trace the causes,—not difficult, I think, to be traced,—which may have led Wordsworth to this exaggeration, a critic may with advantage seize an occasion for trying his own conscience, and for asking himself of what real service at any given moment the practice of criticism either is or may be made to his own mind and spirit, and to the minds and spirits of others.

The critical power is of lower rank than the creative. True; but in assenting to this proposition, one or two things are to be kept in mind. It is undeniable that the exercise of a creative power, that a free creative activity, is the highest function of man; it is proved to be so by man's finding in it his true happiness. But it is undeniable, also, that men may have the sense of exercising this free creative activity in other ways than in producing great works of literature or art; if it were not so, all but a very few men would be shut out from the true happiness of all men. They may have it in well-doing, they may have it in learning, they may have it even in criticizing. This is one thing to be kept in mind. Another is, that the exercise of the creative power in the production of great works of literature or art, however high this exercise of it may rank, is not at all epochs and under all conditions possible; and that therefore labor may be vainly spent in attempting it, which might with more fruit be used in preparing for it, in rendering it possible. This creative power works with elements, with materials; what if it has not those materials, those elements, ready for its use? In that case it must surely wait till they are ready. Now, in literature,—I will limit myself to literature, for it is about literature that the question arises,—the elements with which the creative power works are ideas; the best ideas on every matter which literature touches, current at the time. At any rate we may lay it down as certain that in modern literature no manifestation of the creative power not working with these can be very important or fruitful. And I say *current* at the time, not merely accessible at the time; for creative literary genius does not principally show itself in discovering new ideas, that is rather the business of the philosopher. The grand work of literary genius is a work of synthesis and exposition, not of analysis and discovery; its gift lies in the faculty of being happily inspired by a certain intellectual and spiritual atmosphere, by a certain order of ideas, when it finds itself in them; of dealing divinely with these ideas, presenting them in the most effective and attractive combinations,—making beautiful works with them, in short. But it must have the atmosphere, it must find itself amidst the order of ideas, in order to work freely; and these it is not so easy to command. This is why great creative epochs in literature are so rare, this is why there is so much that is unsatisfactory in the productions of many men of real genius; because, for the creation of a master-work of literature two powers must concur, the power of the man and the power of the moment, and the man is not enough without the moment; the creative power has, for its happy exercise, appointed elements, and those elements are not in its own control.

Nay, they are more within the control of the critical power. It is the business of the critical power, as I said in the words already quoted, "in all branches of knowledge, theology, philosophy, history, art, science, to see the object as in itself it really is." Thus it tends, at last, to make an intellectual situation of which the creative power can profitably avail itself. It tends to establish an order of ideas, if not absolutely true, yet true by comparison with that which it displaces; to make the best ideas prevail. Presently these new ideas reach society, the touch of truth is the touch of life, and there is a stir and growth everywhere; out of this stir and growth come the creative epochs of literature.

Or, to narrow our range, and quit these considerations of the general march of genius and of society,—considerations which are apt to become too abstract and impalpable,—every one can see that a poet, for instance, ought to know life and the world before dealing with them in poetry; and life and the world being in modern times very complex things, the creation of a modern poet, to be worth much, implies a great critical effort behind it; else it must be a comparatively poor, barren, and short-lived affair. This is why Byron's poetry had so little endurance in it, and Goethe's so much; both Byron and Goethe had a great productive power, but Goethe's was nourished by a great critical effort providing the true materials for it, and Byron's was not; Goethe knew life and the world, the poet's necessary subjects, much more comprehensively and thoroughly than Byron. He knew a great deal more of them, and he knew them much more as they really are.

It has long seemed to me that the burst of creative activity in our literature, through the first quarter of this century, had about it in fact something prema-

ture; and that from this cause its productions are doomed, most of them, in spite of the sanguine hopes which accompanied and do still accompany them to prove hardly more lasting than the productions of far less splendid epochs. And this prematureness comes from its having proceeded without having its proper data, without sufficient materials to work with. In other words, the English poetry of the first quarter of this century, with plenty of energy, plenty of creative force, did not know enough. This makes Byron so empty of matter, Shelley so incoherent, Wordsworth even, profound as he is, yet so wanting in completeness and variety. Wordsworth cared little for books, and disparaged Goethe. I admire Wordsworth, as he is, so much that I cannot wish him different; and it is vain, no doubt, to imagine such a man different from what he is, to suppose that he *could* have been different. But surely the one thing wanting to make Wordsworth an even greater poet than he is,—his thought richer, and his influence of wider application,—was that he should have read more books, among them, no doubt, those of that Goethe whom he disparaged without reading him.

But to speak of books and reading may easily lead to a misunderstanding here. It was not really books and reading that lacked to our poetry at this epoch; Shelley had plenty of reading, Coleridge had immense reading. Pindar and Sophocles —as we all say so glibly, and often with so little discernment of the real import of what we are saying—had not many books; Shakespeare was no deep reader. True; but in the Greece of Pindar and Sophocles, in the England of Shakespeare, the poet lived in a current of ideas in the highest degree animating and nourishing to the creative power; society was, in the fullest measure, permeated by fresh thought, intelligent and alive. And this state of things is the true basis for the creative power's exercise, in this it finds its data, its materials, truly ready for its hand; all the books and reading in the world are only valuable as they are helps to this. Even when this does not actually exist, books and reading may enable a man to construct a kind of semblance of it in his own mind, a world of knowledge and intelligence in which he may live and work. This is by no means an equivalent to the artist for the nationally diffused life and thought of the epochs of Sophocles or Shakespeare; but besides that it may be a means of preparation for such epochs, it does really constitute, if many share in it, a quickening and sustaining atmosphere of great value. Such an atmosphere the many-sided learning and the long and widely-combined critical effort of Germany formed for Goethe, when he lived and worked. There was no national glow of life and thought there as in the Athens of Pericles or the England of Elizabeth. That was the poet's weakness. But there was a sort of equivalent for it in the complete culture and unfettered thinking of a large body of Germans. That was his strength. In the England of the first quarter of this century there was neither a national glow of life and thought, such as we had in the age of Elizabeth, nor yet a culture and a force of learning and criticism such as were to be found in Germany. Therefore the creative power of poetry wanted, for success in the highest sense, materials and a basis; a thorough interpretation of the world was necessarily denied to it.

At first sight it seems strange that out of the immense stir of the French Revolution and its age should not have come a crop of works of genius equal to that which came out of the stir of the great productive time of Greece, or out of that of the Renascence, with its powerful episode the Reformation. But the truth is that the stir of the French Revolution took a character which essentially distinguished it from such movements as these. These were, in the main, disinterestedly intellectual and spiritual movements; movements in which the human spirit looked for its satisfaction in itself and in the increased play of its own activity. The French Revolution took a political, practical character. The movement, which went on in France under the old *régime* from 1700 to 1789, was far more really akin than that of the Revolution itself to the movement of the Renascence; the France of Voltaire and Rousseau told far more powerfully upon the mind of Europe than the France of the Revolution. Goethe reproached this last expressly with having "thrown quiet culture back." Nay, and the true key to how much in our Byron, even in our Wordsworth, is this!—that they had their source in a great movement of feeling, not in a great movement of mind. The French Revolution, however,—that object of so much blind love and so much blind hatred,—found undoubtedly its motive-power in the intelligence of men, and not in their practical sense; this is what distinguishes it from the English Revolution of Charles the First's time. This is what makes it a more spiritual event than our Revolution, an event of much more powerful and world-wide interest, though practically less successful; it appeals to an order of ideas which are universal, certain, permanent. 1789 asked of a thing, Is it rational? 1642 asked of a thing, Is it legal? or, when it went furthest, Is it according to conscience? This is the English fashion, a fashion to be treated, within its own sphere, with the highest respect; for its success, within its own sphere, has been prodigious. But what is law in one place is not law in another; what is law here to-day is not law even here to-morrow; and as for conscience, what is binding on one man's conscience is not binding on another's: The old woman who threw her stool at the head of the surpliced minister in St. Gile's Church at Edinburgh obeyed an impulse to which millions of the human race may be permitted to remain strangers. But the prescriptions of reason are absolute, unchanging, of universal validity; *to count by tens is the easiest way of counting*—that is a proposition of which every one, from here to the Antipodes, feels the force; at least I should say so if we did not live in a country where it is not impossible that any morning we may find a letter in the *Time.* declaring that a decimal coinage is an absurdity. That a whole nation should have been penetrated with an enthu siasm for pure reason, and with an ardent zeal for making its prescriptions triumph, is a very remarkable thing, when we consider how little of mind, or anything so worthy and quickening as mind, comes into the motives which alone, in general, impel great masses of men. In spite of the extravagant direction given to this enthusiasm, in spite of the crimes and follies in which it lost itself, the French Revolution derives from the force, truth, and universality of the ideas which it took for its law, and from the passion with which it could inspire a multitude for these ideas, a unique and still living power; it is—it will probably long remain—the greatest, the most animating event in history. And as no sincere passion for the things of the mind, even though it turn out in many respects an unfortunate passion, is ever quite thrown away and quite barren of good, France has reaped from hers one fruit— the natural and legitimate fruit though not precisely the grand fruit she expected: she is the country in Europe where *the people* is most alive.

But the mania for giving an immediate political and practical application to all these fine ideas of the reason was fatal. Here an Englishman is in his element: on this theme we can all go on for hours. And all we are in the habit of saying on it has undoubtedly a great deal of truth. Ideas cannot be too much prized in and for themselves, cannot be too much lived with; but to transport them abruptly into the world of politics, and practice, violently to revolutionize this world to their bidding,—that is quite another thing. There is the world of ideas and there is the world of practice; the French are often for suppressing the one and the English the other; but neither is to be suppressed. A member of the House of Commons said to me the other day: "That a thing is an anomaly, I consider to be no objection to it whatever." I venture to think he was wrong; that a thing is an anomaly *is* an objection to it, but absolutely and in the sphere of ideas: it is not necessarily, under such and such circumstances, or at such and such a moment, an objection to it in the sphere

of politics and practice. Joubert has said beautifully: "C'est la force et le droit qui règlent toutes choses dans le monde; la force en attendant le droit." (Force and right are the governors of this world; force till right is ready.) *Force till right is ready*; and till right is ready, force, the existing order of things, is justified, is the legitimate ruler. But right is something moral, and implies inward recognition, free assent of the will; we are not ready for right,—*right*, so far as we are concerned, *is not ready*,—until we have attained this sense of seeing it and willing it. The way in which for us it may change and transform force, the existing order of things, and become, in its turn, the legitimate ruler of the world, should depend on the way in which, when our time comes, we see it and will it. Therefore for other people enamored of their own newly discerned right, to attempt to impose it upon us as ours, and violently to substitute their right for our force, is an act of tyranny, and to be resisted. It sets at naught the second great half of our maxim, *force till right is ready*. This was the grand error of the French Revolution; and its movement of ideas, by quitting the intellectual sphere and rushing furiously into the political sphere, ran, indeed, a prodigious and memorable course, but produced no such intellectual fruit as the movement of ideas of the Renascence, and created, in opposition to itself, what I may call an *epoch of concentration*. The great force of that epoch of concentration was England; and the great voice of that epoch of concentration was Burke. It is the fashion to treat Burke's writings on the French Revolution as superannuated and conquered by the event; as the eloquent but unphilosophical tirades of bigotry and prejudice. I will not deny that they are often disfigured by the violence and passion of the moment, and that in some directions Burke's view was bounded, and his observation therefore at fault. But on the whole, and for those who can make the needful corrections, what distinguishes these writings is their profound, permanent, fruitful, philosophical truth. They contain the true philosophy of an epoch of concentration, dissipate the heavy atmosphere which its own nature is apt to engender round it, and make its resistance rational instead of mechanical.

But Burke is so great because, almost alone in England, he brings thought to bear upon politics, he saturates politics with thought. It is his accident that his ideas were at the service of an epoch of concentration, not of an epoch of expansion; it is his characteristic that he so lived by ideas, and had such a source of them welling up within him, that he could float even an epoch of concentration and English Tory politics with them. It does not hurt him that Dr. Price and the Liberals were enraged with him; it does not even hurt him that George the Third and the Tories were enchanted with him. His greatness is that he lived in a world which neither English Liberalism nor English Toryism is apt to enter; —the world of ideas, not the world of catchwords and party habits. So far is it from being really true of him that he "to party gave up what was meant for mankind," that at the very end of his fierce struggle with the French Revolution after all his invectives against its false pretensions, hollowness, and madness, with his sincere conviction of its mischievousness, he can close a memorandum on the best means of combating it, some of the last pages he ever wrote,— the *Thoughts on French Affairs*, in December 1791,— with these striking words:—

"The evil is stated, in my opinion, as it exists. The remedy must be where power, wisdom, and information, I hope, are more united with good intentions than they can be with me. I have done with this subject, I believe, forever. It has given me many anxious moments for the last two years. *If a great change is to be made in human affairs, the minds of men will be fitted to it; the general opinions and feelings will draw that way. Every fear, every hope will forward it; and then they who persist in opposing this mighty current in human affairs, will appear rather to resist the decrees of Providence itself, than the mere designs of men. They will not be resolute and firm, but perverse and obstinate.*"

That return of Burke upon himself has always seemed to me one of the finest things in English literature, or indeed in any literature. That is what I call living by ideas: when one side of a question has long had your earnest support, when all your feelings are engaged, when you hear all around you no language but one, when your party talks this language like a steam-engine and can imagine no other,—still to be able to think, still to be irresistibly carried, if so it be, by the current of thought to the opposite side of the question, and, like Balaam, to be unable to speak anything *but what the Lord has put in your mouth.* I know nothing more striking, and I must add that I know nothing more un-English.

For the Englishman in general is like my friend the Member of Parliament, and believes, point-blank, that for a thing to be an anomaly is absolutely no objection to it whatever. He is like the Lord Auckland of Burke's day, who, in a memorandum on the French Revolution, talks of "certain miscreants, assuming the name of philosophers, who have presumed themselves capable of establishing a new system of society." The Englishman has been called a political animal, and he values what is political and practical so much that ideas easily become objects of dislike in his eyes, and thinkers "miscreants," because ideas and thinkers have rashly meddled with politics and practice. This would be all very well if the dislike and neglect confined themselves to ideas transported out of their own sphere, and meddling rashly with practice; but they are inevitably extended to ideas as such, and to the whole life of intelligence; practice is everything, a free play of the mind is nothing. The notion of the free play of the mind upon all subjects being a pleasure in itself, being an object of desire, being an essential provider of elements without which a nation's spirit, whatever compensations it may have for them, must, in the long run, die of inanition, hardly enters into an Englishman's thoughts. It is noticeable that the word *curiosity*, which in other languages is used in a good sense to mean, as a high and fine quality of man's nature, just this disinterested love of a free play of the mind on all subjects, for its own sake,—it is noticeable, I say, that this word has in our language no sense of the kind, no sense but a rather bad and disparaging one. But criticism, real criticism is essentially the exercise of this very quality. It obeys an instinct prompting it to try to know the best that is known and thought in the world, irrespectively of practice, politics, and everything of the kind; and to value knowledge and thought as they approach this best, without the intrusion of any other considerations whatever. This is an instinct for which there is, I think, little original sympathy in the practical English nature, and what there was of it has undergone a long benumbing period of blight and suppression in the epoch of concentration which followed the French Revolution.

But epochs of concentration cannot well endure forever; epochs of expansion, in the due course of things, follow them. Such an epoch of expansion seems to be opening in this country. In the first place all danger of a hostile forcible pressure of foreign ideas upon our practice has long disappeared; like the traveler in the fable, therefore, we begin to wear our cloak a little more loosely. Then, with a long peace, the ideas of Europe steal gradually and amicably in, and mingle, though in infinitesimally small quantities at a time, with our own notions. Then, too, in spite of all that is said about the absorbing and brutalizing influence of our passionate material progress, it seems to me indisputable that this progress is likely, though not certain, to lead in the end to an apparition of intellectual life; and that man, after he has made himself perfectly comfortable and has now to determine what to do with himself next, may begin to remember that he has a mind, and that the mind may be made the source of great pleasure. I grant it is mainly the privilege of faith, at present, to discern this end to our railways, our business, and our fortune-making; but we shall see if, here as elsewhere, faith is not in the end the true prophet. Our ease, our traveling, and our unbounded liberty to hold just as hard and securely as we please to the practice to which our notions have given birth, all tend to beget an inclination to deal a little more freely with these notions themselves, to canvass them a little, to penetrate a little into their real nature. Flutterings of curiosity, in the foreign sense of the word, appear amongst us, and it is in these that criticism must look to find its account. Criticism first; a time of true creative activity, perhaps,—which, as I have said, must inevitably be preceded amongst us by a time of criticism,—hereafter, when criticism has done its work.

It is of the last importance that English criticism should clearly discern what rule for its course, in order to avail itself of the field now opening to it, and to produce fruit for the future, it ought to take. The rule may be summed up in one word,—*disinterestedness*. And how is criticism to show disinterestedness? By keeping aloof from what is called "the practical view of things;" by resolutely following the law of its own nature, which is to be a free play of the mind on all subjects which it touches. By steadily refusing to lend itself to any of those ulterior, political, practical considerations about ideas, which plenty of people will be sure to attach to them, which perhaps ought often to be attached to them, which in this country at any rate are certain to be attached to them quite sufficiently, but which criticism has really nothing to do with. Its business is, as I have said, simply to know the best that is known and thought in the world, and by in its turn making this known, to create a current of true and fresh ideas. Its business is to do this with inflexible honesty, with due ability; but its business is to do no more, and to leave alone all questions of practical consequences and applications, questions which will never fail to have due prominence given to them. Else criticism, besides being really false to its own nature, merely continues in the old rut which it has hitherto followed in this country, and will certainly miss the chance now given to it. For what is at present the bane of criticism in this country? It is that practical considerations cling to it and stifle it. It subserves interests not its own. Our organs of criticism are organs of men and parties having practical ends to serve, and with them those practical ends are the first thing and the play of mind the second; so much play of mind as is compatible with the prosecution of those practical ends is all that is wanted. An organ like the *Révue des Deux Mondes*, having for its main function to understand and utter the best that is known and thought in the world, existing, it may be said, as just an organ for a free play of the mind, we have not. But we have the *Edinburgh Review*, existing as an organ of the old Whigs, and for as much play of the mind as may suit its being that; we have the *Quarterly Review*, existing as an organ of the Tories, and for as much play of mind as may suit its being that; we have the *British Quarterly Review*, existing as an organ of the political Dissenters, and for as much play of mind as may suit its being that; we have the *Times*, existing as an organ of the common, satisfied, well-to-do Englishman, and for as much play of mind as may suit its being that. And so on through all the various factions, political and religious, of our society; every faction has, as such, its organ of criticism, but the notion of combining all factions in the common pleasure of a free disinterested play of mind meets with no favor. Directly this play of mind wants to have more scope, and to forget the pressure of practical considerations a little, it is checked, it is made to feel the chain. We saw this the other day in the extinction, so much to be regretted, of the *Home and Foreign Review*. Perhaps in no organ of criticism in this country was there so much knowledge, so much play of mind; but these could not save it. The *Dublin Review* subordinates play of mind to the practical business of English and Irish Catholicism, and lives. It must needs be that men should act in sects and parties, that each of these sects and parties should have its organ, and should make this organ subserve the interests of its action; but it would be well, too, that there should be a criticism, not the min-

ister of these interests, not their enemy, but absolutely and entirely independent of them. No other criticism will ever attain any real authority or make any real ways towards its end,—the creating a current of true and fresh ideas.

It is because criticism has so little kept in the pure intellectual sphere, has so little detached itself from practice, has been so directly polemical and controversial, that it has so ill accomplished in this country, its best spiritual work; which is to keep man from a self-satisfaction which is retarding and vulgarizing to lead him towards perfection, by making his mind dwell upon what is excellent in itself, and the absolute beauty and fitness of things. A polemical practical criticism makes men blind even to the ideal imperfection of their practice makes them willingly assert its ideal perfection, in order the better to secure it against attack: and clearly this is narrowing and baneful for them. If they were reassured on the practical side speculative considerations of ideal perfection they might be brought to entertain, and their spiritual horizon would thus gradually widen. Sir Charles Adderley says to the Warwickshire farmers: "Talk of the improvement of breed Why, the race we ourselves represent the men and women, the old Anglo-Saxon race, are the best breed in the whole world. . . . The absence of a too enervating climate, too unclouded skies and a too luxurious nature, has produced so vigorous a race of people and ha rendered us so superior to all the world." Mr. Roebuck says to the Sheffield cutlers: "I look around me and ask what is the state of England? Is not property safe Is not every man able to say what he likes? Can you not walk from one end o England to the other in perfect security I ask you whether, the world over or in past history, there is anything like it Nothing. I pray that our unrivaled happiness may last."

Now obviously there is a peril for poo human nature in words and thoughts o such exuberant self-satisfaction, until we find ourselves safe in the streets of the Celestial City.

"Das wenige verschwindet leicht dem Blicke
  Der vorwärts sieht, wie viel noch übrig
    bleibt—"

says Goethe; "the little that is done seems nothing when we look forward and see how much we have yet to do." Clearly this is a better line of reflection for weak humanity, so long as it remains on this earthly field of labor and trial.

But neither Sir Charles Adderley nor Mr. Roebuck is by nature inaccessible to considerations of this sort. They only lose sight of them owing to the controversial life we all lead, and the practical form which all speculation takes with us. They have in view opponents whose aim is not ideal, but practical; and in their zeal to uphold their own practice against these innovators, they go so far as even to attribute to this practice an ideal perfection. Somebody has been wanting to introduce a six-pound franchise, or to abolish church-rates, or to collect agricultural statistics by force, or to diminish local self-government. How natural, in reply to such proposals, very likely improper or ill-timed, to go a little beyond the mark and to say stoutly, "Such a race of people as we stand, so superior to all the world! The old Anglo-Saxon race, the best breed in the whole world! I pray that our unrivaled happiness may last! I ask you whether, the world over or in past history, there is anything like it?" And so long as criticism answers this dithyramb by insisting that the old Anglo-Saxon race would be still more superior to all others if it had no church-rates, or that our unrivaled happiness would last yet longer with a six-pound franchise, so long will the strain. "The best breed in the whole world!" swell louder and louder, everything ideal and refining will be lost out of sight, and both the assailed and their critics will remain in a sphere, to say the truth, perfectly unvital, a sphere in which spiritual progression is impossible. But let

criticism leave church-rates and the franchise alone, and in the most candid spirit, without a single lurking thought of practical innovation, confront with our dithyramb this paragraph on which 'I stumbled in a newspaper immediately after reading Mr. Roebuck:—

"A shocking child murder has just been committed at Nottingham. A girl named Wragg left the workhouse there on Saturday morning with her young illegitimate child. The child was soon afterwards found dead on Mapperly Hills, having been strangled. Wragg is in custody."

Nothing but that; but, in juxtaposition with the absolute eulogies of Sir Charles Adderley and Mr. Roebuck, how eloquent, how suggestive are those few lines! "Our old Anglo-Saxon breed, the best in the whole world!"—how much that is harsh and ill-favored there is in this best! *Wragg!* If we are to talk of ideal perfection of "the best in the whole world," has any one reflected what a touch of grossness in our race, what an original short-coming in the more delicate spiritual perceptions, is shown by the natural growth amongst us of such hideous names.—Higginbottom, Stiggins, Bugg! In Ionia and Attica they were luckier in this respect than "the best race in the world"; by the Ilissus there was no Wragg, poor thing! And "our unrivaled happiness";—what an element of grimness, bareness, and hideousness mixes with it and blurs it; the workhouse, the dismal Mapperly Hills,—how dismal those who have seen them will remember;—the gloom, the smoke, the cold, the strangled illegitimate child! "I ask you whether, the world over or in past history, there is anything like it?" Perhaps not, one is inclined to answer; but at any rate, in that case, the world is very much to be pitied. And the final touch, —short, bleak and inhuman: *Wragg is in custody.* The sex lost in the confusion of our unrivaled happiness; or (shall I say?) the superfluous Christian name lopped off by the straightforward vigor of our old Anglo-Saxon breed! There is profit for the spirit in such contrasts as this; criticism serves the cause of perfection by establishing them. By eluding sterile conflict, by refusing to remain in the sphere where alone narrow and relative conceptions have any worth and validity, criticism may diminish its momentary importance, but only in this way has it a chance of gaining admittance for those wider and more perfect conceptions to which all its duty is really owed. Mr. Roebuck will have a poor opinion of an adversary who replies to his defiant songs of triumph only by murmuring under his breath, *Wragg is in custody*; but in no other way will these songs of triumph be induced gradually to moderate themselves, to get rid of what in them is excessive and offensive, and to fall into a softer and truer key.

It will be said that it is a very subtle and indirect action which I am thus prescribing for criticism, and that, by embracing in this manner the Indian virtue of detachment and abandoning the sphere of practical life, it condemns itself to a slow and obscure work. Slow and obscure it may be, but it is the only proper work of criticism. The mass of mankind will never have any ardent zeal for seeing things as they are; very inadequate ideas will always satisfy them. On these inadequate ideas reposes, and must repose, the general practice of the world. That is as much as saying that whoever sets himself to see things as they are will find himself one of a very small circle; but it is only by this small circle resolutely doing its own work that adequate ideas will ever get current at all. The rush and roar of practical life will always have a dizzying and attracting effect upon the most collected spectator, and tend to draw him into its vortex; most of all will this be the case where that life is so powerful as it is in England. But it is only by remaining collected, and refusing to lend himself to the point of view of the practical man, that the critic can do the practical man any service; and it is only by the greatest sincerity in pursuing his own course, and by at last convincing even the prac-

tical man of his sincerity, that he can escape misunderstandings which perpetually threaten him.

For the practical man is not apt for fine distinctions, and yet in these distinctions truth and the highest culture greatly find their account. But it is not easy to lead a practical man,—unless you reassure him as to your practical intentions, you have no chance of leading him,—to see that a thing which he has always been used to look at from one side only, which he greatly values, and which, looked at from that side, quite deserves, perhaps, all the prizing and admiring which he bestows upon it,—that this thing, looked at from another side, may appear much less beneficent and beautiful, and yet retain all its claims to our practical allegiance. Where shall we find language innocent enough, how shall we make the spotless purity of our intentions evident enough, to enable us to say to the political Englishman that the British Constitution itself, which, seen from the practical side, looks such a magnificent organ of progress and virtue, seen from the speculative side,—with its compromises, its love of facts, its horror of theory, its studied avoidance of clear thoughts,—that, seen from this side, our august Constitution sometimes looks,—forgive me, shade of Lord Somers!—a colossal machine for the manufacture of Philistines? How is Cobbett to say this and not be misunderstood, blackened as he is with the smoke of a lifelong conflict in the field of political practice? how is Mr. Carlyle to say it and not be misunderstood, after his furious raid into this field with his *Latter-day Pamphlets*? how is Mr. Ruskin, after his pugnacious political economy? I say, the critic must keep out of the region of immediate practice in the political, social, humanitarian sphere, if he wants to make a beginning for that more free speculative treatment of things, which may perhaps one day make its benefits felt even in this sphere, but in a natural and thence irresistible manner.

Do what he will, however, the critic will still remain exposed to frequent misunderstandings, and nowhere so much as in this country. For here people are particularly indisposed even to comprehend that without this free disinterested treatment of things, truth and the highest culture are out of the question. So immersed are they in practical life, so accustomed to take all their notions from this life and its processes, that they are apt to think that truth and culture themselves can be reached by the processes of this life, and that it is an impertinent singularity to think of reaching them in any other. "We are all *terrae filii*," cries their eloquent advocate; "all Philistines together. Away with the notion of proceeding by any other course than the course dear to the Philistines; let us have a social movement, let us organize and combine a party to pursue truth and new thought, let us call it *the liberal party*, and let us all stick to each other, and back each other up. Let us have no nonsense about independent criticism, and intellectual delicacy, and the few and the many. Don't let us trouble ourselves about foreign thought; we shall invent the whole thing for ourselves as we go along. If one of us speaks well, applaud him; if one of us speaks ill, applaud him too; we are all in the same movement, we are all liberals, we are all in pursuit of truth." In this way the pursuit of truth becomes really a social, practical, pleasurable affair, almost requiring a chairman, a secretary, and advertisements; with the excitement of an occasional scandal, with a little resistance to give the happy sense of difficulty overcome; but, in general, plenty of bustle and very little thought. To act is so easy, as Goethe says: to think is so hard! It is true that the critic has many temptations to go with the stream, to make one of the party movement, one of these *terrae filii*; it seems ungracious to refuse to be a *terrae filius*, when so many excellent people are; but the critic's duty is to refuse, or, if resistance is vain, at least to cry with Obermann: *Périssons en résistant*.

How serious a matter it is to try and resist, I had ample opportunity of ex-periencing when I ventured some time ago to criticize the celebrated first volume of Bishop Colenso.[2] The echoes of the storm which was then raised I still, from time to time, hear grumbling around me. That storm arose out of a misunderstanding almost inevitable. It is a result of no little culture to attain to a clear perception that science and religion are two wholly different things. The multitude will for ever confuse them; but happily that is of no great real importance, for while the multitude imagines itself to live by its false science, it does really live by its true religion. Dr. Colenso, however, in his first volume did all he could to strengthen the confusion,[3] and to make it dangerous. He did this with the best intentions, I freely admit, and with the most candid ignorance that this was the natural effect of what he was doing; but, says Joubert, "Ignorance, which in matters of morals extenuates the crime, is itself, in intellectual matters, a crime of the first order." I criticized Bishop Colenso's speculative confusion. Immediately there was a cry raised: "What is this? here is a liberal attacking a liberal. Do not you belong to the movement? are not you a friend of truth? Is not Bishop Colenso in pursuit of truth? then speak with proper respect of his book. Dr. Stanley is another friend of truth, and you speak with proper respect of his book; why make these invidious differences? both books are excellent, admirable, liberal; Bishop Colenso's perhaps the most so, because it is the boldest, and will have the best

[2] So sincere is my dislike to all personal attack and controversy, that I abstain from reprinting, at this distance of time from the occasion which called them forth, the essays in which I criticized Dr. Colenso's book; I feel bound, however, after all that has passed, to make here a final declaration of my sincere impenitence for having published them. Nay, I cannot forbear repeating yet once more, for his benefit and that of his readers, this sentence from my original remarks upon him: *There is truth of science and truth of religion: truth of science does not become truth of religion till it is made religious.* And I will add: Let us have all the science there is from the men of science; from the men of religion let us have religion.

[3] It has been said I make it "a crime against literary criticism and the higher culture to attempt to inform the ignorant." Need I point out that the ignorant are not informed by being confirmed in a confusion?

practical consequences for the liberal cause. Do you want to encourage to the attack of a brother liberal his, and your, and our implacable enemies, the *Church and State Review* or the *Record*,—the High Church rhinoceros and the Evangelical hyena? Be silent, therefore; or rather speak, speak as loud as ever you can! and go into ecstasies over the eighty and odd pigeons."

But criticism cannot follow this coarse and indiscriminate method. It is unfortunately possible for a man in pursuit of truth to write a book which reposes upon a false conception. Even the practical consequences of a book are to genuine criticism no recommendation of it, if the book is, in the highest sense, blundering. I see that a lady who herself, too, is in pursuit of truth, and who writes with great ability, but a little too much, perhaps, under the influence of the practical spirit of the English liberal movement, classes Bishop Colenso's book and M. Renan's together, in her survey of the religious state of Europe, as facts of the same order, works, both of them, of "great importance"; "great ability, power, and skill"; Bishop Colenso's, perhaps, the most powerful; at least, Miss Cobbe gives special expression to her gratitude that to Bishop Colenso "has been given the strength to grasp, and the courage to teach, truths of such deep import." In the same way, more than one popular writer has compared him to Luther. Now it is just this kind of false estimate which the critical spirit is, it seems to me, bound to resist. It is really the strongest possible proof of the low ebb at which, in England, the critical spirit is, that while the critical hit in the religious literature of Germany is Dr. Strauss's book, in that of France M. Renan's book, the book of Bishop Colenso is the critical hit in the religious literature of England. Bishop Colenso's book reposes on a total misconception of the essential elements of the religious problem, as that problem is now presented for solution. To criticism, therefore, which seeks to have the best that is known and thought on this problem, it is, however well meant, of no importance whatever. M. Renan's book attempts a new synthesis of the elements furnished to us by the Four Gospels. It attempts, in my opinion, a synthesis, perhaps premature, perhaps impossible, certainly not successful. Up to the present time, at any rate, we must acquiesce in Fleury's sentence on such recastings of the Gospel-story: *Quiconque s'imagine la pouvoir mieux écrire, ne l'entend pas.* M. Renan had himself passed by anticipation a like sentence on his own work, when he said: "If a new presentation of the character of Jesus were offered to me, I would not have it; its very clearness would be, in my opinion, the best proof of its insufficiency." His friends may with perfect justice rejoin that at the sight of the Holy Land, and of the actual scene of the Gospel-story, all the current of M. Renan's thoughts may have naturally changed, and a new casting of that story irresistibly suggested itself to him; and that this is just a case for applying Cicero's maxim; Change of mind is not inconsistency—*nemo doctus unquam mutationem consilii inconstantiam dixit esse.* Nevertheless, for criticism, M. Renan's first thought must still be the truer one, as long as his new casting so fails more fully to commend itself, more fully (to use Coleridge's happy phrase about the Bible) to *find* us. Still M. Renan's attempt is, for criticism, of the most real interest and importance, since, with all its difficulty, a fresh synthesis of the New Testament *data*,—not a making war on them, in Voltaire's fashion, not a leaving them out of mind, in the world's fashion, but the putting a new construction upon them, the taking them from under the old, traditional, conventional point of view and placing them under a new one,—is the very essence of the religious problem, as now presented and only by efforts in this direction can it receive a solution.

Again, in the same spirit in which she judges Bishop Colenso, Miss Cobbe, like so many earnest liberals of our practical race, both here and in America, herself sets vigorously about a positive reconstruction of religion, about making a religion of the future out of hand, or at least setting about making it. We must not rest, she and they are always thinking and saying, in negative criticism, we must be creative and constructive; hence we have such works as her recent *Religious Duty*, and works still more considerable, perhaps, by others, which will be in every one's mind. These works often have much ability; they often spring out of sincere convictions, and a sincere wish to do good; and they sometimes, perhaps, do good. Their fault is (if I may be permitted to say so) one which they have in common with the British College of Health, in the New Road. Every one knows the British College of Health; it is that building with the lion and the statue of the Goddess Hygeia before it; at least I am sure about the lion, though I am not absolutely certain about the Goddess Hygeia. This building does credit, perhaps, to the resources of Dr. Morrison and his disciples; but it falls a good deal short of one's idea of what a British College of Health ought to be. In England, where we hate public interference and love individual enterprise, we have a whole crop of places like the British College of Health; the grand name without the grand thing. Unluckily, creditable to individual enterprise as they are, they tend to impair our taste by making us forget what more grandiose, noble, or beautiful character properly belongs to a public institution. The same may be said of the religions of the future of Miss Cobbe and others. Creditable, like the British College of Health, to the resources of their authors, they yet tend to make us forget what more grandiose, noble, or beautiful character properly belongs to religious constructions. The historic religions, with all their faults, have had this; it certainly belongs to the religious sentiment, when it truly flowers, to have this; and we impoverish our spirit if we allow a religion of the future without it. What then is the duty of criticism here? To take the practical point of view, to applaud the liberal movement and all its works,—its New Road religions of the future into the bargain,—for their general utility's sake? By no means; but to be perpetually dissatisfied with these works, while they perpetually fall short of a high and perfect ideal.

For criticism, these are elementary laws; but they never can be popular, and in this country they have been very little followed, and one meets with immense obstacles in following them. That is a reason for asserting them again and again. Criticism must maintain its independence of the practical spirit and its aims. Even with well-meant efforts of the practical spirit it must express dissatisfaction, if in the sphere of the ideal they seem impoverishing and limiting. It must not hurry on to the goal because of its practical importance. It must be patient, and know how to wait; and flexible, and know how to attach itself to things and how to withdraw from them. It must be apt to study and praise elements that for the fulness of spiritual perfection are wanted, even though they belong to a power which in the practical sphere may be maleficent. It must be apt to discern the spiritual shortcomings or illusions of powers that in the practical sphere may be beneficent. And this without any notion of favoring or injuring, in the practical sphere, one power or the other; without any notion of playing off, in this sphere, one power against the other. When one looks, for instance, at the English Divorce Court—an institution which perhaps has its practical conveniences, but which in the ideal sphere is so hideous; an institution which neither makes divorce impossible nor makes it decent, which allows a man to get rid of his wife, or a wife of her husband, but makes them drag one another first, for the public edification, through a mire of unutterable infamy,—when one looks at this charming institution, I say, with its crowded trials, its newspaper reports, and its money compensations, this institution in which the gross unregenerate British Philistine has indeed stamped an image of himself,—one may be permitted to find the marriage theory of Catholicism refreshing and elevating. Or when Protestantism, in virtue of its supposed rational and intellectual origin, gives the law to criticism too magisterially, criticism may and must remind it that its pretensions, in this respect, are illusive and do it harm; that the Reformation was a moral rather than an intellectual event; that Luther's theory of grace no more exactly reflects the mind of the spirit than Bossuet's philosophy of history reflects it; and that there is no more antecedent probability of the Bishop of Durham's stock of ideas being agreeable to perfect reason than of Pope Pius the Ninth's. But criticism will not on that account forget the achievements of Protestantism in the practical and moral sphere; nor that, even in the intellectual sphere, Protestantism, though in a blind and stumbling manner, carried forward the Renascence, while Catholicism threw itself violently across its path.

I lately heard a man of thought and energy contrasting the want of ardor and movement which he now found amongst young men in this country with what he remembered in his own youth, twenty years ago. "What reformers we were then!" he exclaimed; "What a zeal we had! how we canvassed every institution in Church and State, and were prepared to remodel them all on first principles!" He was inclined to regret, as a spiritual flagging, the lull which he saw. I am disposed rather to regard it as a pause in which the turn to a new mode of spiritual progress is being accomplished. Everything was long seen, by the young and ardent amongst us, in inseparable connection with politics and practical life. We have pretty well exhausted the benefits of seeing things in this connection, we have got all that can be got by so seeing them. Let us try a more disinterested mode of seeing them; let us betake ourselves more to the serener life of the mind and spirit. This life, too, may have its excesses and dangers; but they are not for us at present. Let us think of quietly enlarging our stock of true and fresh ideas, and not, as soon as we get an idea or half an idea, be running out with it into the street, and try-

ing to make it rule there. Our ideas will, in the end, shape the world all the better for maturing a little. Perhaps in fifty years' time it will in the English House of Commons be an objection to an institution that it is an anomaly, and my friend the Member of Parliament will shudder in his grave. But let us in the meanwhile rather endeavor that in twenty years' time it may, in English literature, be an objection to a proposition that it is absurd. That will be a change so vast, that the imagination almost fails to grasp it. *Ab integro saeclorum nascitur ordo.*[4]

If I have insisted so much on the course which criticism must take where politics and religion are concerned, it is because, where these burning matters are in question, it is most likely to go astray. I have wished, above all, to insist on the attitude which criticism should adopt towards things in general; on its right tone and temper of mind. But then comes another question as to the subject-matter which literary criticism should most seek. Here, in general, its course is determined for it by the idea which is the law of its being; the idea of a disinterested endeavor to learn and propagate the best that is known and thought in the world, and thus to establish a current of fresh and true ideas. By the very nature of things, as England is not all the world, much of the best that is known and thought in the world cannot be of English growth, must be foreign; by the nature of things, again, it is just this that we are least likely to know, while English thought is streaming in upon us from all sides, and takes excellent care that we shall not be ignorant of its existence. The English critic of literature, therefore, must dwell much on foreign thought, and with particular heed on any part of it, which, while significant and fruitful in itself, is for any reason specially likely to escape him. Again, judging is often spoken of as the critic's one business, and so in some sense it is; but the judgment which almost insensibly forms itself in a fair and clear mind, along with fresh knowledge, is the

---

4 The world's great age begins anew.

valuable one; and thus knowledge, and ever fresh knowledge, must be the critic's great concern for himself. And it is by communicating fresh knowledge, and letting his own judgment pass along with it,—but insensibly, and in the second place, not the first, as a sort of companion and clue, not as an abstract lawgiver,—that the critic will generally do most good to his readers. Sometimes, no doubt, for the sake of establishing an author's place in literature, and his relation to a central standard (and if this is not done, how are we to get at our *best in the world?*) criticism may have to deal with a subject-matter so familiar that fresh knowledge is out of the question, and then it must be all judgment; an enunciation and detailed application of principles. Here the great safeguard is never to let oneself become abstract, always to retain an intimate and lively consciousness of the truth of what one is saying, and, the moment this fails us, to be sure that something is wrong. Still, under all circumstances, this mere judgment and application of principles is, in itself, not the most satisfactory work to the critic; like mathematics, it is tautological, and cannot well give us, like fresh learning, the sense of creative activity.

But stop, some one will say; all this talk is of no practical use to us whatever; this criticism of yours is not what we have in our minds when we speak of criticism; when we speak of critics and criticism, we mean critics and criticism of the current English literature of the day; when you offer to tell criticism its function, it is to this criticism that we expect you to address yourself. I am sorry for it, for I am afraid I must disappoint these expectations. I am bound by my own definition of criticism: *a disinterested endeavor to learn and propagate the best that is known and thought in the world*. How much of current English literature comes into this "best that is known and thought in the world?" Not very much I fear; certainly less, at this moment, than of the current literature of France or Germany. Well, then, am I to alter my definition of criticism, in order to meet the requirements of a

number of practising English critics, who, after all, are free in their choice of a business? That would be making criticism lend itself just to one of those alien practical considerations, which, I have said, are so fatal to it. One may say, indeed, to those who have to deal with the mass—so much better disregarded—of current English literature, that they may at all events endeavor, in dealing with this, to try it, so far as they can, by the standard of the best that is known and thought in the world; one may say, that to get anywhere near this standard, every critic should try and possess one great literature, at least, besides his own; and the more unlike his own, the better. But, after all, the criticism I am really concerned with,—the criticism which alone can much help us for the future, the criticism which, throughout Europe, is at the present day meant, when so much stress is laid on the importance of criticism and the critical spirit,—is a criticism which regards Europe as being, for intellectual and spiritual purposes, one great confederation, bound to a joint action and working to a common result; and whose members have, for their proper outfit, a knowledge of Greek, Roman, and Eastern antiquity, and of one another. Special, local, and temporary advantages being put out of account, that modern nation will in the intellectual and spiritual sphere make most progress, which most thoroughly carries out this program. And what is that but saying that we too, all of us, as individuals, the more thoroughly we carry it out, shall make the more progress?

There is so much inviting us!—what are we to take? what will nourish us in growth towards perfection? That is the question which, with the immense field of life and of literature lying before him, the critic has to answer; for himself first, and afterwards for others. In this idea of the critic's business the essays brought together in the following pages have had their origin; in this idea, widely different as are their subjects, they have, perhaps, their unity.

I conclude with what I said at the beginning: to have the sense of creative activity is the great happiness and the great proof of being alive, and it is not denied to criticism to have it; but then criticism must be sincere, simple, flexible, ardent, ever widening its knowledge. Then it may have, in no contemptible measure, a joyful sense of creative activity; a sense which a man of insight and conscience will prefer to what he might derive from a poor, starved, fragmentary, inadequate creation. And at some epochs no other creation is possible.

Still, in full measure, the sense of creative activity belongs only to genuine creation; in literature we must never forget that. But what true man of letters ever can forget it? It is no such common matter for a gifted nature to come into possession of a current of true and living ideas, and to produce amidst the inspiration of them, that we are likely to underrate it. The epochs of Aeschylus and Shakespeare make us feel their preeminence. In an epoch like those is, no doubt, the true life of literature; there is the promised land, towards which criticism can only beckon. That promised land it will not be ours to enter, and we shall die in the wilderness: but to have desired to enter it, to have saluted it from afar, is already, perhaps, the best distinction among contemporaries; it will certainly be the best title to esteem with posterity.

The Study of Poetry (1880)

"The future of poetry is immense, because in poetry, where it is worthy of its high destinies, our race, as time goes on, will find an ever surer and surer stay. There is not a creed which is not shaken, not an accredited dogma which is not shown to be questionable, not a received tradition which does not threaten to dissolve. Our religion has materialized itself in the fact, in the supposed fact; it has attached its emotion to the fact, and now the fact is failing it. But for poetry the idea is everything; the rest is a world of illusion, of divine illusion. Poetry attaches its emotion to the idea; the idea *is* the fact. The strongest part of our religion to-day is its unconscious poetry."

Let me be permitted to quote these words of my own, as uttering the thought which should, in my opinion, go with us and govern us in all our study of poetry. In the present work it is the course of one great contributory stream to the world-river of poetry that we are invited to follow. We are here invited to trace the stream of English poetry. But whether we set ourselves, as here, to follow only one of the several streams that make the mighty river of poetry, or whether we seek to know them all, our governing thought should be the same. We should conceive of poetry worthily, and more highly than it has been the custom to conceive of it. We should conceive of it as capable of higher uses, and called to higher destinies, than those which in general men have assigned to it hitherto. More and more mankind will discover that we have to turn to poetry to interpret life for us, to console us, to sustain us. Without poetry, our science will appear incomplete; and most of what now passes with us for religion and philosophy will be replaced by poetry. Science, I say, will appear incomplete without it. For finely and truly does Wordsworth call poetry "the impassioned expression which is in the countenance of all science"; and what is a countenance without its expression? Again, Wordsworth finely and truly calls poetry "the breath and finer spirit of all knowledge": our religion, parading evidences such as those on which the popular mind relies now; our philosophy, pluming itself on its reasonings about causation and finite and infinite being; what are they but the shadows and dreams and false shows of knowledge? The day will come when we shall wonder at ourselves for having trusted to them, for having taken them seriously; and the more we perceive their hollowness, the more we shall prize "th

First published as the General Introduction to *The English Poets*, edited by T. H. Ward (1880).

breath and finer spirit of knowledge" offered to us by poetry.

But if we conceive thus highly of the destinies of poetry, we must also set our standard for poetry high, since poetry, to be capable of fulfilling such high destinies, must be poetry of a high order of excellence. We must accustom ourselves to a high standard and to a strict judgment. Sainte-Beuve relates that Napoleon one day said, when somebody was spoken of in his presence as a charlatan: "Charlatan as much as you please; but where is there *not* charlatanism?"—"Yes," answers Sainte-Beuve, "in politics, in the art of governing mankind, that is perhaps true. But in the order of thought, in art, the glory, the eternal honor is that charlatanism shall find no entrance; herein lies the inviolableness of that noble portion of man's being." It is admirably said, and let us hold fast to it. In poetry, which is thought and art in one, it is the glory, the eternal honor, that charlatanism shall find no entrance; that this noble sphere be kept inviolate and inviolable. Charlatanism is for confusing or obliterating the distinctions between excellent and inferior, sound and unsound or only half-sound, true and untrue or only half-true. It is charlatanism, conscious or unconscious, whenever we confuse or obliterate these. And in poetry, more than anywhere else, it is unpermissible to confuse or obliterate them. For in poetry the distinction between excellent and inferior, sound and unsound or only half-sound, true and untrue or only half-true, is of paramount importance because of the high destinies of poetry. In poetry, as a criticism of life under the conditions fixed for such a criticism by the laws of poetic truth and poetic beauty, the spirit of our race will find, we have said, as time goes on and as other helps fail, its consolation and stay. But the consolation and stay will be of power in proportion to the power of the criticism of life. And the criticism of life will be of power in proportion as the poetry conveying it is excellent rather than inferior, sound rather than unsound or half-sound, true rather than untrue or half-true.

The best poetry is what we want; the best poetry will be found to have a power of forming, sustaining, and delighting us, as nothing else can. A clearer, deeper sense of the best in poetry, and of the strength and joy to be drawn from it, is the most precious benefit which we can gather from a poetical collection such as the present. And yet in the very nature and conduct of such a collection there is inevitably something which tends to obscure in us the consciousness of what our benefit should be, and to distract us from the pursuit of it. We should therefore steadily set it before our minds at the outset, and should compel ourselves to revert constantly to the thought of it as we proceed.

Yes; constantly in reading poetry, a sense for the best, the really excellent, and of the strength and joy to be drawn from it, should be present in our minds and should govern our estimate of what we read. But this real estimate, the only true one, is liable to be superseded, if we are not watchful, by two other kinds of estimate, the historic estimate and the personal estimate, both of which are fallacious. A poet or a poem may count to us historically, they may count to us on grounds personal to ourselves, and they may count to us really. They may count to us historically. The course of development of a nation's language, thought, and poetry, is profoundly interesting; and by regarding a poet's work as a stage in this course of development we may easily bring ourselves to make it of more importance as poetry than in itself it really is, we may come to use a language of quite exaggerated praise in criticising it; in short, to over-rate it. So arises in our poetic judgments the fallacy caused by the estimate which we may call historic. Then, again, a poet or a poem may count to us on grounds personal to ourselves. Our personal affinities, likings, and circumstances, have great power to sway our estimate of this or that poet's work, and to make us attach more importance to it as poetry than in itself it really possesses, because to us it is, or has been, of high importance. Here also we over-rate the object of our interest, and apply to it a language of praise which is quite exaggerated. And thus we get the source of a second fallacy in our poetic judgments—the fallacy caused by an estimate which we may call personal.

Both fallacies are natural. It is evident how naturally the study of the history and development of a poetry may incline a man to pause over reputations and works once conspicuous but now obscure, and to quarrel with a careless public for skipping, in obedience to mere tradition and habit, from one famous name or work in its national poetry to another, ignorant of what it misses, and of the reason for keeping what it keeps, and of the whole process of growth in its poetry. The French have become diligent students of their own early poetry, which they long neglected; the study makes many of them dissatisfied with their so-called classical poetry, the court-tragedy of the seventeenth century, a poetry which Pellisson long ago reproached with its want of the true poetic stamp, with its *politesse stérile et rampante*, but which nevertheless has reigned in France as absolutely as if it had been the perfection of classical poetry indeed. The dissatisfaction is natural; yet a lively and accomplished critic, M. Charles d'Héricault, the editor of Clément Marot, goes too far when he says that "the cloud of glory playing round a classic is a mist as dangerous to the future of a literature as it is intolerable for the purposes of history." "It hinders," he goes on, "it hinders us from seeing more than one single point, the culminating and exceptional point; the summary, fictitious and arbitrary, of a thought and of a work. It substitutes a halo for a physiognomy, it puts a statue where there was once a man, and hiding from us all trace of the labor, the attempts, the weaknesses, the failures, it claims not study but veneration; it does not show us how the thing is done, it imposes upon us a model. Above all, for the historian this creation of classic personages is inadmissible; for it withdraws the poet from his time, from his proper life, it breaks historical relationships, it blinds criticism by conventional admiration, and renders the investigation of literary origins unacceptable. It gives us a human personage no longer, but a God seated immovable amidst His perfect work, like Jupiter on Olympus; and hardly will it be possible for the young student, to whom such work is exhibited at such a distance from him, to believe that it did not issue ready made from that divine head."

All this is brilliantly and tellingly said, but we must plead for a distinction. Everything depends on the reality of a poet's classic character. If he is a dubious classic, let us sift him; if he is a false classic, let us explode him. But if he is a real classic, if his work belongs to the class of the very best (for this is the true and right meaning of the word *classic*, *classical*), then the great thing for us is to feel and enjoy his work as deeply as ever we can, and to appreciate the wide difference between it and all work which has not the same high character. This is what is salutary, this is what is formative; this is the great benefit to be got from the study of poetry. Everything which interferes with it, which hinders it, is injurious. True, we must read our classic with open eyes, and not with eyes blinded with superstition; we must perceive when his work comes short, when it drops out of the class of the very best, and we must rate it, in such cases, at its proper value. But the use of this negative criticism is not in itself, it is entirely in its enabling us to have a clearer sense and a deeper enjoyment of what is truly excellent. To trace the labor, the attempts, the weaknesses, the failures of a genuine classic, to acquaint oneself with his time and his life and his historical relationships, is mere literary dilettantism unless it has that clear sense and deeper enjoyment for its end. It may be said that the more we know about a classic the better we shall enjoy him; and, if we lived as long as Methuselah and had all of us heads of perfect clearness and wills of perfect steadfastness, this might be true in fact as it is plausible in theory. But the case here is much the same as the case with the Greek and Latin studies of our schoolboys. The elaborate philological groundwork which we require them to lay is in theory an admirable preparation for appreciating the Greek and Latin authors worthily. The more thoroughly we lay the groundwork, the better we shall be able, it may be said, to enjoy the authors. True, if time were not so short, and schoolboys' wits not so soon tired and their power of attention exhausted; only, as it is, the elaborate philological preparation goes on, but the authors are little known and less enjoyed. So with the investigator of "historic origins" in poetry. He ought to enjoy the true classic all the better for his investigations; he often is distracted from the enjoyment of the best, and with the less good he over-busies himself, and is prone to over-rate it in proportion to the trouble which it has cost him.

The idea of tracing historic origins and historical relationships cannot be absent from a compilation, like the present. And naturally the poets to be exhibited in it will be assigned to those persons for exhibition who are known to prize them highly, rather than to those who have no special inclination towards them. Moreover the very occupation with an author, and the business of exhibiting him, disposes us to affirm and amplify his importance. In the present work, therefore, we are sure of frequent temptation to adopt the historic estimate, or the personal estimate, and to forget the real estimate; which latter, nevertheless, we must employ if we are to make poetry yield us its full benefit. So high is that benefit, the benefit of clearly feeling and of deeply enjoying the really excellent, the truly classic in poetry, that we do well, I say, to set it fixedly before our minds as our object in studying poets and poetry, and to make the desire of attaining it the one principle to which, as the *Imitation* says, whatever we may read or come to know, we always return. *Cum multa legeris et cognoveris, ad unum semper oportet redire principium.*

The historic estimate is likely in especial to affect our judgment and our language when we are dealing with ancient poets; the personal estimate when we are dealing with poets our contemporaries, or at any rate modern. The exaggerations due to the historic estimate are not in themselves, perhaps, of very much gravity. Their report hardly enters the general ear; probably they do not always impose even on the literary men who

adopt them. But they lead to a dangerous abuse of language. So we hear Caedmon, amongst our own poets, compared to Milton. I have already noticed the enthusiasm of one accomplished French critic for "historic origins." Another eminent French critic, M. Vitet, comments upon that famous document of the early poetry of his nation, the *Chanson de Roland.* It is indeed a most interesting document. The *joculator* or *jongleur* Taillefer, who was with William the Conqueror's army at Hastings, marched before the Norman troops, so said the tradition, singing "of Charlemagne and of Roland and of Oliver, and of the vassals who died at Roncevaux"; and it is suggested that in the *Chanson de Roland* by one Turoldus or Théroulde, a poem preserved in a manuscript of the twelfth century in the Bodleian Library at Oxford, we have certainly the matter, perhaps even some of the words, of the chant which Taillefer sang. The poem has vigor and freshness; it is not without pathos. But M. Vitet is not satisfied with seeing in it a document of some poetic value, and of very high historic and linguistic value; he sees in it a grand and beautiful work, a monument of epic genius. In its general design he finds the grandiose conception, in its details he finds the constant union of simplicity with greatness, which are the marks, he truly says, of the genuine epic, and distinguish it from the artificial epic of literary ages. One thinks of Homer; this is the sort of praise which is given to Homer, and justly given. Higher praise there cannot well be, and it is the praise due to epic poetry of the highest order only, and to no other. Let us try, then, the *Chanson de Roland* at its best. Roland, mortally wounded, lays himself down under a pine-tree, with his face turned towards Spain and the enemy—

"De plusurs choses à remembrer li prist,
De tantes teres cume li bers cunquist,
De dulce France, des humes de sun lign,
De Carlemagne sun seignor ki l'nurrit." [1]

[1] "Then began he to call many things to remembrance,—all the lands which his valour conquered, and pleasant France, and the men of his lineage, and Charlemagne his liege lord who nourished him."— *Chanson de Roland,* iii. 939-942.

That is primitive work, I repeat, with an undeniable poetic quality of its own. It deserves such praise, and such praise is sufficient for it. But now turn to Homer—

> Ὣς φάτο· τοὺς δ ἤδη κατέχεν φυσίζοος αἶα
> ἐ Λακεδαίμονι αὖθι, φίλῃ ἐν πατρίδι λαίῃ [2]

We are here in another world, another order of poetry altogether; here is rightly due such supreme praise as that which M. Vitet gives to the *Chanson de Roland*. If our words are to have any meaning, if our judgments are to have any solidity, we must not heap that supreme praise upon poetry of an order immeasurably inferior.

Indeed there can be no more useful help for discovering what poetry belongs to the class of the truly excellent, and can therefore do us most good, than to have always in one's mind lines and expressions of the great masters, and to apply them as a touchstone to other poetry. Of course we are not to require this other poetry to resemble them; it may be very dissimilar. But if we have any tact we shall find them, when we have lodged them well in our minds, an infallible touchstone for detecting the presence or absence of high poetic quality, and also the degree of this quality, in all other poetry which we may place beside them. Short passages, even single lines, will serve our turn quite sufficiently. Take the two lines which I have just quoted from Homer, the poet's comment on Helen's mention of her brothers;—or take his

> Ἆ δειλώ, τί σφῶϊ δόμεν Πηλῆϊ ἄνακτι
> θνητᾷ; ὑμεῖς δ' ἐστὸν ἀγήρω τ' ἀθανάτω τε,
> ἦ ἵνα δυστήνοισι μετ' ἀνδράσιν ἄλγε' ἔχητον; [3]

the address of Zeus to the horses of Peleus;—or take finally his

> Καί σέ, γέρον, τὸ πρίν μὲν ἀκούομεν ὄλβιον
> εἶναι· [4]

the words of Achilles to Priam, a suppliant before him. Take that incomparable line and a half of Dante, Ugolino's tremendous words—

> "Io no piangeva; sì dentro impietri.
> Piangevan elli . . ." [5]

take the lovely words of Beatrice to Virgil—

> "Io son fatta da Dio, sua mercè,
>   tale,
> Che las vostra miseria non mi
>   tange,
> Nè fiamma d'esto incendio non
>   m'assale . . ." [6]

take the simple, but perfect, single line—

> "In la sua volontade è nostra pace." [7]

Take of Shakespeare a line or two of Henry the Fourth's expostulation with sleep—

> "Wilt thou upon the high and giddy mast
> Seal up the ship-boy's eyes, and rock his
>   brains
> In cradle of the rude imperious surge . . ."

and take, as well, Hamlet's dying request to Horatio—

> "If thou didst ever hold me in thy heart,
> Absent thee from felicity awhile,
> And in this harsh world draw thy breath in
>   pain
> To tell my story . . . "

Take of Milton that Miltonic passage—

>   "Darken'd so, yet shone
> Above them all the archangel; but his face
> Deep scars of thunder had intrench'd, and
>   care
> Sat on his faded cheek . . ."

add two such lines as—

> "And courage never to submit or yield
> And what is else not to be overcome . . ."

---

[2] "So said she; they long since in Earth's soft arms were reposing,
There, in their own dear land, their fatherland, Lacedaemon."
Iliad, iii. 243,244 (translated by Dr. Hawtry).

[3] "Ah, unhappy pair, why gave we you to King Peleus, to a mortal? but ye are without old age, and immortal. Was it that with men born to misery ye might have sorrow?"—*Iliad*, xvii. 443-445.

[4] "Nay, and thou too, old man, in former days wast, as we hear, happy."—*Iliad*, xxiv. 543.

[5] "I wailed not, so of stone grew I within;—*they wailed.*"—*Inferno*, xxxiii. 39, 40.

[6] "Of such sort hath God, thanked be His mercy, made me, that your misery toucheth me not, neither doth the flame of this fire strike me."—*Inferno*, ii. 91-93.

[7] "In His will is our peace."—*Paradiso*, iii. 85.

and finish with the exquisite close to the loss of Proserpine, the loss

> ". . . which cost Ceres all that pain
> To seek her through the world."

These few lines, if we have tact and can use them, are enough even of themselves to keep clear and sound our judgments about poetry, to save us from fallacious estimates of it, to conduct us to a real estimate.

The specimens I have quoted differ widely from one another, but they have in common this: the possession of the very highest poetical quality. If we are thoroughly penetrated by their power, we shall find that we have acquired a sense enabling us, whatever poetry may be laid before us, to feel the degree in which a high poetical quality is present or wanting there. Critics give themselves great labor to draw out what in the abstract constitutes the characters of a high quality of poetry. It is much better simply to have recourse to concrete examples;—to take specimens of poetry of the high, the very highest quality, and to say: The characters of a high quality of poetry are what is expressed *there*. They are far better recognized by being felt in the verse of the master, than by being perused in the prose of the critic. Nevertheless if we are urgently pressed to give some critical account of them, we may safely, perhaps, venture on laying down, not indeed how and why the characters arise, but where and in what they arise. They are in the matter and substance of the poetry, and they are in its manner and style. Both of these, the substance and matter on the one hand, the style and manner on the other, have a mark, an accent, of high beauty, worth, and power. But if we are asked to define this mark and accent in the abstract, our answer must be: No, for we should thereby be darkening the question, not clearing it. The mark and accent are as given by the substance and matter of that poetry, by the style and manner of that poetry, and of all other poetry which is akin to it in quality.

Only one thing we may add as to the substance and matter of poetry, guiding ourselves by Aristotle's profound observation that the superiority of poetry over history consists in its possessing a higher truth and a higher seriousness ($\phi\iota\lambda o\sigma o\phi\acute\omega\tau\epsilon\rho o\nu$ $\kappa\alpha\grave\iota$ $\sigma\pi o\upsilon\delta\alpha\iota\acute o\tau\epsilon\rho o\nu$). Let us add, therefore, to what we have said, this: that the substance and matter of the best poetry acquire their special character from possessing, in an eminent degree, truth and seriousness. We may add yet further, what is in itself evident, that to the style and manner of the best poetry their special character, their accent, is given by their diction, and, even yet more, by their movement. And though we distinguish between the two characters, the two accents, of superiority, yet they are nevertheless vitally connected one with the other. The superior character of truth and seriousness, in the matter and substance of the best poetry, is inseparable from the superiority of diction and movement marking its style and manner. The two superiorities are closely related, and are in steadfast proportion one to the other. So far as high poetic truth and seriousness are wanting to a poet's matter and substance, so far also, we may be sure, will a high poetic stamp of diction and movement be wanting to his style and manner. In proportion as this high stamp of diction and movement, again, is absent from a poet's style and manner, we shall find, also, that high poetic truth and seriousness are absent from his substance and matter.

So stated, these are but dry generalities; their whole force lies in their application. And I could wish every student of poetry to make the application of them for himself. Made by himself, the application would impress itself upon his mind far more deeply than made by me. Neither will my limits allow me to make any full application of the generalities above propounded; but in the hope of bringing out, at any rate, some significance in them, and of establishing an important principle more firmly by their means, I will, in the space which remains to me, follow rapidly from the commencement the course of our English poetry with them in my view.

Once more I return to the early po-

etry of France, with which our own poetry, in its origins, is indissolubly connected. In the twelfth and thirteenth
centuries, that seed-time of all modern
language and literature, the poetry of
France had a clear predominance in Europe. Of the two divisions of that poetry,
its productions in the *langue d'oil* and its
productions in the *langue d'oc*, the poetry of the *langue d'oc*, of southern
France, of the troubadours, is of importance because of its effect on Italian
literature;—the first literature of modern Europe to strike the true and grand
note, and to bring forth, as in Dante and
Petrarch it brought forth, classics. But
the predominance of French poetry in
Europe, during the twelfth and thirteenth centuries, is due to its poetry of
the *langue d'oil*, the poetry of northern
France and of the tongue which is now
the French language. In the twelfth century the bloom of this romance-poetry
was earlier and stronger in England, at
the court of our Anglo-Norman kings,
than in France itself. But it was a bloom
of French poetry; and as our native poetry formed itself, it formed itself out of
this. The romance-poems which took
possession of the heart and imagination
of Europe in the twelfth and thirteenth
centuries are French; "they are," as
Southey justly says, "the pride of French
literature, nor have we anything which
can be placed in competition with them."
Themes were supplied from all quarters;
but the romance-setting which was common to them all, and which gained the
ear of Europe, was French. This constituted for the French poetry, literature,
and language, at the height of the Middle Age, an unchallenged predominance.
The Italian Brunetto Latini, the master
of Dante, wrote his *Treasure* in French
because, he says, "la parleure en est plus
délitable et plus commune à toutes gens."
In the same century, the thirteenth, the
French romance-writer, Christian of
Troyes, formulates the claims, in chivalry
and letters, of France, his native country,
as follows:—

"Or vous ert par ce livre apris,
Que Gresse ot de chevalerie

Le premier los et de clergie;
Puis vint chevalerie à Rome,
Et de la clergie la some,
Qui ore est en France venue.
Diex doinst qu'ele i soit retenu
Et que li lius li abelisse
Tant que de France n'isse
L'onor qui s'i est arestée!"

"Now by this book you will learn that
first Greece had the renown for chivalry
and letters: then chivalry and the primacy in letters passed to Rome, and
now it is come to France. God grant it
may be kept there; and that the place
may please it so well, that the honor
which has come to make stay in France
may never depart thence!"

Yet it is now all gone, this French
romance-poetry, of which the weight of
substance and the power of style are
not unfairly represented by this extract
from Christian of Troyes. Only by means
of the historic estimate can we persuade
ourselves now to think that any of it is
of poetical importance.

But in the fourteenth century there
comes an Englishman nourished on this
poetry; taught his trade by this poetry,
getting words, rhyme, meter from this
poetry; for even of that stanza which the
Italians used, and which Chaucer derived immediately from the Italians, the
basis and suggestion was probably given
in France. Chaucer (I have already
named him) fascinated his contemporaries, but so too did Christian of Troyes and
Wolfram of Eschenbach. Chaucer's
power of fascination, however, is enduring; his poetical importance does not
need the assistance of the historic estimate; it is real. He is a genuine source
of joy and strength, which is flowing still
for us and will flow always. He will be
read, as time goes on, far more generally
than he is read now. His language is a
cause of difficulty for us; but so also, and
I think in quite as great a degree, is the
language of Burns. In Chaucer's case, as
in that of Burns, it is a difficulty to be
unhesitatingly accepted and overcome.

If we ask ourselves wherein consists the
immense superiority of Chaucer's poetry
over the romance-poetry—why it is that
in passing from this to Chaucer we sud-

denly feel ourselves to be in another world, we shall find that his superiority is both in the substance of his poetry and in the style of his poetry. His superiority in substance is given by his large, free, simple, clear yet kindly view of human life,—so unlike the total want, in the romance-poets, of all intelligent command of it. Chaucer has not their helplessness; he has gained the power to survey the world from a central, a truly human point of view. We have only to call to mind the Prologue to *The Canterbury Tales*. The right comment upon it is Dryden's: "It is sufficient to say, according to the proverb, that *here is God's plenty*." And again: "He is a perpetual fountain of good sense." It is by a large, free, sound representation of things, that poetry, this high criticism of life, has truth of substance; and Chaucer's poetry has truth of substance.

Of his style and manner, if we think first of the romance-poetry and then of Chaucer's divine liquidness of diction, his divine fluidity of movement, it is difficult to speak temperately. They are irresistible, and justify all the rapture with which his successors speak of his "gold dew-drops of speech." Johnson misses the point entirely when he finds fault with Dryden for ascribing to Chaucer the first refinement of our numbers, and says that Gower also can show smooth numbers and easy rhymes. The refinement of our numbers means something far more than this. A nation may have versifiers with smooth numbers and easy rhymes, and yet may have no real poetry at all. Chaucer is the father of our splendid English poetry; he is our "well of English undefiled," because by the lovely charm of his diction, the lovely charm of his movement, he makes an epoch and founds a tradition. In Spenser, Shakespeare, Milton, Keats, we can follow the tradition of the liquid diction, the fluid movement, of Chaucer; at one time it is his liquid diction of which in these poets we feel the virtue, and at another time it is his fluid movement. And the virtue is irresistible.

Bounded as in space, I must yet find room for an example of Chaucer's virtue, as I have given examples to show the virtue of the great classics. I feel disposed to say that a single line is enough to show the charm of Chaucer's verse; that merely one line like this—

"O martyr souded [8] in virginitee!"

has a virtue of manner and movement such as we shall not find in all the verse of romance-poetry;—but this is saying nothing. The virtue is such as we shall not find, perhaps, in all English poetry, outside the poets whom I have named as the special inheritors of Chaucer's tradition. A single line, however, is too little if we have not the strain of Chaucer's verse well in our memory; let us take a stanza. It is from *The Prioress's Tale*, the story of the Christian child murdered in a Jewry—

"My throte is cut unto my nekke-bone
    Saidè this child, and as by the way of kinde
I should have dyed, yea, longè time agone
But Jesu Christ, as ye in bookès finde,
Will that his glory last and be in minde,
And for the worship of his mother dere
Yet may I sing O Alma loud and clere."

Wordsworth has modernized this Tale, and to feel how delicate and evanescent is the charm of verse, we have only to read Wordsworth's first three lines of this stanza after Chaucer's—

"My throat is cut unto the bone, I trow,
    Said this young child, and by the law of kind
I should have died, yea, many hours ago."

The charm is departed. It is often said that the power of liquidness and fluidity in Chaucer's verse was dependent upon a free, a licentious dealing with language, such as is now impossible; upon a liberty, such as Burns too enjoyed, of making words like *neck*, *bird*, into a dissyllable by adding to them, and words like *cause*, *rhyme*, into a dissyllable by sounding the *e* mute. It is true that Chaucer's fluidity is conjoined with this liberty, and is admirably served by it; but we ought not to say that it was dependent upon it.

---

[8] The French *soudé*: soldered, fixed fast.

It was dependent upon his talent. Other poets with a like liberty do not attain to the fluidity of Chaucer; Burns himself does not attain to it. Poets, again, who have a talent akin to Chaucer's, such as Shakespeare or Keats, have known how to attain to his fluidity without the like liberty.

And yet Chaucer is not one of the great classics. His poetry transcends and effaces, easily and without effort, all the romance-poetry of Catholic Christendom; it transcends and effaces all the English poetry contemporary with it, it transcends and effaces all the English poetry subsequent to it down to the age of Elizabeth. Of such avail is poetic truth of substance, in its natural and necessary union with poetic truth of style. And yet, I say, Chaucer is not one of the great classics. He has not their accent. What is wanting to him is suggested by the mere mention of the name of the first great classic of Christendom, the immortal poet who died eighty years before Chaucer,—Dante. The accent of such verse as

"In la sua volontade è nostra pace . . ."

is altogether beyond Chaucer's reach; we praise him, but we feel that this accent is out of the question for him. It may be said that it was necessarily out of the reach of any poet in the England of that stage of growth. Possibly; but we are to adopt a real, not a historic, estimate of poetry. However we may account for its absence, something is wanting, then, to the poetry of Chaucer, which poetry must have before it can be placed in the glorious class of the best. And there is no doubt what that something is. It is the σπουδαιότης, the high and excellent seriousness, which Aristotle assigns as one of the grand virtues of poetry. The substance of Chaucer's poetry, his view of things and his criticism of life, has largeness, freedom, shrewdness, benignity; but it has not this high seriousness. Homer's criticism of life has it, Dante's has it, Shakespeare's has it. It is this chiefly which gives to our spirits what they can rest upon; and with the increasing demands of our modern ages upon

poetry, this virtue of giving us what we can rest upon will be more and more highly esteemed. A voice from the slums of Paris, fifty or sixty years after Chaucer, the voice of poor Villon out of his life of riot and crime, has at its happy moments (as, for instance, in the last stanza of *La Belle Heaulmière*[9]) more of this important poetic virtue of seriousness than all the productions of Chaucer. But its apparition in Villon, and in men like Villon, is fitful; the greatness of the great poets, the power of their criticism of life, is that their virtue is sustained.

To our praise, therefore, of Chaucer as a poet there must be this limitation; he lacks the high seriousness of the great classics, and therewith an important part of their virtue. Still, the main fact for us to bear in mind about Chaucer is his sterling value according to that real estimate which we firmly adopt for all poets. He has poetic truth of substance, though he has not high poetic seriousness, and corresponding to his truth of substance he has an exquisite value of style and manner. With him is born our real poetry.

For my present purpose I need not dwell on our Elizabethan poetry, or on the continuation and close of this poetry in Milton. We all of us profess to be agreed in the estimate of this poetry; we all of us recognize it as great poetry, our greatest, and Shakespeare and Milton as our poetical classics. The real estimate, here, has universal currency. With the next age of our poetry divergency and difficulty began. An historic estimate of that poetry has established itself; and the

[9] The name *Heaulmière* is said to be derived from a headdress (helm) worn as a mark by courtesans. In Villon's ballad, a poor old creature of this class laments her days of youth and beauty. The last stanza of the ballad runs thus—

"Ainsi le bon temps regretons
Entre nous, pauvres vieilles sott
Assises bas, à croppetons,
Tout en ung tas comme pelottes;
A petit feu de chenevottes
Tost allumées, tost estainctes,
Et jadis fusmes si mignottes!
Ainsi en prend à maintz et maintes."

"Thus amongst ourselves we regret the good time, poor silly old things, low-seated on our heels, all in a heap like so many balls; by a little fire of hemp-stalks, soon lighted, soon spent. And once we were such darlings! So fares it with many and many a one."

question is, whether it will be found to coincide with the real estimate.

The age of Dryden, together with our whole eighteenth century which followed it, sincerely believed itself to have produced poetical classics of its own, and even to have made advance, in poetry, beyond all its predecessors. Dryden regards as not seriously disputable the opinion "that the sweetness of English verse was never understood or practised by our fathers." Cowley could see nothing at all in Chaucer's poetry. Dryden heartily admired it, and, as we have seen, praised its matter admirably; but of its exquisite manner and movement all he can find to say is that "there is the rude sweetness of a Scotch tune in it, which is natural and pleasing, though not perfect." Addison, wishing to praise Chaucer's numbers, compares them with Dryden's own. And all through the eighteenth century, and down even into our own times, the stereotyped phrase of approbation for good verse found in our early poetry has been, that it even approached the verse of Dryden, Addison, Pope, and Johnson.

Are Dryden and Pope poetical classics? Is the historic estimate, which represents them as such, and which has been so long established that it cannot easily give way, the real estimate? Wordsworth and Coleridge, as is well known, denied it; but the authority of Wordsworth and Coleridge does not weigh much with the young generation, and there are many signs to show that the eighteenth century and its judgments are coming into favor again. Are the favorite poets of the eighteenth century classics?

It is impossible within my present limits to discuss the question fully. And what man of letters would not shrink from seeming to dispose dictatorially of the claims of two men who are, at any rate, such masters in letters as Dryden and Pope; two men of such admirable talent, both of them, and one of them, Dryden, a man, on all sides, of such energetic and genial power? And yet, if we are to gain the full benefit from poetry, we must have the real estimate of it. I cast about for some mode of arriving, in the present case, at such an estimate without offence. And perhaps the best way is to begin, as it is easy to begin, with cordial praise.

When we find Chapman, the Elizabethan translator of Homer, expressing himself in his preface thus: "Though truth in her very nakedness sits in so deep a pit, that from Gades to Aurora and Ganges few eyes can sound her, I hope yet those few here will so discover and confirm that, the date being out of her darkness in this morning of our poet, he shall now gird his temples with the sun,"—we pronounce that such a prose is intolerable. When we find Milton writing: "And long it was not after, when I was confirmed in this opinion, that he, who would not be frustrate of his hope to write well hereafter in laudable things, ought himself to be a true poem,"—we pronounce that such a prose has its own grandeur, but that it is obsolete and inconvenient. But when we find Dryden telling us: "What Virgil wrote in the vigor of his age, in plenty and at ease, I have undertaken to translate in my declining years; struggling with wants, oppressed with sickness, curbed in my genius, liable to be misconstrued in all I write,"—then we exclaim that here at last we have the true English prose, a prose such as we would all gladly use if we only knew how. Yet Dryden was Milton's contemporary.

But after the Restoration the time had come when our nation felt the imperious need of a fit prose. So, too, the time had likewise come when our nation felt the imperious need of freeing itself from the absorbing preoccupation which religion in the Puritan age had exercised. It was impossible that this freedom should be brought about without some negative excess, without some neglect and impairment of the religious life of the soul; and the spiritual history of the eighteenth century shows us that the freedom was not achieved without them. Still, the freedom was achieved; the preoccupation, an undoubtedly baneful and retarding one if it had continued, was got rid of. And as with religion amongst us at that period, so it was also with letters. A fit prose was a necessity; but it was impossible that a fit prose should establish itself amongst us without some touch of frost to the imaginative life of the soul. The needful qualities for a fit prose are regularity, uniformity, precision, balance. The men of letters, whose destiny it may be to bring their nation to the attainment of a fit prose, must of necessity, whether they work in prose or in verse, give a predominating, an almost exclusive attention to the qualities of regularity, uniformity, precision, balance. But an almost exclusive attention to these qualities involves some repression and silencing of poetry.

We are to regard Dryden as the puissant and glorious founder, Pope as the splendid high priest, of our age of prose and reason, of our excellent and indispensable eighteenth century. For the purposes of their mission and destiny their poetry, like their prose, is admirable. Do you ask me whether Dryden's verse, take it almost where you will, is not good?

"A milk-white Hind, immortal and unchanged,
Fed on the lawns and in the forest ranged."

I answer: Admirable for the purposes of the inaugurator of an age of prose and reason. Do you ask me whether Pope's verse, take it almost where you will, is not good?

"To Hounslow Heath I point, and Banstead
Down;
Thence comes your mutton, and these chicks
my own."

I answer: Admirable for the purposes of the high priest of an age of prose and reason. But do you ask me whether such verse proceeds from men with an adequate poetic criticism of life, from men whose criticism of life has a high seriousness, or even, without that high seriousness, has poetic largeness, freedom, insight, benignity? Do you ask me whether the application of ideas to life in the verse of these men, often a powerful application, no doubt, is a powerful *poetic* application? Do you ask me whether the

poetry of these men has either the matter or the inseparable manner of such an adequate poetic criticism; whether it has the accent of

"Absent thee from felicity awhile . . ."

or of

"And what is else not to be overcome . . ."

or of

"O martyr souded in virginitee!"

I answer: It has not and cannot have them; it is the poetry of the builders of an age of prose and reason. Though they may write in verse, though they may in a certain sense be masters of the art of versification, Dryden and Pope are not classics of our poetry, they are classics of our prose.

Gray is our poetical classic of that literature and age; the position of Gray is singular, and demands a word of notice here. He has not the volume or the power of poets who, coming in times more favorable, have attained to an independent criticism of life. But he lived with the great poets, he lived, above all, with the Greeks, through perpetually studying and enjoying them; and he caught their poetic point of view for regarding life, caught their poetic manner. The point of view and the manner are not self-sprung in him, he caught them of others; and he had not the free and abundant use of them. But whereas Addison and Pope never had the use of them, Gray had the use of them at times. He is the scantiest and frailest of classics in our poetry, but he is a classic.

And now, after Gray, we are met, as we draw towards the end of the eighteenth century, we are met by the great name of Burns. We enter now on times where the personal estimate of poets begins to be rife, and where the real estimate of them is not reached without difficulty. But in spite of the disturbing pressures of personal partiality, of national partiality, let us try to reach a real estimate of the poetry of Burns.

By his English poetry Burns in general belongs to the eighteenth century, and has little importance for us.

"Mark ruffian Violence, distain'd with crimes.
Rousing elate in these degenerate times;
View unsuspecting Innocence a prey,
As guileful Fraud points out the erring way;
While subtle Litigation's pliant tongue
The life-blood equal sucks of Right and
    Wrong!"

Evidently this is not the real Burns, or his name and fame would have disappeared long ago. Nor is Clarinda's love-poet, Sylvander, the real Burns either. But he tells us himself: "These English songs gravel me to death. I have not the command of the language that I have of my native tongue. In fact, I think that my ideas are more barren in English than in Scotch. I have been at *Duncan Gray* to dress it in English, but all I can do is desperately stupid." We English turn naturally, in Burns, to the poems in our own language, because we can read them easily; but in those poems we have not the real Burns.

The real Burns is of course in his Scotch poems. Let us boldly say that of much of this poetry, a poetry dealing perpetually with Scotch drink, Scotch religion, and Scotch manners, a Scotchman's estimate is apt to be personal. A Scotchman is used to this world of Scotch drink, Scotch religion, and Scotch manners; he has a tenderness for it; he meets its poet half way. In this tender mood he reads pieces like the *Holy Fair* or *Halloween*. But this world of Scotch drink, Scotch religion, and Scotch manners is against a poet, not for him, when it is not a partial countryman who reads him; for in itself it is not a beautiful world, and no one can deny that it is of advantage to a poet to deal with a beautiful world. Burns's world of Scotch drink, Scotch religion, and Scotch manners, is often a harsh, a sordid, a repulsive world; even the world of his *Cotter's Saturday Night* is not a beautiful world. No doubt a poet's criticism of life may have such truth and power that it triumphs over its world and delights us. Burns may triumph over his world, often

he does triumph over his world, but let us observe how and where. Burns is the first case we have had where the bias of the personal estimate tends to mislead; let us look at him closely, he can bear it.

Many of his admirers will tell us that we have Burns, convivial, genuine, delightful, here—

"Leeze me on drink! it gies us mair
    Than either school or college;
It kindles wit, it waukens lair,
    It pangs us fou o' knowledge.
Be't whisky gill or penny wheep
    Or ony stronger potion,
It never fails, on drinking deep,
    To kittle up our notion
                By night or day."

There is a great deal of that sort of thing in Burns, and it is unsatisfactory, not because it is bacchanalian poetry, but because it has not that accent of sincerity which bacchanalian poetry, to do it justice, very often has. There is something in it of bravado, something which makes us feel that we have not the man speaking to us with his real voice; something, therefore, poetically unsound.

With still more confidence will his admirers tell us that we have the genuine Burns, the great poet, when his strain asserts the independence, equality, dignity, of men, as in the famous song *For a' that and a' that*—

"A prince can mak' a belted knight,
    A marquis, duke, and a' that;
But an honest man's aboon his might,
    Guid faith he mauna fa' that!
    For a' that, and a' that,
        Their dignities, and a' that,
    The pith o' sense, and pride o' worth,
    Are higher rank than a' that."

Here they find his grand, genuine touches; and still more, when this puissant genius, who so often set morality at defiance, falls moralizing—

"The sacred lowe o' weel-placed love
    Luxuriantly indulge it;
But never tempt th' illicit rove,
    Tho' naething should divulge it.
I waive the quantum o' the sin,
    The hazard o' concealing,

But och! it hardens a' within,
  And petrifies the feeling."

Or in a higher strain—

"Who made the heart, 'tis He alone
  Decidedly can try us;
He knows each chord, its various tone;
  Each spring its various bias.
Then at the balance let's be mute,
  We never can adjust it;
What's *done* we partly may compute,
  But know not what's resisted."

Or in a better strain yet, a strain, his admirers will say, unsurpassable—

"To make a happy fire-side clime
        To weans and wife,
That's the true pathos and sublime
        Of human life."

There is criticism of life for you, the admirers of Burns will say to us; there is
the application of ideas to life! There is,
undoubtedly. The doctrine of the last-
quoted lines coincides almost exactly
with what was the aim and end, Xenophon tells us, of all the teaching of Socrates. And the application is a powerful
one; made by a man of vigorous understanding, and (need I say?) a master of
language.

But for the supreme poetical success
more is required than the powerful application of ideas to life; it must be an
application under the conditions fixed
by the laws of poetic truth and poetic
beauty. Those laws fix as an essential
condition, in the poet's treatment of
such matters as are here in question, high
seriousness;—the high seriousness which
comes from absolute sincerity. The accent of high seriousness, born of absolute sincerity, is what gives to such
verse as

"In la sua volontade è nostra pace . . ."

to such criticism of life as Dante's, its
power. Is this accent felt in the passages
which I have been quoting from Burns?
Surely not; surely, if our sense is quick,
we must perceive that we have not in
those passages a voice from the very inmost soul of the genuine Burns; he is
not speaking to us from these depths, he
is more or less preaching. And the compensation for admiring such passages less,
from missing the perfect poetic accent in
them, will be that we shall admire more
the poetry where that accent is found.

No; Burns, like Chaucer, comes short
of the high seriousness of the great classics, and the virtue of matter and manner
which goes with that high seriousness is
wanting to his work. At moments he
touched it in a profound and passionate
melancholy, as in those four immortal
lines taken by Byron as a motto for *The
Bride of Abydos*, but which have in them
a depth of poetic quality such as resides
in no verse of Byron's own—

"Had we never loved sae kindly,
Had we never loved sae blindly,
Never met, or never parted,
We had ne'er been broken-hearted."

But a whole poem of that quality Burns
cannot make; the rest, in the *Farewell
to Nancy*, is verbiage.

We arrive best at the real estimate of
Burns, I think, by conceiving his work as
having truth of matter and truth of manner, but not the accent or the poetic
virtue of the highest masters. His genuine
criticism of life, when the sheer poet in
him speaks, is ironic; it is not—

"Thou Power Supreme, whose mighty scheme
    These woes of mine fulfil,
  Here firm I rest, they must be best
    Because they are Thy will!"

It is far rather: *Whistle owre the lave o't*!
Yet we may say of him as of Chaucer,
that of life and the world, as they come
before him, his view is large, free,
shrewd, benignant,—truly poetic, therefore; and his manner of rendering what
he sees is to match. But we must note,
at the same time, his great difference
from Chaucer. The freedom of Chaucer
is heightened, in Burns, by a fiery, reckless energy; the benignity of Chaucer
deepens, in Burns, into an overwhelming
sense of the pathos of things;—of the
pathos of human nature, the pathos, also,

of non-human nature. Instead of the fluidity of Chaucer's manner, the manner of Burns has spring, bounding swiftness. Burns is by far the greater force, though he has perhaps less charm. The world of Chaucer is fairer, richer, more significant than that of Burns; but when the largeness and freedom of Burns get full sweep, as in *Tam o' Shanter,* or still more in that puissant and splendid production, *The Jolly Beggars,* his world may be what it will, his poetic genius triumphs over it. In the world of *The Jolly Beggars* there is more than hideousness and squalor, there is bestiality; yet the piece is a superb poetic success. It has a breadth, truth, and power which make the famous scene in Auerbach's Cellar, of Goethe's *Faust,* seem artificial and tame beside it, and which are only matched by Shakespeare and Aristophanes.

Here, where his largeness and freedom serve him so admirably, and also in those poems and songs where to shrewdness he adds infinite archness and wit, and to benignity infinite pathos, where his manner is flawless, and a perfect poetic whole is the result,—in things like the address to the mouse whose home he had ruined, in things like *Duncan Gray, Tam Glen, Whistle and I'll come to you my Lad, Auld Lang Syne* (this list might be made much longer),—here we have the genuine Burns, of whom the real estimate must be high indeed. Not a classic, nor with the excellent σπουδαιότης of the great classics, nor with a verse rising to a criticism of life and a virtue like theirs; but a poet with thorough truth of substance and an answering truth of style, giving us a poetry sound to the core. We all of us have a leaning towards the pathetic, and may be inclined perhaps to prize Burns most for his touches of piercing, sometimes almost intolerable, pathos; for verse like—

"We twa hae paidl't i' the burn
　　From mornin' sun till dine;
　But seas between us braid hae roar'd
　　Sin auld lang syne . . ."

where he is as lovely as he is sound. But

perhaps it is by the perfection of soundness of his lighter and archer masterpieces that he is poetically most wholesome for us. For the votary misled by a personal estimate of Shelley, as so many of us have been, are, and will be,—of that beautiful spirit building his many-colored haze of words and images

　"Pinnacled dim in the intense inane"—

no contact can be wholesomer than the contact with Burns at his archest and soundest. Side by side with the

"On the brink of the night and the morning
　My coursers are wont to respire,
But the Earth has just whispered a warning
　That their flight must be swifter than
　　fire . . ."

of *Prometheus Unbound,* how salutary, how very salutary, to place this from *Tam Glen*—

　"My minnie does constantly deave me
　　And bids me beware o' young men;
　They flatter, she says, to deceive me;
　　But wha can think sae o' Tam Glen?"

But we enter on burning ground as we approach the poetry of times so near to us—poetry like that of Byron, Shelley, and Wordsworth—of which the estimates are so often not only personal, but personal with passion. For my purpose, it is enough to have taken the single case of Burns, the first poet we come to of whose work the estimate formed is evidently apt to be personal, and to have suggested how we may proceed, using the poetry of the great classics as a sort of touchstone, to correct this estimate, as we had previously corrected by the same means the historic estimate where we met with it. A collection like the present, with its succession of celebrated names and celebrated poems, offers a good opportunity to us for resolutely endeavoring to make our estimates of poetry real. I have sought to point out a method which will help us in making them so, and to exhibit it in use so far as to put any one who likes in a way of applying it for himself.

At any rate the end to which the method and the estimate are designed to lead, and from leading to which, if they do lead to it, they get their whole value, —the benefit of being able clearly to feel and deeply to enjoy the best, the truly classic, in poetry,—is an end, let me say it once more at parting, of supreme importance. We are often told that an era is opening in which we are to see multitudes of a common sort of readers, and masses of a common sort of literature; that such readers do not want and could not relish anything better than such literature, and that to provide it is becoming a vast and profitable industry. Even if good literature entirely lost currency with the world, it would still be abundantly worth while to continue to enjoy it by oneself. But it never will lose currency with the world, in spite of momentary appearances; it will never lose supremacy. Currency and supremacy are insured to it, not indeed by the world's deliberate and conscious choice, but by something far deeper,—by the instinct of self-preservation in humanity.

HENRY JAMES

(1843-1916)

Henry James devoted a lifetime to the craft of literature and to reflections on its form and meaning. The fullest expression of his views appears in "The Art of Fiction" (1884; 1888), an essay remarkable for its perceptive discussion of many questions that have continued to interest modern critics. Among these are the importance of theory to the artist; the relation of literature to reality, truth, and morals; the nature of organic form and its necessary correspondence with what James called "the strange irregular rhythm" of the life of a given time and place. James also provided a critical commentary on his own fiction in the prefaces to the New York Edition of his works (1907-09); these have been collected in *The Art of the Novel* (ed. R. P. Blackmur, 1934). Other collections of James's critical writings include *Literary Reviews and Essays: American, English, and French Literature* (ed. Albert Mordell, 1957) and *The Scenic Art, Notes on Acting and the Drama* (ed. Allan Wade, 1948).

The Art of Fiction (1884; 1888)

I should not have affixed so comprehensive a title to these few remarks, necessarily wanting in any completeness upon a subject the full consideration of which would carry us far, did I not seem to discover a pretext for my temerity in the interesting pamphlet lately published under this name by Mr. Walter Besant. Mr. Besant's lecture at the Royal Institution—the original form of his pamphlet—appears to indicate that many persons are interested in the art of fiction, and are not indifferent to such remarks as those who practice it may attempt to make about it. I am therefore anxious not to lose the benefit of this favorable association, and to edge in a few words

From *Partial Portraits* by Henry James (London, 1888). First published in *Longman's Magazine* (September, 1884).

under cover of the attention which Mr. Besant is sure to have excited. There is something very encouraging in his having put into form certain of his ideas on the mystery of storytelling.

It is a proof of life and curiosity—curiosity on the part of the brotherhood of novelists as well as on the part of their readers. Only a short time ago it might have been supposed that the English novel was not what the French call *discutable*. It had no air of having a theory, a conviction, a consciousness of itself behind it—of being the expression of an artistic faith, the result of choice and comparison. I do not say it was necessarily the worse for that: it would take much more courage than I possesss to intimate that the form of the novel as Dickens and Thackeray (for instance) saw it had any taint of incompleteness. It was, however, *naif* (if I may help myself out with another French word); and evidently if it be destined to suffer in any way for having lost its *naïveté* it has now an idea of making sure of the corresponding advantages. During the period I have alluded to there was a comfortable, good-humored feeling abroad that a novel is a novel, as a pudding is a pudding, and that our only business with it could be to swallow it. But within a year or two, for some reason or other, there have been signs of returning animation—the era of discussion would appear to have been to a certain extent opened. Art lives upon discussion, upon experiment, upon curiosity, upon variety of attempt, upon the exchange of views and the comparison of standpoints; and there is a presumption that those times when no one has anything particular to say about it, and has no reason to give for practice or preference, though they may be times of honor, are not times of development—are times, possibly even, a little of dullness. The successful application of any art is a delightful spectacle, but the theory too is interesting; and though there is a great deal of the latter without the former I suspect there has never been a genuine success that has not had a latent core of conviction. Discussion,

suggestion, formulation, these things are fertilizing when they are frank and sincere. Mr. Besant has set an excellent example in saying what he thinks, for his part, about the way in which fiction should be written, as well as about the way in which it should be published; for his view of the "art," carried on into an appendix, covers that too. Other laborers in the same field will doubtless take up the argument, they will give it the light of their experience, and the effect will surely be to make our interest in the novel a little more what it had for some time threatened to fail to be—a serious, active, inquiring interest, under protection of which this delightful study may, in moments of confidence, venture to say a little more what it thinks of itself.

It must take itself seriously for the public to take it so. The old superstition about fiction being "wicked" has doubtless died out in England; but the spirit of it lingers in a certain oblique regard directed toward any story which does not more or less admit that it is only a joke. Even the most jocular novel feels in some degree the weight of the proscription that was formerly directed against literary levity: the jocularity does not always succeed in passing for orthodoxy. It is still expected, though perhaps people are ashamed to say it, that a production which is after all only a "make-believe" (for what else is a "story"?) shall be in some degree apologetic—shall renounce the pretension of attempting really to represent life. This, of course, any sensible, wide-awake story declines to do, for it quickly perceives that the tolerance granted to it on such a condition is only an attempt to stifle it disguised in the form of generosity. The old evangelical hostility to the novel, which was as explicit as it was narrow, and which regarded it as little less favorable to our immortal part than a stage play, was in reality far less insulting. The only reason for the existence of a novel is that it does attempt to represent life. When it relinquishes this attempt, the same attempt that we see on the canvas of the painter, it will have arrived at a very strange pass. It is not expected of the picture that it will make itself humble in order to be forgiven; and the analogy between the art of the painter and the art of the novelist is, so far as I am able to see, complete. Their inspiration is the same, their process (allowing for the different quality of the vehicle) is the same, their success is the same. They may learn from each other, they may explain and sustain each other. Their cause is the same, and the honor of one is the honor of another. The Mahometans think a picture an unholy thing, but it is a long time since any Christian did, and it is therefore the more odd that in the Christian mind the traces (dissimulated though they may be) of a suspicion of the sister art should linger to this day. The only effectual way to lay it to rest is to emphasize the analogy to which I just alluded—to insist on the fact that as the picture is reality, so the novel is history. That is the only general description (which does it justice) that we may give of the novel. But history also is allowed to represent life; it is not, any more than painting, expected to apologize. The subject matter of fiction is stored up likewise in documents and records, and if it will not give itself away, as they say in California, it must speak with assurance, with the tone of the historian. Certain accomplished novelists have a habit of giving themselves away which must often bring tears to the eyes of people who take their fiction seriously. I was lately struck, in reading over many pages of Anthony Trollope, with his want of discretion in this particular. In a digression, a parenthesis or an aside, he concedes to the reader that he and this trusting friend are only "making believe." He admits that the events he narrates have not really happened, and that he can give his narrative any turn the reader may like best. Such a betrayal of a sacred office seems to me, I confess, a terrible crime; it is what I mean by the attitude of apology, and it shocks me every whit as much in Trollope as it would have shocked me in Gibbon or Macaulay. It implies that the novelist is

less occupied in looking for the truth (the truth, of course I mean, that he assumes, the premises that we must grant him, whatever they may be) than the historian, and in doing so it deprives him at a stroke of all his standing room. To represent and illustrate the past, the actions of men, is the task of either writer, and the only difference that I can see is, in proportion as he succeeds, to the honor of the novelist, consisting as it does in his having more difficulty in collecting his evidence, which is so far from being purely literary. It seems to me to give him a great character, the fact that he has at once so much in common with the philosopher and the painter; this double analogy is a magnificent heritage.

It is of all this evidently that Mr. Besant is full when he insists upon the fact that fiction is one of the *fine* arts, deserving in its turn of all the honors and emoluments that have hitherto been reserved for the successful profession of music, poetry, painting, architecture. It is impossible to insist too much on so important a truth, and the place that Mr. Besant demands for the work of the novelist may be represented, a trifle less abstractly, by saying that he demands not only that it shall be reputed artistic, but that it shall be reputed very artistic indeed. It is excellent that he should have struck this note, for his doing so indicates that there was need of it, that his proposition may be to many people a novelty. One rubs one's eyes at the thought; but the rest of Mr. Besant's essay confirms the revelation. I suspect in truth that it would be possible to confirm it still further, and that one would not be far wrong in saying that in addition to the people to whom it has never occurred that a novel ought to be artistic, there are a great many others who, if this principle were urged upon them, would be filled with an indefinable mistrust. They would find it difficult to explain their repugnance, but it would operate strongly to put them on their guard. "Art," in our Protestant communities, where so many things have got so strangely twisted about, is supposed in certain circles to have some vaguely injurious effect upon those who make it an important consideration, who let it weigh in the balance. It is assumed to be opposed in some mysterious manner to morality, to amusement, to instruction. When it is embodied in the work of the painter (the sculptor is another affair!) you know what it is: it stands there before you, in the honesty of pink and green and a gilt frame; you can see the worst of it at a glance, and you can be on your *guard*. But when it is introduced into literature it becomes more insidious—there is danger of its hurting you before you know it. Literature should be either instructive or amusing, and there is in many minds an impression that these artistic preoccupations, the search for form, contribute to neither end, interfere indeed with both. They are too frivolous to be edifying, and too serious to be diverting; and they are moreover priggish and paradoxical and superfluous. That, I think, represents the manner in which the latent thought of many people who read novels as an exercise in skipping would explain itself if it were to become articulate. They would argue, of course, that a novel ought to be "good," but they would interpret this term in a fashion of their own, which indeed would vary considerably from one critic to another. One would say that being good means representing virtuous and aspiring characters, placed in prominent positions; another would say that it depends on a "happy ending," on a distribution at the last of prizes, pensions, husbands, wives, babies, millions, appended paragraphs, and cheerful remarks. Another still would say that it means being full of incident and movement, so that we shall wish to jump ahead, to see who was the mysterious stranger, and if the stolen will was ever found, and shall not be distracted from this pleasure by any tiresome analysis or "description." But they would all agree that the "artistic" idea would spoil some of their fun. One would hold it accountable for all the description, another would see it revealed in the absence of sympathy. Its

hostility to a happy ending would be evident, and it might even in some cases render any ending at all impossible. The "ending" of a novel is, for many persons, like that of a good dinner, a course of dessert and ices, and the artist in fiction is regarded as a sort of meddlesome doctor who forbids agreeable aftertastes. It is therefore true that this conception of Mr. Besant's of the novel as a superior form encounters not only a negative but a positive indifference. It matters little that as a work of art it should really be as little or as much of its essence to supply happy endings, sympathetic characters, and an objective tone, as if it were a work of mechanics: the association of ideas, however incongruous, might easily be too much for it if an eloquent voice were not sometimes raised to call attention to the fact that it is at once as free and as serious a branch of literature as any other.

Certainly this might sometimes be doubted in presence of the enormous number of works of fiction that appeal to the credulity of our generation, for it might easily seem that there could be no great character in a commodity so quickly and easily produced. It must be admitted that good novels are much compromised by bad ones, and that the field at large suffers discredit from overcrowding. I think, however, that this injury is only superficial, and that the superabundance of written fiction proves nothing against the principle itself. It has been vulgarized, like all other kinds of literature, like everything else today, and it has proved more than some kinds accessible to vulgarization. But there is as much difference as there ever was between a good novel and a bad one: the bad is swept with all the daubed canvases and spoiled marble into some unvisited limbo, or infinite rubbish yard beneath the back windows of the world, and the good subsists and emits its light and stimulates our desire for perfection. As I shall take the liberty of making but a single criticism of Mr. Besant, whose tone is so full of the love of his art, I may as well have done with it at once.

He seems to me to mistake in attempting to say so definitely beforehand what sort of an affair the good novel will be. To indicate the danger of such an error as that has been the purpose of these few pages; to suggest that certain traditions on the subject, applied *a priori,* have already had much to answer for, and that the good health of an art which undertakes so immediately to reproduce life must demand that it be perfectly free. It lives upon exercise, and the very meaning of exercise is freedom. The only obligation to which in advance we may hold a novel, without incurring the accusation of being arbitrary, is that it be interesting. That general responsibility rests upon it, but it is the only one I can think of. The ways in which it is at liberty to accomplish this result (of interesting us) strike me as innumerable, and such as can only suffer from being marked out or fenced in by prescription. They are as various as the temperament of man, and they are successful in proportion as they reveal a particular mind, different from others. A novel is in its broadest definition a personal, a direct impression of life: that, to begin with, constitutes its value, which is greater or less according to the intensity of the impression. But there will be no intensity at all, and therefore no value, unless there is freedom to feel and say. The tracing of a line to be followed, of a tone to be taken, of a form to be filled out, is a limitation of that freedom and a suppression of the very thing that we are most curious about. The form, it seems to me, is to be appreciated after the fact: then the author's choice has been made, his standard has been indicated; then we can follow lines and directions and compare tones and resemblances. Then in a word we can enjoy one of the most charming of pleasures, we can estimate quality, we can apply the test of execution. The execution belongs to the author alone; it is what is most personal to him, and we measure him by that. The advantage, the luxury, as well as the torment and responsibility of the novelist, is that there is no limit to what he may attempt as an executant—no limit to his possible experiments, efforts, discoveries, successes. Here it is especially that he works, step by step, like his brother of the brush, of whom we may always say that he has painted his picture in a manner best known to himself. His manner is his secret, not necessarily a jealous one. He cannot disclose it as a general thing if he would; he would be at a loss to teach it to others. I say this with a due recollection of having insisted on the community of method of the artist who paints a picture and the artist who writes a novel. The painter *is* able to teach the rudiments of his practice, and it is possible, from the study of good work (granted the aptitude), both to learn how to paint and to learn how to write. Yet it remains true, without injury to the *rapprochement,* that the literary artist would be obliged to say to his pupil much more than the other, "Ah, well, you must do it as you can!" It is a question of degree, a matter of delicacy. If there are exact sciences, there are also exact arts, and the grammar of painting is so much more definite that it makes the difference.

I ought to add, however, that if Mr. Besant says at the beginning of his essay that the "laws of fiction may be laid down and taught with as much precision and exactness as the laws of harmony, perspective, and proportion," he mitigates what might appear to be an extravagance by applying his remark to "general" laws, and by expressing most of these rules in a manner with which it would certainly be unaccommodating to disagree. That the novelist must write from his experience, that his "characters must be real and such as might be met with in actual life"; that "a young lady brought up in a quiet country village should avoid descriptions of garrison life," and "a writer whose friends and personal experiences belong to the lower middle class should carefully avoid introducing his characters into society"; that one should enter one's notes in a commonplace book; that one's figures should be clear in outline; that making them clear by some trick of speech or of carriage is a bad method, and "describing them at length" is a worse one; that English fiction should have a "conscious moral purpose"; that "it is almost impossible to estimate too highly the value of careful workmanship —that is, of style"; that "the most important point of all is the story," that "the story is everything": these are principles with most of which it is surely impossible not to sympathize. That remark about the lower middle-class writer and his knowing his place is perhaps rather chilling; but for the rest I should find it difficult to dissent from any one of these recommendations. At the same time, I should find it difficult positively to assent to them, with the exception, perhaps, of the injunction as to entering one's notes in a commonplace book. They scarcely seem to me to have the quality that Mr. Besant attributes to the rules of the novelist—the "precision and exactness" of "the laws of harmony, perspective, and proportion." They are suggestive, they are even inspiring, but they are not exact, though they are doubtless as much so as the case admits of: which is a proof of that liberty of interpretation for which I just contended. For the value of these different injunctions—so beautiful and so vague —is wholly in the meaning one attaches to them. The characters, the situation, which strike one as real will be those that touch and interest one most, but the measure of reality is very difficult to fix. The reality of Don Quixote or of Mr. Micawber is a very delicate shade; it is a reality so colored by the author's vision that, vivid as it may be, one would hesitate to propose it as a model: one would expose one's self to some very embarrassing questions on the part of a pupil. It goes without saying that you will not write a good novel unless you possess the sense of reality; but it will be difficult to give you a recipe for calling that sense into being. Humanity is immense, and reality has a myriad forms; the most one can affirm is that some of the flowers of fiction have the odor of it, and others have not; as for

telling you in advance how your nosegay should be composed, that is another affair. It is equally excellent and inconclusive to say that one must write from experience; to our supposititious aspirant such a declaration might savor of mockery. What kind of experience is intended, and where does it begin and end? Experience is never limited, and it is never complete; it is an immense sensibility, a kind of huge spiderweb of the finest silken threads suspended in the chamber of consciousness, and catching every air-borne particle in its tissue. It is the very atmosphere of the mind; and when the mind is imaginative— much more when it happens to be that of a man of genius—it takes to itself the faintest hints of life, it converts the very pulses of the air into revelations. The young lady living in a village has only to be a damsel upon whom nothing is lost to make it quite unfair (as it seems to me) to declare to her that she shall have nothing to say about the military. Greater miracles have been seen than that, imagination assisting, she should speak the truth about some of these gentlemen. I remember an English novelist, a woman of genius, telling me that she was much commended for the impression she had managed to give in one of her tales of the nature and way of life of the French Protestant youth. She had been asked where she learned so much about this recondite being, she had been congratulated on her peculiar opportunities. These opportunities consisted in her having once, in Paris, as she ascended a staircase, passed an open door where, in the household of a *pasteur*, some of the young Protestants were seated at table round a finished meal. The glimpse made a picture; it lasted only a moment, but that moment was experience. She had got her direct personal impression, and she turned out her type. She knew what youth was, and what Protestantism; she also had the advantage of having seen what it was to be French, so that she converted these ideas into a concrete image and produced a reality. Above all, however, she was blessed with the faculty which when

you give it an inch takes an ell, and
which for the artist is a much greater
source of strength than any accident of
residence or of place in the social scale.
The power to guess the unseen from the
seen, to trace the implication of things,
to judge the whole piece by the pattern,
the condition of feeling life in general
so completely that you are well on your
way to knowing any particular corner of
it—this cluster of gifts may almost be
said to constitute experience, and they
occur in country and in town, and in the
most differing stages of education. If experience consists of impressions, it may
be said that impressions *are* experience,
just as (have we not seen it?) they are
the very air we breathe. Therefore, if I
should certainly say to a novice, "Write
from experience and experience only," I
should feel that this was rather a tantalizing monition if I were not careful immediately to add, "Try to be one of the
people on whom nothing is lost!"

I am far from intending by this to
minimize the importance of exactness—
of truth of detail. One can speak best
from one's own taste, and I may therefore venture to say that the air of reality
(solidity of specification) seems to me to
be the supreme virtue of a novel—the
merit on which all its other merits (including that conscious moral purpose of
which Mr. Besant speaks) helplessly
and submissively depend. If it be not
there, they are all as nothing, and if
these be there, they owe their effect to
the success with which the author has
produced the illusion of life. The cultivation of this success, the study of this
exquisite process, form, to my taste, the
beginning and the end of the art of the
novelist. They are his inspiration, his despair, his reward, his torment, his delight. It is here in very truth that he
competes with life; it is here that he
competes with his brother the painter in
his attempt to render the look of things,
the look that conveys their meaning, to
catch the color, the relief, the expression,
the surface, the substance of the human
spectacle. It is in regard to this that Mr.
Besant is well inspired when he bids him
take notes. He cannot possibly take too

many, he cannot possibly take enough
All life solicits him, and to "render" the
simplest surface, to produce the mos'
momentary illusion, is a very complicated business. His case would be easier
and the rule would be more exact, if
Mr. Besant had been able to tell him
what notes to take. But this, I fear, he
can never learn in any manual; it is the
business of his life. He has to take a
great many in order to select a few, he
has to work them up as he can, and
even the guides and philosophers who
might have most to say to him must
leave him alone when it comes to the
application of precepts, as we leave the
painter in communion with his palette
That his characters "must be clear in
outline," as Mr. Besant says—he feel:
that down to his boots; but how he shal'
make them so is a secret between his
good angel and himself. It would be
absurdly simple if he could be taught
that a great deal of "description" would
make them so, or that on the contrary
the absence of description and the culti
vation of dialogue, or the absence of
dialogue and the multiplication of "incident," would rescue him from his diffi
culties. Nothing, for instance, is more
possible than that he be of a turn o
mind for which this odd, literal opposi
tion of description and dialogue, inci
dent and description, has little meaning
and light. People often talk of these
things as if they had a kind of interne
cine distinctness, instead of melting into
each other at every breath, and being
intimately associated parts of one gen
eral effort of expression. I cannot imag
ine composition existing in a series o
blocks, nor conceive, in any novel worth
discussing at all, of a passage of descrip
tion that is not in its intention narrative
a passage of dialogue that is not in it
intention descriptive, a touch of truth
of any sort that does not partake of the
nature of incident, or an incident that
derives its interest from any other source
than the general and only source of the
success of a work of art—that of being
illustrative. A novel is a living thing, al
one and continuous, like any other or
ganism, and in proportion as it lives wil

it be found, I think, that in each of the parts there is something of each of the other parts. The critic who over the close texture of a finished work shall pretend to trace a geography of items will mark some frontiers as artificial, I fear, as any that have been known to history. There is an old-fashioned distinction between the novel of character and the novel of incident which must have cost many a smile to the intending fabulist who was keen about his work. It appears to me as little to the point as the equally celebrated distinction between the novel and the romance—to answer as little to any reality. There are bad novels and good novels, as there are bad pictures and good pictures; but that is the only distinction in which I see any meaning, and I can as little imagine speaking of a novel of character as I can imagine speaking of a picture of character. When one says picture one says of character, when one says novel one says of incident, and the terms may be transposed at will. What is character but the determination of incident? What is incident but the illustration of character? What is either a picture or a novel that is *not* of character? What else do we seek in it and find in it? It is an incident for a woman to stand up with her hand resting on a table and look out at you in a certain way; or if it be not an incident I think it will be hard to say what it is. At the same time it is an expression of character. If you say you don't see it (character in *that—allons donc!*), this is exactly what the artist who has reasons of his own for thinking he *does* see it undertakes to show you. When a young man makes up his mind that he has not faith enough after all to enter the church as he intended, that is an incident, though you may not hurry to the end of the chapter to see whether perhaps he doesn't change once more. I do not say that these are extraordinary or startling incidents. I do not pretend to estimate the degree of interest proceeding from them, for this will depend upon the skill of the painter. It sounds almost puerile to say that some incidents are intrinsically much more important

than others, and I need not take this precaution after having professed my sympathy for the major ones in remarking that the only classification of the novel that I can understand is into that which has life and that which has it not.

The novel and the romance, the novel of incident and that of character—these clumsy separations appear to me to have been made by critics and readers for their own convenience, and to help them out of some of their occasional queer predicaments, but to have little reality or interest for the producer, from whose point of view it is of course that we are attempting to consider the art of fiction. The case is the same with another shadowy category which Mr. Besant apparently is disposed to set up—that of the "modern English novel"; unless indeed it be that in this matter he has fallen into an accidental confusion of standpoints. It is not quite clear whether he intends the remarks in which he alludes to it to be didactic or historical. It is as difficult to suppose a person intending to write a modern English as to suppose him writing an ancient English novel: that is a label which begs the question. One writes the novel, one paints the picture, of one's language and of one's time, and calling it modern English will not, alas! make the difficult task any easier. No more, unfortunately, will calling this or that work of one's fellow artist a romance—unless it be, of course, simply for the pleasantness of the thing, as for instance when Hawthorne gave this heading to his story of *Blithedale*. The French, who have brought the theory of fiction to remarkable completeness, have but one name for the novel, and have not attempted smaller things in it, that I can see, for that. I can think of no obligation to which the "romancer" would not be held equally with the novelist; the standard of execution is equally high for each. Of course it is of execution that we are talking—that being the only point of a novel that is open to contention. This is perhaps too often lost sight of, only to produce interminable confusions and cross purposes. We must grant the artist his subject, his idea, his *donnée*: Our criticism is applied only to what he makes of it. Naturally I do not mean that we are bound to like it or find it interesting: in case we do not, our course is perfectly simple—to let it alone. We may believe that of a certain idea even the most sincere novelist can make nothing at all, and the event may perfectly justify our belief; but the failure will have been a failure to execute, and it is in the execution that the fatal weakness is recorded. If we pretend to respect the artist at all, we must allow him his freedom of choice, in the face, in particular cases, of innumerable presumptions that the choice will not fructify. Art derives a considerable part of its beneficial exercise from flying in the face of presumptions, and some of the most interesting experiments of which it is capable are hidden in the bosom of common things. Gustave Flaubert has written a story about the devotion of a servant girl to a parrot, and the production, highly finished as it is, cannot on the whole be called a success. We are perfectly free to find it flat, but I think it might have been interesting; and I, for my part, am extremely glad he should have written it; it is a contribution to our knowledge of what can be done—or what cannot. Ivan Turgenev has written a tale about a deaf and dumb serf and a lap dog, and the thing is touching, loving, a little masterpiece. He struck the note of life where Gustave Flaubert missed it—he flew in the face of a presumption and achieved a victory.

Nothing, of course, will ever take the place of the good old fashion of "liking" a work of art or not liking it: the most improved criticism will not abolish that primitive, that ultimate test. I mention this to guard myself from the accusation of intimating that the idea, the subject, of a novel or a picture, does not matter. It matters, to my sense, in the highest degree, and if I might put up a prayer it would be that artists should select none but the richest. Some, as I have already hastened to admit, are much more remunerative than others, and it would be a world happily arranged in which persons intending to treat them should be exempt from confusions and mistakes. This fortunate condition will arrive only, I fear, on the same day that critics become purged from error. Meanwhile, I repeat, we do not judge the artist with fairness unless we say to him, "Oh, I grant you your starting point, because if I did not I should seem to prescribe to you, and heaven forbid I should take that responsibility. If I pretend to tell you what you must not take, you will call upon me to tell you then what you must take; in which case I shall be prettily caught. Moreover, it isn't till I have accepted your data that I can begin to measure you. I have the standard, the pitch; I have no right to tamper with your flute and then criticize your music. Of course I may not care for your idea at all; I may think it silly, or stale, or unclean; in which case I wash my hands of you altogether. I may content myself with believing that you will not have succeeded in being interesting, but I shall, of course, not attempt to demonstrate it, and you will be as indifferent to me as I am to you. I needn't remind you that there are all sorts of tastes: who can know it better? Some people, for excellent reasons, don't like to read about carpenters; others, for reasons even better, don't like to read about courtesans. Many object to Americans. Others (I believe they are mainly editors and publishers) won't look at Italians. Some readers don't like quiet subjects; others don't like bustling ones. Some enjoy a complete illusion, others the consciousness of large concessions. They choose their novels accordingly, and if they don't care about your idea they won't *a fortiori*, care about your treatment."

So that it comes back very quickly, as I have said, to the liking: in spite of M. Zola, who reasons less powerfully than he represents, and who will not reconcile himself to this absoluteness of taste, thinking that there are certain things that people ought to like, and that they can be made to like. I am quite at a loss to imagine anything (at any rate in this matter of fiction) that people *ought* to like or to dislike. Selection will be sure to take care of itself, for it has a constant motive behind it. That motive is simply experience. As people feel life, so they will feel the art that is most closely related to it. This closeness of relation is what we should never forget in talking of the effort of the novel. Many people speak of it as a factitious, artificial form, a product of ingenuity, the business of which is to alter and arrange the things that surround us, to translate them into conventional, traditional molds. This, however, is a view of the matter which carries us but a very short way, condemns the art to an eternal repetition of a few familiar *clichés*, cuts short its development, and leads us straight up to a dead wall. Catching the very note and trick, the strange irregular rhythm of life, that is the attempt whose strenuous force keeps Fiction upon her feet. In proportion as in what she offers us we see life *without* rearrangement do we feel that we are touching the truth; in proportion as we see it *with* rearrangement do we feel that we are being put off with a substitute, a compromise and convention. It is not uncommon to hear an extraordinary assurance of remark in regard to this matter of rearranging, which is often spoken of as if it were the last word of art. Mr. Besant seems to me in danger of falling into the great error with his rather unguarded talk about "selection." Art is essentially selection, but it is a selection whose main care is to be typical, to be inclusive. For many people art means rose-colored windowpanes, and selection means picking a bouquet for Mrs. Grundy. They will tell you glibly that artistic considerations have nothing to do with the disagreeable, with the ugly; they will rattle off shallow commonplaces about the province of art and the limits of art till you are moved to some wonder in return as to the province and the limits of ignorance. It appears to me that no one can ever have made a seriously artistic attempt without becoming conscious of an immense increase—a kind of revelation—of freedom. One perceives in that case—by the light of a heavenly ray—that the province of art is all life, all feeling, all observation, all vision. As Mr. Besant so justly intimates, it is all experience. That is a sufficient answer to those who maintain that it must not touch the sad things of life, who stick into its divine unconscious bosom little prohibitory inscriptions on the end of sticks, such as we see in public gardens—"It is forbidden to walk on the grass; it is forbidden to touch the flowers; it is not allowed to introduce dogs or to remain after dark; it is requested to keep to the right." The young aspirant in the line of fiction whom we continue to imagine will do nothing without taste, for in that case his freedom would be of little use to him; but the first advantage of his taste will be to reveal to him the absurdity of the little sticks and tickets. If he have taste, I must add, of course he will have ingenuity, and my disrespectful reference to that quality just now was not meant to imply that it is useless in fiction. But it is only a secondary aid; the first is a capacity for receiving straight impressions.

Mr. Besant has some remarks on the question of "the story" which I shall not attempt to criticize, though they seem to me to contain a singular ambiguity, because I do not think I understand them. I cannot see what is meant by talking as if there were a part of a novel which is the story and part of it which for mystical reasons is not—unless indeed the distinction be made in a sense in which it is difficult to suppose that anyone should attempt to convey anything. "The story," if it represents anything, represents the subject, the idea, the *donnée* of the novel; and there is surely no "school"—Mr. Besant speaks of a school —which urges that a novel should be all treatment and no subject. There must assuredly be something to treat; every school is intimately conscious of that. This sense of the story being the idea, the starting point, of the novel, is the only one that I see in which it can be spoken of as something different from its organic whole; and since in proportion as the work is successful the idea permeates and penetrates it, informs and animates it, so that every word and every punctuation point contribute directly to the expression, in that proportion do we lose our sense of the story being a blade which may be drawn more or less out of its sheath. The story and the novel, the idea and the form, are the needle and thread, and I never heard of a guild of tailors who recommended the use of the thread without the needle, or the needle without the thread. Mr. Besant is not the only critic who may be observed to have spoken as if there were certain things in life which constitute stories, and certain others which do not. I find the same odd implication in an entertaining article in the *Pall Mall Gazette*, devoted, as it happens, to Mr. Besant's lecture. "The story is the thing!" says this graceful writer, as if with a tone of opposition to some other idea. I should think it was, as every painter who, as the time for "sending in" his picture looms in the distance, finds himself still in quest of a subject—as every belated artist not fixed about his theme will heartily agree. There are some subjects which speak to us and others which do not, but he would be a clever man who should undertake to give a rule—an index expurgatorius—by which the story and the no-story should be known apart. It is impossible (to me at least) to imagine any such rule which shall not be altogether arbitrary. The writer in the *Pall Mall* opposes the delightful (as I suppose) novel of *Margot la Balafrée* to certain tales in which "Bostonian nymphs" appear to have "rejected English dukes for psychological reasons." I am not acquainted with the romance just designated, and can scarcely forgive the *Pall Mall* critic for not mentioning the name of the author, but the title appears to refer to a lady who may have received a scar in some heroic adventure. I am inconsolable at not being acquainted with this episode, but am utterly as a loss to see why it is a story when the rejection (or acceptance) of a duke is not, and why a reason, psychological or other, is not a subject when a cicatrix is. They are all particles of the multitudinous life with which the novel deals, and surely no dogma which pretends to make it lawful to touch the one and unlawful to touch the other will stand for a moment on its feet. It is the special picture that must stand or fall, according as it seem to possess truth or to lack it. Mr. Besant does not, to my sense, light up the subject by intimating that a story must, under penalty of not being a story, consist of "adventures." Why of adventures more than of green spectacles? He mentions a category of impossible things, and among them he places "fiction without adventure." Why without adventure, more than without matrimony, or celibacy, or parturition, or cholera, or hydropathy, or Jansenism? This seems to me to bring the novel back to the hapless little role of being an artificial, ingenious thing—bring it down from its large, free character of an immense and exquisite correspondence with life. And what *is* adventure, when it comes to that, and by what sign is the listening pupil to recognize it? It is an adventure—an immense one—for me to write this little article; and for a Bostonian nymph to reject an English duke is an adventure only less stirring, I should say, than for an English duke to be rejected by a Bostonian nymph. I see dramas within dramas in that, and innumerable points of view. A psychological reason is, to my imagination, an object adorably pictorial; to catch the tint of its complexion—I feel as if that idea might inspire one to Titianesque effort. There are few things more exciting to me, in short, than a psychological reason, and yet, I protest, the novel seems to me the most magnificent form of art. I have just been reading, at the same time, the delightful story of *Treasure Island,* By Mr. Robert Louis Stevenson and, in a manner less consecutive, the last tale from M. Edmond de Goncourt, which is entitled *Chérie.* One these works treats of murders, mysteries islands of dreadful renown, hairbreadth escapes, miraculous coincidences, and buried doubloons. The other treats of little French girl who lived in a fine house in Paris, and died of wounds sensibility because no one would marry her. I call *Treasure Island* delightful because it appears to me to have succeeded wonderfully in what it attempts; and I venture to bestow no epithet upon *Chérie*, which strikes me as having failed deplorably in what it attempts—that is, in tracing the development of the moral consciousness of a child. But one of these productions strikes me as exactly as much of a novel as the other, and as having a "story" quite as much. The moral consciousness of a child is as much a part of life as the islands of the Spanish Main, and the one sort of geography seems to me to have those "surprises" of which Mr. Besant speaks quite as much as the other. For myself (since it comes back in the last resort, as I say, to the preference of the individual), the picture of the child's experience has the advantage that I can at successive steps (an immense luxury, near to the "sensual pleasure" of which Mr. Besant's critic in the *Pall Mall* speaks) say Yes or No, as it may be, to what the artist puts before me. I have been a child in fact, but I have been on a quest for a buried treasure only in supposition, and it is a simple accident that with M. de Goncourt I should have for the most part to say No. With George Eliot, when he painted that country with a far other intelligence, I always said Yes.

The most interesting part of Mr. Besant's lecture is unfortunately the briefest passage—his very cursory allusion to the "conscious moral purpose" of the novel. Here again it is not very clear whether he be recording a fact or laying down a principle; it is a great pity that in the latter case he should not have developed his idea. This branch of the subject is of immense importance, and Mr. Besant's few words point to considerations of the widest reach, not to be lightly disposed of. He will have treated the art of fiction but superficially who is not prepared to go every inch of the way that these considerations will carry him. It is for this reason that at the beginning of these remarks I was careful to notify the reader that my reflections on so large a theme have no

pretension to be exhaustive. Like Mr. Besant, I have left the question of the morality of the novel till the last, and at the last I find I have used up my space. It is a question surrounded with difficulties, as witness the very first that meets us, in the form of a definite question, on the threshold. Vagueness, in such a discussion, is fatal, and what is the meaning of your morality and your conscious moral purpose? Will you not define your terms and explain how (a novel being a picture) a picture can be either moral or immoral? You wish to paint a moral picture or carve a moral statue: will you not tell us how you would set about it? We are discussing the Art of Fiction; questions of art are questions (in the widest sense) of execution; questions of morality are quite another affair, and will you not let us see how it is that you find it so easy to mix them up? These things are so clear to Mr. Besant that he has deduced from them a law which he sees embodied in English fiction, and which is "a truly admirable thing and a great cause for congratulation." It is a great cause for congratulation indeed when such thorny problems become as smooth as silk. I may add that in so far as Mr. Besant perceives that in point of fact English fiction has addressed itself preponderantly to these delicate questions he will appear to many people to have made a vain discovery. They will have been positively struck, on the contrary, with the moral timidity of the usual English novelist; with his (or with her) aversion to face the difficulties with which on every side the treatment of reality bristles. He is apt to be extremely shy (whereas the picture that Mr. Besant draws is a picture of boldness), and the sign of his work, for the most part, is a cautious silence on certain subjects. In the English novel (by which of course I mean the American as well), more than in any other, there is a traditional difference between that which people know and that which they agree to admit that they know, that which they see and that which they speak of, that which they feel to be a part of life and that which they allow to enter into literature. There is the great difference, in short, between what they talk of in conversation and what they talk of in print. The essence of moral energy is to survey the whole field, and I should directly reverse Mr. Besant's remark and say not that the English novel has a purpose, but that it has a diffidence. To what degree a purpose in a work of art is a source of corruption I shall not attempt to inquire; the one that seems to me least dangerous is the purpose of making a perfect work. As for our novel, I may say lastly on this score that as we find it in England today it strikes me as addressed in a large degree to "young people," and that this in itself constitutes a presumption that it will be rather shy. There are certain things which it is generally agreed not to discuss, not even to mention, before young people. That is very well, but the absence of discussion is not a symptom of the moral passion. The purpose of the English novel—"a truly admirable thing, and a great cause for congratulation"—strikes me therefore as rather negative.

There is one point at which the moral sense and the artistic sense lie very near together; that is in the light of the very obvious truth that the deepest quality of a work of art will always be the quality of the mind of the producer. In proportion as that intelligence is fine will the novel, the picture, the statue partake of the substance of beauty and truth. To be constituted of such elements is, to my vision, to have purpose enough. No good novel will ever proceed from a superficial mind; that seems to me an axiom which, for the artist in fiction, will cover all needful moral ground: if the youthful aspirant take it to heart it will illuminate for him many of the mysteries of "purpose." There are many other useful things that might be said to him, but I have come to the end of my article, and can only touch them as I pass. The critic in the *Pall Mall Gazette*, whom I have already quoted, draws attention to the danger, in speaking of the art of fiction, of generalizing. The danger that he has in mind is rather, I imagine, that of

particularizing, for there are some com prehensive remarks which, in additio to those embodied in Mr. Besant's sug gestive lecture, might without fear o misleading him be addressed to the in genuous student. I should remind him first of the magnificence of the form tha is open to him, which offers to sight s few restrictions and such innumerabl opportunities. The other arts, in com parison, appear confined and hampered the various conditions under which the are exercised are so rigid and definite But the only condition that I can thin of attaching to the composition of the novel is, as I have already said, that be sincere. This freedom is a splendi privilege, and the first lesson of th young novelist is to learn to be worth of it. "Enjoy it as it deserves," I shoul say to him; "take possession of it, ex plore it to its utmost extent, publish i rejoice in it. All life belongs to you, an do not listen either to those who woul shut you up into corners of it and te you that it is only here and there tha art inhabits, or to those who would per suade you that this heavenly messenge wings her way outside of life altogethe breathing a superfine air, and turnin away her head from the truth of thing There is no impression of life, no man ner of seeing it and feeling it, to whic the plan of the novelist may not offer place; you have only to remember tha talents so dissimilar as those of Alexan dre Dumas and Jane Austen, Charle Dickens and Gustave Flaubert hav worked in this field with equal glor Do not think too much about optimism and pessimism; try and catch the colo of life itself. In France today we see prodigious effort (that of Emile Zola to whose solid and serious work no ex plorer of the capacity of the novel ca allude without respect), we see an ex traordinary effort vitiated by a spirit o pessimism on a narrow basis. M. Zol is magnificent, but he strikes an Englis reader as ignorant; he has an air o working in the dark; if he had as muc light as energy, his results would be o the highest value. As for the aberratio of a shallow optimism, the ground (o

English fiction especially) is strewn with their brittle particles as with broken glass. If you must indulge in conclusions, let them have the taste of a wide knowl-edge. Remember that your first duty is to be as complete as possible—to make as perfect a work. Be generous and deli-cate and pursue the prize."

WILLIAM DEAN HOWELLS

(1837-1920)

A prolific novelist and essayist, Howells was the leading spokesman for literary real-ism in America during the years from 1870 to the turn of the century. His critical and literary opinions are most fully expressed in *Criticism and Fiction* (1891), *My Literary Passions* (1895), and *Literature and Life* (1902). Although somewhat con-strained by the genteel conventions of his time, Howells recognized and generously supported younger writers in the naturalistic tradition like Stephen Crane and Frank Norris. Like Whitman, many of whose ideas he adapted, Howells empha-sized the responsibility of the American writer and critic to support democratic ideals and values. His theory is thus distinguished by its assertion of the moral and didactic functions of literature.

From *Criticism and Fiction* (1891)

XVIII

. . . More and more not only the criti-cism which prints its opinions, but the infinitely vaster and powerfuler criticism which thinks and feels them merely, will make this demand. I confess that I do not care to judge any work of the imagi-nation without first of all applying this test to it. We must ask ourselves before we ask anything else, Is it true?—true to the motives, the impulses, the principles that shape the life of actual men and women? This truth, which necessarily includes the highest morality and the highest artistry—this truth given, the book cannot be wicked and cannot be weak; and without it all graces of style and feats of invention and cunning of construction are so many superfluities of naughtiness. It is well for the truth

Reprinted from *Criticism and Fiction* (1891) by Will-iam Dean Howells by permission of William Howells.

to have all these, and shine in them, but for falsehood they are merely mere-tricious, the bedizenment of the wanton; they atone for nothing, they count for nothing. But in fact they come naturally of truth, and grace it without solicita-tion; they are added unto it. In the whole range of fiction we know of no true picture of life—that is, of human nature—which is not also a masterpiece of literature, full of divine and natural beauty. It may have no touch or tint of this special civilization or of that; it had better have this local color well ascer-tained; but the truth is deeper and finer than aspects, and if the book is true to what men and women know of one another's souls it will be true enough, and it will be great and beautiful. It is the conception of literature as some-thing apart from life, superfinely aloof, which makes it really unimportant to the great mass of mankind, without a message or a meaning for them; and it is the notion that a novel may be false in its portrayal of causes and effects that makes literary art contemptible even to those whom it amuses, that forbids them to regard the novelist as a serious or right-minded person. If they do not in some moment of indignation cry out against all novels, as my correspondent does, they remain besotted in the fume of the delusions purveyed to them, with no higher feeling for the author than such maudlin affection as the habitué of an opium-joint perhaps knows for the attendant who fills his pipe with the drug.

Or, as in the case of another correspondent who writes that in his youth he "read a great many novels, but always regarded it as an amusement, like horse-racing and card-playing," for which he had no time when he entered upon the serious business of life, it renders them merely contemptuous. His view of the matter may be commended to the brotherhood and sisterhood of novelists as full of wholesome if bitter suggestion; and we urge them not to dismiss it with high literary scorn as that of some Boeotian dull to the beauty of art. Refuse it as we may, it is still the feeling of the vast majority of people for whom life is earnest, and who find only a distorted and misleading likeness of it in our books. We may fold ourselves in our scholars' gowns, and close the doors of our studies, and affect to despise this rude voice; but we cannot shut it out. It comes to us from wherever men are at work, from wherever they are truly living, and accuses us of unfaithfulness, of triviality, of mere stage-play; and none of us can escape conviction except he prove himself worthy of his time—a time in which the great masters have brought literature back to life, and filled its ebbing veins with the red tides of reality. We cannot all equal them; we need not copy them; but we can all go to the sources of their inspiration and their power; and to draw from these no one need go far—no one need really go out of himself.

Fifty years ago, Carlyle, in whom the truth was always alive, but in whom it was then unperverted by suffering, by celebrity, and by despair, wrote in his study of Diderot: "Were it not reasonable to prophesy that this exceeding great multitude of novel-writers and such like must, in a new generation, gradually do one of two things: either retire into the nurseries, and work for children, minors, and semi-fatuous persons of both sexes, or else, what were far better, sweep their novel-fabric into the dust-cart, and betake themselves with such faculty as they have to understand and record what is true, of which surely there is, and will forever be, a whole infinitude unknown to us of infinite importance to us? Poetry, it will more and more come to be understood, is nothing but higher knowledge; and the only genuine Romance (for grown persons), Reality."

If, after half a century, fiction still mainly works for "children, minors, and semi-fatuous persons of both sexes," it is nevertheless one of the hopefulest signs of the world's progress that it has begun to work for "grown persons," and if not exactly in the way that Carlyle might have solely intended in urging its writers to compile memoirs instead of building the "novel-fabric," still it has, in the highest and widest sense, already made Reality its Romance. I cannot judge it, I do not even care for it, except as it has done this; and I can hardly conceive of a literary self-respect in these days compatible with the old trade of make-believe, with the production of the kind of fiction which is too much honored by classification with card-playing and horse-racing. But let fiction cease to lie about life; let it portray men and women as they are, actuated by the motives and the passions in the measure we all know; let it leave off painting dolls and working them by springs and wires; let it show the different interests in their true proportions; let it forbear to preach pride and revenge, folly and insanity, egotism and prejudice, but frankly own these for what they are, in whatever figures and occasions they appear; let it not put on fine literary airs; let it speak the dialect, the language, that most

Americans know—the language of unaffected people everywhere—and there can be no doubt of an unlimited future, not only of delightfulness but of usefulness, for it.

XXI

. . . I will not say they [American novels] are all good, or that any of them is wholly good; but I find in nearly every one of them a disposition to regard our life without the literary glasses so long thought desirable, and to see character, not as it is in other fiction, but as it abounds outside of all fiction. This disposition sometimes goes with poor enough performance, but in some of our novels it goes with performance that is excellent; and at any rate it is for the present more valuable than evenness of performance. It is what relates American fiction to the only living movement in imaginative literature, and distinguishes by a superior freshness and authenticity any group of American novels from a similarly accidental group of English novels, giving them the same good right to be as the like number of recent Russian novels, French novels, Spanish novels, Italian novels, Norwegian novels.

It is the difference of the American novelist's ideals from those of the English novelist that gives him his advantage, and seems to promise him the future. The love of the passionate and the heroic, as the Englishman has it, is such a crude and unwholesome thing, so deaf and blind to all the most delicate and important facts of art and life, so insensible to the subtle values in either that its presence or absence makes the whole difference, and enables one who is not obsessed by it to thank Heaven that he is not as that other man is.

There can be little question that many refinements of thought and spirit which every American is sensible of in the fiction of this continent, are necessarily lost upon our good kin beyond seas, whose thumb-fingered apprehension requires something gross and palpable for its assurance of reality. This is not their fault, and I am not sure that it is wholly their misfortune: they are made so as not to miss what they do not find, and they are simply content without those subtleties of life and character which it gives us so keen a pleasure to have noted in literature. If they perceive them at all it is as something vague and diaphanous, something that filmily wavers before their sense and teases them, much as the beings of an invisible world might mock one of our material frame by intimations of their presence. It is with reason, therefore, on the part of an Englishman, that Mr. Henley complains of our fiction as a shadow-land, though we find more and more in it the faithful report of our life, its motives and emotions, and all the comparatively etherealized passions and ideals that influence it.

In fact, the American who chooses to enjoy his birthright to the full, lives in a world wholly different from the Englishman's, and speaks (too often through his nose) another language: he breathes a rarefied and nimble air full of shining possibilities and radiant promises which the fog-and-soot-clogged lungs of those less-favored islanders struggle in vain to fill themselves with. But he ought to be modest in his advantage, and patient with the coughing and sputtering of his cousin who complains of finding himself in an exhausted receiver on plunging into one of our novels. To be quite just to the poor fellow, I have had some such experience as that myself in the atmosphere of some of our more attenuated romances.

Yet every now and then I read a book with perfect comfort and much exhilaration, whose scenes the average Englishman would gasp in. Nothing happens; that is, nobody murders or debauches anybody else; there is no arson or pillage of any sort; there is not a ghost, or a ravening beast, or a hair-breadth escape, or a shipwreck, or a monster of self-sacrifice, or a lady five thousand years old in the whole course of the story; "no promenade, no band of music, nossing!" as Mr. Du Maurier's Frenchman said of the meet for a fox-hunt. Yet it is all alive with the keenest interest for those who enjoy the study of individual traits and general conditions as they make themselves known to American experience.

These conditions have been so favorable hitherto (though they are becoming always less so) that they easily account for the optimistic faith of our novel which Mr. Hughes notices. It used to be one of the disadvantages of the practice of romance in America, which Hawthorne more or less whimsically lamented, that there were so few shadows and inequalities in our broad level of prosperity; and it is one of the reflections suggested by Dostoïevsky's novel, The Crime and the Punishment, that whoever struck a note so profoundly tragic in American fiction would do a false and mistaken thing—as false and as mistaken in its way as dealing in American fiction with certain nudities which the Latin peoples seem to find edifying. Whatever their deserts, very few American novelists have been led out to be shot, or finally exiled to the rigors of a winter at Duluth; and in a land where journeyman carpenters and plumbers strike for four dollars a day the sum of hunger and cold is comparatively small, and the wrong from class to class has been almost inappreciable, though all this is changing for the worse. Our novelists, therefore, concern themselves with the more smiling aspects of life, which are the more American, and seek the universal in the individual rather than the social interests. It is worth while, even at the risk of being called commonplace, to be true to our well-to-do actualities; the very passions themselves seem to be softened and modified by conditions which formerly at least could not be said to wrong any one, to cramp endeavor, or to cross lawful desire. Sin and suffering and shame there must always be in the world, I suppose, but I believe that in this new world of ours it is still mainly from one to another one, and oftener still from one to one's self. We have death too in America, and a great deal of disagreeable and painful disease, which the multiplicity of our patent medicines does not seem to cure; but this is tragedy that comes in the very nature of things, and is not peculiarly American, as the large, cheerful average of health and success and happy life is. It will not do to boast, but it is well to be true to the facts, and to see that, apart from these purely mortal troubles, the race here has enjoyed conditions in which most of the ills that have darkened its annals might be averted by honest work and unselfish behavior. . . .

XXII

. . . We may comfort ourselves, however, unless we prefer a luxury of grief, by remembering that no language is ever old on the lips of those who speak it, no matter how decrepit it drops from the pen. We have only to leave our studies, editorial and other, and go into the shops and fields to find the "spacious times" again; and from the beginning Realism, before she had put on her capital letter, had divined this near-at-hand truth along with the rest. Mr. Lowell, almost the greatest and finest realist who ever wrought in verse, showed us that Elizabeth was still Queen where he heard Yankee farmers talk. One need not invite slang into the company of its betters, though perhaps slang has been dropping its "s" and becoming language ever since the world began, and is certainly sometimes delightful and forcible beyond the reach of the dictionary. I would not have any one go about for new words, but if one of them came aptly, not to reject its help. For our novelists to try to write Americanly, from any motive, would be a dismal error, but being born Americans, I would have them use "Americanisms" whenever these serve their turn; and when their characters speak, I should like to hear them speak true American, with all the varying Tennesseean, Philadelphian, Bostonian, and New York accents. If we bother ourselves to write what the critics imagine to be "English," we shall be priggish and artificial, and still more so if we make our Americans talk "English." There is also this serious disadvantage about "English," that if we wrote the best "English" in the world, probably the English themselves would not know it, or, if they did, certainly would not own it. It has always been supposed by grammarians and purists that a language can be kept as they find it; but languages, while they live, are perpetually changing. God apparently meant them for the common people—whom Lincoln believed God liked because he had made so many of them; and the common people will use them freely as they use other gifts of God. On their lips our continental English will differ more and more from the insular English, and I believe that this is not deplorable, but desirable.

In fine, I would have our American novelists be as American as they unconsciously can. Matthew Arnold complained that he found no "distinction" in our life, and I would gladly persuade all artists intending greatness in any kind among us that the recognition of the fact pointed out by Mr. Arnold ought to be a source of inspiration to them, and not discouragement. We have been now some hundred years building up a state on the affirmation of the essential equality of men in their rights and duties, and whether we have been right or wrong the gods have taken us at our word, and have responded to us with a civilization in which there is no "distinction" perceptible to the eye that loves and values it. Such beauty and such grandeur as we have is common beauty, common grandeur, or the beauty and grandeur in which the quality of solidarity so prevails that neither distinguishes itself to the disadvantage of anything else. It seems to me that these conditions invite the artist to the study and the appreciation of the common, and to the portrayal in every art of those finer and higher aspects which unite rather than sever humanity, if he would thrive in our new order of things. The talent that is robust enough to front the every-day world and catch the charm of its work-worn, care-worn, brave, kindly face, need not fear the encounter, though it seems terrible to the sort nurtured in the superstition of the romantic, the bizarre, the heroic, the distinguished, as the things alone worthy of painting or carving or writing. The arts must become democratic, and then we shall have the expression of America in art; and the reproach which Mr. Arnold was half right in making us shall have no justice in it any longer; we shall be "distinguished."

XXVIII

But if the humanitarian impulse has mostly disappeared from Christmas fiction, I think it has never so generally characterized all fiction. One may refuse to recognize this impulse; one may deny that it is in any greater degree shaping life than ever before, but no one who has the current of literature under his eye can fail to note it there. People are thinking and feeling generously, if not living justly, in our time; it is a day of anxiety to be saved from the curse that is on selfishness, of eager question how others shall be helped, of bold denial that the conditions in which we would fain have rested are sacred or immutable. Especially in America, where the race has gained a height never reached before, the eminence enables more men than ever before to see how even here vast masses of men are sunk in misery that must grow every day more hopeless, or embroiled in a struggle for mere life that must end in enslaving and imbruting them.

Art, indeed, is beginning to find out that if it does not make friends with Need it must perish. It perceives that to take itself from the many and leave them no joy in their work, and to give itself to the few whom it can bring no joy in their idleness, is an error that kills. This has long been the burden of Ruskin's message: and if we can believe William Morris, the common people have heard him gladly, and have felt the truth of what he says. "They see the prophet in him rather than the fantastic rhetorician, as more superfine audiences do"; and the men and women who do the hard work of the world have learned from him and from Morris that they have a right to pleasure in their toil, and that when justice is done them they will have it. In all ages poetry has affirmed something of this sort, but it remained for ours to perceive it and express it somehow in every form of literature. But this is only one phase of the devotion of the best literature of our time to the service of humanity. No book written with a low or cynical motive could succeed now, no matter how brilliantly written; and the work done in the past to the glorification of mere passion and power, to the deification of self, appears monstrous and hideous. The romantic spirit worshipped genius, worshipped heroism, but at its best, in such a man as Victor Hugo, this spirit recognized the supreme claim of the lowest humanity. Its error was to idealize the victims of society, to paint them impossibly virtuous and beautiful; but truth, which has succeeded to the highest mission of romance, paints these victims as they are, and bids the world consider them not because they are beautiful and virtuous, but because they are ugly and vicious, cruel, filthy, and only not altogether loathsome because the divine can never wholly die out of the human. The truth does not find these victims among the poor alone, among the hungry, the houseless, the ragged; but it also finds them among the rich, cursed with the aimlessness, the satiety, the despair of wealth, wasting their lives in a fool's paradise of shows and semblances, with nothing real but the misery that comes of insincerity and selfishness.

It is needless for me to say, either to the many whom my opinions on this point incense or to the few who accept them, that I do not think the fiction of our own time even always equal to this work, or perhaps more than seldom so. But as I have before expressed, to the still-reverberating discontent of two continents, fiction is now a finer art than it has ever been hitherto, and more nearly meets the requirements of the infallible standard. I have hopes of real usefulness in it, because it is at last building on the only sure foundation; but I am by no means certain that it will be the ultimate literary form, or will remain as important as we believe it is destined to become. On the contrary, it is quite imaginable that when the great mass of readers, now sunk in the foolish joys of mere fable, shall be lifted to an interest in the meaning of things through the faithful portrayal of life in fiction, then fiction the most faithful may be superseded by a still more faithful form of contemporaneous history. I willingly leave the precise character of this form to the more robust imagination of readers whose minds have been nurtured upon romantic novels, and who really have an imagination worth speaking of, and confine myself, as usual, to the hither side of the regions of conjecture.

The art which in the mean time disdains the office of teacher is one of the last refuges of the aristocratic spirit which is disappearing from politics and society, and is now seeking to shelter itself in aesthetics. The pride of caste is becoming the pride of taste; but as before, it is averse to the mass of men; it consents to know them only in some conventionalized and artificial guise. It seeks to withdraw itself, to stand aloof, to be distinguished, and not to be identified. Democracy in literature is the reverse of all this. It wishes to know and to tell the truth, confident that consolation and delight are there; it does not care to paint the marvellous and impossible for the vulgar many, or to sentimentalize and falsify the actual for the vulgar few. Men are more like than unlike one another: let us make them know one another better, that they may all be humbled and strengthened with a sense of their fraternity. Neither art nor letters, nor sciences, except as they somehow, clearly or obscurely, tend to make the race better and kinder, are to be regarded as serious interests; they are all lower than the rudest crafts that feed and house and clothe, for except they do this office they are idle; and they cannot do this except from and through the truth.

EZRA POUND

(b. 1885)

Ezra Pound, poet and expatriate, has exerted a shaping influence on modern literature and criticism as a leader of revolutionary movements like Imagism and Vorticism, as a friend and adviser to a generation of modern writers, as an editor of literary magazines, and as the author of many articles and books. Reacting against Victorian conventionality and impressionistic subjectivity, Pound helped establish a new tradition of close technical criticism. His followers in this endeavor came to include T. S. Eliot and the later New Critics. Pound is distinguished from the latter, however, by his emphasis on the public role of literature and the responsibility of the artist for the cleanliness and force of common language. His critical views are set forth in many essays, including *Gaudier-Brzeska* (1916), *Pavannes and Divisions* (1918), *Instigations* (1920), *How to Read* (1931), *The ABC of Reading* (1934), *Make It New* (1934), *Polite Essays* (1937), *Guide to Kulchur* (1938). Other valuable sources include *Literary Essays of Ezra Pound* (ed. T. S. Eliot, 1954) and *The Letters of Ezra Pound* (ed. D. D. Paige, 1950).

From The Serious Artist (1913)

I

It is curious that one should be asked to rewrite Sidney's *Defence of Poesy* in the year of grace 1913. During the intervening centuries, and before them, other centres of civilization had decided that good art was a blessing and that bad art was criminal, and they had spent some time and thought in trying to find means whereby to distinguish the true art from the sham. But in England now, in the age of Gosse as in the age of Gosson we are asked if the arts are moral. We are asked to define the relation of the arts to economics, we are asked what position the arts are to hold in the ideal republic. And it is obviously the opinion of many people less objectionable than the Sydney Webbs that the arts had better not exist at all.

I take no great pleasure in writing prose about aesthetic. I think one work of art is worth forty prefaces and as many apologiae. Nevertheless I have been questioned earnestly and by a person certainly of good will. It is as if one said to me: what is the use of open spaces in this city, what is the use of rose-trees and why do you wish to plant trees and lay out parks and gardens? There are some who do not take delight in these things. The rose springs fairest from some buried Caesar's throat and the dogwood with its flower of four petals (our dogwood, not the tree you call by that name) is grown from the heart of Aucassin, or perhaps this is only fancy. Let us pursue the matter in ethic.

It is obvious that ethics are based on the nature of man, just as it is obvious that civics are based upon the nature of men when living together in groups.

It is obvious that the good of the greatest number cannot be attained until we know in some sort of what that good must consist. In other words we must know what sort of an animal man is, before we can contrive his maximum happiness, or before we can decide what percentage of that happiness he can have without causing too great a percentage of unhappiness to those about him.

The arts, literature, poesy, are a science, just as chemistry is a science. Their subject is man, mankind and the individual. The subject of chemistry is matter considered as to its composition.

The arts give us a great percentage of the lasting and unassailable data regarding the nature of man, of immaterial man, of man considered as a thinking and sentient creature. They begin where the science of medicine leaves off or rather they overlap that science. The borders of the two arts overcross.

From medicine we learn that man thrives best when duly washed, aired and sunned. From the arts we learn that man is whimsical, that one man differs from another. That men differ among themselves as leaves upon trees differ. That they do not resemble each other as do buttons cut by machine.

From the arts also we learn in what ways man resembles and in what way he differs from certain other animals. We learn that certain men are often more akin to certain animals than they are to other men of different composition. We learn that all men do not desire the same things and that it would therefore be inequitable to give to all men two acres and a cow.

It would be manifestly inequitable to treat the ostrich and the polar bear in the same fashion, granted that it is not unjust to have them pent up where you can treat them at all.

An ethic based on a belief that men are different from what they are is manifestly stupid. It is stupid to apply such an ethic as it is to apply laws and morals designed for a nomadic tribe, or for a tribe in the state of barbarism, to a people crowded into the slums of a modern metropolis. Thus in the tribe it is well to beget children, for the more

strong male children you have in the tribe the less likely you are to be bashed on the head by males of the neighbouring tribes, and the more female children the more rapidly the tribe will increase. Conversely it is a crime rather worse than murder to beget children in a slum, to beget children for whom no fitting provision is made, either as touching their physical or economic wellbeing. The increase not only afflicts the child born but the increasing number of the poor keeps down the wage. On this count the bishop of London, as an encourager of this sort of increase, is a criminal of a type rather lower and rather more detestable than the souteneur.

I cite this as an example of inequity persisting because of a continued refusal to consider a code devised for one state of society, in its (the code's) relation to a different state of society. It is as if, in physics or engineering, we refused to consider a force designed to affect one mass, in its relation (i.e. the force's) to another mass wholly differing, or in some notable way differing, from the first mass.

As inequities can exist because of refusals to consider the actualities of a law in relation to a social condition, so can inequities exist through refusal to consider the actualities of the composition of the masses, or of the individuals to which they are applied.

If all men desired above everything else two acres and a cow, obviously the perfect state would be that state which gave to each man two acres and a cow.

If any science save the arts were able more precisely to determine what the individual does not actually desire, then that science would be of more use in providing the data for ethics.

In the like manner, if any science save medicine and chemistry were more able to determine what things were compatible with physical wellbeing, then those sciences would be of more value for providing the data of hygiene.

This brings us to the immorality of bad art. Bad art is inaccurate art. It i art that makes false reports. If a scientist falsifies a report either deliberately or through negligence we consider him as either a criminal or a bad scientist according to the enormity of his offence, and he is punished or despised accordingly.

If he falsifies the reports of a maternity hospital in order to retain his position and get profit and advancement from the city board, he may escape detection. If he declines to make such falsification he may lose financial rewards, and in either case his baseness or his pluck may pass unknown and unnoticed save by a very few people. Nevertheless one does not have to argue his case. The layman knows soon enough on hearing it whether the physician is to be blamed or praised.

If an artist falsifies his report as to the nature of man, as to his own nature, as to the nature of his ideal of the perfect, as to the nature of his ideal of this, that or the other, of god, if god exist, of the life force, of the nature of good and evil, if good and evil exist, of the force with which he believes or disbelieves this, that or the other, of the degree in which he suffers or is made glad; if the artist falsifies his reports on these matters or on any other matter in order that he may conform to the taste of his time, to the proprieties of a sovereign, to the conveniences of a preconceived code of ethics, then that artist lies. If he lies out of deliberate will to lie, if he lies out of carelessness, out of laziness, out of cowardice, out of any sort of negligence whatsoever, he nevertheless lies and he should be punished or despised in proportion to the seriousness of his offence. His offence is of the same nature as the physician's and according to his position and the nature of his lie he is responsible for future oppressions and for future misconceptions. Albeit his lies are known to only a few, or his truth-telling to only a few. Albeit he may pass without censure for one and without praise for the other. Albeit he can only be punished on the plane of his crime and by nothing save the contempt of those who know of his crime. Perhaps it is caddish-

ness rather than crime. However there is perhaps nothing worse for a man than to know that he is a cur and to know that someone else, if only one person, knows it.

We distinguish very clearly between the physician who is doing his best for a patient, who is using drugs in which he believes, or who is in a wilderness, let us say, where the patient can get no other medical aid. We distinguish, I say, very clearly between the failure of such a physician, and the act of that physician, who ignorant of the patient's disease, being in reach of more skilful physicians, deliberately denies an ignorance of which he is quite conscious, refuses to consult other physicians, tries to prevent the patient's having access to more skilful physicians, or deliberately tortures the patient for his own ends.

One does not need to read black print to learn this ethical fact about physicians. Yet it takes a deal of talking to convince a layman that bad art is 'immoral'. And that good art however 'immoral' it is, is wholly a thing of virtue. Purely and simply that good art can NOT be immoral. By good art I mean art that bears true witness, I mean the art that is most precise. You can be wholly precise in representing a vagueness. You can be wholly a liar in pretending that the particular vagueness was precise in its outline. If you cannot understand this with regard to poetry, consider the matter in terms of painting.

If you have forgotten my statement that the arts bear witness and define for us the inner nature and conditions of man, consider the Victory of Samothrace and the Taj of Agra. The man who carved the one and the man who designed the other may either or both of them have looked like an ape, or like two apes respectively. They may have looked like other apelike or swinelike men. We have the Victory and the Taj to witness that there was something within them differing from the contents of the apes and of the other swinelike men. Thus we learn that humanity is a species or genus of animals capable of a variation that will produce the desire

for a Taj or a Victory, and moreover
capable of effecting that Taj or Victory
in stone. We know from other testimony
of the arts and from ourselves that the
desire often overshoots the power of efficient presentation; we therefore conclude that other members of the race
may have desired to effect a Taj or a
Victory. We even suppose that men
have desired to effect more beautiful
things although few of us are capable of
forming any precise mental image of
things, in their particular way, more
beautiful than this statue or this building. So difficult is this that no one has
yet been able to effect a restoration for
the missing head of the Victory. At least
no one has done so in stone, so far as I
know. Doubtless many people have stood
opposite the statue and made such heads
in their imagination.

As there are in medicine the art of
diagnosis and the art of cure, so in the
arts, so in the particular arts of poetry
and of literature, there is the art of diagnosis and there is the art of cure. They
call one the cult of ugliness and the
other the cult of beauty.

The cult of beauty is the hygiene, it
is sun, air and the sea and the rain and
the lake bathing. The cult of ugliness,
Villon, Baudelaire, Corbière, Beardsley
are diagnosis. Flaubert is diagnosis.
Satire, if we are to ride this metaphor to
staggers, satire is surgery, insertions and
amputations.

Beauty in art reminds one what is
worth while. I am not now speaking of
shams. I mean beauty, not slither, not
sentimentalizing about beauty, not telling people that beauty is the proper and
respectable thing. I mean beauty. You
don't argue about an April wind, you
feel bucked up when you meet it. You
feel bucked up when you come on a
swift moving thought in Plato or on a
fine line in a statue.

Even this pother about gods reminds
one that something is worth while. Satire reminds one that certain things are
not worth while. It draws one to consider time wasted.

The cult of beauty and the delineation of ugliness are not in mutual opposition.

II

I have said that the arts give us our best
data for determining what sort of creature man is. As our treatment of man
must be determined by our knowledge
or conception of what man is, the arts
provide data for ethics.

These data are sound and the data of
generalizing psychologists and social
theoricians are usually unsound, for the
serious artist is scientific and the theorist
is usually empiric in the medieval fashion. That is to say a good biologist will
make a reasonable number of observations of any given phenomenon before
he draws a conclusion, thus we read
such phrases as 'over 100 cultures from
the secretions of the respiratory tracts of
over 500 patients and 30 nurses and
attendants'. The results of each observation must be precise and no single observation must in itself be taken as determining a general law, although, after
experiment, certain observations may be
held as typical or normal. The serious
artist is scientific in that he presents the
image of his desire, of his hate, of his
indifference as precisely that, as precisely the image of his own desire, hate
or indifference. The more precise his
record the more lasting and unassailable his work of art.

The theorist, and we see this constantly illustrated by the English writers
on sex, the theorist constantly proceeds
as if his own case, his own limits and
predilections were the typical case, or
even as if it were the universal. He is
constantly urging someone else to be
have as he, the theorist, would like to
behave. Now art never asks anybody to
do anything, or to think anything, or to
be anything. It exists as the trees exist,
you can admire, you can sit in the
shade, you can pick bananas, you can
cut firewood, you can do as you jolly
well please.

Also you are a fool to seek the kind
of art you don't like. You are a fool to
read classics because you are told to and
not because you like them. You are a
fool to aspire to good taste if you haven't
naturally got it. If there is one place

where it is idiotic to sham that place is before a work of art. Also you are a fool not to have an open mind, not to be eager to enjoy something you might enjoy but don't know how to. But it is not the artist's place to ask you to learn, or to defend his particular works of art, or to insist on your reading his books. Any artist who wants your particular admiration is, by just so much, the less artist.

The desire to stand on the stage, the desire of plaudits has nothing to do with serious art. The serious artist may like to stand on the stage, he may, apart from his art, be any kind of imbecile you like, but the two things are not connected, at least they are not concentric. Lots of people who don't even pretend to be artists have the same desire to be slobbered over, by people with less brains than they have.

The serious artist is usually, or is often as far from the aegrum vulgus as is the serious scientist. Nobody has heard of the abstract mathematicians who worked out the determinants that Marconi made use of in his computations for the wireless telegraph. The public, the public so dear to the journalistic heart, is far more concerned with the shareholders in the Marconi company.

The permanent property, the property given to the race at large is precisely these data of the serious scientist and of the serious artist; of the scientist as touching the relations of abstract numbers, of molecular energy, of the composition of matter, etc.; of the serious artist, as touching the nature of man, of individuals.

Men have ceased trying to conquer the world[1] and to acquire universal knowledge. Men still try to promote the ideal state. No perfect state will be founded on the theory, or on the working hypothesis that all men are alike. No science save the arts will give us the requisite data for learning in what ways men differ.

The very fact that many men hate the arts is of value, for we are enabled by finding out what part of the arts they hate, to learn something of their nature. Usually when men say they hate the arts we find that they merely detest quackery and bad artists.

In the case of a man's hating one art and not the others we may learn that he is of defective hearing or of defective intelligence. Thus an intelligent man may hate music or a good musician may detest very excellent authors.

And all these things are very obvious.

Among thinking and sentient people the bad artist is contemned as we would contemn a negligent physician or a sloppy, inaccurate scientist, and the serious artist is left in peace, or even supported and encouraged. In the fog and the outer darkness no measures are taken to distinguish between the serious and the unserious artist. The unserious artist being the commoner brand and greatly outnumbering the serious variety, and it being to the temporary and apparent advantage of the false artist to gain the rewards proper to the serious artist, it is natural that the unserious artist should do all in his power to obfuscate the lines of demarcation.

Whenever one attempts to demonstrate the difference between serious and unserious work, one is told that 'it is merely a technical discussion'. It has rested at that—in England it has rested at that for more than three hundred years. The people would rather have patent medicines than scientific treatment. They will occasionally be told that art as art is not a violation of God's most holy laws. They will not have a specialist's opinion as to what art is good. They will not consider the 'problem of style'. They want 'The value of art to life' and 'Fundamental issues'.

As touching fundamental issues: The arts give us our data of psychology, of man as to his interiors, as to the ratio of his thought to his emotions, etc., etc., etc.

The touchstone of an art is its precision. This precision is of various and complicated sorts and only the specialist can determine whether certain works of art possess certain sorts of precision. I don't mean to say that any intelligent person cannot have more or less sound

[1] *Blind Optimism* A.D. 1913.

judgement as to whether a certain work of art is good or not. An intelligent person can usually tell whether or not a person is in good health. It is none the less true that it takes a skilful physician to make certain diagnoses or to discern the lurking disease beneath the appearance of vigour.

It is no more possible to give in a few pages full instructions for knowing a masterpiece than it would be to give full instructions for all medical diagnosis.

Vorticism (1914)

"It is no more ridiculous that a person should receive or convey an emotion by means of an arrangement of shapes, or planes, or colours, than that they should receive or convey such emotion by an arrangement of musical notes."

I suppose this proposition is self-evident. Whistler said as much, some years ago, and Pater proclaimed that "All arts approach the conditions of music."

Whenever I say this I am greeted with a storm of "Yes, but . . ." "But why isn't this art futurism?" "Why isn't?" "Why don't?" and above all: "What, in Heaven's name, has it got to do with your Imagiste poetry?"

Let me explain at leisure, and in nice, orderly, old-fashioned prose.

We are all futurists to the extent of believing with Guillaume Appollonaire that "On ne peut pas porter *partout* avec soi le cadavre de son père." But "futurism," when it gets into art, is, for the most part, a descendant of impressionism. It is a sort of accelerated impressionism.

There is another artistic descent *via* Picasso and Kandinsky; *via* cubism and expressionism. One does not complain of neoimpression or of accelerated impressionism and "simultaneity," but one is not wholly satisfied by them. One has perhaps other needs.

It is very difficult to make generalities about three arts at once. I shall be, perhaps, more lucid if I give, briefly, the history of the vorticist art with which I am most intimately connected, that is to say, vorticist poetry. Vorticism has been announced as including such and such painting and sculpture and "Imagisme" in verse. I shall explain "Imagisme," and then proceed to show its inner relation to certain modern paintings and sculpture.

Imagisme, in so far as it has been known at all, has been known chiefly as a stylistic movement, as a movement of criticism rather than of creation. This is natural, for, despite all possible celerity of publication, the public is always, and of necessity, some years behind the artists' actual thought. Nearly anyone is ready to accept "Imagisme" as a department of poetry, just as one accepts "lyricism" as a department of poetry.

There is a sort of poetry where music, sheer melody, seems as if it were just bursting into speech.

There is another sort of poetry where painting or sculpture seems as if it were "just coming over into speech."

The first sort of poetry has long been called "lyric." One is accustomed to distinguish easily between "lyric" and "epic" and "didactic." One is capable of finding the "lyric" passages in a drama or in a long poem not otherwise "lyric." This division is in the grammars and school books, and one has been brought up to it.

The other sort of poetry is as old as the lyric and as honourable, but, until recently, no one had named it. Ibycus and Liu Ch'e presented the "Image." Dante is a great poet by reason of this faculty, and Milton is a wind-bag because of his lack of it. The "image" is the furthest possible remove from rhetoric. Rhetoric is the art of dressing up

First published in *Fortnightly Review*, XCVI (September 1, 1914), 461-471. Reprinted by permission of the author.

some unimportant matter so as to fool the audience for the time being. So much for the general category. Even Aristotle distinguishes between rhetoric, "which is persuasion," and the analytical examination of truth. As a "critical" movement, the "Imagisme" of 1912 to '14 set out "to bring poetry up to the level of prose." No one is so quixotic as to believe that contemporary poetry holds any such position. . . . Stendhal formulated the need in his *De L'Amour*:—

"La poésie avec ses comparaisons obligées, sa mythologie que ne croit pas le poète, sa dignité de style à la Louis XIV. et tout l'attirail de ses ornements appelé poétique, est bien au dessous de la prose dès qu'il s'agit de donner une idée claire et précise des mouvements du coeur, or dans ce genre on n'émeut que par la clarté."

Flaubert and De Maupassant lifted prose to the rank of a finer art, and one has no patience with contemporary poets who escape from all the difficulties of the infinitely difficult art of good prose by pouring themselves into loose verses.

The tenets of the Imagiste faith were published in March, 1913, as follows:—

I. Direct treatment of the "thing," whether subjective or objective.

II. To use absolutely no word that does not contribute to the presentation.

III. As regarding rhythm: to compose in sequence of the musical phrase, not in sequence of the metronome.

There followed a series of about forty cautions to beginners, which need not concern us here.

The arts have indeed "some sort of common bond, some inter-recognition." Yet certain emotions or subjects find their most appropriate expression in some one particular art. The work of art which is most "worth while" is the work which would need a hundred works of any other kind of art to explain it. A fine statue is the core of a hundred poems. A fine poem is a score of symphonies. There is music which would need a hundred paintings to express it. There is no synonym for the *Victory of Samothrace* or for Mr. Epstein's flemites. There is no painting of Villon's *Frères*

Humains. Such works are what we call works of the "first intensity."

A given subject or emotion belongs to that artist, or to that sort of artist who must know it most intimately and most intensely before he can render it adequately in his art. A painter must know much more about a sunset than a writer, if he is to put it on canvas. But when the poet speaks of "Dawn in russet mantle clad," he presents something which the painter cannot present.

I said in the preface to my *Guido Cavalcanti* that I believed in an absolute rhythm. I believe that every emotion and every phase of emotion has some toneless phrase, some rhythm-phrase to express it.

(This belief leads to *vers libre* and to experiments in quantitative verse.)

To hold a like belief in a sort of permanent metaphor is, as I understand it, "symbolism" in its profounder sense. It is not necessarily a belief in a permanent world, but it is a belief in that direction.

Imagisme is not symbolism. The symbolists dealt in "association," that is, in a sort of allusion, almost of allegory. They degraded the symbol to the status of a word. They made it a form of metronomy. One can be grossly "symbolic," for example, by using the term "cross" to mean "trial." The symbolist's *symbols* have a fixed value, like numbers in arithmetic, like 1, 2, and 7. The imagiste's images have a variable significance, like the signs *a, b,* and *x* in algebra.

Moreover, one does not want to be called a symbolist, because symbolism has usually been associated with mushy technique.

On the other hand, Imagisme is not Impressionism, though one borrows, or could borrow, much from the impressionist method of presentation. But this is only negative definition. If I am to give a psychological or philosophical definition "from the inside," I can only do so autobiographically. The precise statement of such a matter must be based on one's own experience.

In the "search for oneself," in the search for "sincere self-expression," one gropes, one finds some seeming verity. One says "I am" this, that, or the other, and with the words scarcely uttered one ceases to be that thing.

I began this search for the real in a book called *Personae*, casting off, as it were, complete masks of the self in each poem. I continued in long series of translations, which were but more elaborate masks.

Secondly, I made poems like "The Return," which is an objective reality and has a complicated sort of significance, like Mr. Epstein's "Sun God," or Mr. Brzeska's "Boy with a Coney." Thirdly, I have written "Heather," which represents a state of consciousness, or "implies," or "implicates" it.

A Russian correspondent, after having called it a symbolist poem, and having been convinced that it was not symbolism, said slowly: "I see, you wish to give people new eyes, not to make them see some new particular thing."

These two latter sorts of poems are impersonal, and that fact brings us back to what I said about absolute metaphor. They are Imagisme, and in so far as they are Imagisme, they fall in with the new pictures and the new sculpture.

Whistler said somewhere in the *Gentle Art*: "The picture is interesting not because it is Trotty Veg, but because it is an arrangement in colour." The minute you have admitted that, you let in the jungle, you let in nature and truth and abundance and cubism and Kandinsky, and the lot of us. Whistler and Kandinsky and some cubists were set to getting extraneous matter out of their art; they were ousting literary values. The Flaubertians talk a good deal about "constatation." "The 'nineties" saw a movement against rhetoric. I think all these things move together, though they do not, of course, move in step.

The painters realise that what matters is form and colour. Musicians long ago learned that programme music was not the ultimate music. Almost anyone can realise that to use a symbol *with an ascribed or intended meaning* is, usually, to produce very bad art. We all remember crowns, and crosses, and rainbows, and what not in atrociously mumbled colour.

The Image is the poet's pigment.[1] The painter should use his colour because he sees it or feels it. I don't much care whether he is representative or non-representative. He should *depend*, of course, on the creative, not upon the mimetic or representational part in his work. It is the same in writing poems, the author must use his *image* because he sees it or feels it, *not* because he thinks he can use it to back up some creed or some system of ethics or economics.

An *image*, in our sense, is real because we know it directly. If it have an age-old traditional meaning this may serve as proof to the professional student of symbology that we have stood in the deathless light, or that we have walked in some particular arbour of his traditional paradiso, but that is not our affair. It is our affair to render the *image* as we have perceived or conceived it.

Browning's "Sordello" is one of the finest *masks* ever presented. Dante's "Paradiso" is the most wonderful *image*. By that I do not mean that it is a perseveringly imagistic performance. The permanent part is Imagisme, the rest, the discourses with the calendar of saints and the discussions about the nature of the moon, are philology. The form of sphere above sphere, the varying reaches of light, the minutiae of pearls upon foreheads, all these are parts of the Image. The image is the poet's pigment; with that in mind you can go ahead and apply Kandinsky, you can transpose his chapter on the language of form and colour and apply it to the writing of verse. As I cannot rely on your having read Kandinsky's *Ueber das Geistige in der Kunst*, I must go on with my autobiography.

Three years ago in Paris I got out of a "metro" train at La Concorde, and saw suddenly a beautiful face, and then another and another, and then a beautiful child's face, and then another beautiful woman, and I tried all that day to find words for what this had meant to

[1] The image has been defined as "that which presents an intellectual and emotional complex in an instant of time."

me, and I could not find any words that seemed to me worthy, or as lovely as that sudden emotion. And that evening, as I went home along the Rue Raynouard, I was still trying, and I found, suddenly, the expression. I do not mean that I found words, but there came an equation . . . not in speech, but in little splotches of colour. It was just that—a "pattern," or hardly a pattern, if by "pattern" you mean something with a "repeat" in it. But it was a word, the beginning, for me, of a language in colour. I do not mean that I was unfamiliar with the kindergarten stories about colours being like tones in music. I think that sort of thing is nonsense. If you try to make notes permanently correspond with particular colours, it is like tying narrow meanings to symbols.

That evening, in the Rue Raynouard, I realised quite vividly that if I were a painter, or if I had, often, *that kind* of emotion, or even if I had the energy to get paints and brushes and keep at it, I might found a new school of painting, of "non-representative" painting, a painting that would speak only by arrangements in colour.

And so, when I came to read Kandinsky's chapter on the language of form and colour, I found little that was new to me. I only felt that someone else understood what I understood, and had written it out very clearly. It seems quite natural to me that an artist should have just as much pleasure in an arrangement of planes or in a pattern of figures, as in painting portraits of fine ladies, or in portraying the Mother of God as the symbolists bid us.

When I find people ridiculing the new arts, or making fun of the clumsy odd terms that we use in trying to talk of them amongst ourselves; when they laugh at our talking about the "iceblock quality" in Picasso, I think it is only because they do not know what thought is like, and that they are familiar only with argument and gibe and opinion. That is to say, they can only enjoy what they have been brought up to consider enjoyable, or what some essayist has talked about in mellifluous phrases. They think only "the shells of thought," as De Gourmont calls them; the thoughts that have been already thought out by others.

Any mind that is worth calling a mind must have needs beyond the existing categories of language, just as a painter must have pigments or shades more numerous than the existing names of the colours.

Perhaps this is enough to explain the words in my "Vortex":—[2]

"Every concept, every emotion, presents itself to the vivid consciousness in some primary form. It belongs to the art of this form."

That is to say, my experience in Paris should have gone into paint. If instead of colour I had perceived sound or planes in relation, I should have expressed it in music or in sculpture. Colour was, in that instance, the "primary pigment"; I mean that it was the first adequate equation that came into consciousness. The Vorticist uses the "primary pigment." Vorticism is art before it has spread itself into flaccidity, into elaboration and secondary applications.

What I have said of one vorticist art can be transposed for another vorticist art. But let me go on then with my own branch of vorticism, about which I can probably speak with greater clarity. All poetic language is the language of exploration. Since the beginning of bad writing, writers have used images as ornaments. The point of Imagisme is that it does not use images as *ornaments*. The image is itself the speech. The image is the word beyond formulated language.

I once saw a small child go to an electric light switch and say, "Mamma, can I *open* the light?" She was using the age-old language of exploration, the language of art. It was a sort of metaphor, but she was not using it as ornamentation.

One is tired of ornamentations, they are all a trick, and any sharp person can learn them.

The Japanese have had the sense of exploration. They have understood the

2 Appearing in the July number of *Blast*.

beauty of this sort of knowing. A Chinaman said long ago that if a man can't
say what he has to say in twelve lines
he had better keep quiet. The Japanese
have evolved the still shorter form of
the *hokku*.

"The fallen blossom flies back to its branch:
    A butterfly."

That is the substance of a very well-
known *hokku*. Victor Plarr tells me that
once, when he was walking over snow
with a Japanese naval officer, they came
to a place where a cat had crossed the
path, and the officer said, "Stop, I am
making a poem." Which poem was,
roughly, as follows:—

"The footsteps of the cat upon the snow:
    (are like) plum-blossoms."

The words "are like" would not occur in
the original, but I add them for clarity.

The "one image poem" is a form of
super-position, that is to say it is one
idea set on top of another. I found it
useful in getting out of the impasse in
which I had been left by my metro emotion. I wrote a thirty-line poem, and destroyed it because it was what we call
work "of second intensity." Six months
later I made a poem half that length;
a year later I made the following *hokku*-
like sentence:—

"The apparition of these faces in the crowd:
    Petals, on a wet, black bough."

I dare say it is meaningless unless one has
drifted into a certain vein of thought.[3]
In a poem of this sort one is trying to
record the precise instant when a thing
outward and objective transforms itself,
or darts into a thing inward and subjective.

This particular sort of consciousness
has not been identified with impressionist art. I think it is worthy of attention.

The logical end of impressionist art
is the cinematograph. The state of mind

[3] Mr. Flint and Mr. Rodker have made longer poems
depending on a similar presentation of matter. So also
have Richard Aldington, in his *In Via Sestina*, and
"H.D." in her *Oread*, which latter poems express
much stronger emotions than that in my lines here
given.

of the impressionist tends to become
cinematographical. Or, to put it another
way, the cinematograph does away with
the need of a lot of impressionist art.

There are two opposed ways of thinking of a man; firstly, you may think of
him as that toward which perception
moves, as the toy of circumstance, as the
plastic substance *receiving* impressions;
secondly, you may think of him as directing a certain fluid force against circumstance, as *conceiving* instead of
merely reflecting and observing. One
does not claim that one way is better
than the other, one notes a diversity of
the temperament. The two camps always
exist. In the 'eighties there were symbolists opposed to impressionists, now you
have vorticism, which is, roughly speaking, expressionism, neo-cubism, and imagism gathered together in one camp
and futurism in the other. Futurism is
descended from impressionism. It is, in
so far as it is an art movement, a kind
of accelerated impressionism. It is a
spreading, or surface art, as opposed to
vorticism, which is intensive.

The vorticist has not this curious tic
for destroying past glories. I have no
doubt that Italy needed Mr. Marinetti
but he did not set on the egg that
hatched me, and as I am wholly opposed
to his aesthetic principles I see no reason
why I, and various men who agree with
me, should be expected to call ourselves
futurists. We do not desire to evade
comparison with the past. We prefer
that the comparison be made by some
intelligent person whose idea of "the
tradition" is not limited by the conventional taste of four or five centuries and
one continent.

Vorticism is an intensive art. I mean
by this, that one is concerned with the
relative intensity, or relative significance
of different sorts of expression. One desires the most intense, for certain form
of expression *are* "more intense" than
others. They are more dynamic. I do
not mean they are more emphatic, or
that they are yelled louder. I can explain my meaning best by mathematics.

There are four different intensities of
mathematical expression known to the
ordinarily   intelligent   undergraduate

namely: the arithmetical, the algebraic, the geometrical, and that of analytical geometry.

For instance, you can write

$$3 \times 3 + 4 \times 4 = 5 \times 5,$$

or, differently, $3^2 + 4^2 = 5^2$.

That is merely conversation or "ordinary common sense." It is a simple statement of one fact, and does not implicate any other.

Secondly, it is true that

$$3^2 + 4^2 = 5^2, 6^2 + 8^2 = 10^2,$$
$$9^2 + 12^2 = 15^2, 39^2 + 52^2 = 65^2$$

These are all separate facts, one may wish to mention their underlying similarity; it is a bore to speak about each one in turn. One expresses their "algebraic relation" as

$$a^2 + b^2 = c^2.$$

That is the language of philosophy. IT MAKES NO PICTURE. This kind of statement applies to a lot of facts, but it does not grip hold of Heaven.

Thirdly, when one studies Euclid one finds that the relation of $a^2 + b^2 = c^2$ applies to the ratio between the squares on the two sides of a right-angled triangle and the square on the hypotenuse. One still writes it $a^2 + b^2 = c^2$, but one has begun to talk about form. Another property or quality of life has crept into one's matter. Until then one had dealt only with numbers. But even this statement does not *create* form. The picture is given you in the proposition about the square on the hypotenuse of the right-angled triangle being equal to the sum of the squares on the two other sides. Statements in plane or descriptive geometry are like talk about art. They are a criticism of the form. The form is not created by them.

Fourthly, we come to Descartian or "analytical geometry." Space is conceived as separated by two or by three axes (depending on whether one is treating form in one or more planes). One refers points to these axes by a series of coefficients. Given the idiom, one is able *actually to create.*

Thus, we learn that the equation $(x — a)^2 + (y — b)^2 = r^2$ governs the circle. It is the circle. It is not a particular circle, it is any circle and all circles. It is nothing that is not a circle. It is the circle free of space and time limits. It is the universal, existing in perfection, in freedom from space and time. Mathematics is dull as ditchwater until one reaches analytics. But in analytics we come upon a new way of dealing with form. It is in this way that art handles life. The difference between art and analytical geometry is the difference of subject-matter only. Art is more interesting in proportion as life and the human consciousness are more complex and more interesting than forms and numbers.

This statement does not interfere in the least with "spontaneity" and "intuition," or with their function in art. I passed my last *exam.* in mathematics on sheer intuition. I saw where the line *had* to go, as clearly as I ever saw an image, or felt *caelestem intus vigorem.*

The statements of "analytics" are "lords" over fact. They are the thrones and dominations that rule over form and recurrence. And in like manner are great works of art lords over fact, over race-long recurrent moods, and over to-morrow.

Great works of art contain this fourth sort of equation. They cause form to come into being. By the "image" I mean such an equation; not an equation of mathematics, not something about *a, b,* and *c,* having something to do with form, but about *sea, cliffs, night,* having something to do with mood.

The image is not an idea. It is a radiant node or cluster; it is what I can, and must perforce, call a VORTEX, from which, and through which, and into which, ideas are constantly rushing. In decency one can only call it a VORTEX. And from this necessity came the name "vorticism." *Nomina sunt consequentia rerum,* and never was that statement of Aquinas more true than in the case of the vorticist movement.

It is as true for the painting and the sculpture as it is for the poetry. Mr. Wadsworth and Mr. Lewis are not using words, they are using shape and colour. Mr. Brzeska and Mr. Epstein are using "planes in relation," they are dealing with a relation of planes different from the sort of relation of planes dealt with in geometry, hence what is called "the need of organic forms in sculpture."

I trust I have made clear what I mean by an "intensive art." The vorticist movement is not a movement of mystification, though I dare say many people "of good will" have been considerably bewildered.

The organisation of forms is a much more energetic and creative action than the copying or imitating of light on a haystack.

There is undoubtedly a language of form and colour. It is not a symbolical or allegorical language depending on certain meanings having been ascribed, in books, to certain signs and colours.

Certain artists working in different media have managed to understand each other. They know the good and bad in each other's work, which they could not know unless there were a common speech.

As for the excellence of certain contemporary artists, all I can do is to stand up for my own beliefs. I believe that Mr. Wyndham Lewis is a very great master of design; that he has brought into our art new units of design and new manners of organisation. I think that his series "Timon" is a great work. I think he is the most articulate expression of my own decade. If you ask me what his "Timon" means, I can reply by asking you what the old play means. For me his designs are a creation on the same *motif*. That *motif* is the fury of intelligence baffled and shut in by circumjacent stupidity. It is an emotional *motif*. Mr. Lewis's painting is nearly always emotional.

Mr. Wadsworth's work gives me pleasure, sometimes like the pleasure I have received from Chinese and Japanese prints and painting; for example, I derive such pleasure from Mr. Wadsworth's "Khaki." Sometimes his work gives me a pleasure which I can only compare to the pleasure I have in music, in music as it was in Mozart's time. If an outsider wishes swiftly to understand this new work, he can do worse than approach it in the spirit wherein he approaches music.

"Lewis is Bach." No, it is incorrect to say that "Lewis is Bach," but our feeling is that certain works of Picasso and certain works of Lewis have in them something which is to painting what certain qualities of Bach are to music. Music was vorticist in the Bach-Mozart period, before it went off into romance and sentiment and description. A new vorticist music would come from a new computation of the mathematics of harmony, not from a mimetic representation of dead cats in a fog-horn, alias noise-tuners.

Mr. Epstein is too well known to need presentation in this article. Mr. Brzeska's sculpture is so generally recognised in all camps that one does not need to bring in a brief concerning it. Mr. Brzeska has defined sculptural feeling as "the appreciation of masses in relation," and sculptural ability as "the defining of these masses by planes." There comes a time when one is more deeply moved by that form of intelligence which can present "masses in relation" than by that combination of patience and trickery which can make marble chains with free links and spin out bronze until it copies the feathers on a general's hat. Mr. Etchells still remains more or less of a mystery. He is on his travels, whence he has sent back a few excellent drawings. It cannot be made too clear that the work of the vorticists and the "feeling of inner need" existed before the general noise about vorticism. We worked separately, we found an underlying agreement, we decided to stand together.[4]

4 I am often asked whether there can be a long imagiste or vorticist poem. The Japanese, who evolved the hokku, evolved also the Noh plays. In the best "Noh" the whole play may consist of one image. I mean it is gathered about one image. Its unity consists in one image, enforced by movement and music. I see nothing against a long vorticist poem.

On the other hand, no artist can possibly get a vortex into every poem or picture he does. One would like to do so, but it is beyond one. Certain things seem to demand metrical expression, or expression in a rhythm more agitated than the rhythms acceptable to prose, and these subjects, though they do not contain a vortex, may have some interest, an interest as "criticism of life" or of art. It is natural to express these things and a vorticist or imagiste writer may be justified in presenting a certain amount of work which is not vorticism or imagisme, just as he might be justified in printing a purely didactic prose article. Unfinished sketches and drawings have a similar interest; they are trials and attempts toward a vortex.

From *How to Read* (1931)

Has literature a function in the state, in the aggregation of humans, in the republic, in the *res publica*, which ought to mean the public convenience (despite the slime of bureaucracy, and the execrable taste of the populace in selecting its rulers)? It has.

And this function is *not* the coercing or emotionally persuading, or bullying or suppressing people into the acceptance of any one set or any six sets of opinions as opposed to any other one set or half-dozen sets of opinions.

It has to do with the clarity and vigour of 'any and every' thought and opinion. It has to do with maintaining the very cleanliness of the tools, the health of the very matter of thought itself. Save in the rare and limited instances of invention in the plastic arts, or in mathematics, the individual cannot think and communicate his thought, the governor and legislator cannot act effectively or frame his laws, without words, and the solidity and validity of these words is in the care of the damned and despised *litterati*. When their work goes rotten—by that I do not mean when they express indecorous thoughts —but when their very medium, the very essence of their work, the application of word to thing goes rotten, i.e. becomes slushy and inexact, or excessive or bloated, the whole machinery of social and of individual thought and order goes to pot. This is a lesson of history, and a lesson not yet half learned.

The great writers need no debunking. The pap is not in them, and doesn't need to be squeezed out. They do not lend themselves to imperial and sentimental exploitations. A civilization was founded on Homer, civilization not a mere bloated empire. The Macedonian domination rose and grew after the sophists. It also subsided.

It is not only a question of rhetoric, of loose expression, but also of the loose use of individual words. What the renaissance gained in direct examination of natural phenomena, it in part lost in

From *Literary Essays of Ezra Pound*, ed. T. S. Eliot. Copyright 1954 by New Directions. Reprinted by permission of New Directions, Publishers.

losing the feel and desire for exact descriptive terms. I mean that the medieval mind had little but words to deal with, and it was more careful in its definitions and verbiage. It did not define a gun in terms that would just as well define an explosion, nor explosions in terms that would define triggers.

Misquoting Confucius, one might say: It does not matter whether the author desire the good of the race or acts merely from personal vanity. The thing is mechanical in action. In proportion as his work is exact, i.e., true to human consciousness and to the nature of man, as it is exact in formulation of desire, so is it durable and so is it 'useful'; I mean it maintains the precision and clarity of thought, not merely for the benefit of a few dilettantes and 'lovers of literature', but maintains the health of thought outside literary circles and in non-literary existence, in general individual and communal life.

Or *'dans ce genre on n'émeut que par la clarté'*. One 'moves' the reader only by clarity. In depicting the motions of the 'human heart' the durability of the writing depends on the exactitude. It is the thing that is true and stays true that keeps fresh for the new reader.

With this general view in mind, and subsequent to the events already set forth in this narrative, I proposed (from the left bank of the Seine, and to an American publishing house), not the twelve-volume anthology, but a short guide to the subject. That was after a few years of 'pause and reflection'. The subject was pleasantly received and considered with amity, but the house finally decided that it would pay neither them to print nor me to write the book, because we 'weren't in the text-book ring'. For the thing would have been a textbook, its circulation would have depended on educators, and educators have been defined as 'men with no intellectual interests'.

Hence, after a lapse of four years, this essay, dedicated to Mr. Glenn Frank, and other starters of ideal universities, though not with any great hope that it will rouse them.

T. S. ELIOT

(b. 1888)

Perhaps the most influential man of letters in the English-speaking world during the first half of this century, T. S. Eliot has distinguished himself as an editor, playwright, and social philosopher in addition to being the chief poet and literary essayist of his age. While Eliot's first volume of criticism is an important document in behalf of the technical revolutions instituted by "modern" poetry, his larger critical achievement is that of an arbiter rather than a technicalist. His personal judgments have been remarkable in their power to disturb and modify the judgments, even the perceptions, of an entire literary culture, as in his influential essays on the French symbolists, Dante, Donne, the Elizabethan drama, Milton, Dryden, and certain of the romantics and Victorians. He is of course a traditionalist, in temperament and conviction, as announced in his famous introduction to the volume *For Lancelot Andrewes*, a viewpoint that has been expressed again and again in his essays, though with some access of mellowness in recent years. But Eliot has all along been something of a radical modern in viewpoint, too, especially in his belief that the culture of the past can "live" for the present only if it is understood essentially from a present point of view. This principle has provided the tenor, for the most part, of his numerous critical revaluations of writers from the past. His acute historical sense and his commitment to "culture" and the continuity of history, combined with his profound involvement in the stresses and distresses of the life of his time, make him a kind of twentieth century Arnold. In fact, the opposition between Eliot's orthodoxy, monarchism, and classicism and Arnold's agnostic liberal humanism seems relatively unimportant and incidental when one considers the likeness not only of their thought and judgments but also of the literary roles and manners which they assumed before their publics. Eliot's chief volumes of criticism include *The Sacred Wood* (1920), *Dante* (1929), *The Use of Poetry and the Use of Criticism* (1933), *Elizabethan Essays* (1934), and *Essays Ancient and Modern* (1936); much of his important criticism is contained in the two summary volumes, *Selected Essays* (1932; 1950), and *On Poetry and Poets* (1957). A number of scattered pamphlets, essays, and prefaces remain uncollected.

Tradition and the Individual Talent (1919)

In English writing we seldom speak of tradition, though we occasionally apply its name in deploring its absence. We cannot refer to "the tradition" or to "a

tradition"; at most, we employ the adjective in saying that the poetry of So and-so is "traditional" or even "too traditional." Seldom, perhaps, does the word appear except in a phrase of censure. If otherwise, it is vaguely approbative, with the implication, as to th work approved, of some pleasing archaeological reconstruction. You can hardly make the word agreeable to English ears without this comfortable reference to the reassuring science of archaeology.

Certainly the word is not likely to appear in our appreciations of living or dead writers. Every nation, every race, has not only its own creative, but its own critical turn of mind; and is even more oblivious of the shortcomings and limitations of its critical habits than of those of its creative genius. We know, or think we know, from the enormous mass of critical writing that has appeared in the French language the critical method or habit of the French; we only conclude (we are such unconscious people) that the French are "more critical" than we, and sometimes even plume ourselves a little with the fact, as if the French were the less spontaneous. Perhaps they are; but we might remind ourselves that criticism is as inevitable as breathing, and that we should be none the worse for articulating what passes in our minds when we read a book and feel an emotion about it, for criticizing our own minds in their work of criticism. One of the facts that might come to light in this process is our tendency to insist, when we praise a poet, upon those aspects of his work in which he least resembles any one else. In these aspects or parts of his work we pretend to find what is individual, what is the peculiar essence of the man. We dwell with satisfaction upon the poet's difference from his predecessors, especially his immediate predecessors; we endeavour to find something that can be isolated in order to be enjoyed. Whereas if we approach a poet without this prejudice we shall often find that not only the best, but the most individual parts of his work may be those in which the dead poets, his ancestors, assert their immortality most vigorously. And I do not mean the impressionable period of adolescence, but the period of full maturity.

Yet if the only form of tradition, of handing down, consisted in following the ways of the immediate generation before us in a blind or timid adherence to its successes, "tradition" should positively be discouraged. We have seen many such simple currents soon lost in the sand; and novelty is better than repetition. Tradition is a matter of much wider significance. It cannot be inherited, and if you want it you must obtain it by great labour. It involves, in the first place, the historical sense, which we may call nearly indispensable to any one who would continue to be a poet beyond his twenty-fifth year; and the historical sense involves a perception, not only of the pastness of the past, but of its presence; the historical sense compels a man to write not merely with his own generation in his bones, but with a feeling that the whole of the literature of Europe from Homer and within it the whole of the literature of his own country has a simultaneous existence and composes a simultaneous order. This historical sense, which is a sense of the timeless as well as of the temporal and of the timeless and of the temporal together, is what makes a writer traditional. And it is at the same time what makes a writer most acutely conscious of his place in time, of his own contemporaneity.

No poet, no artist of any art, has his complete meaning alone. His significance, his appreciation is the appreciation of his relation to the dead poets and artists. You cannot value him alone; you must set him, for contrast and comparison, among the dead. I mean this as a principle of aesthetic, not merely historical, criticism. The necessity that he shall conform, that he shall cohere, is not onesided; what happens when a new work of art is created is something that happens simultaneously to all the works of art which preceded it. The existing monuments form an ideal order among themselves, which is modified by the introduction of the new (the really new) work of art among them. The existing order is complete before the new work arrives; for order to persist after the supervention of novelty, the *whole* existing order must be, if ever so slightly, altered; and so the relations, proportions, values of each work of art toward the whole are readjusted; and this is conformity between the old and the new. Whoever has approved this idea of order, of the form of European, of English literature will not find it preposterous that the past should be altered by the present as much as the present is directed by the past. And the poet who is aware of this will be aware of great difficulties and responsibilities.

In a peculiar sense he will be aware also that he must inevitably be judged by the standards of the past. I say judged, not amputated, by them; not judged to be as good as, or worse or better than, the dead; and certainly not judged by the canons of dead critics. It is a judgment, a comparison, in which two things are measured by each other. To conform merely would be for the new work not really to conform at all; it would not be new, and would therefore not be a work of art. And we do not quite say that the new is more valuable because it fits in; but its fitting in is a test of its value—a test, it is true, which can only be slowly and cautiously applied, for we are none of us infallible judges of conformity. We say: it appears to conform, and is perhaps individual, or it appears individual, and many conform; but we are hardly likely to find that it is one and not the other.

To proceed to a more intelligible exposition of the relation of the poet to the past: he can neither take the past as a lump, an indiscriminate bolus, nor can he form himself wholly on one or two private admirations, nor can he form himself wholly upon one preferred period. The first course is inadmissible, the second is an important experience of youth, and the third is a pleasant and highly desirable supplement. The poet must be very conscious of the main current, which does not at all flow invariably through the most distinguished reputations. He must be quite aware of the obvious fact that art never improves, but that the material of art is never

quite the same. He must be aware that the mind of Europe—the mind of his own country—a mind which he learns in time to be much more important than his own private mind—is a mind which changes, and that this change is a development which abandons nothing en route, which does not superannuate either Shakespeare, or Homer, or the rock drawing of the Magdalenian draughtsmen. That this development refinement perhaps, complication certainly, is not, from the point of view o the artist, any improvement. Perhap not even an improvement from the point of view of the psychologist or no to the extent which we imagine; per haps only in the end based upon a com plication in economics and machinery But the difference between the presen and the past is that the conscious pres ent is an awareness of the past in a wa and to an extent which the past's aware ness of itself cannot show.

Some one said: "The dead writers ar remote from us because we *know* s much more than they did." Precisely and they are that which we know.

I am alive to a usual objection t what is clearly part of my programm for the *métier* of poetry. The objectio is that the doctrine requires a ridiculo amount of erudition (pedantry), a clai which can be rejected by appeal to th lives of poets in any pantheon. It wi even be affirmed that much learnin deadens or perverts poetic sensibilit While, however, we persist in believin that a poet ought to know as much will not encroach upon his necessa receptivity and necessary laziness, it not desirable to confine knowledge whatever can be put into a useful sha for examinations, drawing-rooms, or t still more pretentious modes of publici Some can absorb knowledge, the mo tardy must sweat for it. Shakespea acquired more essential history fro Plutarch than most men could from t whole British Museum. What is to insisted upon is that the poet must velop or procure the consciousness the past and that he should continue develop this consciousness throughout his career.

What happens is a continual surrender of himself as he is at the moment to something which is more valuable. The progress of an artist is a continual self-sacrifice, a continual extinction of personality.

There remains to define this process of depersonalization and its relation to the sense of tradition. It is in this depersonalization that art may be said to approach the condition of science. I, therefore, invite you to consider, as a suggestive analogy, the action which takes place when a bit of finely filiated platinum is introduced into a chamber containing oxygen and sulphur dioxide.

II

Honest criticism and sensitive appreciation are directed not upon the poet but upon the poetry. If we attend to the confused cries of the newspaper critics and the *susurrus* of popular repetition that follows, we shall hear the names of poets in great numbers; if we seek not Blue-book knowledge but the enjoyment of poetry, and ask for a poem, we shall seldom find it. I have tried to point out the importance of the relation of the poem to other poems by other authors, and suggested the conception of poetry as a living whole of all the poetry that has ever been written. The other aspect of this Impersonal theory of poetry is the relation of the poem to its author. And I hinted, by an analogy, that the mind of the mature poet differs from that of the immature one not precisely in any valuation of "personality," not being necessarily more interesting, or having "more to say," but rather by being a more finely perfected medium in which special, or very varied, feelings are at liberty to enter into new combinations.

The analogy was that of the catalyst. When the two gases previously mentioned are mixed in the presence of a filament of platinum, they form sul-

phurous acid. This combination takes place only if the platinum is present; nevertheless the newly formed acid contains no trace of platinum, and the platinum itself is apparently unaffected; has remained inert, neutral, and unchanged. The mind of the poet is the shred of platinum. It may partly or exclusively operate upon the experience of the man himself; but, the more perfect the artist, the more completely separate in him will be the man who suffers and the mind which creates; the more perfectly will the mind digest and transmute the passions which are its material.

The experience, you will notice, the elements which enter the presence of the transforming catalyst, are of two kinds: emotions and feelings. The effect of a work of art upon the person who enjoys it is an experience different in kind from any experience not of art. It may be formed out of one emotion, or may be a combination of several; and various feelings, inhering for the writer in particular words or phrases or images, may be added to compose the final result. Or great poetry may be made without the direct use of any emotion whatever: composed out of feelings solely. Canto XV of the *Inferno* (Brunetto Latini) is a working up of the emotion evident in the situation; but the effect, though single as that of any work of art, is obtained by considerable complexity of detail. The last quatrain gives an image, a feeling attaching to an image, which "came," which did not develop simply out of what precedes, but which was probably in suspension in the poet's mind until the proper combination arrived for it to add itself to. The poet's mind is in fact a receptacle for seizing and storing up numberless feelings, phrases, images, which remain there until all the particles which can unite to form a new compound are present together.

If you compare several representative passages of the greatest poetry you see how great is the variety of types of combination, and also how completely any semi-ethical criterion of "sublimity" misses the mark. For it is not the "greatness," the intensity, of the emotions, the components, but the intensity of the artistic process, the pressure, so to speak, under which the fusion takes place, that counts. The episode of Paolo and Francesca employs a definite emotion, but the intensity of the poetry is something quite different from whatever intensity in the supposed experience it may give the impression of. It is no more intense, furthermore, than Canto XXVI, the voyage of Ulysses, which has not the direct dependence upon an emotion. Great variety is possible in the process of transmutation of emotion: the murder of Agamemnon, or the agony of Othello, gives an artistic effect apparently closer to a possible original than the scenes from Dante. In the *Agamemnon*, the artistic emotion approximates to the emotion of an actual spectator; in *Othello* to the emotion of the protagonist himself. But the difference between art and the event is always absolute; the combination which is the murder of Agamemnon is probably as complex as that which is the voyage of Ulysses. In either case there has been a fusion of the elements. The ode of Keats contains a number of feelings which have nothing particular to do with the nightingale, but which the nightingale, partly, perhaps, because of its attractive name, and partly because of its reputation, served to bring together.

The point of view which I am struggling to attack is perhaps related to the metaphysical theory of the substantial unity of the soul: for my meaning is, that the poet has, not a "personality" to express, but a particular medium, which is only a medium and not a personality, in which impressions and experiences combine in peculiar and unexpected ways. Impressions and experiences which are important for the man may take no place in the poetry, and those which become important in the poetry may play quite a negligible part in the man, the personality.

I will quote a passage which is un-familiar enough to be regarded with fresh attention in the light—or darkness—of these observations:

And now methinks I could e'en chide myself
For doating on her beauty, though her death
Shall be revenged after no common action.
Does the silkworm expend her yellow labours
For thee? For thee does she undo herself?
Are lordships sold to maintain ladyships
For the poor benefit of a bewildering minute?
Why does yon fellow falsify highways,
And put his life between the judge's lips,
To refine such a thing—keeps horse and men
To beat their valours for her? ...

In this passage (as is evident if it is taken in its context) there is a combination of positive and negative emotions: an intensely strong attraction toward beauty and an equally intense fascination by the ugliness which is contrasted with it and which destroys it. This balance of contrasted emotion is in the dramatic situation to which the speech is pertinent, but that situation alone is inadequate to it. This is, so to speak, the structural emotion, provided by the drama. But the whole effect, the dominant tone, is due to the fact that a number of floating feelings, having an affinity to this emotion by no means superficially evident, have combined with it to give us a new art emotion.

It is not in his personal emotions, the emotions provoked by particular events in his life, that the poet is in any way remarkable or interesting. His particular emotions may be simple, or crude, or flat. The emotion in his poetry will be a very complex thing, but not with the complexity of the emotions of people who have very complex or unusual emotions in life. One error, in fact, of eccentricity in poetry is to seek for new human emotions to express; and in this search for novelty in the wrong place it discovers the perverse. The business of the poet is not to find new emotions, but to use the ordinary ones and, in working them up into poetry, to express feelings which are not in actual emotions at all. And emotions which he has never experienced will serve his turn as well as those familiar to him. Consequently, we must believe that "emotion recollected in tranquillity" is an inexact formula. For it is neither emotion, nor recollection, nor, without distortion of meaning, tranquillity. It is a concentration, and a new thing resulting from the concentration, of a very great number of experiences which to the practical and active person would not seem to be experiences at all; it is a concentration which does not happen consciously or of deliberation. These experiences are not "recollected," and they finally unite in an atmosphere which is "tranquil" only in that it is a passive attending upon the event. Of course this is not quite the whole story. There is a great deal, in the writing of poetry, which must be conscious and deliberate. In fact, the bad poet is usually unconscious where he ought to be conscious, and conscious where he ought to be unconscious. Both errors tend to make him "personal." Poetry is not a turning loose of emotion, but an escape from emotion; it is not the expression of personality, but an escape from personality. But, of course, only those who have personality and emotions know what it means to want to escape from these things.

III

ὁ δὲ νοῦς ἴσως θειότερόν τι καὶ ἀπαθές ἐστιν.

This essay proposes to halt at the frontier of metaphysics or mysticism, and confine itself to such practical conclusions as can be applied by the responsible person interested in poetry. To divert interest from the poet to the poetry is a laudable aim: for it would conduce to a juster estimation of actual poetry, good and bad. There are many people who appreciate the expression of sincere emotion in verse, and there is a smaller number of people who can appreciate technical excellence. But very few know when there is an expression of *significant* emotion, emotion which has its life in the poem and not in the history of the poet. The emotion of art is impersonal. And the poet cannot reach this impersonality without surrendering himself wholly to the work to be done. And he is not likely to know what is to be done unless he lives in what is not merely the present, but the present moment of the past, unless he is conscious, not of what is dead, but of what is already living.

The Metaphysical Poets (1921)

By collecting these poems [1] from the work of a generation more often named than read, and more often read than profitably studied, Professor Grierson has rendered a service of some importance. Certainly the reader will meet with many poems already preserved in other anthologies, at the same time that he discovers poems such as those of Aurelian Townshend or Lord Herbert of Cherbury here included.

But the function of such an anthology as this is neither that of Professor Saintsbury's admirable edition of Caroline poets nor that of the *Oxford Book of English Verse*. Mr. Grierson's book is in itself a piece of criticism and a provocation of criticism; and we think that he was right in including so many poems of Donne, elsewhere (though not in many editions) accessible, as documents in the case of "metaphysical poetry." The phrase has long done duty as a term of abuse or as the label of a quaint and pleasant taste. The question is to what extent the so-called metaphysicals formed a school (in our own time we should say a "movement"), and how far this so-called school

From *Selected Essays: New Edition* by T. S. Eliot, copyright 1932, 1936, 1950 by Harcourt, Brace & World, Inc.; copyright, 1960, by T. S. Eliot. Reprinted by permission of the publishers.
[1] *Metaphysical Lyrics and Poems of the Seventeenth Century:* Donne to Butler. Selected and edited, with an Essay, by Herbert J. C. Grierson (Oxford: Clarendon Press. London: Milford). [*Author's note.*]

or movement is a digression from the main current.

Not only is it extremely difficult to define metaphysical poetry, but difficult to decide what poets practice it and in which of their verses. The poetry of Donne (to whom Marvell and Bishop King are sometimes nearer than any of the other authors) is late Elizabethan, its feeling often very close to that of Chapman. The "courtly" poetry is derivative from Jonson, who borrowed liberally from the Latin; it expires in the next century with the sentiment and witticism of Prior. There is finally the devotional verse of Herbert, Vaughan, and Crashaw (echoed long after by Christina Rossetti and Francis Thompson); Crashaw, sometimes more profound and less sectarian than the others, has a quality which returns through the Elizabethan period to the early Italians. It is difficult to find any precise use of metaphor, simile, or other conceit, which is common to all the poets and at the same time important enough as an element of style to isolate these poets as a group. Donne, and often Cowley, employ a device which is sometimes considered characteristically "metaphysical"; the elaboration (contrasted with the condensation) of a figure of speech to the farthest stage to which ingenuity can carry it. Thus Cowley develops the commonplace comparison of the world to a chess-board through long stanzas (*To Destiny*), and Donne, with more grace, in *A Valediction*, the comparison of two lovers to a pair of compasses. But elsewhere we find, instead of the mere explication of the content of a comparison, a development by rapid association of thought which requires considerable agility on the part of the reader.

> On a round ball
> A workman that hath copies by, can lay
> An Europe, Afrique, and an Asia,
> And quickly make that, which was nothing,
>   All,
> So doth each teare,
> Which thee doth weare,
> A globe, yea, world by that impression grow,
> Till thy tears mixt with mine doe overflow
> This world, by waters sent from thee, my
>   heaven dissolved so.

Here we find at least two connections which are not implicit in the first figure, but are forced upon it by the poet: from the geographer's globe to the tear and the tear to the deluge. On the other hand, some of Donne's most successful and characteristic effects are secured by brief words and sudden contrasts:

> A bracelet of bright hair about the bone,

where the most powerful effect is produced by the sudden contrast of associations of "bright hair" and of "bone." This telescoping of images and multiplied associations is characteristic of the phrase of some of the dramatists of the period which Donne knew: not to mention Shakespeare, it is frequent in Middleton, Webster, and Tourneur, and is one of the sources of the vitality of their language.

Johnson, who employed the term "metaphysical poets," apparently having Donne, Cleveland, and Cowley chiefly in mind, remarks of them that "the most heterogeneous ideas are yoked by violence together." The force of this impeachment lies in the failure of the conjunction, the fact that often the ideas are yoked but not united; and if we are to judge of styles of poetry by their abuse, enough examples may be found in Cleveland to justify Johnson's condemnation. But a degree of heterogeneity of material compelled into unity by the operation of the poet's mind is omnipresent in poetry. We need not select for illustration such a line as:

> Notre âme est un trois-mâts cherchant son
>   Icarie;

we may find it in some of the best lines of Johnson himself (*The Vanity of Human Wishes*):

> His fate was destined to a barren strand,
> A petty fortress, and a dubious hand;
> He left a name at which the world grew pale
> To point a moral, or adorn a tale—

where the effect is due to a contrast of ideas, different in degree but the same in principle, as that which Johnson mildly reprehended. And in one of the finest poems of the age (a poem which could not have been written in any other age), the *Exequy* of Bishop King, the extended comparison is used with perfect success: the idea and the simile become one, in the passage in which the Bishop illustrates his impatience to see his dead wife, under the figure of a journey:

Stay for me there; I will not faile
To meet thee in that hollow Vale.
And think not much of my delay;
I am already on the way,
And follow thee with all the speed
Desire can make, or sorrows breed.
Each minute is a short degree,
And ev'ry houre a step towards thee.
At night when I betake to rest,
Next morn I rise nearer my West
Of life, almost by eight houres sail,
Than when sleep breath'd his drowsy gale . . .
But heark! My Pulse, like a soft Drum
Beats my approach, tells Thee I come;
And slow howere my marches be,
I shall at last sit down by Thee.

(In the last few lines there is that effect of terror which is several times attained by one of Bishop King's admirers, Edgar Poe.) Again, we may justly take these quatrains from Lord Herbert's Ode, stanzas which should, we think, be immediately pronounced to be of the metaphysical school:

So when from hence we shall be gone,
    And be no more, nor you, nor I,
    As one another's mystery,
Each shall be both, yet both but one.

This said, in her up-lifted face,
    Her eyes, which did that beauty crown,
    Were like two starrs, that having faln down,
Look up again to find their place:

While such a moveless silent peace
    Did seize on their becalmed sense,
    One would have thought some influence
Their ravished spirits did possess.

There is nothing in these lines (with the possible exception of the stars, a simile not at once grasped, but lovely and justified) which fits Johnson's gen-

eral observations on the metaphysical poets in his essay on Cowley. A good deal resides in the richness of association which is at the same time borrowed from and given to the word "becalmed"; but the meaning is clear, the language simple and elegant. It is to be observed that the language of these poets is as a rule simple and pure; in the verse of George Herbert this simplicity is carried as far as it can go—a simplicity emulated without success by numerous modern poets. The *structure* of the sentences, on the other hand, is sometimes far from simple, but this is not a vice; it is a fidelity to thought and feeling. The effect, at its best, is far less artificial than that of an ode by Gray. And as this fidelity induces variety of thought and feeling, so it induces variety of music. We doubt whether, in the eighteenth century, could be found two poems in nominally the same metre, so dissimilar as Marvell's *Coy Mistress* and Crashaw's *Saint Teresa*; the one producing an effect of great speed by the use of short syllables, and the other an ecclesiastical solemnity by the use of long ones:

Love, thou art absolute sole lord
Of life and death.

If so shrewd and sensitive (though so limited) a critic as Johnson failed to define metaphysical poetry by its faults, it is worth while to inquire whether we may not have more success by adopting the opposite method: by assuming that the poets of the seventeenth century (up to the Revolution) were the direct and normal development of the precedent age; and without prejudicing their case by the adjective "metaphysical," consider whether their virtue was not something permanently valuable, which subsequently disappeared, but ought not to have disappeared. Johnson has hit, perhaps by accident, on one of their peculiarities, when he observes that "their attempts were always analytic"; he would not agree that, after the dissociation, they put the material together again in a new unity.

It is certain that the dramatic verse
of the later Elizabethan and early Jacobean poets expresses a degree of development of sensibility which is not
found in any of the prose, good as it
often is. If we except Marlowe, a man
of prodigious intelligence, these dramatists were directly or indirectly (it is at
least a tenable theory) affected by Montaigne. Even if we except also Jonson
and Chapman, these two were notably
erudite, and were notably men who incorporated their erudition into their
sensibility: their mode of feeling was
directly and freshly altered by their
reading and thought. In Chapman
especially there is a direct sensuous apprehension of thought, or a re-creation
of thought into feeling, which is exactly
what we find in Donne:

. . . in this one thing, all the discipline
Of manners and of manhood is contained;
A man to join himself with th' Universe
In his main sway, and make in all things fit
One with that All, and go on, round as it;
Not plucking from the whole his wretched
    part,
And into straits, or into nought revert,
Wishing the complete Universe might be
Subject to such a rag of it as he;
But to consider great Necessity.

We compare this with some modern
passage:

No, when the fight begins within himself,
A man's worth something. God stoops o'er his
    head,
Satan looks up between his feet—both tug—
He's left, himself, i' the middle; the soul wakes
And grows. Prolong that battle through his
    life!

It is perhaps somewhat less fair, though
very tempting (as both poets are concerned with the perpetuation of love by
offspring), to compare with the stanzas
already quoted from Lord Herbert's
Ode the following from Tennyson:

One walked between his wife and child,
With measured footfall firm and mild,
And now and then he gravely smiled.
    The prudent partner of his blood
Leaned on him, faithful, gentle, good,
Wearing the rose of womanhood.

And in their double love secure,
The little maiden walked demure,
Pacing with downward eyelids pure.
These three made unity so sweet,
My frozen heart began to beat,
Remembering its ancient heat.

The difference is not a simple differenc
of degree between poets. It is something
which had happened to the mind o
England between the time of Donne o
Lord Herbert of Cherbury and the tim
of Tennyson and Browning; it is th
difference between the intellectual poe
and the reflective poet. Tennyson an
Browning are poets, and they think
but they do not feel their thought a
immediately as the odour of a rose. /
thought to Donne was an experience; i
modified his sensibility. When a poet'
mind is perfectly equipped for its worl
it is constantly amalgamating disparat
experience; the ordinary man's experi
ence is chaotic, irregular, fragmentary
The latter falls in love, or reads Spinoz;
and these two experiences have nothin
to do with each other, or with the nois
of the typewriter or the smell of cook
ing; in the mind of the poet these ex
periences are always forming new
wholes.

We may express the difference by th
following theory: The poets of the se
enteenth century, the successors of th
dramatists of the sixteenth, possessed
mechanism of sensibility which coul
devour any kind of experience. The
are simple, artificial, difficult, or fa
tastic, as their predecessors were; n
less nor more than Dante, Guido Cava
canti, Guinzelli, or Cino. In the seve
teenth century a dissociation of sens
bility[2] set in, from which we have neve
recovered; and this dissociation, as
natural, was aggravated by the influ
ence of the two most powerful poets
the century, Milton and Dryden. Eac
of these men performed certain poet
functions so magnificently well that th
magnitude of the effect concealed th
absence of others. The language we

[2] On the phrase "dissociation of sensibility," whi
Eliot coined in his essay on Dryden, see Eliot's lat
qualifying comment in his "Milton," *Sewanee Revie
56 (Spring, 1948), 193-194; reprinted in *On Poetry a
Poets* (1957), pp. 152-153. [*Editor's note.*]

on and in some respects improved; the best verse of Collins, Gray, Johnson, and even Goldsmith satisfies some of our fastidious demands better than that of Donne or Marvell or King. But while the language became more refined, the feeling became more crude. The feeling, the sensibility, expressed in the *Country Churchyard* (to say nothing of Tennyson and Browning) is cruder than that in the *Coy Mistress*.

The second effect of the influence of Milton and Dryden followed from the first, and was therefore slow in manifestation. The sentimental age began early in the eighteenth century, and continued. The poets revolted against the ratiocinative, the descriptive; they thought and felt by fits, unbalanced; they reflected. In one or two passages of Shelley's *Triumph of Life*, in the second *Hyperion*, there are traces of a struggle toward unification of sensibility. But Keats and Shelley died, and Tennyson and Browning ruminated.

After this brief exposition of a theory —too brief, perhaps, to carry conviction—we may ask, what would have been the fate of the "metaphysical" had the current of poetry descended in a direct line from them, as it descended in a direct line to them? They would not, certainly, be classified as metaphysical. The possible interests of a poet are unlimited; the more intelligent he is the better; the more intelligent he is the more likely that he will have interests: our only condition is that he turn them into poetry, and not merely meditate on them poetically. A philosophical theory which has entered into poetry is established, for its truth or falsity in one sense ceases to matter, and its truth in another sense is proved. The poets in question have, like other poets, various faults. But they were, at best, engaged in the task of trying to find the verbal equivalent for states of mind and feeling. And this means both that they are more mature, and that they wear better, than later poets of certainly not less literary ability.

It is not a permanent necessity that poets should be interested in philosophy, or in any other subject. We can only say that it appears likely that poets in our civilization, as it exists at present, must be *difficult*. Our civilization comprehends great variety and complexity, and this variety and complexity, playing upon a refined sensibility, must produce various and complex results. The poet must become more and more comprehensive, more allusive, more indirect, in order to force, to dislocate if necessary, language into his meaning. (A brilliant and extreme statement of this view, with which it is not requisite to associate oneself, is that of M. Jean Epstein, *La Poésie d'aujourd'hui*.) Hence we get something which looks very much like the conceit—we get, in fact, a method curiously similar to that of the "metaphysical poets," similar also in its use of obscure words and of simple phrasing.

O géraniums diaphanes, guerroyeurs sortilèges,
Sacrilèges monomanes!
Emballages, dévergondages, douches! O
  pressoirs
Des vendanges des grands soirs!
Layettes aux abois,
Thyrses au fond des bois!
Transfusions, représailles,
Relevailles, compresses et l'éternal potion,
Angélus! n'en pouvoir plus
De débâcles nuptiales! de débâcles nuptiales!

The same poet could write, also simply:

Elle est bien loin, elle pleure,
Le grand vent se lamente aussi . . .

Jules Laforgue, and Tristan Corbière in many of his poems, are nearer to the "school of Donne" than any modern English poet. But poets more classical than they have the same essential quality of transmuting ideas into sensations, of transforming an observation into a state of mind.

Pour l'enfant, amoureux de cartes et
  d'estampes,
L'univers est égal à son vaste appétit.
Ah, que le monde est grand à la clarté des
  lampes!
Aux yeux du souvenir que le monde est petit!

In French literature the great master of the seventeenth century—Racine—and the great master of the nineteenth—Baudelaire—are in some ways more like each other than they are like any one else. The greatest two masters of diction are also the greatest two psychologists, the most curious explorers of the soul. It is interesting to speculate whether it is not a misfortune that two of the greatest masters of diction in our language, Milton and Dryden, triumph with a dazzling disregard of the soul. If we continued to produce Miltons and Drydens it might not so much matter, but as things are it is a pity that English poetry has remained so incomplete. Those who object to the "artificiality" of Milton or Dryden sometimes tell us to "look into our hearts and write." But that is not looking deep enough; Racine or Donne looked into a good deal more than the heart. One must look into the cerebral cortex, the nervous system, and the digestive tracts.

May we not conclude, then, that Donne, Crashaw, Vaughan, Herbert and Lord Herbert, Marvell, King, Cowley at his best, are in the direct current of English poetry, and that their faults should be reprimanded by this standard rather than coddled by antiquarian affection? They have been enough praised in terms which are implicit limitation because they are "metaphysical" or "witty," "quaint" or "obscure," though at their best they have not these attributes more than other serious poets. On the other hand, we must not reject the criticism of Johnson (a dangerous person to disagree with) without having mastered it, without having assimilated the Johnsonian canons of taste. In reading the celebrated passage in his essay on Cowley we must remember that by wit he clearly means something more serious than we usually mean today; in his criticism of their versification we must remember in what a narrow discipline he was trained, but also how well trained; we must remember that Johnson tortures chiefly the chief offenders, Cowley and Cleveland. I would be a fruitful work, and one requiring a substantial book, to break up the classification of Johnson (for there has been none since) and exhibit these poets in all their difference of kind and of degree, from the massive music of Donne to the faint, pleasing tinkle of Aurelian Townshend—whose *Dialogue Between a Pilgrim and Time* is one of the few regrettable omissions from the excellent anthology of Professor Grierson.

Religion and Literature (1935)

What I have to say is largely in support of the following propositions: Literary criticism should be completed by criticism from a definite ethical and theological standpoint. In so far as in any age there is common agreement on ethical and theological matters, so far can literary criticism be substantive. In ages like our own, in which there is no such common agreement, it is the more necessary for Christian readers to scrutinize their reading, especially of works of imagination, with explicit ethical and theological standards. The "greatness" of literature cannot be determined solely by literary standards; though we must remember that whether it is literature or not can be determined only by literary standards.[1]

We have tacitly assumed, for some centuries past, that there is *no* relation between literature and theology. This is not to deny that literature—I mean again, primarily works of imagination—has been, is, and probably always will be judged by some moral standards. But

From *Selected Essays: New Edition* by T. S. Eliot, copyright 1932, 1936, 1950, by Harcourt, Brace & World, Inc.; copyright, 1960, by T. S. Eliot. Reprinted by permission of the publishers.

[1] As an example of literary criticism given greater significance by theological interests, I would call attention to Theodor Haecker: *Virgil* (Sheed and Ward).

moral judgements of literary works are made only according to the moral code accepted by each generation, whether it lives according to that code or not. In an age which accepts some precise Christian theology, the common code may be fairly orthodox: though even in such periods the common code may exalt such concepts as "honour," "glory" or "revenge" to a position quite intolerable to Christianity. The dramatic ethics of the Elizabethan Age offers an interesting study. But when the common code is detached from its theological background, and is consequently more and more merely a matter of habit, it is exposed both to prejudice and to change. At such times morals are open to being altered *by* literature; so that we find in practice that what is "objectionable" in literature is merely what the present generation is not used to. It is a commonplace that what shocks one generation is accepted quite calmly by the next. This adaptability to change of moral standards is sometimes greeted with satisfaction as an evidence of human perfectibility: whereas it is only evidence of what unsubstantial foundations people's moral judgements have.

I am not concerned here with religious literature but with the application of our religion to the criticism of any literature. It may be as well, however, to distinguish first what I consider to be the three senses in which we can speak of "religious literature." The first is that of which we say that it is "religious literature" in the same way that we speak of "historical literature" or of "scientific literature." I mean that we can treat the Authorized translation of the Bible, or the works of Jeremy Taylor, as literature, in the same way that we treat the historical writing of Clarendon or of Gibbon—our two great English historians—as literature; or Bradley's *Logic*, or Buffon's *Natural History*. All of these writers were men who, incidentally to their religious, or historical, or philosophic purpose, had a gift of language which makes them delightful to read to all those who can enjoy language well written, even if they are un-

concerned with the objects which the writers had in view. And I would add that though a scientific, or historical, or theological, or philosophic work which is also "literature," may become superannuated as anything but literature, yet it is not likely to be "literature" unless it had its scientific or other value for its own time. While I acknowledge the legitimacy of this enjoyment, I am more acutely aware of its abuse. The persons who enjoy these writings *solely* because of their literary merit are essentially parasites; and we know that parasites, when they become too numerous, are pests. I could fulminate against the men of letters who have gone into ecstasies over "the Bible as literature," the Bible as "the noblest monument of English prose." Those who talk of the Bible as a "monument of English prose" are merely admiring it as a monument over the grave of Christianity. I must try to avoid the by-paths of my discourse: it is enough to suggest that just as the work of Clarendon, or Gibbon, or Buffon, or Bradley would be of inferior literary value if it were insignificant as history, science and philosophy respectively, so the Bible has had a *literary* influence upon English literature *not* because it has been considered as literature, but because it has been considered as the report of the Word of God. And the fact that men of letters now discuss it as "literature" probably indicates the *end* of its "literary" influence.

The second kind of relation of religion to literature is that which is found in what is called "religious" or "devotional" poetry. Now what is the usual attitude of the lover of poetry—and I mean the person who is a genuine and first-hand enjoyer and appreciator of poetry, not the person who follows the admirations of others—towards this department of poetry? I believe, all that may be implied in his calling it a *department*. He believes, not always explicitly, that when you qualify poetry as "religious" you are indicating very clear limitations. For the great majority of people who love poetry, "*religious poetry*" is a variety of *minor* poetry:

the religious poet is not a poet who is
treating the whole subject matter of
poetry in a religious spirit, but a poet
who is dealing with a confined part of
this subject matter: who is leaving out
what men consider their major passions,
and thereby confessing his ignorance of
them. I think that this is the real attitude of most poetry lovers towards such
poets as Vaughan, or Southwell, or
Crashaw, or George Herbert, or Gerard
Hopkins.

But what is more, I am ready to admit that up to a point these critics are
right. For there is a kind of poetry, such
as most of the work of the authors I
have mentioned, which is the product
of a special religious awareness, which
may exist without the general awareness
which we expect of the major poet. In
some poets, or in some of their works,
this general awareness may have existed;
but the preliminary steps which represent it may have been suppressed, and
only the end-product presented. Between these, and those in which the religious or devotional genius represents
the *special* and limited awareness, it
may be very difficult to discriminate. I
do not pretend to offer Vaughan, or
Southwell, or George Herbert, or Hopkins as major poets:[2] I feel sure that the
first three, at least, are poets of this
limited awareness. They are not great
religious poets in the sense in which
Dante, or Corneille, or Racine, even in
those of their plays which do not touch
upon Christian themes, are great Christian religious poets. Or even in the
sense in which Villon and Baudelaire,
with all their imperfections and delin-
quencies, are Christian poets. Since the
time of Chaucer, Christian poetry (in
the sense in which I shall mean it) has
been limited in England almost exclusively to minor poetry.

I repeat that when I am considering
Religion and Literature, I speak of
these things only to make clear that I

am not concerned primarily with Re
ligious Literature. I am concerned wit
what should be the relation betwee
Religion and all Literature. Therefor
the third type of "religious literature
may be more quickly passed over. I mea
the literary works of men who are sin
cerely desirous of forwarding the caus
of religion: that which may come unde
the heading of Propaganda. I am thin
ing, of course, of such delightful fictio
as Mr. Chesterton's *Man Who Wa
Thursday*, or his *Father Brown*. No on
admires and enjoys these things mor
than I do; I would only remark tha
when the same effect is aimed at b
zealous persons of less talent than Mr
Chesterton the effect is negative. Bu
my point is that such writings do no
enter into any serious consideration c
the relation of Religion and Literature
because they are conscious operation
in a world in which it is assumed tha
Religion and Literature are not relatec
It is a conscious and limited relating
What I want is a literature whic
should be *un*consciously, rather than de
liberately and defiantly, Christian: be
cause the work of Mr. Chesterton ha
its point from appearing in a worl
which is definitely not Christian.

I am convinced that we fail to realiz
how completely, and yet how irration
ally, we separate our literary from ou
religious judgements. If there could b
a complete separation, perhaps it migh
not matter: but the separation is no
and never can be, complete. If we ex
emplify literature by the novel—for th
novel is the form in which literatur
affects the greatest number—we may re
mark this gradual secularization of lit
erature during at least the last thre
hundred years. Bunyan, and to som
extent Defoe, had moral purposes: th
former is beyond suspicion, the latte
may be suspect. But since Defoe th
secularization of the novel has bee
continuous. There have been three chie
phases. In the first, the novel took th
Faith, in its contemporary version, fo
granted, and omitted it from its pictur
of life. Fielding, Dickens and Thack
eray belong to this phase. In the second

2 I note that in an address delivered in Swansea some
years later (subsequently published in *The Welsh Review* under the title of "What Is Minor Poetry?") I
stated with some emphasis my opinion that Herbert is
a major, not a minor poet. I agree with my later
opinion. [1949]

it doubted, worried about, or contested the Faith. To this phase belong George Eliot, George Meredith and Thomas Hardy. To the third phase, in which we are living, belong nearly all contemporary novelists except Mr. James Joyce. It is the phase of those who have never heard the Christian Faith spoken of as anything but an anachronism.

Now, do people in general hold a definite opinion, that is to say religious or anti-religious; and do they read novels, or poetry for that matter, with a separate compartment of their minds? The common ground between religion and fiction is behaviour. Our religion imposes our ethics, our judgement and criticism of ourselves, and our behaviour toward our fellow men. The fiction that we read affects our behaviour towards our fellow men, affects our patterns of ourselves. When we read of human beings behaving in certain ways, with the approval of the author, who gives his benediction to this behaviour by his attitude toward the result of the behaviour arranged by himself, we can be influenced towards behaving in the same way.[3] When the contemporary novelist is an individual thinking for himself in isolation, he may have something important to offer to those who are able to receive it. He who is alone may speak to the individual. But the majority of novelists are persons drifting in the stream, only a little faster. They have some sensitiveness, but little intellect.

We are expected to be broadminded about literature, to put aside prejudice or conviction, and to look at fiction as fiction and at drama as drama. With what is inaccurately called "censorship" in this country—with what is much more difficult to cope with than an official censorship, because it represents the opinions of individuals in an irresponsible democracy, I have very little sympathy; partly because it so often suppresses the wrong books, and partly because it is little more effective than Prohibition of Liquor; partly because it is

one manifestation of the desire that state control should take the place of decent domestic influence; and wholly because it acts only from custom and habit, not from decided theological and moral principles. Incidentally, it gives people a false sense of security in leading them to believe that books which are *not* suppressed are harmless. Whether there *is* such a thing as a harmless book I am not sure: but there very likely are books so utterly unreadable as to be incapable of injuring anybody. But it is certain that a book is not harmless merely because no one is consciously offended by it. And if we, as readers, keep our religious and moral convictions in one compartment, and take our reading merely for entertainment, or on a higher plane, for aesthetic pleasure, I would point out that the author, whatever his conscious intentions in writing, in practice recognizes no such distinctions. The author of a work of imagination is trying to affect us wholly, as human beings, whether he knows it or not; and we are affected by it, as human beings, whether we intend to be or not. I suppose that everything we eat has some other effect upon us than merely the pleasure of taste and mastication; it affects us during the process of assimilation and digestion; and I believe that exactly the same is true of anything we read.

The fact that what we read does not concern merely something called our *literary taste*, but that it affects directly, though only amongst many other influences, the whole of what we are, is best elicited, I think, by a conscientious examination of the history of our individual literary education. Consider the adolescent reading of any person with some literary sensibility. Everyone, I believe, who is at all sensible to the seductions of poetry, can remember some moment in youth when he or she was completely carried away by the work of one poet. Very likely he was carried away by several poets, one after the other. The reason for this passing infatuation is not merely that our sensibility to poetry is keener in adolescence

[3] Here and later I am indebted to Montgomery Belgion. *The Human Parrot* (chapter on The Irresponsible Propagandist).

than in maturity. What happens is a kind of inundation, of invasion of the undeveloped personality by the stronger personality of the poet. The same thing may happen at a later age to persons who have not done much reading. One author takes complete possession of us for a time; then another; and finally they begin to affect each other in our mind. We weigh one against another; we see that each has qualities absent from others, and qualities incompatible with the qualities of others: we begin to be, in fact, critical; and it is our growing critical power which protects us from excessive possession by any one literary personality. The good critic—and we should all try to be critics, and not leave criticism to the fellows who write reviews in the papers—is the man who, to a keen and abiding sensibility, joins wide and increasingly discriminating reading. Wide reading is not valuable as a kind of hoarding, an accumulation of knowledge, or what sometimes is meant by the term "a well-stocked mind." It is valuable because in the process of being affected by one powerful personality after another, we cease to be dominated by any one, or by any small number. The very different views of life, cohabiting in our minds, affect each other, and our own personality asserts itself and gives each a place in some arrangement peculiar to ourself.

It is simply not true that works of fiction, prose or verse, that is to say works depicting the actions, thoughts and words and passions of imaginary human beings, *directly* extend our knowledge of life. Direct knowledge of life is knowledge directly in relation to ourselves, it is our knowledge of *how* people behave in general, of *what* they are like in general, in so far as that part of life in which we ourselves have participated gives us material for generalization. Knowledge of life obtained through fiction is only possible by another stage of self-consciousness. That is to say, it can only be a knowledge of other people's knowledge of life, not of life itself. So far as we are taken up with the happenings in any novel in

the same way in which we are taken up with what happens under our eyes, we are acquiring at least as much falsehood as truth. But when we are developed enough to say: "This is the view of life of a person who was a good observer within his limits, Dickens, or Thackeray, or George Eliot, or Balzac; but he looked at it in a different way from me, because he was a different man; he even selected rather different things to look at, or the same things in a different order of importance, because he was a different man; so what I am looking at is the world as seen by a particular mind"—then we are in a position to gain something from reading fiction. We are learning *something* about life from these authors direct, just as we learn something from the reading of history direct; but these authors are only really helping us when we can see, and allow for, their differences from ourselves.

Now what we get, as we gradually grow up and read more and more, and read a greater diversity of authors, is a variety of views of life. But what people commonly assume, I suspect, is that we gain this experience of other men's views of life only by "improving reading." This, it is supposed, is a reward we get by applying ourselves to Shakespeare, and Dante, and Goethe, and Emerson, and Carlyle, and dozens of other respectable writers. The rest of our reading for amusement is merely killing time. But I incline to come to the alarming conclusion that it is just the literature that we read for "amusement," or "purely for pleasure" that may have the greatest and least suspected influence upon us. It is the literature which we read with the least effort that can have the easiest and most insidious influence upon us. Hence it is that the influence of popular novelists, and of popular plays of contemporary life, requires to be scrutinized most closely. And it is chiefly *contemporary* literature that the majority of people ever read in this attitude of "purely for pleasure," of pure passivity.

The relation to my subject of what I

have been saying should now be a little more apparent. Though we may read literature merely for pleasure, of "entertainment" or of "aesthetic enjoyment," this reading never affects simply a sort of special sense: it affects us as entire human beings; it affects our moral and religious existence. And I say that while individual modern writers of eminence can be improving, contemporary literature as a whole tends to be degrading. And that even the effect of the better writers, in an age like ours, may be degrading to some readers; for we must remember that what a writer does to people is not necessarily what he intends to do. It may be only what people are capable of having done to them. People exercise an unconscious selection in being influenced. A writer like D. H. Lawrence may be in his effect either beneficial or pernicious. I am not sure that I have not had some pernicious influence myself.

At this point I anticipate a rejoinder from the liberal-minded, from all those who are convinced that if everybody says what he thinks, and does what he likes, things will somehow, by some automatic compensation and adjustment, come right in the end. "Let everything be tried," they say, "and if it is a mistake, then we shall learn by experience." This argument might have some value, if we were always the same generation upon earth; or if, as we know to be not the case, people ever learned much from the experience of their elders. These liberals are convinced that only by what is called unrestrained individualism will truth ever emerge. Ideas, views of life, they think, issue distinct from independent heads, and in consequence of their knocking violently against each other, the fittest survive, and truth rises triumphant. Anyone who dissents from this view must be either a mediaevalist, wishful only to set back the clock, or else a fascist, and probably both.

If the mass of contemporary authors were really individualists, every one of them inspired Blakes, each with his separate vision, and if the mass of the contemporary public were really a mass of *individuals* there might be something to be said for this attitude. But this is not, and never has been, and never will be. It is not only that the reading individual today (or at any day) is not enough an individual to be able to absorb all the "views of life" of all the authors pressed upon us by the publishers' advertisements and the reviewers, and to be able to arrive at wisdom by considering one against another. It is that the contemporary authors are not individuals enough either. It is not that the world of separate individuals of the liberal democrat is undesirable; it is simply that this world does not exist. For the reader of contemporary literature is not, like the reader of the established great literature of all time, exposing himself to the influence of divers and contradictory personalities; he is exposing himself to a mass movement of writers who, each of them, think that they have something individually to offer, but are really all working together in the same direction. And there never was a time, I believe, when the reading public was so large, or so helplessly exposed to the influences of its own time. There never was a time, I believe, when those who read at all, read so many more books by living authors than books by dead authors; there never was a time so completely parochial, so shut off from the past. There may be too many publishers; there are certainly too many books published; and the journals ever incite the reader to "keep up" with what is being published. Individualistic democracy has come to high tide: and it is more difficult today to be an individual than it ever was before.

Within itself, modern literature has perfectly valid distinctions of good and bad, better and worse: and I do not wish to suggest that I confound Mr. Bernard Shaw with Mr. Noel Coward, Mrs. Woolf and Miss Mannin. On the other hand, I should like it to be clear that I am not defending a "high"-brow against a "low"-brow literature. What I do wish to affirm is that the whole of modern literature is corrupted by what I call Secularism, that it is simply unaware of, simply cannot understand the meaning of, the primacy of the supernatural over the natural life: of something which I assume to be our primary concern.

I do not want to give the impression that I have delivered a mere fretful jeremiad against contemporary literature. Assuming a common attitude between my readers, or some of my readers, and myself, the question is not so much, what is to be done about it? as, how should we behave towards it?

I have suggested that the liberal attitude towards literature will not work. Even if the writers who make their attempt to impose their "view of life" upon us were really distinct individuals, even if we as readers were distinct individuals, what would be the result? It would be, surely, that each reader would be impressed, in his reading, merely by what he was previously prepared to be impressed by; he would follow the "line of least resistance," and there would be no assurance that he would be made a better man. For literary judgement we need to be acutely aware of two things at once: of "what we like," and of "what we *ought* to like." Few people are honest enough to know either. The first means knowing what we really feel: very few know that. The second involves understanding our shortcomings; for we do not really know what we ought to like unless we also know why we ought to like it, which involves knowing why we don't yet like it. It is not enough to understand what we ought to be, unless we know what we are; and we do not understand what we are, unless we know what we ought to be. The two forms of self-consciousness, knowing what we are and what we ought to be, must go together.

It is our business, as readers of literature, to know what we like. It is our business, as Christians, *as well as* readers of literature, to know what we ought to like. It is our business as honest men not to assume that whatever we like is

what we ought to like; and it is our business as honest Christians not to assume that we do not like what we ought to like. And the last thing I would wish for would be the existence of two literatures, one for Christian consumption and the other for the pagan world. What I believe to be incumbent upon all Christians is the duty of maintaining consciously certain standards and criteria of criticism over and above those applied by the rest of the world; and that by these criteria and standards everything that we read must be tested. We must remember that the greater part of our current reading matter is written for us by people who have no real belief in a supernatural order, though some of it may be written by people with individual notions of a supernatural order which are not ours. And the greater part of our reading matter is coming to be written by people who not only have no such belief, but are even ignorant of the fact that there are still people in the world so "backward" or so "eccentric" as to continue to believe. So long as we are conscious of the gulf fixed between ourselves and the greater part of contemporary literature, we are more or less protected from being harmed by it, and are in a position to extract from it what good it has to offer us.

There are a very large number of people in the world today who believe that all ills are fundamentally economic. Some believe that various specific economic changes alone would be enough to set the world right; others demand more or less drastic changes in the social as well, changes chiefly of two opposed types. These changes demanded, and in some places carried out, are alike in one respect, that they hold the assumptions of what I call Secularism: they concern themselves only with changes of a temporal, material, and external nature; they concern themselves with morals only of a collective nature. In an exposition of one such new faith I read the following words:

"In our morality the one single test of any moral question is whether it impedes or destroys in any way the power of the individual to serve the State. [The individual] must answer the questions: 'Does this action injure the nation? Does it injure other members of the nation? Does it injure my ability to serve the nation?' And if the answer is clear on all those questions, the individual has absolute liberty to do as he will."

Now I do not deny that this is a kind of morality, and that it is capable of great good within limits; but I think that we should all repudiate a morality which had no higher ideal to set before us than that. It represents, of course, one of the violent reactions we are witnessing, against the view that the community is solely for the benefit of the individual; but it is equally a gospel of this world, and of this world alone. My complaint against modern literature is of the same kind. It is not that modern literature is in the ordinary sense "immoral" or even "amoral"; and in any case to prefer that charge would not be enough. It is simply that it repudiates, or is wholly ignorant of, our most fundamental and important beliefs; and that in consequence its tendency is to encourage its readers to get what they can out of life while it lasts, to miss no "experience" that presents itself, and to sacrifice themselves, if they make any sacrifice at all, only for the sake of tangible benefits to others in this world either now or in the future. We shall certainly continue to read the best of its kind, of what our time provides; but we must tirelessly criticize it according to our own principles, and not merely according to the principles admitted by the writers and by the critics who discuss it in the public press.

I. A. RICHARDS

(b. 1893)

I. A. Richards was, with T. S. Eliot, one of the chief originators of the school of modern criticism that came to be known as the "New Criticism." But where Eliot was in reaction against the secular actualities of the modern world, Richards not only accepted their inevitability but attempted to apply creatively the principles of the modern science of psychology to the critical study of literature. Richards' training in psychology at Cambridge and his early interest in the work of William James prepared him eventually to see, as he has said, "what a truly portentous fore-runner Coleridge was." Coleridge is certainly the chief of several influences on Richards' critical thought. In fact, the bulk of Richards' work as a theorist may be understood fairly enough as a various and continuing adaptation of Coleridge's ideas about the structure and action of the human mind not only to modern criticism, but to the much larger problems of modern education and the proper utilization of mass communication, and ultimately even to the question of the good society. As far as the New Criticism is concerned, if moralist Eliot is its Plato, theorist-technicalist Richards seems to be its Aristotle. And if the two critics are in almost every way different in the nature of their critical interests and achievements, their work is at least complementary rather than contradictory, and began in a common ground of dissatisfaction with the critical *status quo* as they found it. Richards' principal works of literary theory and criticism include *The Foundations of Aes-*

thetics (with C. K. Ogden and J. Wood, 1921), *Principles of Literary Criticism* (1924), *Science and Poetry* (1925), *Practical Criticism* (1929), *Coleridge on Imagination* (1935), and *The Philosophy of Rhetoric* (1936). Most of Richards' work of the Forties and Fifties has only indirect relevance for literary criticism and theory, with the exception of certain essays in *Speculative Instruments* (1955).

From *Principles of Literary Criticism* (1924)
Chapter XXXIV. The Two Uses of Language

The intelligible forms of ancient poets
The fair humanities of old religion . . .
They live no longer in the faith of reason:
But still the heart doth need a language, still
Doth the old instinct bring back the old names.
Coleridge, *Piccolomini.*

There are two totally distinct uses of language. But because the theory of language is the most neglected of all studies they are in fact hardly ever distinguished. Yet both for the theory of poetry and for the narrower aim of understanding much which is said about poetry a clear comprehension of the differences between these uses is indispensable. For this we must look somewhat closely at the mental processes which accompany them.

It is unfortunate but not surprising that most of the psychological terms which we naturally employ tend to blur the distinction. 'Knowledge', 'belief', 'assertion', 'thought', and 'understanding', for example, as ordinarily used, are ambiguous in a fashion which disguises and obscures the point which must be brought out. They record distinctions which are oblique to the distinctions required, they are cross-cuts of analysis made in the wrong place and in the wrong direction, useful enough for some purposes no doubt, but for this present purpose very confusing. We shall do well to put them out of mind for a while if possible.

The chief departure made from current conceptions in the sketch of the

Reprinted by permission of Harcourt, Brace & World, Inc.

mind given in Chapter XI lay in the substitution of the *causes*, the *characters* and the *consequences* of a mental event, for its aspects as *thought, feeling* and *will*. This treatment was introduced with a view to the analysis which now occupies us. Among the causes of most mental events, we urged, two sets may be distinguished. On the one hand there are the present stimuli reaching the mind through the sensory nerves, and, in co-operation with these, the effects of past stimuli associated with them. On the other hand is a set of quite different factors, the state of the organism, its needs, its readiness to respond to this or that kind of stimulus. The impulses which arise take their character and their course from the interaction of these two sets. We must keep them clearly distinguished.

The relative importance of the two sets of factors varies enormously. A sufficiently hungry man will eat almost anything which can be chewed or swallowed. The nature of the substance, within these limits, has very little effect upon his behaviour. A replete person, by contrast, will only eat such things as he expects will taste pleasant, or regards as possessing definite beneficial properties, for example, medicines. His behaviour, in other words, depends almost entirely upon the character of his optical or olfactory stimulation.

So far as an impulse owes its character to its stimulus (or to such effects of past accompanying or connected stimuli as are revived) so far is it a *reference*, to use the term which we introduced in Chapter XI, to stand for the property of mental events which we substitute for thought or cognition.[1] It is plain that the independent internal conditions of the organism usually intervene to distort reference in some degree. But very many of our needs can only be satisfied if the impulses are left undistorted. Bitter experience has taught us to leave some of them alone, to let them reflect or correspond with external states of affairs as much as they can, undisturbed as far as possible by internal states of affairs, our needs and desires.

In all our behaviour can be distinguished stimuli we receive, and the ways in which we use them. What we receive may be any kind of stimulus, but only when the reaction we make to it tallies with its nature and varies with it in quasi-independence of the uses we make of it does reference occur.

Those to whom visual images are of service in considering complex matters may find it convenient at this point to imagine a circle or sphere constantly bombarded by minute particles (stimuli). Within the sphere may be pictured complex mechanisms continually changing for reasons having nothing to do with the external stimuli. These mechanisms by opening little gateways select which of the stimuli shall be allowed to come in and take effect. So far as the subsequent convulsions are due to the nature of the impacts and to lingering effects of impacts which have accompanied similar impacts in the past, the convulsions are referential. So far as they are due to the independent motions of the internal mechanisms themselves, reference fails. This diagrammatic image may possibly be of convenience to some. By those who distrust such things it may with advantage be disregarded. It is not introduced as a contribution to neurol-

ogy, and is in no way a ground for the author's view.

The extent to which reference is interfered with by needs and desires is underestimated even by those who, not having yet forgotten the events of 1914-1918, are most sceptical as to the independence of opinions and desires. Even the most ordinary and familiar objects are perceived as it pleases us to perceive them rather than as they are, whenever error does not directly deprive us of advantages. It is almost impossible for anyone to secure a correct impression of his own personal appearance or of the features of anyone in whom he is personally interested. Nor is it perhaps often desirable that he should.

For the demarcation of the fields where impulse should be as completely as possible dependent upon and correspondent with external situation, those in which reference should take prior place from those in which it may be subordinated to appetencies with advantage, is not a simple matter. On many views of the good and of what should be, themselves results of subordinating reference to emotional satisfactions, there could be no question. Truth, it would be said, has claims prior to all other considerations. Love not grounded upon knowledge would be described as worthless. We ought not to admire what is not beautiful and if our mistress be not really beautiful when impartially considered we ought, so the doctrine runs, to admire her, if at all, for other reasons. The chief points of interest about such views are the confusions which make them plausible. Beauty as an internal quality of things is usually involved, as well as Good the unanalysable Idea. Both are special twists given to some of our impulses by habits deriving ultimately from desires. They linger in our minds because to think of a thing as Good or Beautiful gives more *immediate* emotional satisfaction than to *refer* to it as satisfying our impulses in one special fashion (cf. Chapter VII) or another (cf. Chapter XXXII).

To think about Good or Beauty is

---

[1] The reader who is a psychologist will notice many points in this statement at which elaboration and qualifications are required. For example, when we are 'introspecting' factors normally belonging to the second set may enter the first. But he will be able, if he grasps the general theory, to supply these complications himself. I did not wish to burden the text with unnecessary intricacies.

not necessarily to refer to anything. For the term 'thinking' covers mental operations in which the impulses are so completely governed by internal factors and so out of control of stimulus that no reference occurs. Most 'thinking of' includes reference in some degree, of course, but not all, and similarly much reference would not commonly be described as thinking. When we drop something which is too hot to hold we would not usually be said to have done so through thinking. The two terms overlap, and their definitions, if there be a definition of 'thinking' as commonly used, are of different types. This is why 'Thought' was on an earlier page described as marking an oblique distinction.

To return, the claims of reference are by no means easy to adjust with other claims. An immense extension of our powers of referring has recently been made. With amazing swiftness Science has opened out field after field of possible reference. Science is simply the organisation of references with a view solely to the convenience and facilitation of reference. It has advanced mainly because other claims, typically the claims of our religious desires, have been set aside. For it is no accident that Science and Religion conflict. They are different principles upon which impulses may be organised, and the more closely they are examined the more inevitable is the incompatibility seen to be. Any so-called reconciliation which is ever effected will involve bestowing the name Religion upon something utterly different from any of the systematisations of impulses which it now denotes, for the reason that the belief elements present would have a different character.

Many attempts have been made to reduce Science to a position of subjection to some instinct or emotion or desire, to curiosity for example. A special passion for knowledge for its own sake has even been invented. But in fact all the passions and all the instincts, all human needs and desires may *on occasion* supply the motive force for Science. There is no human activity which may not on occasion require undistorted

reference. The essential point, however, is that Science is autonomous. The impulses developed in it are modified only by one another, with a view to the greatest possible completeness and systematisation, and for the facilitation of further references. So far as other considerations distort them they are not yet Science or have fallen out of it.

To declare Science autonomous is very different from subordinating all our activities to it. It is merely to assert that so far as any body of references is undistorted it belongs to Science. It is not in the least to assert that no references may be distorted if advantage can thereby be gained. And just as there are innumerable human activities which require undistorted references if they are to be satisfied, so there are innumerable other human activities not less important which equally require distorted references or, more plainly, *fictions*.

The use of fictions, the imaginative use of them rather, is not a way of hoodwinking ourselves. It is not a process of pretending to ourselves that things are not as they are. It is perfectly compatible with the fullest and grimmest recognition of the exact state of affairs on all occasions. It is no make-believe. But so awkwardly have our references and our attitudes become entangled that such pathetic spectacles as Mr. Yeats trying desperately to believe in fairies or Mr. Lawrence impugning the validity of solar physics, are all too common. To be forced by desire into any unwarrantable belief is a calamity. The state which ensues is often extraordinarily damaging to the mind. But this common misuse of fictions should not blind us to their immense services provided we do not take them for what they are not, degrading the chief means by which our attitudes to actual life may be adjusted into the material of a long-drawn delirium.[2]

[2] Revelation Doctrines when once given a foothold tend to interfere everywhere. They serve as a kind of omnipotent major premise justifying any and every conclusion. A specimen: "Since the function of Art is to pierce through to the Real World, then it follows that the artist cannot be too definite in his outlines, and that good drawing is the foundation of all good art." —Charles Gardner, *Vision and Vesture*, p. 54.

If we knew enough it might be possible that all necessary attitudes could be obtained through scientific references alone. Since we do not know very much yet, we can leave this very remote possibility, once recognised, alone.

Fictions whether aroused by statements or by analogous things in other arts may be used in many ways. They may be used, for example, to deceive. But this is not a characteristic use in poetry. The distinction which needs to be kept clear does not set up fictions in opposition to verifiable truths in the scientific sense. A statement may be used for the sake of the *reference,* true or false, which it causes. This is the *scientific* use of language. But it may also be used for the sake of the effects in emotion and attitude produced by the reference it occasions. This is the *emotive* use of language. The distinction once clearly grasped is simple. We may either use words for the sake of the references they promote, or we may use them for the sake of the attitudes and emotions which ensue. Many arrangements of words evoke attitudes without any reference being required *en route.* They operate like musical phrases. But usually references are involved *as conditions* for, or *stages in,* the ensuing development or attitudes, yet it is still the attitudes not the references which are important. It matters not at all in such cases whether the references are true or false. Their sole function is to bring about and support the attitudes which are the further response. The questioning, verificatory way of handling them is irrelevant, and in a competent reader it is not allowed to interfere. "Better a plausible impossibility than an improbable possibility" said Aristotle very wisely; there is less danger of an inappropriate reaction.

The differences between the mental processes involved in the two cases are very great, though easily overlooked. Consider what failure for each use amounts to. For scientific language a difference in the references is itself failure: the end has not been attained. But for emotive language the widest differences in reference are of no impor-

tance if the further effects in attitude and emotion are of the required kind.

Further, in the scientific use of language not only must the references be correct for success, but the connections and relations of references to one another must be of the kind which we call logical. They must not get in one another's way, and must be so organised as not to impede further reference. But for emotive purposes logical arrangement is not necessary. It may be and often is an obstacle. For what matters is that the series of attitudes due to the references should have their own proper organisation, their own emotional interconnection, and this often has no dependence upon the logical relations of such references as may be concerned in bringing the attitudes into being.

A few notes of the chief uses of the word 'Truth' in Criticism may help to prevent misunderstanding:—

1. The scientific sense that, namely, in which references, and derivatively statements symbolising references, are true, need not delay us. A reference is true when the things to which it refers are actually together in the way in which it refers to them. Otherwise it is false. This sense is one very little involved by any of the arts. For the avoidance of confusions it would be well if the term 'true' could be reserved for this use. In purely scientific discourse it could and should be, but such discourse is uncommon. In point of fact the emotive power which attaches to the word is far too great for it to be abandoned in general discussion; the temptation to a speaker who needs to stir certain emotions and evoke certain attitudes of approval and acceptance is overwhelming. No matter how various the senses in which it may be used, and even when it is being used in no sense whatever, its effects in promoting attitudes will still make it indispensable; people will still continue to use the word with the same promiscuity as ever.

2. The most usual other sense is that of acceptability. The 'Truth' of *Robinson Crusoe* is the acceptability of the things we are told, their acceptability in the interests of the effects of the narra-

tive, not their correspondence with any actual facts involving Alexander Selkirk or another. Similarly the falsity of happy endings to *Lear* or to *Don Quixote*, is their failure to be acceptable to those who have fully responded to the rest of the work. It is in this sense that 'Truth' is equivalent to 'internal necessity' or rightness. That is 'true' or 'internally necessary' which completes or accords with the rest of the experience, which co-operates to arouse our ordered response, whether the response of Beauty or another. "What the Imagination seizes as Beauty must be Truth", said Keats, using this sense of 'Truth', though not without confusion. Sometimes it is held that whatever is redundant or otiose, whatever is not required, although not obstructive or disruptive, is also false. "Surplusage!" said Pater, "the artist will dread that, as the runner on his muscles"[3] himself perhaps in this instance sweating his sentence down too finely. But this is to make excessive demands upon the artist. It is to apply the axe of retrenchment in the wrong place. Superabundance is a common characteristic of great art, much less dangerous than the preciousness that too contrived an economy tends to produce. The essential point is whether what is unnecessary interferes or not with the rest of the response. If it does not, the whole thing is all the better probably for the extra solidity which it thereby gains.

This internal acceptability or 'convincingness' needs to be contrasted with other acceptabilities. Thomas Rymer, for example, refused to accept Iago for external reasons: "To entertain the audience with something new and surprising against common sense and nature, he would pass upon us a close, dissembling rascal, instead of an openhearted, frank, plain-dealing Souldier, a character constantly born by them for some thousands of years in the World." "The truth is" he observes "this author's head was full of villainous, unnatural images".[4]

He is remembering no doubt Aristotle's remark that "the artist must preserve the type and yet ennoble it", but interpreting it in his own way. For him the type is fixed simply by convention and his acceptances take no note of internal necessities but are governed merely by accordance with external canons. His is an extreme case, but to avoid his error in subtler matters is in fact sometimes the hardest part of the critic's undertaking. But whether our conception of the type is derived in some such absurd way, or taken, for example, as from a handbook of zoology, is of slight consequence. It is the taking of any *external* canon which is critically dangerous. When in the same connection Rymer objects that there never was a Moorish General in the service of the Venetian Republic, he is applying another external canon, that of historic fact. This mistake is less insidious, but Ruskin used to be particularly fond of the analogous mistake in connection with the 'truth' of drawing.

3. Truth may be equivalent to Sincerity. This character of the artist's work we have already touched upon briefly in connection with Tolstoy's theory of communication (Chapter XXIII). It may perhaps be most easily defined from the critic's point of view negatively, as the absence of any apparent attempt on the part of the artist to work effects upon the reader which do not work for himself. Too simple definitions must be avoided. It is well known that Burns in writing '*Ae fond kiss*' was only too anxious to escape *Nancy's* (Mrs. Maclehose's) attentions, and similar instances could be multiplied indefinitely. Absurdly naïve views upon the matter[5] exemplified by the opinion that Bottomley must have believed himself to be inspired or he would not have moved his audiences, are far too common. At the level at which Bottomley harangued any kind of exaltation in the orator, whether due to pride or to champagne, would make his stuff effective. But at Burns' level a

[3] *Essay on Style*, p. 19.
[4] *A Short View of Tragedy*.

[5] Cf. A. Clutton-Brock, *The Times*, 11th July 1922, p. 13.

very different situation arises. Here his probity and sincerity *as an artist* are involved; external circumstances are irrelevant, but there is perhaps internal evidence in the poem of a flaw in its creating impulse. Compare as a closely similar poem in which there is no flaw, Byron's *'When we two parted'*.

From *Coleridge on Imagination* (1935)
Chapter IX. The Bridle of Pegasus

Be not as the horse, or the mule, who have no understanding; whose mouth must be held in with bit and bridle, lest they come near unto thee.—*Psalm* xxxii.

This same stede shal bere you ever-more
With-outen harm, til ye be ther yow leste.

.   .   .   .   .   .

Of sondry doutes thus they jangle and trete
As lewed peple demeth comunly
Of thinges that ben maad more subtilly
Than they can in her lewedness comprehende;
They demen gladly to the badder ende.
The Squieres Tale.

May I invite attention to a few paragraphs from a representative present-day critic on Wordsworth's doctrine and practice of the interpretation of Nature? They will show us where much current opinion is, in this matter. And they provide a convenient specimen for the study of reading ability.

What claim, for instance, is Wordsworth making for his feelings in these lines, from the *Excursion?*

Far and wide the clouds were touched
And in their silent faces could he read
Unutterable love. Sound needed none
Nor any voice of joy; his spirit drank
The spectacle: sensation, soul, and form,
All melted into him; they swallowed up
His animal being; in them did he live
And by them did he live; they were his life.
In such access of mind, in such high hour
Of visitation from the living God,
Thought was not; in enjoyment it expired.
No thanks he breathed, he proffered no
    request:
Rapt into still communion that transcends
The imperfect offices of prayer and praise. . . .

These last are daring words and more definite perhaps than any others in Wordsworth, in what they claim. He is not merely equalling, but transcending the offices of prayer and praise. Wordsworth is presumably asking us to take him seriously; and if we take him seriously we cannot let such phrases slip by, all merged in one gush of emotion. And once we are asked to consider a theological issue some elementary questions arise.

First, why is this different from pantheism? Does Wordsworth by any denial of his poetic art or of his joy in things suggest that he is communing with a personal God, entirely distinct from his joy in the clouds: or is God, like the poet Donne, merely preaching to him 'from a cloud, but in none'? Herbert tells us that God is not to be found in stars or clouds or any aspect of nature, but in 'the sweet original joy sprung from Thine eye.'

Again, how are we to know that Wordsworth really felt these very emotions when he looked at the cloud, and that some of them did not rather arrive later when he wrote the poem? And if we pass over this difficulty, it is possible, of course, that the presence, which Wordsworth felt was in the cloud, existed only in his own mind as a result of looking at the cloud. If so, God is an attribute of Wordsworth's brain or exists somewhere in the relation between Wordsworth's brain and the cloud. And even if a higher reality, beyond the usual grasp of the human brain, is in truth communicating to Wordsworth from the cloud, this might still have been some biological harmony having no spiritual significance at all.

But suppose we say that this is all cavilling; suppose we say that Wordsworth's emotion is so sublime and impressive that we accept his use of the word God in this passage, what does it mean? Why the living God? What could God be if not merely 'alive', but eternal? The epithet suggests that Wordsworth must be referring to some deity other than the one personal God of the Christian Gospels, a kind of deity who could be either dead or alive. If so, what God? We are not told. And if Wordsworth is really referring to the personal God of Christianity, whom Herbert worshipped, we arrived at his meaning in spite of rather than because of his words. And if this is his meaning, how does the contemplation of a cloud transcend the offices of prayer? Can Wordsworth, then, only communicate with God under certain meteorological conditions?

This passage is taken from a recent number of *The Criterion* (Oct. 1932). I may remark to begin with that it is uncomfortably *not* surprising that this new Defender of the Faith, writing on Nicholas Ferrar and George Herbert, in a periodical known for its Anglo-Catholic tendency, should show himself ignorant of the language of the Book of Common Prayer. 'Why the living God?' Because Wordsworth knew his Psalms:

Like as the hart desireth the water-brooks,
So longeth my soul after thee, O God.
My soul is athirst for God, yea even for the living God;
When shall I come to appear before the presence of God?

> (Psalm 42, *Quemadmodum*, The Evening of the 8th Day.)

In the First Prayer Book of Edward VI this psalm was part of the order for the burial of the dead.[1] And is Matthew xvi. 16 too recondite a reference?

We may note now, first, that Wordsworth's poem does not claim to transcend prayer and praise. An experience is described in it as doing so—that is all. As to whether Wordsworth 'really felt these very emotions' and when: is the distinction between a poem and an autobiographical note, or an *affidavit*, really so difficult as this? And, as to the next set of difficulties: what is there about Wordsworth's lines which specially invites them? These are 'elementary questions' indeed, so elementary that any human utterance of any kind brings them up. Nothing in Herbert or Donne, or any other poet, is a whit more immune from them. They must be reflected on by anyone who would read

any poetry with sincerity. But to use them as missiles in this fashion is merely to show lack of acquaintance with them *as questions,* as 'preliminary steps of the Methodical scale, at the top of which sits the author, and at the bottom the critic' (*Treatise on Method*, Snyder 32).

However, this writer has been making some attempts to find out about these things. He continues on a later page:

Emotion in itself has no religious significance: an emotion is merely a reaction of feeling in the mental plane, as spontaneous as feelings of the physical senses. The *Encyclopaedia of Religion and Ethics,* in summing up the view of emotion so far given by moral philosophy, says that emotion cannot in itself be moral or immoral, religious or irreligious: it only is the manner in which the intellect judges and the will controls the emotions, that can have a place among religious values. In another place in the *Prelude,* Wordsworth does attempt to give some such comment on the emotions, with the following result. He is describing a child listening to a singing shell:

. . . and his countenance soon
Brightened with joy; for from within were heard
Murmurings, whereby the monitor expressed
Mysterious union with its native sea.
Even such a shell the universe itself
Is to the ear of Faith: and there are times,
I doubt not, when to you it doth import
Authentic tidings of invisible things;
Of ebb and flow, and ever during power;
And central peace, subsisting at the heart
Of endless agitation.

But what is it in fact that a child hears, or you hear, when a shell is put to the ear? Not murmurings by which the monitor expresses mysterious union with the sea, but in actual fact murmurings which are the blood circulation in the listener's *own* head. To apply Wordsworth's illustration, as he asks us to apply it, what then are these 'authentic tidings' that he draws from nature? Something, for which a buzzing in his own head is his own chosen simile.

Had Wordsworth paused to reflect and to judge, instead of being swept away by emotions, he could never have misapplied this elementary fact at this crucial moment. Had he reflected and judged, he would have rather written with Hopkins:

---

[1] It remains, in Latin, in the Roman Catholic Office for the Dead. The phrase may also be found in the Canon of the Mass.

Elected silence sing to me
And beat upon my whirled ear.

And once the mind appreciates the collapse of meaning, it can only turn from this passage and from all the other passages that it represents, with something of sense of failure and frustration, and even a loss of pleasure in the poetry itself.

The 'collapse of meaning' however, is not in Wordsworth but in this critic's reading of him. The passage cited is, of course, on Coleridge's Wind Harp theme again, an allegorical presentation of the central problem of philosophy. The reader has missed Wordsworth's deep self-critical humour, and so laughs *at* the lines when he should smile with them. To suggest that Wordsworth did not 'pause to reflect and judge' shows an odd ignorance of this poet's habits in composition.

It is amusing to observe that he gives, 'by way of comparison', as an example of 'exact and careful reflection', this image, which refers to Herbert's own power of thought:

Mark how the fire in flints doth quiet lie,
Content and warm to itself alone.
But when it would appear to other's eye
Without a knock it never shone.

If Wordsworth had written this, how easily would the reader have pointed out that the fire is not in the flint but in the detached particle!

I have lingered with this example partly because it shows the kind of comment which Coleridge's doctrine, in my interpretation of it, must expect, but chiefly because it illustrates both erratic reading and lack of reflection upon the problems of symbolisation. There is a connection between these to-day which perhaps did not hold in former times. The capacity to read intelligently seems undoubtedly to have been greater among educated men in Coleridge's time than it is to-day. Three reasons at least may be suggested for this. More rigorous translation exercises in the schools; less shoddy reading material in

our daily intake of printed matter; a greater homogeneity in the intellectual tradition. Only this last concerns us here. Intellectual tradition tells us, among other things, *how literally* to read a passage. It guides us in our metaphorical, allegorical, symbolical modes of interpretation. The hierarchy of these modes is elaborate and variable; and to read aright we need to shift with an at present indescribable adroitness and celerity from one mode to another. Our sixteenth- and seventeenth-century literature, supported by practice in listening to sermons and by conventions in speech and letter-writing which made 'direct' statement rare to a point which seems to us unnatural, gave an extraordinary training[2] in this skill. But it was skill merely; it was not followed up by theory. With the eighteenth century, the variety of the modes of metaphor in speech and in writing rapidly declined. Dr. Johnson, for example, can show, at times, strange obtuseness in distinguishing between degrees of metaphor. It was this which made Donne seem artificial, absurd, unimpassioned and bewildering to him. But at the same time it is Johnson perhaps who shows us best the first steps of that reflective analytical scrutiny and comparison of the structures of meanings in poetry which is later to take a vast stride in Coleridge. For example, on these lines of Denham,

O could I flow like thee, and make thy stream
My great example as it is my theme!
Though deep, yet clear; though gentle, yet not
   dull;
Strong without rage, without o'erflowing full.

he remarks, "The lines are in them-

2 As Coleridge was among the first to point out, "Shakespeare's time, when the English Court was still foster-mother of the State and the Muses; and when, in consequence, the courtiers and men of rank and fashion affected a display of wit, point, and sententious observation, that would be deemed intolerable at present—but in which a hundred years of controversy, involving every great political, and every dear domestic interest, had trained all but the lowest classes to participate. Add to this the very style of the sermons of the time, and the eagerness of the Protestants to distinguish themselves by long and frequent preaching, and it will be found that, from the reign of Henry VIII to the abdication of James II, no country ever received such a national education as England." (Raysor, I, 93.)

selves not perfect; for most of the words thus artfully opposed, are to be understood simply on one side of the comparison, and metaphorically on the other; and, if there be any language which does not express intellectual operations by material images, into that language they cannot be translated." There is, of course, no such language; but that Johnson should be applying such reflections to the analysis of poetry is instructive. A more persistent examination would have shown him that the transferences here were sometimes primary, sometimes secondary, sometimes went from the river to the mind, sometimes from the mind to the river. And, with that, the assumptions behind his first remark would have been broken down. Naturally enough an age which, partly through false theory, partly through social causes, is losing its skill in interpretation, begins the reflective inquiry which may lead to a theory by which the skill may be regained—this time as a less vulnerable and more deeply grounded, because more consciously recognized, endowment.

With Coleridge's generation came a recovery of skill, both in readers and writers. It was maintained—for modes of meaning close in structure to those in Wordsworth, Shelley or Keats—until towards the end of the nineteenth century. Then came a sudden decline in performance. Twentieth-century criticism has been marked not so much by any enlightening reaction against the biassed preferences of the nineteenth century, as by the betrayal of general inability to read anything with safety on the part of most of those who have anything to say. Scholars and textual critics escape this generalization; but then professional students rarely have much to say. 'The true atheist is he whose hands are cauterized with holy things.' Their work is probably better in quality than any in the past—but we must recall that, like men of science, they have a cumulative advantage in technique, and they are also in closer contact with the records of tradition. Unluckily they have usually so much

the less touch with its new shoots. And they rarely have voices that can be heard—a fact which may be a gain to the world. For if one asks, 'What can a lifetime of literary studies do towards judgment of the new?" the answer must, I fear, be a grim one. Thus the criticism that shapes public taste, and that may indirectly here and there influence original writing, is written by men of letters who are not primarily scholars. And it is this criticism that shows, I think demonstrably—though I decline the invidious task of demonstration—an alarming general drop in the capacity to construe the poetry which it discusses. Our 'Neo-Classic' age is repeating those feats of its predecessor which we least applaud. It is showing a fascinating versatility in travesty. And the poets of the 'Romantic' period provide for it what Shakespeare, Milton and Donne were to the early eighteenth-century grammarians and emendators—effigies to be shot at because what they represent is no longer understood. So the Chinese student bicycles to-day gaily and ribaldly round on the Altar of Heaven.

My point, however, is more general than these graceless and querulous remarks would suggest. It is that a great diversity in our current intellectual tradition, sharp opposition between its different branches, discontinuity in the process by which readers find themselves living in and with one or other of them, quick changes between them, insufficiently realized as they occur—in short, a general heterogeneity in our recent growth has disordered the conduct of reading. This shows itself most clearly, I think, in the frequency with which new and old-fashioned critics alike now pretend that their own inability to understand a poem is a sound argument against it. The conservatives use this plea against the new-fanglers quite as naïvely as do these against Shelley, Keats or Wordsworth. Both, of course, claim to be thereby upholding tradition. And both, to an onlooker, add sanction to Coleridge's adage, "Until you understand a writer's ignorance, presume yourself ignorant of his understanding."

The explanation of this embarrassing situation is not, I believe, in any fundamental difference in outlook between, say, Mr. T. S. Eliot and Mr. F. L. Lucas. No such gap separates them as divided Shelley from Dr. Johnson. Yet something impenetrably shrouds Mr. Eliot's constant preoccupation with the sources of nobility from Mr. Lucas' eye; and something has at times hidden from Mr. Eliot even those purposes of some romantic poetry which most resembled his own. I am tempted to connect these obstructions, to trace them to a common origin in divergent attitudes to language, to different ways in which words are used, and in which they are assumed to work.

Contemporary poetry (and very much of the poetry of other times in which contemporary readers are most interested) is generally supposed to be difficult. It will be fitting to conclude this examination of Coleridge's critical theories by considering what light they can throw upon this 'difficulty'. For it seems probable that in a large measure it derives from differences between the *actual* structures of the meanings of the poetry and the structures which, in various ways, are *supposed* to be natural and necessary to poetry, the structures which from habit and implicit theory are expected in its meanings.

But we must not confuse changes in the structures of poetic meanings with changes in the theories historically connected with them. Most theorizing upon meanings only very distantly reflects them. And this is our difficulty—with which Coleridge may help us. The technique of comparing the structures of meanings is still embryonic and much impeded by immature theories, due to the poets and others, as to what different kinds of poetry try to do and how they try to do it. In almost all familiar formulations, unreal problems of the *what* and of the *how* are distressingly entangled.

It is with deceptive ease, indeed, that the inquiry divides into questions about the *what* and the *how*. Or into questions about the *methods* a poet uses and the *feats* he thereby achieves. Or into questions about his *means* and his *ends*. Or about the *way* of his work and the *whither*. This ease is deceptive because, although for some purposes the division is necessary and for others convenient, in an examination of poetic structure the distinction prevents all advance by destroying the specimens we would examine.

How it does so may be best shown, perhaps, by taking the last of these formulations—between the *way* and the *whither* of a poem—and making the metaphor in it as explicit as possible, undeterred by any charges of 'intoxication by the obvious' that may be occasioned.

The metaphor is that of a path leading to some destination, or of a missile (arrow or boomerang) going to some mark; but let us exercise a trifling ingenuity in inventing journeys without destinations—movements of the earth, the pigeons' flight, the tacking of a boat, an ant's tour of the spokes of a wheel—or in considering the different trajectories which an arrow will take in shifting winds, or that most illuminating instance here, the rocket; and we shall see clearly how unnecessary, as applying to poems, the assumptions behind any division between a *way* and a *whither* may be. However widely we generalize it (as means and ends) the division is here an impeding product of abstraction. From the *total meaning* of the poem, we have singled out some component to be treated as its *whither* and to be set over against the rest as its *way*. We have chosen something to be, in a narrower sense, its 'meaning' and left the rest to be either the vehicle of this meaning or our further response to it. And until and unless we are explicitly aware of these processes of singling-out partial meanings we can make no progress in comparative studies of poetic structures.

Traditionally or conventionally the *whither* of a poem has often been taken to be 'what it says': and this, when thus singled out, has as often, in recent times, been regarded as of minor importance. As Professor Housman put it in his Leslie Stephen Lecture (*The Name and Nature of Poetry*, p. 37), "Poetry is not the thing said but a way of saying it." But this 'thing said', if we try with most poetry to separate it from the 'way of saying it', shows itself to be a most arbitrary thing. Unless we are unreasonably stern with it (or hold indefensible views on synonymity) we have to admit that even very slight changes in a way of saying anything *in poetry* change the thing said—and usually in evident and analysable respects. Only in abstracter matters than poetry ever touches is 'the same thought' able to be uttered with different words. But by taking 'the same thought' in a loose indefinite sense—as thoughts linked by a mere resemblance of topic— we can sometimes deceive ourselves and make the division between 'the thing said' and the 'way of saying it' seem useful and applicable.

" 'But no man may deliver his brother, nor make agreement unto God for him', that," said Mr. Housman, "is to me poetry so moving that I can hardly keep my voice steady in reading it. And that this is the effect of language I can ascertain by experiment: the same thought in the Bible version, 'None of them can by any means redeem his brother, nor give to God a ransom for him', I can read without emotion" (p.37). That this is the effect of language we may grant without misgiving, but in what sense of *thought* that could be relevant do they utter the same thought? *Deliver—redeem; make agreement unto—give a ransom for*: the dominant metaphors are changed, and a defined explicit transaction has taken the place of a crowd of various or conflicting possibilities. It is surprising that so severe a textual critic and so rigorous an upholder of precision in literary studies as Mr. Housman should permit himself such an opinion. The ambiguity of *thought* and its power to mislead even the most wary could not be better shown.

This 'thing said' is an abstraction from the whole meaning, and we may abstract it in various ways, taking a smaller or larger part of the whole meaning to be thus set over against the rest, and to be labelled, if we like, the poem's 'thought' or 'prose-sense'. Mr. Housman calls it sometimes the 'intellectual content' sometimes simply the 'meaning'. Whatever the name, it is clear both that different readers will, with the same poem, separate different parts of the total meaning as this prose-sense; and that different poems invite different kinds of division in this respect. Sometimes the prose-sense seems to be the source, sometimes a tributary, sometimes a mere bank or dyke for the rest. These variations, from poem to poem, in the place and functions of the prose-sense, thought or 'meaning'—are by far the most accessible and examinable aspects of poetic structure. Yet to these differences the difficulty of 'understanding' poetry seems chiefly due. To understand a poem, in this sense, would be to permit the varied components of its total meaning to take their rightful places within it.

The besetting vice of all criticism is thus described by Coleridge—perhaps more clearly than by any other writer:

We call, for we see and feel, the swan and the dove both transcendently beautiful. As absurd as it would be to institute a comparison between their separate claims to beauty from any abstract rule common to both, without reference to the life and being of the animals themselves—say rather if, having first seen the dove, we abstracted its outlines, gave them a false generalization, called them principle or ideal of bird-beauty and then proceeded to criticize the swan or the eagle—not less absurd is it to pass judgement on the works of a poet on the mere ground that they have been called by the same class-name with the works of other poets of other times and circumstances, or any ground indeed save that of their inappropriateness to their own end and being, their want of significance, as symbol and physiognomy (Raysor, I, 196).

The next step is to explore further the physiology, as it were, of poetry. In what we are apt to regard as the normal standard case, the prose-sense appears to be the source of the rest of our response.

The Curfew tolls the knell of parting day,
   The lowing herd wind slowly o'er the lea,
The plowman homeward plods his weary way,
   And leaves the world to darkness and to me.

Here everything which we need to think of is named by the words and described by the syntax, and any inferences we may add—that the poet is not weary as the ploughman is, or that the death of the day is to be compared with the end of their day of life for those lying in the churchyard—are fully prepared by this prose-sense. And, though it is, of course, merely by a figure of speech that we say that any one kind of component in a total meaning comes *before* another, it is clear that almost all the rest can be properly regarded as dependent from and controlled by the prose-sense here.

Now let us take a different case, Blake's song:

   Memory, hither come,
     And tune your merry notes:
   And, while upon the wind
     Your music floats,
   I'll pore upon the stream,
   Where sighing lovers dream,
   And fish for fancies as they pass
   Within the watery glass.

It is not hard to see that this has in some way a different structure. What is hard—but still must be attempted—is to say without exaggeration how its structure differs.

Some differences may be shown by these observations: that, if we abstract a plain sense from it, what we get is something very unlike, if separately considered, anything we are distinctly aware of in reading the words as poetry; secondly, that what prose-sense we obtain will be to some degree optional, will depend upon how we choose to interpret certain of the words in it. For example, *tune* may be read as 'sing, utter' or as 'accord, bring into order', *the stream* may be the 'mere river' or 'the stream of life, or time', or desire, and *glass* may show merely the translucency of the water or turn it into an image-making reflection of things, as with a crystal we gaze into. But still, whatever we get from the poem as its *Sense*—whether, at one extreme, we make it merely an announcement of an intended revery, or, at the other, we load it with symbolic interpretations and make it a commentary on the theme, 'The Temporal the All'—what we get still stands over against the actual whole poetic meaning which any good reader knows as he reads it. The sense, however elaborated, remains something which does not *explain* the poetic meaning as the sense in the lines from the *Elegy* does explain their poetic meaning.

There is another fashion, of course, in which the sense may 'explain' the meaning. If we were asked, for example, 'How did Napoleon do all he did?' and replied, 'Because he was a great man!' our answer would not be an explanation in the stricter sense. But it might be an 'explanation' in the sense of being another way of saying how what he did strikes us as remarkable. Most explanations of poems are perhaps to be regarded as parallel to this, they are comments upon, not accounts of, the total meaning.

Observing this inadequacy or seeming irrelevance of the prose-sense, we shall perhaps be tempted to say that the poem has no sense, no meaning, no intellectual content. The strength of the temptation is shown by the fact that so strict a reader as Mr. Housman—for I have taken this example from him—did very nearly say this. He said (p. 43):

That answers to nothing real; memory's merry notes and the rest are empty phrases, not things to be imagined; the stanza does but entangle the reader in a net of thoughtless delight.

But are there really any 'empty phrases' in it; and is the delight so 'thoughtless' after all? For, granting that no prose-sense we can extract from it is an adequate reflection of it, it is undeniable that all the main words in it have sense. And that their senses are directly relevant to the total meaning is shown by this: that if we change in the least their susceptibility to take certain senses the whole poem collapses. Though experience shows that such experiments are highly resented by some (but any temporary damage to the poem is slight and evanescent in healthy minds) let us try replacing *stream* by *steam*. Or let us read *watery glass* in a sense consonant rather with Bass than with a rivulet. Who will doubt, after such trials, that these words *in the poem* have very definite senses in delicate interaction with those of the other words? But this is not to say that the whole poem derives simply from the articulation of these senses (as was almost the case with Gray); that would be to go too far in the opposite direction. The senses of the words here come to them as much from their feelings (to use this term as a convenient abbreviation for 'the rest of their powers upon us') as their feelings come from their senses. The interchange here seems nearly equal. But even in a case where feeling wholly dominates sense, it would not be true to say that the words, if they did receive some sense from feeling, were empty phrases. And cases where no sense, by whatever means, is given to the words, are extremely rare if indeed they occur at all. Of course, to use a sense in our reading is not the same thing as to be aware in reflection that we are doing so.

Not until we have set aside these two opposite misconceptions: that the whole meaning of a poem is or should be always simply derivative from its articulated prose-sense (if it has one): and that it can consist (for any length) of 'empty phrases'; can we examine poetic structures with any hope of discovering what may be happening.

Of the two errors the second is, at present, by far the most probable. It derives from that ambiguity of the word 'meaning' which leads us to suppose that if a poem has no articulated prose-sense (or none of independent importance) it has no meaning—confusing this narrower use with a wider use of 'meaning'. In the wider sense there are no meaningless poems, as, in the nar-

rower sense, there are few meaningless words, even in the least articulated poems.

Blake's song, more perhaps even than most songs, is *dramatic*. That is, someone other than the poet is speaking (or the poet as other than the man.) To take a long shot in a field to which guesses only are admitted, the melancholy Jacques is speaking. For is not this song a quintessence of *As You Like It*, as *The Mad Song* is of the Storm Scene of *King Lear*, or Mr. de la Mare's *Mad Prince's Song* is of *Hamlet*? However this may be, some poems are obviously more dramatic than others. By some we are invited to identify their voices with their authors'; others lend a character to or take one from other spokesmen yet others, transcending personality seem utterable only by

> Miracle, bird or golden handiwork.

Behind these large and apparent differences hosts of contributory and derivative microscopic changes of structure may well be suspected. For example, so abstruse a poem as Mr. Yeats' magnificent *Byzantium*[3] might, if we were to take Mr. Yeats to be speaking—and if the poem had not passed 'into the artifice of eternity'—challenge us to request explanations. But since the Superhuman, the Death-in-Life and Life-in-Death, is speaking, if we cannot 'understand' it, there will be no help for us from less authorities. The impersonality should there protect us from the impertinences and pedantries of our lesser selves.

All poetry (as all utterances) can of course be looked on as dramatic; but some poems more invite such reading than others and when so read are best understood. For example, Hopkins is most often non-dramatic, he speaks for himself. Mr. Eliot's poems, on the other hand, are almost always dramatic. It is evident that if we simply and uniformly

---

[3] I agree with Mr. Eliot, *The Use of Poetry*, p. 140 that in *Science and Poetry* I did not properly appreciate Mr. Yeats' later work. I can plead that I wrote before *The Tower* was published.

identify with the poet all poetry not plainly labelled 'Dramatic' we shall perpetrate much misreading—especially with modern poets. This is so patent that I am almost ashamed to write it, and I sympathize with my reader if it irks him; but such points cannot be taken for granted when critics of repute complain, for example, that Mr. Eliot is far too young a man to compare himself with an 'aged eagle' (*Ash Wednesday*), or that he actually wishes to be a live lobster,[4] or that, since he is self-confessed a Hollow Man, 'headpiece stuffed with straw', no one should pay attention to him. And if these points of structure are so misconceived it will not be surprising if over-simple views prevail on finer points.

Many such critical preconceptions can be traced to mistaken endeavours to exalt poetry. 'It should come from the heart,' *i.e.* the poet is unpacking his heart in words. Or 'The more mysterious its action, the finer it probably is', *i.e.* explanation is belittling. This last seems often to favour the neglect of the prose-sense of poetry even when it is perfectly plain and evidently active in the meaning. A curious, but not uncommon, case is when the evident sense is accepted in the poetic reading but denied in the account afterwards given of it. I choose my example from Mr. Housman (*The Name and Nature of Poetry*, p. 46).

In these six simple words of Milton:
Nymphs and shepherds, dance no more—
What is it that can draw tears, as I know it can, to the eyes of more readers than one? What in the world is there to cry about? Why have the mere words the physical effect of pathos when the sense of the passage is blithe and gay? I can only say, because they are poetry, and find their way to something in man which is obscure and latent, something older than the present organization of his nature, like the patches of fen which still linger here and there in the drained lands of Cambridgeshire.

4 *Prufrock:*
    I should have been a pair of ragged claws
      Scuttling across the floors of silent seas
—it should be a crab, I think, for crabs go sideways, which is the point.

Surely there is much more to say than this? Are these words really inexplicable in their effect or even at all hard to explain? And is 'the sense of the passage' really 'blithe and gay'? To say so, seems to me to overlook all the force of the words 'no more'. Lear's 'Thou'lt come no more' is the supreme instance. As Shenstone remarked (in 1761): "the words 'no more' have a singular pathos reminding us at once of past pleasure and the future exclusion of it." And the Nymphs and Shepherds that Milton pretends are going now to dance in England; we know, as he knew, that it is a pretence, that they have vanished; all that is over; and the dances in his *Masque* are no substitutes. Is the line lessened if we notice this? Is it not better to recognize that words work in intelligible (if intricate) ways than to appeal to a modern taste for primitiveness? And yet this very appeal has here taken a form which inversely reflects the very sense Milton put into his line.

While I am at this point, let me demur to one other implication in Mr. Housman's treatment. Of Blake's

Hear the voice of the Bard!

he says, "that mysterious grandeur would be less grand if it were less mysterious; if the embryo ideas which are all that it contains should endue form and outline, and suggestion condense itself into thought."
'Embryo ideas' would be undeveloped ideas. There is a slighting implication in this description of them, whether or no we recall Milton's list of the destined contents of Limbo:

Embryos, and Idiots, Eremits and Friers
White, Black and Grey, with all their
    trumperie.

An embryo is at least a piteous and helpless thing, and commonly a parasite. And it is not certain at all here that the thought is dependent. Is it not equally likely that the ideas from which this poem derives its mysterious gran-

deur are not less but more fully developed as we receive them in the poem?
I would suggest seriously that in the
greater poems of great poets the ideas
there brought into being in the mind
are completer, not less complete; and
that the process which extricates them
by abstraction denatures them rather
than develops them. The extracted abstract doctrine (if we arrive at any such)
is a skeleton of the living knowledge,
deformed and schematized for the legitimate purposes of comparison (as
well as for the irrelevant purposes of
argument). In the poem they are autonomous, sanctioned by their acceptability to the whole being of the reader.
Out of the poem, they are doctrine
merely, and a temptation to dispute.

But this perhaps is not so different as
it seems from something Mr. Housman
may have been implying. I have wished
only to protest, on Blake's behalf,
against an arrogant 'intellectualist' assumption that the word 'embryo' *may*
introduce. Blake knew what he was
doing when he wrote about these things
in verse, not prose. But we do not know
what he was doing if we think he was
not speaking—for and to the whole
man, not the abstractive analytic intellect only—about the most important
things in the world,

Of what is past, or passing, or to come.

To return to the division of the *way*
and the *whither*; however we divide
them, whether we make thoughts the
way to the rest of the poem, or the rest
of it the way to the thought—we shall,
if we put the value of the poem either
in the way or the whither, for most
poems misconceive it. We may *read*
them aright but we shall describe them
wrongly. No great matter in itself perhaps; but, as we may see, these errors
are small-scale models for enormous
evils. As we habitually mistake our lesser
myths, so we warp our world-picture by
attempting amiss to 'understand' it, or
by denying it all intelligibility, all meaning, because it lacks a certain sub-variety
of meaning in the place in which we

crave it. And, as with poetry, so with
every mode of the mythopoeic activity
by which we live, shape universes to live
in, reshape, inquire, in a thousand varying ways, seek

                          patiently to bend
Our mind to sifting reason, and clear light
That strangely figured in our soul doth wend,
Shifting its forms, still playing in our sight
Till something it present that we shall take for
    right.[5]

We wrong it and thus ourselves if we
take, as its 'point', some singled-out
component only and disregard the rest.
Yet having done this, by tradition, so
long, we must now by conscious reflection compare the structures of different
kinds of experience as of different kinds
of poetry. Tradition, never really very
successful in this, can no longer teach
us even what it could—now that we live
in a confluence of so many and such
different streams. Our remedy, if we are
not increasingly to misunderstand one
another (thus misunderstanding ourselves), is the dangerous one of analysis
but it is dangerous only when we take
the divisions we make as established
insurmountably in the order of things
and not as introduced to assist us to
compare.

What I have been urging as to the
opposition of the 'thing said' and the
'way of saying it' holds good, I think, of
every other division we may make in
comparing the structure of poems. They
are useful if we do not then segregate
the value of the poem into some com
partment thus created. To do so is like
saying that the point of an elephant is
his strength. (See Coleridge's remark
about the dove and the swan, cited
above.) Apart from some forms of ap
plied poetry—some satires or some de
votional poems for example—poetr
has no whither as opposed to a way
As Coleridge said in his description of
'just poem' (*B. L.*, II, II):

The reader should be carried forward, n
merely or chiefly by the mechanical impul
of curiosity, or a restless desire to arrive at t

5 Henry More, *Song of the Soul.*

inal solution; but by the pleasurable activity of mind excited by the attractions of the journey itself.

With the best poetry there is nowhere to arrive, no final solution. The poem is no ticket to the Fortunate Isles, or even to Purgatory, or even to Moscow. The journey is its own end, and it will not, by having no destination, any less assist the world to become what Moscow should be.

Poems which have a destination, a final solution—whether it be the enunciation of a supposed truth, or suasion to a policy, or the attainment of an end-state of consciousness, or some temporary or permanent exclusive attitude to the world, to society, or to the self, have only a subordinate value. Instead of establishing, as the best poetry does, the norms of value, they have to be judged by standards more inclusive than themselves—a consideration very relevant to the supposed 'difficulty' of much good poetry where this difficulty is conceived as an objection to it. As Coleridge put it:

The elder languages were fitter for poetry because they expressed only prominent ideas with clearness, the others but darkly. . . . Poetry gives most pleasure when only generally and not perfectly understood. It was so by me with Gray's "Bard" and Collins' Odes. The "Bard" once intoxicated me, and now I read without pleasure. From this cause it is that that I call metaphysical poetry gives me so much delight (*Anima Poetae*, p. 5).

'The elder languages' I take, perhaps arbitrarily, to be 'Elizabethan' English, for example; and 'prominent ideas' are not necessarily the most important.

It would be extremely interesting to know just what Coleridge included in 'what I call metaphysical poetry' here. It was not what Johnson and others have called by that name, Cowley being excluded but not Donne, and much of Wordsworth, almost undoubtedly, being added. 'Only generally and not perfectly understood' is a phrase full of dangers, of course. Shift the sense of 'understood' only a little and it is an excuse

for every vague, undisciplined and erratic type of reading, for the merest misty indulgence in unformed 'sentimental' revery. But no one who knows his Coleridge will suppose that he meant this. What he is pointing to is the superiority of the characteristic Shakespearian structure of meaning over the characteristic later eighteenth-century structures, or of Blake's over Southey's. And we may equally take him as pointing to the superiority of the poetic structures used by Mr. Yeats in his recent poetry, in his best poetry by Mr. Eliot, by Mr. Auden or Mr. Empson at their best, or by Hopkins—very different though these structures are—their superiority to, let us say, the characteristic structures used by Rupert Brooke or the chief representatives of 'Georgian Poetry'. The point of contrast can be put shortly by saying that Rupert Brooke's verse, in comparison with Mr. Eliot's, has no *inside*. Its ideas and other components, however varied, are all expressed with prominence; lovely though the display may be, it is a display, the reader is visiting an Exhibition of Poetic Products.

An idea which is expressed 'but darkly' need be neither a dim nor a vague one—but it will be one which we have to look for. It is sometimes thought that this very process of 'looking into' a poem is destructive of the poetic virtue. But whether this is so of course depends upon how we 'look in'—upon what sort of a process this is. Certainly the detective intelligence, or the Cross-word Puzzler's technique, are not proper methods in reading poetry. Something resembling them was, perhaps, a suitable mode of preparation for reading some of Mr. Eliot's earlier poems, *Burbank* or *A Cooking Egg* or some parts of *The Waste Land* for example. Those who went through it, however, found that what they thus discovered—though its discovery may have been necessary for them—was no essential part of the poetry when this came to life. That it can nearly all be forgotten without loss to the poetry, shows perhaps that it was scaffolding for the poet, as well as for the reader. But apart altogether from this play of extrinsic explicit conjecture, there is another way of 'looking into' abstruse poetry—a receptive submission, which will perhaps *be reflected* in conjectures but into which inferences among these conjectures do not enter. For example, the differences between the opening lines of the first and last sections of Mr. Eliot's *Ash Wednesday*:

> Because I do not hope to turn again

and

> Although I do not hope to turn again

in their joint context and their coterminous subcontexts, will come into full being for very few readers without movements of exploration and resultant ponderings that I should not care to attempt to reflect in even the most distant prose translation. And yet these very movements—untrackable as they perhaps are, and uninducible as they almost certainly are by any other words—are the very life of the poem. In these searchings for meanings of a certain sort its being consists. The poem is a quest, and its virtue is not in anything said by it, or in the way in which it is said, or in a meaning which is found, or even in what is passed by in the search. For in this poem—to quote two lines from Coleridge's *Constancy to an Ideal Object* which is a meditation on the same theme—as in so much of the later poetry of Mr. Yeats,

> like strangers sheltering from a storm
> Hope and Despair meet in the porch of Death.

And though from their encounter comes

> strength beyond hope or despair
> Climbing the third stair

there is no account, in other terms than those of poetry, to be given of how it comes. Again the resemblance to the symbolism of Mr. Yeats' *The Winding Stair* is of more than slight or accidental

interest. Is it not remarkable that not only Mr. Yeats, in his later poetry, and Mr. Eliot in his public penances for the sins of every generation,

> Now at this birth season of decease

but Mr. Auden also,

> O watcher in the dark, you wake
> Our dream of waking,

Mr. Empson, with his

> So Semele desired her Deity

and D. H. Lawrence, in all his last poetry,

> Turning to death as I turn to beauty

should be 'thus devoted, concentrated in purpose'?

When Mr. Eliot discusses, in prose the place of meanings in poetry and the bearing of false expectations about them on this alleged 'difficulty' of modern poetry, what he says, though very helpful, needs to be read with a lively awareness of the ambiguities of the word *meaning* and a clear understanding of the narrowed sense in which he is using it. I will quote the whole passage in which he discusses these points:

The difficulty of poetry (and modern poetry is supposed to be difficult) may be due to one of several reasons. First, there may be personal causes which make it impossible for a poet to express himself in any but an obscure way; while this may be regrettable, we should be glad, I think, that the man has been able to express himself at all. Or difficulty may be due just to novelty: we know the ridicule accorded in turn to Wordsworth, Shelley and Keats, Tennyson and Browning—but must remark that Browning was the first to be *called* difficult; hostile critics of the earlier poets found them difficult, but called them silly. Or difficulty may be caused by the reader's having been told, or having suggested to himself, that the poem is going to prove difficult. The ordinary reader, when warned against the obscurity of a poem, is apt to be thrown into a state of consternation very unfavourable to poetic receptivity. Instead of beginning, as he should, in a state of sensitivity, he obfuscates his senses by the desire to be clever and to look very hard for something, he doesn't know what—or else by the desire not to be taken in. There is such a thing as stage fright, but what such readers have is pit or gallery fright. The more seasoned reader, he who has reached, in these matters, a state of greater *purity*, does not bother about understanding; not, at least, at first. I know that some of the poetry to which I am most devoted is poetry which I did not understand at first reading; some is poetry which I am not sure I understand yet: for instance, Shakespeare's. And finally, there is the difficulty caused by the author's having left out something which the reader is used to finding; so that the reader, bewildered, gropes about for what is absent, and puzzles his head for a kind of 'meaning' which is not there, and is not meant to be there.

The chief use of the 'meaning' of a poem, in the ordinary sense, may be (for here again I am speaking of some kinds of poetry and not all) to satisfy one habit of the reader, to keep his mind diverted and quiet, while the poem does its work upon him: much as the imaginary burglar is always provided with a bit of nice meat for the house-dog. This is a normal situation of which I approve. But the minds of all poets do not work that way; some of them, assuming that there are other minds like their own, become impatient of this 'meaning' which seems superfluous, and perceive possibilities of intensity through its elimination.

The 'state of consternation', it may be remarked, wears off quickly for most readers—for those readers at least who would be likely, if not handicapped by it, to 'understand' the poem in the end. And the *purer* reader, if he does not, in one sense, 'bother about understanding' is still, in another sense, occupied with nothing else. But the modes of understanding are as many and as varied as the structures of meanings.

If we turn now from the mere recognition that no prepossessions that we can form can *prescribe* a structure for the meanings in poetry—and yet every poem is a fabric of meaning—a recognition to which Coleridge's account of Imagination inevitably leads us; and from the speculative analysis of the possibilities of diverse poetic structures—a

task for the criticism of the future—to speculations upon the causes of changes in the structures most employed by poets of successive generations and from these to an attempt to divine the general direction of these changes, we shall find further reasons for thinking that Coleridge's 'philosophic' approach to criticism is helpful.

That there has been a general drift in human interests in the West through the last four centuries—in the modes of our current mythology and in the functions of its parts—is hardly to be doubted. It shows itself in innumerable ways: in the growth of Science and History, in our changing attitudes to Authority in all its forms, to the Bible, to Tradition (as a body of truth to be received because of its source), to custom (to be accepted because established), to parental opinion. . . . It shows itself conspicuously in the philosophic movement from Descartes to Kant and on again to modern pragmatism and dialectic materialism; less conspicuously perhaps in the change from Locke's psychology to Freud's; less conspicuously still in the widespread increase in the aptitude of the average mind for self-dissolving introspection, the generally heightened awareness of the goings on of our own minds, merely *as goings on*, not as transitions from one well-known and linguistically recognized moral or intellectual condition to another. And together with this last (it is an aspect of the same change) it shows itself in the startling enhancement of our interest in the *sensory* detail and *nuance* of the visible scene as opposed to the practically useful information about things which these perceptions can give us.

In these last modifications of consciousness we may see more clearly and less debatably than with the others what has been happening. They witness to a change in the focus of what Coleridge called 'the primary imagination . . . the living Power and prime Agent of all human Perception' (*B. L.*, I, 202) and are clearly enough reflected in those activities of character-drawing and description which are so large a part of the work of the 'secondary imagination' of the Novelist. I have in view a very obvious contrast between the modes of depicting both character and the landscape practised by the best seventeenth- and eighteenth-century writers and the best modern novelists. George Moore somewhere in *Avowals*, wishing to say something derogatory of *Tom Jones*, described it, if memory serves me, as 'an empty book without a glimpse of the world without or a hint of the world within'. The remark is perfectly true. There is neither an outer nor an inner world in *Tom Jones* as these are to be found in the work of modern novelists. We can hunt through it in vain to find either a scene described primarily in terms of its appearance, or however short a stretch of the 'stream of consciousness' given with the sensuous detail that any of a dozen modern writers could give it for us. And what is true of Fielding is true, with very rare exceptions, of all the greater seventeenth- and eighteenth-century writers. Defoe, for example, though he has plenty of descriptions, is never interested in the appearances of things for the sake of the appearances themselves or the reverberations of their *sensory* qualities in the percipient's mind. He is interested in the things and their condition, the help or hindrance they can be to man. To turn from his accounts of Crusoe's seashore to Mr. Joyce's description of Sandymount strand is to realize how great a change in man's interests (and perhaps in his perceptions themselves) has occurred. And to turn from Crusoe's moralizing self-examinations to those of Stephen Dedalus is to notice the same change. As Crusoe's eyes, looking outwards, see things where Stephen's see symbols of his own moods; so, when he looks into his own heart he finds a clear-cut world of hopes and fears, doubts and faiths—complex indeed but as well defined in their interrelations as chessmen. There is no uncertainty as to which movements belong to which side. But Stephen's inner world is as phantasmagoric as his outer, being composed

of images which shift and flow and merge with an intricacy beyond the survey of any moral principles and too subtle to be described in the terms o any hitherto conceived psychology. The nomenclature of the faculties, of the virtues and the vices, of the passions, o the moods, the whole machinery through which self-examination with a view to increased order could be conducted by Defoe, has lapsed.

We may suspect, with Coleridge, that for some time it has been no such loss as it may appear; and that some dissolu tion of it must precede a reconstruction

The "King And No King" too, is extremel spirited in all its Characters; Arbaces holds up a Mirror to all Men of Virtuous Principles but violent Passions: hence he is, as it were, at once Magnanimity and Pride, Patience and Fury, Gentleness and Rigor, Chastity and In cest, and is one of the finest Mixtures of Vir tues and Vices that any Poet has drawn, &c (*Preface to Seward's Edition of Beaumon and Fletcher*, 1750).

"These," Coleridge comments, "ar among the endless instances of the abject state to which psychology had sunk from the reign of Charles I to the middle of the present reign of George III; and even now it is but just awak ing." As chief awakener, he can speak with authority. Since his time the dis solution has gone further. The ol vocabulary, from being a framework indispensable, but not necessarily suffi cient, for orientation, has become a mere supply of words which, because of their past history, can be used as tinc tures in the composition of states o mind to which none of them apply.

We are apt to regard this change as a great new conquest of literature ove the unexplored land of ordinary human consciousness, overlooking perhaps the other possibility that ordinary human consciousness may not, until recently have had a form which could be thus represented. And we are ready to ac claim the descriptions of the visibl scene which Katherine Mansfield, Stell Benson or Virginia Woolf can give u as showing a subtlety in the observatio of its sensory aspects and their emotional significance which is disappointingly absent in earlier writers. On one interpretation of the change, they have improved the descriptive technique of prose, have caught something always present which writers in the past could not (or did not wish to) catch; on another interpretation something new in the modes of perception has come into being for them to describe. The two accounts are not perhaps so opposed as they may seem, and I have no desire to decide between them. On either account man's interest in his own consciousness, whether of things without him or of the movements of his own mind, has changed, and with it the mode of an important part of his mythology.

That this change should show itself most clearly in prose is to be expected. For such prose as Mr. Joyce's or Mrs. Woolf's is a dilution (or better, an expansion, 'like gold to ayery thinnesse beate') of a use of words that has in most ages been within the range of poetry. What is new is the composition of whole books with meanings of a structure which in poetry is found only in phrases or single lines supported by quite other structures. And these other structures are strengthened by just those other components which George Moore overlooked in reading *Tom Jones*. Empty though it is of 'glimpses of the world without or hints of the world within' it contains judgment, a moral order, and action, with all that these entail. It contains *ideas*, not as stimulants to revery and whimsy, but as assured forms of mental activity with which coherent purpose may be maintained. And though, as we have seen with the ideas (or doctrines) that may be extracted from Coleridge's Wind Harp image, we must not identify the abstracted idea with the idea *in* the poem, yet ideas in the completeness they have in poetry are commonly main components in its structure. *Tom Jones*, of course, is not a poem; but the components which enter into its prose-fabric and give it its power are of kinds which do not enter into *Jacob's Room* or *Ulysses*; and,

otherwise disposed and interrelated, they are more essential parts of the structure of great poetry than those which do. For these are, as Coleridge would say, only 'the rudiments of imagination's power'.

The dissolution of consciousness exhibited in such prose, at its best as much as in merely imitative writing, forces the task of reconstituting a less relaxed, a less adventitious order for the mind upon contemporary poetry. There can be no question of a return to any mythologic structures prevailing before the seventeenth century. The depth of the changes that then took place (they are described with admirable detachment and clarity in Mr. Basil Willey's *The Seventeenth Century Background*) prevents return. Poetry can no more go back on its past than a man can.

But the waning of any one mode of order—a traditional morality, or a religious sanction or symbolization for it —is not the loss of all possibilities of order. The traditional schemas by which man gave an account of himself and the world in which he lived were made by him, and though they have lost their power to help him as they formerly helped him, he has not lost his power to make new ones. It is easy to represent what has been occurring as a course of error, as due to the pernicious influence of arrogant science, or of Cartesianism or of Rousseau; as an infection of the mind by 'heresies', or as departure from a norm to which, if man is to become again a noble animal, he must return. Dramas in which the proper balance of our faculties has been destroyed by exorbitant claims from one or other of them, in which science displaces religious belief, or sentiment ousts reason, or dreams cloud Reality,

> What will be forever
> What was from of old,

—by corruption from which disasters we now wander, a lost generation, in a wrecked universe—are not hard to invent.

> It was man did it, man
> Who imagined imagination;
> And he did what man can
> He uncreated creation

as Mr. R. G. Eberhart exclaimed. But these dramatic pictures of our predicament are utterances of distress. Though they may sometimes pretend to be diagnoses, they are myths reflecting our unease. What they profess to describe is too vast a matter to be handled by that other system of myths (those of Science and History) to which diagnoses belong, and in which verification is possible. And as philosophic myths they are not of the kind which contribute directly to a new order. For the concepts they use belong to the order which has passed, and they are disqualified by the movement they describe. It is better, as an alternative philosophic myth, to suppose that the great drift is not due merely to internal conflicts between sub-orders of our mythology but rather to an inevitable growth of human awareness—inevitable because time goes on and he retains, in recent centuries, increasing touch with his past.

To put the burden of constituting an order for our minds on the poet may seem unfair. It is not the philosopher, however, or the moralist who puts it on him, but birth. And it is only another aspect of the drift by which knowledge in all its varieties—scientific, moral, religious—has come to seem a vast mythology with its sub-orders divided according to their different pragmatic sanctions, that the poet should thus seem to increase so inordinately in importance. (There is a figure of speech here, of course, for the burden is not on individual poets but upon the poetic function. With Homer, Dante and Shakespeare in mind, however, the importance of the single poet is not to be under-estimated.) For while any part of the world-picture is regarded as not of mythopoeic origin, poetry—earlier recognized as mythopoeic—could not but be given a second place. If philosophic contemplation, or religious experience, or science gave us Reality, then poetry gave us something of less consequence, at best some sort of shadow. If we grant that all is myth, poetry, as the myth-making which most brings 'the whole soul of man into activity' (*B. L.*, II, 12), and as working with words, 'parts and germinations of the plant' and, through them, in 'the medium by which spirits communicate with one another' (*B. L.*, I, 168) becomes the necessary channel for the reconstitution of order.

But this last phrase is tainted also with a picturesque mock-desperate dramatization of our situation. The mind has never been in order. There is no vanished perfection of balance to be restored. The great ages of poetry have mostly been times torn by savage and stupid dissension, intolerant, unreasonable, and confused in other aspects of human endeavour.

> Allas, allas! now may men wepe and crye!
> For in our dayes nis but covetyse
> And doublenesse, and tresoun and envye,
> Poysoun, manslauhtre, and mordre in sondry
>   wyse.

In all this our own age may be preparing to emulate them; but that is no more a reason to anticipate a new great age for poetry than the new possibility of a material paradise now offered by science is a reason for thinking that the day of poetry is over. Eras that produced no poetry that is remembered have been as disordered as ours. There are better reasons, in the work of modern poets, to hope that a creative movement is beginning and that poetry, freed from a mistaken conception of its limitations and read more discerningly than heretofore, will remake our minds and with them our world. Such an estimate of the power of poetry may seem extravagant; but it was Milton's no less than Shelley's, Blake's or Wordsworth's. It has been the opinion of many with whom we need not be ashamed to agree: "The study of poetry (if we will trust Aristotle) offers to mankind a certain rule, and pattern, of living well and happily; disposing us to all civil offices of society. If we will believe

Tully, it nourisheth and instructeth our youth; delights our age; adorns our prosperity; comforts our adversity; entertains us at home . . . insomuch as the widest and best learned have thought her the absolute mistress of manners, and nearest of kin to virtue." Ben Jonson here may merely be repeating commonplaces from antiquity; he may be writing a set piece without concern for what he is saying—but this is unlikely; he may not have been aware of the reasons for such opinions; they were left for Coleridge to display; but he was certainly well placed to judge whether they were creditable opinions or not. Neither the authorities he cites, nor 'this robust, surly, and observing dramatist' himself, may be thought insufficiently acquainted with ordinary lives, or with the forces that may amend them.

Poetry may have these powers and yet, for removable and preventable causes, the study of poetry be of no great use to us. A candid witness must declare, I fear, that its benefits are often unobtrusive where we would most expect them. But the study of poetry, for those born in this age, is more arduous than we suppose. It is therefore rare. Many other things pass by its name and are encouraged to its detriment.

To free it from distracting trivialities, from literary chit-chat, from discussion of form which does not ask what has the form, from flattening rationalization, from the clouds of unchecked sensibility and unexamined interpretations is a minor duty of criticism. But there is a more positive task: to recall that poetry is the supreme use of language, man's chief co-ordinating instrument, in the service of the most integral purposes of life; and to explore, with thoroughness, the intricacies of the modes of language as working modes of the mind.

The sage may teach a doctrine without words; but, if so, it is a doctrine about another world than ours and for another life. Our world and our life have grown and taken what order they have for us through separated meanings which we can only hold together or keep apart through words. The sage may avoid words because our power of controlling certain kinds of meaning through them is too slight; but without the use of words in the past he would have had no doctrine to teach. The meanings sufficient for the dumb creatures are not enough for man.

Because all objects which we can name or otherwise single out—the simplest objects of the senses and the most recondite entities that speculation can conjecture, the most abstract constructions of the intellect and the most concrete aims of passion alike—are projections of man's interests; because the Universe as it is known to us is a fabric whose forms, as we can alone know them, have arisen in and through reflection; and because that reflection, whether made by the intellect in science or by 'the whole soul of man' in poetry, has developed through language—and, apart from language, can neither be continued nor maintained—the study of the modes of language becomes, as it attempts to be thorough, the most fundamental and extensive of all inquiries. It is no preliminary or preparation for other profounder studies, which though they use language more or less trustfully, may be supposed to be autonomous, uninfluenced by verbal processes. The very formation of the objects which these studies propose to examine takes place through the processes (of which imagination and fancy are modes) by which the words they use acquire their meanings.

Criticism is the science of these meanings and the meanings which larger groups of words may carry. It is no mere account of what men have written or how they have written it, taken as questions to be judged by borrowed standards or to be asked without inquiry into the little that we can yet surmise about the growth of the mind and therewith the expansion of our outlook on the world.

Thus the more traditional subjects of criticism, Coleridge's differentiation of imagination from fancy, and his still abstruser ponderings on objectification and the living word, unite with the analysis of the ambiguities and confusions that are overt or latent in all cases of metaphor, transference or projection to form one study. It is embryonic still, through which its possibilities are the less restricted. It offers little intellectual rest or satisfaction; but should we look for satisfaction here where all the problems meet? What it does offer is an immense opportunity for improving our technique of understanding.

With Coleridge we step across the threshold of a general theoretical study of language capable of opening to us new powers over our minds comparable to those which systematic physical inquiries are giving us over our environment. The step across was of the same type as that which took Galileo into the modern world. It requires the shift from a preoccupation with the What and Why to the How of language. The problems of Poetry became for Coleridge, sometimes, interesting as problems with a structure of their own. They ceased to be mere voids waiting to be filled. The interest shifted from the answers to the questions; and, with that, a new era for criticism began. Beyond the old tasks of reaffirming ancient conclusions and defending them from foolish interpretations, an illimitable field of work has become accessible.

The change would have been delayed if Coleridge had not been a philosopher as well as a critic. And it has this consequence, that critics in the future must have a theoretical equipment of a kind which has not been felt to be necessary in the past. (So physicists may at times sigh for the days in which less mathematics was required by them.) But the critical equipment will not be *primarily* philosophical. It will be rather a command of the methods of general linguistic analysis. As the theory of Poetry develops, what is needed will be disengaged from philosophy much as the methodology of physics has been disengaged.

I have tried here to further this development by presenting Coleridge's Theory of Imagination for more detailed consideration than it has hitherto received, and by adding suggestions towards extensions of his method of analysis. These must perhaps await fuller exposition before they become effective. But, with the history of opinions on Coleridge before us, it seemed but just that an account of his work should be attempted before new derivations from it again obscure our debt.

ARTHUR O. LOVEJOY

(1873-1962)

A member of the faculty of Philosophy at The Johns Hopkins University until his retirement in 1938, Arthur O. Lovejoy is an important figure in modern historical and critical thought for his contribution to establishing the "history of ideas" as a type of study appropriate to several of the traditional humanistic disciplines. His work has stimulated close attention to works and writers of secondary importance for the purpose of establishing the background of assumption informing the work of major writers. Lovejoy's studies, and the type of intellectual inquiry they represent, have been particularly fruitful in the investigation of homogeneous ranges or periods of literature that are not pervaded by overtly institutionalized orders of belief—for example, American literature and eighteenth century English literature. Lovejoy's main work is contained in *The Great Chain of Being* (1936) and *Essays in the History of Ideas* (1948).

On the Discrimination of Romanticisms[1] (1924)

I

We approach a centenary not, perhaps, wholly undeserving of notice on the part of this learned company. It was apparently in 1824 that those respected citizens of La-Ferté-sous-Jouarre, MM. Dupuis and Cotonet, began an enterprise which was to cause them, as is recorded, "twelve years of suffering," and to end in disillusionment—the enterprise of discovering what Romanticism is, by collecting definitions and characterizations of it given by eminent authorities. I conjecture, therefore, that one of the purposes of the Committee in inviting me to speak on this subject was perhaps to promote a Dupuis and Cotonet Centennial Exhibition, in which the later varieties of definitions of Romanticism, the fruit of a hundred years' industry on the part of literary critics and professors of modern literature, might be at least in part displayed. Certainly there is no lack of material; the contemporary collector of such articles, while paying tribute to the assiduity and the sufferings of those worthy pioneers of a century ago, will chiefly feel an envious sense of the relative simplicity of their task. He will find, also, that the apparent incongruity of the senses in which the term is employed has fairly kept pace with their increase in number; and that the singular po-

tency which the subject has from the first possessed to excite controversy and breed divisions has in no degree diminished with the lapse of years.

For if some Dupuis of to-day were to gather, first, merely a few of the more recent accounts of the origin and age of Romanticism, he would learn from M. Lassere[2] and many others that Rousseau was the father of it; from Mr. Russell[3] and Mr. Santayana[4] that the honor of paternity might plausibly be claimed by Immanuel Kant; from M. Seillière that its grandparents were Fénelon and Madame Guyon;[5] from Professor Babbitt that its earliest well-identified forebear was Francis Bacon;[6] from Mr. Gosse that it originated in the bosom of the Reverend Joseph Warton;[7] from the late Professor Ker that it had "its beginnings in the seventeenth-century" or a little earlier, in such books as "the *Arcadia* or the *Grand Cyrus*";[8] from Mr. J. E. G. de Montmorency that it "was born in the eleventh century, and sprang from that sense of aspiration which runs through the Anglo-French, or rather, the Anglo-Norman Renaissance";[9] from Professor Grierson that St. Paul's "irruption into Greek religious thought and Greek prose" was an essential example of "a romantic movement," though the "first great romantic" was Plato;[10] and from Mr. Charles Whibley that the Odyssey is romantic in its "very texture and essence," but that, with its rival, Romanticism was "born in the

From *Essays in the History of Ideas* by Arthur O. Lovejoy. Copyright 1948 by The Johns Hopkins University Press. Reprinted by permission of The Johns Hopkins University Press.

[1] An address delivered at the fortieth Annual Meeting of the Modern Language Association of America, December 27, 1923; published in *PMLA*, XXXIX (1924), 229-253. The reference in the first paragraph is to Alfred de Musset's *Lettres de Dupuis et Cotonet*, 1836. In reprinting the address a few later definitions or characterizations of "Romanticism" have been added.

[2] *Le Romantisme français* (1919), 141 and *passim*.
[3] *Jour. of Philosophy*, XIX (1922), 645.
[4] *Egotism in German Philosophy*, 11-20, 54-64.
[5] *Mme Guyon et Fénelon précurseurs de Rousseau*, 1918.
[6] "Schiller and Romanticism"; *Mod. Lang. Notes*, XXXVII, 267 (1922), n. 28.
[7] *Proc. Brit. Acad.*, 1915-16, 146-7.
[8] *The Art of Poetry* (1923), 79-80.
[9] *Contemporary Review*, April, 1919, p. 473.
[10] *Classical and Romantic* (1923), 32, 31.

Garden of Eden" and that "the Serpent was the first romantic."[11] The inquirer would, at the same time, find that many of these originators of Romanticism— including both the first and last mentioned, whom, indeed, some contemporaries are unable to distinguish— figure on other lists as initiators or representatives of tendencies of precisely the contrary sort.

These differing versions of the age and lineage of Romanticism are matched by a corresponding diversity in the descriptions offered by those of our time who have given special care to the observation of it. For Professor Ker Romanticism was "the fairy way of writing,"[12] and for Mr. Gosse it is inconsistent with "keeping to the facts";[13] but for Mr. F. Y. Eccles[14] (following M. Pellissier) "the romantic system of ideas" is the direct source of "the realistic error," of the tendency to conceive of psychology as "the dry notation of purely physiological phenomena" and consequently to reduce the novel and the drama to the description of "the automaton-like gestures of *la bête humaine*." To Professor Ker, again, "romantic" implies "reminiscence": "the romantic schools have always depended more or less on the past."[15] Similarly Mr. Geoffrey Scott finds "its most typical form" to be "the cult of the extinct."[16] But Professor Schelling tells us that "the classic temper studies the past, the romantic temper neglects it; . . . it leads us forward and creates new precedents";[17] while for some of the French "Romantic" critics of the 1820s and 1830s, the slogan of the movement was *il faut être de son temps*.[18] Mr. Paul Elmer More defines Romanticism as "the illusion of beholding the infinite within the stream of nature itself, instead of apart from that stream"—in short, as an apotheosis of

the cosmic flux;[19] but a special studen of German Romanticism cites as typica Romantic utterances Friedrich Schlegel' "alles Sichtbare hat nur die Wahrhei einer Allegorie," and Goethe's "alle Vergängliche ist nur ein Gleichnis";[?] and for a recent German author th deepest thing in Romanticism is "ein Religion die dieses Leben hasst . . Romantik will die gerade Verbindun des Menschslichen mit dem Uberir dischen."[21] Among those for whom th word implies, *inter alia*, a social an political ideology and temper, on writer, typical of many, tells us tha "Romanticism spells anarchy in ever domain . . . a systematic hostility t everyone invested with any particle o social authority—husband or *pater familias*, policeman or magistrate, pries or Cabinet minister";[22] but Professo Goetz Briefs finds "the climax of politi cal and economic thought within th Romantic movement" in the doctrine o Adam Müller, which sought to vindicat the sanctity of established social au thority embodied in the family and th state; "by an inescapable logic th Romanticist ideology was drawn int the camp of reaction."[23] From M. Seil lière's most celebrated work it appear that the Romantic mind tends to be af fected with an inferiority-complex, "un impression d'incomplètude, de solitud morale, et presque d'angoisse";[24] fror other passages of the same writer w learn that Romanticism is the "imperia istic" mood, whether in individuals o nations—a too confident assertion of th will-to-power, arising from "the mysti feeling that one's activities have the ad vantages of a celestial alliance."[25] Th function of the human mind which

[11] Editor's Introduction to *Essays in Romantic Literature* by George Wyndham, (1919), p. xxxiii.
[12] *The Art of Poetry*, 79.
[13] *Aspects and Impressions* (1922), 5.
[14] *La Liquidation du Romantisme* (1919), 14 f.
[15] *The Art of Poetry*, 50.
[16] *The Architecture of Humanism* (1914), 39.
[17] *P. M. L. A.*, XIII, 222.
[18] Cf. George Boas in *Journal of Aesthetics*, I (1941), 52-65.

[19] *The Drift of Romanticism* (1913), xiii, 247.
[20] Marie Joachimi, *Die Weltanschauung der Roma tik* (1905), 52.
[21] Julius Bab, *Fortinbras, oder der Kampf des 1 Jahrhunderts mit dem Geiste der Romantik*.
[22] G. Chatterton-Hill, *Contemporary Rev.* (1942 720.
[23] *Journal of the History of Ideas*, II (1941), 279
[24] *Le mal romantique*, 1908, vii.
[25] Cf. R. Gillouin, *Une nouvelle philosophie l'histoire moderne et française*, 1921, 6 ff.; Seillièr *Le péril mystique*, etc., 2-6.

to be regarded as peculiarly "romantic" is for some "the heart as opposed to the head,"[26] for others, "the Imagination, as contrasted with Reason and the Sense of Fact"[27]—which I take to be ways of expressing a by no means synonymous pair of psychological antitheses. Typical manifestations of the spiritual essence of Romanticism have been variously conceived to be a passion for moonlight, for red waistcoats, for Gothic churches, for futurist paintings;[28] for talking exclusively about oneself, for hero-worship, for losing oneself in an ecstatic contemplation of nature.

The offspring with which Romanticism is credited are as strangely assorted as its attributes and its ancestors. It is by different historians—sometimes by the same historians—supposed to have begotten the French Revolution and the Oxford Movement; the Return to Rome and the Return to the State of Nature; the philosophy of Hegel, the philosophy of Schopenhauer, and the philosophy of Nietzsche—than which few other three philosophies more nearly exhaust the rich possibilities of philosophic disagreement; the revival of neo-Platonic mysticism in a Coleridge or an Alcott, the Emersonian transcendentalism, and scientific materialism; Wordsworth and Wilde; Newman and Huxley; the Waverly novels, the *Comédie Humaine*, and *Les Rougon-Macquart*. M. Seillière and Professor Babbitt have been especially active in tracing the progeny of Romanticism in the past century; the extraordinary number and still more extraordinary diversity of the descendants of it discovered by their researches are known to all here, and it therefore suffices to refer to their works for further examples.

All this is a mere hint, a suggestion by means of random samples, of the richness of the collection which might be brought together for our Centennial Exposition. The result is a confusion of

terms, and of ideas, beside which that of a hundred years ago—mind-shaking though it was to the honest inquirers of La-Ferté-sous-Jouarre—seems pure lucidity. The word "romantic" has come to mean so many things that, by itself, it means nothing. It has ceased to perform the function of a verbal sign. When a man is asked, as I have had the honor of being asked, to discuss Romanticism, it is impossible to know what ideas or tendencies he is to talk about, when they are supposed to have flourished, or in whom they are supposed to be chiefly exemplified. Perhaps there are some who think the rich ambiguity of the word not regrettable. In 1824, as Victor Hugo then testified, there were those who preferred to leave *à ce mot de romantique un certain vague fantastique et indéfinissable qui en redouble l'horreur*, and it may be that the taste is not extinct. But for one of the philosopher's trade, at least, the situation is embarrassing and exasperating; for philosophers, in spite of a popular belief to the contrary, are persons who suffer from a morbid solicitude to know what they are talking about.

Least of all does it seem possible, while the present uncertainty concerning the nature and *locus* of Romanticism prevails, to take sides in the controversy which still goes on so briskly with respect to its merits, the character of its general influence upon art and life. To do so would be too much like consenting to sit on a jury to try a criminal not yet identified, for a series of apparently incompatible crimes, before a bench of learned judges engaged in accusing one another of being accessories to whatever mischief has been done. It is to be observed, for example, that Messrs. Lasserre, Seillière, Babbitt and More (to mention no others) are engaged in arguing that something called Romanticism is the chief cause of the spiritual evils from which the nineteenth century and our own have suffered; but that they represent at least three different opinions as to what these evils are and how they are to be reme-

[26] Wernaer, *Romanticism and the Romantic School in Germany*, p. 3.
[27] Neilson, *Essentials of Poetry*, 1912, ch. III.
[28] For the last mentioned, cf. Gosse in *Proc. Brit. Acad.*, 1915-16, 151.

died. M. Lasserre, identifying Romanticism with the essential spirit of the French Revolution, finds the chief cause of our woes in that movement's breach with the past, in its discarding of the ancient traditions of European civilization; and he consequently seeks the cure in a return to an older faith and an older political and social order, and in an abandonment of the optimistic fatalism generated by the idea of progress. M. Seillière, however, holds that "the spirit of the Revolution in that in which it is rational, Stoic, Cartesian, classical . . . is justified, enduring, assured of making its way in the world more and more";[29] and that, consequently, the ill name of Romanticism should be applied to the revolutionary movement only where it has deviated from its true course, in "the social mysticism, the communistic socialism of the present time." He therefore intimates that the school of opinion which M. Lasserre ably represents is itself a variety of Romanticism.[30] But it is equally certain that M. Seillière's own philosophy is one of the varieties of Romanticism defined by Mr. Babbitt and Mr. More; while Mr. Babbitt, in turn, has been declared by more than one of the critics of his last brilliant book, and would necessarily be held by M. Seillière, to set forth therein an essentially Romantic philosophy. Thus Professor Herford says of it (justly or otherwise) that its "temper is not that of a 'positivist' of any school, but of a mystic," and that "it is as foreign to Homer and Sophocles, the exemplars of true classicism if any are, as it is to Aristotle."[31]

What, then, can be done to clear up, or to diminish, this confusion of terminology and of thought which has for a century been the scandal of literary history and criticism, and is still, as it would not be difficult to show, copiously productive of historical errors and of dangerously undiscriminating diagnoses of the moral and aesthetic maladies of our age? The one really radical remedy —namely, that we should all cease talking about Romanticism—is, I fear, certain not to be adopted. It would probably be equally futile to attempt to prevail upon scholars and critics to restrict their use of the term to a single and reasonably well-defined sense. Such a proposal would only be the starting-point of a new controversy. Men, and especially philologists, will doubtless go on using words as they like, however much annoyance they cause philosophers by this unchartered freedom. There are, however, two possible historical inquiries which, if carried out more thoroughly and carefully than has yet been done, would, I think, do much to rectify the present muddle, and would at the same time promote a clearer understanding of the general movement of ideas, the logical and psychological relations between the chief episodes and transitions in modern thought and taste.

One of these measures would be somewhat analogous to the procedure of contemporary psychopathologists in the treatment of certain types of disorder. It has, we are told, been found that some mental disturbances can be cured or alleviated by making the patient explicitly aware of the genesis of his troublesome "complex," i.e., by enabling him to reconstruct those processes of association of ideas through which it was formed. Similarly in the present case, I think, it would be useful to trace the associative processes through which the word "romantic" has attained its present amazing diversity, and consequent uncertainty, of connotation and denotation; in other words, to carry out an adequate semasiological study of the term. For one of the few things certain about Romanticism is that the name of it offers one of the most complicated, fascinating, and instructive of all problems in semantics. It is, in short, a part of the task of the historian of ideas when he applies himself to the study of the thing or things called Romanticism, to render it, if possible, psychologically

---

[29] *Le mal romantique*, xli.

[30] "Il y a même beaucoup de romantique dans la façon dont le combattent certains traditionalistes imprudents, dont M. Lasserre paraît avoir quelquefois écouté les suggestions dangereuses" (*loc. cit.*).

[31] *Essays and Studies by Members of the English Association*, VIII (1923).

ntelligible how such manifold and dis-
crepant phenomena have all come to
receive one name. Such an analysis
would, I am convinced, show us a large
mass of purely verbal confusions opera-
ive as actual factors in the movement
of thought in the past century and a
quarter; and it would, by making these
confusions explicit, make it easier to
avoid them.

But this inquiry would in practice,
for the most part, be inseparable from
a second, which is the remedy that I
wish, on this occasion, especially to
recommend. The first step in this second
mode of treatment of the disorder is
that we should learn to use the word
"Romanticism" in the plural. This, of
course, is already the practice of the
more cautious and observant literary
historians, in so far as they recognize
that the "Romanticism" of one country
may have little in common with that of
another, and at all events ought to be
defined in distinctive terms. But the discrimination of the Romanticisms which
have in mind is not solely or chiefly
a division upon lines of nationality or
language. What is needed is that any
study of the subject should begin with a
recognition of a *prima-facie* plurality of
Romanticisms, of possibly quite distinct
thought-complexes, a number of which
may appear in one country. There is no
hope of clear thinking on the part of
the student of modern literature, if—as,
alas! has been repeatedly done by eminent writers—he vaguely hypostatizes
the term, and starts with the presumption that "Romanticism" is the heaven-
appointed designation of some single
real entity, or type of entities, to be
found in nature. He must set out from
the simple and obvious fact that there
are various historic episodes or movements to which different historians of
our own or other periods have, for one
reason or another, given the name.
There is a movement which began in
Germany in the seventeen-nineties—
the only one which has an indisputable
title to be called Romanticism, since it
invented the term for its own use. There
is another movement which began

pretty definitely in England in the
seventeen-forties. There is a movement
which began in France in 1801. There
is another movement which began in
France in the second decade of the century, is linked with the German movement, and took over the German name.
There is the rich and incongruous collection of ideas to be found in Rousseau. There are numerous other things
called Romanticism by various writers
whom I cited at the outset. The fact
that the same name has been given by
different scholars to all of these episodes
is no evidence, and scarcely even establishes a presumption, that they are identical in essentials. There may be some
common denominator of them all; but if
so, it has never yet been clearly exhibited, and its presence is not to be assumed *a priori*. In any case, each of
these so-called Romanticisms was a
highly complex and usually an exceedingly unstable intellectual compound;
each, in other words, was made up of
various unit-ideas linked together, for
the most part, not by any indissoluble
bonds of logical necessity, but by alogical
associative processes, greatly facilitated
and partly caused, in the case of the
Romanticisms which grew up after the
appellation "Romantic" was invented,
by the congenital and acquired ambiguities of the word. And when certain of
these Romanticisms have in truth significant elements in common, they are
not necessarily the same elements in
any two cases. Romanticism A may
have one characteristic presupposition
or impulse, X, which it shares with
Romanticism B, another characteristic,
Y, which it shares with Romanticism C,
to which X is wholly foreign. In the
case, moreover, of those movements or
schools to which the label was applied
in their own time, the contents under
the label sometimes changed radically
and rapidly. At the end of a decade or
two you had the same men and the
same party appellation, but profoundly
different ideas. As everyone knows, this
is precisely what happened in the case
of what is called French Romanticism.
It may or may not be true that, as M.

A. Viatte has sought to show,[32] at the beginning of this process of transformation some subtle leaven was already at work which made the final outcome inevitable; the fact remains that in most of its practically significant sympathies and affiliations of a literary, ethical, political, and religious sort, the French "Romanticism" of the eighteen-thirties was the antithesis of that of the beginning of the century.

But the essential of the second remedy is that each of these Romanticisms—after they are first thus roughly discriminated with respect to their representatives or their dates—should be resolved, by a more thorough and discerning analysis than is yet customary, into its elements—into the several ideas and aesthetic susceptibles of which it is composed. Only after these fundamental thought-factors or emotive strains in it are clearly discriminated and fairly exhaustively enumerated, shall we be in a position to judge of the degree of its affinity with other complexes to which the same name has been applied, to see precisely what tacit preconceptions or controlling motives or explicit contentions were common to any two or more of them, and wherein they manifested distinct and divergent tendencies.

II

Of the needfulness of such analytic comparison and discrimination of the Romanticisms let me attempt three illustrations.

1. In an interesting lecture before the British Academy a few years since, Mr. Edmund Gosse described Joseph Warton's youthful poem, *The Enthusiast*, written in 1740, as the first clear manifestation of "the great romantic movement, such as it has enlarged and dwindled down to our day. . . . Here for the first time we find unwaveringly emphasized and repeated what was entirely new in literature, the essence of romantic hysteria. *The Enthusiast* is the earliest expression of complete revolt

against the classical attitude which had been sovereign in all European literature for nearly a century. So completely is this expressed by Joseph Warton that it is extremely difficult to realize that he could not have come under the fascination of Rosseau, . . . who was not to write anything characteristic until ten years later."[33] Let us, then, compare the ideas distinctive of this poem with the conception of *romantische Poesie* formulated by Friedrich Schlegel and his fellow-Romanticists in Germany after 1796. The two have plainly certain common elements. Both are forms of revolt against the neo-classical aesthetics; both are partly inspired by an ardent admiration for Shakespeare; both proclaim the creative artist's independence of "rules." It might at first appear, therefore, that these two Romanticisms, in spite of natural differences of phraseology, are identical in essence—are separate outcroppings of the same vein of metal, precious or base, according to your taste.

But a more careful scrutiny shows a contrast between them not less important—indeed, as it seems to me, more important—than their resemblance. The general theme of Joseph Warton's poem (of which, it will be remembered, the sub-title is "The Lover of Nature") is one which had been a commonplace for many centuries: the superiority of "nature" to "art." It is a theme which goes back to Rabelais's contrast of Physis and Antiphysie. It had been the inspiration of some of the most famous passages of Montaigne. It had been attacked by Shakespeare. Pope's *Essay on Man* had been full of it. The "natural" in contrast with the artificial meant, first of all, that which is not man-made; and within man's life, it was supposed to consist in those expressions of human nature which are most spontaneous, unpremeditated, untouched by reflection or design, and free from the bondage of social convention. "Ce n'est pas raison," cried Montaigne, "que l'art gagne le point d'honneur sur notre grande et

---

[32] *Le Catholicisme chez les Romantiques*, 1922.

[33] "Two Pioneers of Romanticism," *Proc. Brit. Acad.*, 1915, pp. 146-8.

puissante mère Nature. Nous avons tant rechargé la beauté et richesse de ses ouvrages par nos inventions, que nous l'avons tout à fait étouffée." There follows the *locus classicus* of primitivism in modern literature, the famous passage on the superiority of wild fruits and savage men over those that have been "bastardized" by art.[34]

Warton, then, presents this ancient theme in various aspects. He prefers to all the beauties of the gardens of Versailles

> Some pine-topt precipice
> Abrupt and shaggy.

He rhetorically inquires:

> Can Kent design like Nature?

He laments

> That luxury and pomp . . .
> Should proudly banish Nature's simple charms.

He inquires why "mistaken man" should deem it nobler

> To dwell in palaces and high-roof'd halls
> Than in God's forests, architect supreme?

All this, if I may be permitted the expression, was old stuff. The principal thing that was original and significant in the poem was that Warton boldly applied the doctrine of the superiority of "nature" over conscious art to the theory of poetry:

> What are the lays of artful Addison,
> Coldly correct, to Shakespeare's warblings wild?

That Nature herself was wild, untamed, was notorious, almost tautological; and it was Shakespeare's supposed "wildness," his non-conformity to the conventional rules, the spontaneous free-

dom of his imagination and his expression, that proved him Nature's true pupil.

Now this aesthetic inference had not, during the neo-classical period, ordinarily been drawn from the current assumption of the superiority of nature to art. The principle of "following nature" had in aesthetics usually been taken in another, or in more than one other, of the several dozen senses of the sacred word.[35] Yet in other provinces of thought an analogous inference had long since and repeatedly been suggested. From the first the fashion of conceiving of "nature" (in the sense in which it was antithetic to "art") as norm had made for antinomianism, in some degree or other—for a depreciation of restraint, for the ideal of "letting yourself go." There seems to be an idea current that an antinomian temper was, at some time in the eighteenth century, introduced into aesthetic theory and artistic practise by some Romanticist, and that it thence speedily spread to moral feeling and social conduct.[36] The historic sequence is precisely the opposite. It was Montaigne again—not usually classified as a Romanticist—who wrote:

> J'ai pris bien simplement et crûment ce précepte ancien: 'que nous ne saurions faillir à suivre Nature' . . . Je n'ai pas corrigé, comme Socrate, par la force de la raison, mes complexions naturelles, je n'ai aucunement troublé, par art, mon inclination; je me laisse aller comme je suis venu; je ne combats rien.[37]

It was Pope who asked:

> Can that offend great Nature's God
> Which Nature's self inspires?

and who spoke of

> Wild Nature's vigor working at the root

---

[34] *Essais*, I, 31. There is a certain irony in the fact that the sort of naturalism here expressed by Montaigne was to be the basis of a Shakespeare-revival in the eighteenth century. For Shakespeare's own extreme antipathy to the passage is shown by the fact that he wrote two replies to it—a humorous one in *The Tempest*, a serious and profound one in *The Winter's Tale*.

[35] This is not rhetorical exaggeration; more than sixty different senses or applications of the notion of "nature" can be clearly distinguished.

[36] So apparently Mr. Gosse: "When the history of the [Romantic] school comes to be written, there will be a piquancy in tracing an antinomianism down from the blameless Warton to the hedonist essays of Oscar Wilde and the frenzied anarchism of the futurists" (*op. cit.*, 15).

[37] *Essais*, III. 12.

as the source of the passions in which all the original and vital energies of men are contained.

Aside from a certain heightening of the emotional tone, then, the chief novelty of Warton's poem lay in its suggesting the application of these ideas to a field from which they had usually been curiously and inconsistently excluded, in its introduction of antinomianism, of a rather mild sort, into the conception of poetic excellence.[38] But this extension was obviously implicit from the outset in the logic of that protean "naturalism" which had been the most characteristic and potent force in modern thought since the late Renaissance; it was bound to be made by somebody sooner or later. Nor was Warton's the first aesthetic application of the principle; it had already been applied to an art in the theory and practice of which eighteenth-century Englishmen were keenly interested—the art of landscape design. The first great revolt against the neo-classical aesthetics was not in literature at all, but in gardening; the second, I think, was in architectural taste; and all three were inspired by the same ideas.[39] Since, the "artful Addison" had observed, "artificial works receive a greater advantage from their resemblance of such as are natural," and since Nature is distinguished by her "rough, careless strokes," the layer-out of gardens should aim at "an artificial rudeness much more charming than that neatness and elegancy usually met with."[40] This horticultural Romanticism had been preached likewise by Sir William Temple, Pope, Horace Walpole, Batty Langley, and others, and ostensibly exemplified in the work of Kent, Brown, and

Bridgman. Warton in the poem in question describes Kent as at least doing his best to imitate in his gardens the wildness of Nature:

> He, by rules unfettered, boldly scorns
> Formality and method; round and square
> Disdaining, plans irregularly great.

It was no far cry from this to the rejection of the rules in the drama, to a revulsion against the strait-laced regularity and symmetry of the heroic couplet, to a general turning from convention, formality, method, artifice, in all the arts.

There had, however, from the first been a curious duality of meaning in the antithesis of "nature" and "art"— one of the most pregnant of the long succession of confusions of ideas which make up much of the history of human thought. While the "natural" was, on the one hand, conceived as the wild and spontaneous and "irregular," it was also conceived as the simple, the naïve, the unsophisticated. No two words were more fixedly associated in the mind of the sixteenth, seventeenth, and early eighteenth centuries than "Nature" and "simple." Consequently the idea of preferring nature to custom and to art usually carried with it the suggestion of a program of simplification, of reform by elimination; in other words, it implied primitivism. The "natural" was a thing you reached by going back and by leaving out. And this association of ideas—already obvious in Montaigne, in Pope, and scores of other extollers of "Nature"—is still conspicuous in Warton's poem. It was the "bards of old" who were "fair Nature's friends." The poet envies

> The first of men, ere yet confined
> In smoky cities.

He yearns to dwell in some

> Isles of innocence from mortal view
> Deeply retired beneath a plantane's shade,
> Where Happiness and Quiet sit enthroned,
> With simple Indian swains.

[38] The title of the poem and some elements of its thought and feeling—especially its note of religious "enthusiasm" for "Nature" in the sense of the visible universe—are akin to, and probably derivative from, Shaftesbury's *Moralists*. But in Shaftesbury there is no opposition of "nature" to "art" and no antinomian strain, either ethical or aesthetic; "decorum," "order," "balance," and "proportion" are among his favorite words.

[39] Cf. the essay on "The First Gothic Revival," *etc.*, above.

[40] *Spectator*, No. 144.

For one term of the comparison, then, I limit myself, for brevity's sake, to this poem to which Mr. Gosse has assigned so important a place in literary history. There were, of course, even in the writings of the elder Warton, and still more in other phenomena frequently called "Romantic," between the 1740's and the 1790's, further elements which cannot be considered here. There is observable, for example, in what it has become the fashion to classify as the early phases of English Romanticism, the emergence of what may be called gothicism, and the curious fact of its partial and temporary fusion with naturalism. It is one of the interesting problems of the analytic history of ideas to see just how and why naturalism and gothicism became allied in the eighteenth century in England, though little, if at all, in France. But for the present purpose it suffices to take *The Enthusiast* as typical, in one especially important way, of a great deal of the so-called Romanticism before the seventeen-nineties—a Romanticism, namely, which, whatever further characteristics it may have had, was based upon naturalism (in the sense of the word which I have indicated) and was associated with primitivism of some mode or degree.

2. For in this fundamental point this earlier "Romanticism" differed essentially from that of the German aesthetic theorists and poets who chose the term "Romantic poetry" as the most suitable designation for their own literary ideals and program. The latter "Romanticism" is in its very essence a denial of the older naturalistic presuppositions, which Warton's poem had manifested in a special and somewhat novel way. The German movement, as I have elsewhere shown, received its immediate and decisive impetus from Schiller's essay *On Naïve and Sentimental Poetry*; and what it derived from that confused work was the conviction that "harmony with nature," in any sense which implied an opposition to "culture," to "art," to reflection and

self-conscious effort, was neither possible nor desirable for the modern man or the modern artist. The *Frühromantiker* learned from Schiller, and partly from Herder, the idea of an art which should look back no more to the primitive than to the classical—the notions of which, incidentally, Schiller had curiously fused—for its models and ideals; which should be the appropriate expression, not of a *natürliche* but of a *künstliche Bildung*; which, so far from desiring simplification, so far from aiming at the sort of harmony in art and life which is to be attained by the method of leaving out, should seek first fullness of content, should have for its program the adequate expression of the entire range of human experience and the entire reach of the human imagination. For man, the artificial, Friedrich Schlegel observed, *is* "natural." "Die Abstraktion ist ein künstlicher Zustand. Dies ist kein Grund gegen sie, denn es ist dem Menschen gewiss natürlich, sich dann und wann auch in künstliche Zustände zu versetzen." And again: "Eine nur im Gegensatz der Kunst und Bildung natürliche Denkart soll es gar nicht geben." To be unsophisticated, to revert to the mental state of "simple Indian swains," was the least of the ambitions of a German Romantic—though, since the unsophisticated is one type of human character, his art was not, at least in theory, indifferent even to that. The Shakespeare whom he admired was no gifted child of nature addicted to "warblings wild." Shakespeare, said A. W. Schlegel, is not "eine blindes wildlaufendes Genie"; he had "a system in his artistic practise and an astonishingly profound and deeply meditated one." The same critic seems to be consciously attacking either Joseph Warton's or Gray's famous lines about Shakespeare when he writes: "Those poets whom it is customary to represent as carefree nurslings of nature, without art and without schooling, if they produce works of genuine excellence, give evidence of exceptional cultivation (*Kultur*) of their mental powers, of practised art, of ripely pondered and just designs." The greatness of Shakespeare, in the eyes of *these* Romantics, lay in his *Universalität*, his sophisticated insight into human nature and the many-sidedness of his portrayal of character; it was this, as Friedrich Schlegel said, that made him "wie der Mittelpunkt der romantischen Kunst." It may be added that another trait of the Romanticism found by Mr. Gosse in Joseph Warton, namely, the feeling that didactic poetry is not poetic, was also repudiated by early German Romanticism: "How," asked F. Schlegel again, "can it be said that ethics (*die Moral*) belongs merely to philosophy, when the greatest part of poetry relates to the art of living and to the knowledge of human nature?"[41]

The difference, then, I suggest, is more significant, more pregnant, than the likeness between these two Romanticisms. Between the assertion of the superiority of "nature" over conscious "art" and that of the superiority of conscious art over mere "nature"; between a way of thinking of which primitivism is of the essence and one of which the idea of perpetual self-transcendence is of the essence; between a fundamental preference for simplicity—even though a "wild" simplicity—and a fundamental preference for diversity and complexity; between the sort of ingenuous naïveté characteristic of *The Enthusiast* and the sophisticated subtlety of the conception of romantic irony: between these the antithesis is one of the most radical that modern thought and taste have to show. I don't deny anyone's right to call both these things Romanticism, if he likes; but I cannot but observe that the fashion of giving both the same name has led to a good deal of unconscious falsification of the history of ideas. The elements of the one Romanticism tend to be read into the other; the nature and profundity of the oppositions between them tend to be overlooked; and the relative

importance of the different changes o preconceptions in modern thought, an of susceptibilities in modern taste, tend to be wrongly estimated. I shall not at tempt to cite here what seem to m examples of such historical errors; bu the sum of them is, I think, far fron negligible.

Between the "Romanticism" which i but a special and belated manifestatio of the naturalism that had flourishe since the Renaissance (and before it and the "Romanticism" which bega at the end of the eighteenth century i Germany (as well as that which ap peared a little later in France) there another difference not less significan This is due to the identification of th meaning of "Romantic" in the late movement with "Christian"—and main ly with the medieval implications that term. This was not the central ide in the original notion of "Romanti poetry" as conceived by Friedric Schlegel. Primarily, as I have elsewher tried to show,[42] the adjective meant fo him and the entire school "das eigentüm lich Moderne" in contrast with "da eigentümlich Antike." But it early oc curred to him that the principal histori cause of the supposed radical differer tiation of modern from classical art coul lie only in the influence of Christianity He wrote in 1796, before his own con version to what he had already define as the "Romantic," *i.e.*, modern, poir of view:

So lächerlich und geschmacklos sich diese Trachten nach dem Reich Gottes in der chris lichen Poesie offenbaren möchte; so wird dem Geschichtsforscher doch eine sehr mer würdige Erscheinung, wenn er gewahr wir dass eben dieses Streben, das absolut Vollkon mene und Unendliche zu realisiren, eine unt dem unaufhörlichen Wechsel der Zeiten un bei der grössten Verschiedenheit der Völk bleibende Eigenschaft dessen ist, was man m dem besten Rechte modern nennen darf. [43]

When, after reading Schiller's essa

---

[41] Quotations in this paragraph from F. Schlegel are from *Athenaeum*, II, 1, p. 29; III, 1, p. 12; I, 2, p. 68; III, 1, p. 19. Those from A. W. Schlegel have already been cited by Marie Joachimi, *Weltanschauung der Romantik*, 179-183.

[42] Cf. the essay on "The Meaning of Romantic. etc.

[43] Review of Herder's *Humanitätsbriefe;* in Minc *Fr. Schlegel, 1794-1802.*

chlegel himself became a devotee of
hose aesthetic ideals which he had
reviously denounced, he wrote (1797):

Nachdem die vollendete natürliche Bildung
er Alten entschieden gesunken, und ohne
ettung ausgeartet war, ward durch den Ver-
st der endlichen Realität und die Zerrüttung
ellendeter Form ein Streben nach unendlicher
ealität veranlasst, welches bald allgemeiner
on des Zeitalters wurde. [44]

"Romantic" art thus came to mean—
or one thing—an art inspired by or
xpressive of some idea or some ethical
mper supposed to be essential in
hristianity. "Ursprung und Charakter
er ganzen neuern Poesie lässt sich so
icht aus dem Christentume ableiten,
ass man die romantische eben so gut
e christliche nennen könnte," [45] said
ichter in 1804, repeating what had by
iat time become a commonplace. But
ie nature of the essentially Christian,
nd therefore essentially Romantic,
oirit was variously conceived. Upon
ie characteristic of it there was, in-
eed, rather general agreement among
ie German Romanticists: the habit of
iind introduced by Christianity was
istinguished by a certain insatiability;
aimed at infinite objectives and was
icapable of lasting satisfaction with
ny goods actually reached. It became a
ivorite platitude to say that the Greeks
nd Romans set themselves limited ends
o attain, were able to attain them, and
vere thus capable of self-satisfaction
nd finality; and that modern or "ro-
iantic" art differed from this most fun-
amentally, by reason of its Christian
rigin, in being, as Schiller had said, a
Kunst des Unendlichen. "Absolute
.bstraktion, Vernichtung des Jetzigen,
.potheose der Zukunft, dieser eigentlich
essern Welt!; dies ist der Kern des
eheisses des Christentums," declared
Iovalis. In its application to artistic
ractice this "apotheosis of the future"
ieant the ideal of endless progress, of
eine progressive Universalpoesie" in
ie words of Fr. Schlegel's familiar defi-

nition; it implied the demand that art
shall always go on bringing new provinces of life within its domain and
achieving ever fresh and original effects.
But anything which was, or was supposed to be, especially characteristic of
the Christian *Weltanschauung* tended to
become a part of the current connotation of "Romantic," and also a part of
the actual ideals of the school. Preoccupation with supersensible realities
and a feeling of the illusoriness of ordinary existence was thus often held to be
a distinctive trait of Romantic art, on
the ground that Christianity is an other-
worldly religion: "in der christlichen
Ansicht," said A. W. Schlegel, "die
Anschauung des Unendlichen hat das
Endliche vernichtet; das Leben ist zur
Schattenwelt und zur Nacht gewor-
den." [46] Another recognized characteristic of Christianity, and therefore of the
"Romantic," was ethical dualism, a
conviction that there are in man's constitution two natures ceaselessly at war.
The Greek ideal, in the elder Schlegel's
words, was "volkommene Eintracht und
Ebenmass aller Kräfte, natürliche Har-
monie. Die Neueren hingegen sind zum
Bewusstsein der inneren Entzweiung
gekommen, welche ein solches Ideal
unmöglich macht." [47] Directly related to
this, it was perceived, was the "inwardness" of Christianity, its preoccupation
with "the heart" as distinguished from
the outward act, its tendency to introspection; and hence, as Mme de Stael
and others observed, "modern" or
"Romantic" art has discovered, and has
for its peculiar province, the inexhaustible realm of the inner life of man:

Les anciens avaient, pour ainsi dire, une
âme corporelle, dont tous les mouvements
étaient forts, directs, et conséquents; il n'en
est pas de même du coeur humain développé
par le christianisme: les modernes ont puisé
dans le repentir chrétien l'habitude de se rep-
lier continuellement sur eux-mêmes. Mais, pour
manifester cette existence tout intérieure, il
faut qu'une grande variété dans les faits pré-

[44] Vorrede, *Die Griechen und Romer*, in Minor, *op.
t.*, I, 82.
[45] *Vorschule der Aesthetik*, I, Programm V, §23.

[46] *Vorlesungen über dramatische Kunst und Literatur*,
1809-11, in *Werke*, 1846, V, 16. Cf. also Novalis's
Hymnen an die Nacht.
[47] *Op. cit.*, V, 17.

sente sous toutes les formes les nuances infinies de ce qui se passe dans l'âme. [48]

It is one of the many paradoxes of the history of the word, and of the controversies centering about it, that several eminent literary historians and critics of our time have conceived the moral essence of Romanticism as consisting in a kind of "this-worldliness" and a negation of what one of them has termed "the Christian and classical dualism." Its most deplorable and dangerous error, in the judgment of these critics, is its deficient realization of the "civil war in the cave" of man's soul, its belief in the "natural goodness" of man. They thus define "Romanticism" in terms precisely opposite to those in which it was often defined by the writers who first called their own ideals "Romantic"; and this fashion, I cannot but think, has done a good deal to obscure the palpable and important historical fact that the one "Romanticism" which (as I have said) has an indisputable title to the name was conceived by those writers as a rediscovery and revival, for better or worse, of characteristically Christian modes of thought and feeling, of a mystical and otherworldly type of religion, and a sense of the inner moral struggle as the distinctive fact in human experience—such as had been for a century alien to the dominant tendencies in 'polite' literature. The new movement was, almost from the first, a revolt against what was conceived to be paganism in religion and ethics as definitely as against classicism in art. The earliest important formulation of its implications for religious philosophy was Schleiermacher's famous *Reden* (1799) addressed "to the cultivated contemners of religion," a work profoundly—sometimes, indeed, morbidly—dualistic in its ethical temper. Christianity, declares Schleiermacher, is *durch und durch polemisch*; it knows no truce in the warfare of the spiritual with the natural man, it finds no end in the task of in-

ner self-discipline. [49] And the *Reden*, must be remembered, were (in th words of a German literary historian "greeted by the votaries of Romanticis as a gospel." [50]

Now it is not untrue to describe th ethical tendency of the "Romanticism which had its roots in naturalism—tha is, in the assumption of the sole exce lence of what in man is native, prim tive, "wild," attainable without othe struggle than that required for emanc pation from social conventions and art ficialities—as anti-dualistic and esser tially non-moral. This aspect of it ca be seen even in the poem of the "blame less Warton," when he describes the lif of the state of nature for which h yearns. But as a consequence of th prevalent neglect to discriminate th Romanticisms, the very movemer which was the beginning of a deliberat and vigorous insurrection against th naturalistic assumptions that had bee potent, and usually dominant, in mod ern thought for more than three cen turies, is actually treated as if it were continuation of that tendency. Thes and antithesis have, partly through acc dents of language and partly through lack of careful observation on the par of historians of literature, been calle

[48] *De l'Allemagne* Pt. II, chap. XI.

[49] Cf. *Fünfte Rede:* "Nirgends is die Religion vollkommen idealisiert als im Christentum und durc die ursprüngliche Voraussetzung desselben; und ebe damlt ist immerwährendes Streiten gegen alles Wir liche in der Religion als eine Aufgabe hingestellt, d nie völlig Genüge geleistet werden kann. Eben we überall das Ungöttliche ist und wirkt, und weil all Wirkliche zugleich als unbeilig erscheint, ist eine unen liche Heiligkeit das Ziel des Christentums. Nie zufri den mit dem Erlangten, sucht es auch in seinen rei sten Erzeugnissen, auch in seinen heiligsten Gefühle noch die Spuren des Irreligiösen und der der Einhe des Ganzen entegengesetzten und die von ihm abg wandten Tendenz alles Endlichen."

[50] Typical is the review of the book in the *Athe aeum*, II, 299: "Fur mich ist das Christentum und d Art wie es eingeleitet und das, was ewig bleiben soll ihm, gesetzt wird, mit das Grässte im ganzen Werk. Cf. also Schlegel's defense of Fichte against the charg of having "attacked religion": "Wenn das Interesse a Uebersinnlichen das Wesen der Religion ist, so ist sein ganze Lehre Religion in Form der Philosophie." The are, undeniably, also occasional manifestations of conflicting strain in the *Frühromantiker*, especially Novalis; but these are not the usual, dominant, inn vating and characteristic things in the body of ideas the school; they are rather vestigial structures, such are to be found remaining in all new developments.

by the same name, and consequently have frequently been assumed to be the same thing. An ideal of ceaseless striving towards goals too vast or too exacting ever to be wholly attained has been confused with a nostalgia for the untroubled, because unaspiring, indolent, and unselfconscious life of the man of nature. Thus one of the widest and deepest-reaching lines of cleavage in modern thought has been more or less effectually concealed by a word.

3. This cleavage between naturalistic and anti-naturalistic "Romanticism" crosses national lines; and it manifestly cuts, so to say, directly through the person of one great writer commonly classed among the initiators of the Romantic movement in France. The author of the *Essai sur les révolutions* and of the earlier-written parts of *Atala* may perhaps properly be called a Romantic; the author of the later-written parts of the latter work and of the *Génie du Christianisme* may perhaps properly be called a Romantic; but it is obvious that the word has, in most important respects, not merely different but antithetic senses in these two applications of it to the same person. Chateaubriand before 1799 represented in some sort the culmination of the naturalistic and primitivistic Romanticism of which Mr. Gosse sees the beginning in Joseph Warton;[51] he had not only felt intensely but had even gratified the yearning to live "with simple Indian swains." That the Chateaubriand of 1801 represents just as clearly a revolt against this entire tendency is suffi-

[51] There are, for example, passages in the penultimate section of the *Essai sur les révolutions* which present a close parallel to some in *The Enthusiast*; e.g.: "O homme de la nature, c'est toi seul qui me fait me glorifier d'être homme! Ton coeur ne connait point la dépendance; tu ne sais ce que de ramper dans une cour ou de caresser un tigre populaire. Que t'importent nos arts, notre luxe, nos villes? As-tu besoin de spectacle, tu te rends au temple de la nature, à la religieuse forêt . . . Mais il n'y a donc point de gouvernement, point de liberté? De liberté? si: une délicieuse, une céleste, celle de la nature. Et quelle est-elle, cette liberté? . . . Qu'on vienne passer une nuit avec moi chez les sauvages du Canada, peut-être alors parviendrai-je à donner quelque idée de cette espèce de liberté."

ciently evident from the repudiation of primitivism in the first preface to *Atala*:

Je ne suis point, comme M. Rousseau, un enthousiaste des sauvages; . . . je ne crois point que la *pure nature* soit la plus belle chose du monde. Je l'ai toujours trouvée fort laide partout où j'ai eu occasion de la voir . . . Avec ce mot de nature on a tout perdu. [52]

Thus the magic word upon which the whole scheme of ideas of the earlier writing had depended is now plainly characterized as the fruitful source of error and confusion that it was. And in his views about the drama the Chateaubriand of 1801 was opposed *both* to the movement represented by *The Enthusiast* and to the German Romanticism of his own time. Shakespeare was (though mainly, as we have seen, for differing reasons) the idol of both; but Chateaubriand in his *Essai sur la littérature anglaise*[53] writes of Shakespeare in the vein, and partly in the words, of Voltaire and Pope. In point of natural genius, he grants, the English dramatist was without a peer in his own age, and perhaps in any age: "je ne sais si jamais homme a jeté des regards plus profonds sur la nature humaine." But Shakespeare knew almost nothing of the requirements of the drama as an art:

Il faut se persuader d'abord qu' écrire est un art; que cet art a nécessairement ses genres, et que chaque genre a ses règles. Et qu'on ne dise pas que les genres et les règles sont arbitraires; ils sont nés de la nature même; l'art a seulement séparé ce que la nature a confondu . . . On peut dire que Racine, dans toute l'excellence de son art, est plus naturel que Shakespeare.

Chateaubriand here, to be sure, still finds the standard of art in "nature"; but it is "nature" in the sense of the neo-classical critics, a sense in which it is not opposed, but equivalent, to an

[52] On the two strains in *Atala*, cf. Chinard, *L'Exotisme américain dans l'oeuvre de Chateaubriand*, 1918, ch. ix.

[53] The section on Shakespeare was published in April, 1801 (*Mélanges politiques et littéraires*, 1854, pp. 390 ff.).

art that rigorously conforms to fixed rules. And the "great literary paradox of the partisans of Shakespeare," he observes, is that their arguments imply that "there are *no* rules of the drama," which is equivalent to asserting "that an art is not an art." Voltaire rightly felt that "by banishing all rules and returning to *pure nature*, nothing was easier than to equal the *chefs-d'oeuvre* of the English stage"; and he was well advised in recanting his earlier too enthusiastic utterances about Shakespeare, since he saw that "en relevant les beautés des barbares, il avait séduit des hommes qui, comme lui, ne sauraient séparer l'alliage de l'or." Chateaubriand regrets that "the *Cato* of Addison is no longer played" and that consequently "on ne se délasse au théâtre anglais des monstruosités de Shakespeare que par les horreurs d'Otway." "Comment," he exclaims, "ne pas gémir de voir une nation éclairée, et qui compte parmi ses critiques les Pope et les Addison, de la voir s'extasier sur le portrait de l'apothicaire dans *Roméo et Juliette*. C'est le burlesque le plus hideux et le plus dégoûtant." The entire passage might almost have been written with Warton's poem in mind, so completely and methodically does this later "Romanticist" controvert the aesthetic principles and deride the enthusiasm of the English "Romanticist" of 1740. It is worth noting, also, that Chateaubriand at this time thinks almost as ill of Gothic architecture as of Shakespeare and of *la pure nature*:

> Une beauté dans Shakespeare n'excuse pas ses innombrables défauts; un monument gothique peut plaire par son obscurité et la difformité même de ses proportions, mais personne ne songe á bâtir un palais sur son modèle. [54]

We have, then, observed and compared—very far from exhaustively, of course, yet in some of their most fundamental and determinative ideas—three "Romanticisms." In the first and

second we have found certain common elements, but still more significant oppositions; in the second and third we have found certain other common elements, but likewise significant oppositions. But between the first and third the common elements are very scanty; such as there are, it could, I think, be shown, are not the same as those subsisting between either the first and second or the second and third; and in their ethical preconceptions and implications and the crucial articles of their literary creeds, the opposition between them is almost absolute.

All three of these historic episodes, it is true, are far more complex than I have time to show. I am attempting only to illustrate the nature of a certain procedure in the study of what is called Romanticism, to suggest its importance, and to present one or two specific results of the use of it. A complete analysis would qualify, without invalidating, these results, in several ways. It would (for one thing) bring out certain important connections between the revolt against the neo-classical aesthetics (common to two of the episodes mentioned) and other aspects of eighteenth-century thought. It would, again, exhibit fully certain *internal* oppositions in at least two of the Romanticisms considered. For example, in German Romanticism between 1797 and 1800 there grew up, and mainly from a single root, *both* an "apotheosis of the future" and a tendency to retrospection —a retrospection directed, not, indeed, towards classical antiquity or towards the primitive, but towards the medieval. A belief in progress and a spirit of reaction were, paradoxically, joint offspring of the same idea, and were nurtured for a time in the same minds. But it is just these internal incongruities which make it most of all evident, as it seems to me, that any attempt at a *general* appraisal even of a single chronologically determinate Romanticism—still more, of "Romanticism" as a whole—is a fatuity. When a Romanticism has been analyzed into the distinct "strains" or ideas which compose it, the true philosophic affinities and the even-

---

[54] It is somewhat difficult to reconcile this with the eloquent passage on the Gothic church in the *Génie du Christianisme* (V, Ch. 8); yet even there, while ascribing to the Gothic style "une beauté qui lui est particulière," Chateaubriand also refers to its "proportions barbares."

tual practical influence in life and art of these several strains will usually be found to be exceedingly diverse and often conflicting. It will, no doubt, remain abstractly possible to raise the question whether the preponderant effect, moral or aesthetic, of one or another large movement which has been called by the name was good or bad. But that ambitious inquiry cannot even be legitimately begun until a prior task of analysis and detailed comparison—of the sort that I have attempted here to indicate—has been accomplished. And when this has been done, I doubt whether the larger question will seem to have much importance or meaning. What will then appear historically significant and philosophically instructive will be the way in which *each* of these distinguishable strains has worked itself out, what its elective affinities for other ideas, and its historic consequences,

have shown themselves to be. The categories which it has become customary to use in distinguishing and classifying "movements" in literature or philosophy and in describing the nature of the significant transitions which have taken place in taste and in opinion, are far too rough, crude, undiscriminating—and none of them so hopelessly so as the category "Romantic." It is not any large *complexes* of ideas, such as that term has almost always been employed to designate, but rather certain simpler, diversely combinable, intellectual and emotional components of such complexes, that are the true elemental and dynamic factors in the history of thought and of art; and it is with the genesis, the vicissitudes, the manifold and often dramatic interactions of these, that it is the task of the historian of ideas in literature to become acquainted.

IRVING BABBITT

(1865-1933)

With Paul Elmer More as his most influential ally, Irving Babbitt was the leader and guiding spirit of the New Humanist movement, which originated in the first decade of the century and reached its greatest prestige during the 1920's. Anti-modernist, anti-scientific, and anti-democratic, the New Humanists opposed the traditions of both romanticism and naturalism in their assertion of the dualism of man and nature. They also argued for the freedom of the will and the law of restraint, operating through the "inner check." Their practical criticism is strongly colored by their concern for the moral function of literature. Babbitt's humanist position on educational, literary, and social questions is fully represented in five of his many books: *Literature and the American College* (1908), *The New Laokoön* (1910), *The Masters of Modern French Criticism* (1912), *Rousseau and Romanticism* (1919), and *Democracy and Leadership* (1924).

Humanism: An Essay at Definition (1930)

I

The art of defining is so indispensable that one needs to define the limits of

From *Humanism and America* (1930) edited by Norman Foerster. Reprinted by permission of Holt, Rinehart and Winston, Inc.

definition itself. A very eminent humanist, Erasmus, showed his awareness of these limits when he complained of the attempts of the theologians of the Reformation to formulate deity that every definition was a disaster. Though the humanist does not seek to define God and is in general chary of ultimates, he is wont in more mundane matters to put the utmost emphasis on definition. This Socratic emphasis would seem especially needed at a time like the present which has probably surpassed all previous epochs in its loose and irresponsible use of general terms. Unless this tendency is corrected, the day may come when, outside of words that stand for the measurements of science or the objects of sense, communication between men will be well-nigh impossible. The exchange of ideas regarding those aspects of life that fall outside the merely quantitative and material may become as difficult as economic exchanges would be with coins that have no definite value.

This growing debasement of the intellectual coinage may be illustrated from the word humanism itself. The boundaries of a genuine humanism are broad and flexible. It is plain, however, that the word is being appropriated for points of view that cannot be brought within these boundaries, however generously extended. As a preliminary to pointing out some of the more serious of the resulting confusions it would seem desirable to build up the historical background. For what a word actually has meant should surely throw light on what it ought to mean.

As is well known, the word humanist was applied, first in the Italy of the fifteenth century, and later in other European countries, to the type of scholar who was not only proficient in Greek and Latin, but who at the same time inclined to prefer the humanity of the great classical writers to what seemed to him the excess of divinity in the mediaevals. This contrast between humanity and divinity was often conceived very superficially. However, the best of the humanists were not content with opposing a somewhat external imitation of the Ciceronian or Virgilian elegance to the scholastic carelessness of form. They actually caught a glimpse of the fine proportionateness of the ancients at their best. They were thus encouraged to aim at a harmonious development of their faculties in this

world rather than at an other-worldly felicity. Each faculty, they held, should be cultivated in due measure without one-sidedness or over-emphasis, whether that of the ascetic or that of the specialist. "Nothing too much" is indeed the central maxim of all genuine humanists, ancient and modern.

In a world of ever-shifting circumstance, this maxim is not always of easy application. Whoever has succeeded in bridging the gap between the general precept and some particular emergency has to that extent achieved the fitting and the decorous. Decorum is simply the law of measure in its more concrete aspects. For every type of humanist decorum is, in Milton's phrase, the "grand masterpiece to observe." Actually this observation may rest on deep insight, as it did in the case of Milton himself, or it may degenerate into empty formalism. The adjustment of which I have spoken between the variable and the permanent elements in human experience requires spiritual effort and most men are spiritually indolent. For genuine adjustment they tend to substitute outer conformity so that decorum itself finally comes to seem a mere veneer, something that has no deep root in the nature of things. Moreover the notions of decent behaviour to which men have conformed at any particular period have always been more or less local and relative. It is easy to take the next step and assume that they have been *only* local and relative, an assumption subversive not merely of decorum but of humanism itself. Humanism, one of our modernists has argued, may have done very well for other times and places, but under existing circumstances, it is at best likely to prove only a "noble anachronism." A similar objection to humanism is that it has its source in a psychology of "escape," that it is an attempt to take flight from the present into a past that has for the modern man become impossible. But humanism is not to be identified with this or that body of traditional precepts. The law of measure on which it depends becomes meaningless unless it can be shown to be one of the "laws unwritten in the heavens" of which Antigone had the immediate perception, laws that are "not of today or yesterday," that transcend in short the temporal process. The final appeal of the humanist is not to any historical convention but to intuition.

It does not follow that the humanist is ready to abandon history to the relativist. The main conventions that have prevailed in the past reveal important identities as well as differences. These identities cannot be explained as due to their common derivation from some previous convention. The Chinese made an independent discovery of the law of measure.[1] An important task, indeed, that awaits some properly qualified scholar, preferably a Chinese, is a comparison of Confucian humanism with occidental humanism as it appears, for example, in the *Ethics* of Aristotle. The announcement was made recently in the press that a Harvard astronomer had discovered the "centre of the universe" (more strictly the centre of our galactic system). In the meanwhile the far more important question is being neglected whether human nature itself has any centre. One's faith in the existence of such a centre increases when one finds the best commentary on Pascal's dictum that the great man is he who combines in himself opposite virtues and occupies all the space between them, in a Confucian book the very title of which, literally rendered, means the "universal norm" or "centre."[2] Here and elsewhere the Confucian books reveal a deep and direct insight into the law of measure. Legge's translation of the Chinese word for decorum (*li*) as "the rules of propriety" has been rightly censured as unduly prim and formalistic; though it must be admitted that a formalistic element is very marked at times even in the older Confucian writings.

Practically the assertion of a "universal centre" means the setting up of some pattern or model for imitation. The idea of imitation goes even deeper than that of decorum, but is an idea that humanism shares with religion. Humanism, however, differs from religion in putting at the basis of the pattern it sets up, not man's divinity, but the something in his nature that sets him apart simply as man from other animals and that Cicero defines as a "sense of order and decorum and measure in deeds and words."[3] It dwells on the danger of any attempt to pass too abruptly to the religious level; it holds, if I may be pardoned for quoting myself, that the world would have been a better place if more persons had made sure that they were human before setting out to be superhuman. The virtue that results from a right cultivation of one's humanity, in other words from moderate and decorous living, is poise. Perfect poise is no doubt impossible: not even Sophocles succeeded in seeing life steadily and seeing it whole. The difference is none the less marked between the man who is moving towards poise and the man who is moving away from it. Since the break with the somewhat artificial decorum of the eighteenth century most men have been moving away from it. It would not be easy to argue with any plausibility that the typical modernist is greatly concerned with the law of measure; his interest, as a glance at our newspapers should suffice to show, is rather in the doing of stunts and the breaking of records, in "prodigies, feats of strength and crime,"[4] the very topics that, according to the traditional report, Confucius banished from his conversation. "Let us confess it," says Nietzsche, speaking not merely for the rank and file but for the leaders, "proportionateness is foreign to us." It is foreign to us because we no longer refer our experience to any centre. With the growth of the naturalistic temper, the normal has come to have less appeal than the novel. The pursuit of poise has tended to give way to that of uniqueness, spontaneity, and above

---

[1] For an outline of Chinese humanism, see the article by Chang Hsin-Hai in the *Hibbert Journal* for April, 1928 ("The Essentials of Confucian Wisdom").

[2] See *The Conduct of Life*, translation of the *Tsung Yung* by Ku Hung Ming (Wisdom of the East series), p. 55.

[3] "Unum hoc animal sentit quid sit ordo, quid sit quod deceat, in factis dictisque qui modus." *De Officiis*, Lib. I.

[4] See *Analects* (Wisdom of the East series), p. 109.

all intensity. "The last remnant of God on earth," says Nietzsche himself, "are the men of great longing, of great loathing, of great satiety." Once grant that there is no constant element in life and one might agree with Walter Pater that a man's highest ambition should be "to burn with a hard gem-like flame," to get "as many pulsations as possible into the given time."[5] Aesthetic perceptiveness is an excellent thing, but thus to set it up as an end in itself is almost at the opposite pole from humanism. Yet Pater has been called a humanist. One might so regard him if one accepted his view that the distinctive humanistic trait is an all-embracing curiosity.[6] Humanism appears primarily, not in the enlargement of comprehension and sympathy, desirable though this enlargement may be, but in the act of selection, in the final imposition on mere multiplicity of a scale of values. Matthew Arnold, with his striving for centrality, has far better claims to be regarded as a humanist than Pater—and that in spite of his inadequacy on the side of religion. The model that Arnold sets up for imitation in the name of culture is a constant corrective of everything that is one-sided and out of proportion. "I hate," he says, speaking not only for himself but for all true humanists, "all overpreponderance of single elements."

II

We have seen thus far that the word humanist has two main meanings—an historical meaning in its application to the scholars who turned away from the Middle Ages to the Greeks and Romans, and a psychological meaning, as one may say, that derives directly from the historical one: humanists in this latter sense are those who, in any age, aim at proportionateness through a cultivation of the law of measure. Keeping this definition in mind, we should now be prepared to deal with the confusions in the use of the word of which I spoke at the beginning. These confusions have arisen from its misapplication to various types of naturalists and supernaturalists, especially the former.

For example, the eminent orientalist, M. Sylvain Lévi, has in a recent book used the term humanism in speaking of persons as far apart as Buddha and Rousseau.[7] Buddha, it is true, had his humanistic side: he recommended that one follow a *via media* between asceticism and self-indulgence. But, unlike Confucius, he is in his primary emphasis not humanistic, but religious. The association of humanism with Rousseau is especially unjustifiable. Rousseau was, in the current sense of the word, a highly vital individual, but he cannot be properly regarded as either religious or humanistic. He attacked both humanism and religion in their traditional forms, and instead of working out some modern equivalent for these forms, helped to usher in the era of free naturalistic expansion in the midst of which we are still living. He was above all for free temperamental expansion. He was himself emotionally expansive to a degree that was incompatible not only with artificial but with real decorum. He encouraged the humanitarian hope that brotherhood among men may be based on emotional overflow. In general the most serious confusion in the use of the word humanist has arisen from its appropriation by the humanitarians. Walt Whitman was, for instance, highly Rousseauistic in his notion of brotherhood. We should therefore know what to think of the assertion of Mr. Lewis Mumford that Walt Whitman was a true humanist; also of the assumption of the term by the left-wing Unitarians and other Protestants who have been moving towards humanitarianism.[8]

The humanitarian has favoured not only temperamental expansion; he has also, as a rule, favoured the utmost ex-

[5] "Conclusion" to his volume *The Renaissance*.
[6] For Pater's definition of humanism see the end of his essay on Pico della Mirandola (*The Renaissance*).

[7] See *L'Inde et le Monde*, pp. 32, 165.
[8] See, for example, the symposium entitled *Humanist Sermons* edited by C. W. Reese (1927). On page 60 of this volume one encounters the statement that "all Americans are humanists"! For a fuller elucidation of the distinction between the humanist and the humanitarian see the opening chapters of my book *Literature and the American College* (1908).

pansion of scientific knowledge with a view to realising the Baconian ideal. Perhaps indeed the chief driving power behind the humanitarian movement has been the confidence inspired in man by the progressive control physical science has enabled him to acquire over the forces of nature. It goes without saying that the humanist is not hostile to science as such but only to a science that has overstepped its due bounds, and in general to every form of naturalism, whether rationalistic or emotional, that sets up as a substitute for humanism or religion. In the case of such encroachments there is not only a quarrel between the naturalist and the humanist, but a quarrel of first principles. When first principles are involved the law of measure is no longer applicable. One should not be moderate in dealing with error. I have pointed out elsewhere the danger of confounding the humanistic attitude with that of the Laodicean.[9]

The reason for the radical clash between the humanist and the purely naturalistic philosopher is that the humanist requires a centre to which he may refer the manifold of experience; and this the phenomenal world does not supply. In getting his centre the humanist may appeal primarily to tradition, or as I have said, to intuition. In the latter case he will need to submit to a searching Socratic dialectic the word intuition itself—to distinguish between intuitions of the One and intuitions of the Many. Otherwise he will run the risk of not being a modern but only a modernist. The contrast between modern and modernist is not unlike that between Socrates and the sophists. Both modern and modernist are under compulsion to accept in some form the ancient maxim that man is the measure of all things.[10] Only, the measure of the modern is based on a perception of the something in himself that is set above the flux and that he possesses in common with other men; whereas the per-

ception with which the modernist is chiefly concerned, to the subversion of any true measure whatsoever, is of the divergent and the changeful both within and without himself. The present menace to humanism, it has been said, is less from its enemies than from those who profess to be its friends. Thus Mr. F. C. S. Schiller of Oxford proclaims himself a humanist, and at the same time seeks to show that the true humanist was not Socrates but that precursor of recent "flowing" philosophers, Protagoras.

It should be noted that many of our votaries of change and mobility are more emotional than Protagoras or any other Greek sophist. They tend to make, not their own thoughts, but their own feelings the measure of all things. This indulgence in feeling has been encouraged by the sentimentalists who have discovered in feeling not only the quintessentially human element, but, as I have said in speaking of Rousseau, the ultimate ground of fraternal union. In our own time, partly perhaps as a result of the psycho-analytical probing of the sources of the emotional life in the subconscious, there is a growing distrust of the sentimentalist. To be sure, one may, according to the psycho-analyst, turn the emotions to good account by a process of "sublimation." Why not escape still more completely from one's complexes and infantile survivals by adjusting oneself to the cosmic order that is revealed to the scientific investigator in his laboratory? One may thus cease to be ego-centric and become truly mature and disinterested. This is the attitude that Mr. Walter Lippmann recommends in *A Preface to Morals*, and it is this attitude that, by a flagrant misuse of the word, he terms "humanism." It is well that a man should adjust himself to the reality of the natural order and, as a preliminary, should strive to be objective in the scientific sense; but humanism calls for an adjustment to a very different order that is also "real" and "objective" in its own way. It insists in short that there is a "law for man" as well as a "law for thing," and is in this

[9] See my book *Democracy and Leadership*, p. 25.
[10] For the different meanings that this maxim may ~~h~~ave see the last chapter of my book *The Masters of ~~M~~odern French Criticism*.

sense dualistic. Mr. Lippmann's attempt to base ethics on monistic postulates is, from either a religious or humanistic point of view, a revival of the stoical error. Yet he would have us believe that any one who has become disinterested after the scientific fashion has got the equivalent not only of humanism but of "high religion." By thus dissimulating the gap between the wisdom of the ages and the wisdom of the laboratory, he is flattering some of the most dangerous illusions of the present time. He escapes from the main humanitarian tendency to give to feeling a primacy that does not belong to it, only to encourage its other main tendency to accord to physical science a hegemony to which it is not entitled.

It is self-evident that humanitarianism of the scientific or utilitarian type, with its glorification of the specialist who is ready to sacrifice his rounded development, if only he can contribute his mite to "progress," is at odds with the humanistic ideal of poise and proportion. The religious pretensions of humanitarianism of this type are even more inacceptable, at least if one understands by religion anything resembling the great traditional faiths. The Baconian has inclined from the outset to substitute an outer for an inner working—the effort of the individual upon himself—that religion has, in some form or other, always required. The result has been to encourage the acquisitive life and also the pursuit of material instead of spiritual "comfort." A typical example of this utilitarian trend is Professor T. N. Carver's *Religion Worth Having*, in which he so exalts the "productive life" that religion is all but identified with thrift. At this rate it may soon be possible to get one's religion securely tucked away in a safe-deposit drawer! One should, however, be grateful to Professor Carver for not having called himself a humanist.

It does not seem possible to supply from the sentimental or Rousseauistic side of the humanitarian movement the elements that are, religiously speaking, absent from its utilitarian side. The nature to which the Rousseauist invites

one to return, is, as I have sought to show elsewhere, only a projection of the idyllic imagination. In the state of nature or some similar state thus projected, in other words in Arcadia, man is "good." Practically this has meant that there is in the natural man an altruistic impulse that may prevail over his egoism. The upshot of this myth of man's natural goodness has been to discredit the traditional controls, both humanistic and religious. Humility, conversion, decorum, all go by the board in favour of unrestricted temperamental overflow. The crucial question is whether the immense machinery of power that has resulted from the efforts of the utilitarians can be made, on this basis of unlimited expansion, to serve disinterested ends. Everything converges indeed on both sides of the humanitarian movement upon the idea of service. If it can be shown that there has been no vital omission in the passage from the service of God to the service of man, one may safely side with all the altruists from the third Earl of Shaftesbury to John Dewey. Unfortunately a formidable mass of evidence has been accumulating (the Great War was for many a convincing demonstration) that, in the natural man as he exists in the real world and not in some romantic dreamland, the will to power is more than a match for the will to service.

The benefits that have ensued from the major concentration upon the natural order that has been under way since the Renaissance have been numerous and dazzling. We are still celebrating these benefits under the name of progress. It is no longer possible, however, to allay the suspicion that the price which has been paid for progress of this type has been a growing superficiality in dealing with the still more important problems of the human order. "Nothing is more certain," says Burke in a well-known passage, "than that our manners, our civilisation, and all the good things which are connected with manners and with civilisation, have, in this European world of ours, depended for ages upon two principles; and were indeed the result of both combined; I mean the spirit of a gentleman and the spirit of religion." The whole debate would seem to narrow down to the question whether it is possible to secure on utilitarian-sentimental lines a valid equivalent for Burke's two principles. As for the "spirit of a gentleman," its decline is so obvious as scarcely to admit of argument. It has even been maintained that in America, the country in which the collapse of traditional standards has been most complete, the gentleman is at a positive disadvantage in the world of practical affairs; he is likely to get on more quickly if he assumes the "mucker pose."[11] According to William James, usually taken to be the representative American philosopher, the very idea of the gentleman has about it something slightly satanic. "The prince of darkness," says James, "may be a gentleman, as we are told he is, but, whatever the God of earth and heaven is, he can surely be no gentleman."

As for the "spirit of religion," I have already glanced at its humanitarian substitute. The humanitarian maintains that the spirit that appears in Christianity will, if disengaged from mere dogma, be found to be something very similar to his own spirit of service. One should at least be able to understand the position of the person who has become convinced that there is a supernatural element in genuine Christianity, lost in the passage from the old dispensation to the new, for which mere altruism is no substitute, and who therefore takes his stand on the side of tradition. Dogmatic and revealed religion, he argues, was alone capable of rescuing the ancient world from a decadent naturalism. It alone affords an avenue of escape from the analogous situation that confronts the world to-day.

III

The relation of the humanist to this religious traditionalist can scarcely be defined too carefully. Between the humanist and the humanitarian, I have said, there is a clash of first principles. Between the humanist and the authentic Christian, on the other hand, there is room for important co-operation. To be sure, many of the leaders of the early Church were satisfied with nothing short of a stark supernaturalism and inclined to reject the genuinely humanistic elements of the ancient civilisation along with its naturalistic errors. But the orthodox attitude has, in spite of the difficulties of reconciling otherworldliness with a merely secular wisdom, come to be one of friendliness to the classical humanities.[12] Mr. T. S. Eliot is probably close to this attitude when he maintains that humanism is of very great value, but only in subordination to the historical Church. As an independent doctrine, at least in any large way, it is, he maintains, ineffective. A broad survey of the past does not, however, confirm the view that humanism is thus either precarious or parasitical. The two most notable manifestations of the humanistic spirit that the world has seen, that in ancient Greece and that in Confucian China, did not have the support of Christianity or any other form of revealed religion. Take again the humanism of seventeenth-century France: the ideal of the finely poised gentleman who "does not plume himself on anything" was often allied with Christianity ("devout humanism"), but it was also found among the free-thinkers ("libertines") who were hostile to every form of belief in the supernatural.

In general, why should not the humanist, it may be asked, devote himself quietly to his own task—that of effecting an adjustment between the law of measure and the ever-novel emergencies of actual living, and at the same time refuse to take sides too decisively in the great debate between the naturalists and the supernaturalists? If pressed too hard by the supernaturalists

[11] See "The Mucker Pose" by James Truslow Adams, *Harper's Magazine*, November, 1928; reprinted in *Our Business Civilisation* (1929).

[12] For the early hostility of certain Christians to Graeco-Roman culture and the final reconciliation between this culture and the Church, see E. K. Rand's *Founders of the Middle Ages, passim*. Cf. also P.E. More's "Paradox of Oxford" (*Shelburne Essays*, Vol. IX).

in particular, why should he not reply in the words of Pope:

"Presume not God to scan;
The proper study of mankind is man"?

One must, however, admit an element of truth in the assertion of Plato that things human cannot be properly known without a previous insight into things divine. Another thinker, Pascal, who had this religious insight in a high degree, though combined with a form of dogma peculiarly alien to most modern men, declared that unless man has the support of the supernatural, unless in short he attains to true humility, he will fall fatally either into the stoic pride or else, through the intermediary stage of scepticism, into the epicurean relaxation. The whole question bristles with difficulties: one thinks of the immense and, on the whole, salutary influence that two Roman humanists, Cicero and Horace, have exercised on occidental culture, though, to adopt Pascal's classification, the humanism of Cicero leaned unduly to the stoical side, that of Horace to the epicurean. Yet I believe that the humanist will finally be forced to recognise that there is truth in Pascal's contention, that he will have to take sides in the debate between naturalists and supernaturalists, however much he may deplore the frequent failure of both of these fell antagonists to do justice to the immense range of human experience that is subject primarily to the law of measure.

For my own part, I range myself unhesitatingly on the side of the supernaturalists. Though I see no evidence that humanism is necessarily ineffective apart from dogmatic and revealed religion, there is, as it seems to me, evidence that it gains immensely in effectiveness when it has a background of religious insight. One is conscious of such a background, for example, in Sophocles, who ranks high among occidental humanists, as well as in Confucius, the chief exponent of the humanistic idea in the Orient. The phrase religious insight is in itself vague. Is it not possible to give the phrase a definite content without departing from the critical attitude? One may be helped to such a definition by asking oneself what element has tended to fall out of the life of the modern man with the decline of the traditional disciplines. According to Mr. Walter Lippmann, the conviction the modern man has lost is that "there is an immortal essence presiding like a king over his appetites." But why abandon the affirmation of such an "essence" or higher will, to the mere traditionalist? Why not affirm it first of all as a psychological fact, one of the immediate data of consciousness, a perception so primordial that, compared with it, the deterministic denials of man's moral freedom are only a metaphysical dream? One would thus be in a position to perform a swift flanking movement on the behaviourists and other naturalistic psychologists who are to be regarded at present as among the chief enemies of human nature. One might at the same time be in a fair way to escape from the modernist dilemma and become a thoroughgoing and complete modern.

The philosophers have often debated the question of the priority of will or intellect in man. The quality of will that I am discussing and that rightly deserves to be accounted supernatural, has, however, been associated in traditional Christianity not primarily with man's will, but with God's will in the form of grace. The theologians have indulged in many unprofitable subtleties apropos of grace. One cannot afford, however, as has been the modern tendency, to discard the psychological truth of the doctrine along with these subtleties. The higher will must simply be accepted as a mystery that may be studied in its practical effects, but that in its ultimate nature, is incapable of formulation. Herein the higher will is not peculiar. "All things," according to the scholastic maxim, "end in a mystery" (*Omnia exeunt in mysterium*). The man of science is increasingly willing to grant that the reality behind the phenomena he is studying not only eludes him, but must in the nature of the case ever elude him. He no longer holds, for example, as his more dogmatic forebears of the nineteenth century inclined to do, that the mechanistic hypothesis, valuable as it has proved itself to be as a laboratory technique, is absolutely true; its truth is, he admits, relative and provisional.

The person who declines to turn the higher will to account until he is sure he has grasped its ultimate nature is very much on a level with the man who should refuse to make practical use of electrical energy until he is certain he has an impeccable theory of electricity. Negatively one may say of the higher will, without overstepping the critical attitude, that it is not the absolute, nor again the categorical imperative; not the organic and still less the mechanical; finally, not the "ideal" in the current sense of that term. Positively one may define it as the higher immediacy that is known in its relation to the lower immediacy—the merely temperamental man with his impressions and emotions and expansive desires—as a power of vital control (*frein vital*). Failure to exercise this control is the spiritual indolence that is for both Christian and Buddhist a chief source, if not the chief source, of evil. Though Aristotle, after the Greek fashion, gives the primacy not to will but to mind, the power of which I have been speaking is surely related to his "energy of soul," the form of activity distinct from a mere outer working, deemed by him appropriate for the life of leisure that he proposes as the goal of a liberal education. Happiness, which is for him the end of ends, is itself, he tells us, "a kind of working." Here is a difference, one may note in passing, between a true humanist like Aristotle and the epicurean who also has his doctrine of moderation and so often sets up as a humanist. It is no doubt well, as the epicurean urges, so to indulge in present pleasures that they may not be injurious to future ones. To employ the trivial illustration, it is well to avoid overeating at dinner lest one impair one's appetite for supper. But

the meaning of the Aristotelian working is that one should not be content with transitory pleasure at all, but should be striving constantly to rise from a lower to a higher range of satisfactions. The energy of soul that has served on the humanistic level for mediation appears on the religious level in the form of meditation. Religion may of course mean a great deal more than meditation. At the same time humanistic mediation that has the support of meditation may correctly be said to have a religious background. Mediation and meditation are after all only different stages in the same ascending "path" and should not be arbitrarily separated.

This question comes up especially in connection with the rôle of enthusiasm. Humanism is not primarily enthusiastic, whereas religion is. There is a touch of enthusiasm even in Aristotle, in general one of the coolest and most detached of thinkers, when he comes to the passage from the humanistic to the religious level. "We should not," he says, "pay heed to those who bid us think as mortals, but should, as far as may be, seek to make ourselves immortal." At the same time it must be admitted that even a true religious enthusiasm is hard to combine with poise and that this true enthusiasm has many counterfeits. "For one inspired, ten thousand are possessed," wrote the Earl of Roscommon, having in mind the religious zealots of the English seventeenth century. The neo-classic gentleman was therefore as a rule distinctly unfriendly to the enthusiast. The humanist, however, should not deny enthusiasm but merely insist on defining it. He cannot afford to be an enthusiast in Rousseau's sense; on the other hand, he should not neglect the truth of Rousseau's saying that "cold reason has never done anything illustrious."

Though one should, in my judgment, side with the oriental as against Aristotle and the Greeks in giving priority to the higher will over mind,[13] especially

[13] See Ch. V of *Democracy and Leadership* ("Europe and Asia"); also Appendix A ("Theories of the Will").

if one attaches importance to the supreme religious virtue, humility, it yet remains true that this will must be exercised intelligently. Granted that the existence in man of a power of control may be affirmed, quite apart from any dogma, as a psychological fact, the individual must nevertheless go beyond this fact if he is to decide rightly how far he needs to exercise control in any particular instance: in short, he needs standards. In getting his standards the humanist of the best type is not content to acquiesce inertly in tradition. He is aware that there is always entering into life an element of vital novelty and that the wisdom of the past, invaluable though it is, cannot therefore be brought to bear too literally on the present. He knows that, though standards are necessary, they should be held flexibly and that, to accomplish this feat, he must make the most difficult of all mediations, that between the One and the Many. The chief enemies of the humanist are the pragmatists and other philosophers of the flux who simplify this problem for themselves by dismissing the One, which is actually a living intuition, as a metaphysical abstraction.

Whatever reality man achieves in his dealings with either the human or the natural order, is dependent, I have tried to show elsewhere, on the degree to which he establishes a correct relationship between the part of himself that perceives, the part that conceives, and the part that discriminates. The part that conceives, that reaches out and seizes likenesses and analogies, may be defined as imagination; the part that discriminates and tests the unity thus apprehended from the point of view of its truth may be defined as analytical reason; the part that perceives is, in the case of the humanist, primarily concerned with the something in man that is set above the phenomenal order and that I have already defined as a power of control. One may say therefore that standards result from a co-operation between imagination and reason, dealing with the more specifically human aspects of experience, and that

these standards should be pressed into the service of the higher will with a view to imposing a right direction on the emotions and expansive desires of the natural man. The supreme goal of ethical endeavour, as Plato pointed out long ago, is that one should come to like and dislike the right things.

IV

Humanism, even humanism of the distinctly individualistic type I have been outlining, may, as I have already suggested, work in harmony with traditional religion. In that case there must be a careful determination of boundaries. Though humanism and religion both lie on the same ascending path from the naturalistic flux, one must insist that each has its separate domain. It is an error to hold that humanism can take the place of religion. Religion indeed may more readily dispense with humanism than humanism with religion. Humanism gains greatly by having a religious background in the sense I have indicated; whereas religion, for the man who has actually renounced the world, may very conceivably be all in all. On the other hand, the man who sets out to live religiously in the secular order without having recourse to the wisdom of the humanist is likely to fall into vicious confusions—notably, into a confusion between the things of God and the things of Caesar. The Catholic Church has therefore been well inspired in rounding out its religious doctrine with the teaching of Aristotle and other masters of the law of measure. It can scarcely fail to recognise that the position of the positive and critical humanist is sound *as far as it goes*. It follows that the Catholic and the non-Catholic should be able to co-operate on the humanistic level. A like co-operation should be possible between the humanist and the members of other Christian communions who have not as yet succumbed entirely to humanitarianism.

I have tried to show that the weakness of humanitarianism from both the humanistic and the religious point of view is that it holds out the hope of securing certain spiritual benefits—for example, peace and brotherhood—without any ascent from the naturalistic level. The positive and critical humanist would seem to have a certain tactical superiority over the religious traditionalist in dealing with the defects of the humanitarian programme. In the battle of ideas, as in other forms of warfare, the advantage is on the side of those who take the offensive. The modernists have broken with tradition partly because it is not sufficiently immediate, partly because it is not sufficiently experimental. Why not meet them on their own ground and, having got rid of every ounce of unnecessary metaphysical and theological baggage, oppose to them something that is both immediate and experimental—namely the presence in man of a higher will or power of control? I use the word experimental deliberately by way of protest against the undue narrowing of this word by the scientific naturalists to observation of the phenomenal order and of man only in so far as he comes under this order. One should also protest against the restriction of the term reality to observation of this type. Some of the most monstrous mutilations of reality that the world has ever seen are being perpetrated at this moment—for example, by the behaviouristic psychologists—in the name of the "real." At all events everything in the modernist movement will be found to converge either upon the rôle of feeling or upon the rôle of experiment, and the final question raised in either case is that of the will. As a result of the combined influence of the various types of naturalists, the present age is at once more emotional and more mechanical than any other of which we have historical record. By mechanical I refer primarily not to the multiplication of machines in the outer world but to the mechanising of mind itself. An effective procedure is, as I have said, to meet the mechanist on his own ground and point out to him that he is unduly dogmatic, if he holds that his hypothesis is absolutely valid even for the natural order, and that, if he goes further and seeks to make it cover the whole of experience, to impose a deterministic nightmare on the human spirit itself, he is abandoning the experimental attitude for an even more objectionable form of dogmatism.

Similarly one should meet the emotionalist on his favourite ground of immediacy. Inasmuch as the higher immediacy has been largely associated in the Christian occident with the operation of God's will, the substitution for it of the lower immediacy has meant practically the setting up of a subrational parody of grace. In order to make this parody plausible, the emotionalist has had recourse to the usual arts of the sophist, chief among which are a juggling with half-truths and a tampering with general terms. I have commented elsewhere on the way in which words like "virtue" and "conscience" have been so twisted from their traditional meaning as to eliminate the dualistic element that both humanism and religion require. If there is to be any recovery of the truths of dualism, at least along critical lines, a battle royal will need to be fought over the word "nature" itself; here, if anywhere, one needs to practise a Socratic dichotomy.

The half-truth that has been used to compromise religion in particular is that, though religion is in itself something quite distinct from emotion, it is in its ordinary manifestations very much mixed up with emotion. I give an example of this error in its latest and fashionable form. In a very learned and, in some respects, able book,[14] the Rev. N. P. Williams seeks to show that St. Augustine's experience of grace or, what amounts to the same thing, his love of God, was only a "sublimation" of his "lust." St. Augustine was a very passionate man and his passionateness no doubt enters into his love of God. But if it could be shown that the love of God was in St. Augustine or any other of the major saints merely emotion, sublimated or unsublimated, reli-

14 *The Ideas of the Fall and of Original Sin* (Bampton Lectures for 1924). See p. 331.

gion would be only the "illusion" that Freud himself has declared it to be. The psycho-analytical divine, who is, I am told, a fairly frequent type in England, is about the worst *mélange des genres* that has appeared even in the present age of confusion.

One may be helped in escaping from this confusion by considering, so far as possible from a strictly psychological point of view, what the exercise of the higher will has actually meant in genuine religion. One must admit at the outset the difficulty of determining what is genuine religion. Religion, not merely to-day but always, has been subject to extraordinary perversions. It has ever been the chosen domain of self-deception and "wishful" thinking. When one reflects on the fanaticism, casuistry, obscurantism, and hypocrisy that have defaced the history of Christianity itself, one is tempted at times to acquiesce in the famous exclamation of Lucretius.[15] Yet one must insist that religion is in its purity the very height of man. As to where this pure religion is to be found, we should keep in mind the saying of Joubert that in matters religious it is a bad sign when one differs from the saints. Let us then turn to the saints in whom there is some authentic survival of the spirit of the Founder. This spirit surely appears in the author of the *Imitation* when he writes: "Know for certain that thou must lead a dying life; and the more a man dies to himself the more he begins to live in God." Moreover the author of the *Imitation* is at one here not only with Christ but with Buddha, the chief source of sanctity in the Far East.

The point on which Christ and Buddha are in accord is the need of renunciation. It should be abundantly plain from all I have said that the higher will is felt in its relation to the expansive desires as a will to refrain. The humanist does not carry the exercise of this will beyond a subduing of his desires to the law of measure; but it may be carried much further until it amounts to a turning away from the

[15] "Tantum religio potuit suadere malorum."

desires of the natural man altogether— the "dying to the world" of the Christian.

With this background in mind, we should know what to think of the humanistic and religious claims of the modernist movement. This movement has, from the eighteenth century and in some respects from the Renaissance, been marked by a growing discredit of the will to refrain. The very word renunciation has been rarely pronounced by those who have entered into the movement. The chief exception that occurs to one is Goethe (echoed at times by Carlyle). Any one who thinks of the series of Goethe's love affairs prolonged into the seventies, is scarcely likely to maintain that his *Entsagung* was of a very austere character even for the man of the world, not to speak of the saint. The humanitarians in particular, whether of the utilitarian or of the sentimental type, have put slight emphasis on the inner control of appetite. They have encouraged, either directly or through the ineffectiveness of the substitutes they have offered for this control, a multiplication and complication of desires that is in flat contradiction with the wisdom of the ages. Judged by the standards of the great traditional faiths, the religion of "progress" or "service" or "humanity" merely illustrates on a vast scale the truth of the old Latin adage that "the world wishes to be deceived." The various naturalistic philosophies that have been built up on the ruins of tradition should, at all events, whatever their merits or demerits, be made to stand on their own feet. It should be one's ambition to develop so keen a Socratic dialectic, supported by such a wealth of historical illustration, that it will not be easy for the Walter Lippmanns of the future to propose some form of naturalism as the equivalent of "humanism" and "high religion."

In his attempt to show the inadequacy of humanism apart from dogmatic and revealed religion, Mr. T. S. Eliot has painted a picture of the humanist exercising in a sort of psychic solitude self-control purely for the sake of control. It is evident however that the real humanist consents, like Aristotle, to limit his desires only in so far as this limitation can be shown to make for his own happiness. This primary reference to the individual and his happiness is something with which we are nowadays rather unfamiliar. Our preoccupation, one is almost tempted to say our obsession, is, at least in our official philosophy, with society and its supposed interests. A study of humanism from the sociological point of view would call for a separate essay. I may, however, indicate briefly the main issue: the individual who is practising humanistic control is really subordinating to the part of himself which he possesses in common with other men, that part of himself which is driving him apart from them. If several individuals submit to the same or a similar humanistic discipline, they will become psychically less separate, will, in short, move towards a communion. A group that is thus getting together on a sound ethical basis will be felt at once as an element of social order and stability.

No doubt a still more perfect communion may be achieved on the religious level. There are however differences of dogma and ecclesiastical discipline that make a meeting on this plane difficult even for the various denominations of Christians. If one's survey is extended, as it should be in these days of universal and facile material communication, to include Mahometans and Hindus and Chinese, the obstacles in the way of a union among men that is primarily religious are seen to be well-nigh insuperable. It might, for example, be conducive to the peace of the world if everybody, East and West, accepted the authority of the Pope. The chances of such universal acceptance are, however, short of some very "visible upset of grace," practically negligible. One can scarcely remind oneself too often that the great traditional faiths, notably Christianity and Buddhism,[16] have their humanistic side where closer agreement

16 Confucianism is of course primarily humanistic.

may be possible. If the leaders of the various national and cultural groups could bring themselves to display in their dealings with one another moderation, common sense and common decency, they would accomplish a great deal—vastly more than they have been accomplishing of late. The difficulties in the way of an understanding, even on this humanistic basis, not to speak of any deeper religious understanding, have been augmented by the fact that large numbers in the Christian occident as well as in the orient, especially in China, are falling away from their traditional disciplines into spiritual anarchy. The dangers of this anarchy, combined, as it is, with the accumulation of a formidable mass of machinery that, in the abeyance of any higher will, is likely to be pressed into the service of the will to power, are appalling.

The first step, if there is to be an effective opposition to spiritual anarchy of the current type, must be, as I remarked at the outset, right definition. The idea is becoming fairly widespread that there is needed at present a reaction from the romantic movement and that this reaction should assume a religious or a humanistic character. This idea will not in itself take us very far. Even Benedetto Croce, whose philosophy would seem to be in its underlying postulates almost at the opposite pole from a genuinely religious or humanistic position, has declared that we need a "new Christianity" or a "new humanism," if we are to escape "from intellectual anarchy, from unbridled individualism, from sensualism, from scepticism, from pessimism, from every aberration which for a century and a half has been harassing the soul of man and the society of mankind under the name of Romanticism."

Occasional humanists may appear under existing conditions, but if there is to be anything deserving to be called a humanistic movement, it will be necessary that a considerable number of persons get at least within hailing distance of one another as to the definition of the word humanism itself and the nature of the discipline that this definition entails. This preliminary understanding once established, they could then proceed, in the literal sense of that unjustly discredited term, to work out a convention. Their next concern would almost inevitably be with education. Education is, as Professor Gass has remarked, the one altruistic activity of the humanist. The reason is that if the humanistic goal is to be achieved, if the adult is to like and dislike the right things, he must be trained in the appropriate habits almost from infancy. The whole question should be of special interest to Americans. Economic and other conditions are more favourable in this country than elsewhere for the achievement of a

truly liberal conception of education with the idea of leisure enshrined at its very centre. In the meanwhile, our educational policies, from the elementary grades to the university, are being controlled by humanitarians. They are busy at this very moment, almost to a man, proclaiming the gospel of service. It will be strange indeed if dissatisfaction with this situation is not felt by a growing minority, if a demand does not arise for at least a few institutions of learning that are humanistic rather than humanitarian in their aims. One is at all events safe in affirming that the battle that is to determine the fate of American civilisation will be fought out first of all in the field of education.

MAUD BODKIN

An English psychologist and critic, Miss Bodkin has greatly influenced American myth criticism of the past twenty years through her *Archetypal Patterns in Poetry, Psychological Studies of Imagination* (1934), in which she applies C. G. Jung's theory of archetypes to the study of poetry. Unlike some myth critics, Miss Bodkin does not make use of the rebirth archetype as a Procrustean pattern but rather interprets recurrent literary themes in the broadest possible context of contemporary experience—explaining them in psychological terms and emphasizing the collective nature of readers' responses. Her continuing interest in literature as a source of group values lost in the decay of traditional religious faiths appears in her more recent *Studies of Type-Images in Poetry, Religion and Philosophy* (1951).

Archetypal Patterns in Tragic Poetry (1934)

I

In an article, 'On the relation of analytical psychology to poetic art',[1] Dr. C. G. Jung has set forth an hypothesis in regard to the psychological significance of poetry. The special emotional signifi-

From *Archetypal Patterns in Poetry, Psychological Studies of Imagination* (1934), pp. 1-25, by Maud Bodkin. Reprinted by permission of Oxford University Press.
[1] Included in *Contributions to Analytical Psychology*, trans. H. G. and C. F. Baynes (Kegan Paul, 1928).

cance possessed by certain poems—a significance going beyond any definite meaning conveyed—he attributes to the stirring in the reader's mind, within or beneath his conscious response, of unconscious forces which he terms 'primordial images', or archetypes. These archetypes he describes as 'psychic residua of numberless experiences of the same type', experiences which have happened not to the individual but to his ancestors, and of which the results are inherited in the structure of the brain, *a priori* determinants of individual experience.

It is the aim of our present writer to examine this hypothesis, testing it in regard to examples where we can bring together the recorded experience and reflection of minds approaching the matter from different standpoints. It is hoped that, in this way, something may be done towards enriching the formulated theory of the systematic psychologist through the insight of more intuitive thinkers, while at the same time the intuitive thinker's results may receive somewhat more exact definition.

My first illustration I shall take from an essay by Professor Gilbert Murray,[2] where the effect of great poetic drama is described in language somewhat similar to that of Jung. Gilbert Murray has been comparing the tragedies of *Hamlet* and of *Orestes*, noting the curious similarities between them, and how the theme that underlies them seems to have shown an 'almost eternal durability'. When such themes as stirred the interest of primitive man move us now, he says, 'they will tend to do so in ways which we recognize as particularly profound and poetical' (p. 238). Gilbert Murray apologizes for the metaphor of which he cannot keep clear when he says that such stories and situations are 'deeply implanted in the memory of the race, stamped as it were upon our physical organism'. We say that such themes 'are strange to us. Yet there is that within us which leaps at the sight of them, a cry of the blood which tells us we have known them always' (p. 239). And again: 'In plays like *Hamlet* or the *Agamemnon* or the *Electra* we have certainly fine and flexible character-study, a varied and well-wrought story, a full command of the technical instruments of the poet and the dramatist; but we have also, I suspect, a strange, unanalysed vibration below the surface, an undercurrent of desires and fears and passions, long slumbering yet eternally familiar, which have for thousands of

[2] 'Hamlet and Orestes', in *The Classical Tradition in Poetry* (Oxford, 1927).

years lain near the root of our most intimate emotions and been wrought into the fabric of our most magical dreams. How far into past ages this stream may reach back, I dare not even surmise; but it seems as if the power of stirring it or moving with it were one of the last secrets of genius' (pp. 239-40).

We have here an expression, itself somewhat imaginative and poetical, of an experience in presence of poetry which we may submit to closer examination—and this in two ways. We may study the themes that show this persistence within the life of a community or race, and may compare the different forms which they assume; also we may study analytically in different individuals the inner experience of responding to such themes.

The inquiry is plainly of a subtlety and complexity apt to discourage at the outset those who prefer to avoid all questions that cannot be investigated in accordance with a strict technique. There is little possibility here for experiment, since the kind of emotional experience which it is desired to investigate cannot be commanded at will under test conditions. A profound response to great poetic themes can be secured only by living with such themes, dwelling and brooding upon them, choosing those moments when the mind seems spontaneously to open itself to their influence. We must take where we can find it the recorded experience of those who have such acquaintance with poetry.

To the present writer it appears, however, that it is by the study of such deeper experience that psychology at the present time particularly needs enrichment. We might almost say that academic psychologists have been routed by the attack of those medical writers who claim access to the deeper layers of the mind, just because the demand for exact verifiable results has held academic psychologists to the mere outworks or surface of the mind they set out to study. If inexactness of thought or one-sided emphasis has characterized the medical writers, this can be established only by following them along the obscure paths they have opened into the concrete human psyche, and bringing to bear, if possible, a wider ranging interest and a more exact and cautious scrutiny.

The student who seeks to explore the imaginative response of present-day minds to the great themes of poetry may profit by considering the work not only of the medical psychologists, but also of the anthropologists who have attempted to study scientifically the reactions of more primitive minds. In studying the reception by a people of new cultural elements anthropologists have made use of the term 'cultural pattern' to designate the pre-existing 'configuration', or order of arrangement, of tendencies which determines the response of members of the group to the new element. In discussing the value for our 'conceptual explorations' of 'the culture pattern concept', Goldenweiser[3] has noted its relation to the concept of form and system in the arts and cultural disciplines; and L. L. Bernard, in the same work, has undertaken a classification of different kinds of environment, distinguishing the psycho-social environment, which includes such systems of symbols as are preserved in books, and in which he says 'psychic processes reach the highest type of their objectified development'. Such stored symbolic content can at any time become effective in activating the corresponding patterns in the minds of members of the group whose collective product and possession the symbols are.

It is within the general field of anthropology or social psychology that I conceive the inquiry to lie which I am here attempting to pursue. I shall use the term 'archetypal pattern' to refer to that within us which, in Gilbert Murray's phrase, leaps in response to the effective presentation in poetry of an ancient theme. The hypothesis to be examined is that in poetry—and here we are to consider in particular tragic poetry—we may identify themes having a particular form or pattern which persists amid variation from age to age, and which corresponds to a pattern or configuration of emotional tendencies in the minds of those who are stirred by the theme.

In Jung's formulation of the hypothesis, and in the more tentative metaphorical statement of Gilbert Murray, it is asserted that these patterns are 'stamped upon the physical organism', 'inherited in the structure of the brain'; but of this statement no evidence can be considered here. Jung believes himself to have evidence of the spontaneous production of ancient patterns in the dreams and fantasies of individuals who had no discoverable access to cultural material in which the patterns were embodied. This evidence is, however, hard to evaluate; especially in view of the way in which certain surprising reproductions, in trance states, of old material, have been subsequently traced to forgotten impressions of sense in the lifetime of the individual.

Of more force in the present state of our knowledge is the general argument that where forms are assimilated from the environment upon slight contact only, predisposing factors must be present in mind and brain. Whoever has experienced and reflected upon the attempt to convey an idea, especially an idea of intimate and emotional character, to a mind unprepared to receive it, will have realized that it is not mere contact with an idea's expression that secures its assimilation. Some inner factor must co-operate. When it is lacking, the experienced futility of attempted communication is the most convincing proof that it is, as Mr. F. C. Bartlett has said, 'not fanciful to hold' that for the capture of objects complete, by the assimilative imagination, there must stir within us 'larger systems of feeling, of memory, of ideas, of aspirations'.[4] Such systems may be cultural patterns confined to a particular group at a certain time, or may characterize a

3 *The Social Sciences and their Interrelations*, edited by W. F. Ogburn and A. Goldenweiser (Allen & Unwin, 1928).

4 'Types of Imagination', *J. of Philos. Studies*, iii, part 9, p. 80.

particular individual; but there are others of much wider range. Our question is whether there are some whose 'almost eternal durability', in Gilbert Murray's phrase, justifies us in applying to them the term archetypal, and renders them of special interest and importance to the student of psychology and of literature.

II

We come nearer to our particular subject in raising the question: What is the distinctive advantage of having recourse to poetry for the study of these patterns?

Such a theme as that discussed by Gilbert Murray existed as a traditional story in ancient Greece before Aeschylus, and in Northern Europe before Shakespeare handled it. In that form it was already, as A. C. Bradley says of another traditional theme, 'an inchoate poem': 'such a subject, as it exists in the general imagination, has some aesthetic value before the poet touches it'; 'it is already in some degree organized and formed'.[5] Enriched by the poet's touch, the traditional story lives on in our imagination, a memory with aesthetic value, but fading into formlessness, when, as perhaps now in the mind of the reader, the reference to Orestes or to Hamlet excites only a faint recollection of what was once a vivid poetic experience. When, therefore, we desire to examine psychologically the emotional pattern corresponding to a poetic theme, we may sometimes avail ourselves of references to the mere tales recalled in outline, but for closer examination there is need that the actual poetic experience be recovered, since it is in the imaginative experience actually communicated by great poetry that we shall find our fullest opportunity of studying the patterns that we seek—and this from the very nature of poetic experience.

In the writings of Professor Spearman, which have had so much influence in the determining of psychological

method, there are references to imagination—one particularly to imagination as exercised in poetry[6]—in which he asserts that imagination in its intellectual aspect does not differ essentially from any other logical process in which new content may also be said to be generated, as when, from a given term, say 'good', and a knowledge of the nature of verbal opposition, we pass to the term, 'bad'. Such a treatment of imagination illustrates the kind of abstraction that makes psychology, to some thinkers, appear so unreal and empty a study. A student who is interested in imaginative activity as exercised in poetry cannot accept the view that its intellectual aspect can be separated from its emotional nature and covered by any such logical formula as Spearman proposes.

Of the three laws of cognition which Professor Spearman formulates it would seem to be the first which most nearly concerns the poetic imagination. This law is stated: 'Any lived experience tends to evoke immediately a knowing of its characters and experiences.' A note adds: 'The word "immediately" means here the absence of any mediating process.'[7] It is perhaps within this mediating process, denied by Spearman, that we may find a distinctive place for imagination as exercised in poetry.

When psychologists have raised the question: How does lived experience come to awareness? they have usually been content to assert that it happens through introspection, and to leave to philosophers any further investigation of the question. It is here that difficulty has arisen between the academic and the medical psychologists; since the latter believe themselves to have discovered large ranges of lived experience, of conative character, of which introspection can give no account—a discovery that seems surprising to those who believe that in introspection we have direct access to the nature of our desires.

Professor S. Alexander,[8] examining

---

[5] *Oxford Lectures on Poetry* (Macmillan, 1909), pp. 11-12.

[6] *The Nature of Intelligence and the Principles of Cognition* (Macmillan, 1927), pp. 334-6.
[7] *Ibid.*, p. 48.
[8] *Space, Time, and Deity* (Macmillan, 1920).

the question as a philosopher, concludes that lived experience, which is of conative character—as distinct from sensations and images, the objects of the mind—can only be 'enjoyed'; it cannot be contemplated. Introspection, he says, is 'enjoyment' lived through, together with 'a whole apparatus of elaborated speech' (i. 18), which causes the elements of the experience enjoyed to stand out in 'subtly dissected form' (p. 19). 'It is small wonder,' he adds, 'that we should regard our introspection as turning our minds into objects, seeing how largely the language which expresses our mental state has been elaborated in pursuit of practical interests and in contact with physical objects.'

If this view is accepted, we see that the mediating process necessary before lived experience can come to awareness is the linking of such experience with actions and objects that affect the senses and can be contemplated, and with words that recall these objects in all their variety of human perspective. It is in the process of fantasy that the contemplated characters of things are broken from their historical setting and made available to express the needs and impulses of the experiencing mind. The recent study of dreams appears to have made it certain that the bewildering sequence of the images thrown up by the sleeping mind is due to processes of interaction between emotional dispositions lacking the customary control. In individual waking fantasy, and in myth and legend, we have other sequences of images which emotional patterns determine, and which seem to us strange as dreams, when, repeating them in the words used also for the results of logical reflection, we are led to contrast these incompatible renderings of experience.

When a great poet uses the stories that have taken shape in the fantasy of the community, it is not his individual sensibility alone that he objectifies. Responding with unusual sensitiveness to the words and images which already express the emotional experience of the community, the poet arranges these so as to utilize to the full their evocative power. Thus he attains for himself vision and possession of the experience engendered between his own soul and the life around him, and communicates that experience, at once individual and collective, to others, so far as they can respond adequately to the words and images he uses.

We see, then, why, if we wish to contemplate the emotional patterns hidden in our individual lives, we may study them in the mirror of our spontaneous actions, so far as we can recall them, or in dreams and in the flow of waking fantasy; but if we would contemplate the archetypal patterns that we have in common with men of past generations, we do well to study them in the experience communicated by the great poetry that has continued to stir emotional response from age to age. In studying such poetry here, we are not asking what was in the mind of Aeschylus or of Shakespeare when he fashioned the figure of Orestes or of Hamlet, nor do we ask how these figures affected a Greek or an Elizabethan audience. The question is between the writer and the reader of this book: what do the figures of Orestes and Hamlet stand for in the experience communicated to us, as we see, read, or vividly recall the Greek or Shakespearian tragedy?

III

A preliminary difficulty, already touched on, must be considered in more detail. How can we secure that the experience communicated by a great play shall be present to us with such completeness and intensity that we can make adequate study of it?

A parallel question has been discussed by Percy Lubbock[9] in regard to the study of the form of a novel. Critical perception, he says, is of no use to us if we cannot retain the image of a book, and the book reaches us as a passage of experience never present in its completeness. The task of the reader, before he can criticize, is to refashion the novel

[9] *The Craft of Fiction* (The Travellers' Library, 1926).

ut of the march of experience as it
assed. The procession 'must be mar-
halled and concentrated somewhere'
p. 15).

In watching a play adequately inter-
reted upon the stage, we find, perhaps
nore readily than in the silent reading
f a novel, that the procession of experi-
nce is marshalled and concentrated at
ertain points; so that, recalling the
mages of these, we can look back
pon the whole play as a living unity.
The powerful emotional impression thus
ttained may persist while the play is
ead and recurred to again and again,
nd the individual impression clarified
y comparison with the reflective re-
ults of critics and scholars. Central pas-
ages, while the play is thus lived with,
row ever richer in meaning, becoming
ntertwined with the emotional experi-
nce of one's own life.

Some such experience of *Hamlet* I
nust presume in the reader, since I can-
ot afford space to recall the play at all
ully. I will venture, however, to refer
o that passage in which for me the
ignificance of the whole play seems
nost concentrated.

From the experience of seeing *Hamlet*
erformed some thirty years ago, there
as remained with me the memory of
he strange exaltation and wonder of
eauty that attended the words of the
ying Hamlet to Horatio:

If thou didst ever hold me in thy heart,
Absent thee from felicity awhile,
And in this harsh world draw thy breath in
    pain,
To tell my story.

This is one of the passages chosen by
Matthew Arnold[10] as 'touchstones' for
poetry—passages possessing both in style
and substance supreme poetic quality,
the Aristotelian high truth and seriousness, beyond that of history or ordinary
speech. I would suggest that this 'high
truth' of which Matthew Arnold speaks
—like that character attributed by
Lascelles Abercrombie to great poetry,
'a confluence of all kinds of life into a

single flame of consciousness'—belongs
to the lines not as isolated, but as grown
familiar in their setting—the unified experience of the play converging upon
them and the incantation of their music
carrying them ever deeper into the
secret places of the mind that loves
them.

One may make some attempt to
analyse that 'incantation',[11] or enchantment, in which rhythm and sound of
words evidently play a part. It seems
to me that the enchantment of the line,
'Absent thee from felicity awhile', is
heightened by the later echoing of its
sounds in the lines spoken by Horatio:

Good night, sweet prince,
And flights of angels sing thee to thy rest!

Against this music of heaven we feel
more poignantly the contrast of the
words, 'in this harsh world draw thy
breath in pain', that move, labouring,
toward their goal in the words, 'to tell
my story'. Through their power of incantation these words, as they fall in
their place, seem to gather up all the
significance of that struggle of a powerful impulse to action against an obscure
barrier, all the impotent anger and perplexity, and longing for justification
and release, that make up the story of
Hamlet as Shakespeare tells it, and
make also of Hamlet, and of these
lines, a symbol for whatever such struggle and longing has tortured the mind
that is responding to Hamlet's words.

IV

Before attempting to compare, with
reference to underlying emotional pattern, *Hamlet* and the plays concerned
with Orestes, we may consider briefly
the study made of *Hamlet* by Dr. Ernest
Jones.[12]

Dr. Jones, in exploring the nature of
Hamlet's conflict, has to some extent
followed the same line of inquiry that
I am pursuing here. For what is it that

10 'The study of poetry', *Essays in Criticism*, 2nd
series, 1889.

11 Cf. Lascelles Abercrombie, *The Idea of Great
Poetry*, 1925, p. 19.
12 'A psycho-analytic study of *Hamlet*', included in
Essays in Applied Psychoanalysis, 1923.

the critic is actually doing when he traces the motives of a character in a play?

In projecting the figure of a man of a certain disposition and analysing the forces behind his behaviour, the critic is inevitably using the emotional experience which he himself undergoes in living through the play. Having experienced, as communicated by the speeches of Hamlet, a certain psychological movement in which a strong impulse to action is aroused, and again and again sinks back into apathy and despair—a movement which, while imaginatively experiencing it, the reader imputes to the fictitious speaker—afterwards, in reviewing the total impression so received, with analysis and synthesis of its successive movements, the critic discerns, so far as his thought does not deceive him, within the fictitious personality of Hamlet, the reflected pattern of the emotional forces that have operated within his own imaginative activity.

To Dr. Jones the conflict of Hamlet appears an example of the working of the Oedipus complex. Hamlet cannot whole-heartedly will the slaying of his uncle, because 'his uncle incorporates the deepest and most buried part of his own personality'. The repressed desire for the death of his father and the sexual enjoyment of his mother, persisting unconsciously from infancy, has produced an unwitting identification by Hamlet of himself and his guilty uncle, so that only at the point of death, 'when he has made the final sacrifice . . . is he free . . . to slay his other self' (p. 57).

This psychological hypothesis, contributed by Freud and elaborated by Dr. Jones, has been welcomed by certain literary critics. Herbert Read, referring to the view of J. M. Robertson, that *Hamlet* is 'not finally an intelligible drama as it stands'—that Shakespeare could not make a psychologically consistent play out of his barbaric plot and supersubtle hero—urges that however baffling to critics the play may have proved, nevertheless in experiencing it we are aware of a personal intensity of expression, a *consistent* intensity, giving

the play a unity which the older academic critics lacked means to explore.[13] Dr. Jones's hypothesis, he considers does serve to explain this acceptance by our feeling of any difficulties and incoherence which our thought may find Using the terms I have suggested, we might say that the hypothesis of the Oedipus complex—i.e. of a persistent unconscious wish, hostile to the father and dishonouring to the mother, in conflict with the sentiment of filial love and loyalty—offers to our thought an emotional pattern which does correspond to the play of feeling stimulated during a full imaginative participation in the drama. Professor Bradley has spoken of *Hamlet* as deserving the title of 'tragedy of moral idealism',[14] because of the intensity, both of idealizing love and of horror at betrayal of love, that we feel in Hamlet's speeches. He dwells upon the shock to such a moral sensibility as Hamlet's of witnessing the faithlessness of his mother and uncle, yet there seems a discrepancy between the horror and disgust that a sensitive mind might naturally feel at such faithlessness in others and the overwhelming disgust that Hamlet feels, at himself, his whole world and his attempted action, unless we realize that he feels the treachery of his mother and uncle echo within himself, and within the sentiment of loyal love to his father that is his strongest conscious motive. If, in reviewing the experience communicated by the play, we conceive a loyal love undermined, as it were, by a bewildered sense of treachery within as well as without, we must, I think, agree that the Freudian hypothesis does throw some light upon that intimate immediate experience which is the final touchstone of critical theory.

V

Perhaps the most important contribution that has been made by the Freudian theory of dream interpretation to the

[13] Herbert Read, *Reason and Romanticism* (Faber & Gwyer), p. 101.
[14] *Shakespearian Tragedy* (Macmillan, 1912), p. 113.

understanding of the emotional symbolism of poetic themes is that concerned with the 'splitting' of type figures. In comparing the Hamlet story with the story of Oedipus, Dr. Jones asserts that both are variants of the same *motif*, but in one the father figure remains single, while in the other it is 'split into two'—the father loved and revered, and the hated tyrannical usurper.

This assertion involves two elements of hypothesis:

1. The fundamental assumption—implied also in the statements of Jung and Gilbert Murray, with which this discussion opened—that these ancient stories owe their persistence, as traditional material of art, to their power of expressing or symbolizing, and so relieving, typical human emotions.

2. That the emotion relieved is in this case the two-sided—ambivalent—attitude of the son towards the father. Let us examine this latter hypothesis more closely.

It appears to be characteristic of the relation between father and son that the father should excite in the son both feelings of admiration, love, and loyalty, and also impulses of anger, jealousy, and self-assertion. The more the son learns to 'idolize' his father, developing what Shand has called the 'conscience of the sentiment', so that any muttering of jealousy or hostile criticism is suppressed as disloyal, the more acute will become the tension of the inner attitude. It is such an attitude that can find relief in imaginative activity wherein both the love and the repressed hostility have play. In the story of Oedipus, according to the Freudian hypothesis, a repressed persistent impulse to supplant the father and enjoy the mother finds expression in the first part of the action; then in the latter part, in the hero's remorse and suffering, appears the expression of the sentiment of respect and loyalty. In the Hamlet legend—as it appears, e.g. in the Amleth Saga—combined fear and hostile self-assertion against the father find expression through all the incidents of simulated stupidity, and secret bitter word-play, and at last in the achievement of the plotted slaying of the usurper; while at the same time the sentiment of love and loyalty is triumphantly expressed in that same act of filial vengeance. It is Shakespeare only who appears to have brought into the rendering of the ancient story the subtle factor of the division and paralysis of the will of the hero, by the intuitive apprehension that the impulse that drove his uncle against his father was one with that present in himself.

The story of Orestes may be considered as another example of the imaginative expression of the ambivalent attitude of child toward parent. In this story, as presented by the three great Attic tragedians, there is a wealth of material illustrating the manner in which inner forces of emotion may, through shapes created by imagination, become palpable to sense. But we must be content here to consider briefly only the outline of the story.

Considered as a variant of the Hamlet theme, its distinctive note is that the usurper upon whom the son's fierce self-assertion and craving for vengeance strike is not alone the male kinsman, but also the queen-mother, who has betrayed, and with her own hands murdered the father. Therefore the moment of triumphant self-assertion, when the son has proved his manhood, and vindicated his loyalty upon his father's enemies, is also the moment when there awakens the palpable, pursuing horror of the outraged filial relation—since this enemy was also a parent, the mother of the slayer.

The conflict presented in the Orestes dramas is plainly concerned not directly with sex, but with combined love and hate of either son or daughter converging upon a parent figure which may be either father or mother. It is the enduring conflict between the generations which continues to find expression in the story, when more temporary questions—such as that between patriarchy and mother-right, which may have been present in Athenian minds—are no longer urgent. That this theme of conflict between the generations had great significance within the sensibility that found expression in Shakespeare's plays, is evident from the tragedy of *King Lear*.

In this drama the emotional conflict between the generations is communicated from the standpoint of the old man, the father who encounters in separate embodiment in his natural successors, the extremes of bestial self-seeking, and of filial devotion. Bradley has noted how the play illustrates 'the tendency of imagination to analyse and subtract, to decompose human nature into its constituent factors'.[15] This mode of thought, he suggests,[16] is responsible for 'the incessant references to the lower animals' which occur throughout the play. Thus Goneril is likened to a kite, a serpent, a boar, a dog, a wolf, a tiger. This analysing work of the imagination, separating the bestial and the angelic in human nature and giving them distinct embodiment, in the wicked daughters and Cordelia (and again in Edmund and Edgar, the cruel and the loyal sons of Gloucester), presents another instance of what we have already observed in the 'splitting' of the father figure. The splitting in this play is from the point of view of the parent; as, in the Orestes or Hamlet story, it is from the point of view of the child. As, to the feeling of the child, the parent may be both loved protector and unjustly obstructing tyrant, and these two aspects find their emotional symbolism in separate figures in the play; so, to the feeling of the parent, the child may be both loving support of age and ruthless usurper and rival, and these two aspects find expression in separate figures, such as the tender and the wicked daughters of Lear.

VI

We have considered, so far, the emotional pattern corresponding to a particular theme—the conflict between the generations—which, though a recurring one, is by no means co-extensive with

the realm of tragic drama. Can we identify an archetypal pattern corresponding to tragedy itself—its universal idea or form?

Gilbert Murray, taking the 'essential tragic idea' to be that of 'climax followed by decline, or pride by judgement', and attempting a closer analysis of this sequence, maintains that what is 'really characteristic' of the tragic conflict is 'an element of mystery derived ultimately from the ancient religious concepts of *katharsis* and atonement'.[17] The death or fall of the tragic hero has in some sense the character of a purifying or atoning sacrifice.

In considering this conception we may first remedy an inadequacy that the reader has probably noticed in the previous discussion of the dramas of Hamlet and Lear, Orestes and Oedipus. We have so far ignored the royal status of the father and son concerned in the tragic conflict. Yet the kingly status has great significance for the feeling expressed in the play.

Consider, for instance, the tragedy of *King Lear*. 'The master movement of the play,' says Granville-Barker, is Lear's passing 'from personal grievance to the taking upon him, as great natures may, of the imagined burden of the whole world's sorrow'.[18] It is Lear's royal status that helps to make this movement possible. King Lear is at once 'a poor, infirm, weak, and despised old man'—a father broken to tears and madness by his daughters' cruelty, and also in his sufferings a superhuman figure—one who can bid the 'all shaking thunder strike flat the thick rotundity of the world' in vengeance for his wrongs. It is in part the association with which history, and pre-history, has invested the name and image of king that make it possible for us, under the spell of Shakespeare's verse, to accept the figure of Lear as in this way exalted in his agony beyond human stature. His madness, his pitiful humanity, appear according to that comment which

---

[15] *Shakespearian Tragedy*, p. 264.
[16] *Ibid.*, p. 266.

[17] *Op. cit.*, 'Drama', p. 66.
[18] H. Granville-Barker, *Prefaces to Shakespeare* (1927), 1st series, p. 171.

Shakespeare puts into the mouth of an attendant, on behalf of all onlookers, 'a sight . . . past speaking in a king'. The word 'king' is here, through its position in the play, loaded with a significance for the sources of which we must go far back in the story of the race and of the individual.

It is probably because, to the mind of the young child, the father appears of unlimited power that in the life-history of the individual imagination the figures of father and king tend to coalesce. Legends and fairy stories that reflect the feelings of more primitive people towards their king are interpreted by the child in the light of his own earlier feeling towards his father. In the case both of the child and of the primitive individual the same process seems to take place—an emerging of the consciousness of self from out a matrix of less differentiated awareness, which may be called collective or group-consciousness. The figures of both father and king tend to retain within those deeper levels of the mind to which poetry may penetrate, something of the *mana* that invested the first representative of a power akin to, but vastly beyond, that of the individual emerging into self-consciousness.

It is this supernatural aspect which the father-king of tragic drama has for the kindled imagination that is of importance when we try to understand the element of religious mystery which is characteristic of tragedy—plainly in the past, and, as Gilbert Murray holds, in some subtler fashion still in our experience to-day.

Upon this character of tragedy and the tragic hero it is possible, I think, to gain a certain fresh light from a consideration of the conclusions at which Dr. Jung has arrived through his study of fantasy figures appearing in personal analysis.

In *The Psychology of the Unconscious*, in the chapter entitled 'The Sacrifice', he examines the symbol of the dying hero as it appears in individual fantasy, representing, according to his interpretation, an inflated infan-

tile personality—a childish self that must be sacrificed, if the libido is to move forward into active life—and in a later work he discusses, under the title of the 'Mana Personality',[19] a hero figure which he finds appearing with a richer content at late stages of analysis.

It is especially at times when barriers of personal repression are removed and images of 'cosmic' character are arising freely, that the fantasy figure may appear of some great prophet or hero who tends to assume control of the personality.[20] If the conscious or practical personality is poorly developed there is the greater likelihood that it will be overwhelmed when such powerful images rise from the unconscious.

As a literary example of such a case, parallel to actual ones within his experience, Jung accepts H. G. Wells's story of Preemby,[21] 'a small, irrelevant, fledgling of a personality', to whom is presented in dream and fantasy the figure of Sargon, King of Kings, in such compelling fashion that he is led to identify himself with it. Jung observes that here 'the author depicts a really classical type of compensation',[22] and we may compare it with the type of compensation which occurs in connexion with what we have already considered as the ambivalent attitude towards a parent.

If, within the conscious life, in relation to a parent, only reactions of admiration and affection are recognized, while other reactions, of hostile character, excited within the brain, are repressed, it is these latter that tend to present in dreams a parent figure as object of violence or contempt. Similarly, if within the conscious life the personal self comes to be known only as 'an onlooker, an ineffective speech-

---

[19] *Two Essays on Analytical Psychology*, 1928, trans. by H. G. and C. F. Baynes, Essay II, ch. iv.

[20] An interesting autobiographical account of this condition may be found in the writings of E. Maitland (*The Story of Anna Kingsford and Edward Maitland and of the New Gospel of Interpretation*, 1st ed., 1893). See especially the passage where he describes the first arrival of the authoritative 'presence', and the voice distinctly heard: 'at last I have found a man through whom I can speak.'

[21] *Christina Alberta's Father*, 1925.

[22] *Op. cit.*, p. 193.

less man', utterly insignificant; while yet, within the life that animates that particular brain, strong reactions are excited of sympathetic exultation and delight at imaginative representations of human achievement—as the little Preemby of Wells thrilled at 'the mystery of Atlantis and of the measurements of the Pyramids'—then there may arise, as compensatory to the belittled self, the figure of a hero-self, or *mana* personality, fashioned, as it were, from the stuff of these imaginative reactions; just as the figure of the hated father was fashioned from the energy of the repressed hostility, in compensation for the over-idealizing love.

The Preemby of Wells's story is saved from his delusion, after many sufferings, by learning to think of his vision as of the spirit of man and its achievements —an inheritance belonging no more to him personally than to every other man. In the same manner every individual in whose fantasy such mighty ghosts arise, with their superhuman claims and relationships, must learn to distinguish such claims from those of the personal self; while yet the personal self may be enriched through the conscious experience of its relation to the great forces which such figures represent.

In this way, according to the view of Jung—by interpreting and giving conscious direction to the 'pure nature-process'[23] of fantasy in which compensatory images arise—such fantasy can become instrumental to the purging of the individual will and its reconciliation with itself. Is it in some such fashion as this that tragic drama, deeply experienced, now or in the past, exercises the function of purgation or atonement in relation to the passions of the spectator? With this question in view, we may examine a little further the nature of the emotional experience of tragic art, still using the examples of *Hamlet* and of *King Lear*.

Professor Bradley, in examining the experience of tragedy, cites these dramas as examples of tragedies at whose close we feel pain mingled with something

[23] *Op. cit.*, p. 258.

like exultation. There is present, he declares, 'a glory in the greatness of the soul', and awareness of an 'ultimate power' which is 'no mere fate', but spiritual, and to which the hero 'was never so near . . . as in the moment when it required his life'.[24]

I quote these statements of Bradley, not, of course, as universally acceptable, but as the attempt of one eminent critic to render his own deeply pondered experience of tragic drama. The experience is rendered in terms rather of philosophy or religion than of psychology. Can we translate it into any more psychological terms? What is this spiritual power, akin to the characters, and, in some sense, a whole of which they are 'parts, expressions, products'?[25] I would propose (following the view set forth by F. M. Cornford) the psychological hypothesis that this power is the common nature lived and immediately experienced by the members of a group or community—'the collective emotion and activity of the group'.[26] This common nature can, in Alexander's phrase, be enjoyed, but never directly contemplated. As unfathomable to introspection, it is termed by Jung the Collective Unconscious—the life-energy that in its spontaneous movement toward expression generates alike the hero figures of myth and legend and the similar figures that, appearing in individual fantasy, may overwhelm the personal consciousness.

According to Bradley, the tragic exultation that we feel at the close of *Hamlet* is connected with our sense that the spiritual power of which Hamlet is in some manner the expression or product, is receiving him to itself. It would be this same sense that, as Bradley observes,[27] demands, and is satisfied by, the words of Horatio, introducing, against Shakespeare's custom, the reference to another life: 'flights of angels sing thee to thy rest'. If, as I suggest, the spiritual power, which the philosopher analysing

[24] *Oxford Lectures on Poetry*, p. 84.
[25] *Shakespearian Tragedy*, p. 37.
[26] F. M. Cornford, *From Religion to Philosophy* (Arnold, 1912), p. 78.
[27] *Op. cit.*, p. 147.

his poetic experience is constrained to represent, be conceived psychologically as the awakened sense of our common nature in its active emotional phase, then our exultation in the death of Hamlet is related in direct line of descent to the religious exultation felt by the primitive group that made sacrifice of the divine king or sacred animal, the representative of the tribal life, and, by the communion of its shed blood, felt that life strengthened and renewed. Hamlet, though he dies, is immortal, because he is the representative and creature of the immortal life of the race. He lives, as he desired to live, in the story with which he charged Horatio—and us who, having participated in that story, descend from the poetic ecstasy to draw breath again in the harsh world of our straitened separate personalities.

The insight of Nietzsche, who knew at once the intoxication of the artist and the analytic urge of the philosopher, discerned the essential nature of tragedy as a vision generated by a dance.[28] The dance of rhythmical speech, like the dance of the ancient chorus, excites the Dionysian ecstasy wherein arises, serene and clear, the Apollonian vision of the imaged meanings the dancing words convey.

The painful images within the vision are at once intimately known and felt, and also 'distanced' like the objects in a far stretching landscape, 'estranged by beauty'. So far as the memory material used by the imaginative activity comes from personal experience, it has undergone 'separation . . . from the concrete personality of the experiencer' and 'extrusion of its personal aspects';[29] but experience is also used which has never been connected with the personal self—as when, in *King Lear*, Shakespeare causes the actor to 'impersonate Lear and the storm together',[30] and in the storm 'it is the powers of the tormented soul that we hear and see'.[31] Here, dramatist, actor, and spectator are

using experience which was never personal, but shaped through previous apprehension of physical storms into which was imaginatively projected that same impersonal emotional energy from which the daemonic figure of the hero is now fashioned.

To the impersonal, 'distanced', vision corresponds, in Schopenhauer's phrase, 'a Will-free subject', one indifferent to the aims and fears of the ego—not held to its private perspective.[32]

This felt release, and Dionysian union with a larger whole, would seem to constitute that element of religious mystery—of purgation and atonement—traditionally connected with the idea of tragedy.

VII

If now, summing up our results, we recur to the question: what determining emotional pattern corresponds to the form of tragedy? we may answer first, in accordance with our earlier discussion, that the pattern consists of emotional tendencies of opposite character which are liable to be excited by the same object or situation, and, thus conflicting, produce an inner tension that seeks relief in the activity either of fantasy, or of poetic imagination, either originally or receptively creative. The nature of the opposed tendencies that find relief through diverse renderings of the essential tragic theme, the death or fall of a hero, it is not easy to describe at once with conciseness and adequacy. But we may attempt this through the concept of an ambivalent attitude toward the self.

In the gradual fashioning and transforming, through the experience of life, of an idea of the self, every individual must in some degree experience the

---

[28] See *The Birth of Tragedy*, Section 8.
[29] E. Bullough, 'Distance as an aesthetic principle', *Brit. J. of Psychol.* v. part 2, p. 116.
[30] Granville-Barker, *Prefaces to Shakespeare*, p. 142.
[31] A. C. Bradley, *Shakespearian Tragedy*, p. 270.

[32] This character of the aesthetic experience is vividly expressed, in imaginative form, in the lines of de la Mare:

> When music sounds, all that I was I am
> Ere to this haunt of brooding dust I came.

Here we have the felt contrast between the subject of the aesthetic experience—'all that I was I am'—and the self that is bounded in space and time by the bodily organism—'this haunt of brooding dust'.

contrast between a personal self—a limited ego, one among many—and a self that is free to range imaginatively through all human achievement. In infancy and in the later years of those who remain childish, a comparatively feeble imaginative activity together with an undisciplined instinct of self-assertion may present a fantasy self—the image of an infantile personality—in conflict with the chastened image which social contacts, arousing the instinct of submission, tend to enforce. In the more mature mind that has soberly taken the measure of the personal self as revealed in practical life, there remains the contrast between this and the self revealed in imaginative thought—wellnigh limitless in sympathy and aspiration.

Within what McDougall calls the self-regarding sentiment these contrasting images, and the impulses that sustain and respond to them, may bring about persistent tension. The experience of tragic drama both gives in the figure of the hero an objective form to the self of imaginative aspiration, or to the power-craving, and also, through the hero's death, satisfies the counter movement of feeling toward the surrender of personal claims and the merging of the ego within a greater power—the 'community consciousness'.

Thus the archetypal pattern corresponding to tragedy may be said to be a certain organization of the tendencies of self-assertion and submission. The self which is asserted is magnified by that same collective force to which finally submission is made; and from the tension of the two impulses and their reaction upon each other, under the conditions of poetic exaltation, the distinctive tragic attitude and emotion appears to arise.

The theme of the conflict between the generations—considered earlier, in relation to Hamlet and Orestes, as corresponding to an ambivalent attitude toward a parent figure—is plainly related to this more general theme and pattern; since, as we saw, the same underlying emotional associations cling to the images of father and of king. In experiencing imaginatively the conflict of the generations, the spectator is identified with the hero both as son, in his felt solidarity with the father and revolt against him, and again, when, making reparation for the 'injustice' against his predecessor, he gives place to a successor, and is reunited with that whole of life whence he emerged.[33]

One or two points in regard to the argument may be briefly reviewed.

The question is sometimes asked whether the creative activity of the poet and the imaginative response of the reader are sufficiently alike, psychologically, to be considered together. Here I have been concerned primarily with imaginative response, and have not attempted to consider the distinctive activity of original composition. In so far, however, as the poet's work, e.g. a play of Shakespeare, does reveal his imaginative response to material communicated to him by others and by him to us, I have of course been concerned with the poet's experience.

The concept of racial experience enters the present essay in two ways: (1) all those systems or tendencies which appear to be inherited in the constitution of mind and brain may be said to be due to racial experience in the past. It is not necessary for our purpose to determine exactly the method of this 'biological inheritance' from our ancestors. Of more importance for our purpose is the question concerning (2) the racial experience which we may 'enjoy' in responding to that 'social inheritance' of meanings stored in language which also comes to us from our ancestors, and wakens into activity the potentialities of our inherited nature. In such racial or collective experience as we have discussed in relation to tragic poetry, so far as there is reference to an experiencer, this seems to be not an individual, but rather that larger whole from which what we know as the indi-

33 Cf. the mystic saying of Anaximander, concerning the cycle of birth and death, wherein things 'give reparation to one another and pay the penalty of their injustice', and the discussion of it by F. M. Cornford *op. cit.* See especially pp. 8, 147,176.

vidual, or personal, self has been differentiated, and which remains with us as the sense, either latent or active, of a greater power.

In the present paper it is maintained that racial experience in this sense is an important factor in the total experience of tragic drama, at the present day, as in the ritual dance from which drama arose. In regard to this question further examination of the imaginative experience can alone be decisive.

JOHN CROWE RANSOM

(b. 1888)

Poet and literary essayist, John Crowe Ransom was also founding editor of *The Kenyon Review* and one of the four founding Fellows of the Kenyon School of English (later the School of Letters at Indiana University). His criticism, which is primarily aesthetic in orientation, is nevertheless based on a definite social philosophy. As Southerner, Agrarian, and leader of the group that published *The Fugitive* at Nashville during the early Twenties, Ransom is a conservative whose social ideal is modeled on the myth of the landed Old South aristocracy as a symbol of a way of life in which the abstract political and social machineries of the modern world are replaced by an organic body of social, intellectual, and moral traditions which would function together to create a true "culture." But in the modern world, where such a regressive cultural ideal can be little more than a myth, the arts are almost the sole means of sustaining an approximation of the human values implied by that ideal. Ransom's criticism, well-known for its use of such apparent technicalisms as "texture," "structure," "ontology," "concrete universal," is nevertheless bent always toward rediscovering the values of aesthetic experience, the enrichment in the mere contemplation of beauty "for its own sake," in a love of the "nature" and of the arts' images of it, the full possession of which keep men human in a world where the dehumanization of experience has become almost a necessity of simple survival. Many of Ransom's chief critical works are included in *The World's Body* (1938), *The New Criticism* (1941), and *Poems and Essays* (1955), although some essays remain uncollected. Ransom has also edited *The Kenyon Critics* (1951) and *The Selected Poems of Thomas Hardy* (1961).

Poetry: A Note on Ontology (1934)

A poetry may be distinguished from a poetry by virtue of subject-matter, and subject-matter may be differentiated with respect to its ontology, or the

reality of its being. An excellent variety of critical doctrine arises recently out of this differentiation, and thus perhaps criticism leans again upon ontological analysis as it was meant to do by Kant. The recent critics remark in effect that some poetry deals with things, while some other poetry deals with ideas. The two poetries will differ from each other as radically as a thing differs from an idea.

The distinction in the hands of critics is a fruitful one. There is apt to go along with it a principle of valuation, which is the consequence of a temperament, and therefore basic. The critic likes things and intends that his poet shall offer them: or likes ideas and intends that he shall offer them: and approves him as he does the one or the other. Criticism cannot well go much deeper than this. The critic has carried to the last terms his analysis of the stuff of which poetry is made, and valued it frankly as his temperament or his need requires him to value it.

So philosophical a critic seems to be highly modern. He is; but this critic as a matter of fact is peculiarly on one side of the question. (The implication is unfavorable to the other side of the question.) He is in revolt against the tyranny of ideas, and against the poetry which celebrates ideas, and which may be identified—so far as his usual generalization may be trusted—with the hateful poetry of the Victorians. His bias is in favor of the things. On the other hand the critic who likes Victorian verse, or the poetry of ideas, has probably not thought of anything of so grand a simplicity as electing between the things and the ideas, being apparently not quite capable of the ontological distinction. Therefore he does not know the real or constitutional ground of his liking, and may somewhat ingenuously claim that his predilection is for those poets who give him inspiration, or comfort, or truth, or honest metres, or something else equally "worth while." But Plato, who was not a modern, was just as clear as we are about the basic distinction between the ideas and the things, and yet stands far apart from the aforesaid conscious modern in passionately preferring the ideas over the things. The weight of Plato's testimony would certainly fall on the side of the Victorians, though they may scarcely have thought of calling him as their witness. But this con-

sideration need not conclude the hearing.

1. PHYSICAL POETRY

The poetry which deals with things was much in favor a few years ago with the resolute body of critics. And the critics affected the poets. If necessary, they became the poets, and triumphantly illustrated the new mode. The Imagists were important figures in the history of our poetry, and they were both theorists and creators. It was their intention to present things in their thinginess, or *Dinge* in their *Dinglichkeit*; and to such an extent had the public lost its sense of *Dinglichkeit* that their redirection was wholesome. What the public was inclined to seek in poetry was ideas, whether large ones or small ones, grand ones or pretty ones, certainly ideas to live by and die by, but what the Imagists identified with the stuff of poetry was, simply, things.

Their application of their own principle was sufficiently heroic, though they scarcely consented to be as extreme in the practice as in the theory. They had artistic talent, every one of the original group, and it was impossible that they should make of poetry so simple an exercise as in doctrine they seemed to think it was. Yet Miss Lowell wrote a poem on *Thompson's Lunch Room, Grand Central Station*; it is admirable if its intention is to show the whole reach of her courage. Its detail goes like this:

> Jagged greenwhite bowls of pressed glass
> Rearing snow-peaks of chipped sugar
> Above the lighthouse-shaped castors
> Of gray pepper and gray-white salt.

For most of us as for the public idealist, with his "values," this is inconsequential. Unhappily it seems that the things as things do not necessarily interest us, and that in fact we are not quite constructed with the capacity for a disinterested interest. But it must be noted even here that the things are on their good behavior, looking rather well, and arranged by lines into something approaching a military formation. More technically, there is cross-imagery in the snow-peaks of sugar, and in the lighthouse-shaped castors, and cross-imagery involves association, and will presently involve dissociation and thinking. The metre is but a vestige, but even so it means something, for metre is a powerful intellectual determinant marshalling the words and, inevitably, the things. The *Dinglichkeit* of this Imagist specimen, or the realism, was therefore not pure. But it was nearer pure than the world was used to in poetry, and the exhibit was astonishing.

For the purpose of this note I shall give to such poetry, dwelling as exclusively as it dares upon physical things, the name Physical Poetry. It is to stand opposite to that poetry which dwells as firmly as it dares upon ideas.

But perhaps thing *versus* idea does not seem to name an opposition precisely. Then we might phrase it a little differently: image *versus* idea. The idealistic philosophies are not sure that things exist, but they mean the equivalent when they refer to images. (Or they may consent to perceptions; or to impressions, following Hume, and following Croce, who remarks that they are pre-intellectual and independent of concepts. It is all the same, unless we are extremely technical.) It is sufficient if they concede that image is the raw material of idea. Though it may be an unwieldy and useless affair for the idealist as it stands, much needing to be licked into shape, nevertheless its relation to idea is that of a material cause, and it cannot be dispossessed of its priority.

It cannot be dispossessed of a primordial freshness, which idea can never claim. An idea is derivative and tamed. The image is in the natural or wild state, and it has to be discovered there, not put there, obeying its own law and none of ours. We think we can lay hold of image and take it captive, but the docile captive is not the real image but only the idea, which is the image with its character beaten out of it.

But we must be very careful: idealists are nothing if not dialectical. They ob-

ject that an image in an original state of innocence is a delusion and cannot exist, that no image ever comes to us which does not imply the world of ideas, there is "no percept without a concept." There is something in it. Every property discovered in the image is a universal property, and nothing discovered in the image is marvellous in kind though it may be pinned down historically or statistically as a single instance. But there is this to be understood too: the image which is not remarkable in any particular property is marvellous in its assemblage of many properties, a manifold of properties, like a mine or a field, something to be explored for the properties; yet science can manage the image, which is infinite in properties, only by equating it to the one property with which the science is concerned: for science at work is always *a science*, and committed to a special interest. It is not by refutation but by abstraction that science destroys the image. It means to get its "value" out of the image, and we may be sure that it has no use for the image in its original state of freedom. People who are engrossed with their pet "values" become habitual killers. Their game is the images, or the things, and they acquire the ability to shoot them as far off as they can be seen, and do. It is thus that we lose the power of imagination, or whatever faculty it is by which we are able to contemplate things as they are in their rich and contingent materiality. But our dreams reproach us, for in dreams they come alive again. Likewise our memory; which makes light of our science by recalling the images in their panoply of circumstance and with their morning freshness upon them.

It is the dream, the recollection, which compels us to poetry, and to deliberate aesthetic experience. It can hardly be argued, I think, that the arts are constituted automatically out of original images, and arise in some early age of innocence. (Though Croce seems to support this view, and to make art a pre-adult stage of experience.) Art is based on second love, not first love. In it we make a return to something which we had wilfully alienated. The child is occupied mostly with things, but it is because he is still unfurnished with systematic ideas, not because he is a ripe citizen by nature and comes along already trailing clouds of glory. Images are clouds of glory for the man who has discovered that ideas are a sort of darkness. Imagism, that is, the recent historical movement, may resemble a naïve poetry of mere things, but we can read the theoretical pronouncements of Imagists, and we can learn that Imagism is motivated by a distaste for the systematic abstractedness of thought. It presupposes acquaintance with science; that famous activity which is "constructive" with respect to the tools of our economic role in this world, and destructive with respect to nature. Imagists wish to escape from science by immersing themselves in images.

Not far off the simplicity of Imagism was, a little later, the subtler simplicity of Mr. George Moore's project shared with several others, in behalf of "pure poetry." In Moore's house on Ebury Street they talked about poetry, with an after-dinner warmth if not an early-morning discretion, and their tastes agreed almost perfectly and reinforced one another. The fruit of these conversations was the volume *Pure Poetry*. It must have been the most exclusive anthology of English poetry that had yet appeared, since its room was closed to all the poems that dallied visibly with ideas, so that many poems that had been coveted by all other anthologists do not appear there. Nevertheless the book is delicious, and something more deserves to be said for it.

First, that "pure poetry" is a kind of Physical Poetry. Its visible content is a thing-content. Technically, I suppose, it is effective in this character if it can exhibit its material in such a way that an image or set of images and not an idea must occupy the foreground of the reader's attention. Thus:

> Full fathom five thy father lies
> Of his bones are coral made.

Here it is difficult for anybody (except the perfect idealist who is always theoretically possible and who would expect to take a return from anything whatever) to receive any experience except that of a very distinct image, or set of images. It has the configuration of image, which consists in being sharp of edges, and the modality of image, which consists in being given and non-negotiable, and the density, which consists in being full, a plenum of qualities. What is to be done with it? It is pure exhibit; it is to be contemplated; perhaps it is to be enjoyed. The art of poetry depends more frequently on this faculty than on any other in its repertory; the faculty of presenting images so whole and clean that they resist the catalysis of thought.

And something else must be said, going in the opposite direction. "Pure poetry," all the same, is not as pure as it is claimed to be, though on the whole it is Physical Poetry. (All true poetry is a phase of Physical Poetry.) It is not as pure as Imagism is, or at least it is not as pure as Imagism would be if it lived up to its principles; and in fact it is significant that the volume does not contain any Imagist poems, which argues a difference in taste somewhere. Imagism may take trifling things for its material; presumably it will take the first things the poet encounters, since "importance" and "interest" are not primary qualities which a thing possesses but secondary or tertiary ones which the idealist attributes to it by virtue of his own requirements. "Pure poetry" as Moore conceives it, and as the lyrics of Poe and Shakespeare offer it, deals with the more dramatic materials, and here dramatic means human, or at least capable of being referred to the critical set of human interests. Employing this sort of material the poet cannot exactly intend to set the human economists in us actually into motion, but perhaps he does intend to comfort us with the fleeting sense that it is potentially our kind of material.

In the same way "pure poetry" is nicely metred, where Imagism was free. Technique is written on it. And by the way the anthology contains no rugged anonymous Scottish ballad either, and probably for a like reason: because it would not be technically finished. Now both Moore and de la Mare are accomplished conservative artists, and what they do or what they approve may be of limited range but it is sure to be technically admirable, and it is certain that they understand what technique in poetry is though they do not define it. Technique takes the thing-content and metres and orders it. Metre is not an original property of things. It is artificial, and conveys the sense of human control, even if it does not wish to impair the thinginess of the things. Metric is a science, and so far as we attend to it we are within the scientific atmosphere. Order is the logical arrangement of things. It involves the dramatic "form" which selects the things, and brings out their appropriate qualities, and carries them through a systematic course of predication until the total impression is a unit of logic and not merely a solid lump of thing-content. The "pure poems" which Moore admires are studied, though it would be fatal if they looked studious. A sustained effort of ideation effected these compositions. It is covered up, and communicates itself only on a subliminal plane of consciousness. But experienced readers are quite aware of it; they know at once what is the matter when they encounter a realism shamelessly passing for poetry, or a well-planned but blundering poetry.

As critics we should have every good will toward Physical Poetry: it is the basic constituent of any poetry. But the product is always something short of a pure or absolute existence, and it cannot quite be said that it consists of nothing but physical objects. The fact is that when we are more than usually satisfied with a Physical Poetry our analysis will probably disclose that it is more than usually impure.

II. PLATONIC POETRY

The poetry of ideas I shall denominate: Platonic Poetry. This also has grades of purity. A discourse which employed only abstract ideas with no images would be a scientific document and not a poem at all, not even a Platonic poem. Platonic Poetry dips heavily into the physical. If Physical Poetry tends to employ some ideation surreptitiously while still looking innocent of idea, Platonic Poetry more than returns the compliment, for it tries as hard as it can to look like Physical Poetry, as if it proposed to conceal its medicine, which is the idea to be propagated, within the sugar candy of objectivity and *Dinglichkeit*. As an instance, it is almost inevitable that I quote a famous Victorian utterance:

> The year's at the spring
> And day's at the morn;
> Morning's at seven;
> The hill-side's dew-pearled;
> The lark's on the wing;
> The snail's on the thorn:
> God's in his heaven—
> All's right with the world!

which is a piece of transparent homiletics; for in it six pretty, co-ordinate images are marched, like six little lambs to the slaughter, to a colon and a powerful text. Now the exhibits of this poetry in the physical kind are always large, and may take more of the attention of the reader than is desired, but they are meant mostly to be illustrative of the ideas. It is on this ground that idealists like Hegel detect something unworthy, like a pedagogical trick, in poetry after all, and consider that the race will abandon it when it has outgrown its childishness and is enlightened.

The ablest arraignment of Platonic Poetry that I have seen, as an exercise which is really science but masquerades as poetry by affecting a concern for physical objects, is that of Mr. Allen Tate in a series of studies recently in *The New Republic*.[1] I will summarize. Platonic Poetry is allegory, a discourse in things, but on the understanding that they are translatable at every point into ideas. (The usual ideas are those which constitute the popular causes, patriotic,

[1] "Three Types of Poetry." Reprinted in *Reactionary Essays* (1936). Reprinted in *On the Limits of Poetry* (1948). [*Editor's Note.*]

religious, moral, or social.) Or Platonic Poetry is the elaboration of ideas as such, but in proceeding introduces for ornament some physical properties after the style of Physical Poetry; which is rhetoric. It is positive when the poet believes in the efficacy of the ideas. It is negative when he despairs of their efficacy, because they have conspicuously failed to take care of him, and utters his personal wail:

> I fall upon the thorns of life! I bleed!

This is "Romantic Irony," which comes at occasional periods to interrupt the march of scientific optimism. But it still falls under the category of Platonism; it generally proposes some other ideas to take the place of those which are in vogue.

But why Platonism? To define Platonism we must remember that it is not the property of the historical person who reports dialogues about it in an Academy, any more than "pure poetry" is the property of the talkers who describe it from a house on Ebury Street. Platonism, in the sense I mean, is the name of an impulse that is native to us all, frequent, tending to take a too complete possession of our minds. Why should the spirit of mortal be proud? The chief explanation is that modern mortal is probably a Platonist. We are led to believe that nature is rational and that by the force of reasoning we shall possess it. I have read upon high authority: "Two great forces are persistent in Plato: the love of truth and zeal for human improvement." The forces are one force. We love to view the world under universal or scientific ideas to which we give the name truth; and this is because the ideas seem to make not for righteousness but for mastery. The Platonic view of the world is ultimately the predatory, for it reduces to the scientific, which we know. The Platonic Idea becomes the Logos which science worships, which is the Occidental God, whose minions we are, and whose children, claiming a large share in His powers for patrimony.

Now the fine Platonic world of ideas fails to coincide with the original world of perception, which is the world populated by the stubborn and contingent objects, and to which as artists we fly in shame. The sensibility manifested by artists makes fools of scientists, if the latter are inclined to take their special and quite useful form of truth as the whole and comprehensive article. A dandified pagan worldling like Moore can always defeat Platonism; he does it every hour; he can exhibit the savor of his fish and wines, the fragrance of his coffee and cigars, and the solidity of the images in his favorite verse. These are objects which have to be experienced, and cannot be reported, for what is their simple essence that the Platonist can abstract? Moore may sound mystical but he is within the literal truth when he defends "pure poetry" on the ground that the things are constant, and it is the ideas which change—changing according to the latest mode under which the species indulges its grandiose expectation of subjugating nature. The things are constant in the sense that the ideas are never emancipated from the necessity of referring back to them as their original; and the sense that they are not altered nor diminished no matter which ideas may take off from them as a point of departure. The way to obtain the true *Dinglichkeit* of a formal dinner or a landscape or a beloved person is to approach the object as such, and in humility; then it unfolds a nature which we are unprepared for if we have put our trust in the simple idea which attempted to represent it.

The special antipathy of Moore is to the ideas as they put on their moral complexion, the ideas that relate everything to that insignificant centre of action, the human "soul" in its most Platonic and Pharisaic aspect. Nothing can darken perception better than a repetitive moral earnestness, based on the reputed superiority and higher destiny of the human species. If morality is the code by which we expect the race to achieve the more perfect possession of nature, it is an incitement to a more heroic science, but not to aesthetic experience, nor religious; if it is the code of humility, by which we intend to know nature as nature is, that is another matter; but in an age of science morality is inevitably for the general public the former; and so transcendent a morality as the latter is now unheard of. And therefore:

> O love, *they* die in yon rich sky,
> *They* faint on hill or field or river;
> *Our* echoes roll from soul to soul,
> And grow forever and forever.

The italics are mine. These lines conclude an otherwise innocent poem, a candidate for the anthology, upon which Moore remarks: "The Victorian could never reconcile himself to finishing a poem without speaking about the soul, and the lines are particularly vindictive." Vindictive is just. By what right did the Laureate exult in the death of the physical echoes and call upon his love to witness it, but out of the imperiousness of his savage Platonism? Plato himself would have admired this ending, and considered that it redeemed an otherwise vicious poem.

Why do persons who have ideas to promulgate risk the trial by poetry? If the poets are hired to do it, which is the polite conception of some Hegelians, why do their employers think it worth the money, which they hold in public trust for the cause? Does a science have to become a poetry too? A science is the less effective as a science when it muddies its clear waters with irrelevance, a sermon becomes less cogent when it begins to quote the poets. The moralist, the scientist, and the prophet of idealism think evidently that they must establish their conclusions in poetry, though they reach these conclusions upon quite other evidence. The poetry is likely to destroy the conclusions with a sort of death by drowning, if it is a free poetry.

When that happens the Platonists may be cured of Platonism. There are probably two cures, of which this is the better. One cure is by adversity, by the failure of the ideas to work, on account of treachery or violence, or the contingencies of weather, constitution, love, and economics; leaving the Platonist defeated and bewildered, possibly humbled, but on the other hand possibly turned cynical and worthless. Very much preferable is the cure which comes by education in the fine arts, erasing his Platonism more gently, leading him to feel that that is not a becoming habit of mind which dulls the perceptions.

The definition which some writers have given to art is: the reference of the idea to the image. The implication is that the act is not for the purpose of honest comparison so much as for the purpose of proving the idea by image. But in the event the idea is not disproved so much as it is made to look ineffective and therefore foolish. The ideas will not cover the objects upon which they are imposed, they are too attenuated and threadlike; for ideas have extension and objects have intension, but extension is thin while intension is thick.

There must be a great deal of genuine poetry which started in the poet's mind as a thesis to be developed, but in which the characters and the situations have developed faster than the thesis, and of their own accord. The thesis disappears; or it is recaptured here and there and at the end, and lodged sententiously with the reader, where every successive reading of the poem will dislodge it again. Like this must be some plays, even some play out of Shakespeare, whose thesis would probably be disentangled with difficulty out of the crowded pageant; or some narrative poem with a moral plot but much pure detail; perhaps some "occasional" piece by a Laureate or official person, whose purpose is compromised but whose personal integrity is saved by his wavering between the sentiment which is a public duty and the experience which he has in his own right; even some proclaimed allegory, like Spenser's, unlikely as that may seem, which does not remain transparent and everywhere translatable into idea but makes excursions into the territory of objectivity. These are hybrid perform-ances. They cannot possess beauty of design, though there may be a beauty in detailed passages. But it is common enough, and we should be grateful. The mind is a versatile agent, and unex-pectedly stubborn in its determination not really to be hardened in Platonism. Even in an age of science like the nine-teenth century the poetic talents are not so loyal to its apostolic zeal as they and it suppose, and do not deserve the un-qualified scorn which it is fashionable to offer them, now that the tide has turned, for their performance is qualified.

But this may be not stern enough for concluding a note on Platonic Poetry. I refer again to that whose Platonism is steady and malignant. This poetry is an imitation of Physical Poetry, and not really a poetry. Platonists practise their bogus poetry in order to show that an image will prove an idea, but the litera-ture which succeeds in this delicate mis-sion does not contain real images but illustrations.

III. METAPHYSICAL POETRY

"Most men," Mr. Moore observes, "read and write poetry between fifteen and thirty and afterwards very seldom, for in youth we are attracted by ideas, and modern poetry being concerned al-most exclusively with ideas we live on duty, liberty, and fraternity as chame-leons are said to live on light and air, till at last we turn from ideas to things, thinking that we have lost our taste for poetry, unless, perchance, we are classi-cal scholars."

Much is conveyed in this characteris-tic sentence, even in proportion to its length. As for the indicated chronology, the cart is put after the horse, which is its proper sequence. And it is pleasant to be confirmed in the belief that many men do recant from their Platonism and turn back to things. But it cannot be exactly a *volte-face*, for there are quali-fications. If pure ideas were what these men turn from, they would have had no

poetry at all in the first period, and if pure things were what they turn to, they would be having not a classical poetry but a pure imagism, if such a thing is possible, in the second.

The mind does not come unscathed and virginal out of Platonism. Onto-logical interest would have to develop curiously, or wastefully and discontinu-ously, if men through their youth must cultivate the ideas so passionately that upon its expiration they are done with ideas forever and ready to become as little (and pre-logical) children. Be-cause of the foolishness of idealists are ideas to be taboo for the adult mind? And, as critics, what are we to do with those poems (like *The Canonization* and *Lycidas*) which could not obtain admission by Moore into the anthology but which very likely are the poems we cherish beyond others?

The reputed "innocence" of the aesthetic moment, the "knowledge with-out desire" which Schopenhauer praises, must submit to a little scrutiny, like any-thing else that looks too good to be true. We come into this world as aliens come into a land which they must conquer if they are to live. For native endowment we have an exacting "biological" con-stitution which knows precisely what it needs and determines for us our inevita-ble desires. There can be no certainty that any other impulses are there, for why should they be? They scarcely be-long in the biological picture. Perhaps we are simply an efficient animal spe-cies, running smoothly, working fast, finding the formula of life only too easy, and after a certain apprenticeship piling up power and wealth far beyond the capacity of our appetites to use. What will come next? Perhaps poetry, if the gigantic effort of science begins to seem disproportionate to the reward, according to a sense of diminishing re-turns. But before this pretty event can come to pass, it is possible that every act of attention which is allowed us is con-ditioned by a gross and selfish interest. Where is innocence then? The aes-thetic moment appears as a curious moment of suspension; between the

Platonism in us, which is militant, always sciencing and devouring, and a starved inhibited aspiration towards innocence which, if it could only be free, would like to respect and know the object as it might of its own accord reveal itself.

The poetic impulse is not free, yet it holds out stubbornly against science for the enjoyment of its images. It means to reconstitute the world of perceptions. Finally there is suggested some such formula as the following:

Science gratifies a rational or practical impulse and exhibits the minimum of perception. Art gratifies a perceptual impulse and exhibits the minimum of reason.

Now it would be strange if poets did not develop many technical devices for the sake of increasing the volume of the percipienda or sensibilia. I will name some of them.

First Device: metre. Metre is the most obvious device. A formal metre impresses us as a way of regulating very drastically the material, and we do not stop to remark (that is, as readers) that it has no particular aim except some nominal sort of regimentation. It symbolizes the predatory method, like a sawmill which intends to reduce all the trees to fixed unit timbers, and as business men we require some sign of our business. But to the Platonic censor in us it gives a false security, for so long as the poet appears to be working faithfully at his metrical engine he is left comparatively free to attend lovingly to the things that are being metered, and metering them need not really hurt them. Metre is the gentlest violence he can do them, if he is expected to do some violence.

Second Device: fiction. The device of the fiction is probably no less important and universal in poetry. Over every poem which looks like a poem is a sign which reads: This road does not go through to action: fictitious. Art always sets out to create an "aesthetic distance" between the object and the subject, and art takes pains to announce that it is not history. The situation treated is not quite an actual situation, for science is likely to have claimed that field, and exiled art; but a fictive or hypothetical one, so that science is less greedy and perception may take hold of it. Kant asserted that the aesthetic judgment is not concerned with the existence or non-existence of the object, and may be interpreted as asserting that it is so far from depending on the object's existence that it really depends on the object's non-existence. Sometimes we have a certain melancholy experience. We enjoy a scene which we receive by report only, or dream, or meet with in art; but subsequently find ourselves in the presence of an actual one that seems the very same scene; only to discover that we have not now the power to enjoy it, or to receive it aesthetically, because the economic tension is upon us and will not indulge us in the proper mood. And it is generally easier to obtain our aesthetic experience from art than from nature, because nature is actual, and communication is forbidden. But in being called fictive or hypothetical the art-object suffers no disparagement. It cannot be true in the sense of being actual, and therefore it may be despised by science. But it is true in the sense of being fair or representative, in permitting the "illusion of reality"; just as Schopenhauer discovered that music may symbolize all the modes of existence in the world; and in keeping with the customary demand of the readers of fiction proper, that it shall be "true to life." The defenders of art must require for it from its practitioners this sort of truth, and must assert of it before the world this dignity. If jealous science succeeds in keeping the field of history for its own exclusive use, it does not therefore annihilate the arts, for they reappear in a field which may be called real though one degree removed from actuality. There the arts perform their function with much less interference, and at the same time with about as much fidelity to the phenomenal world as history has.

Third Device: tropes. I have named two important devices; I am not prepared to offer the exhaustive list. I mention but one other kind, the device which comprises the figures of speech. A proper scientific discourse has no intention of employing figurative language for its definitive sort of utterance. Figures of speech twist accidence away from the straight course, as if to intimate astonishing lapses of rationality beneath the smooth surface of discourse, inviting perceptual attention, and weakening the tyranny of science over the senses. But I skip the several easier and earlier figures, which are timid, and stop on the climactic figure, which is the metaphor: with special reference to its consequence, a poetry which once in our history it produced in a beautiful and abundant exhibit, called Metaphysical Poetry.

And what is Metaphysical Poetry? The term was added to the official vocabulary of criticism by Johnson, who probably took it from Pope, who probably took it from Dryden, who used it to describe the poetry of a certain school of poets, thus: "He [John Donne] affects the metaphysics, not only in his satires, but in his amorous verses, where nature only should reign. . . . In this Mr. Cowley has copied him to a fault." But the meaning of metaphysical which was common in Dryden's time, having come down from the Middle Ages through Shakespeare, was simply: supernatural; *miraculous*. The context of the Dryden passage indicates it.

Dryden, then, noted a miraculism in poetry and repudiated it; except where it was employed for satire, where it was not seriously intended and had the effect of wit. Dryden himself employs miraculism wittily, but seems rather to avoid it if he will be really committed by it; he may employ it in his translations of Ovid, where the responsibility is Ovid's and not Dryden's, and in an occasional classical piece where he is making polite use of myths well known to be pagan errors. In his "amorous" pieces he finds the reign of nature sufficient, and it is often the worse for his amorous pieces. He is not many removes from a naturalist. (A naturalist is a person who studies nature not because he loves it but because he wants to use it, approaches it from the standpoint of common sense, and sees it thin and not thick.) Dryden might have remarked that Donne himself had a change of heart and confined his miraculism at last to the privileged field of a more or less scriptural revelation. Perhaps Dryden found his way to accepting Milton because Milton's miraculism was mostly not a contemporary sort but classical and scriptural, pitched in a time when the age of miracles had not given way to the age of science. He knew too that Cowley had shamefully recanted from his petty miraculism, which formed the conceits, and turned to the scriptural or large order of miraculism to write his heroic (but empty) verses about David; and had written a Pindaric ode in extravagant praise of "Mr. Hobs," whose naturalistic account of nature seemed to render any other account fantastic if not contrary to the social welfare.

Incidentally, we know how much Mr. Hobbes affected Dryden too, and the whole of Restoration literature. What Bacon with his disparagement of poetry had begun, in the cause of science and protestantism, Hobbes completed. The name of Hobbes is critical in any history that would account for the chill which settled upon the poets at the very moment that English poetry was attaining magnificently to the fullness of its powers. The name stood for common sense and naturalism, and the monopoly of the scientific spirit over the mind. Hobbes was the adversary, the Satan, when the latter first intimidated the English poets. After Hobbes his name is legion.

"Metaphysics," or miraculism, informs a poetry which is the most original and exciting, and intellectually perhaps the most seasoned, that we know in our literature, and very probably it has few equivalents in other literatures. But it is evident that the metaphysical effects may be large-scale or they may be small-scale. (I believe that generically, or ontologically, no distinction is to be made between them.) If

Donne and Cowley illustrate the small-scale effects, Milton will illustrate the large-scale ones, probably as a consequence of the fact that he wrote major poems. Milton, in the *Paradise Lost*, told a story which was heroic and miraculous in the first place. In telling it he dramatized it, and allowed the scenes and characters to develop of their own native energy. The virtue of a long poem on a "metaphysical" subject will consist in the dramatization or substantiation of all the parts, the poet not being required to devise fresh miracles on every page so much as to establish the perfect "naturalism" of the material upon which the grand miracle is imposed. The *Paradise Lost* possesses this virtue nearly everywhere:

Thus *Adam* to himself lamented loud
Through the still Night, not now, as ere man fell,
Wholsom and cool, and mild, but with black Air
Accompanied, with damps and dreadful gloom,
Which to his evil Conscience represented
All things with double terror: On the ground
Outstretcht he lay, on the cold ground, and oft
Curs'd his Creation, Death as oft accus'd
Of tardie execution, since denounc't
The day of his offence. Why comes not Death,
Said hee, with one thrice acceptable stroke
To end me?

This is exactly the sort of detail for a large-scale metaphysical work, but it would hardly serve the purpose with a slighter and more naturalistic subject: with "amorous" verses. For the critical mind Metaphysical Poetry refers perhaps almost entirely to the so-called "conceits" that constitute its staple. To define the conceit is to define small-scale Metaphysical Poetry.

It is easily defined, upon a little citation. Donne exhibits two conceits, or two branches of one conceit in the familiar lines:

Our hands were firmly cemented
By a fast balm which thence did spring;
Our eye-beams twisted, and did thread
Our eyes upon one double string.

The poem which follows sticks to the topic; it represents the lovers in precisely that mode of union and no other. Cowley is more conventional yet still bold in the lines:

Oh take my Heart, and by that means you'll prove
Within, too stor'd enough of love:
Give me but yours, I'll by that change so thrive
That Love in all my parts shall live.
So powerful is this my change, it render can,
My outside Woman, and your inside Man.

A conceit originates in a metaphor; and in fact the conceit is but a metaphor if the metaphor is meant; that is, if it is developed so literally that it must be meant, or predicated so baldly that nothing else can be meant. Perhaps this will do for a definition.

Clearly the seventeenth century had the courage of its metaphors, and imposed them imperially on the nearest things, and just as clearly the nineteenth century lacked this courage, and was half-heartedly metaphorical, or content with similes. The difference between the literary qualities of the two periods is the difference between the metaphor and the simile. (It must be admitted that this like other generalizations will not hold without its exceptions.) One period was pithy and original in its poetic utterance, the other was prolix and predictable. It would not quite commit itself to the metaphor even if it came upon one. Shelley is about as vigorous as usual when he says in *Adonais*:

Thou young Dawn,
Turn all thy dew to splendour . . .

But splendor is not the correlative of dew, it has the flat tone of a Platonic idea, while physically it scarcely means more than dew with sunshine upon it. The seventeenth century would have said: "Turn thy dew, which is water, into fire, and accomplish the transmutation of the elements." Tennyson in his boldest lyric sings:

Come into the garden, Maud,
For the black bat, night, has flown.

and leaves us unpersuaded of the bat. The predication would be complete without the bat, "The black night has flown," and a flying night is not very remarkable. Tennyson is only affecting a metaphor. But later in the same poem he writes:

The red rose cries, "She is near, she is near";
   And the white rose weeps, "She is late";
The larkspur listens, "I hear, I hear";
   And the lily whispers, "I wait."

and this is a technical conceit. But it is too complicated for this author, having a plurality of images which do not sustain themselves individually. The flowers stand for the lover's thoughts, and have been prepared for carefully in an earlier stanza, but their distinctness is too arbitrary, and these are like a schoolgirl's made-up metaphors. The passage will not compare with one on a very similar situation in *Green Candles*, by Mr. Humbert Wolfe:

"I know her little foot," gray carpet said:
"Who but I should know her light tread?"
"She shall come in," answered the open door,
"And not," said the room, "go out any more."

Wolfe's conceit works and Tennyson's does not, and though Wolfe's performance seems not very daring or important, and only pleasant, he employs the technique of the conceit correctly: he knows that the miracle must have a basis of verisimilitude.

Such is Metaphysical Poetry; the extension of a rhetorical device; as one of the most brilliant successes in our poetry, entitled to long and thorough examination; and even here demanding somewhat by way of a more ontological criticism. I conclude with it.

We may consult the dictionary, and discover that there is a miraculism or supernaturalism in a metaphorical assertion if we are ready to mean what we say, or believe what we hear. Or we may read Mr. Hobbes, the naturalist, who was very clear upon it: "II. The second cause of absurd assertions I ascribe to the giving of names of 'bodies' to 'accidents,' or of 'accidents' to 'bodies,' as they do that say 'faith is infused' or 'inspired,' when nothing can be 'poured' or 'breathed' into anything but body . . . and that 'phantasms' are 'spirits,' etc." Translated into our present terms, Hobbes is condemning the confusion of single qualities with whole things; or the substitution of concrete images for simple ideas.

Specifically, the miraculism arises when the poet discovers by analogy an identity between objects which is partial, though it should be considerable, and proceeds to an identification which is complete. It is to be contrasted with the simile, which says "as if" or "like," and is scrupulous to keep the identification partial. In Cowley's passage above, the lover is saying, not for the first time in this literature: "She and I have exchanged out hearts." What has actually been exchanged is affections, and affections are only in a limited sense the same as hearts. Hearts are unlike affections in being engines that pump blood and form body; and it is a miracle if the poet represents the lady's affection as rendering her inside into man. But he succeeds, with this mixture, in depositing with us the image of a very powerful affection.

From the strict point of view of literary criticism it must be insisted that the miraculism which produces the humblest conceit is the same miraculism which supplies to religions their substantive content. (This is said to assert the dignity not of the conceits but of the religions.) It is the poet and nobody else who gives to the God a nature, a form, faculties, and a history; to the God, most comprehensive of all terms, which, if there were no poetic impulse to actualize or "find" Him, would remain the driest and deadest among Platonic ideas, with all intension sacrificed to infinite extension. The myths are conceits, born of metaphors. Religions are periodically produced by poets and destroyed by naturalists. Religion depends for its ontological validity upon a literary understanding, and that is why it is frequently misunderstood.

The metaphysical poets, perhaps like their spiritual fathers the mediaeval schoolmen, were under no illusions about this. They recognized myth, as they recognized the conceits, as a device of expression; its sanctity as the consequence of its public or social importance.

But whether the topics be Gods or amorous experiences, why do poets resort to miraculism? Hardly for the purpose of controverting natural fact or scientific theory. Religion pronounces about God only where science and philosophy is negative; for a positive is wanted, that is, a God who has his being in the physical world as well as in the world of principles and abstractions. Likewise with the little secular enterprises of poetry. Not now are the poets so brave, not for a very long time have they been so brave, as to dispute the scientists on what they call their "truth"; though it is a pity that the statement cannot be turned round. Poets will concede that every act of science is legitimate, and has its efficacy. The metaphysical poets of the seventeenth century particularly admired the methodology of science, and in fact they copied it, and their phrasing is often technical, spare, and polysyllabic, though they are not repeating actual science but making those metaphorical substitutions that are so arresting.

The intention of Metaphysical Poetry is to complement science, and improve discourse. Naturalistic discourse is incomplete, for either of two reasons. It has the minimum of physical content and starves the sensibility, or it has the maximum, as if to avoid the appearance of evil, but is laborious and pointless. Platonic Poetry is too idealistic, but Physical Poetry is too realistic and realism is tedious and does not maintain interest. The poets therefore introduce the psychological device of the miracle. The predication which it permits is clean and quick but it is not a scientific predication. For scientific predication concludes an act of attention but miraculism initiates one. It leaves us looking, marvelling, and revelling in the thick *dinglich* substance that has just received its strange representation.

Let me suggest as a last word, in deference to a common Puritan scruple, that the predication of Metaphysical Poetry is true enough. It is not true like history, but no poetry is true in that sense, and only a part of science. It is true in the pragmatic sense in which some of the generalizations of science are true: it accomplishes precisely the sort of representation that it means to. It suggests to us that the object is perceptually or physically remarkable, and we had better attend to it.

EDMUND WILSON

(b. 1895)

A professional man of letters best known for his literary criticism, Edmund Wilson helped to introduce such "moderns" as Yeats, Joyce, and Eliot to a wide audience through his influential study of the symbolist movement, *Axel's Castle: A Study of the Imaginative Literature of 1870-1930* (1931). From the beginning Wilson has thought of literary criticism as "a history of man's ideas and imaginings in the setting of the conditions which have shaped them." Wilson's critical essays, which are distinguished by a lucidity, comprehensiveness, and concern for the social and historical context of literature, have been collected in *The Triple Thinkers* (1938;

rev. 1948), *The Boys in the Back Room* (1941), *The Wound and the Bow* (1941), *Classics and Commercials: a Literary Chronicle of the Forties* (1950), *The Shore of Light; a Literary Chronicle of the Twenties and Thirties* (1952), *Eight Essays* (1954), and *A Piece of My Mind* (1956). His principal works of political and cultural history are *To the Finland Station, a Study in the Writing and Acting of History* (1940) and *The Scrolls from the Dead Sea* (1955). Books of travel and social commentary include *The American Jitters* (1932), *Travels in Two Democracies* (1936), and *Europe without Baedeker* (1947). Wilson has also edited *The Shock of Recognition* (1943; 1955), a collection of essays on American literature by American writers, and *The Crack-Up* (1945), a documentary account of the later years of his Princeton friend and fellow writer, F. Scott Fitzgerald.

The Historical Interpretation of Literature (1941; 1948)

I want to talk about the historical interpretation of literature—that is, about the interpretation of literature in its social, economic and political aspects.

To begin with, it will be worth while to say something about the kind of criticism which seems to be furthest removed from this. There is a kind of comparative criticism which tends to be non-historical. The essays of T. S. Eliot, which have had such an immense influence in our time, are, for example, fundamentally non-historical. Eliot sees, or tries to see, the whole of literature, so far as he is acquainted with it, spread out before him under the aspect of eternity. He then compares the work of different periods and countries, and tries to draw from it general conclusions about what literature ought to be. He understands, of course, that our point of view in connection with literature changes, and he has what seems to me a very sound conception of the whole body of writing of the past as something to which new works are continually being added, and which is not thereby merely increased in bulk but modified as a whole—so that Sophocles is no longer precisely what he was for Aristotle, or Shakespeare what he was for Ben Jonson or for Dryden or for Dr. Johnson, on account of all the later

literature that has intervened between them and us. Yet at every point of this continual accretion, the whole field may be surveyed, as it were, spread out before the critic. The critic tries to see it as God might; he calls the books to a Day of Judgment. And, looking at things in this way, he may arrive at interesting and valuable conclusions which could hardly be reached by approaching them in any other way. Eliot was able to see, for example—what I believe had never been noticed before—that the French Symbolist poetry of the nineteenth century had certain fundamental resemblances to the English poetry of the age of Donne. Another kind of critic would draw certain historical conclusions from these purely aesthetic findings, as the Russian D. S. Mirsky did; but Eliot does not draw them.

Another example of this kind of non-historical criticism, in a somewhat different way and on a somewhat different plane, is the work of the late George Saintsbury. Saintsbury was a connoisseur of wines; he wrote an entertaining book on the subject. And his attitude toward literature, too, was that of the connoisseur. He tastes the authors and tells you about the vintages; he distinguishes the qualities of the various wines. His palate was as fine as could be, and he possessed the great qualification that he knew how to take each book on its own terms without expect-

From *The Triple Thinkers* by Edmund Wilson. Copyright 1948 by Edmund Wilson. Reprinted by permission of the author.

ng it to be some other book and was thus in a position to appreciate a great variety of kinds of writing. He was a man of strong social prejudices and peculiarly intransigent political views, but, so far as it is humanly possible, he kept them out of his literary criticism. The result is one of the most agreeable and most comprehensive commentaries on literature that have ever been written in English. Most scholars who have read as much as Saintsbury don't have Saintsbury's discriminating taste. Here is a critic who has covered the whole ground like any academic historian, yet whose account of it is not merely a chronology but a record of fastidious enjoyment. Since enjoyment is the only thing he is looking for, he does not need to know the causes of things, and the historical background of literature does not interest him very much.

There is, however, another tradition of criticism which dates from the beginning of the eighteenth century. In the year 1725, the Neapolitan philosopher Vico published *La Scienza Nuova*, a revolutionary work on the philosophy of history, in which he asserted for the first time that the social world was certainly the work of man, and attempted what is, so far as I know, the first social interpretation of a work of literature. This is what Vico says about Homer: "Homer composed the *Iliad* when Greece was young and consequently burning with sublime passions such as pride, anger and vengeance—passions which cannot allow dissimulation and which consort with generosity; so that she then admired Achilles, the hero of force. But, grown old, he composed the *Odyssey*, at a time when the passions of Greece were already somewhat cooled by reflection, which is the mother of prudence—so that she now admired Ulysses, the hero of wisdom. Thus also, in Homer's youth, the Greek people liked cruelty, abuse, savagery, fierceness, ferocity; whereas, when Homer was old, they were already enjoying the luxuries of Alcinoüs, the delights of Calypso, the pleasures of Circe, the songs of the sirens and the pastimes of

the suitors, who went no further in aggression and combat than laying siege to the chaste Penelope—all of which practices would appear incompatible with the spirit of the earlier time. The divine Plato is so struck by this difficulty that, in order to solve it, he tells us that Homer had foreseen in inspired vision these dissolute, sickly and disgusting customs. But in this way he makes Homer out to have been but a foolish instructor for Greek civilization, since, however much he may condemn them he is displaying for imitation these corrupt and decadent habits which were not to be adopted till long after the foundation of the nations of Greece, and accelerating the natural course which human events would take by spurring the Greeks on to corruption. Thus it is plain that the Homer of the *Iliad* must have preceded by many years the Homer who wrote the *Odyssey*; and it is plain that the former must belong to the northeastern part of Greece, since he celebrates the Trojan War, which took place in his part of the country, whereas the latter belongs to the southeastern part, since he celebrates Ulysses, who reigned there."

You see that Vico has here explained Homer in terms both of historical period and of geographical origin. The idea that human arts and institutions were to be studied and elucidated as the products of the geographical and climatic conditions in which the people who created them lived, and of the phase of their social development through which they were passing at the moment, made great progress during the eighteenth century. There are traces of it even in Dr. Johnson, that most orthodox and classical of critics—as, for example, when he accounts for certain characteristics of Shakespeare by the relative barbarity of the age in which he lived, pointing out, just as Vico had done, that "nations, like individuals, have their infancy." And by the eighties of the eighteenth century Herder, in his *Ideas on the Philosophy of History*, was writing of poetry that it was a kind of "Proteus among the people, which is always changing its form in response to the languages, manners, and habits, to the temperaments and climates, nay even to the accents of different nations." He said—what could still seem startling even so late as that—that "language was not a divine communication, but something men had produced themselves." In the lectures on the philosophy of history that Hegel delivered in Berlin in 1822-23, he discussed the national literatures as expressions of the societies which had produced them—societies which he conceived as great organisms continually transforming themselves under the influence of a succession of dominant ideas.

In the field of literary criticism, this historical point of view came to its first complete flower in the work of the French critic Taine, in the middle of the nineteenth century. The whole school of historian-critics to which Taine belonged—Michelet, Renan, Sainte-Beuve—had been occupied in interpreting books in terms of their historical origins. But Taine was the first of these to attempt to apply these principles systematically and on a large scale in a work devoted exclusively to literature. In the introduction to his *History of English Literature*, published in 1863, he made his famous pronouncement that works of literature were to be understood as the upshot of three interfusing factors: *the moment, the race and the milieu*. Taine thought he was a scientist and a mechanist, who was examining works of literature from the same point of view as the chemist in experimenting with chemical compounds. But the difference between the critic and the chemist is that the critic cannot first combine his elements and then watch to see what they will do; he can only examine phenomena which have already taken place. The procedure that Taine actually follows is to pretend to set the stage for the experiment by describing the moment, the race and the milieu, and then to say: "such a situation demands such and such a kind of writer." He now goes on to describe the kind of writer that the situation demands, and the reader finds himself at

the end confronted with Shakespeare or Milton or Byron or whoever the great figure is—who turns out to prove the accuracy of Taine's prognosis by precisely living up to the description.

There was thus a certain element of imposture in Taine; but it was the rabbits he pulled out that saved him. If he had really been the mechanist that he thought he was, his work on literature would have had little value. The truth was that Taine loved literature for its own sake—he was at his best himself a brilliant artist—and he had very strong moral convictions which give his writing emotional power. His mind, to be sure, was an analytical one, and his analysis, though terribly oversimplified, does have an explanatory value. Yet his work was what we call creative. Whatever he may say about chemical experiments, it is evident when he writes of a great writer that the moment, the race and the milieu have combined, like the three sounds of the chord in Browning's poem about Abt Vogler, to produce not a fourth sound but a star.

To Taine's set of elements was added, dating from the middle of the century, a new element, the economic, which was introduced into the discussion of historical phenomena mainly by Marx and Engels. The non-Marxist critics themselves were at the time already taking into account the influence of the social classes. In his chapters on the Norman conquest of England, Taine shows that the difference between the literatures produced respectively by the Normans and by the Saxons was partly the difference between a ruling class, on the one hand, and a vanquished and oppressed class, on the other. And Michelet, in his volume on the Regency, which was finished the same year that the *History of English Literature* appeared, studies the *Manon Lescaut* of the Abbé Prévost as a document representing the point of view of the small gentry before the French Revolution. But Marx and Engels derived the social classes from the way that people made or got their livings—from what they alled the *methods of production*; and they tended to regard these economic rocesses as fundamental to civilization. The Dialectical Materialism of Marx nd Engels was not really so materialis- c as it sounds. There was in it a large lement of the Hegelian idealism that Marx and Engels thought they had got id of. At no time did these two amous materialists take so mechanistic view of things as Taine began by pro- essing; and their theory of the relation f works of literature to what they alled the *economic base* was a good eal less simple than Taine's theory of he moment, the race and the milieu. They thought that art, politics, religion, hilosophy and literature belonged to hat they called the *superstructure* of uman activity; but they saw that the ractitioners of these various professions ended also to constitute social groups, nd that they were always pulling away om the kind of solidarity based on conomic classes in order to establish a rofessional solidarity of their own. urthermore, the activities of the super- ructure could influence one another, nd they could influence the economic ase. It may be said of Marx and Engels general that, contrary to the popular npression, they were tentative, con- used and modest when it came down to hilosophical first principles, where a materialist like Taine was cocksure. Marx once made an attempt to explain hy the poems of Homer were so good hen the society that produced them as from his point of view—that is, om the point of view of its industrial evelopment—so primitive; and this ave him a good deal of trouble. If we ompare his discussion of this problem ith Vico's discussion of Homer, we e that the explanation of literature in erms of a philosophy of social history becoming, instead of simpler and asier, more difficult and more complex. Marx and Engels were deeply im- ued, moreover, with the German ad- iration for literature, which they had earned from the age of Goethe. It ould never have occurred to either of hem that *der Dichter* was not one of

the noblest and most beneficent of humankind. When Engels writes about Goethe, he presents him as a man equipped for "practical life," whose career was frustrated by the "misery" of the historical situation in Germany in his time, and reproaches him for allow- ing himself to lapse into the "cautious, smug and narrow" philistinism of the class from which he came; but Engels regrets this, because it interfered with the development of the "mocking, de- fiant, world-despising genius," "der geni- ale Dichter," "der gewaltige Poet," of whom Engels would not even, he says, have asked that he should have been a political liberal if Goethe had not sacri- ficed to his bourgeois shrinkings his truer esthetic sense. And the great critics who were trained on Marx—Franz Mehring and Bernard Shaw—had all this reverence for the priesthood of lit- erature. Shaw deplores the absence of political philosophy and what he regards as the middle-class snobbery in Shake- speare; but he celebrates Shakespeare's poetry and his dramatic imagination almost as enthusiastically as Swinburne did, describing even those potboiling comedies—*Twelfth Night* and *As You Like It*—the themes of which seem to him most trashy—as "the Crown Jewels of English dramatic poetry." Such a critic may do more for a writer by showing him as a real man dealing with a real world at a definite moment of time than the impressionist critic of Swinburne's type who flourished in the same period of the late nineteenth cen- tury. The purely impressionist critic ap- proaches the whole literature as an ex- hibit of belletristic jewels, and he can only write a rhapsodic catalogue. But when Shaw turned his spotlight on Shakespeare as a figure in the Shavian drama of history, he invested him with a new interest as no other English critic had done.

The insistence that the man of letters should play a political role, the dis- paragement of works of art in compari- son with political action, were thus originally no part of Marxism. They only became associated with it later. This happened by way of Russia, and it was due to special tendencies in that country that date from long before the Revolution or the promulgation of Marxism itself. In Russia there have been very good reasons why the political implications of literature should particularly occupy the critics. The art of Pushkin itself, with its marvelous power of implication, had certainly been partly created by the censorship of Nicholas I, and Pushkin set the tradition for most of the great Russian writers that followed him. Every play, every poem, every story, must be a parable of which the moral is *implied*. If it were stated, the censor would suppress the book as he tried to do with Pushkin's *Bronze Horseman*, where it was merely a question of the packed implications protruding a little too plainly. Right down through the writings of Chekhov and up almost to the Revolution, the imaginative literature of Russia presents the peculiar paradox of an art that is technically objective and yet charged with social messages. In Russia under the Tsar, it was inevitable that social criticism should lead to political conclusions, because the most urgent need from the point of view of any kind of improvement was to get rid of the tsarist regime. Even the neo-Christian moralist Tolstoy, who pretended to be non-political, was to exert a subversive influence, because his independent preaching was bound to embroil him with the Church, and the Church was an integral part of the tsardom. Tolstoy's pamphlet called *What Is Art?*, in which he throws overboard Shakespeare and a large part of modern literature, including his own novels, in the interest of his intransigent morality, is the example which is most familiar to us of the moralizing Russian criticism; but it was only the most sensational expression of a kind of approach which had been prevalent since Belinsky and Chernyshevsky in the early part of the century. The critics, who were usually journalists writing in exile or for a contraband press, were always tending to demand of the imagi-native writers that they should drama-tize bolder morals.

Even after the Revolution had de-stroyed the tsarist government, this state of things did not change. The old habit of censorship persisted in the new social-ist society of the Soviets, which was necessarily made up of people who had been stamped by the die of the despot-ism. We meet here the peculiar phe-nomenon of a series of literary groups that attempt, one after the other, to obtain official recognition or to make themselves sufficiently powerful to estab-lish themselves as arbiters of literature. Lenin and Trotsky and Lunacharsky had the sense to oppose these attempts; the comrade-dictators of Proletcult or Lev or Rapp would certainly have been just as bad as the Count Benckendorf who made Pushkin miserable, and when the Stalin bureaucracy, after the death of Gorky, got control of this department as of everything else, they instituted a system of repression that made Bencken-dorff and Nicholas I look like Lorenzo de' Medici. In the meantime, Trotsky, who was Commissar of War but him-self a great political writer with an in-terest in belles-lettres, attempted, in 1924, apropos of one of these move-ments, to clarify the situation. He wrote a brilliant and valuable book called *Literature and Revolution*, in which he explained the aims of the government, analyzed the work of the Russian writers, and praised or rebuked the lat-ter as they seemed to him in harmony or at odds with the former. Trotsky is intelligent, sympathetic; it is evident that he is really fond of literature and that he knows that a work of art does not fulfill its function in terms of the formulas of party propaganda. But Mayakovsky, the Soviet poet, whom Trotsky had praised with reservations, expressed himself in a famous joke when he was asked what he thought of Trot-sky's book—a pun which implied that a Commissar turned critic was inevitably a Commissar still;[1] and what a foreigner

[1] *The first pancake lies like a narkom . . .* (people's commissar)—a parody of the Russian saying, *. . . The first pancake lies like a lump.*

annot accept in Trotsky is his assump-
ion that it is the duty of the govern-
nent to take a hand in the direction of
terature.

This point of view, indigenous to
Russia, has been imported to other
ountries through the permeation of
Communist influence. The Communist
ress and its literary followers have re-
ected the control of the Kremlin in all
he phases through which it has passed,
own to the wholesale imprisonment of
oviet writers which has been taking
lace since 1935. But it has never been
part of the American system that our
Republican or Democratic administra-
ion should lay down a political line for
he guidance of the national literature.
A recent gesture in this direction on the
art of Archibald MacLeish, who
eemed a little carried away by his posi-
ion as Librarian of Congress, was any-
hing but cordially received by serious
American writers. So long as the United
tates remains happily a non-totalitarian
ountry, we can very well do without
his aspect of the historical criticism of
terature.

Another element of a different order
as, however, since Marx's time been
dded to the historical study of the
rigins of works of literature. I mean
he psychoanalysis of Freud. This ap-
ears as an extension of something
vhich had already got well started be-
ore, which had figured even in John-
on's *Lives of the Poets*, and of which
he great exponent has been Sainte-
Beuve: the interpretation of works of
iterature in the light of the personalities
ehind them. But the Freudians made
his interpretation more exact and more
ystematic. The great example of the
sychoanalysis of an artist is Freud's
wn essay on Leonardo da Vinci; but
his has little critical interest: it is an
ttempt to construct a case history. One
f the best examples I know of the ap-
lication of Freudian analysis to litera-
ure is in Van Wyck Brooks' book, *The
Ordeal of Mark Twain*, in which Mr.
Brooks uses an incident of Mark Twain's
oyhood as a key to his whole career.

Mr. Brooks has since repudiated the
method he resorted to here, on the
ground that no one but an analyst can
ever know enough about a writer to
make a valid psychoanalytic diagnosis.
This is true, and it is true of the method
that it has led to bad results where the
critic has built a Freudian mechanism
out of very slender evidence, and then
given us merely a romance exploiting
the supposed working of this mechanism,
in place of an actual study that sticks
close to the facts and the documents of
the writer's life and work. But I believe
that Van Wyck Brooks really had hold
of something important when he fixed
upon that childhood incident of which
Mark Twain gave so vivid an account
to his biographer—that scene at the
deathbed of his father when his mother
had made him promise that he would
not break her heart. If it was not one of
those crucial happenings that are supposed to determine the complexes of
Freud, it has certainly a typical significance in relation to Mark Twain's
whole psychology. The stories that people tell about their childhood are likely
to be profoundly symbolic even when
they have been partly or wholly made
up in the light of later experience. And
the attitudes, the compulsions, the emotional "patterns" that recur in the work of
a writer are of great interest to the historical critic.

These attitudes and patterns are em-
bedded in the community and the historical moment, and they may indicate
its ideals and its diseases as the cell
shows the condition of the tissue. The
recent scientific experimentation in the
combining of Freudian with Marxist
method and of psychoanalysis with
anthropology, has had its parallel development in criticism. And there is thus
another element added to our equipment for analyzing literary works, and
the problem grows still more complex.

The analyst, however, is of course
not concerned with the comparative
values of his patients any more than
the surgeon is. He cannot tell you why
the neurotic Dostoevsky produces work
of immense value to his fellows while

another man with the same neurotic pattern would become a public menace. Freud himself emphatically states in his study of Leonardo that his method can make no attempt to account for Leonardo's genius. The problems of comparative artistic value still remain after we have given attention to the Freudian psychological factor just as they do after we have given attention to the Marxist economic factor and to the racial and geographical factors. No matter how thoroughly and searchingly we may have scrutinized works of literature from the historical and biographical points of view, we must be ready to attempt to estimate, in some such way as Saintsbury and Eliot do, the relative degrees of success attained by the products of the various periods and the various personalities. We must be able to tell good from bad, the first-rate from the second-rate. We shall not otherwise write literary criticism at all, but merely social or political history as reflected in literary texts, or psychological case histories from past eras, or, to take the historical point of view in its simplest and most academic form, merely chronologies of books that have been published.

And now how, in these matters of literary art, do we tell the good art from the bad? Norman Kemp Smith, the Kantian philosopher, whose courses I was fortunate enough to take at Princeton twenty-five years ago, used to tell us that this recognition was based primarily on an emotional reaction. For purposes of practical criticism this is a safe assumption on which to proceed. It is possible to discriminate in a variety of ways the elements that in any given department go to make a successful work of literature. Different schools have at different times demanded different things of literature: *unity, symmetry, universality, originality, vision, inspiration, strangeness, suggestiveness, improving morality, socialist realism,* etc. But you could have any set of these qualities that any school of writing has called for and still not have a good play, a good novel, a good poem, a

good history. If you identify the essence of good literature with any one of the elements or with any combination of them, you simply shift the emotional reaction to the recognition of the element or elements. Or if you add to your other demands the demand that the writer must have *talent*, you simply shift this recognition to the talent. Once people find some grounds of agreement in the coincidence of their emotional reactions to books, they may be able to discuss these elements profitably; but if they do not have this basic agreement the discussion will make no sense.

But how, you may ask, can we identify this élite who know what they are talking about? Well, it can only be said of them that they are self-appointed and self-perpetuating, and that they will compel you to accept their authority. Impostors may try to put themselves over, but these quacks will not last. The implied position of the people who know about literature (as is also the case in every other art) is simply that they know what they know, and that they are determined to impose their opinions by main force of eloquence or assertion on the people who do not know. This is not a question, of course, of professional workers in literature—such as editors, professors and critics, who very often have no real understanding of the products with which they deal—but of readers of all kinds in all walks of life. There are moments when a first-rate writer, unrecognized or out of fashion with the official chalkers-up for the market, may find his support in the demand for his work of an appreciative cultivated public.

But what is the cause of this emotional reaction which is the critic's divining rod? This question has long been a subject of study by the branch of philosophy called esthetics, and it has recently been made a subject of scientific experimentation. Both these lines of inquiry are likely to be prejudiced in the eyes of the literary critic by the fact that the inquiries are sometimes conducted by persons who are obviously deficient in literary feeling or taste. You one should not deny the possibility that something of value might result from the speculations and explorations of men of acute minds who take as their given data the esthetic emotions of other men.

Almost everybody interested in literature has tried to explain to himself the nature of these emotions that register our approval of artistic works; and I of course have my own explanation.

In my view, all our intellectual activity, in whatever field it takes place, is an attempt to give a meaning to our experience—that is, to make life more practicable; for by understanding things we make it easier to survive and get around among them. The mathematician Euclid, working in a convention of abstractions, shows us relations between the distances of our unwieldy and cluttered-up environment upon which we are able to count. A drama of Sophocles also indicates relations between the various human impulses, which appear so confused and dangerous, and it brings out a certain justice of Fate—that is to say, of the way in which the interaction of these impulses is seen in the long run to work out—upon which we can also depend. The kinship, from this point of view, of the purposes of science and art appears very clearly in the case of the Greeks, because not only do both Euclid and Sophocles satisfy us by making patterns, but they make much the same kind of patterns. Euclid's *Elements* takes simple theorems and by a series of logical operations builds them up to a climax in the square on the hypotenuse. A typical drama of Sophocles develops in a similar way.

Some writers (as well as some scientists) have a different kind of explicit message beyond the reassurance implicit in the mere feat of understanding life or of moulding the harmony of artistic form. Not content with such an achievement as that of Sophocles—who has one of his choruses tell us that it is better not to be born, but who, by representing life as noble and based on law, makes its tragedy easier to bear—such writers attempt, like Plato, to think out and rec-

ommend a procedure for turning it into something better. But other departments of literature—lyric poetry such as Sappho's, for example—have *less* philosophical content than Sophocles. A lyric gives us nothing but a pattern imposed on the expression of a feeling; but this pattern of metrical quantities and of consonants and vowels that balance has the effect of reducing the feeling, however unruly or painful it may seem when we experience it in the course of our lives, to something orderly, symmetrical and pleasing; and it also relates this feeling to the more impressive scheme, works it into the larger texture, of the body of poetic art. The discord has been resolved, the anomaly subjected to discipline. And this control of his emotion by the poet has the effect at second-hand of making it easier for the reader to manage his own emotions. (Why certain sounds and rhythms gratify us more than others, and how they are connected with the themes and ideas that they are chosen as appropriate for conveying, are questions that may be passed on to the scientist.)

And this brings us back again to the historical point of view. The experience of mankind on the earth is always changing as man develops and has to deal with new combinations of elements; and the writer who is to be anything more than an echo of his predecessors must always find expression for something which has never yet been expressed, must master a new set of phenomena which has never yet been mastered. With each such victory of the human intellect, whether in history, in philosophy or in poetry, we experience a deep satisfaction: we have been cured of some ache of disorder, relieved of some oppressive burden of uncomprehended events.

This relief that brings the sense of power, and, with the sense of power, joy, is the positive emotion which tells us that we have encountered a first-rate piece of literature. But stay! you may at this point warn: are not people often solaced and exhilarated by literature of the trashiest kind? They are: crude and limited people do certainly feel some such emotion in connection with work that is limited and crude. The man who is more highly organized and has a wider intellectual range will feel it in connection with work that is finer and more complex. The difference between the emotion of the more highly organized man and the emotion of the less highly organized one is a matter of mere graduation. You sometimes discover books —the novels of John Steinbeck, for example—that seem to mark precisely the borderline between work that is definitely superior and work that is definitely bad. When I was speaking a little while back of the genuine connoisseurs who establish the standards of taste, I meant, of course, the people who can distinguish Grade A and who prefer it to the other grades.

KENNETH BURKE

(b. 1897)

Although often grouped with the New Critics, Burke differs from most of them in his use of terms and concepts from extra-literary disciplines to relate literature to its social environment. Building on the idea of art as symbolic action within a community, Burke has striven to develop a synthetic "dramatistic" theory of literature and criticism under which such diverse systems as those of Marx and Freud might be reconciled as basically similar "conversion" processes that resolve social and personal conflicts. For Burke the aesthetic prototype of all such processes is the ritual drama in which a rebirth is enacted. Burke's theory, liberally illustrated by acute and often ingenious "readings," has been developed through a succession of volumes including *Counter-Statement* (1931; 1953), *Permanence and Change* (1935; 1954), *Attitudes Toward History* (2 vols., 1937), *The Philosophy of Literary Form: Studies in Symbolic Action* (1941), *A Grammar of Motives* (1945), *A Rhetoric of Motives* (1950), and *The Rhetoric of Religion; Studies in Logology* (1961). Burke has defined literary form in terms of the psychology of the audience, and throughout his works an interest in both the social and the psychological values of literature is a continuing emphasis. A prolific coiner of terms, Burke has contributed to the vocabularies of many of his fellow critics, while his fondness for categorization is a trait he shares with the neo-Aristotelian genre critics.

Literature as Equipment for Living (1941)

Here I shall put down, as briefly as possible, a statement in behalf of what might be catalogued, with a fair degree of accuracy, as a *sociological* criticism of literature. Sociological criticism in itself is certainly not new. I shall here try to suggest what partially new elements or emphasis I think should be added to this old approach. And to make the "way in" as easy as possible, I shall begin with a discussion of proverbs.

1

Examine random specimens in *The Oxford Dictionary of English Proverbs.*

You will note, I think, that there is no "pure" literature here. Everything is "medicine." Proverbs are designed for consolation or vengeance, for admonition or exhortation, for foretelling.

Or they name typical, recurrent situations. That is, people find a certain social relationship recurring so frequently that they must "have a word for it." The Eskimos have special names for many different kinds of snow (fifteen, if I remember rightly) because variations in the quality of snow greatly affect their living. Hence, they must "size up" snow much more accurately than we do. And the same is true of social phenomena. Social structures give rise to "type" situations, subtle subdivisions of the relationships involved in competitive and coöperative acts. Many proverbs seek to chart, in more or less homey and picturesque ways, these "type" situations. I submit that such naming is done, not for the sheer glory of the thing, but because of its bearing upon human welfare. A different name for snow implies a different kind of hunt. Some names for snow imply that one should not hunt at all. And similarly, the names for typical, recurrent social situations are not developed out of "disinterested curiosity," but because the names imply a command (what to expect, what to look out for).

To illustrate with a few representative examples:

Proverbs designed for consolation: "The sun does not shine on both sides of the hedge at once." "Think of ease, but work on." "Little troubles the eye, but far less the soul." "The worst luck now, the better another time." "The wind in one's face makes one wise." "He that hath lands hath quarrels." "He knows how to carry the dead cock home." "He is not poor that hath little, but he that desireth much."

For vengeance: "At length the fox is brought to the furrier." "Shod in the cradle, barefoot in the stubble." "Sue a beggar and get a louse." "The higher the ape goes, the more he shows his tail." "The moon does not heed the barking of dogs." "He measures an-

other's corn by his own bushel." "He shuns the man who knows him well." "Fools tie knots and wise men loose them."

Proverbs that have to do with foretelling: (The most obvious are those to do with the weather.) "Sow peas and beans in the wane of the moon, Who soweth them sooner, he soweth too soon." "When the wind's in the north, the skilful fisher goes not forth." "When the sloe tree is as white as a sheet, sow your barley whether it be dry or wet." "When the sun sets bright and clear, An easterly wind you need not fear. When the sun sets in a bank, A westerly wind we shall not want."

In short: "Keep the weather eye open": be realistic about sizing up today's weather, because your accuracy has bearing upon tomorrow's weather. And forecast not only the meteorological weather, but also the social weather: "When the moon's in the full, then wit's in the wane." "Straws show which way the wind blows." "When the fish is caught, the net is laid aside." "Remove an old tree, and it will wither to death." "The wolf may lose his teeth, but never his nature." "He that bites on every weed must needs light on poison." "Whether the pitcher strikes the stone, or the stone the pitcher, it is bad for the pitcher." "Eagles catch no flies." "The more laws, the more offenders."

In this foretelling category we might also include the recipes for wise living, sometimes moral, sometimes technical: "First thrive, and then wive." "Think with the wise but talk with the vulgar." "When the fox preacheth, then beware your geese." "Venture a small fish to catch a great one." "Respect a man, he will do the more."

In the class of "typical, recurrent situations" we might put such proverbs and proverbial expressions as: "Sweet appears sour when we pay." "The treason is loved but the traitor is hated." "The wine in the bottle does not quench thirst." "The sun is never the worse for shining on a dunghill." "The lion kicked by an ass." "The lion's share." "To catch one napping." "To smell a rat."

"To cool one's heels."

By all means, I do not wish to suggest that this is the only way in which the proverbs could be classified. For instance, I have listed in the "foretelling" group the proverb, "When the fox preacheth, then beware your geese." But it could obviously be "taken over" for vindictive purposes. Or consider a proverb like, "Virtue flies from the heart of a mercenary man." A poor man might obviously use it either to console himself for being poor (the implication being, "Because I am poor in money I am rich in virtue") or to strike at another (the implication being, "When he got money, what else could you expect of him but deterioration?"). In fact, we could even say that such symbolic vengeance would itself be an aspect of solace. And a proverb like "The sun is never the worse for shining on a dunghill" (which I have listed under "typical recurrent situations") might as well be put in the vindictive category.

The point of issue is not to find categories that "place" the proverbs once and for all. What I want is categories that suggest their active nature. Here there is no "realism for its own sake." There is realism for promise, admonition, solace, vengeance, foretelling, instruction, charting, all for the direct bearing that such acts have upon matters of welfare.

2

Step two: Why not extend such analysis of proverbs to encompass the whole field of literature? Could the most complex and sophisticated works of art legitimately be considered somewhat as "proverbs writ large"? Such leads, if held admissible, should help us to discover important facts about literary organization (thus satisfying the requirements of technical criticism). And the kind of observation from this perspective should apply beyond literature to life in general (thus helping to take literature out of its separate bin and give it a place in a general "sociological" picture).

The point of view might be phrased in this way: Proverbs are *strategies* for dealing with *situations*. In so far as situations are typical and recurrent in a given social structure, people develop names for them and strategies for handling them. Another name for strategies might be *attitudes*.

People have often commented on the fact that there are contrary *proverbs*. But I believe that the above approach to proverbs suggests a necessary modification of that comment. The apparent contradictions depend upon differences in *attitude*, involving a correspondingly different choice of *strategy*. Consider, for instance, the *apparently* opposite pair: "Repentance comes too late" and "Never too late to mend." The first is admonitory. It says in effect: "You'd better look out, or you'll get yourself too far into this business." The second is consolatory, saying in effect: "Buck up, old man, you can still pull out of this."

Some critics have quarreled with me about my selection of the word "strategy" as the name for this process. I have asked them to suggest an alternative term, so far without profit. The only one I can think of is "method." But if "strategy" errs in suggesting to some people an overly *conscious* procedure, "method" errs in suggesting an overly *"methodical"* one. Anyhow, let's look at the documents:

Concise Oxford Dictionary: "Strategy: Movement of an army or armies in a campaign, art of so moving or disposing troops or ships as to impose upon the enemy the place and time and conditions for fighting preferred by oneself" (from a Greek word that refers to the leading of an army).

New English Dictionary: "Strategy: The art of projecting and directing the larger military movements and operations of a campaign."

André Cheron, *Traité Complet d'Echecs*: *"On entend par stratégie les manoeuvres qui ont pour but la sortie et le bon arrangement des pièces."*

Looking at these definitions, I gain courage. For surely, the most highly alembicated and sophisticated work of art, arising in complex civilizations, could be considered as designed to organize and command the army of one's thoughts and images, and to so organize them that one "imposes upon the enemy the time and place and conditions for fighting preferred by oneself." One seeks to "direct the larger movements and operations" in one's campaign of living. One "maneuvers," and the maneuvering is an "art."

Are not the final results one's "strategy"? One tries, as far as possible, to develop a strategy whereby one "can't lose." One tries to change the rules of the game until they fit his own necessities. Does the artist encounter disaster? He will "make capital" of it. If one is a victim of competition, for instance, if one is elbowed out, if one is willy-nilly more jockeyed against than jockeying, one can by the solace and vengeance of art convert this very "liability" into an "asset." One tries to fight on his own terms, developing a strategy for imposing the proper "time, place, and conditions."

But one must also, to develop a full strategy, be *realistic*. One must *size things up* properly. One cannot accurately know how things *will be*, what is promising and what is meanacing, unless he accurately knows how things *are*. So the wise strategist will not be content with strategies of merely a self-gratifying sort. He will "keep his weather eye open." He will not too eagerly "read into" a scene an attitude that is irrelevant to it. He won't sit on the side of an active volcano and "see" it as a dormant plain.

Often, alas, he will. The great allurement in our present popular "inspirational literature," for instance, may be largely of this sort. It is a strategy for easy consolation. It "fills a need," since there is always a need for easy consolation—and in an era of confusion like our own the need is especially keen. So people are only too willing to "meet a

man halfway" who will *play down* the realistic naming of our situation and *play up* such strategies as make solace cheap. However, I should propose a reservation here. We usually take it for granted that people who consume our current output of books on "How to Buy Friends and Bamboozle Oneself and Other People" are reading as *students* who will attempt applying the recipes given. Nothing of the sort. *The reading of a book on the attaining of success is in itself the symbolic attaining of that success.* It is *while they read* that these readers are "succeeding." I'll wager that, in by far the great majority of cases, such readers make no serious attempt to apply the book's recipes. The lure of the book resides in the fact that the reader, while reading it, is then living in the aura of success. What he wants is *easy* success; and he gets it in symbolic form by the mere reading itself. To attempt applying such stuff in real life would be very difficult, full of many disillusioning difficulties.

Sometimes a different strategy may arise. The author may remain realistic, avoiding too easy a form of solace—yet he may get as far off the track in his own way. Forgetting that realism is an aspect for foretelling, he may take it as an end in itself. He is tempted to do this by two factors: (1) an *ill-digested* philosophy of science, leading him mistakenly to assume that "relentless" naturalistic "truthfulness" is a proper end in itself, and (2) a merely *competitive* desire to outstrip other writers by being "more realistic" than they. Works thus made "efficient" by tests of competition internal to the book trade are a kind of academicism not so named (the writer usually thinks of it as the *opposite* of academicism). Realism thus stepped up competitively might be distinguished from the proper sort by the name of "naturalism." As a way of "sizing things up," the naturalistic tradition tends to become as inaccurate as the "inspirational" strategy, though at the opposite extreme.

Anyhow, the main point is this: A

work like *Madame Bovary* (or its homely American translation, *Babbitt*) is the strategic naming of a situation. It singles out a pattern of experience that is sufficiently representative of our social structure, that recurs sufficiently often *mutandis mutatis,* for people to "need a word for it" and to adopt an attitude towards it. Each work of art is the addition of a word to an informal dictionary (or, in the case of purely derivative artists, the addition of a subsidiary meaning to a word already given by some originating artist). As for *Madame Bovary,* the French critic Jules de Gaultier proposed to add it to our *formal* dictionary by coining the word "Bovarysme" and writing a whole book to say what he meant by it.

Mencken's book on *The American Language,* I hate to say, is splendid. I console myself with the reminder that Mencken didn't write it. Many millions of people wrote it, and Mencken was merely the amanuensis who took it down from their dictation. He found a true "vehicle" (that is, a book that could be greater than the author who wrote it). He gets the royalties, but the job was done by a collectivity. As you read that book, you see a people who were up against a new set of typical recurrent situations, situations typical of their business, their politics, their criminal organizations, their sports. Either there were no words for these in standard English, or people didn't know them, or they didn't "sound right." So a new vocabulary arose, to "give us a word for it." I see no reason for believing that Americans are unusually fertile in word-coinage. American slang was not developed out of some exceptional gift. It was developed out of the fact that new typical situations had arisen and people needed names for them. They had to "size things up." They had to console and strike, to promise and admonish. They had to describe for purposes of forecasting. And "slang" was the result. It is, by this analysis, simply *proverbs not so named,* a kind of "folk criticism."

3

With what, then, would "sociological criticism" along these lines be concerned? It would seek to codify the various strategies which artists have developed with relation to the naming of situations. In a sense, much of it would even be "timeless," for many of the "typical, recurrent situations" are not peculiar to our own civilization at all. The situations and strategies framed in Aesop's Fables, for instance, apply to human relations now just as fully as they applied in ancient Greece. They are, like philosophy, sufficiently "generalized" to extend far beyond the particular combination of events named by them in any one instance. They name an "essence." Or, as Korzybski might say, they are on a "high level of abstraction." One doesn't usually think of them as "abstract," since they are usually so concrete in their stylistic expression. But they invariably aim to discern the "general behind the particular" (which would suggest that they are good Goethe).

The attempt to treat literature from the standpoint of situations and strategies suggests a variant of Spengler's notion of the "contemporaneous." By "contemporaneity" he meant corresponding stages of different cultures. For instance, if modern New York is much like decadent Rome, then we are "contemporaneous" with decadent Rome, or with some corresponding decadent city among the Mayas, etc. It is in this sense that situations are "timeless," "non-historical," "contemporaneous." A given human relationship may be at one time named in terms of foxes and lions, if there are foxes and lions about; or it may now be named in terms of salesmanship, advertising, the tactics of politicians, etc. But beneath the change in particulars, we may often discern the naming of the one situation.

So sociological criticism, as here understood, would seek to assemble and codify this lore. It might occasionally lead us to outrage good taste, as we ometimes found exemplified in some great sermon or tragedy or abstruse work of philosophy the same strategy as we found exemplified in a dirty joke. At this point, we'd put the sermon and the dirty joke together, thus "grouping by situation" and showing the range of possible particularizations. In his exceptionally discerning essay, "A Critic's Job of Work," R. P. Blackmur says, "I think on the whole his (Burke's) method could be applied with equal fruitfulness to Shakespeare, Dashiell Hammett, or Marie Corelli." When I got through convincing, I had to admit that Blackmur was right. This article is an attempt to say for the method what can be said. As a matter of fact, I'll go a step further and maintain: You can't properly put Marie Corelli and Shakespeare apart until you have first put them together. First genus, then differentia. The strategy in common is the genus. The *range* or *scale* or *spectrum* of particularizations is the differentia.

Anyhow, that's what I'm driving at. And that's why reviewers sometimes find in my work "intuitive" leaps that are dubious as "science." They are not "leaps" at all. They are classifications, groupings, made on the basis of some strategic element common to the items grouped. They are neither more nor less "intuitive" than *any* grouping or classification of social events. Apples can be grouped with bananas as fruits, and they can be grouped with tennis balls as round. I am simply proposing, in the social sphere, a method of classification with reference to *strategies*.

The method has these things to be said in its favor: It gives definite insight into the organization of literary works; and it automatically breaks down the barriers erected about literature as a specialized pursuit. People can classify novels by reference to three kinds, eight kinds, seventeen kinds. It doesn't matter. Students patiently copy down the professor's classification and pass examinations on it, because the range of possible academic classifications is endless. Sociological classification, as herein suggested, would derive its relevance from the fact that it should apply both to works of art and to social situations outside of art.

It would, I admit, violate current pieties, break down current categories, and thereby "outrage good taste." But "good taste" has become *inert*. The classifications I am proposing would be *active*. I think that what we need is active categories.

These categories will lie on the bias across the categories of modern specialization. The new alignment will outrage in particular those persons who take the division of faculties in our universities to be an exact replica of the way in which God himself divided up the universe. We have had the Philosophy of the Being; and we have had the Philosophy of the Becoming. In contemporary specialization, we have been getting the Philosophy of the Bin. Each of these mental localities has had its own peculiar way of life, its own values, even its own special idiom for seeing, thinking, and "proving." Among other things, a sociological approach should attempt to provide a reintegrative point of view, a broader empire of investigation encompassing the lot.

What would such sociological categories be like? They would consider works of art, I think, as strategies for selecting enemies and allies, for socializing losses, for warding off evil eye, for purification, propitiation, and desanctification, consolation and vengeance, admonition and exhortation, implicit commands or instructions of one sort or another. Art forms like "tragedy" or "comedy" or "satire" would be treated as *equipments for living*, that size up situations in various ways and in keeping with correspondingly various attitudes. The typical ingredients of such forms would be sought. Their relation to typical situations would be stressed. Their comparative values would be considered, with the intention of formulating a "strategy of strategies," the "over-all" strategy obtained by inspection of the lot.

W. K. WIMSATT, JR., and MONROE C. BEARDSLEY

(b. 1907)   (b. 1915)

W. K. Wimsatt, Jr. is the author, with the philosopher Monroe C. Beardsley, o[f] two of the best known modern essays in prescriptive critical theory, "Th[e] Intentional Fallacy" and "The Affective Fallacy." Though Wimsatt is a specialis[t] in eighteenth century literature, his philosophical interest—strongly influenced, i[t] would appear, by Thomist thought—in the nature of expressive language has mad[e] him an important spokesman for the contextualist, or New Critical, approach t[o] criticism and theory. His scholarly and critical works include *The Prose Style o[f] Samuel Johnson* (1941), *Philosophic Words, a Study of Style and Meaning in th[e] 'Rambler' and Dictionary of Samuel Johnson* (1948), *The Verbal Icon: Studies i[n] the Meaning of Poetry* (1954), and *Literary Criticism; a Short History* (wit[h] Cleanth Brooks, 1957).

The Intentional Fallacy (1946)

He owns with toil he wrote the following
scenes;
But, if they're naught, ne'er spare him for his
pains:
Damn him the more; have no commiseration
For dullness on mature deliberation.
—WILLIAM CONGREVE, Prologue to
The Way of the World

The claim of the author's "intention" upon the critic's judgment has been challenged in a number of recent discussions, notably in the debate entitled *The Personal Heresy*, between Professors Lewis and Tillyard. But it seems doubtful if this claim and most of its romantic corollaries are as yet subject to any widespread questioning. The present writers, in a short article entitled "Intention" for a *Dictionary*[1] of literary criticism, raised the issue but were unable to pursue its implications at any length. We argued that the design or intention of the author is neither available nor desirable as a standard for judging the success of a work of literary

From *The Verbal Icon* by W. K. Wimsatt, Jr. and Monroe C. Beardsley. Copyright 1954 by the University of Kentucky Press. Reprinted by permission of the authors and the University of Kentucky Press.

[1] *Dictionary of World Literature*, Joseph T. Shipley, ed. (New York, 1942) p. 326-29.

art, and it seems to us that this is [a] principle which goes deep into some dif[-] ferences in the history of critical atti[-] tudes. It is a principle which accepte[d] or rejected points to the polar opposite[s] of classical "imitation" and romantic ex[-] pression. It entails many specific truth[s] about inspiration, authenticity, biogra[-] phy, literary history and scholarship, an[d] about some trends of contemporary po[-] etry, especially its allusiveness. There [is] hardly a problem of literary criticism i[n] which the critic's approach will not b[e] qualified by his view of "intention."

"Intention," as we shall use the ter[m] corresponds to *what he intended* in [a] formula which more or less explicitl[y] has had wide acceptance. "In order t[o] judge the poet's performance, we mu[st] know *what he intended*." Intention [is] design or plan in the author's mind. I[n-] tention has obvious affinities for th[e] author's attitude toward his work, th[e] way he felt, what made him write.

We begin our discussion with a seri[es] of propositions summarized and ab[-] stracted to a degree where they seem t[o] us axiomatic.

1. A poem does not come into exis[t-] ence by accident. The words of a poe[m]

as Professor Stoll has remarked, come out of a head, not out of a hat. Yet to insist on the designing intellect as a *cause* of a poem is not to grant the design or intention as a *standard* by which the critic is to judge the worth of the poet's performance.

2. One must ask how a critic expects to get an answer to the question about intention. How is he to find out what the poet tried to do? If the poet succeeded in doing it, then the poem itself shows what he was trying to do. And if the poet did not succeed, then the poem is not adequate evidence, and the critic must go outside the poem—for evidence of an intention that did not become effective in the poem. "Only one *caveat* must be borne in mind," says an eminent intentionalist[2] in a moment when his theory repudiates itself; "the poet's aim must be judged at the moment of the creative act, that is to say, by the art of the poem itself."

3. Judging a poem is like judging a pudding or a machine. One demands that it work. It is only because an artifact works that we infer the intention of an artificer. "A poem should not mean but be." A poem can *be* only through its *meaning*—since its medium is words—yet it *is*, simply *is*, in the sense that we have no excuse for inquiring what part is intended or meant. Poetry is a feat of style by which a complex of meaning is handled all at once. Poetry succeeds because all or most of what is said or implied is relevant; what is irrelevant has been excluded, like lumps from pudding and "bugs" from machinery. In this respect poetry differs from practical messages, which are successful if and only if we correctly infer the intention. They are more abstract than poetry.

4. The meaning of a poem may certainly be a personal one, in the sense that a poem expresses a personality or state of soul rather than a physical object like an apple. But even a short lyric poem is dramatic, the response of a speaker (no matter how abstractly conceived) to a situation (no matter how universalized). We ought to impute the thoughts and attitudes of the poem immediately to the dramatic *speaker*, and if to the author at all, only by an act of biographical inference.

5. There is a sense in which an author, by revision, may better achieve his original intention. But it is a very abstract sense. He intended to write a better work, or a better work of a certain kind, and now has done it. But it follows that his former concrete intention was not his intention. "He's the man we were in search of, that's true," says Hardy's rustic constable, "and yet he's not the man we were in search of. For the man we were in search of was not the man we wanted."

"Is not a critic," asks Professor Stoll, "a judge, who does not explore his own consciousness, but determines the author's meaning or intention, as if the poem were a will, a contract, or the constitution? The poem is not the critic's own." He has accurately diagnosed two forms of irresponsibility, one of which he prefers. Our view is yet different. The poem is not the critic's own and not the author's (it is detached from the author at birth and goes about the world beyond his power to intend about it or control it). The poem belongs to the public. It is embodied in language, the peculiar possession of the public, and it is about the human being, an object of public knowledge. What is said about the poem is subject to the same scrutiny as any statement in linguistics or in the general science of psychology.

A critic of our *Dictionary* article, Ananda K. Coomaraswamy, has argued[3] that there are two kinds of inquiry about a work of art: (1) whether the artist achieved his intentions; (2) whether the work of art "ought ever to have been undertaken at all" and so "whether it is worth preserving." Number (2), Coomaraswamy maintains, is not "criticism of any work of art *qua* work of art," but is rather moral criticism; number (1)

[2] J. E. Spingarn, "The New Criticism," in *Criticism* *America* (New York, 1924), 24-25.

[3] Ananda K. Coomaraswamy, "Intention," in *American Bookman*, I (1944), 41-48.

is artistic criticism. But we maintain that (2) need not be moral criticism: that there is another way of deciding whether works of art are worth preserving and whether, in a sense, they "ought" to have been undertaken, and this is the way of objective criticism of works of art as such, the way which enables us to distinguish between a skillful murder and a skillful poem. A skillful murder is an example which Coomaraswamy uses, and in his system the difference between the murder and the poem is simply a "moral" one, not an "artistic" one, since each if carried out according to plan is "artistically" successful. We maintain that (2) is an inquiry of more worth than (1), and since (2) and not (1) is capable of distinguishing poetry from murder, the name "artistic criticism" is properly given to (2).

II

It is not so much a historical statement as a definition to say that the intentional fallacy is a romantic one. When a rhetorician of the first century A.D. writes: "Sublimity is the echo of a great soul," or when he tells us that "Homer enters into the sublime actions of his heroes" and "shares the full inspiration of the combat," we shall not be surprised to find this rhetorician considered as a distant harbinger of romanticism and greeted in the warmest terms by Saintsbury. One may wish to argue whether Longinus should be called romantic, but there can hardly be a doubt that in one important way he is.

Goethe's three questions for "constructive criticism" are "What did the author set out to do? Was his plan reasonable and sensible, and how far did he succeed in carrying it out?" If one leaves out the middle question, one has in effect the system of Croce—the culmination and crowning philosophic expression of romanticism. The beautiful is the successful intuition-expression, and the ugly is the unsuccessful; the intuition or private part of art is *the* aesthetic fact, and the medium or public part is not the subject of aesthetic at all.

The Madonna of Cimabue is still in the Church of Santa Maria Novella; but does she speak to the visitor of to-day as to the Florentines of the thirteenth century?

Historical interpretation labours . . . to reintegrate in us the psychological conditions which have changed in the course of history. It . . enables us to see a work of art (a physical object) as its *author saw it* in the moment of production. [4]

The first italics are Croce's, the second ours. The upshot of Croce's system is an ambiguous emphasis on history. With such passages as a point of departure a critic may write a nice analysis of the meaning or "spirit" of a play by Shakespeare or Corneille—a process that involves close historical study but remains aesthetic criticism—or he may, with equal plausibility, produce an essay in sociology, biography, or other kinds of non-aesthetic history.

III

I went to the poets; tragic, dithyrambic, and all sorts. . . . I took them some of the most elaborate passages in their own writings, and asked what was the meaning of them. . . Will you believe me? . . . there is hardly a person present who would not have talked better about their poetry than they did themselves. Then I knew that not by wisdom do poets write poetry, but by a sort of genius and inspiration.

That reiterated mistrust of the poet which we hear from Socrates may have been part of a rigorously ascetic view in which we hardly wish to participate, yet Plato's Socrates saw a truth about the poetic mind which the world no longer commonly sees—so much criticism, and that the most inspirational and most affectionately remembered, has proceeded from the poets themselves.

[4] It is true that Croce himself in his *Ariosto, Shakspeare and Corneille* (London, 1920), chap. VII, "The Practical Personality and the Poetical Personality," and in his *Defence of Poetry* (Oxford, 1933), 24, and elsewhere, early and late, has delivered telling attacks on emotive geneticism, but the main drive of the *Aesthetic* is surely toward a kind of cognitive intentionalism.

Certainly the poets have had something to say that the critic and professor could not say; their message has been more exciting: that poetry should come as naturally as leaves to a tree, that poetry is the lava of the imagination, or that it is emotion recollected in tranquillity. But it is necessary that we realize the character and authority of such testimony. There is only a fine shade of difference between such expressions and a kind of earnest advice that authors often give. Thus Edward Young, Carlyle, Walter Pater:

I know two golden rules from *ethics*, which are no less golden in *Composition*, than in life. 1. *Know thyself*; 2dly, *Reverence thyself*.

This is the grand secret for finding readers and retaining them: let him who would move and convince others, be first moved and convinced himself. Horace's rule, *Si vis me flere*, is applicable in a wider sense than the literal one. To every poet, to every writer, we might say: Be true, if you would be believed.

Truth! there can be no merit, no craft at all, without that. And further, all beauty is in the long run only *fineness* of truth, or what we call expression, the finer accommodation of speech to that vision within.

And Housman's little handbook to the poetic mind yields this illustration:

Having drunk a pint of beer at luncheon—beer is a sedative to the brain, and my afternoons are the least intellectual portion of my life—I would go out for a walk of two or three hours. As I went along, thinking of nothing in particular, only looking at things around me and following the progress of the seasons, there would flow into my mind, with sudden and unaccountable emotion, sometimes a line or two of verse, sometimes a whole stanza at once.

This is the logical terminus of the series already quoted. Here is a confession of how poems were written which would do as a definition of poetry just as well as "emotion recollected in tranquillity" —and which the young poet might equally well take to heart as a practical rule. Drink a pint of beer, relax, go walking, think on nothing in particular, look at things, surrender yourself to yourself, search for the truth in your own soul, listen to the sound of your own inside voice, discover and express the *vraie vérité*.

It is probably true that all this is excellent advice for poets. The young imagination fired by Wordsworth and Carlyle is probably closer to the verge of producing a poem than the mind of the student who has been sobered by Aristotle or Richards. The art of inspiring poets, or at least of inciting something like poetry in young persons, has probably gone further in our day than ever before. Books of creative writing such as those issued from the Lincoln School are interesting evidence of what a child can do.[5] All this, however, would appear to belong to an art separate from criticism—to a psychological discipline, a system of self-development, a yoga, which the young poet perhaps does well to notice, but which is something different from the public art of evaluating poems.

Coleridge and Arnold were better critics than most poets have been, and if the critical tendency dried up the poetry in Arnold and perhaps in Coleridge, it is not inconsistent with our argument, which is that judgment of poems is different from the art of producing them. Coleridge has given us the classic "anodyne" story, and tells what he can about the genesis of a poem which he calls a "psychological curiosity," but his definitions of poetry and all of the poetic quality "imagination" are to be found elsewhere and in quite other terms.

It would be convenient if the passwords of the intentional school, "sincerity," "fidelity," "spontaneity," "authenticity," "genuineness," "originality," could be equated with terms such as "integrity," "relevance," "unity," "function," "maturity," "subtlety," "ade-

[5] See Hughes Mearns, *Creative Youth* (Garden City, 1925), esp. 10, 27–29. The technique of inspiring poems has apparently been outdone more recently by the study of inspiration in successful poets and other artists. See, for instance, Rosamond E. M. Harding, *An Anatomy of Inspiration* (Cambridge, 1940); Julius Portnoy, *A Psychology of Art Creation* (Philadelphia, 1942); Rudolf Arnheim and others, *Poets at Work* (New York, 1947); Phyllis Bartlett, *Poems in Process* (New York, 1951); Brewster Ghiselin (ed.), *The Creative Process: A Symposium* (Berkeley and Los Angeles, 1952).

quacy," and other more precise terms of evaluation—in short, if "expression" always meant aesthetic achievement. But this is not so.

"Aesthetic" art, says Professor Curt Ducasse, an ingenious theorist of expression, is the conscious objectification of feelings, in which an intrinsic part is the critical moment. The artist corrects the objectification when it is not adequate. But this may mean that the earlier attempt was not successful in objectifying the self, or "it may also mean that it was a successful objectification of a self which, when it confronted us clearly, we disowned and repudiated in favor of another."[6] What is the standard by which we disown or accept the self? Professor Ducasse does not say. Whatever it may be, however, this standard is an element in the definition of art which will not reduce to terms of objectification. The evaluation of the work of art remains public; the work is measured against something outside the author.

IV

There is criticism of poetry and there is author psychology, which when applied to the present or future takes the form of inspirational promotion; but author psychology can be historical too, and then we have literary biography, a legitimate and attractive study in itself, one approach, as Professor Tillyard would argue, to personality, the poem being only a parallel approach. Certainly it need not be with a derogatory purpose that one points out personal studies, as distinct from poetic studies, in the realm of literary scholarship. Yet there is danger of confusing personal and poetic studies; and there is the fault of writing the personal as if it were poetic.

There is a difference between internal and external evidence for the meaning of a poem. And the paradox is only verbal and superficial that what is (1) internal is also public: it is discovered

through the semantics and syntax of a poem, through our habitual knowledge of the language, through grammars, dictionaries, and all the literature which is the source of dictionaries, in general through all that makes a language and culture; while what is (2) external is private or idiosyncratic; not a part of the work as a linguistic fact: it consists of revelations (in journals, for example, or letters or reported conversations) about how or why the poet wrote the poem—to what lady, while sitting on what lawn, or at the death of what friend or brother. There is (3) an intermediate kind of evidence about the character of the author or about private or semiprivate meanings attached to words or topics by an author or by a coterie of which he is a member. The meaning of words is the history of words, and the biography of an author his use of a word, and the associations which the word had for *him*, are part of the word's history and meaning.[7] But the three types of evidence, especially (2) and (3), shade into one another so subtly that it is not always easy to draw a line between examples, and hence arises the difficulty for criticism. The use of biographical evidence need not involve intentionalism, because while it may be evidence of what the author intended, it may also be evidence of the meaning of his words and the dramatic character of his utterance. On the other hand, it may not be all this. And a critic who is concerned with evidence of type (1) and moderately with that of type (3) will in the long run produce a different sort of comment from that of the critic who is concerned with (2) and with (3) where it shades into (2).

The whole glittering parade of Professor Lowes' *Road to Xanadu*, for instance, runs along the border between types (2) and (3) or boldly traverses the romantic region of (2). " 'Kubla Khan,' " says Professor Lowes, "is the fabric of a vision, but every image that rose up in its weaving had passed that

---

[6] Curt Ducasse, *The Philosophy of Art* (New York, 1929), 116.

[7] And the history of words *after* a poem is written may contribute meanings which if relevant to the original pattern should not be ruled out by a scruple about intention.

way before. And it would seem that there is nothing haphazard or fortuitous in their return." This is not quite clear —not even when Professor Lowes explains that there were clusters of associations, like hooked atoms, which were drawn into complex relation with other clusters in the deep well of Coleridge's memory, and which then coalesced and issued forth as poems. If there was nothing "haphazard or fortuitous" in the way the images returned to the surface, that may mean (1) that Coleridge could not produce what he did not have, that he was limited in his creation by what he had read or otherwise experienced, or (2) that having received certain clusters of associations, he was bound to return them in just the way he did, and that the value of the poem may be described in terms of the experiences on which he had to draw. The latter pair of propositions (a sort of Hartleyan associationism which Coleridge himself repudiated in the *Biographia*) may not be assented to. There were certainly other combinations, other poems, worse or better, that might have been written by men who had read Bartram and Purchas and Bruce and Milton. And this will be true no matter how many times we are able to add to the brilliant complex of Coleridge's reading. In certain flourishes (such as the sentence we have quoted) and in chapter headings like "The Shaping Spirit," "The Magical Synthesis," "Imagination Creatrix," it may be that Professor Lowes pretends to say more about the actual poems than he does. There is a certain deceptive variation in these fancy chapter titles; one expects to pass on to a new stage in the argument, and one finds—more and more sources, more and more about "the streamy nature of association." [8]

"Wohin der Weg?" quotes Professor Lowes for the motto of his book. "Kein Weg! Ins Unbetretene." Precisely because the way is *unbetreten*, we should say, it leads away from the poem. Bartram's *Travels* contains a good deal of

the history of certain words and of certain romantic Floridian conceptions that appear in "Kubla Khan." And a good deal of that history has passed and was then passing into the very stuff of our language. Perhaps a person who has read Bartram appreciates the poem more than one who has not. Or, by looking up the vocabulary of "Kubla Khan" in the *Oxford English Dictionary*, or by reading some of the other books there quoted, a person may know the poem better. But it would seem to pertain little to the poem to know that *Coleridge* had read Bartram. There is a gross body of life, of sensory and mental experience, which lies behind and in some sense causes every poem, but can never be and need not be known in the verbal and hence intellectual composition which is the poem. For all the objects of our manifold experience, for every unity, there is an action of the mind which cuts off roots, melts away context—or indeed we should never have objects or ideas or anything to talk about.

It is probable that there is nothing in Professor Lowes' vast book which could detract from anyone's appreciation of either *The Ancient Mariner* or "Kubla Khan." We next present a case where preoccupation with evidence of type (3) has gone so far as to distort a critic's view of a poem (yet a case not so obvious as those that abound in our critical journals):

In a well known poem by John Donne appears this quatrain:

Moving of th' earth brings harmes and feares,
　Men reckon what it did and meant,
But trepidation of the spheares,
　Though greater farre, is innocent.

A recent critic in an elaborate treatment of Donne's learning has written of this quatrain as follows:

He touches the emotional pulse of the situation by a skillful allusion to the new and the old astronomy. . . . Of the new astronomy, the "moving of the earth" is the most radical principle; of the old, the "trepidation of the

---

[8] Chaps. VIII, "The Pattern," and XVI, "The Known and Familiar Landscape," will be found of most help to the student of the poem.

spheres" is the motion of the greatest complexity. . . . The poet must exhort his love to quietness and calm upon his departure; and for this purpose the figure based upon the latter motion (trepidation), long absorbed into the traditional astronomy, fittingly suggests the tension of the moment without arousing the "harmes and feares" implicit in the figure of the moving earth. [9]

The argument is plausible and rests on a well substantiated thesis that Donne was deeply interested in the new astronomy and its repercussions in the theological realm. In various works Donne shows his familiarity with Kepler's *De Stella Nova*, with Galileo's *Siderius Nuncius*, with William Gilbert's *De Magnete*, and with Clavius' commentary on the *De Sphaera* of Sacrobosco. He refers to the new science in his Sermon at Paul's Cross and in a letter to Sir Henry Goodyer. In *The First Anniversary* he says the "new philosophy calls all in doubt." In the *Elegy on Prince Henry* he says that the "least moving of the center" makes "the world to shake."

It is difficult to answer argument like this, and impossible to answer it with evidence of like nature. There is no reason why Donne might not have written a stanza in which the two kinds of celestial motion stood for two sorts of emotion at parting. And if we become full of astronomical ideas and see Donne only against the background of the new science, we may believe that he did. But the text itself remains to be dealt with, the analyzable vehicle of a complicated metaphor. And one may observe: (1) that the movement of the earth according to the Copernican theory is a celestial motion, smooth and regular, and while it might cause religious or philosophic fears, it could not be associated with the crudity and earthiness of the kind of commotion which the speaker in the poem wishes to discourage; (2) that there is another moving of the earth, an earthquake, which has just these qualities and is to be associated with the tear-floods and

[9] Charles M. Coffin, *John Donne and the New Philosophy* (New York, 1927), 97-98.

sigh-tempests of the second stanza of the poem; (3) that "trepidation" is an appropriate opposite of earthquake, because each is a shaking or vibratory motion; and "trepidation of the spheres" is "greater far" than an earthquake, but not much greater (if two such motions can be compared as to greatness) than the annual motion of the earth; (4) that reckoning what it "did and meant" shows that the event has passed, like an earthquake, not like the incessant celestial movement of the earth. Perhaps a knowledge of Donne's interest in the new science may add another shade of meaning, an overtone to the stanza in question, though to say even this runs against the words. To make the geocentric and heliocentric antithesis the core of the metaphor is to disregard the English language, to prefer private evidence to public, external to internal.

V

If the distinction between kinds of evidence has implications for the historical critic, it has them no less for the contemporary poet and his critic. Or since every rule for a poet is but another side of a judgment by a critic, and since the past is the realm of the scholar and critic, and the future and present that of the poet and the critical leaders of taste, we may say that the problems arising in literary scholarship from the intentional fallacy are matched by others which arise in the world of progressive experiment.

The question of "allusiveness," for example, as acutely posed by the poetry of Eliot, is certainly one where a false judgment is likely to involve the intentional fallacy. The frequency and depth of literary allusion in the poetry of Eliot and others has driven so many in pursuit of full meanings to the *Golden Bough* and the Elizabethan drama that it has become a kind of commonplace to suppose that we do not know what a poet means unless we have traced him in his reading—a supposition redolent with intentional implications. The stand taken by F. O. Matthiessen is a sound one and partially forestalls the difficulty.

If one reads these lines with an attentive ear and is sensitive to their sudden shifts in movement, the contrast between the actual Thames and the idealized vision of it during an age before it flowed through a megalopolis is sharply conveyed by that movement itself, whether or not one recognizes the refrain to be from Spenser.

Eliot's allusions work when we know them—and to a great extent even when we do not know them, through their suggestive power.

But sometimes we find allusions supported by notes, and it is a nice question whether the notes function more as guides to send us where we may be educated, or more as indications in themselves about the character of the allusions. "Nearly everything of importance . . . that is apposite to an appreciation of 'The Waste Land,' " writes Matthiessen of Miss Weston's book, "has been incorporated into the structure of the poem itself, or into Eliot's Notes." And with such an admission it may begin to appear that it would not much matter if Eliot invented his sources (as Sir Walter Scott invented chapter epigraphs from "old plays" and "anonymous" authors, or as Coleridge wrote marginal glosses for *The Ancient Mariner*). Allusions to Dante, Webster, Marvell, or Baudelaire doubtless gain something because these writers existed, but it is doubtful whether the same can be said for an allusion to an obscure Elizabethan:

The sound of horns and motors, which shall bring
Sweeney to Mrs. Porter in the spring.

"Cf. Day, *Parliament of Bees:*" says Eliot,

When of a sudden, listening, you shall hear,
A noise of horns and hunting, which shall bring
Actaeon to Diana in the spring,
Where all shall see her naked skin.

The irony is completed by the quotation itself; had Eliot, as is quite conceivable, composed these lines to furnish his own background, there would be no loss of validity. The conviction may grow as one reads Eliot's next note: "I do not know the origin of the ballad from which these lines are taken: it was reported to me from Sydney, Australia." The important word in this note—on Mrs. Porter and her daughter who washed their feet in soda water—is "ballad." And if one should feel from the lines themselves their "ballad" quality, there would be little need for the note. Ultimately, the inquiry must focus on the integrity of such notes as parts of the poem, for where they constitute special information about the meaning of phrases in the poem, they ought to be subject to the same scrutiny as any of the other words in which it is written. Matthiessen believes the notes were the price Eliot "had to pay in order to avoid what he would have considered muffling the energy of his poem by extended connecting links in the text itself." But it may be questioned whether the notes and the need for them are not equally muffling. F. W. Bateson has plausibly argued that Tennyson's "The Sailor Boy" would be better if half the stanzas were omitted, and the best versions of ballads like "Sir Patrick Spens" owe their power to the very audacity with which the minstrel has taken for granted the story upon which he comments. What then if a poet finds he cannot take so much for granted in a more recondite context and rather than write informatively, supplies notes? It can be said in favor of this plan that at least the notes do not pretend to be dramatic, as they would if written in verse. On the other hand, the notes may look like unassimilated material lying loose beside the poem, necessary for the meaning of the verbal symbol, but not integrated, so that the symbol stands incomplete.

We mean to suggest by the above analysis that whereas notes tend to seem to justify themselves as external indexes to the author's *intention*, yet they ought to be judged like any other parts of a composition (verbal arrangement special to a particular context), and when so judged their reality as parts of the poem, or their imaginative integration with the rest of the poem, may come into question. Matthiessen, for instance, sees that Eliot's titles for poems and epigraphs are informative apparatus, like the notes. But while he is worried by some of the notes and thinks that Eliot "appears to be mocking himself for writing the note at the same time that he wants to convey something by it," Matthiessen believes that the "device" of epigraphs "is not at all open to the objection of not being sufficiently structural." "The *intention*," he says, "is to enable the poet to secure a condensed expression in the poem itself." "In each case the epigraph is *designed* to form an integral part of the effect of the poem." And Eliot himself, in his notes, has justified his poetic practice in terms of intention.

The Hanged Man, a member of the traditional pack, fits my purpose in two ways: because he is associated in my mind with the Hanged God of Frazer, and because I associate him with the hooded figure in the passage of the disciples to Emmaus in Part V. . . . The man with Three Staves (an authentic member of the Tarot pack) I associate, quite arbitrarily, with Fisher King himself.

And perhaps he is to be taken more seriously here, when off guard in a note, than when in his Norton Lectures he comments on the difficulty of saying what a poem means and adds playfully that he thinks of prefixing to a second edition of *Ash Wednesday* some lines from *Don Juan*:

I don't pretend that I quite understand
My own meaning when I would be *very* fine;
But the fact is that I have nothing planned
Unless it were to be a moment merry.

If Eliot and other contemporary poets have any characteristic fault, it may be in *planning* too much.

Allusiveness in poetry is one of several critical issues by which we have illustrated the more abstract issue of intentionalism, but it may be for today the most important illustration. As a poetic practice allusiveness would appear to be in some recent poems an extreme corol-lary of the romantic intentionalist assumption, and as a critical issue it challenges and brings to light in a special way the basic premise of intentionalism. The following instance from the poetry of Eliot may serve to epitomize the practical implications of what we have been saying. In Eliot's "Love Song of J. Alfred Prufrock," toward the end, occurs the line: "I have heard the mermaids singing, each to each," and this bears a certain resemblance to a line in a Song by John Donne, "Teach me to heare Mermaides singing," so that for the reader acquainted to a certain degree with Donne's poetry, the critical question arises: Is Eliot's line an allusion to Donne's? Is Prufrock thinking about Donne? Is Eliot thinking about Donne? We suggest that there are two radically different ways of looking for an answer to this question. There is (1) the way of poetic analysis and exegesis, which inquires whether it makes any sense if Eliot-Prufrock *is* thinking about Donne. In an earlier part of the poem, when Prufrock asks, "Would it have been worth while, . . . To have squeezed the universe into a ball," his words take half their sadness and irony from certain energetic and passionate lines of Marvel "To His Coy Mistress." But the exegetical inquirer may wonder whether mermaids considered as "strange sights" (to hear them is in Donne's poem analogous to getting with child a mandrake root) have much to do with Prufrock's mermaids, which seem to be symbols of romance and dynamism, and which incidentally have literary authentication, if they need it, in a line of a sonnet by Gérard de Nerval. This method of inquiry may lead to the conclusion that the given resemblance between Eliot and Donne is without significance and is better not thought of, or the method may have the disadvantage of providing no certain conclusion. Nevertheless, we submit that this is the true and objective way of criticism, as contrasted to what the very uncertainty of exegesis might tempt a second kind of critic to undertake: (2) the way of biographical or genetic inquiry, in which, taking advantage of the fact that

Eliot is still alive, and in the spirit of a man who would settle a bet, the critic writes to Eliot and asks what he meant, or if he had Donne in mind. We shall not here weigh the probabilities—whether Eliot would answer that he meant nothing at all, had nothing at all in mind —a sufficiently good answer to such a question—or in an unguarded moment might furnish a clear and, within its limit, irrefutable answer. Our point is that such an answer to such an inquiry would have nothing to do with the poem "Prufrock"; it would not be a critical inquiry. Critical inquiries, unlike bets, are not settled in this way. Critical inquiries are not settled by consulting the oracle.

RENÉ WELLEK

(b. 1903)

A student of literary theory and history and of comparative literature, René Wellek is best known for his *Theory of Literature* (1949), written in collaboration with Austin Warren. This influential work supported the New Critical distinction between historical or "extrinsic" and formalist or "intrinsic" methods of literary study and presented Wellek's "perspectivist" theory of literary form, most fully defined in his Chapter 12, "The Analysis of the Literary Work of Art." Wellek's other works include *Kant in England* (1931), *The Rise of English Literary History* (1941), and *A History of Modern Criticism* (2 vols., 1955).

From The Analysis of the Literary Work of Art (1949)

. . . An answer to our question in terms of individual or social psychology cannot be found. A poem, we have to conclude, is not an individual experience or a sum of experiences, but only a potential cause of experiences. Definition in terms of states of mind fails because it cannot account for the normative character of the genuine poem, for the simple fact that it might be experienced correctly or incorrectly. In every individual experience only a small part can be considered as adequate to the true poem. Thus, the real poem must be conceived as a structure of norms, realized only partially in the actual experience of its many readers. Every single experience (reading, reciting, and so forth) is only an attempt—more or less successful and complete—to grasp this set of norms or standards.

The term "norms" as used here should not, of course, be confused with norms which are either classical or romantic, ethical or political. The norms we have in mind are implicit norms which have to be extracted from every individual experience of a work of art and together make up the genuine work of art as a whole. It is true that if we compare works of art among themselves, similarities or differences between these norms will be ascertained, and from the similarities themselves it ought to be possible to proceed to a classification of works of art according to the type of norms they embody. We may finally arrive at theories of genres and ultimately at theories of literature in general. To deny this as it has been denied by those who, with some justification, stress the uniqueness of every work of art, seems to push the conception of individuality so far that every work of art would become completely isolated from tradition and thus finally both incommunicable and incomprehensible. Assuming that we have to start with the analysis of an individual work of art, we still can scarcely deny that there must be some links, some similarities, some common elements or factors which would approximate two or more given works of art and thus would open the door to a transition from the analysis of one individual work of art to a type such as Greek tragedy and hence to tragedy in general, to literature in general, and finally to some all-inclusive structure common to all arts.

But this is a further problem. We, however, have still to decide where and how these norms exist. A closer analysis of a work of art will show that it is best to think of it as not merely one system of norms but rather of a system which is made up of several strata, each implying its own subordinate group. The Polish philosopher, Roman Ingarden, in an ingenious highly technical analysis of the literary work of art, has employed the methods of Husserl's "Phenomenology" to arrive at such distinctions of strata. We need not follow him in every detail to see that his general distinctions are sound and useful: there is, first, the sound-stratum which is not, of course, to be confused with the actual sounding of the words, as our preceding argument must have shown. Still, this pattern is indispensable, as only on the basis of sounds can the second stratum arise: the units of meaning. Every single word will have its meaning, will combine into units in the context, into syntagmas and sentence patterns. Out of this syntactic structure arises a third stratum, that of the objects represented, the "world" of a novelist, the characters, the setting. Ingarden adds two other strata which may not have to be distinguished as separable. The stratum of the "world" is seen from a particular viewpoint, which is not necessarily stated but is implied. An event presented in literature can be, for example, presented as "seen" or as "heard": even the same event, for example, the banging of a

door; a character can be seen in its "inner" or "outer" characteristic traits. And finally, Ingarden speaks of a stratum of "metaphysical qualities" (the sublime, the tragic, the terrible, the holy) of which art can give us contemplation. This stratum is not indispensable, and may be missing in some works of literature. Possibly the two last strata can be included in the "world," in the realm of represented objects. But they also suggest very real problems in the analysis of literature. The "point of view" has, at least in the novel, received considerable attention since Henry James and since Lubbock's more systematic exposition of the Jamesian theory and practice. The stratum of "metaphysical qualities" allows Ingarden to reintroduce questions of the "philosophical meaning" of works of art without the risk of the usual intellectualist errors.

It is useful to illustrate the conception by the parallel which can be drawn from linguistics. Linguists such as the Geneva School and the Prague Linguistic Circle carefully distinguish between *langue* and *parole*, the system of language and the individual speech-act; and this distinction corresponds to that between the individual experience of the poem and the poem as such. The system of language is a collection of conventions and norms whose workings and relations we can observe and describe as having a fundamental coherence and identity in spite of very different, imperfect, or incomplete pronouncements of individual speakers. In this respect at least, a literary work of art is in exactly the same position as a system of language. We as individuals shall never realize it completely, for we shall never use our own language completely and perfectly. The very same situation is actually exhibited in every single act of cognition. We shall never know an object in all its qualities, but still we can scarcely deny the identity of objects even though we may see them from different perspectives. We always grasp some "structure of determination" in the object which makes the act of cognition not an act of arbitrary invention or subjective distinction but the recognition of some norms imposed on us by reality. Similarly, the structure of a work of art has the character of a "duty which I have to realize." I shall always realize it imperfectly, but in spite of some incompleteness, a certain "structure of determination" remains, just as in any other object of knowledge.

Modern linguists have analyzed the potential sounds as phonemes; they can also analyze morphemes and syntagmas. The sentence, for instance, can be described not merely as an *ad hoc* utterance but as a syntactic pattern. Outside of phonemics, modern functional linguistics is still comparatively undeveloped; but the problems, though difficult, are not insoluble or completely new: they are rather restatements of the morphological and syntactical questions as they were discussed in older grammars. The analysis of a literary work of art encounters parallel problems in units of meaning and their specific organization for aesthetic purposes. Such problems as those of poetic semantics, diction, and imagery are reintroduced in a new and more careful statement. Units of meaning, sentences, and sentence structures refer to objects, construct imaginative realities such as landscapes, interiors, characters, actions, or ideas. These also can be analyzed in a way which does not confuse them with empirical reality and does not ignore the fact that they inhere in linguistic structures. A character in a novel grows only out of the units of meaning, is made of the sentences either pronounced by the figure or pronounced about it. It has an indeterminate structure in comparison with a biological person who has his coherent past. These distinctions of strata have the advantage of superseding the traditional, misleading distinction between content and form. The content will reappear in close contact with the linguistic substratum, in which it is implied and on which it is dependent.

But this conception of the literary work of art as a stratified system of norms still leaves undetermined the actual mode of existence of this system.

To deal with this matter properly we should have to settle such controversies as those of nominalism versus realism, mentalism versus behaviorism—in short, all the chief problems of epistemology. For our purposes, however, it will be sufficient to avoid two opposites, extreme Platonism and extreme nominalism. There is no need to hypostatize or "reify" this system of norms, to make it a sort of archetypal idea presiding over a timeless realm of essences. The literary work of art has not the same ontological status as the idea of a triangle, or of a number, or a quality like "redness." Unlike such "subsistences," the literary work of art is, first of all, created at a certain point in time and, secondly, is subject to change and even to complete destruction. In this respect it rather resembles the system of language, though the exact moment of creation or death is probably much less clearly definable in the case of language than in that of the literary work of art, usually an individual creation. On the other hand, one should recognize that an extreme nominalism which rejects the concept of a "system of language" and thus of a work of art in our sense, or admits it only as a useful fiction or a "scientific description," misses the whole problem and the point at issue. The narrow assumptions of behaviorism define anything to be "mystical" or "metaphysical" which does not conform to a very limited conception of empirical reality. Yet to call the phoneme a "fiction," or the system of language merely a "scientific description of speech-acts," is to ignore the problem of truth. We recognize norms and deviations from norms and do not merely devise some purely verbal descriptions. The whole behaviorist point of view is, in this respect, based on a bad theory of abstraction. Numbers or norms are what they are, whether we construct them or not. Certainly I perform the counting, I perform the reading; but number presentation or recognition of a norm is not the same as the number or norm itself. The pronouncement of the sound *h* is not the phoneme *h*. We recognize a structure of norms within reality and do not simply invent verbal constructs. The objection that we have access to these norms only through individual acts of cognition, and that we cannot get out of these acts or beyond them, is only apparently impressive. It is the objection which has been made to Kant's criticism of our cognition, and it can be refuted with the Kantian arguments.

It is true we are ourselves liable to misunderstandings and lack of comprehension of these norms, but this does not mean that the critic assumes a superhuman role of criticizing our comprehension from the outside or that he pretends to grasp the perfect whole of the system of norms in some act of intellectual intuition. Rather, we criticize a part of our knowledge in the light of the higher standard set by another part. We are not supposed to put ourselves into the position of a man who, in order to test his vision, tries to look at his own eyes, but into the position of a man who compares the objects he sees clearly with those he sees only dimly, makes then generalizations as to the kinds of objects which fall into the two classes, and explains the difference by some theory of vision which takes account of distance, light, and so forth.

Analogously, we can distinguish between right and wrong readings of a poem, or between a recognition or a distortion of the norms implicit in a work of art, by acts of comparison, by a study of different false or incomplete realizations. We can study the actual workings, relations, and combinations of these norms, just as the phoneme can be studied. The literary work of art is neither an empirical fact, in the sense of being a state of mind of any given individual or of any group of individuals, nor is it an ideal changeless object such as a triangle. The work of art may become an object of experience; it is, we admit, accessible only through individual experience, but it is not identical with any experience. It differs from ideal objects such as numbers precisely because it is only accessible through the empirical part of its structure, the sound-system, while a triangle or a number can be intuited directly. It also differs from ideal objects in one important respect. It has something which can be called "life." It arises at a certain point of time, changes in the course of history, and may perish. A work of art is "timeless" only in the sense that, if preserved, it has some fundamental structure of identity since its creation, but it is "historical" too. It has a development which can be described. This development is nothing but the series of concretizations of a given work of art in the course of history which we may, to a certain extent, reconstruct from the reports of critics and readers about their experiences and judgments and the effect of a given work of art on other works. Our consciousness of earlier concretizations (readings, criticisms, misinterpretations) will affect our own experience: earlier readings may educate us to a deeper understanding or may cause a violent reaction against the prevalent interpretations of the past. All this shows the importance of the history of criticism or, in linguistics, of historical grammar, and leads to difficult questions about the nature and limits of individuality. How far can a work of art be said to be changed and still remain identical? The *Iliad* still "exists"; that is, it can become again and again effective and is thus different from a historical phenomenon like the battle of Waterloo which is definitely past, though its course may be reconstructed and its effects may be felt even today. In what sense can we, however, speak of an identity between the *Iliad* as the contemporary Greeks heard or read it and the *Iliad* we now read? Even assuming that we know the identical text, our actual experience must be different. We cannot contrast its language with the everyday language of Greece, and cannot therefore feel the deviations from colloquial language on which much of the poetic effect must depend. We are unable to understand many verbal ambiguities which are an essential part of every poet's meaning. Obviously it requires in addition some imaginative effort, which can have only very partial success, to think ourselves back into the Greek belief in gods, or the Greek scale of moral values. Still, it could be scarcely denied that there is a substantial identity of "structure" which has remained the same throughout the ages. This structure, however, is dynamic: it changes throughout the process of history while passing through the minds of its readers, critics, and fellow artists. Thus the system of norms is growing and changing and will remain, in some sense, always incompletely and imperfectly realized. But this dynamic conception does not mean mere subjectivism and relativism. All the different points of view are by no means equally right. It will always be possible to determine which point of view grasps the subject most thoroughly and deeply. A hierarchy of viewpoints, a criticism of the grasp of norms, is implied in the concept of the adequacy of interpretation. All relativism is ultimately defeated by the recognition that "the Absolute is in the relative, though not finally and fully in it."

The work of art, then, appears as an object of knowledge *sui generis* which has a special ontological status. It is neither real (like a statue) nor mental (like the experience of light or pain) nor ideal (like a triangle). It is a system of norms of ideal concepts which are intersubjective. They must be assumed to exist in collective ideology, changing with it, accessible only through individual mental experiences based on the sound-structure of its sentences.

We have not discussed the question of artistic values. But the preceding examination should have shown that there is no structure outside norms and values. We cannot comprehend and analyze any work of art without reference to values. The very fact that I recognize a certain structure as a "work of art" implies a judgment of value. The error of pure phenomenology is in the assumption that such a dissociation is possible, that values are superimposed on structure, "inhere" on or in structures. This error of analysis vitiates the penetrating book of Roman Ingarden, who tries to analyze the work of art without reference to values. The root of the matter lies, of course, in the phenomenologist's assumption of an eternal, non-temporal order of "essences" to which the empirical individualizations are added only later. By assuming an absolute scale of values we necessarily lose contact with the relativity of individual judgments. A frozen Absolute faces a valueless flux of individual judgments.

The unsound thesis of absolutism and the equally unsound antithesis of relativism must be superseded and harmonized in a new synthesis which makes the scale of values itself dynamic, but does not surrender it as such. "Perspectivism," as we have termed such a conception, does not mean an anarchy of values, a glorification of individual caprice, but a process of getting to know the object from different points of view which may be defined and criticized in their turn. Structure, sign, and value form three aspects of the very same problem and cannot be artificially isolated.

RICHARD CHASE

(1914-1962)

A well-known critic and university teacher, Richard Chase drew upon myth, folklore, psychology, history, and other sources of knowledge in his studies of American literary subjects. He was chiefly concerned, however, with a historical perspective from which the writer and his work are seen as involved in the irresolvable contradictions of a complex social process. The preface to his *Herman Melville* (1949) expresses the point of view of the New Liberalism of the post World War II period.

An interest in myth prompted the historical study, *Quest for Myth* (1949), but Chase commented on the limitations of myth criticism in the discussion of "Romance, the Folk Imagination, and Myth Criticism" appended to *The American Novel and Its Tradition* (1957). His other works include *Emily Dickinson* (1953), *Walt Whitman Reconsidered* (1955), *The Democratic Vista* (1958), and *Walt Whitman* (1961); he was also the editor of *Melville, a Collection of Critical Essays* (1962).

Preface to *Herman Melville* (1949)

My first purpose in writing this book is to set the works of Herman Melville before the reader in something like their full imperfect glory. My second purpose is to contribute a book on Melville to a movement which may be described (once again) as the new liberalism— that newly invigorated secular thought at the dark center of the twentieth century which, whatever our cultural wreckage and disappointment, now begins to ransom liberalism from the ruinous sellouts, failures, and defeats of the thirties. The new liberalism must justify its claims to superiority over the old liberalism. It must present a vision of life capable, by a continuous act of imaginative criticism, of avoiding the old mistakes: the facile ideas of progress and "social realism," the disinclination to examine human motives, the indulgence of wish-fulfilling rhetoric, the belief that historical reality is merely a question of economic or ethical values, the idea that literature should participate directly in the economic liberation of the masses, the equivocal relationship to communist totalitarianism and power politics. Translate all this back into the nineteenth century and you will see that these problems were also Melville's, and that his work was in its time just the continuous act of imaginative criticism which we now need to perform ourselves. I have the conviction that if our liberalism is serious about its new vision of life, if it has the necessary will to survive, it must come to terms with Herman Melville.

For Melville is one of our fathers. He stood opposed to the social pieties of transcendentalism very much as we must now oppose the progressive liberalism which was born fifteen or twenty years ago—and which now ventures into the perilous future unarmed by either passion or intellect, still marching toward the terrific unknown as confidently as if the unknown were only a well meaning "common man" extending his hand in brotherhood.

Now there is, of course, some semantic difficulty in using the words "liberal" and "progressive" to refer to certain kinds of contemporary thought and also to the thought of Melville and his time. Since Melville's day, these words have undergone various changes in connotation. As for the word "liberal," I use it literally and generally. It means a kind of thought which cherishes freedom and is free, free of dogma and absolutism; a kind of thought which is bounteous, in the sense that it is open-minded, skeptical, and humanist. Thus it is a large term, for one may remain a liberal and be more or less conservative in one's particular opinions, or more or less religious. But the word does denote a general kind of modern thought despite its historical vicissitudes, despite the different meanings it has acquired by being connected with, say, abolitionism or Stalinism. And in modern times liberalism has been repeatedly traduced in fundamentally the same way: by the pharisaism and power worship to which liberalism has itself been prone.

One may distinguish between "liberal" and "progressive." Melville was a liberal in questions of politics, morals, and religion. But he was a progressive only in a very limited sense of the word. To be sure, he wanted man to progress, to improve his lot; but he did not believe that progress was the principle of the universe or that man could do anything which would make progress inevitable—and he had a name for the pious and irresponsible progressive: he called him "the confidence man." Although Melville entertained larger social aspirations than his friend Hawthorne, he would have seen the truth in what Hawthorne wrote in his campaign biography of President Pierce: "There is no instance in all history of the human will and intellect having perfected any great moral reform by methods which it adapted to that end." Is this reactionary? Does it mean no progress is possible? We can hardly think so, for it simply states the truth that progress can be advanced only with difficulty and by indirection and a variety of means in a world timelessly imperfect. As the well known dictum tells us, "Politics is the art of the possible." So is morality, and life itself. So is art.

In sloughing off a facile idea of progress, Melville accepted what that sloughing-off implied: a tragic view of life. No view of life can protect itself against the attritions of history if it cannot see man's lot as a tragedy—that is, if it cannot see that civilization, precious on any terms, is the fruit of human suffering and anguish, as well as of human joy. Melville thought of man's destiny in this way. And it is a true measure of the inadequacy of the progressive critics that they should have called him, on this score, "morbid," "pessimistic," and bemused by "metaphysical irrelevancies." Melville's work is an enormous cultural fact. It is one of the many facts we can no longer afford to ignore or misinterpret because they do violence to our bland hopes or our stances of moral rectitude.

I do not wish to present Melville as primarily a political thinker. I am interested in his views of personality, culture, art, and morals. And the great thing about his specifically political ideas is that they do not subsist in an ethical void; they are never cut off or abstracted from the full context of his thought. The relevance of Melville to our modern thinking is extensive and intricate. Melville knew many ways of seeking moral truth and he knew that moral truth must be sought in many ways. Mr. Lionel Trilling has suggested that genius is the ability to "counterattack nightmare," and we may be sure that the enemy which the moral intelligence counterattacks will not be reduced by marching single-file against only one of his redoubts. The counterattack must take various forms and be launched on a broad front—a fact which both the intelligent Communist and the intelligent conservative have understood more clearly than has the progressive.

Liberal-progressive thinking in America has been remarkable for the magnitude of the rejections it has made. Ahab himself was a progressive American. Where but in *Moby-Dick* shall we find such a terrifying picture of a man rejecting all connection with his family, his culture, his own sexuality even, expunging the colors from the rainbow, rejecting the stained imperfections of life for a vision of spotless purity and rectitude attainable only in death, drifting into the terrible future, jamming himself on, like a father turned into a raging child, toward a catastrophe which annihilates a whole world?

If the way of Ahab is death, that is because he sets himself up as a spiritual leader without being able to make himself the symbol of a culture. Melville's strong young heroes—the Jack Chases, Bulkingtons, and Ethan Allens—are preeminently culture heroes. Let them be the test. They are Melville's "common man." They are men of epic size, great in heart, in sensibility, and in the quality of endurance; they are companions, storytellers, defenders of freedom, revolutionaries; their brotherhood with other men is open, frank, and based on the deepest ties of common humanity; they are, in their way, pure; but their purity is in their sensitiveness and in their longing for brotherhood and fatherhood; their purity is not the righteous monomania of Ahab. If it is true that one's liberalism stands or falls with one's image of the common man, can we any longer wish to apotheosize the common man of the contemporary liberal-progressive vision: this mindless, heartless, unsexed, and remote youth who stands—a dummy already dead and wonderful in his righteousness—in the midst of historical catastrophe?

2

In his *Essays in Criticism*, Matthew Arnold remarks that Byron lacked the "intellectual equipment" needed by a genuinely "supreme" modern writer. From the annotations in his copy of Arnold's book, we gather that Melville was anxious to know if he would be judged to have had the necessary "intellectual equipment." And well he might wonder! For his critics—progressive and nonprogressive—have in various ways denied him exactly what he was himself so jealous of having. When his reputation was salvaged from obscurity in the 1920's, Melville was pictured as a kind of primitive man—a natural or unconscious genius, as Van Wyck Brooks intimated—whose great creative powers, after *Moby-Dick*, were ruined by the callous indifference of the Gilded Age and by Melville's own temperament: his obscure, abiding neurosis and his ultimately subliterary, subintellectual talents. From the criticism of the twenties, we have inherited the partly true but finally misleading idea of Melville as a heroic failure, a baffled Titan or wounded Prometheus who could do no more than cry out with his agonized rhetoric and his mindless rage against the chains that bound him. Brooks pictures Melville as he did Mark Twain: as a frustrated genius who suffered and failed, not as a thinking and developing artist who achieved a series of imperfect successes. Brooks's theory of the "ordeal" of the American artist is still potent in literary criticism, and it still underesti-

mates, because it cannot objectively see, the artist's works.

Melville studies after the twenties began to present a completer picture, partly by resuscitating the later works and trying to assess Melville's whole contribution in the light of these. Even so, the two later works which tell us most about Melville's mind—*The Confidence Man* and *Clarel*—were generally ignored or misunderstood. In the 1930's progressive writers like Granville Hicks brought Parrington's earlier strictures up to date and attacked Melville because he failed to "participate" and because the moral center of his thinking (which Hicks mistakenly supposed to be a doctrinal concern with evil) could not be immediately stated in economic terms. Do we not see in this attitude a disinclination or inability to perceive what was in fact a most crucial "participation" in American culture? In the 1940's two books—William Ellery Sedgwick's *Herman Melville* and F. O. Matthiessen's *American Renaissance*—added an unresolved religious strain to the earlier progressivism. And in this uneasy amalgam we see Melville in his later works modifying his earlier theological "titanism" and coming gradually to a "religious acceptance of life," apparently involving in *Billy Budd* an apotheosis of the common man as Christ.

The progressive critics have finally been unable to see one of the central intellectual facts about their author; namely, that he was a profound and prophetic critic of liberal-progressivism, that he demanded to be seen with a kind of awareness which the theoretical social orthodoxies of the 1930's automatically prohibited. This blind spot of the progressive critics could not help obscuring whole ranges of Melville's "intellectual equipment."

Those critics of the last twenty years who have not subscribed to the progressive doctrines—the Southern writers, the New Critics—have made no sustained effort to understand Melville. Those concerned with precise textual and structural analysis, with order and concentration, have seen only Melville's sometimes unruly emotions—emotions in excess of their occasions—or his vagueness or his lack of system. If the New Criticism applies itself to the task, however, it may determine the future of Melville studies. An intense verbal analysis might tell us much about *Moby-Dick*. It might give us the "Word" and form the "New Testament" of Melville criticism. On the whole I remain in the "Old Testament" and am interested in the man, the artist, his works, his idols, his myths, his gods, his laws, his history, his prophecies, and his morals.

Academic critics have been more aware of Melville's ideas. But they have generally been guilty of that common academic fallacy—the rationalist fallacy —which makes every artist into a would-be philosopher. Thus *Moby-Dick, Pierre,* and *The Confidence Man* are presented to us as philosophic quests for ultimate truth. This approach ignores the fact that for Melville, as for any artist, ideas have profound aesthetic value, that an artist's "position" is an aesthetic device or context which he uses in his art, besides being a set of explicit intellectual attitudes. A study of Melville's "intellectual equipment" cannot be conceived apart from a study of his art. And Melville was not so much interested in philosophical truth as in man and his culture.

Melville is still the least known of our great writers. Even people with wide literary knowledge are not likely to know very much about *Redburn* or *Pierre* or

The Confidence Man or *Clarel,* to say nothing of *Cock-a-doodle-do* or *Jimmy Rose.* In this book I have tried to set the works of Melville before the reader and to ask: What do these works say within themselves and in relation to one another? and: What do they say to us in our time of troubles?

I have tried to be continually aware of the development of Melville's mind, from his birth to his death, in so far as his writings permit this and sketchy as the evidence on long periods of his life still is. My method, therefore, has been partly biographical, especially in the opening and closing pages; but, of course, the book is not primarily a biography. An artist's "intellectual equipment" is a complex armory—for Melville was eminently an "armed man" —of recurring and developing images, symbols, ideas, and moral attitudes; and these are what I am after.

It may be that my estimate of Melville as an artist is too high; I am sure that, as the professional practice of art goes, he belongs somewhat below Hawthorne and Henry James. But Melville had great qualities which Hawthorne and James lacked, qualities of pathos and lyricism and pity, of range and acceptance and courage.

One of Melville's persistent themes was the search for a father—by which he meant not God but a cultural ideal, a great man in a great culture. Our effort to understand Melville ought to be a similar cultural quest.

Romance, the Folk Imagination, and Myth Criticism (1957)

In the preceding chapters there have been several occasions for referring to the folk mind or folk imagination, especially whenever the question of romance has come up. It is not a good idea to try to define too closely either the archetypes of the folk mind or the romance that sometimes embodies them. Neither,

From *The American Novel and Its Tradition* by Richard Chase. Copyright © 1957 by Richard Chase. Reprinted by permission of the author.

fortunately, is capable of being reduced to a single formula. The closest I have come to a formula is to speak repeatedly, though I think by no means exclusively, of a presumed archetypal symbolic drama of light and dark which has certainly been always widespread if not universal in folklore. The conflicts thus symbolized have been many; they may be suggested by such contraries as life and death, good and evil, male and female, angel and demon, God and Satan, summer and winter. This formula has the imprecision which is inevitable if it is to remain relevant to the manifold uses of the folk imagination in the American romance-novels. That the light-dark archetype *is* relevant to the American romance-novels I have tried to show not only by examining some of them but by following the lead of those critics, like D. H. Lawrence, Yvor Winters, and Leslie Fiedler, who have thought that certain forces and institutions in American society have tended to confirm and sustain, and yet to modify in the life of the imagination, this archetype. I am only too painfully aware, in all this, of the necessity of sacrificing a semblance of specific clarity of definition in order that what I have had to say should refer, illuminatingly as I hope, to many different facets of the novel—and to many different kinds of novel.

In order to suggest what would be lost by a more limited formula, I now confront the objection to my procedure which, as I am well aware, will be brought against it by what have become known as the "myth critics." (I am not myself a "myth critic," although I have been interested in myth, as in one way or another every student of literature must be, and although my first book, *Quest for Myth*, was a historical study of the subject.) These critics, whose influence has been considerable in the last fifteen years, will immediately and mistakenly equate romance with myth. In the critical practice of this school of thought, if not strictly in theory, there is only one myth—namely, the death and rebirth of a god. This archetype is thought to constitute the essential action of tragedy especially, but also of comedy, elegy, and perhaps ultimately all valuable literary forms. It is thought, as one gathers, to be eternally recreated in man's unconscious, and also to be prescribed, in some unexplained manner, by the nature of literature itself—so that in various guises it is always cropping up in different writers and different cultures, irrespective of context, time, or routes of transmission. The characteristic American form of the mythic archetype is thought to be the fall from innocence and the initiation into life—an action of the soul that entails a symbolic dying and rebirth.

I think it has already been sufficiently shown in the preceding chapters that American literature does not often mirror forth this dramatic action. Instead it pictures human life in a context of unresolved contradictions—contradictions which, for better or for worse, are not absorbed, reconciled, or transcended.

The myth critic gets from the rigidity and formal abstractness of his approach a very biased view of American literature. He seems to know only the "late" works of a given author, which are also, by comparison, the lesser and more eccentric works. He is interested in *The Marble Faun* but not *The Scarlet Letter*, *Billy Budd* but not *Moby-Dick*, *The Golden Bowl* but not *The Bostonians*, *The Old Man and the Sea* but not *A Farewell to Arms*, *The Bear* but not *The Sound and the Fury*. The special gains of this approach are outweighed by its apparent denigration of the greater and more characteristic work of whatever author may be in question. Many readers have in recent years formed a distaste for works of literature which are radically involved with the dilemmas of their time and their place and which draw too directly on the reality and the moral contradictions of human experience. As I pointed out in the Introduction, romance as the American novelists have used it does not necessarily incapacitate the novel for a radical involvement with human dilemmas and may in fact enhance this involvement. On the other hand, an exclusive interest in myth, as defined by the myth critics, seems infallibly to lead to an exaggerated opinion of works which avoid this involvement and promise the immanence of grace, of final harmony and reconciliation, in a world whose contradictions it seems no longer possible to bear.

A corollary tendency of the myth critic is that he always sees a novel from above. According to his theory the novel is merely one more of the several literary forms in which the mythic archetype has manifested itself, more or less as God is said to embody Himself in the temporal order. Although there is some historical justification for this idea, in the sense that a novel of Scott or Fielding may be regarded as a descendant of medieval romance or ancient myth, generalizations of this sort lead to little but themselves. They ignore the whole reality of time and place and the whole illuminating cultural context, which more than other literary forms the novel reflects. I have been mindful of this in saying that realism is the fundamental distinguishing quality of the novel and in going on to speak of romance as something that in the novel arises from and modifies realism rather than of realism as something that in the novel romance condescends to become. This procedure is not historical in the most general sense. But it is in the limited and concrete sense, and that is the one that counts in our appreciation and judgment of the novel.

RONALD S. CRANE

(b. 1886)

A leader of the neo-Aristotelian movement centered at the University of Chicago, Crane worked during the 1930's toward the end of establishing literary criticism as an accepted academic discipline in the university—an objective shared by the New Critics. The neo-Aristotelians objected, however, to the New Critics' preoccupation with verbal analysis and neglect of classical tradition. In place of the formalist analysis of the individual work as a self-contained language system, the Chicago critics recommended a "part-whole" study relating the work to a larger system of genres and sought to develop a modern body of critical theory based on the *Poetics* of Aristotle. The neo-Aristotelian position is most fully set forth in the collection of essays edited by Crane and entitled *Critics and Criticism: Ancient and Modern* (1952)—of which an abridged paperback edition has also been published—and in Crane's *The Languages of Criticism and the Structure of Poetry* (1953).

Toward a More Adequate Criticism of Poetic Structure (1953)

We can judge of the adequacy of any procedure in practical criticism only by considering the concepts and the

I have omitted the notes and a few passages in the text and have made a number of verbal corrections. For a fuller development and more specific applications of the general approach to critical problems outlined here, see Elder Olson, *The Poetry of Dylan Thomas* (Chicago, 1954) and *Tragedy and the Theory of Drama* (Detroit, 1961) and Wayne C. Booth, *The Rhetoric of Fiction* (Chicago, 1961). [R.S.C.]

Reprinted from *The Languages of Criticism and the Structure of Poetry* by Ronald S. Crane (University of Toronto Press, 1953), pp. 140-194, by permission of the author and the publishers.

methods of reasoning which it presupposes and asking what important aspects, if any, of the objects we are examining they force us to leave out of account. And when this test is applied not merely to the two contemporary schools of criticism discussed in the last lecture but to the long tradition of critical language from which they have emerged, it becomes apparent, I think, that there are nowhere present in this tradition any means for dealing precisely and particularly with what I shall call the forming principle or immediate shaping cause of structure in individual poems.

The principle operates in much the same way in all the arts; and there is nothing mysterious about it—nothing which any one who has ever written anything, however unpoetic, cannot verify for himself by reflecting upon his own experience. The process of literary composition has often been rather crudely divided, especially by authors of textbooks on English writing, into two stages: a stage of preparatory reading, thinking, planning, incubation, and a stage of putting the materials thus assembled into words; and what happens in the second stage has usually been represented as a direct transference to paper of the ideas or images which the writer has come into possession of in the first stage—as a simple matter, that is, of giving to an acquired content an appropriate verbal form. I have myself taught this easy doctrine to students; but never since I began to meditate on the disturbing fact that all too frequently, when I have attempted to write an essay after a long and interested concentration on the subject, the noting of many exciting ideas and patterns of key terms, and the construction of what looked like a perfect outline, I have found myself unable to compose the first sentence, or even to know what it ought to be about, or, having forced myself to go on, to bring the thing to a satisfying conclusion; whereas, on other occasions, with no more complete preparation, no greater desire to write, and no better state of nerves, I have discovered, to my delight, that nearly everything fell speedily into place, the right words came (or at any rate words which I couldn't change later on), and the sentences and paragraphs followed one another with scarcely a hitch and in an order that still seemed to me the inevitable one when I came to reread the essay in cold blood.

I have had so many more experiences of the first sort than of the second that I have tried to isolate the reason for the difference. The best way I can explain it is to say that what I failed to attain in the former cases and did attain somehow, at one moment or another of the process, in the latter was a kind of intuitive glimpse of a possible subsuming form for the materials, which I had assembled in my mind and notes —a form sufficiently coherent and intelligible, as a form in my mind, so that I could know at once what I must or could do, and what I need not or ought not to do, in what order and with what emphasis in the various parts, in developing my arguments and putting them into words. I have never been able to write anything which seemed to me, in retrospect, to possess any quality of organic wholeness, however uninteresting or thin, except in response to such a synthesizing idea. It is more than a general intention, more than a "theme," and more than an outline in the usual sense of that word; it is, as I have said, a shaping or directing cause, involving at the same time, and in some sort of correlation, the particular form my subject is to take in my essay, the particular mode of argument I am to use in discussing it, and the particular end my discussion is to serve: I must know, in some fashion, at least these three things before I can proceed with any ease or success. As a conception my idea may be tight or loose, complex or simple; I call it a shaping cause for the very good reason that, once such a principle has come to me for a particular essay, it generates consequences and problems in the detailed working out of my subject which I cannot well escape so long as I remain committed to writing the essay as I see it ought to be written. It exerts, that is, a kind of impersonal and objective power, which is at once compulsive and suggestive, over everything I attempt to do, until in the end I come out with a composition which, if my execution has been adequate, is quite distinct, as an ordered whole, from anything I myself completely intended or foresaw when I began to write, so that afterwards I sometimes wonder, even when I applaud, how I could ever have come to say what I have said.

I do not believe that this experience of mine is unique among writers of prose, and I have been told by friends who are novelists, playwrights, or lyric poets that something like this is a true description of what happens also to them whenever they are successfully creative. The point indeed has often been hinted at by artists in the too infrequent moments when they talk in practical terms, undistorted by *a priori* critical doctrines, about their own or others' work. Most of the published criticism of T. S. Eliot has been more concerned with the qualities of poets than with the construction of poems, but what I have been saying about the all-importance and compulsive power of formal causes in writing is at least adumbrated in his famous "impersonal theory of poetry" and more than adumbrated in his remark, in an early essay, that "No artist produces great art by a deliberate attempt to express his personality. He expresses his personality indirectly through concentrating upon a task which is a task in the same sense as the making of an efficient engine or the turning of a jug or a table-leg." There is testimony to the same effect, too, in some observations by Joyce Cary on the writing of novels. "Every professional artist," he says, "has met the questioner who asks of some detail: 'Why did you do it so clumsily like that, when you could have done it so neatly like this?' And smiles, as on a poor dreamer without logic or understanding, when he gets the answer: 'It might have been better your way, but I couldn't do it because it wouldn't have belonged.'" This is well understood, he adds, by critics like Horace and Boileau, who, being also artists, had "learned in practice that there are rules of construction, mysterious relations in technique, which exist apparently in the nature of the art itself"—or, as I should say, in the nature of the particular work of art in hand—"and which oblige the artist to respect them," though these are by no means the same as the abstract notions of literary kinds which most critics insist upon when they discuss, for instance, the novel.

Here then—in the artist's intuition of a form capable of directing whatever he does with his materials in a particular work—is an essential cause of poetic structure, the most decisive, indeed, of all the causes of structure in poetry because it controls in an immediate way the act of construction itself. Without it, no poetic whole; with it, a poetic whole of a certain kind and emotional quality, which will be excellent in proportion to the intrinsic possibilities of the form the poet has conceived and to his success in doing with his materials in his medium all that it requires or permits him to do if its full possibilities, as a form of a certain kind, are to be realized.

If form, however, in this sense of the word, is thus an indispensable first principle for writers, it would seem that it might also be taken, with fruitful results, as a first principle in the criticism of their works. Unfortunately, although I have looked widely in the criticism of the past and present, I do not find that this has been systematically done by any of the critics, in the tradition I have been speaking of in the last two lectures, who have thought the problem of structure in poetry to be an important concern. And there are at least two reasons why this has been so.

In the first place, the shaping cause of any given literary work —the principle which determines for its writer the necessities and opportunities he must consider in composing it—is something over and above and, as a principle, causally distinct from any of the potentialities attributable in advance to either the materials he has assembled in his mind or the technical devices at his disposal. He can know what he can do, in fact, only after he has done it; and the doing is an act of synthesis which, if it is successful, inevitably imposes a new character on the materials and devices out of which it is effected. If we are to talk, therefore, about formal principles in poetry and be able to trace their consequences in the structures of particular poems, we must have terms in our criticism for more than the materials of subject-matter and language which poets use and the technical procedures possible in their art. Yet it is almost wholly on the basis of assumptions limited to these non-formal aspects of poetry that the critics in the tradition we have been discussing have undertaken to deal with problems of structure in poems. Some of them have confined their attention to questions of technique in the sense either of devices or prosody or diction (the rest of poetry being thought of as a matter of inspiration, invention, or subject-matter) or of representational devices in the drama and the novel (the problem of what is represented or why being thought of either as the business of particular writers or as not amenable to art): a good example of both the virtues and limitations of this latter approach is Percy Lubbock's *The Craft of Fiction*, in which the problem of structure or "form" in the novel is reduced to the problem of the different possible ways—some of them assumed to be intrinsically better than others—in which stories may be told.

For the many other critics in the modern tradition whose preoccupations have been not so much technical as aesthetic, the approach to poetic structure has been by way of a dialectic in which the properties of poetic thought and expression have been derived by analogies from the known or assumed characteristics of other modes of discourse, with the result that these critics have been able to distinguish only such attributes of form in poetry as can be discovered by asking how the elements of any discourse can be related to one another in a composition. They have given us in this way many approximations to poetic form, which fail nevertheless, since they necessarily consist merely in possible or observed configurations of the poetic matter, to constitute in any complete sense shaping principles of structure. Some of the approximations have been very general indeed; as when structure, or the best structure, in poetry is identified with abstract relations of symmetry or balance (or their

artful avoidance), of repetition with variation, or of oppositions reconciled, and the structural analysis of particular poems is directed to the subsumption of their details of content and diction under one or another of these schemes; or as when some figure of speech, such as metaphor, synecdoche, or irony, is fixed upon as the basic model of poetic structure and the analysis of poems determined accordingly. The approximations, however, can easily be more specific than these. A good many poetic patterns, thus, have been derived by deduction from the known possibilities of grammatical or rhetorical arrangement in discourse of whatever kind; such is Mr. Yvor Winters' resolution of possible modes of organization in poetry into seven major types: the method of repetition, the logical method, the narrative method, pseudo-reference, qualitative progression, alternation of method, and double mood; the significant thing about these and other similar classifications is their equal applicability to writings which the critics who make them would undoubtedly hold to be non-poetic. And other relatively particularized formulas have been arrived at by finding correspondences between the arrangement of parts in poems and the arrangement of parts in paintings or musical compositions; by analogizing poetic organization to the simpler and more evident structures of rituals or myths; and very often, especially among the historical critics, by imputing to poems, as structural principles, whatever conventions of design can be attributed to the earlier works which served their writers as models. Whether general or particular, however, what these expedients give us are merely signs or manifestations or qualities of order in poems rather than the principles from which, in individual poems, the order springs; they call attention to "patterns" in poems of often great intrinsic interest, but they provide no means, since none are available in the critical language these critics are using, for helping us to understand why the "patterns" are there or what their precise function is. For this we require something more than any method can supply that is content to infer conceptions of form solely from the characteristics and possibilities of poetic materials.

In the second place, the question of shaping principles in poetry is a question not of deductive theory but of empirical fact; the problem, in any given poem, is what actually was, for its poet, the primary intuition of form which enabled him to synthesize his materials into an ordered whole. Until we have some idea of that we cannot proceed to inquire into its consequences in the poet's invention and rendering of details; and this means that the first principle of our analysis must be an induction of which the only warrant is the evidence of the poem itself. We may be assisted in making this by our knowledge of other poems, and we need general concepts, moreover, to guide us, since it is only through concepts that we can understand particular things. But what we are looking for is, first of all, a fact—possibly a fact of a kind that has no complete parallel in the earlier or later history of poetry, inasmuch as it is the mark of good poets that they try to avoid repeating too often the inventions of others. It is fatal therefore to think that we can know the shaping principle of any poem in advance or, what amounts to the same thing in practice, that we can get at it in terms of any predetermined conception or model of what structure in poetry or in this or that special branch of poetry in general either is or ought to be. Yet this is what most of the critics who have concerned themselves with questions of structure have attempted to do. They have come to poems equipped, so to speak, with paradigms of poetry, or of epic, tragedy, lyric, and so on, and hence with more or less definite specifications concerning the nature of the structural patterns they ought to look for; and they have as a consequence been unable to see any structural principles in poems except those already contained in their preferred definitions and models.

Let me give one more example of this paradigm method in operation; I take it from a recent essay on *Othello* by Professor Robert Heilman. Now the question of the structure of *Othello* could surely be approached inductively through a comparison of the material data of action, character, and motive supplied to Shakespeare by Cinthio's *novella* with what happened to these in the completed play. We could then ask what particular shaping principle, among principles possible in serious dramas, we must suppose to have governed Shakespeare's construction of the tragedy if we are to account with a maximum completeness and economy both for the new uses to which he put his borrowed materials and for the differences between the succession of our expectations and desires when we read the *novella* and when we witness or read *Othello*. This is not, however, where Mr. Heilman starts. His problem is not to develop a hypothesis which will explain the structural peculiarities of this play but to read the play in the light of a hypothesis (of the "abstract" sort) already formed in his mind and previously used as the basis of his interpretation of *King Lear*. *Othello* he knows is a "poetic drama" (since it is a dramatic representation in which the verse and diction are obviously important parts); it must therefore have the characteristic structure of "poetic drama," which is to say, according to Mr. Heilman, a structure composed of two elements— "drama" and "poetry"—which operate in "collusion," as two "languages" or "bearers of meaning," to the end of expressing symbolically a "total meaning" relative to a given subject or "theme." The argument of his essay is accordingly an application of this paradigm to the facts of the text which it enables him to select as significant data. "The most obvious approach to the structure of drama," he remarks in the beginning, "is to equate structure with plot and then to describe plot in terms of those familiar and yet somewhat elusive elements sometimes called rising action, climax, dénouement, etc." This would give us a number of observations, or guesses, about the stages of the action, the location of the climax, and so on, which might be true enough but which would yield at best, as he says, "only superficial information." Such information, we can agree, might well be superficial for any critic; what makes it seem superficial to Mr. Heilman is the hypothesis he is engaged in applying. For if *Othello* is not merely a drama but a "poetic drama," then its structure must be "equated" with something else than plot—namely, the interaction of its "drama" and its "poetry." The subject of the dramatic action, he says, is primarily not jealousy (as many have supposed) but love; the advantage of this view is that it not only names the dominant theme but indicates "the forces which give the play a composition of a certain kind," inasmuch as the "central tension is between the love of Othello and the hate of Iago, the specific forms taken in this play"—and here we meet the familiar reduction terms—"by good and evil." This "dramatic structure," however, is constantly modified in the course of the play by the parallel and (in Mr. Heilman's sense) strictly "poetic" structure constituted, in the speeches, by the many patterns of imagery that turn on symbolic oppositions of black and white, darkness and light, hell and heaven, foul and fair, chaos and order. These, we are told, are not so many static antitheses merely, but form a kind of dialectical action, corresponding to and enriching the dramatic action, through the successive permutations and shifts which the basic pairs of terms, at least in Mr. Heilman's exposition, are made to undergo. Much of this is illuminating and provocative; one would not care to embark upon a discussion of the structure of *Othello* without first taking account of Mr. Heilman's observations. I do not think, however, that he comes very close to defining any principle of structure for *Othello* that could conceivably have guided Shakespeare in constructing the poetic whole which arouses in us such poignant tragic emotions. What he exhibits are rather some of the material antecedents of the tragic structure in the conceptions of love and jealousy which the writing of the play presupposed and some of

the consequences of the structure in the imagery and thought by which it is made effective in the words; and his only warrant for "equating" the combination of these aspects with the structure of the play is his prior assumption that the structure of *Othello* must be of this sort.

These are the main reasons, then, why the dominant languages of modern criticism, for all the many insights into poetry which those who use them have attained, are inadequate means for dealing with the causes and aspects of structure in particular poems that have their bases in the productive acts of poets. We need for this purpose, if the question happens to interest or seem important to us, a language in which we can view our questions as questions of fact rather than of relations of ideas (such as "drama" and "poetry" or "poetry" and "prose"); in which we can talk about the internal necessities and possibilities in poems and the problems these posed for their poets rather than merely about the necessities and problems defined for us by our special choice of dialectical premises; in which we can develop terms for distinguishing the formal principles of poems from their material constituents and technical mechanisms; and in which, finally, we can achieve a precision of differentiation in speaking of the structures of different poems which is not glaringly incommensurate with the formal inventiveness of poets. The only near approach to such a critical language, however, is that made long ago by Aristotle; it would be foolish not to avail ourselves of his contribution, in its methodological aspects, so far as possible; and we have therefore to consider to what extent we can still profit, in practical criticism, by attempting to adapt to our current needs the principles and analytical devices which he was the first and almost the last to use.

II

It is not a question of regarding the *Poetics*, in Mr. Blackmur's phrase, as a "sacred book" and certainly not of looking upon ourselves, in any exclusive sense, as forming an "Aristotelian" or "Neo-Aristotelian" school. It would be desirable, indeed, if we could do away with "schools" in criticism as they have been done away with in most of the disciplines in which learning as distinguished from doctrine has been advanced. But our loyalty at any rate should be to problems rather than to ancient masters; and if it happens that we have problems for which Aristotle can give us the means, or some of the means, of solution, we should be prepared to benefit from his initiative in precisely the same way as many of our contemporaries have benefited from the more recent initiatives of Coleridge, Richards, Frazer, and Freud without necessarily becoming disciples of any of these men. And it is not difficult to see what there is in Aristotle, or what we can develop out of him, that is immediately pertinent to the problem of poetic structure in the particular form in which I defined it at the beginning of this lecture.

I should put first the conception of poetic works as "concrete wholes." Anything is a concrete whole the unity of which can be adequately stated only by saying that it "is such and such a form embodied in this or that matter, or such and such a matter with this or that form; so that its shape and structure must be included in our description" as well as that out of which it is constituted or made. And of the two natures which must join in any such whole, or in our account of it, "the formal nature is of greater importance than the material nature" inasmuch as the "form" of any individual object, such as a man or a couch, is the principle or cause "by reason of which the matter is some definite thing." In spite of the unfamiliar language in which the conception is stated in Aristotle, the underlying insight is one that we can easily translate into the terms of common experience. I take, for instance, a piece of modelling clay. There are many things which I cannot do with it—of which, as Aristotle

would say, it cannot be the matter; but on the other hand the potentialities it does hold out, within these limits, are indefinite in number: I can make of it, if I wish, a geographical globe, with all its continents, or the model of a house, or the bust of a sinister-looking man, and so on through a range of similar possibilities that is bounded only by my invention and skill. In any of these realizations the thing I make remains a thing of clay, having all the permanent characteristics of such a thing; but it remains this only in a partial sense; in itself, as a particular object to which we may respond practically or aesthetically, it is at the same time something else—a globe, a house, a sinister-looking man; and any description we may give of it, though it must obviously specify its clayness—that is, its material nature— would be of no use to anybody unless it also specified the definite kind of thing into which the clay has been shaped— that is, its formal nature. And the latter is clearly more important than the former since it is what accounts, in any particular case, for the clay being handled thus and not otherwise and for our response being of such and such a quality rather than any other.

It is not hard to see how the conception fits the work of the poet or of any other writer. Here is a poem, the material nature of which is comprised in the following sequence of happenings:

A young Italian duke, influenced by his idle companions, dismisses the wise counsellor his father had recommended to him, refuses the advice of his fiancée, and devotes himself to a life of private pleasure and neglect of public duty. A Turkish corsair takes advantage of this situation to storm the Duke's castle and to reduce him and all his court to slavery; and the Duke falls into despair when he learns that his fiancée is destined for the conqueror's harem. She, however, deceives the corsair into giving her a delay of three days and a chance to speak to her lover. She uses this time to rouse the Duke to repentance for his past errors and to work out with him a plan whereby he and his father's counsellor will attempt a rescue before the three days are up. The plan succeeds; the Duke and his friends overcome the corsair's troops and make him prisoner. The Duke's false companions then demand that the Turk be executed; but the Duke, grateful for the lesson his captivity has taught him, responds by banishing them and allowing the corsair to depart unharmed; he then marries his fiancée and resolves to rule more wisely in the future.

As an action this is clearly not without some form, being a coherent and complete chain of possible events, to which we are likely to respond by taking sides with the Duke and the girl against their captors. I am sure, however, that anyone who now reads *The Duke of Benevento* for the first time will think that I have given a very indefinite account of what happens in Sir John Henry Moore's poem and hence misled him completely as to the poem's distinctive nature and effect. He will probably be prepared to read a vaguely tragicomic romance or drama of a kind common enough in the 1770's; what he will actually find is a short piece of 204 lines beginning as follows:

I hate the prologue to a story
Worse than the tuning of a fiddle,
   Squeaking and dinning;
Hang order and connection,
I love to dash into the middle;
   Exclusive of the fame and glory,
There is a comfort on reflection
   To think you've done with the beginning.

And so at supper one fine night,
   Hearing a cry of Alla, Alla,
The Prince was damnably confounded,
   And in a fright,
But more so when he saw himself surrounded
By fifty Turks; and at their head the fierce
   Abdalla,

And then he look'd a little grave
To find himself become a slave, ...

And so on consistently to the end, in a rapidly narrated episode of which the formal nature is the kind of anti-romantic comedy clearly foreshadowed in these lines—a form that is only potentially in the story of the poem (since this could yield several other forms) and is created out of it, partly indeed by Moore's pre-Byronic language and manner of narration, but also, as a read-

ing of the whole poem will show, by the notably unheroic qualities of character and thought which he gives to his hero and heroine, with the result that we are unable to take their predicament any more tragically than they themselves do.

It is clear how such a conception of the internal relations of form and matter in a "concrete whole" differs from the later and much commoner analytic in which form or art is set over against content or subject-matter in one or another of the many ways we have already illustrated. A poem, on the view of its structure suggested by Aristotle, is not a composite of *res* and *verba* but a certain matter formed in a certain way or a certain form imposed upon or wrought out of a certain matter. The two are inseparable aspects of the same individual thing, though they are clearly distinct analytically as principles or causes, and though, of the two, the formal nature is necessarily the more important as long as our concern is with the poem as a concrete object. On the one hand, we do not cease to talk about the matter of a poem when we examine its formal structure, and, on the other hand, there is a sense in which nothing in a completed poem, or any distinguishable part thereof, is matter or content merely, in relation to which something else is form. In a well-made poem, everything is formed, and hence rendered poetic (whatever it may have been in itself), by virtue simply of being made to do something definite in the poem or to produce a definitely definable effect, however local, which the same materials of language, thought, character-traits, or actions would be incapable of in abstraction from the poem, or the context in the poem, in which they appear. We are not speaking poetically but only materially of anything in a poem, therefore, when we abstract it from its function or effect in the poem; we speak poetically, or formally, only when we add to a description of the thing in terms of its constituent elements (for example, the content of a metaphor or the events of a plot) an indication of the definite quality it possesses or of that in the poem for the sake of which it is there. In an absolute sense, then, nothing in a successful poem is non-formal or non-poetic; but it is also true that structure of any kind necessarily implies a subordination of some parts to others; and in this relative sense we may intelligibly say of one formed element of a poem that it is material to something else in the same poem, the existence and specific effectiveness of which it makes possible. We may thus speak of the words of a poem as the material basis of the thought they express, although the words also have form as being ordered in sentences and rhythms; and similarly we may speak of thought as the matter of character, of character and thought in words as the matter of action or emotion, and so on up to but not including the overall form which synthesizes all these subordinate elements, formally effective in themselves, into a continuous poetic whole. Or we can reverse the order of consideration, and ask what matter of action, character, and thought a poem requires if its plot or lyric structure is to be formally of a certain kind, or what kind of character a speech ought to suggest if it is to serve adequately its function in a scene, or what selection and arrangement of words will render best or most economically a given state of mind.

Here then is an intelligible, universally applicable, and analytically powerful conception of the basic structural relations in poems which we can take over from Aristotle without committing ourselves to the total philosophy in which it was evolved. We can also take over, in the second place, his special manner of considering questions of poetic value. As things made by and for men, poems can have a great variety of uses and be judged in terms of many different criteria, moral, political, intellectual, rhetorical, historical. To judge them *as* poems, however, is to judge them in their distinctive aspect as wholes of certain kinds, in the light of the assumption that the poet's end—the end which makes him a poet—is simply the perfecting of the poem as a beautiful or intrinsically excellent thing. I do not mean that poems are ever perfected in an absolute sense. We can agree with R. G. Collingwood when he remarks, in his *Autobiography*, that as a boy living in a household of artists he "learned to think of a picture not as a finished product exposed for the admiration of virtuosi, but as the visible record, lying about the house, of an attempt to solve a definite problem in painting, so far as the attempt has gone." "I learned," he adds, "what some critics and aestheticians never know to the end of their lives, that no 'work of art' is ever finished, so that in that sense of the phrase there is no such thing as a 'work of art' at all. Work ceases upon the picture or manuscript, not because it is finished, but because sending-in day is at hand, or because the printer is clamorous for copy, or because 'I am sick of working at this thing' or 'I can't see what more I can do to it.'" This is sound sense, which critics and aestheticians ought to learn if they do not know it; but it is clearly not incompatible with the assumption that what a poet seeks to do, as a poet, is to make as good a work poetically speaking as he can; and this goodness, we can surely agree with Aristotle, must always consist in a mean between doing too much and not doing enough in his invention and handling of all its parts. The criterion, again, is not an absolute one; the mean in art, as in morals, is a relative mean, which has to be determined in adjustment to the particular necessities and possibilities of the form the artist is trying to achieve. And just as the poet can know these only by trial and error plus reflection upon the general conditions of his art and on what other poets have been able to do, so the critic can know them, and the ends to which they are relative, only by similar *ex post facto* means. He must therefore leave to other critics with less strictly "poetic" preoccupations the task of formulating criteria for poetry on the basis of general "abstract" principles; his business is to take the point of view of the poet and his problems and to judge what he has done, as sympathetically as possible, in terms of what must and what might be done *given* the distinctive form which the poet is trying to work out of his materials. And here, once more, the procedure of Aristotle can be of use.

We can still profit, moreover, not merely from these general features of his approach but likewise from some of the more particular applications of his method in the *Poetics*, including, first of all, the fundamental distinction, on which the treatise is based, between poetry which is "imitation" and poetry which is not. The former, for Aristotle, is poetry in the most distinctive sense, since its principles are not the principles of any other art; but to insist on this is not to preclude the possibility of discussing as "poetry" other kinds of works of which the materials and devices, though not the forms, are those of poems in the stricter meaning of the word; the difference is not one of relative dignity or value but purely of constructive principle, and hence of the kinds of hypotheses and terms that are required, respectively, for the analysis and judgment of works belonging to each. The distinction, as Aristotle understood it, has played no important part in the subsequent history of criticism. A class of "didactic" poems has, it is true, been more or less constantly recognized, but the differentiation between these and other poems has most often been made in terms of purpose, content, and technique rather than of matter and form, a "didactic" poem being distinguished sometimes as one in which the end of instruction is more prominent than that of delight, sometimes as one that uses or springs from or appeals to the reason rather than the imagination, sometimes as one that relies mainly on precepts instead of fictions and images or that uses direct rather than indirect means of expression. This breakdown of the original distinction was natural enough in the periods of criticism in which the ends of poetry were defined broadly as instruc-

tion and pleasure, and it is still natural in a period, such as our own, when the great preoccupation is with "meaning" and with poetry as a special kind of language for expressing special modes of signification. In both periods, although some classes of poems have been set apart as "didactic" in a peculiar and frequently pejorative sense, all poetry, or all poetry except that which can be described as "entertainment" merely, has tended to assume an essentially didactic character and function. The prevalence nowadays of "thematic analysis" as a method of discussion applicable to all poetic works that can be taken seriously at all is a clear sign of this, as is also the currency of "archetypal" analogies. The result, however, has been to banish from criticism, or to confuse beyond clear recognition, a distinction which has as much validity now as when it was first made and which has not been supplanted by any of the later distinctions since these all rest on quite different bases of principle. The distinction is simply between works, on the one hand, in which the formal nature is constituted of some particular human activity or state of feeling qualified morally and emotionally in a certain way, the beautiful rendering of this in words being the sufficient end of the poet's effort, and works, on the other hand (like the *Divine Comedy, Absalom and Achitophel, Don Juan, 1984,* etc.), in which the material nature is "poetic" in the sense that it is made up of parts similar to those of imitative poems and the formal nature is constituted of some particular thesis, intellectual or practical, relative to some general human interest, the artful elaboration and enforcement of this by whatever means are available and appropriate being the sufficient end of the poet's effort. Great and serious works can be and have been written on either of these basic principles of construction, but the principles themselves, it must be evident, are sharply distinct, and the difference is bound to be reflected, in innumerable subtle as well as obvious ways, in everything that poets have to do or can do in the two major kinds. To continue to neglect the distinction, therefore, is merely to deprive ourselves unnecessarily of an analytical device—however hard to apply in particular cases—which can serve, when intelligently used, to introduce greater exactness into our critical descriptions and greater fairness into our critical judgments.

Of the other distinctions and concepts in the *Poetics* which are still valid and useful—at least for the kind of discussion of poetic structure we are concerned with here—nearly all are limited, in their strict applicability, to imitative works. For any inquiry into such forms we cannot neglect, to begin with, the all-important distinctions of object, means, manner, and *dynamis* upon which the definition of tragedy in Chapter 6 is based. They are the essential and basic determinants of the structure of any species of imitative works when these are viewed as concrete wholes. We can conceive adequately of such a whole only when we consider as precisely as possible what kind of human experience is being imitated, by the use of what possibilities of the poetic medium, through what mode of representation, and for the sake of evoking and resolving what particular sequence of expectations and emotions relative to the successive parts of the imitated object. It is always some definite combination of these four things that defines, for the imitative writer, the necessities and possibilities of any work he may have in hand; for what he must and can do at any point will differ widely according as he is imitating a character, a state of passion, or an action, and if an action (with character, thought, and passion inevitably involved), whether one of which the central figures are men and women morally better than we are, or like ourselves, or in some sense worse; and according as he is doing this in verse of a certain kind or in prose or in some joining of the two; and according as he is doing it in a narrative or a dramatic or a mixed manner; and according, finally, as he is shaping his incidents and characters and their thoughts

and feelings, his language, and his technique of representation (whatever it may be) so as to give us, let us say, the peculiar kind of comic pleasure we get from *Tom Jones* or that we get from *The Alchemist* or, to add still another possible nuance of comic effect, from *Volpone*. These, then, are indispensable distinctions for the critic who wishes to grasp the principles of construction and the consequences thereof in any imitative work; and he will be sacrificing some of the precision of analysis possible to him if he fails to take them all into consideration as independent variables—if he talks, for instance, about the plot of a novel or the pattern of images in a lyric poem without specifying the emotional "working or power" which is its controlling form, or if, in dealing with any kind of imitative work, he neglects to distinguish clearly between the "things" being imitated, upon which the *dynamis* primarily depends, and the expedients of representational manner by which the writer has sought to clarify or maximize their peculiar effect.

There remains, lastly, the detailed analytic of imitative forms which is represented in the *Poetics* by the chapters on tragedy and epic. I need not repeat what I said in the second lecture about Aristotle's distinctive conceptions —which have largely vanished from later criticism—of plot, character, thought, and diction—or about the relationships of causal subordination in which these "parts" are made to stand to one another in the tragic and epic structures, so that the last three, while being capable of form themselves, have the status of necessary material conditions of the plot, which, in the most specific sense of the synthesis of things done and said in a work as determined to a certain "working or power," is the principal part or controlling form of the whole. I have explained why this analysis seems to me sound, given the assumptions on which it is based and its limited applicability to works of which the subjects are actions of the more or less extended sort Aristotle here had in mind. We can therefore still use it, and the many constituent definitions and distinctions it involves, in the criticism of the larger poetic forms. We can profit particularly, I think, from the discussion of tragic plot-form in Chapter 13, not only because it gives us a clue to the structure of many later "tragic" works (this plot-form is clearly the formula, for example, of *Othello*, though not quite of *Macbeth*, and certainly not of *Richard III*) but also, and chiefly, because it suggests the four general questions we have to ask about any work having a plot as its principle of construction if we are to see clearly what problems its writer faced in composing it: as to precisely what the change is, from what it starts and to what it moves; in what kind of man it takes place; by reason of what causes in the man's thoughts and actions or outside him; and with what succession of emotional effects in the representation.

III

We should be merely "Aristotelians," however, rather than independent scholars were we to remain content with what we can thus extract from Aristotle for present-day critical use; and we should be able to deal only crudely and inadequately with a great many of the most interesting structural problems raised by modern works. We need therefore to push the Aristotelian type of theoretical analysis far beyond the point where Aristotle himself left off, and this in several different directions.

There are, to begin with, the many non-imitative species of poetry or imaginative literature with which the *Poetics* does not deal at all. A large number of these have been roughly distinguished in the nomenclature and theories of subsequent criticism under such heads as: philosophical poems, moral essays, epigrams, treatises in verse, occasional poems; Horatian satires, Juvenalian satires, Varronian or Menippean satires; allegories, apologues, fables, parables, exempla, thesis or propaganda dramas and novels. But though a vast deal of critical and his-

torical discussion has been devoted to these forms, we have as yet only fragmentary beginnings of a usable inductive analytic of their structural principles as distinguished from their material conventions.

Again, there are all the shorter imitative forms, most of them later in origin or artistic development than Aristotle, which we commonly group together as lyric poems; much of the best criticism of these has been concerned either with their techniques and fixed conventional patterns or with a dialectical search for the qualities of subject-matter and expression which are thought to differentiate lyric poetry, as a homogeneous type, from other poetic kinds. What we need to have, therefore, is a comprehensive study, free from "abstract" assumptions, of the existing species of such poems in terms both of the different "proper pleasures" achievable in them and of the widely variant material structures in which the pleasures may inhere. Lyrics, it is plain, do not have plots, but any successful lyric obviously has something analogous to a plot in the sense of a specific form which synthesizes into a definite emotional whole what is said or done in the poem and conditions the necessities and probabilities which the poet must embody somehow in his lines; and the nature of this formal principle—whether it is, for example, a man in an evolving state of passion interpreted for him by his thought (as in the "Ode to a Nightingale") or a man adjusting himself voluntarily to an emotionally significant discovery about his life (as in the "Ode on Intimations of Immortality")—has to be grasped with some precision if we are to be able to speak appropriately and adequately about the poem's construction in all its parts and the degree of its artistic success. And here too most of the necessary analytical work still remains to be done.

We are much better off, thanks to Aristotle, with respect to the full-length imitative forms of narrative and drama; but even in this field there are many outstanding questions. Except for one suggestive paragraph in Chapter 5 on the general nature of the ridiculous, the *Poetics* as we have it is silent on comedy; and although there is much to be learned from the innumerable later discussions, especially since the eighteenth century, the insights these make available still have to be translated out of the rhetorical and psychological languages in which they are, for the most part, embodied into the more consistently "poetic" language we are committed to using. That there are a good many distinguishable comic plot-forms, both in drama and in narrative, must be evident to every one; but as to what they are, and what different artistic necessities and possibilities each of them involves, we have as yet, I think, only rather vague general notions; and the problem has not been greatly advanced by the traditional classifications into comedy of intrigue, comedy of manners, comedy of character, and so on. The same thing is true of the many intermediate forms between comedy in the stricter sense and tragedy proper: of tragicomedy, for example, or the "serious" and "tender" comedy which emerged in the eighteenth century, or the kind of domestic novel which Jane Austen wrote in *Pride and Prejudice*, *Mansfield Park*, and *Persuasion*, or the adventure romance in its earlier as well as its contemporary forms, or even the detective novel, much as has been written about the "poetics" of that. Nor is tragedy itself in much better case. What the *Poetics* gives us is an analytic of only one among the many plot-forms which the critical opinion as well as the common sense of later times has thought proper to call "tragic"; and it is one of the unfortunate results of the respect which Aristotle has always commanded that critics have tended to blur the distinctive principles of construction and effect, or to impair the artistic integrity, of these "non-Aristotelian" tragic forms in their eagerness to bring them in some fashion under his definition. We need therefore a fresh attempt at analysis, by the same method but in more appropriate terms, for such plot-forms,

among others, as are represented severally by *Richard III* and *The Duchess of Malfi*, by *The Orphan*, by *The Brothers Karamazov*, and by *A Passage to India*.

It is not merely of the forms of drama and narrative, however, that we require a better theory but also of many of their characteristic structural devices. We still tend to think of plot in its material aspects in the limited terms in which it is treated in the *Poetics* on the basis of the somewhat elementary practice of the Greeks, with the result that when we have to deal with works that combine in various ways many lines of action or concern themselves primarily not with external actions but with changes in thought and feeling or with the slow development or degeneration of moral character or with the fortunes of groups rather than of individuals, we often fall into the confusion which has led many modern critics to reject the concept of plot altogether. This is clearly no solution, but the remedy can be only a more comprehensive and discriminating induction of possible dramatic and narrative structures than Aristotle was able to provide. And there is also the complex question of how plots of whatever kind, or their equivalents in other forms, have to be or can be represented in the words —the question, in short, of imitative manner in a sense that goes beyond, while still depending upon, Aristotle's distinction of the three manners in his third chapter. Of all the topics I have mentioned, this is perhaps the one on which the largest body of precise and useful observation has been accumulated, by all those critics from the Renaissance to our day who have devoted themselves to the "techniques" first of the drama and epic and then of the novel, short-story, and lyric. Even here, however, much remains to be done; and one of the chief requisites, I think, is a clearer posing of the whole problem in such a way as to correlate the many devices of manner which these critics have discriminated, as well as others that have escaped them, with the distinguishable functions which manner has to serve with

respect to form. I have touched upon
some of these functions in the second
lecture, and I will add only the suggestion
that there are likely to be, in all richly
developed imitative works, incidents,
characters, speeches, and images which
are not parts of the plot-form but must
be viewed by the critic as elements of
"thought" in a sense akin to but distinct
from that intended by Aristotle in
Chapters 6 and 19. We may treat as
"thought" of this kind anything permitting of inference in a poetic work, over
and above the direct working of the
imitated object, that functions as a
device, vis-à-vis the audience, for disclosing or hinting at relevant traits of character or situation, awakening or directing expectations, conditioning states of
mind, emphasizing essential issues, suggesting in what light something is to be
viewed, or, more broadly still, setting
the action or some part of it in a larger
context of ideas or analogies so that it
may come to seem, in its universal implications for human beings, not simply
the particular and untypical action it
might otherwise be taken to be. Every
novelist or dramatist—or lyric poet, for
that matter—who reflects on his own
work will understand what this means;
but the conception has still to become
widely recognized among critics, or it
surely would have been applied long
since to such things as the apparently
superfluous episodes and characters and
the recurrent general words and patterns of images in Shakespeare—the
dialectic of "Nature" in *King Lear*, for
instance—concerning which most recent writers have thought it necessary
to offer much more profound explanations.

It would be well, finally, if we could
carry our method of inductive and causal
analysis into some of the larger questions of theory—common to both imitative and non-imitative poetry—to which
these writers and other contemporary
critics have given special prominence:
we could profit greatly, for example,
from a re-examination of poetic images,
of the elements and functions of diction in poetry, of the various modes and

uses of symbols, and of the structural
characteristics of myths.

We need not wait, however, for the
completion of these possible studies before beginning to use such theory of
poetic forms as we now possess in the
service of practical criticism. There is
after all a close mutual interdependence,
in the method we are considering, between theoretical analysis and the investigation of particular works; and as
our attempts at application become
more numerous and more varied in their
objects, so will our grasp of the necessary general distinctions and principles
tend to improve.

IV

In these attempts, we shall be making
a pretty complete break with the tradition of practical criticism discussed in
the last two lectures—a tradition in
which it has always been necessary, before individual works of poetic art can
be analysed or judged, to conceive of
poetry as a homogeneous whole and to
define its nature in some kind of dialectical relation to other modes of discourse or thought. We shall not need,
for our purposes, to commit ourselves to
any critical theory of this sort. We shall
not need to worry about how poetry
differs from science or prose, or about
what its mission is in the modern
world. We shall not need to decide in
advance of our studies of poems whether
poetry in general is best defined as a
kind of language or a kind of subject-
matter; whether its end is pleasure or
some species of knowledge or practical
good; whether its proper domain includes all the kinds of imaginative writing or only some of these; whether it is
most closely akin to rhetoric and dialectic or to ritual, myth, or dream; or
whether it is or is not a separable element in prose fiction and drama. Nor
shall we need to assume that all good
poems have "themes" or that poetic expression is always indirect, metaphorical,
and symbolic. Not merely would such
speculative commitments be useless to
us, given our empirical starting-point

but they would be fatal, in proportion as we allowed our analyses to be directed by them, to our very effort, since they would inevitably blind us to all those aspects of our problem which our particular doctrine of poetry failed to take into account.

I do not mean that we shall not have to make some assumptions of our own, but only that these need not and ought not to be particularized assumptions about the intrinsic nature and necessary structure of our objects considered as a unitary class of things. We shall have to assume that any poetic work, like any other production of human art, has, or rather is, a definite structure of some kind which is determined immediately by its writer's intuition of a form to be achieved in its materials by the right use of his medium, and, furthermore, that we can arrive at some understanding of what this form actually is and use our understanding as a principle in the analysis and criticism of the work. We shall have to come to some agreement, moreover, as to what we will mean by "poetic works"; but here again the fewer specifications we impose on ourselves in advance the better. It will be sufficient for all our purposes if we begin, simply, by taking as "poems" or "works of literary art" all those kinds of productions which have been commonly called such at different times, but without any supposition that, because these have the same name, they are all "poems" or "works of literary art" in the same fundamental structural sense—that the art necessary to write *The Divine Comedy* or *The Faerie Queene* is the same art, when viewed in terms of its peculiar principles of form, as the art which enabled Shakespeare to write *King Lear* and *Othello*. And for such productions we shall need to assume, in addition, only one common characteristic: that they are all works which, in one degree or another, justify critical consideration primarily for their own sake, as artistic structures, rather than merely for the sake of the knowledge or wisdom they express or the practical utility we may derive from

them, though either or both of these other values may be importantly involved in any particular case.

The problem of structure, for any individual work of this kind, is the problem—to give it its most general statement—of how the material nature of the work is related to its formal nature, when we understand by form that principle, or complex of principles, which gives to the subject-matter the power it has to affect our opinions and emotions in a certain definite way. The question, as I have said, is primarily one of fact and cause; and it is answered, for a given work, when we have made as intelligible as we can the fashion in which its material elements of whatever kind—words, images, symbols, thoughts, character-traits, incidents, devices of representation—are made to function in relation to a formal whole which we can warrantably assert was the actual final cause of its composition. By "actual final cause" I mean simply a principle without the assumption of which, as somehow effective in the writing, the observable characteristics of the parts, their presence in the poem, their arrangement and proportioning, and their interconnections cannot be adequately understood. In discovering what this shaping principle is in any work we must make use of such evidence as there may be concerning the history of its conception and writing, including any statements the writer may have made about his intentions. Our task, however, is not to explain the writer's activity but the result thereof; our problem is not psychological but artistic; and hence the causes that centrally concern us are the internal causes of which the only sufficient evidence is the work itself as a completed product. What we want to know is not the actual process but the actual rationale of the poem's construction in terms of the poetic problems the writer faced and the reasons which determined his solutions. And in looking for these we shall assume that if the poem holds together as an intelligibly effective whole, in which a certain form is realized in a certain matter which never before had this form, the result can be understood fully only by supposing that such and such problems were involved and were solved by the writer in accordance with reasons which, in part at least, we can state; and this clearly does not commit us to holding that the problems and reasons we uncover in our analysis, as necessarily implied by the completed poem, must have presented themselves to the writer explicitly as such in a continuous movement of self-conscious deliberation; it will be sufficient if we can show that the poem could hardly have been written as it is or have the effect it does on our minds had the writer not done, somehow or at some time, what these particular problems and reasons dictate.

We can never, of course, know such things directly, but only by inference from the consequences of the conceived form, whether of the whole or of any of its parts, in the details of the completed work; and there can be no such inference except by way of hypotheses which both imply and are implied by the observable traits of the work. There are, however, hypotheses and hypotheses, and the character of those we need to make is determined by the nature of our problem. We propose to consider poems as unique existent things the structural principles of which are to be discovered, rather than as embodiments of general truths about the structure of poetry already adequately known. Hence our procedure must be the reverse of that procedure by way of preferred paradigms or models of structure which we have seen to be so characteristic of contemporary practical criticism. Our task is not to show the reflection in poems of complex or "ironical" attitudes, interactions of prose and poetry or of logical structure and irrelevant texture, patterns of ritual drama, or basic mythical themes, on the assumption that if the poem is a good poem it will inevitably have whichever of these or other similar general structures we happen to be interested in finding examples of; it is rather the task of making formal sense out of any poetic work

before us on the assumption that it may in fact be a work for whose peculiar principles of structure there are nowhere any usable parallels either in literary theory or in our experience of other works. The hypotheses we have to make, therefore, will not be of the fixed and accredited kind which scientists employ only when their problem is not to find out something still unknown but to "demonstrate" a classic experiment to beginners, but rather of the tentative kind—to be modified or rejected altogether at the dictation of the facts—which are the proper means to any serious inductive inquiry. They will be particular working hypotheses for the investigation of the structures of individual poems, not general hypotheses about such things as poetry or "poetic drama" in which the specific nature of the individual structures to be examined is already assumed.

Such hypotheses will be of two sorts according as the questions to which they are answers relate to the principles by which poetic works have been constructed as wholes of certain definite kinds or to the reasons which connect a particular part of a given work, directly or indirectly, with such a principle by way of the poetic problems it set for the writer at this point. And there can be no good practical criticism in this mode in which both sorts are not present; for although the primary business of the critic is with the particulars of any work he studies down to its minuter details of diction and rhythm, he can never exhibit the artistic problems involved in these or find other than extra-poetic reasons for their solutions without the guidance of an explicit definition of the formal whole which they have made possible.

A single work will suffice to illustrate both kinds of critical hypotheses as well as the relation between them, and I will begin by considering what idea of the governing form of *Macbeth* appears to accord best with the facts of that play and the sequence of emotions it arouses in us. I need not say again why it seems to me futile to look for an adequate structural formula for *Macbeth* in any of the more "imaginative" directions commonly taken by recent criticism; I shall assume, therefore, without argument, that we have to do, not with a lyric "statement of evil" or an allegory of the workings of sin in the soul and the state or a metaphysical myth of destruction followed by re-creation or a morality play with individualized characters rather than types, but simply with an imitative tragic drama based on historical materials. To call it an imitative tragic drama, however, does not carry us very far; it merely limits roughly the range of possible forms we have to consider. Among these are the contrasting plot-forms embodied respectively in *Othello* and in *Richard III*: the first a tragic plot-form in the classic sense of Aristotle's analysis in *Poetics* 13; the second a plot-form which Aristotle rejected as non-tragic but which appealed strongly to poets in the Renaissance—a form of serious action designed to arouse moral indignation for the deliberately unjust and seemingly prospering acts of the protagonist and moral satisfaction at his subsequent ruin. The plot-form of *Macbeth* clearly involves elements which assimilate it now to the one and now to the other of both these kinds. The action of the play is twofold, and one of its aspects is the punitive action of Malcolm, Macduff, and their friends which in the end brings about the protagonist's downfall and death. The characters here are all good men, whom Macbeth has unforgivably wronged, and their cause is the unqualifiedly just cause of freeing Scotland from a bloody tyrant and restoring the rightful line of kings. All this is made clear in the representation not only directly through the speeches and acts of the avengers but indirectly by those wonderfully vivid devices of imagery and general thought in which modern critics have found the central value and meaning of the play as a whole; and our responses, when this part of the action is before us, are such as are clearly dictated by the immediate events and the poetic commentary: we desire,

that is, the complete success of the counter-action and this as speedily as possible before Macbeth can commit further horrors. We desire this, however —and that is what at once takes the plot-form out of the merely retributive class—not only for the sake of humanity and Scotland but also for the sake of Macbeth himself. For what most sharply distinguishes our view of Macbeth from that of his victims and enemies is that, whereas they see him from the outside only, we see him also, throughout the other action of the play —the major action—from the inside, as he sees himself; and what we see thus is a moral spectacle the emotional quality of which, for the impartial observer, is not too far removed from the tragic *dynamis* specified in the *Poetics*. This is not to say that the main action of *Macbeth* is not significantly different, in several respects, from the kind of tragic action which Aristotle envisages. The change is not merely from good to bad fortune, but from a good state of character to a state in which the hero is almost, but not quite, transformed into a monster; and the tragic act which initiates the change, and still more the subsequent unjust acts which this entails, are acts done—unlike Othello's killing of Desdemona—in full knowledge of their moral character. We cannot, therefore, state the form of this action in strictly Aristotelian terms, but the form is none the less one that involves, like tragedy in Aristotle's sense, the arousal and catharsis of painful emotions for, and not merely with respect to, the protagonist—emotions for which the terms pity and fear are not entirely inapplicable.

Any adequate hypothesis about the structure of *Macbeth*, then, would have to take both of these sets of facts into account. For both of the views we are given of the hero are true: he is in fact, in terms of the nature and objective consequences of his deeds, what Macduff and Malcolm say he is throughout Acts IV and V, but he is also—and the form of the play is really the interaction of the two views in our opinions and emotions—what we ourselves see him to be as we witness the workings of his mind before the murder of Duncan, then after the murder, and finally when, at the end, all his illusions and hopes gone, he faces Macduff. He is one who commits monstrous deeds without becoming wholly a monster, since his knowledge of the right principle is never altogether obscured, though it is almost so in Act IV. We can understand such a person and hence feel fear and pity of a kind for him because he is only doing upon a grander scale and with deeper guilt and more terrifying consequences for himself and others what we can, without too much difficulty, imagine ourselves doing, however less extremely, in circumstances generally similar. For the essential story of *Macbeth* is that of a man, not naturally depraved, who has fallen under the compulsive power of an imagined better state for himself which he can attain only by acting contrary to his normal habits and feelings; who attains this state and then finds that he must continue to act thus, and even worse, in order to hold on to what he has got; who persists and becomes progressively hardened morally in the process; and who then, ultimately, when the once alluring good is about to be taken away from him, faces the loss in terms of what is left of his original character. It is something like this moral universal that underlies, I think, and gives emotional form and power to the main action of *Macbeth*. It is a form that turns upon the difference between what seemingly advantageous crime appears to be in advance to a basically good but incontinent man and what its moral consequences for such a man inevitably are; and the catharsis is effected not merely by the man's deserved overthrow but by his own inner suffering and by his discovery, before it is too late, of what he had not known before he began to act. If we are normal human beings we must abhor his crimes; yet we cannot completely abhor but must rather pity the man himself, and even when he seems most the monster (as Macbeth does in Act IV) we must

still wish for such an outcome as wil be best, under the circumstances, no merely for Scotland but for him.

But if this, or something close to it, i indeed the complex emotional structur intended in *Macbeth*, then we have basis for defining with some precisio the various problems of incident, char acter, thought, imagery, diction, an representation which confronted Shake speare in writing the play, and hence starting-point for discussing, in detai the rationale of its parts. Consider—t take only one instance—the final scene In the light of the obvious consequence of the form I have attributed to th play as a whole, it is not hard to stat what the main problems at this poin are. If the catharsis of the tragedy is t be complete, we must be made to fee both that Macbeth is being killed in just cause and that his state of min and the circumstances of his death ar such as befit a man who, for all hi crimes, has not altogether lost our pit and goodwill. We are of course pre pared for this double response by al that has gone before, and, most im mediately, in the earlier scenes of Act V by the fresh glimpses we are give of the motivation of the avenger and by Macbeth's soliloquies. Bu it will clearly be better if the dua effect can be sustained until the ver end; and this requires, on the one hand that we should be vividly reminded onc more of Macbeth's crimes and the justi fied hatred they have caused and of th prospect of a new and better time whicl his death holds out for Scotland, and on the other hand, that we should b allowed to take satisfaction, at last, i the manner in which Macbeth himsel behaves. The artistic triumph of th scene lies in the completeness wit which both problems are solved: th first in the words and actions of Mac duff, the speeches about young Siward and Malcolm's closing address; the sec ond by a variety of devices, both of in vention and of representation, the ap propriateness of which to the neede effect can be seen if we ask what w would not want Macbeth to do at thi moment. We want him to be killed, as I have said, for his sake no less than that of Scotland; but we would not want him either to seek out Macduff or to flee the encounter when it comes or to "play the Roman fool"; we would not want him to show no recognition of the wrongs he has done Macduff or, when his last trust in the witches has gone, to continue to show fear or to yield or to fight with savage animosity; and he is made to do none of these things, but rather the contraries of all of them, so that he acts in the end as the Macbeth whose praises we have heard in the second scene of the play. And I would suggest that the cathartic effect of these words and acts is reinforced indirectly, in the representation, by the analogy we can hardly help drawing between his conduct now and the earlier conduct of young Siward, for of Macbeth too it can be said that "he parted well and paid his score"; the implication of this analogy is surely one of the functions, though not the only one, which the lines about Siward are intended to serve.

Such are the kinds of hypotheses we need to make if we are to have critical knowledge of the shaping principles of poetic works or of the artistic reasons governing the character and interrelation of their parts. They are working suppositions which, as I have said, both imply and are implied by the particulars of the works for which they are constructed; and they can never be made well by any critic who is not naturally sensitive to such particulars and in the habit of observing them closely. These, however, though indispensable, are not sufficient conditions. It never happens in any inquiry into matters of fact that the particulars we observe determine their own meaning automatically; the concrete or the individual is never intelligible except through the general and the abstract; if we are to allow the facts to speak for themselves, we must in some fashion supply them with a language in which to talk. Hypotheses, in short, are not made out of nothing, but presuppose on the part of the inquirer who forms them a systematic body of concepts relative to the subject-matter with which he is dealing. The critic who proposes to explore hypothetically the structures of poems is in the same predicament; he must bring to his task, inescapably, general ideas about poetic structure, or he can never construct a workable hypothesis about the structure of any poem.

Hence the crucial importance for the practical critic of poetic forms, in the sense we are now giving to this term, of the kind of analytic of poetry outlined earlier in this lecture. From the point of view of the criticism of individual poems, the concepts and distinctions involved in that analytic differ from those which most contemporary critics have been content to use: they supply, not a unified set of terms for constituting structural patterns in poems (like Mr. Heilman's formula for "poetic drama" or the theories that make all good poetry a species of "ironical" or "paradoxical" structure), but a great variety of terms designating distinct and alternative principles, devices, and functions in poetry from which the critic need select only such combinations as appear to be relevant to the poems he is examining. What he thus acquires are not hypotheses ready formed but elements out of which he may form such hypotheses as the facts of his poems seem to warrant—in short, knowledge of structural possibilities only, resting on inductive inquiry into the principles poets have actually used in building poems and hence expanding with the development and progressive differentiation of poetry itself, so that he brings to the discussion of individual poems merely conceptual materials for framing pertinent questions about them without any predetermination of his answers; much as a physician uses the alternatives given him by medical theory in diagnosing symptoms in one of his patients. In the other mode of criticism the relation of theory to a particular poem is the relation of a previously selected idea or pattern of structure to its embodiment or reflection in a given work; here the relation is one of many known possibilities of structural patterning in poetry to the actualization in the poem examined of some one or more of these.

The more extensive and discriminating such general knowledge, therefore, the better the critic's hypotheses are likely to be. But it is also the nature of this kind of theoretical knowledge to be always inadequate, though in varying degrees, to the particulars we use it to illuminate. We can never know in advance all the possibilities, and we can never, consequently, form a hypothesis about a work of any artistic complexity or even about many simpler works without making a shorter or longer inductive leap from the words and sentences before us to the peculiar combination of universals which define their poetic form. And that is why, in this mode of criticism, we can make no real separation between theory and application, the latter being possible only if the former already exists at least up to a certain point and the former being constantly refined and enlarged as we proceed with the latter.

Application, however, is our main problem here, and its success depends upon the extent to which the universal terms of our hypotheses and the perceived and felt particulars of the texts for which they are constructed can be made to fit together. The general conditions are two: first, our ability to keep our explanatory formulas fluid and to submit them to constant revisions in principle or in detail before we transform them into conclusions; second, our willingness to use systematically what has been called "the method of multiple working hypotheses." We have to remember, that is, that the value of a hypothesis is always relative, not merely to the facts it is intended to explain, but to all the other variant hypotheses which the same facts might suggest if only we gave them a chance; that the best hypothesis is simply the best among several possible hypotheses, relevant to the same work or problem, with which

we have actually compared it; and that unless we make such comparisons a regular part of our procedure, we always court the danger of missing either slightly or altogether what our author was really attempting to do.

There are also, in addition to these very general rules, several more particular criteria. Our aim is an explanation and judgment of poetic works in terms of their structural principles; hence, in the first place, the necessity of framing our hypotheses so that they are not descriptive formulas merely but clearly imply practical artistic consequences, in what the writers must or cannot or might well do in the act of writing, for the details of the works they are being used to explain; that is the character, for example, of Aristotle's definition of tragic plot-form in *Poetics* 13, and I have tried to impart a similar character to the statements above about *Macbeth*. The ideal is to have a central principle of explanation that will enable us to see precisely the functional relations between all the particular problems a writer has attempted to solve and the form of his work as a whole, even though we may have to conclude, in some cases, that the relation is a very tenuous one. In the second place, our aim is an explanation and judgment in terms adapted as closely as possible to the peculiar structure and power of the work before us. Hence the necessity of trying to go beyond formulas that imply the work as a whole or any of its parts only generically; as when, for instance, we neglect to distinguish between the different material structures possible in lyrics and treat a particular lyric without regard to such distinctions, or as when we discuss a work like Jane Austen's *Emma* merely as a comedy, failing to see how little this can tell us about its distinctive comic construction. In the third place, we aspire to completeness of explanation; and this means that in framing a hypothesis about any work we must consider everything in the text as significant evidence that involves in any way a free choice on the writer's part between possible alternative things to be done with his materials or ways of doing them at any point. The hypothesis must therefore be complex rather than simple; it must recognize that the same parts may have different functions, including that of mere adornment; and, above all, it cannot be arrived at by giving a privileged position, on *a priori* grounds, to a particular variety of signs of artistic intention, in a complex work, to the exclusion of other and often conflicting signs of the same thing. This last is conspicuously the error of those interpreters of *Macbeth* who have inferred the central form of that play chiefly from the thought and imagery that serve to emphasize the "unnatural" character of the hero's crimes and the inevitability of a just retribution, without attempting to correlate with this the many signs, both in the construction of the plot and in its extraordinarily artful representation, of the distinctive moral quality of Macbeth's actions when these are seen from the inside. There will always be incompleteness in any hypothesis, moreover, that leaves out of account, as one of the crucial facts, the peculiar sequence of emotions we feel when we read the work unbiased by critical doctrine; for, as we have seen, the most important thing about any poetic production is the characteristic power it has to affect us in this definite way rather than that. Completeness, however, is impossible without coherence; hence our hypotheses, in the fourth place, must aim at a maximum of internal unity, on the assumption that, although many works are episodic and although many predominantly imitative works, for example, also have didactic or topical parts, this can best be seen if we begin by presuming that literary artists usually aim at creating wholes.

The only proof there can be of a hypothesis about any particular thing lies in its power of completeness and coherence of explanation within the limits of the data it makes significant—and this always relatively to the other hypotheses pertinent to the same data with which it has been compared. We must be guided, however, in choosing among alternative hypotheses, by a further criterion—the classic criterion of economy: that that hypothesis is the best, other things being equal, which requires the fewest supplementary hypotheses to make it work or which entails the least amount of explaining away; it is no recommendation, thus, for Mr. L. C. Knights's interpretation of *Macbeth* that he says of the emotion aroused in most readers as well as in Bradley by Macbeth's soliloquies in Act V, that this is mere "conventional 'sympathy for the hero,'" which ought not to be allowed to distort that dialectical system of values in the play that is for him "the pattern of the whole." And we must be careful, further, not to construe our "data" in too narrow a sense and so be satisfied with hypotheses that clearly conflict with facts external to the works we are considering but relevant nevertheless to their interpretation; I mean not only such particular evidences as we can often find of writers' intentions—for example, Coleridge's statements about the kind of poem he designed *The Rime of the Ancient Mariner* to be—but also such general probabilities with respect to the works of a given period or genre or with respect to poetic works of any kind or age as are supplied by either our historical knowledge or our common sense. It is not likely, for instance, that a Shakespearean tragedy intended for the popular stage should really have a kind of basic structure which practising playwrights of any time would find it difficult or impossible to make effective for their audiences. Nor is it ever a sensible thing in a critic to cultivate indifference to common opinion about the works he is discussing. The opinion may be wrong or, as often happens, it may need to be corrected and refined; but in such conflicts—at least when they involve the larger aspects and effects of works—the burden of proof is on him. For the secrets of art are not, like the secrets of nature, things lying deeply hid, inaccessible to the perception and understanding of all who have not mastered the special techniques their discovery requires. The critic does, indeed, need special techniques, but for the sake of building upon common sense apprehensions of his objects, not of supplanting these; and few things have done greater harm to the practice and repute of literary criticism in recent times than the assumption that its discoveries, like those of the physical sciences, must gain in importance and plausibility as they become more and more paradoxical in the ancient sense of that word: as if—to adapt a sharp saying of Professor Frank Knight about social studies—now that everybody is agreed that natural phenomena are not like works of art, the business of criticism must be to show that works of art are like natural phenomena.

It remains, finally, to consider the bearing of all this on judgments of poetic value. And the first thing to observe is that, if our hypothesis concerning the shaping principle of any work is adequate, it will give us a basis for saying with some precision (as my example of Act V of *Macbeth* may perhaps suggest) what are the necessities which such a form imposes on any artist whose aim is its successful realization in his materials. Some of them will be necessities common to all self-contained poetic works of no matter what kind, such as the necessity, if the parts are to cohere, of devices for effecting continuity from beginning through middle to end; others will be more and more specific necessities determined by the nature of the form we assume to have been intended, such as the necessity, if a comic effect like that of *Tom Jones* is to be obtained, of keeping the ridiculous mistakes of the hero from obscuring the sympathetic traits that make us wish him ultimate good fortune. These will all be consequences inferable from our basic definition of the form, and our primary task will be to trace them, in detail, throughout the particulars of the work at all its levels from plot or lyric situation down to the imagery and words. A kind of judgment of value will thus emerge in the very process of our analysis: if the

writer has indeed done, somehow, all the essential things he would need to do on the assumption that he is actually writing the kind of work we have defined, then to that extent the work is good, or at least not artistically bad; and we should have to use very little rhetoric in addition to make this clear. But this is only half of the problem, for it is true of most mediocre writers that they usually do, in some fashion, a great part or all of the things their particular forms require, but do little more besides. The crucial question, therefore, concerns not so much the necessities of the assumed form as its possibilities. What is it that the writer might have done, over and above the minimum requirements of his task, which he has not done, or what is it that we have not expected him to do which he has yet triumphantly accomplished? These are the things our analyses ought peculiarly to attend to if they are to be adequate to their objects.

The possible in this sense, as distinguished from the necessary, is that which tends to perfect—to warrant praise of a positive rather than a merely negative kind. We can know it in two ways: by having our minds stored with memories of what both the most and the least perfect of artists have done when confronted with similar problems of invention, representation, and writing; and by considering theoretically the conditions under which any particular effect aimed at in a given work might be better or worse achieved—by asking, for instance, what would in general make a predicament like that of Tom Jones on the discovery of his first affair with Molly seem most completely comic, and then discussing the episode, as it is actually developed by Fielding, in these terms. Both methods are comparative, but the comparisons, if they are not to result in unfair impositions on the writer whose work we are considering, must take account of the fact that the desirable or admirable in literature is never something absolute but is always relative, in any given part of a work, to the requirements of the over-all form and to the function of the part as only one part along with many others: forgetting this, we should make the mistake of Joyce Cary's critic and demand neatness where clumsiness is what "belongs," vividness and particularity where faintness and generality are needed, doing more than is done when this would be doing too much.

The judgments of value we should thus be trying to make would for this reason always be judgments in kind, grounded on a prior definition of the writer's problems as problems peculiar, at least in their concrete determination, to the formal nature of the work he is writing. They would also be judgments in terms of intentions—what is it that the writer aimed to do here and how well has he succeeded in doing it?—but the intentions we should take as principles would not be those, except accidentally, which the writer had stated explicitly before or after writing or those which can be defined for the writer by saying that he must have intended to write this work because this is what he has written. The common objections to criticism based on "intention" in either of these senses are unanswerable. They do not hold, however, when we identify intention with the hypothesized form of a poetic work and then consider how fully what we know of the necessities and possibilities of this form are achieved in the work, on the assumption that, if the work shows any serious concern with art at all, the writer must have wished or been willing to be judged in this way. There is nothing unfair to the writer in such an approach, inasmuch as we are not engaged in a judicial process of bringing his work under a previously formulated general theory of literary value but in a free inquiry whose aim is simply the discovery of those values in his work—among them, we always hope, unprecedented values— which he has been able to put there. They will always be values incident to the relation between the form of the work and its matter at all of its structural levels; and it will be appropriate to interpret what we find in terms of a distinction between three classes of works considered from this point of view: works that are well conceived as wholes but contain few parts the formal excellence of which remains in our memory or invites us to another reading; works that are rich in local virtues but have only a loose or tenuous over-all form; and works that satisfy Coleridge's criterion for a poem, that it aims at "the production of as much immediate pleasure in parts, as is compatible with the largest sum of pleasure in the whole." These last are the few relatively perfect productions in the various literary kinds, and as between the other two we shall naturally prefer the second to the first.

V

All methods, in any field of study, have their characteristic corruptions when they fall into the hands of incompetent practitioners. The corruption of the historical critic is typically some kind of antiquarian irrelevance, as when texts are annotated more learnedly than they need to be or with only a loose pertinence to the problems and difficulties they present. The corruption of the literary critic in the modes of criticism we are chiefly familiar with at the present time is most commonly perhaps a cult of the paradoxical, along with which go, often enough, an addiction to irresponsible analogizing, a preference for metaphorical over literal statement, and a tendency to substitute rhetoric for inquiry as a guiding aim. The critic whose portrait I am drawing in this lecture is less likely, I think, to give way to any of these perversions than to certain others which, though different in kind, are no less to be deplored. In his concern with form, he can all too easily become merely formalistic, attending less to what gives life to poems than to the mechanism of their structural parts; in his concern with poetic wholes, he can be tempted to forget that the wholes have no existence apart from the words through which they are made actual; in his concern with development of theory, he can readily persuade himself that the enunciation of theory, however well established, is more important than the solution of the concrete problems to which it is relevant and so fall into a methodological pedantry as bad as the factual pedantry of the antiquarians.

I do not think, however, that these are inevitable faults, given a certain flexibility of mind, a sensitivity to literary particulars, an ability to resist the spirit of routine and self-satisfaction, and an understanding of the right relation between methods and problems. And when they are not allowed to distort the results, I should contend that the approach I have been describing is capable of giving us more nearly adequate insights into the structural principles and characteristics of poetic works than any of the other modes of critical language with which we have compared it. We may say of these other methods, in terms borrowed from our own, that what they have chiefly concentrated on, in their analyses of structure, has been the matter of poetic works and its generic figurations and techniques rather than their forms. These are essential aspects of the problem, but they are aspects with which we too can deal. We can consider how any element in a poem "works with the other elements to create the effect intended by the poet"; we can discuss the "meaning" of poems in the sense of the thought that is presupposed by or expressed through any of their characteristic devices of statement and representation; we can treat of images and patterns of images and of the subtleties of poetic diction and rhythm; we can find a place for what is sound in the distinction between "structure" and "texture"; and we can make use of all that the "archetypal" critics can tell us about the cultural and psychological universals which poems imply. We can do all these things; but we can also do more, and as a consequence be able to do these things with greater precision and intelligibility.

For we possess what these other methods have conspicuously lacked: a means of isolating and defining those principles of structure in individual poems which distinguish them from other poems or kinds of poems and determine thus in highly specific ways what their distinctive elements are and the artistic reasons that justify the particular configurations we observe them to have. In contrast with our constructive and differentiating procedure, the procedures of these other critical schools have been, in varying degrees, generalizing and reductive. There is reduction, and hence a loss of explanatory particularity, whenever the only terms critics use in talking about literary structures are terms applicable primarily to the writer as distinct in some way from his product (as in F. R. Leavis' discussions of novels as direct reflections of the "complexity" of the novelists' "interests") or whenever the only source of terms is the psychology of readers (as in Miss Bodkin's definition of the "archetypal pattern" of rebirth evoked for her by *The Ancient Mariner*): what can be discovered in such cases is merely a kind of structure that many poems can have, or even other species of writing. There is reduction similarly in any method that draws its only structural formulas from such things as the common figures of poetical or rhetorical language (as in Cleanth Brooks and the Shakespearean critics who speak of plays as "metaphors"), or the nonpoetic forms of myth and ritual, or the supposed patterns of psychic activity. And there is still reduction, though of a less extreme variety, in the critics who equate poetic structure, in all except the most general sense of "aesthetic pattern," exclusively with the conventions of verbal form or thematic arrangement which poets derive from earlier poetic tradition; in the critics, again, who look for fixed and unitary definitions of the poetic genres and discuss individual tragedies, comedies, epics, novels, and lyrics as more or less typical or perfect examples of these various quasi-Platonic forms; in the critics who identify the principles of structure in poems with the "themes" which are either their germinal ideas or moral bases or their underlying schemes of probability; and in the many critics, lastly, who fix their attention on some part of the total structure —on one phase of the action or on the framework of its representation, on a principal character, a "key" passage of thought, a conspicuous train of imagery —and proceed to derive from this their formula for the whole.

What these critics all leave out is thus the very principle we have taken as our starting-point: the shaping principle of form and emotional "power" without which no poem could come into existence as a beautiful and effective whole of a determinate kind. We can therefore talk with a fullness and precision of distinction impossible to them about the particular and widely variant relations which exist in different poems between their formal and their material natures. We are not limited to any one conception of poetic unity or to any one set of concepts for defining structure. We are not forced to speak of the working together of the parts of a poem merely in terms of simple contrarieties of theme or tone or in a vocabulary of which the most exact words are expressions like "goes with," is "associated with," or is "related to" or "carries out," "reflects," "repeats," "qualifies," "balances," "contrasts with," "contradicts," and so on. We are not compelled, in order to show our recognition that the best poetry is not indifferent to thought or "meaning," to interpret all poetic masterpieces in which ideas are contained or evoked as if they were compositions of the same order as *The Divine Comedy,* or, at any rate, in some sense or in some degree, metaphorical or symbolic expressions, or, at the very least, "studies" of something or other. We shall be aware that there are indeed many poetic works to which such descriptions can be applied, but we shall go on the assumption—which all experience and literary history surely warrant—that ideas can function in poems in radically different ways: sometimes as sources of inspiration, sometimes as formal and shaping ends, sometimes as means for constituting the characters, purposes, or states of mind of the *dramatis personae,* sometimes as choric devices for enhancing or universalizing the actions; and the distinctions of our theoretic analysis, and notably our distinction between imitative and nonimitative forms, will enable us to discriminate these various uses when we come upon them and to judge of the significance of the thought in any poem or passage according as one or another of them is its primary cause. And finally, in dealing with the problems of imagery that have been so prominent during the past generation, especially in the criticism of Shakespeare, we are not restricted to either a merely material classification and psychological interpretation of images (as in Miss Spurgeon and her followers) or to a merely generalized and indefinite discussion of their functions in drama (as in some of the more recent Shakespeareans): with our basic distinction of object, manner, and means and our more specific devices for relating the parts of individual works to their controlling forms, we should be able, at the very least, to introduce greater particularity and artistic intelligibility into the subject than are apparent in most of the current discussions.

I look upon this approach, therefore, as one likely to repay a more concentrated effort of research and application than it has received in modern times. It is not a method that lends itself too easily, perhaps, to the immediate purposes of reviewers and professional critics of current productions, but it is not without its utility even here. There must be many readers of such criticism who would be grateful for more precise indications than they usually get of what are the formal as well as the material and technical novelties to be found in the latest serious novels, plays, and volumes of verse, and above all of the kinds of "peculiar pleasure" they are fitted to give us and why. The method is undoubtedly better suited, however, to the more ample and considered criticism of the literature of the past or of contemporary literature when this is made an object of elaborated study; and there is excellent reason to think that the writing of literary history in particular might be radically transformed, and to great advantage, through the inclusion of what I have called the immediate artistic causes of literary productions along with the relatively more external and remote causes to which historians of literature have mainly confined themselves.

And there is another realm in which these principles might be expected to yield benefits—that of literary education. They can give us, for one thing, the basis of a teachable discipline of reading and appreciation which would be exempt, on the one hand, from mere impressionism and the evocation of irresponsible opinion and, on the other hand, from the imposition on students of ready-made literary doctrines or canons of taste. Its essence would be simply the communication to students of a comprehensive scheme of questions to be asked about all the different kinds of literary works they might be studying and of criteria for discussing the appropriateness and adequacy of the answers in the light of the particulars of texts and of the students' responses as human beings to what is going on in them. The development of such a discipline, centered in the statement and free comparison of hypotheses, would help to bring into literary studies something they have commonly lacked—a subject-matter, namely, in the sense not merely of facts but of general concepts for their interpretation; concepts, moreover, that can be translated into habits of observation and reflection such as will tend to make the student independent of his teacher: a potential scholar in criticism rather than a disciple or member of a school, and a scholar who would do credit to his training precisely in proportion as he was able to correct and develop further the things he had been taught. I think that this could be done by a kind of practical and inductive teaching which would keep the student's mind centred on the concrete aspects of

works and his feelings about them rather than on theoretical matters as such and which would, at the same time, build up in him an increasingly clear understanding of what it means to give a reasoned and warranted answer to a critical question and also, to an extent greater than has been common in the teaching of criticism, of how essential it is, if the answer is to be valid, that it accord with whatever truths the student has learned in the linguistic and historical parts of his education. For it is hard to see how the training I am suggesting could be carried on successfully without bringing criticism and these other disciplines into closer mutual relations than have existed between them for a long time.

We might expect, moreover, that such training would encourage a kind of appreciation of literary masterpieces that has been largely neglected in the critical tradition upon which our teaching has hitherto, in the main, been founded. The strength of that tradition has been its sensitiveness to the qualities and values which literary works share with one another or with other modes of expression—to these rather than to the differentiated characteristics of works which are what they are by virtue primarily of their writers' individual acts of poetic making. And it is not at all to minimize the importance of analogies and common principles in criticism to suggest that any literary culture is incomplete that does not lead also to a discriminating understanding, such as the training I propose is suited to give, of the peculiar principles of construction that contribute to make poetry the complex and richly diversified experience we all feel it to be. We may say indeed that what chiefly distinguishes the genius of literary study, as of the humanities in general, from the genius of science is that it naturally aspires to this kind of completion, not being permanently satisfied with reductions of the individual and the specific to the common, and perpetually feeling the need for distinctions and methods that will help us to do justice to the inventiveness of man and the uniqueness of his works.

And along with this would go a third benefit, in the capacity of our principles to maintain the integrity of literary appreciation without cutting it off formalistically from the life which literary works represent or attempt to guide. It is difficult to keep this balance in any of the critical languages in which the basic distinction for the analysis and judgment of works is some variant of the ancient dichotomy of *verba* and *res*; for if we distinguish thus between art and what art expresses, between poetic language and poetic thought, structure and idea, technique and meaning, symbol and concept, "presentment" and the moral "interests" of writers, we inevitably tend to regard one or the other of these two aspects as primary in importance. Our teaching of literature, consequently, in so far as it is "literary," appears far removed from common experience and human emotion, and in so far as it throws the emphasis on content, on questions of knowledge and behavior, runs the risk of becoming merely an amateur branch of ethics, psychology, sociology, anthropology, or the history of ideas.

These disadvantages very largely disappear, I think, when we bring to the discussion of poetic works our radically different distinction of matter and form. For form as we conceive it is simply that which gives definite shape, emotional power, and beauty to the materials of man's experience out of which the writer has composed his work. Hence it cannot be separated as mere "form" from the matter in which it exists, nor can we talk about it adequately (as I have tried to illustrate in my discussion of *Macbeth*) without talking at the same time about the human qualities of the actions, persons, feelings, and thoughts the work brings before us and the very human, but no less poetic, responses these evoke in our minds. There can thus be no good "literary" criticism, in this language, that does not presuppose a constant making of moral and psychological discrimina-

tions and a constant concern with nuances of thought, as well as with subtleties of language and technique; what keeps it "literary" or "poetic" and prevents it from degenerating into either "studies in character" or excursions into philosophy and social history is the direction imposed on our questions about the "content" of works by our hypotheses concerning their shaping principles of form. We can agree, therefore, with the critics who hold that we ought to deal with poetry as poetry and not another thing, and we can agree no less with those who insist that one of the main tasks of criticism is to show the "relevance" of poems to "life"; only these, for us, are not two tasks but one. And I would state a further point in the same connection, the bearing of which will be evident to those who have grown impatient with the current tendency to reduce all questions of morals and politics to questions of ideologies and beliefs. The counterpart of this "rationalism" in literary studies is the assumption that "relevance to life" in poetry is a matter primarily of "themes" and "imaginative visions," so that no imaginative work can be taken seriously from which we cannot extract a "total meaning" over and above the human particulars it exhibits, which we then set forth as what the work is intending to say. From this narrowing of the scope of literary values to such values as only earnest modern intellectuals can think of greater importance than the spectacle of individual men doing and suffering, we have, fortunately, an effective way of escape in our distinction between imitative and didactic forms. We can accord a proper appreciation, in their own terms, to works of which the formal principles are clearly ideas. But we are free to discuss the others, including notably the tragedies of Shakespeare, in a way that fully respects their seriousness, and the implication of universals in the working out of their plots, without being committed to the dehumanizing supposition that the moral habits and dispositions of individual persons and the qualities and circumstances of their actions are things less valuable for us, as men and citizens, to contemplate in literature than the pale abstractions by which they have been overlaid in the prevailing modes of interpretation. And so we might contribute not only to a more discriminating understanding of what literature as literature can do but to a kind of training in concrete moral and social perception, unbiased by doctrine, such as all who live in a free society would be the better for having.

VI

When all this is said, however, it is still true that what I have been talking about in this lecture is only one out of many possible legitimate approaches to the question of poetic structure, not to speak of the innumerable other questions with which critics can profitably concern themselves. I should not want to leave the impression, therefore, that I think it the only mode of criticism seriously worth cultivation at the present time by either teachers of literature or critics, but simply that its development, along with the others, might have many fruitful consequences for our teaching and criticism generally. What distinguishes it from the other modes is its preoccupation with the immediate constructive problems of writers in the making of individual works and with the artistic reasoning necessarily involved in their successful solution. Its claim to consideration is that it can deal with these matters more precisely and adequately, and with a more complete reliance on the canons of inductive inquiry, unhampered by doctrinal preconceptions, than any of the other existing critical languages. It can give us, consequently, a body of primary literary facts about literary works, in their aspect as concrete wholes, in the light of which we can judge the relevance and validity —or see the precise bearing—of such observations and statements of value as result from the application to the same works of other critical principles and

procedures: if the structural principles of *Macbeth* are actually what we have taken them to be, then whatever else may be truly said about this work, in answer to other questions or in the context of other ways of reasoning about them, must obviously be capable of being brought into harmony with this prior factual knowledge of the distinctive how and why of their construction. Here is something, therefore, which critics who prefer a more generalizing or a more speculative approach to literary works can hardly neglect if they wish to be responsible students of literature rather than merely rhetoricians bent on exploiting favorite theses at any cost. For though it is true enough, for example, that what writers do is conditioned by their personal lives and complexes, their social circumstances, and their literary traditions, there is always a risk that exclusive explanations of literary peculiarities in terms of such remoter causes will collapse and seem absurd as soon as we consider, for any work to which they have been applied, what are the immediate artistic exigencies which its writer faced because of his choice of form or manner in this particular work. These exigencies can never be safely disregarded so long as the genetic relation between art and its sources and materials in life remains the very indirect relation we know it is; and it is perhaps not the least of the utilities to be found in the criticism of forms that its cultivation, in a context of the many other kinds of critical inquiry, would help to keep critics of all schools constantly reminded of their existence and importance.

But the other kinds ought to be there. Of the truth about literature, no critical language can ever have a monopoly or even a distant approach to one; and there are obviously many things which the language I have been speaking of cannot do. It is a method not at all suited, as is criticism in the grand line of Longinus, Coleridge, and Matthew Arnold, to the definition and appreciation of those general qualities of writing—mirroring the souls of writers—for the sake of which most of us read or at any rate return to what we have read. It is a method that necessarily abstracts from history and hence requires to be supplemented by other very different procedures if we are to replace the works we study in the circumstances and temper of their times and see them as expressions and forces as well as objects of art. It is a method, above all, that fails, because of its essentially differentiating character, to give us insights into the larger moral and political values of literature or into any of the other organic relations with human nature and human experience in which literature is involved. And yet who will say that these are not as compelling considerations for criticism as anything comprised in the problem of poetic structure as we have been discussing it in these lectures? The moral is surely that we ought to have at our command, collectively at least, as many different critical methods as there are distinguishable major aspects in the construction, appreciation, and use of literary works. The multiplicity of critical languages is therefore something not to be deplored but rather rejoiced in, as making possible a fuller exploration of our subject in its total extent than we could otherwise attain; and for my part I have as fond a regard for Longinus and for the masters of historical criticism as I have for Aristotle, and as strong a conviction of their continuing utility. Nor will there ever cease to be use for criticism of the less rigorous or more imaginative types—in directing attention to aspects of poems which only a new model or analogy can bring into view, in formulating and promoting new ideals of poetic excellence or new poetic styles, in suggesting to poets unrealized possibilities in subject-matter and language, in relating poetry, for readers, to large non-poetic human contexts of emotion and meaning, in keeping the life of poetry and of taste from declining into orthodoxy and routine.

The best hope for criticism in the future, indeed, lies in the perpetuation of this multiplicity; nothing could be more damaging than the practical success of any effort to define authoritatively the frontiers and problems of our subject or to assign to each of its variant languages a determinate place in a single hierarchy of critical modes. Better far than that the chaos of schools and splinter parties we have with us now! But there need be no such choice; for the great obstacle to advance in criticism is not the existence of independent groups of critics each pursuing separate interests, but the spirit of exclusive dogmatism which keeps them from learning what they might from one another; and for that the only effective remedy, I think, is to take to heart the two lessons which the persistence throughout history of many distinct critical languages ought to teach us. The first is the lesson of self-knowledge. We can attempt to become more clearly aware than we have usually been of just what it is that we ourselves are doing—and why—when we make critical statements of any kind, and at the same time try to extend that clarity, in as intellectually sympathetic a way as possible, to the statements of other critics, and especially to those that appear to be most inconsistent with our own. And it will be all the easier to attain this self-understanding, with its natural discouragements to doctrinal prejudice, if we also learn the second lesson, and come habitually to think of the various critical languages of the past and present, including our own, no longer as rival attempts to foreclose the "real" or "only profitable" truth about poetry, so that we have to choose among them as we choose among religious dogmas or political causes, but simply as tools of our trade—as so many distinct conceptual and logical means, each with its peculiar capacities and limitations, for solving truly the many distinct kinds of problems which poetry, in its magnificent variety of aspects, presents to our view.

NORTHROP FRYE

(b. 1912)

A scholar critic well known for his studies of symbol and myth in literature, Northrop Frye is the author of *Fearful Symmetry, a Study of William Blake* (1947). His *Anatomy of Criticism, Four Essays* (1957) is a theoretical work aiming at a synoptic view of interrelated categories of historical, ethical, archetypal, and rhetorical criticism. The foundation of Frye's theory is a conception of the archetype which is modified and extended beyond its formulation by C. G. Jung.

Anagogic Phase: Symbol as Monad (1957)

In tracing the different phases of literary symbolism, we have been going up a sequence parallel to that of medieval criticism. We have, it is true, established a different meaning for the word "literal." It is our second or descriptive level that corresponds to the historical or literal one of the medieval scheme, or at any rate of Dante's version of it. Our third level, the level of commentary and interpretation, is the second or allegorical level of the Middle Ages. Our fourth level, the study of myths, and of poetry as a technique of social communication, is the third medieval level of moral and tropological meaning, concerned at once with the social and the figurative aspect of meaning. The medieval distinction between the allegorical as what one believes (*quid credas*) and the moral as what one does (*quid agas*) is also reflected in our conception of the formal phase as aesthetic or speculative and the archetypal phase as social and part of the continuum of work. We have now to see if we can establish a modern parallel to the medieval conception of anagogy or universal meaning.

Again, the reader may have noticed a parallelism gradually shaping up between the five modes of our first essay and the phases of symbolism in this one.

Literal meaning, as we expounded it, has much to do with the techniques of thematic irony introduced by *symbolisme*, and with the view of many of the "new" critics that poetry is primarily (i.e., literally) an ironic structure. Descriptive symbolism, shown at its most uncompromising in the documentary naturalism of the nineteenth century, seems to bear a close connection with the low mimetic, and formal symbolism, most easily studied in Renaissance and neo-Classical writers, with the high mimetic. Archetypal criticism seems to find its center of gravity in the mode of romance, when the interchange of ballads, folk tales, and popular stories was at its easiest. If the parallel holds, then, the last phase of symbolism will still be concerned, as the previous one was, with the mythopoeic aspect of literature, but with myth in its narrower and more technical sense of fictions and themes relating to divine or quasi-divine beings and powers.

We have associated archetypes and myths particularly with primitive and popular literature. In fact we could almost define popular literature, admittedly in a rather circular way, as literature which affords an unobstructed view of archetypes. We can find this quality on every level of literature: in fairy tales and folk tales, in Shakespeare (in most of the comedies), in the Bible (which would still be a popular book if it were not a sacred one), in

unyan, in Richardson, in Dickens, in
'oe, and of course in a vast amount of
phemeral rubbish as well. We began
his book by remarking that we cannot
orrelate popularity and value. But there
s still the danger of reduction, or as-
uming that literature is *essentially*
rimitive and popular. This view had a
reat vogue in the nineteenth century,
nd is by no means dead yet, but if we
vere to adopt it we should cut off a
hird and most important source of sup-
ly for archetypal criticism.

We notice that many learned and
econdite writers whose work requires
atient study are explicitly mythopoeic
vriters. Instances include Dante and
penser, and in the twentieth century
mbrace nearly all the "difficult" writers
n both poetry and prose. Such work,
vhen fictional, is often founded on a
asis of naive drama (*Faust, Peer Gynt*)
r naive romance (Hawthorne, Mel-
ille: one may compare the sophisticated
llegories of Charles Williams and C. S.
.ewis in our day, which are largely
ased on the formulas of the Boy's Own
'aper). Learned mythopoeia, as we have
: in the last period of Henry James and
n James Joyce, for example, may be-
ome bewilderingly complex; but the
omplexities are designed to reveal and
ot to disguise the myth. We cannot
ssume that a primitive and popular
ayth has been swathed like a mummy
n elaborate verbiage, which is the as-
umption that the fallacy of reduction
ould lead to. The inference seems to
e that the learned and the subtle, like
ne primitive and the popular, tend to-
vard a center of imaginative experience.
Knowing that *The Two Gentlemen of
'erona* is an early Shakespeare comedy
nd *The Winter's Tale* a late one, the
:udent would expect the later play to
e more subtle and complex; he might
ot expect it to be more archaic and
rimitive, more suggestive of ancient
ayths and rituals. The later play is also
nore popular, though not popular of
ourse in the sense of giving a lower-
niddle class audience what it thinks it
vants. As a result of expressing the
nner forms of drama with increasing
orce and intensity, Shakespeare arrived

in his last period at the bedrock of
drama, the romantic spectacle out of
which all the more specialized forms of
drama, such as tragedy and social
comedy, have come, and to which they
recurrently return. In the greatest
moments of Dante and Shakespeare, in,
say *The Tempest* or the climax of the
Purgatorio, we have a feeling of converging significance, the feeling that here
we are close to seeing what our whole
literary experience has been about, the
feeling that we have moved into the still
center of the order of words. Criticism
as knowledge, the criticism which is
compelled to keep on talking about the
subject, recognizes the fact that there *is*
a center of the order of words.

Unless there is such a center, there is
nothing to prevent the analogies supplied by convention and genre from
being an endless series of free associations, perhaps suggestive, perhaps even
tantalizing, but never creating a real
structure. The study of archetypes is the
study of literary symbols as parts of a
whole. If there are such things as archetypes at all, then, we have to take yet
another step, and conceive the possibility of a self-contained literary universe. Either archetypal criticism is a
will-o'-the-wisp, an endless labyrinth
without an outlet, or we have to assume
that literature is a total form, and not
simply the name given to the aggregate
of existing literary works. We spoke before of the mythical view of literature as
leading to the conception of an order of
nature as a whole being imitated by a
corresponding order of words.

If archetypes are communicable symbols, and there is a center of archetypes, we should expect to find, at that
center, a group of universal symbols.
I do not mean by this phrase that there
is any archetypal code book which has
been memorized by all human societies
without exception. I mean that some
symbols are images of things common
to all men, and therefore have a communicable power which is potentially
unlimited. Such symbols include those
of food and drink, of the quest or
journey, of light and darkness, and of
sexual fulfilment, which would usually

take the form of marriage. It is inadvisable to assume that an Adonis or Oedipus myth is universal, or that certain associations, such as the serpent with the phallus, are universal, because when we discover a group of people who know nothing of such matters we must assume that they did know and have forgotten, or do know and won't tell, or are not members of the human race. On the other hand, they may be confidently excluded from the human race if they cannot understand the conception of food, and so any symbolism founded on food is universal in the sense of having an indefinitely extensive scope. That is, there are no limits to its intelligibility.

In the archetypal phase the work of literary art is a myth, and unites the ritual and the dream. By doing so it limits the dream: it makes it plausible and acceptable to a social waking consciousness. Thus as a moral fact in civilization, literature embodies a good deal of the spirit which in the dream itself is called the censor. But the censor stands in the way of the impetus of the dream. When we look at the dream as a whole, we notice three things about it. First, its limits are not the real, but the conceivable. Second, the limit of the conceivable is the world of fulfilled desire emancipated from all anxieties and frustrations. Third, the universe of the dream is entirely within the mind of the dreamer.

In the anagogic phase, literature imitates the total dream of man, and so imitates the thought of a human mind which is at the circumference and not at the center of its reality. We see here the completion of the imaginative revolution begun when we passed from the descriptive to the formal phase of symbolism. There, the imitation of nature shifted from a reflection of external nature to a formal organization of which nature was the content. But in the formal phase the poem is still contained by nature, and in the archetypal phase the whole of poetry is still contained within the limits of the natural, or plausible. When we pass into anagogy, nature becomes, not the container, but the thing contained, and the archetypal universal symbols, the city, the garden, the quest, the marriage, are no longer the desirable forms that man constructs inside nature, but are themselves the forms of nature. Nature is now inside the mind of an infinite man who builds his cities out of the Milky Way. This is not reality, but it is the conceivable or imaginative limit of desire, which is infinite, eternal, and hence apocalyptic. By an apocalypse I mean primarily the imaginative conception of the whole of nature as the content of an infinite and eternal living body which, if not human, is closer to being human than to being inanimate. "The desire of man being infinite," said Blake, "the possession is infinite and himself infinite." If Blake is thought a prejudiced witness on this point, we may cite Hooker: "That there is somewhat higher than either of these two (sensual and intellectual perfection), no other proof doth need than the very process of man's desire, which being natural should be frustrate, if there were not some farther thing wherein it might rest at the length contented, which in the former it cannot do."

If we turn to ritual, we see there an imitation of nature which has a strong element of what we call magic in it. Magic seems to begin as something of a voluntary effort to recapture a lost rapport with the natural cycle. This sense of a deliberate recapturing of something no longer possessed is a distinctive mark of human ritual. Ritual constructs a calendar and endeavors to imitate the precise and sensitive accuracy of the movements of the heavenly bodies and the response of vegetation to them. A farmer must harvest his crop at a certain time of the year, but because he must do this anyway, harvesting itself is not precisely a ritual. It is the expression of a will to synchronize human and natural energies at that time which produces the harvest songs, harvest sacrifices, and harvest folk customs that we associate with ritual. But the impetus of the magical element in ritual is clearly toward a universe in which a stupid and ndifferent nature is no longer the container of human society, but is contained by that society, and must rain or shine at the pleasure of man. We notice too the tendency of ritual to become not only cyclical but encyclopaedic, as already noted. In its anagogic phase, then, poetry imitates human action as total ritual, and so imitates the action of an omnipotent human society that contains all the powers of nature within itself.

Anagogically, then, poetry unites total ritual, or unlimited social action, with total dream, or unlimited individual thought. Its universe is infinite and boundless hypothesis: it cannot be contained within any actual civilization or set of moral values, for the same reason that no structure of imagery can be restricted to one allegorical interpretation. Here the *dianoia* of art is no longer a *mimesis logou,* but the Logos, the shaping word which is both reason and, as Goethe's Faust speculated, *praxis* or creative act. The *ethos* of art is no longer a group of characters within a natural setting, but a universal man who is also a divine being, or a divine being conceived in anthropomorphic terms.

The form of literature most deeply influenced by the anagogic phase is the scripture or apocalyptic revelation. The god, whether traditional deity, glorified hero, or apotheosized poet, is the central image that poetry uses in trying to convey the sense of unlimited power in a humanized form. Many of these scriptures are documents of religion as well, and hence are a mixture of the imaginative and the existential. When they lose their existential content they become purely imaginative, as Classical mythology did after the rise of Christianity. They belong in general, of course, to the mythical or theogonic mode. We see the relation to anagogy also in the vast encyclopaedic structure of poetry that seems to be a whole world in itself, that stands in its culture as an inexhaustible storehouse of imaginative suggestion, and seems, like theories of gravitation or relativity in the physical universe, to be applicable to, or have analogous connec-tions with, every part of the literary universe. Such works are definitive myths, or complete organizations of archetypes. They include what in the previous essay we called analogies of revelation: the epics of Dante and Milton and their counterparts in the other modes.

But the anagogic perspective is not to be confined only to works that seem to take in everything, for the principle of anagogy is not simply that everything is the subject of poetry, but that anything may be the subject of a poem. The sense of the infinitely varied unity of poetry may come, not only explicitly from an apocalyptic epic, but implicitly from any poem. We said that we could get a whole liberal education by picking up one conventional poem, *Lycidas* for example, and following its archetypes through literature. Thus the center of the literary universe is whatever poem we happen to be reading. One step further, and the poem appears as a microcosm of all literature, an individual manifestation of the total order of words. Anagogically, then, the symbol is a monad, all symbols being united in a single infinite and eternal verbal symbol which is, as *dianoia,* the Logos, and, as *mythos,* total creative act. It is this conception which Joyce expresses, in terms of subject-matter, as "epiphany," and Hopkins, in terms of form, as "inscape."

If we look at *Lycidas* anagogically, for example, we see that the subject of the elegy has been identified with a god who personifies both the sun that falls into the western ocean at night and the vegetable life that dies in the autumn. In the latter aspect Lycidas is the Adonis or Tammuz whose "annual wound," as Milton calls it elsewhere, was the subject of a ritual lament in Mediterranean religion, and has been incorporated in the pastoral elegy since Theocritus, as the title of Shelley's *Adonais* shows more clearly. As a poet, Lycidas's archetype is Orpheus, who also died young, in much the same role as Adonis, and was flung into the water. As priest, his archetype is Peter, who would have drowned on the "Galilean lake" without the help of

Christ. Each aspect of *Lycidas* poses the question of premature death as it relates to the life of man, of poetry, and of the Church. But all of these aspects are contained within the figure of Christ, the young dying god who is eternally alive, the Word that contains all poetry, the head and body of the Church, the good Shepherd whose pastoral world sees no winter, the Sun of righteousness that never sets, whose power can raise Lycidas, like Peter, out of the waves, as it redeems souls from the lower world, which Orpheus failed to do. Christ does not enter the poem as a character, but he pervades every line of it so completely that the poem, so to speak, enters him.

Anagogic criticism is usually found in direct connection with religion, and is to be discovered chiefly in the more uninhibited utterances of poets themselves. It comes out in those passages of Eliot's quartets where the words of the poet are placed within the context of the incarnate Word. An even clearer statement is in a letter of Rilke, where he speaks of the function of the poet as revealing a perspective of reality like that of an angel, containing all time and space, who is blind and looking into himself. Rilke's angel is a modification of the more usual god or Christ, and his statement is all the more valuable because it is explicitly not Christian, and illustrates the independence of the anagogic perspective, of the poet's attempt to speak from the circumference instead of from the center of reality, from the acceptance of any specific religion. Similar views are expressed or implied in Valéry's conception of a total intelligence which appears more fancifully in his figure of M. Teste; in Yeats's cryptic utterances about the artifice of eternity, and, in *The Tower* and elsewhere, about man as the creator of all creation as well as of both life and death; in Joyce's non-theological use of the theological term epiphany; in Dylan Thomas's exultant hymns to a universal human body. We may note in passing that the more sharply we distinguish the poetic and the critical functions, the easier it is for us to take seriously what great writers have said about their work.

The anagogic view of criticism thus leads to the conception of literature as existing in its own universe, no longer a commentary on life or reality, but containing life and reality in a system of verbal relationships. From this point of view the critic can no longer think of literature as a tiny palace of art looking out upon an inconceivably gigantic "life." "Life" for him has become the seed-plot of literature, a vast mass of potential literary forms, only a few of which will grow up into the greater world of the literary universe. Similar universes exist for all the arts. "We make to ourselves pictures of facts," says Wittgenstein, but by pictures he means representative illustrations, which are not pictures. Pictures as pictures are themselves facts, and exist only in a pictorial universe. "Tout, au monde," says Mallarmé, "existe pour aboutir à un livre."

So far we have been dealing with symbols as isolated units, but clearly the unit of relationship between two symbols, corresponding to the phrase in music, is of equal importance. The testimony of critics from Aristotle on seems fairly unanimous that this unit of relationship is the metaphor. And the metaphor, in its radical form, is a statement of identity of the "A is B" type, or rather, putting it into its proper hypothetical form, of the "let X be Y" type (letters altered for euphony). Thus the metaphor turns its back on ordinary descriptive meaning, and presents a structure which literally is ironic and paradoxical. In ordinary descriptive meaning, if A is B then B is A, and all we have really said is that A is itself. In the metaphor two things are identified while each retains its own form. Thus if we say "the hero was a lion" we identify the hero *with* the lion, while at the same time both the hero and the lion are identified *as* themselves. A work of literary art owes its unity to this process of identification *with*, and its variety, clarity, and intensity to identification *as*.

On the literal level of meaning, metaphor appears in its literal shape, which is simple juxtaposition. Ezra Pound, in explaining this aspect of the metaphor, uses the illustrative figure of the Chinese ideogram, which expresses a complex image by throwing a group of elements together without predication. In Pound's famous blackboard example of such a metaphor, the two-line poem "In a Station of the Metro," the images of the faces in the crowd and the petals on the black bough are juxtaposed with no predicate of any kind connecting them. Predication belongs to assertion and descriptive meaning, not to the literal structure of poetry.

On the descriptive level we have the double perspective of the verbal structure and the phenomena to which it is related. Here meaning is "literal" in the common sense which we explained would not do for criticism, an unambiguous alignment of words and facts. Descriptively, then, all metaphors are similes. When we are writing ordinary discursive prose and use a metaphor, we are not asserting that A is B; we are "really" saying that A is in some respects comparable with B; and similarly when we are extracting the descriptive or paraphrasable meaning of a poem. "The hero was a lion," then, on the descriptive level, is a simile with the word "like" omitted for greater vividness, and to show more clearly that the analogy is only a hypothetical one. In Whitman's poem *Out of the Cradle Endlessly Rocking*, we find shadows "twining and twisting as if they were alive," and the moon swollen "as if with tears." As there is no *poetic* reason why shadows should not be alive or the moon tearful, we may perhaps see in the cautious "as if" the working of a low mimetic discursive prose conscience.

On the formal level, where symbols are images or natural phenomena conceived as matter or content, the metaphor is an analogy of natural propor-

tion. Literally, metaphor is juxtaposition; we say simply "A; B." Descriptively, we say "A is (like) B." But formally we say "A is as B." An analogy of proportion thus requires four terms, of which two have a common factor. Thus "the hero was a lion" means, as a form of expression which has nature for its internal content, that the hero is to human courage as the lion is to animal courage, courage being the factor common to the third and fourth terms.

Archetypally, where the symbol is an associative cluster, the metaphor unites two individual images, each of which is a specific representative of a class or genus. The rose in Dante's *Paradiso* and the rose in Yeats's early lyrics are identified *with* different things, but both stand for all roses—all poetic roses, of course, not all botanical ones. Archetypal metaphor thus involves the use of what has been called the concrete universal, the individual identified with its class, Wordsworth's "tree of many one." Of course there are no *real* universals in poetry, only poetic ones. All four of these aspects of metaphor are recognized in Aristotle's discussion of metaphor in the *Poetics*, though sometimes very briefly and elliptically.

In the anagogic aspect of meaning, the radical form of metaphor, "A is B," comes into its own. Here we are dealing with poetry in its totality, in which the formula "A is B" may be hypothetically applied to anything, for there is no metaphor, not even "black is white," which a reader has any right to quarrel with in advance. The literary universe, therefore, is a universe in which everything is potentially identical with everything else. This does not mean that any two things in it are separate and very similar, like peas in a pod, or in the slangy and erroneous sense of the word in which we speak of identical twins. If twins were really identical they would be the same person. On the other hand, a grown man feels identical with himself at the age of seven, although the two manifestations of this identity, the man and the boy, have very little in common as regards similarity or likeness. In form, matter, personality, time, and space, man and boy are quite unlike. This is the only type of image I can think of that illustrates the process of identifying two independent forms. All poetry, then, proceeds as though all poetic images were contained within a single universal body. Identity is the opposite of similarity or likeness, and total identity is not uniformity, still less monotony, but a unity of various things.

Finally, identification belongs not only to the structure of poetry, but to the structure of criticism as well, at least of commentary. Interpretation proceeds by metaphor as well as creation, and even more explicitly. When St. Paul interprets the story of Abraham's wives in Genesis, for instance, he says that Hagar "is" Mount Sinai in Arabia. Poetry, said Coleridge, is the identity of knowledge.

The universe of poetry, however, is a literary universe, and not a separate existential universe. Apocalypse means revelation, and when art becomes apocalyptic, it reveals. But it reveals only on its own terms, and in its own forms: it does not describe or represent a separate content of revelation. When poet and critic pass from the archetypal to the anagogic phase, they enter a phase of which only religion, or something as infinite in its range as religion, can possibly form an external goal. The poetic imagination, unless it disciplines itself in the particular way in which the imaginations of Hardy and Housman were disciplined, is apt to get claustrophobia when it is allowed to talk only about human nature and subhuman nature; and poets are happier as servants of religion than of politics, because the transcendental and apocalyptic perspective of religion comes as a tremendous emancipation of the imaginative mind. If men were compelled to make the melancholy choice between atheism and superstition, the scientist, as Bacon pointed out long ago, would be compelled to choose atheism, but the poet would be compelled to choose supersti-

tion, for even superstition, by its ver[y] confusion of values, gives his imagina[-] tion more scope than a dogmatic denia[l] of imaginative infinity does. But th[e] loftiest religion, no less than the grosses[t] superstition, comes to the poet, *qu[a]* poet, only as the spirits came to Yeat[s] to give him metaphors for poetry.

The study of literature takes us to[-] ward seeing poetry as the imitation o[f] infinite social action and infinite hum[an] thought, the mind of a man who is a[ll] men, the universal creative word whic[h] is all words. About this man and wor[d] we can, speaking as critics, say only on[e] thing ontologically: we have no reaso[n] to suppose either that they exist or tha[t] they do not exist. We can call the[m] divine if by divine we mean the un[-] limited or projected human. But th[e] critic, *qua* critic, has nothing to say fo[r] or against the affirmations that a rel[i-] gion makes out of these conceptions. [If] Christianity wishes to identify the inf[i-] nite Word and Man of the literary uni[-] verse with the Word of God, the perso[n] of Christ, the historical Jesus, the Bib[le] or church dogma, these identification[s] may be accepted by any poet or criti[c] without injury to his work—the accept[-] ance may even clarify and intensify h[is] work, depending on his temperame[nt] and situation. But they can never be ac[-] cepted by poetry as a whole, or by crit[i-] cism as such. The literary critic, like th[e] historian, is compelled to treat every re[-] ligion in the same way that religion[s] treat each other, as though it were [a] human hypothesis, whatever else h[e] may in other contexts believe it to b[e.] The discussion of the universal Word a[t] the opening of the Chhandogya Upan[-] ishad (where it is symbolized by th[e] sacred word "Aum") is exactly as rele[-] vant and as irrelevant to literary criti[-] cism as the discussion at the opening o[f] the Fourth Gospel. Coleridge was righ[t] in thinking that the "Logos" was th[e] goal of his works as a critic, but no[t] right in thinking that his poetic Logo[s] would so inevitably be absorbed int[o] Christ as to make literary criticism [a] kind of natural theology.

The total Logos of criticism by itself can never become an object of faith or an ontological personality. The conception of a total Word is the postulate that there is such a thing as an order of words, and that the criticism which studies it makes, or could make, complete sense. Aristotle's *Physics* leads to the conception of an unmoved first mover at the circumference of the physical universe. This, in itself, means essentially that physics *has* a universe. The systematic study of motion would be impossible unless all phenomena of motion could be related to unifying principles, and those in their turn to a total unifying principle of movement which is not itself merely another phenomenon of motion. If theology identifies Aristotle's unmoved mover with a creating God, that is the business of theology; physics as physics will be unaffected by it. Christian critics may see their total Word as an analogy of Christ, as medieval critics did, but as literature itself may be accompanied in culture by any religion, criticism must detach itself accordingly. In short, the study of literature belongs to the "humanities," and the humanities, as their name indicates, can take only the human view of the superhuman.

The close resemblance between the conceptions of anagogic criticism and those of religion has led many to assume that they can only be related by making one supreme and the other subordinate. Those who choose religion, like Coleridge, will, like him, try to make criticism a natural theology; those who choose culture, like Arnold, will try to reduce religion to objectified cultural myth. But for the purity of each the autonomy of each must be guaranteed. Culture interposes, between the ordinary and the religious life, a total vision of possibilities, and insists on its totality —for whatever is excluded from culture by religion or state will get its revenge somehow. Thus culture's essential service to a religion is to destroy intellectual idolatry, the recurrent tendency in religion to replace the object of its worship with its present understanding and forms of approach to that object. Just as no argument in favor of a religious or political doctrine is of any value unless it is an intellectually honest argument, and so guarantees the autonomy of logic, so no religious or political myth is either valuable or valid unless it assumes the autonomy of culture, which may be provisionally defined as the total body of imaginative hypothesis in a society and its tradition. To defend the autonomy of culture in this sense seems to me the social task of the "intellectual" in the modern world: if so, to defend its subordination to a total synthesis of any kind, religious or political, would be the authentic form of the *trahison des clercs*.

Besides, it is of the essence of imaginative culture that it transcends the limits both of the naturally possible and of the morally acceptable. The argument that there is no room for poets in any human society which is an end in itself remains unanswerable even when the society is the people of God. For religion is also a social institution, and so far as it is one, it imposes limitations on the arts just as a Marxist or Platonic state would do. Christian theology is no less of a revolutionary dialectic, or indissoluble union of theory and social practice. Religions, in spite of their enlarged perspective, cannot as social institutions *contain* an art of unlimited hypothesis. The arts in their turn cannot help releasing the powerful acids of satire, realism, ribaldry, and fantasy in their attempt to dissolve all the existential concretions that get in their way. The artist often enough has to find that, as God says in *Faust*, he "muss als Teufel schaffen," which I suppose means rather more than that he has to work like the devil. Between religion's "this is" and poetry's "but suppose *this* is," there must always be some kind of tension, until the possible and the actual meet at infinity. Nobody wants a poet in the perfect human state, and, as even the poets tell us, nobody but God himself can tolerate a poltergeist in the City of God.

FRANK KERMODE

(b. 1919)

An English university professor and critic, Frank Kermode is well known as both a Renaissance scholar and a student of modern literature. The essay "Dissociation of Sensibility" also appears in modified form in his *Romantic Image* (1957), a reappraisal of the literary and critical theory of the modern symbolist tradition. Mr. Kermode's other works include *The Living Milton* (1961), *Wallace Stevens* (1960), and *Puzzles and Epiphanies* (1962).

Dissociation of Sensibility (1957)

The "dissociation of sensibility" has lately been wilting under well-directed criticism, and it may seem gratuitous at this stage to examine the concept in so much detail. But although it is "going out," like Donne, there are two good reasons for paying it this attention. The first is that, though it may soon be bad form for anybody to use the term, a whole generation has grown up believing in a pattern, applicable not only to poetry but to general intellectual history, formed and codified by the expression "dissociation of sensibility"; in other words we are still likely to have the effects of the doctrine though the doctrine itself is démodé. There are plenty of signs that critics whose "line" is heavily committed to the "dissociation of sensibility" are burning the flag without abandoning the position; the new, extraordinarily bad, volume in the Pelican Guide to English Literature (a publication dominated by such critics) contains amusing evidence of this. Now if it is, in its historical aspect, a fallacious doctrine, some effort should be made to say so definitely, otherwise a mere change of title will perpetuate the error. The second good reason is that we don't, by proving it wrong, find out how and why the doctrine has been such a success; and the fact that it is apparently in de-

cline itself suggests the present as a good moment for doing this job; an important job, I think, because the doctrine *was* so influential, and we ought to know why it seemed so satisfactory.

Nobody reading this will need to be told about the origin of the expression, nor of how it has come to be used, but it will be convenient to have set down here a few lines from the essay on "The Metaphysical Poets" (1921) in which Mr. Eliot first used it, and a much later passage from his Lecture on Milton, in which he qualified what he had said in the light of a quarter-century's thinking about it. The first passage, as printed in *Selected Essays*, and in the heart of every undergraduate, runs like this. Mr. Eliot has been saying that the dramatic verse of the late Elizabethans and early Jacobeans "expresses a degree of development of sensibility" which is not found in any of the prose. . . . In Chapman especially there is "a direct sensuous apprehension of thought, or a recreation of thought into feeling, which is exactly what we find in Donne. . . ." He then compares a passage of Chapman's and one by Lord Herbert of Cherbury with bits of Tennyson and Browning, and comments:

The difference is not a simple difference of degree between poets. It is something which had happened to the mind of England between the time of Donne or Lord Herbert of Cher-

From *Kenyon Review*, XIX (1957), 169-194. Copyright 1961 by Frank Kermode. Reprinted by permission of the author and the editors of *Kenyon Review*.

bury, and the time of Tennyson and Browning; it is the difference between the intellectual poet and the reflective poet. Tennyson and Browning are poets, and they think; but they do not feel their thought as immediately as the odor of a rose. A thought to Donne was an experience; it modified his sensibility. When a poet's mind is perfectly equipped for its work, it is constantly amalgamating disparate experience; the ordinary man's experience is chaotic, irregular, fragmentary. The latter falls in love, or reads Spinoza, and these two experiences have nothing to do with each other, or with the noise of the typewriter or the smell of cooking; in the mind of the poet these experiences are always forming new wholes.

We may express the difference by the following theory: The poets of the seventeenth century, the successors of the dramatists of the sixteenth, possessed a mechanism of sensibility which could devour any kind of experience. They are simple, artificial, difficult, or fantastic, as their predecessors were; no less nor more than Dante, Guido Cavalcanti, Guinicelli, or Cino. In the seventeenth century a dissociation of sensibility set in, from which we have never recovered; and this dissociation, as is natural, was aggravated by the influence of the two most powerful poets of the century, Milton and Dryden.

Of course there are other loci in Mr. Eliot's earlier criticism that amplify this, but we will content ourselves with his last pronouncement on the subject:

I believe that the general affirmation represented by the phrase "dissociation of sensibility" . . . retains some validity; but . . . to lay the burden on the shoulders of Milton and Dryden was a mistake. If such a dissociation did take place, I suspect that the causes are too complex and profound to justify our accounting for the change in terms of literary criticism. All we can say is, that something like this did happen; that it had something to do with the Civil War; that it would be unwise to say it was caused by the Civil War, but that it is a consequence of the same cause which brought about the Civil War; that we must seek the causes in Europe, not in England alone; and for what these causes were, we may dig and dig until we get to a depth at which words and concepts fail us.

In this passage Mr. Eliot seems to be recommending, as a desideratum, what had in fact already been done; for by 1947 supplementary enquiries into the dissociation had long ceased to be conducted entirely in terms of literary criticism. Almost every conceivable aspect of 17th Century life had been examined by scholars anxious to validate the concept, and much historical investigation that had been conducted from quite different and unrelated points of view was dragooned into service. Admittedly the scholars involved nearly all belonged to English Faculties, sometimes venturing outside their own disciplines to find support in Weber and Tawney, for instance, or in the medievalism of modern Catholic theology; sometimes seeking it nearer home, in the precise investigations of such scholars as R. F. Jones. But who, after all, is in a better position to spread such a doctrine than professors of English? It is certainly to them that the doctrine owes its success. Yet they are not alone in their love for simplicity and design in history; many others are equally attracted to the notion of a pregnant historical crisis, of great importance in every conceivable sphere of human activity. And there was a predisposition to locate this crisis in the 17th Century. So there was an attentive audience for G. Williamson when he gave a full account of it from the point of view of the historian of poetry; for F. R. Leavis when he developed the extremely influential theory of the Line of Wit, evaluating all later poetry in terms of the criteria declared appropriate for that of the early 17th Century; for L. C. Knights when he invoked and interpreted the economic history of the period in support of the doctrine; and for Basil Willey when he provided, in a book which has had an enormous influence in England, formulations of the theory to fit almost every aspect of the thought of the whole period. And of course one could mention many more contributions. A period which frankly confessed that it thought and felt by turns did homage to a period when men did these things simultaneously: a double-minded period measured itself by a serenely single-minded one. Intellect deferred to imagination; the slaves of second to the devotees of first causes: men habituated to asking *how* longed for a period when the proper question was *why*? Poets tried once more to be concrete, to banish ratiocination, to be "physical" rather than "platonic," to charge their thinking with passion and their passion with thought; to restore to poetry a truth independent of the presumptuous intellect. They looked admiringly toward those early years of the 17th Century when this was normal; and the scholars attended them with explanations of why it was so, and why it ceased to be so. There was an implicit parallel with the Fall; man's soul, since 1650, had been divided against itself, and it would never be the same again, though correct education might achieve something.

It is indeed a measure of Mr. Eliot's extraordinary persuasiveness that thinkers in this tradition have accepted the 17th Century as the period in which the disaster occurred. As we see from his second pronouncement, he himself has stuck to his position, although he advises us to look back into earlier history for fuller explanations. Nor is his attitude difficult to understand; it is animated by a rich nostalgia for the great period of Anglican divinity, the period when the Church of England, beset on all sides by determined recusancy, confidently proposed itself as truly Catholic and apostolic—looking back, itself, to a vague past when the folly and arrogance of human intellect had not yet begun the process of dissociating Christianity. This period ended with the Civil War; and the end of the first Anglo-Catholicism coincided with the end of an admired poetry and a great drama, both affected, to some extent, by ecclesiastically-determined literary attitudes, the drama remembering (but how faintly!) its devout origins, "metaphysical poetry" the *concetto predicabile*. In the view that the Civil War was historically and culturally decisive he had the support of Marvell and Dryden, as well as of those historians who explain the particular evils of the modern world as stemming from the dissidence of the early dissenters. Yet it must be confessed that, if we look to Europe and not to England alone, there was never a reasonable chance that the claims of the Church of England would be universally recognized, and that "something" had presumably "happened" long before to predispose people against their acceptance. And when one considers the position of those who say everything was all right before Bacon, or before Descartes, one is forced to a very similar conclusion, namely that the kind of wrongness these philosophers represent, for scholars anxious to show how the modern mind got split, is observable in earlier thought.

In itself, this is an old story, but it has to be told when someone makes a case for the absolutely decisive historical importance of a particular event or idea. Even Milton's Adam had to allow passion to get the better of reason before he ate the fruit, and so fall before the Fall. But in fact there is a great deal more to be said against the theory than that its supporters simply got the date wrong; though for the moment we are simply looking at the particular period that has been regarded as crucial, and asking whether it was so, in any of the ways proposed. (At present I am leaving poetry out of account.) One often hears the term "dissociation of sensibility" used as if it stood for a real historical event, like, say, Pride's Purge; after it, feeling disappeared from certain mental transactions, leaving a rump of intellect, with which we are still conducting our business. (It is this last inference that will survive the nominal death of the doctrine.) A lot of the blame naturally falls on the Royal Society, because of its interest in the accurate notation of observation and experiment without constant recourse to that First Cause which, they felt, often invalidated earlier philosophical argument. Certainly they took, quite early in their career, a great beating from Swift and his friends, who interpreted the modern fixation of interest on "nature" as a wanton violation of what seemed to them the proper order of human studies, in which ethics, economics and politics, theology and poetry, all ranked above anything that

Wotton's intellect, unaided by earlier accumulations of wisdom, could produce. And there is no doubt that Swift and Pope (even in his assault on Bentley and Theobald) were protesting against an abuse of human learning and tradition which is somewhat like a "dissociation of sensibility," though they would hardly have understood the expression. So were Blake and Coleridge and Wordsworth and Lamb and Keats. . . . But there is no point, as yet, in looking forward; the theory itself says that the lamented condition was never cured. The truth is that it is difficult to find a time when a roughly similar situation did not exist. In other words, the chronological placing of the "dissociation" is suspect.

This becomes clear when one considers such aspects of the doctrine as the dissociative force of science and the un-dissociated condition of pre-Baconian and pre-Cartesian philosophy and theology, basic antipositivist positions and always, by the dissociator, connected with a specifically 17th Century collapse.

The achievements of pre-Baconian science in England had been consistently undervalued until less than twenty years ago, but it is now quite clear that experiment and observation, notably in optics and astronomy, had proceeded very effectively on a basis of mathematics and with an infusion of Platonic mysticism. There was no automatic ecclesiastical objection to this; God the geometer was acceptable to churchmen as well as to scientists, and astronomy was a way of understanding the heavens' declaration of the glory of God. Most scientists were ready enough to emphasize that their discipline was ancillary to theology and in fact they rejoiced that mathematics could illuminate the doctrine of the Trinity and glorify the God who made the world in number, weight and measure. Everybody knows of Kepler's devoutness; and his was a scientific type that lived on into the 18th Century. The 16th Century in England was perfectly familiar with this type, which never proposed to

set the human reason against faith, any more than Bacon did ("as we are to obey his law, though we find a reluctation in our will, so we are to believe his word, though we find a reluctation in our reason. For if we believe only that which is agreeable unto our sense, we give consent to the matter, and not to the author; which is no more than we would do towards a suspected and discredited witness"). So long as the scientist labored for the greater glory of God he would not incur the condemnation of the Church for impiety of intellect—a sure symptom of "dissociation." But there were two ways in which he might be held to be working against God; he might develop his Platonism to the point of heresy, like Dee, or he might carry on with his work without sufficiently indicating that he had the proper end in view which was "atheism"; and there was a growing number of such men. "The quiet indifference" of such scientists, as Mr. P. Kocher has said, "was to work worse mischief to religion in the long run than the conjuring of a Dee or the blaspheming of a Marlowe." Both types, in their different ways, were guilty of the sin of *curiositas*, of "seeking knowledge merely to be known," as Greville said, or of seeking it in order to gain power by forbidden knowledge, a sort of witchcraft. (Incidentally, the Royal Society's supposedly indiscriminate thirst for, and allowance of, human learning, might be supposed to have liberalized the views of members on the black arts; but in fact the attitude of Glanville, for example, was superstitious and fearful—whereas Reginald Scot, living in the old pre-dissociation days, was a healthy rationalist.) The Church did not on the whole feel obliged to condemn new knowledge unless acquired for improper ends. So Copernicus evaded condemnation for decades. But when another authority was preferred to that of the Scriptures and the Church, or when the human intellect grew so self-centered as to omit its duty to God, there followed all that obscure disturbance which characterizes the intellectual life of the later part of

Elizabeth's reign; charges of scientific "atheism" invade literary life, where other "naturalisms," like the political naturalism of Machiavelli and the ethical naturalism of Montaigne, were already setting in. All this, of course, was going on before Donne, whose importance to the theory of dissociation I shall discuss later, was fully mature; and when the political strength of Puritanism was still half a century short of war (this has to be mentioned because, fundamentally, the dissociator's emphasis on the Civil War implies an allegory with Parliament as Pride of Intellect and Charles as Spiritual Unity—that is why Mr. Eliot says it "has never been concluded"). In Elizabethan science there were men guilty of precisely the sins of the Royal Society; and in every other department of life there were plain indications of a conflict between "naturalism" and "custom," which last word was already used to mean irrational authoritarianism in any sphere. Perhaps the "split" should be placed earlier, in the last quarter of the 16th Century?

But the merest glance backwards— and here I come to my second point— makes it clear that this won't do. Sixteenth century science owed much, we are told, to the intellectual traditions of the University of Padua; and dominant in these was a variety of Aristotelianism. It is indeed obvious that, in some sense, the rediscovery of Aristotle, which was the cause of what we understand as medieval philosophy, necessarily involved a dissociation in Christian thought. Aquinas did present a whole and consistent view, but even that was admittedly a laborious synthesis with little promise of stability; the decade of his death was marked by ecclesiastical condemnations, notably that of 1277, of a philosophic tendency to exalt reason independently of faith, and from these condemnations St. Thomas himself was not completely exempted. It was not merely that there were necessarily points of doctrine upon which Aristotle and the Scriptures were incompatible, as in their pronouncements on the creation

and the nature of the soul; such dif culties dissolve in Aquinas because Ari totle can always be called wrong, as worked by the light of nature. The re problem arises when philosophers (di ferentiated from theologians but not, v may remember, from scientists) flat declare that the intellect of a Christia guided by the rules of reason, can d termine certain matters in a mann totally contradictory to revealed religio and let the issue rest there; that is, the suggestion that there are two kin of truth. Now the controversy abo "double-truth," habitually associate with a 17th Century "dissociation," endemic throughout the supposedly u dissociated Middle Ages. There is a hi of it much earlier in Christian though notoriously indeed in Tertullian; but the height of the scholastic period it always likely to crop up when philos phers are trying to cope with the Ari totelian tradition as Averroes and followers represented it.

The theologians of the period we on the whole unwilling to explain t difference in the findings of philosopl and revelation by arguing that huma reason had been hopelessly obscured the Fall, or to restate the old argume that there was more merit in believir what was apparently untrue; both the answers as a matter of fact were offer in the 17th Century apologetics whe the same sort of problem arose, and is surely not without interest that t Middle Ages were more reluctant surrender the intellect than their su cessors and admirers. First Bonaventu and then the Bishop of Paris co demned all those points of Averroist philosophy that would have been fl heresy had they not been protected the doctrine of the double-truth; b Bonaventure also sought the root these errors in the thought of Aristotl that is, attempted an intellectual refut tion, in addition to abusing the philos phers for vain learning (the usual rea tion right up to the end of the 17 Century from those who would not e tirely give up human learning) and f the *specialized* pursuit of philosophy

olation from theology. The situation is
much the same as in the late 16th Century. Finally in 1277 there was a wholesale Papal condemnation of the Aver-
oist positions, which M. Gilson calls a
critical date in the history of philosophy
because henceforth "a spirit of suspicion
towards the 'philosophers' began to replace . . . the spirit of friendly and
confident collaboration with philosophy
which had generally prevailed, from the
beginning of the century, in the minds
of the theologians." The fact that the
condemnation of 1277 was not confined
to Averroism, but treated that body of
doctrine as an aspect of what M. Gilson
calls "a sort of polymorphic naturalism
stressing the rights of pagan nature"
(Andreas Capellanus came in for some
hostile comment) is perhaps proof that
the dissociation is not merely a matter
of philosophy and theology, but affects
the whole emotional and intellectual life
of the 13th Century. Certainly the distinction between *scientia* and *sapientia*
is not unknown outside the field of scholastic philosophy, and the condemnation
of *curiositas* was to develop into a literary convention. From this time on, right
up to Pomponazzi, who invoked the
double-truth clause in his opposition to
both Neo-Platonic and Christian thought,
denying on philosophical grounds the
immortality of the soul, and to Cremonini,
that very influential friend of Mr. Eliot's
un-dissociated Lord Herbert, Padua continued to produce its rationalist Aver-
oists, and, as we now know, to lay the
foundations of modern science. Having
split the truth, it was possible to ignore,
for all practical purposes, revelation; and
theologians, suspicious of philosophy, devoted their attention, as M. Gilson says, to
the elimination of the naturalism of Greek
thought, and the necessitarianism of
Graeco-Arabic divinity. Is this not the
historical locus of the great dissociation?
Alas, it is clearly not so; for example, Averroes takes us back to Aristotle
and Athens, where we find similar conflicts. Perhaps a philologist would suggest that unless we are looking for a
very primitive society we shall never
find a state of culture in which language

refuses to admit thinking that is not
numinous; in which there is no
possibility of a naturalist assault on the
society's beliefs. The Christian "West"
has never wanted to be as primitive even
as the Song of Solomon, and its whole
immense allegorical tradition is the result of applying intellectual instruments
to the dissection of writings in which
thought and feeling are, if anywhere,
inseparable.

I have taken the liberty of discussing,
doubtless in an over-elementary way,
these two matters, Elizabethan "atheism" and that "naturalism" we associate
with Averroes and Padua, simply to
show that the theory of dissociation has
difficulty, outside poetry, in choosing its
period. The fact seems to be that it is
normal for what we may loosely call
"naturalism" to threaten an establishment which claims supernatural sanction. And however this threat is countered—by denunciations *ex cathedra*
that reason cannot possibly conflict with
faith, or that the intellect is a fallacious
instrument—it cannot be suppressed. I
have drawn attention to its occurrence
in the 13th and 16th Centuries. Of
course it happened in the 17th also;
and the success of the doctrine of "dissociation of sensibility" is testimony that
it is still happening in the 20th. And it
would not be difficult to provide many
more examples from other periods. The
17th Century conflict is well-documented
and easily to hand, but it was not the
peculiar catastrophe that supporters of
the doctrine argue for.

But of course poetry is the heart of
the theory, and I have been wasting my
time showing that the "dissociation of
sensibility" doesn't belong to the 17th
Century if I can't do for poetry what I
have tried to do for these purely secondary matters. In point of fact this is far
easier to do, because the poets and
critics responsible for the development
of the theory have themselves not always agreed about where and when the
great split occurred; and for that reason
I propose to vary the method followed
so far, and instead of taking historical

samples, to consider this question of the genesis of the theory.

Full consideration would fill a book, in which the "dissociation of sensibility" would be merely one chapter; but the short answer is that the "dissociation of sensibility"—it has not always gone under that name—is an attempt to project upon the history of poetry a modern theory of the image. This theory owes something to Blake, and something to Coleridge; through the French Symbolists it owes something to Schopenhauer, and through Hulme something to Bergson. Before Mr. Eliot made his particular projection of it, it was familiar to Yeats (who got it directly from Blake and indirectly through Symons) and to Pound, who got it from Symons and de Gourmont and the French poets themselves. Ultimately this image is the product of over a century of continuous anti-positivist poetic speculation, defining and defending the poet's distinct and special way of knowing truth. It involves a theory of form which excludes or strictly subordinates all intellectual speculation, and which finds in music, and better still in the dance, an idea of what art should be: entirely free of discursive content, thinking in quite a different way from the scientists; as Donne said of Elizabeth Drury, in a passage much favored by writers in the tradition, "Her body thought." Form and meaning are coessential, and the image belongs not to the mechanical world of intellect, but to the vital world of intuition; it is the aesthetic monad of the Symbolists, the Image of the Imagists, the Vortex of the Vorticists, and finally the ideogram of Pound. It is anti-positivist above all; for Symons and Yeats it was even frankly magical, having a function very similar to that of the magician's seal; that is, a complete representation, with occult powers over the otherwise unimaginable matters represented. All the emphasis is on the inseparability of formal, intellectual and emotional aspects of the image or symbol, and this is as true of Pound and Eliot as it is of Blake and Mallarmé. The image is the philosopher's stone of

the whole movement of poetry from Blake and the early German Romantics to the present day. It has been described in many different ways, but it is recognizably the same thing, and occasionally even men wild with excitement about their discovery of it will perceive a resemblance to an earlier formula, as Hulme grudgingly quotes Coleridge, and Wyndham Lewis quotes Pater. The full story of this Image cannot be told here; it is enough to say that its in-dissociability is its prime quality—much as for Aristotle form and matter could not be separated except by intellectual abstraction—so that one now speaks of the "heresy" of paraphrase: that is, the wickedness of separating out the intellectual content of a poem. This indissociability is, in the end, proposed as the poet's only but infallible defense in a world of naturalists, his only hope in what is otherwise a universe of death. The price he pays is that nothing binds him to society but a mutual hatred.

It is reasonable to recall Coleridge's part in the early stages of the development of this theory, because apart from Blake he was the first Englishman to see the importance of a complete break with empiricist aesthetics. But mention of him may also remind us that in the movement we call Romantic there is another well-recognized characteristic relevant to this argument, and that is its medievalism. And it is hardly surprising that an anti-intellectual view of poetry, which insists upon special ends and values for the art, seeks in the past some epoch, some golden age, when the prevalent mode of knowing was not positivist and anti-imaginative; some age when the Image, the intuited, creative reality, was habitually known and respected; when art was not permanently on the defensive against mechanical and systematic modes of enquiry; when the truth of poetry, which resides in the Image, was a truth of self-evident importance. As the order of reality postulated as the proper study of the poet tends, in one way or another, to be granted supernatural attributes, the ideal epoch is usually a religious ne. Hence the medievalism or Byzan-inism of Hulme and the Decadents, of Yeats and Henry Adams. On such a view the extraordinary unease of Cow-ey, his shifty concern about what you an say in poetry and expect people to believe, is a direct consequence of a cer-ain Renaissance development which ulminates catastrophically in Hobbes; he later religious poetry of Dryden ex-ibits the new, defensive fideism; the trange confusions of the *Essay on Man* ndicate that a point has been reached t which the poet, out of mere igno-ance of his birthright, sells himself to he enemy—a Catholic poet writing ra-ional theology. The revolt of Coleridge gainst Hartley saves poetry because ven in the hands of its most skilful pologists the aesthetics of empiricism ould not restore the autonomy of the mage; Coleridge himself tried in the ld way, but soon discovered that he nust make a clean break; and on his wn showing his mentors (who were o speak in the ear of all Romantic hought) were the mystics of Renais-ance hermeticism, proclaiming in an ge of reason the magical oneness of the world and the powerlessness of the dis-ursive intellect to understand it. One as to go back to a point earlier than he moment when philosophy developed n exclusive interest in second causes.

Somewhere in the past, then, there nust have been a time when the poet's vay of knowing, by images in the full ymbolist sense, was the normal human vay, when the full play of the whole nind—not merely of the reason—in nowing, was taken for granted. The nly question for the historiographers of he Image is when this golden age really vas. There is a passage in Pound's *Make It New* that illuminates the prob-em.

When the late T. E. Hulme was trying to be a hilosopher . . . and fussing about Sorel and ergson . . . I spoke to him one day of the ifference between Guido's precise interpreta-ve metaphor, and the Petrarchian fustian and rnament, pointing out that Guido thought in ccurate terms; that the phrases correspond to efinite sensations undergone. . . . Hulme took

some time over it in silence, and then finally said; "That is very interesting"; and after a pause: "That is more interesting than any-thing anyone ever said to me. It is more inter-esting than anything I ever read in a book."

The only aspects of this odd interchange that I wish to discuss are those which are relevant to what I am trying to say about the historiography of modern Symbolist aesthetics. One is that Pound is describing Cavalcanti as a poet of the integral image, and contrasting him with Petrarch, a poet of the ornamental image, the image appended to discourse, the flower stuck in sand. In the one there is (to use the well-known formula) a unification of thought and feeling; in the other, a dissociation of them. An-other is concerned with Hulme's reac-tion to what Pound said. The general idea could not have been unfamiliar to him; after all, it was the reason why he was fussing about Bergson. But a man is never more impressed by an argu-ment than when it seems to provide unexpected support for opinions he al-ready holds; and Hulme could not have been other than charmed to discover that Petrarch of all people—the First Man of that Renaissance he blamed so strenuously—already exhibited the symp-toms of error which characterized the whole period, whereas Cavalcanti, an older contemporary of Dante, habituated to the hallowed concept of discontinuity, brought up on Original Sin, had pre-cisely those Imagist qualities, that re-luctance to glide away into abstraction, which for Hulme was the index of true art. Somewhere between Cavalcanti and Petrarch a dissociation of sensibility, it would seem, had set in; and from it, Hulme was doubtless willing to add, we have never recovered.

But we have now to remind ourselves that Mr. Eliot claimed for the poets of the 17th Century the very qualities of Dante, Cavalcanti, and Cino; and that after *them* this dissociation set in. It is not in the nature of the concept of dis-sociation, any more than it is of the Fall, that it should occur more than once—only Yeats with his cyclic theory of history imagines that it can. What are we to conclude from this confusion?

The fact is that Mr. Eliot's argument for a historical dissociation that can be detected in art is meant to satisfy precisely the same need as Hulme's. Hulme, powerfully influenced by Worringer's historical projection of the doctrine of empathy, and by the desire to justify a new abstract art, looked back into the past for a period of "life-alien" art, produced by a "life-denying" society; such art will be quasi-geometrical, emancipated "from all the contingency and temporality of the world-picture," non-organic, inhuman. For Hulme this was the society that existed before the Renaissance destroyed the belief in Original Sin. After that, art was empathy; it was anti-religious, anthropocentric, organic, preferring life to the truth that exists discontinuously from it, accessible only to a special intuitive act that Renaissance attitudes discouraged. The right kind of art is Egyptian and Byzantine; the wrong kind Greek and Renaissance. In the right kind, Hulme found his Image, free of the meddling human intellectual pride; in the wrong, a characteristic irreligious formlessness, the sloppiness and sentiment of the modern denial of limit. For him the Renaissance (though he is vague about when this was), is the critical moment since when nothing has been the same. Romanticism is just the new disease at the stage of mania; hence Hulme's utterly misleading description of himself as a classicist, when all his thinking is completely in the Romantic tradition. With Yeats, the case is not radically different. For him, there was a great moment in history (celebrated in some of his most splendid prose) when soul and body were one—nobody more explicitly relates the aesthetic and the historical than he does. His date is 1550: for a century before that there was a tense perfection; but after that everything changed. Of course he did believe it all happened before, and found a similar dissociation in the history of ancient art. Yeats, indeed, wrote his history in terms of this doctrine, and

wrote it in a world that offended h socially and imaginatively, a world "shopkeeping logicians," the very exi ence of which he had to explain by e haustive glosses on every conceivab aspect of the idea of dissociation. N own belief is that Yeats's expression the whole aesthetic-historical complex by far the most satisfactory and, terms of poetry, by far the most fruitf But my immediate point is that all the writers search history for a critic moment after which everything we wrong; and because they share, to large extent, the same poetic heritag they are looking for much the sar kinds of rightness and wrongness. Th seek, in short, a historical period po sessing the qualities that postulate f the image of art—unity, in-dissociabilit qualities, which though passionately d sired are, as they say, uniquely hard come by in the modern world.

Two consequences are to be noted, think, if it is conceded that Eliot's "d sociation" differs from the others only that it has gained wide currency. T first is that the formula is absolute useless historically. It will not do to s. that it is partly true, or true in a slight different way, as people are now clair ing. A once-for-all event cannot ha pen every few years; there cannot be, the term is to retain the significance has acquired, dissociations between t archaic Greeks and Phidias, betwee Catullus and Virgil, between Guido ar Petrarch, between Donne and Milto "Dissociated in sensibility" some mig still find a possible, though very nast *stylistic* description; but as a way speaking about "periods" it is much le useful than even "baroque." At its wor it is merely a way of saying which poe one likes—as the Symbolists, with mo justification because they were profes edly using aesthetic and not historic criteria, held that all the great poet of the past was Symbolist. At its bes the doctrine is an interesting primiti ism, looking for an unmodern virtue n as the noble savage was sought in th impossibly remote past or in Tahiti, b in Christian Europe right up to son moment in, or shortly after, what is vaguely called the Renaissance.

The second consequence is that the period or the poets chosen to illustrate the pre- and post-dissociated conditions are bound to be perversely treated; you must misrepresent them if you propose to make them illustrate a false doctrine. And this is precisely what has happened in recent years to Donne and Milton.

It is common knowledge that these two poets somehow got involved in an unhappy relationship existing only in the minds of historians, the long and short of which was that one of them—Milton, in fact—had to be occulted to enable Donne to light up (and we note that Mr. Eliot's change of opinion on Donne was followed by an upward revision of his estimate of Milton). At the very time when Donne was being admired for thinking freely, Milton was being despised for writing monuments to dead ideas in a dead language. Milton, self-conscious post-lapsarian that he was, obstinately thought and discoursed about feeling, divorcing the body and soul, the form and matter, of the image. Donne, writing before the same Fall, had his intellect at the tips of his senses.

Or so it proved possible, for a considerable length of time, to argue. Superficially, the argument was attractive because it gave major status to an obscure poet whose diction was inartificial, even colloquial; and because he was a poet who lived in times supposed to be very like modern times, in that the established order was already being threatened by those "naturalist" forces which eventually dissociated sensibility.

There is, of course, a contradiction here somewhere. Donne is admired because he was deeply troubled, or so they say, by the new philosophy, and also because he was lucky enough to live just before it became really troublesome. There is also an error of fact; Donne alludes frequently enough to the "new philosophy," but nobody who has coolly examined these allusions in their context can seriously believe he was much put out by it, and considering his religious views it would indeed be surprising if he had been. It might have been useful for the dissociationist argument if somebody had been prepared to capitalize this point, by way of emphasizing Donne's pre-dissociation status; but there seems to have been a heavy commitment to the view that Donne was important to modern poets because of the ways in which his world resembled theirs, as well as because it was completely different from theirs. As usual, the history is feeble. But pure criticism has had very similar difficulties: Miss Tuve's famous demonstration that Donne's images have a logical, or at any rate a pseudo-logical function, was a direct affront to the basis of the theory that he was a poet of the modern image; but it can scarcely have surprised anybody who had read Donne open-eyed and seen how much he depends on dialectical conjuring of various kinds, arriving at the point of wit by subtle syllogistic misdirections, inviting admiration by slight though totally destructive perversities of analogue, which re-route every argument to paradox. Some of this Mr. Eliot perhaps felt when he prematurely prophesied the demise of Donne during the tercentenary celebration of 1931, and showed how far he had gone towards excluding Donne from the category of unified sensibility, saying outright that in him "there is a manifest fissure of thought and sensibility." And to say the least, Donne is a doubtful ally. The ambiguous quality of his contribution can be seen at a glance; consider a poem where most people would be inclined to say he is near his best, "Batter my heart, three-person'd God. . . ." It is certainly unusual at such a moment of sensibility to qualify the vocative with a reference to the Trinity, and it may be that this is the measure of Donne's ability to marry his incessant intellectual activity to powerful feeling. On the other hand, it is hard to answer the charge—a charge Herbert might have supported—that this is indecorous, a mere grotesquerie, with no point unless it be that three Persons can batter better than One. Mr. Eliot, one feels, had come down on this side by 1931. On the whole, although the doctrine of "dissociation of sensibility" is inextricably involved with the Donne revival, one might be excused for wondering how he ever got mixed up with it.

In attempting a partial explanation of this, I also come to the point where I can wind up this essay. Mr. Bateson has noticed in passing how little separates Mr. Eliot's formula from the conventional 19th Century view, which he exemplifies by Stopford Brooke's teaching that the Restoration saw the end "of a poetry in which emotion always accompanied thought." After Grosart's edition of 1872 some people were already remarking that in Donne the note of passion, the true voice of feeling, was audible in love poems unpromisingly couched in terms of alchemy, astronomy and law. And it was this discovery of the true voice of feeling in such surroundings that led to what was in effect a late Romantic glorification of Donne. This was contemporary with the Blake revival, the teaching of Pater, and finally with the assimilation of the parallel but more important phenomenon of French Symbolism—in short, with the emergence of the modern poetic image as it was understood by Symons (a great champion of Donne and the Jacobean Drama), and those who came under his influence: Yeats, and later Pound and Eliot. One can watch the older thought-and-feeling formula developing from a Romantic into a characteristically Symbolist hypothesis. George Eliot, who knew Donne by the time she wrote *Middlemarch*, assumes like her master Wordsworth that the true voice comes from artists of higher organic sensibility than other men, but can say in that novel—doubtless unconscious of her role as critical pioneer— that the poet is "quick to discern," but also "quick to feel" because he possesses "a soul in which knowledge passes instantaneously into feeling, and feeling flashes back as a new organ of knowledge."

A paper recently published by Mr. J. E. Duncan in the *Journal of English and Germanic Philosophy* is relevant here. Any one who has used the Victorian editions upon which so much of our reading in 17th Century poetry still depends must have occasionally felt, if obscurely, that there was some hallucinatory resemblance between certain observations made by these enthusiastic clerical editors and those of Mr. Eliot. Mr. Duncan has collected a great deal of evidence to show, not only that Donne was well and truly revived long before Eliot's essays, and indeed Grierson's edition, but that even seventy years ago people were talking about the poet in what we recognize as the modern way. Grosart's edition of 1872 launched the revival, and by 1911 Courthope, in his *History*, was already complaining that it had probably gone too far. Grierson's great edition of the following year was accepted as merely setting the seal on Donne's reputation. But what is more interesting than this mere setting back of the starting post is the terminology which the Victorian critics, pleased with their rediscovery of the conceit and of hard-thinking poetry, devised in order to praise the Metaphysical poets. They speak of its intellectual cunning *and* its power of "sensibility" and then quite early, we find ourselves approaching, with a sort of unconscious inevitability, the modern formula which combines these two qualities as two sides of a coin. Grosart says that Crashaw's thinking "was so emotional as almost always to tremble into feeling"; Cowley's thought is "made to pulsate with feeling." Symons finds that Donne's "senses speak with unparalleled directness"; Schelling that Donne's contribution to the English lyric was "intellectualized emotion." Poets began to find Donne-like qualities in their own work in so doing, Francis Thompson spoke of his own "sensoriness instinct with mind," and the parallel was supported by Symons and by Mrs. Meynell. The familiar comparison between the 17th and 20th Centuries began as early as 1900; after that it was easy to play the game of parallel poets, and both Brooke and Bridges were credited with resem

lances to Donne. Gosse and Grierson
alike saw the similarities between Donne
and Baudelaire, and briefly hinted at
the parallel between English-Jacobean
and French-Symbolist which Mr. Eliot
was to find so fertile. Arthur Symons in
fact developed the parallel to a considerable extent; he is, as I have suggested, a crucial figure, combining as he
does in a speculative synthesis all that
Pater had taught, all he himself had
learned from Blake and Coleridge, with
the fullest information of anybody in
England about French Symbolism; he
was not only indispensable to Yeats, but
he admitted, though somewhat despised,
mentor of both Eliot and Pound on this
last subject. He is the link between 19th
and 20th Century orthodoxies of the
Image or Symbol, and Donne and the
17th Century.

Long before the great edition of
Grierson, which made Donne relatively
easy to read, and long before Mr. Eliot's
phrase had its remarkable success in the
world, powerful aesthetic interests were
being satisfied by a process of converting an almost unknown poet into an
early English Laforgue; and the same
interests demanded a catastrophic start
to the modern world shortly after the
death of Donne, and before *Paradise
Lost*, that great dissociated poem which
you must, said Mr. Eliot, read once for
the meaning and once for the verse, and
which is therefore of no use either to
poetry or to that illiterate audience he
desiderates for his unified Symbolist po-
try, nor for the next best thing, a highly
cultivated audience that also likes its art
undissociated. The strangest irony in all
this—and it is all I have to say about
the other perverted poet—is that Milton,
rather exceptionally, actually believed in
and argued for the unity of the soul
(a continuum of mind and sensibility);
allowed his insistence on the inseparability of form and matter to lead him
into heresy; and believed that poetry
took precedence over other activities of
the soul because it was simple (undissociated by intellect), sensuous and passionate. But unfortunately he wrote long
poems; this alone disqualifies him as, on
the Symbolist view, long poems are impossible.

In fact, the history of these distortions is the history of 19th and early
20th Century aesthetic, the projection
onto an historical scale of a developed
Romantic-Symbolist view of the Image.

It is necessary, now, for the sake of
whatever completeness this paper can
pretend to, to allude a little more fully
to Mr. Bateson's attack on the doctrine,
which was delivered from another
quarter altogether. I don't think he
goes so far as I do in denying absolutely
the value of the hypothesis; but he does,
as I have consequently refrained from
doing, analyse the idea itself—what, if
you look closely at it, does the phrase
"dissociation of sensibility" mean? I
have tried to show that it is only a way
of rewriting history to emphasize the
importance of poets you happen to like
—a very extravagant way; that it is a
way of talking about poems and poets
which satisfy certain aesthetic criteria
(notably that discourse should be purged
from poems so that the poet doesn't
appear merely to be thinking about
something he felt, or worse still feeling
about something he thought; the whole
thing has to happen at once). But, as several critics have said, it is not very helpful
to talk about *thought* and *feeling* here—
these are the terms used for those elements which add up to a *sensibility*
capable of receiving the Image. Yet the
reason for the choice of the words is
clear enough; they are used in a Romantic way as being not only opposed
to each other, but subject to combination only under unusual circumstances
and in a most exceptional person. There
is even a kind of primitivism involved;
just as Mill argued that Shelley was,
virtually, in a blessedly backward state
of intellectual development, getting sensations straight into words without any
intervening intellection, so Gourmont, as
Mr. Bateson has brilliantly reminded
us, was speaking of a sort of happy
immaturity in Laforgue when he wrote
the essay upon which Mr. Eliot drew.
"Laforgue's intelligence, Gourmont says,

. . . was closely connected with his sensibility; he adds that Laforgue died before he acquired the scepticism which would have enabled him to dissociate his intelligence from his sensibility (*dissocier son intelligence de sa sensibilité*)." (I quote Mr. Bateson). In other words, Laforgue could still *feel* his thought as immediately as the odor of a rose. Laforgue was a poet Mr. Eliot admired, and here he found a way of talking about him as the older critics had talked about Donne; but Mr. Bateson shows that he draws more from Gourmont than this. For Gourmont "thinking was only a kind of sensation," and he held that

our mental activities can be divided into three separate segments or stages. The first stage is from sensations to images (*mots-images*). The second stage is from images to ideas (*mots-idées*). The third stage is from ideas to emotions (*mots-sentiments*). The cycle then closes in action. The literary sensibility, therefore, straddles the first two of Gourmont's stages. Not only does it build up the sensation into an image, but it at least begins the process by which the image is crystallized into the idea. It is at this transitional point, according to Gourmont, that the best thinking is done.

After this explanation, says Mr. Bateson, we can see Mr. Eliot's theory in perspective. "What he has done . . . has been to transfer to the nation de Gourmont's analysis of the mental processes of the individual"; a remark which chimes well with my earlier observation. Mr. Bateson was ably challenged by Mr. Eric Thompson, who showed how much F. H. Bradley must have been in Mr. Eliot's mind when he used this terminology; but Mr. Bateson is right in replying that one would never guess it. All we can see is an attempt (very sophisticated and of course highly qualified) to block out poetry between 1650 and the critic's own time; Blake and Wordsworth had made roughly similar attempts in the interest of their own kind of poetry.

The age of pre-dissociated sensibility is, then, the Golden Age of Romantic-Symbolist thought, the time before somebody ruined England. For many of the prophets, the moment in which they themselves live is the point at which a series of new times begin; it was so for Blake and, up to a point, Wordsworth; the young Yeats thought so; so did Hulme; and there is a hint of it in Pound. The Astraea of the Image is to return, with all manner of beneficial results upon life at large; out of the Image will come, perhaps, many other benefits appropriate to an age of unified sensibility—Catholicism, the abolition of usury and so on.

So we look back nostalgically to archaic Greece, to the early epoch of Ravenna, to Guido and to Donne; and such is the power of this primitivist urge that it succeeds, for a moment, in representing Milton as a kind of magnificent disaster. There can be no doubt that the success of Mr. Eliot's formula which happens not to be a very good way of putting something that had been put many times, is due in part to the fact that he was the first Symbolist poet in England to achieve wide recognition as distinctively "modern," and in part to the respect rightly accorded to the criticism of distinguished poets. Also his version, if not in its formulation then in its application, has the air of being more moderate and reasonable than Hulme's or Pound's and he was directing attention to Donne and the Jacobean drama at a moment when they were easily available, and when the work of his contemporaries, as well as his own, had removed some of the extra-literary objections to such reading. But it is important to remember also the great accumulated flood of Romantic thinking that swept into the channel of Symbolism. Symons, for instance, was a poet who announced himself as deriving from the French Symbolists and from the Jacobean Drama; but the time was not ripe. When it was, the flood that fertilized the land in which Mr. Eliot as poet sowed his seed came from sources in Coleridge and Blake and Pater, in German Romantic thought and its French developments; and the sluice gate through which it poured happened to be labelled "disociation of sensibility." The landscape of English poetry was for a while curiously changed; now the waters are subsiding. Fine crops grow, though some crocodiles were generated. Now we may wonder about the form of the next catastrophe, and hope it won't be drought.

There is no good reason why the history of poetry should not be rewritten from time to time in terms of a powerful new historical myth. If we think of "dissociation of sensibility" as that, it will seem that the vagueness of the expression itself was part of its strength. It gave plenty of scope to the team of laboring historians who sought to establish it where Mr. Eliot had simply made a sketch. But now it is clear that it has done its work, and in so far as people continue to behave as though it constituted a valid way of talking about history, it is a nuisance. So it is worth trying to show that it really is untenable as a way of talking about the 17th Century, and to show where its importance lies. It does not refer to a moment when Bacon or somebody else ruined England, but to a necessary attempt on the part of Symbolists to find an historical justification for their poetics.

JOHN GASSNER

(b. 1903)

John Gassner is well known for his scholarly and critical writings on dramatic literature, especially for his interest in the practical problems involved in turning plays into "theater." His books include *The Theatre in Our Times* (1954), *Form and Idea in Modern Theatre* (1956), and *Theatre at the Crossroads; Plays and Playwrights of the Mid-Century American Stage* (1960). His critical edition of Aristotle's *Poetics* (1951) is widely used.

Tragic Perspectives: A Sequence of Queries (1958)

I

'It is about time someone wrote a new *Poetics*," my friend said. He was thinking of Tragedy, of course, and he looked hopefully at me, or so my vanity led me to believe. And it occurred to me at once how easy it would be to join this enterprise of drafting new or modified "laws" for tragedy, and how difficult to extricate oneself from it. There hasn't been a generation since the fifteenth century that

Reprinted from *Tulane Drama Review*, Vol. II (May, 1958), pp. 7-22, by permission of the author and the editors of *Tulane Drama Review*.

hasn't tried to rewrite Aristotle's text whether by interpretation or augmentation. Yet nothing absolute has ever been said on the subject that went perceptibly beyond the prejudices or ambitions of a period, a nation, a species of litterateur, or a class of play-goers and readers. The very effort to define the limits of tragedy appears to have introduced more confusion into criticism and playwriting than it has eradicated. Surely, tragedy is never quite the same thing from place to place, from one playwright's work to another. Even Sophocles, the ideal tragedian of most critics, did not conform to any "tragic blueprint." Only the most superficial reading could fail to disclose glaring differences between *Ajax* and *Antigone*. In the former, for example, the hero's *hamartia* is a decisive factor whereas the heroine's in the latter is of small consequence, if any. (And from one point of view she can be said to have none, while from another point of view her *hamartia* is her chief glory, and idealists or romanticists right up to Anouilh cannot but endorse it whereas the "tragic flaw" was surely not intended for praise, least of all in the *Ajax*.) How different, too, is tragedy if the model we take is *Oedipus at Colonus* rather than either of the aforementioned plays. And are there not differences between tragic form if the protagonist is overthrown, as in *Oedipus the King*, or triumphant, as in *Electra*. How insecure would be the tragic status of the latter if it had to be validated as a tragedy solely by analysis rather than by our feelings. The temptation to generalize has been too strong to be resisted by reasonably active critics. But we have reached such fluidity in theory and practice that a "new" *Poetics* could have only a tangential relevance. It has always been necessary to evaluate plays as separate entities, and we surely have more reason now than ever before to examine individual works with a view to ascertaining their uniqueness rather than degree of conformity to *genre*.

II

If it is no longer customary to lay down dogmatic principles for tragedy, there is still a tendency to cherish some "ideal" of tragedy. *Oedipus the King* represents it in Aristotle's thought and can still do so in the opinion of contemporary critics. Carried to the point of idolatry, however, respect for "ideal tragedy" becomes inhibitory. It conduces to the notion that a single work or single conception of drama contains all the possibilities of tragic art. This conclusion, latent in every definition of ideal tragedy (the definitions imply an ideal), is made absurd by the facts. *Hamlet* includes elements of tragic experience and perception not contained in *Oedipus the King*, just as Sophocles' play includes tragic qualities absent in *Hamlet*. And *Phèdre* has a concentration of feeling lacking in the *Hippolytus*, just as Euripides' play has a dimension of idea absent in Racine's. This much will probably be granted, but literary warfare is sure to be declared whenever we look to modern drama on its altitudes or plateaus. We are in difficulties, for instance, whenever we suggest that treatments of destructive femininity, as *Hedda Gabler* and *The Father*, have added tragic elements not contained in the *Phèdre* and the *Hippolytus*. I would not hesitate to make this claim myself, with the understanding, of course, that the addition of a new dramatic element or dimension does not necessarily make a late play superior to an early one. It is even possible to assert that an Oedipus play so far below Sophocles' masterpiece as Cocteau's *The Infernal Machine* has enriched the tragic action in at least one respect; I refer to the psychological element—the fatal attraction of Jocasta and Oedipus for each other—that deepens the husband-son and wife-mother relationship in the Cocteau version.

Another danger latent in idealization of *one* type of tragedy is the danger of our regarding every other kind of play as a necessary descent from some isolated individual achievement (*Oedipus the King*, probably) or some golden age (the fifth century Attic period, no doubt), never recovered or recoverable. This viewpoint seems to me altogether too rigid and fatalistic for dramatic art. Consistently maintained, this view would leave too little room for the appearance of *Hamlet, Macbeth,* or *King Lear* and the emergence of an Elizabethan age of tragedy two thousand years after the death of Sophocles. It would make the writing of "true" tragedy conditional upon the recovery of esthetic and social norms that prevailed only once, centuries or millenia ago. It would predicate failure for all contemporary efforts to attain tragic art and forbid the mobility that is the life of the theatre.

III

A major source of error may be our tendency to certify one work as *more* tragic than another, as if quantitative measures could possibly be as valid in art as they are in physical science. To formulate judgments on the drama on this basis is to create a false hierarchy of values. For playwrights to think in terms of making themselves tragical at all is to court academicism in the worst sense of the term. It would encourage epigonal tendencies rather than the spontaneously creative spirit of the theatre. Maxwell Anderson has especially favored the epigonal approach in most of his verse plays, but his popular success with *Elizabeth the Queen* or *Mary of Scotland* has had no effect on dramatic writing in our time. He had a number of predecessors in the nineteenth century theatre such as George Henry Boker and Stephen Philips, but none of these succeeded in revitalizing tragedy by adopting Elizabethan and romantic modes of drama. To worry about how much more tragic one piece is than another can be utterly misleading. A question not only relevant but seminal would be not "how much *more* tragic" but "how *differently* tragic."

Common sense would suggest, of course, that we employ a theory of limits as an alternative to dogmatism. That is, we are to assume that some dramatic works are completely tragic whereas other works are only incompletely so. And from this view it is only a step to predicating gradations of tragedy until we reach a borderline between the tragic and the melodramatic. If this meant nothing more than that we rate some tragedies higher than others there would be no problem of definition. We would be saying nothing more than that we like one play better than another because its content, structure, or style impresses us more. But if we say that we like one play better than another because it is "more tragic," or that one play is less meritorious than another because it is less tragic, then we only compound our difficulties in arriving at judgment.

In the first place, we omit too many values by making tragicality a major criterion. Maxwell Anderson's verse play *Elizabeth the Queen* meets many long-accepted criteria for tragedy. The exalted lovers Elizabeth and Essex have all the nobility, all the "tragic stature," that has long been required of the protagonists of a tragedy, and their action has "magnitude" in almost any sense of the term. A well defined *hamartia* produces the downfall of Essex and the unhappiness of the Queen. The "reversal of fortune" in their case is the most tragic of possible reversals. It is caused, moreover, by their own strong will; *proairesis* is in good order here, for the chief characters make critical choices and are highly aware of the consequences of their decisions; their *dianoia* and *ethos* dominate the action. Neither their intellectual nor ethical bent can be considered revolting, and their conduct does not outrage our sensibilities even at the point of highest tension. The "tragic rhythm" of "purpose, passion, and perception," Kenneth Burke's well known formulation, determines the movement of the action quite satisfactorily, and when Essex dies he departs from life in a manner obviously calculated to elevate the public. The "dignity of man" is affirmed by his refusal to save his neck, and I would suppose that an audience affected by Essex and Elizabeth about as much as the public was moved (by "pity" and "fear"?) when Alfred Lunt and Lynn Fontanne played the leading roles in the successful Theatre Guild production of 1930, would experience a *katharsis*—if, after having written extensively on the subject, we really knew what *katharsis* is.

We have no difficulty in certifying *Elizabeth the Queen* as a tragedy, whereas the same cannot be said of Euripides' *Electra*, at which we have looked askance for a long time. It does not, however, follow that the latter is the inferior —that is, the less penetrating and stirring —play. In calling *Electra* a melodrama in his noteworthy book on Greek tragedy, Professor Kitto did not indeed deny that the play had an excellence of its own that was not to be slighted simply because he would not validate it as a "tragedy." And, to move on to our own times, *A Streetcar Named Desire* is not to be considered inferior to *Elizabeth the Queen.*

It is entirely conceivable that a play may be non-tragic and yet more absorbing than a work we can easily certify as a tragedy. Can there be any doubt about this matter when we compare, let us say, the *Paolo and Francesca* of Stephen Phillips or any of the poetic tragedies of our English romantic and Victorian poets with *The Cherry Orchard,* which its author called a "Comedy," or *Juno and the Paycock*, in which the admixture of comic and tragic elements can be disconcerting only to purists. Then there are, of course, all the modern plays from *Ghosts* to *Death of a Salesman* whose tragic status has been sharply questioned; how shall we account for their relative excellence and their patent superiority to many tragedies? If there are more obvious reflections than these I am sure they have not occurred to me, but they remain heretical; they cannot be countenanced by those for whom tragedy is an honorific term. It would seem that they cannot abide the thought that a tragedy may be inferior to a non-tragic work. For them, above all, there seems to be no such thing as a *bad* tragedy, even if the Elizabethan and Jacobean theatre abounded with exalted rubbish, as did the neo-classic theatres of France, England, and Germany after *Athalie*. The manner of reasoning is flagrantly circular; it amounts to saying that if the play is bad it cannot be a tragedy, and if it is a tragedy it cannot be bad.

Reasoning of this sort turns "tragedy" into a value rather than a *genre*. A rejected tragedy is then called a "melodrama." Even though it is apparent that the authors of such plays as *The Spanish Tragedy* or *The Revenger's Tragedy* had only the genre of tragedy in mind, it becomes necessary to find a separate pigeonhole for them in order to preserve the ideal of Tragedy from debasement or criticism. But what if we should differ as to the excellence of a play, then one man's tragedy will become another man's

melodrama. John Webster was dismissed by Bernard Shaw as a "Tussaud laureate." Those who agree with this judgment and use the term tragedy honorifically have no choice but to deny that Webster was a tragic poet. The honorific view of tragedy, moreover, is conducive to imitative and inflationary writing. Why should Maxwell Anderson be made to think that he has to fit *Winterset* to the pattern of *Hamlet*? His first "journalistic" treatment of the Sacco and Vanzetti case, *Gods of the Lightning*, had a truer ring and possessed more integrity in action and dialogue than a play in which a gangster speaks diluted Elizabethan verse and a mobster-melodrama, combined with a jettisoned exposé of social injustice, blossoms at the end into a rabbinical sermon on the tragic dignity of man. And the *reductio ad absurdum* materializes when, having come to the conclusion that the writing of a social drama is not a passport to immortality, the playwright tries to make doubly or trebly sure that his treatment will have the requisite tragic "nobility" and "universality" by combining the *Hamlet* theme with the *Romeo and Juliet* and the "mad Lear" motifs that have been traced in *Winterset*. It is indeed a tribute to Maxwell Anderson's abilities that the fragments coalesce as well as they do and produce a tolerably unified impression. But the danger is manifest in trying to write tragedy as the high art that assures "significance," if not indeed immortality, instead of simply writing a play. Tragedy should be the end-result of a writer's struggle with his matter rather than a collection of previously assembled attitudes, caveats, and aspirations to which the playwright endeavors to conform with a view to uplifting the theatre.

IV

What is the use of devising finely ground definitions of tragedy unless they can be serviceable to one's own time?

I cannot but agree that the current definitions can increase our understanding and appreciation of the work of other periods than our own. Even a vital theatre has to rely on classics as well as on more or less newly hatched writing. Do the definitions help? To some degree they do in elementary approaches to specific plays. But never so much as the study of the play as a *play* rather than as a *tragedy*. Besides, there is little that is new or penetrating to be said about the masterpieces of the past by confining ourselves to *genre* or giving it preference over other considerations. What we can say about Euripides' *Electra* after noting that it is not a tragedy is more important, because it deals with more essential aspects of the play, than does the mere "proof" that the play is untragic. It may have been more valuable and necessary to have written an untragic *Electra* at a certain point in the Attic period than to have written a version that would conform to conventional requirements for Tragedy. (Conventional requirements of a later period, of course. There is no evidence of rules in Euripides' time that invalidated unheroic, "clinical," or even tragicomic plays as "tragedy.") For an art to remain vital and to give birth to viable offspring it is necessary for it to be constantly violated.

Genre is, so to speak, an *a posteriori* postulate. First come the specific works, then comes the classification; and the classification undergoes modification in accordance with modifications in the works we presume to classify. *Genre* is something we can usually determine meaningfully only after we have noted enough significant resemblance between works that at the same time also display significant variety. And *genre* tends to stagnate unless an individual genius of a later period violates it, as he fortunately does from time to time. There is no surer way to destroy a genre than to venerate it. (What a holocaust in the English theatre from the veneration of blank-verse tragedy, for example!) What have we accomplished, besides, in determining that T. S. Eliot's *The Family Reunion* is a tragedy? The question of its merit or success as a play still remains to be determined, as would also be the case if we classified *The Family Reunion* as a

"divine comedy" or a symbolic comedy of salvation. As Eliot discerned, the essential question, from the viewpoint of literature, would concern the texture of the writing; and the prime problem, so far as the theatre is concerned, would involve not the tragic quality of the theme and the main character, but the degree to which they have been credibly and vividly activated as an effective "imitation of an action."

Another concession I am prepared to make is that the tragic measure is a handy one to have around. With it we can threaten to take the height and width of some plays that have been stretched artificially by sensation-mongering play-wrights and stage directors. With it we can take soundings, too, to ascertain whether there is any depth in a contemporary work presented to us with an air of profundity, whereas there is usually a false bottom to it. For such purposes as these, it is good to have a measure that does not shrink opportunistically to suit the marketplaces of art, ideas and ethics. Our concept of tragedy must not be cheapened to conform to cheapness in our feelings, ideas, and social values. But opportunism is not the sole alternative to dogmatism, and works of art are never wholly measurable. The negative value of tragic absolutism in detecting false coinage is greater than its positive value. Above all, our problem is how to maintain reasonable standards without atrophying dramatic art by preventing the theatre from responding to new knowledge, new awareness, and new issues. Yes, new *issues*, too, since "the universal" has to be embodied in the concrete if it is to be perceived at all as something more than an abstraction of little use to the theatre. Timeless drama, in an absolute sense, is a romantic delusion; issueless drama is an academic illusion.

Ultimately, we shall come to realize, I believe, that, so far as tragedy is concerned, no standard interpretation of the *Poetics* and no "new" *Poetics* will have positive value for us unless it can give support and guidance to our century's major ventures in serious playwriting—

"psychological drama" and "social drama." Psychological and social elements we have always had in the drama. But in their preponderance since about 1870 they have eventuated as more or less distinct types of plays, and these have usually been denied certification (sometimes justly) as tragedies even when their action has included the extreme suffering or death of the protagonist. With validation, moreover, may come the clarification, as well as the encouragement, that will translate "psychology" and "journalism" into universal tragic terms—and this not by means of rhetorical inflation of language after evisceration of the psychological or social content. Acceptance of new knowledge need not compel abdication from tragic eminence if new knowledge can be assimilated into old principle.

A review of Ernest Jones's third volume of *The Life and Work of Sigmund Freud* (by David Baken in the December 9, 1957 issue of *The New Republic*) opens as follows:

Freud once wrote that the world had experienced blows to its narcissism: the cosmological blow from Copernicus, the biological blow at the hands at [*sic*] Darwin, and the psychological blow from psychoanalysis. Each of these, from the vantage point of 1957, has had a paradoxical effect. In spite of the seeming abasement of man, each has, in its turn, increased man's power over the forces that govern him, and has thus served to enhance man's dignity.

Combined with the greater sense of reality and the greater courage demanded of men deprived of comforting ignorance, the increase in man's awareness can be viewed as a factor in making tragic art more, rather than less, possible. "Blows to narcissism" may be interpreted as incentives, rather than deterrents, to tragic art. The tragic art of past ages would have been pinchbeck indeed if it had subsisted on our narcissism rather than on men's sense of reality and readiness to face it. (The many respects in which Tragedy is our most realistic art, indeed, would fill a separate long essay.) We can face reality—or at least we should be able to face it—even with new knowledge undermining old egotism and security. When everything else fails us, it may be that our oldest support—to wit, our sense of tragedy—will continue to prop us up.

V

Why indeed cannot "social drama" be tragedy?

It can be that (and what does this mean other than that the work can have an effect called tragic . . .) if the protagonist looms humanly large among his fellow-creatures of the play and if his values, however deplorable in their particular results, magnify rather than diminish him as human being. If the sympathies asserted by the author favoring the common man and emphasizing social causation do not cheapen life! And if the struggle involving the principal characters has in view issues whose references are not less personal than social.

Hebbel's *Maria Magdalena,* which meets these provisions, is virtually the *locus classicus* of "social tragedy"—a term preferable in many ways to "middle class tragedy" even though the milieu is indubitably that of the provincial bourgeoisie. So long as the individual is not dwarfed by the social analysis or transformed into the puppet of social forces "theme" is in little danger of being reduced to "thesis." So long as theme is not whittled down to thesis, there is little danger of the characters being reduced to puppets. The real impediments to the writing of social drama are want of talent and want of intelligence. Want of talent will result in the absence of life in the work, in abortive character-creation or even total absence of individualization. Want of intelligence will result in failure to surmount thesis. The playwright will be incapable of realizing the implications of the social situation and of letting his mind carry the initial social issue beyond its journalistic immediacy. The playwright will see case histories rather than humanity, problems rather than the human condition; he will be unable to see the forest for the trees.

He will, we may also say, fail to apprehend the *moral* nature of the issues, contenting himself *exclusively* with their political and social character or their news value. The tragic imagination is essentially a moral one, though by no means a moralizing one—unless, as in the *Agamemnon*, the moralizer employs dramatic agents and his moral is the dramatic action itself.

One reason why so spirited a social drama as John Wexley's Scottsboro case play about racial prejudice, *They Shall Not Die*, could not be tragedy is that the author seemed to be content with indignation instead of being willing to give scope to the moral imagination. Mr. Wexley expressed his sense of morality in attacking social injustice with vigor and clarity; beyond that he did not go and, considering the vogue of propaganda-drama in the nineteen-thirties, did not think it necessary to go. Indignation carries us only as far as condemnation, as a result of which we are enabled only to see the issue, the victim, and the culprit rather than human beings. Imagination begins where the clear-cut issue fades, where "Victim" and "Culprit" conclude their roles and begin to live, ideally also acquiring some degree of insight as sentient and rational members of the human race.

The great limitation of our writers of ordinary social drama has been a limitation of the creative imagination, which is also a limitation of moral insight. Condemnation is especially limiting because it simplifies everything to the point of banality. The greatest of all moral tragedians was Aeschylus. But Aeschylus would have had little stature as a tragic poet if the *Agamemnon* had amounted to nothing more than a demonstration that it is wrong for a woman to murder her husband, or if the *raison d'être* of *The Libation Bringers* had been simply to assure Greek audiences that it is a crime to kill one's mother. Too many modern social dramas have been focussed on the demonstration of the obvious, too much effort has been expended upon proving that which it requires no creative effort to prove. The moral imagination is a form of understanding,

whereas indignation is judgment signed and sealed. Tragedy, with its largeness of spirit, is an estate possible to social drama whenever the moral imagination takes precedence over the indictments humanity invites at all times and never more so than during the travail of social and political transitions.

Even thesis drama is not unalterably antipodal to tragedy, as the Oresteian trilogy alone would suggest. But theme and thesis must then be fused in one imaginative conception, so that "myth" and "argument" become the same thing, as in the Oresteian trilogy or in *Hippolytus* and *The Bacchae*. (That is, if we can agree that these are thesis plays in which Aphrodite and Dionysus symbolize natural forces that wreak destruction when denied and thwarted.) The difficulty of perceiving tragic possibilities in thesis drama has been due largely to the fact that thesis is the prose of drama whereas tragedy is its poetry. The difficulty vanishes when the prose of argument is interfused with the poetry of feeling. Whenever that is the rare case, as it is in Tolstoy's peasant-drama *The Power of Darkness*, it should not be anomalous to actually speak of "thesis tragedy."

Another difficulty has been the tendency in thesis drama—indeed, generally in modern social drama—to present error and suffering as wholly eradicable by legislation or by a formal change in opinion, custom, or education, and as neither involving any fundamental change in human nature nor encountering human nature as an insuperable obstacle. Or, for that matter, encountering other impediments of a non-sociological character such as moral law, divine caprice, Tychê, or Fate in the universe.

Genuine tragedy has always been more realistic than melioristic drama—or, for that matter, than moralistic drama. Tragedy has extended recognition to a "built-in" capacity for disaster in man and his world, and tragedians have given evidence of knowing that life has its "impossibilities" whereas reformers have ever been concerned, as they should be, with life's "possibilities." Tragedy may therefore be less *useful* than comedy, farce, and even melodrama. And the tragic sense of life might well be useless to humanity in periods of moral reformation, uplift, and reorganization, as in the period of the establishment of the Christian Church. Had there been any vogue of tragedy in St. Augustine's time, the great Bishop of Hippo would probably have had to regard it as subversive as Manicheism, unless he could have moralized tragedy and employed it to demonstrate "original sin." The author of the *Confessions* might well have done so, but original sin is, of course, precisely what modern progressive writers, scions of the 18th century Enlightenment, would have discounted before undertaking to produce thesis drama. Tragedy indeed may be the one luxury a society urgently in need of reformation cannot afford. Only perhaps to discover, after piling up blasted hopes, that tragedy is the one luxury it *can* afford!

VI

Realism? It is often maintained that the vogue of realism has destroyed tragic drama. But can we really place the onus on *realism of outlook*, which is the essence of the tragic sense of life? It is true that some contemporaries write about tragedy as though its outlook had to be almost desperately romantic. They give that impression when they refer to tragic art as idealistic, spiritual, elevating, or consolatory. Maxwell Anderson, for instance, sounded a familiar note in *The Essence of Tragedy* by declaring that the tragedian "must so arrange his story that it will prove to the audience that men pass through suffering purified, that, animal though we are, despicable though we are in many ways, there is in us all some divine, incalculable fire that urges us to be better than we are." And other writers, practicing critics such as Joseph Wood Krutch and John Mason Brown among them, have entertained more or less romantic interpretations, with the former going so far in *The Modern Temper* as to regard the tragic outlook as *ersatz*-belief for the religious faith that scientific thought has allegedly made untenable. Yet no one has seriously invalidated the hard realism of tragedy that connects life with suffering, crime with expiation, disequilibrium (in the individual and in society) with painfully arrived at restorations of equilibrium. Even the most romantically disposed writers would agree that nobody escapes from the consequences of his conduct and that even the "innocent" may suffer (from the disorder of other individuals or the disorder of the world) in tragic drama.

"Realism" is held culpable, in the main, as the literary and theatrical movement that has given primacy to *verisimilitude, illusionism,* and *intellectualism* or *rationalism*. There is something to this indictment, which is not of recent origin in fact; it was made as early as the last quarter of the fifth century B.C. and applied to Euripides. Yet the indictment is not really air-tight. *Verisimilitude* is not intrinsically anti-tragic. What did the Greek audiences get when they saw the blinded Oedipus or the Furies at the close of *The Libation Bringers* but verisimilitude? And consider the impact of Lear's dying line, "Pray you, undo this button." *Illusionism* is something even the Attic and Elizabethan, not to mention the French neo-classic and the Baroque, stages endeavored to effectuate in some respects. Illusionism, like verisimilitude, is a highly relativistic concept. Technical devices and a manner of acting that would strike us as anything but illusionistic today provided sufficient "illusion of reality" for their own times. Garrick's Shakespearian acting would undoubtedly impress us as exaggerated or "ham," whereas his contemporaries acclaimed it as the high-water mark of realistic performance. *Intellectualism* or *rationalism* is not inconsistent with passionateness or with a concern with the passions, as the example of Euripides and Racine would go far to prove. Did not Aristotle, who would have been the last person in Greece to overlook Euripides' intellectualism, call him the "most tragic" of the Greek poets.

What else has realism been blamed for? *Prose drama* and the so-called *fourth-wall convention*. But do these factors really destroy the possibility of writing tragedy? As for prose drama, the fact that it came into vogue long before Ibsen introduced genuine realism into the theatre is to be considered. To be considered, too, is the fact that the prevalence of verse drama has not assured the successful writing of tragedy in many periods. *Verse* may provide a certain degree of formalism that can dignify a dramatic composition and provide considerably more "esthetic distance" than colloquial prose can do. But tragedy needs a great deal more than "dignity" and "esthetic distance." Much formalistic drama has been patently untragic. Formalism may even militate against the art of tragedy by destroying the reality of the characters through whose agony and its consequences tragedy is produced. *Poetry* is another matter: Its absence is apt to be accompanied by lack of imaginativeness, universalization, and "reverberation" (the failure of the surface action to start vibrations below and above the surface), and without these qualities a play, however serious and catastrophic the action, will be untragic. But it is no secret that it has been possible to write poetic drama without composing dialogue in verse. And realism, far from discouraging poetic prose in the theatre has been favorable to its employment, as may be observed in plays by Chekhov, Synge, O'Casey, Maeterlinck, Andreyev, Masefield, Lorca, Obey, Giraudoux, Anouilh, Zuckmayer, and many others. For anyone familiar with their writing, the charge that realism, or "naturalism," destroyed poetic writings in the theatre must seem a tiresome canard. Those who persist in making the charge draw up their indictment on insufficient evidence.

As for the "fourth-wall" convention of realism, it may have limited the articulateness of dramatic characters by virtually outlawing soliloquies. Hamlet without his soliloquies would certainly be that much less than Hamlet. But it does not follow that articulateness in the theatre depends upon the actor's addressing the audience directly. Too much blame has been attached to the fourth-wall convention that bans direct address. As a matter of fact, a psychological wall between the drama's characters and the drama's audiences was bound to be established in almost any sort of theatre the moment the actors played a scene with each other. Nor has it mattered much whether the play has been staged in the open or in an enclosed theatre, within a box-set or on a platform stage, with scenery or without, and whether or not there were three other "walls." The moment the actors are "in scene" or, shall we say, "in action"—the moment they are truly interacting—they belong to themselves and not to the public, so that they are psychologically shut off from those who watch the performance. Actors indeed have had to especially stylize their performance, they have had to adopt a "sophisticated" attitude and break their concentration upon each other in order to speak to the audience. They used to violate their self-containedness and break through the psychological wall only by employing "asides," a crude device at best for tragedy.

In tragedy, the characters play "for keeps" rather than for the audience. With few exceptions, such as Iago's and Richard III's speeches, in which the effect is one of wit or comedy however sultry or diabolical, even the soliloquies are likely to establish a wall around the character. "To be or not to be" or "Tomorrow and tomorrow and tomorrow" and similar speeches were surely not intended to be plumped into the lap of the audience as a bouquet. The characters are perhaps never more isolated than when they give their soliloquies, and the isolation of the protagonist has contributed greatly to the power and significance of tragedy. Great tragedians such as Sophocles, Shakespeare, and Racine appear to have made a special effort to effect the "tragic isolation" of their protagonists. We may observe, for example, the lack of rapport between Antigone and the Chorus or between Hamlet and his mother. Isolation is also an integral factor in minor tragedies such as Schiller's *Maria Stuart* and *Wallensteins Tod*. But it is unnecessary to pursue this argument further when it is apparent that expressiveness can be achieved *without* soliloquy. If necessary, the protagonist can address himself even at great length to other characters, as Hickey does in a fifteen-minute harangue to his friends in *The Iceman Cometh*. This monologue, and the actor delivers it without any need to address the audience, is the most memorable episode of O'Neill's play, which is never more genuinely tragic than at that point. Dialogue, of course, invariably allows expression of viewpoint or of inner stress at considerable length behind the "wall." Anouilh, who did not hesitate to reach across the proscenium arch and break the "picture-frame" in his *Antigone* with a Narrator who even lectures the audience on the subject of Tragedy, actually reached the peak of his effectiveness in the play with a behind-the-fourth-wall discussion between the heroine and Creon.

So much for regarding the "fourth-wall" as an impediment to tragedy. There is no reason to fear that the protagonist's *état d'âme* will remain hidden behind that "wall." The really pertinent question is whether the playwright actually has an *état d'âme* to express or one that is interesting enough to be worth expressing.

That question is another matter, and much thought has been expended upon it. Joseph Wood Krutch's essay "The Tragic Fallacy," published in 1920 in *The Modern Temper*, expressed doubts as to the survival of the tragic spirit in the modern world, and it has not yet been possible to allay them entirely. Into the quicksands of that controversy, which would entail evaluations of the "modern soul," few of us can venture with any competence. I am sure *I* cannot. But I doubt that realism *per se* must destroy the "tragic spirit"; the realism of Tolstoy and Dostoevsky, surely the greatest literary realism of the past century, did not do so. Realism can be considered intrinsically anti-tragic only by identifying it narrowly with materialism and mechanism, an identification that literary realists have never really had to accept and that exponents of contemporary scientific philosophy have actually rejected. Besides, man is often a paradox; the less reason he has to think well of himself the better he thinks of himself. Men did not

consider themselves insignificant even when nineteenth-century mechanism and determinism found the widest theoretical acceptance.

The resilience of the human spirit tends to be underestimated whenever we assert that this or that outlook, this or that philosophy, is destroying man's "tragic sense of life." It is certainly true, moreover, that the tragic character has been a paradox in any case; with his noble and ignoble elements existing in delicate balance he could hardly be anything else. If a particular era, our own not the least, depletes the supply of tragic values available to a generation, the talented playwright's sympathy and insight can still supply restorative and redemptive elements. He may, of course, be under the influence of his times, but no creative writer is exclusively under that influence. He may be the child of his own age, but he is also the proud heir of past ages of humanism. The creation of art is not a conditioned reflex. Tragedy especially must be thought of as a thing consciously *made*—made by the tragedian in collaboration with the whole human estate as well as with his age. And the tragic character, incidentally, is usually shown *making himself tragic* or, as in the case of Oedipus, making himself more tragic.

Still, in representing inner conflicts or in clashing with characters holding opposed values, the protagonist brings the common and ignoble elements of a society, as well as of human nature, into the tragic action. Every age, in brief, contributes its meanness as well as its nobility to the tragedies written in its time. The meanness and the gross values of our own age, I would conclude, cannot be regarded as an inexorable injunction against the existence of tragic art. The meanness and evil of modern times, on the contrary, *belong* to modern tragedy, just as the deplorable aspects of the Renaissance belonged to Elizabethan tragedy.

Without incorporating the unadmirable qualities of men and their times, indeed, tragic literature would be literature in a void. We tend to see the heroic element without the antiheroic in the old masterpieces. We ennoble the "tragic flaw" and play down that which is shameful about it or about the milieu that produced it. I like, therefore, Cedric Whitman's reference to "the self-slain greatness" of the tragic character and William McCollom's statement in his recent book, *Tragedy* (page 167), that "the hero's shame is the corollary of his genius." But the role of the "unnoble" element in drama has yet to be explored. We have to pick up the clue that Nietzsche left us in juxtaposing Dionysian and Apollonian aspects in *The Birth of Tragedy*.

The heroic element or the "genius" of the tragic character should, of course, also receive due weight. But we must come to understand it a little better than we usually do in the case of contemporary characters such as Willy Loman, the salesman-hero of *Death of a Salesman*. Arthur Miller has insisted upon the tragic worth of this greatly flawed character, and anybody familiar with the struggles of the little man and not too sheltered or snobbish to be capable of sympathy should know what heroism is required of the Willy Lomans of the world. Or if this appeal is too "common" for some members of the literary and academic world perhaps they will respond to the monitions of the poem by Goethe in which admission to the Moslem paradise of heroes is claimed on the grounds that it was heroic enough to be a human being. Willy Loman indeed makes himself a tragic hero of sorts by his abundant capacity for suffering in the present action; by his fine resentment of slights, by his battle for self-respect, and by his refusal to surrender all expectations of triumph for, and through, his son. Willy is passionately unwilling to resign himself to failure and the cheat of days. His very agony gives him tragic stature within the recognizable world of middle-class realities, and it is surely true that the tragic hero is not tragic by status prior to his action in a play. Tragedy is no one's prerogative; it is rather, *earned* damnation and redemption. The tragic hero *makes himself* tragic—by his struggle and suffering.

Moreover, he makes himself tragic *differently* in different societies. Even awareness on the hero's part, the "tragic awareness" upon which so much stress has been placed of late, is bound to be different in the case of different characters differently conditioned by the social situation. Miller would be justified in insisting that, within limits that are themselves valid dramatic factors in *Death of a Salesman*, Willy does arrive at self-realization—that is, at a degree of self-realization that can be convincingly Willy's. And I, for one, fail to perceive any virtue in recognitions that are conspicuously out of character and have been imposed upon the play from without—that is, from the author's philosophy of tragedy or from "literature," as in the case of *Winterset*.

The most convincing and, to my mind, also the most significant characters make themselves tragic in collaboration with their world. In tragedy, as William McCollom has rightly observed, there is both "self-determination" and "social determination." In various scenes set in the present and the past, Willy seeks the truth about himself and his situation. The search is his, for we must not ignore the fact that all the flashbacks and hallucinations in *Death of a Salesman* are in Willy's own anguished consciousness. Willy pursues the "truth" and struggles against it within his personal and social limits no less arduously and catastrophically than Oedipus. It is possible to say, then, that Miller's protagonist brings both personal and social meanness into his play, but that he also brings personal stature and heroism into it.

The one thing Miller could not do—that Miller's scrupulousness indeed would not have allowed him to do—is to give Willy *an interesting mind*. And it is chiefly this limitation, along with a limitation of language (because the character is an urban commoner while the author is rarely a poet), that has made me contemplate the use of such a term as "low tragedy," my intention being to distinguish modern democratic drama from the aristocratic "high tragedy" of earlier ages. Perhaps indeed the genius of our century resides precisely in "low tragedy," if we are to allow ourselves a generalization concerning the taste and aptitude of the age. For there is a difference in the degree of tragic exaltation and exhilaration, of tragic realization and liberation or catharsis, as well as a difference in tone such as appears when we contrast the relative informality of discourse by a Giraudoux or Cocteau with tragic dialogue by Marlowe, Shakespeare, and Racine. "Low tragedy" is the only term that seems sufficiently descriptive of *The Lower Depths* and *The Iceman Cometh, The Tragedy of Nan* and *Desire Under the Elms, The Three Sisters* and *The House of Bernarda Alba, The Weavers* and *The Plough and the Stars, Drayman Henschel* and *Death of a Salesman, Rosmersholm* and *John Gabriel Borkman,* and even Giraudoux' *Electra* and Cocteau's *The Infernal Machine.*

If "low tragedy" were employed descriptively rather than pejoratively, it could become useful in calling attention to a modern type of tragedy different from the typical forms of classic and Elizabethan tragic writing. And surely the term does not have to be derogatory; powerful dramatic impressions have been created, for instance, by O'Casey's colloquial passionateness and O'Neill's prosaic masonry. When I use the terms "low comedy" and "high comedy" to describe the work of Plautus and Terence respectively, I certainly do not intend a slur on Plautine comedy. It is possible to describe differences without establishing hierarchies. And when I nevertheless, accept the superiority of *Hamlet* to, let us say, *Death of a Salesman,* it is not because I think of Shakespeare's tragedy as "more tragic," but because I consider it more expressive, and *more beautiful.*

MARK SPILKA

(b. 1925)

Mark Spilka is a scholar-critic who has written essays on a wide range of literary figures and works. He combines an interest in theory with the exercise of practical criticism in which formalist analysis is supported by the use of psychology, social theory, and literary history. He is the author of *The Love Ethic of D. H. Lawrence* (1955) and *Dickens and Kafka* (1963) and the editor of *D. H. Lawrence, A Collection of Critical Essays* (1963).

The Necessary Stylist: A New Critical Revision (1960-61)

The progress of the New Criticism is relatively simple to graph: a steady upward climb, from about 1930 to 1950, then a sudden levelling off for the next decade, with noticeable bumps and ruffles near the sixties. Though the success of the

"The Necessary Stylist: A New Critical Revision" by Mark Spilka. From *Modern Fiction Studies,* VI (Winter, 1960-61), 283-297. Revised by Mark Spilka for publication in this volume, and reprinted by his permission and that of the Purdue Research Foundation.

movement is undeniable, it seems to have lost its initial force and direction and now threatens to decline for lack of generative ideas. For critics trained in the fifties, however, it remains a major source of intellectual ferment. For this generation especially it functions as the formative approach to literature, more challenging and absorbing than other current theories. If the movement is to acquire new strength, these new adherents must provide it. The founding fathers have had their say; the unruly or subservient sons—Jarrell, Fiedler, Hyman, Stallman—have gone their different ways, and the fate of the movement lies with younger men. This being the case, the nature of its appeal for them is worth exploring.

Irving Howe has argued that criticism has become "a problem in mechanics, the tools, methods and trade secrets of which can be picked up, usually during the summer, from the more experienced operatives" (*Partisan Review,* XXI, 27-28). As a representative summer product, let me vouch for this as partial truth. For better or worse, the New Criticism does attract the novice with its methodology which resembles "mechanics" in its thoroughness and objectivity: but it also offers him a ready-made aesthetic, a set of easily mastered concepts which subtly redirect its method. This blend of theory and practice is called "explicative holism" by W. K. Wimsatt, who means by this the careful analysis of specific texts, considered as autonomous wholes (*The Verbal Icon* [New York, 1954], p. 237). The word "autonomous" is, of course, an abstraction, like "universal" or "eternal"; but, unlike these older aesthetic terms, it puts space around a novel, poem, or story, and lends solidity to the work within; it outlines and substantiates a forbidden realm of knowledge, and thus opens it to explication.

In a positivistic age this strategy has its merits: it gives literature some status in reality, without raising metaphysical issues; and it saves it from absorption into origins and effects, as mere history and impression. Like other useful metaphors—"organic form," "the verbal icon," "the objective correlative"—it grants imagined life to words upon a page. Nor is this merely to hypostatize the work for critical practice; instead the term connects us with realities which we all affirm, but are hard put to defend against the realities of science. The New Critics defend them for us in two ways: by their own objective method, which

is itself "scientific" and hence competitive in function; and by covert and protective metaphors, like autonomy and organic form, which begin in biology but end in metaphysics, since they point to knowledge of a kind not reached by science. These knowledge-claims are seldom boldly asserted; but all the major formalists—Brooks, Warren, Tate, Ransom, Vivas—seem to assume them; in fact, there is considerable ground for calling formalism a disguise for spiritual concern with literature (*cf.* Richard Foster, *Hudson Review,* XII, 232-246). For my own generation this has always been the secret appeal of the movement: its promise of something like objective certainty about subjective truths—their order, worth and meaning—as revealed through verbal forms. We are even somewhat impatient with our elders here. As Hyatt Waggoner confirms, young men "are likely to feel that the new criticism does not attack value questions directly or determinedly enough, that it tries . . . too hard to be objective and so ends by keeping its largest assumptions out of sight" (*Criticism,* I, 219). We feel the need, in short, to re-examine those assumptions.

If it was once necessary to hide them, so that literature might appear as respectable and real as science, it seems important now to exhume them and to face their implications squarely. The movement, having won all major battles, has become its own worst enemy: its problems are internal, not external, and strategies designed to rout scientists and "old scholars" will not resolve them. The defect here is narrowness of a special order. To remove it, some recent theorists would buttress formalism with an eclectic or synoptic mixture of methods (*cf.* Waggoner, 211-225, and Northrop Frye, *Anatomy of Criticism* [Princeton, 1957]). Others would strike at theory itself: they would broaden the base of formalism by showing that quality in verbal art depends partly on external elements, like history and language, and on shared awareness of those elements (*cf.* Roy Harvey Pearce, *Kenyon Review,* XX, 554-591, and Walter Sutton, *Jour-*

nal of Aesthetics and Art Criticism,
XVII, 219-229). This connection between *form* and broader contexts seems
to me exactly right. New Critical narrowness is internal; it will not be cured by
added methods; but the movement might
transcend its limits, and achieve its promise, through expansion and revision of
its formal concepts. Among them is the
concept of the author, which bears importantly on such issues as autonomy, intention, response and objectivity. If we
can connect the author *formally* with his
works, rather than historically or bio-
graphically, we can begin to make some
headway in connecting literature with
life.

II

The concept of the author is conspicuous, in New Critical thought, by
its absence. Sometimes this absence
means an actual blank space on the page,
as in experimental texts where poems
appear by number only and poets' names
are exiled to the index (*e.g.,* Richards'
Practical Criticism and Thomas and
Brown's *Reading Poems* [New York,
1955]). But generally speaking, names
are given their usual task of identification. New Critics are even well-informed
about authors' lives and times, and will
use such knowledge freely, if "unfor-
mally," when it adds to meaning. They
are not averse to scholarship, *per se,* but
to its critical sins. When they first reacted
against those sins, they did so to excess
and created latent troubles of their own.
Still, the initial step was badly needed.

According to Roy Harvey Pearce, historians had so confused works with setting that works became for them "just
dim spots on the historical horizon—so
dim that it [didn't] seem worthwhile to
distinguish one from another; so dim
that critical explication [was] at best an
adventure in uncontrolled impressionism" (562). To correct that trend, early
theorists tried to isolate and brighten
works by calling them autonomous and
organic; then later theorists defined two
kinds of fallacies, the intentional and the
affective, which made for further isola-

tion, if not for greater brightness. By
these definitions it was wrong to derive
standards of critical judgment from
authors' aims or readers' feelings; it was
right to derive them from the work itself,
conceived as verbal object. Rigidity and
exclusiveness began here, I think, with
definitions which were clear on sin but
vague on virtue, and which made extremely sharp distinctions between feeling and idea. What is the role of feeling,
for instance, in literary judgment? Do we
abandon it, with Wellek and Austin Warren, and settle for "the perceptions of
emotions" (*Theory of Literature* [New
York, 1956], p. 25)? Or do we translate
"formulas of emotion," with Wimsatt
and Beardsley, so that others may respond to them (Wimsatt, pp. 34, 37)?
In either case, it seems to me impossible
to have perceptions, much less formulas,
without using actual feelings to confirm
them.

Discernment and response work
hand-in-hand, in critical practice, though
with varying predominance and intensity; but for most of the New Critics
these elements remain estranged. Literature, for them, embodies feeling, while
criticism disembodies thought: witness
Richards' spurious distinction between
scientific and emotive use of language; or
Eliot's odd belief that poets never
"think"—they find emotional equivalents
for thought; or Wimsatt's admonition
that understanding and evaluation are as
far apart for cognitive as for emotive
critics. Yet feeling and idea are seldom
disconnected in this manner; the inter-
flow between them is psychological fact
(*cf.* Lionel Trilling, *The Liberal Imagination* [New York, 1953], p. 273). When
New Critics hold, to the contrary, that
emotion plays no role in critical discernment, they invite affective chaos. For in
their view we need never question our
emotions nor doubt the purity of our perceptions: as objective critics, we have
already eschewed subjective judgments;
but if complete detachment happens to
be impossible, such judgments must return without our conscious knowledge. In
other words, the affective fallacy, as a
warning concept, has not eliminated im-

pressionism; it has simply driven it underground.

But our chief argument is with the intentional fallacy, which has led to much the same results. As everyone knows, authors are suspicious figures, victims of inspiration, drugs, drink, neurosis, vanity and self-deception; they are fallible, that is, and critics have rightly questioned their pronouncements of intention. Ideally, the work itself reveals *achieved* intention—the only kind which matters, since it indicates where judgment must begin. At this level of discussion, we might add one rule of thumb: if outside evidence corrects or assists objective judgment, there is no point in ignoring it, provided that achievement (not intention) is the test of relevance (*cf.* Waggoner, pp. 220-221, and Henry David Aiken, *Journal of Philosophy*, LII, pp. 742-753). This is common sense, and most New Critics would accept it. The real trouble lies elsewhere, in their failure to accommodate the author's role as stylist.

One critic, Wimsatt, does allude to the poet as "sayer," "maker," or "accomplisher" (pp. xviii, 263). His terms are undefined, however, and he never demonstrates their value. He seems almost to equate the poet with his finished work. More likely, he detaches him completely, since equation might suggest a formal bond, an interfusion, a personal invasion of an otherwise impersonal and autonomous realm. But isn't this a definition of style—that personal element which seems so tangibly *there*, in arts like painting, where we identify a Rembrandt or Renoir by visible characteristics, ways of arranging light, shadow, color and shape to achieve *organic wholes*? Such distinctive traits are less apparent in literature, but they do exist in Austen, Conrad or Fitzgerald novels, in poems by Wyatt, Milton, Hardy, Yeats. And if we mean by style two things—a characteristic use of language and (more difficult to define) a characteristic way of arranging experience for aesthetic ends—then these and other writers have recognizable styles. If we mean, beyond this double definition, that style adapts itself to

theme, or to an author's working vision of existence, then it affects the very quality and form of single works, and, through it, authors too connect with works in formal ways. In this sense, authors are that common element which persists, even in changing aspects, throughout their whole production: they inform specific works yet at the same time stand outside them; they are the shapers, makers and accomplishers whom critics *must* consult if they would analyze organic wholes.

Because they have concerned themselves, so frequently, with single poems, and because their rescue work has made them concentrate on isolation, New Critics have forgotten that each verbal object lives in company with others like itself. We read the *novels* of Joyce and Lawrence, the *plays* of Shakespeare, the *poems* of Keats: we seldom stop with one creation. And because we familiarize ourselves with *works*, we see the common element which unites them, the personal dimension which informs them, the stylist who creates them. To ignore the stylist, it seems to me, is to ignore the very principle of form—the creative principle, which invests each work with its uniqueness. Style ought to be our foremost clue to that uniqueness, that achieved intention which we also call "organic form." We use such clues in practice, where knowledge of related works improves our grasp of single texts. But New Critics treat such knowledge as mere preparation for analysis: they do the same with history and biography, as if autonomy were absolute and all else relative and inert. Yet autonomy itself is relative: all works of art exist within surrounding contexts, on which their quality depends.

We say of poetry, for instance, that it suffers in translation, which violates the subtle interconnections of image, rhythm, sound and idea. This inviolateness demonstrates the autonomy of specific poems, but it also highlights their dependence on a given language, a social and historical medium in which their very form inheres. In the same vein, Walter Sutton holds that poems depend for their effects upon reference to things outside the poems: they appeal to common experience and shared value; they proceed from and are received in contexts broader than themselves (pp. 226-229). The responsible critic must accept these broader contexts and account for their effect on form. His maxim here might run: no work of art is an island, entire of itself; no organism exists which is not dependent, in the most vital way, on its surroundings (a maxim drawn, incidentally, from Aiken and Sutton). When those surroundings consist of similar creations, their common maker reasserts his formal role. As stylist, he controls the quality of language, the arrangement of experience for aesthetic ends, the expression of a total vision. Accordingly, the critic must consult the general contours of his work, his phases and progressions, his favorite themes and methods, the kinds of problems which he can or cannot solve. Biography and history enter, not as background, but as contexts which add knowledge of the stylist. Intention now becomes involved with critical judgment, since the maker's aims are manifest in form, in conscious and unconscious fusion. In short, the total process is organic, from biography through art to judgment, if we confirm the author's role as stylist and the supporting role of felt response.

If, on the other hand, we minimize the author's role, as we persistently minimize response, the penalties are these: the critic will become the author, he will supply his own intention (plus his own emotions) and rewrite the story; and he will do this with impunity, since there is no stylist to rebuff him, no maker to deny his reading: he is, after all, an objective critic, a master of autonomous wholes, who contemplates his text within the vacuum which surrounds it, or at the most, within inert surroundings. Wimsatt argues against such penalties, saying that works belong neither to authors nor to critics, but to the public (p. 5); but if an author does *inform* (rather than own) his works, and no one grants his role, the critic will assume it. The temptation is too great, in an age when creativity is

scarce and precious; critics are as apt to steal it as biographers were before them. Indeed, we might even see a wave of New Intentionalists and Impressionists, of critics who twist stories to their liking and seem insensitive to affective quality. Such critics will commit what I would call the Objective Fallacy: the belief in objectivity without recourse to feeling or informing style. But of course we all commit that fallacy these days, as critics and teachers reared on formalist doctrines. Whatever our critical talents, we all project assumptions into texts; we acquire the gloss of objectivity from method, from thorough sifting of evidence and from close analysis, which guarantee our virtue; when contradictions arise, ingenuity removes them—the mind has patterns to enforce which override the text, the searching heart, or that biographical myth, the creative writer. Because such lapses are so common, we must all learn how to avoid them, or more pertinently, how to strengthen the movement which unwittingly invites them.

III

What are we to say, for instance, when sensitive, intelligent formalists reveal the co-existence, in "After Apple-Picking," of nightmares with contemplative delights? or when they postulate a "shorter happy life" for Mrs. Macomber, an access of renewed devotion as she attempts to save her husband but accidentally kills him? One is reminded here of Randall Jarrell's complaint of 1952, that "Criticism will soon have reached the state of scholarship, and the most obviously absurd theory—if it is maintained intensively, exhaustively, and professionally—will do the theorist no harm in the eyes of his colleagues" (*Partisan Review,* XIX, 193). Apparently that state has come to pass. The above-mentioned readings *are* maintained "intensively, exhaustively, and professionally"; they seem exemplary in thoroughness and objectivity, in modesty and detachment: yet the whole effect is of methodology gone berserk. Confronted by such readings, we cannot merely explicate the same details more sensibly and rest our case. Inclusiveness and coherence, those touchstones of objective certainty, will not avail us: our opponents have achieved inclusive and coherent readings (give or take a few absurdities), and there is no way to refute them from the isolated text. Objective readings, equally exhaustive and consistent, merely cancel out when diametrically opposed, and objectivity itself reverts to armed impressionism. If we can grant, however, that texts extend to human contexts, through creation and response, we may begin to validate objective readings. We may show, for instance, how critics violate the stylist's mode of operation, distort his plain assumptions, neglect his characteristic weightings and arrangements, ignore the limits of his diction, or appeal to other works for *corroboration*—but never to define the author's vision; and we may expose their affective blindness, their insensitivity to tonal quality, and their own disguised impressionism. If, on the other hand, we neglect these aspects of creation and response, we have no way to combat exemplary madness—and no way to prevent its certain spread. Our passion for the verbal object, and for objective criticism, is right and central; but without provision for the stylist, and for the emotionally responsive reader, our claim to objectivity will collapse—indeed, is now collapsing.

I am speaking here of an advanced stage of critical practice, not of introductory methods; and I am speaking of an advanced stage of the New Criticism, which, in its early missionary zeal, produced a permanent body of objective readings and worked a vital revolution in the academies through stress on explication. There is a point, however, when an objective mode becomes defensive, becomes an evasion of those inner depths which justify its use, and which it first sought to preserve. At such a point methods can rigidify or turn destructive: adherents, in their sophistication, can abuse them with humane intentions, or use them to disguise their own impressions. We are all familiar with such

readings, which destroy or cancel meaning through exhaustive ingenuity. To avoid them, or simply to counteract their damage, we need acts of critical imagination, attempts to reconstruct the terms of an author's vision, and to define its limits and capacities (*cf.* E. D. Hirsch, Jr., *PMLA,* LXXV, 463-479, for corroborative views). Such acts can only proceed, of course, through cumulative insights, drawn from tentative and wisely selective reading, and from scholarly research. Once these requirements are met, the return to single texts should be rewarding. The need for sheer intelligence remains, but granting this necessity, the process fosters several virtues: it operates by open and demonstrable assumptions, which, even if they are wrong, are nonetheless open; it broadens critical outlook and so overcomes myopic trends in current practice; and finally, it works on human as well as formal grounds, since the imaginative act embraces human contexts and forces judgment of the stylist's aims, powers, and values—his vision of significant life.

We must commit ourselves, I think, to such analysis as we explicate specific texts. We can do so with confidence, if we use imaginative reconstructions to support (rather than supplant) objective methods, and to reinforce their cognitive role—their role, that is, in revealing patterns of experiential truth. Once methodology rescued verbal works from science, and preserved them as forbidden realms of knowledge; now it threatens to destroy them, since we worship it as an end and forget its instrumental function. In our extreme objectivity, we have reduced the reading process to an experience of isolated forms. In itself this is harmless, since those forms are rich with qualitative knowledge, and to experience them has immediate value. But method, used in isolation, will eventually betray the reader and destroy that value; we *must* connect those forms with human contexts—with stylists and responsive readers—to keep their worth (indeed, their *sense*) intact. The need is urgent in a changing academic world. The mass influx of students, in the postwar period, has created teaching jobs for young New Critics, or, at the least, young "explicative holists." Together with the "old" New Critics, this group has met the American middle class head on, or met its brighter children, and has taught them how to read good literature. This is a unique achievement, unparalleled in critical history; there has never been a semi-popular movement which could so affect the quality of our culture. But if method is its burden, the duration of effect seems doubtful and its depth uncertain. The New Critics are not "empty formalists," as so often charged; at their worst, they are self-defeating formalists who continue to use tough-minded scientific attitudes to rescue art from science. The great irony here is to defeat oneself by imitating positivists. The great challenge is to be humanists—to acquire subjective knowledge through objective methods, and so change the quality of American culture.

ALFRED KAZIN

(b. 1915)

Alfred Kazin has been an editor, reporter, college instructor, and public lecturer at various times during his career as a literary critic. His critical viewpoint was conditioned early by his deep sense of identification with the life of New York City, where he was born, reared, and educated, and about which he has written in his autobiographical *A Walker in the City* (1951). He views literature as deriving its human importance primarily from its intellectual and moral functions, a view nurtured by his early interest in the work of such critics as Sainte-Beuve, Matthew Arnold, Van Wyck Brooks, and Edmund Wilson. As might be expected, he views criticism as an essentially public and societal rather than coterie activity. The critic, according to Kazin's ideal, is an intellectual journalist whose responsibility is to judge literature in the light of the social and political needs of his moment in history, and to judge, in turn, the life of his time in the light of literature's moral and intellectual illumination of it. *On Native Grounds* (1942), which Kazin has described as "a moral history of America from the dark days of the 1880's up to the present," is still his best known book. *The Inmost Leaf* (1953) and *Contemporaries* (1962) are collections of critical essays and reviews originally published in various American magazines and symposia. Kazin has edited several collections, including *The Portable William Blake* (1946), *F. Scott Fitzgerald: the Man and His Work* (1951), and *The Stature of Theodore Dreiser* (with Charles Shapiro, 1955).

The Function of Criticism Today (1960)

Some years ago, in a course I was giving on European novels, a student handed in a paper in which he described Emile

Reprinted from *Commentary*, October, 1960, Copyright American Jewish Committee, by permission of *Commentary* and the author. Reprinted in *Contemporaries* (1962), pp. 494-509.

Zola's *Germinal*—that powerful but old-fashioned novel of French miners struggling for their rights—as characterized by *paradox, tension,* and *ambiguity.* Since these terms were brought into modern criticism to characterize the tensely wrought and ambivalent verse of the 17th-century metaphysicals, and then the poetry of those (like T. S. Eliot) who absorbed a style, a manner, from these Hamlet-like literary intellectuals, I explained that Zola's rather large and florid prose style—the style a French naturalist needs to get himself through a shelf of documentary novels describing the ravages of alcoholism and syphilis on all the descendants of a French family— could not possibly be compared to those highly artful poets. Zola's style certainly has its share of grandiloquent poetry, and Zola liked, in the manner of the epic-writing romantics, to sign himself *poète*. But *Germinal*, in both its crudity and its passion, its violent sexual metaphors and its indignant description of the oppressed, is so far from the language and subject of an Eliot that, properly speaking, it makes no sense to find in 19th-century naturalistic fiction the attributes of what is, even for our time, only one kind of poetry.

My student insisted on his point. He had been instructed in *paradox, tension,* and *ambiguity* in a course called "Introduction to Literature," and with the very text of *Germinal* before him, he was so concerned with showing that he knew how to read his book with a modish approach to literature, that he simply could not recognize the most obvious quality of Zola's great novel—which was its force. He felt no necessary connection between his experience and that described in the novel, but he had brought in wholly arbitrary connections, couched in a critical vocabulary that he had learned by rote, whose historical applications and limitations he did not understand. He was like a tourist in a foreign country; he could imitate the language but he did not understand it. There was no community of interest between himself and the novel, but he did not even realize this, he was not even thinking of the novel he was reading, so busy was he plastering *paradox, tension,* and *ambiguity* over Zola's astonished face.

Now this quality of making arbitrary connections, this lack of historical aware-

ness, often of historical information rudimentary enough to supply guideposts and danger signals in going through the country of Zola, this false sophistication —this is what troubles me about many students who have been taught to read critically, as the saying goes, but who do not really read at all, who do not enjoy reading, who have no interest in literature. But equally, I'm troubled by the editors who print my essays but are utterly unconcerned with my ideas and values, with the readers who come up to say how much they have "enjoyed" a piece but who never discuss the argument in it. There's something wrong, some basic element missing, in the relationship of the audience to the critic in America today, and I see this wrongness in the professional journals for which you don't have to take the trouble to write well and in the Sunday book supplements that exist only to sell books, in the lack of general magazines publishing serious criticism, and in the very absence of any responsible and authoritative evaluation of contemporary literature. There are a great many rewarding and fruitful sides to being a literary critic, but one of the things that we don't talk about, that some of us never even notice, is the absence of echo to our work, the uncertainty of response, the confusion of basic terms in which we deal. It's not that we lack an audience; it's that the audience doesn't know what it wants, is not sure of what it thinks, is fundamentally uneasy with literature, even afraid of it, and wants to control the beast rather than to live with it.

This situation is what characterizes criticism in a mass society—mass communications in themselves have changed nothing and determine nothing. As soon as you get people who do not read themselves but who feel that they need criticism to make contact with literature, as soon as the educated public (which used to test its own opinions on the critic's) breaks up into the self-declared mass that wants things to be explained, then you get the critic-as-popularizer, the critic consciously mediating between the work of art and the public. But no critic who is any good sets out deliberately to enlighten someone else; he writes to put his own ideas in order; to possess, as a critic, through the integral force of his intelligence, the work of art that someone else had created. Of course he will elucidate, he will analyze, he will define and locate and explain, but all the things he does for his reader he does first for himself.

What the critic does for his reader, for the public, he does on the flood tide, so to speak, of his excitement with a particular book, a brave new insight, an evaluation, a theory. A critic is not an artist, except incidentally; he is a thinker, and it is the force, the exactness, the extension—perhaps the originality—of his thinking, that gets him to say those things that the artist himself may value as an artist, the reader as a reader. To the true critic insights are valuable for themselves, and different members of the audience may use them in different ways. But no critic who works for the pleasure and excitement of his task writes just to instruct the writer he is reviewing and for the sake exclusively of the public that reads him. For the interest of criticism lies in itself, in the thinking that it practices.

Criticism affects the artist only as the artist is himself a member of the educated public that reads criticism. A writer will often get better advice about a book from his editor or his wife, or his literary agent, than from a critic. But the critic, if he is interesting and deep enough, will affect the writer far more profoundly than would specific technical criticism of a book—by making him see the significance of his efforts. At its best, true literary criticism may actually suggest new subjects, can enliven the imagination. This is the great tradition of criticism, a part of the general criticism of established values which must go on in every age. Its greatest single attribute is its force, its passionate declaration of the true nature of man and what his proper destiny must be. In America itself, this was the kind of criticism that Emerson wrote in his great essay on The Poet and

that Whitman created in *Democratic Vistas*, John Jay Chapman in his essay on Emerson, and the young Van Wyck Brooks in *America's Coming of Age* and his much underrated book on Mark Twain. The greatest examples of such criticism in modern times were Arnold's essays on poetry and culture, Proust's attack on Sainte-Beuve, and Nietzsche's on Wagner. To me this is the most valuable kind of criticism—the kind that Baudelaire wrote in dealing with art, Shaw in dealing with drama, and that before them had been practiced by Goethe in his remarks on the Age of Prose, by Schiller in his letters on aesthetics, by Blake in his personal manifestoes, by Wordsworth in his preface to *Lyrical Ballads*. It is the kind of criticism that I always think of as *histoire morale,* that sums up the spirit of the age in which we live and then asks us to transcend it, that enables us to see things in the grand perspective, and that in the way of Marx on Greek philosophy, of Kierkegaard on Mozart, of Nietzsche on the birth of tragedy, of Shaw on Ibsen, of Lawrence on American literature, asks us—not only in the light of man's history but of his whole striving—to create a future in keeping with man's imagination.

It is precisely because he once wrote criticism of this kind that Eliot has had his influence—Eliot, when asked by Paul Elmer More why his poetry and criticism were written in such different tones, replied that poetry deals with the world as it is, criticism with the world as it ought to be. It is because of his grounding in the historical ideals of self-liberation which we associate with Marx and Freud that Lionel Trilling has remained so steadily a moral influence, an Emersonian teacher of the tribe, and it is because of his constant awareness that books make revolutions in the public history as well as in the private sensibility of men that Edmund Wilson has been able to write with equal insight of Proust and John O'Hara, Michelet and Edna St. Vincent Millay, Tolstoy and Lincoln, the Hebrew Bible and the Marquis de Sade. The Van Wyck Brooks who, at least in 1915, wrote with such verve and exhilaration against the plaster gods of American life worked constantly with this sense of being sent forward by an irresistible movement of social criticism in all fields. And as I write I seem to see this image not in any young American critic but in the young British drama critic, Kenneth Tynan, who before he left this country was summoned up before a secret Congressional session for his dangerous thoughts. Tynan's rule for drama criticism is, "Rouse tempers, goad, lacerate, raise whirlwinds," and I must say that his sense of art as something dramatically and effectively involved in the affairs of men is one which any serious critic of drama must have, for on the stage, at least, the passions of men as makers of history are inescapable.

The essence of such criticism is that it is concerned explicitly, fightingly, with an ideal of man, with a conception of what man is seeking to become, with what he must become. The dynamic sense of values, the electric and constantly demanding sense of his age which such a critic has—this is the quality that makes him a particularly keen and demanding analyst of concrete values, of aesthetic differences. For there is a significant distinction between what I would call passive "taste," as a social category concerned only with success of execution, and the critic's judgment, which says that so-and-so is a good writer, but not good enough, or that it is because he is a good writer that he is also a dangerous writer, such a narrowing or stultifying influence. By keeping alive the spirit of criticism in the sense in which the Enlightenment gave it to us—the "modern spirit," as Matthew Arnold called it, which subjects everything handed down to us, all institutions and beliefs, to critical examination, we no longer limit our aesthetic categories to the beautiful, the sublime, the merely correct. Goethe, in his essay on art and the classic, identified the modern age with what he called the age of prose, and lamented that "the all too radical attempt of the age of philosophy (18th century) at a 'humanization' and ration-

alization of the mysterious ends in a perverted miracle. The mystery, cheated of its rightful place, goes underground, reverting to its primeval, unholy and barbarous stage. No center holds the human world together and men must lose their bearings." This is virtually the language of Yeats's "The Second Coming," and in one form or another of most of the criticism that has been modeled on Eliot's well-known laments for Catholic order. But Goethe himself, as a poet, a dramatist, as a speculative free-wheeling scientist, found his new forms, new interests, a brave new future for himself, in exactly this modern spirit. And criticism, in our modern sense of it, examining works not for their classic theory or neoclassic correctness, but for their fulfillment of the goals which they have independently set, has led to an awareness of aesthetic possibility and of individual vision which unites *all* modern poets, novelists, and painters, whether they acknowledge it or not, whether they want it or not, as children of the Romantic movement. The point of this modern spirit in art is not that everyone agrees on the value of the modern movement, but that everyone must work in its atmosphere of freedom and individual discovery—Catholic artists as well as secularist artists, the haters of the modern spirit as well as its most pragmatist admirers. There are no longer any aesthetic goals which we can name outside the individual works of art that give us our fertile and experimental sense of aesthetic achievement. Marcel Proust wrote an essay attacking Sainte-Beuve's naturalistic conception of art, and in the middle of this essay virtually began to sketch the first pages of his famous novel. He had discovered his own necessary vision, his artistic credo, in attacking as a profound danger to the imaginative life of humanity Sainte-Beuve's "neo-scientific" view of life. But out of this necessary "chaos" of positions, as Goethe thought of it, had come not merely Proust's discovery of himself as an original and major artist but his discovery, through the profound revelation afforded by the inner consciousness, of the new vision of the eternal open to modern artists. The possibilities opened up to us by creative memory became Proust's idea of the future.

To use Jacques Barzun's significant phrase, the "energies of art" are revealed to us, and so can be described and judged, only when they are seen against the background of man's striving, man's belief that *he* can help create the future he wants. There is no energy where there is no hope—no energy, no wit, no passion, no involvement, no lightness. Our individual sense of the future is the dimension in which we breathe, or as Emily Dickinson put it, "*I dwell in Possibility— / A fairer house than Prose.*" We can judge what things are like because in our hearts we know what we really want; we judge by the direction, the vector of forces, along which life seems to be moving. If a writer believes in his own vision of things, no matter how idiosyncratic it may seem, that is all the future he may need. But he must believe in it, as Blake believed in his visions, Dostoevsky in the redemption of sinners, and Marx in the holy city that would be created by communism. This sense of the eventual vindication of life by the imagination is what gives meaning to every great artist's life, and it is the critic's job to support this belief, to delineate it, to fight for it. Through this dimension of the imaginative future alone can we understand what literature is for. And to bring this kind of imagination, this historical sense of what has been, what is now, what must be—to bring this into play, in the immediate confrontation and analysis of works of art, is to make evaluation significant—one might almost say, possible. There is in every true work of art a tendency pressing for recognition, pressing a work of art together, and without recognizing what the work of art is itself striving to be, in the light of what man himself is always striving to become, our evaluation becomes a question of frigid correctness.

So strongly committed are we by now to the idea of a work of art as created from a wholly individual standpoint, and

measurable by the goals which the work itself has set, that anyone who really practices critical judgment, who is constantly engaged in confronting new and unforeseen works of art, actually finds his own physical energies challenged and changed by the energies of art. He cannot save himself from the sometimes painful new experience that a new work presents. This does not mean that he is an impressionist, taking his own prejudices and limitations as the only values. It means that his skill begins by noticing his intuitive reactions and building up from them; he responds to the matter in hand with perception at the pitch of passion, as Henry James puts it; the unity of thinking and feeling actually exists in the passionate operation of the critic's intelligence. Judgment can be a very physical matter indeed. A false or strained work of art can make you literally sick. Anyone who is serious about criticism, for whom judgment is an active factor in his daily awareness, will have an intensely sensory and tactile response to poems, stories, novels, dramas, essays. In some way, the critic's sense of his existing balance is challenged by that new balance of forces that is a work of art, and in this downright challenge to our physical being that a new work of art can represent, the critic will recognize how much he has been advanced, and how much not, by a work that can be as real to him as sex and his daily bread.

There is no discrimination without partisanship to an ideal. It is undesirable to have a perfect taste, to respond properly to all the masterpieces. Unless we approach literature demandingly, as I say, unless we respect it for its influence, we fall into the attitude of the dilettante, the epicurean, on the style of the late Bernard Berenson, who by trying to prove that his taste was equal to the best that has been thought and said, made culture look like a table set with tidbits. The critic who has the equipment to be a force, the critic who can set up standards for his age, must be a partisan of one kind of art and a bitter critic of another. Like Johnson, he will be unfair to the metaphysicals; like Goethe, to Hölderlin; like Sainte-Beuve, to Flaubert; like Arnold, to Whitman; like Emerson, to Dickens; like Henry James, to Tolstoy; like Eliot, to Shelley; like Wilson, to Kafka; like Trilling, to Dreiser. Such a critic will be not only unfair, he will pursue his prejudice to the point of absurdity, setting up a straw figure that will serve to bear all his dislike and even his hatred of a certain kind of art. And significantly, the critic who sees himself setting standards for his age may stimulate new works of art by helping to create the climate of discussion, by revealing the hidden issues that give a writer a hint of new subjects.

Above all, the critic who works with this sense of the age in his bones, who sees himself working toward the future that man must build for himself, is always a writer. He writes for the public, not to a few imagined co-specialists; he writes to convince, to argue, to establish his argument; he writes dramatically, marshaling his evidence in a way that pure logic would never approve and pure scholarship would never understand, but which is justifiable, if it succeeds, as moral argument in the great tradition of literature. The critic who writes well is the critic who lives in literature, who is involved himself and therefore sees the involvement of literature in our conduct, our thinking, our pleasures, our human fate. Some of the best criticism has been communicated in talk, like Hazlitt's, Goethe's, Alfred Whitehead's, but we know this only because someone wrote it down. Criticism that is not *written*, in the best sense, communicable as literature, is only advice—and if you read the actual letters to authors of such famous editors as Maxwell Perkins, you see immediately the difference between editing and criticism. Some great criticism has been written in private letters, like Ezra Pound's to Laurence Binyon on the latter's translation of *The Divine Comedy*; some as inserts in novels, as in Goethe's *Wilhelm Meister* and Joyce's *A Portrait of the Artist as a Young Man*; a good deal of really valuable criticism has, of course, been written in the form

of verse. But it has to be written so that we can read it—that is, like Plato's philosophy and Marx's sociology and Freud's psychology, it has to explain itself and be read for itself. Criticism should never be so professional that only professionals can read it, for the trouble with writing for professionals is that you don't take the trouble to write well. I have been staggered lately by the absolutely worthless essays in so many recent academic journals devoted to modern literature and criticism. Eliot and Faulkner and Salinger haven't smiled on their anxious elucidators at all. The scholarly journal, in this sense, is no more an organ for criticism than is the *Saturday Review*.

Criticism exists as literature only when it has a great argument to present, and to this I would add that the critic knows his argument in full only by writing it, by coming to grips with his own mind. Arnold's essays are a prime example, and indeed Arnold's essays are far greater than his poetry precisely because even his best poems give the effect of a mind too quickly made up against the modern age and lamenting its loneliness, whereas in his essays, those incomparably noble essays on the study of poetry, on translating Homer, you feel that the subject under discussion has taken him in hand and is directing and searching him out. Eliot's essays seem to me most valuable not for their general prejudices but for the thinking that goes on in them line by line. I have always found it hard to understand how people who dislike Eliot's general line, and I myself certainly do—people like F. R. Leavis and Kenneth Rexroth and Karl Shapiro— can overlook the exciting and moving quality of concern, the level of actual critical thinking, that goes on in Eliot's essays. Eliot, in his essay on Blake, managed to say exactly the right things about Blake's imaginative independence, and to draw the wrong conclusions. But who cares about Eliot's disapproving conclusion so long as we have his exhilarating analysis of Blake's mind? Like everyone else, Eliot has changed his mind about so many things that his conclusions, as such, have no more authority than has Henry James's ignorant assumption that Russian writers never have any style. But Eliot working out a line of critical thinking about the character of Othello, or the conflict between Pascal and Montaigne, creates superb criticism by thinking, how shall I say, not conclusively, as a philosopher might, but critically—making us see all the elements of the literary experience before him.

This has always been Edmund Wilson's special gift, and it is because of the excitement that a particular essay by Wilson can generate, not necessarily by the taste that he upholds, that he can give so much pleasure to people who distrust his opinions. For ironically, it is because Wilson is *not* the mediator between artist and public (except incidentally) he often declares himself to be, it is because in his best work he thinks and thinks, almost desperately, to put his own thoughts in order, that the resulting tension and passion make him effective to the general reader. Similarly, Lionel Trilling's *The Liberal Imagination* comes out of a deep personal drive to set in order the underlying conflict that must possess a radical mind that has seen so many radical values abandoned, misused, and converted into the very opposite of these values. Any critic who is any good is going to write out of a profound inner struggle between what has been and what must be, the values he is used to and those which presently exist, between the past and the present out of which the future must be born.

This struggle with oneself as well as with the age, out of which something must be written and which therefore can be read—this is my test for a critic, and it is for this reason that I admire critics in themselves so different as Shaw and Mencken and Chesterton, Santayana and Eliot, Wilson and Trilling. Of the newer critics writing in English, I admire the dramatic criticism of Kenneth Tynan and Eric Bentley and Lionel Abel, the essays on Whitman and Frost by Randall Jarrell and on the American novel by

Richard Chase. W. H. Auden's poetry seems to me terribly impoverished in recent years, but his critical essays are often profound—yet always written in the great English and Continental tradition of the *feuilleton*, the weekly article. I once heard Professor Harry Levin say disparagingly of the English critics that they have the amateur spirit, but I would reverse the term and say that a critic should be able to write well enough to get paid and so lose his amateur standing.

I like criticism to be as serious as possible in content, but as personal and even idiosyncratic in style as possible—thus reversing the usual academic recipe of the trivial point and the heavy style. Have we forgotten under what conditions so much of the most powerful criticism has originated? Poe wrote his greatest critical essays for general magazines, in the same way that Coleridge and Hazlitt wrote for newspapers. Arnold lectured to audiences so large that many could not hear him. Sainte-Beuve wrote his greatest pieces week after week for newspapers. Eliot wrote his best early essays as a reviewer for English weeklies. Proust wrote his own first essays for frivolous Parisian papers. In our time perhaps the most valuable new interpretation of Lincoln appeared in the *New Yorker*. It was the *Seven Arts*, the old *Nation* and *New Republic*, the *Freeman*, the *Dial*, the *Liberator, Poetry*, the old *Masses*, that published the essays of Randolph Bourne and Van Wyck Brooks and Edmund Wilson, Conrad Aiken and Santayana, William Carlos Williams and Ezra Pound. It was the *American Mercury* that made Mencken one of the prime critical influences on the 20's, and it was in such magazines that Eliot and Pound, Frost and O'Neill, were defended, explained, established. Go back and recall that Emerson's great essays were popular lectures, that Henry James's famous essay on "The Art of Fiction" appeared in a popular magazine, as did his best fiction, that Howells's essays on realism and his marvellous essay on Mark Twain all came out first in magazines. In England, the most significant essays of Beerbohm, Shaw, Wilde, were written as dramatic criticism for magazines, just as Virginia Woolf and Orwell, Lawrence, Chesterton, Ford Madox Ford, and more recently C. P. Snow, Angus Wilson, V. S. Pritchett, have been read in the *New Statesman*, the *Spectator*, the *Sunday Times*, the *Observer*, the *Manchester Guardian Weekly*, the *Times Literary Supplement*, the *Tribune*. This kind of critic sees himself not as a hack, but as a man seizing the largest possible audience for his ideas, and in the weekly dialogue he holds with his readers, he establishes standards, sets up a forum around which ideas gather, where neglected important figures can be revived and new writers recognized.

Behind this tradition of criticism lay the common conviction that there were issues to be fought out, that terms might be shared and understood but that there was no agreement over the solutions. Criticism was still seen as part of the general debate over the ends of man in our age. This was the struggle between Chesterton and Shaw, and earlier, between Wells and Henry James; in America, between the new experimental writers of the 20's and the bitterly resisting old guard represented by the New Humanists. Criticism cannot live without dispute over the terms of art and the significance of certain kinds of art, and dispute was possible because the critic and *his* critics—and the audience which criticized them all—were somehow alive to the same issues and shared the same culture, so they were free to disagree about the necessary ends to be reached.

Now it is my impression that for some time critics in America have had too easy a time of it, that their readers no longer make any great demand on them. And I believe the reason for this is the growing assumption that literature cannot affect our future, that the future is in other hands. It is my impression that there is not much belief that literature can exercise its classic functions of providing ideas central to social policy and moral behavior.

Literature no longer seems to exercise much influence. The reason for this, I think, is the pervasive feeling that our freedom is being taken away from us, that the new society now being built up by the technological revolution and collectivism may no longer leave room for the old-fashioned individual in literary pursuits. C. P. Snow, in *The Two Cultures*, insists that so long as our most sensitive poets and distinguished literary intelligences refuse to become literate in science, the prime maker and shaper of our lives, literature must continue to dwindle into insignificance. Last summer when I visited the Soviet Union in a delegation of American writers, I discovered that in *that* science-worshiping society, delegates at the Congress of Soviet Writers applauded Khrushchev's open contempt for their efforts, and that in public, at least, the only function of literature in a totalitarian and technological society was journalism and propaganda. If the Russian literature of the 19th century made the revolution possible, the new Communist society has turned literature into advertising. Gomulka's Poland even grants avant-garde poets and writers artistic latitude, permits them to write like Wallace Stevens or to paint like Jackson Pollock, so long as they do not tamper with politics. And to speak here only of our own country, you can see that the enormous increase in our population, the predominating influence of an inflationary prosperity, the widespread leisure so often absorbed by television and the cheapest magazines, have accelerated the division into classes that are culturally haves and have-nots. You have more and more people who are indifferent to literature, who positively prefer cheap or bad literature, who are certain that literature has nothing to say to our age. Then you have all the people who, though they profess an interest in literature, know very little about it and cannot make up their own minds about a book. Yet at the same time, those who in a sense are most intimately involved with literature, who care most about it, are in such despair over the future of our society that you have, in the most prosperous and still relatively the most open society in the world, whole battalions of what the Russians call internal emigrés and what we call the beat movement—people who simply don't see the connection between their personal striving and the country at large, and who have holed up in their pads, made a fetish of external spontaneity, in order, even if they cannot write, to live like writers and so preserve what they think of as the last possible portion of their freedom.

Much of this seems to be a phenomenon of economic prosperity rather than of political despair, yet it cannot be denied that the kind of intellectual clan which we now associate with another expansive period, the 20's, and which has always been characteristic of imperial wealth and influence like ours, tends to be muffled in anxieties of one kind or another. I myself believe that we, like everyone else, are now going through such a constantly accelerating historical advance that we are unable to seize the moment properly, to see all that is happening and where it will end. Our whole sense of time has to be changed, but since the only real measure of time is our daily biological cycle, we feel ourselves being constantly exploded into the sky like rockets. We are rushing into our future so fast that no one can say who is making it, or what is being made; all we know is that *we* are not making it, and there is no one, no matter what his age is, who does not in his heart feel that events have been taken out of his hands.

Yet ironically enough, the great idea systems of the past have been so outdistanced by events that very often the only check we have on events at all is contemporary literature. Often enough now it is not Marx, or even Freud, but Eliot, Hemingway, and Faulkner, and more recently J. D. Salinger, by whom an American undergraduate tries to read the plight of the individual today. The literature that we have come to think of as modern literature, the literature that began in the idealism of the early 20th century and that perished only in the depression, the literature of 1914-1935 that now seems to us as almost the last proud assertion of man's will in a still liberal and confident society—this literature has become the great text of our teaching. From it we compose our introduction to literature for students who are separated from the last modern generation not by frustration but by the irresistible momentum of a continually changing society. As English schoolboys once learned history from Homer, so American undergraduates now learn it from Eliot and Hemingway and Faulkner.

The enormous interest in contemporary literature that one finds everywhere in American colleges today stems from this awareness that contemporary literature somehow records our fate—that not only *The Hollow Men, The Bear,* but pressingly now, "A Perfect Day for Bananafish" and *Augie March* and *The Deer Park* provide a text in which we still read our hopes and our fate. No matter how negative Augie March or Seymour Glass or Charles Frances Eitel may seem to be, these heroes of contemporary American literature are still human in the classic manner —they suffer, they are comic, they aim at a world in which human beings can live. I would even say, from my experience as a teacher, that probably nothing else in the liberal curriculum now so much touches on the lives and real thinking of American students as these stories and novels and poems which have kept the unforgettable impression of man's effort to apply his understanding and to assert his will. In many American colleges and universities just now we have virtually no other way of approaching fundamental questions except through the materials furnished by contemporary literature.

And it has been my experience that the critic who teaches literature is now the focus for values and influence that in other cultures are furnished by the family, religion, political ideologies. Randall Jarrell once said that in America today many intellectual couples turn to criticism for the sort of guidance they used to get from a minister. Look at the way the stories of Salinger have been taken up by students, at the frenzied interest in the Beats, at the way various paperbacks become the bible of the student intellectuals. Students in America are starved for what one can only call enlightenment, for the literature that will bring the hidden issues out into the open. Just as America alone has turned psychoanalysis from a clinical method into an ethical system for living, so we fasten on contemporary literature with the same avid need.

Yet the most obvious thing about criticism in America today is that it is not consciously related to any literary movement. It does not consciously work toward a future. Look at much of the criticism that concentrates on Joyce, Eliot, Faulkner, Stevens. Are these essays written so as to suggest new possibilities for art, to welcome new writers, or are they written to explain a point in *Ulysses* that no one else has mentioned? The rebels of the little magazines, the crazy men of *transition* and the *Dial*, have become the staple of the curriculum. If you take the kind of essay defending Faulkner that Conrad Aiken wrote for the *Atlantic Monthly* in 1939, to justify him when he was being ruthlessly attacked, and compare it with the latest essay on Faulkner's orthodoxy of sensibility, indistinguishable from other essays on the same subject, you will see that criticism of modern authors likes to regard them as safe authors, classic authors, and often misrepresents the rebelliousness and iconoclasm that give these authors their force. Faulkner, like everybody else, is a moralist, but he should not be used year after year to buttress Southern nostalgia. No one has ever shown quite so conclusively how dead the old South is. When Faulkner's profoundly heretical and important book, *A Fable*, came out in 1954, was struck with how much the advanced critics joined with the professional philistines of the daily book reviews to attack it. The remarkable appreciation of the novel published by the poet Delmore Schwartz stands out in interesting contrast both to the attacks on the book and to the fawning and derivative essays still being published on *The Sound and the Fury*. *A Fable* is a fantastic

book, literally a fantasy, for it is about peace in our time, a peace that very few really now believe in. No one accustomed to moving in the safe grooves of literary criticism was prepared for a book about the First World War by an author whose experience, like that of his generation, is attached to the last time when men went from peace to war knowing they would never return.

The trouble with all of us who teach and explain so much of modern literature is that we are too far from the kind of historical confidence, the élan, the historical swagger, that made it possible. A critic like Edmund Wilson has a kind of independence, constitutes a personal resistance movement in himself, that critics who come after him can hardly understand. Once, when I heard a professor at the Salzburg Seminar explain in good English-35 fashion that *The Great Gatsby* represents a search for the Holy Grail, I thought of Fitzgerald and Zelda diving into the Plaza fountain in New York, and was ashamed to think that no one roughly of a later generation, not even Allen Ginsberg, would do it just for fun. No one could ever confuse a poem by Eliot with one by Stevens, or an essay by Wilson with one by Kenneth Burke. These writers are all originals, and you always know where you are with them. But when, as critics and teachers, we pass on to our students, with all the latest modern methods, *The Waste Land, In Our Time*, "Sunday Morning," "My Father Moved through Dooms of Love," we can't help distorting such works by omitting something. What we omit is our own experience of the unselfconscious individuality, the relaxed independence, the natural sauciness and sassiness and exuberance of style that gives these works still—as Fitzgerald said of his own—the stamp that goes into them so that we can read them like braille. Step by step the great confidence that man could understand his time and build from it, the feeling that provides the energy of modern art, has gone out of us, and we are left teaching such books as if they were models of correctness rather than rare moments of spirit.

This is why, properly speaking, there can never be a consciously ignorant, a mass psychology, in regard to modern literature. For the essence of the modern movement is that it represents a permanent revolution of consciousness, an unending adventure into freedom. In the deepest sense, we can never study modern literature or art; we can only be part of it. That is why criticism is important. We must practice criticism on the older writers lest they harden into the only acceptable writers. We must learn to practice criticism on the newer writers in order to bind them more truly to our own experience. We must practice criticism on our age while it is still here to show us its possibilities.

PART TWO · Practice

Introduction

The organization of Part Two of this anthology is a guiding scheme designed to provide one among many possible perspectives on what may be done by a practicing critic, as well as what has in fact been done, in compendious variety, by modern critics generally. It is meant not as dogma, but rather as a way of suggesting, in the broadest and most open way, what kinds of questions modern critics ask, what "approaches" are available to them, what their typical subjects are.

Certain critics, most often those who are professional scholars and academicians, are interested primarily in the "origins" of literature—how it comes into being. Some, like M. H. Abrams in his comprehensive study of English romanticism, *The Mirror and the Lamp*, approach the job of interpreting a whole period by examining its general historical context for the chief intellectual currents and counter-currents that helped to form the general sensibility of the time. Such a study is rather like a "biography" of a period or a movement. Other commentators concentrate on the literal biographies of individual writers, or on some limited aspect of them, as a key to the critical understanding of their works, as Van Wyck Brooks did in his controversial *The Ordeal of Mark Twain* and as Ford Madox Ford did, rather more informally, in his books on Conrad and James and his many personal essays on his contemporaries. And still other critics limit their inquiry to questions of immediate and more or less direct literary and intellectual influences and sources. Again the range is wide, from such narrowly intensive studies as John Livingston Lowes's famous investigation of Coleridge's reading in *The Road to Xanadu* to such broader studies of continuities and influences as R. W. B. Lewis's *The American Adam*.

But most modern critics are less interested in the causal influences upon literature than in the results of those influences, perhaps especially as they are manifested in the "content" or meaning of literature as an expression of ideas and values. From the single analysis appearing in a critical or scholarly journal to broad interpretations of whole periods, such as F. O. Matthiessen's *American Renaissance*, the intention is usually to elucidate ideas rather than to evaluate them. But perhaps the more memorable criticism of this kind—in the present collection the essays of Rahv, Howe, Trilling and Tate would be notable examples—is rather strongly flavored with the critic's "viewpoint." And some critics—for example, T. S. Eliot on the right and George Orwell on the left—seem to analyze only in order to be able to judge, finally, from the point of view of their own strong value-commitments and convictions, the ideas and values embodied in the works before them.

A third general critical emphasis, one that is sometimes, though by no mean
always, part of a larger program of eschewing and condemning the genetic and
ideological approaches, focuses primarily on the aesthetic or formal properties o
literature. It tends to concentrate on texts, whether few considered dissectively o
many synoptically, and it usually tries to show how some one element or group o
elements contributes to the organic nature, the "wholeness," of a work of art, or o
art itself. And again the spectrum of possibility is wide—from such work as Arnol
Stein's analysis of the prosody of a single poet, to Francis Fergusson's pursuit of th
complex meaning of *Hamlet* through an exhaustive examination of the elements tha
contribute to its structure, to Northrop Frye's defining of the "structure" of litera
ture itself on the basis of a theoretically unlimited range of types and examples.*

But to organize a collection of examples of practical criticism in this way is no
the same thing as saying what criticism, modern criticism in particular, "is." To tr
to define the "essential" nature of criticism as something like a discrete discipline
or modern criticism as a special form of it, is another matter entirely. How do w
know a piece of literary criticism when we see one? What differentiates it, in th
nature of its dealings with its proper subject matter, from a piece of history o
philosophy or scientific exposition? The answers to these questions lie somewher
in the fact that criticism is informed always by a judgmental motive, even whe
that judgment is only implicit. Criticism *judges* its subjects. And unlike related an
parallel disciplines it judges them absolutely rather than relativistically or prag
matically. Criticism is an immediate *act* of judgment, furthermore, rather than
record of judgments.

Some clarification of this view of criticism can perhaps be elicited from a pert
nent negative example. Dr. Ernest Jones's famous little book on *Hamlet* is strikingl
unusual, perhaps especially when the intellectual partisanship of its author is cor
sidered, in its apparent lack of the judgmental motive, its lack of any commitmer
or responsiveness to its subject as anything but a solvable puzzle. The book is a
entirely cool-minded, patient, and systematically thorough job of reasoning fror
given assumptions through data toward Truth. And even the particular assump
tions (Freudian) are justified rationally, rather than preferentially or provisionall
as a "point of view," in that they are proffered as the only remaining grounds fo
proceeding after Dr. Jones has shown that all the other explanations for Hamlet
delay, and the assumptions upon which those explanations are based, are inadequa
or faulty. The remarkable thing is that Dr. Jones's book, so essentially mechanica
and "neutral" in its dealings with its subject, should at the same time be so richl
suggestive. Its tone and method are in basic disharmony with its perceptions an
ideas. And so, to read it is to feel some speculative excitement at the insights pre
sented at the same time one feels dimly puzzled by one's sense that the author him
self does not quite care about them, nor even quite grasp them, in the light of

---

* That Frye's work appears in this collection as an example of "theory," and that the sam
work can also validly serve, as in this discussion, as an example of a certain kind of practic
criticism indicates how the placing or typing of critics is often a matter of deciding wher
among perhaps several possibilities, a defining emphasis should be placed. As an archetypal
Frye might as properly have appeared as a practical example under the heading "ideas a
values."

ally realized experience of the play. Perhaps the answer is that Freud is the real critic in the background, with Dr. Jones serving as his somewhat obfuscating, somewhat deadening medium.

This is often the case when a creative thinker inspires followers. We are familiar enough with the kind of journal article that begins by announcing that it is about to apply Kenneth Burke's concept of the scene-word relationship to Eliot's "Ash Wednesday" or that it will attempt a reading of *What Maisie Knew* in terms of the archetypes of night-journey and *rite de passage*. Some of these exercises are as genuinely valuable and illuminating as is Dr. Jones's study of *Hamlet*. But that most of them, however useful they may be, are items of information or illustration in which the work of art as an experience is subordinated to the machinery of assumption and proof, is perhaps suggested by the fact that we tend often to describe the kinds of work they are by other words than "criticism"—for example, "explication," "analysis," "scholarship." They are workouts—workouts, perhaps, that will help future real critics to learn their craft and come to some awareness of what they really believe in and care for. But what we call "criticism," particularly when we are referring to modern criticism, is the kind of work in which we listen to a man *thinking* about a significant work of art. His words characteristically carry some note of personality, some note of involvement with his subject that says, "Listen. What I am explaining is *important*."

Matthew Arnold, who was all but an anti-Aristotelian, though he was warmly devoted to the "hellenic" aspects of Western tradition, was quite insistent about criticism's being viewed as a "creative" activity, a sentiment echoed by an impressive number of our most important modern critics—for example, Trilling, Tate, Ransom, Fiedler, Kazin, to name only some of them. It is this element of involvement, this arousing of a personal energy in an intellectual engagement with a work of art as a meaningful experience, that both Arnold and his successors see as the basis for claiming some continuity between criticism and the artist's "creativity." And it is perhaps one of the grounds, too, for distinguishing "modern" criticism, at least quantitatively if not qualitatively, from the traditional criticism of the past. Most classical, Renaissance, and neoclassical criticism consists in the unexcepting application of "rules" to art. But Dr. Johnson is a critic whose personal responses to literature are often discomfitingly at odds with the received dogmas of tradition. As a result, most of his criticism, as in the preface to his edition of Shakespeare and his *Lives of the English Poets*, carries the note of an independent search for viable critical judgments that do no violence to the art experience whether it is the product of tradition or innovation. And of course the *causes* of "modern" criticism, of which the heroically earnest and clear-sightedly honest Dr. Johnson is one of the earliest true practitioners, are one with that wide and deep stream of destructive and liberating causes that brought about the much larger and much less limitable phenomenon that we call the "modern" world.

If the note of individual engagement with literature, of skeptical but committed searching of it, is the characteristic note of modern criticism, we may perhaps legitimately go on to ask what is characteristically being sought, or even what is found. Dr. Jones's use of Freud's theories is at least suggestive of a general direction that modern critics tend to take. An interest in the "mind," with works of litera-

ture, in their quality of organic wholeness, implicitly discerned as symbols of, o
even keys to, the mind's energies and principles of action, seems to be a motive i
most modern criticism. And it is the characteristic purpose not just of specialis
critics such as Dr. Jones on *Hamlet* or Dr. Rosenzweig on Henry James but also o
such obviously non-psychoanalytical critics as the New Critics, whose critical pe
suasion is usually thought of as "contextualist" or "formalist" in kind. The work o
Cleanth Brooks, for example, whose usual intention is to elucidate meanings tha
underlie, or transcend, and thus subtly qualify and enrich the statement-meaning
in which they inhere, could be validly described as that of a critic concerned with poetr
as the utterance not only of full consciousness, but also of the "subconscious" o
"arational" or "suprarational" parts of the mind. It could even be said that suc
critics as Kenneth Burke and William Empson are so interested in the mind tha
they sometimes come close to losing interest in literature "for its own sake" (exem
plified in their occasional specialist's interest in sub-literary matter, as in Empson
essay, included in this volume, on *Alice in Wonderland*). They have been accuse
more than once, in fact, of trying to turn literary criticism into the paths of "sc
ence"; and both, especially Burke, rear great scientific-looking terminological struc
tures that are hard to understand and harder to use. But in context this very striv
ing for definitiveness and precision is an unmistakable expression of responsivene
to particular works of literature. And "hard" as they are, these critics write wel
with a lively directness and not infrequent humor that lightens the burden of the
analytical machineries. They *are* writing criticism. Their tendency to turn discussio
of literature into descriptions of "mind-actions" is their way of recognizing tha
works of art are at once the richest, the most disinterested and unencumbered ex
pressions of our most valuable, and at the same time least knowable, human po
sessions—our minds. Though certainly less consciously schematized than Burke an
Empson, and with less conscious intention of "using" literature as a key to th
mind's mysteries and energies, even much important historical criticism seem
aimed at illuminating literature as a sequential manifestation of the mind's unde
currents—in this case, the "mind" of a culture as it develops in time. Roy Harve
Pearce's historical narrative of the "continuity" of American poetry, M. H. Abrams
examination of the ideology and symbol-systems of English Romanticism, C. I
Barber's study of the socio-psychological nature of early Shakespearean comedy—
all these are attempts to illuminate *un*conscious forms of thought and feeling o
larger scope, unconscious until history provided perspectives and vocabularies b
means of which they could be understood and described.

Modern practical criticism has been considered so far largely in terms of its ana
lytical and descriptive functions. But we are reminded by such a work as Law
rence's *Studies in Classic American Literature*, in which judgment and interpretatio
are so closely intertwined as to be almost inextricable, that evaluation is an equall
important function of practical criticism. One has only to recall a few of the mo
important names in recent criticism—Tate, Trilling, Wilson—to see how vigorousl
alive, in this age of supposed predominantly "technical" criticism, the tradition
role of the critic as judge and arbiter is. Consider Yvor Winters: he is remarkabl
as a technical critic, but especially as a technical critic whose analyses are chara
teristically subordinated (as in his exposition presented here of Hawthorne's inte

lectual inadequacies) to the articulation of a code of moral reason by which literary value is ultimately to be judged. Or F. R. Leavis (represented here by his brief defense of the moral energies of D. H. Lawrence) whose skills of technical criticism have been employed as devices of progressive cultural warfare against bourgeois illiberalism and non-culture. Or T. S. Eliot, the great Cham of the age, the suave arbiter, as in the essays on "Tradition and the Individual Talent" and "Religion and Literature," who judges artistic proprieties in terms of historically and theologically derived cultural norms. All of these critics are finally judges, and they may all be seen as judging, in their different ways, the same thing—the "modern mind" as it expresses itself in literature. Even a specialist-scholar like C. S. Lewis, whose career has been devoted to publicizing the virtues of the hard-to-take classics of our pre- and post-Renaissance Christian heritage, is in the end a lively moral and aesthetic critic—as in his account here of the limitations of Donne's poetry—of the "modern mind."

Of course, the interpretation of modern criticism being proposed in this introduction is offered in the spirit of hypothesis. But to see modern criticism as characteristically concerned, if often indirectly, with the mysteriously creative potentialities of the mind, the half-unconscious impulses, sensings, and knowledges that it transforms into the formal properties of literary art, seems at least true enough to be useful as an interpretive viewpoint. It helps one to understand what is "modern" about modern criticism. This implicit interest in the mind as both a mystery and a power is what has sent critics to such widely varying fields of inquiry—from Leslie Fiedler's psychoanalytic mythography to Christopher Caudwell's Marxist historicism—in search of new techniques of understanding. It is this individualism and eclecticism that distinguishes modern criticism from classical, mediaeval, Renaissance, and neoclassical criticism, where critics were executants of "laws" rather than skeptical but searching investigators of forms and meanings. In our world—which in literary criticism we might date from Dr. Johnson and would certainly date from Coleridge—the mind has the problem of discovering, even of creating, its own laws of judgment, argument, art. This is because at the same time we have lost faith in most traditional fixities and absolutes we have also happened upon an awareness of the imagination as one of the mind's unmeasured, and perhaps immeasurable powers. Our literary criticism may be seen as an exhibit of the ways that we try intellectually to encounter, describe, understand, and sometimes master, for the good of the other human powers which it complements and to which it contributes, the human imagination.

It is just this characteristically modern interest in the hidden powers of the mind that leads to the question of the relation of critical theory to critical practice. Because theory is implicitly concerned with absolutes rather than with accidents, with the derivation of "principles" rather than with the description of experiences, it tends to become, by its very nature, prescriptive. The historical transformation of Aristotle's work from percept into precept—from practical criticism into "theory"— is a case in point. Until the end of the seventeenth century, what *should* be, in literary criticism, was pretty much identical with what *was*. Usage was consonant with rule, and as a consequence theory, except perhaps for an occasional settling of some nical point or other, was essentially a matter of confirmatory rhetoric. Sidney's

"Apology" for poetry was one of the liveliest and most elegant examples of this kin of critical theory, and it was also one of the last.

Though the sureties of Sidney's viewpoint continued to be expressed until we into the eighteenth century, they were expressed with less and less vitality an more and more qualification. It was as if the new and radical creative powers c Sidney's age, symbolically concentrated in the creative genius of Shakespeare, ha made rule criticism, a criticism in which theory and practice are hardly distir guishable, forever irrelevant to actuality. Johnson emerges as the first great "moc ern" critic in English, as we have observed already, in that he dealt with literatur as a *person* rather than as an instrument. In Johnson's work the bifurcation of prac tice and theory becomes evident in the pragmatic and essentially relativistic view h takes of critical principles. He was the first major critic to attempt to formulate, o the basis of the free *experiencing* of works of art, viable theoretical justifications f the right of the individual creative mind to overthrow the conventions and rule imposed upon it by tradition. From the time of Wordsworth and Coleridge—an in this connection the influence of Coleridge's German contemporaries and fore runners must also be given recognition—literary and critical theory has been cor stituted primarily by an effort to understand and describe the principles of th mind's creativity rather than to catalogue and sustain the typologies of the work it produces.

Modern critical theory has been on the whole "heuristic"; and when it has n been that—as in, for example, the neo-Aristotelianism that sprang up during th Forties in opposition to the domination of the New Criticism—it has tended to b barren, like Renaissance and neoclassical criticism, of significant results in practica criticism. The drift of modern criticism, in spite of the fact that the systemati procedures of the modern natural and social sciences have left their unmistakabl marks upon it, has been always away from homogeneity of method, always towar multeity. In fact, the history of modern criticism is a history of revolutions an counterrevolutions with, it seems, ever-diminishing cycles of peace and harmony i between. This is because in criticism as in the arts themselves, motive is neve wholly encompassed or enabled by method. Interest—not problem-solving, as in th sciences, but interest—is the motive of criticism. The modern critic especially, how ever systematic much of his work may be, is ultimately engaged in an expressiv activity in much the way that the artist is, and like the modern artist, he work independently, often in defiance of accepted norms and judgments. He is constantl in search of a language that will adequately, in terms of his interest, express hi insight and understanding and justify his judgment. Practical criticism is th immediate record of that search, critical theory the understanding of the signifi cance of its success—the "criticism," perhaps, of it. As long as the imaginatior remains "free," as long as the literary mind identifies the chief promise of valu with its own indeterminate powers of creativity rather than with the known an measured world "outside," it seems unlikely that modern criticism will be mor homogeneous, stable, unitary than it has been for the last couple of centuries, o indeed, than we could wish it to be.

R. F.

Origins

C. S. LEWIS

(b. 1898)

C. S. Lewis is a poet, prose fantasist, religious essayist, and author of children's books, as well as a literary scholar and critic. His avocation of Christian apologetics underlies his scholarly interest in the literature of the middle ages and Renaissance as the implicit justification for his steady defense of its more formal, artificial, and conventionally didactic elements. Lewis's mission as a scholar and critic has been to illuminate for skeptical modern readers the pleasures and profundities of such unappreciated conventional expressions of traditional culture and a Christian world-view as pastoral, romance, decadent epic, and allegory. Lewis's principal critical and scholarly books are *The Allegory of Love* (1936), *A Preface to Paradise Lost* (1942), *English Literature in the Sixteenth Century* (1954), and *Experiment in Criticism* (1961).

Donne and Love Poetry in the Seventeenth Century (1938)

'Little of Manfred (but not very much of him)'   w. s. GILBERT.

I have seen an old history of literature in which the respective claims of Shelley and Mrs. Hemans to be the greatest lyrist of the nineteenth century were seriously weighed; and Donne, who was so inconsiderable fifty years ago, seems at the moment to rank among our greatest poets.

If there were no middle state between absolute certainty and what Mr. Kellett calls the whirligig of taste, these fluctuations would make us throw up criticism in despair. But where it is impossible to go quite straight we may yet resolve to reel as little as we can. Such phenomena as the present popularity of Donne or the growing unpopularity of Milton are not to be deplored; they are rather to be explained. It is not impossible to see why Donne's poetry should be overrated in

Reprinted from *Seventeenth Century Studies Presented to Sir Herbert Grierson*, by permission of The Clarendon Press, Oxford. Copyright 1938 by The Clarendon Press.

the twentieth and underrated in the eighteenth century; and in so far as we detect these temporary disturbing factors and explain the varying appearances of the object by the varying positions of the observers, we shall come appreciably nearer to a glimpse of Donne *simpliciter*. I shall concern myself in what follows chiefly with his love poetry.

In style this poetry is primarily a development of one of the two styles which we find in the work of Donne's immediate predecessors. One of these is the mellifluous, luxurious, 'builded rhyme', as in Spenser's *Amoretti*: the other is the abrupt, familiar, and consciously 'manly' style in which nearly all Wyatt's lyrics are written. Most of the better poets make use of both, and in *Astrophel and Stella* much of Sidney's success depends on deliberate contrast between such poetry as

That golden sea whose waves in curls are broken

and such poetry as

He cannot love: no, no, let him alone.

355

But Wyatt remains, if not the finest, yet much the purest example of the plainer manner, and in reading his songs, with their conversational openings, their surly (not to say sulky) defiances, and their lack of obviously poetic ornament, I find myself again and again reminded of Donne. But of course he is a Donne with most of the genius left out. Indeed, the first and most obvious achievement of the younger poet is to have raised this kind of thing to a much higher power; to have kept the vividness of conversation where Wyatt too often had only the flatness; to sting like a lash where Wyatt merely grumbled. The difference in degree between the two poets thus obscures the similarity in kind. Donne has so far surpassed not only Wyatt but all the Elizabethans in what may be called their Wyatt moments, and has so generally abstained from attempting to rival them in their other vein, that we hardly think of him as continuing one side of their complex tradition; he appears rather as the innovator who substituted a realistic for a decorated kind of love poetry.

Now this error is not in itself important. In an age which was at all well placed for judging the comparative merits of the two styles, it would not matter though we thought that Donne had invented what in fact he only brought to perfection. But our own age is not so placed. The mellifluous style, which we may agree to call Petrarchan though no English poet is very like Petrarch, has really no chance of a fair hearing. It is based on a conception of poetry wholly different from that of the twentieth century. It descends from old Provençal and Italian sources and presupposes a poetic like that of Dante. Dante, we may remember, thinks of poetry as something to be made, to be 'adorned as much as possible', to have its 'true sense' hidden beneath a rich vesture of 'rhetorical colouring'. The 'Petrarchan' sonneteers are not trying to make their work sound like the speaking voice. They are not trying to communicate faithfully the raw, the merely natural, impact of actual passion. The passion for them is not a specimen of 'nature' to be followed so much as a lump of ore to be refined: they

ask themselves not 'How can I record it with the least sophistication?' but 'Of its bones what coral can I make?', and to accuse them of insincerity is like calling an oyster insincere because it makes its disease into a pearl. The aim of the other style is quite different. It wishes to be convincing, intimate, naturalistic. It would be very foolish to set up these two kinds of poetry as rivals, for obviously they are different and both are good. It is a fine thing to hear the living voice, the voice of a man like ourselves, whispering or shouting to us from the printed page with all the heat of life; and it is a fine thing, too, to see such life—so pitiably like our own, I doubt not, in the living —caught up and transfigured, sung by the voice of a god into an ecstasy no less real though in another dimension.[1] There is no necessary quarrel between the two. But there are many reasons why one of them should start with overwhelming odds in its favour at the present moment. For many years our poetics have been becoming more and more expressionistic. First came Wordsworth with his theory, and we have never quite worked it out of our system; even in the crude form that 'you should write as you talk', it works at the back of much contemporary criticism. Then came the final break-up of aristocracy and the consequent, and still increasing, distaste for arduous disciplines of sentiment—the wholesale acceptance of the merely and unredeemedly natural. Finally, the psychological school of criticism overthrew what was left of the old conception of a poem as a construction and set up instead the poem as 'document'. In so far as we admire Donne for being our first great practitioner in one of the many possible kinds of lyric, we are on firm ground; but the conception of him as liberator, as one who substituted 'real' or 'live' or 'sincere' for 'artificial' or 'conventional' love lyric, begs all the questions and is simply a prejudice *de siècle*.

[1] Those who object to 'emotive terms' in criticism may prefer to read '. . . used by an accomplished poet to produce an attitude relevant not directly to outer experience but to the central nucleus of the total attitude-and-belief-feeling system'. It must not be supposed, however, that the present writer's theory of either knowledge or value would permit him, in the long run, to accept the restatement.

But of course when we have identified the Wyatt element in Donne, we have still a very imperfect notion of his manner. We have described 'Busie old foole' and 'I wonder by my troth' and 'For Godsake hold your tongue, and let me love'; but we have left out the cleaving remora, the triple soul, the stiff twin compasses, and a hundred other things that were not in Wyatt. There were indeed a great many things not in Wyatt, and his manly plainness can easily be over-praised—'pauper videri Cinna vult et est pauper'. If Donne had not reinforced the style with new attractions it would soon have died of very simplicity. An account of these reinforcements will give us a rough notion of the unhappily named 'metaphysical' manner.

The first of them is the multiplication of conceits—not conceits of any special 'metaphysical' type but conceits such as we find in all the Elizabethans. When Donne speaks of the morning coming from his mistress's eyes, or tells how they wake him like the light of a taper, these fanciful hyperboles are not, in themselves, a novelty. But side by side with these, we find, as his second characteristic, what may be called the difficult conceit. This is clearly a class which no two readers will fill up in quite the same way. An example of what I mean comes at the end of *The Sunne Rising* where the sun is congratulated on the fact that the two lovers have shortened his task for him. Even the quickest reader will be checked, if only for an infinitesimal time, before he sees how and why the lovers have done this, and will experience a kind of astonished relief at the unexpected answer. The pleasure of the thing, which can be paralleled in other artistic devices, perhaps in rhyme itself, would seem to depend on recurrent tension and relaxation. In the third place, we have Donne's characteristic choice of imagery. The Petrarchans (I will call them so for convenience) had relied for their images mainly on mythology and on natural objects. Donne uses both of these sparingly —though his sea that 'Leaves embroider'd works upon the sand' is as fine an image from nature as I know—and taps new sources such as law, science, philosophy, and the commonplaces of urban life. It is this that has given the Metaphysicals their name and been much misunderstood. When Johnson said that they were resolved to show their learning he said truth in fact, for there is an element of pedantry, of dandyism, an *odi profanos* air, about Donne—the old printer's address not to the *readers* but to the *understanders* is illuminating. But Johnson was none the less misleading. He encouraged the idea that the abstruse nature of some of Donne's similes was poetically relevant for good or ill. In fact, of course, when we have once found out what Donne is talking about —that is, when Sir Herbert Grierson has told us—the learning of the poet becomes unimportant. The image will stand or fall like any other by its intrinsic merit— its power of conveying a meaning 'more luminously and with a sensation of delight'. The matter is worth mentioning only because Donne's reputation in this respect repels some humble readers and attracts some prigs. What is important for criticism is his avoidance of the obviously poetical image; whether the intractable which he is determined to poetize is fetched from Thomas Aquinas or from the London underworld, the method is essentially the same. Indeed it would be easy to exaggerate the amount of learned imagery in his poems and even the amount of his learning. He knows much, but he seems to know even more because his knowledge so seldom overlaps with our own; and some scraps of his learning, such as that of angelic consciousness or of the three souls in man, come rather too often—like the soldiers in a stage army, and with the same result. This choice of imagery is closely connected with the surprising and ingenious nature of the connexions which Donne makes between the image and the matter in hand, thus getting a double surprise. No one, in the first place, expects lovers to be compared to compasses; and no one, even granted the comparison, would guess in what respect they are going to be compared.

But all these characteristics, in their mere enumeration, are what Donne would have called a 'ruinous anatomie'.

They might all be used—indeed they all are used by Herbert—to produce a result very unlike Donne's. What gives their peculiar character to most of the *Songs and Sonets* is that they are dramatic in the sense of being addresses to an imagined hearer in the heat of an imagined conversation, and usually addresses of a violently argumentative character. The majority of lyrics, even where nominally addressed to a god, a woman, or a friend, are meditations or introspective narratives. Thus Herbert's 'Throw away thy rod' is formally an apostrophe; in fact, it is a picture of Herbert's own state of mind. But the majority of the *Songs and Sonets*, including some that are addressed to abstractions like Love, present the poet's state of mind only indirectly and are ostensibly concerned with badgering, wheedling, convincing, or upbraiding an imagined hearer. No poet, not even Browning, buttonholes us or, as we say, 'goes for' us like Donne. There are, of course, exceptions. *Goe and catche a falling starre*, though it is in the form of an address, has not this effect; and *Twicknam Garden* or the *Nocturnall* are in fact, as well as in pretension, soliloquies. These exceptions include some of Donne's best work; and indeed, one of the errors of contemporary criticism, to my mind, is an insufficient distinction between Donne's best and Donne's most characteristic. But I do not at present wish to emphasize this. For the moment it is enough to notice that the majority of his love lyrics, and of the *Elegies*, are of the type I have described. And since they are, nearly always, in the form of arguments, since they attempt to extort something from us, they are poetry of an extremely exacting kind. This exacting quality, this urgency and pressure of the poet upon the reader in every line, seems to me to be the root both of Donne's weakness and his strength. When the thing fails it exercises the same dreadful fascination that we feel in the grip of the worst kind of bore—the hot-eyed, unescapable kind. When it succeeds it produces a rare intensity in our enjoyment —which is what a modern critic meant (I fancy) when he claimed that Donne made all other poetry sound less 'serious'. The point is worth investigation.

For, of course, in one sense these poems are not serious at all. Poem after poem consists of extravagant conceits woven into the preposterous semblance of an argument. The preposterousness is the point. Donne intends to take your breath away by the combined subtlety and impudence of the steps that lead to his conclusion. Any attempt to overlook Donne's 'wit' in this sense, or to pretend that his rare excursions into the direct expression of passion are typical, is false criticism. The paradox, the surprise, are essential; if you are not enjoying these you are not enjoying what Donne intended. Thus *Womans Constancy* is of no interest as a document of Donne's 'cynicism'—any fool can be promiscuously unchaste and any fool can say so. The merit of the poem consists in the skill with which it leads us to expect a certain conclusion and then gives us precisely the opposite conclusion, and that, too, with an appearance of reasonableness. Thus, again, the art of *The Will* consists in keeping us guessing through each stanza what universal in the concluding triplet will bind together the odd particulars in the preceding six lines. The test case is *The Flea*. If you think this very different from Donne's other poems you may be sure that you have no taste for the real Donne. But for the accident that modern cleanliness by rendering this insect disgusting has also rendered it comic, the conceit is exactly on the same level as that of the tears in *A Valediction: of weeping*.

And yet the modern critic was right. The effect of all these poems is somehow serious. 'Serious' indeed is the only word. Seldom profound in thought, not always passionate in feeling, they are none the less the very opposite of gay. It is as though Donne performed in deepest depression those gymnastics which are usually a sign of intellectual high spirits. He himself speaks of his *'concupiscence of wit'*. The hot, dark word is well chosen. We are all familar—at least if we have lived in Ireland—with the type of mind which combines furious anger with a revelling delight in eloquence, may grows more rhetorical as anger increases. In the same way, wit and the delight in wit are, for Donne, not only compatible with, but actually provoked by, the most uneasy passions—by contempt and self-contempt and unconvinced sensuality. His wit is not so much the play as the irritability of intellect. But none the less, like the angry Irishman's *clausulae*, it is still enjoyed and still intends to produce admiration; and if we do not hold our breaths as we read, wondering in the middle of each complication how he will resolve it, and exclaiming at the end 'How ever did you think of *that*?' (Carew speaks of his 'fresh invention'), we are not enjoying Donne.

Now this kind of thing can produce a very strong and a very peculiar pleasure. Our age has nothing to repent of in having learned to relish it. If the Augustans, in their love for the obviously poetical and harmonious, were blind to its merits, so much the worse for them. At the same time it is desirable not to overlook the special congeniality of such poetry to the twentieth century, and to beware of giving to this highly specialized and, in truth, very limited kind of excellence, a place in our scheme of literary values which it does not deserve. Donne's rejection of the obviously poetical image was a good method—for Donne; but if we think that there is some intrinsic superiority in this method, so that all poetry about pylons and *non obstantes* must needs be of a higher order than poetry about lawns and lips and breasts and orient skies, we are deceived—deceived by the fact that we, like Donne, happen to live at the end of a great period of rich and nobly obvious poetry. It is natural to want your savoury after your sweets; but you must not base a philosophy of cookery on that momentary preference. Again, Donne's obscurity and occasional abstruseness have sometimes (not always) produced magnificent results, and we do well to praise them. But, as I have hinted, an element of dandyism was present in Donne himself—he would have no such readers as he could teach'—and we must be very cautious

here lest shallow call to shallow. There is a great deal of dandyism (largely of Franco-American importation) in the modern literary world. And finally, what shall we say of Donne's 'seriousness', of that persistency, that nimiety, that astringent quality (as Boehme would have said) which makes him, if not the saddest, at least the most uncomfortable, of our poets? Here, surely, we find the clearest and most disturbing congeniality of all. It would be foolish not to recognize the growth in our criticism of something that I can only describe as literary Manichaeism—a dislike of peace and pleasure and heartsease simply as such. To be bilious is, in some circles, almost the first qualification for a place in the Temple of Fame.[2] We distrust the pleasures of imagination, however hotly and unmerrily we preach the pleasures of the body. This seriousness must not be confused with profundity. We do not like poetry that essays to be wise, and Chaucer would think we had rejected 'doctryne' and 'solas' about equally. We want, in fact, just what Donne can give us—something stern and tough, though not necessarily virtuous, something that does not conciliate. Born under Saturn, we do well to confess the liking complexionally forced upon us; but not to attempt that wisdom which dominates the stars is pusillanimous, and to set up our limitation as a norm—to believe, against all experience, in a Saturnocentric universe—is folly.

Before leaving the discussion of Donne's manner I must touch, however reluctantly, on a charge that has been brought against him from the time of Ben Jonson till now. Should he, or should he not, be hanged for not keeping the accent? There is more than one reason why I do not wish to treat this subject. In the first place, the whole nature of Donne's stanza, and of what he does within the stanza, cannot be profitably discussed except by one who knows much more than I do about the musical history

[2] In this we have been anticipated. See *Emma*, ch. 25: 'I know what worthy people they are. Perry tells me that Mr. Cole never touches malt liquor. You would not think it to look at him, but he is bilious— Mr. Cole is very bilious.'

of the time. *Confined Love,* for example, is metrically meaningless without the tune. But I could make shift with that difficulty: my real trouble is of quite a different kind. In discussing Donne's present popularity, the question of metre forces me to a statement which I do not make without embarrassment. Some one must say it, but I do not care for the office, for what I have to say will hardly be believed among scholars and hardly listened to by any one else. It is simply this—that the opinions of the modern world on the metre of any poet are, in general, of no value at all, because most modern readers of poetry do not know how to scan. My evidence for this amazing charge is twofold. In the first place I find that very many of my own pupils —some of them from excellent schools, most of them great readers of poetry, not a few of them talented and (for their years) well-informed persons—are quite unable, when they first come to me, to find out from the verse how Marlowe pronounced Barabas or Mahomet. To be sure, if challenged, they will say that they do not believe in syllable-counting or that the old methods of scansion have been exploded, but this is only a smoke screen. It is easy to find out that they have not got beyond the traditional legal fiction of longs and shorts and have never even got so far: they are in virgin ignorance. And my experience as an examiner shows me that this is not peculiar to my own pupils. My second piece of evidence is more remarkable. I have heard a celebrated belle-lettrist—a printed critic and poet—repeatedly, in the same lecture, so mispronounce the name of a familiar English poem as to show that he did not know a decasyllabic line when he met it. The conclusion is unavoidable. Donne may be metrically good or bad, in fact; but it is obvious that he might be bad to any degree without offending the great body of his modern admirers. On that side, his present vogue is worth precisely nothing. No doubt this widespread metrical ignorance is itself a symptom of some deeper change; and I am far from suggesting that the appearance of *vers libre* is simply a result of the ignorance.

More probably the ignorance, and the deliberate abandonment, of accentual metres are correlative phenomena, and both the results of some revolution in our whole sense of rhythm—a revolution of great importance reaching deep down into the unconscious and even perhaps into the blood. But that is not our business at the moment.

The sentiment of Donne's love poetry is easier to describe than their manner and its charm for modern readers easier to explain. No one will deny that the twentieth century, so far, has shown an extraordinary interest in the sexual appetite and has been generally marked by a reaction from the romantic idealization of that appetite. We have agreed with the romantics in regarding sexual love as a subject of overwhelming importance, but hardly in anything else. On the purely literary side we are wearied with the floods of uxorious bathos which the romantic conception undoubtedly liberated. As psychologists we are interested in the new discovery of the secreter and less reputable operations of the instinct. As practical philosophers we are living in an age of sexual experiment. The whole subject offers us an admirable field for the kind of seriousness I have just described. It seems odd, at first sight, that a sixteenth-century poet should give us so exactly what we want; but it can be explained.

The great central movement of love poetry, and of fiction about love, in Donne's time is that represented by Shakespeare and Spenser. This movement consisted in the final transmutation of the medieval courtly love or romance of adultery into an equally romantic love that looked to marriage as its natural conclusion. The process, of course, had begun far earlier—as early, indeed, as the *Kingis Quhair*—but its triumph belongs to the sixteenth century. It is most powerfully expressed by Spenser, but more clearly and philosophically by Chapman in that under-estimated poem, his *Hero and Leander.* These poets were engaged, as Professor Vinaver would say, in reconciling Carbonek and Camelot, virtue and courtesy, divine and human love; and incidentally in laying down the lines which love poetry was to follow till the nineteenth century. We who live at the end of the dispensation which they inaugurated and in reaction against it are not well placed for evaluating their work. Precisely what is revolutionary and creative in it seems to us platitudinous, orthodox, and stale. If there were a poet, and a strong poet, alive in their time who was failing to move with them, he would inevitably appear to us more 'modern' than they.

But was Donne such a poet? A great critic has assigned him an almost opposite role, and it behoves us to proceed with caution. It may be admitted at once that Donne's work is not, in this respect, all of a piece; no poet fits perfectly into such a scheme as I have outlined—it can be true only by round and by large. There are poems in which Donne attempts to sing a love perfectly in harmony with the moral law, but they are not very numerous and I do not think they are usually his best pieces. Donne never for long gets rid of a medieval sense of the sinfulness of sexuality; indeed, just because the old conventional division between Carbonek and Camelot is breaking up, he feels this more continuously and restively than any poet of the Middle Ages.

Donne was bred a Roman Catholic. The significance of this in relation to his learned and scholastic imagery can be exaggerated; scraps of Calvin, or, for that matter, of Euclid or Bacon, might have much the same poetical effect as his scraps of Aquinas. But it is all-important for his treatment of love. This is not easily understood by the modern reader, for later-day conceptions of the Puritan and the Roman Catholic stand in the way. We have come to use the word 'Puritan' to mean what should rather be called 'rigorist' or 'ascetic', and we stand to assume that the sixteenth-century Puritans were 'puritanical' in this sense. Calvin's rigorist theocracy at Geneva lends colour to the error. But there is no understanding the period of the Reformation in England until we have grasped the fact that the quarrel between

the Puritans and the Papists was not primarily a quarrel between rigorism and indulgence, and that, in so far as it was, the rigorism was on the Roman side. On many questions, and specially in their view of the marriage bed, the Puritans were the indulgent party; if we may without disrespect so use the name of a great Roman Catholic, a great writer, and a great man, they were much more Chestertonian than their adversaries. The idea that a Puritan was a repressed and repressive person would have astonished Sir Thomas More and Luther about equally. On the contrary, More thought of a Puritan as one who 'loved no lenten fast nor lightly no fast else, saving breakfast and eat fast and drink fast and luske fast in their lechery'—a person only too likely to end up in the 'abominable heresies' of the Anabaptists about communism of goods and wives. And Puritan theology, so far from being grim and gloomy, seemed to More to err in the direction of fantastic optimism. 'I could for my part', he writes, 'be very well content that sin and pain and all were as shortly gone as Tindall telleth us: but I were loth that he deceved us if it be not so.' More would not have understood the idea, sometimes found in the modern writers, that he and his friends were defending a 'merry' Catholic England against sour precisions; they were rather defending necessary severity and sternly realistic theology against wanton labefaction—penance and 'works' and vows of celibacy and mortification and Purgatory against the easy doctrine, the mere wishfulfilment dream, of salvation by faith. Hence when we turn from the religious works of More to Luther's *Table-talk* we are at once struck by the geniality of the latter. If Luther is right, we have waked from nightmare into sunshine: if he is wrong, we have entered a fools' paradise. The burden of his charge against the Catholics is that they have needlessly tormented us with scruples; and, in particular, that 'Antichrist will regard neither God nor the love of women'. 'On what pretence have they forbidden us marriage? 'Tis as though we were forbidden to eat, to drink, to sleep.'

'Where women are not honoured, temporal and domestic government are despised.' He praises women repeatedly: More, it will be remembered, though apparently an excellent husband and father, hardly ever mentions a woman save to ridicule her. It is easy to see why Luther's marriage (as he called it) or Luther's 'abominable bichery' (if you prefer) became almost a symbol. More can never keep off the subject for more than a few pages.

This antithesis, if once understood, explains many things in the history of sentiment, and many differences, noticeable to the present day, between the Protestant and the Catholic parts of Europe. It explains why the conversion of courtly love into romantic monogamous love was so largely the work of English, and even of Puritan, poets; and it goes far to explain why Donne contributes so little to that movement.

I trace in his poetry three levels of sentiment. On the lowest level (lowest, that is, in order of complexity), we have the celebration of simple appetite, as in *Elegy XIX*. If I call this a pornographic poem, I must be understood to use that ugly word as a descriptive, not a dyslogistic, term. I mean by it that this poem, in my opinion, is intended to arouse the appetite it describes, to affect not only the imagination but the nervous system of the reader.[3] And I may as well say at once—but who would willingly claim to be a judge in such matters?—that it seems to me to be very nearly perfect in its kind. Nor would I call it an immoral poem. Under what conditions the reading of it could be an innocent act is a real moral question; but the poem itself contains nothing intrinsically evil.

On the highest, or what Donne supposed to be the highest, level we have the poems of ostentatiously virtuous love, *The Undertaking, A Valediction: forbidding mourning,* and *The Extasie*. It is

here that the contrast between Donne and his happier contemporaries is most marked. He is trying to follow them into the new age, to be at once passionate and innocent; and if any reader will make the experiment of imagining Beatrice or Juliet or Perdita, or again, Amoret or Britomart, or even Philoclea or Pamela, as the auditress throughout these poems, he will quickly feel that something is wrong. You may deny, as perhaps some do, that the romantic conception of 'pure' passion has any meaning; but certainly, if there is such a thing, it is not like this. It does not prove itself pure by talking about purity. It does not keep on drawing distinctions between spirit and flesh to the detriment of the latter and then explaining why the flesh is, after all, to be used. This is what Donne does, and the result is singularly unpleasant. The more he labours the deeper 'Dun is in the mire', and it is quite arguable that *The Extasie* is a much nastier poem than the nineteenth *Elegy*. What any sensible woman would make of such a wooing it is difficult to imagine—or would be difficult if we forgot the amazing protective faculty which each sex possesses of not listening to the other.

Between these two extremes falls the great body of Donne's love poetry. In certain obvious, but superficial, respects, it continues the medieval tradition. Love is still a god and lovers his 'clergie'; oaths may be made in 'reverentiall feare' of his 'wrath'; and the man who resists him is 'rebell and atheist'. Donne can even doubt, like Soredamors, whether those who admit Love after a struggle have not forfeited his grace by their resistance, like

Small townes which stand stiffe, til great shot
Enforce them.

He can personify the attributes of his mistress, the 'enormous gyant' her Disdain and the 'enchantress *Honor*', quite in the manner of *The Romance of the Rose*. He writes *Albas* for both sexes, and in the *Holy Sonnets* repents of his love poetry, writing his palinode, in true med-

---

[3] The restatement of this in terms acceptable to the Richardsian school (for whom all poetry equally is addressed to the nervous system) should present no difficulty. For them it will be a distinction between parts, or functions, of the system.

ieval fashion. A reader may wonder, at first, why the total effect is so foreign to the Middle Ages: but Donne himself has explained this when he says, speaking of the god of Love,

If he wroung from mee a teare, I brin'd it so
With scorne or shame, that him it nourish'd
    not.

This admirable couplet not only tells us, in brief, what Donne has effected but shows us that he knew what he was doing. It does not, of course, cover every single poem. A few pieces admittedly express delighted love and they are among Donne's most popular works; such are *The Good-morrow* and *The Anniversarie*—poems that again remind us of the difference between his best and his typical. But the majority of the poems ring the changes on five themes, all of them, grim ones—on the sorrow of parting (including death), the miseries of secrecy, the falseness of the mistress, the fickleness of Donne, and finally on contempt for love itself. The poems of parting stand next to the poems of happy love in general popularity and are often extremely affecting. We may hear little of the delights of Donne's loves, and dislike what we hear of their 'purity'; the pains ring true. The song *Sweetest love, I do not goe* is remarkable for its broken, but haunting, melody, and nowhere else has Donne fused argument, conceit, and classical imitation into a more perfect unity. *The Feaver* is equally remarkable, and that for a merit very rare in Donne —its inevitability. It is a single jet of music and feeling, a straight flight without appearance of effort. The remaining four of our five themes are all various articulations of the 'scorne or shame' with which Donne 'brines' his reluctantly extorted tributes to the god of Love; monuments, unparalleled outside Catullus, to the close kinship between certain kinds of love and certain kinds of hate. The faithlessness of women is sometimes treated, in a sense, playfully; but there is always something—the clever surprise in *Womans Constancy* or the grotesque in *Goe and catch a falling starre*—which stops

these poems short of a true Anacreontic gaiety. The theme of faithlessness rouses Donne to a more characteristic, and also a better, poetry in such a hymn of hate as *The Apparition*, or in the sad mingling of fear, contempt, and self-contempt in *A Lecture upon the Shadow*. The pains of secrecy give opportunity for equally fierce and turbulent writing. I may be deceived when I find in the sixteenth *Elegy*, along with many other nauseas and indignations, a sickened male contempt for the whole female world of nurses and 'midnight startings' and hysterics; but *The Curse* is unambiguous. The ending here is particularly delicious just because the main theme—an attack on *Jalosie* or the 'lozengiers'—is so medieval and so associated with the 'honour of love'. Of the poet's own fickleness one might expect, at last, a merry treatment; and perhaps in *The Indifferent* we get it. But I am not sure. Even this seems to have a sting in it. And of *Loves Usury* what shall I say? The struggle between lust and reason, the struggle between love and reason, these we know; but Donne is perhaps the first poet who has ever painted lust holding love at arm's length, in the hope 'that there's no need to trouble himself with any such thoughts yet'—and all this only as an introduction to the crowning paradox that in old age even a reciprocated love must be endured. The poem is, in its way, a masterpiece, and a powerful indirect expression of Donne's habitual 'shame and scorne'. For, in the long run, it must be admitted that 'the love of hatred and the hate of love' is the main, though not the only theme of the *Songs and Sonets*. A man is a fool for loving and a double fool for saying so in 'whining poetry'; the only excuse is that the sheer difficulty of drawing one's pains through rhyme's vexation 'allays' them. A woman's love at best will be only the 'spheare' of a man's—inferior to it as the heavenly spheres are to their intelligences or air to angels. Love is a spider that can transubstantiate all sweets into bitter: a devil who differs from his fellow devils at court by taking the soul and giving nothing in exchange. The mystery which the Petrarchans or their medieval predecessors made of it is 'imposture all', like the claims of alchemists. It is a very simple matter (*foeda et brevis voluptas*), and all it comes to in the end is

> that my man
> Can be as happy as I can.

Unsuccessful love is a plague and tyranny; but there is a plague even worse —Love might try

> A deeper plague, to make her love mee too!

Love enjoyed is like gingerbread with the gilt off. What pleased the whole man now pleases one sense only—

> And that so lamely, as it leaves behinde
> A kinde of sorrowing dulnesse to the minde.

The doctors say it shortens life.

It may be urged that this is an unfair selection of quotations, or even that I have arrived at my picture of Donne by leaving out all his best poems, for one reason or another, as 'exceptions', and then describing what remains. There is one sense in which I admit this. Any account of Donne which concentrates on his love poetry must be unfair to the poet, for it leaves out much of his best work. By hypothesis, it must neglect the dazzling sublimity of his best religious poems, the grotesque charm of *The Progresse of the Soule*, and those scattered, but exquisite, patches of poetry that appear from time to time amidst the insanity of *The First and Second Anniversaries*. Even in the *Epistles* there are good passages. But as far as concerns his love poetry, I believe I am just. I have no wish to rule out the exceptions, provided that they are admitted to be exceptions. I am attempting to describe the prevailing tone of his work, and in my description no judgment is yet implied.

To judgment let us now proceed. Here is a collection of verse describing with unusual and disturbing energy the torments of a mind which has been baffled in its relation to sexual love by certain temporary and highly special conditions. What is its value? To admit the 'unusual and disturbing energy' is, of course, to admit that Donne is a poet; he has, in the modern phrase, 'put his stuff across'. Those who believe that criticism can separate inquiry into the success of communication from that into the value of the thing communicated will demand that we should now proceed to evaluate the 'stuff'; and if we do so, it would not be hard to point out how transitory and limited and, as it were, accidental the appeal of such 'stuff' must be. But something of the real problem escapes under this treatment. It would not be impossible to imagine a poet dealing with this same stuff, marginal and precarious as it is, in a way that would permanently engage our attention. Donne's real limitation is not that he writes *about*, but that he writes *in*, a chaos of violent and transitory passions. He is perpetually excited and therefore perpetually cut off from the deeper and more permanent springs of his own excitement. But how is this to be separated from his technique—the nagging, nudging, quibbling stridency of his manner? If a man writes thus, what can he communicate but excitement? Or again, if he finds nothing but excitement to communicate, how else should he write? It is impossible here to distinguish cause from effect. Our concern, in the long run, must be with the actual poetry (the 'stuff' *thus* communicated, this communication of *such* 'stuff') and with the question how far that total phenomenon is calculated to interest human imagination. And to this question I can see only one answer: that its interest, save for a mind specially predisposed in its favour, must be short-lived and superficial, though intense. Paradoxical as it may seem, Donne's poetry is too simple to satisfy. Its complexity is all on the surface—an intellectual and fully conscious complexity that we soon come to the end of. Beneath this we find nothing but a limited series of 'passions'—explicit, mutually exclusive passions which can be instantly and adequately labelled as such —things which can be readily talked about, and indeed, must be talked about because, in silence, they begin to lose their hard outlines and overlap, to betray themselves as partly fictitious. That is why Donne is always arguing. There are puzzles in his work, but we can solve them all if we are clever enough; there is none of the depth and ambiguity of real experience in him, such as underlies the apparent simplicity of *How sleep the brave* or *Songs of Innocence,* or even Αἰαῖ Λεωψύδριον.[4] The same is true for the most part, of the specifically 'metaphysical' comparisons. One idea has been put into each and nothing more can come out of it. Hence they tend to die on our hands, where some seemingly banal comparison of a woman to a flower or God's anger to flame can touch us at innumerable levels and renew its virginity at every reading. Of all literary virtues 'originality', in the vulgar sense, has, for this reason, the shortest life. When we have once mastered a poem by Donne there is nothing more to do with it. To use his own simile, he deals in earthquakes, not in that 'trepidation of the spheres' which is so much less violent but 'greater far'.

Some, of course, will contend that his love poems should interest me permanently because of their 'truth'. They will say that he has shown me passion with the mask off, and catch at my word 'uncomfortable' to prove that I am running away from him because he tells me more truth than I can bear. But this is the mere frenzy of anti-romanticism. Of course, Donne is true in the sense that passions such as he presents do occur in human experience. So do a great many other things. He makes his own selection, like Dickens, or Gower, or Herrick, and his world is neither more nor less 'real' than theirs; while it is obviously less real than the world of Homer, or Virgil, or Tolstoy. In one way, indeed, Donne's love poetry is less true than that of the Petrarchans, in so far as it largely omits the very thing that all the pother is

about. Donne shows us a variety of sorrows, scorns, angers, disgusts, and the like which arise out of love. But if any one asked 'What is all this *about*? What is the attraction which makes these partings so sorrowful? What is the peculiarity about this physical pleasure which he speaks of so contemptuously, and how has it got tangled up with such a storm of emotions?', I do not know how we could reply except by pointing to some ordinary love poetry. The feeblest sonnet, almost, of the other school would give us an answer with coral lips and Cupid's golden wings and the opening rose, with perfumes and instruments of music, with some attempt, however trite, to paint that iridescence which explains why people write poems about love at all. In this sense Donne's love poetry is parasitic. I do not use this word as a term of reproach; there are so many good poets, by now, in the world that one particular poet is entitled to take for granted the depth of a passion and deal with its froth. But as a purely descriptive term, 'parasitic' seems to me true. Donne's love poems could not exist unless love poems of a more genial character existed first. He shows us amazing shadows cast by love upon the intellect, the passions, and the appetite; to learn of the substance which casts them we must go to other poets, more balanced, more magnanimous, and more humane. There are, I well remember, poems (some two or three) in which Donne himself presents the substance; and the fact that he does so without much luxury of language and symbol endears them to our temporarily austere taste. But in the main, his love poetry is *Hamlet* without the prince.

Donne's influence on the poets of the seventeenth century is a commonplace of criticism. Of that influence at its best, as it is seen in the great devotional poetry of the period, I have not now to speak. In love poetry he was not, perhaps, so dominant. His *nequitiae* probably encouraged the cynical and licentious songs of his successors, but, if so, the imitation is very different from the model. Suck-

---

[4] The superficial simplicity here is obvious; the deeper ambiguity becomes evident if we ask whether Lipsydrion is an object of detestation or of nostalgic affection.

ling's impudence, at its best, is light-hearted and very unlike the ferocity of Donne; and Suckling's chief fault in this vein—a stolid fleshliness which sometimes leads him to speak of his mistress's body more like a butcher than a lecher—is entirely his own. The more strictly metaphysical elements in Donne are, of course, lavishly reproduced; but I doubt if the reproduction succeeds best when it is most faithful. Thus Carew's stanzas *When thou, poor Excommunicate* or Lovelace's *To Lucasta, going beyond the Seas* are built up on Donne's favourite plan, but both, as it seems to me, fail in that startling and energetic quality which this kind of thing demands. They have no edge. When these poets succeed it is by adding something else to what they have learned from Donne—in fact by reuniting Donne's manner with something much more like ordinary poetry. Beauty (like cheerfulness) is always breaking in. Thus the conceit of asking where various evanescent, beautiful phenomena go when they vanish and replying that they are all to be found in one's mistress is the sort of conceit that Donne might have used; and, starting from that end, we could easily work it up into something tolerably like bad Donne. As thus:

Oh fooles that aske whether of odours burn'd
The seminall forme live, and from that death
Conjure the same with chymique arte—'tis
　　turn'd
To that quintessence call'd her Breath!

But if we use the same idea as Carew uses it we get a wholly different effect:

Ask me no more where Jove bestows
When June is past, the fading rose:
For in your beauty's orient deep
These flowers, as in their causes, sleep.

The idea is the same. But the choice of the obvious and obviously beautiful rose, instead of the recondite seminal form of vegetables, the great regal name of Jove, the alliteration, the stately voluptuousness of a quatrain where all the accented syllables are also long in quantity (a secret little known)—all this smothers the sharpness of thought in sweetness. Compared with Donne, it is almost soporific; compared with it, Donne is shrill. But the conceit is there; and 'as in their causes, sleep' which looks at first like a blunder, is in fact a paradox that Donne might have envied. So again, the conceit that the lady's hair outshines the sun, though not much more than an Elizabethan conceit, might well have appeared in the *Songs and Sonets*; but Donne would neither have wished, nor been able, to attain the radiance of Lovelace's

But shake your head and scatter day!

This process of enchanting, or, in Shakespeare's sense, 'translating' Donne was carried to its furthest point by Marvell. Almost every element of Donne—except his metrical roughness—appears in the *Coy Mistress*. Nothing could be more like Donne, both in the grimness of its content and in its impudently argumentative function, than the conceit that

worms shall try
That long preserved virginity.

All the more admirable is the art by which this, and everything else in that poem, however abstruse, dismaying, or sophistical, is subordinated to a sort of golden tranquillity. What was death to Donne is mere play to Marvell. 'Out of the strong', we are tempted to say, 'has come sweetness', but in reality the strength is all on Marvell's side. He is an Olympian, ruling at ease for his own good purposes, all that intellectual and passionate mobility of which Donne was the slave, and leading Donne himself, bound, behind the chariot.

From all this we may conclude that Donne was a 'good influence'—a better influence than many greater poets. It would hardly be too much to say that the final cause of Donne's poetry is the poetry of Herbert, Crashaw, and Marvell; for the very qualities which make Donne's kind of poetry unsatisfying poetic food make it a valuable ingredient.

M. H. ABRAMS

(b. 1912)

M. H. Abrams has distinguished himself as a major contributor to the historical understanding of English romanticism through his interpretive studies of the key images and metaphors in which the romantics cast their speculations about the mind and the imagination. He is the author of *The Milk of Paradise* (1934) and *The Mirror and the Lamp: Romantic Theory and the Critical Tradition* (1953).

Newton's Rainbow and the Poet's (1953)

Keats was one among the lovers of poetry to whom it seemed that matter of fact or science is not only the opposite but the enemy of poetry, in a war in which the victory, even the survival, of poetry is far from certain. Keats's utterances on poetry are written with the unphilosophical informality and the volatility of mood proper to the personal letter; it is difficult to interpret many of them, and perilous to take any one as his ultimate judgment. But it is clear that in one recurrent frame of mind, Keats could not accept Wordsworth's opinion that the valid aim of poetry is to treat things 'as they *appear*.' To the younger poet, either poetry treats things as they are, or it is a delusion.

'Kean! Kean!' exclaimed Keats, reviewing a Shakespearean performance in December of 1817. 'Have a carefulness of thy health . . . in these cold and enfeebling times! . . . for romance lives but in books. The goblin is driven from the hearth, and the rainbow is robbed of its mystery.'[1] Only a week later, at Benjamin Haydon's 'immortal dinner,' Charles Lamb, as chance would have it, introduced the same subject. In 'a strain

of humour beyond description,' Lamb abused the painter for putting Newton's head into his 'Jerusalem.' 'And then he and Keats agreed that [Newton] had destroyed all the poetry of the rainbow by reducing it to the prismatic colors.'[2] If the toast of 'confusion to mathematics' which they drank on that occasion was a Bacchic whimsy, the idea nevertheless haunted Keats, and after some eighteen months, he presented it again, entirely seriously, in *Lamia*. The central figure of the serpent-woman in that poem is a complex and equivocal symbol, but the familiar passage on Newton's rainbow demonstrates that in part it signifies the poet's vision, in opposition to the scrutiny of 'cold philosophy,' which, Keats says, will 'empty the haunted air' and 'unweave the rainbow.' The opinion that Newton's analysis of the rainbow in his *Opticks* is of special concern to the poet had a long history, but the opinion that this analysis was a threat to poetry was much later in origin. A summary of the poetic fortunes of Newton's rainbow will clarify both Keats's ideas and the romantic shift in the concept of poetry.

Various seventeenth-century theorists agreed that the new philosophy had eliminated from the poet's world the

[1] *Complete Works*, ed. H. B. Forman (Glasgow, 1901), III, 232.

[2] *The Autobiography and Memoirs of Benjamin Haydon*, ed. Aldous Huxley (London, 1926), I, 269.

materials of myth and superstition; but, it was held, if science took something away from literature, it gave something more valuable in return. It is high time, as Thomas Sprat said, to dismiss the wit of ancient fable and religion, especially since 'they were only *Fictions* at first: whereas *Truth* is never so well express'd or amplify'd, as by those Ornaments which are *Tru* and *Real* in themselves.' He adds:

It is now therefore seasonable for *Natural Knowledge* to come forth, and to give us the *understanding* of new *Virtues* and *Qualities* of things. . . . This charitable assistance *Experiments* will soon bestow. [3]

Various writers of the following century consented to both these observations. As late as 1777, for example, John Aikin wrote *An Essay on the Application of Natural History to Poetry* in which, on the principle that 'nothing can be really beautiful which has not truth for its basis,' he decried modern use of 'the trite and hackneyed fables of ancient poets,' and recommended instead 'the accurate and scientific study of nature.' [4] Accordingly, the physical discoveries of Newton, far from being viewed as inimical to poetry, were embraced as a rich source of poetic material which combined the rare advantages of novelty and the best scientific sanction. In *Newton Demands the Muse*, Marjorie Nicolson shows the extent to which eighteenth-century poets joyously pillaged Newton's *Opticks*. The enlightened few, wrote James Thomson in *The Seasons*, are above 'superstitious horrors,' and poetry, fortunately, is now tutored by philosophy, 'Effusive source of evidence and truth.' [5] These days only the ignorant swain views the rainbow as a 'bright Enchantment,' for thanks to Newton, the sage-instructed eye sees it as a 'showery Prism,' unfolding the 'various Twine of Light.' [6] And in his poem 'To the Memory of Sir Isaac Newton,' Thomson declares that the rainbow is but the more poetic, now that its mystery has sur-

rendered to intellect, on the apparent principle that Newton alone has looked on beauty bare:

Did ever poet image ought so fair,
Dreaming in whispering groves by the hoarse brook?
. . . .
How just, how beauteous the refractive law. [7]

In the same poem, Thomson himself exemplifies the process of transforming Newton's refractive law into poetry. Newton had written:

This Image or Spectrum PT was colored, being red at its least refracted end T, and violet at its most refracted end P, and yellow green and blue in the intermediate Spaces. [8]

Poetized, this becomes: Newton 'Untwisted all the shining robe of day,' and

To the charm'd eye educed the gorgeous train
Of parent-colours. First the flaming Red
Sprung vivid forth; the tawny Orange next . . .
. . . and then, of sadder hue,
Emerged the deepen'd Indigo, as when
The heavy-skirted evening droops with frost;
While the last gleamings of refracted light
Died in the fainting Violet away.

Truth is made poetry through the current device of 'ornamenting' statements by means of simile, personification, and incipient allegory. In this way, Thomson put back into the prismatic phenomena the sensuousness and drama—even, in the implied figure of the scientist as a magician, the mystery and enchantment —which Newton had methodically excluded from his experimental observations.

But some amateurs of romance, acknowledging the efficacy of the new philosophy in dispelling what are admitted illusions, were not so certain the gains outweighed the losses. For 'a great

---

[3] *The History of the Royal Society*, pp. 414, 416.
[4] (Warrington and London, 1777), pp. 24, 32-3.
[5] 'Summer' (ed. of 1746), II. 1711-13, 1730-54.
[6] 'Spring' (ed. of 1746), II. 208-15.

[7] 'To the Memory of Sir Isaac Newton,' II. 96-124. Cf. Akenside, *Pleasures of Imagination* (1744), I, II. 103ff.; and see Marjorie H. Nicolson, *Newton Demands the Muse* (Princeton University Press, 1946), pp. 30-33.
[8] *Optiks* (3d ed.; London, 1721), p. 27. For an exposition of the way a Poet is able 'to inlist Imagination under the banner of Science,' through converting abstract into visual terms by means of such devices as personification and allegory, see Erasmus Darwin, *The Botanic Garden* (4th ed.; London, 1799), I, 'Advertisement,' and II, 63, 65.

deal of good sense,' Bishop Hurd wrote in 1762, we have exchanged 'a world of fine fabling; the illusion of which is so grateful to the *charmed Spirit.* . . .'[9] Thomas Warton maintained that the improvement of society in general is at the expense of poetry. For 'ignorance and superstition . . . are the parents of imagination'; and by 'the force of reason and inquiry,' poetry gained 'much good sense, good taste, and good criticism,' but at the cost of parting 'with incredibilities that are more acceptable than truth, and with fictions that are more valuable than reality.'[10]

Before the end of the eighteenth century, we begin also to hear suggestions that not only scientific skepticism, but the scientific description of natural phenomena, is the enemy rather than the benefactor of poetry. Mrs. Montagu in 1769 agreed with Hurd that the new philosophy, by dispelling fables, destroyed the golden age of poetry; she also indicated her doubt about Thomson's assertion that by 'untwisting' light and the rainbow, Newton had opened new materials for poetry. 'Echo, from an amorous nymph, fades into voice, and nothing more; the very threads of Iris's scarf are untwisted. . . .'[11] Twenty years later, a writer who signed himself 'ghm,' defining poetry as 'the language of passion and feeling,' attributed its decline both to the loss of a 'strong propensity to the marvellous' and to the incompatibility between the habitual perceptions of scientist and poet. In a statement anticipating passages in both Wordsworth and Keats, he said that, as opposed to poetical description,

philosophical description exhibits objects as they really are; their reasons and causes, not as they appear to be. . . . Thus a botanist disregards the beauty of a flower, and is only intent upon its internal construction.

For this reason poetry was at its height when writers described the 'beauty of the works of nature, before Newton discovered the true system of the world.' 'As soon as men begin to philosophise, they become less fit for works of imagination.'[12]

In the next century, the Utilitarian opponents of poetry, as we saw, accepted the proposition that the progress of reason and imagination, of science and poetry, must be inversely related, and merely modulated the threnody into a song of thanksgiving. One man who was both historian and poet put this theory of cultural history in its most unqualified form, and explicitly on the grounds that the scientific and poetic descriptions of the sensible world are not reconcilable. 'We think,' wrote Macaulay in 1825, 'that, as civilisation advances, poetry almost necessarily declines.' The progress of knowledge is from 'particular images to general terms,' and from concrete perception to generalization, but 'analysis is not the business of the poet. His office is to portray, not to dissect.' After his apodeictic fashion, Macaulay leaves us no alternative. No person in these enlightened times can write or even enjoy poetry 'without a certain unsoundness of mind.' The truth of poetry is 'the truth of madness. The reasonings are just; but the premises are false.'

We cannot unite the incompatible advantages of reality and deception, the clear discernment of truth and the exquisite enjoyment of fiction.[13]

In this historical context, we can discriminate the separate strands in Keats's indictment of science in *Lamia.*

> Do not all charms fly
> At the mere touch of cold philosophy?
> There was an awful rainbow once in heaven:
> We know her woof, her texture; she is given
> In the dull catalogue of common things.
> Philosophy will clip an Angel's wings,
> Conquer all mysteries by rule and line,
> Empty the haunted air, and gnomed mine—
> Unweave a rainbow, as it erewhile made
> The tender-person'd Lamia melt into a shade.

[9] *Letters on Chivalry and Romance*, Letter XI, pp. 154-5.
[10] *The History of English Poetry* (ed. of 1824), III, 284-6. See also William Duff, *Critical Observations* (London, 1770), p. 303n.
[11] *An Essay on the Writings and Genius of Shakespear* (4th ed.; London, 1777), pp. 149-50.

[12] 'Thoughts on Ancient and Modern Poetry,' *The General Magazine and Impartial Review*, III (1789), 532-4.
[13] 'Milton,' *Critical and Historical Essays*, I, 153-6.

First, cold philosophy dispels the charms of myth and fairy-lore—it empties 'the haunted air, and gnomed mine'—but like Hurd and Warton, Keats cannot agree with James Thomson that such materials are easily spared. Also, philosophy breaks down the rainbow into its physical components and causes; 'we know her woof, her texture,' and this knowledge 'unweaves' the rainbow, and substitutes a dull, abstract thing for the beauty and mystery of concrete perception. In maintaining, with Lamb, that Newton 'had destroyed all the poetry of the rainbow by *reducing* it to the prismatic colors,' Keats accedes to the fallacy (in which he has been joined by numerous professional philosophers) that, when a perceptual phenomenon is explained by correlating it with something more elementary than itself, the explanation discredits and replaces the perception—that only the explanation is real, and the perception illusory. And to Keats, if not to Thomson, the ability to versify and dramatize the new scientific 'truths' was no adequate payment for the 'life of sensations,' and the 'indolent' surrender to the sensuous concrete which is integral to his characteristic poetry.

As a consequence, the presumed conflict between the poet's vision and the scrutiny of the scientist raises the question not merely, as in Hurd and Warton, of poetic decline, but, as in Macaulay, of poetic survival. For Keats, in his moments of depression, accepts the exclusive disjunction of some contemporary positivists: either science or poetry; if Newton describes reality, then the poet's rainbow is an illusion; if science in general is true, then poetry in general is false. The basic theme in *Lamia*, as in so many of Keats's major poems, is that of illusion against reality. And after all, as Keats himself sets up the story, Apollonius, the cold philosopher, was right. Lamia was indeed, as he said, a serpent; and all her furniture, according to the passage from Burton's *Anatomy of Melancholy* which Keats quoted as his source, 'no substance but mere illusions.' So far as Lamia and her phantom palace symbolize the poet's view of the world, they reflect Keats's opposition of the 'authenticity of the imagination' to 'consequitive reasonings,' and his recurrent fear that the subject matter of his poetry is the vestige of a magical view of the world, vulnerable to the cold stare of reason.

Keats exemplifies a romantic tendency to shift the debate about the discrepancy between science and poetry from the question of poetic myth and fable to the difference between the visible universe of concrete imaginative observation and that of scientific analysis and explanation. Whether they agreed or disagreed with Keats's conclusions, many writers followed his procedure by pointing to an object traditionally consecrated to poets —if not the rainbow, then the glowworm, the lily, the star, or the cloud— in order to contrast its traditional poetic depiction to its description in the science of optics, biology, astronomy, or meteorology.

In the same year that *Lamia* appeared (1820), Thomas Campbell's 'To the Rainbow' gave further evidence that the happy marriage of poetry and Newton's *Opticks* was ending in recriminations and divorce. 'I ask not proud Philosophy,' Campbell cried, 'To teach me what thou art.'

> Can all that optics teach, unfold
>   Thy form to please me so,
> As when I dreamt of gems and gold
>   Hid in thy radiant bow?
> When Science from Creation's face
>   Enchantment's veil withdraws,
> What lovely visions yield their place
>   To cold material laws!

Nine years later Poe's sonnet 'To Science' echoed phrases from *Lamia*, and posed even more bitterly the conflict between the 'dull realities' of Science with its 'peering eyes,' and the consecration and the poet's dream.

> Hast thou not torn the Naiad from her flood,
> The Elfin from the green grass, and from me
> The summer dream beneath the tamarind
>   tree? [14]

[14] Cf. Emily Dickinson's 'Arcturus is his other name,' as well as: 'I pull a flower from the woods,—/A monster with a glass/Computes the stamens in a breath/And has her in a class.'/

Almost all the important romantic theorists commented on the disparity between imaginative and scientific perception, and deplored the disproportionate development of the latter in recent times. It is important to recognize, however, that by far the greater number refused to admit that there is any inherent and inescapable conflict between science and poetry, or that scientific progress necessarily entails poetic decline. The most common procedure was to regard these, when properly employed, as parallel and complementary ways of seeing, and to hold that while analysis yields truth, this is not the whole truth, and cannot, in vigorous and flexible minds, unweave the poet's rainbow.

Wordsworth, for example, had been present at Haydon's famous dinner, but with customary prudence had refused, pending further inquiry, to drink Keats's toast. 'And don't you remember,' Haydon wrote to Wordsworth, many years after the event, 'Keats proposing "Confusion to the memory of Newton," and upon your insisting on an explanation before you drank it, his saying: "Because he destroyed the poetry of the rainbow by reducing it to a prism." ' [15] The caution is understandable in a poet who had a Renaissance responsiveness to the grandeur of man's intellectual exploration of the universe, and who was also aware of the contributions of the 'nature-study' fostered by science to the power of exact description which he held to be a necessary, if not sufficient condition for poetry. Later Wordsworth was to expand a brief allusion to Newton's statue at Cambridge into three lines surpassing all the windy panegyrics of the preceding century—

Newton with his prism and silent face,
The marble index of a mind for ever
Voyaging through strange seas of Thought, alone.[16]

We must not mistake Wordsworth's contempt, in his *Lyrical Ballads*, for the 'meddling intellect' which murders to dissect, and for the 'philosopher' who would peep and botanize on his mother's grave, for a general attack against science. Other passages make it clear that these lines are to be read only as his judgments against the fallacy of misplaced abstraction, and against the scientist whose laboratory habits are so indurate that he continues to analyze where only imagination and feeling are relevant.[17] In the Preface to these *Ballads*, Wordsworth said that poetry, being grounded in man's emotional nature, incorporates, and has nothing to fear from the narrower 'knowledge' of science: 'Poetry is the first and last of all knowledge—it is as immortal as the heart of man.' In this passage of sustained eloquence, he not only echoes the opinion of Sprat and the eighteenth-century enthusiasts that poetry will assimilate 'the remotest discoveries of the Chemist, the Botanist, or Mineralogists,' but passes beyond them to herald the poetry of *machinisme* and the industrial revolution. 'If the labours of Men of science should ever create any material revolution . . . in our condition,' the poet 'will be at his side, carrying sensation into the midst of the objects of the science itself.' [18] I must add Wordsworth's comment to Isabella Fenwick, which can be read as a belated rebuttal to Keats's toast at the Haydon dinner:

Some are of the opinion that the habit of analysing, decomposing, and anatomizing is inevitably unfavourable to the perception of beauty. . . . We are apt to ascribe to them that insensibility of which they are in truth the effect and not the cause. . . . The beauty in form of a plant or an animal is not made less but more apparent as a whole by more accurate insight into its constituent properties and powers. [19]

Wordsworth's published comments

[15] 16 Oct. 1842, in *Correspondence and Table-Talk*, with a Memoir by Frederick Wordsworth Haydon (London, 1876), II, 54-5.
[16] *Prelude* (1850 ed.), III, 62-3. The passage was added after 1830.
[17] 'The Tables Turned,' 'The Poet's Epitaph'; cf. *The Excursion*, IV, 961-2; also IV, 620ff., 1251ff. And see Douglas Bush, *Science and English Poetry* (New York, 1950), pp. 88-97.
[18] *Wordsworth's Literary Criticism*, pp. 27-8. For Wordsworth's comment on the good and ill effects of the industrialization of England, see *The Excursion*, VIII, 87ff.; and for one of his own attempts at the poetry of the machine, the sonnet called 'Steamboats, Viaducts, and Railways.'
[19] Note to 'This Lawn, a carpet all alive,' in *Poetical Works*, ed. de Selincourt, IV, 425.

established the common pattern of his day for resolving the supposed conflict between poetry and science. Shelley, who was as saturated in scientific fact as any eighteenth-century versifier of physics or botany, held no commerce with the opinion that what he called 'Science and her sister Poesy,' need be at odds. Scientific developments, he admits, have momentarily outgrown the assimilative capacity of our imagination and creative faculty; but he follows Wordsworth, although on other philosophical grounds, in envisioning poetry as the larger class 'which comprehends all science, and that to which all science must be referred.'[20] And in America, William Cullen Bryant, writing in 1825, refused to deplore the supersession of 'mysteries,' myth, and superstition by the 'new wonders and glories' of science, nor see any reason that, 'because the chemist prosecutes his science successfully, therefore the poet should lose his inspiration.'[21]

To Coleridge the threat of science to poetry lay, more profoundly, in the mistaken and unbounded metaphysical pretensions of atomism and mechanism—in Coleridge's view, a useful working hypothesis for physical research which had been illicitly converted first into fact, and then into a total world-view. In his alternative statement in terms of faculties and their functions: that which produced the diverse errors and *malaises* of the mechanistic eighteenth century, in politics, morals, and art, was 'the growing alienation and self-sufficiency of the understanding,' which, as the faculty of 'the science of *phenomena*,' is properly employed only 'as a tool or organ.'[22] But Coleridge, who was himself an amateur biologist, of course proposes not the disjunctive, 'Either poetry or science,' but the conjunctive, 'Both poetry and sci-

ence.' Though a poem is opposed in aim to 'works of science,' the highest poetry is the largest, most inclusive utterance— 'the whole soul of man [in] activity'— including both the emotional and the rational elements, and involving the faculty productive of science as an integral though subordinate part of the mind' whole working: 'with the subordination of the faculties to each other, according to their relative worth and dignity.'[23]

Of special interest to us are writers who, like Keats, contrast the poetic and scientific descriptions of the same natural object, but use the instance to demonstrate that the two outlooks are compatible and mutually invulnerable. In a passage which Keats probably remembered while writing *Lamia*, Hazlitt admitted that, as a matter of historical fact, 'it cannot be concealed' that the progress of knowledge and experimental philosophy 'has a tendency to circumscribe the limits of the imagination, and to clip the wings of poetry'; yet, he added, scientific and poetic observation are not exclusive alternatives. His example is the glowworm, which the naturalist carries home to find it 'nothing but a little grey worm.' The poet visits it at evening when

it has built itself a palace of emerald light This is also one part of nature, one appearance which the glow-worm presents, and that no the least interesting; so poetry is one part o the history of the human mind, though it i neither science nor philosophy.[24]

Leigh Hunt preferred the lily as hi example:

Poetry begins where matter of fact or of science ceases to be merely such, and to exhibit a fur ther truth; that is to say, the connexion i has with the world of emotion, and its powe to produce imaginative pleasure. Inquiring o a gardener, for instance, what flower it is tha we see yonder, he answers, 'a lily.' This is mat ter of fact. The botanist pronounces it to be o the order of 'Hexandria Monogynia.' This i a matter of science. . . .

[20] *The Revolt of Islam*, II. 2254-5; 'Defence of Poetry,' *Shelley's Literary and Philosophical Criticism*, pp. 151-2.
[21] *Lectures on Poetry*, in *Prose Writings*, ed. Parke Godwin (New York, 1889), I, 27-31. Cf. George Moir, article 'Poetry,' *Encyclopaedia Britannica* (7th ed., 1830), XVIII, 145.
[22] *Aids to Reflection*, pp. 268-9; *Lay Sermons*, pp. 63, 71-2; 80ff.

[23] *Biographia*, II, 10-12.
[24] 'On Poetry in General' (1818), *Complete Works* V, 9.

The plant and flower of *light*,

says Ben Jonson; and poetry then shows us the beauty of the flower in all its mystery and splendor.

That the ghost of Newton's *Opticks* continues to haunt this issue Hunt indicates by setting out to prove, through a most tenuous argument, that as 'light, undecomposed, is white; and as the lily is white . . . the two things, so far, are not merely similar, but identical.' [25] Hunt returned to the problem repeatedly in his essays; and his championship of Keats did not restrain him from taking strong issue, the year after his friend's death, with the rainbow passage in *Lamia*. He does not agree, Hunt says, 'that modern experiment has done a deadly thing to poetry,' for the man who thinks he is no poet 'as soon as he finds out the physical cause of the rainbow . . . need not alarm himself; he was none before.' [26]

To cite one other instance: Soon after his own conversion to Wordsworth and poetry, John Stuart Mill was confronted with the argument of John Roebuck, the Benthamite, that to cultivate feelings through imagination 'was only cultivating illusions.' 'In vain I urged on him,' Mill tells us, 'that the imaginative emotion which an idea, when vividly conceived, excites in us, is not an illusion, but a fact, as real as any of the other qualities of objects.' To demonstrate the possibility of alternative perspectives, as each becomes relevant, Mill chose for his representative example the cloud.

The intensest feeling of the beauty of a cloud lighted by the setting sun, is no hindrance to my knowing that the cloud is vapour of water, subject to all the laws of vapours in a state of suspension; and I am just as likely to allow for, and act on, these physical laws whenever there is occasion to do so, as if I had been incapable of perceiving any distinction between beauty and ugliness. [27]

To validate the natural object seen by the poet, as against the object described by the natural scientist, became almost routine in Victorian criticism. 'The difference,' wrote Ruskin, 'between the mere botanist's knowledge of plants, and the great poet's or painter's knowledge of them' is that 'the one notes their distinctions for the sake of swelling his herbarium, the other, that he may render them vehicles of expression and emotion.' [28] In Matthew Arnold's version:

It is not Linnaeus or Cavendish or Cuvier who gives us the true sense of animals, or water, or plants, who seizes their secret for us, who makes us participate in their life; it is Shakespeare, with his

> 'daffodils
> That come before the swallow dares, and take
> The winds of March with beauty. . . .' [29]

The belief, nevertheless, persists, even in our day, that the advances of science must shrink the province of poetry; and we still hear echoes of Keats's fallacy, that scientific description discredits the phenomena for which it is intended to account. As Keats had lamented the rainbow and the haunted air, so D. H. Lawrence has lamented:

'Knowledge' has killed the sun, making it a ball of gas, with spots; 'knowledge' has killed the moon. . . . How are we to get back Apollo and Attis, Demeter, Persephone, and the halls of Dis? [30]

[25] 'What Is Poetry?' (1844), *Imagination and Fancy* (New York, 1848), p. 3.
[26] Review of *Lamia*, in *The Indicator* (2 Aug. 1822); in Edmund Blunden, *Leigh Hunt's 'Examiner' Examined* (London, 1928), p. 147. In an essay written in 1824, Hunt again attacked the 'favorite remark with a pretty numerous set of writers' that knowledge of the nature of optical delusions has put poetry at a stand (*Men, Women, and Books*, London, 1876, pp. 3-4).

[27] *Autobiography*, pp. 106-7.
[28] Preface to *Modern Painters*, 2d ed., 1844, *The Complete Works of John Ruskin*, ed. Cook and Wedderburn (London, 1903), III, 36.
[29] 'Maurice De Guerin,' *Essays in Criticism* (London, 1891), p. 82.
[30] *A Propos of Lady Chatterley's Lover* (London, 1931), pp. 86-7.

WILLIAM CARLOS WILLIAMS

(1883-1963)

Dr. Williams is best known for his volumes of verse and his major poem, *Paterson*
but he also wrote much on literature and American culture. *In the American
Grain* (1925) is a collection of essays on the American past, written in an artist'
prose. In "Edgar Allan Poe" Williams explains the work of the earlier writer, which
had often been dismissed as exotic and even "un-American," as an expression of
Poe's time and place. Other sources of Williams' criticism and literary opinions are
Selected Essays of William Carlos Williams (1954), *The Selected Letters of William
Carlos Williams* (ed. J. C. Thirlwall, 1957), and *I Wanted to Write a Poem* (ed
Edith Heal, 1958).

Edgar Allan Poe (1925)

Poe was not "a fault of nature," "a find
for French eyes," ripe but unaccountable,
as through our woollyheadedness we've
sought to designate him, but a genius intimately shaped by his locality and time.
It is to save our faces that we've given
him a crazy reputation, a writer from
whose classic accuracies we have not
known how else to escape.

The false emphasis was helped by his
Parisian vogue and tonal influence on
Baudelaire, but the French mind was
deeper hit than that. Poe's work strikes
by its scrupulous originality, *not* "originality" in the bastard sense, but in its
legitimate sense of solidity which goes
back to the ground, a conviction that he
can judge within himself. These things
the French were *ready* to perceive and
quick to use to their advantage: a new
point from which to readjust the trig-
onometric measurements of literary form.

It is the New World, or to leave that
for the better term, it is a *new locality*
that is in Poe assertive; it is America,
the first great burst through to expression of a re-awakened genius of *place*.

Poe gives the sense for the first time in
America, that literature is *serious*, not a
matter of courtesy but of truth. (See
Maria Lucretia Davidson.)

The aspects of his critical statements
as a whole, from their hundred American
titles to the inmost structure of his sentences, is that of a single gesture, not
avoiding the trivial, to sweep all worthless chaff aside. It is a movement, first
and last to clear the GROUND.

There is a flavor of provincialism that
IS provincialism in the plainness of his
reasoning upon elementary grammatical
syntactical and prosodic grounds which
awakened Lowell's derision. But insistence upon primary distinctions, that
seems coldly academic, was in this case
no more than evidence of a strong impulse to begin at the beginning. Poe was
unsophisticated, when contrasted with
the puerile sophistications of a Lowell
It is a *beginning* he has in mind, a
juvenescent *local* literature. By this he
avoids the clownish turn of trying to
join, contrary to every reasonable impul-
sion, a literature (the English) with
which he had no actual connection and
which might be presumed, long since, to
have passed that beginning which to the

new condition was requisite.

But Mr. Lowell's comment had to be answered:

"Here comes Poe with his Raven, like Barnaby Rudge—
Three fifths of him genius, and two fifths sheer fudge;
Who talks like a book of iambs and pentameters
In a way to make all men of common sense damn meters
Who has written some things far the best of their kind;
But somehow the heart seems squeezed out by the mind."

It brings a technical retort from Poe upon the grounds that, "We may observe here that *profound* ignorance on any particular topic is always sure to manifest itself by some allusion to 'common sense' as an all-sufficient instructor." Then he tears L.'s versification to pieces, adding, "Mr. L. should not have meddled with the anapestic rhythm: it is exceedingly awkward in the hands of one who knows nothing about it and who *will* persist in fancying that he can write it by ear." But, previously, he had nailed the matter in a different vein. Lowell "could not do a better thing than to take the advice of those who mean him well, and leave prose, with satiric verse, to those who are better able to manage them; while he contents himself with that class of poetry for which, and for which alone, he seems to have an especial vocation—the poetry of *sentiment*." But Poe might have added finally, in his own defense, what he says elsewhere, concerning the accusation in L.'s last two lines: "The *highest* order of the imaginative intellect is always preëminently mathematical—"

The whole passage is noteworthy not only for the brilliance of such a statement as that, but also because of its use of the provincial "we" (*Mr. Griswold and the Poets*): "That we are not a poetical people has been asserted so often and so roundly, both at home and abroad that the slander, through mere dint of repetition, has come to be received as truth. Yet nothing can be farther removed from it. The mistake is but a portion, or corollary, of the old dogma, that the calculating faculties are at war with the ideal; while, in fact, it may be demonstrated that the two divisions of mental power are never to be found in perfection apart. The highest order of the imaginative intellect is always preëminently mathematical; and the converse."

"The idiosyncrasy of our political position has stimulated into early action whatever practical talent we possessed. Even in our national infancy we evinced a degree of utilitarian ability which put to shame the mature skill of our forefathers. While yet in leading strings we proved ourselves adepts in all the arts and sciences which promoted the *comfort* of the animal man. But the arena of exertion, and of consequent distinction, into which our first and most obvious wants impelled us, has been regarded as the field of our deliberate choice. Our necessities have been taken for our propensities. Having been forced to make railroads, it has been deemed impossible that we should make verse. Because it suited us to construct an engine in the first instance, it has been denied that we could compose an epic in the second. Because we are not all Homers in the beginning, it has been somewhat rashly taken for granted that we shall be all Jeremy Benthams to the end."

"But this is purest insanity . . ."

In the critical note upon *Francis Marryat*, the distinction between "nationality in letters," which Poe carefully slights, and the preëminent importance, in letters as in all other branches of imaginative creation, of the *local*, which is his constant focus of attention, is to be noted.

Poe was NOT, it must be repeated, a Macabre genius, *essentially* lost upon the grotesque and the arabesque. If we have appraised him a morass of "lolling lilies," *that* is surface only.

The local causes shaping Poe's genius were two in character: the necessity for a fresh beginning, backed by a native vigor of extraordinary proportions,— with the corollary, that all "colonial imitation" must be swept aside. This was the conscious force which rose in Poe as innumerable timeless insights resulting, by his genius, in firm statements on the character of form, profusely illustrated by his practices; and, *second* the immediate effect of the locality upon the first, upon his nascent impulses, upon his original thrusts; tormenting the depths into a surface of bizarre designs by which he's known and which are *not at all* the major point in question.

Yet BOTH influences were determined by the locality, which, in the usual fashion, finds its mind swayed by the results of its stupidity rather than by a self-interest bred of greater wisdom. As with all else in America, the value of Poe's genius TO OURSELVES must be *uncovered* from our droppings, or at least uncovered from the "protection" which it must have raised about itself to have survived in any form among us—where everything is quickly trampled.

Poe "saw the end"; unhappily he saw his own despair at the same time, yet he continued to attack, with amazing genius seeking to discover, and discovering, points of firmness by which to STAND and grasp, against the slipping way they had of holding on in his locality. Either the New World must be mine as I will have it, or it is a worthless bog. There can be no concession. His attack was *from the center out*. Either I exist or I do not exist and no amount of pap which I happen to be lapping can dull me to the loss. It was a doctrine, anti-American. Here everything was makeshift, everything was colossal, in profusion. The frightened hogs or scared birds feeding on the corn— It left, in 1840, the same mood as ever dominant among us. Take what you can get. What you lack, copy. It was a population puffed with braggadocio, whom Poe so beautifully summarizes in many of his prose tales. To such men, all of them, the most terrible experience in the world is to be shown up. This Poe did, in his criticisms, with venomous accuracy. It was a gesture to BE CLEAN. It was a wish to HAVE the world or leave it. It was the truest instinct in America demanding to be satisfied, and an end to makeshifts, self deceptions and grotesque excuses. And yet the grotesque inappropriateness of the life about him forced itself in among his words.

One is forced on the conception of the New World as a woman. Poe was a new De Soto. The rest might be content with little things, not he.

"Rather the ice than their way."

His attack upon the difficulty which faced him was brilliantly conceived, faultlessly maintained and successful. The best term is perhaps: immaculate.

What he wanted was connected with no particular place; therefore it *must* be where he *was*.

"We have at length arrived at that epoch when our literature may and must stand on its own merits, or fall through its own defects. We have snapped asunder the leading-strings of our British Grandmama, and, better still, we have survived the first hours of our novel freedom,—the first licentious hours of hobbledehoy braggadocio and swagger. A last, then, we are in a condition to be criticized—even more, to be neglected; . . ."

What Poe says gains power by his no diminishing his force for the slightness o the object; it is a sense of an inevitable impartial tide. "We have *no* design to b bitter. We notice this book at all, onl because it is an unusually large one o its kind, because it is lying here upon ou table, and because, whether justly or un justly, whether for good reason or fo none, it has attracted some portion o the attention of the public." There is n softening for the department of name old or new, but a sense of the evidenc examined, as it lies on the page, by faultless mechanism which he bring from the rear of his head for the tria

Lowell, Bryant, etc., concerned poetr with literature, Poe concerned it with th soul; hence their differing conceptions o the use of language. With Poe, word were not hung by usage with association the pleasing wraiths of former masterie this is the sentimental trap-door to b ginnings. With Poe words were figure an old language truly, but one fro which he carried over only the most el mental qualities to his new purpos which was, to find a way to tell his sou Sometimes he used words so playful his sentences seem to fly away from sense, the destructive! with the conserving abandon, foreshadowed, of a Gertrude Stein. The particles of language must be clear as sand. (See *Diddling*.)

This was an impossible conception for the gluey imagination of his day. Constantly he labored to detach SOMETHING from the inchoate mass—That's it:

His concern, the apex of his immaculate attack, was to detach a "method" from the smear of common usage—it is the work of nine tenths of his criticism. He struck to lay low the "*niaiseries*" of form and content with which his world abounded. It was a machine-gun fire; even in the slaughter of banality he rises to a merciless distinction. (See *Rufus Dawes*.) He sought by stress upon construction to hold the loose-strung mass off even at the cost of an icy coldness of appearance; it was the first need of his time, an escape from the formless mass he hated. It is the very sense of a beginning, as *it is the impulse which drove him to the character of all his tales*; to get from sentiment to form, a backstroke from the swarming "population."

He has a habit, borrowed perhaps from algebra, of balancing his sentences in the middle, or of reversing them in the later clauses, a sense of play, as with objects, or numerals which he *has* in the original, disassociated, that is, from other literary habit; separate words which he feels and turns about as if he fitted them to his design with *some* sense of their individual quality: "those who belong properly to books, and to whom books, perhaps, do not quite so properly belong."

The strong sense of a beginning in Poe is in *no one* else before him. What he says, being thoroughly local in origin, has some chance of being universal in application, a thing they never dared conceive. Made to fit a *place* it will have that actual quality of *things* antimetaphysical——

About Poe there is—

No supernatural mystery—

No extraordinary eccentricity of fate——

He is American, understandable by a simple exercise of reason; a light in the morass—which *must* appear eerie, even to himself, by force of terrific contrast, an isolation that would naturally lead to drunkenness and death, logically and simply—by despair, as the very final evidence of a too fine seriousness and devotion.

It is natural that the French (foreigners, unacquainted with American conditions) should be attracted by the SURFACE of his genius and copy the wrong thing, (but the expressive thing), the strange, the bizarre (the recoil) without sensing the actuality, of which that is the complement,—and we get for Poe a REPUTATION for eccentric genius, maimed, the curious, the sick—at least the unexplainable crop-up, unrelated to his ground—which has become his inheritance.

* * *

"The fiery serpent that bit the children of Israel when they wandered through the wilderness was possibly the guinea worm, which enters the body as a water flea, develops, and ultimately, lies coiled under the skin, from one to six feet in length. It formerly was coaxed out by winding it on a stick little by little each day. Then the zoologist found that it seeks water in which to lay its eggs, and will naively crawl out if the affected leg or arm is simply submerged in water for a few hours.

"The mysterious is so simple when revealed by science!"

* * *

On him is FOUNDED A LITERATURE— typical; an anger to sweep out the unoriginal, that became ill-tempered, a monomaniacal driving to destroy, to annihilate the copied, the slavish, the FALSE literature about him: this the major impulse in his notes—darkening as he goes, losing the battle, as he feels himself going under—he emerges as the ghoulish, the driven back. It is the crudeness with which he was attacked in his own person, scoffed at—

He declares, maintains himself, presupposes himself and IS first rate. FIRST! —madly, valiantly battling for the right to BE first—to hold up his ORIGINALITY—

"If a man—if an Orphicist—or SEER

—or whatever else he may choose to call himself, while the rest of the world calls him an ass—if this gentleman have an idea which he does not understand himself, the best thing he can do is to say nothing about it; . . . but if he have any idea which is actually intelligible to himself, and if he sincerely wishes to render it intelligible to others, we then hold it as indisputable that he should employ those forms of speech which are the best adapted to further his object. He should speak to the people in that people's ordinary tongue. He should arrange words such as are habitually employed for the preliminary and introductory ideas to be conveyed—he should arrange them in collocations such as those in which we are accustomed to see those words arranged." "Meantime we earnestly ask if *bread-and-butter* be the vast IDEA in question —if *bread-and-butter* be any portion of this vast IDEA? for we have often observed that when a SEER has to speak of even so usual a thing as bread-and-butter, he can never be induced to mention it outright. . . . "

The language of his essays is a remarkable HISTORY of the locality he springs from. There is no aroma to his words, rather a luminosity, that comes of a disassociation from anything else than thought and ideals; a coldly nebulous, side to side juxtaposition of the words as the ideas—It seems to fall back continuously to a bare surface exhausted by having reached no perch in tradition. Seldom a long or sensuous sentence, but with frequent reduplication upon itself as if holding itself up by itself.

Thought, thought, mass—and the sense of SOMETHING over the heads of the composite particles of the logic, the insignificance of the details, WHICH HE DID ACTUALLY achieve. A "childlike," simple deductive reasoning IS his criticism—a sense of BEGINNING—of originality that presupposes an intrinsic WORTH in the reasoner—a sense of *stripped*, being clothed, nevertheless.

Unwilling to concede the necessity for any prop to his logical constructions, save the locality upon which originality is rested, he is the diametric opposite of Longfellow—to say the least. But Longfellow was the apotheosis of all that had preceded him in America, to this extent that he brought over the *most* from "the other side." In "*Longfellow and Other Plagiarists*," Poe looses himself to the full upon them. But what had they done? No more surely than five hundred architects are constantly practicing. Longfellow did it without genius, perhaps, but he did no more and no less than to bring the tower of the Seville Cathedral to Madison Square.

This is the expression of a "good" spirit. It is the desire to have "culture" for America by "finding" it, full blown— somewhere. But we had wandered too far, suffered too many losses for that. Such a conception could be no more than a pathetic reminiscence. It had NOTHING of the New World in it. Yet, it was bred of the wish to bring to the locality what it lacked.

What it lacked, really, was to be cultivated. So they build an unrelated copy upon it; this, as a sign of intelligence,— vigor. That is, to bring out its qualities they cover them. Culture is still the effect of cultivation, to work with a thing until it be rare; as a golden dome among the mustard fields. It implies a solidity capable of cultivation. Its effects are marble blocks that lie perfectly fitted and aligned to express by isolate distinction the rising lusts which threw them off regulated, in moving through the mass of impedimenta which is the world.

This is culture; in mastering them, to burst through the peculiarities of an environment. It is NOT culture to *oppress* a novel environment with the stale, if symmetrical, castoffs of another battle. They are nearly right when they say: Destroy the museums! But that is only the reflection, after all, of minds that fear to be slavish. Poe could look at France, Spain, Greece, and NOT be impelled to copy. He could do this BECAUSE he had the sense within him of a locality of his own, capable of cultivation.

Poe's use of the tags of other culture than his own manages to be novel, interesting, useful, *unaffected*, since it succeeds in giving the impression of being not in the least dragged in by rule or pretence but of a fresh purpose such as I have indicated. There is nothing offensively "learned" there, nothing contemptuous, even in the witty tricks with bogus Latin which he plays on his illiterate public, which by *its* power, in turn, *permits* him an originality, *allows him*, even when he is satiric, an authenticity—— since he is not seeking to destroy but to assert, candidly, and to defend *his own*.

He was the first to realize that the hard, sardonic, truculent mass of the New World, hot, angry—was, in fact, not a thing to paint over, to smear, to destroy —for it WOULD not be destroyed, it was too powerful,—it smiled! That it is NOT a thing to be slighted by men. Difficult, its very difficulty was their strength. It was in the generous bulk of its animal crudity that their every fineness would be found safely imbedded.

Poe conceived the possibility, the sullen, volcanic inevitability of the *place*. He was willing to go down and wrestle with its conditions, using every tool France, England, Greece could give him, —but to use them to original purpose.

This is his anger against Longfellow.

The difficulty is in holding the mind down to the point of seeing the *beginning* difference between Poe and the rest. One cannot expect to see as wide a gap between him and the others as exists between the Greek and the Chinese. It is only in the conception of a *possibility* that he is most distinguished. His greatness is in that he turned his back and faced inland, to originality, with the identical gesture of a Boone.

And for *that* reason he is unrecognized. Americans have never recognized themselves. How can they? It is impossible until someone invent the ORIGINAL terms. As long as we are content to be called by somebody's else terms, we are incapable of being anything but our own dupes.

Thus Poe must suffer by his originality. Invent that which is new, even if it be made of pine from your own yard, and there's none to know what you have done. It is because there's no *name*. This is the cause of Poe's lack of recognition. He was American. He was the astound-

ing, inconceivable growth of his locality. Gape at him they did, and he at them in amazement. Afterward with mutual hatred; he in disgust, they in mistrust. It is only that which is under your nose which seems inexplicable.

Here Poe emerges—in no sense the bizarre, isolate writer, the curious literary figure. On the contrary, in him American literature is anchored, in him alone, on solid ground.

In all he says there is a sense of him *surrounded* by his time, tearing at it, ever with more rancor, but always at battle, taking hold.

But Poe—differing from pioneers in other literatures, the great beginners— due to the nature of the people, *had first to lift his head through* a successful banality. This was a double impost. But he did it, NOT by despising, ignoring, slighting the work that preceded him but by attacking it. "Among all the pioneers of American literature, whether prose or poetical, there is *not one* (Note: In his own estimate even, he begins.) whose productions have not been much overrated by his countrymen."

"But originality, as it is one of the highest, is also one of the rarest of merits. In America it is especially, and very remarkably, rare—this through causes sufficiently well understood."

He abhorred the "excessively opportune."—Of course, he says, to write of the Indians, the forests, the great natural beauty of the New World will be attractive and make a hit—so he counsels writers to AVOID it, for reasons crystal clear and well chosen. (See *Fenimore Cooper*.) His whole insistence has been upon method, in opposition to a nameless rapture over nature. He admired Claude Lorraine. Instead of to hog-fill the copied style with a gross rural sap, he wanted a lean style, rapid as a hunter and with an aim as sure. One way, in the New World, men must go. Bust gut or acute wit. Find the ground, on your feet or on your belly. It is a fight. He counsels writers to *borrow nothing* from the scene, but to put all the weight of effort into the WRITING. Put aside the GRAND scene and get to work to express yourself.

Method, punctuation, grammar—

The local condition of literature FORCED Poe's hand. It is necessary to understand this if his names are to be grasped. By avoiding, of necessity, the fat country itself for its expression; to originate a style that does spring from the local conditions, not of trees and mountains, but of the "soul"—here starved, stricken by loss of liberty, ready to die— he is *forced in certain directions for his subjects.*

But this left him in difficulties. When he had narrowed himself down to a choice of method and subject, when all the meaningless lump of the lush landscape and all that that implies had been swept away, THEN, and only then will he begin to search for a subject. A voluntary lopping off of a NATURAL landscape, forced him into a field which he must have *searched* for, a field of cold logic, of invention, to which his work must still present a natural *appearance*: into his imaginative prose.

His criticism paves the way for what *must* be his prose—illustrating his favorite theory that the theory *includes the practice.*

No better means of transit from the criticism to the tales could be imagined than his discussion of the merits and demerits of Hawthorne as a proseist. He expresses his delight and surprise at finding Hawthorne's work of such excellence, but then he finds a fault:

"He has the purest style, the finest taste, the most available scholarship, the most delicate humor, the most touching pathos, the most radiant imagination, the most consummate ingenuity, and with these varied good qualities he has done well as a mystic. But is there any one of these qualities which would prevent his doing doubly as well in a career of honest, upright, sensible, prehensible, and comprehensible things? Let him mend his pen, get a bottle of visible ink, come out from the Old Manse, cut Mr. Alcott, hang (if possible) the Editor of *The Dial*, and throw out of the window to the pigs all his odd numbers of *The North American Review*."

Hawthorne has no repugnance for handling what Poe purposely avoids, the contamination of the UNFORMED LUMP, the "*monstrum, horrendum, informe, ingens, cui lumen ademptum*." And it is precisely here that lies Hawthorne's lack of importance to our literature when he is compared with Poe; what Hawthorne *loses* by his willing closeness to the life of his locality in its vague humors; his lifelike copying of the New England melancholy; his reposeful closeness to the town pump—Poe *gains* by abhorring; flying to the ends of the earth for "original" material—

By such a simple, logical twist does Poe succeed in being the more American, heeding more the local necessities, the harder structural imperatives—by standing off to SEE instead of forcing himself too close. Whereas Hawthorne, in his tales, by doing what everyone else in France, England, Germany was doing *for his own milieu*, is no more than copying their *method* with another setting; does not ORIGINATE; has not a *beginning* literature at heart that must establish its own rules, own framework,—Poe has realized by adopting a more elevated mien.

This feeling in Poe's tales, that is, the hidden, under, unapparent part, gives him the firmness of INSIGHT into the conditions upon which our literature must rest, always the same, a local one, surely, but not of sentiment or mood, as not of trees and Indians, but of original fibre, the normal toughness which fragility of mood presupposes, if it will be expressive of anything— It is the expression of Poe's clearness of insight into the true difficulty, and his soundess of judgment.

*   *   *

To understand what Poe is driving at in his tales, one should read first NOT the popular, perfect—*Gold Bug, Murders in the Rue Morgue*, etc., which by their brilliancy detract from the observation of his deeper intent, but the less striking tales—in fact all, but especially those where his humor is less certain, his mood lighter, less tightly bound by the incident, where numerous illuminating *faults* are allowed to become expressive. *The Business Man, The Man That Was Used Up,*

Loss of Breath, BonBon, Diddling, The Angel of the Odd—and others of his lesser Tales.

It should be noted how often certain things take place—how often there is death but not that only; it is the body broken apart, dismembered, as in *Loss of Breath*—

Then, as in *Hop Frog, The System of Dr. Tarr and Professor Fether* and the *Murders in the Rue Morgue*—the recurrent image of the ape. Is it his disgust with his immediate associates and his own fears, which cause this frequent use of the figure to create the emotion of extreme terror?—"Your majesty cannot conceive of the *effect* produced, at a masquerade, by eight chained orang-outangs, imagined to be real ones by the most of the company; and rushing in with savage cries, among the crowd of delicately and gorgeously habited men and women. The contrast is inimitable."

Note, in *Silence—a Fable*: "sorrow and weariness and disgust with mankind and a longing for solitude."

Many colloquial words could be detached from Poe's usage if it were worth while, to show how the language he practices varies from English, but such an exercise would be of little value—*hipped, crack,* etc.—it does not touch bottom.

The Tales continue the theories of the criticism, carrying out what they propose:

1. In choice of material, abstract. 2. In method, a logical construction that clips away, in great part, the "scenery" near at hand in order to let the real business of composition *show.* 3. A primitive awkwardness of diction, lack of polish, colloquialism that is, unexpectedly, especially in the dialogues, much in the vein of Mark Twain.

One feels that in the actual composition of his tales there must have been for him, as they embody it in fact, a fascination other than the topical one. The impulse that made him write them, that made him enjoy writing them—cannot have been the puerile one of amazement, but a deeper, logical enjoyment, in keeping with his own seriousness: it is that of PROVING even the most preposterous of

his inventions plausible—that BY HIS METHOD he makes them WORK. They go: they *prove* him potent, they confirm his thought. And by the very extreme of their play, by so much the more do they hold up the actuality of that which he conceives.

If there ever had been another American to use his Greek, Sanscrit, Hebrew, Latin, French, German, Italian and Spanish—in the text—with anything like the unspoiled mastery of Poe, we should have known, long since, what it meant to have a literature of our own.

It is to have a basis, a local stanchion, by which to *bridge over* the gap between present learning and the classical; that asserts the continuity of the common virtues of style; that asserts their aristocratic origin, or their democratic origin, the same, as it has been pointed out recently, since an aristocracy is the flower of a locality and so the *full* expression of a democracy.

Of his method in the Tales, the significance and the secret is: authentic particles, a thousand of which spring to the mind for quotation, taken apart and reknit with a view to emphasize, enforce and make evident, the *method.* Their quality of skill in observation, their heat, local verity, being *over-shadowed* only by the detached, the abstract, the cold philosophy of their joining together; a method springing so freshly from the local conditions which determine it, by their emphasis of firm crudity and lack of co-ordinated structure, as to be worthy of most painstaking study—The whole period, America 1840, could be rebuilt, psychologically (phrenologically) from Poe's "method."

*   *   *

It is especially in the poetry where "death looked gigantically down" that the horror of the formless resistance which opposed, maddened, destroyed him has forced its character into the air, the wind, the blessed galleries of paradise, above a morose, dead world, peopled by shadows and silence, and despair— It is the compelling force of his isolation.

The one earthly island he found where

he might live in something akin to the state he imagined, the love of his wife, had to be single and inviolate. Failing of a more comprehensive passion, which might have possessed him had the place been of favorable omen, only in this narrow cell could he exist at all. Of this the poems are the full effect. He is known as a poet, yet there are but five poems, possibly three.

When she died, there was nothing left. In his despair he had nowhere to turn. It is the very apotheosis of the place and the time.

He died imploring from those about him a love he could not possess, since his own love, as his poems, had been so mingled in character with the iron revenge which completely surrounded him that it could not be repeated once its single object had been lost.

But here, in his poetry least of all, is there a mystery. It is but the accumulation of all that he has expressed, in the criticism, in the prose tales, but made as if so shaken with desire, that it has come off as a flame, destroying the very vial that contained it—and become, against his will almost it would seem,—himself.

It is not by a change in character but by its quickened motion that it has turned from mere heat into light—by its power of penetration that it has been brought to dwell upon love. By its acid power to break down truth that it has been *forced* upon love—

I mean that though in this his "method" has escaped him, yet his poems remain of the single stuff of his great "theory": to grasp the meaning, to understand, to reduce all things to method, to control, lifting himself to power—

And failing, truth turning to love, as if metamorphosed in his hands as he was

about to grasp it—now the full horror of his isolation comes down—

In his prose he could still keep a firm hold, he still held the "arrangement" fast and stood above it, but in the poetry he was at the edge—there was nothing——

Here in poetry, where it is said "we approach the gods," Poe was caught, instead, in his time.

Now, defenseless, the place itself attacked him. Now the thinness of his coat, the terror of his isolation took hold.

Had he lived in a world where love throve, his poems might have grown differently. But living where he did, surrounded as he was by that world of unreality, a formless "population"—drifting and feeding—a huge terror possessed him.

His passion for the refrain is like an echo from a hollow. It is his own voice returning—

His imagery is of the desperate situation of his mind, thin as a flame to mount unsupported, successful for a moment in the love of—not so much his wife—but in the escape she filled for him with her frail person, herself afflicted as by "ghouls."

Disarmed, in his poetry the place itself comes through. This is the New World. It is this that it does, as if——

It is in this wraithlike quality of his poems, of his five poems, that Poe is most of the very ground, hard to find, as if we walked upon a cushion of light pressed thin beneath our feet, that insulates, satirises—while we lash ourselves up and down in a fury of impotence.

Poe stayed against the thin edge, driven to be heard by the battering racket about him to a distant screaming —the pure essence of his locality.

The best poem is *To One in Paradise.*

ALLEN TATE

(b. 1898)

Poet, biographer, novelist, and editor, Allen Tate is perhaps best known as one of the "New Critics." Both Tate's poetry and criticism reflect an intellectual viewpoint that is conservative and traditionalist in the Eliot manner, a viewpoint clarified and intensified by Tate's acute sense of his historical inheritance as a Southerner of the agrarian Old South tradition, and by his conversion, in the early Fifties, to Roman Catholicism. Because of these convictions, Tate's essays, always very personal in tone and reference, tend to put literary criticism into a broader perspective of social, political, and moral criticism of the central "liberal" and technological tendencies of modern life. As Ransom may be said to be the chief "metaphysician" of the Southern Agrarians, Tate is perhaps their chief "moralist." The bulk of Tate's most important criticism can be found in the two summary collections, *The Man of Letters in the Modern World* (New York, 1955) and *Collected Essays* (Denver, 1959).

Our Cousin, Mr. Poe (1949)

When I was about fourteen there were in our house, along with the novels of John Esten Cooke, E. P. Roe, and Augusta Evans, three small volumes of Edgar Allan Poe. That, by my reckoning, was a long time ago. Even then the books were old and worn, whether from use (I suppose not) or from neglect, it did not occur to me to enquire. I remember, or imagine I remember the binding, which was blue, and the size, which was small, and the paper, which was yellow and very thin. One volume contained the Poems, prefaced by Lowell's famous "biography." In this volume I am sure, for I read it more than the others, was the well-known, desperate, and asymmetrical photograph, which I gazed at by the hour and which I hoped that I should some day resemble. Another volume contained most, or at least the most famous of the Tales: "Ligeia," which I liked best (I learned in due time that Poe had, too); "Morella" and "William Wilson," which I now like best; and "The Fall of the House of Usher," which was a little

spoiled for me even at fourteen by the interjection of the "Mad Tryst of Sir Launcelot Canning." Perhaps it was in this volume that I admired "Marginalia," the first "criticism" I remember reading; but I did not discern either the bogus erudition or the sense of high literature which Poe was the first American to distinguish from entertainment and self-improvement through books; the merits as well as the defects went over my head. "Marginalia" could not at any rate have been in the third volume, which was given to a single long work: *Eureka—A Prose Poem*. This astrophilosophical discourse, which the late Paul Valéry took more seriously than any English or American critic ever did, fell in with my readings in popular astronomical books. In the backyard I arranged in a straight line peas, cherries, and oranges, in the proportionate sizes and distances of the sun and planets, and some hundreds of feet away (an inch perhaps to a thousand light-years) an old volley ball of my elder brothers' to represent Alpha Lyrae.

Later, on another occasion, I expect to examine *Eureka* at length, as I read it now, not as I read it at fourteen; yet before I leave it I must mention two other circumstances of my boyhood reading and the feeling that accompanied it. It lives for me as no later experience of ideas lives, because it was the first I had. The "proposition" that Poe undertook to demonstrate has come back to me at intervals in the past thirty-six years with such unpredictable force that now I face it with mingled resignation and dismay. I can write it without looking it up:

In the original unity of the first thing lies the secondary cause of all things, with the germ of their inevitable annihilation.

This is not the place to try to say what Poe meant by it. I could not, at fourteen, have guessed what it meant even after I had read the book; yet it is a fact of my boyhood (which I cannot suppose unique) that this grandiose formula for cosmic cataclysm became a part of my consciousness through no effort of my own but seemed to come to me like a dream, and came back later, like a nursery rhyme, or a tag from a popular song unbidden.

The other circumstance I am surer of because it was a visible fact, a signature in faded brown ink on the fly-leaf of *Eureka*: it told me years later that the three volumes had been printed earlier than 1870, the year the man who had owned them died. He was my great-grandfather. My mother had said, often enough, or on some occasion that fixed it in memory, that her grandfather had "known Mr. Poe." (She was of the era when all eminent men, living or recently dead, were "Mr.") I knew as a boy that my great-grandfather had been a "poet," and in 1880 I found some of his poems, which I forbear to discuss. He had for a while been editor of the *Alexandria Gazette* at about the time of Mr. Poe's death. Both were "Virginians," though Virginians of somewhat different schools and points of view. I can see my great-grandfather in Poe's description of a preacher who called upon him in the summer of 1848: "He stood smiling and bowing at the madman Poe."

I have brought together these scattered memories of my first reading of a serious writer because in discussing any writer, or in coming to terms with him, we must avoid the trap of mere abstract evaluation, and try to reproduce the actual conditions of our relation to him. It would be difficult for me to take Poe up, "study" him, and proceed to a critical judgment. One may give these affairs the look of method, and thus deceive almost everybody but oneself. In reading Poe we are not brought up against a large, articulate scheme of experience, such as we see adumbrated in Hawthorne or Melville, which we may partly sever from personal association, both in the writer and in ourselves. Poe surrounds us with Eliot's "wilderness of mirrors," in which we see a subliminal self endlessly repeated or, turning, a new posture of the same figure. It is not too harsh, I think, to say that it is stupid to suppose that by "evaluating" this forlorn demon in the glass, we dispose of him. For Americans, perhaps for most modern men, he is with us like a dejected cousin: we may "place" him but we may not exclude him from our board. This is the recognition of a relationship, almost of the blood, which we must in honor acknowledge: what destroyed him is potentially destructive of us. Not only this; we must acknowledge another obligation, if, like most men of my generation, we were brought up in houses where the works of Poe took their easy place on the shelf with the family Shakespeare and the early novels of Ellen Glasgow. This is the obligation of loyalty to one's experience: he was in our lives and we cannot pretend that he was not. Not even Poe's great power in Europe is quite so indicative of his peculiar "place" as his unquestioned, if examined, acceptance among ordinary gentle people whose literary culture was not highly developed. The horrors of Poe created not a tremor in the bosoms of young ladies or a moment's anxiety in the eyes of vigilant mothers. I suppose the gentlemen of the South did not read him much after his time; in his time, they could scarcely have got the full sweep and depth of the horror. Nothing that Mr. Poe wrote, it was said soon after his death, could bring a blush to the cheek of the purest maiden.

But I doubt that maidens read very far in the Tales. If they had they would have found nothing to disconcert the image that Miss Susan Ingram recorded from a visit of Poe to her family a few weeks before his death:

Although I was only a slip of a girl and he what seemed to me then quite an old man, and a great literary one at that, we got on together beautifully. He was one of the most courteous gentlemen I have ever seen, and that gave great charm to his manner. None of his pictures that I have ever seen look like the picture of Poe that I keep in my memory . . . there was something in his face that is in none of them. Perhaps it was in the eyes.

If he was a madman he was also a gentleman. Whether or not we accept Mr. Krutch's theory,[1] we know, as this sensible young lady knew, that she was quite safe with him. A gentleman? Well, his manners were exemplary (when he was not drinking) and to the casual eye at any rate his exalted idealization of Woman (even of some very foolish women) was only a little more humorless, because more intense, than the standard cult of Female Purity in the Old South.

What Mr. Poe on his own had done with the cult it was not possible then to know. A gentleman and a Southerner, he was not quite, perhaps, a Southern gentleman. The lofty intellect of Ligeia, of Madeline, of Berenice, or of Eleanora, had little utility in the social and economic structure of Virginia, which had to be perpetuated through the issue of the female body, while the intellect, which was public and political, remained under the supervision of the gentlemen. Although Morella had a child (Poe's only heroine, I believe, to be so compromised), she was scarcely better equipped than Virginia Clemm herself to sustain more than the immaculate half of the vocation of the Southern lady. "But the fires," writes Morella's narrator-husband, "were not of Eros." And we know, at the end of the story, that the daughter is no real daughter but, as Morella's empty "tomb" reveals, Morella herself come back as a vampire to wreak

upon her "lover" the vengeance due him. Why is it due him? Because, quite plainly, the lover lacked, as he always lacked with his other heroines, the "fires of Eros." The soul of Morella's husband "burns with fires it had never before known . . . and bitter and tormenting to my spirit was the gradual conviction that I could in no manner define their unusual meaning, or regulate their vague intensity." Perhaps in the soul of John Randolph alone of Virginia gentlemen strange fires burned. The fires that were not of Eros were generally for the land and oratory, and the two fires were predictably regulated.

Poe's strange fire is his leading visual symbol, but there is not space in an essay to list all its appearances. You will see it in the eye of the Raven; in "an eye large, liquid, and luminous beyond comparison," of Roderick Usher; in the burning eye of the old man in "The Tell-Tale Heart"; in "Those eyes! those large, those shining, those divine orbs," of the Lady Ligeia. Poe's heroes and heroines are always burning with a hard, gem-like flame—a bodyless exaltation of spirit that Poe himself seems to have carried into the drawing-room, where its limited visibility was sufficient guarantee of gentlemanly behavior. But privately, and thus, for him, publicly, in his stories, he could not "regulate its vague intensity."

I cannot go into this mystery here as fully as I should like; yet I may, I think, ask a question: Why did not Poe use explicitly the universal legend of the vampire? Perhaps some instinct for aesthetic distance made him recoil from it; perhaps the literal, business-like way the vampire went about making its living revolted the "ideality" of Poe. At any rate D. H. Lawrence was no doubt right in describing as vampires his women characters; the men, soon to join them as "undead," have by some defect of the moral will, made them so. The mysterious exaltation of spirit which is invariably the unique distinction of his heroes and heroines is not quite, as I have represented it, bodyless. *It inhabits a human body but that body is dead. The spirits prey upon one another*

---

[1] The theory that Poe was sexually impotent.

with destructive fire which is at once pure of lust and infernal. All Poe's characters represent one degree or another in a movement towards an archetypal condition: the survival of the soul in a dead body; but only in "The Facts in the Case of Monsieur Valdemar" is the obsessive subject explicit.

In none of the nineteenth-century comment on "The Fall of the House of Usher" that I have read, and in none of our own period, is there a feeling of shock, or even of surprise, that Roderick Usher is in love with his sister: the relation not being physical, it is "pure." R. H. Stoddard, the least sympathetic of the serious early biographers, disliked Poe's morbidity, but admitted his purity. The American case against Poe, until the first World War, rested upon his moral indifference, or his limited moral range. The range is limited, but there is no indifference; there is rather a compulsive, even a profound, interest in a moral problem of universal concern. His contemporaries could see in the love stories neither the incestuous theme nor what it meant, because it was not represented literally. The theme and its meaning as I see them are unmistakable: the symbolic compulsion that drive through, and beyond, physical incest moves towards the extinction of the beloved's will in complete possession, not of her body, but of her being; there is the reciprocal force, returning upon the lover, of self-destruction. Lawrence shrewdly perceived the significance of Poe's obsession with incestuous love. Two persons of the least dissimilarity offer the least physical resistance to mutual participation in the *fire* of a common being. Poe's most casual reader perceives that his lovers never do anything but contemplate each other, or pore upon the rigmarole of preposterously erudite, ancient books, most of which never existed. They are living in each other's insides, in the hollows of which burns the fire of will and intellect.

The fire is a double symbol; it lights and it burns. It is overtly the "light" of reason but as action it becomes the consuming fire of the abstract intellect, without moral significance, which invades the being of the beloved. It is the fire that, having illuminated, next destroys. Lawrence is again right in singling out for the burden of his insight the epigraph to "Ligeia," which Poe had quoted from Glanvill: "Man does not yield himself to the angels, nor unto death utterly, save through the weakness of his own feeble will." Why do these women of monstrous will and intellect turn into vampires? Because, according to Lawrence, the lovers have not subdued them through the body to the biological level, at which sanity alone is possible, and they retaliate by devouring their men. This view is perhaps only partly right. I suspect that the destruction works both ways, that the typical situation in Poe is more complex than Lawrence's version of it.

If we glance at "The Fall of the House of Usher" we shall be struck by a singular feature of the catastrophe. Bear in mind that Roderick and Madeline are brother and sister, and that the standard hyperaesthesia of the Poe hero acquires in Roderick a sharper reality than in any of the others, except perhaps William Wilson. His naked sensitivity to sound and light is not "regulated" to the forms of the human situation; it is a mechanism operating apart from the moral consciousness. We have here something like a capacity for mere sensation, as distinguished from sensibility, which in Usher is atrophied. In terms of the small distinction that I am offering here, sensibility keeps us in the world; sensation locks us into the self, feeding upon the disintegration of its objects and absorbing them into the void of the ego. The lover, circumventing the body into the secret being of the beloved, tries to convert the spiritual object into an object of sensation: the intellect which knows and the will which possesses are unnaturally turned upon that centre of the beloved which should remain inviolate.

As the story of Usher opens, the Lady Madeline is suffering from a strange illness. She dies. Her brother has, of course, possessed her inner being, and killed her; or thinks he has, or at any rate wishes to think that she is dead. This is all a little vague: perhaps he has deliberately entombed her alive, so that she will die by suffocation—a symbolic action for extinction of being. Why has he committed this monstrous crime? Sister though she is, she is nevertheless not entirely identical with him: she has her own otherness, of however slight degree, resisting his hypertrophied will. He puts her alive, though "cataleptic," into the "tomb." (Poe never uses graves, only tombs, except in "Premature Burial." His corpses, being half dead, are thus only half buried; they rise and walk again.) After some days Madeline breaks out of the tomb and confronts her brother in her bloody cerements. This is the way Poe presents the scene:

". . . Is she not hurrying to upbraid me for my haste? Have I not heard her footsteps on the stair? Do I not distinguish the heavy and horrible beating of her heart? Madman!"—here he sprang furiously to his feet, and shrieked out his syllables, as if in his effort he were giving up his soul—*"Madman! I tell you that she now stands without the door!"*

As if in the superhuman energy of his utterance there had been found the potency of a spell, the huge antique panels to which the speaker pointed threw slowly back, upon the instant, their ponderous and ebony jaws. It was the work of the rushing gust—but then without those doors there *did* stand the lofty and enshrouded figure of the Lady Madeline of Usher. There was blood upon her white robes, and the evidence of some bitter struggle upon every portion of her emaciated frame. For a moment she remained trembling to and fro upon the threshold—then, with a low moaning cry, fell heavily inward upon the person of her brother, and in her violent and now final death-agonies, bore him to the floor a corpse, and a victim to the terrors he had anticipated.

Madeline, back from the tomb, neither dead nor alive, is in the middle state of the unquiet spirit of the vampire, whose heart-beats are "heavy and horrible." There is no evidence that Poe knew any anthropology; yet in some legends of vampirism the undead has a sluggish pulse, or none at all. In falling prone upon her brother she takes the position of the vampire suffocating its victim in a sexual embrace. By these observations I do not suggest that Poe was conscious of what he was doing; had he been, he might have done it even worse. I am not saying, in other words, that Poe is offer-

ing us, in the Lady Madeline, a vampire according to Bram Stoker's specifications. An imagination of any power at all will often project its deepest assumptions about life in symbols that duplicate, without the artist's knowledge, certain meanings, the origins of which are sometimes as old as the race. If a writer ambiguously exalts the "spirit" over the "body," and the spirit must live wholly upon another spirit, some version of the vampire legend is likely to issue as the symbolic situation.

Although the action is reported by a narrator, the fictional point of view is that of Usher: it is all seen through his eyes. But has Madeline herself not also been moving towards the cataclysmic end in the enveloping action outside the frame of the story? Has not her *will to know* done its reciprocal work upon the inner being of her brother? Their very birth had violated their unity of being. They must achieve spiritual identity in mutual destruction. The physical symbolism of the fissured house, of the miasmic air, and of the special order of nature surrounding the House of Usher and conforming to the laws of the spirits inhabiting it—all this supports the central dramatic situation, which moves towards spiritual unity through disintegration.

In the original unity of the first thing lies the secondary cause of all things, with the germ of their inevitable annihilation.

Repeated here, in the context of the recurrent subject of the Tales, the thesis of *Eureka* has a sufficient meaning and acquires something of the dignity that Valéry attributed to it. Professor Quinn adduces quotations from mathematical physicists to prove that Poe, in *Eureka*, was a prophet of science. It is a subject on which I am not entitled to an opinion. But even if Professor Quinn is right, the claim is irrelevant, and is only another version of the attempt today to make religion and the arts respectable by showing that they are semi-scientific. Another sort of conjecture seems to me more profitable: that in the history of the moral imagination in the nineteenth century Poe occupies a special place. No other writer in England or the United States, or, so far as I know, in France, went so far as Poe in his vision of de-humanized man.

His characters are, in the words of William Wilson's double, "dead to the world"; they are machines of sensation and will, with correspondences, in the physical universe, to particles and energy. Poe's engrossing obsession in *Eureka* with the cosmic destiny of man issued in a quasi-cosmology, a more suitable extension of his vision than any mythology, home-made or traditional, could have offered him. The great mythologies are populous worlds, but a cosmology need have nobody in it. In Poe's, the hyper-aesthetic egoist has put all other men into his void: he is alone in the world, and thus dead to it. If we place Poe against the complete Christian imagination of Dante, whom he resembles in his insist-ence upon a cosmic extension of the moral predicament, the limits of his range are apparent, and the extent of his insight within those limits. The quality of Poe's imagination can be located, as I see it, in only two places in Dante's en-tire scheme of the after-life: Cantos XIII and XXXII of the *Inferno*. In Canto XIII, the Harpies feed upon the living trees enclosing the shades of suicides—those "violent against themselves," who will not resume their bodies at the Resur-rection, for "man may not have what he takes from himself." In XXXII, we are in Caïna, the ninth circle, where traitors to their kin lie half buried in ice, up to the pubic shadow—"where the doleful shades were . . . sounding with their teeth like storks." Unmotivated treach-ery, for the mere intent of injury, and self-violence are Poe's obsessive subjects. He has neither Purgatory nor Heaven; and only two stations in Hell.

Let us turn briefly to the question of Poe's style. He has several styles, and it is not possible to damn them all at once. The critical style, which I shall not be able to examine here, is on occasion the best; he is a lucid and dispassionate ex-positor, he is capable of clear and rig-orous logic (even from mistaken prem-ises, as in "The Rationale of Verse"), when he is not warped by envy or the desire to flatter. He is most judicial with his peers, least with his inferiors, whom he either overestimates or wipes out. As for the fictional style, it, too, varies; it is perhaps at its sustained best, in point of sobriety and restraint, in the tales of de-duction. Exceptions to this observation are "Descent into the Maelström," "The Narrative of Arthur Gordon Pym," and perhaps one or two others in a genre which stems from the eighteenth-century "voyage." These fictions demanded a Defoe-like verisimilitude which was ap-parently beyond his reach when he dealt with his obsessive theme. Again I must make an exception: "William Wilson," one of the serious stories (by serious, I mean an ample treatment of the obses-sion), is perspicuous in diction and on the whole credible in realistic detail. I quote a paragraph:

> The extensive enclosure was irregular in form, having many capacious recesses. Of these, three or four of the largest constituted the play-ground. It was level, and covered with a hard fine gravel. I well remember it had no trees, nor benches, nor anything similar within it. Of course it was in the rear of the house. In front lay a small parterre, planted with box and other shrubs, but through this sacred division we passed only upon rare oc-casions indeed—such as a first advent to school or a final departure hence, or perhaps, when a parent or a friend having called upon us, we joyfully took our way home for the Christmas or midsummer holidays.

It is scarcely great prose, but it has an eighteenth-century directness, and even elegance, of which Poe was seldom ca-pable in his stories. I surmise that the playground at Dr. Bransby's school at Stoke-Newington, where, as a child, he was enrolled for five years, recalled one of the few periods of his life which he could detach from the disasters of man-hood and face with equanimity. Now a part of the description of the Lady Ligeia:

> . . . I examined the contour of the lofty and pale forehead—it was faultless—how cold in-deed that word when applied to a majesty so divine!—the skin rivalling the purest ivory, the commanding extent and repose, the gentle prominence of the regions above the temples; and the raven-black, the glossy, the luxuriant,

the naturally curling tresses, setting forth the full force of the Homeric epithet, "hyacinthine." I looked at the delicate outline of the nose. . . .

But I refrain. It is easy enough to agree with Aldous Huxley and Yvor Winters, and dismiss this sort of ungrammatical rubbish as too vulgar, or even too idiotic, to reward the time it takes to point it out. But if Poe is worth understanding at all (I assume that he is), we might begin by asking why the writer of the lucid if not very distinguished passage from "William Wilson" repeatedly fell into the bathos of "Ligeia." I confess that Poe's serious style at its typical worst makes the reading of more than one story at a sitting an almost insuperable task. The Gothic glooms, the Venetian interiors, the ancient winecellars (from which nobody ever enjoys a vintage but always drinks "deep")—all this, done up in a glutinous prose, so fatigues one's attention that with the best will in the world one gives up, unless one gets a clue to the power underlying the flummery.

I have tried in the course of these remarks to point in the direction in which the clue, as I see it, is to be found. I do not see it in the influence of the Gothic novel. This was no doubt there, but no man is going to use so much neo-Gothic, over and over again, unless he means business with it; I think that Poe meant business. If the Gothic influence had not been to hand, he would have invented it, or something equally "unreal" to serve his purpose. His purpose in laying on the thick décor was to simulate sensation. Poe's sensibility, for reasons that I cannot surmise here, was almost completely impoverished. He could feel little but the pressure of his predicament, and his perceptual powers remained undeveloped. Very rarely he gives us a real perception because he is not interested in anything that is alive. Everything in Poe is dead: the houses, the rooms, the furniture, to say nothing of nature and of human beings. He is like a child—all appetite without sensibility; but to be in manhood all appetite, all will, without sensibility, is to be a monster: to feed spiritually upon men without sharing

with them a real world is spiritual vampirism. The description of Ligeia's head is that of a dead woman's.

Does it explain anything to say that this is necrophilism? I think not. Poe's prose style, as well as certain qualities of his verse,[2] expresses the kind of "reality" to which he had access: I believe I have indicated that it is a reality sufficiently terrible. In spite of an early classical education and a Christian upbringing, he wrote as if the experience of these traditions had been lost: he was well ahead of his time. He could not relate his special reality to a wider context of insights—a discipline that might have disciplined his prose. From the literary point of view he combined the primitive and the decadent: primitive, because he had neither history nor the historical sense; decadent, because he was the conscious artist of an intensity which lacked moral perspective.

But writers tend to be what they are; I know of no way to make one kind into another. It may have been a condition of Poe's genius that his ignorance should have been what it was. If we read him as formal critics we shall be ready to see that it was another condition of his genius that he should never produce a poem or a story without blemishes, or a critical essay that, despite its acuteness in detail, does not evince provincialism of judgment and lack of knowledge. We must bear in mind Mr. Eliot's remark that Poe must be viewed as a whole. Even the fiction and the literary journalism that seem without value add to his massive impact upon the reader.

What that impact is today upon other readers I cannot pretend to know. It has been my limited task to set forth here a little of what one reader finds in him,

[2] I expect to examine Poe's verse on another occasion. It may be remarked that his verse rhythms are for the metronome, not the human ear. Its real defects are so great that it is not necessary to invent others, as Mr. T. S. Eliot seems to do in *From Poe to Valéry* (New York, 1949). Thus Mr. Eliot (and I cite only one of his observations that seem to me wrong) complains that "the saintly days of yore" could not be an appropriate time for the Raven to have lived. Elijah was fed by Ravens, a bird which was almost extinct in America in the 1840's. Ravens frequently fed hermits and saints and were in fact a fairly standard feature of saintly equipment.

and to acknowledge in his works the presence of an incentive (again, for one man) to self-knowledge. I do not hesitate to say that had Poe not written *Eureka*, I should have been able, a man of this age, myself to formulate a proposition of "inevitable annihilation." I can only invite others to a similar confession. Back of the preceding remarks lies an ambitious assumption, about the period in which we live, which I shall not make explicit. It is enough to say that, if the trappings of Poe's nightmare strike us as tawdry, we had better look to our own. That particular vision in its purity (Poe was very pure) is perhaps not capable of anything better than Mr. Poe's ludicrous décor. Nor have persons eating one another up and calling it spiritual love often achieved a distinguished style either

in doing it or in writing about it. It was not Ugolino, it was Dante who wrote about Ugolino with more knowledge than Ugolino had. Mr. Poe tells us in one of his simple poems that from boyhood he had "a demon in my view." Nobody then—my great-grandfather, my mother, three generations—believed him. It is time we did. I confess that his voice is so near that I recoil a little, lest he, Montressor, lead me into the cellar, address me as Fortunato, and wall me up alive. I should join his melancholy troupe of the undead, whose voices are surely as low and harsh as the grating teeth of storks. He is so close to me that I am sometimes tempted to enter the mists of pre-American genealogy to find out whether he may not actually be my cousin.

FORD MADOX FORD

(1873-1939)

Novelist, poet, and essayist, Ford (originally Hueffer) is less well-known as a critic, although he published a considerable amount of criticism during his lifetime and was an important critical influence both as editor of *The English Review* and *The Transatlantic Review* and as a personal advisor to many modern writers. His critical books and essays are impressionistic, frequently developing almost in the manner of "stream-of-consciousness"; their content is usually biographical or autobiographical, and it is as often as not apocryphal. But Ford brings to his impressionistic-anecdotal method an acute taste, a profound sense of history, and a special awareness of the predicaments of the serious artist in the modern world. In his hands anecdote, apocryphal or not, can become a remarkably expressive technique of revealing the individuality of writers in the contexts of their times and places. Ford's chief critical writings include *Henry James: A Critical Study* (1913), *The Critical Attitude* (1915), *Joseph Conrad: A Personal Reminiscence* (1924). *The English Novel: from the Earliest Days to the Death of Conrad* (1929), *Portraits from Life* (1937), and *The March of Literature* (1938).

Henry James, the Master (1936)

I will begin this work with a little romance in the style of the Master—for *what* an intrigue he would have made of

From *Portraits from Life* by Ford Madox Ford. Copyright 1936 and 1937. Reprinted by permission of the estate of Ford Madox Ford, and by permission of and arrangement with Houghton Mifflin Company, the authorized publishers.

it if he had heard it at one of the hospitable boards where he so continually picked up what 'I have always recognized on the spot as "germs" '—the central ideas from which sprang his innumerable stories. . . . And it is the innumerability of his stories rather than the involutions of his style and plots that most have struck me in rereading the works of him who must, whether we like to acknowledge it or not, be called the great master of all us novelists of today.

I hasten to avert thunders from my head by saying that I know that there are thousands of novelists of today and here who will swear that they never read a word of Henry James—just as the first words that Mr. H. M. Tomlinson ever said to me were, 'Never heard of the fellow!'—the 'fellow' being Conrad. But one's master is far more an aura in the air than an admonitory gentleman with uplifted forefinger, and one learns as much by reacting against a prevailing tendency as by following in a father's footsteps. . . .

Well, then . . . I was sitting one day in my study in Winchelsea when, from beside the window, on the little verandah, I heard a male voice, softened by the intervening wall, going on and on interminably . . . with the effect of a long murmuring of bees. I had been lost in the search for one just word or other so that the gentle sound had only dreamily penetrated to my attention. When it did so penetrate and after the monologue had gone on much, much longer, a certain irritation took hold of me. Was I not the owner of the establishment? Was I not supposed by long pondering over just words and their subsequent transference to paper to add at least to the credit, if not to the resources of that establishment? Was it not, therefore, understood that chance visitors must *not* be entertained at the front door which was just beside my window? . . . The sound, however, was not harsh or disagreeable and I stood it for perhaps another ten minutes. But at last impatience overcame me and I sprang to my door.

Silhouetted against the light at the end of the little passage were the figures of one of the housemaids and of Mr. Henry James. And Mr. James was uttering the earth-shaking question:

'Would you then advise me . . . for I know that such an ornament decorates your master's establishment and you will therefore from your particular level be able to illuminate me as to the . . . ah . . . smooth functioning of such, if I may use the expression, a wheel in the domestic timepiece—always supposing that you will permit me the image, meaning that, as I am sure in this household is the case, the daily revolution of a really harmonious *chez soi* is as smooth as the passing of shadows over a dial . . . would you then advise me to have . . . in short to introduce into *my* household and employ . . . a . . . that is to say . . . a Lady Help?'

I advanced at that and, as the housemaid with a sigh of relief disappeared amongst the rustlings of her skirts, in the strongest and firmest possible terms assured Mr. James that such an adornment of the household of an illustrious and well-appointed bachelor was one that should very certainly not be employed. He sighed. He appeared worn, thin for him, dry-skinned, unspirited. His liquid and marvellous dark eyes were dulled, the skin over his aquiline nose was drawn tight. He was suffering from a domestic upheaval—his household, that for a generation had, indeed, revolved around him as quietly as the shadows on a dial, with housekeeper, butler, upper housemaid, lower housemaid, tweeny maid, knife-boy, gardener, had suddenly erupted all round him so that for some time he had been forced to content himself with the services of the knife-boy.

That meant that he had to eat in the ancient hostelry, called The Mermaid, that stood beside his door. And, his housekeeper having for thirty years and more sent up, by the imposing if bottle-nosed butler who was her husband, all Mr. James's meals without his ever having ordered a single one—being used to such a halcyon cuisine the Master had not the slightest idea of what foods agreed with him and which did not. So that everything disagreed with him and he had all the appearance of being really ill. . . . The cause of the bottle-nose had been also the occasion of the eruption, all the female servants having one day left in a body on account of the 'carryings-on' of the butler, and the butler himself, together, alas, with his admirable wife, the housekeeper, having, twenty-four hours later, to be summarily and violently ejected by a sympathetic police sergeant.

So the poor Master was not only infinitely worried about finding an appropriate asylum for the butler and his wife, but had had to spend long mornings and afternoons on what he called 'the benches of desolation in purgatorial, if I may allow myself the word, establishments, ill-named, since no one appeared there to register themselves . . . eminently ill-named: *registry-offices* . . .' And there would be a sound like the hiss of a snake as he uttered the compound word. . . .

He would pass his time, he said, interviewing ladies all of a certain age, all of haughty—the French would say *renfrognée*—expressions, all of whom unanimously assure him that, if they demeaned themselves merely by for an instant considering the idea of entering the household of an untitled person like himself, in such a God-forsaken end of the world as the Ancient Town of Rye, they having passed their lives in the families of never anyone less than a belted earl in mansions on Constitution Hill in the shadow of Buckingham Palace . . . if they for a fleeting moment toyed with the idea, it was merely, they begged to assure him . . . 'forthegoodoftheirhealths.' Mr. James having dallied with this sentence would utter the last words with extreme rapidity, raising his eyebrows and his cane in the air and digging the ferrule suddenly into the surface of the road. . . .

How they come back to me after a quarter of a century . . . the savoured, half-humorous, half-deprecatory words, the ironically exaggerated gestures, the workings of the closely shaved lips, the halting to emphasize a point, the sudden scurryings forward, for all the world like the White Rabbit hurrying to the Queen's tea-party . . . along the Rye Road, through the marshes, from Winchelsea. . . . I walking beside him and hardly ever speaking, in the guise of God's strong, silent Englishman—which he took me really to be. . . .

To give the romance, then, its happy ending . . . One of the matrons of Rye had conceived the idea of lodging a dependant orphan niece in poor Mr. James's house and so had recommended him to employ a Lady Help, offering to supply herself that domestic functionary. He had consulted as to the advisability of this step all the doctors', lawyers', and parsons' wives of the neighbourhood, and in addition one of the local great ladies —I think it was Lady Maude Warrender. The commoners' ladies, loyal to the one who wanted to dispose of the dependant niece, had all said the idea was admirable. Her Ladyship was non-committal, going no further than to assure him that the great ladies of the neighbourhood would not refuse to come to tea with him in his garden—that being their, as well as his, favourite way of passing an afternoon—merely because he should shelter an unattached orphan beneath his roof. But she would go no further than that.

So, in his passion for getting, from every possible angle, light on every possible situation—including his own—he had walked over to Winchelsea to consult not only me, but any female member of my household upon whom he should chance, and had kept the appalled and agitated housemaid for a full half hour on the doorstep whilst he consulted her as to the advisability of the step he was contemplating. . . . But I soon put a stop to *that* idea. In practical matters Mr. James did me the honour to pay exact attention to my opinion—I was for him the strong, silent man of affairs.

How long his agony lasted after that I cannot say. His perturbations were so agonizing to witness that it seemed to be a matter of years. And then, one day, he turned up with a faint adumbration of jauntiness. At last he had heard of a lady who gave some promise of being satisfactory. . . . The only shadow appeared to be the nature of her present employment.

'Guess,' he said, 'under whose august roof she is at the moment sheltering? . . . *Je vous le donne en mille.* . . .' He started back dramatically, rolling his fine eyes, and with great speed he exclaimed:

'The Poet Laureate . . . no less a person!'

Now the Poet Laureate occupies in England a position that it is very difficult to explain on this side of the water. By his official situation he is something preposterous and eminent . . . and at the same time he is something obsolescent, harmless, and ridiculous. Southey, Tennyson, and Doctor Bridges have commanded personally a certain respect, but I cannot think of anyone else who was anything else than ridiculous . . . rendered ridiculous by his office. And at the time of which I am speaking the whole literary world felt outragedly that either Swinburne or Mr. Kipling ought to have been the laureate. As it was, the holder of the title was a Mr. Alfred Austin, an obscure, amiable, and harmless poetaster who wrote about manor-houses and gardens and lived in a very beautiful manor-house in a very beautiful garden.

And, two days later Mr. James turned up, radiant. He lifted both hands above his head and exclaimed:

'As the German Emperor is said to say about his mostachio, "*it is accomplished.*" . . . Rejoice—as I am confident you will —with me, my young friend. All from now onwards shall, I am assured, be with me gas and gingerbread. . . . Halcyon, halcyon days. In short, ahem . . .' And he tapped himself lightly on the breast and assumed the air of a traveller returned from the wintry seas. 'I went,' he continued, 'to the house of the Poet Laureate . . . to the back door of course . . . and interviewed a Lady who, except for one trifling—let us not say defect but let us express it "let or hindrance" to what I will permit myself to call the perfect union, the continuing *lune de miel* . . . except for that, then, she appeared the perfect, the incredible, the except for the pure-in-heart, unattainable She . . . But upon delicate enquiry . . . oh, I assure you, enquiry of the *most* delicate . . . for the obstacle was no less than that on reckoning up the tale of her previous "situations" . . . as twenty years with the Earl of Breadalbane, thirty years with Sir Ponsonby Peregrine Perowne, forty with the Right Honourable the Lord Bishop of Tintagel and Camelot . . . on reckoning up the incredible tale of years it appeared that she must be of the combined ages of Methusaleh and the insupportable Mariner—not of your friend Conrad, but of the author of *Kubla Khan.* But upon investigation it appeared

that this paragon and phoenix actually was and in consequence will, to the end of recorded time, remain, exactly the same age as' . . . and he took three precise, jaunty steps to the rear, laid his hand over his heart and made a quick bow . . . 'myself. . . .'

'And,' he resumed, 'an upper housemaid and her sister, the underhousemaid, who had left me in circumstances that I was unable to fathom but that today are only too woefully apparent to me, having offered to return and to provide a what they call tweeny of their own choosing . . . all shall for the future be as I have already adumbrated, not only gas and gingerbread, but cloves and clothes pegs and beatitude and bliss and beauty . . .' And so it proved.

I have taken some time over that Romance because the whole of James, the man, could be evolved from it—and a great deal of James, the writer. For me the strongest note of all in his character was expressed in his precautions. Not his cautions, for in action, as in writing, he was not in the least cautious.

Whether for his looks or life he studied every aspect of the affair on which he was engaged with extraordinary elaboration—the elaboration which he gave to every speech that he uttered. And he was a man of the most amazing vitality, inexhaustible, indefatigable. He consulted everybody from the conductor of the train from Rye Harbor to Rye golf links, to the chauffeur of a royal automobile who, having conveyed his august master to call on the local great lady, spent a disgusted afternoon in the Mermaid expressing rancour at the fact that the stone-deaf old lady who kept the local tollgate should have refused to let her Sovereign pass through except after payment of a shilling. What exact treasures of information Mr. James can have extracted as to either the passengers to the golf links or the travelling habits of Edward VII, or what use he expected to make of that information, I do not know. But he had an extraordinary gift of exacting confidence and even confessions so that his collection of human instances must have been one of the vastest that any man ever had. It made him perhaps feel safe—or at least as safe as it was in his nature to feel. He could feel, that is to say, that he knew his own *milieu*—the coterie of titled, distinguished, and 'good' people in which he and his books moved and had their beings. And in the special English sense the words 'good people' does not mean the virtuous, but all the sufficiently well-born, sufficiently inconspicuous, sufficiently but not too conspicuously opulent, sufficiently but very certainly not too conspicuously intelligent and educated, that supply recruits to the ruling classes of the British Isles. . . .

Of that class he knew the lives and circumstances, at first perhaps rather superficially and with enthusiasm, and at last profoundly and with disillusionment as profound as his knowledge. . . . And it comforted him to know 'things' about the lives of the innumerable not-born that surrounded the manors or the De Vere Street apartments of the people he really knew, in the sense of having them on his calling list—and being on theirs. . . . He saw the 'common people' lying like a dark sea round the raft of the privileged. They excited his piqued wonder, his ardent curiosity, he built the most elaborate theories all over and round them, he observed enough of them to be able to give characteristics, phrases, and turns of mind to the retainers of the Privileged, but he never could be brought to think that he knew enough about them to let him project their lives onto paper. He noted admirably the very phraseology of Mrs. Wicks, the faithful attendant of Maisie who lived forever in fear of being 'spoken to,' and with equal admirableness the point of view of poor Brooksmith, the gentleman's valet who 'never *had* got his spirits up' after the loss of his one wonderful master. But if, as happens to us today, he had been confronted by a Radical Left clamouring that he must write about the proletariat or be lost, he would just for ever have dismissed his faithful amanuensis and relapsed into mournful silence.

He had that conscientiousness—or if you will, that pre-cautiousness . . . and that sense of duty to his public. He set himself up—and the claim was no little one—as directing his reader as to the fine shades of the psychology of a decorative and utterly refined world where it was always five o'clock. He makes the claim with the utmost equanimity again and again in his Prefaces, only abandoning it to say that if the world did not in fact contain any creatures of such hypersensibility and sensitiveness as those he rendered in his later work, the world ought, if it was to lay claim to being civilized, to contain nobody else. . . . Yet he actually knew so many details of the lives of the poorer people about him in Rye that, as I have elsewhere related, I once asked him why he did not for once try his hand at something with at least the local peasantry for a *milieu*. The question was prompted more by wonder at the amazing amount he did know than by any idea that he would possibly consider having a try at it. After all, in masterpieces like *The Spoils of Poynton*, which remains for me the technical high-water mark of all James's work—and can't I remember the rapturous and shouting enthusiasm of Conrad over that story when we first read it together so that that must have been the high-water mark of Conrad's enthusiasm for the work of any other writer? In masterpieces, then, like *The Spoils of Poynton*, James, who fifteen years or so before must have been utterly foreign to the *milieu*, had got completely and mercilessly under the skin of the English ruling classes. So that if he could penetrate one foreignness, why not another? And I cited his other great and impeccable masterpiece, *The Real Thing*, which shows members of the ruling classes reduced by financial disaster to complete pennilessness. He replied, pausing for a moment whilst the heights of Iden with its white, thatched farmhouses formed a background to his male and vigorous personality—for it was always on the Winchelsea Road that we conversed . . . he replied then:

'My dear H, you confuse the analogies. You might say that I came to this country *from* comfortable circumstances *into* comfortably circumstanced circles. Though no further uptown than Washington Square, the Washington Square of my youth was almost infinitely divided, by gulfs, chasms, canyons, from the downtownnesses round Trinity Spire where, you understand, they worked—mysteriously and at occupations as to which we of Washington Square hadn't the very ghost of an inkling. . . . And if, as you have heard me say, the comfortably circumstanced of that day were not by any manner of means luxuriously—or even hardly so much as comfortably caparisoned or upholstered or garnished at table or horse-furnitured when they rode in the buggies . . . or, if in the mecca of good society, internationally of the highest cultivation and nationally of all that the nation had of the illustrious to offer . . . if, then, on descending the steps of the Capitol *on trébuchait sur des vaches* as the Marquis de Sabran-Penthièvre remarked in the seventies, . . . if they still, at Washington, D.C., not Square, they still, to the embarrassment of the feet of visiting diplomatists, pastured cows on the lawns outside of White House, nevertheless the frame of mind . . . the frame of mind, and that's the important thing, was equally, for the supporters of the initials as for those of the Square, that of all the most comfortable that the world had to offer. . . . I do not suppose that, with the exception of the justlanded relatives of my parents' Nancies or Biddies or Bridgets in the kitchen visiting their kinsmaids, I ever saw to speak to a single human being who did not, as the phrase is—and Heaven knows, more than the phrase is and desperate and dark and hideously insupportable the condition must be—the verb's coming now . . . didn't know where their next day's meals were coming from . . . who were, that is to say, of that frame of mind, that, as the lamentable song says: "They lived in a dive and sometimes contrived to pick up a copper or two." . . . For of course, as you were kind enough to say, in *The Real Thing* I have sufficiently well rendered the perturbations of the English comfortable who by financial disaster were reduced, literally, to complete vagueness as to the provenance of their next day's breakfast, lunch, tea, and

dinner. . . . Or, as in the sketch—it isn't sufficiently complete of the more than reduced circumstances of the fathers of Kate Croy in m . . . mmm. . . .' He stopped and surveyed me with a roguish and carefully simulated embarrassment. For it was established sufficiently between us that in the longish, leanish, fairish Englishman who was Merton Densher of *The Wings of the Dove*, he had made an at least external portrait of myself at a time when he had known me only vaguely and hadn't imagined that in the ordinary course of things the acquaintance would deepen. . . . So he began again:

'Consider,' he said with a sort of appalled vehemence, 'what it must be—how desperate and dark and abhorrent—to live in such tenebrousness that all the light that could fall into your cavern must come in through a tiny orifice which, if it were shuttered by a penny, would give you light, warmth, sustenance, society, even . . . and that, if it were absent, that penny would disclose nothing but unmeasured blackness that penetrated to and pervaded your miserable lair. . . . All light, all hope, all chance in life or of heaven dependant from that tiny disk of metal . . . Why, how could you enter into a frame of mind similar to that, and still more, if you were a writer, how could you render such circumstances and all their circumambiences and implications? . . . And you ask me, who *am*, for my sins, of the same vocation as the beautiful Russian genius—who am, I permit myself to say, a renderer of human vicissitudes . . . of a certain conscience, of a certain scrupulousness . . . you ask *me* to mislead my devotees by the rendering of caves as to which I know nothing and as to the penetration or the mere imagination of which I truly shudder? . . . Perish the thought . . . I say perish, perish the damnable thought. . . .' He walked on for some time in a really disturbed silence, muttering every two or three seconds to himself—and then turned on me almost furiously.

'You understand,' he said, 'the damnable thought is not that I might be poor. If I had to be poor I should hope to sup-

port the condition with equanimity. . . .'
And he went on to explain that it wasn't
even the idea of contemplating, of delv-
ing into the poverty of others. What he
shrank from was the temptation to treat
themes that did not come into his province—the province that he considered
the one in which he could work assuredly
and with a quiet conscience.

Once he stopped suddenly on the road
and said, speaking very fast:

'You've read my last volume? . . .
There's a story in it. . . .' He continued
gazing intently at me, then as suddenly
he began again: 'There are subjects one
thinks of treating all one's life. . . . And
one says they are not for one. And one
says one must not treat them . . . all one's
life. All one's life. . . . And then suddenly
. . . one does . . . *Voilà!*' He had been
speaking with almost painful agitation.
He added much more calmly: 'One has
yielded to temptation. One is to that
extent dishonoured. One must make the
best of it.'

That story was *The Great Good Place*,
appearing, I think, in the volume called
The Soft Side. In it he considered that
he had overstepped the bounds of what
he considered proper to treat—in the
way of his sort of mysticism. There were,
that is to say, mysticisms that he considered proper to treat and others whose
depths he thought should not be probed
—at any rate by his pen. For there were
whole regions of his character that he
never exploited in literature, and it would
be the greatest mistake to forget that the
strongest note in that character was a
mysticism different altogether in character from that of the great Catholic
mystics. It resembled rather a perception
of a sort of fourth dimensional penetration of the material world by strata of the
supernatural, of the world of the living
by individuals from among the dead.
You will get a good inkling of what I
mean if you will read again *The Turn of
the Screw* with the constant peepings-in
of the ghosts of the groom and the governess with their sense of esoteric evil—
their constant peepings-in on the haunted
mortals of the story. For him, good and

evil were not presented by acts; they
were something present in the circum-
ambience of the actual world, something
spiritual attendant on actions or words.
As such he rendered them and, once convinced that he had got that sense in, he
was content—he even took an impish
pleasure in leaving out the renderings of
the evil actions.

Of that you can read sufficiently in his
enormous and affrighting Prefaces. . . .
He never specifies in *The Turn of the
Screw* what were the evil deeds of the
ghostly visitants, nor what the nature of
the corruption into which the children
fell. And, says he in the Preface to the
story:

Only make the reader's vision of evil intense enough, I said to myself—and that is
already a charming job—and his own experience, his own sympathy (with the children)
and horror (of their false friends) will supply
him quite sufficiently with all the particulars.
Make him *think* the evil, make him think it
for himself, and you are released from weak
specifications.

It is an admirable artistic maxim. But
it did not—and that is what I am trying
to emphasize as the main note of this
paper—dispense him, in his own mind,
from having all the knowledges, whether
of esoteric sin or the mentality of but-
lers, that were necessary to make him
feel that he knew enough about his subject to influence the reader's vision in the
right direction. As far as I know—and if
diligence in reading the works of James
gives one the right to know, I ought to
have that right—not a single rendering
of esoteric sin, sexual incidents, or shad-
owing of obscenities exists in all the
works of the Master, and his answer to
D. H. Lawrence or to Rabelais would,
for him, have been sufficiently and triumphantly expressed in the sentences I
have just quoted.

But that did not prevent him—when
he considered the occasion to serve—from
making his conversations heroically
Rabelaisian, or, for me, really horrific,
on the topics of esoteric sin or sexual indulgence. I have attended at conversations between him and a queer tiny
being who lay as if crumpled up on the

stately sofa in James's magnificent pan-
elled room in Lamb House—conversations that made the tall wax candles seem
to me to waver in their sockets and the
skin of my forehead and hands to prickle
with sweat. I am in these things rather
squeamish; I sometimes wish I was not,
but it is so and I can't help it. I don't
wish to leave the impression that these
conversations were carried on for purposes of lewd stimulation or irreverent
ribaldry. They occurred as part of the
necessary pursuit of that knowledge that
permitted James to give his reader the
'sense of evil.' . . . And I dare say they
freed him from the almost universal
proneness of Anglo-Saxon writers to indulge in their works in a continually intrusive fumbling in placket-holes as
Sterne called it, or in the lugubrious occupation of composing libidinous Lim-
ericks. James would utter his racy 'Ho-
ho-ho's' and roll his fine eyes whilst
talking to his curious little friend, but
they were not a whit more racy and his
eyes did not roll any more than they did
when he was asking a housemaid or a
parson's wife for advice as to the advisability of employing a Lady's Help, or
than when he was recounting urbane
anecdotes at tea on his lawn to the Ladies
So-and-So and So-and-So. It was all in
the day's work.

Exactly what may have been his intimate conviction as to, say, what should
be the proper relation of the sexes, I
don't profess to know. That he demanded from the more fortunate characters in
his books a certain urbanity of behaviour
as long as that behaviour took place in
the public eye, his books are there to
prove. That either Mr. Beale Farange or
Mrs. Beale committed in the cimcum-
ambience of *What Masie Knew* one or
more adulteries must be obvious, since
they obtained divorces in England. But
the fact never came into the foreground
of the book. And that he had a personal
horror of letting his more august friends
come into contact through him with anyone who might be even remotely suspected of marital irregularities, I know
from the odd, seasonal nature of my relations with him. We met during the win-

ters almost every day, but during the
summers only by, usually telegraphed,
appointment. This was because during
the summer Mr. James's garden overflowed with the titled, the distinguished,
the eminent in the diplomatic world . . .
with all his *milieu*. And, once he had got
it well fixed into his head that I was a
journalist, he conceived the idea that all
my friends must be illegally united with
members of the opposite sex. So that it
was inconceivable that my summer
friends should have any chance to penetrate onto his wonderfully kept lawns.
I do not think that I knew any journalists at all in those days, and I am perfectly certain that, with one very eminent
exception, I did not know anyone who
had been so much as a plaintiff in the
shadow of the divorce courts. I was in
the mood to be an English country gentleman and, for the time being, I was.
. . . It happened, however, that the extraordinarily respectable wives of two
eminent editors were one week-end during a certain summer staying in Winchelsea—which was a well-known tourist resort—and they took it into their heads to
go and call on James at Rye.

I had hardly so much as a bowing
acquaintance with them. But the next
day, happening to go into Rye, I met
the Old Man down by the harbour. Just
at the point where we met was a coal
yard whose proprietor had the same
name as one of the husbands of one of
those ladies. James stopped short and
with a face working with fury pointed his
stick at the coal man's name above the
gate and brought out the exasperated
words:

'A couple of jaded . . . WANTONS!
. . .' and, realizing that I was fairly quick
on the uptake, nothing whatever more.
. . . But, as soon as the leaves fell, there
he was back on my doorstep, asking innumerable advices—as to his invest-
ments, as to what would cure the parasites of a dog, as to brands of cigars, as
to where to procure cordwood, as to the
effects of the Corn Laws on the landed
gentry of England . . . And I would
accompany him, after he had had a cup
of tea, back to his Ancient Town; and

next day I would go over and drink a cup of tea with him and wait whilst he finished dictating one of his sentences to his amanuensis and then he would walk back with me to Winchelsea. . . . In that way we each got a four-mile walk a day. . . .

No, I never did get any knowledge as to how he regarded sexual irregularities. . . . I remember he one day nearly made me jump out of my skin during a one-sided discussion as to the relative merits of Flaubert and Turgenev—the beautiful Russian genius of his youth.

Turgenev was for him perfection—in person, except that his features were a little broad, in the Slav manner; in his books; in his manners; in his social relations, which were of the highest; in what was aristocratic. But Flaubert, James went on and on hating and grumbling at to the end of his days. Flaubert had, as I have elsewhere related, once been rude to the young James. That James never mentioned. But he had subseqently received James and Turgenev in his dressing-gown. . . . It was not, of course, a dressing-gown, but a working garment —a sort of long, loose coat without revers —called a *chandail*. And if a French man of letters received you in his *chandail*, he considered it a sort of showing honour, as if he had admitted you into his working intimacy. But James never forgave that—more perhaps on account of Turgenev than himself. . . . Flaubert for ever afterwards was for him the man who worked, who thought, who received, who lived—and perhaps went to Heaven in—his dressing-gown! . . . In consequence he was a failure. All his books except one were failures—technical and material . . . and that one, *Madame Bovary*, if it was a success in both departments . . . well, it was nothing to write home about. And Flaubert's little *salon* in the Faubourg Saint-Honoré was 'rather bare and provisional,' and Flaubert cared too much for 'form,' and, because he backed bills for a relation, died in reduced circumstances. . . .

Flaubert was in short the sort of untidy colossus whom I might, if I had the chance, receive at Winchelsea, but who would never, never have been received

on the summer lawns of Lamb House at Rye.

And suddenly Mr. James exclaimed, just at the dog-leg bend in the road between the two Ancient Towns:

'But Maupassant!!!! . . .' That man apparently was, for him, the real Prince Fortunatus amongst writers. I don't mean to say that he did not appreciate the literary importance of the author of *La Maison Tellier*—who was also the author of *Ce Cochon de Morin* and, alas, of *Le Horla*, so that whilst in 1888 James was writing of him the words I am about to quote, that poor Prince was already gravitating towards the lunatic asylum. But, writes Mr. James:

What makes M. de Maupassant salient is two facts: the first of which is that his gifts are remarkably strong and definite and the second that he writes directly *from* them. . . . Nothing can exceed the masculine firmness, the quiet force of his style in which every phrase is a close sequence, every epithet a paying piece. Less than anyone today does he beat the air; more than anyone does he hit out from the shoulder . . .

sentiments which seem—but only seem— singular in view of the later convolutions of epithet that distinguished our Master. . . .

And those considerations in his conversation Mr. James completely omitted. On the Rye Road, Maupassant was for him the really prodigious, prodigal, munificent, magnificently rewarded Happy Prince of the Kingdom of Letters. He had yachts, villas on the Mediterranean, 'affairs,' mistresses, wardrobes of the most gorgeous, grooms, the entrée into the historic salons of Paris, furnishings, overflowing bank balances . . . everything that the heart of man could require even to the perfectly authentic *de* to ally him to the nobility and a public that was commensurate with the ends of the earth. . . . And then, as the topstone of that edifice, Mr. James recounted that once, when Mr. James had been invited to lunch with him, Maupassant had received him, not, be assured, in a dressing-gown, but in the society of a naked lady wearing a mask. . . . And Maupassant assured the author of *The Great Good lace* that the lady was a *femme du monde*. And Mr. James believed him. . . . Fortune could go no further than *that*! . . .

Manners, morals, and the point of view have so changed since even 1906 when Mr. James must have recounted that anecdote that I am not going to dilate upon it. And you have to remember that some years after the 1888 in which he wrote the words I have quoted, Mr. James underwent an experience that completely altered his point of view, his methods, and his entire literary practice. His earlier stages, Mr. James the Second contrived entirely—or almost entirely—to obscure in a sort of cuttlefish cloud of interminable phrases. Until the middle nineties nothing could have exceeded the masculine firmness, the quiet force of his writing, and of no one else than himself could it more justly be written that 'less than anyone did he beat the air, more than anyone did he hit out from the shoulder.'

That is amazingly the case. I have more than once proclaimed the fact that there were two Jameses. And yet no one could be more overwhelmed than I at re-reading in their earliest forms, after all these years, his early masterpieces as they were written and before he went over and elaborated their phrases. Thus to re-read is to realize with immense force that more than anyone else, in the matter of approach to his subjects, Maupassant rather than Turgenev must have been the young James's master. *Daisy Miller*; that most wonderful *nouvelle* of all, *The Four Meetings; The Pupil; The Lesson of the Master; The Death of the Lion*, and all the clear, crisp, mordant-stories that went between, right up to *The Real Thing* and *In the Cage*—all these stories are of a complete directness, an economy, even of phrase, that make James one of the great masters of the *nouvelle*, the long or merely longish short story.

But at a given date, after a misfortune that, for the second time, shattered his life and convinced him that his illusions as to the delicacies of his 'good' people of a certain *milieu* were in fact . . . delu-sions; after that he became the creature of infinite precautions that he was when I knew him best. I had, that is to say, a sight—two or three sights—of him in the previous stage. Then he resembled one of those bearded elder statesman—the Marquis of Salisbury, Sir Charles Dilke, or the Prince who was to become Edward VII. He was then slightly magisterial; he cross-questioned rather than questioned you; he was obviously of the *grand monde* and of the daily habit of rubbing, on equal terms, shoulders with the great.

But about the later James, clean-shaven, like an actor, so as to recover what he could of the aspect of youth; nervous; his face for ever mobile; his hands for ever gesturing; there hung continually the feeling of a forced energy, as if of a man conscious of failure and determined to conceal mortification. He had had two great passions—the one for a cousin whom he was to have married and who died of consumption while they were both very young, and the other for a more conspicuous but less satisfactory personage who in the end, at about the time when the break occurred, let him down mercilessly after a period of years. And the tenacity of his attachments was singular and unforgetting.

The Wings of the Dove [he writes in his Preface of 1909 to that novel], published in 1902, represents to my memory a very old— if I shouldn't perhaps say a very young— motive. I can scarcely remember the time when the motive on which this long-drawn fiction mainly rests was not vividly present to me. The idea, reduced to its essence, is that of a young person conscious of a great capacity for life, but early stricken and doomed, condemned to die under short respite while also en-amoured of the world. . . . She was the last fine flower—blooming alone for the fullest attestation of her freedom—of an old New York stem, the happy congruities thus pre-served being matters that I may not now go into, although the fine association . . . shall yet elsewhere await me. . . .

I do not know anywhere words more touching. . . . And I do not think that, in spite of the later obscuration, the image of the Milly Theale of that book was ever very far away from his thoughts. I remember that when, in 1906, I told him that I was coming to this country, his immediate reaction was to ask me to visit his cousins, the Misses Mason at Newport, Rhode Island, and to take a certain walk along the undercliff beneath Ocean Avenue and there pay, as it were, vicarious honour to the spot where, for the last time, he had parted from his dead cousin. It was the most romantic—it was the only one that was romantic—of the many small jobs that I did for him. . . . And in one of the fits of apologizing that would occasionally come over him—for having physically drawn myself in the portrait of Merton Densher, who was, to be sure, no hero if he wasn't more than only very subterraneously discreditable—he once said:

'After all you've got to remember that I was to fabricate a person who could decently accompany, if only in the pages of my book, another person to whom I was—and remain, and remain, Heaven knows—let us say, most tenderly attached. . . .' As if to say that, in fabricating such a person, his mind would not let him portray someone who was completely disagreeable.

The other attachment was completely detrimental to him. Its rupture left him the person of infinite precautions that I have here rather disproportionately limned. It was as if, from then on, he was determined that nobody or nothing—no society coterie, no tramconductor, no housemaid, no *femme du monde*—should ever have the chance, either in life or in his books, to let him down. And it was as if he said the very same thing to the phrases that he wrote. If he was continuously parenthetic, it was in the determination that no word he wrote should ever be misinterpreted, and if he is, in his later work, bewildering, it was because of the almost panicked resolve to be dazzlingly clear. Because of that he could never let his phrases alone. . . . How often when waiting for him to go for a walk haven't I heard him say whilst dictating the finish of a phrase:

'No, no, Miss Dash . . . that is not clear. . . . Insert before "we all are" . . . Let me see. . . . Yes, insert "not so much

locally, though to be sure we're here; but temperamentally, in a manner of speaking." ' . . . So that the phrase, blindingly clear to him by that time, when completed would run:

So that here, not so much locally, though to be sure we're here, but at least temperamentally in a manner of speaking, we all are.

No doubt the habit of dictating had something to do with these convolutions and the truth of the matter is that during these later years he wrote far more for the ear of his amanuensis than for the eye of the eventual reader. So that, if you will try the experiment of reading him aloud and with expression, you will find his even latest pages relatively plain to understand. But, far more than that, the underlying factor in his later work was the endless determination to add more and more detail, so that the exact illusions and the exact facts of life may appear, and so that everything may be blindingly clear even to a little child. . . . For I have heard him explain with the same profusion of detail as he gave to my appalled and bewildered housemaid—I have heard him explain to Conrad's son of five why he wore a particular hat whose unusual shape had attracted the child's attention. He was determined to present to the world the real, right thing.

I will quote, to conclude, the description of myself as it appears in *The Wing of the Dove* so that you may have some idea of what was James's image of the rather silent person who walked so often beside him on the Rye Road.

He was a longish, leanish [alas, alas!], fairish young Englishman, not unamenable on certain sides to classification—as for instance being a gentleman, by being rather specifically one of the educated, one of the generally sound and generally civil; yet, though to that degree neither extraordinary nor abnormal, he would have failed to play straight into an observer's hands. He was young for the House of Commons; he was loose for the Army. He was refined, as might have been said, for the City and, quite apart from the cut of his cloth, sceptical, it might have been felt, for the Church. On the other hand he was credulous for diplomacy, or perhaps even for science, while he was perhaps at the same time too much in his real senses for poetry and yet too little in them for art. . . . The difficulty with Densher was that he looked vague without looking weak—idle without looking empty. It was the accident possibly of his long legs which were apt to stretch themselves; of his straight hair and well-shaped head, never,

the latter neatly smooth and apt into the bargain . . . to throw itself suddenly back and, supported behind by his uplifted arms and interlocked hands, place him for unconscionable periods in communion with the ceiling, the tree-tops, the sky. . . .

That, I suppose, was the young man that James rather liked.

SAUL ROSENZWEIG

(b. 1907)

A professor of psychology specializing in the field of personality theory and psychodynamics, Dr. Rosenzweig has long been an interested student of the creative process, especially in literature. In "The Ghost of Henry James" (1943; rev. 1963), originally subtitled "A Study in Thematic Apperception," he brings the resources of psychology to the analysis of literary theme. Dr. Rosenzweig has also written of the psychic interrelationship of Henry James, his father, and his brother William in "The Jameses' Stream of Consciousness," *Contemporary Psychology*, III (September, 1958), 250-257.

The Ghost of Henry James: Revised, with a Postscript, 1962

To the "total recall" of James Thurber, fellow-admirer of Henry James.

"To call a man healthy nowadays is almost an insult—invalids learn so many secrets. But the health of the intellect is often promoted by physical disability." Henry James: Review of "The Earthly Paradise" by William Morris, 1868; reprinted in *Views and Reviews*, edited by Le Roy Phillips, 1908 (p. 80).

The method of analysis to be employed in this essay is that of *idiodynamics*—a point of view refined out of psychodynamics in which the life of a personality is construed as a universe of events

"The Ghost of Henry James: Revised with a Postscript, 1962" copyright © 1963 by Dr. Saul Rosenzweig, St. Louis, Missouri. The original version was published a centenary commemoration in *Character and Personality*, XII (December, 1943), 79-100, and was printed with minor changes in *Partisan Review* (Fall, 1944). The present version is printed for the first time this volume by arrangement with the author and permission of Duke University Press.

(idioverse) with its own inherent structure and trends. These, in turn, are rooted in the biological (constitutional and familial) *Anlage* and the cultural or social *Umwelt* (situation). The idioverse is explored to discover those individual norms in terms of which the person approaches and creatively reconstitutes his ongoing life. The method has many approximate predecessors.

The subject of the study is Henry James. While his longer novels continue to be a notorious stumbling-block for the average reader, his short stories are by no means difficult and deserve to be more widely read. It is these latter tales that play the larger part in the present attempt to interweave the author's life experience with certain of his productions in the exploration of his idioverse.

Among the tales of Henry James is a supernatural series composed during the final third of his life and peopled by ghosts of a character utterly Jamesian. It is the peculiarity of these wraiths which merits special attention at this centenary of the author's birth; for, unlike the ordinary creatures of their kind, they fail to represent the remnants of once-lived lives but point instead to the irrepressible unlived life. To consider these ghosts in their significance for him is a fitting expression of interest in James's immortality.

Weirdly enough, these apparitions lead back to their point of origin in James's first published and signed tale, "The Story of a Year," which appeared in the pages of the *Atlantic Monthly* for March, 1865. Here at the very outset was announced that "death" which spoke more elusively in his early writings, and more explicitly provided toward the end the basis for his literary specters. It was, in short, the story of his own life—written prophetically, and published at the early age of twenty-two; complemented in too perfect a fashion for other interpretation by the tales of his later years; and clarified autobiographically in the last full book he lived to complete. Singularly this tale has never been reprinted, though, as every reader of James is aware, most of his other short stories have appeared in collected form once at least; many of them more than once.[1]

The story may be more significantly reviewed after some facts of James's early life have been recalled. The second child of Henry James, the theological and semiphilosophical writer (William James, the famous psychologist, having been by but a little over a year the first), Henry James, the novelist, spent his earliest days

[1] "The Story of a Year," unnoticed in the literature on Henry James prior to this essay (1943), was first reprinted from the *Atlantic Monthly* of 1865 in 1947 in *The American Novels and Stories of Henry James*, edited by F. O. Matthiessen (New York: Knopf, pp. 3-36). It was later included in *Eight Uncollected Tales of Henry James*, edited by Edna Kenton (New Brunswick: Rutgers University Press, 1950, pp. 23-64). The interested reader may now conveniently find it in either of these books.

in a household richly gifted with intellectual fare and gracious cheer. The father (cf. 17) was a strongly individual student of cosmic problems which for a period brought him into close association with the transcendentalist group of Concord and Boston. Emerson was a close friend, as were also many other literary and scholarly figures of the time. His books dealt with religious questions, such as the nature of evil, and with social problems, like those of marriage and divorce, in which the relation of the individual to society occupied a central place. His views were distinctly unconventional. Though he was at various times an enthusiastic student of Fourier and Swedenborg, he was never a mere disciple—the individualistic stamp was too strong on all he thought and wrote. Indeed, this markedly idiosyncratic bias made his books, despite their vivid language and command of style, accessible to a very limited audience. The majority tended to be of a mind with the reviewer who said of "The Secret of Swedenborg" that the elder James had not only written about the secret of Swedenborg but that he had kept it. One is inevitably reminded of the similar quips with which the works of his son and namesake were later received; for example, the comment in *Life* expressing the hope that Henry James would sharpen his point of view and then stick himself with it, and Mark Twain's avowal that he would rather be damned to John Bunyan's heaven than have to read *The Bostonians*.

The early life of the elder James is not without interest in the present context, especially as concerns an accident which befell him at the age of thirteen and which left its mark upon him for the rest of his life. While a schoolboy at the Albany Academy, he formed one of a group who used to meet in a near-by park for experiments in balloon flying. The motive power for the balloon was furnished by a ball of tow soaked in turpentine. The ball would drop when the balloon caught fire, and the boy would then kick the ball around for their amusement. During one of these expe-ments, when Henry's pantaloons had by chance got sprinkled with turpentine, one of the balls came flying through the open window of a stable. The boy in an attempt to put out the fire, which would otherwise have consumed the building, rushed to the hayloft and stamped out the flame. In doing so he burnt his leg severely and had to remain in bed for the next two years. A double amputation above the knee proved necessary. He had a wooden leg in later years and was prevented by his infirmity from leading a very active life. Fortunately he had inherited sufficient money from his father—an influential and wealthy citizen of Albany—to obviate any routine means of earning a livelihood. Accordingly, the children of Henry James were much more closely companioned by him than would otherwise have been possible, and it is thus easier to understand that the strength of character which he had should have left so strong an impression upon their young personalities. In the *Notes of a Son and Brother* (p. 192), the son Henry refers to his father's handicap and couples the latter's acceptance of it with a further resignation to the lack of worldly recognition the message of his books received. The similarity to the son's own fate is again noteworthy, not merely for their both having been neglected by the general public—a circumstance already mentioned—but for their common lot of infirmity.

The particular infirmity of the son must at the very outset be recognized as having established itself upon fertile soil. Henry was apparently always unsure of himself. As a boy his incapacity for athletics and for schoolwork stood out equally in his impressions although he occupied the place of favorite in his mother's affections. He was especially aware of a certain inferiority to his older and more energetic brother William—he has said as much—and William has in counterpart written in one of his letters (cf. 16, Vol. I, p. 288) about "innocent and at bottom very powerless-feeling Harry." But the accident which offered his general orientation a specific date

and place for its disclosure is still inescapably important.

No better description of it could possibly be given than that which the victim has himself provided. He is speaking in *Notes of a Son and Brother* of his year at the Harvard Law School, and of the inception of his literary career. He continues (pp. 296 ff.) :

Two things and more had come up—the biggest of which, and very wondrous as bearing on any circumstance of mine, as having a grain of weight to spare for it, was the breaking out of the [Civil] War. The other, the infinitely small affair in comparison, was a passage of personal history the most entirely personal, but between which, as a private catastrophe or difficulty, bristling with embarrassments, and the great public convulsion that announced itself in bigger terms each day, I felt from the very first an association. of the closest, yet withal, I fear, almost of the least clearly expressible. Scarce at all to be stated, to begin with, the queer fusion or confusion established in my consciousness during the soft spring of '61 by the firing on Fort Sumter, Mr. Lincoln's instant first call for volunteers and a physical mishap, already referred to as having overtaken me at the same dark hour, and the effects of which were to draw themselves out incalculably and intolerably. Beyond all present notation the interlaced, undivided way in which what had happened to me, by a turn of fortune's hand, in twenty odious minutes, kept company of the most unnatural—I can call it nothing less—with my view of what was happening, with the question of what might still happen, to everyone about me, to the country at large: it so made of these marked disparities a single vast visitation. One had the sense, I mean, of a huge comprehensive ache, and there were hours at which one could scarce have told whether it came from one's own poor organism, still so young and so meant for better things, but which had suffered particular wrong, or from the enclosing social body, a body rent with a thousand wounds and that thus treated one to the honour of a sort of tragic fellowship. The twenty minutes had sufficed, at all events, to establish a relation—a relation to everything occurring round me not only for the next four years but for long afterward—that was at once extraordinarily intimate and quite awkwardly irrelevant. I must have felt in some befooled way in presence of a crisis—the smoke of Charleston Bay still so acrid in the air—at which the likely young should be up and doing or, as familiarly put, lend a hand much wanted; the willing youths, all round, were mostly starting to their feet, and to have trumped up a lameness at such a juncture could be made to pass in no light for graceful. Jammed into the acute angle between two high fences, where the rhythmic play of my arms, in tune with that of several other pairs, but at a dire disadvantage of position, induced a rural, a rusty, a quasi-extemporised old engine to work and a saving stream to flow, I had done myself, in face of a shabby conflagration, a horrid even if an obscure hurt; and what was interesting from the first was my not doubting in the least its duration—though what seemed equally clear was that I needn't as a matter of course adopt and appropriate it, so to speak, or place it for increase of interest on exhibition. The interest of it, I very presently knew, would certainly be of the greatest, would even in conditions kept as simple as I might make them become little less than absorbing. The shortest account of what was to follow for a long time after is therefore to plead that the interest never did fail. It was naturally what is called a painful one, but it consistently declined, as an influence at play, to drop for a single instant. Circumstances, by a wonderful chance, overwhelmingly favoured it—*as* an interest, an inexhaustible, I mean; since I also felt in the whole enveloping tonic atmosphere a force promoting its growth. Interest, the interest of life and of death, of our national existence, of the fate of those, the vastly numerous, whom it closely concerned, the interest of the extending War, in fine, the hurrying troops, the transfigured scene, formed a cover for every sort of intensity, made tension itself in fact contagious—so that almost any tension would do, would serve for one's share.

Two points stand out in these stirring words: first, James did not doubt from the beginning that his hurt would involve much and last long; and, second, he could not view it as a merely personal experience but found it indissolubly united with the war which was at that moment engulfing the entire nation. The former consideration shows clearly that somewhere in his personality the seed had been sown for what had now transpired, despite the appearance of mere accident, just as in his later tale, "The Beast in the Jungle," the hero knew without any statable basis that he would one day suffer some extremity of disaster from which

his life would acquire its significance. I may be conjectured from what has a ready been said regarding the accidenta crippling of the father at the age c thirteen that the dire experience of th son at eighteen was in some sense a rep etition—that by one of those deviou paths of identification which create strange needs in sensitive personalitie Henry James, the son, while likewise er gaged in extinguishing a fire may, if onl for a moment, have suffered a lapse c attention or alertness, due possibly t some glimmering association about h father's accident on a so similar occasior and that thus favored, the accident too effect.[2] It seems not unlikely that but fc this momentary inco-ordination, the ir jury—described somewhere as a sprain— would not have been sustained. Such psychological moment can surely not b underestimated by any sympatheti reader of James since he himself made c just such minutiae the essence of his ar How much the proximity of the rhytl mically moving men may have contrib uted to the mental association with th father and the "lapse" must remain lik the lapse itself a matter of conjectur But the presumed relationship to th father's accident seems to explain th son's avowed receptivity for the ever and his certainty as to its consequence

These considerations also shed son light upon the nature of the injury, esp cially in its psychological significanc James himself describes it as "the mo entirely personal" and as "a horrid eve if an obscure hurt." It is known also th it in some way affected his back. But th physical aspect which has on occasic been stressed is of purely secondary in portance. Paramount is the subjectiv depth of the injury as James experience

[2] The coincidence between the accidents of Hen James, Sr., and his son Henry is amazingly parallel by a similar duplication of experience between th father and the son William. In this latter case psychological catastrophe rather than a physical inju is involved, but the powerful relationship betwe father and son is again inescapable. For a descriptio of the experiences, compare William James, *Varieties Religious Experience* (New York, 1902), pp. 160-16 with the footnote reference to the work of Hen James, Sr. (*Society: the Redeemed Form of Ma* Boston, 1879, p. 43ff.), where the father's case equally sudden terror is recounted.

. Occurring at the very outbreak of
he war, the event may well have caused
im to suspect himself as an unconscious
malingerer. A complex of guilt could
hus have remained. Coming as it did at
time when *men* were needed by the
country and were, like his own brothers
Wilky and Robertson, answering the call,
he injury even more surely constituted a
roof of his powerlessness and crystallized
sense of impotence from which he
ever fully recovered. The avoidance of
assion and the overqualification in his
ater writings are largely traceable to
uch an implicit attitude of combined
guilt and inferiority; as are also some of
is subsequent actions including, as will
e pointed out presently, his participation
n World War I.

In such a context is understandable
lso his consternation after having re-
ealed his problem at finding it "treated
ut to a comparative pooh-pooh—an
mpression I long looked back to as a
harp parting of the ways, with an adop-
on of the wrong one distinctly deter-
ined" (7, p. 330). The great surgeon
o whom his father conducted him for
onsultation in Boston might at least
ave offered some warning of what was
n store. Obviously, the surgeon, with a
ot uncommon lack of interest in psy-
hological implications, did not even
egin to fathom the depths to
which the experience of his patient
eached, and the patient, feeling much
om these depths, was the more appalled
t the medical advice he received. Cor-
esponding to this negative aspect is a
ositive one—the orientation which
ames tells of adopting toward his injury
n trying to come to terms with it. In the
ate summer of 1861 he visited a camp
f invalid and convalescent troops in
.hode Island. He had here his "first and
ll but sole vision of the American soldier
n his multitude, and above all—for that
as markedly the colour of the whole
ning—in his depression, his wasted mel-
ncholy almost; an effect that somehow
orresponds for memory, I bethink my-
elf, with the tender elegiac tone in which
Valt Whitman was later on so admirably
o commemorate him" (7, pp. 310 f.).

James tells of talking with the soldiers
and comforting them as he could, not
only with words but by "such pecuniary
solace as I might at brief notice draw on
my poor pocket for. Yet again, as I indulge this memory, do I feel that I might
if pushed a little rejoice in having to
such an extent coincided with, not to say
perhaps positively anticipated, dear old
Walt—even if I hadn't come armed like
him with oranges and peppermints. I
ministered much more summarily,
though possibly in proportion to the time
and thanks to my better luck more
pecuniarily; but I like to treat myself to
making out that I can scarce have
brought to the occasion (in proportion to
the time again and to other elements of
the case) less of the consecrating sentiment than he" (7, pp. 314 f.). As he
sailed back to Newport that night feeling
considerably the worse for his exertion in
his "impaired state," there established
itself in his mind, "measuring wounds
against wounds," a correspondence between himself and the soldiers "less ex-
altedly than wastefully engaged in the
common fact of endurance" (7, p. 318).

Another heartening aspect presented
itself at the Harvard Law School, which
he at this time attended for some months,
where the "bristling horde of . . . comrades fairly produced the illusion of a
mustered army. The Cambridge campus
was tented field enough for a conscript
starting so compromised; and I can
scarce say moreover how easily it let me
down that when it came to the point one
had still fine fierce young men, in great
numbers, for company, there being at the
worst so many such who hadn't flown to
arms" (7, pp. 301-302).

His new orientation entailed a constructive step forward. In the months
which followed, James turned to the art
of fiction. His first published tale was, as
has already been mentioned, "The Story
of a Year." Needless to say, the story
should be read in its original form to be
fully appreciated. Unfortunately it is not
easy of access since it was never reprinted, but a synopsis, however lacking
artistically, may convey certain essentials
of the plot which are needed here.

John Ford has a second lieutenancy in the Northern Army and is about to leave for the war. On a long walk just before his departure he proposes marriage to the ward of his widowed mother. The girl is named Elizabeth, or Lizzie, Crowe. She is a simple, pretty creature who is overjoyed at the prospect of marriage, but he exacts from her the promise that if anything should happen to him in the war, she will forget him and accept the love of another. He also cautions that, to avoid gossip, it may be better to keep the engagement a secret, but he does not bind her on this point. On getting home the girl goes to her room, while he tells his mother of the engagement. Mrs. Ford is definitely against the match because she thinks Elizabeth shallow and not good enough for him. (The author suggests that, having been a good mother, Mrs. Ford would have liked for her son to choose a woman on her own model.) He refuses to accept his mother's judgment about the girl, but tries to avoid contention on his last night at home. He asks his mother not to discuss the matter with Elizabeth.

After he is gone the two women say nothing about the engagement to each other at any time, but the mother has her secret plans. When Elizabeth's first blush of excitement is over, she is sent by Mrs. Ford on a visit to a friend in another city and there, decked out in finery of her guardian's making, she soon wins another suitor—Bruce. When she leaves for home, he comes to the train to see her off and accidentally shows her the newspaper which contains the announcement of Ford's having been severely wounded. Elizabeth is in great conflict and now avoids Bruce, who would accompany her to the next station. When Elizabeth reaches home, Mrs. Ford states her intention of going to nurse her son—the very thing the girl had planned to do herself; but Lizzie is strangely relieved by this shift of responsibility. She stays at home, while Mrs. Ford goes off.

Elizabeth now dreams one night that she is walking with a tall dark man who calls her wife. In the shadow of a tree they find an unburied male corpse covered with wounds. Elizabeth proposes that a grave be dug, but as they lift the corpse it suddenly opens its eyes and says "Amen." She and her companion place it in the grave and stamp the earth down with their feet.

Various changes occur—Ford gets better, gets worse, etc., and at one point when it seems he is dying, Elizabeth accepts Bruce, who is visiting in the town at the time. But Ford unexpectedly has a turn for the better and is brought home to be nursed. His mother manages to keep Elizabeth away from him for some time. When first rejected at his door, Lizzie wraps a blanket around herself and goes out on the steps. Bruce comes by, but she will not talk with him and leaves him standing there stupefied. The next day she manages to get into Jack's room, and he appears to recognize her. When Mrs. Ford learns of this visit, she is very angry, but Jack asks for Elizabeth to come again. This time he explains to her that he knows he is going to die. He is, however, glad that she has found someone else and blesses them both. He asks Elizabeth to be kind to his mother. He dies. The next day Elizabeth encounters Bruce, but she is willing only to say farewell. She says she must do justice to her old love. She forbids Bruce to follow her. "But for all that he went in" (12, p. 281).

The story has today a timely interest of a general sort since it embodies a type of problem confronting many young men and women in the confused contemporary world. But it obviously goes deeper by bringing home the manner in which events on a national, or even international, scale may have a peculiarly personal significance for the individual which is timeless in character. Thus James says (12, pp. 263 f.): "I have no intention of following Lieutenant Ford to the seat of war. The exploits of his campaign are recorded in the public journals of the day, where the curious may still peruse them. My own taste has always been for unwritten history, and my present business is with the reverse of the picture."

As a first step in interpretation mu

be noted the facts that the hero foresees his own death, is wounded, and dies. In foreseeing his death, he makes his sweetheart promise that she will forget him and choose another if need be. The mother opposes the match, and the girl in the case is represented as abandoning the hero well before his own physical wounds have doomed him. It is hardly possible to escape the conclusion that those wounds were not meant to be fatal without the contribution of the unhappy love motif. The wounds of the hero are, in other words, not those of a patriot who dies of what befalls him in military combat. They are those of a lover forsaken by his psychological fate. The personal significance of the war as opposed to its national or external one is emphasized. The war serves merely as a screen upon which the deeply private problem can be projected.

At this point one comes readily to see that this tale of the Civil War and the author's description of his civilian injury at the time of its outbreak are closely related. The correspondence which had established itself in his mind between the wounded soldiers in Rhode Island and his own impaired state is expressed imaginatively in this first story. But the author's view takes precedence over the soldier's even in the fiction, since it is the implication of the wounds for love rather than for war that is stressed. The death of the hero in "The Story of a Year" is thus a representation of James's own passional death as implied in the *Notes of a Son and Brother*.

The dream of Elizabeth is one of the highlights of the tale and clearly illustrates James's early mastery of certain psychological processes which have been more formally described by professional psychologists only recently. Not only is the dream prophetic—that would be banal—but it portrays in clear images the conflict in the dreamer's mind and the inevitable solution she will adopt in keeping with her deepest wishes. Such a reading of the dream indicates unmistakably that the hero's fate was sealed not by the wounds he sustained in battle, but by the psychological forces in the situation. Among such forces were not only the faithlessness of the girl but also the opposition of the mother and the hero's own self-doubt. The banter with which his early conversation with the girl is embellished—the references to the possibility of the hero's looking like a woman instead of a man after he returns with his wounds—is of considerable interest as indicating the presence of certain feminine elements in his personality to which his self-doubt and the anticipated injury may bear some relationship.

Certain details of the story might with further knowledge of James's own life lend themselves to a fuller interpretation. Thus, for instance, the possessive character of the mother in relation to the son; the heroine's being a ward of the mother—a "cousin" of the hero; and the personality of the successful rival Bruce—all raise interesting problems regarding possible intimates in James's environment. Perhaps even more significant is the absence of a father—the widowed state of Mrs. Ford. If Henry James's own father is here in question, the filial relationship may have been sensed as "too sacred" for exposure. The depth of identification between father and son in terms of their common infirmity, already discussed, agrees with such a view. This construction is, moreover, borne out by the fiction itself if the father's death existing as a given fact when the story opens is taken as corresponding to the death of the son at its close. The identity of their fates may be regarded as symbolizing their psychological identification. Paramount, however, is the other equivalence of Henry James's blight and John Ford's death. For from this "death" came the ghost which was to appear again and again in the later tales.

Before turning to the subject of this specter, attention must be paid to some intermediate stages of development. As if to materialize the "death," James actually left America to take up residence in England in 1875. The fantasy had for a time been adequate as a form of adjustment, but in the end it yielded as a forecast to the actual physical withdrawal. For this often discussed self-

exile seems to have represented an escape
from a world disagreeable before and
now no longer tolerable. Most of James's
tales and novels were written while he was
living abroad, and a great number of
them, from *A Passionate Pilgrim* (1871)
to *The Ambassadors* (1903), present the
problems of the expatriate and the allied
contrast between Old and New Worlds.
He returned twice to his native land in
the early eighties. His mother died during the first visit, and his father's sudden
and final illness brought him back almost
immediately. He then remained away
again for over twenty years. After a decade, however,—in the early nineties—
he began writing a series of supernatural
tales to which allusion has already been
made. "Sir Edmund Orme" (11), which
was copyrighted in 1891 and appears to
have been the first, concerns the fate of a
lover who as a prerequisite to his marriage must rid himself of a ghost that
represents an early jilted suitor of his
prospective mother-in-law. The uncanny
relationship between the older woman
and young man, with the apparition of
an unloved youth as intermediary, unmistakably revives the situation in "The
Story of a Year." There, it will be recalled, the subordination of John Ford
to his mother's judgment eventually coincided with his own presentiment of death
and made together for what could on the
surface well be taken for a jilting by his
sweetheart. The supernatural tale, however, records the triumph of the hero
over the ghost and thus sounds the keynote of James's new orientation. The
same restorative tendency is even more
obviously at work in "Owen Wingrave"
(9), which appeared in 1893. Owen has
been preparing for a military career—the
traditional profession of his family—when
at the eleventh hour he decides to brave
every misunderstanding, even that of
cowardice, and keep faith with his deepest convictions by giving up his plans. In
the stormy days that follow he accepts
the challenge of the girl who, somewhat
like Elizabeth Crowe in the case of John
Ford, had been his childhood playmate
and a dependent of his family. To prove
his courage, he allows her to lock him

for the night in a haunted chamber
where his great-great-grandfather had
mysteriously died after having accidentally caused the death of his own young
son by an angry blow. Like his ancestor,
Owen *wins* his *grave* in that room. "He
looked like a young soldier on a battle
field" (9, p. 220). In this instance the
relationship of the hero to the paternal
figure, rather than the maternal one—as
in "Sir Edmund Orme"—is portrayed
and, similarly, the emphasis is laid upon
aggression (or war) rather than upon
love. The other aspect of John Ford's
problem seems thus to be bared—the role
of the father figure as an inhibitor of aggression. The integrity of the hero is in
the end established even if, like his sire
before him, he has to yield his life to the
ghost of an accidental violence. As a presentation of James's personal problem at
the outbreak of the Civil War, including
even the relation of his injury to that of
his father, this tale is once more clearly
autobiographical. As in "Sir Edmund
Orme," the vindicating theme is again
dominant. For the ghosts which haunted
their author from the undying past (as
a return of the repressed) could only be
exorcised by the achievement of some
solution.

After a series of such tales had for
over ten years proclaimed his deep preoccupation with the past, James began
to plan eagerly for an American visit of
six or eight months. His supernatural
fantasies had foretold this revisit even as
"The Story of a Year" had previously
forecast the departure for Europe. The
counterpart to the defensive escape was
to be a compulsive return. The need he
felt was strong. His brother William tried
to dissuade him, in order doubtless to
spare him the pain which the exposure
would inflict upon his sensitive nature.
But Henry insisted that he actually
needed "shocks." How he experienced
these in 1904-1905 is vividly recorded in
The American Scene (2), which he
wrote on his return to England.

The itinerary of his American trip a
reflected in the chapters of this book is in
itself instructive. The "repatriated ab

sentee" or "restless analyst," as he variously styles himself, went first to New England. He then saw New York, Newport, Boston, Concord, and Salem; Philadelphia, Baltimore, Washington, and the South—Richmond, Charleston, and Florida. He traveled also to the Far West, but his book concludes with Florida. The sequel he planned was never written, and it strikes one that, with the South accounted for, the rest was to him merely appendix.

At any rate, his visits to Richmond and Charleston—where he had never been before—stand out as especially significant. He says, in speaking of his "going South," that it somehow corresponded now to what in ancient days the yearning for Europe seemed romantically to promise. Early in the chapter on Richmond he alludes to the outbreak of the Civil War and describes the city almost purely in terms of its having been the Confederate capital. He characterizes it (2, p. 358, *passim*) as "the haunted scene" and "the tragic ghost-haunted city," full of an "adorable weakness" that evokes a certain "tenderness" in the visitor. The gist of his impression he gives in an image: "I can doubtless not sufficiently tell why, but there was something in my whole sense of the South that projected at moments a vivid and painful image—that of a figure somehow blighted or stricken, discomfortably, impossibly seated in an invalid-chair, and yet fixing one with strange eyes that were half a defiance and half a deprecation of one's noticing, and much more of one's referring to, an abnormal sign" (2, p. 362). A strong suspicion arises that the image here projected is that of James himself in 1861. For confirmation one need only recall his own description of the manner in which his youthful injury had united itself indissolubly in his mind with the Civil War. As his own inner turmoil had corresponded then to the internal conflict of the country, so now his highly sympathetic and tender response to the vanquished faction seems builded on an understanding of his quite similar fate.

This view is borne out by his impressions of Charleston. Here, again, the war of North and South dominates his field of vision, but, unlike the Northern friend who accompanied him, he finds himself concentrating on the "bled" condition and his heart fails to harden even against the treachery at Fort Sumter. Once more a synoptic image emerges, this time of feminization: "The feminization is there just to promote for us some eloquent antithesis; just to make us say that whereas the ancient order was masculine, fierce and moustachioed, the present is at the most a sort of sick lioness who has so visibly parted with her teeth and claws that we may patronizingly walk all round her. . . . This image really gives us the best word for the general effect of Charleston. . . ." (2, pp. 401 f.). One recalls almost with a start the bantering conversation in "The Story of a Year" of forty years earlier between the hero and the heroine as to the possibility of his looking like a "lady" when he returns from the war with his wounds. John Ford carries on the figure by saying that even if he grows a moustache, as he intends to do, he will be altering his face as women do a misfitting garment—taking in on one side and letting out on the other—insofar as he crops his head and cultivates his chin.

In general, then, the impression seems sustained that Henry James's visit to America in 1904-1905, after twenty years of absence, was largely actuated by an impulse to repair, if possible, the injury and to complete the unfinished experience of his youth. He was, as it were, haunted by the ghost of his own past and of this he wished to disabuse his mind before actual death overtook him. Since the Civil War had played so vital a part in his early blight, he now visited the South for the first time and received there those impressions which bear so strong a mark of personal projection.

The plausibility of this reconstruction and of the preceding interpretation of "The Story of a Year" is strengthened by a psychological reading of the later supernatural tales, especially "The Jolly Corner" (5). This short story was first published in the *English Review* for

December, 1908, shortly after his visit to the United States. It is the story of Spencer Brydon who as a man of fifty-six returns to America after many years of residence in Europe. He has come to look at his property—the house on the Jolly Corner—where he was born and grew up. Before long he becomes absorbed in the old house to the point of visiting it nightly in the strange hope of encountering there his own alter ego—the ghost of his former self. When he finally does succeed and is confronted by the specter he has been seeking, he notes among other things that two fingers on its right hand are missing. He cannot endure to face the image before him—he refuses to recognize himself there—and overwhelmed by the extremity of his emotion, he falls unconscious. When he revives, Alice Staverton, whom he had known in his early days before taking up residence abroad and whom he has been seeing since his return, is standing over him. She, too, has seen the ghost—in a dream—and thus knew that Spencer had made the encounter. He protests to her that the shape he has met was not himself till she quite simply declares, "Isn't the whole point that you'd have been different?" (5, p. 483.) It is clear from the context that the heroine could have been in love with the rejected personality (the ghost) since she understood it. She is, however, equally ready to accept Brydon as he is today and reconcile him, perhaps, to those unacknowledged aspects of himself which have kept him from her all these years—which have driven him abroad to escape himself.

The specter in this tale is typical of Henry James. Unlike the ghosts of other writers, the creatures of James's imagination represent not the shadows of lives once lived, but the immortal impulses of the unlived life. In the present story the ghost of Spencer Brydon is obviously his rejected self. Moreover, an injury—the two lost fingers—here stands in some relation to the fact that the life was not lived or that, in other words, a kind of psychological death had occurred. Finally, the injury and the related incompletion have entailed an unfulfilled love. The hero has

fled the heroine because he could not face himself.

At this point one is obviously but a step from "The Story of a Year," written forty years earlier than "The Jolly Corner." To repeat what has more than once been implied: with the death of John Ford the ghost of Spencer Brydon came into existence. The story of the latter is a complement to that of the former. As Henry James—or Ford—left America to reside abroad, Brydon returns to confront his former self. The identity of the characters is established by the injuries each suffered—James's "obscure hurt," Ford's wounds, and Brydon's missing fingers. But like James during his visit in 1904-1905, Brydon is obviously attempting to rectify the past—to face it again and test the answer previously given. There is thus represented here not merely a harking back with vain regrets but an obvious effort to overcome old barriers and pass beyond them. It is in this spirit that the woman in the case, Alice Staverton, now likewise appears as a complement to Elizabeth Crowe. Whereas Elizabeth had been faithless, Alice is ever faithful and still ready to accept her lover both as he was and as he is. Even the device of the dream recurs—the dream of Elizabeth having presaged her abandonment of Ford, while that of Alice brings her through her empathy to the scene of Brydon's overwhelming encounter with his ghost.

The complementary relationship of these two tales, standing at the very beginning and all but the end of James's creative work, is so striking that one is impelled to believe that the second was intentionally written as a counterpart to the first. This conjecture is supported by chronological considerations. When James toured America in 1904-1905, memories of the Civil War were vividly revived for him, as has already been mentioned. "The Story of a Year" must surely have been recalled at that time in sharp relief. But one of the more practical reasons for the journey was to arrange for the publication of the definitive New York Edition (8) of his collected fiction. After completing *The American*

Scene on his return to England, he spent the next two years in re-reading, selecting, and meticulously revising his novels and tales. Critics have assailed the rigorous censorship to which the earlier writings were subjected in this process, but James's action is understandable if one compares the revision and the revisit as attempts equally to reclaim the past and reshape it while there was yet time. In the careful review of all his past work which the preparation of the collected edition entailed, James must again have come upon "The Story of a Year"—this time paginally. But he did not include this tale. What one does find there— psychologically instead—is a new story, "The Jolly Corner," which was first published in 1908 and was probably written during the arduous process of the collective revision. This tale was plainly based on the American visit, yet it no doubt also represented a retelling of the omitted "The Story of a Year"—the most radical revision of them all. For in "The Jolly Corner" one finds a coalescence of revisit and revision which satisfactorily explains the complementary relationship of this story to the very first one. Through marking the persistence of the trend one comes to see that, despite the wishful reworking, "The Story of a Year" was nevertheless the story of a life.

Towards the end of 1909 and for nearly a year thereafter, James suffered from a severe nervous depression which completely incapacitated him for work. This illness must in the foregoing context be taken as a reaction to the failure of his restitutive efforts. Neither the supernatural tales nor the American return nor the definitive revision of his works had achieved the solution he desperately sought, and despair overtook him. His brother William's death toward the end of 1910 removed a mainstay of his life and deepened his misery. Further illness in 1912 made the end seem tragically near.

But through everything he held on, actuated still by the same forward impetus that had unfailingly declared itself before. He was unwittingly preparing for the final and highest adventure of his life. For with the outbreak of World War I in 1914, this reticent man of seventy-one, until now without any obvious interest in political affairs, of a sudden identified himself with *social action*. He recognized the cost that might be involved when he compared himself to the quiet dweller in a tenement upon whom the question of "structural improvements" is thrust and he feared for his "house of the spirit" where everything had become for better or worse adjusted to his familar habits and use. But this "vulgar apprehension" could not deter him; and, as he says, "I found myself before long building on additions and upper stories, throwing out extensions and protrusions, indulging even, all recklessly, in gables and pinnacles and battlements—things that had presently transformed the unpretending place into I scarce know what to call it, a fortress of the faith, a palace of the soul, an extravagant, bristling, flag-flying structure which had quite as much to do with the air as with the earth" (13, pp. 19 f.).

His efforts for the Allied cause knew no bounds. He visited army hospitals and refugee encampments (as he had on a certain earlier occasion visited a military camp of invalids in Rhode Island); made pecuniary contributions and wrote articles for war charities; supported movements like the American Volunteer Ambulance Corps; and performed a host of lesser tasks as a daily routine from the beginning of the war until his death. His friends were amazed—even as they were inspired—by the fervor of this notoriously passionless writer. As Percy Lubbock, the editor of James's *Letters*, well says: "To all who listened to him in those days it must have seemed that he gave us what we lacked—a voice; there was a trumpet note in it that was heard nowhere else and that alone rose to the height of the truth. For a while it was as though the burden of age had slipped from him; he lived in the lives of all who were acting and suffering—especially of the young, who acted and suffered most. His spiritual vigour bore a strain that was the greater by the whole weight of his towering imagination; but the time came at last when his bodily endurance failed. He died resolutely confident of the victory that was still so far off" (6, Vol. II, p. 379). Edmund Gosse, among others, expressed the opinion (14) that James's death early in 1916 was definitely hastened by his profligate expenditure of energy in war service.

In these days when the centenary of Henry James's birth coincides with World War II, the significance of his death during World War I well lends itself to further examination. Without detracting in the least from the positive significance of the contribution, one may still trace the line of its descent from the earlier record already revealed. Is it too much to suggest that the unparalleled fervor of his actions is to some extent explained by a belated compensation for his failure at the time of the Civil War? In favor of such a view is the fact that the last book he lived to complete—*Notes of a Son and Brother*—and the one in which he recounted the memories of his youth, including his injury, was published in 1914. His early experiences were thus unusually fresh in his mind at the outbreak of the war. But to this inference may be added his own testimony as found in the opening sentences of the little volume, *Within the Rim* (13), in which are collected his wartime essays: "The first sense of it all to me after the first shock and horror was that of a sudden leap back into life of the violence with which the American Civil War broke upon us, at the North, fifty-four years ago, when I had a consciousness of youth which perhaps equalled in vivacity my present consciousness of age. . . . The analogy quickened and deepened with every elapsing hour; the drop of the balance under the invasion of Belgium reproduced with intensity the agitation of the New England air by Mr. Lincoln's call to arms, and I went about for a short space as with the queer secret locked in my breast of at least already knowing how such occasions helped and what a big war was going to mean" (13, pp. 11 f.). The analogy of the wars in his own consciousness thus attested, it is not difficult to believe that a common

motivational tie was at least implicitly at work. He might have been found wanting in 1861, but he would not be found so on this second and doubtless final occasion. At that earlier time he had adjusted to his personal wounds by withdrawal and by such constructive acts as the art of fiction permitted. But now a positive participation in real social action would provide the solution for the problem which had haunted him through life. Instead of hanging his head as a war disability, he would stand forth as a war hero; England, which had been for him a refuge of escape, would become a citadel of his true assertion; and America, which had exhibited him as weak, would now be exhibited by him as weak.

In this setting becomes intelligible the mooted question of James's assumption of British citizenship a few months before his death. He had, on the one hand, been adding to his numerous activities in the Allied interest repeated statements of his consternation that America did not enter the war at once. On the other hand, his fervent identification with the English cause increased daily. Thus in July, 1915, he at last became a naturalized British subject. By this stroke he changed for himself the orientation of a lifetime. His haven of refuge was transformed into the many-flagged and turreted embattlements of which he well might write with a surge of liberated passion. From these heights he could in the end look down upon America hanging back in the distance. His own words—in a letter to his nephew—again at this point offer direct confirmation: "I have testified to my long attachment here in the only way I could—though I certainly shouldn't have done it, under the inspiration of our Cause, if the U. S. A. had done it a little more *for* me. Then I should have thrown myself back on that and been content with it; but as this, at the end of a year, hasn't taken place, I have had to act for myself, and I go so far as quite to think, I hope not fatuously, that I shall have set an example and shown a little something of the way" (6, Vol. II, p. 491).

It seems not improbable that this excessive expenditure of energy in a man over seventy brought on a death premature by some months or even years. But he must surely have felt that the reward had been worth the cost. And regarding these final events in the terms not of what they may have been surmounting in his past, but, as from the vantage point of the present, they appear progressively to mean, one can respond in full accord; since James by the active assertion of that period re-established vital contact with contemporary social realities.

So at last the pattern of the genius which was Henry James emerges. Suffering since childhood from a keen sense of inadequacy, he experienced in his eighteenth year an injury that sharply crystalized this attitude into a passional death. The ghost which as an apotheosis of his unlived life appears repeatedly in his later tales was liberated from this "death." Many aspects of his experience and work up to the very time of his actual death were oriented as movements back to and forward from this nucleus.

The broader application of the inherent pattern is familiar to readers of Edmund Wilson's volume, *The Wound and the Bow* (18). This title paraphrases the *Philoctetes* of Sophocles in which the hero's rare skill with the bow is portrayed as having a mysterious, if not supernatural, relationship to his stubbornly persistent wound—a snake bite to the foot. Abandoned in his illness for years on the island of Lemnos, Philoctetes is finally conducted to Troy, where he fights and kills Paris in single combat, thus becoming one of the great heroes of the Trojan War. Reviewing the experience and works of several well-known literary masters, Wilson discloses the sacrificial roots of their power on the model of the Greek legend. In the case of Henry James the present account not only provides a similar insight into the unhappy sources of his genius but reveals the aptness of the Philoctetes pattern even to the point where the bow of the wounded and exiled archer is at the last enlisted literally in a crucial military cause.

EPICRISIS

In the jargon of psychoanalysis the story just sketched could be retold as follows. The Oedipus situation of Henry James included a highly individualistic father—a cripple—and a gifted sibling rival (William) who together dwarfed the boy in his own eyes beyond hope of ever attaining their stature. A severe inferiority complex resulted. The problematic relationship to father and brother was solved submissively by a profound repression of aggressiveness.

At the age of eighteen, in the earliest days of the Civil War, Henry sustained a persistent physical injury. A keen sense of created impotence, combined with a possible suspicion of unconscious malingering, now crystallized his early sense of inferiority into "castration anxiety." The "obscure but intimate hurt" was experienced as involving not only the manliness of war, then socially so moot, but also the virility of love, which was focal in the adolescent stage of his individual development. Identification with the crippled ("castrated") but powerful father could have figured in the trauma both through the son's remarkably similar accident and in their common incapacitation. At the same time, the injury, interpreted more deeply, may have been unconsciously embraced as a token of filial submission: the acknowledged weakness was at once peculiarly appropriated as "an inexhaustible interest." Introversion in which both aggression and sexuality were repressed was now established as a *modus vivendi*.

The possible role of constitutional bisexuality should be noted in passing, even if only speculatively. Injuries like the one experienced by James may be conceived to subdue the more active and masculine components of personality and accentuate as a counterpoise the more passive and feminine ones. The creative drive of genius seems often to be enhanced even as its capacity is paradoxically also limited by such a destiny.

It was, at any rate, after his injury that James turned to the art of fiction. His writing served him both as an escape from frustration by way of fantasy and as a partial means of solving his problems through sublimation. But the fantasied escape proved insufficient, and he therefore soon abandoned the American scene that had become to him intolerable. During most of his life he lived in England. His various novels and tales written both before and after the departure from America acquired their notorious peculiarities—precious overqualification of style and restraint of sexual passion—from the repressed pattern of his life. The acute psychological insights in which his work abounds sprang in part, however, from the introspective vigilance allied with these "defects."

As James began to enter the final third of his life, a resurgence of his buried drives occurred. The supernatural stories which began to come from his pen during this period testify to this "return of the repressed." His ghosts consistently represent an apotheosis of the unlived life. This fictional attempt to face again the early unsolved problems was followed compulsively by an actual revisit to America. As the criminal returns to the scene of his crime, James now went back to the haunts of his catastrophe. But the neurotic repression failed to yield, and a severe nervous depression that expressed his sense of defeat ensued.

With the outbreak of World War I soon following, when he was already over seventy, came a final effort at solution—now not by sublimation in fiction, by escape or return, but in relationships to the real social world. It is not surprising that a note of overcompensation was present in these war activities, especially in the assumption of British citizenship, and that his end was probably hastened by his profligate expenditure of energy. But in large measure he re-established contact with the realities of his environment by these acts and in the same degree he thus succeeded in laying the ghost of his unlived past before death overtook him.

Three wars are thus spanned by the ghost of Henry James: the Civil War, which evoked it mortally in his youth; World War I, which permitted it to be laid before his death; and World War II, which, occurring during the centenary of his birth, recalls it anew in the immortal sense.

REFERENCES

Works by Henry James

1. *The Ambassadors.* New York: Harpers, 1903.
2. *The American Scene.* New York: Harpers, 1907.
3. "The Beast in the Jungle" in *The Better Sort.* New York: Scribners, 1903. Pp. 189-244.
4. *The Bostonians.* New York: Macmillan, 1886.
5. "The Jolly Corner" in *Novels and Tales.* New York Edition. New York: Scribners, 1909. Vol. XVII, pp. 433-485.
6. *Letters.* Edited by Percy Lubbock. New York: Scribners, 1920. 2 vols.
7. *Notes of a Son and Brother.* New York: Scribners, 1914.
8. *Novels and Tales.* New York Edition. New York: Scribners, 1907-1917. 26 vols.
9. "Owen Wingrave" in *The Wheel of Time.* New York: Harpers, 1893. Pp. 147-220.
10. *A Passionate Pilgrim and Other Tales.* Boston: James R. Osgood, 1875.
11. "Sir Edmund Orme" in *The Lesson of the Master and Other Tales.* New York: Macmillan, 1892. Pp. 266-302.
12. "The Story of a Year," *Atlantic Monthly,* 1865, 15, 257-281.
13. *Within the Rim.* London: Collins, 1918.

Works by Others

14. Gosse, Edmund. *Aspects and Impressions.* New York: Scribners, 1922. Pp. 17-53.
15. James, Henry, Sr. *The Secret of Swedenborg.* Boston: Houghton Mifflin, 1869.
16. James, William. *Letters.* Edited by his son Henry James. Boston: Atlantic Monthly Press, 1920. 2 vols.
17. Warren, Austin. *The Elder Henry James.* New York: Macmillan, 1934.
18. Wilson, Edmund. *The Wound and the Bow.* Boston: Houghton Mifflin, 1941.

POSTSCRIPT, 1962

The use of the present study by Leon Edel in the first volume of his biography *Henry James* (Philadelphia: Lippincott, 1953) affords an instructive example of one mode of assimilating certain insights —the cautious mode. In Edel's chapter "An Obscure Hurt" (pp. 167-183) the accident of 1861 is recounted with considerable new factual detail. The biographer acknowledges the evidence, first adduced in this essay, that James was psychologically prepared for this injury. When, however, he comes to the evaluation of its implication for the novelist's life and work, the mentioned caution prevails. There is, first, the substitution of "A Most Extraordinary Case," a story of 1868, for the distinctly more proximate and telling one of 1865, "The Story of a Year." As an addition "A Most Extraordinary Case" is clearly relevant but as a substitute it seems to pave the way for the second, and far more consequential, omission found at the end of the chapter. Here (p. 183) one reaches the biographer's appraisal of the "obscure hurt" and reads that "This is reflected in all his early stories and contributed to the quite extraordinarily literal assumption by the critics that Henry James 'castrated' himself in the accident. Of such substance are legends sometimes compounded." The biographer then proceeds to demolish the legend by noting James's active physical life, his monumental productiveness, and his uninhibited use of the word *eunuch* —all offered as evidence that physical castration is out of the question. But then the chapter comes to an end with not a word said about another kind of "castration"—the psychological—which the argument of the present study did not obscure. (Edel might well have introduced this view if on no other basis than to illustrate, as can so aptly be done in this case, that legends of *fact* are often symptomatic of unconscious psychological *insights*.) James may not have been physically castrated, but the psychological

equivalent in his life and work is difficult to repudiate (if considered).[3]

In 1956 Edel discovered an earlier tale —*the* first—by James published anonymously a year before "The Story of a Year" under the title "A Tragedy of Errors" (cf. *New England Quarterly,* September, 1956, Vol. 29, 291-317). As an unexpected and striking confirmation, this pristine production, in a French setting, adumbrates James's idioverse even more neatly than its successor. In it also the hero-lover (author) dies prematurely (psychological castration). The characters naively reproduce the family constellation of young Henry James. The dubious heroine of the triangular affair, a faithless wife, is the mother. The older rival, husband of the heroine, is the father (depicted in the story as lame even as was Henry James, Sr.). The globe-trotting assassin, hired by the heroine, who mistakenly kills the lover instead of the husband (the error of the tragedy), is shaped on the prototype of the writer's extraverted and mercurial brother William (member-to-be of the imminent Agassiz Expedition to the Amazon). The alliance of the heroine with her tool to constitute the composite villain of the piece exposes Henry's ambivalence toward his mother as well as his intense sibling rivalry. The crippled husband has a completely passive role in the plot and the lover's fated interchange with him represents the unconscious father-son identification. ("Meyrau," the hero's surname, becomes recognizable as an anagram of the given name "Henry" once the latter is translated into and pronounced in the French.) The reader is given only one indirect glimpse of the cuckold—in the last sentence of the story when the wife suspensefully waits to welcome kismet's survivor: ". . . she saw a figure emerge from below the terrace, and come limp-

---

[3] To complete the record it is possible now to state that in the third volume of his James biography, published after this essay went to press, Edel included an interpretation of some of his hero's male characters as "symbolically castrated." (See *Henry James: The Middle Years: 1882-1895,* [Philadelphia, Lippincott, 1962] p. 144.)

ing toward her with outstretched arms."
"A Tragedy of Errors," ironically titled
after Shakespeare's comedy, is thus even
more closely autobiographical than "The
Story of a Year"—one patent reason
why it was concealed in anonymity and
never revived or acknowledged by its
author.

The idioverse of Henry James has been
further explored in the writer's article
"The Jameses' Stream of Consciousness,"
Contemporary Psychology, 1958, Vol. 3,

250-257. The theory and practice of the
stream is there examined with focal attention on the concinnity of the three
Jameses and marginal notation of the
historical context out of which emerged
both the artistic fictions of Henry James
and the scientific fantasies[4] of Sigmund
Freud.

[4] For Freud's own avowal to this effect, see "Analysis Terminable and Interminable" in his *Collected
Papers* (London, 1950), Vol. 5, p. 326.

Ideas and Values

ERNEST JONES

(1879-1958)

A student of Sigmund Freud's, Dr. Ernest Jones is best known as a psychoanalytic theorist and as the author of *The Life and Works of Sigmund Freud* (1953-1957). Though *Hamlet and Oedipus* (1910, 1923; rev. 1949) is his only significant application of Freudian psychoanalytic principles to literature, *On the Nightmare* (1931), partly because of its publication by Leonard and Virginia Woolf at the Hogarth Press, has interest for students of literature.

Hamlet: The Psycho-analytical Solution (1947)

We are compelled then to take the position that there is some cause for Hamlet's vacillation which has not yet been fathomed. If this lies neither in his incapacity for action in general, nor in the inordinate difficuty of the particular task in question, then it must of necessity lie in the third possibility—namely, in some special feature of the task that renders it repugnant to him. This conclusion, that Hamlet at heart does not want to carry out the task, seems so obvious that it is hard to see how any open-minded reader of the play could avoid making it.[1] Some of the direct evidence for it furnished in the play will presently be brought forward when we discuss the problem of the cause of the repugnance, but it will first be necessary to mention some of the views that have been expressed on the subject.

The first writer clearly to recognize that Hamlet was a man not baffled in his endeavours but struggling in an internal conflict was Ulrici,[2] in 1839. The details of Ulrici's hypothesis, which like Klein's originated in the Hegelian views of morality, are not easy to follow, but the essence of it is the contention that Hamlet gravely doubted the moral legitimacy of revenge. He was thus plunged into a struggle between his natural tendency to avenge his father and his highly developed ethical and Christian views, which forbade the indulging of this instinctive desire. This hypothesis has been further developed on moral, ethical, and religious planes by Tolman,[3] Arndt,[4] Egan,[5] Wright,[6] Liebau,[7] Mézières,[8] Gerth,[9] Baumgart,[10] Robertson,[11] and Ford.[12] VonBerger[13] says that the task laid on him is beneath Hamlet's dignity: "He is too wise and too noble for this

Reprinted from *Hamlet and Oedipus* by Ernest Jones, M.D. by permission of W. W. Norton & Co., Inc. Copyright 1949 by Ernest Jones.
[1] Anyone who doubts this conclusion is recommended to read Loening's convincing chapter (XII), "Hamlet's Verhalten gegen seine Aufgabe".
[2] Ulrici: *Shakespeare's dramatische Kunst; Geschichte und Charakteristik des Shakespeare'schen Dramas*, 1839.

[3] Tolman: "A View of the Views about 'Hamlet' ", *Publications of the Modern Language Association of America*, 1898, p. 155.
[4] Wilhelm Arndt: "Hamlet, der Christ", *Die Zukunft*. 1896, S. 275.
[5] M. F. Egan: "The Puzzle of Hamlet" in *The Ghost in Hamlet and Other Essays*, 1906.
[6] W. B. Wright: "Hamlet", *Atlantic Monthly*, 1902, p. 686.
[7] Liebau: *Studien über William Shakespeares Trauerspiel Hamlet*. Date not stated.
[8] Mézières: *Shakespeare, ses oeuvres et ses critiques*, 1860.
[9] Gerth: *op. cit.*
[10] Baumgart: *op. cit.*
[11] J. M. Robertson: *Montaigne and Shakspere*, 1897, p. 129.
[12] Ford: *Shakespeare's Hamlet: A New Theory*, 1900.
[13] A. von Berger: "*Hamlet*" in *Dramaturgische Vorträge*, 1890.

pernicious world". Foss[14] thinks that the motive for Hamlet's delay is to gain time so as to think out how he can sinlessly commit a great sin; his conscience tells him it was wrong even to think of assassination, and that what he should do was to denounce Claudius. Kohler[15] ingeniously transferred the conflict to the sphere of jurisprudence, maintaining that Hamlet represented a type in advance of his time in recognizing the superiority of legal punishment over private revenge or family vendetta and was thus a fighter in the van of progress; he writes:[16] "Hamlet is a corner-stone in the evolution of law and morality". A similar view has been developed by Rubinstein.[17] This special pleading has been effectually refuted by Loening[18] and Fuld;[19] it is contradicted by all historical considerations. Finally, Schipper,[20] Gelber,[21] and, more recently, Stoll[22] have suggested that the conflict was a purely intellectual one, Hamlet being unable to satisfy himself of the adequacy or reliability of the Ghost's evidence. In his interesting work Figgis combines these views by insisting that the play is a tragedy of honour, Hamlet's main instinct: "In striking at the King without a full assurance of his guilt, was to him not only to strike at the legal monarch of the realm, but also to seem as though he was seizing a pretext to strike for the throne, he being the next in succession":[23] "What seems like indecision in the early portion of the play is really the honourable desire not to let his mere hatred of the King prick him into a capital action against an innocent man, to prove that the apparition of his father

was no heated fantasy, and, above all, not to take action till he was assured that his action would not involve his mother".[24]

The obvious question that one puts to the upholders of any of the hypotheses just mentioned is: why did Hamlet in his monologues give us no indication whatsoever of the nature of the conflict in his mind? As we shall presently note, he gave several pretended excuses for his hesitancy, but never once did he hint at any doubt about what his duty was in the matter. He was always clear enough about what he *ought* to do; the conflict in his mind ranged about the question why he couldn't bring himself to do it. If Hamlet had at any time been asked whether it was right for him to kill his uncle, or whether he really intended to do so, no one can seriously doubt what his instant answer would have been. Throughout the play we see his mind irrevocably made up on the desirability of a given course of action, which he fully accepts as being his bounden duty; indeed, he would have resented the mere insinuation of doubt on this point as an untrue slur on his filial piety. Ulrici, Baumgart, and Kohler try to meet this difficulty by assuming that the ethical objection to personal revenge was never clearly present to Hamlet's mind; it was a deep and undeveloped feeling which had not fully dawned. I would agree that only in some such way as this can the difficulty be logically met, and further that in recognizing Hamlet's non-consciousness of the cause of his repugnance to his task we are nearing the core of the mystery. In fact Hamlet tells us so himself in so many words (in his bitter cry—Act IV, Sc. 3—*I do not know why*, etc.). But an insurmountable obstacle in the way of accepting any of the causes of repugnance suggested above is that the nature of them is such that a keen and introspective thinker, as Hamlet was, would infallibly have recognized some indication of their presence, and would have openly debated them instead of deceiving himself with a number of

[14] G. R. Foss: *What the Author Meant*, 1932, p. 13.
[15] Kohler: *Shakespeare vor dem Forum der Jurisprudenz*, 1883; and *Zur Lehre von der Blutrache*, 1885. See also *Zeitschrift für vergleichende Rechtswissenschaft*, Bd. V, S. 330.
[16] Kohler: *Shakespeare* etc.; *op. cit.*, S. 189.
[17] Rubinstein: *Hamlet als Neurastheniker*, 1896.
[18] Loening: *Zeitschrift für die gesamte Strafrechtswissenschaft*, Bd. V, S. 191.
[19] Fuld: "Shakespeare und die Blutrache", *Dramaturgische Blätter und Bühnen-Rundschau*, 1888, Nr. 44.
[20] Schipper: *Shakespeare's Hamlet; ästhetische Erläuterung des Hamlet*, 1862.
[21] Gelber: *Shakespeare'sche Probleme, Plan und Einheit im Hamlet*, 1891.
[22] Stoll: *op. cit.* (1919).
[23] Figgis: *op. cit.*, p. 213.

[24] Idem: *op. cit.*, p. 232.

false pretexts in the way we shall presently recall. Loening[25] well states this in the sentence: "If it had been a question of a conflict between the duty of revenge imposed from without and an inner *moral* or *juristic* counter-impulse, this discord and its cause *must* have been brought into the region of reflection in a man so capable of thought, and so accustomed to it, as Hamlet was".

In spite of this difficulty the hint of an approaching solution encourages us to pursue more closely the argument at that point. The hypothesis just stated may be correct up to a certain stage and then have failed for lack of special knowledge to guide it further. Thus Hamlet's hesitancy may have been due to an internal conflict between the impulse to fulfil his task on the one hand and some special cause of repugnance to it on the other; further, the explanation of his not disclosing this cause of repugnance may be that he was not conscious of its nature; and yet the cause may be one that doesn't happen to have been considered by any of the upholders of this hypothesis. In other words, the first two stages in the argument may be correct, but not the third. This is the view that will now be developed, but before dealing with the third stage of the argument it is first necessary to establish the probability of the first two—namely, that Hamlet's hesitancy was due to some special cause of repugnance for his task and that he was unaware of the nature of this repugnance.

A preliminary obstruction to this line of thought, based on some common prejudices on the subject of mental dynamics, may first be considered. If Hamlet was not aware of the nature of his inhibition, doubt may be felt concerning the possibility of our penetrating to it. This pessimistic thought was expressed by Baumgart[26] as follows: "What hinders Hamlet in his revenge is for him himself a problem and *therefore* it must remain a problem for us all". Fortunately for our investigation, however, psycho-analytic

studies have demonstrated beyond doubt that mental trends hidden from the subject himself may come to external expression in ways that reveal their nature to a trained observer, so that the possibility of success is not to be thus excluded. Loening[27] has further objected to this hypothesis that the poet himself has not disclosed this hidden mental trend, or even given any indication of it. The first part of his objection is certainly true—otherwise there would be no problem to discuss, but we shall presently see that the second is by no means true. It may be asked: why has the poet not put in a clearer light the mental trend we are trying to discover? Strange as it may appear, the answer is probably the same as with Hamlet himself—namely, he could not because he was unaware of its nature. We shall later deal with this question is connection with the relation of the poet to the play.

As Trench well says:[28] "We find it hard, with Shakespeare's help, to understand Hamlet: even Shakespeare, perhaps, found it hard to understand him: Hamlet himself finds it impossible to understand himself. Better able than other men to read the hearts and motives of others, he is yet quite unable to read his own". I know of no more authentic statement than this in the whole literature on the Hamlet problem. But, if the motive of the play is so obscure, to what can we attribute its powerful effect on the audience, since, as Kohler[29] asks, "Who has ever seen Hamlet and not felt the fearful conflict that moves the soul of the hero?" This can only be because the hero's conflict finds its echo in a similar inner conflict in the mind of the hearer, and the more intense is this already present conflict the greater is the effect of the drama.[30] Again, it is certain that the hearer himself does not know the inner cause of the conflict in his own mind, but experiences only the outer manifesta-

[25] Loening: *Die Hamlet-Tragödie Shakespeares*, 1893, S. 78.
[26] Baumgart: *op. cit.*, S. 48.
[27] Loening: *op. cit.*, S. 78, 79.
[28] Trench: *op. cit.*, p. 115.
[29] Kohler: *Shakespeare vor dem Forum der Jurisprudenz*, 1883, S. 195.
[30] It need hardly be said that the play, like most others, appeals to its audience in a number of different respects. We are here considering only the main appeal, the central conflict in the tragedy.

tions of it. So we reach the apparent paradox that the hero, the poet, and the audience are all profoundly moved by feelings due to a conflict of the source of which they are unaware.

The fact, however, that such a conclusion should appear paradoxical is in itself a censure on popular ignorance of the actual workings of the human mind, and before undertaking to sustain the assertions made in the preceding paragraph it will first be necessary to make a few observations on the prevailing views of motive and conduct in general. The new science of clinical psychology stands nowhere in sharper contrast to the older attitudes towards mental functioning than on this very matter. Whereas the generally accepted view of man's mind, usually implicit and frequently explicit in psychological writings and elsewhere, regards it as an interplay of various processes that are for the most part known to the subject, or are at all events accessible to careful introspection on his part, the analytic methods of clinical psychology have on the contrary decisively proved that a far greater number of these processes than is commonly surmised arises from origins that he never even suspects. Man's belief that he is a self-conscious animal, alive to the desires that impel or inhibit his actions, is the last stronghold of that anthropomorphic and anthropocentric outlook on life which has so long dominated his philosophy, his theology, and, above all, his psychology. In other words, the tendency to take man at his own valuation is rarely resisted, and we assume that the surest way of finding out why a person commits a given act is simply to ask him, relying on the knowledge that he, as we ourselves would in a like circumstance, will feel certain of the answer and will almost infallibly provide a plausible reason for his conduct. Special objective methods of penetrating into the more obscure mental processes, however, disclose the most formidable obstacles in the way of this direct introspective route, and reveal powers of self-deception in the human mind to which a limit has yet to be found. If I may quote from a former paper:[31] "We are beginning to see man not as the smooth, self-acting agent he pretends to be, but as he really is, a creature only dimly conscious of the various influences that mould his thought and action, and blindly resisting with all the means at his command the forces that are making for a higher and fuller consciousness".

That Hamlet is suffering from an internal conflict the essential nature of which is inaccessible to his introspection is evidenced by the following considerations. Throughout the play we have the clearest picture of a man who sees his duty plain before him, but who shirks it at every opportunity and suffers in consequence the most intense remorse. To paraphrase Sir James Paget's well-known description of hysterical paralysis: Hamlet's advocates say he cannot do his duty, his detractors say he will not, wheras the truth is that he cannot will. Further than this, the deficient will-power is localized to the one question of killing his uncle; it is what may be termed a *specific aboulia*. Now instances of such specific aboulias in real life invariably prove, when analyzed, to be due to an unconscious replusion against the act that cannot be performed (or else against something closely associated with the act, so that the idea of the act becomes also involved in the repulsion). In other words, whenever a person cannot bring himself to do something that every conscious consideration tells him he should do—and which he may have the strongest conscious desire to do—it is always because there is some hidden reason why a part of him doesn't want to do it; this reason he will not own to himself and is only dimly if at all aware of. That is exactly the case with Hamlet. Time and again he works himself up, points out to himself his obvious duty, with the cruelest self-reproaches lashes himself to agonies of remorse—and once more falls away into inaction. He eagerly seizes at every excuse for occupying himself with any other matter than the performance of his duty—even in the last scene of the last

[31] "Rationalization in Every Day Life", *Journal of Abnormal Psychology*, 1908, p. 168.

act entering on the distraction of a quite irrelevant fencing-match with a man who he must know wants to kill him, an eventuality that would put an end to all hope of fulfilling his task: just as on a lesser plane a person faced with a distasteful task, e.g. writing a difficult letter, will whittle away his time in arranging, tidying, and fidgeting with any little occupation that may serve as a pretext for procrastination. Bradley[32] even goes so far as to make out a case for the view that Hamlet's self-accusation of "bestial oblivion" is to be taken in a literal sense, his unconscious detestation of his task being so intense as to enable him actually to forget it for periods.

Highly significant is the fact that the grounds Hamlet gives for his hesitancy are grounds none of which will stand any serious consideration, and which continually change from one time to another. One moment he pretends he is too cowardly to perform the deed, at another he questions the truthfulness of the ghost, at another—when the opportunity presents itself in its naked form—he thinks the time is unsuited, it would be better to wait till the King was at some evil act and then to kill him, and so on. They have each of them, it is true, a certain plausibility—so much so that some writers have accepted them at face value; but surely no pretext would be of any use if it were not plausible. As Madariaga[33] truly says: "The argument that the reasons given by Hamlet not to kill the king at prayers are cogent is irrelevant. For the man who wants to procrastinate cogent arguments are more valuable than mere pretext." Take, for instance, the matter of the credibility of the ghost. There exists an extensive and very interesting literature concerning Elizabethan beliefs in supernatural visitation. It was doubtless a burning topic, a focal point of the controversies about the conflicting theologies of the age, and moreover, affecting the practical question of how to treat witches. But there is no evidence of Hamlet (or Shakespeare!) being specially interested in theology, and

from the moment when the ghost confirms the slumbering suspicion in his mind ("O, my prophetic soul! My uncle!") his intuition must indubitably have convinced him of the ghost's veridical nature. He never really doubted the villainy of his uncle.

When a man gives at different times a different reason for his conduct it is safe to infer that, whether consciously or not, he is concealing the true reason. Wetz,[34] discussing a similar problem in reference to Iago, truly observes: "Nothing proves so well how false are the motives with which Iago tries to persuade himself as *the constant change in these motives*". We can therefore safely dismiss all the alleged motives that Hamlet propounds, as being more or less successful attempts on his part to blind himself with self-deception. Loening's[35] summing-up of them is not too emphatic when he says: "They are all mutually contradictory; *they are one and all false pretexts*". The alleged motives excellently illustrate the psychological mechanisms of evasion and rationalization I have elsewhere described.[36] It is not necessary, however, to discuss them here individually, for Loening has with the greatest perspicacity done this in full detail and has effectually demonstrated how utterly untenable they all are.[37]

Still, in his moments of self-reproach Hamlet sees clearly enough the recalcitrancy of his conduct and renews his efforts to achieve action. It is noticeable how his outbursts of remorse are evoked by external happenings which bring back to his mind that which he would so gladly forget, and which, according to Bradley, he does at times forget: particularly effective in this respect are incidents that contrast with his own conduct, as when the player is so moved over the fate of Hecuba (Act II, Sc. 2), or when Fortinbras takes the field and "finds quarrel in a straw when honour's at the stake" (Act IV, Sc. 4). On the

---

[32] Bradley: *op. cit.*, pp. 125, 126, 410, 411.
[33] Madariaga: *op. cit.*, p. 98.

[34] Wetz: *Shakespeare vom Standpunkt der vergleichenden Litteraturgeschichte*, 1890, Bd. I, S. 186.
[35] Loening: *op. cit.*, S. 245.
[36] *op. cit.*, p. 161.
[37] See especially his analysis of Hamlet's pretext for non-action in the prayer scene: *op. cit.*, S. 240-2.

former occasion, stung by the monstrous way in which the player pours out his feeling at the thought of Hecuba, he arraigns himself in words which surely should effectually dispose of the view that he has any doubt where his duty lies.

What's Hecuba to him, or he to Hecuba,
That he should weep for her? What would he do,
Had he the motive and the cue for passion
That I have? He would drown the stage with tears
And cleave the general ear with horrid speech,
Make mad the guilty and appal the free,
Confound the ignorant, and amaze indeed
The very faculties of eyes and ears; yet I,
A dull and muddy-mettled rascal, peak
Like John-a-dreams, unpregnant of my cause, [38]
And can say nothing; no, not for a king,
Upon whose property and most dear life
A damn'd defeat was made: Am I a coward?
Who calls me villain, breaks my pate across,
Plucks off my beard and blows it in my face,
Tweaks me by the nose, gives me the lie i' the throat
As deep as to the lungs? Who does me this?
Ha, 'swounds, I should take it: for it cannot be
But I am pigeon-liver'd, and lack gall
To make oppression bitter, or ere this
I should ha' fatted all the region kites
With this slave's offal. Bloody, bawdy villain!
Remorseless, treacherous, lecherous, kindless villain!
O, vengeance!
Why, what an ass am I! This is most brave,
That I, the son of a dear father murder'd,
Prompted to my revenge by heaven and hell,
Must like a whore unpack my heart with words,
And fall a-cursing like a very drab;
A scullion! [39]

The readiness with which his guilty conscience is stirred into activity is again evidenced on the second appearance of the Ghost, when Hamlet cries,

Do you not come your tardy son to chide,
That lapsed in time and passion lets go by

[38] How the essence of the situation is conveyed in these four words.
[39] Dover Wilson considers this a misprint for "stallion".

Th'important acting of your dread command?
O, say!

The Ghost at once confirms this misgiving by answering,

Do not forget! this visitation
Is but to whet thy almost blunted purpose.

In short, the whole picture presented by Hamlet, his deep depression, the hopeless note in his attitude towards the world and towards the value of life, his dread of death,[40] his repeated reference to bad dreams, his self-accusations, his desperate efforts to get away from the thoughts of his duty, and his vain attempts to find an excuse for his procrastination: all this unequivocally points to a *tortured conscience*, to some hidden ground for shirking his task, a ground which he dare not or cannot avow to himself. We have, therefore, to take up the argument again at this point, and to seek for some evidence that may serve to bring to light the hidden counter-motive.

The extensive experience of the psycho-analytic researches carried out by Freud and his school during the past half-century has amply demonstrated that certain kinds of mental processes show a greater tendency to be inaccessible to consciousness (put technically, to be "repressed") than others. In other words, it is harder for a person to realize the existence in his mind of some mental trends than it is of others. In order therefore to gain a proper perspective it is necessary briefly to inquire into the relative frequency with which various sets of mental processes are "repressed". Experience shows that this can be correlated with the degree of compatibility of these various sets with the ideals and standards accepted by the conscious ego; the less compatible they are with these

[40] Tieck (*Dramaturgische Blätter*, II, 1826) saw in Hamlet's cowardly fear of death a chief reason for his hesitancy in executing his vengeance. How well Shakespeare understood what this fear was like may be inferred from Claudio's words in *Measure for Measure*:
The weariest and most loathed worldly life
That age, ache, penury and imprisonment
Can lay on nature is a paradise
To what we fear of death.

the more likely are they to be "repressed". As the standards acceptable to consciousness are in considerable measure derived from the immediate environment, one may formulate the following generalization: those processes are most likely to be "repressed" by the individual which are most disapproved of by the particular circle of society to whose influence he has chiefly been subjected during the period when his character was being formed. Biologically stated, this law would run: "That which is unacceptable to the herd becomes unacceptable to the individual member", it being understood that the term herd is intended here in the sense of the particular circle defined above, which is by no means necessarily the community at large. It is for this reason that moral, social, ethical, or religious tendencies are seldom "repressed", for, since the individual originally received them from his herd, they can hardly ever come into conflict with the dicta of the latter. This merely says that a man cannot be ashamed of that which he respects; the apparent exceptions to this rule need not be here explained.

The language used in the previous paragraph will have indicated that by the term "repression" we denote an active dynamic process. Thoughts that are "repressed" are actively kept from consciousness by a definite force and with the expenditure of more or less mental effort, though the person concerned is rarely aware of this. Further, what is thus kept from consciousness typically possesses an energy of its own; hence our frequent use of such expressions as "trend", "tendency", etc. A little consideration of the genetic aspects of the matter will make it comprehensible that the trends most likely to be "repressed" are those belonging to what are called the innate impulses, as contrasted with secondarily acquired ones. Loening[41] seems very discerningly to have grasped this, for, in commenting on a remark of Kohler's to the effect that "where a feeling impels us to action or to omission, it

[41] Loening: *op. cit.*, S. 245, 246.

is replete with a hundred reasons—with reasons that are as light as soap-bubbles, but which through self-deception appear to us as highly respectable and compelling motives, because they are hugely magnified in the (concave) mirror of our own feeling", he writes: "But this does not hold good, as Kohler and others believe, when we are impelled by *moral* feelings of which reason *approves* (for these we admit to ourselves, they need no excuse), only for feelings that arise from our *natural man*, those the gratification of which is *opposed by our reason*". It only remains to add the obvious corollary that, as the herd unquestionably selects from the "natural" instincts the sexual one on which to lay its heaviest ban, so it is the various psycho-sexual trends that are most often "repressed" by the individual. We have here the explanation of the clinical experience that the more intense and the more obscure is a given case of deep mental conflict the more certainly will it be found on adequate analysis to centre about a sexual problem. On the surface, of course, this does not appear so, for, by means of various psychological defensive mechanisms, the depression, doubt, despair, and other manifestations of the conflict are transferred on to more tolerable and permissible topics, such as anxiety about worldly success or failure, about immortality and the salvation of the soul, philosophical considerations about the value of life, the future of the world, and so on.

Bearing these considerations in mind, let us return to Hamlet. It should now be evident that the conflict hypotheses discussed above, which see Hamlet's conscious impulse towards revenge inhibited by an unconscious misgiving of a highly ethical kind, are based on ignorance of what actually happens in real life, since misgivings of this order belong in fact to the more conscious layers of the mind rather than to the deeper, unconscious ones. Hamlet's intense self-study would speedily have made him aware of any such misgivings and, although he might subsequently have ignored them, it would almost certainly have been by the aid of some process of rationalization which would have enabled him to deceive himself into believing that they were ill-founded; he would in any case have remained conscious of the nature of them. We have therefore to invert these hypotheses and realize—as his words so often indicate—that the positive striving for vengeance, the pious task laid on him by his father, was to him the moral and social one, the one approved of by his consciousness, and that the "repressed" inhibiting striving against the act of vengeance arose in some hidden source connected with his more personal, natural instincts. The former striving has already been considered, and indeed is manifest in every speech in which Hamlet debates the matter: the second is, from its nature, more obscure and has next to be investigated.

This is perhaps most easily done by inquiring more intently into Hamlet's precise attitude towards the object of his vengeance, Claudius, and towards the crimes that have to be avenged. These are two: Claudius' incest with the Queen,[42] and his murder of his brother. Now it is of great importance to note the profound difference in Hamlet's attitude towards these two crimes. Intellectually of course he abhors both, but there can be no question as to which arouses in him the deeper loathing. Whereas the murder of his father evokes in him indignation and a plain recognition of his obvious duty to avenge it, his mother's guilty conduct awakes in him the intensest horror. Furnivall[43] remarks, in speaking of the Queen, "Her disgraceful adultery and incest, and treason to his noble father's memory, Hamlet has felt in his inmost soul. Compared to their ingrain die, Claudius' murder of his father—notwithstanding all his protestations—is only a skin-deep stain".

Now, in trying to define Hamlet's attitude towards his uncle we have to guard against assuming off-hand that this is a simple one of mere execration, for there is a possibility of complexity arising in the following way: The uncle has not merely committed *each* crime, he has committed *both* crimes, a distinction of considerable importance, since the *combination* of crimes allows the admittance of a new factor, produced by the possible inter-relation of the two, which may prevent the result from being simply one of summation. In addition, it has to be borne in mind that the perpetrator of the crimes is a relative, and an exceedingly near relative. The possible inter-relationship of the crimes, and the fact that the author of them is an actual member of the family, give scope for a confusion in their influence on Hamlet's mind which may be the cause of the very obscurity we are seeking to clarify.

Let us first pursue further the effect on Hamlet of his mother's misconduct. Before he even knows with any certitude, however much he may suspect it, that his father has been murdered he is in the deepest depression, and evidently on account of this misconduct. The connection between the two is unmistakable in the monologue in Act I, Sc. 2, in reference to which Furnivall[44] writes: "One must insist on this, that before any revelation of his father's murder is made to Hamlet, before any burden of revenging that murder is laid upon him, he thinks of suicide as a welcome means of escape from this fair world of God's, made abominable to his diseased and weak imagination by his mother's lust, and the dishonour done by her to his father's memory."

O that this too too solid [45] flesh would melt,
Thaw and resolve itself into a dew,
Or that the Everlasting had not fix'd
His canon 'gainst self-slaughter, O God, God,
How weary, stale, flat, and unprofitable
Seem to me all the uses of this world!
Fie on 't, O fie, 'tis an unweeded garden
That grows to seed, things rank and gross in nature
Possess it merely, that it should come to this,
But two months dead, nay, not so much, not two,

[42] Had this relationship not counted as incestuous, then Queen Elizabeth would have had no right to the throne; she would have been a bastard, Katherine of Aragon being still alive at her birth.
[43] Furnivall: Introduction to the "Leopold" Shakespeare, p. 72.
[44] Furnivall: *op. cit.*, p. 70.
[45] Dover Wilson (*Times Literary Supplement*, May 16, 1908) brings forward excellent reasons for thinking that this word is a misprint for "sullied", I use the Shakespearean punctuation he has restored.

So excellent a king; that was to this
Hyperion to a satyr, so loving to my mother,
That he might not beteem the winds of ·
     heaven
Visit her face too roughly—heaven and
     earth
Must I remember? why, she would hang on
     him
As if increase of appetite had grown
By what it fed on, and yet within a month,
Let me not think on 't; frailty thy name is
     woman!
A little month or ere those shoes were old
With which she follow'd my poor father's
     body
Like Niobe all tears, why she, even she—
O God, a beast that wants discourse of
     reason
Would have mourn'd longer—married with
     my uncle,
My father's brother, but no more like my
     father
Than I to Hercules, within a month,
Ere yet the salt of most unrighteous tears
Had left the flushing in her galled eyes,
She married. O most wicked speed . . . to
     post
With such dexterity to incestuous sheets!
It is not, nor it cannot come to good,
But break my heart, for I must hold my
     tongue.

According to Bradley,[46] Hamlet's melncholic disgust at life was the cause of ¡is aversion from "any kind of decided ·ction". His explanation of the whole ·roblem of Hamlet is "the moral shock ·f the sudden ghastly disclosure of his ¡other's true nature",[47] and he regards ¡he effect of this shock, as depicted in the ·lay, as fully comprehensible. He says:[48] Is it possible to conceive an experience ¡ore desolating to a man such as we ¡ave seen Hamlet to be; and is its result ¡nything but perfectly natural? It brings ·ewildered horror, then loathing, then ¡espair of human nature. His whole mind ¡ poisoned . . . A nature morally blunter ¡ould have felt even so dreadful a revlation less keenly. A slower and more ¡mited and positive mind might not have ¡xtended so widely through the world the ¡isgust and disbelief that have entered ¡".

But we can rest satisfied with this ¡eemingly adequate explanation of Ham-

let's weariness of life only if we accept unquestioningly the conventional standards of the causes of deep emotion. Many years ago Connolly,[49] a well-known psychiatrist, pointed out the disproportion here existing between cause and effect, and gave as his opinion that Hamlet's reaction to his mother's marriage indicated in itself a mental instability, "a predisposition to actual unsoundness;" he writes: "The circumstances are not such as would at once turn a healthy mind to the contemplation of suicide, the last resource of those whose reason has been overwhelmed by calamity and despair." In T. S. Eliot's[50] opinion, also, Hamlet's emotion is in *excess* of the facts as they appear, and he specially contrasts it with Gertrude's negative and insignificant personality. Wihan[51] attributes the exaggerated effect of his misfortunes to Hamlet's "Masslosigkeit" (lack of moderation), which is displayed in every direction. We have unveiled only the exciting cause, not the predisposing cause. The very fact that Hamlet is apparently content with the explanation arouses our misgiving, for, as will presently be expounded, from the very nature of the emotion he cannot be aware of the true cause of it. If we ask, not what ought to produce such soul-paralysing grief and distaste for life, but what in actual fact does produce it, we are compelled to go beyond this explanation and seek for some deeper cause. In real life speedy second marriages occur commonly enough without leading to any such result as is here depicted, and when we see them followed by this result we invariably find, if the opportunity for an analysis of the subject's mind presents itself, that there is some other and more hidden reason why the event is followed by this inordinately great effect. The reason always is that the event has awakened to increased activity mental processes that have been "repressed" from the subject's consciousness. His mind has been specially prepared for the catastrophe by previous mental processes with which those directly resulting from

46 Bradley: *op. cit.*, p. 122.
47 *Idem: op. cit.*, p. 117.
48 *Idem: op. cit.*, p. 119.
49 Connolly: *A Study of Hamlet*, 1863, pp. 22, 23.
50 T. S. Eliot: *loc. cit.*
51 J. Wihan: "Die Hamletfrage", in *Leipziger Beiträge zur englischen Philologie*, 1921, S. 89.

the event have entered into association. This is perhaps what Furnivall means when he speaks of the world being made abominable to Hamlet's "diseased imagination". In short, the special nature of the reaction presupposes some special feature in the mental predisposition. Bradley himself has to qualify his hypothesis by inserting the words "to a man such as we have seen Hamlet to be".

We come at this point to the vexed question of Hamlet's sanity, about which so many controversies have raged. Dover Wilson[52] authoritatively writes: "I agree with Loening, Bradley and others that Shakespeare meant us to imagine Hamlet as suffering from some kind of mental disorder throughout the play". The question is what kind of mental disorder and what is its significance dramatically and psychologically. The matter is complicated by Hamlet's frequently displaying simulation (the Antic Disposition),[53] and it has been asked whether this is to conceal his real mental disturbance or cunningly to conceal his purposes in coping with the practical problems of this task? This is a topic that presently will be considered at some length, but there can be few who regard it as a comprehensive statement of Hamlet's mental state. As T. S. Eliot[54] has neatly expressed it, "Hamlet's 'madness' is less than madness and more than feigned".

But what of the mental disorder itself? In the past this little problem in clinical diagnosis seems to have greatly exercised psychiatrists. Some of them, e.g. Thierisch,[55] Sigismund,[56] Stenger,[57] and many others, have simply held that Hamlet was insane, without particularizing the form of insanity. Rosner[58] labelled Hamlet as a hysteroneurasthenic, an opinion contradicted by Rubinstein[59] and Land-

mann.[60] Most, however, including K[ellog,[61] de Boismon,[62] Heuse,[63] Nicholsor and others, have committed themselv to the view that Hamlet was sufferi from melancholia, though there are r failing psychiatrists, e.g. Ominus,[65] w reject this. Schücking[66] attributes the c lay in his action to Hamlet's being pa alysed by melancholia. Laehr[67] has a pa ticularly ingenious hypothesis whi maintains that Shakespeare, having tak over the Ghost episode from the earl play, was obliged to depict Hamlet as melancholiac because this was theat cally the most presentable form of sanity in which hallucinations occu Long ago Dowden made it seem pro able that Shakespeare had made use an important study of melancholia Timothe Bright,[68] but, although he m have adapted a few phrases to his o use, the clinical picture of Hamlet diff notably from that delineated by Brig

More to the point is the actual accou given in the play by the King, t Queen, Ophelia, and above all, Po nius.[69] In his description, for example, note—if the Elizabethan language translated into modern English—t symptoms of dejection, refusal of foc insomnia, crazy behaviour, fits of c lirium, and finally of raving madne Hamlet's poignant parting words Polonius ("except my life", etc.) can mean other than a craving for dea These are undoubtedly suggestive of c tain forms of melancholia, and the li ness to manic-depressive insanity, which melancholia is now known to but a part, is completed by the occ rence of attacks of great excitement t would nowadays be called " hypomani

52 Dover Wilson: *What Happens* etc., p. 217.
53 Cp. R. Alexander: "Hamlet, the Classical Malingerer", *Medical Journal and Record*, Sept. 4, 1929, p. 287.
54 T. S. Eliot: *Selected Essays*, 1932, p. 146.
55 Thierisch: *Nord und Süd*, 1878, Bd. VI.
56 Sigismund: *Jahrbuch der Deutschen Shakespeare-Gesellschaft*, 1879, Jahrg. XVI.
57 E. Stenger: *Der Hamlet Charakter. Eine psychiatrische Shakespeare-Studie*, 1883.
58 Rosner: *Shakespeare's Hamlet im Lichte der Neuropathologie*, 1895.
59 Rubinstein: *op. cit.*

60 Landmann: *Zeitschrift für Psychologie*, 1896, XI.
61 Kellog: *Shakespeare's Delineation of Insanity*, 1
62 De Boismon: *Annales médico-psychologiques*, 1 4e série, 12e fasc.
63 Heuse: *Jahrbuch der deutschen Shakespe Gesellschaft*, 1876, Jahrg. XIII.
64 Nicholson: *Transactions of the New Shakesp Society*, 1880-5, Part II.
65 Ominus: *Revue des Deux Mondes*, 1876, 3e 14e fasc.
66 Schücking: *Character Problems in Shakespe Plays*, 1922, p. 162.
67 Laehr: *Die Darstellung krankhafter Geisteszustä in Shakespeare's Dramas*, 1898, S. 179, etc.
68 Timothe Bright: *A Treatise of Melancholia*, 1
69 Act 2, Sc. 2. "Fell into a sadness", etc.

f which Dover Wilson[70] counts no fewer than eight. This modern diagnosis has indeed been suggested, e.g. by Brock,[71] Somerville,[72] and others. Nevertheless, the rapid and startling oscillations between intense excitement and profound depression do not accord with the accepted picture of this disorder, and if I had to describe such a condition as Hamlet's in clinical terms—which I am not particularly inclined to—it would have to be as a severe case of hysteria on a cyclothymic basis.

All this, however, is of academic interest only. What we are essentially concerned with is the psychological understanding of the dramatic effect produced by Hamlet's personality and behaviour. That effect would be quite other were the central figure in the play to represent merely a "case of insanity". When that happens, as with Ophelia, such a person passes beyond our ken, is in a sense no more human, whereas Hamlet successfully claims our interest and sympathy to the very end. Shakespeare certainly never intended us to regard Hamlet as insane, so that the "mind o'erthrown" must have some other meaning than its literal one. Robert Bridges[73] has described the matter with exquisite delicacy:

> Hamlet himself would never have been
> aught to us, or we
> To Hamlet, wer't not for the artful balance
> whereby
> Shakespeare so gingerly put his sanity in
> doubt
> Without the while confounding his Reason.

I would suggest that in this Shakespeare's extraordinary powers of observation and penetration granted him a degree of insight that it has taken the world three subsequent centuries to reach. Until our generation (and even now in the juristic sphere) a dividing line separated the sane and responsible from the irresponsible insane. It is now becoming more and more widely recognized that much of mankind lives in an intermediate and unhappy state charged with what Dover Wilson[74] well calls "that sense of frustration, futility and human inadequacy which is the burden of the whole symphony" and of which Hamlet is the supreme example in literature. This intermediate plight, in the toils of which perhaps the greater part of mankind struggles and suffers, is given the name of psychoneurosis, and long ago the genius of Shakespeare depicted it for us with faultless insight.

Extensive studies of the past half century, inspired by Freud, have taught us that a psychoneurosis means a state of mind where the person is unduly, and often painfully, driven or thwarted by the "unconscious" part of his mind, that buried part that was once the infant's mind and still lives on side by side with the adult mentality that has developed out of it and should have taken its place. It signifies *internal* mental conflict. We have here the reason why it is impossible to discuss intelligently the state of mind of anyone suffering from a psychoneurosis, whether the description is of a living person or an imagined one, without correlating the manifestations with what must have operated in his infancy and is *still operating*. That is what I propose to attempt here.

For some deep-seated reason, which is to him unacceptable, Hamlet is plunged into anguish at the thought of his father being replaced in his mother's affections by someone else. It is as if his devotion to his mother had made him so jealous for her affection that he had found it hard enough to share this even with his father and could not endure to share it with still another man. Against this thought, however, suggestive as it is, may be urged three objections. First, if it were in itself a full statement of the matter, Hamlet would have been aware of the jealousy, whereas we have concluded that the mental process we are seeking is hidden from him. Secondly, we see in it no evidence of the arousing of an old and forgotten memory. And, thirdly, Hamlet is being deprived by Claudius of no greater share in the Queen's affection

70 Dover Wilson: *op. cit.*, p. 213.
71 J. H. E. Brock: *The Dramatic Purpose of Hamlet*, 35.
72 H. Somerville: *Madness in Shakespearean Tragedy*, 29.
73 Robert Bridges: *The Testament of Beauty*, I. 577.
74 Dover Wilson: *op. cit.*, p. 261.

than he had been by his own father, for the two brothers made exactly similar claims in this respect—namely, those of a loved husband. The last-named objection, however, leads us to the heart of the situation. How if, in fact, Hamlet had in years gone by, as a child, bitterly resented having had to share his mother's affection even with his own father, had regarded him as a rival, and had secretly wished him out of the way so that he might enjoy undisputed and undisturbed the monopoly of that affection? If such thoughts had been present in his mind in childhood days they evidently would have been "repressed", and all traces of them obliterated, by filial piety and other educative influences. The actual realization of his early wish in the death of his father at the hands of a jealous rival would then have stimulated into

activity these "repressed" memori which would have produced, in the fo of depression and other suffering, obscure aftermath of his childhood's cc flict. This is at all events the mechani that is actually found in the real Haml who are investigated psychologically.[7]

The explanation, therefore, of the c lay and self-frustration exhibited in t endeavour to fulfil his father's dema for vengeance is that to Hamlet t thought of incest and parricide combin is too intolerable to be borne. One p of him tries to carry out the task, t other flinches inexorably from t thought of it. How fain would he b it out in that "bestial oblivion" whi unfortunately for him his conscience cc temns. He is torn and tortured in insoluble inner conflict.

[75] See, for instance, Wulf Sachs: *Black Hamlet*, 1

C. L. BARBER
(b. 1913)

Cesar Lombardi Barber combines an interest in analytical criticism and historie scholarship. In *Shakespeare's Festive Comedy, A Study of Dramatic Form and Relation to Social Custom* (1959) he interprets six of Shakespeare's plays by referen to their complex social environment—including popular holiday celebrations a sophisticated dramatic conventions—and thus demonstrates the interrelationships literary form and culture. Barber has also prepared the Laurel edition of Shakespear *Sonnets* (1960) and contributed a discussion of Eliot's later criticism and plays the expanded third edition of F. O. Matthiessen's *The Achievement of T. S. El* (1935; rev. 1947, 1958). He is the author of *More Power to Them: A Report Faculty and Student Experience in the Encouragement of Student Initiative* (196 and co-author of *The New College Plan* (1958).

May Games and Metamorphoses on a Midsummer Night (1959)

> Such shaping fantasies, that apprehend
> More than cool reason ever comprehends.

If Shakespeare had called *A Midsummer Night's Dream* by a title that referred to

This essay is a revised and condensed version of Chapter 6 of *Shakespeare's Festive Comedy, A Study of Dramatic Form and Its Relation to Social Custom* by C. L. Barber. Copyright 1959 by Princeton University Press. Reprinted by permission of the author and Princeton University Press. The book is also available in a Meridian paperback edition.

pageantry and May games, the aspects it with which I shall be chiefly concern would be more often discussed. To hor a noble wedding, Shakespeare gather up in a play the sort of pageantry whi was usually presented piece-meal aristocratic entertainments, in park a court as well as in hall. And the M game, everybody's pastime, gave the p tern for his whole action, which mov

from the town to the grove" and back
gain, bringing in summer to the bridal.
'hese things were familiar and did not
eed to be stressed by a title.

Shakespeare's young men and maids,
ke those the Puritan Phillip Stubbes
escribed in May games, "run gadding
ver night to the woods, . . . where they
pend the whole night in pleasant pas-
mes—" and in the fierce vexation which
ften goes with the pastimes of falling in
nd out of love and threatening to fight
bout it. "And no marvel," Stubbes ex-
laimed about such headlong business,
for there is a great Lord present among
hem, as superintendent and Lord over
heir pastimes and sports, namely, Satan,
rince of hell." [1] In making Oberon,
rince of fairies, into the May king,
hakespeare urbanely plays with the no-
ion of a supernatural power at work in
oliday: he presents the common May
ame presided over by an aristocratic
arden god. Titania is a Summer Lady
rho "waxeth wounder proud":

am a spirit of no common rate,
'he summer still doth tend upon my state . . .

nd Puck, as jester, promotes the
night-rule" version of misrule over
rhich Oberon is superintendent and lord
1 the "haunted grove." The lovers orig-
nally meet

in the wood, a league without the town,
Vhere I did meet thee once with Helena
'o do observance to a morn of May.

Next morning, when Theseus and Hip-
olyta find the lovers sleeping, it is after
heir own early "observation is per-
ormed"—presumably some May-game
bservance, of a suitably aristocratic
ind, for Theseus jumps to the conclu-
ion that

o doubt they rose up early to observe
he rite of May; and, hearing our intent,
ame here in grace of our solemnity.

'hese lines need not mean that the play's
ction happens on May Day. Shake-

speare does not make himself accountable for exact chronological inferences;
the moon that will be new according to
Hippolyta will shine according to Bottom's almanac. And in any case, people
went Maying at various times, "Against
May, Whitsunday, and other time" is the
way Stubbes puts it. This Maying can be
thought of as happening on a midsummer night, even on Midsummer Eve itself, so that its accidents are complicated
by the delusions of a magic time. (May
Week at Cambridge University still comes
in June.) The point of the allusions is
not the date, but the *kind* of holiday occasion. The Maying is completed when
Oberon and Titania with their trains
come into the great chamber to bring the
blessing of fertility. They are at once
common and special, a May king and
queen making their good luck visit to the
manor house, and a pair of country gods,
half-English and half-Ovid, come to
bring their powers in tribute to great
lords and ladies.

The play's relationship to pageantry
is most prominent in the scene where the
fairies are introduced by our seeing their
quarrel. This encounter is the sort of
thing that Elizabeth and the wedding
party might have happened on while
walking about in the park during the
long summer dusk. The fairy couple accuse each other of the usual weakness of
pageant personages—a compelling love
for royal personages:

Why art thou here,
Come from the farthest steep of India,
But that, forsooth, the bouncing Amazon,
Your buskin'd mistress and your warrior love,
To Theseus must be wedded, and you come
To give their bed joy and prosperity?

Oberon describes an earlier entertainment, very likely one in which the family
of the real-life bride or groom had been
concerned:

My gentle Puck, come hither. Thou
    rememb'rest
Since once I sat upon a promontory
And heard a mermaid, on a dolphin's back . . .
That very time I saw (but thou couldst not)
Flying between the cold moon and the earth
Cupid, all arm'd. A certain aim he took

---

[1] *The Anatomie of Abuses . . . in Ailgna* (1538), ed.
V. Furnival (London, 1877-82), p. 149.

At a fair Vestal, throned by the West,
And loos'd his love-shaft smartly from his
  bow,
As it should pierce a hundred thousand
  hearts.
But I might see young Cupid's fiery shaft
Quench'd in the chaste beams of the wat'ry
  moon,
And the imperial vot'ress passed on,
In maiden meditation, fancy-free.

At the entertainment at Elvetham in 1591, Elizabeth was throned by the west side of a garden lake to listen to music from the water; the fairy queen came with a round of dancers and spoke of herself as wife to Auberon. These and other similarities make it quite possible, but not necessary, that Shakespeare was referring to the Elvetham occasion. What is not in doubt is the *kind* of occasion Oberon's speech refers to, the kind of occasion Shakespeare's scene is shaped by. The speech describes, in retrospect, just such a joyous overflow of pleasure into music and make-believe as is happening in Shakespeare's own play. The fact that what Shakespeare handled with supreme skill was commonplace no doubt contributes to our inability to connect what he produced with particular historical circumstances.

It was commonplace to imitate Ovid. Ovidian fancies pervade *A Midsummer Night's Dream*, and especially the scene of the fairy quarrel: the description of the way Cupid "loos'd his love shaft" at Elizabeth parallels the Metamorphoses' account of the god's shooting "his best arrow, with the golden head" at Apollo; Helena, later in the scene, exclaims that "The story shall be chang'd: / Apollo flies, and Daphne holds the chase"—and proceeds to invert animal images from Ovid. The game was not so much to lift things gracefully from Ovid as it was to make up fresh things in Ovid's manner, as Shakespeare here, by playful mythopoesis, explains the bad weather by his fairies' quarrel and makes up a metamorphosis of the little Western flower to motivate the play's follies and place Elizabeth superbly above them. The pervasive Ovidian influence accounts for The-

seus' putting fables and fairies in th[e] same breath when he says, punning o[n] ancient and antic,

> I never may believe
> These antique fables nor these fairy toys.

The humor of the play relates super[-]stition, magic and passionate delusion a[s] "fancy's images." The title emphasizes [a] sceptical attitude by calling the comed[y] a "dream." It seems unlikely that th[e] title's characterization of the dream, "[a] midsummer night's dream," implie[s] association with the specific customs [of] Midsummer Eve, the shortest night [of] the year, except as "midsummer night[s]" would carry suggestions of a magic time[.] The observance of Midsummer Eve i[n] England centered on building bonfires o[r] "bonefires," of which there is nothing i[n] Shakespeare's moonlight play. It was [a] time when maids might find out wh[o] their true love would be by dreams o[r] divinations. There were customs of deck[-]ing houses with greenery and hangin[g] lights, which just possibly might con[-]nect with the fairies' torches at th[e] comedy's end. And when people gath[-]ered fern seed at midnight, sometime[s] they spoke of spirits whizzing invisibl[y] past. In the absence of evidence, there [is] no way to settle just how much come[s] from tradition. But what *is* clear is tha[t] Shakespeare was not *simply* writing ou[t] folklore which he heard in his youth, a[s] Romantic critics liked to assume. On th[e] contrary, his fairies are produced by [a] complex fusion of pageantry and popula[r] game, as well as popular fancy. More[-]over, as we shall see, they are not seriou[s] in the menacing way in which th[e] people's fairies were serious. Instead the[y] are serious in a very different way, a[s] embodiments of the May-game expe[-]rience of eros in men and women an[d] trees and flowers, while any superstitiou[s] tendency to believe in their literal realit[y] is mocked. The whole night's action i[s] presented as a release of shaping fantas[y] which brings clarification about the trick[s] of strong imagination. We watch [a] dream; but we are awake, thanks t[o] pervasive humor about the tendency to take fantasy literally, whether in love, in superstition, or in Bottom's mechanical dramatics. In the course of an inclusive release of imagination, the folly of fantasy becomes the general subject, echoed back and forth between the strains of the play's imitative counterpoint.

The Fond Pageant

We can best follow first the strain of the lovers; then the fairies, their persuasive and then their humorous aspects; and finally the broadly comic strain of the clowns. We feel what happens to the young lovers in relation to the wedding of the Duke. Theseus and Hippolyta have a quite special sort of role: they are principals without being protagonists; the play happens for them rather than to them. This relation goes with their being stand-ins for the noble couple whose marriage the play originally honored. In expressing the prospect of Theseus' marriage, Shakespeare can fix in ideal form, so that it can be felt later at performance in the theater, the mood that would obtain in a palace as the "nuptial hour / Draws on apace." Theseus looks towards the hour with masculine impatience, Hippolyta with a woman's happy willingness to dream away the time. Theseus gives directions for the "four happy days" to his "usual manager of mirth," his Master of the Revels, Philostrate:

> Go, Philostrate,
> Stir up the Athenian youth to merriments,
> Awake the pert and nimble spirit of mirth,
> Turn melancholy forth to funerals;
> The pale companion is not for our pomp.

The whole community is to observe a decorum of the passions, with Philostrate as choreographer of a pageant where Melancholy's float will not appear. After the war in which he won Hippolyta, the Duke announces that he is going to wed her

> in another key,
> With pomp, with triumph, and with revelling.

But his large, poised line is interrupted by Egeus, panting out vexation. After the initial invocation of nuptial festivity, we are confronted by the sort of tension from which merriment is a release. Here is Age, standing in the way of Athenian youth; here are the locked conflicts of everyday. By the dwelling here on "the sharp Athenian law," on the fate of nuns "in shady cloister mew'd," we are led to feel the outgoing to the woods as an escape from the inhibitions imposed by parents and the organized community. And this sense of release is also prepared by looking for just a moment at the tragic potentialities of passion. Lysander and Hermia, left alone in their predicament, speak a plaintive, symmetrical duet on the theme, learned "from tale or history," that "The course of true love never did run smooth":

> *Lysander.* But, either it was different in blood—
> *Hermia.* O cross! too high to be enthrall'd to low!
> *Lysander.* Or else misgraffed in respect of years—
> *Hermia.* O spite! too old to be engag'd to young!

Suddenly the tone changes, as Lysander describes in little the sort of tragedy presented in *Romeo and Juliet*, where Juliet exclaimed that their love was "Too like the lightning, which doth cease to be / Ere one can say 'It lightens' " (II.ii.119-120).

> *Lysander.* Or, if there were a sympathy in choice,
> War, death, or sickness did lay siege to it,
> Making it momentany as a sound,
> Swift as a shadow, short as any dream,
> Brief as the lightning in the collied night,
> That, in a spleen, unfolds both heaven and earth,
> And ere a man hath power to say 'Behold!'
> The jaws of darkness do devour it up:
> So quick bright things come to confusion.

But Hermia shakes herself free of the tragic vision, and they turn to thoughts of stealing forth tomorrow night to meet in the Maying wood and go on to the dowager aunt, where "the sharp Athenian law / Cannot pursue us."

If they had reached the wealthy aunt, the play would be a romance. But it is a change of heart, not a change of fortune, which lets love have its way. The merriments Philostrate was to have directed happen inadvertently, the lovers walking into them blind, so to speak. The roles which the young people might play in a wooing game, they carry out in earnest. And nobody is shown setting about to play the parts of Oberon or Titania. Instead the pageant fictions are presented as "actually" happening—at least so it seems at first glance.

We see the fairies meet by moonlight in the woods before we see the lovers arrive there, and so are prepared to see the mortals lose themselves. In *The Winter's Tale*, Perdita describes explicitly the transforming and liberating powers of the spring festival which in *A Midsummer Night's Dream* are embodied in the nightwood world the lovers enter. After Perdita has described the spring flowers, she concludes with

> O, these I lack
> To make you garlands of; and my sweet friend,
> To strew him o'er and o'er!
> *Florizel.*　　　　　What, like a corse?
> *Perdita.* No, like a bank for love to lie and play on;
> Not like a corse; or if—not to be buried,
> But quick, and in mine arms. Come, take your flow'rs.
> Methinks I play as I have seen them do
> In Whitsun pastorals. Sure this robe of mine
> Does change my disposition.

Her recovery is as exquisite as her impulse towards surrender: she comes back to herself by seeing her gesture as the expression of the occasion. She makes the festive clothes she wears mean its transforming power. Florizel has told her that

> These your unusual weeds to each part of you
> Do give a life—no shepherdess but Flora
> Peering in April's front!

Holiday disguising, her humility suggests, would be embarrassing but for the license of the sheep-shearing feast:

> But that our feasts
> In every mess have folly, and the feeders
> Digest it with a custom, I should blush
> To see you so attired.

The lovers in *A Midsummer Night's Dream* play "as in Whitsun pastorals," but they are entirely without this sort of consciousness of their folly. They are unreservedly *in* the passionate protestation which they rhyme at each other as they change partners:

> *Helena.* Lysander, if you live, good sir, awake.
> *Lysander.* And run through fire I will for thy sweet sake
> Transparent Helena!

The result of this lack of consciousness is that they are often rather dull and undignified, since however energetically they elaborate conceits, there is usually no qualifying irony, nothing withheld. And only accidental differences can be exhibited, Helena tall, Hermia short. Although the men think that "reason says" now Hermia, now Helena, is "the worthier maid," personalities have nothing to do with the case: it is the flowers that bloom in the spring. The life in the lovers' parts is not to be caught in individual speeches, but by regarding the whole movement of the farce, which swings and spins each in turn through a common pattern, an evolution that seems to have an impersonal power of its own. The lovers' evolutions are like a dance, but they have a headlong and helpless quality that depends on their not being *intended* as dance. The farce is funniest and most meaningful, in the climactic scene where the lovers are most unwilling, where they try their hardest to use personality to break free, and still are willy-nilly swept along to end in pitch darkness, trying to fight. When both men have arrived at wooing Helena, she assumes it must be voluntary mockery, a "false sport" fashioned "in spite." She appeals to Hermia on the basis of their relation as particular individuals, their "sister's vows." But Hermia is at sea, too; names no longer work: "Am I not Hermia? Are not you Lysander?" So in the end Hermia too, though she has held off, is swept into the whirl, attacking Helena as a thief of love. She grasps at straws to explain what has happened by something manageably related to their individual identities:

> *Helena.* Fie, fie! You counterfeit, you puppet you.
> *Hermia.* Puppet? Why so! Ay, that way goes the game.
> Now I perceive that she hath made compare
> Between our statures; she hath urg'd her height . . .
> How low am I, thou painted maypole? Speak!

In exhibiting a drastic helplessness of will and mind, this farce conveys a sense of people being tossed about by a force which puts them beside themselves to take them beyond themselves. The change that happens is presented simply, with little suggestion that it involves a growth in insight—Demetrius is not led to realize something false in his diverted affection for Hermia. But one psychological change, fundamental in growing up, is presented. Helena tries at first to move Hermia by an appeal to "schooldays friendship, childhood innocence," described at length in lovely, generous lines:

> So we grew together,
> Like to a double cherry, seeming parted,
> But yet an union in partition—
> Two lovely berries molded on one stem . . .
> And will you rent our ancient love asunder
> To join with men in scorning your poor friend?

"To join with men" has a plaintive girlishness about it. But before the scramble is over, the two girls have broken the double-cherry bond, to fight each without reserve for her man. So they move from the loyalties of one stage of life to those of another. When it has happened, when they wake up, the changes in affections seem mysterious. So Demetrius says

But, my good lord, I wot not by what power

> (But by some power it is) my love to Hermia,
> Melted as the snow, seems to me now
> As the remembrance of an idle gaud
> Which in my childhood I did dote upon . . .

The comedy's irony about love's motives and choices expresses love's power not as an attribute of special personality but as an impersonal force beyond the persons concerned. The tragedies of love, by isolating Romeo and Juliet, Antony and Cleopatra, enlist our concern for love as it enters into unique destinies, and convey its subjective immensity in individual experience. The festive comedies, in presenting love's effect on a group, convey a different sense of its power, less intense but also less precarious.

In *Love's Labour's Lost* it was one of the lovers, Berowne, who was aware, in the midst of folly's game, that it was folly and a game; such consciousness, in *A Midsummer Night's Dream*, is lodged outside the lovers, in Puck. It is he who knows "which way goes the game," as poor Hermia only thought she did. As a jester, and as Robin Goodfellow, games and practical jokes are his great delight: his lines express for the audience the mastery that comes from seeing folly as a pattern:

> Then will two at once woo one.
> That must needs be sport alone.

Like Berowne, he counts up the sacks as they come to Cupid's mill:

> Yet but three? Come one more.
> Two of both kinds makes up four.
> Here she comes, curst and sad.
> Cupid is a knavish lad
> Thus to make poor females mad.

Females, ordinarily a graceless word, works nicely here because it includes *every* girl. The same effect is got by using the names Jack and Jill, *any* boy and *any* girl:

> And the country proverb known,
> That every man should take his own,
> In your waking shall be shown:
> Jack shall have Jill;
> Nought shall go ill:
> The man shall have his mare again and all shall be well.

The trailing off into rollicking doggerel is exactly right to convey a country-proverb confidence in common humanity and in what humanity have in common. A festive confidence that things will ultimately go right supports the perfect gaiety and detachment with which Puck relishes the preposterous course they take:

> Shall we their fond pageant see?
> Lord, what fools these mortals be!

The pageant is "fond" because the mortals do not realize they are in it, nor that it is sure to come out right, since nature will have its way.

Bringing in Summer to the Bridal

Spenser's *Epithalamion*, written at about the same time as *A Midsummer Night's Dream*, about 1595, is very like Shakespeare's play in the way it uses a complex literary heritage to express native English customs. In the course of fetching the bride to church and home again, Spenser makes the marriage a fulfillment of the whole countryside and community:

> So goodly all agree with sweet consent,
> To this dayes merriment.

A gathering in, like that of the May game, is part of this confluence. The church of course is decked with garlands, and the bride, "being crowned with a girland greene," seems "lyke some mayden Queene." It is Midsummer. The pervasive feeling for the kinship of men and nature is what rings in the refrain:

> That all the woods them answer and their echo
> ring.

Shakespeare, in developing a Maygame action at length to express the will in nature that is consummated in marriage, brings out underlying magical meanings of the ritual while keeping always a sense of what it is humanly, as an experience. The way nature is felt is shaped by the things that are done in encountering it. The woods are a region of passionate excitement where, as Berowne said, love "adds a precious seeing to the eye." This precious seeing was talked about but never realized in *Love's Labour's Lost*; instead we got wit. But now it is realized; we get poetry. Poetry conveys the experience of amorous tendency diffused in nature; and poetry, dance, gesture, dramatic fiction, combine to create, in the fairies, creatures who employ the passionate mind's elated sense of its own omnipotence. The woods are established as a region of metamorphosis, where in liquid moonlight or glimmering starlight, things can change, merge and melt into each other. Metamorphosis expresses both what love sees and what it seeks to do.

The opening scene, like an overture, announces this theme of dissolving, in unobtrusive but persuasive imagery. Hippolyta says that the four days until the wedding will "quickly *steep* themselves in night" and the nights "quickly *dream* away the time"—night will dissolve day in dream. Then an imagery of wax develops as Egeus complains that Lysander has bewitched his daughter Hermia, "stol'n the *impression* of her fantasy." Theseus backs up Egeus by telling Hermia that

> To you your father should be as a god;
> One that compos'd your beauties; yea, and one
> To whom you are but as a form in wax,
> By him imprinted, and within his power
> To leave the figure, or disfigure it.

The supposedly mortal threat is incongruously communicated in lines that relish the joy of composing beauties and suggests a god-like, almost inhuman freedom to do as one pleases in such creation. The metaphor of sealing as procreation is picked up again when Theseus requires Hermia to decide "by the next new moon, / The sealing day betwixt my love and me." The consummation in prospect with marriage is envisaged as a melting into a new form and a new meaning Helena says to Hermia that she would give the world "to be to you translated," and in another image describes meaning

hat melt from love's transforming
power:

> ere Demetrius look'd on Hermia's eyes,
> He hail'd down oaths that he was only mine;
> And when this hail some heat from Hermia
>   felt,
> So he dissolv'd, and show'rs of oaths did melt.

The most general statement, and one
that perfectly fits what we are to see in
the wood when Titania meets Bottom, is

> Things base and vile, holding no quantity,
> Love can transpose to form and dignity.

"The glimmering . night" promotes
transpositions by an effect not simply of
light, but also of a half-liquid medium in
or through which things are seen:

> Tomorrow night, when Phoebe doth behold
> Her silver visage in the wat'ry glass,
> Decking with liquid pearl the bladed grass,
> (A time that lovers' flights doth still
>   conceal) . . .

The liquid imagery conveys an experience of the skin, as well as the eye's
confusion by refraction. The moon "looks
with a wat'ry eye" and "washes all the
air"; its sheen, becoming liquid pearl as
it mingles with dew, seems to get onto
the eyeballs of the lovers, altering them
to reshape what they see, like the juice
of the flower with which they are
"streaked" by Oberon and Puck. The
climax of unreason comes when Puck
overcasts the night to make it "black as
Acheron"; the lovers now experience
only sound and touch, running blind over
uneven ground, through bog and brake,
"bedabbled with the dew and torn with
briers." There is nothing more they can
do until the return of light permits a return of control: light is anticipated as
"comforts from the East," "the Morning's love." The sun announces its coming in a triumph of red and gold over
salt green, an entire change of key from
the moon's "silver visage in her wat'ry
glass":

> the eastern gate, all fiery red,
> Opening on Neptune, with fair blessed beams
> Turns into yellow gold his salt green streams.

Finally Theseus comes with his hounds
and his horns in the morning, and the
lovers are startled awake. They find as
they come to themselves that

> These things seem small and undistinguishable,
> Like far-off mountains turned into clouds.

The teeming metamorphoses which we
encounter are placed, in this way, in a
medium and in a moment where the
perceived structure of the outer world
breaks down, where the body and its environment interpenetrate in unaccus-
tomed ways, so that the seeming separate-
ness and stability of identity is lost.

The action of metaphor is itself a process of transposing, a kind of metamorphosis. There is less direct description of
external nature *in* the play than one
would suppose: much of the effect of
being in nature comes from imagery
which endows it with anthropomorphic
love, hanging a wanton pearl in every
cowslip's ear. Titania laments that

>   the green corn
> Hath rotted ere his youth attain'd a beard;

while

>   Hoary-headed frosts
> Fall in the fresh lap of the crimson rose . . .

By a complementary movement of imagination, human love is treated in terms
of growing things. Theseus warns Hermia
against becoming a nun, because

>   earthlier happy is the rose distill'd
> Than that which, withering on the virgin
>   thorn
> Grows, lives and dies in single blessedness.

Titania, embracing Bottom, describes
herself in terms that fit her surroundings
and uses the association of ivy with
women of songs traditional at Christmas:

> So doth the woodbine the sweet honeysuckle
> Gently entwist; the female ivy so
> Enrings the barky fingers of the elm.

One could go on and on in instancing

metamorphic metaphors. But one of the most beautiful bravura speeches can serve as an epitome of the metamorphic action in the play, Titania's astonishing answer when Oberon asks for the change-ling boy:

> Set your heart at rest.
> The fairyland buys not the child of me.
> His mother was a vot'ress of my order;
> And in the spiced Indian air, by night,
> Full often hath she gossip'd by my side,
> And sat with me on Neptune's yellow sands,
> Marking th'embarked traders on the flood;
> When we have laugh'd to see the sails
>   conceive
> And grow big-bellied with the wanton wind;
> Which she, with pretty and with swimming
>   gait
> Following (her womb then rich with my
>   young squire)
> Would imitate, and sail upon the land
> To fetch me trifles, and return again,
> As from a voyage, rich with merchandise.
> But she, being mortal, of that boy did die,
> And for her sake do I rear up her boy;
> And for her sake I will not part from him.

The memory of a moment seemingly so remote expresses with plastic felicity the present moment when Titania speaks and we watch. It suits Titania's immediate mood, for it is a glimpse of women who gossip alone, apart from men and feeling now no need of them, rejoicing in their own special part of life's power. At such moments, the child, not the lover, is their object—as this young squire is still the object for Titania, who "crowns him with flowers, and makes him all her joy." The passage conveys a wanton joy in achieved sexuality, in fertility; and a gay acceptance of the waxing of the body (like joy in the varying moon). At leisure in the spiced night air, when the proximate senses of touch and smell are most alive, this joy finds sport in projecting images of love and growth where they are not. The mother, having laughed to see the ship a woman with child, imitates it so as to go the other way about and herself become a ship. She fetches trifles, but she is also actually "rich with merchandise," for her womb is "rich with my young squire." The secure quality of the play's pleasure is conveyed by hav-

ing the ships out on the flood while sh᎑ sails, safely, upon the *land*, with a prett᎑ and swimming gait that is an overflowin᎑ of the security of make-believe. The nex᎑ line brings a poignant glance out beyon᎑ this gamesome world:

> But she, being mortal, of that boy did die.

It is when the flower magic lead᎑ Titania to find a new object that sh᎑ gives up the child (who goes now fror᎑ her bower to the man's world of Ober᎑ on). So here is another sort of chang᎑ of heart that contributes to the expressio᎑ of what is consummated in marriage᎑ this one a part of the rhythm of adul᎑ life, as opposed to the change in th᎑ young lovers that goes with growing up᎑ Once Titania has made this transition᎑ their ritual marriage is renewed:

> Now thou and I are new in amity,
> And will to-morrow midnight solemnly
> Dance in Duke Theseus' house triumphant᎑
> And bless it to all fair prosperity.

The final dancing blessing of th᎑ fairies, "Through the house with glim᎑ mering light," after the lovers are abed᎑ has been given meaning by the symboli᎑ action we have been describing: th᎑ fairies have been made into tutelar᎑ spirits of fertility, so that they can prom᎑ ise that

> the blots of Nature's hand
> Shall not in their issue stand.

Puck's broom is his property as ᎑ housemaid's sprite, "to sweep the dus᎑ behind the door"; also it permits him t᎑ make "room," in the manner of the pre᎑ senter of a holiday mummers' group᎑ And with the dust, out go evil spirits᎑ Puck refers to "evil sprites" let forth b᎑ graves, developing a momentary sense o᎑ midnight terrors, of spirits that walk b᎑ night; then he promises that no mous᎑ shall disturb "this hallowed house." Th᎑ exorcism of evil powers complements th᎑ invocation of good. With their "field dev᎑ consecrate," the fairies enact a lustration᎑ Fertilizing and beneficent virtues are i᎑

stival custom persistently attributed to
ew gathered on May mornings. Shake-
peare's handling of nature has infused
ew in this play with the vital spirit of
oist and verdant woods. The dew is
consecrate" in this sense. But the re-
gious associations inevitably attaching to
he word suggest also the sanctification
f love by marriage. It was customary for
he clergy, at least in important mar-
ages, to bless the bed and bridal couple
ith holy water. The benediction in-
uded exorcism, in the Manual for the
se of Salisbury a prayer to protect them
om what Spenser called "evill sprights"
nd "things that be not" (*ab omnibus
ntasmaticis demonum illusionibus*).
his custom may itself be an ecclesiasti-
al adaptation of a more primitive bridal
stration, a water charm of which dew-
athering on May Day is one variant.
uch a play as *A Midsummer Night's
ream* is possible because the May and
ummer Spirit, despite its pagan af-
nities, is not conceived as necessarily in
pposition to the wholeness of traditional
hristian life.

agic as Imagination: The Ironic Wit

In promoting the mastery of passion by
xpression, dramatic art can provide a
vilized equivalent for exorcism. The
corcism represented as magically ac-
omplished at the conclusion of the
omedy is accomplished, in another sense,
y the whole dramatic action, as it keeps
oving through release to clarification.
y embodying in the fairies the mind's
roclivity to court its own omnipotence,
hakespeare draws this tendency, this
pirit," out into the open. They have
he meaning they do only because we see
hem in the midst of the metamorphic
gion we have just considered—removed
om this particular wood, most of their
gnificance evaporates, as for example in
ymphidia and other pretty floral min-
tures. One might summarize their role
y saying that they represent the power
f imagination. But to say what they *are*
to short-circuit the life of them and the
umor. They present themselves moment
y moment as actual persons; the humor

keeps *recognizing* that the person is a
personification, that the magic is imagination.

The sceptical side of the play has been
badly neglected because romantic taste,
which first made it popular, wanted to
believe in fairies. Romantic criticism
usually praised *A Midsummer Night's
Dream* on the assumption that its spell
should be complete, and that the absolute
persuasiveness of the poetry should be
taken as the measure of its success. The
result is the nineteenth-century's characteristic misreading, which regards "the
play" as a series of real supernatural
events, with a real ass's head and real
fairies, and, by excluding all awareness
that "the play" is a play, misses its most
important humor.

The extravagant subject matter actually led the dramatist to rely more
heavily than elsewhere on a flexible attitude toward representation. The circumstances of the original production
made this all the more inevitable: Puck
stood in a hall familiar to the audience.
In holiday shows, it was customary to
make game with the difference between
art and life by witty transitions back and
forth between them. The aim was not to
make the auditors "forget they are in a
theater," but to extend reality into fiction. The general Renaissance tendency
frankly to accept and relish the artificiality of art, and the vogue of formal
rhetoric and "conceited" love poetry, also
made for sophistication about the artistic
process. Shakespeare's auditors had not
been conditioned by a century and a half
of effort to achieve sincerity by denying
art. Coleridge has a remark about the
advantages that Shakespeare enjoyed as
a dramatist which is particularly illuminating in connection with this feeling
for art in *A Midsummer Night's Dream*.
He observes that "the circumstances of
acting were altogether different from
ours; it was more of recitation," with the
result that "the idea of the poet was
always present." The nearly bare stage
worked as Proust observed that the bare
walls of an art gallery work, to isolate
"the essential thing, the act of mind."
It is "the act of mind" and "the idea

of the poet" which are brought into focus when, at the beginning of the relaxed fifth act, Theseus comments on what the lovers have reported of their night in the woods. I shall quote the passage in full, despite its familiarity, to consider the complex attitude it conveys:

The lunatic, the lover, and the poet
Are of imagination all compact.
One sees more devils than vast hell can hold:
That is the madman. The lover, all as frantic,
Sees Helen's beauty in a brow of Egypt.
The poet's eye, in a fine frenzy rolling,
Doth glance from heaven to earth, from earth to heaven;
And as imagination bodies forth
The forms of things unknown, the poet's pen
Turns them to shapes, and gives to airy nothing
A local habitation and a name.
Such tricks hath strong imagination
That, if it would but apprehend some joy,
It comprehends some bringer of that joy;
Or in the night, imagining some fear,
How easy is a bush suppos'd a bear!

The description of the power of poetic creation is so beautiful that these lines are generally taken out of context and instanced simply as glorification of the poet. But the praise of the poet is qualified in conformity with the tone Theseus adopts towards the lover and the madman. In his comment there is wonder, wonderfully expressed, at the power of the mind to create from airy nothing; but also recognition that the creation may be founded, after all, merely on airy nothing. Neither awareness cancels out the other. A sense of the plausible life and energy of fancy goes with the knowledge that often its productions are more strange than true.

Scepticism is explicitly crystallized out in the *détente* of Theseus' speech; but scepticism is in solution throughout the play. There is a delicate humor about the unreality of the fairies even while they are walking about in a local habitation with proper names. The usual production, even now, rides rough-shod over this humor by trying to act the fairies in a "vivid" way that will compel belief—

with much fluttery expressiveness that has led many to conclude that the fairies are naïve and silly. Quite the contrary— the fairy business is exceedingly sophisticated. The literal and figurative aspects of what is presented are both deliberately kept open to view. The effect is well described by Hermia's remark when she looks back at her dream:

Methinks I see these things with parted eye
When everything seems double.

As we watch the dream, the doubleness is made explicit to keep us aware that strong imagination is at work:

And I serve the Fairy Queen,
To dew her orbs upon the green.
The cowslips tall her pensioners be;
In their gold coats spots you see.
Those be rubies, fairy favours;
In those freckles live their savours.

These conceits, half botany, half personification, are explicit about remaking nature's economy after the pattern of man's: "spots you see. / Those be rubies . . . " The same conscious double vision appears when Puck introduces himself:

sometime lurk I in a gossip's bowl
In very likeness of a roasted crab . . .
The wisest aunt, telling the saddest tale,
Sometime for three-foot stool mistaketh me;

The plain implication of the lines, though Puck speaks them, is that Puck does not really exist—that he is a figment of naïve imagination, projected to motivate the little accidents of household life.

This scepticism goes with social remoteness from the folk whose superstitions the poet is here enjoying. Puck's description has the aloof detachment of genre painting, where the grotesqueries of the subject are seen across lines of class difference. As a matter of fact there is much less popular lore in these fairies than is generally assumed in talking about them. The fairies do, it is true, show all the main characteristics of fairies in popular belief: they appear in the forest, at midnight, and leave at sunrise they take children, dance in ringlets. But as I have remarked already, their whole quality is drastically different from that of the fairies "of the villagery," creatures who, as Dr. Minor White Latham has shown, were dangerous to meddle with, large enough to harm, often malicious, sometimes the consorts of witches.[2] One can speak of Shakespeare's having changed the fairies of popular superstition, as Miss Latham does. Or one can look at what he did in relation to the traditions of holiday and pageantry and see his creatures as pageant nymphs and holiday celebrants, colored by touches from popular superstition, but shaped primarily by a very different provenance. Most of the detailed popular lore concerns Puck, not properly a fairy at all; even he is several parts Cupid and several parts mischievous stage page (a cousin of Moth in *Love's Labour's Lost* and no doubt played by the same small, agile boy). And Puck is only *using* the credulity of the folk as a jester, to amuse a king.

Titania and Oberon and their trains are very different creatures from the *gemütlich* fairies of middleclass folklore enthusiasm in the nineteenth century. The spectrum of Shakespeare's imagination includes some of the warm domestic tones which the later century cherished. But the whole attitude of self-abnegating humility before the mystery of folk imagination is wrong for interpreting this play. His fairies are creatures of pastoral, varied by adapting folk superstitions so as to make a new sort of arcadia. Though they are not shepherds, they lead a life similarly occupied with the pleasures of song and dance and, for king and queen, the vexations and pleasures of love. They have not the pastoral "labours" of tending flocks, but equivalent duties are suggested in the tending of nature's fragile

beauties, killing "cankers in the muskrose buds." They have a freedom like that of shepherds in arcadias, but raised to a higher power: they are free not only of the limitations of place and purse but of space and time.

The settled content of regular pastoral is possible because it is a "low" content, foregoing wealth and position; Shakespeare's fairies too can have their fine freedom because their sphere is limited. At times their tiny size limits them, though this is less important than is generally suggested by summary descriptions of Shakespeare's fairy race. The poet plays the game of diminution delightfully, but never with Titania and Oberon, only with their attendants, and not all the time with them. It seems quite possible that Peaseblossom, Cobweb, Moth, and Mustardseed were originally played by children of the family—their parts seem designed to be foolproof for little children: "Ready.—And I.—And I.—And I." Diminutiveness is *the* characteristic of the Queen Mab Mercutio describes in *Romeo and Juliet*, and it quickly became the hallmark of the progeny of literary fairies that followed; but it is only occasionally at issue in *A Midsummer Night's Dream*. More fundamental is their limited time. Oberon can boast that, by contrast with horrors who must wilfully exile themselves from light,

> we are spirits of another sort.
> I with the Morning's love have oft made sport. . . .

But for all his pride, full daylight is beyond him: "But notwithstanding, haste; . . . We must effect this business yet ere day." The enjoyment of any sort of pastoral depends on an implicit recognition that it presents a hypothetical case as if it were actual. Puck's lines about the way the fairies run

> From the presence of the sun,
> Following darkness like a dream,

summarize the relation between their special time and their limited sort of existence.

---

[2] *The Elizabethan Fairies, The Fairies of Folklore and the Fairies of Shakespeare* (New York, 1930), Ch. V. and passim. Professor Latham's excellent study points out in detail how Shakespeare, in keeping such features of popular superstition as, say, the taking of changelings, entirely alters the emphasis, so as to make the fairies either harmless or benign, as Titania is benign in rearing up the child of her dead vot'ress "for her sake." Dr. Latham emphasizes that, in addition to being malicious, the fairies of common English belief were large enough to be menacing.

This explicit summary comes at the close, when the whole machinery is being distanced to end with "If we shadows have offended. . . ." But the consciousness and humor which I am concerned to underline are present throughout the presentation of the fairies. It has been easy for production and criticism to ignore, just because usually amusement is not precipitated out in laughter but remains in solution with wonder and delight. In the scene of the quarrel between Titania and Oberon, the fragility of the conceits corresponds finely to the half-reality of their world and specialness of their values. The factitiousness of the causes Titania lays out for the weather is gently mocked by the repeated *therefore's*: "Therefore the winds . . . Therefore the moon . . . The ox hath therefore. . . ." Her account makes it explicit that she and Oberon are tutelary gods of fertility, but with an implicit recognition like Sidney's about Cupid's dart—"an image . . . which for ourselves we carve." And her emphasis makes the wheat blight a disaster felt most keenly not for men who go hungry but for the green wheat itself, because it never achieves manhood. Her concern for the holiday aspect of nature is presented in lines which are poised between sympathy and amusement:

The human mortals want their winter cheer;
No night is now with hymn or carol blest . . .
The seasons alter. Hoary-headed frosts
Fall in the fresh lap of the crimson rose;
And on old Hiems' thin and icy crown
An odorous chaplet of sweet summer buds
Is, as in mockery, set.

Part of the delight of this poetry is that we can enjoy without agitation imaginative action of the highest order. It is like gazing in a crystal: what you see is clear and vivid, but on the other side of the glass. Almost unnoticed, the lines have a positive effect through the amorous suggestion implicit in the imagery, even while letting it be manifest that those concerned are only personifications of flowers and a pageant figure wearing the livery of the wrong season. Titania can speak of "the human mortals" as very far off indeed; the phrase crystallizes what has been achieved in imaginative distance and freedom. But Titania is as far off from us as we are from her.

The effect of wit which in such passages goes along with great imaginative power is abetted by the absence of any compelling interest in passion or plot. Producers utterly ruin the scene when they have the fairy couple mouth their lines at each other as expressively as possible. Titania, after all, leaves before that point is reached: "Fairies, away! / We shall chide downright if I longer stay." At moments of dramatic intensity, the most violent distortion can go unnoticed; what the poet is doing is ignored in responding to what his people are doing. But here a great part of the point is that we *should* notice the distortion, the action of the poet, the wit. Plot tension launches flights of witty poetry which use it up, so to speak, just as the tensions in broad comedy are discharged in laughter. Rhetorical schematizations, or patterns of rhyme, are often used in *A Midsummer Night's Dream* to mark off the units of such verse. But blank verse paragraphs are also constructed so as to form autonomous bravura passages which reach a climax and come to rest while actor and audience catch their breath. Oberon's description of the mermaid and his tribute to Elizabeth are two such flights, each a rhythmical unit, the first punctuated by Puck's "I remember," the second by Oberon's change of tone at "Yet mark'd I where the bolt of Cupid fell." The formal and emotional isolation of the two passages is calculated to make the audience respond with wonder to the effortless reach of imagination which brings the stars madly shooting from their spheres. In a tribute to Elizabeth, the prominence of "the idea of the poet" in the poetry obviously was all to the good. By Oberon's remark to Puck, "that very time I saw, but thou couldst not," courtly Shakespeare contrived to place the mythology he was creating about Elizabeth on a level appropriately more sublime and occult than that about the mermaid.

Moonlight and Moonshine: The Ironic Burlesque

The consciousness of the creative or poetic act itself, which pervades the main action, explains the subject-matter of the burlesque accompaniment provided by the clowns. If Shakespeare were chiefly concerned with the nature of love, the clowns would be in love, after their fashion. But instead, they are putting on play. That some commoners should honor the wedding, in their own way, along with the figures from pageantry, is of course in keeping with the purpose of gathering into a play the several sorts of entertainments usually presented separately. But an organic purpose is served too: the clowns provide a broad burlesque of the mimetic impulse to become something by acting it, the impulse which in the main action is fulfilled by imagination and understood by humor. Bottom feels he can be anything: "What is Pyramus, a lover, or a tryant? . . . An I may hide my face, let me play Thisby too . . . let me play the lion too." His soul would like to fly out into them all; but he is *not* stuck! In dealing with dramatic illusion, he and the other mechanicals are invincibly literal-minded, carrying to absurdity the tendency to treat the imaginary as though it were real. They exhibit just the all-or-nothing attitude towards fancy which would be fatal to the play as a whole.

When the clowns think that Bottom's transformation has deprived them of their chief actor, their lament seems pointedly allusive to Shakespeare's company and their play.

Snug. Masters, the Duke is coming from the temple, and there is two or three lords and ladies more married. If our sport had gone forward, we had all been made men.
Flute. O sweet bully Bottom! Thus hath he lost sixpence a day during his life. He could not have scaped sixpence a day. An the Duke had not given him sixpence a day for playing Pyramus, I'll be hanged! He would have deserved it. Sixpence a day in Pyramus, or nothing!

The repetition of "sixpence a day" seems loaded: if Bottom in Pyramus is worth sixpence, what is Kempe in Bottom worth? For Bottom is to Theseus as Kempe was to the nobleman for whom the play was first produced. The business about moonshine brings this out:

Quince. . . . But there is two hard things: that is, to bring the moonlight into a chamber; for, you know, Pyramus and Thisby meet by moonlight.
Snout. Doth the moon shine that night we play our play?
Bottom. A calendar, a calendar! Look in the almanac. Find out moonshine, find out moonshine!
Quince. Yes, it doth shine that night.
Bottom. Why, then may you leave a casement of the great chamber window, where we play, open, and the moon may shine in at the casement.
Quince. Ay; or else one must come in with a bush of thorns and a lantern, and say he comes to disfigure, or to present, the person of Moonshine.

Shakespeare, in *his* play, triumphantly accomplishes just this hard thing, "to bring the moonlight into a chamber." The moonshine, here and later, shows how aware Shakespeare was of what his plastic imagination was doing with moonlight. Since the great chamber Bottom speaks of was, at the initial private performance, the very chamber in which the Chamberlain's men were playing, "Pyramus and Thisby" adorns Theseus' fictitious wedding just as *A Midsummer Night's Dream* adorns the real wedding. Bottom's proposal to open a casement reduces the desire for realism to the absurdity of producing the genuine article. Translated out of irony, it suggests, that "if you want real moonlight, you put yourself in Bottom's class." It is amusing how later producers have labored with ever greater technical resources to achieve Bottom's ideal. Hollywood's Max Reinhardt version omitted most of the poetry to make room for cellophane-spangled fairies standing in rows on ninety-foot moonbeams.

The difference between art and life is also what the clowns forget in their parlous fear lest "the ladies be afeared of the lion" and the killing. Bottom's solution is to tell the ladies in plain language that fiction is not fact:

Write me a prologue; and let the prologue seem to say, we will do no harm with our swords, and that Pyramus is not kill'd indeed; and for the more better assurance, tell them that I Pyramus am not Pyramus, but Bottom the weaver. This will put them out of fear.

Now this expresses Bottom's vanity, too. But producers and actors, bent on showing "character," can lose the structural, ironic point if they let the lines get lost in Bottom's strutting. What the clowns forget, having "never labour'd in their minds till now," is that a killing or a lion in a play, however plausibly presented, is a mental event. Because, like children, they do not discriminate between imaginary and real events, they are literal about fiction. But they are not *un*imaginative: on the contrary they embody the stage of mental development before the discipline of facts has curbed the tendency to equate what is "in" the mind with what is "outside" it. They apply to drama the same sort of mentality that supports supersitition—it is in keeping that the frightening sort of folk beliefs about changelings are for them an accepted part of life: "Out of doubt he is transported." Because this uncritical imaginativeness is the protoplasm from which all art develops, the clowns are as delightful and stimulating as they are ridiculous. Even while we are laughing at them, we recover sympathetically the power of fantasy enjoyed by children, who, like Bottom, can be anything, a train, an Indian or a lion.

In the performance of *Pyramus and Thisby*, Shakespeare captures the naïveté of folk dramatics and makes it serve his controlling purpose as a final variant of imaginative aberration. The story from Ovid, appropriate for a burlesque in an Ovidian play, is scarcely the kind of thing the simple people would have presented in life; but their method and spirit in putting it on, and the spirit in which the noble company take it, are not unlike that of the bride-ale show at Kenilworth. "If we imagine no worse of them than they of themselves," Theseus observes of the Athenian artisans, "they may pass for

excellent men." The comedy of the piece centers not so much on what is acted in it as in the continual failure to translate actor into character. Shakespeare's skill is devoted to keeping both the player and their would-be play before us at the same time, so that we watch, not Pyramus alone, nor Bottom alone, but Bottom "in Pyramus," the fact of the one doing violence to the fiction of the other.

Almost half of *Pyramus and Thisby* is taken up with prologues of the sort one gets in the mummers' plays:

> I am king of England,
> As you may plainly see. [3]

Such prologues suit Shakespeare's purpose, because they present the performer openly climbing in the window of aesthetic illusion, where he can get stuck midway:

In this same enterlude it doth befall
That I, one Snout by name, present a wall . .
This loam, this roughcast, and this stone doth show
That I am that same wall. The truth is so.

"The truth is so," by warranting that fiction is fact, asks for a laugh, as does the Prologue's "At the which let no man wonder," or Moon's

Myself the man i' the moon *do seem to be.*

The incarnation of Wall is a particularly "happy-unhappy" inspiration, because the more Wall does, the less he is a wall and the more he is Snout.

There is a great deal of incidental amusement in the parody and burlesque with which *Pyramus and Thisby* is loaded. It burlesques the substance of the death scene in *Romeo and Juliet* in a style which combines ineptitudes from Golding's translation of Ovid with locutions from the crudest doggerel drama. What is most remarkable about it, however, is the way it fits hilarious fun into the whole comedy's development of attitude and understanding. After the exigent poise of the humorous fantasy, laughs now explode one after another and yet they are still on the subject, even though now we are romping reassuringly

[3] J. M. Manly, *Specimens of Pre-Shakespearean Drama* (Boston, 1897), I, 293, from *The Lutterworth Christmas Play.*

through easy-to-make distinctions. The-seus can say blandly

The best in this kind are but shadows; and the worst are no worse, if imagination amend them.

Although we need not agree (Hippolyta says, "It must be your imagination then, and not theirs."), Theseus expresses part of our response—a growing detachment towards imagination, moving towards the distance from the dream expressed in Puck's epilogue.

The meeting in the woods of Bottom and Titania is the climax of the poly-phonic interplay; it comes in the middle of the dream, when the humor has the most work to do. Bottom in the ass's head provides a literal metamorphosis, and in the process brings in the element of grotesque fantasy, a comic version of an animal-headed dancer or of the sort of figure Shakespeare used in Herne the Hunter, "with great ragged horns," at the oak in *The Merry Wives of Windsor*. At the same time he is the theatrical company's clown "thrust in by head and shoulder to play a part in majestical matters" and remaining up-roariously literal and antipoetic as he does so. Titania and he are fancy against fact, not beauty and the beast. She makes all the advances while he remains very respectful, desiring nothing bestial but "a peck of provender." Clownish oblivion to languishing beauty is sure-fire comedy on any vaudeville stage. Here it is elaborated in such a way that when Titania is frus-trated, so is the transforming power of poetry:

Titania. I pray thee, gentle mortal, sing again.
Mine ear is much enamoured of thy note;
So is mine eye enthralled to thy shape;
And thy fair virtue's force (perforce) doth move me,
On the first view, to say, to swear, I love thee.
Bottom. Methinks, mistress, you should have little reason for that. And yet, to say the truth, reason and love keep little com-pany together now-a-days. The more the pity that some honest neighbours will not

make them friends. Nay, I can gleek, upon occasion.
Titania. Thou art as wise as thou art beautiful.
Bottom. Not so, neither . . .

From a vantage below romance, the clown makes the same point as sceptical Theseus, that reason and love do not go together. Titania tells him that she

. . . will purge thy mortal grossness so
That thou shalt like an airy spirit go.

But even her magic cannot "transpose" Bottom.

The "low" or "realistic" effect which he produces when juxtaposed with her is much less a matter of accurate imitation of common life than one assumes at first glance. Of course the homely touches are telling—forms of address like "Methinks, mistress" or words like *gleek* suggest a social world remote from the elegant queen's. But the realistic effect does not depend on Bottom's being like real weav-ers, but on the *détente* of imaginative tension, on a downward movement which counters imaginative lift. This antipoetic action involves, like the poetic, a high degree of abstraction from real life, in-cluding the control of rhythm which can establish a blank verse movement in as little as a single line, "Thou art as wise as thou art beautiful," and so be able to break the ardent progression of the queen's speech with "Not so, neither." When Bottom encounters the fairy at-tendants, he reduces the fiction of their existence to fact:

Bottom. I cry your worship's mercy, heartily. I beseech your worship's name.
Cobweb. Cobweb.
Bottom. I shall desire you of more acquaint-ance, good Master Cobweb. If I cut my finger, I shall make bold with you.

Cobwebs served the Elizabethans for ad-hesive plaster, so that when Bottom proposes to "make bold with" Cobweb, he treats him as a *thing*, undoing the per-sonification on which the little fellow's life depends. To take hold of Cobweb in this way is of course a witty thing to do, when one thinks about it. But since the wit is in the service of a literal tendency, we can take it as the expression of a "hempen homespun." There is usually a similar incongruity between the "stupidity" of a clown and the imagination and wit required to express such stupidity. Bottom's charming combination of ignorant exuberance and oblivious imaginativeness make him the most humanly credible and appealing personality Shakespeare had yet created from the incongruous qualities required for the clown's role. The only trouble with the part, in practice, is that performers become so preoccupied with bringing out the weaver's vanity as an actor that they lose track of what the role is expressing as part of the larger imaginative design.

For there is an impersonal, imaginative interaction between the clowning and the rest of the play which makes the clowns mean more than they themselves know and more than they are as personalities. Bottom serves to represent, in so aware a play, the limits of awareness, limits as limitations—and also, at moments, limits as form and so strength.

> *Bottom.* Where are these lads? Where are these hearts?
> *Quince.* Bottom! O most courageous day! O most happy hour!
> *Bottom.* Masters, I am to discourse wonders; but ask me not what. For if I tell you, I am no true Athenian. I will tell you everything, right as it fell out.
> *Quince.* Let us hear, sweet Bottom.
> *Bottom.* Not a word of me. All that I will tell you is, that the Duke hath dined. Get your apparel together, good strings to your beards . . .

It is ludicrous for Bottom to be so utterly unable to cope with the "wonders," especially where he is shown boggling in astonishment as he wordlessly remembers them: "I have had a most rare vision. I have had a dream past the wit of man to say what dream it was." But there is something splendid, too, in the way he exuberantly rejoins "these lads" and takes up his particular, positive, life as a "true Athenian." Metamorphosis cannot faze him for long. His imperviousness, indeed, is what is most delightful about

him with Titania: he remains so completely himself, even in her arms, and despite the outward change of his head and ears; his confident, self-satisfied tone is a triumph of consistency, persistence, existence.

The Sense of Reality

The value of humor, and the finest pleasure in it, depends on the seriousness of what it makes into fun. It is easy to be gay by taking a trivial theme, or by trivializing an important theme. The greatness of comedy, as of every other art form, must rest, to use Henry James' phrase, on the amount of "felt life" with which it deals in its proper fashion. After examining the structure and artifice of *A Midsummer Night's Dream*, we can now ask how much reality it masters by its mirth. This comedy is the first that is completely, triumphantly successful; but it has the limitations, as well as the strength, of a youthful play.

The role of imagination in experience is a major preoccupation in other plays of the same period. Dreams are several times presented as oracles of irrational powers shaping life, and inspire dread and awe. In the death scene of Clarence, in *Richard III*, the poet had presented the experience of oppression and helplessness on waking from the grip of nightmare. *A Midsummer Night's Dream* presents a resolution of the dream forces which so often augur conflict. To indulge dreamlike irrationality with impunity is, as Freud pointed out, one of the basic satisfactions of wit. The action of *A Midsummer Night's Dream* shows the same pattern on a large scale: it suggests the compulsion of dream, and then reconciles night's motives with the day's as the lovers conclude, "Why then, we are awake":

> *Demetrius.* These things seem small and undistinguishable,
> Like far-off mountains turned into clouds . . .
> *Helena.* And I have found Demetrius like a jewel,
> Mine own, and not mine own.
> *Demetrius.* Are you sure

That we are awake? It seems to me
That yet we sleep, we dream. Do not you think
The Duke was here, and bid us follow him?
Hermia. Yea, and my father.
Helena. And Hippolyta.
Lysander. And he did bid us follow to the temple.
Demetrius. Why then, we are awake.
Let's follow him,
And by the way let us recount our dreams.

The fun which Mercutio makes of dreams and fairies in *Romeo and Juliet* is an attempt to do in a single speech what the whole action does in *A Midsummer Night's Dream*. His excursion on Queen Mab is designed to laugh away Romeo's dream-born misgivings about their fatal visit to the Capulets. Romeo's dream, however, in spite of Mercutio, is not to be dismissed so easily as airy nothing:

. . . my mind misgives
Some consequence, yet hanging in the stars . . .

A Midsummer Night's Dream is a play in the spirit of Mercutio: the dreaming in it includes the knowledge "that dreamers often lie." The comedy and tragedy are companion pieces: the one moves away from sadness as the other moves away from mirth.

One can feel, indeed, that, as compared with Shakespeare's later works, mastery comes a little too easily, because the imaginary and the real are too easy to separate, in the comedy as well as in other plays of the period, notably *Titus Andronicus* and *Romeo and Juliet*. In *Richard II*, however, the simple shadow-substance antithesis becomes something more: the divine right of kings gives one sort of objective validity to Richard's imaginings—although his guardian angels are ineffective immediately, they are grounded in moral perception, and Bolingbroke eventually finds their avenging power. Later in Shakespeare's work, the imagination becomes in its own right a way of knowing "more things in heaven and earth" than cool reason ever comprehends. Contrasts between real and imaginary are included in and superseded by contrasts between appearance and reality, as these unfold at various levels of awareness. How different Shakespeare's sense of reality finally became is evident if we set the proud scepticism of Theseus beside the humble scepticism of Prospero. The presiding genius of Shakespeare's latest fantasy also turns from a pageant-like work of imagination to reflect on its relation to life. But for him life itself is like the insubstantial pageant, and *we,* not just the Titanias and Oberons, are such stuff as dreams are made on.

The greater profundity of the later work, however, should not blind us to the different virtues of the earlier. The confident assumption dominant in *A Midsummer Night's Dream,* that substance and shadow can be kept separate, determines the peculiarly unshadowed gaiety of the fun it makes with fancy. Its organization by polarities—everyday-holiday, town-grove, day-night, waking-dreaming—provides a remarkable resource for mastering passionate experience. By a curious paradox, the full dramatization of holiday affirmations permitted "that side" of experience to be boxed off by Theseus. If we take our stand shoulder to shoulder with Theseus, the play can be an agency for distinguishing what is merely "apprehended" from what is "comprehended." Shakespeare's method of structuring is as powerful, in its way, as Descartes' distinction between mind and body, the formidable engine by which the philosopher swept away "secondary qualities" so that mathematical mind might manipulate geometrical extension. If we do not in our age want to rest in Theseus' rationalistic position (any more than in Descartes'), it remains a great achievement to have got there, and wherever we are going in our sense of reality, we have come via that standing place.

Theseus, moreover, does not quite have the last word, even in this play: his position in only one stage in a dialectic. Hippolyta will not be reasoned out of her wonder, and answers her new Lord with

But all the story of the night told over,

And all their minds transfigur'd so together,
More witnesseth than fancy's images
And grows to something of great constancy;
But howsoever, strange and admirable.

Did it happen, or didn't it happen? The doubt is justified by what Shakespeare has shown us. We are not asked to think that fairies exist. But imagination, by

presenting these figments, has reached to something, a creative tendency and process. What is this process? Where is it? What shall we call it? It is what happens in the play. It is what happens in marriage. To name it requires many words, words in motion—the words of *A Midsummer Night's Dream.*

CHRISTOPHER CAUDWELL

(1907-1937)

Christopher St. John Sprigg, who published his serious work under the name of Caudwell, was a young upper-middle-class Englishman who became a Marxist and who died in battle in Spain as a member of the International Brigade. A prolific writer of popular fiction and of scientific treatises, Caudwell is best known as a literary critic for his *Illusion and Reality: A Study of the Sources of Poetry* (1937), a Marxist analysis of the development of English poetry as the result of social and economic forces. His other essays on literary and cultural subjects have been collected in *Studies in a Dying Culture* (1938) and *Further Studies in a Dying Culture* (1949).

English Poets
The Period of Primitive Accumulation (1937)

1

Capitalism requires two conditions for its existence—masses of capital and "free"—*i.e.* expropriated—wage labourers. Once the movement has started, capitalism generates its own conditions for further development. The sum of constant capital grows by accumulation and aggregates by amalgamation, and this amalgamation, by continually expropriating artisans and other petty bourgeoisie, produces the necessary supply of wage-labourers.

A period of primitive accumulation is therefore necessary before these conditions can be realised. This primitive ac-

cumulation must necessarily be violent and forcible, for the bourgeoisie, not yet a ruling class, has not yet created the political conditions for its own expansion: the State is not yet a bourgeois state.

In England during this period the bourgeoisie and that section of the nobility which had gone over to the bourgeoisie, seized the Church lands and treasure and created a horde of dispossessed vagrants by the enclosure of common lands, the closing of the monasteries, the extension of sheep-farming and the final extinction of the feudal lords with their retainers. The seizure of gold and silver from the New World also played an important part in providing a base for capitalism. This movement was possible because the monarchy, in its fight with the feudal nobil-

From *Illusion and Reality: A Study of the Sources of Poetry* (1937) by Christopher Caudwell, pp. 75-89. Reprinted by permission of the publisher, Macmillan and Co. Ltd.

ity, leant on the bourgeois class and in turn rewarded them for their support. The Tudor monarchs were autocrats in alliance with the bourgeoisie and bourgeoisified nobility.

In this period of primitive accumulation the conditions for the growth of the bourgeois class are created lawlessly. To every bourgeois it seems as if his instincts—his "freedom"—are intolerably restricted by laws, rights and restraints, and that beauty and life can only be obtained by the violent expansion of his desires.

Intemperate will, "bloody, bold and resolute", without norm or measure, is the spirit of this era of primitive accumulation. The absolute individual will overriding all other wills is therefore the principle of life for the Elizabethan age. Marlowe's Faust and Tamburlaine express this principle in its naïvest form.

This life principle reaches its highest embodiment in the Renaissance "prince". In Italy and England—at this time leaders in primitive accumulation—life reaches its most poignant issue in the absolute will of the prince—this figure of the prince expresses most clearly the bourgeois illusion, just as in real society the prince is the necessary means of realising the conditions for bourgeois expansion. To break the moulds of feudalism and wrench from them capital requires the strength and remorselessness of an absolute monarch. Any established bound or let to the divine right of his will would be wrong, for such bounds or lets, being established and traditional, could only be feudal, and would therefore hold back the development of the bourgeois class.

Elizabethan poetry in all its grandeur and insurgence is the voice of this princely will, the absolute bourgeois will whose very virtue consists in breaking all current conventions and realising itself. That is why all Shakespeare's heroes are princely; why kingliness is the ideal type of human behaviour at this time.

Marlowe, Chapman, Greene, but above all Shakespeare, born of bourgeois parents, exactly express the cyclonic force of the princely bourgeois will in

this era, in all its vigour and recklessness. Lear, Hamlet, Macbeth, Antony, Troilus, Othello, Romeo and Coriolanus, each in his different way knows no other obligation than to be the thing he is, to realise himself to the last drop, to give out in its purest and most exquisite form the aroma of self. The age of chivalry appears, not as it sees itself, but discredited and insulted, as the bourgeois class sees it, in the person of Hotspur, Falstaff and Armado, English cousins of Don Quixote.

Even the meanest creature, the empty, discredited, braggart Parolles, realises this unbounded self-realisation to be the law of his stage existence and in some sort the justification of his character:

> Simply to be the thing I am
> Shall make me live.

In this intemperate self-expression, by which they seem to expand and fill the whole world with their internal phantasmagoria, lies the significance of Shakespeare's heroes. That even death does not end their self-realisation, that they are most essentially themselves in death —Lear, Hamlet, Cleopatra and Macbeth—in this too is both the secret of their death and the solution of the tragedy.

The depth with which Shakespeare moved in the bourgeois illusion, the greatness of his grasp of human society, is shown by the fact that he is ultimately a tragedian. This unfettered realisation of human individualities involves for him the equally unfettered play of Necessity. The contradiction which is the driving force of capitalism finds its expression again and again in Shakespeare's tragedies. In *Macbeth* the hero's ambitions are realised—inverted. In *King Lear* the hero wrecks himself against the equally untempered expression of his daughters' will and also against Nature, whose necessity is expressed in a storm. The power of the storm symbolism lies in the fact that in a thunderstorm Nature seems to conduct herself, not as an inexorable machine but like a human being in an ungovernable passion. In *Othello* man's love, which realises the best in himself, yet by the free play of that realisation "kills the thing it loves". In *Hamlet* the problem of a conflict of unmeasured wills is posed in yet another form—here a man's will is divided against itself, and therefore even though nothing "external" can oppose or reflect it, it can yet struggle with itself and be wrecked. This "doubleness" of a single will is aptly symbolised by the poisoned swords and goblet in which the one aim is as it were two-faced, and secures opposite ends. In *Antony and Cleopatra* and in *Romeo and Juliet* the fulfilment of the simplest and most violent instinct is to love without bound or compass, and this love ensures the destruction of the lovers, who are justified simply because the love is unbounded, and scorns patriotism, family loyalty, reason and self-interest. Such deaths are tragic because at this era the intemperate realisation of the self is heroic; it is the life principle of history. We feel that the death is necessary and is what must have been: "Nothing is here for tears".

At this stage the strength and vigour of the bourgeois depends on his cohesion as a class under monarchist leadership. In many parts already a self-armed, self-acting commune, the bourgeoisie in England, has as its spear-head the court. The court is the seat of progress, and its public collective life is for the moment the source of bourgeois progress and fountain of primitive accumulation. The court itself is not bourgeois: it seeks the coercive imposition of its will like a feudal overlord, but it can only do so by allying itself with the bourgeoisie for whom the "absoluteness" of the monarch, although feudal in its essence, is bourgeois in its outcome because it is creating the conditions for their development.

Hence we find Shakespeare, although expressing the bourgeois illusion, is an official of the court or of the bourgeois nobility. Players are the "Queen's Servants". He is not a producer for the bourgeois market or "public". He has a feudal *status*. Hence his art is not in its form individualistic: it is still collective.

It breathes the collective life of the court. As player and as dramatist he lived with his audience in one simultaneous public world of emotion. That is why Elizabethan poetry is, in its greatest expression, drama—real, acted drama. It can still remain social and public and yet be an expression of the aspirations of the bourgeois class because of the alliance of the monarchy with the bourgeoisie.

Elizabethan poetry tells a story. The story always deals with men's individualities as realised in economic functions—it sees them from the outside as "characters" or "types". It sites them in a real social world seen from the outside. But in the era of primitive accumulation, bourgeois economy has not differentiated to an extent where social "types" or "norms" have been stabilised. Bourgeois man believes himself to be establishing an economic rôle by simply realising his character, like a splay foot. The instinctive and the economic seem to him naturally one: it is only the feudal rôles which seem to him forced and "artificial". Hence the story and poetry are not yet antagonistic: they have not yet separated out.

In this era of primitive accumulation all is fluid and homogeneous. Bourgeois society has not created its elaborate division of labour, to which the elaborate complexity of culture corresponds. To-day psychology, biology, logic, philosophy, law, poetry, history, economics, novel-writing, the essay, are all separate spheres of thought, each requiring specialisation for their exploration and each using a specialised vocabulary. But men like Bacon and Galileo and da Vinci did not specialise, and their language reflects this lack of differentiation. Elizabethan tragedy speaks a language of great range and compass, from the colloquial to the sublime, from the technical to the narrative, because language itself is as yet undifferentiated.

Like all great language, this has been bought and paid for. Tyndale paid for it with his life; the English prose style as a simple and clear reality, fit for poetry, was written in the fear of death, by heretics for whom it was a religious but also a revolutionary activity demanding a bareness and simplicity which scorned all trifling ornament and convention. Nothing was asked of it but the truth.

These facts combined make it possible for Elizabethan poetry to be drama and story, collective and undifferentiated, and yet express with extraordinary power the vigour of the bourgeois illusion in the era of primitive accumulation.

Shakespeare could not have achieved the stature he did if he had not exposed, at the dawn of bourgeois development, the whole movement of the capitalist contradiction, from its tremendous achievement to its mean decline. His position, his feudal "perspective", enabled him to comprehend in one era all the trends which in later eras were to separate out and so be beyond the compass of one treatment.[1] It was not enough to reveal the dewy freshness of bourgeois love in *Romeo and Juliet*, its fatal empire-shattering drowsiness in *Antony and Cleopatra*, or the pageant of individual human wills in conflict in *Macbeth, Hamlet, Lear* and *Othello*. It was necessary to taste the dregs, to anticipate the era of *surréalisme* and James Joyce and write *Timon of Athens*, to express the degradation caused by the whole movement of capitalism, which sweeps away all feudal loyalties in order to realise the human spirit, only to find this spirit the miserable prisoner of the cash-nexus— to express this not symbolically, but with burning precision:

Gold! yellow, glittering, precious gold! No, gods,
I am no idle votarist. Roots, you clear heavens!
Thus much of this will make black white, foul fair,
Wrong right, base noble, old young, coward valiant.
Ha! you gods, why this? What this, you gods?
Why this

Will lug your priests and servants from your sides,
Pluck stout men's pillows from below their heads:
This yellow slave
Will knit and break religions; bless the accurs'd;
Make the hoar leprosy ador'd; place thieves,
And give them title, knee, and approbation,
With senators on the bench; this is it
That makes the wappen'd widow wed again;
She, whom the spital-house and ulcerous sores
Would cast the gorge at, this embalms and spices
To the April day again. Come, damned earth,
Thou common whore of mankind, that putt'st odds
Among the rout of nations, I will make thee
Do thy right nature.

James Joyce's characters repeat the experience of Timon:

all is oblique,
There's nothing level in our cursed natures
But direct villainy. Therefore, be abhorred
All feasts, societies, and throngs of men!
His semblable, yea, *himself*, Timon disdains.
Destruction, fang mankind!

From the life-thoughts of Elizabethan poetry to the death-thoughts of the age of imperialism is a tremendous period of development but all are comprehended and cloudily anticipated in Shakespeare's plays.

Before he died Shakespeare had cloudily and phantastically attempted an *untragic* solution, a solution without death. Away from the rottenness of bourgeois civilisation, in the island of *The Tempest*, man attempts to live quietly and nobly, alone with his thoughts. Such an existence still retains an Elizabethan reality—there is an exploited class—Caliban, the bestial serf, and a "free" spirit who serves only for a time —Ariel, apotheosis of the free wage-labourer. This heaven cannot endure. The actors return to the real world. The magic wand is broken. And yet, in its purity and childlike wisdom, there is a bewitching quality about *The Tempest* and its magic world, in which the forces of Nature are harnessed to men's service in a bizarre forecast of communism.

---

[1] In the same way More, from his feudal perspective, anticipates the development of capitalism into communism in his *Utopia*.

2

As primitive accumulation gradually generates a class of differentiated bourgeois producers, the will of the monarch, which in its absoluteness had been a creative force, now becomes anti-bourgeois and feudal. Once primitive accumulation has reached a certain point, what is urgently desired is not capital but a set of conditions in which the bourgeois can realise the development of his capital. This is the era of "manufacture"—as opposed to factory development.

The absolute monarchy, by its free granting of monopolies and privileges, becomes as irksome as the old network of feudal loyalties. It is, after all, itself feudal. A cleavage appears between the monarchy and the class of artisans, merchants, farmers and shopkeepers.

The court supports the big landowner or noble who is already parasitic. He is allied with the court to exploit the bourgeoisie and the court rewards him with monopolies, privileges or special taxes which hamper the development of the overwhelming majority of the rising bourgeois class. Thus the absolute "will" of the prince, now that the era of primitive accumulation is over, no longer expresses the life principle of the bourgeois class at this stage.

On the contrary the court appears as the source of evil. Its glittering corrupt life has a smell of decay; foulness and mean deeds are wrapped in silk. Bourgeois poetry changes into its opposite and by a unanimous movement puritanically draws its skirt's hem away from the dirt of the court life. The movement which at first was a reaction of the Reformed Church against the Catholic Church is now a reaction of the puritan against the Reformed Church.

The Church, expressing the absolute will of the monarch and the privileges of the nobility, is met by the individual "conscience" of the puritan, which knows no law but the Spirit—his own will idealised. His thrift reflects the need, now that primitive accumulation is over, to amass the capital in which freedom and virtue inheres by "saving"

and not by gorgeous and extravagant robbery.

Donne expresses the transition, for he is torn by it. At first captivated by the sensuality and glittering brilliance of the court, the insolent treatment he receives produces a movement away from it, into repentance. The movement is not complete. In Donne's last years, filled as they are with death-thoughts and magniloquent hatred of life, the pride of the flesh still tears at his heart.

Poetry, drawing away from the collective life of the court, can only withdraw into the privacy of the bourgeois study, austerely furnished, shared only with a few chosen friends, surroundings so different from the sleeping and waking publicity of court life that it rapidly revolutionises poetic technique. Crashaw, Herrick, Herbert, Vaughan—all the poetry of this era seems written by shy, proud men writing alone in their studies —appealing from court life to the country or to heaven. Language reflects the change. Lyrics no longer become something that a gentleman could sing to his lady; conceits are no longer something which could be tossed off in courtly conversation. Poetry is no longer something to be roared out to a mixed audience. It smells of the library where it was produced. It is a learned man's poetry: student's poetry. Poetry is read, not declaimed: it is correspondingly subtle and intricate.

But Suckling and Lovelace write court poetry, the simple, open poetry of their class. They stand in antagonism to puritan poetry, and maintain the tradition of the Elizabethan court lyric.

The collective drama, born of the collective spirit of the court, necessarily perishes. Webster and Tourneur express the final corruption, the malignantly evil and Italianate death of the first stage of the bourgeois illusion.

3

The transitional period moves towards Revolution. The bourgeoisie revolt against the monarchy and the privileged nobility in the name of Parliament, liberty and the "Spirit" which is nothing but the bourgeois will challenging the monarchical. This is the era of armed revolution, of civil war, and with it emerges England's first openly revolutionary poet, Milton.

Revolutionary in style, revolutionary in content. The bourgeois now enters a stage of the illusion where he sees himself as defiant and lonely, challenging the powers that be. With this therefore goes an artificial and *consciously* noble style, an isolated style, the first of its kind in English poetry.

Bourgeois revolutions, which are only accomplished by the help of the people as a whole, always reach a stage where it is felt that they have "gone too far". The bourgeois demand for unlimited freedom is all very well until the "have-nots" too demand unlimited freedom, which can only be obtained at the expense of the "haves". Then a Cromwell or Robespierre steps in to hold back coercively the progress of the Revolution.

Such a bourgeois halt must always lead to a reaction, for the bourgeois class thus destroys its own mass basis. A Robespierre gives place to a Directory and then a Napoleon; at an earlier stage a Cromwell gives place to a Monk and a Charles II. The wheel does not come back full circle: there is a compromise.

To those who expressed directly the interests of the petty bourgeois, the puritans, this final stage of reaction is a betrayal of the Revolution. Therefore in *Paradise Lost* Milton sees himself as Satan overwhelmed and yet still courageous: damned and yet revolutionary. In *Paradise Regained* he has already rejected power in this world in exchange for power in the next. He scorns the temples and towers of this world; his reward is in the next because he will not compromise. Hence this poem is defeatist, and lacks the noble defiance of *Paradise Lost*. In *Samson Agonistes* Milton recovers his courage. He hopes for the day when he can pull the temple down on the luxury of his wanton oppressors and wipe out the Philistine court.

Did he consciously figure himself as Satan, Jesus and Samson? Only consciously perhaps as Samson. But when he came to tackle the bourgeois theme of how man, naturally good, is everywhere bad, and to give the familiar answer—because of Adam's fall from natural goodness as a result of temptation, he was led to consider the tempter, Satan and *his* fall. And Satan's struggle being plainly a revolution, he filled it with his revolutionary experience and made the defeated revolutionary a puritan, and the reactionary God a Stuart. Thus emerged the towering figure of Satan, which by its unexpected disproportion shows that Milton's theme had "run away with him".

In *Paradise Regained* Milton tries to believe that to be defeated temporally is to win spiritually, to win "in the long run". But Milton was a real active revolutionary and in his heart he finds this spiritual satisfaction emptier than real defeat—as the unsatisfactoriness of the poem shows. In *Samson Agonistes* he tries to combine defeat and victory.

Of course the choice was already made in *Comus*, where the Lady spurns the luxury of the court and allies herself with the simple virtue of the people.

Note how already the bourgeois illusion is a little self-conscious. Milton is consciously noble—Shakespeare never. The Elizabethans are heroic: the Puritans are not, and therefore have to see themselves as heroic, in an archaistic dress. The verse and vocabulary of the Latin secretary to the Provisional Government well expresses this second movement of the illusion. The theme of the poems cannot at once be noble and in any sense contemporary. Poetry is already isolating itself from the collective daily life, which makes it inevitable that the prose "story" now begins to appear as an opposite pole.

Of course the transition from the court, like all other movements of the bourgeois illusion, is foreshadowed in Shakespeare. In *The Tempest* Prospero withdraws from corrupt court life to the peace of his island study, like a Herbert or a Milton. Shakespeare did the same in life when he retired to Stratford-on-Avon.

But he could not write there. His

magic wand was a collective one. He had broken it with the breaking of his tie with the court, and the cloud-capp'd palaces of his fancy became empty air.

4

The atmosphere of a period of reaction such as that which followed the Puritan Revolution is of good-humoured cynicism. A betrayal of the extreme "ideals" for which the battle had been fought appeared prudent to the majority. Unrestrained liberty and the free following of the spirit, excellent in theory, had in practice been proved to involve awkwardnesses for the very class of whom it was the battle cry. The bourgeois illusion went through a new stage, that of the Restoration.

Such a movement is cynical, because it is the outcome of a betrayal of "ideals" for earthly reasons. It is luxurious because the class with whom the bourgeoisie, having taught it a sharp lesson, now allies itself again—the landed nobility—has no need of thrift to acquire capital. It is collective because there is a return to the public court life and the play. It is not decadent in any real sense; true, the bourgeoisie has allied itself with the old doomed class— but it has breathed new life into that class. Webster, expressing the decadence of the court, gives way to Dryden, expressing its vigour. And Dryden, with his turn-coat life, so different from Milton's rectitude, exactly expresses the confused and rapid movement of the bourgeoisie of the time, from Cromwell to Charles II and from James II to William III. It is a real alliance—there is no question of the feudal régime returning. James II's fate in the "Glorious Revolution" clearly shows the bourgeoisie have come to rule.

The poet must return from his study to court, but it is now a more citified, sensible, less romantic and picturesque court. The court itself has become almost burgher. The language shows the same passage from study to London street, from conscious heroism to business-like common sense. The sectarian bourgeois revolutionary, a little inclined to pose, becomes the sensible man-of-the-world. This is the transition from Milton to Dryden. The idealisation of compromise between rival classes as "order" and "measure"—a familiar feature of reaction—leads to the conception of the Augustan age, which passes by an inevitable transition into eighteenth century nationalism, once the Glorious Revolution has shown that the bourgeoisie are dominant in the alliance.

The self-valuation of this age as Augustan is in fact singularly fitting. Caesar played the rôle of Cromwell and Augustus of Charles II in a similar movement in Rome, where the knightly class at first rebelled against the senatorial and, when it became dangerous to go farther, entered on a road of compromise and reaction.

Elizabethan insurgence, the voice of primitive accumulation, thus turns into its opposite, Augustan propriety, the voice of manufacture. Individualism gives place to good taste. In its early stages bourgeoisdom requires the shattering of all feudal forms, and therefore its illusion is a realisation of the instinct in freedom. In the course of this movement, first to acquire capital, and then to give capital free play, it leans first on the monarchy—Shakespeare—and then on the common people—Milton. But because it is the interests of a class it dare not go too far in its claims, for to advance the interests of all society is to deny its own. It must not only shatter the old forms which maintained the rule of the feudal class, but it must create the new forms which will ensure its own development as a ruling class. This is the epoch of manufacture and of agricultural capitalism. Land, not factories, is still the pivot.

This epoch is not only opposed to that of primitive accumulation, it is also opposed to that of free trade. Capital exists, but the proletariat is as yet barely in existence. The numerous artisans and peasants are not yet proletarianised by the very movement of capital; the State must therefore be invoked to assist the process. The expansive period of capitalism, in which the rapid expropriation of the artisan hurls thousands of free labourers on to the market, has not yet arrived. The vagrants of Elizabethan days have already been absorbed. The bourgeoisie finds that there is a shortage of wage labour which might lead to a rise in the price of labour power over and above its value (*i.e.* its cost of reproduction in food and rent).

Hence there is need for a network of laws to keep down wages and prices and regulate labour in order to secure for the bourgeois class the conditions of his development. He now sees the "impracticable idealism" of his revolutionary demands for liberty. Order, measure, law, good taste and other imposed forms are necessary. Tradition and convention are valuable. Now that the feudal State has perished, these restraints ensure the development of bourgeois economy. Free trade seems the very opposite of desirable to the economists of this era. The bourgeois illusion betrays itself.

5

Therefore, during the eighteenth century, bourgeois poetry expresses the spirit of manufacture, of the petty manufacturing bourgeoisie, beneath the wings of the big landowning capitalists, giving birth to industrial capitalism. The shattering expansion of capitalism has not yet begun. Capitalism still approximates to those economies where "conservation is the first condition of existence" and has not yet fully entered into the state where it "cannot exist without constantly revolutionising the means of production". Capitalism is revolutionising itself, but like a slowly growing plant that needs protection, instead of like an explosion in which the ignition of one part detonates the rest. By the compromise of the Glorious Revolution, the Whig landed aristocracy were prepared to give that protection because they had themselves become bourgeoisified.

It was only when the separation between agricultural and industrial capitalism took place as a result of the rise of the factory that the cleavage between the aristocracy and the bourgeoisie began to have a determining effect on the bourgeois illusion. While the woollen-mill was still no more than a hand-loom and an appendage of the agricultural capitalist's sheep-farm there was no direct antagonism between the classes: it was only as the woollen-mill became a cotton-mill, depending for its raw material on outside sources, and when sheep-farming developed in Australia and provided wool for English mills, that there arose a direct antagonism between agricultural and industrial capitalism which expressed itself ultimately on the side of the industrialists as a demand for Free Trade and the repeal of the Corn Laws.

Pope's poetry, and its "reason"—a reason moving within singularly simple and shallow categories but moving accurately—with its polished language and metre and curt antitheses, is a reflection of that stage of the bourgeois illusion where freedom for the bourgeoisie can only be "limited"—man must be prudent in his demands, and yet there is no reason for despair, all goes well. Life is on the up-grade, but it is impossible to hurry. The imposition of outward forms on the heart is necessary and accepted. Hence the contrast between the elegant corset of the eighteenth-century heroic couplet and the natural luxuriance of Elizabethan blank verse, whose sprawl almost conceals the bony structure of the iambic rhythm inside it.

Pope perfectly expresses the ideals of the bourgeois class in alliance with a bourgeoisified aristocracy in the epoch of manufacture.

It is important to note that even now the poet himself has not been bourgeoisified as a producer. He does not produce as yet for the free market. Almost a court or aristocratic official in the time of Shakespeare, poet is a parson's or scholar's occupation in the ensuing period, and even as late as Pope he is dependent on being patronised, *i.e.* he has a "patriarchal" or "idyllic" relation to the class of whom he is the spokesman in the time of Pope.

Such an "idyllic" relation means that the poet writes non-idyllic poetry. He still sees himself as a man playing a social rôle. This was the case with the primitive poet; it remains true of Pope. It imposes on him the obligation to speak the language of his paymasters or co-poets—in the primitive tribe these constitute the whole tribe, in Augustan society these are the men who form his patron's circle—the ruling class. Johnson—dependent on subscribers—bridges the gap between the poet by status and the poet as producer. Thus poetry remains in this sense collective. It talks a more or less current language, and the poet writes for an audience he has directly in mind, to whom perhaps he will presently read his poems and so be able to watch their effect. Poetry is still for him not so much a poem—a self-subsisting work of art—as a movement from writer to reader, like the movement of emotion in a publicly-acted drama or the movement of a Muse in the minds of men. Hence he realises himself as playing a social rôle: inspirer of humanity or redresser of the follies of mankind. He has not yet become a self-conscious artist.

D. H. LAWRENCE

(1885-1930)

D. H. Lawrence is known primarily as a novelist and poet, though in recent years his work as a literary critic has received increasing attention. Lawrence's literary judgments, based on a wide knowledge of contemporary and traditional literature, are often cantankerous and eccentric. As his novels and stories are characteristically occasions of harsh social criticism derived from an intensely personal and individualist ethic, his literary essays and reviews tend to be centered on the failures of the artist to break loose from the blinding and deadening machineries of conventional society. Lawrence sees the artist as, ideally, a type of prophet, but finds most individual artists to be psychically crippled victims of "civilization" only partially in harmony with their own special powers. Lawrence's criticism, then, is a psychologically, at times almost psychoanalytically, based moral criticism of art's failures and successes in realizing its essentially oracular functions. The chief examples of Lawrence's criticism are contained in *Studies in Classic American Literature* (1923), *Pornography and Obscenity* (1930), *Phoenix* (ed. Aldous Huxley, 1936), *Sex, Literature and Censorship* (ed. Harry T. Moore, 1953), and *Selected Literary Criticism of D. H. Lawrence* (ed. Anthony Beal, 1955). Some of Lawrence's most lively literary pronouncements occur in his letters, which have been edited by Harry T. Moore (1962).

Nathaniel Hawthorne and *The Scarlet Letter* (1923)

Nathaniel Hawthorne writes romance.

And what's romance? Usually, a nice little tale where you have everything

As You Like It, where rain never wets your jacket and gnats never bite your nose and it's always daisy-time. *As You Like It* and *Forest Lovers*, etc. *Morte D'Arthur*.

Hawthorne obviously isn't this kind of romanticist: though nobody has muddy boots in *The Scarlet Letter*, either.

But there is more to it. *The Scarlet Letter* isn't a pleasant, pretty romance. It is a sort of parable, an earthly story with a hellish meaning.

All the time there is this split in the American art and art-consciousness. On the top it is as nice as pie, goody-goody and lovey-dovey. Like Hawthorne being such a blue-eyed darling, in life, and Longfellow and the rest such sucking-doves. Hawthorne's wife said she "never saw him in time", which doesn't mean she saw him too late. But always in the "frail effulgence of eternity".

Serpents they were. Look at the inner meaning of their art and see what demons they were.

You *must* look through the surface of American art, and see the inner diabolism of the symbolic meaning. Otherwise it is all mere childishness.

That blue-eyed darling Nathaniel knew disagreeable things in his inner soul. He was careful to send them out in disguise.

Always the same. The deliberate consciousness of Americans so fair and smooth-spoken, and the under-consciousness so devilish. *Destroy! destroy! destroy!* hums the under-consciousness. *Love and produce! Love and produce!* cackles the upper consciousness. And the world hears only the Love-and-produce cackle. Refuses to hear the hum of destruction underneath. Until such time as it will *have* to hear.

The American has got to destroy. It is his destiny. It is his destiny to destroy the whole corpus of the white psyche, the white consciousness. And he's got to do it secretly. As the growing of a dragon-fly inside a chrysalis or cocoon destroys the larva grub, secretly.

Though many a dragon-fly never gets out of the chrysalis case: dies inside. As America might.

So the secret chrysalis of *The Scarlet Letter*, diabolically destroying the old psyche inside.

Be good! Be good! warbles Nathaniel. *Be good, and never sin! Be sure your sins will find you out.*

So convincingly that his wife never saw him "as in time".

Then listen to the diabolic undertone of *The Scarlet Letter*.

Man ate of the tree of knowledge, and became ashamed of himself.

Do you imagine Adam had never lived with Eve before that apple episode? Yes, he had. As a wild animal with his mate.

It didn't become "sin" till the knowledge-poison entered. That apple of Sodom.

We are divided in ourselves, against ourselves. And that is the meaning of the cross symbol.

In the first place, Adam knew Eve as a wild animal knows its mate, momentaneously, but vitally, in blood-knowledge. Blood-knowledge, not mind-knowledge. Blood-knowledge, that seems utterly to forget, but doesn't. Blood-knowledge, instinct, intuition, all the vast vital flux of knowing that goes on in the dark, antecedent to the mind.

Then came that beastly apple, and the other sort of knowledge started.

Adam began to look at himself. "My hat!" he said. "What's this? My Lord! What the deuce!—And Eve! I wonder about Eve."

Thus starts KNOWING. Which shortly runs to UNDERSTANDING, when the devil gets his own.

When Adam went and took Eve, *after* the apple, he didn't do any more than he had done many a time before, in act. But in consciousness he did something very different. So did Eve. Each of them kept an eye on what they were doing, they watched what was happening to them. They wanted to KNOW. And that was the birth of sin. Not *doing* it, but KNOWING about it. Before the apple, they had shut their eyes and their minds had gone dark. Now, they peeped and pried and imagined. They watched themselves. And they felt uncomfortable after. They felt self-conscious. So they said, "The *act* is sin. Let's hide. We've sinned."

No wonder the Lord kicked them out of the Garden. Dirty hypocrites.

The sin was the self-watching, self-consciousness. The sin, and the doom. Dirty understanding.

Nowadays men do hate the idea of dualism. It's no good, dual we are. The cross. If we accept the symbol, then, virtually, we accept the fact. We are divided against ourselves.

For instance, the blood *hates* being KNOWN by the mind. It feels itself destroyed when it is KNOWN. Hence the profound instinct of privacy.

And on the other hand, the mind and the spiritual consciousness of man simply *hates* the dark potency of blood-acts: hates the genuine dark sensual orgasms, which do, for the time being, actually obliterate the mind and the spiritual consciousness, plunge them in a suffocating flood of darkness.

You can't get away from this.

Blood-consciousness overwhelms, obliterates, and annuls mind-consciousness.

Mind-consciousness extinguishes blood-consciousness, and consumes the blood.

We are all of us conscious in both ways. And the two ways are antagonistic in us.

They will always remain so.

That is our cross.

The antagonism is so obvious, and so far-reaching, that it extends to the smallest thing. The cultured, highly-conscious person of to-day *loathes* any form of physical, "menial" work: such as washing dishes or sweeping a floor or chopping wood. This menial work is an insult to the spirit. "When I see men carrying heavy loads, doing brutal work, it always makes me want to cry," said a beautiful, cultured woman to me.

"When you say that, it makes me want to beat you," said I, in reply. "When I see you with your beautiful head pondering heavy thoughts, I just want to hit you. It outrages me."

My father hated books, hated the sight of anyone reading or writing.

My mother hated the thought that any of her sons should be condemned to manual labour. Her sons must have something higher than that.

She won. But she died first.

He laughs longest who laughs last.

There is a basic hostility in all of u between the physical and the menta the blood and the spirit. The mind "ashamed" of the blood. And the bloo is destroyed by the mind, actuall Hence pale-faces.

At present the mind-consciousne and the so-called spirit triumphs. I America supremely. In America, n body does anything from the blood. A ways from the nerves, if not from th mind. The blood is chemically reduce by the nerves, in American activity.

When an Italian labourer labour his mind and nerves sleep, his bloo acts ponderously.

Americans, when they are *doin* things, never seem really to be doin them. They are "busy about" it. The are always busy "about" something. Bi truly *immersed* in *doing* something, wit the deep blood-consciousness active, tha they never are.

They *admire* the blood-consciou spontaneity. And they want to get it i their heads. "Live from the body," the shriek. It is their last mental shrie *Co-ordinate.*

It is a further attempt still to ratio alise the body and blood. "Think abou such and such a muscle," they say, "an relax there."

And every time you "conquer" th body with the mind (you can say "hea it, if you like) you cause a deeper, moi dangerous complex or tension some where else.

Ghastly Americans, with their bloo no longer blood. A yellow spiritual flui

The Fall.

There have been lots of Falls.

We *fell* into *knowledge* when Eve b the apple. Self-conscious knowledge. Fo the first time the mind put up a figl against the blood. Wanting to UNDE STAND. That is to intellectualise th blood.

The blood must be *shed*, says Jesu Shed on the cross of our own divide psyche.

Shed the blood, and you becon mind-conscious. Eat the body and drin the blood, self-cannibalising, and you become extremely conscious, like Americans and some Hindus. Devour yourself, and God knows what a lot you'll know, what a lot you'll be conscious of.

Mind you don't choke yourself.

For a long time men *believed* that they could be perfected through the mind, through the spirit. They believed, passionately. They had their ecstasy in pure consciousness. They *believed* in purity, chastity, and the wings of the spirit.

America soon plucked the bird of the spirit. America soon killed the *belief* in the spirit. But not the practice. The practice continued with a sarcastic vehemence. America, with a perfect inner contempt for the spirit and the consciousness of man, practises the same spirituality and universal love and KNOWING all the time, incessantly, like a drug habit. And inwardly gives not a fig for it. Only for the *sensation*. The pretty-pretty *sensation* of love, loving all the world. And the nice fluttering aeroplane *sensation* of knowing, knowing, knowing. Then the prettiest of all sensations, the sensation of UNDERSTANDING. Oh, what a lot they understand, the darlings! *So* good at the trick, they are. Just a trick of self-conceit.

The Scarlet Letter gives the show away.

You have your pure-pure young parson Dimmesdale.

You have the beautiful Puritan Hester at his feet.

And the first thing she does is to seduce him.

And the first thing he does is to be seduced.

And the second thing they do is to hug their sin in secret, and gloat over it, and try to understand.

Which is the myth of New England.

Deerslayer refused to be seduced by Judith Hunter. At least the Sodom apple of sin didn't fetch him.

But Dimmesdale was seduced gloatingly. Oh, luscious Sin!

He was such a pure young man.

That he had to make a fool of purity.

The American psyche.

Of course, the best part of the game lay in keeping up pure appearances.

The greatest triumph a woman can have, especially an American woman, is the triumph of seducing a man: especially if he is pure.

And he gets the greatest thrill of all, in falling.—"Seduce me, Mrs. Hercules."

And the pair of them share the subtlest delight in keeping up pure appearances, when everybody knows all the while. But the power of pure appearances is something to exult in. All America gives in to it. *Look* pure!

To seduce a man. To have everybody know. To keep up appearances of purity. Pure!

This is the great triumph of woman.

A. The Scarlet Letter. Adulteress! The great Alpha. Alpha! Adulteress! The new Adam and Adama! American!

A. Adulteress! Stitched with gold thread, glittering upon the bosom. The proudest insignia.

Put her upon the scaffold and worship her there. Worship her there. The Woman, the Magna Mater. *A.* Adulteress! Abel!

Abel! Abel! Abel! Admirable!

It becomes a farce.

The fiery heart. *A.* Mary of the Bleeding Heart. Mater Adolerata! *A.* Capital *A.* Adulteress. Glittering with gold thread. Abel! Adultery. Admirable!

It is, perhaps, the most colossal satire ever penned. *The Scarlet Letter.* And by a blue-eyed darling of a Nathaniel.

Not Bumppo, however.

The human spirit, fixed in a lie, adhering to a lie, giving itself perpetually the lie.

All begins with *A.*

Adulteress. Alpha. Abel, Adam. *A.* America.

The Scarlet Letter.

"Had there been a Papist among the crowd of Puritans, he might have seen in this beautiful woman, so picturesque in her attire and mien, and with the infant at her bosom, an object to remind him of the image of Divine Maternity, which so many illustrious painters have vied with one another to represent; something which should remind him, indeed, but only by contrast, of that sacred image of sinless Motherhood, whose infant was to redeem the world."

Whose infant was to redeem the world indeed! It will be a startling redemption the world will get from the American infant.

"Here was a taint of deepest sin in the most sacred quality of human life, working such effect that the world was only the darker for this woman's beauty, and more lost for the infant she had borne."

Just listen to the darling. Isn't he a master of apology?

Of symbols, too.

His pious blame is a chuckle of praise all the while.

Oh, Hester, you are a demon. A man *must* be pure, just that you can seduce him to a fall. Because the greatest thrill in life is to bring down the Sacred Saint with a flop in the mud. Then when you've brought him down, humbly wipe off the mud with your hair, another Magdalen. And then go home and dance a witch's jig of triumph, and stitch yourself a Scarlet Letter with gold thread, as duchesses used to stitch themselves coronets. And then stand meek on the scaffold and fool the world. Who will all be envying you your sin, and beating you because you've stolen an advantage over them.

Hester Prynne is the great nemesis of woman. She is the KNOWING Ligeia risen diabolic from the grave. Having her own back. UNDERSTANDING.

This time it is Mr. Dimmesdale who dies. She lives on and is Abel.

His spiritual love was a lie. And prostituting the woman to his spiritual love, as popular clergymen do, in his preachings and loftiness, was a tall white lie. Which came flop.

We are so pure in spirit. Hi-tiddly-i-ty!

Till she tickled him in the right place, and he fell.

Flop.

Flop goes spiritual love.

But keep up the game. Keep up appearances. Pure are the pure. To the pure all things, etc.

Look out, Mister, for the Female Devotee. Whatever you do, don't let her start tickling you. She knows your weak spot. Mind your Purity.

When Hester Prynne seduced Arthur Dimmesdale it was the beginning of the end. But from the beginning of the end to the end of the end is a hundred years or two.

Mr. Dimmesdale also wasn't at the end of his resources. Previously, he had lived by governing his body, ruling it, in the interests of his spirit. Now he has a good time all by himself torturing his body, whipping it, piercing it with thorns, macerating himself. It's a form of masturbation. He wants to get a mental grip on his body. And since he can't quite manage it with the mind, witness his fall—he will give it what for, with whips. His will shall *lash* his body. And he enjoys his pains. Wallows in them. To the pure all things are pure.

It is the old self-mutilation process, gone rotten. The mind wanting to get its teeth in the blood and flesh. The ego exulting in the tortures of the mutinous flesh. I, the ego, I *will* triumph over my own flesh. Lash! Lash! I am a grand free spirit. *Lash!* I am the master of my soul! *Lash! Lash!* I am the captain of my soul. *Lash! Hurray!* "In the fell clutch of circumstance," etc., etc.

Good-bye Arthur. He depended on women for his Spiritual Devotees, spiritual brides. So, the woman just touched him in his weak spot, his Achilles Heel of the flesh. Look out for the spiritual bride. She's after the weak spot.

It is the battle of wills.

"For the will therein lieth, which dieth not——"

The Scarlet Woman becomes a Sister of Mercy. Didn't she just, in the late war. Oh, Prophet Nathaniel!

Hester urges Dimmesdale to go away with her, to a new country, to a new life. He isn't having any.

He knows there is no new country, no new life on the globe to-day. It is the same old thing, in different degree everywhere. *Plus ça change, plus c'est le même chose.*

Hester thinks, with Dimmesdale for her husband, and Pearl for her child, in

Australia, maybe, she'd have been perfect.

But she wouldn't. Dimmesdale had already fallen from his integrity as a minister of the Gospel of the Spirit. He had lost his manliness. He didn't see the point of just leaving himself between the hands of a woman and going away to a "new country", to be her thing entirely. She'd only have despised him more, as every woman despises a man who has "fallen" to her; despises him with her tenderest lust.

He stood for nothing any more. So let him stay where he was and dree out his weird.

She had dished him and his spirituality, so he hated her. As Angel Clare was dished, and hated Tess. As Jude in the end hated Sue: or should have done. The women make fools of them, the spiritual men. And when, as men, they've gone flop in their spirituality, they can't pick themselves up whole any more. So they just crawl, and die detesting the female, or the females, who made them fall.

The saintly minister gets a bit of his own back, at the last minute, by making public confession from the very scaffold where she was exposed. Then he dodges into death. But he's had a bit of his own back, on everybody.

" 'Shall we not meet again?' whispered she, bending her face down close to him. 'Shall we not spend our immortal life together? Surely, surely we have ransomed one another with all this woe! Thou lookest far into eternity with those bright dying eyes. Tell me what thou seest!' "

" 'Hush, Hester—hush,' said he, with tremulous solemnity. 'The law we broke!—the sin here so awfully revealed! Let these alone be in thy thoughts. I fear! I fear!' "

So he dies, throwing the "sin" in her teeth, and escaping into death.

The law we broke, indeed. You bet! Whose law?

But it is truly a law, that man must either stick to the belief he has grounded himself on, and obey the laws of that belief, or he must admit the belief itself to be inadequate, and prepare himself for a new thing.

There was no change in belief, either in Hester or in Dimmesdale or in Hawthorne or in America. The same old treacherous belief, which was really cunning disbelief, in the Spirit, in Purity, in Selfless Love, and in Pure Consciousness. They would go on following this belief, for the sake of the sensationalism of it. But they would make a fool of it all the time. Like Woodrow Wilson, and the rest of modern Believers. The rest of modern Saviours.

If you meet a Saviour, to-day, be sure he is trying to make an innermost fool of you. Especially if the saviour be an UNDERSTANDING WOMAN, offering her love.

Hester lives on, pious as pie, being a public nurse. She becomes at last an acknowledged saint, Abel of the Scarlet Letter.

She would, being a woman. She has had her triumph over the individual man, so she quite loves subscribing to the whole spiritual life of society. She will make herself as false as hell, for society's sake, once she's had her real triumph over Saint Arthur.

Blossoms out into a Sister-of-Mercy Saint.

But it's a long time before she really takes anybody in. People kept on thinking her a witch, which she was.

As a matter of fact, unless a woman is held, by man, safe within the bounds of belief, she becomes inevitably a destructive force. She can't help herself. A woman is almost always vulnerable to pity. She can't bear to see anything *physically* hurt. But let a woman loose from the bounds and restraints of man's fierce belief, in his gods and in himself, and she becomes a gentle devil. She becomes subtly diabolic. The colossal evil of the united spirit of Woman. WOMAN, German woman or American woman, or every other sort of woman, in the last war, was something frightening. As every *man* knows.

Woman becomes a helpless, would-be-loving demon. She is helpless. Her very love is a subtle poison.

Unless a man believes in himself and his gods, *genuinely*: unless he fiercely obeys his own Holy Ghost; his woman will destroy him. Woman is the nemesis of doubting man. She can't help it.

And with Hester, after Ligeia, woman becomes a nemesis to man. She bolsters him up from the outside, she destroys him from the inside. And he dies hating her, as Dimmesdale did.

Dimmesdale's spirituality had gone on too long, too far. It had become a false thing. He found his nemesis in woman. And he was done for.

Woman is a strange and rather terrible phenomenon, to man. When the subconscious soul of woman recoils from its creative union with man, it becomes a destructive force. It exerts, willy-nilly, an invisible destructive influence. The woman herself may be as nice as milk, to all appearance, like Ligeia. But she is sending out waves of silent destruction of the faltering spirit in men, all the same. She doesn't know it. She can't even help it. But she does it. The devil is in her.

The very women who are most busy saving the bodies of men, and saving the children: these women-doctors, these nurses, these educationalists, these public-spirited women, these female saviours: they are all, from the inside, sending out waves of destructive malevolence, which eat out the inner life of a man, like a cancer. It is so, it will be so, till men realise it and react to save themselves.

God won't save us. The women are so devilish godly. Men must save themselves in this strait, and by no sugary means either.

A woman can use her sex in sheer malevolence and poison, while she is *behaving* as meek and good as gold. Dear darling, she is really snow-white in her blamelessness. And all the while she is using her sex as a she-devil, for the endless hurt of her man. She doesn't know it. She will never believe it if you tell her. And if you give her a slap in the face for her fiendishness, she will rush to the first magistrate, in indignation. She is so *absolutely* blameless, the she-devil, the dear, dutiful creature.

Give her the great slap, just the same, just when she is being most angelic. Just when she is bearing her cross most meekly.

Oh, woman out of bounds is a devil. But it is man's fault. Woman never *asked*, in the first place, to be cast out of her bit of an Eden of belief and trust. It is man's business to bear the responsibility of belief. If he becomes a spiritual fornicator and liar, like Ligeia's husband and Arthur Dimmesdale, how can a woman believe in him? Belief doesn't go by choice. And if a woman doesn't believe in a *man*, she believes, essentially, in nothing. She becomes, willy-nilly, a devil.

A devil she is, and a devil she will be. And most men will succumb to her devilishness.

Hester Prynne was a devil. Even when she was so meekly going round as a sick-nurse. Poor Hester. Part of her wanted to be saved from her own devilishness. And another part wanted to go on and on in devilishness, for revenge. Revenge! REVENGE! It is this that fills the unconscious spirit of woman to-day. Revenge against man, and against the spirit of man, which has betrayed her into unbelief. Even when she is most sweet and a salvationist, she is her most devilish, is woman. She gives her man the sugar-plum of her own submissive sweetness. And when he's taken this sugar-plum in his mouth, a scorpion comes out of it. After he's taken this Eve to his bosom, oh, so loving, she destroys him inch by inch. Woman and her revenge! She will have it, and go on having it, for decades and decades, unless she's stopped. And to stop her you've got to believe in yourself and your gods, your own Holy Ghost, Sir Man; and then you've got to fight her, and never give in. She's a devil. But in the long run she is conquerable. And just a tiny bit of her wants to be conquered. You've got to fight three-quarters of her, in absolute hell, to get at the final quarter of her that wants a release, at last, from the hell of her own revenge. But it's a long last. And not yet.

"She had in her nature a rich, voluptuous, oriental characteristic—a taste for the gorgeously beautiful." This is Hester. This is American. But she repressed her nature in the above direction. She would not even allow herself the luxury of labouring at fine, delicate stitching. Only she dressed her little sin-child Pearl vividly, and the scarlet letter was gorgeously embroidered. Her Hecate and Astarte insignia.

"A voluptuous, oriental characteristic——" That lies waiting in American women. It is probable that the Mormons are the forerunners of the coming real America. It is probable that men will have more than one wife, in the coming America. That you will have again a half-oriental womanhood, and a polygamy.

The grey nurse, Hester. The Hecate, the hell-cat. The slowly-evolving voluptuous female of the new era, with a whole new submissiveness to the dark, phallic principle.

But it takes time. Generation after generation of nurses and political women and salvationists. And in the end, the dark erection of the images of sex-worship once more, and the newly submissive women. That kind of depth. Deep women in that respect. When we have at last broken this insanity of mental-spiritual consciousness. And the women *choose* to experience again the great submission.

"The poor, whom she sought out to be the objects of her bounty, often reviled the hand that was stretched to succour them."

Naturally. The poor hate a salvationist. They smell the devil underneath.

"She was patient—a martyr indeed—but she forbore to pray for her enemies, lest, in spite of her forgiving aspirations, the words of the blessing should stubbornly twist themselves into a curse."

So much honesty, at least. No wonder the old witch-lady Mistress Hibbins claimed her for another witch.

"She grew to have a dread of children; for they had imbibed from their parents a vague idea of something horrible in this dreary woman gliding silently through the town, with never any companion but only one child."

"A vague idea!" Can't you see her "gliding silently"? It's not a question of a vague idea imbibed, but a definite feeling directly received.

"But sometimes, once in many days, or perchance in many months, she felt an eye—a human eye—upon the ignominious brand, that seemed to give a momentary relief, as if half her agony were shared. The next instant, back it all rushed again, with a still deeper throb of pain; for in that brief interval she had sinned again. Had Hester sinned alone?"

Of course not. As for sinning again, she would go on all her life silently, changelessly "sinning". She never repented. Not she. Why should she? She had brought down Arthur Dimmesdale, that too-too snow-white bird, and that was her life-work.

As for sinning again when she met two dark eyes in a crowd, why of course. Somebody who understood as she understood.

I always remember meeting the eyes of a gipsy woman, for one moment, in a crowd, in England. She knew, and I knew. What did we know? I was not able to make out. But we knew.

Probably the same fathomless hate of this spiritual-conscious society in which the outcast woman and I both roamed like meek-looking wolves. Tame wolves waiting to shake off their tameness. Never able to.

And again, that "voluptuous, oriental" characteristic that knows the mystery of the ithyphallic gods. She would not betray the ithyphallic gods to this white, leprous-white society of "lovers". Neither will I, if I can help it. These leprous-white, seducing, spiritual women, who "understand" so much. One has been too often seduced, and "understood". "I can read him like a book," said my first lover of me. The book is in several volumes, dear. And more and more comes back to me the gulf of dark hate and *other* understanding, in the eyes of the gipsy woman. So different from the hateful white light of understanding which floats like scum on the eyes of white, oh, so white English and American women, with their understanding voices and their deep, sad words, and their profound, *good* spirits. Pfui!

Hester was scared only of one result of her sin: Pearl. Pearl, the scarlet letter incarnate. The little girl. When women bear children, they produce either devils or sons with gods in them. And it is an evolutionary process. The devil in Hester produced a purer devil in Pearl. And the devil in Pearl will produce—she married an Italian Count—a piece of purer devilishness still.

And so from hour to hour we ripe and ripe.

And then from hour to hour we rot and rot.

There was that in the child "which often impelled Hester to ask in bitterness of heart, whether it were for good or ill that the poor little creature had been born at all."

For ill, Hester. But don't worry. Ill is as necessary as good. Malevolence is as necessary as benevolence. If you have brought forth, spawned, a young malevolence, be sure there is a rampant falseness in the world against which this malevolence must be turned. Falseness has to be bitten and bitten, till it is bitten to death. Hence Pearl.

Pearl. Her own mother compares her to the demon of plague, or scarlet fever, in her red dress. But then, plague is necessary to destroy a rotten, false humanity.

Pearl, the devilish girl-child, who can be so tender and loving and *understanding*, and then, when she has understood, will give you a hit across the mouth, and turn on you with a grin of sheer diabolic jeering.

Serves you right, you shouldn't be *understood*. That is your vice. You shouldn't want to be loved, and then you'd not get hit across the mouth. Pearl will love you: marvellously. And she'll hit you across the mouth: oh, so neatly. And serves you right.

Pearl is perhaps the most modern child in all literature.

Old-fashioned Nathaniel, with his little-boy charm, he'll tell you what's what. But he'll cover it with smarm.

Hester simply *hates* her child, from one part of herself. And from another, she cherishes her child as her one precious treasure. For Pearl is the continuing of her female revenge on life. But female revenge hits both ways. Hits back at its own mother. The female revenge in Pearl hits back at Hester, the mother, and Hester is simply livid with fury and "sadness", which is rather amusing.

"The child could not be made amenable to rules. In giving her existence a great law had been broken; and the result was a being whose elements were perhaps beautiful and brilliant, but all in disorder, or with an order peculiar to themselves, amidst which the point of variety and arrangement was difficult or impossible to discover."

Of course, the order is peculiar to themselves. But the point of variety is this: "Draw out the loving, sweet soul, draw it out with marvellous understanding; and then spit in its eye."

Hester, of course, didn't at all like it when her sweet child drew out her motherly soul, with yearning and deep understanding: and then spit in the motherly eye, with a grin. But it was a process the mother had started.

Pearl had a peculiar look in her eyes: "a look so intelligent, yet so inexplicable, so perverse, sometimes so malicious, but generally accompanied by a wild flow of spirits, that Hester could not help questioning at such moments whether Pearl was a human child."

A little demon! But her mother, and the saintly Dimmesdale, had borne her. And Pearl, by the very openness of her perversity, was more straightforward than her parents. She flatly refuses any Heavenly Father, seeing the earthly one such a fraud. And she has the pietistic Dimmesdale on toast, spits right in his eye: in both his eyes.

Poor, brave, tormented little soul, always in a state of recoil, she'll be a devil to men when she grows up. But the men deserve it. If they'll let themselves be "drawn", by her loving understanding, they deserve that she shall slap them across the mouth the moment they *are* drawn. The chickens! Drawn and trussed.

Poor little phenomenon of a modern child, she'll grow up into the devil of a modern woman. The nemesis of weak-kneed modern men, craving to be love-drawn.

The third person in the diabolic trinity, or triangle, of *The Scarlet Letter*, is Hester's first husband, Roger Chillingworth. He is an old Elizabethan physician, with a grey beard and a long-furred coat and a twisted shoulder. Another healer. But something of an alchemist, a magician. He is a magician on the verge of modern science, like Francis Bacon.

Roger Chillingworth is of the old order of intellect, in direct line from the medieval Roger Bacon alchemists. He has an old, intellectual belief in the dark sciences, the Hermetic philosophies. He is no Christian, no selfless aspirer. He is not an aspirer. He is the old authoritarian in man. The old male authority. But without passional belief. Only intellectual belief in himself and his male authority.

Shakespeare's whole tragic wail is because of the downfall of the true male authority, the ithyphallic authority and masterhood. It fell with Elizabeth. It was trodden underfoot with Victoria.

But Chillingworth keeps on the *intellectual* tradition. He hates the new spiritual aspirers, like Dimmesdale, with a black, crippled hate. He is the old male authority, in intellectual tradition.

You can't keep a wife by force of an intellectual tradition. So Hester took to seducing Dimmesdale.

Yet her only marriage, and her last oath, is with the old Roger. He and she are accomplices in pulling down the spiritual saint.

"Why dost thou smile so at me——" she says to her old, vengeful husband. "Art thou not like the Black Man that haunts the forest around us? Hast thou not enticed me into a bond which will prove the ruin of my soul?"

"Not thy soul!" he answered with another smile. "No, not thy soul!"

It is the soul of the pure preacher, that false thing, which they are after. And the crippled physician—this other healer—blackly vengeful in his old, distorted male authority, and the "loving" woman, they bring down the saint between them.

A black and complementary hatred, akin to love, is what Chillingworth feels for the young, saintly parson. And Dimmesdale responds, in a hideous kind of love. Slowly the saint's life is poisoned. But the black old physician smiles, and tries to keep him alive. Dimmesdale goes in for self-torture, self-lashing, lashing his own white, thin, spiritual saviour's body. The dark old Chillingworth listens outside the door and laughs, and prepares another medicine, so that the game can go on longer. And the saint's very soul goes rotten. Which is the supreme triumph. Yet he keeps up appearances still.

The black, vengeful soul of the crippled, masterful male, still dark in his authority: and the white ghastliness of the fallen saint! The two halves of manhood mutually destroying one another.

Dimmesdale has a "coup" in the very end. He gives the whole show away by confessing publicly on the scaffold, and dodging into death, leaving Hester dished, and Roger as it were, doubly cuckolded. It is a neat last revenge.

Down comes the curtain, as in Ligeia's poem.

But the child Pearl will be on in the next act, with her Italian Count and a new brood of vipers. And Hester greyly Abelling in the shadows, after her rebelling.

It is a marvellous allegory. It is to me one of the greatest allegories in all literature, *The Scarlet Letter*. Its marvellous under-meaning! And its perfect duplicity.

The absolute duplicity of that blue-eyed *Wunderkind* of a Nathaniel. The American wonder-child, with his magical allegorical insight.

But even wonder-children have to grow up in a generation or two.

And even SIN becomes stale.

R. W. B. LEWIS

(b. 1917)

Richard Warrington Baldwin Lewis is one of a number of critics who during the 1950's extended the methods of analytical criticism to the study of literature in its larger cultural and historical setting. In *The American Adam; Innocence, Tragedy, and Tradition in the Nineteenth Century* (1955), Lewis discusses the thematic oppositions of innocence and experience, of nature and society, in American literature in relation to political and social traditions, literary history, mythology, and psychology. In *The Picaresque Saint, Representative Figures in Contemporary Fiction* (1959), he defines the hero's role, as it has been affected by changing social and historical conditions, in contemporary European and American fiction. Lewis is also the editor of *A Melville Reader* (1962), *Th Presence of Walt Whitman* (1962), and *Malraux, A Collection of Critical Essays* (1963).

The Case against the Past (1955)

> Democracy . . . is revolutionary, not formative. It is born of denial. It comes into existence in the way of denying established institutions. Its office is rather to destroy the old world, than fully to reveal the new.
>
> HENRY JAMES, SR., "Democracy and Its Issues" (1853)

In the decade following the end of the War of 1812, an air of hopefulness became apparent in American life and letters. It expressed the sense of enormous possibility that Americans were beginning to share about the future of their new country; but hopefulness at the outset was combined with feelings of impatience and hostility. For believers in the future could not fail to notice, dotted across the American scene, many signs of the continuing power of the past: institutions, social practices, liter-

ary forms, and religious doctrines—carry-overs from an earlier age and a far country and irrelevant obstructions (as it seemed) to the fresh creative task at hand. Emerson, tracing the haphazard movement for social reform in New England, remembered the "noise of denial and protest" which was the first symptom of the reformist spirit; "much was to be resisted," he said, "much was to be got rid of by those who were reared in the old, before they could begin to affirm and to construct." More vehement patriots even regretted that Americans were forced to communicate with one another in an old, inherited language. Indeed, the urge to root out vestiges of the culture and society of the Old World became so intense over the years that a commentator like the elder Henry James was led to identify democracy itself with a program of denial and destruction.

Nothing was to be spared. Thus it was, according to one story, that a huge crowd of people gathered together on some broad western prairie to build an immense bonfire: a cosmic bonfire, upon which was piled all the world's "outworn trumpery." The heraldry of ancient aristocratic families fed the flames, to the crowd's mounting enthusiasm; after that came the robes and scepters of royalty; the scaffold and other symbols of repressive institutions; and finally the total body of European literature and philosophy. "Now," declared the chief celebrant, "we shall get rid of the weight of dead men's thoughts."

The story is a fantasy, to be sure—a fantasy composed by Nathaniel Hawthorne in 1844 and called "Earth's Holocaust." But it was close enough to history, and, like every good story, it was truer than history. Its theme may have been suggested by the historic activities of a religious group known as the "Millerites," though the Millerites were only among the more extreme and disappointed of the age's millennialists. But Hawthorne, as usual, enlarged upon his historical materials; and, in doing so, he managed very accurately to catch in a fable the prevailing impulse to escape from every existing mode of organizing and explaining experience, in order to confront life in entirely original terms. And at the same time, in the divided attitude that gives his story its vital tension, Hawthorne managed to convey the deep reservations that certain Americans felt about the contemporary passion to destroy. A genuine sympathy informs the irony and melancholy of "Earth's Holocaust"; but though one can tell from Hawthorne's notebooks that he too would have set fire to many symbols of injustice, he makes it clear at the end of his story that the true source of oppression—the human heart—has remained untouched by the conflagration: a conclusion Melville was to find at once profound and appalling.

The drama of "Earth's Holocaust" has a ritual quality, and much of its dialogue is incantatory in tone. Behind the story, one sees such ritualistic historic events as the burning of the Bastille, and, beyond that, the recurring human instinct to purge by fire. Hawthorne had articulated the need he detected in the atmosphere of the day for a purgatorial action—preceding, as it were, the life of the new Adam in the new earthly paradise. Thoreau, alert to the ritual aspects of human behavior and the primitive energy of words, gave voice to the same instinctive need while he was reflecting on "the essential facts of life" at Walden Pond. He made semantic fun of a deacon whose dreary effects had been sold at auction: "Instead of a *bonfire,* or purifying destruction of them, there was an *auction,* or increasing of them." This private little joke led Thoreau to wonder whether the tribal customs of "some savage nations" might not be usefully instituted in America—the ceremony of the "busk," for example, which he found described in William Bartram's eighteenth-century travel-book: "When a town celebrates the busk . . . they have previously provided themselves with new clothes, new pots, pans, and other household utensils and furniture, they collect all their worn out clothes and other despicable things, sweep and cleanse their houses, squares and the whole town, of their filth, which with all the remaining grain and other old provisions they cast together into one common heap and consume it with fire." The whole of *Walden,* according to one reading, is a metaphoric expansion of Bartram's busk—the busk of the human spirit, when clothes and pots and pans are discarded as symbols of ambitions and interests.

But the rite of purification was more than a poetic invention. The need for it, in fact, had long been expressed in a series of concrete political and economic proposals, all of them voicing a belief in the need for periodic and radical change in the very structure of American society.

II

The American argument against institutional continuity drew its force and its fervor from the native conviction about the rights of man. For the principle of the rights of *man* led to a restriction on the rights of *men*. In order to insure the freedoms of future men, those of the present (the argument ran) must have only temporary validity; and rights, consequently, were given a time limit. The constant in the argument was "the present generation," and the principle of judgment was the sovereignty of the living.[1] The principle had been formulated and flaunted in the writings of Jefferson and Paine; it helped to ease the painful break with the past that the political situation demanded. "The Creator," Jefferson pronounced, no doubt consciously echoing St. Matthew, "has made the earth for the living, not the dead. Rights and powers can only belong to persons, not to things, not to mere matter, unendowed with will. The dead are not even things." These are metaphysical statements: rights are attributed to that which can be said to be real; and the question of reality turns upon a dialectic of dead and living which is essentially biological. The author of that extraordinary contribution to natural history, *Notes on Virginia*, was among the first to make natural history the queen of the sciences, the new metaphysic, and to turn the inquiry of reality into an investigation of natural processes. In the generation of hope, his logical successor was Oliver Wendell Holmes.

Although we currently all too often employ a pious phrase about our heritage when we mention Thomas Jefferson, he himself was opposed to several kinds of inheritance, finding them, in the name of the sovereign present, mere forms of slavery. He posed the general problem in a letter written to Madison from Paris, in 1789: "The question, whether one generation of men has a right to bind another, seems never to have started on this or our side of the water. Yet it is a question of such consequence as not only to merit decision, but place, also, among the fundamental principles of government. . . . I set out

[1] See the study by Daniel J. Boorstin, *The Lost World of Thomas Jefferson* (New York, 1948), especially the chapter entitled "The Sovereignty of the Present Generation."

on this ground which I suppose to be self-evident, *'that the earth belongs in usufruct to the living'*; that the dead have neither power nor rights over it." Jefferson was even willing to calculate the approximate life-expectancy of any single generation: it amounted to about nineteen years. The arithmetic was applied. The devices by which society orders itself must be introduced and consented to by the living; hence legislation may not endure longer than the estimated life of the consenting generation, and a complete review of all laws should be made every nineteen years. Such a policy would, of course, have meant periodic administrative chaos, and the proposal was not acted upon; though there was administrative chaos enough, as Tocqueville discovered. It was, however, administrative fear that operated against the proposal; an older argument against change in law, which considered the effect of change on the stability of moral habits, scarcely entered the discussion; habit was already a term of abuse.

Jefferson could not have foreseen, nor would he have approved, all the consequences of the principle of the sovereign present. He was attempting to make the practical controls of life dependent upon the voluntary agreement of the living. He did not mean to reject the whole scheme of values of the past, or to assert that each generation in turn should do so. And yet this is what was proposed, stage by stage, over the first half of the nineteenth century. In 1829 the *economic* authority of the living was affirmed with some violence in a book called *The Rights of Man to Property, Being a Proposition To Make It Equal among the Adults of the Present Generation*. The author was one Thomas Skidmore, a leader in the Workingmen's movement in New York and Philadelphia and for a time a follower of Fanny Wright and the progressive laborites. The reforms urged by Skidmore seemed extreme even to his associates; but his manner of reasoning was symptomatic of a deepening sense of the disjunction between generations. Skidmore reflected the contemporary awareness, on which the first tentative efforts toward a labor movement were based, that, without equality of economic opportunity, the great phrases of the Declaration of Independence rang somewhat hollowly. In developing his thesis, Skidmore managed to attack the whole concept of inheritance. "If property is to descend to particular individuals from the previous generations, and if the many are born, having neither parents nor any one else, to give them property, equal in amount to that which the sons of the rich receive, from their fathers or other testators, how is it established that they are created equal?" Transmission in any kind from one generation to another was a fiction: "One generation cannot sell, give or convey, even if it had the right, to another. The reason is, that the one is dead; the other living. The one is present; the other absent. They do not and cannot *meet*, to come to a treaty, to make delivery; to give or receive." The terms "testator" and "heir" should be dispensed with, Skidmore went on; and the question to be answered was simply: "*How long* does a man own property?" Skidmore's general principles were shared far beyond the bounds of the labor movement, and they continued to be enunciated. From the main contention, that denied commerce between generations, the argument could easily be extended beyond the political and economic areas.

To an acute foreign observer, visiting this country a few years after the appearance of Skidmore's polemic, such an extension of principle seemed already to be operative. Alexis de Tocqueville had probably the handsomest talent in the century for sensing the significant drift of contemporary social and intellectual history; and his experience and wisdom told him that the disjunction between generations was inevitably becoming a striking aspect of democracy as such: "for among democratic nations each generation is a new people." The insight followed from Tocqueville's analysis of the intellectual character of democracy in America, in the second volume of his great study (published in translation here in 1840); but it gained additional force from his survey of institutions in the preceding volume (1837).

He had observed there, in a section called "Instability of the Administration in the United States," that "no one cares for what occurred before his time. . . . In America, society seems to live from hand to mouth, like an army in the field. Nevertheless, the art of administration is undoubtedly a science, and no sciences can be improved if the discoveries and observations of successive generations are not connected together in the order in which they occur." On the evidence, Tocqueville could infer that "democracy, pushed to its furthest limits, is . . . prejudicial to the art of government," something the Jeffersonians might cheerfully have confirmed. Tocqueville noticed a similar brevity of life in philosophic theories or literary conventions. Democratic literature, he thought, was not only shorn of received conventions, it was inherently almost incapable of generating its own; "if it should happen that the men of some one period were agreed upon any such rules, that would prove nothing for the following period." That circumstance was to comprise an important part of the artist's dilemma in America.

As the principle of the sovereign present thrust upward from its political and economic roots, it managed to affect not only literature, but educational beliefs, too, and religious doctrines (fifty years before John Dewey elaborated it into a coherent philosophic statement). In the forties, those who favored territorial expansion in the direction of Oregon but who found activity hampered by longstanding laws were able to reiterate Jefferson's suggestions about change in laws with considerably larger confidence.[2] By 1850, when Hawthorne was writing *The House of the Seven Gables*, he could draw a plausible portrait of a young reformer who wanted to apply

[2] Cf. *Manifest Destiny*, by Albert K. Weinberg (New York, 1935), chap. v, especially.

the idea of the sovereign present to every imaginable phase of life:

Shall we never, never get rid of this Past? It lies upon the present like a giant's dead body! In fact, the case is just as if a young giant were compelled to waste all his strength in carrying about the corpse of the old giant his grandfather, who died a long while ago, and only needs to be decently buried. Just think a moment, and it will startle you to see what slaves we are to bygone times,—to Death, if we give the matter the right word! . . . For example, a dead man, if he happen to have made a will, disposes of wealth no longer his own; or, if he died intestate, it is distributed in accordance with the notions of men much longer dead than he. A dead man sits on all our judgment-seats; and living judges do but search out and report his decisions. We read in dead men's books! We laugh at dead men's jokes, and cry at dead men's pathos! We are sick of dead men's diseases, physical and moral, and die of the same remedies with which dead doctors killed their patients! We worship the living Deity according to dead men's forms and creeds. Whatever we do of our free motion, a dead man's icy hand obstructs us. . . . And we must be dead ourselves before we can begin to have our proper influence on our own world, which will then be no longer our world, but the world of another generation, with which we shall have no shadow of right to interfere.

The profession of the speaker, Holgrave, adds to the content of the speech, for this young ex-Fourierite and earnest member of the party of Hope ("How you hate everything old!" his audience, Phoebe Pyncheon, tells him) is not only an artist; he is a practitioner of the peculiarly appropriate new art of photography. The instrument of Daguerre could achieve in art what the hopeful sought for in life: the careful and complete differentiation of the individual in time and space, the image of the single person in all his rugged singularity. Dead forms and conventions of art are implicit in the catalogue of the oppressive past, to be destroyed at set intervals, in the proposition Holgrave brings forward a moment later:

If each generation were allowed and expected to build its own houses, that single change, comparatively unimportant in itself, would imply almost every reform which society is now suffering for. I doubt whether even our public edifices—our capitols, statehouses, courthouses, city-halls and churches—ought to be built of such permanent materials as stone or brick. It were better that they should crumble to ruin once in twenty years or thereabouts, as a hint to people to examine and reform the institutions which they symbolise.

The estimated time-span for the life of institutions is close to Jefferson's; but both of Holgrave's speeches, as their references move forward from money and laws to moral principles and religious doctrines, indicate the expanded application since 1789 of the notion of periodic "purification." According to the opposition party, the real trouble was that the suggestions of the Holgraves had long been put into practice. The immediate had triumphed, someone said in the alert New York weekly, the *Literary World*, in the same year (1850); education was sacrificed to "the immediately practical"; houses were built "which fall into tombs and monuments upon the passer-by; . . . anybody makes a new religion nowadays, a patent Christianity. The old," the article concluded, "was better."

But the physical environment had changed enormously since 1789, and these changes were the warrant urged for the changes in attitude and expression suggested by Holgrave. For example, in a sequence in the *Democratic Review*, there was an article on material progress since 1789 in one issue (October, 1839), and an editorial on the need for new ideas in the next. In the former a German political refugee named Francis Lieber drew up a memorandum for Congress on the statistics of progress over the half-century beginning in 1789 with a now familiar reverence for arithmetic. Lieber found that the territory of the country had tripled and that the population had quadrupled; at the same rate of increase, he went on, the American people would, after one hundred more years, be equal in numbers to all of Europe. He calculated that exports of domestic origin had increased from less than 20,000,000 to nearly 100,000,000 products annually, and tonnage from half a million to three times that much. Miles of post road had multiplied from

1,300 to 134,818, and post offices from 75 to 12,000. Six hundred steamboats had been constructed in thirty years ("The immediate builds steamboats of tinder, and roasts passengers alive," the *Literary World* was to mutter); and 1,000 miles of railroad track had been laid down. It was in the following issue of the *Democratic Review* that there appeared the editorial mentioned in the Prologue: a manifesto of liberation from the past, followed by the demand for an independent literature to communicate the novelty of experience in the New World.

III

"We have the Saint Vitus dance." This was Thoreau's view of the diversion of energies to material expansion and of the enthusiastic arithmetic by which expansion was constantly being measured. Miles of post roads and millions of tons of domestic export did not convince Thoreau that first principles ought to be overhauled; but a close interest in these matters did convince him that first principles had been abandoned. Probably nobody of his generation had a richer sense of the potentiality for a fresh, free, and uncluttered existence; certainly no one projected the need for the ritual burning of the past in more varied and captivating metaphors. This is what *Walden* is about; it is the most searching contemporary account of the desire for a new kind of life. But Thoreau's announcement of a spiritual molting season (one of his favorite images) did not arise from a belief that the building of railroads was proof of the irrelevance of too-well-remembered doctrines. Long before Whitman, himself a devotee of the dazzling sum, attacked the extremes of commercialism in *Democratic Vistas*, Thoreau was insisting that the obsession with railroads did not demonstrate the hope for humanity, but tended to smother it. "Men think it is essential that the *Nation* have commerce, and export ice, and talk through a telegraph and ride thirty miles an hour, without a doubt, whether *they* do or not; but whether we should live like baboons or men is a little uncertain."

Watching the local railroad train as it passed near Walden Pond on the recently laid track between Fitchburg and Boston, Thoreau noticed that while the narrow little cars moved eastward along the ground, the engine smoke drifted skyward, broadening out as it rose. The picture (it occurs in the chapter called "Sounds") provided him with a meaningful glimpse of that wholeness, of interrelated doubleness, which was for Thoreau the required shape of the life that was genuinely lived. The trouble with railroads—he said it, in fancy, to the scores of workmen he saw starting up in protest against him—was that so few persons who rode on them were heading in any definite direction or were aware of a better direction than Boston; quite a few persons were simply run over, while the building of railroads crushed the heart and life out of the builders. The trouble, in general, with expending one's strength on "internal improvements" was that the achievement, like the aim, was partial: there was nothing internal about them. The opportunity that Thoreau looked out upon from his hut at Walden was for no such superficial accomplishment, but for a wholeness of spirit realized in a direct experience of the whole of nature. The words "nature" and "wholeness" have been overworked and devitalized (Thoreau and Emerson are partly to blame), and now they are suspect; but they glow with health in the imaginatively ordered prose of Henry Thoreau.

The narrator of *Walden* is a witness to a truly new world which the speaker alone has visited, from which he has just returned, and which he is sure every individual ought to visit at least once—not the visible world around Walden Pond, but an inner world which the Walden experience allowed him to explore. Thoreau liked to pretend that his book was a purely personal act of private communion. But that was part of his rhetoric, and *Walden* is a profoundly rhetorical book, emerging unmistakably from the long New England preaching tradition; though here the trumpet call announces the best imaginable news rather than apocalyptic warnings. Thoreau, in *Walden,* is a man who has come back down into the cave to tell the residents there that they are really in chains, suffering fantastic punishments they have imposed on themselves, seeing by a light that is reflected and derivative. A major test of the visionary hero must always be the way he can put his experience to work for the benefit of mankind; he demonstrates his freedom in the liberation of others. Thoreau prescribes the following cure: the total renunciation of the traditional, the conventional, the socially acceptable, the well-worn paths of conduct, and the total immersion in nature.

Everything associated with the past should be burned away. The past should be cast off like dead skin. Thoreau remembered with sympathetic humor the pitiful efforts of one John Field, an Irishman living at near-by Baker Farm, to catch perch with shiners: "thinking to live by some derivative old-country mode in this primitive new country." "I look on England today," he wrote, "as an old gentleman who is travelling with a great deal of baggage, trumpery which has accumulated from long housekeeping, which he has not the courage to burn." Thoreau recorded with approval and some envy a Mexican purification rite practiced every fifty-two years; and he added, "I have scarcely heard of a truer sacrament." These periodic symbolic acts of refreshment, which whole societies ought to perform in each generation ("One generation abandons the enterprises of another like stranded vessels"), were valid exactly because they were images of fundamental reality itself. Individuals and groups should enact the rhythmic death and rebirth reflected in the change of season from winter to spring, in the sequence of night and day. "The phenomena of the year take place every day in a pond on a small scale." These were some of the essential facts discovered by Thoreau when he fronted them at Walden; and the experience to which he was to become a witness took its shape, in act and in description, from a desire to live in accordance with these facts. So it was

that he refused the offer of a door-mat lest he should form the habit of shaking it every morning; and, instead, every morning "I got up early and bathed in the pond; that was a religious exercise and one of the best things which I did."

The language tells us everything, as Thoreau meant it to. He had his own sacramental system, his own rite of baptism. But his use of the word "nature" indicates that the function of sacraments was to expose the individual again to the currents flowing through nature, rather than to the grace flowing down from supernature. The ritual of purification was no less for Thoreau than for St. Paul a dying into life; but Thoreau marched to the music he heard; it was the music of the age; and he marched in a direction *opposite* to St. Paul. His familiar witticism, "One world at a time" (made on his deathbed to an eager abolitionist named Pillsbury, who looked for some illumination of the future life from the dying seer) was a fair summary of his position; with this addition, that poetry traditionally taken as hints about what could be seen through a glass darkly about the next world was taken by Thoreau as what had been seen by genius, face to face with this one. He was among the first to see Christian literature as only the purest and most inspiring of the fables about the relation of man to nature and about the infinite capacities of the unaided human spirit. The Bible (Thoreau referred to it simply as "an old book") was the finest poem which had ever been written; it was the same in substance as Homeric or Hindu mythology, but it was richer in metaphor. The Bible spoke more sharply to the human condition. This was why Thoreau, like Whitman, could employ the most traditional or religious phrases and invest them with an unexpected and dynamic new life.

It is not surprising that transcendentalism was Puritanism turned upside down, as a number of critics have pointed out; historically, it could hardly have been anything else. Transcendentalism drew on the vocabularies of European romanticism and Oriental mysticism; but the only available local vocabulary was the one that the hopeful were so anxious to escape from, and a very effective way to discredit its inherited meaning was to serve it up in an unfamiliar context. There was something gratifyingly shocking in such a use of words: "What demon possessed me that I behaved so well?" Thoreau spoke as frequently as he could, therefore, about a *sacrament*, a sacred mystery, such as baptism: in order to define the cleansing, not of St. Paul's natural man, but of the conventional or traditional man; in order, precisely, to bring into being the natural man. For the new tensions out of which insights were drawn and moral choices provoked were no longer the relation of nature and grace, of man and God, but of the natural and the artificial, the new and the old, the individual and the social or conventional. Thoreau had, as he remarked in his other deathbed witticism, no quarrel with God; his concern was simply other.

His concern was with the strangulation of nature by convention. The trouble with conventions and traditions in the New World was that they had come first; they had come from abroad and from a very long way back; and they had been superimposed upon nature. They had to be washed away, like sin, so that the natural could reveal itself again and could be permitted to create its own organic conventions. They had to be renounced, as the first phase of the ritual; and if renunciation was, as Emily Dickinson thought, a piercing virtue, it was not because it made possible an experience of God in an infusion of grace, but because it made possible an experience of self in a bath of nature.

Thoreau had, of course, learned a good deal from Emerson, whose early energy was largely directed toward constructing "an original relation with the universe" and who reverted time and again to the same theme: "beware of tradition"; "forget historical Christianity"; "lop off all superfluity and tradition, and fall back on the nature of things." And what was this nature of things which men were enjoined to fall back on? Lowell understood some of it, in one of the better sentences of his querulous and uneven essay on Thoreau (1865): "There is only one thing better than tradition, and that is the original and eternal life out of which all tradition takes its rise. It was this life which the reformers demanded, with more or less clearness of consciousness and expression, life in politics, life in literature, life in religion." But even in this moment of qualified approval, Lowell makes it sound too pallid, soft, and ethereal. Nature was not merely the mountains and the prairie, any more than it was merely the bees and the flowers; but it was all of those things too, and it must always include them. If nature was partly represented by "Higher Laws," as the title of one chapter in *Walden* tells us, it was represented also by "Brute Neighbors," "Winter Animals," and a "Bean-Field," as we know from the titles of other chapters. Thoreau's nature is bounded by an irony which applies the phrase "Higher Laws" to a chapter that, for all its idealism, talks at some length about fried rats.

Irony too—the doubleness of things —Thoreau could learn from Emerson, as each of them had learned from Coleridge and Plato. "All the universe over," Emerson wrote in his journal (1842), "there is just one thing, this old double." The old double, the ideal and the actual, the higher law and the fried rat, required a double consciousness and found expression in a double criticism; nature could be satisfied with nothing else. Emerson tramped in mud puddles, and Thoreau, more adventurously, swam in Walden Pond; the puddle and the pond were instances of unimpeded nature; but both men searched, in their separate ways, for the spiritual analogues which completed the doubleness of nature. Their ability to address themselves with very nearly equal fluency to both dimensions of consciousness gave later comfort to idealists and nominalists alike, though neither group understood the Emersonian principle that only the whole truth could be true at all. Bronson Alcott was the most high-minded of the contemporary idealists, but Emerson chided him for neglecting the value of the many in his rapture for the one, and thought he had genius but no talent. "The philosophers of Fruitlands," Emerson said in 1843, naming Alcott's experimental community, "have such an image of virtue before their eyes, that the poetry of man and nature they never see; the poetry that is man's life, the poorest pastoral clownish life; the light that shines on a man's hat, in a child's spoon." He was harder, of course, on those who saw only the hat and the spoon: the materialists and the tradesmen whom he excoriated in many essays, and writers who stuck too obstinately to the ordinary (Emerson would say, the "vulgar") aspects of the visible world.

Thoreau's personal purification rite began with the renunciation of old hats and old spoons and went forward to the moment—as he describes himself in the opening paragraph of "Higher Laws"—when the initiate stood fully alive in the midst of nature, eating a woodchuck with his fingers, and supremely aware, at the same instant, of the higher law of virtue. "I love the wild not less than the good," Thoreau admitted, announcing duplicity in his own peculiar accent. The structure of *Walden* has a similar beginning and a similar motion forward. The book starts amid the punishing conventions of Concord, departs from them to the pond and the forest, explores the natural surroundings, and exposes the natural myth of the yearly cycle, to conclude with the arrival of spring, the full possession of life, and a representative anecdote about the sudden bursting into life of a winged insect long buried in an old table of apple-tree wood.[3]

Individual chapters are sometimes carried along to the same rhythm. "Sounds," for example, starts with conventional signs and then looks to nature for more authentic ones; it picks up the cycle of the day, as Thoreau listens to

sounds around the clock; and it concludes with a total surrender to the vitalizing power of unbounded nature. Thoreau had been talking about his reading in the previous chapter; now he reminds us: "While we are confined to books . . . we are in danger of forgetting the language which all things and events speak without metaphor." Sounds are elements of this natural language: the sound of the trains passing in the morning; the church bells from Lincoln, Bedford, or Concord; the lowing of cows in the evening; "regularly at half-past seven," the vesper chant of the whip-poor-wills; the "maniacal hooting of owls," which "represent the stark twilight and unsatisfied thoughts which all have"; "late in the evening . . . the distant rumbling of wagons over bridges, —a sound heard farther than almost any other at night,—the baying of dogs . . . the trump of bullfrogs"; and then at dawn the morning song of the cockerel, the lusty call to awaken of the chanticleer which Thoreau offered on the title-page as the symbol of the book. "To walk in a winter morning, in a wood where these birds abounded . . . think of it! It would put nations on the alert." Finally, in a morning mood, Thoreau closes his chapter rejoicing that his hut has no yard, no fence, but is part of unfenced nature itself.

It was with the ultimate aim of making such an experience possible—a life determined by nature and enriched by a total awareness—that Thoreau insisted so eloquently upon the baptismal or rebirth rite. What he was demanding was that individuals start life all over again, and that in the new world a fresh start was literally and immediately possible to anyone wide enough awake to attempt it. It was in this way that the experience could also appear as a return to childhood, to the scenes and the wonder of that time. In a particularly revealing moment, Thoreau reflected, while adrift on the lake in the moonlight and playing the flute for the fishes, on a boyhood adventure at that very place. "But now," he said, "I made my home by the shore." Thoreau reflected the curious but logical reverence of his

---

[3] I am indebted here to the analysis of *Walden* as a rebirth ritual by Stanley Hyman, "Henry Thoreau in Our Time," *Atlantic Monthly*, CLXXVIII (November, 1946), 137-46. Mr. Hyman acknowledges his own debt, which I share, to F. O. Matthiessen's treatment of Thoreau in *American Renaissance* (New York, 1941).

age for children: "Children, who play life, discern its true law and relations more clearly than men, who fail to live it worthily." Children seemed for Thoreau to possess some secret which had been lost in the deadening process of growing up, some intimation (like Wordsworth's child) which had faded under the routine pressure of everyday life. Emerson found the new attitude of adults toward children the appropriate symbol with which to introduce his retrospective summary of the times (1867): "Children had been repressed and kept in the background; now they were considered, cosseted and pampered." Thoreau thought he knew why: because "every child begins the world again"; every child managed to achieve without conscious effort what the adult could achieve only by the strenuous, periodic act of refreshment. In this sense, the renewal of life was a kind of homecoming; the busks and the burnings were preparatory to recapturing the outlook of children.

Psychologists who have followed Jung's poetic elaboration and doctrinaire schematizing of the guarded suggestions of Freud could make a good deal of the impulse. They might describe it as an impulse to return to the womb; and some support could doubtless be found in the image-clusters of Walden: water, caves, shipwrecks, and the like. This approach might persuasively maintain that the end of the experience narrated by Thoreau was the reintegration of the personality. And since, according to Jung, "the lake in the valley is the unconscious," it is possible to hold that *Walden* enacts and urges the escape from the convention-ridden conscious and the release of the spontaneous energies of personality lying beneath the surface, toward a reuniting of the psychic "old double." An analysis of this sort can be helpful and even illuminating, and it could be applied to the entire program of the party of Hope, substituting terms associated with the unconscious for all the terms associated with Emerson's "Reason." A certain warrant for the psychological interpretation can be found in the novels of Dr. Holmes,

and the methodological issue arises more sharply in that discussion. But we may also remind ourselves that the psychological vocabulary simply manipulates a set of metaphors other than those we normally use. Probably we do not need to go so far afield to grasp what Thoreau was seeking to explain; we may even suspect that he meant what he said. And what he said was that he went to the woods in order to live deliberately, "to front only the essential facts of life"; because human life and human expression were so burdened with unexamined habits, the voice of experience so muffled by an uninvestigated inheritance, that only by a total rejection of those habits and that inheritance and by a recovery of a childlike wonder and directness could anyone find out whether life were worth living at all.

Thoreau, like most other members of the hopeful party, understood dawn and birth better than he did night and death. He responded at once to the cockerel in the morning; the screech owls at night made him bookish and sentimental. And though their wailing spoke to him about "the low spirits and melancholy forebodings of fallen souls," the whole dark side of the world was no more than another guaranty of the inexhaustible variety of nature.[4] Thoreau knew not evil; his American busk would have fallen short, like the bonfire in Hawthorne's fantasy, of the profounder need for the purification of the human heart. He would have burned away the past as the accumulation of artifice, in the name of the natural and the essential. But if the natural looked to him so much more wholesome and so much more dependable than others have since thought it, his account of the recovery of nature was never less than noble: the noblest expression, in fact and in language, of the first great aspiration of the age.

[4] Thoreau goes on to say that the hooting of owls "is a sound admirably suited to swamps and twilight woods which no day illustrates, suggesting a vast and undeveloped nature which men have not yet recognized." The figurative language here is suggestive and may be surprising to anyone who supposes Thoreau unaware of the very existence of the cloacal regions of mind and nature.

F. O. MATTHIESSEN

(1902-1950)

As a critic and a professor of literature at Harvard, Francis Otto Matthiessen was both a perceptive interpreter of literature and a disciplined historical scholar who saw criticism and cultural history as an organically unified process. His early analytical study, *The Achievement of T. S. Eliot, an Essay on the Nature of Poetry* (1935; rev. 1947, 1958), explains Eliot's artistry in relation to the poet's larger literary and social experience. *American Renaissance, Art and Expression in the Age of Emerson and Whitman* (1941) greatly influenced the study of American literature through its definition of a native, culturally conditioned symbolist aesthetic and its discussion of the "tragic vision" of Hawthorne and Melville. Matthiessen's other works include *Sarah Orne Jewett* (1929), *Translation: An Elizabethan Art* (1931), *Henry James: the Major Phase* (1944), *The James Family* (1947), *Theodore Dreiser* (1951), and *The Responsibilities of the Critic, Essays and Reviews* (ed. John Rackliffe, 1952).

The Vision of Evil (1941)

The creation of tragedy demands of its author a mature understanding of the relation of the individual to society, and, more especially, of the nature of good and evil. He must have a coherent grasp of social forces, or, at least, of man as a social being; otherwise he will possess no frame of reference within which to make actual his dramatic conflicts. For the hero of tragedy is never merely an individual, he is a man in action, in conflict with other individuals in a definite social order. It is for such a reason that the most perceptive of recent critics of Shakespeare, Granville-Barker, has remarked that dramatic art in its most fully developed form 'is the working-out . . . not of the self-realization of the individual, but of society itself.'

And unless the author also has a profound comprehension of the mixed nature of life, of the fact that even the most per-fect man cannot be wholly good, any conflicts that he creates will not give the illusion of human reality. Tragedy does not pose the situation of a faultless individual (or class) overwhelmed by an evil world, for it is built on the experienced realization that man is radically imperfect. Confronting this fact, tragedy must likewise contain a recognition that man, pitiful as he may be in his finite weakness, is still capable of apprehending perfection, and of becoming transfigured by that vision. But not only must the author of tragedy have accepted the inevitable co-existence of good and evil in man's nature, he must also possess the power to envisage some reconciliation between such opposites, and the control to hold an inexorable balance. He must be as far from the chaos of despair as he is from ill-founded optimism.

These are the considerations which lie behind my entire treatment of Hawthorne and Melville, and to which I shall frequently refer.

You might judge that the era least likely to have produced a tragic vision of life would have been that dominated by Emerson's doctrine of 'the infinitude of the private man.' The transcendentalists were few in number, but their convictions that human nature should not be regarded as corrupt, in continual need of discipline and rebuke, but should be heartily encouraged to trust itself, to embark on the opening road of limitless freedom, were being acted upon in the eighteen-thirties and forties by many Americans who had never heard Emerson's name. In the era of Jackson, with the prospects of the common man seemingly brighter than they had ever been, and with our economic life just at the outset of its century of confident and reckless expansion, it became increasingly assumed that, as Margaret Fuller said, 'Man is not made for society, but society is made for man.'

Although Emerson was able to recognize that such a centrifugal theory was oversimplified, and was to devote his whole career to trying to effect some adjustment between the claims of society and solitude, his voice vibrated with his deepest conviction when he said that he could not find language of sufficient energy to convey his 'sense of the sacredness of private integrity. All men, all things, the state, the church, yea, the friends of the heart are phantasms and unreal beside the sanctuary of the heart.' He conceived of the heart in such pure isolation that his speculations now seem remote from violent actuality. And even when his belief in the free individual was endowed with flesh and blood in the richest poetry yet to have sprung from American soil, in *Leaves of Grass*, it was destined to call out from Yeats the characteristic view of our own time. Yeats came to feel, in spite of a youthful devotion, that Whitman as well as Emerson 'have begun to seem superficial, precisely because they lack the Vision of Evil.'

Many texts could be cited from Emerson to prove that he was not unconscious that evil existed, but, as always with him, the significant thing to determine is his prevailing tone. The assumptions that stirred emancipated New Englanders of his day were those of 'Spiritual Laws' (1841): 'Our young people are diseased with the theological problems of original sin, origin of evil, predestination and the like. These never presented a practical difficulty to any man,—never darkened across any man's road who did not go out of his way to seek them. These are the soul's mumps and measles . . .' At the time when he had graduated from college and was struggling to find his vocation, he had felt, to be sure, that 'there *is* a huge and disproportionate abundance of *evil* on earth. Indeed the good that is here is but a little island of light amidst the unbounded ocean.' But even then he hoped that America might prove a fresher field. A few years later, shortly after he had been ordained, he noted how Pascal had exposed the contradictions existing in human nature, the paradox of its being both vile and sublime. But Emerson felt that Pascal had emphasized the wrong aspect; for if close to meanness lies grandeur, 'how, then, can man be low? If, on one side, his feet are in the dust, on the other there is nothing between his head and the infinite heavens.'

That is the Emerson who prevailed, who declared in his 'Lecture on the Times' (1841) that the terrors of sin had lost their force: 'Our torment is Unbelief, the Uncertainty as to what we ought to do.' Thinking of *Hamlet*, he had a fleeting perception that poetry could spring out of suffering, but then, in the disarming candor with which he always acknowledged the limitations of his temperament, he said: 'I grieve that grief can teach me nothing.' He could say this in spite of his ample experience of it in the cumulating deaths of his first wife, his two most talented brothers, and his oldest boy. Even this last, most bitter loss was dissolved in the wistful flow of his 'Threnody'; only rarely, most notably in his essay on 'Fate,' did he stick to his observation that 'no picture of life can have any veracity that does not admit the odious facts,' that great men have always been 'perceivers of the terror of life.'

He was sometimes perplexed, as we have seen, at the discrepancy between the world of fact and the world that man thinks. But even at such moments he could feel little doubt which realm to choose as the true. If details are melancholy, if everything is sour as 'seen from experience'; as seen from the vantage point of the mind, the plan of the whole 'is seemly and noble.' He was sure that 'good is positive, evil is merely privative, not absolute,' that in the physical and moral spheres alike, the ugly facts are merely partial and can be transcended. Consequently, no matter how black appearances might be, there could always be found 'a small excess of good, a small balance in brute facts . . . favorable to the side of reason.' All fragmentary sorrow and suffering would disappear in the radiance of good, like mists before the sun over Concord meadows, and Emerson was free to go on and declare that 'the soul refuses limits and always affirms an Optimism, never a Pessimism.'

Henry James, Sr., was baffled by Emerson's habit of fluctuating thus from shrewd observer to seer with so little compulsion to bring the contrasting roles into any coherent relation. James could explain it only by concluding that Emerson 'had no conscience, in fact, and lived by perception, which is an altogether lower or less spiritual faculty.' He added that this made him 'fundamentally treacherous to civilization, without being at all aware himself of the fact.' Perhaps the surest way to sense Emerson's tone on the problem of evil is to test the effect he had on other sympathetic contemporaries who were seriously concerned with it. For James, who was determined, by means of his pungent combination of Swedenborg and Fourier, to break through the constrictions of selfhood into a warm community with all men, was not unique in finding Emerson's response to life less satisfactory than that of 'any average old dame in a horsecar.' He was joined in his objections by the orthodox, both Presbyterian

and Catholic, who were united in pronouncing Emerson's poems 'hymns to the devil,' since in their pride they gave no 'recognition of sin, as actual or even possible.' In addition, friends of Emerson's as diverse as Father Taylor and fastidious Charles Eliot Norton spoke in almost the same terms.

The ex-sailor's opinion of a transcendental sermon was that it would take as many like that 'to convert a human soul as it would quarts of skimmed milk to make a man drunk.' After hearing Emerson preach, he altered his tune only to the extent of saying: 'Mr. Emerson is one of the sweetest creatures God ever made; there is a screw loose somewhere in the machinery, yet I cannot tell where it is, for I never heard it jar. He must go to heaven when he dies, for if he went to hell, the devil would not know what to do with him. But he knows no more of the religion of the New Testament than Balaam's ass did of the principles of the Hebrew grammar.'

Norton, who was a quarter of a century Emerson's junior, came to know him best during the days when they crossed the Atlantic together on Emerson's return from his last visit to Europe in 1873. The younger man had already confessed to grave doubts 'whether our period of economic enterprise, unlimited competition, and unrestrained individualism, is the highest stage of human progress.' The existing conditions of the social order were bad 'for the mass alike of upper and lower classes'; and looking ahead he could envisage only 'outbreak after outbreak of passion and violence.' Thirty years later he had advanced no closer to a belief in any potential social order, for the world looked then as if 'were entering upon a new stage of experience, unlike anything heretofore,' which there must be a new discipline of suffering to fit men for the new conditions.' Thus his accents anticipated Eliot's.

To such a perturbed spirit Emerson's discourse, robbed of the freshness and surprise that had marked his early work, seemed nearly meaningless:

His serene sweetness, the pure whiteness of his soul, the reflection of his soul in his face, were never more apparent to me; but never before in intercourse with him had I been so impressed with the limits of his mind . . . He can accept nothing as a fact that tells against his dogma. His optimism becomes a bigotry, and, though of a nobler type than the common American conceit of the pre-eminent excellence of American things as they are, has hardly less of the quality of fatalism. To him this is the best of all possible worlds, and the best of all possible times. He refuses to believe in disorder or evil. Order is the absolute law; disorder is but a phenomenon; good is absolute, evil but good in the making . . . He is the most innocent, the most inexperienced of men who have lived in and reflected on the world.

Emerson's essay on 'The Tragic' is as unsatisfactory as these comments would lead you to suppose. He approached no subject with less sympathy, unless it was 'The Comic,' for he simply could not accept the confines of a single attitude. He knew that tragedy consists in division, and he was always striving for reconciliation. What Goethe said of himself, that he was incapable of writing tragedies because he could not tolerate discords unresolved, was far truer of Emerson. He started his essay with the firm proposition that no theory of life 'can have any right' if it leaves out of account the values of vice, pain, and fear. But presently he drifted into saying that all sorrow 'is superficial'; and he ended on the note that the intellect and the moral sense 'both ravish us into a region whereunto these passionate clouds . . . cannot rise.' He was confident that no such thing as 'pure malignity' can exist.

How an age in which Emerson's was the most articulate voice could also have given birth to *Moby-Dick* can be accounted for only through reaction. Fortunately it is not necessary to conjecture what Melville might have thought about Emerson, since he has left his own annotated copies of the *Essays*. His penciled remarks hardly constitute finished criticism. Their value lies in the immediate contact they give with a mind that was instinctively unwilling to allow a gap between the spheres of thought and

experience, but was determined to make each stand the scrutiny of the other. Melville reveals here a full glimpse of the forces against which his startling and profound imagination had to make a desperate stand before it could discover any meaning in the life that surrounded him. He felt a strong attraction in the transcendental beliefs; he frequently underscored Emerson's lines with that heavily-freighted nineteenth-century word 'noble.' Yet at the same time his untrained but keen thought was thrashing to get free from many of their implications. On the level of everyday life it was not hard to confute the philosopher, as we have seen in Melville's dismissal of the blithe remarks in 'Prudence' on the unreal 'terrors of the storm.'

Against the metaphysical assumptions of 'Spiritual Laws' Melville made his most determined onslaught. When Emerson tried to establish the merely negative nature of evil by stating: 'The good, compared to the evil' which man sees, 'is as his own good to his own evil,' Melville replied: 'A Perfectly Good being therefore would see no evil.—But what did Christ see? He saw what made him weep . . . To annihilate all this nonsense read the Sermon on the Mount, and consider what it implies.' Seeking for a clue that would enable him to articulate further the ground of his objection, Melville found it in the bland oversimplification that declared, in *The Conduct of Life*: 'The first lesson of history is the good of evil.' To that Melville retorted: 'He still bethinks himself of his optimism—he must make that good somehow against the eternal hell itself.' Melville had already been angered by the analogous pronouncement that the problem of ugliness is solved by the Poet who, 'by a deeper insight, disposes very easily of the most disagreeable facts.' Yet many of Emerson's perceptions about art evoked Melville's warmest assent, particularly the belief in organic expression. He marked the passage that declares how the Poet 'names the thing because he sees it, or comes one step nearer to it than any other. This expression, or naming, is not art, but a second nature, grown out of the first, as a leaf out of a tree.' At the end of that passage Melville wrote his most inclusive comment: 'This is admirable, as many other thoughts of Mr. Emerson's are. His gross and astonishing errors and illusions spring from a self-conceit so intensely intellectual and calm that at first one hesitates to call it by its right name. Another species of Mr. Emerson's errors, or rather, blindness, proceeds from a defect in the region of the heart.'

These annotations were not made until Melville was past forty, since he did not buy these particular volumes of the *Essays* until the first year of the Civil War. But he had reacted with substantially the same mixture of attraction and repulsion at his first contact with Emerson, when he had heard him lecture a dozen years before. He wrote to his friend Duyckinck that he had been 'very agreeably disappointed.' Heretofore he had only glanced at a book of Emerson's once in a bookstore, but 'had heard of him as full of transcendentalisms, myths and oracular gibberish . . . Say what they will, he's a great man . . . I love all men who *dive*.' But as he followed Emerson in his plunge into ideas, he quickly felt himself being suffocated. This philosopher's element was so purely intellectual that it was death to a man who wanted to dilate his lungs and drink in the sustenance of life. In his letter, he got no closer to his objection to Emerson's pale asceticism than to say, 'His belly, Sir, is in his chest, and his brains descend down into his neck.' Melville knew that there was 'a gaping flaw' in all the transcendental yea-sayers to life, that these continual affirmers of perfection were 'all cracked right across the brow.' If he had read it, he would not have considered F. H. Hedge's tribute in *The Christian Examiner* to amount to praise: 'Mephistopheles . . . designates himself as the spirit "that always denies." Mr. Emerson is not one of these spirits. We should characterize him as the spirit that always affirms.' What Melville wanted was a man who could 'say No! in thunder,' who had ex-

perienced not merely the mystery of life, but also its black tragedy. He had 'enough of this Plato who talks thro' his nose.'

It was crucially fortunate that, in the year after he heard Emerson lecture, Melville encountered the work of a contemporary who seemed to him to be richly endowed with the substance that the philosopher lacked. At this time he had been back from his adventures in the Pacific for less than six years, but having married, he had rapidly turned out five books in an attempt to support his family by his pen. His mental and spiritual growth within that concentrated interval had been enormous. As he was himself to reflect a year later 'Until I was twenty-five, I had no development at all. From my twenty-fifth year I date my life. Three weeks have scarcely passed, at any time between then and now, that I have not unfolded within myself.' He had never really read Shakespeare until he was twenty-nine in the same winter when he had listened to Emerson. And now in the summer of 1850, when he was ready for a far greater effort than any he had yet made and was indeed already preoccupied with the theme of The Whale, he fell the spell of Hawthorne. Shortly after settling at Pittsfield, Melville picked up *Mosses from an Old Manse*, which though published four years previously he had hitherto let slide. The fact that Hawthorne, having just emerged into belated fame with *The Scarlet Letter* was now a near neighbor at Lenox, no doubt provided the stimulus for reading him, though at the time the two had not yet met.

Melville poured out his impressions at once. As he confesses part way through his essay, he had begun to write before he had finished the book. Hardly more than with his annotations on Emerson can the result be reckoned as fully rounded criticism. It is something rare, a creative mind disclosing its own ambitions and problems in response to the profound challenge that only a fellow artist can present.

What satisfied him in Hawthorne was the mark of unhurried completion every page, the sustained maturity of thought and style, an Indian-summer mellowness. The pervasive charm seemed to be symbolized in one of Hawthorne's own sentences: 'In the stillest afternoon, if I listened, the thump of a great apple was audible, falling without a breath of wind, from the mere necessity of perfect ripeness.' In reading the *Mosses*, Melville had been stirred for the first time by the sense of living at a moment of ripeness for American life and art. He seized upon the truths for which Cooper, in his insistence on cultural independence, had been battling for a generation. The creator of Leatherstocking had protested angrily against the inaccurate description of himself as 'the American Scott.' Melville echoed almost his very words: 'We want no American Goldsmiths, nay, we want no American Miltons.' At the time of Cooper's death a year later, Melville wrote that his books were among the earliest he could remember from his boyhood as having produced 'a vivid and awakening power' upon his mind. But in the flush of his first experience of Hawthorne's greatness, Melville saw the drastic limitations of our 'appendix to Goldsmith'; and though he did not mention Irving by name, the reference was unmistakable as he went on to describe 'that graceful writer, who perhaps of all Americans has received the most plaudits from his own country for his productions,—that very popular and amiable writer' who, 'however good and self-reliant in many things, perhaps owes his chief reputation to the self-acknowledged imitation of a foreign model, and to the studied avoidance of all topics but smooth ones.' Such facile success meant that the author had not even perceived what Melville formulated now as an axiom: 'He who has never failed somewhere, that man cannot be great. Failure is the true test of greatness.'

He had said practically the same thing when he had pushed off from the safe shores of his narratives of experience and had made his first excited trial of his own creative depths in *Mardi* (1849). He had recently scored, in his copy of *Lear*, Edgar's profound affirma-

tion, 'Ripeness is all.' He sensed now in Hawthorne 'the culmination of his powers,' and thus unconsciously used the very phrase that Emerson had formulated the winter before to characterize the age that had produced Plato, and to express at the same time his hopes for his own day: 'There is a moment in the history of every nation, when, proceeding out of this brute youth, the perceptive powers reach their ripeness and have not yet become microscopic: so that man, at that instant, extends across the entire scale . . . That is the moment of adult health, the culmination of power.'

Within a year after his essay on Hawthorne, Melville himself had grown so far from the young barbarian who had lived among cannibals that he could feel that he had 'come to the inmost leaf of the bulb, and that shortly the flower must fall to the mould.' But in the mixed elation and anguish of finishing *Moby-Dick* not even he could have been fully cognizant of the rare moment of flowering of which he was a part. In a span of a little more than two years there came into being *The Scarlet Letter* (winter, 1850), *The House of the Seven Gables* (spring, 1851), *Moby-Dick* (fall, 1851), *The Blithedale Romance* (spring, 1852), *Pierre* (summer, 1852). Owing partly to the long obscurity of Melville's reputation, the concentrated force of these books as a group and the possible interactions between them have scarcely yet been reckoned with.

Hawthorne's one period of great productivity, coming in his late forties, seems to have been due more than to anything else to the stimulus of finding, with the publication of *The Scarlet Letter*, that he had at last a sufficient audience to serve as a challenge to his fullest energies. At the time when he met Melville, Hawthorne's mind and style were too completely formed to be susceptible of direct influence, but both he and his wife were enormously pleased with the essay on 'Hawthorne and his Mosses' when they read it in Duyckinck's *Literary World*. They did not know who had written it, since Melville had adopted the fanciful anonymity of pretending to be 'a Virginian spending July in Vermont,' but as Mrs. Hawthorne wrote to the editor, here was 'the first person who has ever in *print* apprehended Mr. Hawthorne.'

Hawthorne had read *Typee* when it came out, had liked it 'uncommonly well,' and had written a short notice of it. Now Duyckinck, who arranged for the two to meet just before the essay appeared, played the cagey impresario by sending Hawthorne the rest of Melville's books, but not yet revealing him as the essay's author. Still in ignorance, Hawthorne wrote in the same letter in which he expressed his appreciation for the generous estimate of his *Mosses*: 'I have read Melville's works with a progressive appreciation of the author. No writer ever put the reality before his reader more unflinchingly than he does in *Redburn*, and *White Jacket*. *Mardi* is a rich book, with depths here and there that compel a man to swim for his life. It is so good that one scarcely pardons the writer for not having brooded long over it, so as to make it a great deal better.'

The reserved Hawthorne liked Melville so much on their very first meeting that he asked him to come and stay a few days with him. It would be strange if fervent admiration from the man who talked to him 'about time and eternity, things of this world and of the next,' had not been a contributing cause to the more abundant activity of Hawthorne's talent in these years. Then, after the rapid succession of his three long narratives, he may have felt that he had said his say for the time being. At any rate he knew that he was still unable to live entirely by his pen, so (in 1853) he accepted his friend Pierce's offer of the consulship at Liverpool, and did not write his next book, *The Marble Faun*, until seven years later.

Melville's efflorescence came as an immediate response of his imagination to the possibilities that Hawthorne's had opened before him. Stirred by this evidence of 'the increasing greatness' among American writers, he reflected on other moments of artistic awakening, on the number of dramatists who had sur-

rounded Shakespeare, and wondered, 'Would it, indeed, appear so unreasonable to suppose, that this great fulness and overflowing may be, or may be destined to be, shared by a plurality of men of genius?' His choice of the Elizabethan drama as an example was not accidental, for he had just begun to meditate on Shakespeare more creatively than any other American writer ever has. This meditation brought him to his first profound comprehension of the nature of tragedy. This was the charge that released *Moby-Dick*, and that carried him in *Pierre* to the unbearable desperation of a Hamlet.

With the burden of those books still ahead of him, he could already perceive in Hawthorne the same kind of 'short, quick probings at the very axis of reality' that had so impressed him in Shakespeare. He realized that some of his readers would start at seeing those two names on the same page, that they would say that a lesser comparison 'might have sufficed to elucidate this Hawthorne, this small man of yesterday.' But Melville knew that he could make his contention good. He had himself previously heard Hawthorne admired for his quietness, as 'a pleasant writer, with a pleasant style,—a sequestered harmless man, from whom any deep and weighty thing would hardly be anticipated—a man who means no meanings.' But Melville quickly found this to be false. As he became fixed and fascinated by the haunting blackness in these tales, he discovered that it is often 'the least part of genius' that attracts popular admiration. In fact, he made a whole series of discoveries about Hawthorne, which are of equal value in illuminating himself. He became fully aware that there can be no authentic style unless it has been created by a meaning, by a close response to the complexity of existence. He was sure that Hawthorne's sketches, with their delicate revelations of human nature, could not have been produced by any mere technical skill. 'They argue such a depth of tenderness, such a boundless sympathy with all forms of being, such an omnipresent love, that we must needs say that this Hawthorne is here almost alone in his generation— at least, in the artistic manifestation of these things.' And as Melville conceived it, this power to sympathize with humanity could not exist in the 'high form called genius' without 'the indispensable complement of . . . a great, deep intellect which drops down into the universe like a plummet.' The conception that he was feeling his way towards here was to remain his touchstone for major literature. Both for its creation and for its appreciation there must be such a union of thought and emotion as in Hawthorne, who was 'content with the still rich utterance of a great intellect in repose . . . which sends few thoughts into circulation, except they be arterialized at his large warm lungs and expanded in his honest heart.' When Melville added that 'the great beauty in such a mind is but the product of its strength,' he had already grasped the principle upon which he was to act in evolving the right form for the massive content of *Moby-Dick*.

What made Hawthorne's somber analysis even more compelling to him was his conviction that it must have been the product of personal suffering, since 'this only can enable any man to depict it in others.' Whether there really lurked in Hawthorne, 'perhaps unknown to himself, a touch of Puritanic gloom,' Melville could not altogether tell. But he was certain, in diametrical contrast with Emerson, that 'this great power of blackness in him derives its force from its appeals to that Calvinistic sense of Innate Depravity and Original Sin, from whose visitations, in some shape or

other, no deeply thinking mind is always and wholly free . . . Perhaps no writer has ever wielded this terrific thought with greater terror than this same harmless Hawthorne.' And brooding over 'Young Goodman Brown,' which struck him as the strongest of all the tales, Melville believed it no exaggeration to call it as 'deep as Dante' in its penetration into the mystery of evil.

Such were the qualities that made Melville feel that America had at last found a native voice, and so led him to exult: 'The world is as young to-day as when it was created; and this Vermont morning dew is as wet to my feet, as Eden's dew to Adam's.' His tone of jubilation is quite like Emerson's in *The American Scholar*, though they were rejoicing in very different things. But Melville could enter fully into the satisfaction of self-reliance when it meant that his country was living no longer on borrowed experience, but belonging to itself. He also agreed with Emerson in affirming that 'it is not so much paucity as superabundance of material that seems to incapacitate modern authors.' Out of such a mood he declared, 'It is for the nation's sake, and not for her authors' sake, that I would have America be heedful of the increasing greatness among her writers.' And though he could go to the nationalistic extreme in shouting, 'Let us away with this leaven of literary flunkeyism toward England,' he generally held to a sounder basis in humanity, urging that each of our authors should write first 'like a man, for then he will be sure to write like an American.'

LESLIE FIEDLER

(b. 1917)

A poet and fiction writer as well as a scholar and critic, Leslie Fiedler is best known as a literary and social critic of conservative conviction. In his literary criticism he has been instinctively suspicious of "liberal" viewpoints of most kinds, expressing a pronounced skepticism of traditional American individualism, which he has found characteristically colored by patterns of sexual repression and deviance. Though significantly influenced by Jungian thought, Fiedler's criticism in techniques, temperament, and conviction, seems most often to be modeled on the example of D. H. Lawrence. His most important work is contained in *An End to Innocence* (1955), *Love and Death in the American Novel* (1960), and *No! in Thunder* (1960).

Come Back to the Raft Ag'in, Huck Honey! (1948)

It is perhaps to be expected that the Negro and the homosexual should become stock literary themes in a period when the exploration of responsibility and failure has become again a primary concern of our literature. It is the discrepancy they represent that haunts us, that moral discrepancy before which we are helpless, having no resources (no tradition of courtesy, no honored mode of cynicism) for dealing with a conflict of principle and practice. It used once to be fashionable to think of puritanism as a force in our lives encouraging hypocrisy; quite the contrary, its emphasis upon the singleness of belief and action, its turning of the most prosaic areas of life into arenas where one's state of grace is tested, confuse the outer and the inner and make hypocrisy among us, perhaps more strikingly than ever elsewhere, *visible*, visibly detestable, the cardinal sin. It is not without significance that the shrug of the shoulders (the acceptance of circumstance as a sufficient excuse, the sign of self-pardon before the inevitable lapse) seems in America an unfamiliar, an alien gesture.

And yet before the continued existence of physical homosexual love (our crudest epithets notoriously evoke the mechanics of such affairs), before the blatant ghettos in which the Negro conspicuously creates the gaudiness and stench that offend him, the white American must make a choice between coming to terms with institutionalized discrepancy or formulating radically new ideologies. There are, to be sure, stopgap devices, evasions of that final choice; not the least interesting is the special night club:

the "queer" café, the black-and-tan joint, in which fairy or Negro exhibit their fairy-ness, their Negro-ness as if they were mere divertissements, gags thought up for the laughs and having no reality once the lights go out and the chairs are piled on the tables by the cleaning women. In the earlier minstrel show, a Negro performer was required to put on with grease paint and burnt cork the formalized mask of blackness; while the queer must exaggerate flounce and flutter into the convention of his condition.

The situations of the Negro and the homosexual in our society pose quite opposite problems, or at least problems suggesting quite opposite solutions. Our laws on homosexuality and the context of prejudice they objectify must apparently be changed to accord with a stubborn social fact; whereas it is the social fact, our overt behavior toward the Negro, that must be modified to accord with our laws and the, at least official, morality they objectify. It is not, of course, quite so simple. There is another sense in which the fact of homosexual passion contradicts a national myth of masculine love, just as our real relationship with the Negro contradicts a myth of that relationship; and those two myths with their betrayals are, as we shall see, one.

The existence of overt homosexuality threatens to compromise an essential aspect of American sentimental life: the camaraderie of the locker room and ball park, the good fellowship of the poker game and fishing trip, a kind of passionless passion, at once gross and delicate, homoerotic in the boy's sense, possessing an innocence above suspicion. To doubt for a moment this innocence, which can survive only as *assumed*, would destroy our stubborn belief in a relationship simple, utterly satisfying, yet immune to lust; physical as the handshake is physical, this side of copulation. The nineteenth-century myth of the Immaculate Young Girl has failed to survive in any *felt* way into our time. Rather, in the dirty jokes shared among men in the smoking car, the barracks, or the dormitory, there is a common male revenge against women for having flagrantly betrayed that myth; and under the revenge, the rather smug assumption of the chastity of the revenging group, in so far as if is a purely male society. From what other source could arise that unexpected air of good clean fun which overhangs such sessions? It is this self-congratulatory buddy-buddiness, its astonishing naïveté that breed at once endless opportunities for inversion and the terrible reluctance to admit its existence, to surrender the last believed-in stronghold of love without passion.

It is, after all, what we know from a hundred other sources that is here verified: the regressiveness, in a technical sense, of American life, its implacable nostalgia for the infantile, at once wrong-headed and somehow admirable. The mythic America is boyhood—and who would dare be startled to realize that the two most popular, most *absorbed*, I am sure, of the handful of great books in our native heritage are customarily to be found, illustrated, on the shelves of the children's library. I am referring, of course, to *Moby Dick* and *Huckleberry Finn*, so different in technique and language, but alike children's books or, more precisely, *boys'* books.

There are the Leatherstocking Tales of Cooper, too, as well as Dana's *Two Years Before the Mast* and a good deal of Stephen Crane, books whose continuing favor depends more and more on the taste of boys; and one begins to foresee a similar improbable fate for Ernest Hemingway. Among the most distinguished novelists of the American past, only Henry James completely escapes classification as a writer of juvenile classics; even Hawthorne, who did

write sometimes for children, must in his most adult novels endure, though not as Mark Twain and Melville submit to, the child's perusal. A child's version of *The Scarlet Letter* would seem a rather far-fetched joke if it were not a part of our common experience. Finding in the children's department of the local library what Hawthorne liked to call his "hell-fired book," and remembering that *Moby Dick* itself has as its secret motto "*Ego te baptizo in nomine diaboli,*" one can only bow in awed silence before the mysteries of public morality, the American idea of "innocence." Everything goes except the frank description of adult heterosexual love. After all, boys will be boys!

What, then, do all these books have in common? As boys' books we should expect them shyly, guiltlessly as it were, to proffer a chaste male love as the ultimate emotional experience—and this is spectacularly the case. In Dana, it is the narrator's melancholy love for the *kanaka*, Hope; in Cooper, the lifelong affection of Natty Bumppo and Chingachgook; in Melville, Ishmael's love for Queequeg; in Twain, Huck's feeling for Nigger Jim. At the focus of emotion, where we are accustomed to find in the world's great novels some heterosexual passion, be it "platonic" love or adultery, seduction, rape, or long-drawn-out flirtation, we come instead on the fugitive slave and the no-account boy lying side by side on a raft borne by the endless river toward an impossible escape, or the pariah sailor waking in the tattooed arms of the brown harpooner on the verge of their impossible quest. "*Aloha, aikane, aloha nui,*" Hope cries to the lover who prefers him to all his fellow-whites; and Ishmael in utter frankness tells us: "I found Queequeg's arm thrown over me in the most loving and affectionate manner. You had almost thought I had been his wife . . . he still hugged me tightly, as though naught but death should part us twain . . . Thus, then, in our heart's honeymoon, lay I and Queequeg—a cosy, loving pair . . . he pressed his forehead against mine, clasped me around the waist, and said that henceforth we were married."

In Melville, the ambiguous relationship is most explicitly rendered; almost, indeed, openly explained. Not by a chance phrase or camouflaged symbol (the dressing of Jim in a woman's gown in *Huck Finn*, for instance, which can mean anything or nothing at all), but in a step-by-step exposition, the Pure Marriage of Ishmael and Queequeg is set before us: the initial going to bed together and the first shyness overcome, that great hot tomahawk-pipe accepted in a familiarity that dispels fear; next, the wedding ceremony itself (for in this marriage like so many others the ceremonial follows the deflowering), with the ritual touching of foreheads; then, the queasiness and guilt the morning after the *official* First Night, the suspicion that one has joined himself irrevocably to his own worst nightmare; finally, a symbolic portrayal of the continuing state of marriage through the image of the "monkey rope" which binds the lovers fast waist to waist (for the sake of this symbolism, Melville changes a *fact* of whaling practice—the only time in the book), a permanent alliance that provides mutual protection but also threatens mutual death.

Physical it all is, certainly, yet somehow ultimately innocent. There lies between the lovers no naked sword but a childlike ignorance, as if the possibility of a fall to the carnal had not yet been discovered. Even in the *Vita Nuova* of Dante, there is no vision of love less offensively, more unremittingly chaste; that it is not adult seems beside the point. Ishmael's sensations as he wakes under the pressure of Queequeg's arm, the tenderness of Huck's repeated loss and refinding of Jim, the role of almost Edenic helpmate played for Bumppo by the Indian—these shape us from childhood: we have no sense of first discovering them or of having been once without them.

Of the infantile, the homoerotic aspects of these stories we are, though vaguely, aware; but it is only with an effort that we can wake to a consciousness of how, among us who at the level of adulthood find a difference in color

sufficient provocation for distrust and hatred, they celebrate, all of them, the mutual love of *a white man and a colored*. So buried at a level of acceptance which does not touch reason, so desperately repressed from overt recognition, so contrary to what is usually thought of as our ultimate level of taboo —the sense of that love can survive only in the obliquity of a symbol, persistent, obsessive, in short, an archetype: the boy's homoerotic crush, the love of the black fused at this level into a single thing.

I hope I have been using here a hopelessly abused word with some precision; by "archetype" I mean a coherent pattern of beliefs and feelings so widely shared at a level beneath consciousness that there exists no abstract vocabulary for representing it, and so "sacred" that unexamined, irrational restraints inhibit any explicit analysis. Such a complex finds a formula or pattern story, which serves both to embody it, and, at first at least, to conceal its full implications. Later, the secret may be revealed, the archetype "analyzed" or "allegorically" interpreted according to the language of the day.

I find the complex we have been examining genuinely mythic; certainly it has the invisible character of the true archetype, eluding the wary pounce of Howells or Mrs. Twain, who excised from *Huckleberry Finn* the cussing as unfit for children, but who left, unperceived, a conventionally abhorrent doctrine of ideal love. Even the writers in whom we find it attained it, in a sense, dreaming. The felt difference between *Huckleberry Finn* and Twain's other books must lie in part in the release from conscious restraint inherent in the author's assumption of the character of Huck; the passage in and out of darkness and river mist, the constant confusion of identities (Huck's ten or twelve names; the question of who is the real uncle, who the true Tom), the sudden intrusions into alien violences without past or future, give the whole work, for all its carefully observed detail, the texture of a dream. For *Moby Dick* such a point need scarcely be made. Even

Cooper, despite his insufferable gentlemanliness, his tedium, cannot conceal from the kids who continue to read him the secret behind his overconscious prose: the childish, impossible dream. D. H. Lawrence saw in him clearly the boy's Utopia: the absolute wilderness in which the stuffiness of home yields to the wigwam, and "My Wife" to Chingachgook.

I do not recall ever having seen in the commentaries of the social anthropologist or psychologist an awareness of the role of this profound child's dream of love in our relation to the Negro. (I say Negro, though the beloved in the books I have mentioned is variously Indian and Polynesian, because the Negro has become more and more exclusively for us *the* colored man, the colored man *par excellence*.) Trapped in what have by now become shackling clichés—the concept of the white man's sexual envy of the Negro male, the ambivalent horror of miscegenation—they do not sufficiently note the complementary factor of physical attraction, the archetypal love of white male and black. But either the horror or the attraction is meaningless alone; only together do they make sense. Just as the pure love of man and man is in general set off against the ignoble passion of man for woman, so more specifically (and more vividly) the dark desire which leads to miscegenation is contrasted with the ennobling love of a white man and a colored one. James Fenimore Cooper is our first poet of this ambivalence; indeed, miscegenation is the secret theme of the Leatherstocking novels, especially of *The Last of the Mohicans*. Natty Bumppo, the man who boasts always of having "no cross" in *his* blood, flees by nature from the defilement of all women, but never with so absolute a revulsion as he displays toward the *squaw* with whom at one point he seems at the point of being forced to cohabit; and the threat of the dark-skinned rapist sends pale woman after pale woman skittering through Cooper's imagined wilderness. Even poor Cora, who already has a fatal drop of alien blood that cuts her off from any marriage with a white man, in so far as she is white cannot be mated with Uncas, the noblest of redmen. Only in death can they be joined in an embrace as chaste as that of males. There's no good woman but a dead woman! Yet Chingachgook and the Deerslayer are permitted to sit night after night over their campfire in the purest domestic bliss. So long as there is no mingling of blood, soul may couple with soul in God's undefiled forest.

Nature undefiled—this is the inevitable setting of the Sacred Marriage of males. Ishmael and Queequeg, arm in arm, about to ship out, Huck and Jim swimming beside the raft in the peaceful flux of the Mississippi—here it is the motion of water which completes the syndrome, the American dream of isolation afloat. The notion of the Negro as the unblemished bride blends with the myth of running away to sea, of running the great river down to the sea. The immensity of water defines a loneliness that demands love; its strangeness symbolizes the disavowal of the conventional that makes possible all versions of love. In *Two Years Before the Mast*, in *Moby Dick*, in *Huckleberry Finn* the water is there, is the very texture of the novel; the Leatherstocking Tales propose another symbol for the same meaning: the virgin forest. Notice the adjectives—the virgin forest and the forever inviolable sea. It is well to remember, too, what surely must be more than a coincidence, that Cooper, who could dream this myth, also invented for us the novel of the sea, wrote for the first time in history the sea story proper.

The rude pederasty of the forecastle and the captain's cabin, celebrated in a thousand jokes, is the profanation of a dream; yet Melville, who must have known such blasphemies, refers to them only once and indirectly, for it was *his* dream that they threatened. And still the dream survives; in a recent book by Gore Vidal, an incipient homosexual, not yet aware of the implications of his feelings, indulges in the reverie of running off to sea with his dearest friend. The buggery of sailors is taken for granted everywhere, yet is thought of usually as an inversion forced on men by their isolation from women; though the opposite case may well be true: the isolation sought more or less consciously as an occasion for male encounters. At any rate, there is a context in which the legend of the sea as escape and solace, the fixated sexuality of boys, the myth of the dark beloved, are one. In Melville and Twain at the center of our tradition, in the lesser writers at the periphery, the archetype is at once formalized and perpetuated. Nigger Jim and Queequeg make concrete for us what was without them a vague pressure on the threshold of our consciousness; the proper existence of the archetype is in the realized character, who waits, as it were, only to be asked his secret. Think of Oedipus biding in silence from Sophocles to Freud!

Unwittingly, we are possessed in childhood by these characters and their undiscriminated meaning, and it is difficult for us to dissociate them without a sense of disbelief. What—these household figures clues to our subtlest passions! The foreigner finds it easier to perceive the significances too deep within us to be brought into focus. D. H. Lawrence discovered in our classics a linked mythos of escape and immaculate male love; Lorca in *The Poet in New York* grasped instinctively (he could not even read English) the kinship of Harlem and Walt Whitman, the fairy as bard. But of course we do not have to be conscious of what possesses us; in every generation of our own writers the archetype reappears, refracted, half-understood, but *there*. In the gothic reverie of Capote's *Other Voices, Other Rooms*, both elements of the syndrome are presented, though disjunctively: the boy moving between the love of a Negro maidservant and his inverted cousin. In Carson McCullers' *Member of the Wedding*, another variant is invented: a *female* homosexual romance between the boy-girl Frankie and a Negro cook. This time the Father-Slave-Beloved is converted into the figure of a Mother-Sweetheart-Servant, but remains still, of course, satisfactorily black. It is not strange, after all, to find this archetypal complex in latter-day writers of a frankly homosexual sensibility; but it recurs, too, in such resolutely masculine writers as Faulkner, who evokes the myth in the persons of the Negro and the boy of *Intruder in the Dust*.

In the myth, one notes finally, it is typically in the role of outcast, ragged woodsman, or despised sailor ("Call me Ishmael!"), or unregenerate boy (Huck before the prospect of being "sivilized" cries out, "I been there before!") that we turn to the love of a colored man. But how, we cannot help asking, does the vision of the white American as a pariah correspond with our long-held public status: the world's beloved, the success? It is perhaps only the artist's portrayal of *himself*, the notoriously alienated writer in America, at home with such images, child of the town drunk, the hapless survivor. But no, Ishmael is in all of us, our unconfessed universal fear objectified in the writer's status as in the outcast sailor's: that compelling anxiety, which every foreigner notes, that we may not be loved, that we are loved for our possessions and not our selves, that we are really—*alone*. It is that underlying terror which explains our incredulity in the face of adulation or favor, what is called (once more the happy adjective) our "boyish modesty."

Our dark-skinned beloved will take us in, we assure ourselves, when we have been cut off, or have cut ourselves off, from all others, without rancor or the insult of forgiveness. He will fold us in his arms saying, "Honey" or "Aikane"; he will comfort us, as if our offense against him were long ago remitted, were never truly *real*. And yet we cannot ever really forget our guilt; the stories that embody the myth dramatize as if compulsively the role of the colored man as the victim. Dana's Hope is shown dying of the white man's syphilis; Queequeg is portrayed as racked by fever, a pointless episode except in the light of this necessity; Crane's Negro is disfigured to the point of monstrosity; Cooper's Indian smolders to a hopeless old age conscious of the imminent disappearance of his race; Jim is shown loaded down with chains, weakened by the hundred torments dreamed up by Tom in the name of bulliness. The immense gulf of guilt must not be mitigated any more than the disparity of color (Queequeg is not merely brown but monstrously tattooed; Chingachgook is horrid with paint; Jim is portrayed as the sick A-rab died blue), so that the final reconciliation may seem more unbelievable and tender. The archetype makes no attempt to deny our outrage as fact; it portrays it as meaningless in the face of love.

There would be something insufferable, I think, in that final vision of remission if it were not for the presence of a motivating anxiety, the sense always of a last chance. Behind the white American's nightmare that someday, no longer tourist, inheritor, or liberator, he will be rejected, refused, he dreams of his acceptance at the breast he has most utterly offended. It is a dream so sentimental, so outrageous, so desperate, that it redeems our concept of boyhood from nostalgia to tragedy.

In each generation we *play out* the impossible mythos, and we live to see our children play it: the white boy and the black we can discover wrestling affectionately on any American sidewalk, along which they will walk in adulthood, eyes averted from each other, unwilling to touch even by accident. The dream recedes; the immaculate passion and the astonishing reconciliation become a memory, and less, a regret, at last the unrecognized motifs of a child's book. "It's too good to be true, Honey," Jim says to Huck. "It's too good to be true."

AUSTIN WARREN

(b. 1899)

A scholar-critic with a wide range of interests, Austin Warren has been associated for many years with the New Criticism. His identification with some of its major principles and causes, and his emphasis at the same time upon the historical backgrounds of the religious and moral content of literature, is one indication that the New Criticism cannot be characterized with perfect validity as an "anti-historical," "textual," or "ontological" criticism. Warren's critical and scholarly works include *Alexander Pope as Critic and Humanist* (1929), *The Elder Henry James* (1934), *Richard Crashaw, A Study in Baroque Sensibility* (1939), *Rage for Order* (1948), *Theory of Literature* (with René Wellek, 1949), and *New England Saints* (1956).

The New England Conscience, Henry James, and Ambassador Strether (1962)

The 'NEW ENGLAND CONSCIENCE' I cannot find used by any writer before Henry James used it in his *Notebooks*—an 1895 entry; yet, as James five years later used the phrase in single quotes, it

Reprinted from *The Minnesota Review*, Vol. II (Winter, 1962), pp. 151-61, by permission of the author and the editors of *The Minnesota Review*. Copyright 1962 by *The Minnesota Review*.

was presumably an already current phrase. But it does not appear in Hawthorne or in Mrs. Stowe's New England novels: they describe the phenomenon but never name it. It seems probable that, like 'Puritan', it was first devised by an outside observer or critic,—and that it may have first been used pejoratively,—by those who did not regard the private conscience (if I may be tautological) as both infallible and inexorable. Whether or no this conjecture be accurate, by the end of the nineteenth century New Englanders came to pride themselves on the possession of this high and morbid ethicality.

Such stringency of conscience is, of course, not limited to New Englanders. Matthew Arnold has wise things to say about it in his *Culture and Anarchy* (1869) when he speaks of a "strict conscience" as the pride of English Puritanism,—a term which he chronologically extends to include the Nonconformists of his own time. Recommending that the Hebraic conscience be supplemented by the Hellenic consciousness, he appositely quotes the eighteenth century Anglican Bishop Wilson's maxim, "Never go against the best light you have, [but] take care that your light be not darkness." I understand this maxim to mean—as I think Arnold took it to mean—that conscience is a man's ethical light and moral imperative, and must be followed, but that a second and equal—or better say, almost equal—duty is to regard the conscience as educable.

It would be a mistake also to suppose that over-conscientiousness to be purely a Protestant phenomenon. The Catholic Church knows it and calls it 'scrupulosity'—a perpetual self-scrutiny, such a concern about details of conduct and purity of intention as leaves the penitent always uncertain whether he has confessed all his sins and whether his absolution is valid since he is not sure whether he has been truly or adequately enough penitent.

None the less, the fussy and over-exacting conscience is, in my judgment, commoner among Protestants than among Catholics, and commonest among those who are 'ethnically' rather than theologically Protestant. The seventeenth century Puritan, like the Orthodox Jew, had an intricate and manifold series of duties prescribed by the infallible Bible and the almost infallible clergy; but the latter-day Protestant has no Church to prescribe his major duties and no confessional save his own journals. He is still under the Law, or rather the Laws, and cannot apprehend that Love is the fulfilling of the Law.

Now comes an important distinction. Suffering for conscience's sake is not to be confounded with suffering from conscience. The former,—the lot sometimes unchosen and sometimes rather perversely chosen—by Christians among pagans, by Catholics among Protestants, by Puritans among Anglicans, by Quakers and Seekers among Puritans—consists in being beaten, imprisoned, sent into exile, or put to death, and has its own reward in the martyr's crown. Such persons are what we now call 'conscientious objectors.' They are not tormented by their own consciences but by rival theologies and rival ecclesiasticisms.

The second group are those who suffer interiorly. They are tormented by doubts and scruples, feel the mixed—and, hence, impure—motives which prompt them to perform what, externally considered, are 'good works,' never feel worthy enough to 'join the church,' never, however many duties they may have performed, feel that they have adequately done their Duty, never feel their contrition adequate to the assurance of Divine pardon.

The immigrant Fathers of New England appear to have been untroubled by conscience in this second sense. Converted either from religious indifference or from the 'imperfectly reformed' Church of England, they felt no serious doubt of their being, in the language of St. Paul's Epistle to the Romans, 'saints' and the 'elect.' They had suffered imprisonment or, at any event, silencing at the mandates of Archbishop Laud, suffered again the journey, which they forever compared to the Israelites' journey through the wilderness to Canaan, which brought them to a place where they could found a truly theocratic state; and at last they were, as they delighted to repeat, a "city set upon a hill," an exemplar to the rest of the world.

The Journals of Michael Wiggles

worth, an early Harvard graduate, and of Cotton Mather, grandson of immigrant clergy, show much self-chastisement—and, in the case of Mather—many instances of 'special providences' —self-glorifications viewed as signs of angelic, if not Divine, visitations; but in both cases,—and especially Mather's—it is difficult to distinguish between rhetoric and the desire to edify posterity on the one hand and, on the other, sincere pangs of conscience.

Jonathan Edwards is the beginning of a new theological and ethical era. No one can read his Resolutions and his Diary without feeling that they are straightforward wrestlings of the soul; and I cannot doubt that he was a saint in that more special and Catholic sense unintended by the Pauline and Puritan use of 'saints' as meaning all members of the visible churches of Christ. With Edwards and his *Treatise on the Religious Affections*, and with his disciples, Hopkins, Bellamy and Emmons, the New England conscience as directed against oneself instead of against others begins to take shape. It is manifest in Mrs. Marvyn, a chief figure in Mrs. Stowe's *The Minister's Wooing*—Mrs. Marvyn, who sits weekly under the once famous Dr. Hopkins' Edwardsean sermons, is scrupulous in the performance of every duty, yet can never feel that God has elected her to salvation. It is manifest in Dr. Hopkins' own celebrated test of sanctity: that one should be willing to be damned for the glory of God. That was a test which certainly never occurred to seventeenth century Puritans. Indeed, in the whole period of Edwardsean theology, so distinct from the earlier so-called Calvinism of the immigrant Fathers, one sees conscience turning from the testimony that one is elect to the doubt whether one is not only damned but worthy of damnation.

Unitarianism, of the benign Boston variety, might be expected to mitigate the New England conscience. But here comes another turn of the screw. Legalism and theological system give their own security. To dissolve and discharge them leaves men free to worldliness or to antinomianism or to moralism, but also to self-doubt and self-scrutiny and self-laceration.

Emerson was an innocent antinomian. Says the father of the Jameses, Emerson "never felt a movement of the life of conscience from the day of his birth till that of his death." And James adds, "if we are still to go on cherishing any such luxury as a private conscience toward God, I greatly prefer for my own part that it should be an evil conscience. Conscience was always intended as a rebuke and never as an exhilaration to the private citizen." Emerson knew youthful depression and sense of inferiority, but he never knew either of the two religious realizations of man,—the sense of sin of the Western Church or the sense of finiteness of the Eastern Church. He was, as William James said in *The Varieties*, once-born.

Yet Emerson is not a representative of the New England conscience. Eventually, the New England conscience is left faced, not with serene and blithe innocence but with the impersonal concept of Duty,—not with some naturalistic or humanistic version of Grace but with the Moral Law, a concept and a tyrant more rigid and all-searching, of a rectitude to which one can never attain because it is a perfection both of taste, manners, conduct, and motives. And, as with the ancient Jews, Law does not separate itself from Laws. There are so many high principles to be followed that the high principles themselves conflict, and every case becomes a 'case of conscience'—that is, an attempt to discover which high principle must take precedence over what other high principle. The hedonist may be happy; the saint may say with St. Augustine, "Love and do what you will"; but either the lower or the higher spontaneity is ruled out by the supremacy of Duty.

Howells' novel of 1891 is called *An Imperative Duty*; but to the mind of one like his character, Mrs. Meredith, whom he first met in company of "a serious young clergyman, sojourning in Florence after a journey to the Holy

Land," every duty is in turn an imperative, for she has "a conscience of prodigious magnifying force, cultivated to the last degree by constant training upon the ethical problems of fiction" such as George Eliot's.

Henry James, who was not a New Englander by birth but who was a curious and attentive observer and analyst of its conscience, even before, in 1866, he met Howells, also not of New England origins but a convert to Boston and its conscience, notably employed himself in the definition of something at once alien and repellent but also, with whatever civilized improvements, an ineradicable part of himself.

In that little masterpiece, *The Europeans: A Sketch* (1878), he dealt with the Unitarian New England "upwards of thirty years since"—that is, the 1840's, the age of Channing Unitarianism as well as of Transcendentalism. The 'Europeans' are expatriate Americans whose uncle is the New England gentleman, Mr. Wentworth; and James sees the Wentworths through the expatriates' eyes and the expatriates through the Wentworths' and those of their Unitarian pastor, Mr. Brand. James already anticipates Mr. Wentworth's judgment when he describes expatriate Felix as having a face "at once benevolent and picturesque" but "not at all serious."

Gertrude Wentworth is a rebellious New England girl who is introduced in conjunction with her serious sister and her serious young pastor. It is Sunday morning, and she is not going to church. Her sister is, and when Gertrude criticizes her sister's hairdo, her sister replies, "I don't think one should ever try to look pretty." The clergyman thinks she is staying at home because she is depressed. Gertrude replies, "Depressed. I am never depressed." "Oh, surely, sometimes," he replies, as if he thought this a regrettable account of oneself. "I am never depressed," Gertrude repeats. "But I am sometimes wicked. When I am wicked I am in high spirits."

Reporting his introductory visit to his sister, Felix, the 'European', meets her comment: "They must be Puritans to their fingertips; anything but gay." "No, they are not gay," he admits. "They are sober; they are even severe. They are of a pensive cast; they take things hard . . . they have some melancholy memory or some *depressing expectation*. It's not the epicurean temperament. My uncle, Mr. Wentworth, is a tremendously high-toned old fellow; he looks as if he were undergoing martyrdom, not by fire."

When the sister, morganatic wife of a German Prince, comes to call with her brother, Mr. Wentworth looks "very rigid and grave" and "almost cadaverous"; but Felix's "light imagination had gained a glimpse of Mr. Wentworth's spiritual mechanism, and taught him that the old man being *infinitely conscientious*, the special operating conscience within him announced itself by several of the indications of physical faintness." This is naturally a grave occasion for a man infinitely conscientious: how to treat a lady so aristocratic, so unhappy and also, presumably, as a Catholic and European, so refinedly corrupt.

So much for the Wentworths of the 1840's.

In 1895, a young friend's mention of Howells in Paris, where he "had scarcely been . . . even in former days" and of Howells' sadly serious injunction to the young friend, "Live all you can: it's a mistake not to . . . I haven't done so—and now I'm old. It's too late," starts in James' mind the theme of *The Ambassadors*. His long *Notebook* entry of 1895 and his 20,000 word Prospectus for the novel, sent about 1900 to Harpers and published in the *Notebooks*, made clear the extent to which this novel was James' most serious as well as final dealing with the New England conscience.

The *Notebook* entries are conceptual and explicit in a way James as an artist would never be—and is not—in his novel. His hero, suggested by Howells, the convert to Boston, is a man "who hasn't 'lived,' hasn't at all in the sense of sensations, passions, impulses, pleasures. . . . He has never really enjoyed

—he has lived only for Duty [capitalized] and *conscience—his conception of them*; . . . lived for effort, for surrender, abstention, sacrifice." "He has married very young, and austerely. Happily enough, but charmlessly and oh, so conscientiously: a wife replete with the New England conscience." Now long a widower, he has been taken under the financial and moral protection of a New England and wealthy widow, an imposing figure in her city,—some place like Providence, Worcester, or Hartford. She is, says James, a reflection of Strether's pre-European initiation; and, as befits the American world, the woman is "of the strenuous pattern,"—Strether of the passive. She is will without imagination —unlike "poor Strether," who, despite his conscientiousness, has "imagination," that is, can conceive of other ways of being right than in his own suffering way.

Both Mrs. Newsome and Strether have New England consciences; but their consciences are of different species. Strether is said, in *The Ambassadors*, to arrive in Paris weary, perhaps on the verge of breakdown; but the representation scarcely bears out the assertion: he is, rather, frustrate at the ineffectuality of his life's efforts and mildly puzzled that being good has not made him happy.

Mrs. Newsome has no qualms on that score. She knows that we were not put here on earth to be happy; and her worries are not puzzles about herself. She must expiate, by her philanthropy, the unscrupulous ways by which her late husband left her wealthy; she must save her son, who has been for a few years in Paris, studying art and love, and who is presumably detained from returning to the unscrupulous promotion of her late husband's business by a sordid sexual attachment; she also is a woman of what used to be called 'culture and refinement,' and hence unavoidably distressed by, as well as with familial piety attached to, her daughter, not so cultured and refined, and her daughter's husband, who is even less so.

As a woman of force, Mrs. Newsome is a kind of New England counterpart of Aunt Maud Lowder in *The Wings of the Dove*; but the difference between the two types of Anglo-Saxons is rendered perfectly and—not at all strangely —in accord with Hawthorne's impressions of the two in *Our Old Home*. Mrs. Lowder is untroubled by conscience or nerves: she is Britannia seated on her money-bags and ruling the waves while Mrs. Newsome is a beautiful specimen of one kind of late nineteenth century American woman: when James says, in his characteristic way, that she is "a really remarkable woman" he does not mean to praise her but to delight in her being so remarkably pure a specimen of a type. She is "high, strenuous, nervous, 'intense' (oh, a type)—*full of ideals and activities*"—a delicious phrase. "She is many other things besides; invalidic, exalted, depressed, at once shrill and muffled, at once abounding and extremely narrow . . . she is a particularly intense and energetic invalid," ever active, by virtue of her "restless conscience"—one, of course, directed towards others—in charities, reforms, and good works.

Mrs. Newsome loves Strether, "poor fine melancholy, missing, striving, Strether": all of James' later sensitively passive men are Strethers; but he is not reported in the *Notebooks* as doing more than admiring and esteeming her. Indeed—though James can never bring either himself or Strether to say so, they both almost certainly fear and somewhat dislike her, though James has the advantage over Strether of seeing her as comic as well as—what Strether comes to see her as—narrow and unimaginatively righteous. Talking of her to Maria Gostrey, "his eyes might have been fixing some particularly large iceberg in a cool blue northern sea." Maria rejoins, "There's nothing so magnificent—for making others feel you—as to have no imagination." With full confidence in truth, undeniable in the sense intended, James successfully makes Mrs. Newsome, the unimaginative, present in the novel only through the force she exerts on the imaginative.

At the instigation of Mrs. Newsome, Strether sets out for Paris to rescue Chad from his un-New England ways. The manifest irony is that, finding Chad vastly—and, for the reader, somewhat incredibly—improved over his earlier self,—now indeed, at least temporarily, and in Strether's eyes—Strether is forced to a conception of salvation opposite to that with which he came. To save Chad is not to take him back to Worcester, Mass., but to keep him from returning. In this he finally fails. Chad's somewhat incredible elegance is attributable to the influence upon him of a Catholic noblewoman who, by her code, cannot marry him. As the *Notebooks* make more explicit than the novel, there is much of the unscrupulous late Mr. Newsome in Chad; and at the end of the novel he is fascinatedly studying that peculiarly unsavory American art, the art of advertising, and about to become a successful business man at Worcester.

But Chad's failure to be—only to seem—a man of imagination; the passive, borrowed, and temporary quality of his civilizing—is only incidental to James' book. Its real subject, as well as its point of view, is Strether. Its real theme is the inadequacy of the famous New England conscience. Strether—and apparently Mrs. Newsome—are not even Unitarians; but, as for conscience, each has been accustomed to accuse the other of being "morbid"—that is, overbeset by the sense of guilt and the sense of duty; and they both hold inflexibly to the conception that all adultery is a sin and that happiness is dangerous—if not indeed evil.

What occurs to Strether in his three or four months in Europe can be called either the development of conscience into consciousness,—or the change from the view of conscience as identical with its early presuppositions and mandates to the view that conscience is educable.

James calls his novel *The Ambassadors*, for the sake of the comic and the ironic; but it might, more seriously, have been called *The Instructors* or—had not he earlier used that title with delicate irony for a delicate and masterful *nouvelle,* "The Pupil." The novel is a novel of initiation, a *Bildungsroman.* Strether's instructors are Miss Gostrey, Chad, little Bilham, Mme. de Vionnet.

The first-named is the most explicit and pedagogic. She takes her disciple in hand from his arrival at Liverpool and relinquishes her commentaries only when she feels sure that he can "toddle alone"; and she establishes immediately an intellectual intimacy which makes him feel disloyal to the betrothed Mrs. Newsome.

Miss Gostrey directly sets to work on Strether. Strolling with her through Chester, Strether feels delight in the picturesque, dim memories of his former visit at twenty-five, but also conscience. "It was with Waymarsh he should have shared" this experience; and he was now, then, taking from Waymarsh "something that was his due." His observant mentor quickly comments, "You're doing something that you think not right." The dialogue on the sin of even pleasure goes on, with Strether's question, "Am I enjoying it as much as that?" and Maria's replying, adapting herself to a New Englander by reminding him that pleasure may be a duty, "You're not enjoying it, I think, so much as you ought," and Strether's presently saying, "Woollett [the name finally adopted for Worcester] isn't sure it ought to enjoy." His guide responds, "I wish you would let me show you how" to enjoy.

But, thus committing himself, he confesses to fearing; and he further expands the plight of the man beset by duties: "I'm always considering something else, something else, I mean, than the thing of the moment." Rebuked, he says, he knows he shouldn't. "If only I could! But that's the deuce of it—that I never can."

Paris abounds in surprises for Strether. He attempts to do his manifest duty. He indites long letters to Mrs. Newsome, long ambassadorial reports on things seen and heard; and as regularly for a time receives long replies from Woollett. But the time comes when

Woollett letters cease, and a cable demands the ambassador's immediate return. He defies it, only to learn that his post is to be occupied by newly appointed and more sturdy legates. They come; before they depart, Mrs. Newsome's daughter Sarah summons Strether that he may make his submission. As Mrs. Newsome is "essentially all moral pressure," so, through Sarah, she "reaches him by the lengthened arm of the spirit." Still he resists; and Sarah has to remonstrate against his attitude toward the relation between Chad and Mme. de Vionnet—his acting as though there could be a doubt—as between Chad's loyalties—of Chad's duty. Strether has to ponder not only the question but "the sore abysses it revealed" before he can bravely answer, "Of course they're totally different sorts of duty"—an abstract reply which might be intelligible to the New England mind were it not followed by an affronting explication to the effect that Strether's state of mind, and—by polite, if not ironic, inclusion, pre-European—Sarah's proceeded from "our queer New England ignorance, our queer misconceptions and confusions—from which, since then, an inexorable tide of light seems to have floated us into our perhaps still queerer knowledge."

Sarah and party leave indignantly and virtuously for the Alps: and now Strether faces, in Book XI, a new trial of conscience and consciousness. He has had earlier adjustments to make—for eminent example that it is a married mother and not her daughter with whom Chad is in love. Yet he has been sustained by a formula which he has been careful not to test too rigorously—little Bilham's formula that what was under scrutiny was "an innocent attachment." Now he is called upon to witness not indeed the act of adultery but a situation which can scarcely be interpreted by easy inference as other; and his consciousness is forced to admit both that the relationship between Chad and Mme. de Vionnet has never been purely 'spiritual' and yet that little Bilham's delicate ambiguity of an "innocent at-

tachment" was, in a sense which he can no longer deny, true. If there can be a conflict between duties, so there can be a distinction between sexual relations,—a point made, to Anglo-Saxon distress, by Swedenborg in his book, *Conjugial Love.*

Mme. de Vionnet does her subtle best at face-saving, not for her sake or Chad's but for Strether's; yet he is left with three pains,—the "quantity of make-believe involved, and so vividly exemplified, that most disagreed with his spiritual stomach," and, in one of those "vain vigils," those sleepless nights, so often attributed to 'poor Strether', with the pity that the make-belief should be "so much like lying," and, lastly, with the contrast the intimacy of others thus revealed and his own cold loneliness.

Now Strether's conscience has been educated, stretched, as far as it can go. He has learned to distinguish, in the case of others, tints and shades between white and black. And to this new-found ability to distinguish—or to admit to his consciousness that he can distinguish—he has sacrificed his chance of returning to Woollett, his marriage to Mrs. Newsome, his thus acquired economic security, although perhaps the first two were not severe losses but partly releases. Miss Gostrey must test out whether his knowledge of the "virtuous attachment's" real nature, a knowledge she had all along possessed but felt he was conceivably not ready to take, has made "an arrest of his independence . . . , a revulsion in favor of the principles of Woollett"; she discovers it has not. He has arrived at one of the latest refinements of the New England conscience: that one can charitably allow others to do what one wouldn't do oneself, or, to put it another way, that one's public conscience is emancipated beyond one's private.

There are no very credible reasons why Strether must return to New England. Mme. de Vionnet, represented as to him the most attractive of women, would accept him as her lover; Chad would support him; Maria Gostrey wants to marry him, and in her he would have a sympathetic and intelligent companion. This rejection of Miss Gostrey is not eased for the reader by James' calling her the novel's *ficelle*; and Strether's rejection of her proposal —Strether must always be proposed to —certainly appears—if one wants to phrase it so—as failure to do a duty. But still Strether must return. The only reason he can give Maria is that he must go "to be right" and that "to be right" is, "out of the whole affair, not to have got anything for myself."

The last scenes with both Mme. de Vionnet and Miss Gostrey are masterly in the women's shrewd appraisals of Strether. According to the former, to feel himself victimized is evidently the way he must live. The latter reminds him that he has got something for himself—his "wonderful impressions" but, when reminded that he has not got, be-cause not asked for, her, charmingly asks, "But why should you be so dreadfully right?"

James manages to shift the emphasis in the final lines of dialogue by having Miss Gostrey pun on the word *right*. In her question, *right* meant *good*; and *good* means *self-sacrificing*; in her final and, as James calls it, her "defeated protest," the word shifts its meaning to 'true to type.' "It isn't so much you're being 'right'—it's your horrible sharp eye for what makes you so."

Yet Miss Gostrey's question remains —Why does Strether have to be so "dreadfully right"? And perhaps no less her comment. Strether's emancipated conscience in judging others,—an emancipation painful to him in the process and hardly joyful in the end— has still left him pride—his pride in the supererogatory rigors of his own, his New England, conscience.

PHILIP RAHV

(b. 1908)

A former Marxist and an editor of *The Partisan Review* since its founding in 193 Philip Rahv is an independent socialist in political viewpoint whose primary critic interest has been the study of fiction as an imaginative response to political an social history. Rahv has edited several volumes of criticism and fiction, includir collections of the shorter fiction of James and Tolstoy, and the collection of critic essays, *Literature in America* (1957); his most important essays are collected *Image and Idea* (1949; 1957).

The Cult of Experience in American Writing (1940)

Every attentive reader of Henry James remembers that highly dramatic scene in *The Ambassadors*—a scene singled out by its author as giving away the "whole

From *Image and Idea* by Philip Rahv. Copyright 1940, 1949 by Philip Rahv. Reprinted by permission of the author.

case" of his novel—in which Lambe Strether, the elderly New England ge tleman who had come to Paris on a m sion of business and duty, proclaims conversion to the doctrine of experien Caught in the spell of Paris, the disco ery of whose grace and form is mark for him by a kind of meaning and intensity that can be likened only to the raptures of a mystic vision, Strether feels moved to renounce publicly the morality of abstention he had brought with him from Woollett, Mass. And that mellow Sunday afternoon, as he mingles with the charming guests assembled in the garden of the sculptor Gloriani, the spell of the world capital of civilization is so strong upon the sensitive old man that he trembles with happiness and zeal. It is then that he communicates to little Bilham his newly acquired piety toward life and the fruits thereof. The worst mistake one can make, he admonishes his youthful interlocutor, is not to live all one can.—"Do what you like so long as you don't make my mistake . . . Live! . . . It doesn't so much matter what you do in particular, so long as you have your life. If you haven't had that, what *have* you had? . . . This place and these impressions . . . have had their abundant message for me, have just dropped *that* into my mind. I see it now . . . and more than you'd believe or I can express. . . . The right time is now yours. The right time is any *time* that one is still so lucky as to have . . . Live, Live!"

To an imaginative European, unfamiliar with the prohibitive American past and the long-standing national habit of playing hide and seek with experience, Strether's pronouncements in favor of sheer life may well seem so commonplace as scarcely to be worth the loving concentration of a major novelist. While the idea that one should "live" one's life came to James as a revelation, to the contemporary European writers this idea had long been a thoroughly assimilated and natural assumption. Experience served them as the concrete medium for the testing and creation of values, whereas in James's work it stands for something distilled or selected from the total process of living; it stands for romance, reality, civilization—a self-propelling, autonomous "presence" inexhaustibly alluring in its own right. That is the "presence" which in the imagination of Hyacinth Robin-

son, the hero of *The Princess Casamassima*, takes on a form at once "vast, vague, and dazzling—an irradiation of light from objects undefined, mixed with the atmosphere of Paris and Venice."

The significance of this positive approach to experience and identification of it with life's "treasures, felicities, splendors and successes" is that it represents a momentous break with the then dominant American morality of abstention. The roots of this morality are to be traced on the one hand to the religion of the Puritans and, on the other, to the inescapable need of a frontier society to master its world in sober practice before appropriating it as an object of enjoyment. Such is the historical content of that native "innocence" which in James's fiction is continually being ensnared in the web of European "experience." And James's tendency is to resolve this drama of entanglement by finally accepting what Europe offers on condition that it cleanse itself of its taint of evil through an alliance with New World virtue.

James's attitude toward experience is sometimes overlooked by readers excessively impressed (or depressed) by his oblique methods and effects of remoteness and ambiguity. Actually, from the standpoint of the history of the national letters, the lesson he taught in *The Ambassadors*, as in many of his other works, must be understood as no less than a revolutionary appeal. It is a veritable declaration of the rights of man —not, to be sure, of the rights of the public, of the social man, but of the rights of the private man, of the rights of personality, whose openness to experience provides the sole effective guaranty of its development. Already in one of his earliest stories we find the observation that "in this country the people have rights but the person has none." And in so far as any artist can be said to have had a mission, his manifestly was to brace the American individual in his moral struggle to gain for his personal and subjective life that measure of freedom which, as a citizen of a prosperous and democratic community, he had long been enjoying in the sphere of material and political relations.

Strether's appeal, in curiously elaborated, varied, as well as ambivalent forms, pervades all of James's work; and for purposes of critical symbolization it might well be regarded as the compositional key to the whole modern movement in American writing. No literature, it might be said, takes on the qualities of a truly national body of expression unless it is possessed by a basic theme and unifying principle of its own. Thus the German creative mind has in the main been actuated by philosophical interests, the French by the highest ambitions of the intelligence unrestrained by system or dogma, the Russian by the passionately candid questioning and shaping of values. And since Whitman and James the American creative mind, seizing at last upon what had long been denied to it, has found the terms and objects of its activity in the urge toward and immersion in experience. It is this search for experience, conducted on diverse and often conflicting levels of consciousness, which has been the dominant, quintessential theme of the characteristic American literary productions—from *Leaves of Grass* to *Winesburg, Ohio* and beyond; and the more typically American the writer—a figure like Thomas Wolfe is a patent example—the more deeply does it engulf him.

It is through this preoccupation, it seems to me, that one can account, perhaps more adequately than through any other factor, for some of the peculiarities of American writing since the close of its classic period. A basis is thus provided for explaining the unique indifference of this literature to certain cultural aims implicit in the aesthetic rendering of experience—to ideas generally, to theories of value, to the wit of the speculative and problematical, and, to that new-fashioned sense of irony which at once expresses and modulates the conflicts in modern belief. In his own way even a writer as intensely aware as James shares this indifference. He is the analyst of fine consciences, and fine minds too, but scarcely of minds capable of grasping and acting upon those ineluctable problems that enter so prominently and with such significant results into the literary art developed in Europe during the past hundred years. And the question is not whether James belonged among the "great thinkers"—very few novelists do—but whether he is "obsessed" by those universal problems, whether, in other words, his work is vitally associated with that prolonged crisis of the human spirit to which the concept of modernity is ultimately reducible. What James asks for, primarily, is the expansion of life beyond its primitive needs and elementary standards of moral and material utility; and of culture he conceives as the reward of this expansion and as its unfailing means of discrimination. Hence he searches for the whereabouts of "Life" and for the exact conditions of its enrichment. This is what makes for a fundamental difference between the inner movement of the American and that of the European novel, the novel of Tolstoy and Dostoevsky, Flaubert and Proust, Joyce, Mann, Lawrence, and Kafka, whose problem is invariably posed in terms of life's intrinsic worth and destiny.

The intellectual is the only character missing in the American novel. He may appear in it in his professional capacity —as artist, teacher, or scientist—but very rarely as a person who thinks with his entire being, that is to say, as a person who transforms ideas into actual dramatic motives instead of merely using them as ideological conventions or as theories so externally applied that they can be dispensed with at will. Everything is contained in the American novel except ideas. But what are ideas? At best judgments of reality, at worst substitutes for it. The American novelist's conversion to reality, however, has been so belated that he cannot be baffled by judgments and vexed by substitutes. Thus his work exhibits a singular pattern consisting, on the one hand, of a disinclination to thought and, on the other, of an intense predilection for the real: and the real appears in it as a vast phenomenology swept by waves of sensation and feeling. In this welter there is little room for the intellect, which in the unconscious belief of many imaginative Americans is naturally impervious, if not wholly inimical, to reality.

Consider the literary qualities of Ernest Hemingway, for example. There is nothing Hemingway dislikes more than experience of a make-believe, vague, or frigid nature, but in order to safeguard himself against the counterfeit he consistently avoids drawing upon the more abstract resources of the mind, he snubs the thinking man and mostly confines himself to the depiction of life on its physical levels. Of course, his rare mastery of the sensuous element largely compensates for whatever losses he may sustain in other spheres. Yet the fact remains that a good part of his writing leaves us with a sense of situations unresolved and with a picture of human beings tested by values much too simplified to do them justice. Cleanth Brooks and Robert Penn Warren have recently remarked on the interrelation between qualities of Hemingway's style and his bedazzlement by sheer experience. The following observation in particular tends to bear out the point of view expressed in this essay: "The short simple rhythms, the succession of co-ordinate clauses, the general lack of subordination—all suggest a dislocated and ununified world. The figures which live in this world live a sort of hand-to-mouth existence perceptually, and conceptually, they hardly live at all. Subordination implies some exercise of discrimination—the sifting of reality through the intellect. But Hemingway has a romantic anti-intellectualism which is to be associated with the premium which he places upon experience as such."[1]

But Hemingway is only a specific instance. Other writers, less gifted and not so self-sufficiently and incisively one-sided, have come to grief through this

[1] Cf. "The Killers," by Cleanth Brooks and Robert Penn Warren, in *American Prefaces*, Spring 1942.

same creative psychology. Under its conditioning some of them have produced work so limited to the recording of the unmistakably and recurrently real that it can truly be said of them that their art ends exactly where it should properly begin.

"How can one make the best of one's life?" André Malraux asks in one of his novels. "By converting as wide a range of experience as possible into conscious thought." It is precisely this reply which is alien to the typical American artist, who all too often is so absorbed in experience that he is satisfied to let it "write its own ticket"—to carry him, that is, to its own chance or casual destination.

In the first part of *Faust* Goethe removes his hero, a Gothic dreamer, from the cell of scholastic devotion in order to embroil him in the passions and high-flavored joys of "real life." But in the second part of the play this hero attains a broader stage of consciousness, reconciling the perilous freedom of his newly released personality with the enduring interests of the race, with high art, politics, and the constructive labor of curbing the chaotic forces in man and nature alike. This progress of Faust is foreshadowed in an early scene, when Mephisto promises to reveal to him "the little and then the great world."—*Wir sehen die kleine, dann die grosse Welt.* —The little world is the world of the individual bemused by his personal experience, and his sufferings, guilt-feelings, and isolation are to be understood as the penalty he pays for throwing off the traditional bonds that once linked him to God and his fellow-men. Beyond the little world, however, lies the broader world of man the inhabitant of his own history, who in truth is always losing his soul in order to gain it. Now the American drama of experience constitutes a kind of half-*Faust*, a play with the first part intact and the second part missing. And the Mephisto of this shortened version is the familiar demon of the Puritan morality-play, not at all the Goethian philosopher-sceptic driven by the nihilistic spirit of the modern epoch. Nor is the plot of this half-*Faust* consistent within itself. For its protagonist, playing Gretchen as often as he plays Faust, is evidently unclear in his own mind as to the role he is cast in— that of the seducer or the seduced?

It may be that this confusion of roles is the inner source of the famous Jamesian ambiguity and ever-recurring theme of betrayal. James's heroines—his Isabel Archers and Milly Theales and Maggie Ververs—are they not somehow always being victimized by the "great world" even as they succeed in mastering it? Gretchen-like in their innocence, they none the less enact the Faustian role in their uninterrupted pursuit of experience and in the use of the truly Mephistophelean gold of their millionaire-fathers to buy up the brains and beauty and nobility of the civilization that enchants them. And the later heroes of American fiction—Hemingway's young man, for instance, who invariably appears in each of his novels, a young man posing his virility against the background of continents and nations so old that, like Tiresias, they have seen all and suffered all—in his own way he, too, responds to experience in the schizoid fashion of the Gretchen-Faust character. For what is his virility if not at once the measure of his innocence and the measure of his aggression? And what shall we make of Steinbeck's fable of Lennie, that mindless giant who literally kills and gets killed from sheer desire for those soft and lovely things of which fate has singularly deprived him? He combines an unspeakable innocence with an unspeakable aggression. Perhaps it is not too far-fetched to say that in this grotesque creature Steinbeck has unconsciously created a symbolic parody of a figure such as Thomas Wolfe, who likewise crushed in his huge caresses the delicate objects of the art of life.

The disunity of American literature, its polar division into above and below or paleface and redskin writing, I have noted elsewhere. Whitman and James, who form a kind of fatal antipodes, have served as the standard examples of this dissociation. There is one sense, however, in which the contrast between these two archetypal Americans may be said to have been overdrawn. There is after all, a common ground on which they finally, though perhaps briefly meet—an essential Americanism subsuming them both that is best defined by their mutual affirmation of experience. True, what one affirmed the other was apt to negate; still it is not in their attitudes toward experience as such that the difference between them become crucial but rather in their contradictory conceptions of what constitutes experience. One sought its ideal manifestation in America, the other in Europe. Whitman, plunging with characteristic impetuosity into the turbulent, formless life of the frontier and the big cities, accepted experience in its total ungraded state, whereas James, insisting on a precise scrutiny of its origins and conditions, was endlessly discriminatory, thus carrying forward his ascetic inheritance into the very act of reaching out for the charms and felicities of the great European world. But the important thing to keep in mind here is that this plebeian and patrician are historically associated each in his own incomparable way, in the radical enterprise of subverting the puritan code of stark utility in the conduct of life and in releasing the long compressed springs of experience in the national letters. In this sense, Whitman and James are the true initiators of the American line of modernity.

If a positive approach to experience is the touchstone of the modern, a negative approach is the touchstone of the classic in American writing. The literature of early America is a sacred rather than a profane literature. Immaculate spiritual at the top and local and anecdotal at the bottom, it is essentially, the genteel literary historian Barrett Wendell accurately noted, a "record the national inexperience" marked "instinctive disregard of actual fact For this reason it largely left untouched the two chief experiential media—the novel and the drama. Brockden Brown Cooper, Hawthorne, and Melville were "romancers" and poets rather than novelists. They were incapable of apprehending the vitally new principle of realism by virtue of which the art of fiction in Europe was in their time rapidly evolving toward a hitherto inconceivable condition of objectivity and familiarity with existence. Not until James did a fiction-writer appear in America who was able to sympathize with and hence to take advantage of the methods of George Eliot, Balzac, and Turgenev. Since the principle of realism presupposes a thoroughly secularized relationship between the ego and experience, Hawthorne and Melville could not possibly have apprehended it. Though not religious men themselves, they were nevertheless held in bondage by ancestral conscience and dogma, they were still living in the afterglow of a religious faith that drove the ego, on its external side, to aggrandize itself by accumulating practical sanctions while scourging and inhibiting its intimate side. In Hawthorne the absent or suppressed experience reappears in the shape of spectral beings whose function is to warn, repel, and fascinate. And the unutterable confusion that reigns in some of Melville's narratives (*Pierre, Mardi*) is primarily due to his inability either to come to terms with experience or else wholly and finally to reject it.

Despite the featureless innocence and moral enthusiastic air of the old American books, there is in some of them a peculiar virulence, a feeling of discord that does not easily fit in with the general tone of the classic age. In such worthies as Irving, Cooper, Bryant, Longfellow, Whittier, and Lowell there is scarcely anything more than meets the eye, but in Poe, Hawthorne, and Melville there is an incandescent symbolism, a meaning within meaning, the vitality of which is perhaps only now being rightly appreciated. D. H. Lawrence was close to the truth when he spoke of what serpents they were, of the "inner diabolism of their underconsciousness." Hawthorne, "that blue-eyed darling," as well as Poe and Melville, insisted on a subversive vision of human nature at the same time as cultivated Americans were everywhere relishing the orations of Emerson who, as James put it, was helping them "to take a picturesque view of one's internal possibilities and to find in the landscape of the soul all sorts of fine sunrise and moonlight effects." Each of these three creative men displays a healthy resistance to the sentimentality and vague idealism of his contemporaries; and along with this resistance they display morbid qualities that, aside from any specific biographical factors, might perhaps be accounted for by the contradiction between the poverty of the experience provided by the society they lived in and the high development of their moral, intellectual, and affective natures—though in Poe's case there is no need to put any stress on his moral character. And the curious thing is that whatever faults their work shows are reversed in later American literature, the weaknesses of which are not to be traced to poverty of experience but to an inability to encompass it on a significant level.

The dilemma that confronted these early writers chiefly manifests itself in their frequent failure to integrate the inner and outer elements of their world so that they might stand witness for each other by way of the organic linkage of object and symbol, act and meaning. For that is the linkage of art without which its structure cannot stand. Lawrence thought that *Moby Dick* is profound *beyond* human feeling —which in a sense says as much against the book as for it. Its further defects are dispersion, a divided mind: its real and transcendental elements do not fully interpenetrate, the creative tension between them is more fortuitous than organic. In *The Scarlet Letter* as in a few of his shorter fictions, and to a lesser degree in *The Blithedale Romance*, Hawthorne was able to achieve an imaginative order that otherwise eluded him. A good deal of his writing, despite his gift for precise observation, consists of phantasy unsupported by the conviction of reality.

Many changes had to take place in

America before its spiritual and material levels could fuse in a work of art in a more or less satisfactory manner. Whitman was already in the position to vivify his democratic ethos by an appeal to the physical features of the country, such as the grandeur and variety of its geography, and to the infinite detail of common lives and occupations. And James too, though sometimes forced to resort to makeshift situations, was on the whole successful in setting up a lively and significant exchange between the moral and empiric elements of his subject-matter. Though he was, in a sense, implicitly bound all his life by the morality of Hawthorne, James none the less perceived what the guilt-tossed psyche of the author of *The Marble Faun* prevented him from seeing—that it is not the man trusting himself to experience but the one fleeing from it who suffers the "beast in the jungle" to rend him.

The Transcendentalist movement is peculiar in that it expresses the native tradition of inexperience in its particulars and the revolutionary urge to experience in its generalities. (Perhaps that is what Van Wyck Brooks meant when, long before prostrating himself at his shrine, he wrote that Emerson was habitually abstract where he should be concrete, and vice versa.) On a purely theoretical plane, in ways curiously inverted and idealistic, the cult of experience is patently prefigured in Emerson's doctrine of the uniqueness and infinitude, as well as in Thoreau's equally steep estimate, of the private man. American culture was then unprepared for anything more drastic than an affirmation of experience in theory alone, and even the theory was modulated in a semiclerical fashion so as not to set it in too open an opposition to the dogmatic faith that, despite the decay of its theology, still prevailed in the ethical sphere. "The love which is preached nowadays," wrote Thoreau, "is an ocean of new milk for a man to swim in. I hear no surf nor surge, but the winds coo over it." No wonder, then, that Transcendentalism declared itself most clearly and dramatically in the form of the essay—a form in which one can preach without practicing.

Personal liberation from social taboos and conventions was the war cry of the group of writers that came to the fore in the second decade of the century. They employed a variety of means to formulate and press home this program. Dreiser's tough-minded though somewhat arid naturalism, Anderson's softer and spottier method articulating the protest of shut-in people, Lewis's satire of Main Street, Cabell's florid celebrations of pleasure, Edna Millay's emotional expansiveness, Mencken's worldly wisdom and assaults on the provincial pieties, the early Van Wyck Brooks' high-minded though bitter evocations of the inhibited past, his ideal of creative self-fulfillment—all these were weapons brought to bear by the party of rebellion in the struggle to gain free access to experience. And the secret of energy in that struggle seems to have been the longing for what was then called "sexual freedom"; for at the time Americans seeking emancipation were engaged in a truly elemental discovery of sex whose literary expression on some levels, as Randolph Bourne remarked, easily turned into "caricatures of desire." The novel, the poem, the play—all contributed to the development of a complete symptomatology of sexual frustration and release. In his *Memoirs*, written toward the end of his life, Sherwood Anderson recalled the writers of that period as "a little band of soldiers who were going to free life . . . from certain bonds." Not that they wanted to overplay sex, but they did want "to bring it back into real relation to the life we lived and saw others living. We wanted the flesh back in our literature, wanted directly in our literature the fact of men and women in bed together, babies being born. We wanted the terrible importance of the flesh in human relations also revealed again." In retrospect much of this writing seems but a naive inversion of the dear old American innocence, a turning inside out of inbred fear and reticence, but the qualities of likes in it are its positiveness of statement, its zeal and pathos of the limited view.

The concept of experience was then still an undifferentiated whole. But as the desire for personal liberation, even if only from the less compulsive social pressures, was partly gratified and the tone of the literary revival changed from eagerness to disdain, the sense of totality gradually wore itself out. Since the nineteen-twenties a process of atomization of experience has forced each of its spokesmen into a separate groove from which he can step out only at the risk of utterly disorienting himself. Thus, to cite some random examples, poetic technique became the special experience of Ezra Pound, language that of Gertrude Stein, the concrete object was appropriated by W. C. Williams, super-American phenomena by Sandburg and related nationalists, Kenneth Burke experienced ideas (which is by no means the same as thinking them), Archibald MacLeish experienced public attitudes, F. Scott Fitzgerald the glamor and sadness of the very rich, Hemingway death and virile sports, and so on and so forth. Finally Thomas Wolfe plunged into a chaotic recapitulation of the cult of experience, traversing it in all directions and ending nowhere.

Though the crisis of the nineteen-thirties arrested somewhat the progress of the experiential mode, it nevertheless managed to put its stamp on the entire social-revolutionary literature of the decade. A comparison of European and American left-wing writing of the same period will at once show that whereas Europeans like Malraux and Silone enter deeply into the meaning of political ideas and beliefs, Americans touch only superficially on such matters, as actually their interest is fixed almost exclusively on the class war as an experience which, to them at least, is new and exciting. They succeed in representing incidents of oppression and revolt, as well as sentimental conversions, but conversions of the heart and mind they merely sketch in on the surface or imply in a gratuitous fashion. (What does a radical novel like *The Grapes of Wrath* contain, from an ideological point of view, that agitational journalism cannot communicate with equal heat and facility? Surely its vogue cannot be explained by its radicalism. Its real attraction for the millions who read it lies elsewhere—perhaps in its vivid recreation of "a slice of life" so horridly unfamiliar that it can be made to yield an exotic interest.) The sympathy of these ostensibly political writers with the revolutionary cause is often genuine, yet their understanding of its inner movement, intricate problems, and doctrinal and strategic motives is so deficient as to call into question their competence to deal with political material. In the complete works of the so-called "proletarian school" you will not find a single viable portrait of a Marxist intellectual or of any character in the revolutionary drama who, conscious of his historical role, is not a mere automaton of spontaneous class force or impulse.

What really happened in the nineteen-thirties is that due to certain events the public aspects of experience appeared more meaningful than its private aspects, and literature responded accordingly. But the subject of political art is *history*, which stands in the same relation to experience as fiction to biography; and just as surely as failure to generalize the biographical element thwarts the aspirant to fiction, so the ambition of the literary Left to create a political art was thwarted by its failure to lift experience to the level of history. (For the benefit of those people who habitually pause to insist on what they call "strictly literary values," I might add that by "history" in this connection I do not mean "history books" or anything resembling what is known as the "historical novel" or drama. A political art would succeed in lifting experience to the level of history if its perception of life—any life—were organized around a perspective relating the artist's sense of the *society* of the dead to his sense of the *society* of the living and the as yet unborn.)

Experience, in the sense of "felt life"

rather than as life's total practice, is the main but by no means the total substance of literature. The part experience plays in the aesthetic sphere might well be compared to the part that the materialist conception of history assigns to economy. Experience, in the sense of this analogy, is the substructure of literature above which there rises a superstructure of values, ideas, and judgments —in a word, of the multiple forms of consciousness. But this base and summit are not stationary: they continually act and react upon each other.

It is precisely this superstructural level which is seldom reached by the typical American writer of the modern era. Most of the well-known reputations will bear out my point. Whether you approach a poet like Ezra Pound or novelists like Steinbeck and Faulkner, what is at once noticeable is the uneven, and at times quite distorted, development of the various elements that constitute literary talent. What is so exasperating about Pound's poetry, for example, is its peculiar combination of a finished technique (his special share in the distribution of experience) with amateurish and irresponsible ideas. It could be maintained that for sheer creative power Faulkner is hardly excelled by any living novelist, yet the diversity and wonderful intensity of the experience represented in his narratives cannot entirely make up for their lack of order, of a self-illuminating structure, and obscurity of value and meaning. One might naturally counter this criticism by stating that though Faulkner rarely or never sets forth values directly, they none the less exist in his work by implication. Yes, but implications incoherently expressed are no better than mystifications, and nowadays it is values that we can least afford to take on faith. Moreover, in a more striking manner perhaps than any of his contemporaries, Faulkner illustrates the tendency of the experiential mode, if pursued to its utmost extreme, to turn into its opposite through unconscious self-parody. In Faulkner the excess, the systematic inflation of the horrible is such a parody

of experience. In Thomas Wolfe t[...] same effect is produced by his swoll[...] rhetoric and compulsion to repeat hi[...] self—and repetition is an obvious fo[...] of parody. This repetition-compulsi[...] has plagued a good many Americ[...] writers. Its first and most conspicuo[...] victim, of course, was Whitman, w[...] occasionally slipped into unintentio[...] parodies of himself.

Yet there is a positive side to t[...] primacy of experience in late Americ[...] literature. For this primacy has co[...] ferred certain benefits upon it, of whi[...] none is more bracing than its relati[...] immunity from abstraction and othe[...] worldliness. The stream of life, uni[...] peded by the rocks and sands of id[...] ology, flows through it freely. If inept [...] coping with the general, it particulari[...] not at all badly; and the assumptions [...] sanctity that so many European arti[...] seem to require as a kind of guarar[...] of their professional standing are n[...] readily conceded in the lighter a[...] clearer American atmosphere. "Wh[...] ever may have been the case in ye[...] gone by," Whitman wrote in 1888, "t[...] true use for the imaginative faculty [...] modern times is to give ultimate vivi[...] cation to facts, to science, and to co[...] mon lives, endowing them with glo[...] and glories and final illustriousn[...] which belong to every real thing, a[...] to real things only." As this stateme[...] was intended as a prophecy, it is wor[...] noting that while the radiant endo[...] ments that Whitman speaks of—t[...] "glows and glories and final illustrio[...] ness"—have not been granted, the [...] sired and predicted vivification of fac[...] science, and common lives has in [...] measure been realized, though in t[...] process Whitman's democratic faith h[...] as often been belied as confirmed.

It is not the mere recoil from the [...] hibitions of puritan and neopurit[...] times that instigated the Americ[...] search for experience. Behind it is t[...] extreme individualism of a coun[...] without a long past to brood on, wh[...] bourgeois spirit had not worn itself [...] and been debased in a severe strug[...]

against an old culture so tenacious as to retain the power on occasion to fascinate and render impotent even its predestined enemies. Moreover, in contrast to the derangements that have continually shaken Europe, life in the United States has been relatively fortunate and prosperous. It is possible to speak of American history as "successful" history. Within the limits of the capitalist order—and until the present period the objective basis for a different social order simply did not exist here—the American people have been able to find definitive solutions for the great historical problems that faced them. Thus both the Revolutionary and the Civil Wars were complete actions that virtually abolished the antagonisms which had initially caused the breakdown of national equilibrium. In Europe similar actions have usually led to festering compromises that in the end reproduced the same conflicts in other forms.

It is plain that until very recently there has really been no urgent need in America for high intellectual productivity. Indeed, the American intelligentsia developed very slowly as a semi-independent grouping; and what is equally important, for more than a century now and especially since 1865, it has been kept at a distance from the machinery of social and political power. What this means is that insofar as it has been deprived of certain opportunities, it has also been sheltered and pampered. There was no occasion or necessity for the intervention of the intellectuals—it was not mentality that society needed most in order to keep its affairs in order. On the whole the intellectuals were left free to cultivate private interests, and, once the moral and aesthetic ban on certain types of exertion had been removed, uninterruptedly to solicit individual experience. It is this lack of a sense of extremity and many-sided involvement which explains the peculiar shallowness of a good deal of American literary expression. If some conditions of insecurity have been known to retard and disarm the mind, so have some conditions of security. The question is not whether Americans have suffered less than Europeans, but of the quality of whatever suffering and happiness have fallen to their lot.

The consequence of all this has been that American literature has tended to make too much of private life, to impose on it, to scour it for meanings that it cannot always legitimately yield. Henry James was the first to make a cause, if not a fetish, of personal relations; and the justice of his case, despite his vaunted divergence from the pioneer type, is that of a pioneer too, for while Americans generally were still engaged in "gathering in the preparations and necessities" he resolved to seek out "the amenities and consummations." Furthermore, by exploiting in a fashion altogether his own the contingencies of private life that fell within his scope, he was able to dramatize the relation of the new world to the old, thus driving the wedge of historical consciousness into the very heart of the theme of experience. Later not a few attempts were made to combine experience with consciousness, to achieve the balance of thought and being characteristic of the great traditions of European art. But except for certain narratives of James and Melville, I know of very little American fiction which can unqualifiedly be said to have attained this end.

Since the decline of the regime of gentility many admirable works have been produced, but in the main it is the quantity of felt life comprised in them that satisfies, not their quality of belief or interpretive range. In poetry there is evidence of more distinct gains, perhaps because the medium has reached that late stage in its evolution when its chance of survival depends on its capacity to absorb ideas. The modern poetic styles—metaphysical and symbolist- depend on a conjunction of feeling and idea. But, generally speaking, bare experience is still the *leitmotif* of the American writer, though the literary depression of recent years tends to show that this theme is virtually exhausted. At bottom it was the theme of the individual transplanted from an old culture taking inventory of himself and of his new surroundings. This inventory, this initial recognition and experiencing of oneself and one's surroundings, is all but complete now, and those who persist in going on with it are doing so out of mere routine and inertia.

The creative power of the cult of experience is almost spent, but what lies beyond it is still unclear. One thing, however, is certain: whereas in the pa throughout the nineteenth and well in the twentieth century, the nature American literary life was largely det mined by national forces, now it is i ternational forces that have begun exert a dominant influence. And in t long run it is in the terms of this histor change that the future course of Ame can writing will define itself.

F. R. LEAVIS

(b. 1895)

F. R. Leavis has played a role in modern British criticism somewhat like that Yvor Winters in modern American criticism. A thorough scholar, and a practici academic at Cambridge University for many years, he has nevertheless oppos "academicism" with vigor. A major contributor to the critical revolution of t Thirties and Forties (like Winters he has been labeled a "New Critic") by mea of both his own writing and his long editorship (1932-1953) of *Scrutiny*, he h nevertheless been an independent, a maverick, an irritant within the ranks of mo ern criticism, taking stands and uttering judgments that have often been in defian of congealing critical orthodoxy. An able and perceptive formalist critic of mo ern poetry and fiction, he is ultimately, and again like Winters, a didactic cri whose implicit aesthetic is based on the conviction that literature is the art moral wisdom. While he is perhaps more the "liberal" than Winters, he resen bles Winters in that the power and perceptiveness of his critical responses seem derive largely from the somewhat paradoxical tensions between his deep-runni skepticism and his strenuous moral humanism. His criticism includes *New Bearir in English Poetry* (1932), *For Continuity* (1933), *Revaluation: Tradition a Development in English Poetry* (1936), *The Great Tradition* (1948), *The Comm Pursuit* (1952), and *D. H. Lawrence, Novelist* (1955).

Mr. Eliot and Lawrence (1951)

I live in hopes that Lawrence's recognition is at last to come—to come, after all, in my lifetime; I mean, his recognition for what I am convinced he is: the

Reprinted from *D. H. Lawrence: Novelist* by F. R. Leavis, by permission of Alfred A. Knopf, Inc. Copyright 1955 by F. R. Leavis. Originally published in *Scrutiny* (Vol. XVII, No. 1) as a reveiw of *D. H. Lawrence and Human Existence* by Father William Tiverton (Foreword by T. S. Eliot).

great creative genius of our age, and o of the greatest figures in English liter ture. By "our age" I mean the clima phase (so to speak) in which we st live at present—for, though Lawren died twenty years ago, he may prope be said, I think, to belong to that. M immediate excuse for this sanguine n is the Foreword contributed by Mr.

S. Eliot to Fr. William Tiverton's book. Fr. Tiverton recommends Lawrence as a positively improving author for Christians and Mr. Eliot says that his reason for contributing a preface is that he thinks the book "a serious piece of criticism of Lawrence of a kind for which the time is now due." (He adds that "we need books about him by critics who know him only through his works.")

If Mr. Eliot finds that the time for giving serious critical attention to Lawrence's writings is more due now than it was, say, twenty years ago (or even earlier), the only reason I can think of is that there has been a change in Mr. Eliot. For those of us who, all these years, have steadily contended that the time was due, and overdue, have always known Mr. Eliot as, in various ways, the reverse of an ally. He has lent all his weight and subtlety to the enemy —the enemy that has maligned and slighted and dismissed. In fact, we have had reason for seeing in him the essential opposition in person. So that when so significant and influential a voice suddenly becomes encouraging, we may feel there has been a change worth attending to.

The history the more deserves pondering in that our time, in literature, may fairly be called the age of D. H. Lawrence and T. S. Eliot: the two, in creative pre-eminence, I think, though Lawrence appears to me so immensely the greater genius, will be seen in retrospect to dominate the age together. True respect for genius is to take it seriously and appraise it critically, and it seems to me that Mr. Eliot's attitude towards Lawrence has a significance in respect of himself that, pondered, entails limiting and qualifying criticism of a kind for which the time is now very decidedly due. My business at the moment, of course, is rather with appraising the genius of Lawrence, but to that business, it should be plain, what I have said is immediately relevant. Moreover, history is history, and it is important that this particular history should not go unrecorded.

And indeed it is not yet the history of an outgrown past. For, though the Foreword to which I have referred recommends Lawrence for serious study, it perpetuates the misconceptions, misrepresentations, and misdirections that have already, over so long a period, worked so much mischief. Not only does Mr. Eliot make no recantation; he shows himself to be still unemancipated from his disabling prejudices (for no one, I am convinced, who had been able to *read* what Lawrence wrote could have pronounced as Mr. Eliot does). If they are expressed now less offensively, they are the more insidious—and the more insidious because associated with a recommendatory approach. And to tackle them seems to me to be, at the present moment, very much the way to set about one's work when faced with contending, as effectively as one can, for a just appreciation of Lawrence's genius.

Here, then, is Mr. Eliot in his preface to Fr. Tiverton's *D. H. Lawrence and Human Existence*:

He was an impatient and impulsive man (or so I imagine him to have been; for, like the author of this book, I never knew him). He was a man of fitful and profound insights, rather than of ratiocinative powers; and therefore he was an impatient man; he expressed some of his insights in the form least likely to make them acceptable to most of his contemporaries, and sometimes in a form which almost wilfully encouraged misunderstanding . . . Wrong he often was (I think) from ignorance, prejudice, or drawing the wrong conclusions in his conscious mind from the insights which came to him from below consciousness: it will take time to dissociate the superficial error from the fundamental truth. To me, also, he seems often to write very badly; but to be a writer who had to write often badly in order to write sometimes well. As for his religious attitude . . . we can now begin to see how much was ignorance, rather than hostility; for Lawrence was an ignorant man in the sense that he was unaware of how much he did not know.

These observations in themselves are ill-calculated to remove the preconceptions and obtusenesses that have prevented Lawrence's work from being seen for what it is and have made the shameful history of misrepresentation and abuse possible; and it seems to me very much in place to relate them to those past judgments that Mr. Eliot has never shown regret for and in part now repeats.

Take, for example, that charge of ignorance. It is made twice in the passage quoted. The second time the formulation might seem to give it a special limited, almost esoteric, force that makes it, however grave as addressed to Mr. Eliot's and Fr. Tiverton's special religious connexion, not obviously, perhaps, exceptionable as itself an expression of prejudice and ignorance. But already in this Foreword—in the same paragraph, in fact—the charge has been made in a general form: "Wrong he often was (I think) from ignorance, prejudice." The attendant suggestions—"a man of fitful and profound insights, rather than of ratiocinative powers," "drawing the wrong conclusions in his conscious mind from the insights which came to him from below consciousness," "a writer who had to write often badly in order to write sometimes well"—these attendant suggestions plainly give the charge of "ignorance" an ordinarily unsophisticated and pejorative intention. What Mr. Eliot meant by such criticism in the past was fully explicit; and what has never been withdrawn, and is far from being unsaid now, must be recalled to be refuted. There is no way of getting Lawrence's genius recognized except by dealing with these fallacies and prejudices and misrepresentations.

In the *Cambridge Journal* for February [1951] a writer—and one not at all inclined to the corrective severity that seems to me called for—testifies: "With one or two exceptions"—he mentions only myself—"critics since Lawrence's death have tended to follow the lead of Mr. Eliot in *After Strange Gods*." Let me recall, then, some of the things that Mr. Eliot says in that book. I pick on some judgments and assertions that are immediately relevant to the charge of ignorance. "The point is," we are told, "that Lawrence started life wholly free

from any restriction of tradition or institution. . . ." He suffered "from a lack not so much of information, as of the critical faculties which education should give, and an incapacity for what is ordinarily called thinking." Again Mr Eliot speaks of Lawrence's "lack of intellectual and social training." A reference to Lawrence's mother tells us, I'm afraid, what Mr. Eliot means by this "lack of social training": he speaks of her "vague hymn-singing pietism . . . which does not seem to have provided her with any firm principles by which to scrutinize the conduct of her sons"—Lawrence was working-class, in fact a miner's son; and therefore brought up in the midst of ignorance and uncouthness and spiritual barbarity and moral squalor, disinherited of all the humaner achievements of civilized living. We are to see him as an extreme case of the "crippling effect upon men of letters of not having been brought up in the environment of a living and central tradition."

It is when I come to these things in Mr. Eliot that I find myself saying: "I am a fellow countryman of D. H. Lawrence." Mr. Eliot is not—the fact that is in any case, sufficiently obvious insists here upon recognition. For no educated Englishman of Mr. Eliot's generation and Mr. Eliot's intelligence, I am convinced, could so confidently have expressed such ignorance. And yet there is something familiar about the tone and manner: it is as if, not to the manner born, Mr. Eliot were showing himself to have been impressed by the aplomb with which Lord David Cecil intimates *his* sense of the disadvantages suffered by low-born writers such as Hardy and George Eliot—and D. H. Lawrence. (I well remember the *Spectator* article in which Lord David Cecil put Mr. Lawrence, recently dead, impeccably in his place.)

To be born, with that genius, a miner's son at Eastwood in the eighteen eighties—it is as if destiny, having given him the genius, had arranged also that he should be enabled to develop it to the utmost and qualified to use it for the purpose for which it was meant. If he had not been born into the working class he could not have known working-class life from the inside. As it was, he enjoyed advantages that a writer middle-class born could not have had: the positive experience and a freedom both from illusions and from the debilitating sense of ignorance. On the other hand, gifted as he was, there was nothing to prevent his getting to know life at other social levels.

And the disadvantages, what were they? In education? It seems to me that he had a better education, one better calculated to develop his genius for its most fruitful use, than any other he could have got. That is what strikes one as one reads the admirable *Memoir of D. H. Lawrence* by E. T. I some years ago, in an article (*Scrutiny*, VI, 3)[1] referred to by Fr. Tiverton, discussed the extraordinarily active intellectual life enjoyed by that group of young people of which Lawrence was the centre, and pointed to the obvious fact that, though in all this the initiative and drive of Lawrence's genius must have counted enormously, the initiative and drive could neither have been what they were, nor could they have worked to such effect, if there hadn't been conditions other than personal genius, or "the individual talent," favouring. To examine these conditions adequately would be to go into a large part of English social and cultural history.

It must be enough here to say that the religion of Lawrence's mother does not deserve the contempt with which Mr. Eliot dismisses it. The Chapel, in the Lawrence circle, was the centre of a strong social life, and the focus of a still persistent cultural tradition that had as its main drive the religious tradition of which Mr. Eliot is so contemptuous. To turn, as Lawrence did, the earnestness and moral seriousness of that tradition to the powering of a strenuous intellectual inquiringness was all in the tradition. That the Lawrences were Congregationalists is a relevant point—

[1] "The Wild. Untutored Phoenix," reprinted in *The Common Pursuit*.

their Nonconformity was very far from being the debased tin-chapel salvationism that Mr. Eliot appears to think it. Congregationalism had a peculiarly strong intellectual tradition—in what ways does Mr. Eliot think Unitarianism superior? As for the part played by Nonconformity in English civilization, I suggest that he read Halévy, though books alone will not cure that kind of ignorance.

And for those young people in the eighteen-nineties their intellectual education was intimately bound up with a social training which, even if it didn't give them Wykehamist or Etonian or even Harvard manners, I see no reason for supposing inferior to that enjoyed by Mr. Eliot. Moreover, they met and talked and read in a setting of family life such as, to judge from *The Cocktail Party*, Mr. Eliot cannot imagine to have existed—a family life beset by poverty and the day-to-day exigencies of breadwinning, yet quite finely civilized. And further, with what advantageous consequences for English literature I have pointed out in some detail, Lawrence knew every day of his life in intimate experience the confrontation, the interpenetration, of the old agricultural England with the industrial; the contrast of the organic forms and rhythms and the old beauty of humane adaptation with what had supervened.

As for the intellectual training, *that* Lawrence, I have insisted, did not lack (and Fr. Tiverton says that he has to agree with me here as against Mr. Eliot). Lawrence, we know, was not denied acquaintance with formal academic standards. He says some severe things about Nottingham University College, but he was qualified to make incomparable use of his opportunities, and that he made good use, in formal study, and in informal intercourse intellectual and social with his friends, we know. In short, I cannot see on what grounds Mr. Eliot could assume it to be obvious (if he does—and I don't know what else his tone means) that he himself at twenty-one was better trained intellectually than Lawrence at the same age. He was certainly more sophisticated, and his ability, years older, to proclaim himself, ceremonially, Anglo-Catholic, Royalist, and Classicist, suggests to me that he was certainly less mature.

I have already made my comment on Mr. Eliot's ignorance of the English cultural history, of the English civilization, that is illuminated in E. T.'s *Memoir of D. H. Lawrence*. It will not be found surprising if I sum up on this head of Lawrence's "ignorance" by saying that to take him as an example of "the crippling effect upon men of letters of not having been brought up in the environment of a living and central tradition" seems to me nothing more respectable than an astonishing feat of prejudice—and ignorance.

That Lawrence *was* brought up in a living and central tradition—there, it seems to me, is where to lay the stress. And it seems to me the right answer to the less bluntly repellable form in which Mr. Eliot brings his charge in this recent Foreword: "for Lawrence was an ignorant man in the sense that he was unaware of how much he did not know." Mr. Eliot imputes, in particular, some defects of knowledge about religion and theology, and I cannot forbear concluding this matter of ignorance with a direct retort. I am not, then, impressed by any superiority of religious and theological knowledge in a writer capable of exposing what is to me the shocking essential ignorance that characterizes *The Cocktail Party*—ignorance of the possibilities of life; ignorance of the effect the play must have on a kind of reader or spectator of whose existence the author appears to be unaware: the reader who has, himself, found serious work to do in the world and is able to be unaffectedly serious about it, who knows what family life is and has helped to bring up children, and who, though capable of being interested in Mr. Eliot's poetry, cannot afford cocktail civilization and would reject it, with contempt and boredom, if he *could* afford it.

I come out with these things in order to bring home the force of my insistence that Lawrence *was* brought up in the environment of a living and central tradition. Anything in the nature of *The Cocktail Party* from him is inconceivable, and he, in his good-humoured way (the charge of impatience is very ill-founded), with that light and unstrained but complete seriousness of his, would have made the unanswerable diagnostic comment. (There are two reviews of *The Cocktail Party* I should like to see —one by Lawrence and one by Albert Schweitzer.)

Another damaging suggestion about Lawrence that is propagated by Mr. Eliot is that which is conveyed with the word "insights": "He was a man of . . . profound insights, rather than of ratiocinative powers." In the nineteen-twenties they used commonly to grant that Lawrence had *genius*; but intelligence, which really mattered—for that you must go to Aldous Huxley. I myself have always felt bound to insist— though it should, I can't help thinking, be obvious—that genius in Lawrence was, among other things, supreme intelligence. It is on intelligence, and not on "insight" or "intuition," that I choose to lay the stress; and Mr. Eliot's formulation explains well enough why. "He was a man of fitful and profound insights, rather than of ratiocinative powers"—which amounts to the earlier judgment: "a lack . . . of the critical faculties which education should give and an incapacity for what is ordinarily called thinking."

This account seems to me completely mistaken. Lawrence's "insights" were a matter of being able to see what was there, as only genius can, and they went with an extraordinary power of relating insights, and not only of understanding situations comprising elements difficult to get at and recognize, but of understanding whole comprehensive and complete fields of experience. His thinking in fact, is so much superior to what is ordinarily called thinking that it tends not to be recognized for thinking at all If "ratiocinative powers" means anything worth having, then Lawrence's seem to me superlative; in logical stamina, the power to pursue an organizing process of thought through a wide and difficult tract, with a sustained consistency that is at the same time a delicate fidelity to the complexities of the full concrete experience, Lawrence seems to me to be superior to Mr. Eliot (yes, to the author of *Four Quartets*).

If I wanted to win recognition most readily for the justice of this claim (presuming it not granted), I should turn first to *Psychoanalysis and the Unconscious*. This is the sober prose exposition corresponding to the *Fantasia of the Unconscious*, the work that Mr. Eliot commends in *After Strange Gods*. In *Psychoanalysis and the Unconscious* Lawrence explains his conception of the nature and the function of intelligence, in doing which he exemplifies intelligence, so conceived, in operation.

What he undertakes to do in the book (and I think that he does it with wonderful lucidity and complete convincingness) is to set forth the conditions of health and wholeness in the psyche. I have recently quoted key passages in discussing *Women in Love* in these pages. The relevant stress at this moment is this: Lawrence makes plain that without proper use of intelligence there can be no solution of the problems of mental, emotional, and spiritual health. We are committed, he insists, to consciousness and self-responsibility. The mind—mental consciousness—has its essential part in the prosperous functioning of the psyche; but it cannot, with its will-enforced ideas or ideals, command the sources of life, though it can thwart them. The power of recognizing justly the relation of idea and will to spontaneous life, of using the conscious mind for the attainment of "spontaneous-creative fulness of being," is intelligence. It is intelligence we see at work in the exposition of Lawrence's theme in *Psychoanalysis and the Unconscious*— the intelligence that was necessary for the undertaking just as it is necessary for the attaining and preserving of wholeness in the psyche.

Lawrence's intelligence, in its superlative fineness and vitality, always seems to me—and in the closely argued prose treatise and in the criticism as much as anywhere else—essentially the intelligence of the creative artist. It is significant that Mr. Eliot, who in effect denies the distinction of intelligence, denies the artist too. At least he once—and has never recanted—made a point of the denial, seizing on a statement (quoted in Huxley's introduction to the *Letters*) of what I take to be the truth as a challenge to a counter-demonstration. There is nothing in this recent Foreword to suggest that he has changed his mind,[2] and, whatever Fr. Tiverton's position in the abstract may be, the book itself might have been written by someone quite incapable of perceiving for himself that Lawrence is a great creative writer. And I very much fear that the books about him that Mr. Eliot says we need are not to be any more books of literary criticism than Fr. Tiverton's is. In particular, I view with the gravest distrust the prospect of Lawrence's being adopted for expository appreciation as almost a Christian by writers whose religious complexion is congenial to Mr. Eliot.

What, on such challenges, one has to say in general about Lawrence's genius is this: it manifests itself in an infallible centrality of judgment—that which makes him an incomparable literary critic. I repeat with, if possible, even greater conviction what I have said before: he has an unfailingly sure sense of the difference between that which makes for life and that which makes against it; of the difference between health and that which tends away from health. It is this that makes him a so much better critic than Eliot, whose major value-judgments, when he risks them (especially in the contemporary field), have nearly always been bad— often disastrously bad. But I ought at this point to add that I speak as one

[2] As for Lawrence's writing "often badly," I have allowed that he *sometimes* does. But badness in him is never of the order of the badness of Mr. Eliot's writing (e.g., in *The Use of Poetry and the Use of Criticism*), where it betrays thwarting of intelligence by unrecognized emotional bias, and unwillingness or fear in the author to criticize his self-suspect intentions.

who, when years ago Mr. Eliot wrote in *The Criterion* of the frightful consequences that might have ensued if Lawrence "had been a don at Cambridge, 'rotten and rotting others,'" was widely supposed—at Cambridge, anyway, where it mattered—to share the honour of the intention with Lawrence.

LIONEL TRILLING

(b. 1905)

A short-story writer and novelist as well as a scholar and critic, Trilling's critical viewpoint can be described as "humanist" in a general sense. He typically examines a given literary achievement—sometimes a single work, but more often a larger body of work by a single author—for its quality as a formalized response to the intellectual-moral currents of its moment in history. Trilling is a relativist in that he judges literary worth by his sense of the fullness, intelligence, and seriousness of the writer's response rather than by any set theory or dogma, aesthetic or otherwise. It is a sign of Trilling's intellectual catholicity as a critic, as well as of his representativeness in his time, that two of the most important influences on his thought and criticism have been Matthew Arnold and Sigmund Freud. Trilling's most important work is contained in *Matthew Arnold* (1939; 1949), *E. M. Forster* (1943), *The Liberal Imagination* (1950), *The Opposing Self* (1955), *Freud and the Crisis of Our Culture* (1955), *and A Gathering of Fugitives* (1956).

Reality in America (1940-1946)

I

It is possible to say of V. L. Parrington that with his *Main Currents in American Thought* he has had an influence on our conception of American culture which is not equaled by that of any other writer of the last two decades. His ideas are now the accepted ones wherever the college course in American literature is given by a teacher who conceives himself to be opposed to the genteel and the academic and in alliance with the vigorous and the actual. And whenever the liberal historian of America finds occasion to take account of the national literature, as nowadays he feels it proper to do, it is Parrington who is his standard and guide. Parrington's ideas are the more firmly established because they do not have to be imposed—the teacher or the critic who presents them is likely to find that his task is merely to make articulate for his audience what it has always believed, for Parrington formulated in a classic way the suppositions about our culture which are held by the American middle class so far as that class is at all liberal in its social thought and so far as it begins to understand that literature has anything to do with society.

Parrington was not a great mind; he was not a precise thinker or, except when measured by the low eminences that were about him, an impressive one. Separate Parrington from his informing idea of the economic and social determination of thought and what is left is a simple intelligence, notable for its generosity and enthusiasm but certainly not for its accuracy or originality. Take him even with his idea and he is, once its direction is established, rather too predictable to be continuously interesting; and, indeed, what we dignify with the name of economic and social determinism amounts in his use of it to not much more than the demonstration that most writers incline to stick to their own social class. But his best virtue was real and important—he had what we like to think of as the saving salt of the American mind, the lively sense of the practical, workaday world, of the welter of ordinary undistinguished things and people, of the tangible, quirky, unrefined elements of life. He knew what so many literary historians do not know, that emotions and ideas are the sparks that fly when the mind meets difficulties.

Yet he had after all but a limited sense of what constitutes a difficulty. Whenever he was confronted with a work of art that was complex, personal and not literal, that was not, as it were, a public document, Parrington was at a loss. Difficulties that were complicated by personality or that were expressed in the language of successful art did not seem quite real to him and he was inclined to treat them as aberrations, which is one way of saying what everybody admits, that the weakest part of Parrington's talent was his aesthetic judgment. His admirers and disciples like to imply that his errors of aesthetic judgment are merely lapses of taste, but this is not so. Despite such mistakes as his notorious praise of Cabell, to whom in a remarkable passage he compares Melville, Parrington's taste was by no means bad. His errors are the errors of understanding which arise from his assumptions about the nature of reality.

Parrington does not often deal with abstract philosophical ideas, but whenever he approaches a work of art we are made aware of the metaphysics on which his aesthetics is based. There exists, he believes, a thing called *reality*; it is one and immutable, it is wholly external, it is irreducible. Men's minds may waver, but reality is always reliable, always the same, always easily to be known. And the artist's relation to reality he conceives as a simple one. Reality being fixed and given, the artist has but to let it pass through him, he is the lens in the first diagram of an elementary book on optics: Fig. 1, Reality; Fig. 2, Artist; Fig. 1', Work of Art. Figs. 1 and 1' are normally in virtual correspondence with each other. Sometimes the artist spoils this ideal relation by "turning away from" reality. This results in certain fantastic works, unreal and ultimately useless. It does not occur to Parrington that there is any other relation possible between the artist and reality than this passage of reality through the transparent artist; he meets evidence of imagination and creativeness with a settled hostility the expression of which suggests that he regards them as the natural enemies of democracy.

In this view of things, reality, although it is always reliable, is always rather sober-sided, even grim. Parrington, a genial and enthusiastic man, can understand how the generosity of man's hopes and desires may leap beyond reality; he admires will in the degree that he suspects mind. To an excess of desire and energy which blinds a man to the limitations of reality he can indeed be very tender. This is one of the many meanings he gives to *romance* or *romanticism*, and in spite of himself it appeals to something in his own nature. The praise of Cabell is Parrington's response not only to Cabell's elegance— for Parrington loved elegance—but also to Cabell's insistence on the part which a beneficent self-deception may and even should play in the disappointing fact-bound life of man, particularly in the private and erotic part of his life.[1]

[1] See, for example, how Parrington accounts for the "idealizing mind"—Melville's—by the discrepancy between "a wife in her morning kimono" and "the Helen of his dreams." Vol. II, p. 259.

The second volume of *Main Currents* is called *The Romantic Revolution in America* and it is natural to expect that the word romantic should appear in it frequently. So it does, more frequently than one can count, and seldom with the same meaning, seldom with the sense that the word, although scandalously vague as it has been used by the literary historians, is still full of complicated but not wholly pointless ideas, that it involves many contrary but definable things; all too often Parrington uses the word romantic with the word romance close at hand, meaning a romance, in the sense that *Graustark* or *Treasure Island* is a romance, as though it signified chiefly a gay disregard of the limitations of everyday fact. Romance is refusing to heed the counsels of experience (p. iii); it is ebullience (p. iv); it is utopianism (p. iv); it is individualism (p. vi); it is self-deception (p. 59)— "romantic faith . . . in the beneficent processes of trade and industry" (as held, we inevitably ask, by the romantic Adam Smith?); it is the love of the picturesque (p. 49); it is the dislike of innovation (p. 50) but also the love of change (p. iv); it is the sentimental (p. 192); it is patriotism, and then it is cheap (p. 235). It may be used to denote what is not classical, but chiefly it means that which ignores reality (pp. ix, 136, 143, 147, and *passim*); it is not critical (pp. 225, 235), although in speaking of Cooper and Melville, Parrington admits that criticism can sometimes spring from romanticism.

Whenever a man with whose ideas he disagrees wins from Parrington a reluctant measure of respect, the word romantic is likely to appear. He does not admire Henry Clay, yet something in Clay is not to be despised—his romanticism, although Clay's romanticism is made equivalent with his inability to "come to grips with reality." Romanticism is thus, in most of its significations, the venial sin of *Main Currents*; like carnal passion in the *Inferno*, it evokes not blame but tender sorrow. But it can also be the great and saving virtue which Parrington recognizes. It is ascribed to the transcendental re-formers he so much admires; it is said to mark two of his most cherished heroes, Jefferson and Emerson: "they were both romantics and their idealism was only a different expression of a common spirit." Parrington held, we may say, at least two different views of romanticism which suggest two different views of reality. Sometimes he speaks of reality in an honorific way, meaning the substantial stuff of life, the ineluctable facts with which the mind must cope, but sometimes he speaks of it pejoratively and means the world of established social forms; and he speaks of realism in two ways: sometimes as the power of dealing intelligently with fact, sometimes as a cold and conservative resistance to idealism.

Just as for Parrington there is a saving grace and a venial sin, there is also a deadly sin, and this is turning away from reality, not in the excess of generous feeling, but in what he believes to be a deficiency of feeling, as with Hawthorne, or out of what amounts to sinful pride, as with Henry James. He tells us that there was too much realism in Hawthorne to allow him to give his faith to the transcendental reformers: "he was too much of a realist to change fashions in creeds"; "he remained cold to the revolutionary criticism that was eager to pull down the old temples to make room for nobler." It is this cold realism, keeping Hawthorne apart from his enthusiastic contemporaries, that alienates Parrington's sympathy—"Eager souls, mystics and revolutionaries, may propose to refashion the world in accordance with their dreams; but evil remains, and so long as it lurks in the secret places of the heart, utopia is only the shadow of a dream. And so while the Concord thinkers were proclaiming man to be the indubitable child of God, Hawthorne was critically examining the question of evil as it appeared in the light of his own experience. It was the central fascinating problem of his intellectual life, and in pursuit of a solution he probed curiously into the hidden, furtive recesses of the soul." Parrington's disapproval of the enterprise is unmistakable.

Now we might wonder whether Hawthorne's questioning of the naïve and often eccentric faiths of the transcendental reformers was not, on the face of it, a public service. But Parrington implies that it contributes nothing to democracy, and even that it stands in the way of the realization of democracy. If democracy depends wholly on a fighting faith, I suppose he is right. Yet society is after all something that exists at the moment as well as in the future, and if one man wants to probe curiously into the hidden furtive recesses of the contemporary soul, a broad democracy and especially one devoted to reality should allow him to do so without despising him. If what Hawthorne did was certainly nothing to build a party on, we ought perhaps to forgive him when we remember that he was only one man and that the future of mankind did not depend upon him alone. But this very fact serves only to irritate Parrington; he is put out by Hawthorne's loneliness and believes that part of Hawthorne's insufficiency as a writer comes from his failure to get around and meet people. Hawthorne could not, he tells us, establish contact with the "Yankee reality," and was scarcely aware of the "substantial world of Puritan reality that Samuel Sewall knew."

To turn from reality might mean to turn to romance, but Parrington tells us that Hawthorne was romantic "only in a narrow and very special sense." He was not interested in the world of, as it were, practical romance, in the Salem of the clipper ships; from this he turned away to create "a romance of ethics." This is not an illuminating phrase but it is a catching one, and it might be taken to mean that Hawthorne was in the tradition of, say, Shakespeare; but we quickly learn that, no, Hawthorne had entered a barren field, for although he himself lived in the present and had all the future to mold, he preferred to find many of his subjects in the past. We learn too that his romance of ethics is not admirable because it requires the hard, fine pressing of ideas, and we are told that "a romantic uninterested in adventure and afraid of sex is likely to become

somewhat graveled for matter." In short, Hawthorne's mind was a thin one, and Parrington puts in evidence his use of allegory and symbol and the very severity and precision of his art to prove that he suffered from a sadly limited intellect, for so much fancy and so much art could scarcely be needed unless the writer were trying to exploit to the utmost the few poor ideas that he had.

Hawthorne, then, was "forever dealing with shadows, and he knew that he was dealing with shadows." Perhaps so, but shadows are also part of reality and one would not want a world without shadows, it would not even be a "real" world. But we must get beyond Parrington's metaphor. The fact is that Hawthorne was dealing beautifully with realities, with substantial things. The man who could raise those brilliant and serious doubts about the nature and possibility of moral perfection, the man who could keep himself aloof from the "Yankee reality" and who could dissent from the orthodoxies of dissent and tell us so much about the nature of moral zeal, is of course dealing exactly with reality.

Parrington's characteristic weakness as a historian is suggested by his title, for the culture of a nation is not truly figured in the image of the current. A culture is not a flow, nor even a confluence; the form of its existence is struggle, or at least debate—it is nothing if not a dialectic. And in any culture there are likely to be certain artists who contain a large part of the dialectic within themselves, their meaning and power lying in their contradictions; they contain within themselves, it may be said, the very essence of the culture, and the sign of this is that they do not submit to serve the ends of any one ideological group or tendency. It is a significant circumstance of American culture, and one which is susceptible of explanation, that an unusually large proportion of its notable writers of the nineteenth century were such repositories of the dialectic of their times—they contained both the yes and the no of their culture, and by that token they were prophetic of the future. Parrington said that he had not set up shop as a literary critic; but if a literary critic is simply a reader who has the ability to understand literature and to convey to others what he understands, it is not exactly a matter of free choice whether or not a cultural historian shall be a literary critic, nor is it open to him to let his virtuous political and social opinions do duty for percipience. To throw out Poe because he cannot be conveniently fitted into a theory of American culture, to speak of him as a biological sport and as a mind apart from the main current, to find his gloom to be merely personal and eccentric, "only the atrabilious wretchedness of a dipsomaniac," as Hawthorne's was "no more than the skeptical questioning of life by a nature that knew no fierce storms," to judge Melville's response to American life to be less noble than that of Bryant or of Greeley, to speak of Henry James as an escapist, as an artist similar to Whistler, a man characteristically afraid of stress—this is not merely to be mistaken in aesthetic judgment; rather it is to examine without attention and from the point of view of a limited and essentially arrogant conception of reality the documents which are in some respects the most suggestive testimony to what America was and is, and of course to get no answer from them.

Parrington lies twenty years behind us, and in the intervening time there has developed a body of opinion which is aware of his inadequacies and of the inadequacies of his coadjutors and disciples, who make up what might be called the literary academicism of liberalism. Yet Parrington still stands at the center of American thought about American culture because, as I say, he expresses the chronic American belief that there exists an opposition between reality and mind and that one must enlist oneself in the party of reality.

II

This belief in the incompatibility of mind and reality is exemplified by the doctrinaire indulgence which liberal intellectuals have always displayed toward Theodore Dreiser, an indulgence which becomes the worthier of remark when it is contrasted with the liberal severity toward Henry James. Dreiser and James: with that juxtaposition we are immediately at the dark and bloody crossroads where literature and politics meet. One does not go there gladly, but nowadays it is not exactly a matter of free choice whether one does or does not go. As for the particular juxtaposition itself, it is inevitable and it has at the present moment far more significance than the juxtaposition which once used to be made between James and Whitman. It is not hard to contrive factitious oppositions between James and Whitman, but the real difference between them is the difference between the moral mind, with its awareness of tragedy, irony, and multitudinous distinctions, and the transcendental mind, with its passionate sense of the oneness of multiplicity. James and Whitman are unlike not in quality but in kind, and in their very opposition they serve to complement each other. But the difference between James and Dreiser is not of kind, for both men addressed themselves to virtually the same social and moral fact. The difference here is one of quality, and perhaps nothing is more typical of American liberalism than the way it has responded to the respective qualities of the two men.

Few critics, I suppose, no matter what their political disposition, have ever been wholly blind to James's great gifts, or even to the grandiose moral intention of these gifts. And few critics have ever been wholly blind to Dreiser's great faults. But by liberal critics James is traditionally put to the ultimate question: of what use, of what actual political use, are his gifts and their intention? Granted that James was devoted to an extraordinary moral perceptiveness, granted too that moral perceptiveness has something to do with politics and the social life, of what possible practical value in our world of impending disaster can James's work be? And James's style, his characters, his subjects, and even his own social origin and the manner of his personal life are adduced to show that his work cannot endure the question. To James no quarter is given by American criticism in its political and liberal aspect. But in the same degree that liberal criticism is moved by political considerations to treat James with severity, it treats Dreiser with the most sympathetic indulgence. Dreiser's literary faults, it gives us to understand, are essentially social and political virtues. It was Parrington who established the formula for the liberal criticism of Dreiser by calling him a "peasant": when Dreiser thinks stupidly, it is because he has the slow stubbornness of a peasant; when he writes badly, it is because he is impatient of the sterile literary gentility of the bourgeoisie. It is as if wit, and flexibility of mind, and perception, and knowledge were to be equated with aristocracy and political reaction, while dullness and stupidity must naturally suggest a virtuous democracy, as in the old plays.

The liberal judgment of Dreiser and James goes back of politics, goes back to the cultural assumptions that make politics. We are still haunted by a kind of political fear of the intellect which Tocqueville observed in us more than a century ago. American intellectuals, when they are being consciously American or political, are remarkably quick to suggest that an art which is marked by perception and knowledge, although all very well in its way, can never get us through gross dangers and difficulties. And their misgivings become the more intense when intellect works in art as it ideally should, when its processes are vivacious and interesting and brilliant. It is then that we like to confront it with the gross dangers and difficulties and to challenge it to save us at once from disaster. When intellect in art is awkward or dull we do not put it to the test of ultimate or immediate practicality. No liberal critic asks the question of Dreiser whether *his* moral preoccupations are going to be useful in confronting the disasters that threaten us. And it is a judgment on the proper nature of mind, rather than any actual political meaning that might be drawn

from the works of the two men, which accounts for the unequal justice they have received from the progressive critics. If it could be conclusively demonstrated—by, say, documents in James's handwriting—that James explicitly intended his books to be understood as pleas for co-operatives, labor unions, better housing, and more equitable taxation, the American critic in his liberal and progressive character would still be worried by James because his work shows so many of the electric qualities of mind. And if something like the opposite were proved of Dreiser, it would be brushed aside—as his doctrinaire anti-Semitism has in fact been brushed aside—because his books have the awkwardness, the chaos, the heaviness which we associate with "reality." In the American metaphysic, reality is always material reality, hard, resistant, unformed, impenetrable, and unpleasant. And that mind is alone felt to be trustworthy which most resembles this reality by most nearly reproducing the sensations it affords.

In *The Rise of American Civilization*, Professor Beard uses a significant phrase when, in the course of an ironic account of James's career, he implies that we have the clue to the irrelevance of that career when we know that James was "a whole generation removed from the odors of the shop." Of a piece with this, and in itself even more significant, is the comment which Granville Hicks makes in *The Great Tradition* when he deals with James's stories about artists and remarks that such artists as James portrays, so concerned for their art and their integrity in art, do not really exist: "After all, who has ever known such artists? Where are the Hugh Verekers, the Mark Ambients, the Neil Paradays, the Overts, Limberts, Dencombes, Delavoys?" This question, as Mr. Hicks admits, had occurred to James himself, but what answer had James given to it? "If the life about us for the last thirty years refused warrant for these examples," he said in the preface to volume XII of the New York Edition, "then so much the worse for that life.

. . . There are decencies that in the name of the general self-respect we must take for granted, there's a rudimentary intellectual honor to which we must, in the interest of civilization, at least pretend." And to this Mr. Hicks, shocked beyond argument, makes this reply, which would be astonishing had we not heard it before: "But this is the purest romanticism, this writing about what ought to be rather than what is!"

The "odors of the shop" are real, and to those who breathe them they guarantee a sense of vitality from which James is debarred. The idea of intellectual honor is not real, and to that chimera James was devoted. He betrayed the reality of what is in the interests of what ought to be. Dare we trust him? The question, we remember, is asked by men who themselves have elaborate transactions with what ought to be. Professor Beard spoke in the name of a growing, developing, and improving America. Mr. Hicks, when he wrote *The Great Tradition*, was in general sympathy with a nominally radical movement. But James's own transaction with what ought to be is suspect because it is carried on through what I have called the electrical qualities of mind, through a complex and rapid imagination and with a kind of authoritative immediacy. Mr. Hicks knows that Dreiser is "clumsy" and "stupid" and "bewildered" and "crude in his statement of materialistic monism"; he knows that Dreiser in his personal life—which is in point because James's personal life is always supposed to be so much in point—was not quite emancipated from "his boyhood longing for crass material success," showing "again and again a desire for the ostentatious luxury of the successful business man." But Dreiser is to be accepted and forgiven because his faults are the sad, lovable, honorable faults of reality itself, or of America itself—huge, inchoate, struggling toward expression, caught between the dream of raw power and the dream of morality.

"The liability in what Santayana called the genteel tradition was due to its being the product of mind apart from experience. Dreiser gave us the stuff of our common experience, not as it was hoped to be by any idealizing theorist, but as it actually was in its crudity." The author of this statement certainly cannot be accused of any lack of feeling for mind as Henry James represents it; nor can Mr. Matthiessen be thought of as a follower of Parrington—indeed, in the preface to *American Renaissance* he has framed one of the sharpest and most cogent criticisms of Parrington's method. Yet Mr. Matthiessen, writing in the *New York Times Book Review* about Dreiser's posthumous novel, *The Bulwark*, accepts the liberal cliché which opposes crude experience to mind and establishes Dreiser's value by implying that the mind which Dreiser's crude experience is presumed to confront and refute is the mind of gentility.

This implied amalgamation of mind with gentility is the rationale of the long indulgence of Dreiser, which is extended even to the style of his prose. Everyone is aware that Dreiser's prose style is full of roughness and ungainliness, and the critics who admire Dreiser tell us it does not matter. Of course it does not matter. No reader with a right sense of style would suppose that it does matter, and he might even find it a virtue. But it has been taken for granted that the ungainliness of Dreiser's style is the only possible objection to be made to it, and that whoever finds in it any fault at all wants a prettified genteel style (and is objecting to the ungainliness of reality itself). For instance, Edwin Berry Burgum, in a leaflet on Dreiser put out by the Book Find Club, tells us that Dreiser was one of those who used—or, as Mr. Burgum says, utilized—"the diction of the Middle West, pretty much as it was spoken, rich in colloquialism and frank in the simplicity and directness of the pioneer tradition," and that this diction took the place of "the literary English, formal and bookish, of New England provincialism that was closer to the aristocratic spirit of the mother country than to the tang of everyday life in the new West." This is mere fantasy. Hawthorne, Thoreau, and Emerson were for the most part remarkably colloquial—

they wrote, that is, much as they spoke; their prose was specifically American in quality, and, except for occasional lapses, quite direct and simple. It is Dreiser who lacks the sense of colloquial diction—that of the Middle West or any other. If we are to talk of bookishness, it is Dreiser who is bookish; he is precisely literary in the bad sense; he is full of flowers of rhetoric and shines with paste gems; at hundreds of points his diction is not only genteel but fancy. It is he who speaks of "a scene more distingué than this," or a woman "artistic in form and feature," or of a man who, although "strong, reserved, aggressive, with an air of wealth and experience, was *soi-disant* and not particularly eager to stay at home." Colloquialism held no real charm for him and his natural tendency is always toward the "fine:"

. . . Moralists come and go; religionists fulminate and declare the pronouncements of God as to this; but Aphrodite still reigns. Embowered in the festal depths of the spring, set above her altars of porphyry, chalcedony, ivory and gold, see her smile the smile that is at once the texture and essence of delight, the glory and despair of the world! Dream on, oh Buddha, asleep on your lotus leaf, of an undisturbed Nirvana! Sweat, oh Jesus, your last agonizing drops over an unregenerate world! In the forests of Pan still ring the cries of the worshippers of Aphrodite! From her altars the incense of adoration ever rises! And see, the new red grapes dripping where votive hands new-press them!

Charles Jackson, the novelist, telling us in the same leaflet that Dreiser's style does not matter, remarks on how much still comes to us when we have lost by translation the stylistic brilliance of Thomas Mann or the Russians or Balzac. He is in part right. And he is right too when he says that a certain kind of conscious, supervised artistry is not appropriate to the novel of large dimensions. Yet the fact is that the great novelists have usually written very good prose, and what comes through even a bad translation is exactly the power of mind that made the well-hung sentence of the original text. In literature style is so little the mere clothing of thought—

need it be insisted on at this late date? —that we may say that from the earth of the novelist's prose spring his characters, his ideas, and even his story itself.[2]

To the extent that Dreiser's style is defensible, his thought is also defensible. That is, when he thinks like a novelist, he is worth following—when by means of his rough and ungainly but no doubt cumulatively effective style he creates rough, ungainly, but effective characters and events. But when he thinks like, as we say, a philosopher, he is likely to be not only foolish but vulgar. He thinks as the modern crowd thinks when it decides to think: religion and morality are nonsense, "religionists" and moralists are fakes, tradition is a fraud, what is man but matter and impulses, mysterious "chemisms," what value has life anyway? "What, cooking, eating, coition, job holding, growing, aging, losing, winning, in so changeful and passing a scene as this, important? Bunk! It is some form of titillating illusion with about as much import to the superior forces that bring it all about as the functions and gyrations of a fly. No more. And maybe less." Thus Dreiser at sixty. And yet there is for him always the vulgarly saving suspicion that maybe, when all is said and done, there is Something Behind It All. It is much to the point of his intellectual vulgarity that Dreiser's anti-Semitism was not

[2] The latest defense of Dreiser's style, that in the chapter on Dreiser in the *Literary History of the United States,* is worth noting: "Forgetful of the integrity and power of Dreiser's whole work, many critics have been distracted into a condemnation of his style. He was, like Twain and Whitman, an organic artist; he wrote what he knew—what he was. His many colloquialisms were part of the coinage of his time, and his sentimental and romantic passages were written in the language of the educational system and the popular literature of his formative years. In his style, as in his material, he was a child of his time, of his class. Self-educated, a type or model of the artist of plebeian origin in America, his language, like his subject matter, is not marked by internal inconsistencies." No doubt Dreiser was an organic artist in the sense that he wrote what he knew and what he was, but so, I suppose, is every artist; the question for criticism comes down to *what* he knew and *what* he was. That he was a child of his time and class is also true, but this can be said of everyone without exception; the question for criticism is how he transcended the imposed limitations of his time and class. As for the defense made on the ground of his particular class, it can only be said that liberal thought has come to a strange pass when it assumes that a plebeian origin is accountable for a writer's faults through all his intellectual life.

merely a social prejudice but an idea, a way of dealing with difficulties.

No one, I suppose, has ever represented Dreiser as a masterly intellect. It is even commonplace to say that his ideas are inconsistent or inadequate. But once that admission has been made, his ideas are hustled out of sight while his "reality" and great brooding pity are spoken of. (His pity is to be questioned: pity is to be judged by kind, not amount, and Dreiser's pity—*Jennie Gerhardt* provides the only exception—is either destructive of its object or it is self-pity.) Why has no liberal critic ever brought Dreiser's ideas to the bar of political practicality, asking what use is to be made of Dreiser's dim, awkward speculation, of his self-justification, of his lust for "beauty" and "sex" and "living" and "life itself," and of the showy nihilism which always seems to him so grand a gesture in the direction of profundity? We live, understandably enough, with the sense of urgency; our clock, like Baudelaire's, has had the hands removed and bears the legend, "it is later than you think." But with us it is always a little too late for mind, yet never too late for honest stupidity; always a little too late for understanding, never too late for righteous, bewildered wrath; always too late for thought, never too late for naïve moralizing. We seem to like to condemn our finest but not our worst qualities by pitting them against the exigency of time.

But sometimes time is not quite so exigent as to justify all our own exigency, and in the case of Dreiser time has allowed his deficiencies to reach their logical, and fatal, conclusion. In *The Bulwark* Dreiser's characteristic ideas come full circle, and the simple, didactic life history of Solon Barnes, a Quaker business man, affirms a simple Christian faith, and a kind of practical mysticism, and the virtues of self-abnegation and self-restraint, and the belief in and submission to the hidden powers, those "superior forces that bring it all about"—once, in Dreiser's opinion, so brutally indifferent, now somehow benign. This is not the first occasion on which Dreiser has shown a tenderness toward religion and a responsiveness to mysticism. *Jennie Gerhardt* and the figure of the Reverend Duncan McMillan in *An American Tragedy* are forecasts of the avowals of *The Bulwark*, and Dreiser's lively interest in power of any sort led him to take account of the power implicit in the cruder forms of mystical performance. Yet these rifts in his nearly monolithic materialism cannot quite prepare us for the blank pietism of *The Bulwark*, not after we have remembered how salient in Dreiser's work has been the long surly rage against the "religionists" and the "moralists," the men who have presumed to believe that life can be given any law at all and who have dared to suppose that will or mind or faith can shape the savage and beautiful entity that Dreiser liked to call "life itself." Now for Dreiser the law may indeed be given, and it is wholly simple—the safe conduct of the personal life requires only that we follow the Inner Light according to the regimen of the Society of Friends, or according to some other godly rule. And now the smiling Aphrodite set above her altars of porphyry, chalcedony, ivory, and gold is quite forgotten, and we are told that the sad joy of cosmic acceptance goes hand in hand with sexual abstinence.

Dreiser's mood of "acceptance" in the last years of his life is not, as a personal experience, to be submitted to the tests of intellectual validity. It consists of a sensation of cosmic understanding, of an overarching sense of unity with the world in its apparent evil as well as in its obvious good. It is no more to be quarreled with, or reasoned with, than love itself—indeed, it is a kind of love, not so much of the world as of oneself in the world. Perhaps it is either the cessation of desire or the perfect balance of desires. It is what used often to be meant by "peace," and up through the nineteenth century a good many people understood its meaning. If it was Dreiser's own emotion at the end of his life, who would not be happy that he had achieved it? I am not even sure that our civilization would not be the better for more of us knowing and desiring this emotion of grave felicity. Yet granting the personal validity of the emotion, Dreiser's exposition of it fails, and is, moreover, offensive. Mr. Matthiessen has warned us of the attack that will be made on the doctrine of *The Bulwark* by "those who believe that any renewal of Christianity marks a new 'failure of nerve.' " But Dreiser's religious avowal is not a failure of nerve—it is a failure of mind and heart. We have only to set his book beside any work in which mind and heart are made to serve religion to know this at once. Ivan Karamazov's giving back his ticket of admission to the "harmony" of the universe suggests that *The Bulwark* is not morally adequate, for we dare not, as its hero does, blandly "accept" the suffering of others; and the Book of Job tells us that it does not include enough in its exploration of the problem of evil, and is not stern enough. I have said that Dreiser's religious affirmation was offensive; the offense lies in the vulgar ease of its formulation, as well as in the comfortable untroubled way in which Dreiser moved from nihilism to pietism.[3]

The Bulwark is the fruit of Dreiser's old age, but if we speak of it as a failure of thought and feeling, we cannot suppose that with age Dreiser weakened in mind and heart. The weakness was always there. And in a sense it is not Dreiser who failed but a whole way of dealing with ideas, a way in which we have all been in some degree involved. Our liberal, progressive culture tolerated Dreiser's vulgar materialism with its huge negation, its simple cry of "Bunk!," feeling that perhaps it was not quite intellectually adequate but certainly very

strong, certainly very *real*. And now, almost as a natural consequence, it has been given, and is not unwilling to take, Dreiser's pietistic religion in all its inadequacy.

Dreiser, of course, was firmer than the intellectual culture that accepted him. He *meant* his ideas, at least so far as a man can mean ideas who is incapable of following them to their consequences. But we, when it came to his ideas, talked about his great brooding pity and shrugged the ideas off. We are still doing it. Robert Elias, the biographer of Dreiser, tells us that "it is part of the logic of [Dreiser's] life that he should have completed *The Bulwark* at the same time that he joined the Communists." Just what kind of logic this is we learn from Mr. Elias's further statement. "When he supported left-wing movements and finally, last year, joined the Communist Party, he did so not because he had examined the details of the party line and found them satisfactory, but because he agreed with a general program that represented a means for establishing his cherished goal of greater equality among men." Whether or not Dreiser was following the logic of his own life, he was certainly following the logic of the liberal criticism that accepted him so undiscriminatingly as one of the great, significant expressions of its spirit. This is the liberal criticism, in the direct line of Parrington, which establishes the social responsibility of the writer and then goes on to say that, apart from his duty of resembling reality as much as possible, he is not really responsible for anything, not even for his ideas. The scope of reality being what it is, ideas are held to be mere "details," and, what is more, to be details which, if attended to, have the effect of diminishing reality. But ideals are different from ideas; in the liberal criticism which descends from Parrington ideals consort happily with reality and they urge us to deal impatiently with ideas—a "cherished goal" forbids that we stop to consider how we reach it, or if we may not destroy it in trying to reach it the wrong way.

---

[3] This ease and comfortableness seem to mark contemporary religious conversions. Religion nowadays has the appearance of what the ideal modern house has been called, "a machine for living," and seemingly one makes up one's mind to acquire and use it not with spiritual struggle but only with a growing sense of its practicability and convenience. Compare *The Seven Storey Mountain*, which Monsignor Sheen calls "a twentieth-century form of the *Confessions* of St. Augustine," with the old, the as it were original, *Confessions* of St. Augustine.

GEORGE ORWELL

(1903-1950)

Aptly dubbed "the conscience of his generation," George Orwell (Eric Blair) expresses, in both his fiction and his essays, the viewpoint of an independent and persistently skeptical radical of the left. A disenchanted onetime servant of the Empire in Burma, Orwell became a Marxist and fought with the Loyalists in the Spanish Civil War. After disillusioning experiences with the Communists in Spain and with British labor politics at home he became an acrid critic of party politics of the left as well as of the right. "I am definitely 'left,' " he wrote about himself late in life, "but I believe that a writer can remain honest only if he keeps free of party labels." Orwell's literary criticism is not extensive, but it is notable for its unusual combination of socio-political emphasis and delicacy of insight, and for its ingenious and often profound illumination of unconscious patterns of social and political frustration, trauma, and neurosis in apparently affirmative or innocuous works of popular literature. Orwell's major critical essays are contained in *Inside the Whale* (1940), *Dickens, Dali, and Others* (1946), *Shooting an Elephant* (1950), and *Such, Such, Were the Joys* (1953); and in three sampler volumes, *Critical Essays* (1951), *A Collection of Essays* (1954), and *The Orwell Reader* (ed. Richard H. Rovere, 1956).

Boys' Weeklies (1939)

You never walk far through any poor quarter in any big town without coming upon a small newsagent's shop. The general appearance of these shops is always very much the same: a few posters for the *Daily Mail* and the *News of the World* outside, a poky little window with sweet-bottles and packets of Players, and a dark interior smelling of liquorice allsorts and festooned from floor to ceiling with vilely printed twopenny papers, most of them with lurid cover-illustrations in three colours.

Except for the daily and evening papers, the stock of these shops hardly overlaps at all with that of the big newsagents. Their main selling line is the twopenny weekly, and the number and variety of these are almost unbelievable. Every hobby and pastime— cage-birds, fret-work, carpentering, bees, carrier-pigeons, home conjuring, philately, chess—has at least one paper devoted to it, and generally several. Gardening and livestock-keeping must have at least a score between them. Then there are the sporting papers, the radio papers, the children's comics, the various snippet papers such as *Tit-bits*, the large range of papers devoted to the movies and all more or less exploiting women's legs, the various trade papers, the women's story-papers (the *Oracle*, *Secrets*, *Peg's Paper*, etc. etc.), the needlework papers—these so numerous that a display of them alone will often fill an entire window—and in addition the long series of "Yank Mags" (*Fight Stories, Action Stories, Western Short Stories,* etc.), which are imported shop-soiled from America and sold at two-pence halfpenny or threepence. And the periodical proper shades off into the fourpenny novelette, the *Aldine Boxing Novels,* the *Boys' Friend Library,* the *Schoolgirls' Own Library* and many others.

Probably the contents of these shops is the best available indication of what the mass of the English people really feels and thinks. Certainly nothing half so revealing exists in documentary form. Best-seller novels, for instance, tell one a great deal, but the novel is aimed almost exclusively at people above the £4-a-week level. The movies are probably a very unsafe guide to popular taste, because the film industry is virtually a monopoly, which means that it is not obliged to study its public at all closely. The same applies to some extent to the daily papers, and most of all to the radio. But it does not apply to the weekly paper with a smallish circulation and specialised subject-matter. Papers like the *Exchange and Mart,* for instance, or *Cage-Birds,* or the *Oracle,* or *Prediction,* or the *Matrimonial Times,* only exist because there is a definite demand for them, and they reflect the minds of their readers as a great national daily with a circulation of millions cannot possibly do.

Here I am only dealing with a single series of papers, the boys' twopenny weeklies, often inaccurately described as "penny dreadfuls." Falling strictly within this class there are at present ten papers, the *Gem, Magnet, Modern Boy, Triumph* and *Champion,* all owned by the Amalgamated Press, and the *Wizard, Rover, Skipper, Hotspur* and *Adventure,* all owned by D. C. Thomson & Co. What the circulations of these papers are, I do not know. The editors and proprietors refuse to name any figures, and in any case the circulation of a paper carrying serial stories is bound to fluctuate widely. But there is no ques-tion that the combined public of the ten papers is a very large one. They are on sale in every town in England, and nearly every boy who reads at all goes through a phase of reading one or more of them. The *Gem* and *Magnet,* which are much the oldest of these papers, are of rather different type from the rest, and they have evidently lost some of their popularity during the past few years. A good many boys now regard them as old-fashioned and "slow." Nevertheless I want to discuss them first, because they are more interesting psychologically than the others, and also because the mere survival of such papers into the nineteen-thirties is a rather startling phenomenon.

The *Gem* and *Magnet* are sister-papers (characters out of one paper frequently appear in the other), and were both started more than thirty years ago. At that time, together with *Chums* and the old *B.O.P.,* they were the leading papers for boys, and they remained dominant till quite recently. Each of them carries every week a fifteen- or twenty-thousand-word school story, complete in itself, but usually more or less connected with the story of the week before. The *Gem* in addition to its school story carries one or more adventure serials. Otherwise the two papers are so much alike that they can be treated as one, though the *Magnet* has always been the better known of the two, probably because it possesses a really first-rate character in the fat boy, Billy Bunter.

The stories are stories of what purports to be public-school life, and the schools (Greyfriars in the *Magnet* and St. Jim's in the *Gem*) are represented as ancient and fashionable foundations of the type of Eton or Winchester. All the leading characters are fourth-form boys aged fourteen or fifteen, older or younger boys only appearing in very minor parts. Like Sexton Blake and Nelson Lee, these boys continue week after week and year after year, never growing any older. Very occasionally a new boy arrives or a minor character drops out, but in at any rate the last twenty-five years the personnel has barely altered. All the principal characters in both papers—Bob Cherry, Tom Merry, Harry Wharton, Johnny Bull, Billy Bunter and the rest of them—were at Greyfriars or St. Jim's long before the Great War, exactly the same age as at present, having much the same kind of adventures and talking almost exactly the same dialect. And not only the characters but the whole atmosphere of both *Gem* and *Magnet* has been preserved unchanged, partly by means of very elaborate stylisation. The stories in the *Magnet* are signed "Frank Richards" and those in the *Gem*, "Martin Clifford," but a series lasting thirty years could hardly be the work of the same person every week.[1] Consequently they have to be written in a style that is easily imitated—an extraordinary, artificial, repetitive style, quite different from anything else now existing in English literature. A couple of extracts will do as illustrations. Here is one from the *Magnet*:

> *Groan!*
> "*Shut up, Bunter!*"
> *Groan!*
> *Shutting up was not really in Billy Bunter's line. He seldom shut up, though often requested to do so. On the present awful occasion the fat Owl of Greyfriars was less inclined than ever to shut up. And he did not shut up! He groaned, and groaned, and went on groaning.*
>
> *Even groaning did not fully express Bunter's feelings. His feelings, in fact, were inexpressible.*
>
> *There were six of them in the soup! Only one of the six uttered sounds of woe and lamentation. But that one, William George Bunter, uttered enough for the whole party and a little over.*
>
> *Harry Wharton & Co. stood in a wrathy and worried group. They were landed and stranded, diddled, dished and done!* etc. etc. etc.

Here is one from the *Gem*:

> "*Oh cwumbs!*"
> "*Oh gum!*"
> "*Ooooogh!*"
> "*Urrggh!*"
> *Arthur Augustus sat up dizzily. He grabbed his handkerchief and pressed it to his damaged nose. Tom Merry sat up, gasping for breath. They looked at one another.*
> "*Bai Jove! This is a go, deah boy!*" *gurgled Arthur Augustus.* "*I have been thrown into quite a fluttah! Oogh! The wottahs! The wuffians! The feahful outsidahs! Wow!*" etc. etc. etc.

Both of these extracts are entirely typical; you would find something like them in almost every chapter of every number, to-day or twenty-five years ago. The first thing that anyone would notice is the extraordinary amount of tautology (the first of these two passages contains a hundred and twenty-five words and could be compressed into about thirty), seemingly designed to spin out the story, but actually playing its part in creating the atmosphere. For the same reason various facetious expressions are repeated over and over again: "wrathy," for instance, is a great favourite, and so is "diddled, dished and done." "Ooooogh!", "Grooo!" and "Yaroo!" (stylised cries of pain) recur constantly, and so does "Ha! ha! ha!", always given a line to itself, so that sometimes a quarter of a column or thereabouts consists of "Ha! ha! ha!" The slang ("Go and eat coke!", "What the thump!", "You frabjous ass!", etc. etc.) has never been altered, so that the boys are now using slang which is at least thirty years out of date. In addition, the various nicknames are rubbed in on every possible occasion. Every few lines we are reminded that Harry Wharton & Co. are "the Famous Five," Bunter is always "the fat Owl" or "the Owl of the Remove," Vernon-Smith is always "the Bounder of Greyfriars," Gussy (the Honourable Arthur Augustus D'Arcy) is always "the swell of St. Jim's," and so on and so forth. There is a constant, untiring effort to keep the atmosphere intact and to make sure that every new

[1] 1945. This is quite incorrect. These stories have been written throughout the whole period by "Frank Richards" and "Martin Clifford," who are one and the same person! See articles in *Horizon*, May 1940, and *Summer Pie*, summer 1944.

reader learns immediately who is who. The result has been to make Greyfriars and St. Jim's into an extraordinary little world of their own, a world which cannot be taken seriously by anyone over fifteen, but which at any rate is not easily forgotten. By a debasement of the Dickens technique a series of stereotyped "characters" has been built up, in several cases very successfully. Billy Bunter, for instance, must be one of the best-known figures in English fiction; for the mere number of people who know him he ranks with Sexton Blake, Tarzan, Sherlock Holmes and a handful of characters in Dickens.

Needless to say, these stories are fantastically unlike life at a real public school. They run in cycles of rather differing types, but in general they are the clean-fun, knockabout type of story, with interest centring round horseplay, practical jokes, ragging masters, fights, canings, football, cricket and food. A constantly recurring story is one in which a boy is accused of some misdeed committed by another and is too much of a sportsman to reveal the truth. The "good" boys are "good" in the clean-living Englishman tradition—they keep in hard training, wash behind their ears, never hit below the belt, etc. etc.—and by way of contrast there is a series of "bad" boys, Racke, Crooke, Loder and others, whose badness consists in betting, smoking cigarettes and frequenting public-houses. All these boys are constantly on the verge of expulsion, but as it would mean a change of personnel if any boy were actually expelled, no one is ever caught out in any really serious offence. Stealing, for instance, barely enters as a motif. Sex is completely taboo, especially in the form in which it actually arises at public schools. Occasionally girls enter into the stories, and very rarely there is something approaching a mild flirtation, but it is always entirely in the spirit of clean fun. A boy and a girl enjoy going for bicycle rides together—that is all it ever amounts to. Kissing, for instance, would be regarded as "soppy." Even the bad boys are presumed to be completely sex-

less. When the *Gem* and *Magnet* were started, it is probable that there was a deliberate intention to get away from the guilty sex-ridden atmosphere that pervaded so much of the earlier literature for boys. In the 'nineties the *Boys' Own Paper*, for instance, used to have its correspondence columns full of terrifying warnings against masturbation, and books like *St. Winifred's* and *Tom Brown's Schooldays* were heavy with homosexual feeling, though no doubt the authors were not fully aware of it. In the *Gem* and *Magnet* sex simply does not exist as a problem. Religion is also taboo; in the whole thirty years' issue of the two papers the word "God" probably does not occur, except in "God save the King." On the other hand, there has always been a very strong "temperance" strain. Drinking and, by association, smoking are regarded as rather disgraceful even in an adult ("shady" is the usual word), but at the same time as something irresistibly fascinating, a sort of substitute for sex. In their moral atmosphere the *Gem* and *Magnet* have a great deal in common with the Boy Scout movement, which started at about the same time.

All literature of this kind is partly plagiarism. Sexton Blake, for instance, started off quite frankly as an imitation of Sherlock Holmes, and still resembles him fairly strongly; he has hawklike features, lives in Baker Street, smokes enormously and puts on a dressing-gown when he wants to think. The *Gem* and *Magnet* probably owe something to the school-story writers who were flourishing when they began, Gunby Hadath, Desmond Coke and the rest, but they owe more to nineteenth-century models. In so far as Greyfriars and St. Jim's are like real schools at all, they are much more like Tom Brown's Rugby than a modern public school. Neither school has an O.T.C., for instance, games are not compulsory, and the boys are even allowed to wear what clothes they like. But without doubt the main origin of these papers is *Stalky & Co.* This book has had an immense influence on boys' literature, and it is one of those books which have a sort of traditional reputation among people who have never even seen a copy of it. More than once in boys' weekly papers I have come across a reference to *Stalky & Co.* in which the word was spelt "Storky." Even the name of the chief comic among the Greyfriars masters, Mr. Prout, is taken from *Stalky & Co.* and so is much of the slang; "jape," "merry," "giddy," "bizney" (business), "frabjous," "don't" for "doesn't"—all of them out of date even when *Gem* and *Magnet* started. There are also traces of earlier origins. The name "Greyfriars" is probably taken from Thackeray, and Gosling, the school porter in the *Magnet*, talks in an imitation of Dickens's dialect.

With all this, the supposed "glamour" of public-school life is played for all it is worth. There is the usual paraphernalia—lock-up, roll-call, house matches, fagging, prefects, cosy teas round the study fire, etc. etc.—and constant reference to the "old school," the "old grey stones" (both schools were founded in the early sixteenth century), the "team spirit" of the "Greyfriars men." As for the snob-appeal, it is completely shameless. Each school has a titled boy or two whose titles are constantly thrust in the reader's face; other boys have the names of well-known aristocratic families, Talbot, Manners, Lowther. We are for ever being reminded that Gussy is the Honourable Arthur A. D'Arcy, son of Lord Eastwood, that Jack Blake is heir to "broad acres," that Hurree Jamset Ram Singh (nicknamed Inky) is the Nabob of Bhanipur, that Vernon-Smith's father is a millionaire. Till recently the illustrations in both papers always depicted the boys in clothes imitated from those of Eton; in the last few years Greyfriars has changed over to the blazers and flannel trousers, but St. Jim's still sticks to the Eton jacket, and Gussy sticks to his top-hat. In the school magazine which appears every week as part of the *Magnet*, Harry Wharton writes an article discussing the pocket-money received by the "fellows in the Remove," and reveals that some of them get as

much as five pounds a week! This kind of thing is a perfectly deliberate incitement to wealth-fantasy. And here it is worth noticing a rather curious fact, and that is that the school story is a thing peculiar to England. So far as I know, there are extremely few school stories in foreign languages. The reason, obviously, is that in England education is mainly a matter of status. The most definite dividing-line between the petite-bourgeoisie and the working class is that the former pay for their education, and within the bourgeoisie there is another unbridgeable gulf between the "public" school and the "private" school. It is quite clear that there are tens and scores of thousands of people to whom every detail of life at a "posh" public school is wildly thrilling and romantic. They happen to be outside that mystic world of quadrangles and house-colours, but they yearn after it, day-dream about it, live mentally in it for hours at a stretch. The question is, Who are these people? Who reads the *Gem* and *Magnet*?

Obviously one can never be quite certain about this kind of thing. All I can say from my own observation is this. Boys who are likely to go to public schools themselves generally read the *Gem* and *Magnet*, but they nearly always stop reading them when they are about twelve; they may continue for another year from force of habit, but by that time they have ceased to take them seriously. On the other hand, the boys at very cheap private schools, the schools that are designed for people who can't afford a public school but consider the Council schools "common," continue reading the *Gem* and *Magnet* for several years longer. A few years ago I was a teacher at two of these schools myself. I found that not only did virtually all the boys read the *Gem* and *Magnet*, but that they were still taking them fairly seriously when they were fifteen or even sixteen. These boys were the sons of shopkeepers, office employees and small business and professional men, and obviously it is this class that the *Gem* and *Magnet* are aimed at. But they are certainly read by working-class boys as well. They are generally on sale in the poorest quarters of big towns, and I have known them to be read by boys whom one might expect to be completely immune from public-school "glamour." I have seen a young coal-miner, for instance, a lad who had already worked a year or two underground, eagerly reading the *Gem*. Recently I offered a batch of English papers to some British legionaries of the French Foreign Legion in North Africa; they picked out the *Gem* and *Magnet* first. Both papers are much read by girls,[2] and the Pen Pals department of the *Gem* shows that it is read in every corner of the British Empire, by Australians, Canadians, Palestine Jews, Malays, Arabs, Straits Chinese, etc. etc. The editors evidently expect their readers to be aged around fourteen, and the advertisements (milk chocolate, postage stamps, water pistols, blushing cured, home conjuring tricks, itching powder, the Phine Phun Ring which runs a needle into your friend's hand, etc. etc.) indicate roughly the same age; there are also the Admiralty advertisements, however, which call for youths between seventeen and twenty-two. And there is no question that these papers are also read by adults. It is quite common for people to write to the editor and say that they have read every number of the *Gem* or *Magnet* for the past thirty years. Here, for instance, is a letter from a lady in Salisbury:

I can say of your splendid yarns of Harry Wharton & Co., of Greyfriars, that they never fail to reach a high standard. Without doubt they are the finest stories of their type on the market to-day, which is saying a good deal. They seem to bring you face to face with Nature. I have taken the Magnet *from the start, and have followed the adventures of Harry Wharton & Co. with rapt interest. I have no sons, but*

[2] There are several corresponding girls' papers. The *Schoolgirl* is companion-paper to the *Magnet* and has stories by "Hilda Richards." The characters are interchangeable to some extent. Bessie Bunter, Billy Bunter's sister, figures in the *Schoolgirl*.

two daughters, and there's always a rush to be the first to read the grand old paper. My husband, too, was a staunch reader of the Magnet *until he was suddenly taken away from us.*

It is well worth getting hold of some copies of the *Gem* and *Magnet*, especially the *Gem*, simply to have a look at the correspondence columns. What is truly startling is the intense interest with which the pettiest details of life at Greyfriars and St. Jim's are followed up. Here, for instance, are a few of the questions sent in by readers:

"What age is Dick Roylance?" "How old is St. Jim's?" "Can you give me a list of the Shell and their studies?" "How much did D'Arcy's monocle cost?" "How is it fellows like Crooke are in the Shell and decent fellows like yourself are only in the Fourth?" "What are the Form captain's three chief duties?" "Who is the chemistry master at St. Jim's?" (From a girl) "Where is St. Jim's situated? Could you tell me how to get there, as I would love to see the building? Are you boys just 'phoneys,' as I think you are?"

It is clear that many of the boys and girls who write these letters are living a complete fantasy-life. Sometimes a boy will write, for instance, giving his age, height, weight, chest and bicep measurements and asking which member of the Shell or Fourth Form he most exactly resembles. The demand for a list of the studies on the Shell passage, with an exact account of who lives in each, is a very common one. The editors, of course, do everything in their power to keep up the illusion. In the *Gem* Jack Blake is supposed to write the answers to correspondents, and in the *Magnet* a couple of pages is always given up to the school magazine (the *Greyfriars Herald*, edited by Harry Wharton), and there is another page in which one or other character is written up each week. The stories run in cycles, two or three characters being kept in the foreground for several weeks at a time. First there will be a series of rollicking adventure stories, featuring the Famous Five and Billy Bunter; then a run of stories turning on mistaken identity, with Wibley (the make-up wizard) in the star part; then a run of more serious stories in which Vernon-Smith is trembling on the verge of expulsion. And here one comes upon the real secret of the *Gem* and *Magnet* and the probable reason why they continue to be read in spite of their obvious out-of-dateness.

It is that the characters are so carefully graded as to give almost every type of reader a character he can identify himself with. Most boys' papers aim at doing this, hence the boy-assistant (Sexton Blake's Tinker, Nelson Lee's Nipper, etc.) who usually accompanies the explorer, detective or what not on his adventures. But in these cases there is only one boy, and usually it is much the same type of boy. In the *Gem* and *Magnet* there is a model for very nearly everybody. There is the normal, athletic, high-spirited boy (Tom Merry, Jack Blake, Frank Nugent), a slightly rowdier version of this type (Bob Cherry), a more aristocratic version (Talbot, Manners), a quieter, more serious version (Harry Wharton), and a stolid, "bulldog" version (Johnny Bull). Then there is the reckless, dare-devil type of boy (Vernon-Smith), the definitely "clever," studious boy (Mark Linley, Dick Penfold), and the eccentric boy who is not good at games but possesses some special talent (Skinner, Wibley). And there is the scholarship-boy (Tom Redwing), an important figure in this class of story because he makes it possible for boys from very poor homes to project themselves into the public-school atmosphere. In addition there are Australian, Irish, Welsh, Manx, Yorkshire and Lancashire boys to play upon local patriotism. But the subtlety of characterisation goes deeper than this. If one studies the correspondence columns one sees that there is probably *no* character in the *Gem* and *Magnet* whom some or other reader does not identify with, except the out-and-out comics, Coker, Billy Bunter, Fisher T. Fish (the money-grubbing American boy) and, of course, the masters. Bunter, though in his origin he probably owed something to the fat boy in *Pickwick,* is a real creation. His tight trousers against which boots and canes are constantly thudding, his astuteness in search of food, his postal order which never turns up, have made him famous wherever the Union Jack waves. But he is not a subject for day-dreams. On the other hand, another seeming figure of fun, Gussy (the Honourable Arthur A. D'Arcy, "the swell of St. Jim's"), is evidently much admired. Like everything else in the *Gem* and *Magnet,* Gussy is at least thirty years out of date. He is the "knut" of the early twentieth century or even the "masher" of the 'nineties ("Bai Jove, deah boy!" and "Weally, I shall be obliged to give you a feahful thwashin'!"), the monocled idiot who made good on the fields of Mons and Le Cateau. And his evident popularity goes to show how deep the snob-appeal of this type is. English people are extremely fond of the titled ass (cf. Lord Peter Wimsey) who always turns up trumps in the moment of emergency. Here is a letter from one of Gussy's girl admirers:

I think you're too hard on Gussy. I wonder he's still in existence, the way you treat him. He's my hero. Did you know I write lyrics? How's this—to the tune of "Goody Goody"?

Gonna get my gas-mask, join the A.R.P.
'Cos I'm wise to all those bombs you drop on me.
 Gonna dig myself a trench
 Inside the garden fence;
Gonna seal my windows up with tin
So that the tear gas can't get in;
Gonna park my cannon right outside the kerb
With a note to Adolf Hitler: 'Don't disturb!'
And if I never fall in Nazi hands
That's soon enough for me
Gonna get my gas-mask, join the A.R.P.

P.S.—Do you get on well with girls?

I quote this in full because (dated April 1939) it is interesting as being probably the earliest mention of Hitler in the *Gem*. In the *Gem* there is also a heroic fat boy, Fatty Wynn, as a set-off against Bunter. Vernon-Smith, "the Bounder of the Remove," a Byronic character, always on the verge of the sack, is another great favourite. And even some of the cads probably have their following. Loder, for instance, "the rotter of the Sixth," is a cad, but he is also a highbrow and given to saying sarcastic things about football and the team spirit. The boys of the Remove only think him all the more of a cad for this, but a certain type of boy would probably identify with him. Even Racke, Crooke and Co. are probably admired by small boys who think it diabolically wicked to smoke cigarettes. (A frequent question in the correspondence column: "What brand of cigarettes does Racke smoke?")

Naturally the politics of the *Gem* and *Magnet* are Conservative, but in a completely pre-1914 style, with no Fascist tinge. In reality their basic political assumptions are two: nothing ever changes, and foreigners are funny. In the *Gem* of 1939 Frenchmen are still Froggies and Italians are still Dagoes. Mossoo, the French master at Greyfriars, is the usual comic-paper Frog, with pointed beard, pegtop trousers, etc. Inky, the Indian boy, though a rajah, and therefore possessing snob-appeal, is also the comic babu of the *Punch* tradition. ("'The rowfulness is not the proper caper, my esteemed Bob,' said Inky. 'Let dogs delight in the barkfulness and bitefulness, but the soft answer is the cracked pitcher that goes longest to a bird in the bush, as the English proverb remarks.'") Fisher T. Fish is the old-style stage Yankee ("'Waal, I guess,'" etc.) dating from a period of Anglo-American jealousy. Wun Lung, the Chinese boy (he has rather faded out of late, no doubt because some of the *Magnet's* readers are Straits Chinese), is the nineteenth-century pantomine Chinaman, with saucer-shaped hat, pigtail and pidgin-English. The assumption all along is

not only that foreigners are comics who are put there for us to laugh at, but that they can be classified in much the same way as insects. That is why in all boys' papers, not only the *Gem* and *Magnet*, a Chinese is invariably portrayed with a pigtail. It is the thing you recognise him by, like the Frenchman's beard or the Italian's barrel-organ. In papers of this kind it occasionally happens that when the setting of the story is in a foreign country some attempt is made to describe the natives as individual human beings but as a rule it is assumed that foreigners of any one race are all alike and will conform more or less exactly to the following patterns:

FRENCHMAN: Excitable. Wears beard, gesticulates wildly.

SPANIARD, MEXICAN, etc.: Sinister, treacherous.

ARAB, AFGHAN, etc.: Sinister, treacherous.

CHINESE: Sinister, treacherous. Wears pigtail.

ITALIAN: Excitable. Grinds barrel-organ or carries stiletto.

SWEDE, DANE, etc.: Kindhearted, stupid.

NEGRO: Comic, very faithful.

The working classes only enter into the *Gem* and *Magnet* as comics or semi-villains (race-course touts, etc.). As for class-friction, trade unionism, strikes, slumps, unemployment, Fascism and civil war—not a mention. Somewhere or other in the thirty years' issue of the two papers you might perhaps find the word "Socialism," but you would have to look a long time for it. If the Russian Revolution is anywhere referred to, it will be indirectly, in the word "Bolshy" (meaning a person of violent disagreeable habits). Hitler and the Nazis are just beginning to make their appearance, in the sort of reference I quoted above. The war-crisis of September 1938 made just enough impression to produce a story in which Mr. Vernon-Smith, the Bounder's millionaire father, cashed in on the general panic by buying up country houses in order to sell them to "crisis scuttlers." But that is probably as near to noticing the European situation as the *Gem* and *Magnet* will come, until the war actually starts.[3] That does not mean that these papers are unpatriotic—quite the contrary! Throughout the Great War the *Gem* and *Magnet* were perhaps the most consistently and cheerfully patriotic papers in England. Almost every week the boys caught a spy or pushed a conchy into the army, and during the rationing period "EAT LESS BREAD" was printed in large type on every page. But their patriotism has nothing whatever to do with power-politics or "ideological" warfare. It is more akin to family loyalty, and actually it gives one a valuable clue to the attitude of ordinary people, especially the huge untouched block of the middle class and the better-off working class. These people are patriotic to the middle of their bones, but they do not feel that what happens in foreign countries is any of their business. When England is in danger they rally to its defense as a matter of course, but in between-times they are not interested. After all, England is always in the right and England always wins, so why worry? It is an attitude that has been shaken during the past twenty years, but not so deeply as is sometimes supposed. Failure to understand it is one of the reasons why Left Wing political parties are seldom able to produce an acceptable foreign policy.

The mental world of the *Gem* and *Magnet*, therefore, is something like this:

The year is 1910—or 1940, but it is all the same. You are at Greyfriars, a rosy-cheeked boy of fourteen in posh tailor-made clothes, sitting down to tea in your study on the Remove passage after an exciting game of football which was won by an odd goal in the last half-minute. There is a cosy fire in the study, and outside the wind is whistling. The ivy clusters thickly round the old grey stones. The King is on his throne and the pound is worth a pound. Over in Europe the comic foreigners are jabbering and gesticulating, but the grim grey battleships of the British Fleet are steaming up the Channel and at the outposts of Empire the monocled Englishmen are holding the natives at bay. Lord Mauleverer has just got another fiver and we are all settling down to a tremendous tea of sausages, sardines, crumpets, potted meat, jam and doughnuts. After tea we shall sit round the study fire having a good laugh at Billy Bunter and discussing the team for next week's match against Rockwood. Everything is safe, solid and unquestionable. Everything will be the same for ever and ever. That approximately is the atmosphere.

But now turn from the *Gem* and *Magnet* to the more up-to-date papers which have appeared since the Great War. The truly significant thing is that they have more points of resemblance to the *Gem* and *Magnet* than points of difference. But it is better to consider the differences first.

There are eight of these newer papers, the *Modern Boy, Triumph, Champion, Wizard, Rover, Skipper, Hotspur* and *Adventure*. All of these have appeared since the Great War, but except for the *Modern Boy* none of them is less than five years old. Two papers which ought also to be mentioned briefly here, though they are not strictly in the same class as the rest, are the *Detective Weekly* and the *Thriller*, both owned by the Amalgamated Press. The *Detective Weekly* has taken over Sexton Blake. Both of these papers admit a certain amount of sex-interest into their stories, and though certainly read by boys, they are not aimed at them exclusively. All the others are boys' papers pure and simple, and they are sufficiently alike to be considered together. There does not seem to be any notable difference between Thomson's publications and those of the Amalgamated Press.

As soon as one looks at these papers one sees their technical superiority to the *Gem* and *Magnet*. To begin with, they have the great advantage of not

---

[3] This was written some months before the outbreak of war. Up to the end of September 1939 no mention of the war has appeared in either paper.

being written entirely by one person. Instead of one long complete story, a number of the *Wizard* or *Hotspur* consists of half a dozen or more serials, none of which goes on for ever. Consequently there is far more variety and far less padding, and none of the tiresome stylisation and facetiousness of the *Gem* and *Magnet*. Look at these two extracts, for example:

Billy Bunter groaned.

A quarter of an hour had elapsed out of the two hours that Bunter was booked for extra French.

In a quarter of an hour there were only fifteen minutes! But every one of those minutes seemed inordinately long to Bunter. They seemed to crawl by like tired snails.

Looking at the clock in Class-room No. 10 the fat Owl could hardly believe that only fifteen minutes had passed. It seemed more like fifteen hours, if not fifteen days!

Others fellows were in extra French as well as Bunter. They did not matter. Bunter did! [The Magnet.]

After a terrible climb, hacking out handholds in the smooth ice every step of the way up, Sergeant Lionheart Logan of the Mounties was now clinging like a human fly to the face of an icy cliff, as smooth and treacherous as a giant pane of glass.

An Arctic blizzard, in all its fury, was buffeting his body, driving the blinding snow into his face, seeking to tear his fingers loose from their handholds and dash him to death on the jagged boulders which lay at the foot of the cliff a hundred feet below.

Crouching among those boulders were eleven villainous trappers who had done their best to shoot down Lionheart and his companion, Constable Jim Rogers—until the blizzard had blotted the two Mounties out of sight from below. [The Wizard.]

The second extract gets you some distance with the story, the first takes a hundred words to tell you that Bunter is in the detention class. Moreover, by not concentrating on school stories (in point of numbers the school story slightly predominates in all these papers, except the *Thriller* and *Detective Weekly*), the *Wizard, Hotspur,* etc., have far greater opportunities for sensationalism. Merely looking at the cover illustrations of the papers which I have on the table in front of me, here are some of the things I see. On one a cowboy is clinging by his toes to the wing of an aeroplane in mid-air and shooting down another aeroplane with his revolver. On another a Chinese is swimming for his life down a sewer with a swarm of ravenous-looking rats swimming after him. On another an engineer is lighting a stick of dynamite while a steel robot feels for him with its claws. On another a man in airman's costume is fighting bare-handed against a rat somewhat larger than a donkey. On another a nearly naked man of terrific muscular development has just seized a lion by the tail and flung it thirty yards over the wall of an arena, with the words, "Take back your blooming lion!" Clearly no school story can compete with this kind of thing. From time to time the school buildings may catch fire or the French master may turn out to be the head of an international anarchist gang, but in a general way the interest must centre round cricket, school rivalries, practical jokes, etc. There is not much room for bombs, death-rays, sub-machine guns, aeroplanes, mustangs, octopuses, grizzly bears or gangsters.

Examination of a large number of these papers shows that, putting aside school stories, the favourite subjects are Wild West, Frozen North, Foreign Legion, crime (always from the detective's angle), the Great War (Air Force or Secret Service, not the infantry), the Tarzan motif in varying forms, professional football, tropical exploration, historical romance (Robin Hood, Cavaliers and Roundheads, etc.) and scientific invention. The Wild West still leads, at any rate as a setting, though the Red Indian seems to be fading out. The one theme that is really new is the scientific one. Death-rays, Martians, invisible

men, robots, helicopters and inter-
planetary rockets figure largely; here
and there there are even far-off rumours
of psychotherapy and ductless glands.
Whereas the *Gem* and *Magnet* derive
from Dickens and Kipling, the *Wizard*,
Champion, *Modern Boy*, etc., owe a
great deal to H. G. Wells, who, rather
than Jules Verne, is the father of "Sci-
entifiction." Naturally it is the magical,
Martian aspect of science that is most
exploited, but one or two papers include
serious articles on scientific subjects, besides quantities of informative snippets.
(Examples: "A Kauri tree in Queens-
land, Australia, is over 12,000 years old";
"Nearly 50,000 thunderstorms occur
every day"; "Helium gas costs £1 per
1000 cubic feet"; "There are over 500
varieties of spiders in Great Britain";
"London firemen use 14,000,000 gallons
of water annually," etc. etc.) There is a
marked advance in intellectual curiosity
and, on the whole, in the demand made
on the reader's attention. In practice
the *Gem* and *Magnet* and the past-war
papers are read by much the same public, but the mental age aimed at seems
to have risen by a year or two years—
an improvement probably corresponding
to the improvement in elementary education since 1909.

The other thing that has emerged in
the post-war boys' papers, though not
to anything like the extent one would
expect, is bully-worship and the cult of
violence.

If one compares the *Gem* and *Magnet*
with a genuinely modern paper, the
thing that immediately strikes one is the
absence of the leader-principle. There is
no central dominating character; instead there are fifteen or twenty characters, all more or less on an equality,
with whom readers of different types
can identify. In the more modern papers
this is not usually the case. Instead of
identifying with a schoolboy of more or
less his own age, the reader of the *Skipper*, *Hotspur*, etc., is led to identify with
a G-man, with a Foreign Legionary,
with some variant of Tarzan, with an
air ace, a master spy, an explorer, a
pugilist—at any rate with some single

all-powerful character who dominates
everyone about him and whose usual
method of solving any problem is a sock
on the jaw. This character is intended
as a superman, and as physical strength
is the form of power that boys can best
understand, he is usually a sort of human gorilla; in the Tarzan type of story
he is sometimes actually a giant, eight
or ten feet high. At the same time the
scenes of violence in nearly all these
stories are remarkably harmless and un-
convincing. There is a great difference
in tone between even the most blood-
thirsty English paper and the three-
penny Yank Mags, *Fight Stories*, *Action
Stories*, etc. (not strictly boys' papers,
but largely read by boys). In the Yank
Mags you get real blood-lust, really gory
descriptions of the all-in, jump-on-his-
testicles style of fighting, written in a
jargon that has been perfected by people
who brood endlessly on violence. A
paper like *Fight Stories*, for instance,
would have very little appeal except to
sadists and masochists. You can see the
comparative gentleness of the English
civilisation by the amateurish way in
which prize-fighting is always described
in the boys' weeklies. There is no specialised vocabulary. Look at these four
extracts, two English, two American:

*When the gong sounded, both men
were breathing heavily, and each had
great red marks on his chest. Bill's chin
was bleeding, and Ben had a cut over
his right eye.*

*Into their corners they sank, but when
the gong clanged again they were up
swiftly, and they went like tigers at each
other.* [Rover.]

*He walked in stolidly and smashed a
clublike right to my face. Blood spat-
tered and I went back on my heels, but
surged in and ripped my right under
the heart. Another right smashed full
on Sven's already battered mouth, and,
spitting out the fragments of a tooth, he
crashed a flailing left to my body.* [Fight
Stories.]

*It was amazing to watch the Black
Panther at work. His muscles rippled*

and slid under his dark skin. There was all the power and grace of a giant cat in his swift and terrible onslaught.

He volleyed blows with a bewildering speed for so huge a fellow. In a moment Ben was simply blocking with his gloves as well as he could. Ben was really a past master of defence. He had many fine victories behind him. But the Negro's rights and lefts crashed through openings that hardly any other fighter could have found. [Wizard.]

Haymakers which packed the bludgeoning weight of forest monarchs crashing down under the ax hurled into the bodies of the two heavies as they swapped punches. [Fight Stories.]

Notice how much more knowledgeable the American extracts sound. They are written for devotees of the prize-ring, the others are not. Also, it ought to be emphasised that on its level the moral code of the English boys' papers is a decent one. Crime and dishonesty are never held up to admiration, there is none of the cynicism and corruption of the American gangster story. The huge sale of the Yank Mags in England shows that there is a demand for that kind of thing, but very few English writers seem able to produce it. When hatred of Hitler became a major emotion in America, it was interesting to see how promptly "anti-Fascism" was adapted to pornographic purposes by the editors of the Yank Mags. One magazine which I have in front of me is given up to a long, complete story, "When Hell Came to America," in which the agents of a "blood-maddened European dictator" are trying to conquer the U.S.A. with death rays and invisible aeroplanes. There is the frankest appeal to sadism, scenes in which the Nazis tie bombs to women's backs and fling them off heights to watch them blown to pieces in mid-air, others in which they tie naked girls together by their hair and prod them with knives to make them dance, etc. etc. The editor comments solemnly on all this, and uses it as a plea for tightening up restrictions against immigrants. On another page of the same paper: "LIVES OF THE HOTCHA CHORUS GIRLS. Reveals all the intimate secrets and fascinating pastimes of the famous Broadway Hotcha girls. NOTHING IS OMITTED. Price 10c." "HOW TO LOVE. 10c." "FRENCH PHOTO RING, 25c." "NAUGHTY NUDIES TRANSFERS. From the outside of the glass you see a beautiful girl, innocently dressed. Turn it around and look through the glass and oh! what a difference! Set of 3 transfers 25c.," etc. etc. etc. There is nothing at all like this in any English paper likely to be read by boys. But the process of Americanisation is going on all the same. The American ideal, the "he-man," the "tough guy," the gorilla who puts everything right by socking everybody else on the jaw, now figures in probably a majority of boys' papers. In one serial now running in the *Skipper* he is always portrayed, ominously enough, swinging a rubber truncheon.

The development of the *Wizard, Hotspur*, etc., as against the earlier boys' papers, boils down to this: better technique, more scientific interest, more bloodshed, more leader-worship. But, after all, it is the *lack* of development that is the really striking thing.

To begin with, there is no political development whatever. The world of the *Skipper* and the *Champion* is still the pre-1914 world of the *Magnet* and the *Gem*. The Wild West story, for instance, with its cattle-rustlers, lynch-law and other paraphernalia belonging to the 'eighties, is a curiously archaic thing. It is worth noticing that in papers of this type it is always taken for granted that adventures only happen at the ends of the earth, in tropical forests, in Arctic Wastes, in African deserts, on Western prairies, in Chinese opium dens —everywhere, in fact, except the places where things really *do* happen. That is a belief dating from thirty or forty years ago, when the new continents were in process of being opened up. Nowadays, of course, if you really want adventure, the place to look for it is in Europe. But apart from the picturesque side of the Great War, contemporary history is carefully excluded. And except that Americans are now admired instead of being laughed at, foreigners are exactly the same figures of fun that they always were. If a Chinese character appears, he is still the sinister pigtailed opium-smuggler of Sax Rohmer; no indication that things have been happening in China since 1912—no indication that a war is going on there, for instance. If a Spaniard appears, he is still a "dago" or "greaser" who rolls cigarettes and stabs people in the back; no indication that things have been happening in Spain. Hitler and the Nazis have not yet appeared, or are barely making their appearance. There will be plenty about them in a little while, but it will be from a strictly patriotic angle (Britain *versus* Germany), with the real meaning of the struggle kept out of sight as much as possible. As for the Russian Revolution, it is extremely difficult to find any reference to it in any of these papers. When Russia is mentioned at all it is usually in an information snippet (example: "There are 29,000 centenarians in the U.S.S.R."), and any reference to the Revolution is indirect and twenty years out of date. In one story in the *Rover*, for instance, somebody has a tame bear, and as it is a Russian bear, it is nicknamed Trotsky—obviously an echo of the 1917-23 period and not of recent controversies. The clock has stopped at 1910. Britannia rules the waves, and no one has heard of slumps, booms, unemployment, dictatorships, purges or concentration camps.

And in social outlook there is hardly any advance. The snobbishness is somewhat less open than in the *Gem* and *Magnet*—that is the most one can possibly say. To begin with, the school story, always partly dependent on snob-appeal, is by no means eliminated. Every number of a boys' paper includes at least one school story, these stories slightly outnumbering the Wild Westerns. The very elaborate fantasy-life of the *Gem* and *Magnet* is not imitated and there is more emphasis on extraneous adventure, but the social atmosphere (old grey stones) is much the same. When a new school is introduced at the beginning of a story we are often told in just those words that "it was a very posh school." From time to time a story appears which is ostensibly directed *against* snobbery. The scholarship-boy (cf. Tom Redwing in the *Magnet*) makes fairly frequent appearances, and what is essentially the same theme is sometimes presented in this form; there is great rivalry between two schools, one of which considers itself more "posh" than the other, and there are fights, practical jokes, football matches, etc., always ending in the discomfiture of the snobs. If one glances very superficially at some of these stories it is possible to imagine that a democratic spirit has crept into the boys' weeklies, but when one looks more closely one sees that they merely reflect the bitter jealousies that exist within the white-collar class. Their real function is to allow the boy who goes to a cheap private school (*not* a Council school) to feel that his school is just as "posh" in the sight of God as Winchester or Eton. The sentiment of school loyalty ("We're better than the fellows down the road"), a thing almost unknown to the real working class, is still kept up. As these stories are written by many different hands, they do, of course, vary a good deal in tone. Some are reasonably free from snobbishness, in others money and pedigree are exploited even more shamelessly than in the *Gem* and *Magnet*. In one that I came across an actual *majority* of the boys mentioned were titled.

Where working-class characters appear, it is usually either as comics (jokes about tramps, convicts, etc.), or as prize-fighters, acrobats, cowboys, professional footballers and Foreign Legionaries—in other words, as adventurers. There is no facing of the facts about working-class life, or, indeed, about *working* life of any description. Very occasionally one may come across a realistic description of, say, work in a coal-mine, but in all probability it will only be there as the background of some lurid adventure. In any case the central character is not likely to be a coal-miner. Nearly all the time the boy who reads these papers—in nine cases out of ten a boy who is going to spend his life working in a shop, in a factory or in some subordinate job in an office—is led to identify with people in positions of command, above all with people who are never troubled by shortage of money. The Lord Peter Wimsey figure, the seeming idiot who drawls and wears a monocle but is always to the fore in moments of danger, turns up over and over again. (This character is a great favourite in Secret Service stories.) And, as usual, the heroic characters all have to talk B.B.C.; they may talk Scottish or Irish or American, but no one in a star part is ever permitted to drop an aitch. Here it is worth comparing the social atmosphere of the boys' weeklies with that of the women's weeklies, the *Oracle*, the *Family Star*, *Peg's Paper*, etc.

The women's papers are aimed at an older public and are read for the most part by girls who are working for a living. Consequently they are on the surface much more realistic. It is taken for granted, for example, that nearly everyone has to live in a big town and work at a more or less dull job. Sex, so far from being taboo, is *the* subject. The short, complete stories, the special feature of these papers, are generally of the "came the dawn" type: the heroine narrowly escapes losing her "boy" to a designing rival, or the "boy" loses his job and has to postpone marriage, but presently gets a better job. The changeling fantasy (a girl brought up in a poor home is "really" the child of rich parents) is another favourite. Where sensationalism comes in, usually in the serials, it arises out of the more domestic type of crime, such as bigamy, forgery or sometimes murder; no Martians, death-rays or international anarchist gangs. These papers are at any rate aiming at credibility, and they have a link with real life in their correspondence columns, where genuine problems are being discussed. Ruby M. Ayres's column

of advice in the *Oracle*, for instance, is extremely sensible and well written. And yet the world of the *Oracle* and *Peg's Paper* is a pure fantasy-world. It is the same fantasy all the time; pretending to be richer than you are. The chief impression that one carries away from almost every story in these papers is of a frightful, overwhelming "refinement." Ostensibly the characters are workingclass people, but their habits, the interiors of their houses, their clothes, their outlook and, above all, their speech are entirely middle class. They are all living at several pounds a week above their income. And needless to say, that is just the impression that is intended. The idea is to give the bored factory-girl or worn-out mother of five a dream-life in which she pictures herself—not actually as a duchess (that convention has gone out) but as, say, the wife of a bank-manager. Not only is a five-to-six-pound-a-week standard of life set up as the ideal, but it is tacitly assumed that that is how working-class people really *do* live. The major facts are simply not faced. It is admitted, for instance, that people sometimes lose their jobs; but then the dark clouds roll away and they get better jobs instead. No mention of unemployment as something permanent and inevitable, no mention of the dole, no mention of trade unionism. No suggestion anywhere that there can be anything wrong with the system *as a system*; there are only individual misfortunes, which are generally due to somebody's wickedness and can in any case be put right in the last chapter. Always the dark clouds roll away, the kind employer raises Alfred's wages, and there are jobs for everybody except the drunks. It is still the world of the *Wizard* and the *Gem*, except that there are orange-blossoms instead of machineguns.

The outlook inculcated by all these papers is that of a rather exceptionally stupid member of the Navy League in the year 1910. Yes, it may be said, but what does it matter? And in any case, what else do you expect?

Of course no one in his senses would want to turn the so-called penny dreadful into a realistic novel or a Socialist tract. An adventure story must of its nature be more or less remote from real life. But, as I have tried to make clear, the unreality of the *Wizard* and the *Gem* is not so artless as it looks. These papers exist because of a specialised demand, because boys at certain ages find it necessary to read about Martians, death-rays, grizzly bears and gangsters. They get what they are looking for, but they get it wrapped up in the illusions which their future employers think suitable for them. To what extent people draw their ideas from fiction is disputable. Personally I believe that most people are influenced far more than they would care to admit by novels, serial stories, films and so forth, and that from this point of view the worst books are often the most important, because they are usually the ones that are read earliest in life. It is probable that many people who would consider themselves extremely sophisticated and "advanced" are actually carrying through life an imaginative background which they acquired in childhood from (for instance) Sapper and Ian Hay. If that is so, the boys' twopenny weeklies are of the deepest importance. Here is the stuff that is read somewhere between the ages of twelve and eighteen by a very large proportion, perhaps an actual majority, of English boys, including many who will never read anything else except newspapers; and along with it they are absorbing a set of beliefs which would be regarded as hopelessly out of date in the Central Office of the Conservative Party. All the better because it is done indirectly, there is being pumped into them the conviction that the major problems of our time do not exist, that there is nothing wrong with *laissez-faire* capitalism, that foreigners are unimportant comics and that the British Empire is a sort of charity-concern which will last for ever. Considering who owns these papers, it is difficult to believe that this is unintentional. Of the twelve papers I have been discussing (*i.e.* twelve including the *Thriller* and *Detective Weekly*) seven are the property of the Amalgamated Press, which is one of the biggest press-combines in the world and controls more than a hundred different papers. The *Gem* and *Magnet*, therefore, are closely linked up with the *Daily Telegraph* and the *Financial Times*. This in itself would be enough to rouse certain suspicions, even if it were not obvious that the stories in the boys' weeklies are politically vetted. So it appears that if you feel the need of a fantasy-life in which you travel to Mars and fight lions barehanded (and what boy doesn't?), you can only have it by delivering yourself over, mentally, to people like Lord Camrose. For there is no competition. Throughout the whole of this run of papers the differences are negligible, and on this level no others exist. This raises the question, why is there no such thing as a left-wing boys' paper?

At first glance such an idea merely makes one slightly sick. It is so horribly easy to imagine what a left-wing boys' paper would be like, if it existed. I remember in 1920 or 1921 some optimistic person handing round Communist tracts among a crowd of public-school boys. The tract I received was of the question-and-answer kind:

Q. *Can a Boy Communist be a Boy Scout, Comrade?*
A. *No, Comrade.*
Q. *Why, Comrade?*
A. *Because, Comrade, a Boy Scout must salute the Union Jack, which is the symbol of tyranny and oppression.* Etc. etc.

Now, suppose that at this moment somebody started a left-wing paper deliberately aimed at boys of twelve or fourteen. I do not suggest that the whole of its contents would be exactly like the tract I have quoted above, but does anyone doubt that they would be *something* like it? Inevitably such a paper would either consist of dreary uplift or it would be under Communist influence and given over to adulation of Soviet Russia; in either case no normal boy would ever look at it. Highbrow literature apart, the whole of the existing left-wing Press, in so far as it is at all vigorously "left," is one long tract. The one Socialist paper in England which could live a week on its merits *as a paper* is the *Daily Herald*: and how much Socialism is there in the *Daily Herald*? At this moment, therefore, a paper with a "left" slant and at the same time likely to have an appeal to ordinary boys in their teens is something almost beyond hoping for.

But it does not follow that it is impossible. There is no clear reason why every adventure story should necessarily be mixed up with snobbishness and gutter patriotism. For, after all, the stories in the *Hotspur* and the *Modern Boy* are not Conservative tracts; they are merely adventure stories with a Conservative bias. It is fairly easy to imagine the process being reversed. It is possible, for instance, to imagine a paper as thrilling and lively as the *Hotspur*, but with subject-matter and "ideology" a little more up to date. It is even possible (though this raises other difficulties) to imagine a women's paper at the same literary level as the *Oracle*, dealing in approximately the same kind of story, but taking rather more account of the realities of working-class life. Such things have been done before, though not in England. In the last years of the Spanish monarchy there was a large output in Spain of left-wing novelettes, some of them evidently of anarchist origin. Unfortunately at the time when they were appearing I did not see their social significance, and I lost the collection of them that I had, but no doubt copies would still be procurable. In get-up and style of story they were very similar to the English fourpenny novelette, except that their inspiration was "left." If, for instance, a story described police pursuing anarchists through the mountains, it would be from the point of view of the anarchists and not of the police. An example nearer to hand is the Soviet film *Chapaiev*, which has been shown a number of times in London. Technically, by the standards of the time when it was made, *Chapaiev* is a first-rate film, but mentally, in spite of the unfamiliar Russian background, it is not so very remote from Hollywood. The one thing that lifts it out of the ordinary is the remarkable performance by the actor who takes the part of the White officer (the fat one)—a performance which looks like an inspired piece of gagging. Otherwise the atmosphere is familiar. All the usual paraphernalia is there—heroic fight against odds, escape at the last moment, shots of galloping horses, love interest, comic relief. The film is in fact a fairly ordinary one, except that its tendency is "left." In a Hollywood film of the Russian Civil War the Whites would probably be angels and the Reds demons. In the Russian version the Reds are angels and the Whites demons. That also is a lie, but, taking the long view, it is a less pernicious lie than the other.

Here several difficult problems present themselves. Their general nature is obvious enough, and I do not want to discuss them. I am merely pointing to the fact that, in England, popular imaginative literature is a field that left-wing thought has never begun to enter. *All* fiction from the novels in the mushroom libraries downwards is censored in the interests of the ruling class. And boys' fiction above all, the blood-and-thunder stuff which nearly every boy devours at some time or other, is sodden in the worst illusions of 1910. The fact is only unimportant if one believes that what is read in childhood leaves no impression behind. Lord Camrose and his colleagues evidently believe nothing of the kind, and, after all, Lord Camrose ought to know.

IRVING HOWE

(b. 1920)

Like Philip Rahv and Alfred Kazin, Irving Howe shows the influence of his social background and early life in the nature of his literary criticism, which he characterizes as follows: "I have tried to strike a balance between the social and the literary; to fructify one with the other; yet not to confuse one with the other. Though I believe in the social approach to literature, it seems to me peculiarly open to misuse; it requires particular delicacy and care." Howe is founding editor of the socialist quarterly *Dissent* and a frequent contributor to its pages. In addition to his socio-historical writing, he has published three books of literary criticism, *Sherwood Anderson* (1951), *William Faulkner* (1952; 1962), and *Politics and the Novel* (1957). He has also edited *Modern Literary Criticism* (1961), a collection of critical essays.

Orwell: History as Nightmare (1956)

About some books we feel that our reluctance to return to them is the true measure of our admiration. It is hard to suppose that many people go back, from a spontaneous desire, to reread *1984*: there is neither reason nor need to, no one forgets it. The usual distinctions between forgotten details and a vivid general impression mean nothing here, for the book is written out of one passionate breath, each word is bent to a severe discipline of meaning, everything is stripped to the bareness of terror.

Kafka's *The Trial* is also a book of terror, but it is a paradigm and to some extent a puzzle, so that one may lose oneself in the rhythm of the paradigm and play with the parts of the puzzle. Kafka's novel persuades us that life is inescapably hazardous and problematic, but the very "universality" of this idea

Reprinted from *Politics and the Novel* by Irving Howe, with the permission of the publishers, Horizon Press, Inc. Copyright 1957 by Irving Howe.

helps soften its impact: to apprehend the terrible on the plane of metaphysics is to lend it an almost soothing aura. And besides, *The Trial* absorbs one endlessly in its aspect of enigma.

Though not nearly so great a book, *1984* is in some ways more terrible. For it is not a paradigm and hardly a puzzle; whatever enigmas it raises concern not the imagination of the author but the life of our time. It does not take us away from, or beyond, our obsession with immediate social reality, and in reading the book we tend to say—the linguistic clumsiness conceals a deep truth—that the world of 1984 is "more real" than our own. The book appals us because its terror, far from being inherent in the "human condition," is particular to our century; what haunts us is the sickening awareness that in *1984* Orwell has seized upon those elements of our public life that, given courage and intelligence, were avoidable. How remarkable a book *1984* really is, can be discovered only after a second reading. It offers true testimony, it speaks for our time. And because it derives from a perception of how our time may end, the book trembles with an eschatological fury that is certain to create among its readers, even those who sincerely believe they admire it, the most powerful kinds of resistance. It already has. Openly in England, more cautiously in America, there has arisen a desire among intellectuals to belittle Orwell's achievement, often in the guise of celebrating his humanity and his "goodness." They feel embarrassed before the apocalyptic desperation of the book, they begin to wonder whether it may not be just a little overdrawn and humorless, they even suspect it is tinged with the hysteria of the death-bed. Nor can it be denied that all of us would feel more comfortable if the book could be cast out. It is a remarkable book.

Whether it is a remarkable novel or a novel at all, seems unimportant. It is not, I suppose, really a novel, or at least it does not satisfy those expectations we have come to have with regard to the novel—expectations that are mainly the heritage of nineteenth century romanticism with its stress upon individual consciousness, psychological analysis and the study of intimate relations. One American critic, a serious critic, reviewed the book under the heading, "Truth Maybe, Not Fiction," as if thereby to demonstrate the strictness with which he held to distinctions of literary genre. Actually, he was demonstrating a certain narrowness of modern taste, for such a response to *1984* is possible only when discriminations are no longer made between fiction and the novel, which is but one kind of fiction though the kind modern readers care for most.

A cultivated eighteenth century reader would never have said of *1984* that it may be true but isn't fiction, for it was then understood that fiction, like poetry, can have many modes and be open to many mixtures; the novel had not yet established its popular tyranny.

What is more, the style of *1984*, which many readers take to be drab or uninspired or "sweaty," would have been appreciated by someone like Defoe, since Defoe would have immediately understood how the pressures of Orwell's subject, like the pressures of his own, demand a gritty and hammering factuality. The style of *1984* is the style of a man whose commitment to a dreadful vision is at war with the nausea to which that vision reduces him. So acute is this conflict that delicacies of phrasing or displays of rhetoric come to seem frivolous —*he has no time, he must get it all down.* Those who fail to see this, I am convinced, have succumbed to the pleasant tyrannies of estheticism; they have allowed their fondness for a cultivated style to blind them to the urgencies of prophetic expression. The last thing Orwell cared about when he wrote *1984*, the last thing he should have cared about, was literature.

Another complaint one often hears is that there are no credible or "three-dimensional" characters in the book. Apart from its rather facile identification of credibility with a particular treatment of character, the complaint involves a failure to see that in some books an extended amount of psychological specification or even dramatic incident can be disastrous. In *1984* Orwell is trying to present the kind of world in which individuality has become obsolete and personality a crime. The whole idea of the self as something precious and inviolable is a *cultural* idea, and as we understand it, a product of the liberal era; but Orwell has imagined a world in which the self, whatever subterranean existence it manages to eke out, is no longer a significant value, not even a value to be violated.

Winston Smith and Julia come through as rudimentary figures because they are slowly learning, and at great peril to themselves, what it means to be human. Their experiment in the rediscovery of the human, which is primarily an experiment in the possibilities of solitude, leads them to cherish two things that are fundamentally hostile to the totalitarian outlook: a life of contemplativeness and the joy of "purposeless"—that is, free—sexual passion. But this experiment cannot go very far, as they themselves know; it is inevitable that they be caught and destroyed.

Partly, that is the meaning and the pathos of the book. Were it possible, in the world of 1984, to show human character in anything resembling genuine freedom, in its play of spontaneous desire and caprice—it would not be the world of 1984. So that in a slightly obtuse way the complaint that Orwell's characters seem thin testifies to the strength of the book, for it is a complaint directed not against his technique but against his primary assumptions.

The book cannot be understood, nor can it be properly valued, simply by resorting to the usual literary categories, for it posits a situation in which these categories are no longer significant. Everything has hardened into politics, the leviathan has swallowed man. About such a world it is, strictly speaking, impossible to write a novel, if only because the human relationships taken for granted in the novel are here suppressed.[1] The book must first be approached through politics, yet not as a political study or treatise. It is something else, at once a model and a vision —a model of the totalitarian state in its "pure" or "essential" form and a vision of what this state can do to human life. Yet the theme of the conflict between ideology and emotion, as at times their fusion and mutual reinforcement—a theme that has been noticed repeatedly

in the previous chapters of this book— is still to be found in 1984, as a dim underground motif. Without this theme, there could be no dramatic conflict in a work of fiction dominated by politics. Winston Smith's effort to reconstruct the old tune about the bells of St. Clement is a token of his desire to regain the condition of humanness, which is here nothing more than a capacity for so "useless" a feeling as nostalgia. Between the tune and Oceania there can be no peace.

1984 projects a nightmare in which politics has displaced humanity and the state has stifled society. In a sense, it is a profoundly antipolitical book, full of hatred for the kind of world in which public claims destroy the possibilities for private life; and this conservative side of Orwell's outlook he suggests, perhaps unconsciously, through the first name of his hero. But if the image of Churchill is thus raised in order to celebrate, a little wryly, the memory of the bad (or as Winston Smith comes to feel, the good) old days, the opposing image of Trotsky is raised, a little skeptically, in order to discover the inner meanings of totalitarian society. When Winston Smith learns to think of Oceania as a *problem*—which is itself to commit a "crimethink"—he turns to the forbidden work of Emmanuel Goldstein, *The Theory and Practise of Oligarchical Collectivism*, clearly a replica of Trotsky's *The Revolution Betrayed*. The power and intelligence of 1984 partly derives from a tension between these images; even as Orwell understood the need for politics in the modern world, he felt a profound distaste for the ways of political life, and he was honest enough not to try to suppress one or another side of this struggle within himself.

[1] Some people have suggested that *1984* is primarily a symptom of Orwell's psychological condition, the nightmare of a disturbed man who suffered from paranoid fantasies, was greatly troubled by dirt and feared that sexual contact would bring down punishment from those in authority. Apart from its intolerable glibness, such an "explanation" explains either too much or too little. Almost everyone has nightmares and a great many people have ambiguous feelings about sex, but few manage to write books with the power of *1984*. Nightmare the book may be, and no doubt it is grounded, as are all books, in the psychological troubles of its author. But it is also grounded in his psychological health, otherwise it could not penetrate so deeply the social reality of our time. The private nightmare, if it is there, is profoundly related to, and helps us understand, public events.

II

No other book has succeeded so completely in rendering the essential quality of totalitarianism. 1984 is limited in scope; it does not pretend to investigate the genesis of the totalitarian state, nor the laws of its economy, nor the prospect for its survival; it simply evokes the "tone" of life in a totalitarian society. And since it is not a realistic novel, it can treat Oceania as an *extreme instance*, one that might never actually exist but which illuminates the nature of societies that do exist.[2]

Orwell's profoundest insight is that in a totalitarian world man's life is shorn of dynamic possibilities. The end of life is completely predictable in its beginning, the beginning merely a manipulated preparation for the end. There is no opening for surprise, for that spontaneous animation which is the token of and justification for freedom. Oceanic society may evolve through certain stages of economic development, but the life of its members is static, a given and measured quantity that can neither rise to tragedy nor tumble to comedy. Human personality, as we have come to grasp for it in a class society and hope for it in a classless society, is obliterated; man becomes a function of a process he is never allowed to understand or control. The fetishism of the state replaces the fetishism of commodities.

There have, of course, been unfree societies in the past, yet in most of them it was possible to find an oasis of freedom, if only because none had the resources to enforce total consent. But totalitarianism, which represents a decisive break from the Western tradition, aims to permit no such luxuries; it offers a total "solution" to the problems of the twentieth century, that is, a total distortion of what might be a solution. To be sure, no totalitarian state has been able to reach this degree of "perfection," which Orwell, like a physicist who in his experiment assumes the absence of friction, has assumed for Oceania. But the knowledge that friction can never actually be absent does not make the experiment any the less valuable.

To the degree that the totalitarian state approaches its "ideal" condition, it destroys the margin for unforeseen behavior; as a character in Dostoevsky's *The Possessed* remarks, "only the necessary is necessary." Nor is there a social crevice in which the recalcitrant or independent mind can seek shelter. The totalitarian state assumes that—given modern technology, complete political control, the means of terror and a rationalized contempt for moral tradition—anything is possible. Anything can be done with men, anything with their minds, with history and with words. Reality is no longer something to be acknowledged or experienced or even transformed; it is fabricated according to the need and will of the state, sometimes in anticipation of the future, sometimes as a retrospective improvement upon the past.

But even as Orwell, overcoming the resistance of his own nausea, evoked the ethos of the totalitarian world, he used very little of what is ordinarily called "imagination" in order to show how this ethos stains every aspect of human life. Like most good writers, he understood that imagination is primarily the capacity for apprehending reality, for seeing both clearly and deeply whatever it is that exists. That is why his vision of social horror, if taken as a model rather than a portrait, strikes one as essentially credible, while the efforts of most writers to create utopias or anti-utopias founder precisely on their desire to be scientific or inventive. Orwell understood that social horror consists not in the prevalence of diabolical machines or in the invasion of Martian automatons flashing death rays from mechanical eyes, but in the persistence of inhuman relations among men.

And he understood, as well, the significance of what I can only call the psychology and politics of "one more step." From a bearable neurosis to a crippling psychosis, from a decayed society in which survival is still possible to a totalitarian state in which it is hardly desirable, there may be only

[2] "My novel *1984*," wrote Orwell shortly before his death, "is *not* intended as an attack on socialism, or on the British Labor Party, but as a show-up of the perversions to which a centralized economy is liable. . . . I do not believe that the kind of society I describe necessarily *will* arrive, but I believe . . . that something resembling it *could* arrive."

"one step." To lay bare the logic of that social regression which leads to totalitarianism Orwell had merely to allow his imagination to take . . . one step.

Consider such typical aspects of Oceanic society as telescreens and the use of children as informers against their parents. There are no telescreens in Russia, but there could well be: nothing in Russian society contradicts the "principle" of telescreens. Informing against parents who are political heretics is not a common practice in the United States, but some people have been deprived of their jobs on the charge of having maintained "prolonged associations" with their parents. To capture the totalitarian spirit, Orwell had merely to allow certain tendencies in modern society to spin forward without the brake of sentiment or humaneness. He could thus make clear the relationship between his model of totalitarianism and the societies we know in our experience, and he could do this without resorting to the clap-trap of science fiction or the crude assumption that we already live in 1984. In imagining the world of 1984 he took only one step, and because he knew how long and terrible a step it was, he had no need to take another.

III

Through a struggle of the mind and an effort of the will that clearly left him exhausted, Orwell came to see—which is far more than simply to understand —what the inner spirit or ethos of totalitarianism is. But it was characteristic of Orwell as a writer that he felt uneasy with a general idea or a total vision; things took on reality for him only as they were particular and concrete. The world of 1984 seems to have had for him the hallucinatory immediacy that Yoknapatawpha County has for Faulkner or London had for Dickens, and even as he ruthlessly subordinated his descriptions to the dominating theme of the book, Orwell succeeded in noting the details of Oceanic society with a painstaking and sometimes uncanny accuracy.

There are first the incidental accuracies of mimicry. Take, as an example, Orwell's grasp of the role played by the scapegoat-enemy of the totalitarian world, the rituals of hate for which he is indispensable, and more appalling, the uncertainty as to whether he even exists or is a useful fabrication of the state. Among the best passages in the book are those in which Orwell imitates Trotsky's style in *The Theory and Practise of Oligarchical Collectivism*. Orwell caught the rhetorical sweep and grandeur of Trotsky's writing, particularly his fondness for using scientific references in non-scientific contexts: "Even after enormous upheavals and seemingly irrevocable changes, the same pattern has always reasserted itself, just as a gyroscope will always return to equilibrium, however far it is pushed one way or another." And in another sentence Orwell beautifully captured Trotsky's way of using a compressed paradox to sum up the absurdity of a whole society: "The fields are cultivated with horse plows while books are written by machinery."

Equally skillful was Orwell's evocation of the physical atmosphere of Oceania, the overwhelming gloomy shabbiness of its streets and houses, the tasteless sameness of the clothes its people wear, the unappetizing gray-pink stew they eat, that eternal bureaucratic stew which seems to go with all modern oppressive institutions. Orwell had not been taken in by the legend that totalitarianism is at least efficient; instead of the usual chromium-and-skyscraper vision of the future, he painted London in 1984 as a composite of the city in its dismal grayness during the last (Second) world war and of the modern Russian cities with their Victorian ostentation and rotting slums. In all of his books Orwell had shown himself only mildly gifted at visual description but remarkably keen at detecting loathsome and sickening odors. He had the best nose of his generation—his mind sometimes betrayed him, his nose never. In the world of 1984, he seems to be suggesting, all of the rubbish of the past, together with some that no one had quite been able to foresee, is brought together.

The rubbish survived, but what of the past itself, the past in which men had managed to live and sometimes with a little pleasure? One of the most poignant scenes in the book is that in which Winston Smith, trying to discover what life was like before the reign of Big Brother, talks to an old prole in a pub. The exchange is unsatisfactory to Smith, since the worker can remember only fragments of disconnected fact and is quite unable to generalize from his memories; but the scene itself is a fine bit of dramatic action, indicating that not only does totalitarian society destroy the past through the obliteration of objective records but that it destroys the memory of the past through a disintegration of individual consciousness. The worker with whom Smith talks remembers that the beer was better before Big Brother (a very important fact) but he cannot really understand Smith's question: "Do you feel that you have more freedom now than you had in those days?" To pose, let alone understand, such a question requires a degree of social continuity, as well as a set of complex assumptions, which Oceania is gradually destroying.

The destruction of social memory becomes a major industry in Oceania, and here of course Orwell was borrowing directly from Stalinism which, as the most "advanced" form of totalitarianism, was infinitely more adept at this job than was fascism. (Hitler burned books, Stalin had them rewritten.) In Oceania the embarrassing piece of paper slides down memory hole—and that is all.

Orwell is similarly acute in noticing the relationship between the totalitarian state and what passes for culture. Novels are produced by machine; the state anticipates all wants, from "cleansed" versions of Byron to pornographic magazines; that vast modern industry which we call "popular culture" has become an important state function. Mean-

while, the language is stripped of words that suggest refinements of attitude or gradations of sensibility.

And with feeling as with language, Oceania seeks to blot out spontaneous affection because it assumes, with good reason, that whatever is uncalculated is subversive. Smith thinks to himself:

> It would not have occurred to [his mother] that an action which is ineffectual thereby becomes meaningless. If you loved someone, you loved him, and when you had nothing else to give, you still gave him love. When the last of the chocolate was gone, his mother had clasped the children in her arms. It was no use, it changed nothing, it did not produce more chocolate, it did not avert the child's death or her own; but it seemed natural for her to do it.

IV

At only a few points can one question Orwell's vision of totalitarianism, and even these involve highly problematic matters. If they are errors at all, it is only to the extent that they drive valid observations too hard: Orwell's totalitarian society is at times more *total* than we can presently imagine.

One such problem has to do with the relation between the state and "human nature." Granted that human nature is itself a cultural concept with a history of change behind it; granted that the pressures of fear and force can produce extreme variations in human conduct. There yet remains the question: to what extent can a terrorist regime suppress or radically alter the fundamental impulses of man? Is there a constant in human nature which no amount of terror or propaganda can destroy?

In Oceania the sexual impulse, while not destroyed, has been remarkably weakened among the members of the Outer Party. For the faithful, sexual energy is transformed into political hysteria. There is a harrowing passage in which Smith remembers his sexual relations with his former wife, a loyal party member who would submit herself once a week, as if for an ordeal and resisting even while insisting, in order to procreate for the party. The only thing she did not feel was pleasure.

Orwell puts the matter with some care:

The aim of the Party was not merely to prevent men and women from forming loyalties which it might not be able to control. Its real, undeclared purpose was to remove all pleasure from the sexual act. Not love so much as eroticism was the enemy, inside marriage as well as outside it . . . The only recognized purpose of marriage was to beget children for the service of the Party. Sexual intercourse was to be looked on as a slightly disgusting minor operation, like having an enema . . . The Party was trying to kill the sex instinct, or, if it could not be killed, then to distort it and dirty it . . . And so far as the women were concerned, the Party's efforts were largely successful.

That Orwell has here come upon an important tendency in modern life, that the totalitarian state is inherently an enemy of erotic freedom, seems to me indisputable. And we know from the past that the sexual impulse can be heavily suppressed. In Puritan communities, for example, sex was regarded with great suspicion, and it is not hard to imagine that even in marriage the act of love might bring the Puritans very little pleasure. But it should be remembered that in Puritan communities hostility toward sex was interwoven with a powerful faith: men mortified themselves in behalf of God. By contrast, Oceania looks upon faith not merely as suspect but downright dangerous, for its rulers prefer mechanical assent to intellectual fervor or zealous belief. (They have probably read enough history to know that in the Protestant era enthusiasm had a way of turning into individualism.)

Given these circumstances, is it plausible that the Outer Party members would be able to discard erotic pleasure so completely? Is this not cutting too close to the limit of indestructible human needs? I should think that in a society so pervaded by boredom and grayness as Oceania is, there would be a pressing hunger for erotic adventure, to say nothing of experiments in perversion.

A totalitarian society can force people to do many things that violate their social and physical desires; it may even teach them to receive pain with quiet resignation; but I doubt that it can break down the fundamental, if sometimes ambiguous, distinction between pleasure and pain. Man's biological make-up requires him to obtain food, and, with less regularity or insistence, sex; and while society can do a great deal—it has—to dim the pleasures of sex and reduce the desire for food, it seems reasonable to assume that even when consciousness has been blitzed, the "animal drives" of man cannot be violated as thoroughly as Orwell suggests. In the long run, these drives may prove to be one of the most enduring forces of resistance to the totalitarian state.

Does not Orwell imply something of the sort when he shows Winston Smith turning to individual reflection and Julia to private pleasure? What is the source of their rebellion if not the "innate" resistance of their minds and bodies to the destructive pressures of Oceania? It is clear that they are no more intelligent or sensitive—certainly no more heroic—than most Outer Party members. And if their needs as human beings force these two quite ordinary people to rebellion, may not the same thing happen to others?

A related problem concerns Orwell's treatment of the workers in Oceania. The proles, just because they are at the bottom of the heap and perform routine tasks of work, get off rather better than members of the Outer Party: they are granted more privacy, the telescreen does not bawl instructions at them nor watch their every motion, and the secret police seldom troubles them, except to wipe out a talented or independent worker. Presumably Orwell would justify this by saying that the state need no longer fear the workers, so demoralized have they become as individuals and so powerless as a class. That such a situation might arise in the future it would be foolhardy to deny, and in any case Orwell is deliberately pushing things to a dramatic extreme; but we should also notice that nothing of the kind has yet happened, neither the Nazis nor the Stalinists having ever relaxed their control or surveillance of the workers to any significant extent. Orwell has here made the mistake of taking more than "one step" and thereby breaking the tie between the world we know and the world he has imagined.

But his treatment of the proles can be questioned on more fundamental grounds. The totalitarian state can afford no luxury, allow no exceptions; it cannot tolerate the existence of any group beyond the perimeter of its control; it can never become so secure as to lapse into indifference. Scouring every corner of society for rebels it knows do not exist, the totalitarian state cannot come to rest for any prolonged period of time. To do so would be to risk disintegration. It must always tend toward a condition of self-agitation, shaking and reshaking its members, testing and retesting them in order to insure its power. And since, as Winston Smith concludes, the proles remain one of the few possible sources of revolt, it can hardly seem plausible that Oceania would permit them even the relative freedom Orwell describes.

Finally, there is Orwell's extremely interesting though questionable view of the dynamics of power in a totalitarian state. As he portrays the party oligarchy in Oceania, it is the first ruling class of modern times to dispense with ideology. It makes no claim to be ruling in behalf of humanity, the workers, the nation or anyone but itself; it rejects as naive the rationale of the Grand Inquisitor that he oppresses the ignorant to accomplish their salvation. O'Brien, the representative of the Inner Party, says: "The Party seeks power entirely for its own sake. We are not interested in the good of the others; we are interested solely in power." The Stalinists and Nazis, he adds, had approached this view of power, but only in Oceania has all pretense to serving humanity—that is, all ideology—been discarded.

Social classes have at least one thing in common: an appetite for power. The bourgeoisie sought power, not primarily as an end in itself (whatever that vague phrase might mean), but in order to be free to expand its economic and social activity. The ruling class of the new totalitarian society, especially in Russia, is different, however, from previous ruling classes of our time: it does not think of political power as a means toward a non-political end, as to some extent the bourgeoisie did; it looks upon political power as its essential end. For in a society where there is no private property the distinction between economic and political power becomes invisible.

So far this would seem to bear out Orwell's view. But if the ruling class of the totalitarian state does not conceive of political power as primarily a channel to tangible economic privileges, what *does* political power mean to it?

At least in the West, no modern ruling class has yet been able to dispense with ideology. All have felt an overwhelming need to rationalize their power, to proclaim some admirable objective as a justification for detestable acts. Nor is this mere slyness or hypocrisy; the rulers of a modern society can hardly survive without a certain degree of sincere belief in their own claims. They cling to ideology not merely to win and hold followers, but to give themselves psychological and moral assurance.

Can one imagine a twentieth century ruling class capable of discarding these supports and acknowledging to itself the true nature of its motives? I doubt it. Many Russian bureaucrats, in the relaxation of private cynicism, may look upon their Marxist vocabulary as a useful sham; but they must still cling to some vague assumption that somehow their political conduct rests upon ultimate sanctions. Were this not so, the totalitarian ruling class would find it increasingly difficult, perhaps impossible, to sustain its morale. It would go soft, it would become corrupted in the obvious ways, it would lose the fanaticism that is essential to its survival.

But ideology aside, there remains the

enigma of totalitarian power. And it *is* an enigma. Many writers have probed the origins of totalitarianism, the dynamics of its growth, the psychological basis of its appeal, the economic policies it employs when in power. But none of the theorists who study totalitarianism can tell us very much about the "ultimate purpose" of the Nazis or the Stalinists; in the end they come up against the same difficulties as does Winston Smith in *1984* when he says, "I understand HOW: I do not understand WHY."

Toward what end do the rulers of Oceania strive? They want power; they want to enjoy the sense of exercising their power, which means to test their ability to cause those below them to suffer. Yet the question remains, why do they kill millions of people, why do they find pleasure in torturing and humiliating people they know to be innocent? For that matter, why did the Nazis and Stalinists? What is the image of the world they desire, the vision by which they live?

I doubt that such questions can presently be answered, and it may be that they are not even genuine problems. A movement in which terror and irrationality play so great a role may finally have no goal beyond terror and irrationality; to search for an ultimate end that can be significantly related to its immediate activity may itself be a rationalist fallacy.

Orwell has been criticized by Isaac Deutscher for succumbing to a "mysticism of cruelty" in explaining the behavior of Oceania's rulers, which means, I suppose, that Orwell does not entirely accept any of the usual socio-economic theories about the aims of totalitarianism. It happens, however, that neither Mr. Deutscher nor anyone else has yet been able to provide a satisfactory explanation for that systematic excess in destroying human values which is a central trait of totalitarianism. I do not say that the mystery need remain with us forever, since it is possible that in time we shall be able to dissolve it into a series of problems more easily manageable. Meanwhile, however, it seems absurd to attack a writer for acknowledging with rare honesty his sense of helplessness before the "ultimate" meaning of totalitarianism—especially if that writer happens to have given us the most graphic vision of totalitarianism that has yet been composed. For with *1984* we come to the heart of the matter, the whiteness of the whiteness.

Form

FRANCIS FERGUSSON

(b. 1904)

Poet, playwright, and translator, as well as a critic with a special interest in drama, Francis Fergusson was actively associated with the theater for many years, first as a member of the American Laboratory Theatre in New York during the early Thirties, and then as director of the Bennington College theater from 1934 to 1947. Fergusson's achievement as a critic has been a developing modern "poetics" of drama grounded in a religious conception of man and concerned with the theater's function as a communal enactment of man's nature as it is realized within the structures of society. Fergusson's criticism, then, which is sociological and psychological in the speculative manner of "myth" criticism, has a profoundly philosophical orientation unusual in modern dramatic criticism. Fergusson's important work is to be found in *The Idea of a Theatre, a Study of Ten Plays* (1949), *Dante's Drama of the Mind: a Modern Reading of the Purgatorio* (1953), and *The Human Image in Dramatic Literature* (1957).

From *Hamlet, Prince of Denmark*: The Analogy of Action (1949)

Hamlet as Ritual and Improvisation

If one could see a performance of *Hamlet*, uncut, unbroken by intermissions, and employing the kind of simple make-believe which Shakespeare, with his bare stage, must have intended, we should find much to enthrall us besides the stories themselves. The stories, of course, start at once, and are felt continuously as working themselves out: fate, behind the scenes, makes, from time to time, its sudden pronouncements. But on-stage, the music and the drums and the marching of royal and military pageantry, are directly absorbing, and they assure us that something of great and general significance is going on. From time to time the stage is emptied; the pageantry is gone; the stories seem to

be marking time—and Hamlet emerges, alone, or with one or two interlocutors. Sometimes he suffers his visions before us; sometimes he makes jokes and topical allusions; sometimes he spars with his interlocutors like the gag-man in a minstrel show, or the master of ceremonies in a modern musical.

The scenes of pageantry are all civic or military or religious rituals; the changing of the guard, the formal assembling of the court of Denmark; the funeral of Ophelia. Though they all have their relevance to the interwoven stories of the play and to the discordant purposes of the various characters, their chief function is to show forth the main action or underlying theme, at various stages in its development. At these ritual moments the plot-lines are, as it were, gathered together; the issues are held in suspension, and we are reminded of the traditional social values in which all have some sort of stake.

Hamlet's monologues, and his nimble exchanges with Polonius or Rosencrantz and Guildenstern, his "topical allusions" to drunkenness or to the state of the theater, make a very different kind of theatrical appeal. He steps out of the narrative course of the play, out of the "world of Denmark" which is the basic postulate of the make-believe, refers directly to the parallels between "Denmark" and the England of his audience. From one point of view Shakespeare seems to be counting on the inherent dramatic and theatrical interest which this character has apart from the story —permitting him, like the first violin in a concerto, a cadenza on his own, after which we are returned to the matter in hand. From another point of view, Hamlet's "improvized" moments are carried by our confidence in him as "chief reflector" we look to him, as to the ritual scenes, to show us the underlying theme of the whole.

Both the ritual and the improvisational elements in *Hamlet* are essential —as essential as the stories—in the structure of the whole. The Elizabethan theater, at once as frankly "theatrical" as vaudeville, and as central to the life of its time as an ancient rite, offered Shakespeare two resources, two theatrical "dimensions" which the modern naturalistic tradition of serious drama must try, or pretend, to do without. In the table on the following page I have shown the chief ritual and the chief improvisational scenes in relation to the main parts of the plot.

If one thinks over the succession of ritual scenes as they appear in the play, it is clear that they serve to focus attention on the Danish body politic and its hidden malady: they are ceremonious invocations of the well-being of society, and secular or religious devices for securing it. As the play progresses, the rituals change in character, from the dim but honest changing of the guard, through Ophelia's mock rites, to the black mass of Claudius' last court. And it appears that the improvisational scenes bear a significant and developing relationship to the rituals. In general,

they throw doubt upon the efficacy of the official magic, as when Hamlet refuses to take Claudius' first court at its face value; yet even the most cutting ironies of Hamlet do not disavow the mystery which the rituals celebrate, or reject the purposes that inform them.

The rituals, the stories, and the improvisations together make the peculiar rhythm of *Hamlet* as a performance. Denmark is shown as waiting, as it were, in the darkness of its ineffective ceremonies and hollow communal prayers while the infection, "mining all within," divides every man in secret from every other and bursts forth, from time to time, in savage but brief and ineffective fights.

But before examining the sequence of rituals, with its center in the players' scene, it is necessary to endeavor to support the view that the Elizabethan theater had, in fact, this ritual aspect: that Shakespeare's audience, like that of Sophocles, was prepared to accept his play not only as an exciting story but as the "celebration of the mystery" of human life.

The Globe Theater and the Festival of Dionysos

The main evidence (apart from the play itself) for taking *Hamlet* as a species of ritual drama, is provided by recent studies which show that a great deal of the religious culture of the Middle Ages was still alive in Shakespeare's time. Tilyard's *The Elizabethan World Picture*, for example, makes this clear. Mr. Tilyard quotes Hamlet's famous speech on man: "What a piece of work is a man: how noble in reason; how infinite in faculty; in form and moving how express and admirable; in action how like an angel; in apprehension how like a god; the beauty of the world, the paragon of animals."—"This has been taken," Mr. Tilyard explains, "as one of the great English versions of Renaissance humanism, an assertion of the dignity of man against the asceticisms of medieval misanthropy. Actually it is in the purest medieval tradition: Shake-

THE PARTS OF THE PLOT	RITUAL SCENES	IMPROVISATIONAL ENTERTAINMENT
The Prologue	Act I, sc. 1 The changing of the Guard Act I, sc. 2 Claudius' First Court	
The Agons—development of conflicting purposes of various characters; contrasts of their stories; "purposes mistook"; indecision and fighting in the dark.		Act I, sc. 4 Hamlet's sermon on drunkenness (in Denmark and/or England). Act II, sc. 2 Hamlet exchanges wisecracks with Polonius, Rosencrantz, Guildenstern, and the players. Act III, sc. 2 Hamlet's charge to the players—his opinions on the art of acting.
The Climax, Peripety, and Recognitions; all narrative strands brought together.	RITUAL AND ENTERTAINMENT Act III, sc. 2 The performance of Hamlet's play is both rite and entertainment, and shows the Prince as at once clown and ritual head of the state.	
The Pathos or "sparagmos," both of the state and the individuals, leading to the epiphany or "collective revelation" of the general disease. (Cf. Toynbee's "schism in the state and schism in the soul".)	Act IV, sc. 5 Ophelia's Madness is a mock ritual, a mixture of false and lewd marriage, and false and savage funeral; refers also to the funeral of Hamlet's father and Gertrude's false marriage. Alternates with rebellion in the state.	
The Epiphany, or Final Vision of the underlying truth of the action.	Act V, sc. 1 Ophelia's funeral. A "maimed rite" but a real death. Act V, sc 2 The duel between Hamlet and Laertes. This duel is surrounded with all the ceremonies of Claudius' Court, like the players' scene, and Claudius' other loud and drunken celebrations; but every element in it is false or mistaken: a mockery of invocation; and it eventuates in death, and "resurrection" in the shape of Fortinbras, who, now that Claudius' regime is gone, can appear with his new faith and hope.	Act V Hamlet jokes and moralizes with the Gravedigger and Horatio. He feels like the gag-man and the royal victim in one. Gravedigger corresponds to Polonius.

speare's version of the orthodox encomia of what man, created in God's image, was like in his prelapsarian state and of what ideally he is still capable of being. It also shows Shakespeare placing man in the traditional cosmic setting between the angels and the beasts. It is what the theologians had been saying for centuries." And Mr. Tilyard proceeds to show that most of the "world picture which the Middle Ages inherited" was still tacitly assumed by the Elizabethans: "an ordered universe arranged in a fixed system of hierarchies but modified by man's sin and the hope of his redemption."

The Elizabethan stage itself, that central mirror of the life of its times, was a symbolic representation of this traditional cosmos: it was thus taken both as the physical and as the metaphysical "scene" of man's life. Mr. Kernodle has shown this in detail in his illuminating study, *From Art to Theater*. He traces the genealogy of the symbolic façade of the Elizabethan stage house back through street pageantry to painting and to the architecture of tombs and altars; and thence to the arcade screen of the Greek tragic theater itself. "More than an arrangement of side doors and inner and upper stages, that façade was itself a symbol of castle, throne, triumphal arch, altar, tomb"—in short, an all-purpose, eminently practicable setting, implying the constant elements in the Elizabethan world picture, yet flexible enough to serve the shifting make-believe of the actors. Over the whole was a permanent canopy, painted to represent the heavens, a vault literally "fretted with golden fire."

The symbolic character of this stage seems to imply a conception of the theater akin to that of ritual: the celebration of the mystery of human life. This stage and its drama did not, it is true, develop directly from the Mass; it developed from the secular theater of the Middle Ages and, as Mr. Kernodle shows, from royal and civic pageantry. But in the Renaissance the monarchy and its rites was taking over some of the religious significance of the church

and its rites. The pope tended to be superseded by the prince as vicar, or "type" of Christ, the pageantry and ceremony of the church by the pageantry and ceremony of the national state. The Tudor monarch was the symbol, and the visible center of the traditional world order, so that Donne could write, on the death of Prince Henry:

Of Weight one Centre, one of Greatness is, And Both my Centres feel this Period.

The role of the monarch in Shakespeare's time (and in his plays) was thus very close to that of Sophocles' Oedipus or Creon: he was at once ruler, high priest, and father of the community. And the ceremonies which Shakespeare and Hamlet's Danes engaged in— whether obviously religious, like the funeral, or more secular, like the Court— were taken as celebrating and securing the welfare of the whole, of the monarchy, and of the "lives of many" that depended on it.

The Elizabethan theater may thus be regarded as the heir of the Greek tragic theater with its ritual basis. The Elizabethan cosmos is still that of the great tradition,[1] which the Middle Ages inherited from the city state. The physical stage itself is symbolic in the same way as the tragic stage of the Greeks; and the ritual component in its drama has similar deep and general meanings.

This does not mean, of course, that Shakespeare's audience, or even Shakespeare himself, could have expounded this genealogy and these parallels. If the tradition was alive in Shakespeare's time, it was as a "habit of thought and feeling" rather than as an explicit and integrated philosophy. But Shakespeare seems to have felt the essential elements of this great "theater" as alive still; to have assumed that his audience would respond to them, and to have based his dramaturgy upon them.

If Shakespeare's theater is thus akin to the theater of Sophocles, their drama

---

[1] *The Great Chain of Being*, by Arthur Lovejoy, is a chief source of this view of what the Renaissance inherited.

should be composed on similar principles: appealing in both cases to ancient and publicly accepted values and modes of understanding, rather than preaching, inventing, and arguing in the manner of modern drama. And the comparison should throw some light on both.

The themes of *Oedipus* are, from many points of view, strikingly similar to those of *Hamlet*. Oedipus gave his name to that "complex" to which, as we saw, Ernest Jones reduces *Hamlet*. Whatever one may think of this reduction, it is clear that in both plays a royal sufferer is associated with pollution, in its very sources, of an entire social order. Both plays open with an invocation of the well-being of the endangered body politic. In both, the destiny of the individual and of society are closely intertwined; and in both the suffering of the royal victim seems to be necessary before purgation and renewal can be achieved.

But my purpose here is not to attempt an extended comparison of the two plays; it is, rather, to contrast the structural principles of these two ritual dramas, one from the beginnings of the tradition, the other from the end, at the very brink of the modern world.

The extraordinary unity and clarity of *Oedipus*, in comparison with *Hamlet*, is perhaps due to the fact that it is closer to the form, purpose, and occasion (the Festival of Dionysos) of its ritual source than *Hamlet*, in the Globe Theater, is to its ritual sources. Oedipus is the one and obvious protagonist, his story the literal subject of the play. He is the diagrammatic royal scapegoat, a marked man, from the first. And the parts of the play, which show the stages of his destruction, correspond very closely to the stages of the ancient ritual sacrifice.

In *Hamlet* it is as though every one of these elements had been elaborated by a process of critical analysis. Hamlet himself, though a prince, is without a throne; though a sufferer for the truth, he can appear in public as a mere infatuated or whimsical youth. We have seen how many ironic parallels Shakespeare provides to his story—and to this

I may add that it takes both Hamlet and Claudius to represent the royal victim of the tradition. Though the play has the general shape of the tragic rhythm, and the traditional parts of the plot, each part is presented in several ironically analogous versions. The prologue is in three scenes of contrasting moods. The agon is so complicated that the very purposes of the antagonists are critically seen as false, hidden, or "mistook." It takes all of Act v to represent the epiphany, the final version of death, from all the angles that Shakespeare knows.

Even the ritual process itself is, in *Hamlet*, directly dramatized: i.e., presented in a tragic, ironic light. There are no rituals in *Oedipus*: Oedipus is a ritual. But Hamlet has an extremely modern and skeptical, a Pirandellesque, theatricality as well; Shakespeare plays with the basis of his own make-believe. Sophocles uses the tragic theater with its ritual basis to mirror human life directly. Shakespeare uses the Elizabethan theater in the same way; but at the same time he has another mirror—his own and Hamlet's supermodern awareness—in which the making of the ritual is itself ironically reflected.

Oedipus moves, as it were, straight to its end, in clear figures of the tragic rhythm. But in *Hamlet* there is also a movement of ironic analysis, represented by the analogous versions of the main theme which the interwoven plots embody, and by Hamlet's monologues and wry jokes: improvisations which are beside the story of the play, in closer relationship to the audience. But though Shakespeare thus sees the ritual order of Claudius' Denmark as it were from without, he does not, like Euripides, simply satirize the values and the order of the traditional religion: the movement of analysis is corrected from time to time by a synthesis (a funeral or a Court scene) in which the main theme of the play, and the interdependence of all the dramatis personae, is reaffirmed. These rituals in Hamlet are not simply absurd, as a Euripidean *deus ex machina* is absurd; they are rather tragic failures, like Claudius' private attempt to pray: "Words without thoughts never to heaven go." In spite of the ironic device of the double plot, and the deeper irony of the Pirandellesque improvisation (Is all the world a stage or the stage life itself?) Shakespeare also clings to the conception of the theater as ritual.

Ritual and Improvisation: Hamlet's Play as the Center

Shakespeare's theater, because of its ancient roots and its central place in society, permitted the development of ritual drama—or at least a drama which had this dimension as well as others. In the structure of *Hamlet* the rituals, as distinguished from the plots, serve to present the main action at various points in its development. Shakespeare uses them in much the same way in which Henry James uses his "social occasions" to present the main theme of *The Awkward Age*. The structure of *Hamlet* could be described in Henry James's words: "A circle consisting of a number of small rounds disposed at equal distance about a central object. The central object was my situation, my subject in itself, to which the thing would owe its title, and the small rounds represented so many distinct lamps, as I liked to call them, the function of each of which would be to light up with all due intensity one of its aspects. . . . I revelled in this notion of the Occasion as a thing by itself." That is the most important point: the social rite or occasion is taken as a thing by itself; it enables the author to assemble his dramatis personae in a wider light than any of their individual intelligences could provide. If my analysis of *Hamlet* is correct, the rituals (though they have deeper meanings than James's social gatherings) are also "occasions" of this kind: lamps lighting the rottenness of Denmark (the basic situation of the play) and the many-sided action which results, at various points in its course, and in various aspects.

In the table showing the relation of the plot to the ritual scenes and the improvisations, the players' scene is at the center. It has a ritual aspect, it is Hamlet's most ambitious improvisation, and it is the climax and peripety of the whole complex plot-scheme. If one can understand this scene, one will be close to grasping Shakespeare's sense of the theater, and his direct, profoundly histrionic dramaturgy.

The prologue contains two rituals, the changing of the guard and Claudius' first court. The changing of the guard is conducted by the honest and simple-minded soldiers, in perfect good faith: the welfare of the state is conceived in the most obvious and acceptable terms, and with the solemnity and authority of the military function. The motives of the soldiers are not impugned; and the only ironic angle we get on this scene is due to the arrival of the Ghost, which clearly suggests that the military rite is not an appropriate means for dealing with the actual danger. Claudius' court, on the other hand, is conducted by the new King; and here we feel (both in the light of Hamlet's disabused view of Claudius, and in the light of the visit of the Ghost) that there is something false about Claudius' discharge of the royal function. Together the two scenes establish the fact of danger and the common concern with the threatened welfare of the state. But they throw ironic lights upon each other. The point of view of the regime is in conflict with that of the simple soldiers. Neither the soldiers nor the regime have the magic for dealing with the Ghost; and it appears that the rituals of the state in general are false or mistaken.

The many conflicts, which the prologue presents as it were in suspension, are further developed (though without coming to direct issue) during the rest of the first act, the second act, and the first scene of Act III. Then (bringing the climax, peripety, and recognition) comes Hamlet's improvised ritual, the players scene. Hamlet, as the "chief reflector," the widest consciousness in literature, as Henry James called him, is aware of what the soldiers see, of what Claudius sees, and of what the Ghost sees, and he is torn by all the conflicts implicit in these partial values and myopic vested interests. His "ritual occasion" is thus an answer to both rituals in the prologue; and at the same time (because he has also seen what the Ghost sees) it is an answer to, and a substitute for, the inadequate or false ritual order of Denmark. It is itself a "ritual" in that it assembles the whole tribe for an act symbolic of their deepest welfare; it is false and ineffective, like the other public occasions, in that the Danes do not really understand or intend the enactment which they witness. It is, on the other hand, not a true ritual, but an improvisation—for here the role of Hamlet, as showman, as master of ceremonies, as clown, as night-club entertainer who lewdly jokes with the embarrassed patrons—Hamlet the ironist, in sharpest contact with the audience on-stage and the audience off-stage, yet a bit outside the literal belief in the story: it is here that this aspect of Hamlet's role is clearest. But notice that, if Hamlet is the joking clown, he is also like those improvising Old Testament prophets who, gathering a handful of dust or of little bones, or a damaged pot from the potter's wheel, present to a blind generation a sudden image of their state. It is in the players' scene that the peculiar theatricality of *Hamlet*—ritual as theater and theater as ritual; at once the lightest improvisation and the solemnest occasion—is most clearly visible.

What then is the image, the parable, the "fear in a handful of dust," which Hamlet thus places—with all the pomp of court and all the impudence of the night-club entertainer—in the very center of the public consciousness of Denmark?

The most detailed analysis I know of the players' scene is Mr. Dover Wilson's, in his excellent book, *What Happens in Hamlet*. The reader is referred to that study, and to its companion-piece, Granville-Barker's book on *Hamlet*, for a discussion of the theatrical problems which the scene presents and for an understanding of the complexity of the scene as a whole, wherein the focus of the audience's attention is shifted from Hamlet (the "central reflector") to Horatio, to the Queen, to Ophelia, to the King—as though the play-within-a-play were being lighted from many angles by reflection from many mirrors. My purpose here is only to describe Hamlet's play itself, in order to show how it reveals the malady of the regime in all its ambiguity, mystery, and spreading ramifications. For this little play is indeed an all-purpose mousetrap—and it catches more than the conscience of the King.

First of all the play presents the hidden crime (the murder of a king and the more or less incestuous theft of his queen and his throne) upon which, as in *Oedipus*, all the threads of the interwoven plots depend. It is the presentation of this literal fact which has the immediate effect upon the innocent bystanders of the court and upon the innocent groundlings in the audience, though in Hamlet's violent view none are innocent. Because the security of the regime and the purposes of its supporters depend either upon ignorance or concealment, the public representation of the crime is itself an act of aggression, Hamlet's attack, the turning point in the story. This attack reaches the guilty Claudius first, Gertrude second, Polonius third; then Laertes and Ophelia. And at length it clears the way for Fortinbras, the new faith and the new regime.

But though the fact of murder, incest, and usurpation is clearly presented, the time of the murder—is it still to come? —is vague; and the dramatis personae in the playlet are shifted about in such a way as to leave the identity of the criminal in question, and so to spread the guilt. The actual crime was that of Claudius; but in the play the guilty one is nephew to the King. This could mean (as Polonius and Gertrude seem to think) a direct threat by Hamlet to Claudius; it also means that Hamlet (who had admitted to himself a "weakness and melancholy" which makes him subject to devilish solicitations, and who had assured Ophelia, that "I am myself indifferent honest, yet I could accuse me of such things it were better my mother had not borne me") had granted Claudius, in advance, that he too is at least potentially guilty. Neither Hamlet nor Shakespeare seem to rule out a Freudian interpretation of the tangle; Hamlet comes close to representing himself as the diagrammatic son of the Oedipus complex, killing the father and possessing the mother. Yet his awareness of such motivations lifts the problems from the level of pathology to that of drama; he sees himself, Claudius, Denmark, the race itself, as subject to greeds and lusts which the hypocritical façade of the regime guiltily conceals.

Thus the literal meaning of the playlet is the fact of the crime; but the trope and the anagoge convey a picture of the human in general as weak, guilty, and foolish: the deepest and most sinister version of the malady of Claudius' regime in Denmark. This picture should emerge directly from the staging of the playlet before the corrupt and hypocritical court, under the inspired and triumphant irony of the regisseur-prince. The whining of pipes, the parade of mummers, the wooden gestures of the dumb-show, the tinkle of the rhymes, should have the magical solemnity of a play-party or children's singing-game ("London bridge is falling down"). Yet because of the crimes represented, this atmosphere is felt as unbearably weak and frivolous, a parody of all solemn rites. If this playlet invokes the magic potency of the theater ("the play's the thing") it does so with as much despairing irony as love. The staging is crude and childish: Hamlet's actors vainly take things into their own hands, and the court audience is as condescendingly unperceptive (until the scandal dawns on them) as any cynical crowd at a Broadway opening.

Hamlet's audience on-stage (and perhaps off-stage as well) misses the deeper meanings of his play. Yet he and his author have put it as simply as possible in the weary couplets of the Player-King. The Player-King seems to stand for Hamlet's father, and thus for the Ghost; and he speaks in fact with the clarity but helplessness (in this world) of the dead—addressing the frivolous Player-Queen without much hope of understanding. Since he is Hamlet's puppet, he speaks also for Hamlet, and since he is the King, he stands also for Claudius. Claudius, in the course of the play, will gradually acquire a helplessness like that of the Ghost; a faithlessness and an indecision like that of Hamlet. It is the function of the Player-King to state as directly as possible that gloomy and fatalistic sense of human action which is the subject of the play, and which all the various characters have by analogy.

The way to show this in detail would be to study the action of each character and to show what frivolity and gloomy faithlessness they have in common, but this would take too long. The point may be briefly illustrated by juxtaposing a few utterances of Hamlet and Claudius with analogous couplets of the Player-King:

HAMLET: Act v scene 2	There's a divinity that shapes our ends, Rough-hew them how we will. Was't Hamlet wronged Laertes? Never Hamlet: . . . . .Hamlet denies it. Who does it then? His madness.
CLAUDIUS: Act III scene 3	My stronger guilt defeats my strong intent: And, like a man to double business bound, I stand in pause where I shall first begin, And both neglect.
Act IV scene 7	Not that I think you did not love your father, But that I know love is begun by time, And that I see, in passages of proof, Time qualifies the spark and fire of it. There lives within the very flame of love A kind of wick or snuff that will abate it,

And nothing is at a like good-
ness still,
For goodness, growing to a
plurisy,
Dies in his own too much.
That we would do,
We should do when we would,
for this "would" changes
And hath abatements and de-
lays as many
As there are tongues, are
hands, are accidents;
And then this "should" is like
a spend-thrift sigh,
That hurts by easing.

PLAYER KING: Our wills and fates do so contrary run
That our devices still are
overthrown,
Our thoughts are ours, their
ends none of our own.

What to ourselves in passion
we propose,
The passion ending, doth the
purpose lose.
Purpose is but the slave to
memory
Of violent birth, but poor
validity.

The speeches of Hamlet and Claudius which I have quoted come late in the play, when both of them gain a deathly insight into their destinies—the hidden and uncontrolled springs of their own and others' actions. Even Claudius sees so deeply at this moment that he gets the sense of human action which all the characters have by analogy. His speech to Laertes (Act IV, scene 7) is, more-over, both made more ironic and more general by being addressed to Laertes in order to deceive him into a course which is contrary to his deepest purposes and best interests. As for Hamlet, his sense of pathos, of the suffering of motiva-tions beyond our understanding or con-trol, does not save him from violent out-bursts any more than that of Claudius does. Shakespeare usually grants his vic-tims a moment of great clarity when it is too late—and then shows them re-turning, like automatons, to "ravin down their proper bane" and die. But the chief point I wish to make

here is that the Player-King presents very pithily the basic vision of human action in the play, at a level so deep that it applies to all the characters: the guilty, the free, the principals, the by-standers, those in power and the dis-possessed. This vision of course comes directly from the crime of Claudius and the other "accidental judgements, casual slaughters, purposes mistook" (as Hora-tio describes them when summing up for Fortinbras) upon which the compli-cated plot depends; yet this generalized vision is more terrible than any of the particular crimes, and much more im-portant for understanding Hamlet's motivation. To this point I shall return later.

The immediate effect of Hamlet's play comes by way of the concrete scan-dal which brings the climax and peripety of the narratives. The presentation of the play is Hamlet's attack; it succeeds; it convicts Claudius' regime, and "the lives of many" that depend upon it, of impotence and corruption. After that revelation all is lost (just as Macbeth is lost after the banquet scene)—and the desperate devices of the King and Laertes, the brief folly of Polonius, and the unimpeded progress of Fortinbras, in the healthy rhythm of the march, are seen as clearly fated or doomed.

For this reason also the "rituals" which follow the players' scene have a different quality from those which pre-cede it. Since the regime has lost its manna—been "shown up"—the rituals in Acts IV and V, marking the stages of the collective pathos and epiphany, are clearly presented as mad or evil. Ophelia's mad ritual presents the "spa-ragmos" or tearing asunder of the indi-vidual and society at once ("schism in the state and schism in the soul"); mingling marriage and funeral, lewd-ness and prettiness, love and destruction to the accompaniment of plotting and rebellion. Ophelia's funeral is a real death but a "maimèd rite"; the duel between Hamlet and Laertes is ostensi-bly a ritual and actually a murder. With the assembling of the court and the royal family for the duel, the picture of

Claudius' regime (the collective revelation of his black masses) is complete.

In the succession of "ritual scenes" with its center and climax in Hamlet's little play, it is obvious that Hamlet himself plays a central role. In the two rituals of the prologue he is, like the audience, a mere puzzled and troubled bystander. After the hidden struggles of Acts I, II, and III, he presents, with his play, his own black mass, his own parody of a rite. He does not appear for the "tearing asunder" of Ophelia's madness, for this marks the pathos of the regime, and of the lives that depend directly on it; and his life (wherever it may be) has already withdrawn from all loyalty to Claudius' Denmark. But he returns to record Ophelia's truncated funeral in his cold, spent, but clear awareness; and to take his fated role in the duel at the end. I have endeavored to study the rituals as marking the progress of the "play as a whole"; but it is evident that in the play, and in the order of the rituals, Hamlet is both chief "agonist" and central "reflector." With this in mind it is possible to offer an interpretation of the role of Hamlet in relation to Shakespeare's idea of the theater, and the traditional social values which the play assumes.

An Interpretation of the Role of Hamlet

> "For, by the image of my cause, I see
> The portraiture of his."

Oedipus, as I have pointed out, starts out as the hero, the triumphant human adequate to rule, and ends, like Tiresias, a scapegoat, a witness and a sufferer for the hidden truth of the human condition. The play starts with the conflict and contrast between Oedipus and Tiresias, shows the steps of Oedipus' dismemberment, and ends when he is blind and all-seeing and helpless, as Tiresias was in the beginning. Hamlet is apparently thought of as undergoing a similar transformation, from hero to scapegoat, from "the expectancy and rose of the fair state" to the distracted, suffering witness and victim of Act v. But this development is not neatly laid

out for him according to a publicly understood series of struggles: he feels his way toward it, not with public sanction but against the faithless worldliness of the Danes. It is not until Act v that his martyr-like destiny "feels right" to him.

We see him in the first three acts of the play as a puzzled and, as it were, unconvinced hero and prince. He knows that "the times are out of joint" and that he is born to set them right; he knows that the Prince should be moved by honor and ambition: but he cannot reconcile this worldly code with his sense of evil in Denmark nor with the otherworldly solicitations of his Ghost-father. From Corneille to Dryden the ethical values of "honor" will be taken as sufficient basis for the drama of human life; but Hamlet's sense of his own and Denmark's condition contradicts this simplified philosophy. When he looks at Laertes, that "noble youth," he envies him—envies, at least, his simple and honorable motivations. When he looks at Fortinbras, he envies him the ability to risk his own and other lives for honor—"even for an eggshell." If he could accept this code, he would feel that the murder of Claudius would heal the schism in his own soul and in society; but just as his sense of evil preceded his knowledge of Claudius' literal guilt, so he cannot believe that the literal punishment of Claudius (an eye for an eye) will cure the damage he has done. And so his drama becomes far deeper than a simple revenge play.

If Hamlet is not content with the simple soldierly code of honor, it is because he sees too deeply and skeptically into that cosmic setting of human life which Shakespeare's theater symbolically represented. He sees beyond the tiny human involvements of the foreground to the social order indicated by the stage house façade and, above that, to the order in the stars implied by the canopy over his head. This is especially clear in his first scene with Rosencrantz and Guildenstern (Act II, scene 2). It is in this scene that he makes the great speech on Man which Tilyard quotes as an exposition of the traditional ordered universe. But the speech ends bitterly: "And yet, to me, what is this quintessence of dust?"

Though Hamlet accepts this order, he does not know where he belongs in it; he is not even sure which way is up. He would have felt the force of that remark of Heracleitus which Eliot uses as epigraph to *Burnt Norton*: "The way up and the way down are one and the same." His intellect plays over the world of the religious tradition with an all-dissolving irony like that of Montaigne in the *Apologie de Raimond Sebonde*: a truly double-edged irony, for he can neither do with nor do without the ancient moral and cosmic order.

That is why he has a despairing fellow-feeling for Rosencrantz and Guildenstern. He knows them for little trimmers, neither for God nor for the Devil, but "for themselves," like the dim figures in Dante's Limbo: "indifferent children of the earth," "Fortune's privates," as they call themselves. He is himself anything but indifferent, yet he does not at that moment know how to care, and so he feels himself, like them, lost between "greatness" and the chill of mere bodily "weight" and utter faithlessness at the bottom of the universe. Thus he is troubled with "bad dreams":

GUIL. Which dreams, indeed, are ambition, for the very substance of the ambitious is but the shadow of a dream.
HAM. A dream itself is but a shadow.
ROS. Truly, and I hold ambition of so airy and light a quality that it is but a shadow's shadow.
HAM. Then are our beggars bodies, and our monarchs and outstretched heroes the beggars' shadows. Shall we to the court? for, by my fay, I cannot reason.

Hamlet draws the deduction which troubles *him*, but not Rosencrantz and Guildenstern: if ambition like Fortinbras' is illusory, what, in Denmark, is to show us the way, and prevent us from taking the "shadow of a solid thing"?

It would be an exaggeration to say that Hamlet envies these two as he envies Fortinbras and Laertes. But his fellow-feeling for them—call it sympathy, or a sense of the analogy between them, or seeing their cause as mirroring his—comes, like his envy, from the fact that he himself is lost. Until the success of his play, Hamlet feels his over-quick sympathy as a weakness, and covers it up with murderous sarcasm. On his return from England, he has accepted it, and in Act v his abnormally quick sympathy has acquired some of the quiet of the vision integrated and lived-up-to, some of the breadth of charity.

What has intervened is chiefly the presentation of his play. When the players come, and do a speech for Hamlet, he envies *them*, but at this time it turns out that he has found a real clue to his own action. He cannot act like a simple soldier but he can employ the theater in an equally dangerous, and far more significant, project. He can use it as a trap for the conscience of the King, and at the same time as a test of his own and the Ghost's vision. Thus empirically, or improvisationally, feeling his way through the concrete elements of his situation, he finds his own proper line of action, and a use of the theater very much like that which two other autobiographical characters of Shakespeare make of it.

The two other characters who use the theater in this way are the Duke in *Measure for Measure* and Prospero in *The Tempest*. These two plays are, of course, very different from each other and from *Hamlet*. But the analogies between the three dispossessed rulers, and their attempts to purify the spiritual atmosphere of their societies by means of significant shows, are close enough to throw a good deal of light on the nature of the role of Hamlet.

The "Duke of dark corners" is dispossessed and anonymous much as Hamlet is, even though he himself has rejected the official role of ruler. His theatricality consists in casting Angelo and Claudio and Isabella for tragic roles, and then moving about behind the scenes like a nervous régisseur, to make sure that the moral of the drama is clear, and yet that the real tragedy does not go too far. The play he arranges is almost a practical joke; yet, like Hamlet's play, it both tests and reveals a wider and healthier vision of human society than Vienna publicly accepts. And by this means he proposes to substitute the rule of charity for Angelo's blind and univocal conception of Mosaic justice. *Measure for Measure* has been called a problem comedy, and it has, in fact, a discursive clarity, a kind of modern intellectuality, quite unlike *Hamlet*. But with this reservation, the Duke as regisseur-prince is very closely akin to Hamlet in that role.

The Tempest has neither the analytic naturalism of *Hamlet* nor the "thesis" quality of *Measure for Measure*. It partakes of the qualities of myth, of Medieval allegory, and of dream; as though Shakespeare's mind, at the end of his career, were in that state which Dante knew, in the early morning, at the threshold of the Mount of Purgatory:

Canto IX che la mente nostra, peregrina / più dalla carne e men da' pensier presa, / alle sue vision quasi è divina.	When our mind, wandering farther from the flesh and less caught by thought, is in its visions almost prophetic.

The basic donné of the play is the magic of Prospero. And hence the shows with which he purges the worldly exiles from Milan can be close to the very idea of such shows. Mr. Colin Still (in *The Timeless Theme*) has traced in them many ancient ritual themes. It is in this play that Shakespeare comes to terms with his own imaginative power as a wielder of the theater—indicating its use in the service of truth, and its limitations as a means of salvation. For at the end, when Prospero has demonstrated both the magic power of the theater and its use, he buries his book and staff and prays for grace. He has a ripeness and a clarity and a power which Hamlet lacks, but for that very reason he helps one to see what Hamlet, with his play, was trying to do.

Hamlet, more than either the Duke or Prospero, is defenseless and unin-structed in the midst of life; and if he stumbles on the theater as a means of realizing his vision and his anonymous being, he does not clearly understand what he has accomplished. When the King rises after the play, Hamlet takes his success with almost childish pleasure: "Would not this, sir, and a forest of feathers, if the rest of my fortunes turn Turk with me, with two Provincial roses on my razed shoes, get me a fellowship in a cry of players, sir?" The delight is, of course, partly ironic; moreover he has still to confirm his success with his mother and the King. Even after those two interviews he is puzzled and tormented; he does not really feel that he has done his part, borne his witness, taken his stand, until he returns from England. By that time his testimony has had its effect: the regime is wounded beyond repair, and he himself is doomed.

In Act V, while he records in the graveyard the vision of death—literal death and the death of society, to the accompaniment of the clowns' heartless equivocations—and finally suffers the truncated funeral of Ophelia—he feels that his role, all but the very last episode, has been played. He is still uncertain what this will be, still feels that it must include the killing of Claudius: "Is't not perfect conscience to quit him with this arm?" His personal hatred for the King is still sharp as ever; but he is content, now, to let the fated end come as it will. "It will be short: the interim is mine; and a man's life no more than to say 'one'." He feels, I think, whether he or his author would put it so or not, that he is ready to take the consequences of his revelation, to suffer for that truth: "Thou wouldst not think how ill's all here about my heart; but it is no matter. . . . It is such a kind of gain-giving as would perhaps trouble a woman. . . . The readiness is all." One could say that he feels the poetic rightness of his own death. One could say, with Ernest Jones, that because of his Oedipus complex he had a death-wish all along. Or one could say that his death was the only adequate expiation for the evil of Denmark, according to the ancient emotional logic of the scapegoat; or one could say that only by accepting death to prove it could the truth of his vision be properly affirmed.

However one may interpret it, when his death comes it "feels right," the only possible end for the play. Horatio makes music for his going-off like that which accompanies Oedipus' death at Colonnus: "Good night, sweet prince, and flights of angels sing thee to thy rest." And Fortinbras treats him like one of those honor-seekers that had puzzled him all along, as though in his career the hero had somehow seen subsumed in the martyr: "Let four captains bear Hamlet, like a soldier, to the stage." We are certainly intended to feel that Hamlet, however darkly and uncertainly he worked, had discerned the way to be obedient to his deepest values, and accomplished some sort of purgatorial progress for himself and Denmark.

I am aware that this interpretation of the role of Hamlet is open to the same sort of objections as all other interpretations; there is no substitute for the direct knowledge which a good performance of the play would give. But I think that Shakespeare, in writing the play, was counting on such a performance, and upon the willing make-believe of his audience and his performers. The elements of the Tudor monarchy, of the emblematic stage of the Globe, and of the traditional cosmos they stood for, were accepted for the purposes of the play as real; and within the concrete elements of this scene the role of Hamlet has its own logic.

Analogous Action: An Interpretation of the Play

"For goodness, growing to a plurisy,
Dies in his own too much."

The remark of the King, which he uses as a warning to Laertes, and which I have used to describe Hamlet's over-quick and over-subtle sympathy, applies also to Shakespeare's principles of composition in the play as a whole. Shakespeare's sense of analogy is perhaps too productive, burgeoning too richly in all directions, as though the dramatic life he had got hold of gave him more instances than he needed. Yet it is my belief that the life itself, the germ, the "unity" is there, however overlaid with elaborations and confusingly illumined from many directions.

Miss Caroline Spurgeon discerned this underlying life, quite accurately, as a result of her studies of the metaphors in the play: "To Shakespeare's pictorial imagination," she writes, "the problem in *Hamlet* is not predominantly that of the will and reason, of a mind too philosophic or a nature temperamentally unfitted to act quickly: he sees it pictorially *not as the problem of an individual at all*, but as something greater and even more mysterious, as a *condition* for which the individual himself is apparently not responsible, any more than the sick man is to blame for the infection which strikes and devours him, but which, nevertheless, in its course and development, impartially and relentlessly annihilates him and others, innocent and guilty alike. That is the tragedy of *Hamlet*, and it is perhaps the chief tragic mystery of life."

Miss Spurgeon offers a kind of scientific proof of her view of the play by showing that the predominant metaphors are those of disease. An analysis of the play as the imitation of action gives the same result. The action of the play as a whole is "to identify and destroy the hidden imposthume which is endangering the life of Denmark." But because the source of infection is hidden, and there is no general agreement about its nature or location, the action of the play is predominantly in the passive mode—the suffering of forces not controlled or understood, rather than the consistent drive of an intelligible purpose. *Hamlet* is, like *The Cherry Orchard*, in its essential structure an "ensemble pathos," broken from time to time by the spasmodic moves of one or two of the characters.

This action is realized in many analogous ways in the contrasted characters. Claudius, who identifies the health of Denmark with the safety of his own corrupt regime, and therefore merely wishes to hold what he has, gradually comes to feel that the imposthume which poisons the communal life and his own is Hamlet: "for like the hectic in my blood he rages." Polonius, the chief figure in the comic sub-plot, also identifies the health of the body politic with the status quo; and for him the dis-ease is only the normal but troublesome fires of youth: Laertes' appetite for drabbing and gambling, Hamlet's infatuation for Ophelia—both to be cured by a judicious mixture of discipline and indulgence, which his age and experience can easily concoct.

Gertrude and Ophelia (like other women pictured by Shakespeare) define their actions and their beings only with reference to their men; and since they both have a stake in the regime, and at the same time in the rebellious Hamlet, they suffer the worst of the disease itself. In the economy of the play, they are symbols and measures of the health of the body politic—glamorous signs of what might have been, and torn and dishonored images of what is.

Hamlet himself, as we saw, comes the closest to seeing the whole range of the disease, as it spreads from the immediate guilt of Claudius to ruin all dependent lives. And we have seen that the adequate response to the rottenness of Denmark, as he sees it, is not a simple, purposive course of action, but a bearing-witness and a suffering-for-the-truth.

The characters have not only analogous objects of their actions, they all act in a similar way, indirectly. Polonius has his "windlasses" and his "essays of bias." Claudius acts only through intermediaries: Polonius, Rosencrantz and Guildenstern, Laertes. Ophelia acts as the puppet of her father, and Hamlet by means of his symbolic play. The Gravedigger speaks in equivocations, and Osric in such a "yesty collection" of ornamental clichés that he is barely comprehensible.

In defining the action of the play as a whole, the one underlying "essence" which the actions of the various charac-

ters "adumbrate" in their different ways, the character of Claudius is all important—not because he sees more, or realizes a deeper life, but because as head of the state he is, *de facto*, the one center of "weight" and of "greatness." As Tudor monarch, father, king, and high-priest—the massy wheel upon which the lives of the many depend—he makes, so to speak, the spiritual weather in Denmark. It is his particular kind of spiritual night—his motionless worldly presence, like a wall; his gratified lust ("fat weed on Lethe wharf," "things rank and gross in nature")—which defines the action in *Hamlet*. In such a nonconducting. atmosphere, all purposes are short, hidden, and mistook, and they soon sink into frightened or oblivious stagnation. As long as he rules, "Denmark is a prison," "one of the worst" of the world's many confines, closed away from Dante's "dolce mondo."

From this point of view, Claudius' place in the economy of the play is like that of Macbeth in his play: Shakespeare thinks of the usurper in both cases as defining the "scene" and thereby the action of the play. Macbeth is in his moral being quite unlike Claudius; and he produces a different action and a different rhythm in the play as a whole. Macbeth is like a man running downhill to escape himself: however fast he goes, "the pauser, reason," is still with him. In his depraved career he lays an irrational and obsessive basis for all human thought and intercourse; hence every action is paradoxical and unnatural. Even the peripety, when Macduff, Malcolm, and Ross are forced to take action against Macbeth, is realized as a tissue of denials and paradoxes. The final assault upon the castle is (in spite of its healthy marching rhythm) unreasonable and unnatural too. The wood moves, the leader is unborn of woman, and the soldiers are sustained by the super-rational, the miraculous blessings and graces that hang about King Edward's throne.

Mr. Kenneth Burke has pointed out that "action" may be defined in terms of "scene." This is one of the principles of composition in the *Divine Comedy*: human actions are presented in an orderly succession of scenes which concretely realize and define them. But Dante's tremendous subject was human life and action in general, while the subject of a Shakespearean tragedy is, more immediately, human action under a particular regime, or at a particular historic moment. His dramatis personae are seldom seeking salvation directly, but rather trying to realize a human life in a concrete society. That is why an analysis like Miss Spurgeon's is so suggestive, and takes one so far toward an understanding of the play as a whole—much further, for example, than the attempt to rationalize Hamlet's character, as though Shakespeare had been writing a drama of the individual will and reason only.

Yet there are dangers in an analysis based on metaphor. Such an analysis leaves *Hamlet* at the level of the romantic lyric, as though its "logic" were a logic of feeling only, and its principles of composition those of "association and contrast," as Mr. Burke calls them. Such an analysis works better for *Tristan* than for *Hamlet*, for it leaves out the substantial elements (the beings of the individual characters, the stable elements in the traditional cosmos) which underlie the associated or contrasted *qualities* of their lives, the "atmosphere" or feeling of the play. Miss Spurgeon's lyrical or subjective or qualitative analysis needs to be supported and extended by a more realist analysis, one based for instance on the four levels of Medieval symbolism.

According to this system, the analogous actions of the characters in their attempts to destroy the hidden disease of Denmark would constitute the "trope" or moral meaning of the play. The rottenness of the regime itself, from which they all suffer, could be called the "allegory," for it refers to a particular moment in history when a corrupt regime falsifies the life of the community. We have seen that in *Hamlet*, as in *Macbeth*, Shakespeare takes this historic moment as defining his subject. But Shakespeare is no Spenglerian determinist; in spite of his worldly focus his preoccupation with social order, and his feeling for the "divine sanction" of kingship, he places Claudius' Denmark in a wider setting; and this "placing" of Claudius' regime is the anagoge, the meaning of the play in relation to ultimate values.

Miss Spurgeon records the fact that there is in *Hamlet* a series of images contrasting with those of disease and darkness; and, indeed, from the first we are made to feel that the condition of the Danes is not the human condition *überhaupt* but only a particular version of it. Ophelia's description of Hamlet, "What a noble mind is here o'er-thrown," contrasts his present plight with what she feels to be his natural role: "the expectancy and rose of the fair state." Hamlet's description of his father, in his terrible interview with his mother, has a similar effect—to make us feel that a natural and divinely sanctioned order has been betrayed and lost. And in his famous speech on "man, the paragon of animals," though the context gives it depths of irony, Hamlet unrolls the traditional moral order as both good and true though he has somehow lost a vital relation to it. But it is chiefly in Act v that Claudius' regime is seen for what it is, brought to its temporal end, and placed in a wider and therefore truer scene.

Act v unrolls for us, first of all, a picture of all, a picture of Denmark after it has been torn asunder, its deathliness or its nonentity laid as it were flat and open to the eye of the audience and the eyes of Hamlet. The vision, as usual in Shakespeare, is firmly based upon the most concrete sensory impact (like the darkness of Act I, scene 1) and proceeds then to elaborate ever wider and more complex perspectives. The basic sensual impression is the brutal digging up of skulls; then comes the solemn-joyful equivocating of the clowns—a denial of all meaning, the end result of Claudius' falsity. With this goes a series of hints of social disorder: the dead receive no respect; the professions, especially law, are laughably helpless; "the age is grown so picked that the toe of the peasant comes so near the heel of the courtier, he galls his kibe." As for the courtiers, we shall presently have Osric: "He did comply with his dug before he sucked it." Osric corresponds to Rosencrantz and Guildenstern, a more shameless hypocrite and time-server, much as the clowns correspond to Polonius in their complacent irrelevancy but speak in equivocations where Polonius, less deathly, merely rationalizes upon false premises.

From this opening impression of literal death and meaninglessness in many forms comes the funeral of Ophelia, the "maimèd rite." I have already pointed out its place in the succession of rituals. It is full of cross-references: to the funerals of Hamlet the first and Polonius; to Gertrude's corrupt marriage; to the marriage of Ophelia and Hamlet, which never occurred; and to Ophelia's mad mixture of funeral and marriage.

The second scene of Act v, with the duel between Hamlet and Laertes, shows the denouements of all the intrigues in the play: Polonius is avenged by Laertes; Laertes, like Hamlet, falls victim to Claudius' deceits; Gertrude follows Ophelia; Hamlet kills the King at last, and Fortinbras finally appears upon the Danish scene, the new faith and hope which Claudius no longer prevents. But these events, which literally end the narratives in the play, and bring Claudius' regime to its temporal end, tell us nothing new but the fact: that the sentence, which fate or providence pronounced long since, has now been executed. It is the pageantry, the ceremonial mummery, in short the ritual character of this last scene which makes us feel it as the final epiphany, the showing-forth of the true nature of Claudius' regime.

The staging of this scene is parallel to that of Claudius' first court (Act I, scene 2) and to that of the players' scene. It is the last time we see all the dramatis personae gathered to celebrate the social order upon which they all depend. But whereas we saw Claudius' first court as smooth, plausible, almost majestic, and ostensibly devoted to guarding the welfare of all the subjects, we see this last court, all in mourning, for the death-trap it is. The vision of Claudius' Denmark which Hamlet's play presented as a parable, is now brilliantly and literally visible. As soon as we glimpse it with this literal clarity, it is gone like a bad dream, and we are returned, with the healthy rhythms of young Fortinbras, to the wider world of the order of nature, with the possibility at least of divine sanction.

Thus the "placing" of the play follows immediately upon the completion of its action. Fortinbras is the agent; and in the scheme of the whole the role of Fortinbras, though it is very economically developed, is of major importance.

I have already pointed out that Fortinbras' story is one of the variations on the son-father theme. When we first hear of Fortinbras he, like Hamlet (and later, Laertes) is trying to avenge a dead and dishonored father. Like Hamlet, he has an uncle who stands *in loco parentis*. Like Laertes, he is a simple and noble youth, expending his high spirits upon the worldly code of "honor," yet at the same time he is a "good child," obedient to age—so that when his uncle tells him to, he is quite willing to turn his martial ambitions from the Danes to the Poles. But unlike both Hamlet and Laertes he does not live under Claudius' shadow: his obedience is not (like Laertes' obedience to Claudius) misplaced—and his life works itself out (as we hear) in a reign free of the Danish infection.

Thus the role of Fortinbras, in *Hamlet*, corresponds to those of Malcolm, Macduff, and King Edward in *Macbeth*. Like them, he is felt as a constant, though off-stage, threat to the corrupt regime. Like them, he does not appear in the flesh until after the peripety and, though we feel his approach, does not enter Denmark until Claudius is gone. Like Malcolm and Macduff, he has his own version of the main action of the play. He moves and fights in the dark as much as his contemporaries, Hamlet and Laertes; but his darkness is not the artificial shadow of Claudius but the natural darkness of inexperience. He confronts it with a kind of sanguine natural faith, "exposing all that's mortal and unsure even for an eggshell"—as he could not (Laertes' example is there to prove it) in Denmark. That is why he cannot enter Denmark until the end. In the same way, in *Macbeth*, we are not ready for Macduff's and Malcolm's reception of Grace until Macbeth and his Queen have reached the nightmarish stalemate of the banquet scene. When the avengers appear before Macbeth's castle, they show him that there is another way to "outrun reason"; and when Fortinbras comes in at the end, he places the action we have seen in Denmark, both with reference to the wider world from which he comes, and with reference to his healthier version of "the fight in the dark," the "quest for the unseen danger." Fortinbras' darkness of natural faith is the last variation, this time in a major key, which Shakespeare plays upon his great theme.

This does not mean that Fortinbras, either in his character or in his vision, provides an answer to Hamlet's "problem"—nor does it mean that his example is intended to show that the experience of the play was simply illusory. This experience was "real," just as Dante's experience of Hell was real—though this is the region of low ceilings, and of those who have lost the good of the intellect. Hamlet sees a great deal that Fortinbras will never see; but Hamlet, who has his own limited being, is defined by it, and by the spiritual realm in which he moves; and this is not all of life. Fortinbras does not destroy, he "places" the action of the play by suddenly revealing a new analogue of this action. The effect, once more, is not to provide us with an intellectual key, an explicit philosophy, but to release us from the contemplation of the limited mystery of Denmark by returning us to the wider mystery of life in the world at large.

Thus it seems to me that the elements of Shakespeare's composition (like those of Sophocles and Dante before him) are not qualities, like those of the romantics with their logic of feeling, not abstract concepts, like those of the dramatists of the Age of Reason, with their clear and distinct moral ideas, but beings, real people in a real world, related to each other in a vast and intricate web of analogies.

I know that analogy is a very difficult concept to use with accuracy. I have endeavored to raise some of the questions connected with it in the Appendix. At this point I merely wish to point out that the anagoge, or ultimate meaning of the play, can only be sought through a study of the analogical relationships within the play and between the world of Denmark and the traditional cosmos. There are the analogous actions of all the characters, pointing to the action which is the underlying substance of the play. There are the analogous father-son relationships, and the analogous man-woman relationships. There are the analogous stories, or chains of events, the fated results of the characters' actions. And stretching beyond the play in all directions are the analogies between Denmark and Rome under "the mightiest Julius"; Hamlet's stage and Shakespeare's stage; the theater and life. Because Shakespeare takes all these elements as "real," he can respect their essential mystery, not replacing them with abstractions, nor merely exploiting their qualities as mood-makers, nor confining us in an artificial world with no exit. He asks us to sense the unity of his play through the direct perception of these analogies; he does not ask us to replace our sense of a real and mysterious world with a consistent artifact, "the world of the play."

If Shakespeare's *Hamlet* is realist in the tradition represented by Sophocles and Dante, if he composes by analogy rather than by "qualitative progression" or "syllogistic progression," then the question of *Hamlet* as an artistic success appears in a different light. Because it is rooted in an ancient tradition, and in a theater central to its culture, it is not only a work of art, but a kind of more-than-individual natural growth, like the culture itself, and Shakespeare is not so much its inventor as its god-like recorder: "Cuando amor spira, vo significando." The question is not whether the subject Shakespeare intends is there, but whether it is there in too bewildering a richness and complexity. The besetting sin of the Renaissance, as Pico foresaw, was an overindulgence in the imagination as it discerns analogies of every kind. M. Gilson has explained how even Bonaventura could abuse his gift for analogizing, losing at times the distinction between real analogy and the superficial correspondences which his faith led him to see. And Mr. Scott Buchanan in *Poetry and Mathematics*

asks the suggestive question, at what point in history, and by what process, was the clue to the vast system of Medieval analogies lost, the thread broken, and the way cleared for the centerless proliferations of modern culture?

Of this question too Shakespeare seems to have been prophetically aware. Like Hamlet, he felt, perhaps, too wide a sympathy, too precise a scruple. His endless sense of analogical relationships, though a good, *could* "grow to a plurisy." And *Hamlet* can be regarded as a dramatization of the process which led, in the Renaissance, to the modern world and its fragmentary theaters.

ARNOLD STEIN

(b. 1915)

Arnold Stein is both a poet in his own right and a specialist in seventeenth century poetry. He is particularly interested in the work of Milton and John Donne and in the problems of prosodic description and analysis in criticism. His published criticism includes *Answerable Style: Essays on 'Paradise Lost'* (1953), *Heroic Knowledge; an Interpretation of 'Paradise Regained' and 'Samson Agonistes'* (1957), and *John Donne's Lyrics: The Eloquence of Action* (1962.)

A Note on Meter (1956)

What does meter do in a poem? It is already a kind of form before the poet begins his poem. And what happens finally to meter? Is it absorbed into the shape of the rhythm it has helped create? Or does it stubbornly maintain its own independent form even as part of the final effect? And what are the relations between the two antipodal horizons and the warm, immediate, physical, and various state of the dynamic process which most of the time we think of

From *The Kenyon Review*, Vol. XVIII (1956), pp. 451-460. Reprinted by permission of the author and the editors of *The Kenyon Review*.

as the poem itself, but which cannot alone be the poem?

I cannot, of course, answer these questions, but must apply myself, as well and as reasonably as I can, to the process. That is the area where most can be known, and where most needs to be known. Still, I think it may help to ask, and remember, the more difficult questions.

In the process of the poem meter, the ideal metronomic pattern, creates, or becomes, rhythm. This happens, our first and most general observation tells us, by means of the external interaction between meter and the way the words have to be emphasized. The way the words have to be emphasized is determined in part by the natural rules of language, as the pronunciation of words, which meter may influence, and modify, or strengthen, but not violate. A second and closer observation tells us that the way the words have to be emphasized is also determined by the context, not only the most local rhetorical context governing the pronunciation of combinations of words, but also the context which is being created by the process of the poem—as who is rhetorically saying what, under what cumulative circumstances, under what governing perspectives, etc.

But meter also influences that developing context, for meter is the one continuous element in unbroken contact with everything else in the poem. And so the interaction between meter and context is of at least two kinds: between meter and the context which is already sufficiently created to be *there*, in fact or illusion, and between meter and the context in the dynamic process of becoming context. And we may recognize, as freely moving between both of these kinds of interaction, the accumulating-cumulative effect of a *style* of using meter. That style, once established, can be brought to bear upon situations that range from the familiar to the unique, and with an almost infinite variety of adjustment and combination.

Or let me try to put the main point in another way, and then carry it a step further. There is an external and obvious conflict between the ideal pattern of the meter and the way the words have to be emphasized according to the natural rules of language and according to the established context. There is also an internal conflict which reappears, as it were, inside the developing process of the context. The internal conflict is characterized by subtle, often complex, attractions toward and repulsions from the ideal pattern. Even in the act of modifying the meter, pulling away from it, the elements in conflict are influenced by it. But the very identity of the

rhythm, in all its rich individuality of being, depends upon a separation from the ideal pattern. And so there is a separation, but it is one that maintains an intimate and, as it were, loving tension between meter and rhythm.

Some of these observations are too familiar, or trite, to need any discussion, but perhaps I can illustrate the more difficult points. I take two lines spoken by Milton's Eve as she contemplates what the "sciential sap" of the apple is going to do for her intellectual figure:

Till dieted by thee I grow mature
In knowledge, as the Gods who all things know.

Let us for the moment resist being diverted by the charming Marvellian whimsy of the *dieted*, and let us ignore the confusing of vegetable and rational souls under the resounding metaphor of maturity, while we fix our attention mostly on the bones of the rhythmic structure. The stress of three syllables could be determined naturally: ma*ture*, *knowl*edge, and *di*eted. The influence of the meter, and the rhetorical demands produced by the situation and the attitude of the speaker in that situation— all taken together no doubt require that the following be stressed: *thee, grow, Gods, all, know.* Only two syllables, diet*ed* and *as*, depend entirely upon the meter for their stress.

The external conflict between ideal pattern and the way the words have to be emphasized is not strenuous in this example; that is, the natural does not actively and positively clash with the ideal by wanting to go its own assertive way. Nor does the natural simply coincide with the meter in order to strengthen further an already strong assertion of the natural emphasis. Instead, the words in our example resist negatively, by tending to be flat and unemphatic. If we try to imagine, what can never be quite managed, a prose rendering that is uninfluenced by our previous metrical impression, we shall have a kind of standard by which to measure what has happened: Till dieted by thee I grow mature in knowledge, as the Gods who all things know.

Perhaps it will be useful at this point to digress briefly by citing two examples from Milton that illustrate some of the possibilities for conflict between meter and the way the words have to be emphasized. First, from the early "At a Solemn Musick":

Wéd your divíne soúnds, and mixt power
  employ,
Deád things with ínbreath'd sense áble to
  pierce
And to our high-rais'd phantasie present,
That undisturbed Song of pure concent.

In the above, *sounds* and *able* conflict impressively with the meter. Though the voice and verse being celebrated in this marriage are heavenly and harmonious, they do not unite without a marked energy of resistance. They are "pledges" of heaven's joy, as the preceding lines state, and raise the imagination to the pure, original condition; but they fulfil the conditions of earthly creation, through opposites, and "mixt power," and a conflict between meter and voice. That conflict heightens the energy of the process of creation in the very act of being presented. In doing so, the conflict contributes to the release of energy which is part of the first stage of the imagined miracle. The second stage, of pure return, follows the release of energy. This movement is exalted and tranquil. It is purged of conflict. But if one wants a measure of how important that conflict was, one may try the third and fourth lines by themselves, forgetting what precedes. It will be hard to rescue the beautiful fourth line from a little intrusive thinness and obviousness of beat. But the transitional third line will suffer even more.

This example also provides us with an illustration of the increased emphasis possible by a coincidence of metrical accent and natural stress. The *in* of *in-breath'd* is raised to a height of emphasis quite comparable in effect with the emphasis on *sounds* and *able*, which is achieved by the contrary means of conflict. After its radical departure from

meter, the rhythm returning falls hard on the place cunningly prepared by the rhetoric, and the insignificant syllable is charged with an extraordinary office of meaning. That also constitutes a kind of conflict and surprising transformation of energy. Thus by a quite opposite technique from the emphasis on *sounds* and *able*, the regular *is* is also made radical in effect, and is woven into the complex conflict we have described as the first stage of the imagined miracle.

Let us now look at a somewhat simpler example. Samson is answering the Philistine Officer, and he expresses a sudden fervor of indignation and sense of his own ridiculousness which he has been laboring to master with heroic patience and justice:

Have they not Swórd-pláyers, and ev'ry sort
Of Gymnic Artists, Wrestlers, Riders, Runners,

Júglers and Dancers, Antics, Mummers,
  Mimics,
But they must pick me out with shackles tir'd,
And over-labour'd at thir publick Mill,
To make them sport with blind activity? . . .

Cán they thínk me so broken, so debas'd

With corporal servitude, that mý mind éver
Will condescend to such absurd commands?
Although thir drudge, to be thir fool or jester,

And in my midst of sorrow and heárt-gríef
To show them feats and play before thir
  god. . . .

What is metrically most interesting about this passage is that it is individual and assertive in effect, and seems to put a very great strain upon the meter, as if the strength of the personal passion were tearing at the bonds of the impersonal form. But in fact, except for the few places noted,[1] the natural emphasis of the words and the meter coincide. The apparent conflict, strengthened by some actual conflict, requires that we

[1] I may be conceding too much to the apparent conflict when I recognize a possible stress shift at the beginning of the first line and two stress shifts at the beginning of the seventh line. These interpretations are possible, and are certainly encouraged by the metrical style of the passage, but even more by the rhetorical style. I am inclined to explain my doubt as part of the contrived effect of the passage.

look twice in order to discover how much of the real emphasis derives from the metrical regularity, from the coincidence of angry, personal accent and the impersonal accent of the meter. (To some extent the example resembles that in *inbreath'd*.) One may also see a special kind of deception in the regularity. At three places we have lines that advertise their regularity: "To make them sport with blind activity. . . . Will condescend to such absurd commands. . . . To show them feats and play before their god." The effect, most notable in the first of these lines, is the familiar slow withering of satiric focus. But what chiefly accounts for the apparent difference of the line is not a different relation between metrical and natural emphasis, but a difference in tempo, and, incidentally, the rhetorical and rhythmical placing of the line in the whole passage, with what that does for the reciprocal effect of line on passage and passage on line.

Let us return now to the problems in our chief example:

Till dieted by thee I grow mature
In knowledge, as the Gods who all things know.

I said that the words here resist the meter negatively, by tending to be flat and unemphatic. Our imagined prose rendering, for instance, will demonstrate how the last two syllables of *dieted* will almost disappear if not prevented by the meter. And if we fix our attention on the first line and a half, through *knowledge,* we see that the words react to the meter by being bolstered in their stress. They return from the kind of emphasis heard in their prose rendering toward the stiffened beat of the ideal pattern. The result is a heightened emphasis one could not have expected either from the words themselves or from the meter itself. And as one attends more closely one observes that the return may be toward the pattern but not to it really. For the heightened emphasis is one that rises toward *knowledge,* but meter is regular and holds its level. (Partly, of course, we may recognize the co-operative work of the sense, the context, and the vowel movement, and the friction-release of the consonants *in*-knowledge.)

Something has happened during the process by which these stresses have been drawn toward the ideal pattern, which they have happily missed—to the great improvement of their individuality of rhythm. Perhaps one may see in the artificial propping up of the last syllable of *dieted* the beginning of what has happened. A certain overdependence on the meter at that point helped establish the immediate and extreme need of metrical support for the line.

I lack a proper technical apparatus for making clear precisely what the steps are in the occurrence we have been watching. I cannot do much better here than to point out what I think has come about and to assert that the excessive metrical support does not absorb the rhythm of the line, but instead, somehow, serves to create the actual individuality of the rhythm. But there is a kind of negative test of experiment that will tell us something. What might have happened without that overdependence? Let me invent, though crudely: Till daily fed with thee I grow mature / In knowledge. This kind of return to the basic form is very sad, for almost nothing has happened. The return is completely without transformation, and rhythm has only collapsed back into meter. So perhaps it is possible to say that overdependence may have a virtue not present in plain dependence.

The rest of the second line is very different in its return and transformation. The conflict between the words and the meter, though also negative, is most strenuous. The words themselves, without meter, would tend to disintegrate chaotically, to collapse into a formless non-rhythm: astheGodswhoallthingsknow. But the meter, far more radically than with *dieted* (though no doubt not unmindful of that precedent), will prevent this. The formless becomes marvelously shaped. Indeed, the rise in the pitch of significance (by which I mean a physical, vocal phenomenon, but also a psychological and dramatic and cognitive one), that rise toward *knowledge* is held wonderfully at that plane, for a long sustained moment during which this rhythm may be felt to return toward meter. But that is, luckily, an illusion which is perhaps due to the extreme straining of the formless back to form.

If again we rely on a negative discrimination, we may make the obvious point that if this rhythm were identical with meter the last stress, on *know*, would bob up fatuously, which it does not. The crucial point is *as*, which like the last syllable of *dieted* evokes the immediate and extreme support of the meter. But meter is not allowed to take over and, because of the excessive dependence of one word, to hold as a passive prize the rest of the line. The conflict for individuality reasserts itself, and not less energetically because of the one moment of absolute need. If I try to describe the words prosodically (which I find very difficult to do) I have to say something like this: the resistance to the meter does not express itself by any of the ordinary metrical variations; there are no stress shifts or the like. One could scan as conventionally iambic, without altering the fact that a reading creates a powerful tension between meter and the way the words have to be emphasized. My interpretation is that there is practically no discernible difference in the stress of the last words. They are held at one level, I think, and are modulated by texture, by the movement, not progressive but a movement, of the vowels: *Gods who all things know.* One might in the abstract expect that the artificial order of words ought to strengthen the domination of the meter, as a kind of typical concession to meter. But the natural order—Gods who know all things—besides losing the special effect of *know* and the cunning vowel modulation, would severely reduce the resistance to meter. Then *know* would coincide too closely with the meter, and only *all* would be left to set up some resistance. Besides, much of the effect relies on suspending the syntactical con-

clusion, holding back the *know*, which contributes to the suspense of the whole clause.

Furthermore, our sense of the metrical situation is assisted by our built-up sense of the dramatic context: Eve's identifying herself in a kind of willed (and therefore hallucinatory) mystical union with divine knowledge. That is what Eve is identifying herself with, talking herself deliciously into.[2] The meter provides the form by which a potentially dull scramble of words achieves a distinctive kind of rapt order. The exaltation of rhythm which is created is an integral part of the high, unwavering illusion of mystical motionlessness.

Can we draw any conclusions that may help justify our intensive studying of this one example instead of having followed a more usual procedure of working by means of a broader survey based upon many examples? At least some of the difficult points raised by the preliminary statement have been partly explored, and are now, I hope, somewhat less difficult. If we think back on the two conflicts mentioned in the preliminary statement, we may now with some assurance identify the *external* conflict as that between the relatively shapeless words and the meter. The *internal* conflict is what happens when the shapelessness influenced by the meter is counter-influenced by the process of the context. If our basic formulation is accurate, the meter figures twice, and may be considered the constant, pure, unindividualized form which endows, through conflict, the relatively formless with what is humanly individualized, and more interesting, and more beautiful. If our description has been reasonably accurate, we have seen one example of how the created rhythm can express the warm, various, physical, unique immediacy of the process. For

[2] A rhythmical context can also be set up for reference. When Eve, in the dream that helps rehearse the real temptation, has the apple held to her mouth, it is with these words: "Ascend to Heav'n, by merit thine, and see/What life the Gods live there." The second line is an earlier, and lesser, version of the exalted rhythm we have been considering.

though the meter figures twice, it is the process which is projected.

The only further generalizations I dare attempt I shall sketch as a kind of freehand allegory. The meter is an unchangeable and indifferent form, an unmoved but moving externality. The rhythm in its dynamic and turbulent process of individual experience reacts both toward and against that externality. Inside the struggle there is an effort, wonderfully fruitful in failure, to become identified with the external form.

KENNETH BURKE

Symbolic Action in a Poem by Keats (1945)

We are here set to analyze the "Ode on a Grecian Urn" as a viaticum that leads, by a series of transformations, into the oracle, "Beauty is truth, truth beauty." We shall analyze the Ode "dramatistically," in terms of symbolic action.

To consider language as a means of *information* or *knowledge* is to consider it epistemologically, semantically, in terms of "science." To consider it as a mode of *action* is to consider it in terms of "poetry." For a poem is an act, the symbolic act of the poet who made it— an act of such a nature that, in surviving as a structure or object, it enables us as readers to re-enact it.

"Truth" being the essential word of knowledge (science) and "beauty" being the essential word of art or poetry, we might substitute accordingly. The oracle would then assert, "Poetry is science, science poetry." It would be particularly exhilarating to proclaim them one if there were a strong suspicion that they were at odds (as the assertion that "God's in his heaven, all's right with the world" is really a *counter*-assertion to doubts about God's existence and suspicions that much is wrong). It was the dialectical opposition between the "aesthetic" and the "practical," with "poetry" on one side and utility (business and applied science) on the other that was being ecstatically denied. The

From *A Grammar of Motives by* Kenneth Burke. © 1945 by Prentice-Hall, Inc. Reprinted by permission of the author and publishers. For information about the author, see p. 242 above.

relief in this denial was grounded in the romantic philosophy itself, a philosophy which gave strong recognition to precisely the *contrast* between "beauty" and "truth."

Perhaps we might put it this way: If the oracle were to have been uttered 'in the first stanza of the poem rather than the last, its phrasing proper to that place would have been: "Beauty is *not* truth, truth *not* beauty." The five stanzas of successive transformation were necessary for the romantic philosophy of a romantic poet to transcend itself (raising its romanticism to a new order, or new dimension). An abolishing of romanticism through romanticism! (To transcend romanticism through romanticism is, when all is over, to restore in one way what is removed in another.)

But to the poem, step by step through the five stanzas.

As a "way in," we begin with the sweeping periodic sentence that, before the stanza is over, has swiftly but imperceptibly been transmuted in quality from the periodic to the breathless, a cross between interrogation and exclamation:

Thou still unravish'd bride of quietness,
  Thou foster-child of silence and slow time,
Sylvan historian, who canst thus express
  A flowery tale more sweetly than our rhyme:
What leaf-fring'd legend haunts about thy
    shape
  Of deities or mortals, or of both,
    In Tempe or the dales of Arcady?

What men or gods are these? What maidens
  loth?
  What mad pursuit? What struggle to
    escape?
    What pipes and timbrels? What wild
      ecstasy?

Even the last quick outcries retain
somewhat the quality of the periodic
structure with which the stanza began.
The final line introduces the subject
of "pipes and timbrels," which is developed and then surpassed in Stanza II:

Heard melodies are sweet, but those unheard
  Are sweeter; therefore, ye soft pipes, play
    on;
Not to the sensual ear, but, more endear'd,
  Pipe to the spirit ditties of no tone:
Fair youth, beneath the trees, thou canst not
    leave
  Thy song, nor ever can those trees be bare;
    Bold Lover, never, never canst thou kiss,
Though winning near the goal—yet, do not
    grieve;
  She cannot fade, though thou hast not thy
    bliss,
    Forever wilt thou love, and she be fair!

If we had only the first stanza of this
Ode, and were speculating upon it from
the standpoint of motivation, we could
detect there tentative indications of two
motivational levels. For the lines express
a doubt whether the figures on the urn
are "deities or mortals"—and the motives of gods are of a different order
from the motives of men. This bare hint
of such a possibility emerges with something of certainty in the second stanza's
development of the "pipes and timbrels"
theme. For we explicitly consider a contrast between body and mind (in the
contrast between "heard melodies," addressed "to the sensual ear," and "ditties of no tone," addressed "to the
spirit").

Also, of course, the notion of inaudible sound brings us into the region of
the mystic oxymoron (the term in rhetoric for "the figure in which an epithet
of a contrary significance is added to a
word: e.g., *cruel kindness; laborious
idleness*"). And it clearly suggests a concern with the level of motives-behind-
motives, as with the paradox of the

prime mover that is itself at rest, being
the unmoved ground of all motion and
action. Here the poet whose sounds are
the richest in our language is meditating
upon *absolute* sound, the *essence* of
sound, which would be soundless as the
prime mover is motionless, or as the
"principle" of sweetness would not be
sweet, having transcended sweetness, or
as the sub-atomic particles of the sun are
each, in their isolate purity, said to be
devoid of temperature.

Contrast Keats's unheard melodies
with those of Shelley:

Music, when soft voices die,
Vibrates in the memory—
Odours, when sweet violets sicken,
Live within the sense they quicken.

Rose leaves, when the rose is dead,
Are heaped for the beloved's bed;
And so thy thoughts, when thou art gone,
Love itself shall slumber on.

Here the futuristic Shelley is anticipating retrospection; he is looking forward
to looking back. The form of thought
is naturalistic and temporalistic in terms
of *past* and *future*. But the form of
thought in Keats is mystical, in terms
of an *eternal present*. The Ode is striving to move beyond the region of becoming into the realm of *being*. (This
is another way of saying that we are
here concerned with two levels of motivation.)

In the last four lines of the second
stanza, the state of immediacy is conveyed by a development peculiarly
Keatsian. I refer not simply to translation into terms of the erotic, but rather
to a quality of *suspension* in the erotic
imagery, defining an eternal prolonga-
tion of the state just prior to fulfilment—
not exactly arrested ecstasy, but rather
an arrested pre-ecstasy.[1]

Suppose that we had but this one poem
by Keats, and knew nothing of its author or its period, so that we could treat

[1] Mr. G. Wilson Knight, in *The Starlit Dome*, refers
to "that recurring tendency in Keats to image a poised
form, a stillness suggesting motion, what might be
called a 'tiptoe' effect."

it only in itself, as a series of internal transformations to be studied in their development from a certain point, and without reference to any motives outside the Ode. Under such conditions, I think, we should require no further observations to characterize (from the standpoint of symbolic action) the main argument in the second stanza. We might go on to make an infinity of observations about the details of the stanza; but as regards major deployments we should deem it enough to note that the theme of "pipes and timbrels" is developed by the use of mystic oxymoron, and then surpassed (or given a development-atop-the-development) by the stressing of erotic imagery (that had been ambiguously adumbrated in the references to "maidens loth" and "mad pursuit" of Stanza I). And we could note the quality of *incipience* in this imagery, its state of arrest not at fulfilment, but at the point just prior to fulfilment.

Add, now, our knowledge of the poem's place as an enactment in a particular cultural scene, and we likewise note in this second stanza a variant of the identification between death and sexual love that was so typical of 19th-century romanticism and was to attain its musical monument in the Wagnerian *Liebestod*. On a purely dialectical basis, to die in love would be to be born to love (the lovers dying as individual identities that they might be transformed into a common identity). Adding historical factors, one can note the part that capitalist individualism plays in sharpening this consummation (since a property structure that heightens the sense of individual identity would thus make it more imperiously a "death" for the individual to take on the new identity made by a union of two). We can thus see why the love-death equation would be particularly representative of a romanticism that was the reflex of business.

Fortunately, the relation between private property and the love-death equation is attested on unimpeachable authority, concerning the effect of con-

sumption and consummation in a "mutual flame":

> So between them love did shine,
> That the turtle saw his right
> Flaming in the phoenix' sight;
> Either was the other's mine.
>
> Property was thus appall'd,
> That the self was not the same;
> Single nature's double name
> Neither two nor one was called.

The addition of fire to the equation, with its pun on sexual burning, moves us from purely dialectical considerations into psychological ones. In the lines of Shakespeare, fire is the third term, the ground term for the other two (the synthesis that ends the lovers' roles as thesis and antithesis). Less obviously, the same movement from the purely dialectical to the psychological is implicit in any imagery of a *dying* or a *falling* in common, which when woven with sexual imagery signalizes a "transcendent" sexual consummation. The figure appears in a lover's compliment when Keats writes to Fanny Brawne, thus:

> I never knew before, what such a love as you have made me feel, was; I did not believe in it; my Fancy was afraid of it lest it should burn me up. But if you will fully love me, though there may be some fire, 'twill not be more than we can bear when moistened and bedewed with pleasures.

Our primary concern is to follow the transformations of the poem itself. But to understand its full nature as a symbolic act, we should use whatever knowledge is available. In the case of Keats, not only do we know the place of this poem in his work and its time, but also we have material to guide our speculations as regards correlations between poem and poet. I grant that such speculations interfere with the symmetry of criticism as a game. (Criticism as a game is best to watch, I guess, when one confines himself to the single unit, and reports on its movements like a radio commentator broadcasting the blow-by-blow description of a prizefight.) But linguistic analysis has opened up new possibilities in the correlating of producer and product—and these concerns have such important bearing upon matters of culture and conduct in general that no sheer conventions or ideals of criticism should be allowed to interfere with their development.

From what we know of Keats's illness, with the peculiar inclination to erotic imaginings that accompany its fever (as with the writings of D. H. Lawrence) we can glimpse a particular bodily motive expanding and intensifying the lyric state in Keats's case. Whatever the intense *activity* of his thoughts, there was the material *pathos* of his physical condition. Whatever transformations of mind or body he experienced, his illness was there as a kind of constitutional substrate, whereby all aspects of the illness would be imbued with their derivation from a common ground (the phthisic fever thus being at one with the phthisic chill, for whatever the clear contrast between fever and chill, they are but modes of the same illness, the common underlying substance).

The correlation between the state of agitation in the poems and the physical condition of the poet is made quite clear in the poignant letters Keats wrote during his last illness. In 1819 he complains that he is "scarcely content to write the best verses for the fever they leave behind." And he continues: "I want to compose without this fever." But a few months later he confesses, "I am recommended not even to read poetry, much less write it." Or: "I must say that for 6 Months before I was taken ill I had not passed a tranquil day. Either that gloom overspre[a]d me or I was suffering under some passionate feeling, or if I turn'd to versify that exacerbated the poison of either sensation." Keats was "like a sick eagle looking at the sky," as he wrote of his mortality in a kindred poem, "On Seeing the Elgin Marbles."

But though the poet's body was a *patient,* the poet's mind was an *agent.* Thus, as a practitioner of poetry, he could *use* his fever, even perhaps encouraging, though not deliberately, esthetic habits that, in making for the perfection of his lines, would exact payment in the ravages of his body (somewhat as Hart Crane could write poetry only by modes of living that made for the cessation of his poetry and so led to his dissolution).

Speaking of agents, patients, and action here, we might pause to glance back over the centuries thus: in the Aristotelian grammar of motives, action has its reciprocal in passion, hence *passion* is the property of a *patient.* But by the Christian paradox (which made the martyr's action identical with his passion, as the accounts of the martyrs were called both Acts and Passionals), *patience* is the property of a moral *agent.* And this Christian view, as secularized in the philosophy of romanticism, with its stress upon creativeness, leads us to the possibility of a bodily suffering redeemed by a poetic act.

In the third stanza, the central stanza of the Ode (hence properly the fulcrum of its swing) we see the two motives, the action and the passion, in the process of being separated. The possibility raised in the first stanza (which was dubious whether the level of motives was to be human or divine), and developed in the second stanza (which contrasts the "sensual" and the "spirit"), becomes definitive in Stanza III:

Ah, happy, happy boughs! that cannot shed
  Your leaves, nor ever bid the Spring adieu;
And, happy melodist, unwearied,
  For ever piping songs for ever new;
More happy love! more happy, happy love!
  For ever warm and still to be enjoy'd,
    For ever panting, and for ever young;
All breathing human passion far above,
  That leaves a heart a high-sorrowful and
    cloy'd,
    A burning forehead, and a parching
    tongue.

The poem as a whole makes permanent, or fixes in a state of arrest, a peculiar agitation. But within this fixity, by the nature of poetry as a progressive medium, there must be development. Hence, the agitation that is maintained throughout (as a mood absolutized so that it fills the entire universe of discourse) will at the same time undergo internal transformations. In the third stanza, these are manifested as a clear division into two distinct and contrasted realms. There is a transcendental fever, which is felicitous, divinely above "all breathing human passion." And this "leaves" the other level, the level of earthly fever, "a burning forehead and a parching tongue." From the bodily fever, which is a passion, and malign, there has split off a spiritual activity, a wholly benign aspect of the total agitation.

Clearly, a movement has been finished. The poem must, if it is well-formed, take a new direction, growing out of and surpassing the curve that has by now been clearly established by the successive stages from "Is there the possibility of two motivational levels?" through "there are two motivational levels" to "the 'active' motivational level 'leaves' the 'passive' level."

Prophesying, with the inestimable advantage that goes with having looked ahead, what should we expect the new direction to be? First, let us survey the situation. Originally, before the two strands of the fever had been definitely drawn apart, the bodily passion could serve as the scene or ground of the spiritual action. But at the end of the third stanza, we abandon the level of bodily passion. The action is "far above" the passion, it "leaves" the fever. What then would this transcendent act require, to complete it?

It would require a scene of the same quality as itself. An act and a scene belong together. The nature of the one must be fit with the nature of the other. (I like to call this the "scene-act ratio," or "dramatic ratio.") Hence, the act having now transcended its bodily setting, it will require, as its new setting, a transcendent scene. Hence, prophesying *post eventum*, we should ask that, in Stanza IV, the poem *embody* the transcendental act by endowing it with an appropriate scene.

The scene-act ratio involves a law of dramatic consistency whereby the quality of the act shares the quality of the scene in which it is enacted (the synecdochic relation of container and thing contained). Its grandest variant was in supernatural cosmogonies wherein mankind took on the attributes of gods by acting in cosmic scenes that were themselves imbued with the presence of godhead.[2]

Or we may discern the logic of the scene-act ratio behind the old controversy as to whether "God willed the good because it is good," or "the good is good because God willed it." This strictly theological controversy had political implications. But our primary concern here is with the *dramatistic* aspects of this controversy. For you will note that the whole issue centers in the problem of the *grounds* of God's creative act.

Since, from the purely dramatic point of view, every act requires a scene in which it takes place, we may note that one of the doctrines (that "God willed the good because it is good") is more symmetrical than the other. For by it, God's initial act of creation is itself given a ground, or scene (the objective existence of goodness, which was so real that God himself did not simply make it up, but acted in conformity with its nature when willing it to be the law of his creation). In the scholastic formulas taken over from Aristotle, God was defined as "pure act" (though this pure act was in turn the ultimate ground or *scene* of human acting and willing). And from the standpoint of purely dramatic symmetry, it would be desirable to have some kind of "scene" even for God. This requirement is met, we are suggesting, in the doctrine that "God willed the good *because* it is good." For this word, "because," in assigning a reason for God's willing, gives us in principle a kind of scene, as we may discern in the pun of our word,

[2] In an article by Leo Spitzer, *"Milieu and Ambiance*: An Essay in Historical Semantics"* (September and December 1942 numbers of *Philosophy and Phenomenological Research*), one will find a wealth of material that can be read as illustrative of "dramatic ratio."

"ground," itself, which indeterminately applies to either "place" or "cause."

If even theology thus responded to the pressure for dramatic symmetry by endowing God, as the transcendent act, with a transcendent scene of like quality, we should certainly expect to find analogous tactics in this Ode. For as we have noted that the romantic passion is the secular equivalent of the Christian passion, so we may recall Coleridge's notion that poetic action itself is a "dim analogue of Creation." Keats in his way confronting the same dramatistic requirement that the theologians confronted in theirs, when he has arrived at his transcendent act at the end of Stanza III (that is, when the benign fever has split away from the malign bodily counterpart, as a divorcing of spiritual action from sensual passion), he is ready in the next stanza for the imagining of a scene that would correspond in quality to the quality of the action as so transformed. His fourth stanza will concretize, or "materialize," the act, by dwelling upon its appropriate ground.

Who are these coming to the sacrifice?
To what green altar, O mysterious priest,
Lead'st thou that heifer lowing at the skies,
    And all her silken flanks with garlands
        drest?
What little town, by river or sea shore,
    Or mountain built with peaceful citadel,
    Is emptied of this folk, this pious morn?
And, little town, thy streets for evermore
    Will silent be; and not a soul to tell
    Why thou art desolate, can e'er return.

It is a vision, as you prefer, of "death" or of "immortality." "Immortality," we might say, is the "good" word for "death," and must necessarily be conceived in terms of death (the necessity that Donne touches upon when he writes, " . . . but thinke that I/Am, by being dead, immortall"). This is why, when discussing the second stanza, I felt justified in speaking of the variations of the love-death equation, though the poem spoke not of love and *death*, but of love *for ever*. We have a deathy-deathless scene as the corresponding ground of our transcendent act. The Urn itself, as with the scene upon it, is not merely an immortal act in our pres-

ent mortal scene; it was originally an immortal act in a mortal scene quite different. The imagery, of sacrifice, piety, silence, desolation, is that of communication with the immortal or the dead.[3]

Incidentally, we might note that the return to the use of rhetorical questions in the fourth stanza serves well, on a purely technical level, to keep our contact with the mood of the opening stanza, a music that now but vibrates in the memory. Indeed, one even gets the impression that the form of the rhetorical question had never been abandoned; that the poet's questings had been couched as questions throughout. This is tonal felicity at its best, and something much like unheard tonal felicity. For the actual persistence of the rhetorical questions through these stanzas would have been wearisome, whereas their return now gives us an inaudible variation, by making us feel that the exclamations in the second and third stanzas had been questions, as the questions in the first stanza had been exclamations.

But though a lyric greatly profits by so strong a sense of continuousness, or perpetuity, I am trying to stress the fact that in the fourth stanza we *come upon* something. Indeed, this fourth stanza is related to the three foregoing stanzas quite as the sestet is related to the octave in Keats's sonnet, "On First Looking Into Chapman's Homer":

Much have I travell'd in the realms of gold,
    And many goodly states and kingdoms seen;
    Round many western islands have I been
Which bards in fealty to Apollo hold.
Oft of one wide expanse had I been told

[3] In imagery there is no negation, or disjunction. Logically, we can say, "this *or* that," "this, *not* that." In imagery we can but say "this *and* that," "this *with* that," "this-that," etc. Thus, imagistically considered, a commandment cannot be simply a proscription, but is also latently a provocation (a state of affairs that figures in the kind of stylistic scrupulosity and/or curiosity to which Gide's heroes have been particularly sensitive, as "thou shalt not . . ." becomes imaginatively transformed into "what would happen if . . ."). In the light of what we have said about the deathiness of immortality, and the relation between the erotic and the thought of a "dying," perhaps we might be justified in reading the last line of the great "Bright Star!" sonnet as naming states not simply alternative but also synonymous:

And so live ever—or else swoon to death.

This use of the love-death equation is as startlingly paralleled in a letter to Fanny Brawne:

I have two luxuries to brood over in my walks, your loveliness and the hour of my death. O that I could take possession of them both in the same moment.

That deep-brow'd Homer ruled as his
  demesne;
Yet did I never breathe its pure serene
Till I heard Chapman speak out loud and
  bold;

Then felt I like some watcher of the skies
  When a new planet swims into his ken;
Or like stout Cortez when with eagle eyes
  He stared at the Pacific—and all his men
Look'd at each other with a wild surmise—
  Silent, upon a peak in Darien.

I am suggesting that, just as the sestet in this sonnet, *comes upon a scene*, so it is with the fourth stanza of the Ode. In both likewise we end on the theme of silence; and is not the Ode's reference to the thing that "not a soul can tell" quite the same in quality as the sonnet's reference to a "wild surmise"?

Thus, with the Urn as viaticum (or rather, with the *poem* as viaticum, and *in the name* of the Urn), having symbolically enacted a kind of act that transcends our mortality, we round out the process by coming to dwell upon the transcendental ground of this act. The dead world of ancient Greece, as immortalized on an Urn surviving from that period, is the vessel of this deathy-deathless ambiguity. And we have gone dialectically from the "human" to the "divine" and thence to the "ground of the divine" (here tracing in poetic imagery the kind of "dramatistic" course we have considered, on the purely conceptual plane, in the theological speculations about the "grounds" for God's creative act). Necessarily, there must be certain inadequacies in the conception of this ground, precisely because of the fact that immortality can only be conceived in terms of death. Hence the reference to the "desolate" in a scene otherwise possessing the benignity of the eternal.

The imagery of pious sacrifice, besides its fitness for such thoughts of departure as when the spiritual act splits from the sensual pathos, suggests also a bond of communication between the levels (because of its immortal character in a mortal scene). And finally, the poem, in the name of the Urn, or under the aegis of the Urn, is such a bond. For we readers, by re-enacting it in the reading, use it as a viaticum to transport us into the quality of the scene which it depicts on its face (the scene containing as a fixity what the poem as act extends into a process). The scene *on* the Urn is really the scene *behind* the Urn; the Urn is literally the ground of this scene, but transcendentally the scene is the ground of the Urn. The Urn contains the scene out of which it arose.

We turn now to the closing stanza:

O Attic shape! Fair attitude! with brede
  Of marble men and maidens overwrought,
With forest branches and the trodden weed;
  Thou, silent form, dost tease us out of
    thought
As doth eternity: Cold Pastoral!
  When old age shall this generation waste,
    Thou shalt remain, in midst of other woe
Than ours, a friend to man, to whom thou
    say'st,
  'Beauty is truth, truth beauty,'—that is all
    Ye know on earth, and all ye need to
    know.

In the third stanza we were at a moment of heat, emphatically sharing an imagery of loves "panting" and "for ever warm" that was, in the transcendental order, companionate to "a burning forehead, and a parching tongue" in the order of the passions. But in the last stanza, as signalized in the marmorean utterance, "Cold Pastoral!" we have gone from transcendental fever to transcendental chill. Perhaps, were we to complete our exegesis, we should need reference to some physical step from phthisic fever to phthisic chill, that we might detect here a final correlation between bodily passion and mental action. In any event we may note that, the mental action having departed from the bodily passion, the change from fever to chill is not a sufferance. For, as only the *benign* aspects of the fever had been left after the split, so it is a wholly benign chill on which the poem ends.[4]

---

[4] In a letter to Fanny Brawne, Keats touches upon the fever-chill contrast in a passage that also touches upon the love-death equation, though here the chill figures in an untransfigured state:

I fear that I am too prudent for a dying kind of Lover. Yet, there is a great difference between going off in warm blood like Romeo; and making one's exit like a frog in a frost.

I wonder whether anyone can read the reference to "brede of marble men and maidens overwrought" without thinking of "breed" for "brede" and "excited" for "overwrought." (Both expressions would thus merge notions of sexuality and craftsmanship, the erotic and the poetic.) As for the designating of the Urn as an "Attitude," it fits in admirably with our stress upon symbolic action. For an attitude is an arrested, or incipient *act*—not just an *object*, or *thing*.

Yeats, in *A Vision*, speaks of "the diagrams in Law's *Boehme*, where one lifts a paper to discover both the human entrails and the starry heavens." This equating of the deeply without and the deeply within (as also with Kant's famous remark) might well be remembered when we think of the sky that the "watcher" saw in Keats's sonnet. It is an internal sky, attained through meditations induced by the reading of a book. And so the oracle, whereby truth and beauty are proclaimed as one, would seem to derive from a profound inwardness.

Otherwise, without these introductory mysteries, "truth" and "beauty" were at odds. For whereas "beauty" had its fulfilment in romantic poetry, "truth" was coming to have its fulfilment in science, technological accuracy, accountancy, statistics, actuarial tables, and the like. Hence, without benefit of the rites which one enacts in a sympathetic reading of the Ode (rites that remove the discussion to a different level), the enjoyment of "beauty" would involve an esthetic kind of awareness radically in conflict with the kind of awareness deriving from the practical "truth." And as regards the tactics of the poem, this conflict would seem to be solved by "estheticizing" the true rather than by "verifying" the beautiful.

Earlier in our essay, we suggested reading "poetry" for "beauty" and "science" for "truth," with the oracle deriving its *liberating* quality from the fact that it is uttered at a time when the poem has taken us to a level where earthly contradictions do not operate.

But we might also, in purely conceptual terms, attain a level where "poetry" and "science" cease to be at odds; namely: by translating the two terms into the "grammar" that lies behind them. That is: we could generalize the term "poetry" by widening it to the point where we could substitute for it the term "act." And we could widen "science" to the point where we could substitute "scene." Thus we have:

"beauty" equals "poetry" equals "act"
"truth" equals "science" equals "scene"

We would equate "beauty" with "act," because it is not merely a decorative thing, but an assertion, an affirmative, a creation, hence in the fullest sense an act. And we would equate "truth" or "science" with the "scenic" because science is a knowledge of *what is*—and *all that is* comprises the over-all universal *scene*. Our corresponding transcendence, then, got by "translation" into purely grammatical terms, would be: "Act is scene, scene act." We have got to this point by a kind of purely conceptual transformation that would correspond, I think, to the transformations of imagery leading to the oracle in the Ode.

"Act is scene, scene act." Unfortunately, I must break the symmetry a little. For poetry, as conceived in idealism (romanticism) could not quite be equated with *act*, but rather with *attitude*. For idealistic philosophies, with their stress upon the subjective, place primary stress upon the *agent* (the individual, the ego, the will, etc.). It was medieval scholasticism that placed primary stress upon the *act*. And in the Ode the Urn (which is the vessel or representative of poetry) is called an "attitude," which is not outright an act, but an incipient or arrested act, a *state of mind*, the property of an *agent*. Keats, in calling the Urn an attitude, is *personifying* it. Or we might use the italicizing resources of dialectic by saying that for Keats, beauty (poetry) was not so much "the *act* of an agent" as it was "the act of an *agent*."

Perhaps we can re-enforce this interpretation by examining kindred strategies in Yeats, whose poetry similarly derives from idealistic, romantic sources. Indeed, as we have noted elsewhere,[5] Yeats's vision of immortality in his Byzantium poems but carries one step further the Keatsian identification with the Grecian Urn:

Once out of nature I shall never take
My bodily form from any natural thing,
But such a form as Grecian goldsmiths make
Of hammered gold and gold enamelling . . .

Here certainly the poet envisions immortality as "esthetically" as Keats. For he will have immortality as a golden bird, a fabricated thing, a work of Grecian goldsmiths. Here we go in the same direction as the "overwrought" Urn, but farther along in that direction.

The ending of Yeats's poem, "Among School Children," helps us to make still clearer the idealistic stress upon agent:

Labour is blossoming or dancing where
The body is not bruised to pleasure soul,
Nor beauty torn out of its own despair,
Nor blear-eyed wisdom out of midnight oil.
O chestnut tree, great rooted blossomer,
Are you the leaf, the blossom or the bole?
O body swayed to music, O brightening glance,
How can we know the dancer from the dance?

Here the chestnut tree (as personified agent) is the ground of unity or continuity for all its scenic manifestations; and with the agent (dancer) is merged the act (dance). True, we seem to have here a commingling of act, scene, and agent, all three. Yet it is the *agent* that is "foremost among the equals." Both Yeats and Keats, of course, were much more "dramatistic" in their thinking than romantic poets generally, who usually center their efforts upon the translation of *scene* into terms of *agent* (as the materialistic science that was the dialectical counterpart of romantic idealism preferred conversely to translate *agent* into terms of *scene*, or in other words, to treat "consciousness" in terms

[5] "On Motivation in Yeats" (*The Southern Review*, Winter 1942).

of "matter," the "mental" in terms of the "physical," "people" in terms of "environment").

To review briefly: The poem begins with an ambiguous fever which in the course of the further development is "separated out," splitting into a bodily fever and a spiritual counterpart. The bodily passion is the malign aspect of the fever, the mental action its benign aspect. In the course of the development, the malign passion is transcended and the benign active partner, the intellectual exhilaration, takes over. At the beginning, where the two aspects were ambiguously one, the bodily passion would be the "scene" of the mental action (the "objective symptoms" of the body would be paralleled by the "subjective symptoms" of the mind, the bodily state thus being the other or ground of the mental state). But as the two become separated out, the mental action transcends the bodily passion. It becomes an act in its own right, making discoveries and assertions not grounded in the bodily passion. And this quality of action, in transcending the merely physical symptoms of the fever, would thus require a different ground or scene, one more suited in quality to the quality of the transcendent act.

The transcendent act is concretized, or "materialized," in the vision of the "immortal" scene, the reference in Stanza IV to the original scene of the Urn, the "heavenly" scene of a dead, or immortal, Greece (the scene in which the Urn was originally enacted and which is also fixed on its face). To indicate the internality of this vision, we referred to a passage in Yeats relating the "depths" of the sky without to the depths of the mind within; and we showed a similar pattern in Keats's account of the vision that followed his reading of Chapman's Homer. We suggested that the poet is here coming upon a new internal sky, through identification with the Urn as act, the same sky that he came upon through identification with the enactments of Chapman's translation.

This transcendent scene is the level at which the earthly laws of contradiction no longer prevail. Hence, in the terms of this scene, he can proclaim the unity of truth and beauty (of science and art), a proclamation which he needs to make precisely because here was the basic split responsible for the romantic agitation (in both poetic and philosophic idealism). That is, it was gratifying to have the oracle proclaim the unity of poetry and science because the values of technology and business were causing them to be at odds. And from the perspective of a "higher level" (the perspective of a dead or immortal scene transcending the world of temporal contradictions) the split could be proclaimed once more a unity.

At this point, at this stage of exaltation, the fever has been replaced by chill. But the bodily passion has completely dropped out of account. All is now mental action. Hence, the chill (as in the ecstatic exclamation, "Cold Pastoral!") is proclaimed only in its benign aspect.

We may contrast this discussion with explanations such as a materialist of the Kretschmer school might offer. I refer to accounts of motivation that might treat disease as cause and poem as effect. In such accounts, the disease would not be "passive," but wholly active; and what we have called the mental action would be wholly passive, hardly more than an epiphenomenon, a mere symptom of the disease quite as are the fever and the chill themselves. Such accounts would give us no conception of the essential matter here, the intense linguistic activity.

CLEANTH BROOKS

(b. 1906)

A university professor and critic, Cleanth Brooks was a student and associate of John Crowe Ransom at Vanderbilt University during the late 1920's. As an author of textbook anthologies like *Understanding Poetry* (with R. P. Warren, 1938; rev. 1950, 1960), Brooks contributed to the critical revolution in the teaching of literature. As a New Critic, he followed T. S. Eliot and I. A. Richards in emphasizing wit, ambiguity, and irony as criteria of poetic worth. His books of criticism include *Modern Poetry and the Tradition* (1939), *The Well Wrought Urn: Studies in the Structure of Poetry* (1947), and *Tragic Themes in Western Literature* (1955). He is also the co-author, with W. K. Wimsatt, of *Literary Criticism: A Short History* (1957). Brooks's essay on Keats's "Ode on a Grecian Urn" illustrates his typically New Critical view that the language of paradox is the language of poetry, which expresses through metaphor a complex truth, distinct from that of science or of any prose paraphrase formulated by the critic.

Keats's Sylvan Historian: History without Footnotes (1947)

There is much in the poetry of Keats which suggests that he would have approved of Archibald MacLeish's dic-

tum, "A poem should not mean/But be." There is even some warrant for thinking that the Grecian urn (real or imagined) which inspired the famous ode was, for Keats, just such a poem "palpable and mute," a poem in stone

Hence it is the more remarkable that the "Ode" itself differs from Keats's other odes by culminating in a statement—a statement even of some sententiousness in which the urn itself is made to say that beauty is truth, and—more sententious still—that this bit of wisdom sums up the whole of mortal knowledge.

This is "to mean" with a vengeance —to violate the doctrine of the objective correlative, not only by stating truths, but by defining the limits of truth. Small wonder that some critics have felt that the unravished bride of quietness protests too much.

T. S. Eliot, for example, says that "this line ["Beauty is truth," etc.] strikes me as a serious blemish on a beautiful poem; and the reason must be either that I fail to understand it, or that it is a statement which is untrue." But even for persons who feel that they do understand it, the line may still constitute a blemish. Middleton Murry, who, after a discussion of Keats's other poems and his letters, feels that he knows what Keats meant by "beauty" and what he meant by "truth," and that Keats used them in senses which allowed them to be properly bracketed together, still, is forced to conclude: "My own opinion concerning the value of these two lines *in the context of the poem itself* is not very different from Mr. T. S. Eliot's." The troubling assertion is apparently an intrusion upon the poem—does not grow out of it—is not dramatically accommodated to it.

This is essentially Garrod's objection, and the fact that Garrod does object indicates that a distaste for the ending of the "Ode" is by no means limited to critics of notoriously "modern" sympathies.

But the question of real importance is not whether Eliot, Murry, and Garrod are right in thinking that "Beauty is truth, truth beauty" injures the poem. The question of real importance concerns beauty and truth in a much more general way: what is the relation of the beauty (the goodness, the perfection) of a poem to the truth or falsity of what it seems to assert? It is a question which has particularly vexed our own generation—to give it I. A. Richards' phrasing, it is the problem of belief.

The "Ode," by its bold equation of beauty and truth, raises this question in its sharpest form—the more so when it becomes apparent that the poem itself is obviously intended to be a parable on the nature of poetry, and of art in general. The "Ode" has apparently been an enigmatic parable, to be sure: one can emphasize *beauty* is truth and throw Keats into the pure-art camp, the usual procedure. But it is only fair to point out that one could stress *truth* is beauty, and argue with the Marxist critics of the 'thirties for a propaganda art. The very ambiguity of the statement, "Beauty is truth, truth beauty" ought to warn us against insisting very much on the statement in isolation, and to drive us back to a consideration of the context in which the statement is set.

It will not be sufficient, however, if it merely drives us back to a study of Keats's reading, his conversation, his letters. We shall not find our answer there even if scholarship does prefer on principle investigations of Browning's ironic question, "What porridge had John Keats?" For even if we knew just what porridge he had, physical and mental, we should still not be able to settle the problem of the "Ode." The reason should be clear: our specific question is not what did Keats the man perhaps want to assert here about the relation of beauty and truth; it is rather: was Keats the poet able to exemplify that relation in this particular poem? Middleton Murry is right: the relation of the final statement in the poem to the total context is all-important.

Indeed, Eliot, in the very passage in which he attacks the "Ode" has indicated the general line which we are to take in its defense. In that passage, Eliot goes on to contrast the closing lines of the "Ode" with a line from *King Lear*, "Ripeness is all." Keats's lines strike him as false; Shakespeare's on the other hand, as not clearly false, and as possibly quite true. Shakespeare's generalization, in other words, avoids raising the question of truth. But is it really a question of truth and falsity? One is tempted to account for the difference of effect which Eliot feels in this way: "Ripeness is all" is a statement put in the mouth of a dramatic character and a statement which is governed and qualified by the whole context of the play. It does not directly challenge an examination into its truth because its relevance is pointed up and modified by the dramatic context.

Now, suppose that one could show that Keats's lines, *in quite the same way*, constitute a speech, a consciously riddling paradox, put in the mouth of a particular character, and modified by the total context of the poem. If we could demonstrate that the speech was "in character," was dramatically appropriate, was properly prepared for—then would not the lines have all the justification of "Ripeness is all"? In such case, should we not have waived the question of the scientific or philosophic truth of the lines in favor of the application of a principle curiously like that of dramatic propriety? I suggest that some such principle is the only one legitimately to be invoked in any case. Be this as it may, the "Ode on a Grecian Urn" provides us with as neat an instance as one could wish in order to test the implications of such a maneuver.

It has seemed best to be perfectly frank about procedure: the poem is to be read in order to see whether the last lines of the poem are not, after all, dramatically prepared for. Yet there are some claims to be made upon the reader too, claims which he, for his part, will have to be prepared to honor. He must not be allowed to dismiss the early characterizations of the urn as merely so much vaguely beautiful description. He must not be too much surprised if "mere decoration" turns out to be meaningful symbolism—or if ironies develop where he has been taught to expect only sensuous pictures. Most of all, if the teasing riddle spoken finally by the urn is not to strike him as a bewildering break in tone, he must not be too much disturbed to

have the element of paradox latent in the poem emphasized, even in those parts of the poem which have none of the energetic crackle of wit with which he usually associates paradox. This is surely not too much to ask of the reader—namely, to assume that Keats meant what he said and that he chose his words with care. After all, the poem begins on a note of paradox, though a mild one: for we ordinarily do not expect an urn to speak at all; and yet, Keats does more than this: he begins his poem by emphasizing the apparent contradiction.

The silence of the urn is stressed—it is a "bride of quietness"; it is a "foster-child of silence," but the urn is a "historian" too. Historians tell the truth, or are at least expected to tell the truth. What is a "Sylvan historian"? A historian who is like the forest rustic, a woodlander? Or, a historian who writes histories of the forest? Presumably, the urn is sylvan in both senses. True, the latter meaning is uppermost: the urn can "express/A flowery tale more sweetly than our rhyme," and what the urn goes on to express is a "leaf-fring'd legend" of "Tempe or the dales of Arcady." But the urn, like the "leaf-fring'd legend" which it tells, is covered with emblems of the fields and forests: "Overwrought,/ With forest branches and the trodden weed." When we consider the way in which the urn utters its history, the fact that it must be sylvan in both senses is seen as inevitable. Perhaps too the fact that it is a rural historian, a rustic, a peasant historian, qualifies in our minds the dignity and the "truth" of the histories which it recites. Its histories, Keats has already conceded, may be characterized as "tales"—not formal history at all.

The sylvan historian certainly supplies no names and dates—"What men or gods are these?" the poet asks. What it does give is action—of men *or* gods, of godlike men or of superhuman (though not daemonic) gods—action, which is not the less intense for all that the urn is cool marble. The words "mad" and "ecstasy" occur, but it is the quiet, rigid urn which gives the dynamic picture. And the paradox goes further: the scene is one of violent love-making, a Bacchanalian scene, but the urn itself is like a "still unravish'd bride," or like a child, a child "of silence and slow time." It is not merely like a child, but like a "foster-child." The exactness of the term can be defended. "Silence and slow time," it is suggested, are not the true parents, but foster-parents. They are too old, one feels, to have borne the child themselves. Moreover, they dote upon the "child" as grandparents do. The urn is fresh and unblemished; it is still young, for all its antiquity, and time which destroys so much has "fostered" it.

With Stanza II we move into the world presented by the urn, into an examination, not of the urn as a whole—as an entity with its own form—but of the details which overlay it. But as we enter that world, the paradox of silent speech is carried on, this time in terms of the objects portrayed on the vase.

The first lines of the stanza state a rather bold paradox—even the dulling effect of many readings has hardly blunted it. At least we can easily revive its sharpness. Attended to with care, it is a statement which is preposterous, and yet true—true on the same level on which the original metaphor of the speaking urn is true. The unheard music is sweeter than any audible music. The poet has rather cunningly enforced his conceit by using the phrase, "ye soft pipes." Actually, we might accept the poet's metaphor without being forced to accept the adjective "soft." The pipes might, although "unheard," be shrill, just as the action which is frozen in the figures on the urn can be violent and ecstatic as in Stanza I and slow and dignified as in Stanza IV (the procession to the sacrifice). Yet, by characterizing the pipes as "soft," the poet has provided a sort of realistic basis for his metaphor: the pipes, it is suggested, are playing very softly; if we listen carefully, we can hear them; their music is just below the threshold of normal sound.

This general paradox runs through the stanza: action goes on though the actors are motionless; the song will not cease; the lover cannot leave his song; the maiden, always to be kissed, never actually kissed, will remain changelessly beautiful. The maiden is, indeed, like the urn itself, a "still unravish'd bride of quietness"—not even ravished by a kiss; and it is implied, perhaps, that her changeless beauty, like that of the urn, springs from this fact.

The poet is obviously stressing the fresh, unwearied charm of the scene itself which can defy time and is deathless. But, at the same time, the poet is being perfectly fair to the terms of his metaphor. The beauty portrayed is deathless because it is lifeless. And it would be possible to shift the tone easily and ever so slightly by insisting more heavily on some of the phrasings so as to give them a darker implication. Thus, in the case of "thou canst not leave/ Thy song," one could interpret: the musician cannot leave the song even if he would: he is fettered to it, a prisoner. In the same way, one could enlarge on the hint that the lover is not wholly satisfied and content: "never canst thou kiss,/ . . . *yet, do not grieve.*" These items are mentioned here, not because one wishes to maintain that the poet is bitterly ironical, but because it is important for us to see that even here the paradox is being used fairly, particularly in view of the shift in tone which comes in the next stanza.

This third stanza represents, as various critics have pointed out, a recapitulation of earlier motifs. The boughs which cannot shed their leaves, the unwearied melodist, and the ever-ardent lover reappear. Indeed, I am not sure that this stanza can altogether be defended against the charge that it represents a falling-off from the delicate but firm precision of the earlier stanzas. There is a tendency to linger over the scene sentimentally: the repetition of the word "happy" is perhaps symptomatic of what is occurring. Here, if anywhere, in my opinion, is to be found the blemish on the ode—not in the last two lines. Yet, if we are to attempt a defense of the third stanza, we shall come nearest success by emphasizing the paradoxical implications of the repeated items; for whatever development there is in the stanza inheres in the increased stress on the paradoxical element. For example, the boughs cannot "bid the Spring adieu," a phrase which repeats "nor ever can those trees be bare," but the new line strengthens the implications of speaking: the falling leaves are a gesture, a word of farewell to the joy of spring. The melodist of Stanza II played sweeter music because unheard, but here, in the third stanza, it is implied that he does not tire of his song for the same reason that the lover does not tire of his love —neither song nor love is consummated. The songs are "for ever new" because they cannot be completed.

The paradox is carried further in the case of the lover whose love is "For ever warm and still to be enjoy'd." We are really dealing with an ambiguity here, for we can take "still to be enjoy'd" as an adjectival phrase on the same level as "warm"—that is, "still virginal and warm." But the tenor of the whole poem suggests that the warmth of the love depends upon the fact that it has not been enjoyed—that is, "warm and still to be enjoy'd" may mean also "warm *because* still to be enjoy'd."

But though the poet has developed and extended his metaphors furthest here in this third stanza, the ironic counterpoise is developed furthest too. The love which a line earlier was "warm" and "panting" becomes suddenly in the next line, "All breathing human passion far above." But if it is *above* all breathing passion, it is, after all, outside the realm of breathing passion, and therefore, not human passion at all.

(If one argues that we are to take "All breathing human passion" as qualified by "That leaves a heart high-sorrowful and cloy'd"—that is, if one argues that Keats is saying that the love depicted on the urn is above only that human passion which leaves one cloyed and not above human passion in general, he misses the point. For Keats in the "Ode" is stressing the ironic fact that all human passion *does* leave one cloyed; hence the superiority of art.)

The purpose in emphasizing the ironic undercurrent in the foregoing lines is not at all to disparage Keats—to point up implications of his poem of which he was himself unaware. Far from it: the poet knows precisely what he is doing. The point is to be made simply in order to make sure that we are completely aware of what he *is* doing. Garrod, sensing this ironic undercurrent, seems to interpret it as an element over which Keats was not able to exercise full control. He says: "Truth to his main theme [the fixity given by art to forms which in life are impermanent] has taken Keats farther than he meant to go. The pure and ideal art of this 'cold Pastoral,' this 'silent form,' *has* a cold silentness which in some degree saddens him. In the last lines of the fourth stanza, especially the last three lines . . . every reader is conscious, I should suppose, of an undertone of sadness, of disappointment." The undertone is there, but Keats has not been taken "farther than he meant to go." Keats's attitude, even in the early stanzas, is more complex than Garrod would allow: it is more complex and more ironic, and a recognition of this is important if we are to be able to relate the last stanza to the rest of the "Ode." Keats is perfectly aware that the frozen moment of loveliness is more dynamic than is the fluid world of reality *only* because it is frozen. The love depicted on the urn remains warm and young because it is not human flesh at all but cold, ancient marble.

With Stanza IV, we are still within the world depicted by the urn, but the scene presented in this stanza forms a contrast to the earlier scenes. It emphasizes, not individual aspiration and desire, but communal life. It constitutes another chapter in the history that the "Sylvan historian" has to tell. And again, names and dates have been omitted. We are not told to what god's altar the procession moves, nor the occasion of the sacrifice.

Moreover, the little town from which the celebrants come is unknown; and the poet rather goes out of his way to leave us the widest possible option in locating it. It may be a mountain town, or a river town, or a tiny seaport. Yet, of course, there is a sense in which the nature of the town—the essential character of the town—is actually suggested by the figured urn. But it is not given explicitly. The poet is willing to leave much to our imaginations; and yet the stanza in its organization of imagery and rhythm does describe the town clearly enough; it is small, it is quiet, its people are knit together as an organic whole, and on a "pious morn" such as this, its whole population has turned out to take part in the ritual.

The stanza has been justly admired. Its magic of effect defies reduction to any formula. Yet, without pretending to "account" for the effect in any mechanical fashion, one can point to some of the elements active in securing the effect: there is the suggestiveness of the word "green" in "green altar"—something natural, spontaneous, living; there is the suggestion that the little town is caught in a curve of the seashore, or nestled in a fold of the mountains—at any rate, is something secluded and something naturally related to its terrain; there is the effect of the phrase "peaceful citadel," a phrase which involves a clash between the ideas of war and peace and resolves it in the sense of stability and independence without imperialistic ambition—the sense of stable repose.

But to return to the larger pattern of the poem: Keats does something in this fourth stanza which is highly interesting in itself and thoroughly relevant to the sense in which the urn is a historian. One of the most moving passages in the poem is that in which the poet speculates on the strange emptiness of the little town which, of course, has not been pictured on the urn at all.

The little town which has been merely implied by the procession portrayed on the urn is endowed with a poignance beyond anything else in the poem. Its streets "for evermore/Will silent be," its desolation forever shrouded in a mystery. No one in the figured procession will ever be able to go back to the town to break the silence there, not even one to tell the stranger there why the town remains desolate.

If one attends closely to what Keats is doing here, he may easily come to feel that the poet is indulging himself in an ingenious fancy, an indulgence, however, which is gratuitous and finally silly; that is, the poet has created in his own imagination the town implied by the procession of worshipers, has given it a special character of desolation and loneliness, and then has gone on to treat it as if it were a real town to which a stranger might actually come and be puzzled by its emptiness. (I can see no other interpretation of the lines, "and not a soul to tell/Why thou art desolate can e'er return.") But, actually, of course, no one will ever discover the town except by the very same process by which Keats has discovered it: namely, through the figured urn, and then, of course, he will not need to ask why it is empty. One can well imagine what a typical eighteenth-century critic would have made of this flaw in logic.

It will not be too difficult, however, to show that Keats's extension of the fancy is not irrelevant to the poem as a whole. The "reality" of the little town has a very close relation to the urn's character as a historian. If the earlier stanzas have been concerned with such paradoxes as the ability of static carving to convey dynamic action, of the soundless pipes to play music sweeter than that of the heard melody, of the figured lover to have a love more warm and panting than that of breathing flesh and blood, so in the same way the town implied by the urn comes to have a richer and more important history than that of actual cities. Indeed, the imagined town is to the figured procession as the unheard melody is to the carved pipes of the unwearied melodist. And the poet, by pretending to take the town as real—so real that he can imagine the effect of its silent streets upon the stranger who chances to come into it— has suggested in the most powerful way possible its essential reality for him—and for us. It is a case of the doctor's taking his own medicine: the poet is prepared to stand by the illusion of his own making.

With Stanza V we move back out of the enchanted world portrayed by the urn to consider the urn itself once more as a whole, as an object. The shift in point of view is marked with the first line of the stanza by the apostrophe, "O Attic shape . . ." It is the urn itself as a formed thing, as an autonomous world, to which the poet addresses these last words. And the rich, almost breathing world which the poet has conjured up for us contracts and hardens into the decorated motifs on the urn itself: "with brede/Of marble men and maidens overwrought." The beings who have a life above life—"All breathing human passion far above"—are marble, after all.

This last is a matter which, of course, the poet has never denied. The recognition that the men and maidens are frozen, fixed, arrested, has, as we have already seen, run through the second, third, and fourth stanzas as an ironic undercurrent. The central paradox of the poem, thus, comes to conclusion in the phrase, "Cold Pastoral." The word "pastoral" suggests warmth, spontaneity, the natural and the informal as well as the idyllic, the simple, and the informally charming. What the urn tells is a "flowery tale," a "leaf-fring'd legend," but the "Sylvan historian" works in terms of marble. The urn itself is cold, and the life beyond life which it expresses is life which has been formed, arranged. The urn itself is a "silent form," and it speaks, not by means of statement, but by "teasing us out of thought." It is as enigmatic as eternity is, for, like eternity, its history is beyond time, outside time, and for this very reason bewilders our time-ridden minds: it teases us.

The marble men and maidens of the urn will not age as flesh-and-blood men and women will: "When old age shall this generation waste." (The word "generation," by the way, is very rich. It

means on one level "that which is generated"—that which springs from human loins—Adam's breed; and yet, so intimately is death wedded to men, the word "generation" itself has become, as here, a measure of time.) The marble men and women lie outside time. The urn which they adorn will remain. The "Sylvan historian" will recite its history to other generations.

What will it say to them? Presumably, what it says to the poet now: that "formed experience," imaginative insight, embodies the basic and fundamental perception of man and nature. The urn is beautiful, and yet its beauty is based—what else is the poem concerned with?—on an imaginative perception of essentials. Such a vision is beautiful but it is also true. The sylvan historian presents us with beautiful histories, but they are true histories, and it is a good historian.

Moreover, the "truth" which the sylvan historian gives is the only kind of truth which we are likely to get on this earth, and, furthermore, it is the only kind that we *have* to have. The names, dates, and special circumstances, the wealth of data—these the sylvan historian quietly ignores. But we shall never get all the facts anyway—there is no end to the accumulation of facts. Moreover, mere accumulations of facts—a point our own generation is only beginning to realize—are meaningless. The sylvan historian does better than that: it takes a few details and so orders them that we have not only beauty but insight into essential truth. Its "history," in short, is a history without footnotes. It has the validity of myth—not myth as a pretty but irrelevant make-belief, an idle fancy, but myth as a valid perception into reality.

So much for the "meaning" of the last lines of the "Ode." It is an interpretation which differs little from past interpretations. It is put forward here with no pretension to novelty. What is important is the fact that it can be derived from the context of the "Ode" itself.

And now, what of the objection that the final lines break the tone of the poem with a display of misplaced sententiousness? One can summarize the answer already implied thus: throughout the poem the poet has stressed the paradox of the speaking urn. First, the urn itself can tell a story, can give a history. Then, the various figures depicted upon the urn play music or speak or sing. If we have been alive to these items, we shall not, perhaps, be too much surprised to have the urn speak once more, not in the sense in which it tells a story—a metaphor which is rather easy to accept —but, to have it speak on a higher level, to have it make a commentary on its own nature. If the urn has been properly dramatized, if we have followed the development of the metaphors, if we have been alive to the paradoxes which work throughout the poem, perhaps then, we shall be prepared for the enigmatic, final paradox which the "silent form" utters. But in that case, we shall not feel that the generalization, unqualified and to be taken literally, is meant to march out of its context to compete with the scientific and philosophical generalizations which dominate our world.

"Beauty is truth, truth beauty" has precisely the same status, and the same justification as Shakespeare's "Ripeness is all." It is a speech "in character" and supported by a dramatic context.

To conclude thus may seem to weight the principle of dramatic propriety with more than it can bear. This would not be fair to the complexity of the problem of truth in art nor fair to Keats's little parable. Granted; and yet the principle of dramatic propriety may take us further than would first appear. Respect for it may at least insure our dealing with the problem of truth at the level on which it is really relevant to literature. If we can see that the assertions made in a poem are to be taken as part of an organic context, if we can resist the temptation to deal with them in isolation, then we may be willing to go on to deal with the world-view, or "philosophy," or "truth" of the *poem as a whole* in terms of its dramatic wholeness: that is, we shall not neglect the maturity of attitude, the dramatic tension, the emotional *and* intellectual coherence in favor of some statement of theme abstracted from it by paraphrase. Perhaps, best of all, we might learn to distrust our ability to represent any poem adequately by paraphrase. Such a distrust is healthy. Keats's sylvan historian, who is not above "teasing" us, exhibits such a distrust, and perhaps the point of what the sylvan historian "says" is to confirm us in our distrust.

YVOR WINTERS

(b. 1900)

Although Yvor Winters, poet and scholar-critic, is usually identified with the New Critics because of his practice of close textual analysis, he is distinguished from them by his emphasis on the rational nature of poetic language and structure and upon moral discipline as a function of literature. His volumes of critical essays, collected in *In Defense of Reason* (1947), include *Primitivism and Decadence: A Study of American Experimental Poetry* (1937), *Maule's Curse: Seven Studies in the History of American Obscurantism* (1938), and *The Anatomy of Nonsense*

(1943). Further sources of his criticism are *Edwin Arlington Robinson* (1946), a critical biography, and *The Function of Criticism, Problems and Exercises* (1957). The essay on Hawthorne from *Maule's Curse* reveals Winters' rationalism and aversion to romanticism, traits he shares with the earlier New Humanists.

Maule's Curse,
or Hawthorne and the Problem of Allegory (1938)

"At the moment of execution—with the halter about his neck and while Colonel Pyncheon sat on horseback, grimly gazing at the scene— Maule had addressed him from the scaffold, and uttered a prophecy, of which history as well as fireside tradition, has preserved the very words. 'God,' said the dying man, pointing his finger, with a ghastly look, at the undismayed countenance of his enemy, 'God will give him blood to drink!'"
—The House of the Seven Gables

Of Hawthorne's three most important long works—*The Scarlet Letter, The House of the Seven Gables,* and *The Marble Faun*—the first is pure allegory, and the other two are impure novels, or novels with unassimilated allegorical elements. The first is fautless, in scheme and in detail; it is one of the chief masterpieces of English prose. The second and third are interesting, the third in particular, but both are failures, and neither would suffice to give the author a very high place in the history of prose fiction. Hawthorne's sketches and short stories, at best, are slight performances; either they lack meaning, as in the case of *Mr. Higginbotham's Catastrophe*, or they lack reality of embodiment, as in the case of *The Birthmark*, or, having a measure of both, as does *The Minister's Black Veil*, they yet seem incapable of justifying the intensity of the method, their very brevity and attendant simplification, perhaps, working against them; the best of them, probably, is *Young Goodman Brown*. In his later romances, *Septimius Felton, Dr. Grimshaw's Secret, The Ancestral Footstep,* and *The Dolliver Romance,* and in much of *The Blithedale Romance* as well, Hawthorne

struggles unsuccessfully with the problem of allegory, but he is still obsessed with it.

Hawthorne is, then, essentially an allegorist; had he followed the advice of Poe and other well-wishers, contemporary with himself and posthumous, and thrown his allegorizing out the window, it is certain that nothing essential to his genius would have remained. He appears to have had none of the personal qualifications of a novelist, for one thing: the sombre youth who lived in solitude and in contemplation in Salem, for a dozen years or more, before succumbing to the charms and propinquity of Miss Sophia Peabody and making the spasmodic and only moderately successful efforts to accustom himself to daylight which were to vex the remainder of his life, was one far more likely to concern himself with the theory of mankind than with the chaos, trivial, brutal, and exhausting, of the actuality. Furthermore, as we shall see more fully, the Puritan view of life was allegorical, and the allegorical vision seems to have been strongly impressed upon the New England literary mind. It is fairly obvious in much of the poetry of Emerson, Emily Dickinson, Bryant, Holmes, and even Very—Whittier, a Quaker and a peasant, alone of the more interesting poets escaping; Melville, relatively an outsider, shows the impact of New England upon his own genius as much through his use of allegory as through his use of New England character; and the only important novelist purely a New Englander, aside from Hawthorne, that is, O. W. Holmes, was primarily concerned with the Puritan tendency to allegory, as its one considerable satirist, yet was himself more or less addicted to it.

These matters are speculative. That

New England predisposed Hawthorne to allegory cannot be shown; yet the disposition in both is obvious. And it can easily be shown that New England provided the perfect material for one great allegory, and that, in all likelihood, she was largely to blame for the later failures.

The Puritan theology rested primarily upon the doctrine of predestination and the inefficaciousness of good works; it separated men sharply and certainly into two groups, the saved and the damned, and, technically, at least, was not concerned with any subtler shadings. This in itself represents a long step toward the allegorization of experience, for a very broad abstraction is substituted for the patient study of the minutiae of moral behavior long encouraged by Catholic tradition. Another step was necessary, however, and this step was taken in Massachusetts almost at the beginning of the settlement, and in the expulsion of Anne Hutchinson became the basis of governmental action: whereas the wholly Calvinistic Puritan denied the value of the evidence of character and behavior as signs of salvation, and so precluded the possibility of their becoming allegorical symbols—for the orthodox Calvinist, such as Mrs. Hutchinson would appear to have been, trusted to no witness save that of the Inner Light—it became customary in Massachusetts to regard as evidence of salvation the decision of the individual to enter the church and lead a moral life. "The Puritans," says Parkes, "were plain blunt men with little taste for mysticism and no talent for speculation. A new conception was formulated by English theologians, of whom William Ames was the most influential. The sign of election was not an inner assurance; it was a sober decision to trust in Christ and obey God's law. Those who made this sober decision might feel reasonably confident that they had received God's grace; but the surest proof of it was its fruit in conduct; complete assurance was impossible. It was assumed that all was the work of grace; it was God, without human coöperation, who caused the sober decision to be made. But in actual practice this doctrine had the effect of unduly magnifying man's ability to save himself, as much as Calvin's conception had unduly minimized it; conversion was merely a choice to obey a certain code of rules, and did not imply any emotional change, any love for God, or for holiness, or any genuine religious experience; religion in other words was reduced to mere morality."[1] Objective evidence thus took the place of inner assurance, and the behavior of the individual took on symbolic value. That is, any sin was evidence of damnation; or, in other words, any sin represented all sin. When Hester Prynne committed adultery, she committed an act as purely representative of complete corruption as the act of Faustus in signing a contract with Satan. This view of the matter is certainly not Catholic and is little short of appalling; it derives from the fact, that although, as Parkes states in the passage just quoted, there occurred an exaggeration of the will in the matter of practical existence, this same will was still denied in the matter of doctrine, for according to doctrine that which man willed had been previously willed by God.

The belief that the judgment of a man is predestined by God, and the corollary that the judgment of a good man, since all men are either good or bad, purely and simply, is the judgment of God, may lead in the natural course of events to extraordinary drama; and this the more readily if the actors in the drama are isolated from the rest of the world and believe that the drama in which they take part is of cosmic importance and central in human destiny. Andrews writes: "The belief that God had selected New England as the chosen land was profoundly held by the Puritans who went there. Winthrop himself in 1640 wrote to Lord Saye and Sele of 'this good land which God hath found and given to his people,' adding that 'God had chosen this country to plant his people in.' Cotton in his sermon, *God's Prom-*

[1] *The Puritan Heresy*, by H. B. Parkes, The Hound and Horn, V-2, Jan.-March 1932, pages 173-4. See also *The Pragmatic Test* by H. B. Parkes, The Colt Press, San Francisco.

ise to His Plantation (London, 1634), devotes much space to the same idea—'This place is appointed me of God.' " [2] And Schneider writes on the same subject: "No one can live long in a Holy Commonwealth without becoming sensitive, irritable, losing his sense of values and ultimately his balance. All acts are acts either of God or of the devil; all issues are matters of religious faith; and all conflicts are holy wars. No matter how trivial an opinion might appear from a secular point of view, it became vital when promulgated as a theological dogma; no matter how harmless a fool might be, he was intolerable if he did not fit into the Covenant of Grace; no matter how slight an offense might be, it was a sin against Almighty God and hence infinite. Differences of opinion became differences of faith. Critics became blasphemers, and innovators, heretics."[3] And again: ". . . the mind of the Puritan was singularly unified and his imagination thoroughly moralized. The clergy were, of course, the professional moral scientists, but the laymen were no less dominated by such mental habits. The common man and illiterate shared with the expert this interest in divining God's purposes in the course of events. No event was merely natural; it was an act of God and was hence charged with that 'numinous' quality which gives birth to both prophetic insight and mystic illumination."[4] And again: "Nature was instructive to them only in so far as it suggested the hidden mysterious operations of designing agents. God and devil were both active, scheming, hidden powers, each pursuing his own ends by various ministrations, and natural events were therefore to be understood only in so far as they showed evidence of some divine or diabolical plot."[5]

Now according to the doctrine of predestination, if we interpret it reasonably, Hester merely gave evidence, in committing adultery, that she had always been one of the damned. This point of view, if really understood, could never have led to the chain of events which Hawthorne described in *The Scarlet Letter;* neither could it have led to the events of the actual history of New England. It is at this point that we must consider that fluid element, history, in connection with dogma, for Hester, like the witches who so occupied the Mathers, was treated as if she had wilfully abandoned the ways of God for the ways of Satan. This final illogicality introduces the element of drama into the allegory of *The Scarlet Letter* and into the allegorical morality of the Puritans.

The English Puritans who settled Massachusetts were socially the product of centuries of the type of ethical discipline fostered by the Catholic and Anglo-Catholic Churches. They may have denied the freedom of the will and the efficaciousness of good works by lip, but by habit, and without really grasping the fact, they believed in them and acted upon them. Edwards exhorts sinners to repent while preaching the doctrine of the inability to repent; the Mathers wrestled with demons physically and in broad daylight, and quite obviously felt virtuous for having done so; in fact, to such a pass did Puritanism come, that Melville's Ahab, who wilfully embarks upon the Sea of Unpredictability in order to overtake and slay the Spirit of Evil—an effort in which he is predestined and at the end of which he is predestined to destruction—appears to us merely the heroic projection of a common Puritan type. The Puritan may be said to have conceived the Manicheistic struggle between Absolute Good and Absolute Evil, which he derived through the processes of simplification and misunderstanding which have already been enumerated, as a kind of preordained or mechanical, yet also holy combat, in which his own part was a part at once intense and holy and yet immutably regulated.

There were at least two motives in the new environment which tended to intensify the effect of habit in this con-

[2] *The Colonial Period of American History,* by Charles M. Andrews; Yale University Press, 1934. Vol. I, page 386, note 2.
[3] *The Puritan Mind,* by H. W. Schneider; Henry Holt, 1930, pages 51-2.
[4] *Ibid.,* page 48.
[5] *Ibid.,* pages 42-3.

nection: one was the inevitable impulse given to the will by the exaltation attendant upon a new religious movement; the other was the impulse given by the supremely difficult physical surroundings in which the new colonies found themselves. Foster writes on these points: "The first Puritans, sure in their own hearts that they were the elect of God, found the doctrine necessary to sustain them in the tremendous struggle through which they passed. . . . Hence the doctrine nerved to greater activity; and it produced a similar effect during the first period of the promulgation of Calvinism, among every nation which accepted the system."[6] The force of the will was strengthened at the beginning, then, at the same time that its existence was denied and that reliance upon its manner of functioning (that is, upon good works) was, from a doctrinal standpoint, regarded as sin. The will, highly stimulated, but no longer studied and guided by the flexible and sensitive ethical scholarship of the Roman tradition, might easily result in dangerous action.

Andrews speaks of this subject as follows: "The dynamic agency . . . the driving force which overrode all opposition, legal and otherwise, was the profound conviction of the Puritan leaders that they were doing the Lord's work. They looked upon themselves as instruments in the divine hand for the carrying out of a great religious mission, the object of which was the rebuilding of God's church in a land—the undefiled land of America—divinely set apart as the scene of a holy experiment that should renovate the church at large, everywhere corrupt and falling into ruins. This new and purified community was to be the home of a saving remnant delivered from the wrath to come and was to serve as an example to the mother church of a regenerated form of faith and worship. It was also to become a proselyting center for the conversion of the heathen and the extension of the true gospel among those who

knew it not. In the fulfillment of this mission the Puritans counted obstacles, moral and physical, of no moment. Theirs was a religious duty to frustrate their enemies, to eradicate all inimical opinions, religious and political, and to extend the field of their influence as widely as possible. Once they had determined on their rules of polity and conduct, as laid down in the Bible and interpreted by the clergy, they had no doubts of the justness and rightness of their course. The means employed might savor of harshness and inequity, but at all costs and under all circumstances, error, sin, and idolatry, in whatever form appearing and as determined by themselves, must be destroyed. In the process, as events were to prove, a great many very human motives played an important part in interpreting the law of God, and personal likes and dislikes, hypocrisy, prejudice, and passion got badly mixed with the higher and more spiritual impulses that were actively at work purging the church of its errors."[7]

Over a long period, however, the doctrine of predestination would naturally lead to religious apathy, for it offered no explicit motive to action; and this is precisely that to which it led, for after the Great Awakening of the middle of the eighteenth century, itself a reaction to previous decay in the church, the church lost power rapidly, and by the opening of the nineteenth century was succumbing on every hand to Unitarianism, a mildly moralistic creed, in which the element of supernaturalism was minimized, and which, in turn, yielded rapidly among the relatively intellectual classes to Romantic ethical theory, especially as propounded by the Transcendentalists. "It has never been a good way to induce men to repent," says Foster, "to tell them that they cannot."[8] Or at least the method has never been highly successful except when employed by a rhetorician of the power of Edwards, or by an orator of the effectiveness of Whitefield; and the effect can scarcely be expected long to outlive the immedi-

---

[6] *A Genetic History of the New England Theology*, by Frank Hugh Foster; University of Chicago Press, 1907; page 29.

[7] Charles M. Andrews, *op. cit.*, Vol. I, pages 430-1.
[8] Frank Hugh Foster, *op. cit.*, page 29.

ate presence of the speaker. The Unitarians, in depriving the ethical life of the more impressive aspects of its supernatural sanction, and in offering nothing to take the place of that sanction, all but extinguished intensity of moral conviction, although their own conviction—we may see it portrayed, for example, in *The Europeans*, by Henry James, and exemplified in the lucid and classical prose of W. E. Channing—was a conviction, at least for a period, of the greatest firmness and dignity. Emerson eliminated the need of moral conviction and of moral understanding alike, by promulgating the allied doctrines of equivalence and of inevitable virtue. In an Emersonian universe there is equally no need and no possibility of judgment; it is a universe of amiable but of perfectly unconscious imbeciles; it is likewise a universe in which the art of the fictionist—or for that matter, any other art—can scarcely be expected to flourish. A fictionist who has been in any considerable measure affected by Emersonian or allied concepts, or even who is the product of the historical sequence which gave rise to Emerson, is likely to find himself gravely confused and may even find himself paralyzed; and we have only to read such a document, to cite a single example, as *The New Adam and Eve*, to realize that Hawthorne's own moral ideas, in spite of his intense but conflicting moral sentiments, and in spite of his professed dislike for Emerson's philosophy, were much closer to the ideas of Emerson than to those of Edwards.

Now in examining Hawthorne, we are concerned with two historical centers: that of the first generation of Puritans in New England, in which occurs the action of *The Scarlet Letter*; and that of the post-Unitarian and Romantic intellectuals, in which was passed the life of Hawthorne.

Hawthorne, by nature an allegorist, and a man with a strong moral instinct regardless of the condition of his ideas, found in the early history of his own people and region the perfect material for a masterpiece. By selecting sexual sin as the type of all sin, he was true alike to the exigencies of drama and of history. In the setting which he chose, allegory was realism, the idea was life itself; and his prose, always remarkable for its polish and flexibility, and stripped, for once, of all superfluity, was reduced to the living idea; it intensified pure exposition to a quality comparable in its way to that of great poetry.

The compactness and complexity of the allegory will escape all save the most watchful readers. Let us consider the following passage as a representative example. Hester has learned that the magistrates and clergy are considering whether or not she ought to be separated from her child, and she waits upon Governor Bellingham in order to plead with him:

"On the wall hung a row of portraits, representing the forefathers of the Bellingham lineage, some with armor on their breasts, and others with stately ruffs and robes of peace. All were characterized by the sternness and severity which old portraits so invariably put on; as if they were the ghosts, rather than the pictures, of departed worthies, and were gazing with harsh and intolerant criticism at the pursuits and enjoyments of living men.

"At about the center of the oaken panels, that lined the hall, was suspended a suit of mail, not, like the pictures, an ancestral relic, but of the most modern date; for it had been manufactured by a skillful armorer in London, the same year in which Governor Bellingham came over to New England. There was a steel head-piece, a cuirass, a gorget, and greaves, with a pair of gauntlets and a sword hanging beneath; all, especially the helmet and breastplate, so highly burnished as to glow with white radiance, and scatter an illumination everywhere about the floor. This bright panoply was not meant for mere idle show, but had been worn by the Governor on many a solemn muster and training field, and had glittered, moreover, at the head of a regiment in the Pequot war. For, though bred a lawyer, and accustomed to speak of Bacon, Coke, Noye, and Finch as his professional associates, the exigencies of this new country had transformed Governor Bellingham into a soldier as well as a statesman and ruler.

"Little Pearl—who was as greatly pleased with the gleaming armor as she had been with the glittering frontispiece of the house—spent some time looking into the polished mirror of the breast-plate.

" 'Mother,' cried she, 'I see you here. Look! Look!'

"Hester looked, by way of humoring the child; and she saw that, owing to the peculiar effect of the convex mirror, the scarlet letter was represented in gigantic and exaggerated proportions, so as to be greatly the most prominent feature of her appearance. In truth, she seemed absolutely hidden behind it. Pearl pointed upward, also, at a similar picture in the head-piece; smiling at her mother with the elfish intelligence that was so familiar an expression on her small physiognomy. That look of naughty merriment was likewise reflected in the mirror, with so much breadth and intensity of effect, that it made Hester Prynne feel as if it could not be the image of her own child, but of an imp who was seeking to mold itself into Pearl's shape."

The portraits are obviously intended as an apology for the static portraits in the book, as an illustration of the principle of simplification by distance and by generalization; the new armor, on the other hand, is the new faith which brought the Puritans to New England, and which not only shone with piety— "especially the helmet and breast-plate," the covering of the head and heart—but supported them in their practical struggles with physical adversaries, and which in addition altered their view of the life about them to dogmatic essentials, so that Hester was obliterated behind the fact of her sin, and Pearl transformed in view of her origin. Governor Bellingham, in his combination of legal training with military prowess, is representative of his fellow colonists, who displayed in a remarkable degree a capacity to act with great strength and with absolutely sim-

ple directness upon principles so generalized as scarcely to be applicable to any particular moral problem, which mastered moral difficulties not by understanding them, but by crushing them out.

Historically and relatively considered, Richard Bellingham might conceivably have been spared this function in the story, for of his group he was one of the two or three most humane and liberal; but the qualities represented were the qualities of the group of which he was a leader, and were extremely evident in most of the actions of the colony. Perhaps the best—or in another sense, the worst—embodiment of these qualities is to be found in John Endecott, of whom Andrews gives the following characterization: "Endecott had few lovable qualities. He was stern, unyielding, and on some subjects a zealot. Johnson apostrophizes him as 'strong, valiant John,' whom Christ had called to be his soldier, but the Old Planters, most if not all of whom were Anglicans and demanded service according to the Book of Common Prayer, deemed themselves slaves and took in very bad part his determination to suppress the Church of England in the colony. They preferred Roger Conant, who though a less forcible man was one much easier to get along with. Endecott's later career discloses his attitude toward those who differed with him—the heathen Indian, the Quaker, the prisoner before him for judgment, and the Brownes and other upholders of the Anglican service who were disaffected with the Puritan government. It also shows his dislike of forms and devices that offended him—the Book of Common Prayer, the cross of St. George, and the Maypole. He was hard, intolerant, and at times cruel. Even the Massachusetts government caused him 'to be sadly admonished for his offense' in mutilating the flag at Salem in 1635, charging him with 'rashness, uncharitableness, indiscretion, and exceeding the limits of his calling'; and again in the same year 'committed' him for losing his temper. Endecott once apologized to Winthrop for striking 'goodman Dexter,' acknowledging that he was rash, but saying that Dexter's conduct 'would have provoked a very patient man.' The best that can be said of him has been said by Chapple ('The Public Service of John Endecott,' Historical Collections, Essex Institute), an essay in the best Palfrey manner. It is odd that Endecott should have chosen for his seal a skull and cross-bones."[9] It is interesting to observe in such a passage, as in many others, that the Puritans cannot be discussed, nor can they discuss each other, without the language employed exceeding the limits proper to predestinarians and invoking the traditional morality of the older churches; yet the attempt to ignore this traditional morality as far as might be, and, in the matter of formal doctrine, to repudiate it, unquestionably had much to do with the formation of such characters as Professor Andrews here describes and as Hawthorne in the last passage quoted from him symbolizes. The imperceptive, unwavering brutality of many of the actions committed in the name of piety in the Massachusetts colonies more than justified the curse and prophecy uttered by Matthew Maule, that God would give these Puritans blood to drink; in the name of God, they had violently cut themselves off from human nature; in the end, that is in Hawthorne's generation and in the generation following, more than one of them drank his own heart's blood, as Hawthorne himself must have done in his ultimate and frustrated solitude, and more than one of them shed it.

It is noteworthy that in this passage from *The Scarlet Letter* Hawthorne turns his instrument of allegory, the gift of the Puritans, against the Puritans themselves, in order to indicate the limits of their intelligence; it is noteworthy also that this act of criticism, though both clear and sound, is negative, that he nowhere except in the very general notion of regeneration through repentance establishes the nature of the intelligence which might exceed the intelligence of the Puritans, but rather hints

[9] Charles M. Andrews, *op. cit.*, Vol. I, page 361, note 3.

at the ideal existence of a richer and more detailed understanding than the Puritan scheme of life is able to contain. The strength of *The Scarlet Letter* is in part safe-guarded by the refusal to explore this understanding; the man who was able in the same lifetime to write *The New Adam and Eve*, to conceive the art-colony described in *The Marble Faun*, and to be shocked at the nude statues of antiquity, was scarcely the man to cast a clear and steady light upon the finer details of the soul.

The conception of the book in general is as cleanly allegorical as is the conception of the passage quoted. Hester represents the repentant sinner, Dimmesdale the half-repentant sinner, and Chillingworth the unrepentant sinner. The fact that Chillingworth's sin is the passion for revenge is significant only to the extent that this is perhaps the one passion which most completely isolates man from normal human sympathies and which therefore is most properly used to represent an unregenerate condition.

The method of allegorization is that of the Puritans themselves; the substance of the allegory remained in a crude form a part of their practical Christianity in spite of their Calvinism, just as it remained in their non-theological linguistic forms, just as we can see it in the language of the best poems of so purely and mystically Calvinistic a writer as Jones Very, a living language related to a living experience, but overflowing the limits of Calvinistic dogma; Hawthorne's point of view was naturally more enlightened than that of the Puritans themselves, yet it was insufficiently so to enable him to recover the traditional Christian ethics except in the most general terms and by way of historical sympathy, for had a more complete recovery been possible, he would not have been so narrowly bound to the method of allegory and the frustration of the later romances would scarcely have been so complete.

Once Hawthorne had reduced the problem of sin to terms as general as these, and had brought his allegory to perfect literary form, he had, properly speaking, dealt with sin once and for all; there was nothing further to be said about it. It would not serve to write another allegory with a new set of characters and a different sin as the motive; for the particular sin is not particular in function, but is merely representative of sin in general, as the characters, whatever their names and conditions may be, are merely representative of the major stages of sin—there is no escape from the generality so long as one adheres to the method. There was nothing further, then, to be done in this direction, save the composition of a few footnotes to the subject in the form of sketches.

The only alternative remaining was to move away from the allegorical extreme of narrative toward the specific, that is, toward the art of the novelist. The attempt was made, but fell short of success. In *The House of the Seven Gables* and in *The Marble Faun* alike the moral understanding of the action —and there is a serious attempt at such understanding, at least in *The Marble Faun*—is corrupted by a provincial sentimentalism ethically far inferior to the Manicheism of the Puritans, which was plain and comprehensive, however brutal. And Hawthorne had small gift for the creation of human beings, a defect allied to his other defects and virtues: even the figures in *The Scarlet Letter* are unsatisfactory if one comes to the book expecting to find a novel, for they draw their life not from simple and familiar human characteristics, as do the figures of Henry James, but from the precision and intensity with which they render their respective ideas; the very development of the story is neither narrative nor dramatic, but expository. When, as in *The Marble Faun* or *The House of the Seven Gables*, there is no idea governing the human figure, or when the idea is an incomplete or unsatisfactory equivalent of the figure, the figure is likely to be a disappointing spectacle, for he is seldom if ever a convincing human being and is likely to verge on the ludicrous. Hawthorne had not the rich and profound awareness of immediacy which might have saved a

writer such as Melville in a similar predicament.

His effort to master the novelist's procedure, however, was not sustained, for his heart was not in it. In *The Blithedale Romance*, he began as a novelist, but lost himself toward the close in an unsuccessful effort to achieve allegory; the four unfinished romances represent similar efforts throughout.

His procedure in the last works was startlingly simple; so much so, that no one whom I can recollect has run the risk of defining it.

In *The Scarlet Letter* there occurs a formula which one might name the formula of alternative possibilities. In the ninth chapter, for example, there occurs the following passage: "The people, in the case of which we speak, could justify its prejudice against Roger Chillingworth by no fact or argument worthy of serious refutation. There was an aged handicraftsman, it is true, who had been a citizen of London at the period of Sir Thomas Overbury's murder, now some thirty years agone; he testified to having seen the physician, under some other name, which the narrator of the story had now forgotten, in company with Dr. Forman, the famous old conjuror, who was implicated in the affair of Overbury. Two or three individuals hinted, that the man of skill, during his Indian captivity, had enlarged his medical attainments by joining in the incantations of the savage priests; who were universally acknowledged to be powerful enchanters, often performing seemingly miraculous cures by their skill in the black art. A large number—many of them were persons of such sober sense and practical observation that their opinions would have been valuable in other matters—affirmed that Roger Chillingworth's aspect had undergone a remarkable change while he had dwelt in the town, and especially since his abode with Dimmesdale. At first, his expression had been calm, meditative, scholar-like. Now, there was something ugly and evil in his face, which they had not previously noticed, and which grew still more obvious to sight the oftener they looked upon him. According to the vulgar idea, the fire in his laboratory had been brought from the lower regions, and was fed with infernal fuel; and so, as might be expected, his visage was getting sooty with smoke."

In such a passage as this, the idea conveyed is clear enough, but the embodiment of the idea appears farfetched, and Hawthorne offers it whimsically and apologetically, professing to let you take it or leave it. Another example occurs in the eighteenth chapter; Dimmesdale and Hester are sitting in the forest, planning the flight which ultimately is never to take place, and Pearl, the symbolic offspring of the untamed elements of human nature, and hence akin to the forest, which, in the Puritan mind, was ruled by Satan in person, plays apart: "A fox, startled from his sleep by her light footstep on the leaves, looked inquisitively at Pearl, as doubting whether it were better to steal off or renew his nap on the same spot. A wolf, it is said—but here the tale has surely lapsed into the improbable—came up and smelt of Pearl's robe, and offered his savage head to be patted by her hand. The truth seems to be, however, that the mother-forest, and these wild things which it nourished, all recognized a kindred wildness in the human child." Similarly, in *The Marble Faun*, one never learns whether Donatello had or had not the pointed ears which serve throughout the book as the physical symbol of his moral nature; the book ends with the question being put to Kenyon, who has had opportunities to observe, and with his refusing to reply.

This device, though it becomes a minor cause of irritation through constant recurrence, is relatively harmless, and at times is even used with good effect. If we reverse the formula, however, so as to make the physical representation perfectly clear but the meaning uncertain, we have a very serious situation; and this is precisely what occurs, in some measure toward the close of *The Blithedale Romance*, and without mitigation throughout the four unfinished romances. We have in the last all of the machinery

and all of the mannerisms of the allegorist, but we cannot discover the substance of his communication, nor is he himself aware of it so far as we can judge. We have the symbolic footprint, the symbolic spider, the symbolic elixirs and poisons, but we have not that of which they are symbolic; we have the hushed, the tense and confidential manner, on the part of the narrator, of one who imparts a grave secret, but the words are inaudible. Yet we have not, on the other hand, anything approaching realistic fiction, for the events are improbable or even impossible, and the characters lack all reality. The technique neither of the novelist nor of the allegorist was available to Hawthorne when he approached the conditions of his own experience: he had looked for signals in nature so long and so intently, and his ancestors before him had done so for so many generations, that, like a man hypnotized, or like a man corroded with madness, he saw them; but he no longer had any way of determining their significance, and he had small talent for rendering their physical presence with intensity.

Percy Boynton,[10] in quoting the following passages from *Septimius Felton*, refers to it as a self-portrait: "As for Septimius, let him alone a moment or two, and then they would see him, with his head bent down, brooding, brooding, his eyes fixed on some chip, some stone, some common plant, any commonest thing, as if it were the clew and index to some mystery; and when, by chance startled out of these meditations, he lifted his eyes, there would be a kind of perplexity, a dissatisfied, foiled look in them, as if of his speculations he found no end."

It is in this generation and the next that we see most clearly and bitterly the realization of Maule's prophecy. These men were cut off from their heritage, from their source of significance, and were abnormally sensitive to the influence of European Romanticism. In Em-

[10] *Literature and American Life*, by Percy H. Boynton; Ginn and Co., 1936; page 518.

erson[11] the terms of New England mysticism and of Romantic amoralism were fused and confused so inextricably that we have not yet worked ourselves free of them. In Poe, a man born without a background, New England or any other, Romantic doctrine was introduced directly, in a form free of theological terminology, but in a form none the less which would tend in the long run to support the influence of Emerson. In Melville, the greatest man of his era and of his nation, we find a writer superior at certain points in his career—in books such as *Moby Dick* and *Benito Cereno*, for example—to the confusion and apparently understanding it; at other points—in books like *Mardi* and *Pierre*, —succumbing to the confusion; at all points in his career made to suffer for the confusion of contemporary literary taste; and at the end, settling himself in silence, a figure more difficult to face than the later Hawthorne—more difficult, because more conscious, more controlled, and more nearly indifferent.

In Henry Adams we see the curse at work most clearly: intellectual but inconsecutive, unable to justify any principle of action, yet with a character of the highest, a character which demanded not only just action but its justification, he was damned to a kind of restless torment; in which, though an historian of great learning and of high academic distinction, he transformed the Middle Ages by a process of subtle falsification, into a symbol of his own latter-day New England longing; in which, though a stylist of great power and precision, he propounded the aesthetic theory that modern art must be confused to express confusion;[12] in which, though a philosopher of a sort, he created one of the most unphilosophical theories of history imaginable, as a poetic symbol of his own despair. In the suicide of Henry Adams' wife it is conceivable that we see the logical outcome of his own dilemma, an outcome in his own case prevented by

the inheritance of character, which, like the inheritance of confusion, was bequeathed him by early New England.[13]

In *The Scarlet Letter*, then, Hawthorne composed a great allegory; or, if we look first at the allegorical view of life upon which early Puritan society was based, we might almost say that he composed a great historical novel. History, which by placing him in an anti-intellectual age had cut him off from the ideas which might have enabled him to deal with his own period, in part made up for the injustice by facilitating his entrance, for a brief time, into an age more congenial to his nature. Had he possessed the capacity for criticizing and organizing conceptions as well as for dramatizing them, he might have risen superior to his disadvantages, but like many other men of major genius he lacked this capacity. In turning his back upon the excessively simplified conceptions of his Puritan ancestors, he abandoned the only orderly concepts, whatever their limitations, to which he had access, and in his last work he is restless and dissatisfied. The four last romances are unfinished, and in each successive one he sought to incorporate and perfect elements from those preceding; the last, *The Dolliver Romance*, which he had sought to make the best, had he lived, is a mere fragment, but on the face of it is the most preposterous of all. His dilemma, the choice between abstractions inadequate or irrelevant to experience on the one hand, and experience on the other as far as practicable unilluminated by understanding, is tragically characteristic of the history of this country and of its literature; only a few scattered individuals, at the cost of inordinate labor, and often impermanently, have achieved the permeation of human experience by a consistent moral understanding which results in wisdom and in great art. If art is to be measured by the greatness of the difficulties overcome—and the measure is not wholly unreasonable, for there can

[11] This subject is fully discussed by H. B. Parkes, The Hound and Horn, V-4, July-Sept. 1932, pages 581-601, and *The Pragmatic Test*.

[12] See the last three or four pages of *Mount Saint-Michel and Chartres*.

[13] This idea is very ably defended by Katherine Simonds, the New England Quarterly, December, 1936.

scarcely be virtue without a comprehension of sin, and the wider and more careful the comprehension the richer the virtue—then these few writers are very great indeed. Hawthorne, when he reversed his formula of alternative possibilities, and sought to grope his way blindly to significance, made the choice of the later Romantics; and his groping was met wherever he moved by the smooth and impassive surface of the intense inane.

ROY HARVEY PEARCE

(b. 1919)

A scholar-critic with special interests in literary theory and American literature and culture, Roy Harvey Pearce is a proponent of a return to what he calls "historicism" in literary studies. But Pearce's historicism, a concept that he offers as an alternative to certain more narrowly exclusive modern approaches to literature, is very different from that of Arthur O. Lovejoy, one of his acknowledged mentors. Pearce sees "history" as that self-image which is expressed for a culture by its artists, a self-image made up not only of "facts," but also of the patterns of aspiration and conflict that underlie the culture. He is thus, unlike Lovejoy, interested primarily in the major writer rather than the minor or representative writer because the major writer discovers, even creates, the shape of history as well as confirms it. The utility of this sort of historical awareness is based, for Pearce, on a creative principle of evolutionary humanism—the principle that man must know what he is in order to know what he might become. Besides editing several anthologies and contributing articles to critical and scholarly journals, Pearce has published *The Savages of America, a Study of the Indian and the Idea of Civilization* (1953) and *The Continuity of American Poetry* (1961).

Toward an American Epic (1959)

I

One of the most arresting yet practically unnoticed phenomena in the history of our poetry is the regularity with which there occurs an attempt to write nothing less than an American epic. The regularity is of an intensity such as to indicate a virtual compulsion to make such a poem—which is to say, to create such a form. Indeed, one can now say that this phenomenon is of a much more vital significance for the history of our national imagination than is that com-

Reprinted by permission from *The Hudson Review*, Vol. XII, No. 3, Autumn 1959. Copyright 1959 by The Hudson Review, Inc.

parable phenomenon, the urge to create the great American novel. This is so because in order to do it right, to invent an autochthonous American epic, or—to say the same thing—a genuinely American analogue of the traditional epic, the poet would have to break radically with the very tradition which he would be trying to carry on and reinvigorate. He would indeed have, in Pound's phrase, to make it new. Confronted with a society which supplied him with no authentically American epic material, he would yet have to find that material, to transubstantiate what his society gave him so that he could transform it. And this, one concludes, is exactly what has happened—or, perhaps to put it more accurately—what has been intended to happen.

There is no point, at this stage, in trying to recite the history of the American epic; nor of trying to indicate precisely the limits of its achievement. In the present state of our knowledge, it would seem unlikely that such a history could be written, or if such evaluations could be made. Nonetheless, it is possible to establish the dialectic of that history and to begin to assess its signficance for the more general history of our aspiration toward not only an American epic but an American poetry. I mean to make such an attempt here—to offer what amounts to a theory of the American epic and a summation of the sort of poetics it has striven so hard, so desperately, to put into action. I shall take as my exemplars three poems—*The Columbiad, Song of Myself,* and the *Cantos.*

These are heroic poems, but of a curious sort. For, instead of celebrating, affirming, and memorializing a hero, as the poet of traditional epic had done, the poet of the American epic (or, quite strictly speaking, proto-epic) tried and continues to try to create a hero. And his means to that creation was, and remains, the very act of the poem itself. Barlow's *Columbiad* (1807), so dreary in what it is and so exciting in what it is not, is our first instance—and almost a negative one. *Almost.* For if Barlow could not write an adequate American epic, he could at least desiderate one—indeed, desiderate (and how shocked he would have been to learn this!) poems like *Song of Myself* and the *Cantos.*

As we all know, *The Columbiad* is an enlarged and improved version of Barlow's earlier *Vision of Columbus* (1787). The enlargements were by way of clarifying and articulating the idea of democratic order and progress which totally suffuses the poem. As it stands, the poem, so Barlow tells us in his Preface, is meant to celebrate the establishment of democratic order, inculcate its working in those who participate in it, and

project its glorious possibilities into the future. Its aim, Barlow says, is "altogether of a moral and political nature." Specifically, he insists that his moral object far supersedes his poetical object. Only thus can he write the true modern epic, uncluttered with the base and false values of the traditional epic, those of *The Iliad* for example. His problem, hence, is to find a heroic center for democratic, progressivist values; and inevitably he fails utterly to do so. The poem begins epically ("I sing the Mariner who first unfurl'd/An eastern banner o'er the western world/And taught mankind where future empires lay . . ."). But in fact it is not Columbus's actions which are sung, but rather the inexorable progress of free institutions in the Americas as Columbus is given to envision them. To Columbus, despairing in prison, comes Hesper, the guardian Genius of the western continent, who takes him to a mount of vision. And the poem unfolds in a series of visions in which Columbus cannot be made to take part. Rather, he is tutored by his vision, as a person assuaged by an assurance that all will go off on schedule. He looks on at the origin of the new world, its native populations, Inca heroics, English colonization, the American Revolution—he looks on at all these and, now understanding something of the history and meaning of a national culture, is somehow changed. The vision is meant to do its work on him, as later in *Song of Myself* and the *Cantos,* the vision, the lived-through quality of the poetic experience, is meant to do its work on us. Columbus thus figures the reader, with whom Barlow makes him share his vision, as later Whitman and Pound themselves figure the reader, on whom they make their visions do their work. But, of course—and the contrast with Whitman and Pound makes it all the more obvious—Barlow is not poet enough to give his poetic rendering of Columbus's vision the power to work in this way. The quality of that vision is not substantial enough to make us accept Barlow's Columbus as a hero, as we can accept as heroes—even if we hate to—

Whitman and Pound, or the *personae* who speak to us in *Song of Myself* and the *Cantos*. What is unfolded in the twelve books of *The Columbiad* are tiresome, insistent, intemperate, homogenized descriptions of places, people, and events—all of value only as they aspire (in *The Columbiad*, even the places are made to aspire) toward the reason, freedom, and joy of a new society in a new world. The poem, if we look at it closely enough, would have us see how history, as informing milieu and ambiance, literally creates its protagonists—or what is the same thing, creates the values which, as they are embodied by the protagonists of history, give them their worth.

To say this is indeed to look very closely at the poem. I do so here, and so briefly, because I want to remark those implications of Barlow's theory and practice which point the epic away from its traditional mode and function. If it is undoubtedly true that Barlow could write neither a traditional epic nor an adequate American equivalent of that epic, nonetheless he seems, in the act of writing a poem which fails to do what he wanted it to do, to have had a sense of one of the preconditions of the sort of poem which his hero-less culture needed. This precondition was a new poetics, deriving from a new use of imaginative language, this deriving in turn from a new language itself. Barlow's conception is two or three times removed from that of a poetics which would make the new epic immediately possible; but it is nonetheless there, however vaguely, however subliminally—a product, one assumes, of the very logic of his conception of the relation between the American poet and his new world. It occurs as part of Columbus's utopian vision in Book X:

> At this blest period, when the total race
> Shall speak one language and all truths
>   embrace
> Instruction clear a speedier course shall find,
> And open earlier on the infant mind,
> No foreign terms shall crowd with barbarous
>   rules
> The dull unmeaning pageantry of schools;
> Nor dark authorities nor names unknown

> Fill the learnt head with ignorance not its
>   own;
> But wisdom's eye with beams unclouded shine,
> And simplest rules her native charms define;
> One living language, one unborrow'd dress
> Her boldest flights with fullest force express;
> Triumphant virtue, in the garb of truth
> Win[s] a pure passage to the heart of
>   youth. . . .

This is, on the one hand, an utterly simplistic view of one world as utopia. But it is, in the light of what came after it in the history of American poetry, something more: a description of the sufficient and necessary qualities of a poetic language which, at once carrying a vision like Columbus's and working on its reader as the vision is intended to have worked on him, will have given him a sense of certitude and authenticity, of being fully and creatively at one with his culture, of being defined as a person. This is indeed precisely how Columbus is said to feel at the very end of *The Columbiad*, and presumably how the reader is supposed to feel. It is beyond Barlow's abilities to bring about such a condition, of course. To have done so he would have to have created a radically new kind of epic—an epic which, in its very directness and overwhelming clarity, would have not subordinated poetic to moral purpose but would have made them one; one in which language, transubstantiating and transforming history and milieu, would, in its pure passage to men's hearts, have redefined Columbus's sense of himself and his world, and through him that of Barlow's readers; one which, lacking a traditional hero on which to center, would create him and make the reader participate in that creation. Barlow failed utterly, as we have always known. But we have not known how, in his very failure, he hit upon and tried to understand the necessary and sufficient conditions of an authentic and valid American epic.

II

It is as exemplars of that epic, with all its aspirations, commitments, compulsions, and excesses, that we must finally consider *Song of Myself* and the *Cantos*.

Consider the vexing problem of the form of *Song of Myself*. We have regularly made it out to have been more than it is, or have damned it for not having been so. But if only we consider it in the light of its status as a further stage in the development of that epic which Barlow so painfully desiderated, we can accept the poem for what it is and see how it breaks with all traditional canons of form, just so that it can do the job that an American epic would perforce have to do. It is as if Barlow's Columbus were allowed to have a vision which would demonstrably be his and his alone, not one which had been given to him; as though the structure of that vision were demonstrably the structure of his own native perceptions and his wilful resolution of them into meaning and significance. What the Whitman of *Song of Myself* (he is his own Columbus) does is to survey his whole world, his milieu and his ambiance—but not according to any necessary order and chronology. He looks when he wills and interprets as he wills. There is a dialectic here, but not a form. It is essential to the meaning of the poem that the dialectic be unique; for the dialectic derives from the very motion of the protagonist's sensibility. What is relatively stable and fixed, because it has no end and no beginning, is the world of which that sensibility becomes conscious, the world in and through which that sensibility would discover and define itself. The end of *Song of Myself*, the moral object which synchronizes with its poetic object, is to know that the world is there, and in the knowing, to know itself as there; in effect, through such a transaction to create itself and the possibility for readers to create themselves.

This is, quite briefly, how *Song of Myself* looks when, in gross outline, we trace that dialectic set by the rhythm of the sensibility:

1-5: The initial insight into the creative nature of the self and the initiating of creative power which follows spontaneously upon that insight.

6-16: Recognition of the relation of the self to its world, and a seeking after the creative metamorphosis which follows spontaneously upon that recognition.

17-25: The roles of the self in and through its world; a return to the matter of 1-5, but with this difference—that self-knowledge now exists formally, a product not of sheer inwardness as in 1-5 but of a spontaneously formalized relation between the self and its world. Now the poet is not just a force, but a force defined in terms of its world; now he is fully a person and can even name himself: "Walt Whitman, a kosmos, of Manhattan the son."

26-52: The poet (as person) fully at home in his newly defined world, fully sure of himself and his "procreant urge." He no longer needs to seek his world (as in 6-16); he can openly and lovingly address it as he creates and controls it and as he is created and controlled by it. He is thus a religion, God-like in himself. "I am an acme of things accomplish'd, and I am encloser of things to be."

And this is, quite briefly, how the rhythm of sensibility moves in what we have marked out as the first stage of the poem's total dialectic, in sections 1-5: *Song of Myself* begins epically, but immediately (so sharply in contrast to the traditional epic that one is shocked into awareness of the fact that Whitman has found the tradition inadequate and so has rejected it) turns inward, demanding that its readers do likewise:

I celebrate myself, and sing myself,
And what I assume you shall assume,
For every atom belonging to me as good belongs to you. (1)

The whole first section establishes the dominance of the self when for the first time it is overpoweringly discovered; the language of the section is composed in such a way as to register the overpower. For example, all verbs in the section apply only to the self and its attributes. At the end Whitman writes:

Creeds and schools in abeyance,
Retiring back awhile sufficed at what they are, but never forgotten,
I harbor for good or bad, I permit to speak at every hazard,
Nature without check with original energy.

In this stanza the absence of verbs for the items named in the first and last lines absolutely subordinates them to the newly (or re-) discovered self. What follows in the next sections is a retailing of a complete absorption into the self ("I am mad to be in contact with me" [2]) and a sense that the self possesses "the orgin of all poems"; an elucidation of the timeless "Urge and urge and urge,/Always the procreant urge of the world" (3); a recognition of its difference from other souls ("But they are not the Me myself" [4]); and the final account of how the soul, turning inward upon itself, discovers its true nature:

I mind how once we lay such a transparent
*   summer morning,*
How you settled your head athwart my hips
*   and gently turn'd over upon me,*
And parted the shirt from my bosom-bone, and
*   plunged your tongue to my bare-stript heart,*
And reach'd till you felt my beard, and reach'd
*   till you held my feet. (5)*

The passage of parallelisms which follows takes its energy from this apocalyptic moment. The items that are named are chaotically scattered in their natural habitat; but the force of the parallelisms is to unify and interrelate them by means of the newly initiated powers of the creative self:

Swiftly arose and spread around me the peace
*   and knowledge that pass all the argument*
*   of the earth,*
And I know that the hand of God is the prom-
*   ise of my own,*
And I know that the spirit of God is the
*   brother of my own,*
And that all the men ever born are also my
*   brothers, and the women my sisters and*
*   lovers,*
And that a kelson of the creation is love,
And that limitless are leaves stiff or drooping
*   in the fields,*
And brown ants in the little wells beneath
*   them,*
And mossy scabs of the worm fence, heap'd
*   stones, elder, mullein and poke weed.*

Thus, at the very end of this first phase of the discovery, creation, and transubstantiation of the sensibility, the self begins to turn outward toward its world and to unite with it in a heroic transformation. There begins a unique metamorphosis—unique because through its transformation, the self best discovers what it is as self. The rest of *Song of Myself* projects the sensibility in the process of making that discovery.

I venture this quite foreshortened view of the dialectic of *Song of Myself* and of the rhythm of its first phase, because I want to point out just how the poem seems to be intended to do its job. What is particularly important in this connection is that the poet's heroic quality has come about precisely by virtue of the fact that he has made the sort of poem that he has made—one in which he at once creates and controls his world (including his readers) and is created and controlled by it (including his readers). All that is demanded of the readers is that they yield to the poem, as has the world. This done, the "procreant urge," as Whitman calls the drive towards creativity, will be spontaneously released and the readers will be on their way to their own personal, individuated transformations, to their own achievement of heroic status. Thus, we may say, Whitman worked toward what Pound has called a new Paideuma—"a tangle or complex of unrooted ideas": one entirely of process, of guiding, strengthening, energizing, and redefining the sensible self by putting it into direct contact with the world, only in which it would be free, creative, and whole—a self proper to the American democrat. Such a poetry would, to say it again, not memorialize a hero but rather create one.

Song of Myself does make for a new kind of heroic poetry. In it, the hero comes into being, as, releasing the full creative force of the self, he energizes the *realia* of his world and takes from them his name, his office, and his phenomenal qualities. Unlike Barlow's Columbus, he is not given a vision; he makes one—and making it, he becomes it. Part of his heroic act entails his freeing himself from what he has learned is the false hierarchical heroism of traditional societies. The dialectic of *Song of Myself* articulates this act. And as the act is dynamically invertebrate, so is the dialectic. This new heroic poem, this new epic, is one of ordering, not of order; of creation, not confirmation; of energizing, not memorializing. When in 1872 Whitman wrote *Democratic Vistas* and let the trajectory of *Song of Myself* and what followed it carry him forward toward his utopia, he concluded:

It must still be reiterated . . . that all else in the contributions of nation or age, through its policies, materials, heroic personalities, military eclat &c., remains crude, and defers, in any close and thorough-going estimate, until vitalized by a national, original archetype in literature. They only put the nation in form, finally tell anything—prove, complete anything—perpetrate anything.

Song of Myself, then, as it is the sort of poem which Barlow's Columbus might have envisioned, is such a national, original archetype.

III

The third of my exemplars of the American epic is the *Cantos* of Ezra Pound. Pound, of course, is the ideal type of an anti-Whitmanian poet. Yet this very opposition is quite meaningful, as oppositions in a dialectical series tend inevitably to be. For the question of Whitman has always troubled Pound. Recently we have been told a good deal about Pound's varying appraisals of Whitman: how he seems finally to have come to understand Whitman as a nineteenth-century culture hero who, in Pound's words, went "bail for the nation." But the understanding goes even deeper than that; for in *Canto 82* (one of the Pisan series) Pound finally goes so far as to identify himself with Whitman—both poets, in his view, seeking to understand the deep mystery of birth, death, regeneration as it totally informs man's lonely fate on this earth. It is, however, an identification which we should be careful to limit and define. Pound feels that he too is making the sort of cosmically penetrating poem toward which Whitman aspired; moreover he too feels that he is a culture hero for

modern man and that his poem, when read properly, will exhibit to his readers a sense of the possibility for heroic action in our time and thus will redefine, reintegrate and re-create them as total human beings. But his poetics are almost diametrically opposed to Whitman's.

The crux of the opposition lies in two conceptions of style; which is to say, two conceptions of how poetry acts, hence two poetics. This can be illustrated briefly. Whitman wrote in the 1855 preface to *Leaves of Grass*:

The greatest poet has less a marked style and is more the channel of thoughts and things without increase or diminution, and is the free channel of himself. He swears to his art, I will not be meddlesome, I will not have in my writing any elegance or effect or originality to hang in the way between me and the rest like curtains . . . [my elision]. You shall stand by my side and look in the mirror with me.

And Pound wrote in his *Guide to Kulchur* (1938):

STYLE, the attainment of a style consists of so knowing words that one will communicate the various parts of what one says with the various degrees and weights of importance which one wishes.

It is, in essence, for Pound, a matter of self-expression and decorum at all costs. Pound's belief in decorum ("knowing words") of this sort, indeed, is at bottom the belief which makes possible his conception of the American epic: one in which degrees and weights are so finely managed that communication is exact and exacting knowledge. The end—its fusion of the artistic and the moral object—of the Poundian epic is such knowledge and insight—the new Paideuma which will make the new man. One thing—and I cannot help but think that, in spite of Pound's marvellous internationalism, it is an American thing—Pound has in common with Whitman: He would create, not confirm, the hero of his epic.

And how is he to do so? Which is to ask: What are the *Cantos*? What would they do? How would they do it? Toward the middle of *Canto 85*, these words suddenly leap off the page:

No classics,
　　No American history,
　　　　no centre, no general root,
No prezzo giusto as core.

The *Cantos* are an attempt to remedy this radical defect. They supply, however, not a single center but a series—a constellation of exemplars of *prezzo giusto* and its opposites by means of which the center, and the reader who will seek it, may be defined. The *Cantos* consist of a complex of centers, the perception of which is to be ordered by the absolutely decorous management of "degrees and weights of importance." They may be perceived thus because they are intended to exist as ideograms, as Pound now puts it; units of meaning so clearly articulated that they virtually dispense with abstract, discursive effects. Whereas in Whitman, it was the rhythm of the sensibility which was procreantly to urge the reader toward the wonders of the visible world, in Pound it is the commanding power of the ideograms (or images, or vortexes) which is to define the reader's world and so define the reader himself.

There are, to take a quite brief example, these lines from that section of *Canto 82* to which I have already alluded: Pound has had occasion to speak of the "ignorance of locality," modern man's inability to know himself in relation to the culture in which he lives. He speaks of ancient Greece, where things were better. Then:

Till forty years since, Reithmuller indignant:
"Fvy! in Tdaenmarck efen dh' beasantz gnow
*　　him,"*
　　meaning Whitman, exotic, still suspect
four miles from Camden
　　"O troubled reflection
　　"O Throat, O throbbing heart"
How drawn, O GEA TERRA,
　　what draws as thou drawest
　　　　till one sink into thee by an arm's
　　　　width
　　embracing thee.　Drawest,
　　　truly thou drawest.

　　Wisdom lies next thee,
　　　simple, past metaphor.
Where I lie let the thyme rise

　　　　　　　　and basilicum
　　　let the herbs rise in April abundant
By Ferrara was buried naked, fu Nicolo
　e di qua di la del Po,
wind: ἐμὸν τὸν ἄνδρα
lie into earth to the breast bone, to the left
　　　shoulder
　　Kipling suspected it
　to the height of ten inches or over
man, earth: two halves of the tally . . . .

The work of the Pound exegetes lets us begin to see what this passage comes to. Riethmuller (Pound misspells the name) was a teacher of Pound's at the University of Pennsylvania and the author of a study of "Whitman and the Germans." Recalling his teacher's oral statement, Pound then recalls and echoes "Out of the Cradle." He moves to an address to Gea Terra, and so to a definition of his own situation through that of Whitman and the protagonists of his poem. This is the wisdom "past metaphor." And our sense of that wisdom is further sharpened by the image of the herbs rising out of the grave, of the account of the burial place of Nicolo (one of Pound's culture-bearing Renaissance heroes); of the Greek "my man"—a fragmentary quotation from the second idyll of Theocritus in which a woman asks the goddess of the moon to keep her lover faithful; of the (as yet not totally understood) reference to Kipling on burial; and of the use of the Whitmanian "tally" to indicate the ritualistic significance of "man, earth." The passage goes on in this vein, drawing from widely scattered sources, to force us into a realization of the ultimate loneliness—separated like a lover from his lost or dead beloved—of the role of the hero as artist in our culture. It is not so much that Pound speaks, but that he would make his images, quotations, and citations speak—speak so sharply, infra-linguistically, as to define the sensibility of him who makes and/or reads the *Cantos*.

What emerges (or is intended to emerge) from the *Cantos* is a sense of absolute propaedeutic control; the assemblage of centers that is the poem is for Pound the only proper Paideuma. It is intended to constitute a rediscovery, a making new, of the noblest, truest, and surest elements in culture; a rediscovery so powerful in its stylistic precision that it will irresistably reconstitute the sensibility (and thus the political and economic morality) of him who would give himself over to reading it—someone, in the end, akin to the "cosmic man" whom Pound's friend Wyndham Lewis envisaged for America at the end of the forties. Pound once said of the *Cantos*: "They are openly volitionist, establishing, I think clearly, the effect of the factive personality. . . ." In Pound's hands, the American epic becomes thus openly volitionist and entirely factive—willing and making, through its collocation of ideogrammic centers, a new Paideuma for a new world.

We cannot yet say precisely what the structural principle of the *Cantos* is. Pound has not made up his mind. We can observe, quite briefly (with D. S. Carne-Ross, whose observances I echo here), that there are a series of thematic continuities in the poem: sea-voyages of Odysseus to hell, of Niccolo of Este to the Holy Land, of the Carthaginian Hanno along the west coast of Africa. We can observe, moreover, a reiterated concern with the problem of the artist in society. And we can trace out episodes in early national American history, in that of Renaissance Italy, and of Confucian China. And there are Pound's factive, volitionist heroes, Odysseus, Confucius, Sigismundo, Jefferson, John Adams, and the poet himself—each of whom is marked by a quality of awareness which is transubstantiated by his acts into the monuments of world culture. In all there is the concern to see how the great acts of world history have been acts of creation, not destruction; how such acts have resulted from a resistance to the abstractive, usurous demands which Pound believes the world has put on his heroes. Yet it is not possible to put down even briefly the poem's dialectic; for it has none. That is, it has no

linear, composed, structured form; no rhythmic periodicities; rather it consists of decorously managed, ideogrammically set down instants of insight which are to force themselves beyond abstractness into the reader's consciousness and so to make him new. The *Cantos*, Pound has said, "are the tale of the tribe." The point is that Pound has to re-create the tribe in order to tell its tale. The *Cantos* are that act of creation. If it is but done powerfully enough, there will be no longer a need to tell the tale. For it would be ours—ours in such a way that we would not have to have it told to us. As in Barlow's vision, and as in Whitman's practice, the end of poetry is that reconstitution of man which will entail the withering away of poetry.

IV

Pound once declared that the *Cantos* had a large defect, "the defect inherent in the record of struggle." He did not say, or have to say, that the virtues of the *Cantos* are specifically related to its defects. For they are indeed the virtues of struggle: the struggle to make the poem such a powerful social weapon that it will come to dispense with itself by being itself. And it is thus also with *Song of Myself*. The struggle is one for self-identification and self-preservation, and it is truly the epic subject of modern times, in America and out. The fact that the poet should be obliged to conceive the poetic act as the sole means of self-identification and self-preservation: this is perhaps one of the tragic subjects of modern times. The highest significance that *Song of Myself* and the *Cantos* can have for us is as the most profound of records of that impossible struggle. No poem, I should judge, can do all they are intended to.

And yet I should likewise judge that in the modern world, such poems have to exist just so that they may fail. A sign of their success indeed is their failure. And what is left? A need to question what we have, how far we have come, and how far we may go, I can only think that it is ultimately as an instigator of such questions that the American epic, as given to us by Whitman and Pound (and many others, I should say), has its highest imaginative value for us. Asking such questions, we concern ourselves with the life of our culture; perhaps we will be moved to strive to make it more vital. Doing so, perhaps we will even have one day that kind of community in which we can conceive of an authentic hero, whom the poets among us will finally be able to memorialize and reaffirm in a true epic. We can only hope that he will not be as obtuse as Barlow's Columbus, as manic as Whitman's Whitman, or as distorted from his historical actuality as Pound's Malatesta. Which is to say: We can only hope that he will be a projection of something other than the agonizing desire of his creator to make over the world, and the men in it, in his own heroic image. We would wish him to be a person first and a hero afterwards—a hero in consequence of his bèing a person.

Indeed, if we ever get to the point of knowing how to define ourselves as persons, maybe we will be able to define our community. And maybe it will turn out to be a community with not one image of the hero but many—a community whose heroes' heroism consists in the fact that they can teach us how to resist a community's inevitable urge to coalesce all its heroes into one. What we long for, in many heroes or one, is a strong, assured image of our full possibilities as persons in our community. And it might well be that for us a definition of the person is *per se* a definition of the hero—instead of the other way around; as it seems to have been in the epic and the epic communities of tradition. And it might well be that Barlow's, Whitman's, and Pound's ultimate failure to create a hero adequate to our needs lies in the fact that such a definition was for them intolerable in its restrictiveness. They lusted (Pound still lusts) after a sheer creative power which would not only let them define the modern heroic self but reformulate it, not only make it new but make it. Thus, we can quite safely say, they went too far. But surely

they did what they had to do; and surely we can learn from it. They saw (does Pound still see?) quite clearly what Freud was to see in 1930, in *Civilization and Its Discontents*. Speaking of that "misère psychologique" which is so marked in modern life, he wrote:

This danger is most menacing where the social forces of cohesion consist predominantly of identifications of the individuals in the group with one another, whilst leading personalities fail to acquire the significance that should fall to them in the process of group-formation. The state of civilization in America at the present day offers a good opportunity for studying this injurious effect of civilization which we have reason to dread.

The Columbiad, Song of Myself, and the *Cantos*—each can be made out to be therapeutic in so far as each is to initiate in us something of a clear understanding of the powers and limitations of our own processes of group-formation. The best, as always, must be yet to come.

But this is utopianism. It is a curious fact, and a painful one, that those of us who might want such a society and who cannot struggle for it imaginatively, as do Whitman and Pound, so often, like Barlow, conclude with such bleak, abstractive, fleshless utopianisms. We cannot really believe in heroes, yet we want them, and so want them created for us. Looking for a hero in an epic, we discover, of course, that the author must first of all be his own hero, as his epic is the struggle of his own creative forces to bring into being something which constitutes his central subject. Thus, we see, in some way or other he must tell all; thus he wills himself to be incapable of dissembling, lest something of the creative self be left out. There is ever the ungainliness of his compulsions, which we cannot escape: some of them, like Whitman's homosexuality and his political sentimentality, no longer much disturb or concern us; others, like Pound's paranoia and his antisemitism, are of a dangerousness which we can only hate and fear, even to the point of cutting off part of the *Cantos* from ourselves. We know all this, know it well. Still, as we used to gather around Whitman and form Fellowships, so we now wait upon Pound at St. Elizabeth's and contribute to *Pound Newsletters*. We seem bound to strive to live in our hero's image in cults with no rituals except those of *explication de texte*. We even publish statements like this:

"Leaves of Grass" has a tone peculiarly its own and strange in all the annals of literary creation. Whitman speaks in it as would heaven, making unalterable pronouncements, oracular of the mysteries and powers that pervade and guide all life, all death, all purpose.
(Horace Trauble, in *In Re Walt Whitman*, 1883)

And this:

It would seem that [Pound] has his fingers on the pulse of creation, and like the poet-philosopher Goethe, bequeaths more than he states: a myriad of facets of existence to be explored in coming years, an attempt to understand what this fire is that he . . . kindles in one.
(Louise Myers, in *Pound Newsletter*, 1955)

At second glance, we blush, or should. But then this is our situation; and we all (perhaps secretly, or unknowingly) hope for someone, somewhere, who will make the struggle for us—or at least show us its conditions. Occasionally we find him, as many found Whitman and have found Pound. Whitman and Pound, each knows who the real hero is: himself. This is the root of their virtues and

their defects, of the strength of their epics and of their weakness. Their poems are thus doubly propaedeutic—in their strength and in their weakness, in their virtues and in their defects. If we fail to take the two together, we miss their great meaning for us. It is perhaps useful to recall that the *editio princeps* of *Song of Myself* (in the 1855 *Leaves of Grass*) and of the *Cantos* (and, curiously enough, of *The Columbiad* too) has as frontispiece a portrait of its real hero, its author: he who is perforce our hero because he is, in so far as we can bring ourselves to know and admit it, a projection of ourselves into an ultimate American personality. Looking at our ultimate, marginal selves thus, we are bound either to hate or to adore.

And what, in the long run, is the relation between the American epic and the epic of tradition? It is as though Odysseus, or Aeneas, or Beowulf, or Mio Cid, or even Dante, under the *persona* of Adam (in whose fall/we sinnèd all) had been compelled, out of some deep, dark necessity, to write his own history, and in writing it, to make it. I am reminded of some words of Robert Penn Warren in the prefatory note to *Brother to Dragons*: ". . . if poetry is the little myth we make, history is the big myth we live, and in our living, constantly remake." The struggle to make the big myth into the little one—this is as good a definition as any of the American epic.

WILLIAM EMPSON

(b. 1906)

A student of I. A. Richards at Cambridge in the late 1920's, William Empson specialized in close textual analysis. His first book, *Seven Types of Ambiguity* (1930; 1947) treated paradox and tension as essential qualities of poetry and influenced later New Critical theories of poetic language and structure. Empson differed from the New Critics, however, in his insistence upon the critical relevance of historical and social factors. His sociological interests are clearly apparent in

Some Versions of Pastoral (1935), published in America as *English Pastoral Poetry* (1938). In the essay on *Alice in Wonderland*, Empson draws upon Freudian psychology and many other sources of knowledge to relate the form of Lewis Carroll's classics to their literary context and social environment. Empson's more recent works include *The Structure of Complex Words* (1951) and *Milton's God* (1961).

Alice in Wonderland
The Child as Swain
(1935)

It must seem a curious thing that there has been so little serious criticism of the Alices, and that so many critics, with so militant and eager an air of good taste, have explained that they would not think of attempting it. Even Mr. De La Mare's book, which made many good points, is queerly evasive in tone. There seems to be a feeling that real criticism would involve psychoanalysis, and that the results would be so improper as to destroy the atmosphere of the books altogether. Dodgson was too conscious a writer to be caught out so easily. For instance it is an obvious bit of interpretation to say that the Queen of Hearts is a symbol of 'uncontrolled animal passion' seen through the clear but blank eyes of sexlessness; obvious, and the sort of thing critics are now so sure would be in bad taste; Dodgson said it himself, to the actress who took the part when the thing was acted. The books are so frankly about growing up that there is no great discovery in translating them into Freudian terms; it seems only the proper exegesis of a classic even where it would be a shock to the author. On the whole the results of the analysis, when put into drawing-room language, are his conscious opinions; and if there was no other satisfactory outlet for his feelings but the special one fixed in his books the same is true in a degree of any original artist. I shall use psychoanalysis where it seems relevant, and feel I had better begin by saying what use it is supposed

to be. Its business here is not to discover a neurosis peculiar to Dodgson. The essential idea behind the books is a shift onto the child, which Dodgson did not invent, of the obscure tradition of pastoral. The formula is now '*child*-become-judge,' and if Dodgson identifies himself with the child so does the writer of the primary sort of pastoral with his magnified version of the swain. (He took an excellent photograph, much admired by Tennyson, of Alice Liddell as a ragged beggar-girl, which seems a sort of example of the connection.) I should say indeed that this version was more open to neurosis than the older ones; it is less hopeful and more a return into oneself. The analysis should show how this works in general. But there are other things to be said about such a version of pastoral; its use of the device prior to irony lets it make covert judgments about any matter the author was interested in.

There is a tantalising one about Darwinism. The first Neanderthal skull was found in 1856. *The Origin of Species* (1859) came out six years before *Wonderland*, three before its conception, and was very much in the air, a pervading bad smell. It is hard to say how far Dodgson under cover of nonsense was using ideas of which his set disapproved; he wrote some hysterical passages against vivisection and has a curious remark to the effect that chemistry professors had better not have laboratories, but was open to new ideas and doubted the eternity of hell. The 1860 meeting of the British Association, at which Huxley started his career as publicist and gave that resounding snub to Bishop Wilberforce, was held at Oxford where Dodgson was already in residence. He had met Tennyson in '56, and we hear of Tennyson lecturing him later on the likeness of monkeys' and men's skulls.

The only passage that I feel sure involves evolution comes at the beginning of *Wonderland* (the most spontaneous and 'subconscious' part of the books) when Alice gets out of the bath of tears that has magically released her from the underground chamber; it is made clear (for instance about watering-places) that the salt water is the sea from which life arose; as a bodily product it is also the amniotic fluid (there are other forces at work here); ontogeny then repeats phylogeny, and a whole Noah's Ark gets out of the sea with her. In Dodgson's own illustration as well as Tenniel's there is the disturbing head of a monkey and in the text there is an extinct bird. Our minds having thus been forced back onto the history of species there is a reading of history from the period when the Mouse 'came over' with the Conqueror; questions of race turn into the questions of breeding in which Dodgson was more frankly interested, and there are obscure snubs for people who boast about their ancestors. We then have the Caucus Race (the word had associations for Dodgson with local politics; he says somewhere, 'I never go to a Caucus without reluctance'), in which you begin running when you like and leave off when you like, and all win. The subtlety of this is that it supports Natural Selection (in the offensive way the nineteenth century did) to show the absurdity of democracy, and supports democracy (or at any rate liberty) to show the absurdity of Natural Selection. The race is not to the swift because idealism will not let it be to the swift, and because life, as we are told in the final poem, is at random and a dream. But there is no weakening of human values in this generosity; all the animals win, and Alice because she is Man has therefore to give them comfits, but though they demand this they do not fail to recognise that she is superior. They give her her own ele-

gant thimble, the symbol of her labour, because she too has won, and because the highest among you shall be the servant of all. This is a solid piece of symbolism; the politically minded scientists preaching progress through 'selection' and *laissez-faire* are confronted with the full anarchy of Christ. And the pretence of infantilism allows it a certain grim honesty; Alice is a little ridiculous and discomfited, under cover of charm, and would prefer a more aristocratic system.

In the *Looking-Glass* too there are ideas about progress at an early stage of the journey of growing up. Alice goes quickly through the first square by railway, in a carriage full of animals in a state of excitement about the progress of business and machinery; the only man is Disraeli dressed in newspapers—the new man who gets on by self-advertisement, the newspaper-fed man who believes in progress, possibly even the rational dress of the future.

> . . . to her great surprise, they all *thought* in chorus (I hope you understand what *thinking in chorus* means—for I must confess that *I* don't), 'Better say nothing at all. Language is worth a thousand pounds a word.'
>
> 'I shall dream of a thousand pounds tonight, I know I shall,' thought Alice.
>
> All this time the Guard was looking at her, first through a telescope, then through a microscope, and then through an opera-glass. At last he said, 'You're travelling the wrong way,' and shut up the window and went away.

This seems to be a prophecy; Huxley in the Romanes lecture of 1893, and less clearly beforehand, said that the human sense of right must judge and often be opposed to the progress imposed by Nature, but at this time he was still looking through the glasses.

> But the gentleman dressed in white paper leaned forwards and whispered in her ear, 'Never mind what they all say, my dear, but take a return ticket every time the train stops.'

In 1861 'many Tory members considered that the prime minister was a better representative of conservative opinions than the leader of the opposition' (*D.N.*

B.). This seems to be the double outlook of Disraeli's conservatism, too subtle to inspire action. I think he turns up again as the unicorn when the Lion and the Unicorn are fighting for the Crown; they make a great dust and nuisance, treat the commonsense Alice as entirely mythical, and are very frightening to the poor king to whom the Crown really belongs.

'Indeed I shan't,' Alice said rather impatiently. 'I don't belong to this railway journey at all—I was in a wood just now—and I wish I could get back there!'

When she gets back to the wood it is different; it is Nature in the raw, with no names, and she is afraid of it. She still thinks the animals are right to stay there; even when they know their names 'they wouldn't answer at all, if they were wise.' (They might do well to write nonsense books under an assumed name, and refuse to answer even to that.) All this is a very Kafka piece of symbolism, less at ease than the preceding one; *Wonderland* is a dream, but the *Looking-Glass* is self-consciousness. But both are topical; whether you call the result allegory or 'pure nonsense' it depends on ideas about progress and industrialisation, and there is room for exegesis on the matter.

The beginning of modern child-sentiment may be placed at the obscure edition of *Mother Goose's Melodies* (John Newbury, 1760), with 'maxims' very probably by Goldsmith. The important thing is not the rhymes (Boston boasts an edition of 1719. My impression is that they improved as time went on.) but the appended maxims, which take a sophisticated pleasure in them. Most are sensible proverbs which the child had better know anyway; their charm (mainly for the adult) comes from the unexpected view of the story you must take if they are not to be irrelevant.

Amphion's Song of Eurydice.
I won't be my Father's Jack,
I won't be my Father's Jill,
I won't be the Fiddler's Wife,
And I will have music when I will.

T'other little Tune,
T'other little Tune,
Prithee Love play me
T'other little Tune.

MAXIM.—Those Arts are the most valuable which are of the greatest Use.

It seems to be the fiddler whose art has been useful in controlling her, but then again she may have discovered the art of wheedling the fiddler. The pomp of the maxim and the childishness of the rhyme make a mock-pastoral compound. The pleasure in children here is obviously a derivative of the pleasure in Macheath; the children are 'little rogues.'

Bow wow wow
Whose dog art Thou?
Little Tom Tinker's Dog.
Bow wow wow.

Tom Tinker's Dog is a very good Dog; and an honester Dog than his Master.

Honest ('free from hypocisy' or the patronising tone to a social inferior) and *dog* ('you young dog') have their *Beggar's Opera* feelings here; it is not even clear whether Tom is a young vagabond or a child.

This is a pleasant example because one can trace the question back. Pope engraved a couplet 'on the collar of a dog which I gave to His Royal Highness' —a friendly act as from one gentleman to another resident in the neighbourhood.

I am his Highness' dog at Kew.
Pray tell me, sir, whose dog are you?

Presumably Frederick himself would be the first to read it. The joke carries a certain praise for the underdog; the point is not that men are slaves but that they find it suits them and remain good-humoured. The dog is proud of being the prince's dog and expects no one to take offence at the question. There is also a hearty independence in its lack of respect for the inquirer. Pope took this from Sir William Temple, where it is said by a fool: 'I am the Lord Chamberlain's fool. And whose are you?' was his answer to the nobleman. It is a neat case of the slow shift of this sentiment from fool to rogue to child.

Alice, I think, is more of a 'little rogue' than it is usual to say, or than Dodgson himself thought in later years:

loving as a dog . . . and gentle as a fawn; then courteous,—courteous to *all*, high or low, grand or grotesque, King or Caterpillar . . . trustful, with an absolute trust. . . .

and so on. It depends what you expect of a child of seven.

. . . she had quite a long argument with the Lory, who at last turned sulky, and would only say, 'I am older than you, and must know better'; and this Alice would not allow without knowing how old it was, and as the Lory positively refused to tell its age, there was no more to be said.

Alice had to be made to speak up to bring out the points—here the point is a sense of the fundamental oddity of life given by the fact that different animals become grown-up at different ages; but still if you accept the Lory as a grown-up this is rather a pert child. She is often the underdog speaking up for itself.

A quite separate feeling about children, which is yet at the back of the pertness here and in the Goldsmith, since it is needed if the pertness is to be charming, may be seen in its clearest form in Wordsworth and Coleridge; it is the whole point of the *Ode to Intimations* and even of *We are Seven*. The child has not yet been put wrong by civilisation, and all grown-ups have been. It may well be true that Dodgson envied the child because it was sexless, and Wordsworth because he knew that he was destroying his native poetry by the smugness of his life, but neither theory explains why this feeling about children arose when it did and became so general. There is much of it in Vaughan after the Civil War, but as a general tendency it appeared when the eighteenth-century settlement had come to seem narrow and unescapable; one might connect it with the end of duelling; also when the scien-

tific sort of truth had been generally accepted as the main and real one. It strengthened as the aristocracy became more puritan. It depends on a feeling, whatever may have caused that in its turn, that no way of building up character, no intellectual system, can bring out all that is inherent in the human spirit, and therefore that there is more in the child than any man has been able to keep. (The child is a microcosm like Donne's world, and Alice too is a stoic.) This runs through all Victorian and Romantic literature; the world of the adult made it hard to be an artist, and they kept a sort of tap-root going down to their experience as children. Artists like Wordsworth and Coleridge, who accepted this fact and used it, naturally come to seem the most interesting and in a way the most sincere writers of the period. Their idea of the child, that it is in the right relation to Nature, not dividing what should be unified, that its intuitive judgment contains what poetry and philosophy must spend their time labouring to recover, was accepted by Dodgson and a main part of his feeling. He quotes Wordsworth on this point in the 'Easter Greeting'—the child feels its life in every limb; Dodgson advises it, with an infelicitous memory of the original poem, to give its attention to death from time to time. That the dream books are

Like Pilgrim's withered wreaths of flowers
Plucked in a far-off land

is a fine expression of Wordsworth's sense both of the poetry of childhood and of his advancing sterility. And the moment when she finds herself dancing with Tweedledum and Tweedledee, so that it is difficult to introduce herself afterwards, is a successful interruption of Wordsworthian sentiment into his normal style.

. . . she took hold of both hands at once; the next moment they were dancing round in a ring. This seemed quite natural (she remembered afterwards), and she was not even surprised to hear music playing: it seemed to come from the tree under which they were dancing, and it was done (as well as she could make out) by the branches rubbing one against another, like fiddles and fiddle-sticks. . . . 'I don't know when I began it, but somehow I felt as if I had been singing it a long long time.'

This is presented as like the odd behaviour of comic objects such as souptureens, but it is a directer version of the idea of the child's unity with nature. She has been singing a long long time because she sang with no temporal limits in that imperial palace whence she came. Yet it is the frank selfishness of the brothers, who being little boys are horrid, are made into a satire on war, and will only give her the hands free from hugging each other, that forces her into the ring with them that produces eternity. Even here this puts a subtle doubt into the eternities open to the child.

For Dodgson will only go half-way with the sentiment of the child's unity with nature, and has another purpose for his heroine; she is the free and independent mind. Not that this is contradictory; because she is right about life she is independent from all the other characters who are wrong. But it is important to him because it enables him to clash the Wordsworth sentiments with the other main tradition about children derived from rogue-sentiment. (For both, no doubt, he had to go some way back; the intervening sentiment about children is that the great thing is to repress their Original Sin, and I suppose, though he would not have much liked it, he was among the obscure influences that led to the cult of games in the public schools.)

One might say that the Alices differ from other versions of pastoral in lacking the sense of glory. Normally the idea of including all sorts of men in yourself brings in an idea of reconciling yourself with nature and therefore gaining power over it. The Alices are more self-protective; the dream cuts out the real world and the delicacy of the mood is felt to cut out the lower classes. This is true enough, but when Humpty Dumpty says that glory means a nice knock-down argument he is not far from the central feeling of the book. There is a real feeling of isolation and yet just that is taken as the source of power.

The obvious parody of Wordsworth is the poem of the White Knight, an important figure for whom Dodgson is willing to break the language of humour into the language of sentiment. It takes off *Resolution and Independence*, a genuine pastoral poem if ever there was one; the endurance of the leechgatherer gives Wordsworth strength to face the pain of the world. Dodgson was fond of saying that one parodied the best poems, or anyway that parody showed no lack of admiration, but a certain bitterness is inherent in parody; if the meaning is not 'This poem is absurd' it must be 'In my present mood of emotional sterility the poem will not work, or I am afraid to let it work, on *me*.' The parody here will have no truck with the dignity of the leechgatherer, but the point of that is to make the unwordly dreaminess of the Knight more absurd; there may even be a reproach for Wordsworth in the lack of consideration that makes him go on asking the same question. One feels that the Knight has probably imagined most of the old man's answers, or anyway that the old man was playing up to the fool who questioned him. At any rate there is a complete shift of interest from the virtues of the leechgatherer onto the childish but profound virtues of his questioner.

The main basis of the joke is the idea of absurd inventions of new foods. Dodgson was well-informed about food, kept his old menus and was wine-taster to the College; but ate very little, suspected the High Table of overeating, and would see no reason to deny that he connected overeating with other forms of sensuality. One reason for the importance of rich food here is that it is the child's symbol for all luxuries reserved for grown-ups. I take it that the fascination of Soup and of the Mock Turtle who sings about it was that soup is mainly eaten at dinner, the excitingly grown-up meal eaten after the child has gone to bed. When Alice talks about her dinner she presumably means lunch, and it is rather a boast when she says she has already met whiting. In the White Knight's song and conversation these little jokes based on fear of sensuality are put to a further use; he becomes the scientist, the inventor, whose mind is nobly but absurdly detached from interest in the pleasures of the senses and even from 'good sense.'

'How *can* you go on talking so quietly, head downwards?' Alice asked, as she dragged him out by the feet, and laid him in a heap on the bank.

The Knight looked surprised at the question. 'What does it matter where my body happens to be?' he said. 'My mind goes on working all the same. In fact, the more head downwards I am, the more I keep inventing new things.'

'Now the cleverest thing that I ever did,' he went on after a pause, 'was inventing a new pudding during the meat-course.'

This required extreme detachment; the word 'clever' has become a signal that the mind is being admired for such a reason. The more absurd the assumptions of the thinking, for instance those of scientific materialism, the more vigorous the thought based upon it. 'Life is so strange that his results have the more chance of being valuable because his assumptions are absurd, but we must not forget that they are so.' This indeed is as near the truth as one need get about scientific determinism.

One reason for the moral grandeur of the Knight, then, is that he stands for the Victorian scientist, who was felt to have invented a new kind of Roman virtue; earnestly, patiently, carefully (it annoyed Samuel Butler to have these words used so continually about scientists) without sensuality, without self-seeking, without claiming any but a fragment of knowledge, he goes on labouring at his absurd but fruitful conceptions. But the parody makes him stand also for the poet, and Wordsworth would have been pleased by this; he considered that the poet was essentially one who revived our sense of the original facts of nature, and should use scien-

tific ideas where he could; poetry was the impassioned expression of the face of all science; Wordsworth was as successful in putting life into the abstract words of science as into 'the plain language of men,' and many of the Lyrical Ballads are best understood as psychological notes written in a form that saves one from forgetting their actuality. The Knight has the same readiness to accept new ideas and ways of life, such as the sciences were imposing, without ceasing to be good and in his way sensible, as Alice herself shows for instance when in falling down the rabbit-hole she plans a polite entry into the Antipodes and is careful not to drop the marmalade onto the inhabitants. It is the childishness of the Knight that lets him combine the virtues of the poet and the scientist, and one must expect a creature so finely suited to life to be absurd because life itself is absurd.

The talking animal convention and the changes of relative size appear in so different a children's book as *Gulliver*; they evidently make some direct appeal to the child whatever more sophisticated ideas are piled onto them. Children feel at home with animals conceived as human; the animal can be made affectionate without its making serious emotional demands on them, does not want to educate them, is at least unconventional in the sense that it does not impose its conventions, and does not make a secret of the processes of nature. So the talking animals here are a child-world; the rule about them is that they are always friendly though childishly frank to Alice while she is small, and when she is big (suggesting grown-up) always opposed to her, or by her, or both. But talking animals in children's books had been turned to didactic purposes ever since Aesop; the schoolmastering tone in which the animals talk nonsense to Alice is partly a parody of this—they are really childish but try not to look it. On the other hand, this tone is so supported by the way they can order her about, the firm and surprising way their minds work, the abstract topics they work on, the useless rules they accept with so much conviction, that we take them as real grown-ups contrasted with unsophisticated childhood. 'The grown-up world is as odd as the child-world, and both are a dream.' This ambivalence seems to correspond to Dodgson's own attitude to children; he, like Alice, wanted to get the advantages of being childish and grown-up at once. In real life this seems to have at least occasional disadvantages both ways; one remembers the little girl who screamed and demanded to be taken from the lunch-table because she knew she couldn't solve his puzzles (not, apparently, a usual, but one would think a natural reaction to his mode of approach)—she clearly thought him too grown-up; whereas in the scenes of jealousy with his little girls' parents the grown-ups must have thought him quite enough of a child. He made a success of the process, and it seems clear that it did none of the little girls any harm, but one cannot help cocking one's eye at it as a way of life.

The changes of size are more complex. In Gulliver they are the impersonal eye; to change size and nothing else makes you feel 'this makes one see things as they are in themselves.' It excites Wonder but of a scientific sort. Swift used it for satire on science or from a horrified interest in it, and to give a sort of scientific authority to his deductions, that men seen as small are spiritually petty and seen as large physically loathsome. And it is the small observer, like the child, who does least to alter what he sees and therefore sees most truly. (The definition of potential, in all but the most rigid textbooks of electricity, contents itself with talking about the force on a *small* charge which doesn't alter the field *much*. The objection that the small alteration in the field might be proportional to the small force does not occur easily to the reader.) To mix this with a pious child's type of Wonder made science seem less irreligious and gave you a feeling that you were being good because educating a child; Faraday's talks for children on the chemical history of a candle came out in 1861, so the method was in the air. But these are special uses of a material rich in itself. Children like to think of being so small that they could hide from grown-ups and so big that they could control them, and to do this dramatises the great topic of growing up, which both Alices keep to consistently. In the same way the charm of Jabberwocky is that it is a code language, the language with which grown-ups hide things from children or children from grown-ups. Also the words are such good tongue-gestures, in Sir Richard Paget's phrase, that they seem to carry their own meaning; this carries a hint of the paradox that the conventions are natural.

Both books also keep to the topic of death—the first two jokes about death in *Wonderland* come on pages 3 and 4 —and for the child this may be a natural connection; I remember believing I should have to die before I grew up, and thinking the prospect very disagreeable. There seems to be a connection in Dodgson's mind between the death of childhood and the development of sex, which might be pursued into many of the details of the books. Alice will die if the Red King wakes up, partly because she is a dream-product of the author and partly because the pawn is put back in its box at the end of the game. He is the absent husband of the Red Queen who is a governess, and the end of the book comes when Alice defeats the Red Queen and 'mates' the King. Everything seems to break up because she arrives at a piece of *knowledge*, that all the poems are about fish. I should say the idea was somehow at work at the end of *Wonderland* too. The trial is meant to be a mystery; Alice is told to leave the court, as if a child ought not to hear the evidence, and yet they expect her to give evidence herself.

'What do you know about this business?' the King said to Alice.
'Nothing,' said Alice.
'Nothing *whatever*?' persisted the King.
'Nothing whatever,' said Alice.
'That's very important,' the King said, turning to the jury. They were just beginning to

write this down on their slates, when the White Rabbit interrupted: '*Un*important, your Majesty means, of course,' he said in a very respectful tone, but frowning and making faces as he spoke.

'*Un*important, of course, I meant,' the King hastily said, and went on to himself in an undertone, 'important—unimportant—unimportant—important—' as if he were trying which word sounded best.

There is no such stress in the passage as would make one feel there must be something behind it, and certainly it is funny enough as it stands. But I think Dodgson felt it was important that Alice should be innocent of all knowledge of what the Knave of Hearts (a flashy-looking lady's-man in the picture) is likely to have been doing, and also important that she should not be told she is innocent. That is why the king, always a well-intentioned man, is embarrassed. At the same time Dodgson feels that Alice is right in thinking 'it doesn't matter a bit' which word the jury write down; she is too stable in her detachment to be embarrassed, these things will not interest her, and in a way she includes them all in herself. And it is the refusal to let her stay that makes her revolt and break the dream. It is tempting to read an example of this idea into the poem that introduces the *Looking-Glass*.

> Come, hearken then, ere voice of dread,
>   With bitter summons laden,
> Shall summon to unwelcome bed
>   A melancholy maiden.

After all the marriage-bed was more likely to be the end of the maiden than the grave, and the metaphor firmly implied treats them as identical.

The last example is obviously more a joke against Dodgson than anything else, and though the connection between death and the development of sex is I think at work it is not the main point of the conflict about growing up. Alice is given a magical control over her growth by the traditionally symbolic caterpillar, a creature which has to go through a sort of death to become

grown-up, and then seems a more spiritual creature. It refuses to agree with Alice that this process is at all peculiar, and clearly her own life will be somehow like it, but the main idea is not its development of sex. The butterfly implied may be the girl when she is 'out' or her soul when in heaven, to which she is now nearer than she will be when she is 'out'; she must walk to it by walking away from it. Alice knows several reasons why she should object to growing up, and does not at all like being an obvious angel, a head out of contact with its body that has to come down from the sky, and gets mistaken for the Paradisal serpent of the knowledge of good and evil, and by the pigeon of the Annunciation, too. But she only makes herself smaller for reasons of tact or proportion; the triumphant close of *Wonderland* is that she has outgrown her fancies and can afford to wake and despise them. The *Looking-Glass* is less of a dream-product, less concentrated on the child's situation, and (once started) less full of changes of size; but it has the same end; the governess shrinks to a kitten when Alice has grown from a pawn to a queen, and can shake her. Both these clearly stand for becoming grown-up and yet in part are a revolt against grown-up behaviour; there is the same ambivalence as about the talking animals. Whether children often find this symbolism as interesting as Carroll did is another thing; there are recorded cases of tears at such a betrayal of the reality of the story. I remember feeling that the ends of the books were a sort of necessary assertion that the grown-up world was after all the proper one; one did not object to that in principle, but would no more turn to those parts from preference than to the 'Easter Greeting to Every Child that Loves Alice' (Gothic type).

To make the dream-story from which *Wonderland* was elaborated seem Freudian one has only to tell it. A fall through a deep hole into the secrets of Mother Earth produces a new enclosed soul wondering who it is, what will be its position in the world, and how it can get out. It is in a long low hall, part of the palace of the Queen of Hearts (a neat touch), from which it can only get out to the fresh air and the fountains through a hole frighteningly too small. Strange changes, caused by the way it is nourished there, happen to it in this place, but always when it is big it cannot get out and when it is small it is not allowed to; for one thing, being a little girl, it has no key. The nightmare theme of the birth-trauma, that she grows too big for the room and is almost crushed by it, is not only used here but repeated more painfully after she seems to have got out; the rabbit sends her sternly into its house and some food there makes her grow again. In Dodgson's own drawing of Alice when cramped into the room with one foot up the chimney, kicking out the hateful thing that tries to come down (she takes away its pencil when it is a juror), she is much more obviously in the foetus position than in Tenniel's. The White Rabbit is Mr. Spooner to whom the spoonerisms happened, an undergraduate in 1862, but its business here is as a pet for children which they may be allowed to breed. Not that the clearness of the framework makes the interpretation simple; Alice peering through the hole into the garden may be wanting a return to the womb as well as an escape from it; she is fond, we are told, of taking both sides of an argument when talking to herself, and the whole book balances between the luscious nonsense-world of fantasy and the ironic nonsense-world of fact.

I said that the sea of tears she swims in was the amniotic fluid, which is much too simple. You may take it as Lethe in which the souls were bathed before re-birth (and it is their own tears; they forget, as we forget our childhood, through the repression of pain) or as the 'solution' of an intellectual contradiction through Intuition and a return to the Unconscious. Anyway it is a sordid image made pretty; one need not read Dodgson's satirical verses against babies to see how much he would dislike a child wallowing in its tears in real life. The fondness of small girls

for doing this has to be faced early in attempting to prefer them, possibly to small boys, certainly to grown-ups; to a man idealising children as free from the falsity of a rich emotional life their displays of emotion must be particularly disconcerting. The celibate may be forced to observe them, on the floor of a railway carriage for example, after a storm of fury, dabbling in their ooze; covertly snuggling against mamma while each still pretends to ignore the other. The symbolic pleasure of dabbling seems based on an idea that the liquid itself is the bad temper which they have got rid of by the storm and yet are still hugging, or that they are not quite impotent since they have at least 'done' this much about the situation. The acid quality of the style shows that Dodgson does not entirely like having to love creatures whose narcissism takes this form, but he does not want simply to forget it as he too would like a relief from 'ill-temper'; he sterilises it from the start by giving it a charming myth. The love for narcissists itself seems mainly based on a desire to keep oneself safely detached, which is the essential notion here.

The symbolic completeness of Alice's experience is I think important. She runs the whole gamut; she is a father in getting down the hole, a foetus at the bottom, and can only be born by becoming a mother and producing her own amniotic fluid. Whether his mind played the trick of putting this into the story or not he has the feelings that would correspond to it. A desire to include all sexuality in the girl child, the least obviously sexed of human creatures, the one that keeps its sex in the safest place, was an important part of their fascination for him. He is partly imagining himself as the girl-child (with these comforting characteristics) partly as its father (these together make *it* a father) partly as its lover—so it might be a mother—but then of course it is clever and detached enough to do everything for itself. He told one of his little girls a story about cats wearing gloves over their claws: 'For you see, "gloves" have got "love" inside them—there's none outside, you know.' So far from its dependence, the child's independence is the important thing, and the theme behind that is the self-centred emotional life imposed by the detached intelligence.

The famous cat is a very direct symbol of this ideal of intellectual detachment; all cats are detached, and since this one grins it is the amused observer. It can disappear because it can abstract itself from its surroundings into a more interesting inner world; it appears only as a head because it is almost a disembodied intelligence, and only as a grin because it can impose an atmosphere without being present. In frightening the king by the allowable act of looking at him it displays the soul-force of Mr. Gandhi; it is unbeheadable because its soul cannot be killed; and its influence brings about a short amnesty in the divided nature of the Queen and Duchess. Its cleverness makes it formidable—it has very long claws and a great many teeth—but Alice is particularly at home with it; she is the same sort of thing.

The Gnat gives a more touching picture of Dodgson; he treats nowhere more directly of his actual relations with the child. He feels he is liable to nag at it, as a gnat would, and the gnat turns out, as he is, to be alarmingly big as a friend for the child, but at first it sounds tiny because he means so little to her. It tries to amuse her by rather frightening accounts of other dangerous insects, other grown-ups. It is reduced to tears by the melancholy of its own jokes, which it usually can't bear to finish; only if Alice had made them, as it keeps egging her on to do, would they be at all interesting. That at least would show the child had paid some sort of attention, and he could go away and repeat them to other people. The desire to have jokes made all the time, he feels, is a painful and obvious confession of spiritual discomfort, and the freedom of Alice from such a feeling makes her unapproachable.

'Don't tease so,' said Alice, looking about in vain to see where the voice came from; 'if you're so anxious to have a joke made, why don't you make one yourself?'

The little voice sighed deeply: it was *very* unhappy, evidently, and Alice would have said something pitying to comfort it, 'if it would only sigh like other people!' she thought. But this was such a wonderfully small sigh, that she wouldn't have heard it at all, if it hadn't come *quite* close to her ear. The consequence of this was that it tickled her ear very much, and quite took off her thoughts from the unhappiness of the poor little creature.

I know you are a friend,' the little voice went on; '*a dear friend, and an old friend. And you won't hurt me, though I am an insect.*'

'What kind of insect?' Alice inquired a little anxiously. What she really wanted to know was, whether it could sting or not, but she thought this wouldn't be quite a civil question to ask.

'*What, then you don't—*' the little voice began. . . .

'Don't know who I am! Does anybody not know who I am?' He is afraid that even so innocent a love as his, like all love, may be cruel, and yet it is she who is able to hurt him, if only through his vanity. The implications of these few pages are so painful that the ironical calm of the close, when she kills it, seems delightfully gay and strong. The Gnat is suggesting to her that she would like to remain purely a creature of Nature and stay in the wood where there are no names.

'. . . That's a joke. I wish *you* had made it.'
'Why do you wish *I* had made it?' Alice asked. 'It's a very bad one.'
But the Gnat only sighed deeply, while two large tears came rolling down its cheeks.
'You shouldn't make jokes,' Alice said, 'if it makes you so unhappy.'
Then came another of those melancholy little sighs, and this time the poor Gnat really seemed to have sighed itself away, for, when Alice looked up, there was nothing whatever to be seen on the twig, and, as she was getting quite chilly with sitting so long, she got up and walked on.

The overpunctuation and the flat assonance of 'long—on' add to the effect. There is something charmingly prim and well-meaning about the way she sweeps aside the feelings that she can't deal with.

One need not suppose that Dodgson ever performed this scene, which he can imagine so clearly, but there is too much self-knowledge here to make the game of psychoanalysis seem merely good fun.

The scene in which the Duchess has become friendly to Alice at the garden-party shows Alice no longer separate from her creator; it is clear that Dodgson would be as irritated as she is by the incident, and is putting himself in her place. The obvious way to read it is as the middle-aged woman trying to flirt with the chaste young man.

'The game seems to ·be going on rather better now,' she said.
' 'Tis so,' said the Duchess; 'and the moral of it is—"Oh, 'tis love, 'tis love, that makes the world go round!" '
'Somebody said,' whispered Alice, 'that it's done by everybody minding their own business!'
'Ah, well! It means much the same thing,' said the Duchess, digging her sharp little chin into Alice's shoulder as she added, 'and the moral of *that* is—"Take care of the sense, and the sounds will take care of themselves." '
'How fond she is of finding morals in things,' Alice thought to herself.

Both are true because the generous and the selfish kinds of love have the same name; the Duchess seems to take the view of the political economists, that the greatest public good is produced by the greatest private selfishness. All this talk about 'morals' makes Alice supicious; also she is carrying a flamingo, a pink bird with a long neck. 'The chief difficulty Alice found at first was in managing her flamingo . . . it *would* twist itself round and look up in her face.'

'I dare say you're wondering why I don't put my arm round your waist,' the Duchess said after a pause: 'the reason is, that I'm doubtful about the temper of your flamingo. Shall I try the experiment?'
'He might bite,' Alice cautiously replied, not feeling at all anxious to have the experiment tried.
'Very true,' said the Duchess: 'flamingoes and mustard both bite. And the moral of that is—"Birds of a feather flock together." '

Mustard may be classed with the pepper

that made her 'ill-tempered' when she had so much of it in the soup, so that flamingoes and mustard become the desires of the two sexes. No doubt Dodgson would be indignant at having this meaning read into his symbols, but the meaning itself, if he had been intending to talk about the matter, is just what he would have wished to say.

The Duchess then jumps away to another aspect of the selfishness of our nature.

'It's a mineral, I *think*,' said Alice.
'Of course it is,' said the Duchess, who seemed ready to agree to everything that Alice said; 'there's a large mustard-mine near here. And the moral of that is—"The more there is of mine, the less there is of yours." '

One could put the same meanings in again, but a new one has come forward: 'Industrialism is as merely greedy as sex; all we get from it is a sharper distinction between rich and poor.' They go off into riddles about sincerity and how one can grow into what one would seem to be.

This sort of 'analysis' is a peep at machinery; the question for criticism is what is done with the machine. The purpose of a dream on the Freudian theory is simply to keep you in an undisturbed state so that you can go on sleeping; in the course of this practical work you may produce something of more general value, but not only of one sort. Alice has, I understand, become a patron saint of the Surrealists, but they do not go in for Comic Primness, a sort of reserve of force, which is her chief charm. Wyndham Lewis avoided putting her beside Proust and Lorelei to be danced on as a debilitating child-cult (though she is a bit of pragmatist too); the present-day reader is more likely to complain of her complacence. In this sort of child-cult the child, though a means of imaginative escape, becomes the critic; Alice is the most reasonable and responsible person in the book. This is meant as charmingly pathetic about her as well as satire about her elders, and there is some implication that the sane man can take no other view of the world, even for controlling it, than the child does; but this is kept a good distance from sentimental infantilism. There is always some doubt about the meaning of a man who says he wants to be like a child, because he may want to be like it in having fresh and vivid feelings and senses, in not knowing, expecting, or desiring evil, in not having an analytical mind, in having no sexual desires recognisable as such, or out of a desire to be mothered and evade responsibility. He is usually mixing them up—Christ's praise of children, given perhaps for reasons I have failed to list, has made it a respected thing to say, and it has been said often and loosely—but he can make his own mixture; Lewis's invective hardly shows which he is attacking. The praise of the child in the Alices mainly depends on a distaste not only for sexuality but for all the distortions of vision that go with a rich emotional life; the opposite idea needs to be set against this, that you can only understand people or even things by having such a life in yourself to be their mirror; but the idea itself is very respectable. So far as it is typical of the scientist the books are an expression of the scientific attitude (*e.g.* the bread-and-butter fly) or a sort of satire on it that treats it as inevitable.

The most obvious aspect of the complacence is the snobbery. It is clear that Alice is not only a very well-brought-up but a very well-to-do little girl; if she has grown into Mabel, so that she will have to go and live in that poky little house and have next to no toys to play with, she will refuse to come out of her rabbit-hole at all. One is only surprised that she is allowed to meet Mabel. All through the books odd objects of luxury are viewed rather as Wordsworth viewed mountains; meaningless, but grand and irremovable; objects of myth. The whiting, the talking leg of mutton, the soup-tureen, the tea-tray in the sky, are obvious examples. The shift from the idea of the child's unity with nature is amusingly complete; a mere change in the objects viewed makes it at one with the conventions. But this is still not far from Wordsworth, who made his mountains into symbols of the stable and moral society living among them. In part the

joke of this stands for the sincerity of the child that criticises the folly of convention, but Alice is very respectful to conventions and interested to learn new ones; indeed the discussions about the rules of the game of conversation, those stern comments on the isolation of humanity, put the tone so strongly in favour of the conventions that one feels there is nothing else in the world. There is a strange clash on this topic about the three little sisters discussed at the Mad Tea-party, who lived on treacle. 'They couldn't have done that, you know,' Alice gently remarked, 'they'd have been ill.' 'So they were,' said the Dormouse, '*very* ill.' The creatures are always self-centred and argumentative, to stand for the detachment of the intellect from emotion, which is necessary to it and yet makes it childish. Then the remark stands both for the danger of taking as one's guide the natural desires ('this is the sort of thing little girls would do if they were left alone') and for a pathetic example of a martyrdom to the conventions; the little girls did not mind *how* ill they were made by living on treacle, because it was their rule, and they knew it was expected of them. (That they are refined girls is clear from the fact that they do allegorical sketches.) There is an obscure connection here with the belief of the period that a really nice girl is 'delicate' (the profound sentences implied by the combination of meanings in this word are (*a*) 'you cannot get a woman to be refined unless you make her ill' and more darkly (*b*) 'she is desirable because corpse-like'); Dodgson was always shocked to find that his little girls had appetites, because it made them seem less pure. The passage about the bread-and-butter fly brings this out more frankly, with something of the wilful grimness of Webster. It was a creature of such high refinement that it could only live on weak tea with cream in it (tea being the caller's meal, sacred to the fair, with nothing gross about it).

A new difficulty came into Alice's head.

'Supposing it couldn't find any?' she suggested.

'Then it would die, of course.'

'But that must happen very often,' Alice remarked thoughtfully.

'It always happens,' said the Gnat.

After this, Alice was silent for a minute or two, pondering.

There need be no gloating over the child's innocence here, as in Barrie; anybody might ponder. Alice has just suggested that flies burn themselves to death in candles out of a martyr's ambition to become Snapdragon flies. The talk goes on to losing one's name, which is the next stage on her journey, and brings freedom but is like death; the girl may lose her personality by growing up into the life of convention, and her virginity (like her surname) by marriage; or she may lose her 'good name' when she loses the conventions 'in the woods'—the animals, etc., there have no names because they are out of reach of the controlling reason; or when she develops sex she must neither understand nor name her feelings. The Gnat is weeping and Alice is afraid of the wood but determined to go on. 'It always dies of thirst' or 'it always dies in the end, as do we all'; 'the life of highest refinement is the most deathly, yet what else is one to aim at when life is so brief, and when there is so little in it of any value.' A certain ghoulishness in the atmosphere of this, of which the tight-lacing may have been a product or partial cause,[1] comes out very strongly in Henry James; the decadents pounced on it for their own purposes but could not put more death-wishes into it than these respectables had done already.

The blend of child-cult and snobbery that Alice shares with Oscar Wilde is indeed much more bouncing and cheerful; the theme here is that it is proper for the well-meaning and innocent girl to be worldly, because she, like the world, should know the value of her condition. 'When we were girls we were brought up to know nothing, and very interest-

ing it was'; 'mamma, whose ideas on education are remarkably strict, has brought me up to be extremely short-sighted; so do you mind my looking at you through my glasses?' This joke seems to have come in after the Restoration dramatists as innocence recovered its social value; there are touches in Farquhar and it is strong in the *Beggar's Opera*. Sheridan has full control of it for Mrs. Malaprop.

I don't think so much learning becomes a young woman. . . . But, Sir Anthony, I would send her, at nine years old, to a boarding school, in order to learn a little ingenuity and artifice. Then, sir, she should have a supercilious knowledge in accounts; and as she grew up, I would have her instructed in geometry, that she might learn something of the contagious countries; but above all, Sir Anthony, she should be mistress of orthodoxy, that she might not mis-spell, and mispronounce words so shamefully as girls usually do; and likewise that she might reprehend the true meaning of what she is saying.

Dodgson has an imitation of this which may show, what many of his appreciators seem anxious to deny, that even *Wonderland* contains straight satire. The Mock Turtle was taught at school

Reeling and Writhing, of course, to begin with, and then the different branches of Arithmetic—Ambition, Distraction, Uglification, and Derision . . . Mystery, ancient and modern, with Seaography; then Drawling—the Drawling-master used to come once a week; *he* taught us Drawling, Stretching, and Fainting in Coils.

Children are to enjoy the jokes as against education, grown-ups as against a smart and too expensive education. Alice was not one of the climbers taught like this, and remarks firmly elsewhere that manners are not learnt from lessons. But she willingly receives social advice like 'curtsey while you're thinking what to say, it saves time,' and the doctrine that you must walk away from a queen if you really want to meet her has more point when said of the greed of the climber than of the unselfseeking curiosity of the small girl. Or it applies to both, and allows the climber a sense

---

[1] It was getting worse when the Alices were written. In what Mr. Hugh Kingsmill calls 'the fatal fifties' skirts were so big that the small waist was not much needed for contrast, so it can't be blamed for the literary works of that decade.

of purity and simplicity; I think this was a source of charm whether Dodgson meant it or not. Alice's own social assumptions are more subtle and all-pervading; she always seems to raise the tone of the company she enters, and to find this all the easier because the creatures are so rude to her. A central idea here is that the perfect lady can gain all the advantages of contempt without soiling herself by expressing or even feeling it.

This time there could be no mistake about it; it was neither more nor less than a pig, and she felt that it would be quite absurd for her to carry it any further. So she set the little creature down, and felt quite relieved to see it trot quietly away into the wood. 'If it had grown up,' she said to herself, 'it would have made a dreadfully ugly child, but it makes rather a handsome pig, I think.' And she began thinking over other children she knew, who might do very well as pigs, and was just saying to herself, 'if only one knew the right way to change them—' when she was a little startled by seeing the Cheshire Cat on the bough of a tree a few yards off.

The Cat only grinned when it saw Alice. It looked good-natured, she thought: still it had very long claws and a great many teeth, so she felt that it ought to be treated with respect.

The effect of cuddling these mellow evasive phrases—'a good deal'—'do very well as'—whose vagueness can convey so rich an irony and so complete a detachment, while making so firm a claim to show charming good-will, is very close to that of Wilde's comedy. So is the hint of a delicious slavishness behind the primness, and contrasting with the irony, of the last phrase. (But then Dodgson feels the cat deserves respect as the detached intelligence—he is enjoying the idea that Alice and other social figures have got to respect Dodgson.) I think there is a feeling that the aristocrat is essentially like the child because it is his business to make claims in advance of his immediate personal merits; the child is not strong yet, and the aristocrat only as part of a system; the best he can do if actually asked for his credentials, since it would be indecent to produce his pedigree, is to display charm and hope it will appear unconscious, like the good young

girl. Wilde's version of this leaves rather a bad taste in the mouth because it is slavish; it has something of the naive snobbery of the high-class servant. Whistler meant this by the most crashing of his insults—'Oscar now stands forth unveiled as his own "gentleman" '—when Wilde took shelter from a charge of plagiarism behind the claim that a gentleman does not attend to coarse abuse.

Slavish, for one thing, because they were always juggling between what they themselves thought wicked and what the society they addressed thought wicked, talking about sin when they meant scandal. The thrill of *Pen, Pencil and Poison* is in the covert comparison between Wilde himself and the poisoner, and Wilde certainly did not think his sexual habits as wicked as killing a friend to annoy an insurance company. By their very hints that they deserved notice as sinners they pretended to accept all the moral ideas of society, because they wanted to succeed in it, and yet society only took them seriously because they were connected with an intellectual movement which refused to accept some of those ideas. The Byronic theme of the man unable to accept the moral ideas of his society and yet torn by his feelings about them is real and permanent, but to base it on intellectual dishonesty is to short-circuit it; and leads to a claim that the life of highest refinement must be allowed a certain avid infantile petulance.

Alice is not a slave like this; she is almost too sure that she is good and right. The grown-up is egged on to imitate her not as a privileged decadent but as a privileged eccentric, a Victorian figure that we must be sorry to lose. The eccentric though kind and noble would be alarming from the strength of his virtues if he were less funny; Dodgson saw to it that this underlying feeling about his monsters was brought out firmly by Tenniel, who had been trained on drawing very serious things like the British Lion weeping over Gordon, for *Punch*. Their massive and romantic nobility is, I think, an important element in the effect; Dodgson did not get it in his own drawings (nor, by the way, did he give all the young men eunuchoid legs) but no doubt he would have done if he had been able. I should connect this weighty background with the tone of worldly goodness, of universal but not stupid charity, in Alice's remarks about the pig: 'I shall do my best even for you; of course one will suffer, because you are not worth the efforts spent on you; but I have no temptation to be uncharitable to you because I am too far above you to need to put you in your place'—this is what her tone would develop into; a genuine readiness for self-sacrifice and a more genuine sense of power.

The qualities held in so subtle a suspension in Alice are shown in full blast in the two queens. It is clear that this sort of moral superiority involves a painful isolation, similar to those involved in the intellectual way of life and the life of chastity, which are here associated with it. The reference to *Maud* (1855) brings this out. It was a shocking book; mockery was deserved; and its improper freedom was parodied by the flowers at the beginning of the *Looking-Glass*. A taint of fussiness hangs over this sort of essay, but the parodies were assumed to be obvious (children who aren't forced to learn Dr. Watts can't get the same thrill from parodies of him as the original children did) and even this parody is not as obvious as it was. There is no doubt that the flowers are much funnier if you compare them with their indestructible originals.

> whenever a March-wind sighs
> He sets the jewel-print of your feet
> In violets blue as your eyes . . .
> the pimpernel dozed on the lea;
> But the rose was awake all night for your sake,
> Knowing your promise to me;
> The lilies and roses were all awake . . .
> Queen rose of the rose-bud garden of girls. . . .

> There has fallen a splendid tear
> From the passion-flower at the gate.
> She is coming, my dove, my dear;
> She is coming, my life, my fate;
> The red rose cries, 'She is near, she is near';
> And the white rose weeps, 'She is late';

> The larkspur listens, 'I hear, I hear';
> And the lily whispers, 'I wait.'

'It isn't manners for us to begin, you know,' said the Rose, 'and I really was wondering when you'd speak.' . . . 'How is it that you all talk so nicely?' Alice said, hoping to get it into a better temper by a compliment. . . . 'In most gardens,' the Tiger-Lily said, 'they make the beds too soft, so that the flowers are always asleep.' This sounded a very good reason, and Alice was quite pleased to know it. 'I never thought of that before!' she said. 'It's *my* opinion you never think *at all*,' the Rose said in rather a severe tone. 'I never saw anybody that looked stupider,' a Violet said, so suddenly, that Alice quite jumped; for it hadn't spoken before. . . . 'She's coming!' cried the Larkspur. 'I hear her footstep, thump, thump, along the gravel-walk!' Alice looked round eagerly, and found that it was the Red Queen—

the concentrated essence, Dodgson was to explain, of all governesses. The Tiger-Lily was originally a Passion-Flower, but it was explained to Dodgson in time that the passion meant was not that of sexual desire (which he relates to ill-temper) but of Christ; a brilliant recovery was made after the shock of this, for *Tiger-Lily* includes both the alarming fierceness of ideal passion (chaste till now) and the ill-temper of the life of virtue and self-sacrifice typified by the governess (chaste always). So that in effect he includes all the flowers Tennyson named. The willow-tree that said Bough-Wough doesn't come in the poem, but it is a symbol of hopeless love anyway. The pink daisies turn white out of fear, as the white ones turn pink in the poem out of admiration. I don't know how far we ought to notice the remark about beds, which implies that they should be hard because even passion demands the virtues of asceticism (they are also the earthy beds of the grave); it fits in very well with the ideas at work, but does not seem a thing Dodgson would have said in clearer language.

But though he shied from the Christian association in the complex idea wanted from 'Passion-Flower' the flowers make another one very firmly.

'But that's not *your* fault,' the Rose added kindly: 'you're beginning to fade, you know—and then one can't help one's petals getting a little untidy.' Alice didn't like this idea at all: so, to change the subject, she asked 'Does she ever come out here?' 'I daresay you'll see her soon,' said the Rose. 'She's one of the thorny kind.' 'Where does she wear the thorns?' Alice asked with some curiosity. 'Why, all round her head, of course,' the Rose replied. 'I was wondering *you* hadn't got some too. I thought it was the regular rule.'

Death is never far out of sight in the books. The Rose cannot help standing for desire but its thorns here stand for the ill-temper not so much of passion as of chastity, that of the governess or that involved in ideal love. Then the thorns round the Queen's head, the 'regular rule' for suffering humanity, not yet assumed by the child, stand for the Passion, the self-sacrifice of the most ideal and most generous love, which produces ugliness and ill-temper.

The joke of making romantic love ridiculous by applying it to undesired middle-aged women is less to be respected than the joke of the hopelessness of idealism. W. S. Gilbert uses it for the same timid facetiousness but more offensively. This perhaps specially nineteenth-century trick is played about all the women in the Alices—the Ugly Duchess who had the aphrodisiac in the soup (pepper, as Alice pointed out, produces 'ill-temper') was the same person as the Queen in the first draft ('Queen of Hearts and Marchioness of Mock Turtles') so that the Queen's sentence of her is the suicide of disruptive passion. The Mock Turtle, who is half beef in the picture, with a cloven hoof, suffers from the calf-love of a turtle-dove; he went to a bad school and is excited about dancing. (He is also weeping for his lost childhood, which Dodgson sympathised with while blaming its exaggeration, and Alice thought very queer; this keeps it from being direct satire.) So love is also ridiculous in young men; it is felt that these two cover the whole field (Dodgson was about thirty at the time) so that granted these points the world is safe for

chastity. The danger was from middle-aged women because young women could be treated as pure like Alice. Nor indeed is this mere convention; Gilbert was relying on one of the more permanent jokes played by nature on civilisation, that unless somewhat primitive methods are employed the specific desires of refined women may appear too late. So far as the chaste man uses this fact, and the fact that men are hurt by permanent chastity less than women, in order to insult women, no fuss that he may make about baby women will make him dignified. Dodgson keeps the theme fairly agreeable by connecting it with the more general one of self-sacrifice—which may be useless or harmful, even when spontaneous or part of a reasonable convention, which then makes the sacrificer ridiculous and crippled, but which even then makes him deserve respect and may give him unexpected sources of power. The man playing at child-cult arrives at Sex War here (as usual since, but the comic Lear didn't), but not to the death nor with all weapons.

The same ideas are behind the White Queen, the emotional as against the practical idealist. It seems clear that the Apologia (1864) is in sight when she believes the impossible for half an hour before breakfast, to keep in practice; I should interpret the two examples she gives as immortality and putting back the clock of history, also Mass occurs before breakfast. All through the Wool and Water chapter (milk and water but not nourishing, and gritty to the teeth) she is Oxford; the life of learning rather than of dogmatic religion. Every one recognises the local shop, the sham fights, the rowing, the academic old sheep, and the way it laughs scornfully when Alice doesn't know the technical slang of rowing; and there are some general reflections on education. The teacher wilfully puts the egg a long way off so that you have to walk after it yourself, and meanwhile it turns into something else; and when you have 'paid for' the education its effects, then first known, must be accepted as part of you whether they are good or bad. Oxford as dreamy may be half satire half acceptance of Arnold's 'adorable dreamer' purple patch (1865).

Once at least in each book a cry of loneliness goes up from Alice at the oddity beyond sympathy or communication of the world she has entered—whether that in which the child is shut by weakness, or the adult by the renunciations necessary both for the ideal and the worldly way of life (the strength of the snobbery is to imply that these are the same). It seems strangely terrible that the answers of the White Queen, on the second of these occasions, should be so unanswerable.

By this time it was getting light. 'The crow must have flown away, I think,' said Alice: 'I'm so glad it's gone. I thought it was the night coming on.'

Even in the rhyme the crow may be fear of death. The rhymes, like those other main structural materials, chess and cards, are useful because, being fixed, trivial, odd, and stirring to the imagination, they affect one as conventions of the dream world, and this sets the tone about conventions.

'I wish I could manage to be glad!' the Queen said. 'Only I never can remember the rule. You must be very happy, living in this wood, and being glad whenever you like.'

So another wood has turned out to be Nature. This use of 'that's a rule' is Sheridan's in *The Critic*; the pathos of its futility is that it is an attempt of reason to do the work of emotion and escape the dangers of the emotional approach to life. There may be a glance at the Oxford Movement and dogma. Perhaps chiefly a satire on the complacence of the fashion of slumming, the remark seems to spread out into the whole beauty and pathos of the ideas of pastoral; by its very universality her vague sympathy becomes an obscure self-indulgence.

'Only it is so very lonely here!' Alice said in a melancholy voice; and at the thought of her loneliness two large tears came rolling down her cheeks.

'Oh, don't go on like that,' cried the poor Queen, wringing her hands in despair. 'Consider what a great girl you are. Consider what a long way you've come to-day. Consider what o'clock it is. Consider anything, only don't cry!'

Alice could not help laughing at this, even in the midst of her tears. 'Can you keep from crying by considering things?' she asked.

'That's the way it's done,' the Queen said with great decision; 'nobody can do two things at once, you know. Let's consider your age to begin with—how old are you?'

We are back at once to the crucial topic of age and the fear of death, and pass to the effectiveness of practice in helping one to believe the impossible; for example that the ageing Queen is so old that she would be dead. The helplessness of the intellect, which claims to rule so much, is granted under cover of the counter-claim that since it makes you impersonal you can forget pain with it; we do not believe this about the queen chiefly because she has not enough understanding of other people. The jerk of the return to age, and the assumption that this is a field for polite lying, make the work of the intellect only the game of conversation. Humpty Dumpty has the same embarrassing trick for arguing away a suggestion of loneliness. Indeed about all the rationalism of Alice and her acquaintants there hangs a suggestion that there are after all questions of pure thought, academic thought whose altruism is recognised and paid for, thought meant only for the upper classes to whom the conventions are in any case natural habit; like that suggestion that the scientist is sure to be a gentleman and has plenty of space which is the fascination of Kew Gardens.

The Queen is a very inclusive figure. 'Looking before and after' with the plaintive tone of universal altruism she lives chiefly backwards, in history; the necessary darkness of growth, the mysteries of self-knowledge, the self-contradictions of the will, the antinomies of philosophy, the very Looking-Glass itself, impose this; nor is it mere weakness to attempt to resolve them only in the direct impulse of the child. Gathering the more dream-rushes her love for man becomes the more universal, herself the more like a porcupine. Knitting with more and more needles she tries to control life by a more and more complex intellectual apparatus—the 'progress' of Herbert Spencer; any one shelf of the shop is empty, but there is always something very interesting—the 'atmosphere' of the place is so interesting—which moves up as you look at it from shelf to shelf; there is jam only in the future and our traditional past, and the test made by Alice, who sent value through the ceiling as if it were quite used to it, shows that progress can never reach value, because its habitation and name is heaven. The Queen's scheme of social reform, which is to punish those who are not respectable before their crimes are committed, seems to be another of these jokes about progress:

'But if you *hadn't* done them,' the Queen said, 'that would have been better still; better, and better, and better!' Her voice went higher with each 'better' till it got to quite a squeak at last.

There is a similar attack in the Walrus and the Carpenter, who are depressed by the spectacle of unimproved nature and engage in charitable work among oysters. The Carpenter is a Castle and the Walrus, who could eat so many more because he was crying behind his handkerchief, was a Bishop, in the scheme at the beginning of the book. But in saying so one must be struck by the depth at which the satire is hidden; the queerness of the incident and the characters takes on a Wordsworthian grandeur and aridity, and the landscape defined by the tricks of facetiousness takes on the remote and staring beauty of the ideas of the insane. It is odd to find that Tenniel went on to illustrate Poe in the same manner; Dodgson is often doing what Poe wanted to do, and can do it the more easily because he can safely introduce the absurd. The Idiot Boy of Wordsworth is too milky a moonlit creature to be at home with Nature as she was deplored by the Carpen-

ter, and much of the technique of the rudeness of the Mad Matter has been learned from Hamlet. It is the ground-bass of this kinship with insanity, I think, that makes it so clear that the books are not trifling, and the cool courage with which Alice accepts madmen that gives them their strength.

This talk about the snobbery of the Alices may seem a mere attack, but a little acid may help to remove the slime with which they have been encrusted. The two main ideas behind the snobbery, that virtue and intelligence are alike lonely, and that good manners are therefore important though an absurd confession of human limitations, do not depend on a local class system; they would be recognised in a degree by any tolerable society. And if in a degree their opposites must also be recognised, so they are here; there are solid enough statements of the shams of altruism and convention and their horrors when genuine; it is the forces of this conflict that make a clash violent enough to end both the dreams. In *Wonderland* this is mysteriously mixed up with the trial of the Knave of Hearts, the thief of love, but at the end of the second book the symbolism is franker and more simple. She is a grown queen and has acquired the conventional dignities of her insane world; suddenly she admits their insanity, refuses to be a grown queen, and destroys them.

'I can't stand this any longer!' she cried, as she seized the table-cloth in both hands: one good pull, and plates, dishes, guests, and candles came crashing down together in a heap on the floor.

The guests are inanimate and the crawling self-stultifying machinery of luxury has taken on a hideous life of its own. It is the High Table of Christ Church that we must think of here. The gentleman is not the slave of his conventions because at need he could destroy them; and yet, even if he did this, and all the more because he does not, he must adopt while despising it the attitude to them of the child.

R. P. BLACKMUR

(b. 1904)

A critic best known for his perceptive close analyses of poetic language, Richard Palmer Blackmur has described his approach as "primarily through technique, in the widest sense of that word, of the examples handled." Although he is identified with the New Criticism, Blackmur was a practicing "technical" critic for more than a decade before the emergence of that movement. His many critical essays have been collected in volumes that include *The Double Agent: Essays in Craft and Elucidation* (1935), *The Expense of Greatness* (1940), *Language as Gesture* (1952), and *The Lion and the Honeycomb* (1952). *Form and Value in Modern Poetry* (1957) is a selection of essays from *Language as Gesture*. Blackmur has also edited *The Art of the Novel, Critical Prefaces by Henry James* (1934).

The Later Poetry of W. B. Yeats (1936)

The later poetry of William Butler Yeats is certainly great enough in its kind, and varied enough within its kind, to warrant a special approach, deliberately not the only approach, and deliberately not a complete approach. A body of great poetry will awaken and exemplify different interests on different occasions, or even on the same occasions, as we may see in the contrasting and often contesting literatures about Dante and Shakespeare: even a relation to the poetry is not common to them all. I propose here to examine Yeats's later poetry with a special regard to his own approach to the making of it; and to explore a little what I conceive to be the dominant mode of his insight, the relations between it and the printed poems, and—a different thing—the relations between it and the readers of his poems.

The major facts I hope to illustrate are these: that Yeats has, if you accept

his mode, a consistent extraordinary grasp of the reality of emotion, character, and aspiration; and that his chief resort and weapon for the grasping of that reality is magic; and that if we would make use of that reality for ourselves we must also make some use of the magic that inspirits it. What is important is that the nexus of reality and magic is not by paradox or sleight of hand, but is logical and represents, for Yeats in his poetry, a full use of intelligence. Magic performs for Yeats the same fructifying function that Christianity does for Eliot, or that ironic fatalism did for Thomas Hardy; it makes a connection between the poem and its subject matter and provides an adequate mechanics of meaning and value. If it happens that we discard more of Hardy than we do of Yeats and more of Yeats than we do of Eliot, it is not because Christianity provides better machinery for the movement of poetry than fatalism or magic, but simply because Eliot is a more cautious craftsman. Besides, Eliot's poetry has not even comparatively worn long enough to show what parts are permanent and what merely temporary. The point here is that fatalism, Christianity, and magic are none of them disciplines to which many minds can consciously appeal today, as Hardy, Eliot, and Yeats do, for emotional strength and moral authority. The supernatural is simply not part of our mental furniture, and when we meet it in our reading we say: Here is debris to be swept away. But if we sweep it away without first making sure what it is, we are likely to lose the poetry as well as the debris. It is the very purpose of a supernaturally derived discipline, as used in poetry, to set the substance of natural life apart, to give it a form, a meaning, and a value which cannot be evaded. What is excessive and unwarranted in the discipline we indeed ought to dismiss; but that can be determined only when what is integrating and illuminating is known first. The discipline will in the end turn out to have had only a secondary importance for the reader; but its effect will remain active even when he no longer considers it. That is because for the poet the discipline, far from seeming secondary, had an extraordinary structural, seminal, and substantial importance to the degree that without it he could hardly have written at all.

Poetry does not flow from thin air but requires always either a literal faith, an imaginative faith, or, as in Shakespeare, a mind full of many provisional faiths. The life we all live is not alone enough of a subject for the serious artist; it must be life with a leaning, life with a tendency to shape itself only in certain forms, to afford its most lucid revelations only in certain lights. If our final interest, either as poets or as readers, is in the reality declared when the forms have been removed and the lights taken away, yet we can never come to the reality at all without the first advantage of the form and lights. Without them we should *see* nothing but only glimpse something unstable. We glimpse the fleeting but do not see what it is that fleets.

So it was with Yeats; his early poems are fleeting, some of them beautiful and some that sicken, as you read them, to their own extinction. But as he acquired for himself a discipline, however unacceptable to the bulk of his readers, his poetry obtained an access to reality. So it is with most of our serious poets. It is almost the mark of the poet of genuine merit in our time—the poet who writes serious works with an intellectual aspect which are nonetheless poetry—that he performs his work in the light of an insight, a group of ideas, and a faith, with the discipline that flows from them, which taken together form a view of life most readers cannot share, and which, furthermore, most readers feel as repugnant, or sterile, or simply inconsequential.

All this is to say generally—and we shall say it particularly for Yeats later—that our culture is incomplete with regard to poetry; and the poet has to provide for himself in that quarter where authority and value are derived. It may be that no poet ever found a culture complete for his purpose; it was a welcome and arduous part of his business to make it so. Dante, we may say, completed for poetry the Christian culture of his time, which was itself the completion of centuries. But there was at hand for Dante, and as a rule in the great ages of poetry, a fundamental agreement or convention between the poet and his audience about the validity of the view of life of which the poet deepened the reality and spread the scope. There is no such agreement today. We find poets either using the small conventions of the individual life as if they were great conventions, or attempting to resurrect some great convention of the past, or, finally, attempting to discover the great convention that must lie, willy-nilly, hidden in the life about them. This is a labor, whichever form it takes, which leads as often to subterfuge, substitution, confusion, and failure, as to success; and it puts the abnormal burden upon the reader of determining what the beliefs of the poet are and how much to credit them before he can satisfy himself of the reality which those beliefs envisage. The alternative is to put poetry at a discount—which is what has happened.

This the poet cannot do who is aware of the possibilities of his trade: the possibilities of arresting, enacting, and committing to the language through his poems the expressed value of the life otherwise only lived or evaded. The poet so aware knows, in the phrasing of that prose-addict Henry James, both the sacred rage of writing and the muffled majesty of authorship; and knows, as Eliot knows, that once to have been visited by the muses is ever afterward to be haunted. These are qualities that once apprehended may not be discounted without complete surrender, when the poet is no more than a haunt haunted. Yeats has never put his poetry at a discount. But he has made it easy for his readers to do so—as Eliot has in his way—because the price he has paid for it, the expense he has himself been to in getting it on paper, have been a price most readers simply do not know how to pay and an expense, in time and labor and willingness to understand, beyond any initial notion of adequate reward.

The price is the price of a fundamental and deliberate surrender to magic as the ultimate mode for the apprehension of reality. The expense is the double expense of, on the one hand, implementing magic with a consistent symbolism, and on the other hand, the greatly multiplied expense of restoring, through the *craft* of poetry, both the reality and its symbols to that plane where alone their experience becomes actual—the plane of the quickened senses and the concrete emotions. That is to say, the poet (and, as always, the reader) has to combine, to fuse inextricably into something like an organic unity the constructed or derived symbolism of his special insight with the symbolism animating the language itself. It is, on the poet's plane, the labor of bringing the representative forms of knowledge home to the experience which stirred them: the labor of keeping in mind *what* our knowledge is of: the labor of craft. With the poetry of Yeats this labor is, as I say, doubly hard, because the forms of knowledge,

being magical, do not fit naturally with the forms of knowledge that ordinarily preoccupy us. But it is possible, and I hope to show it, that the difficulty is, in a sense, superficial and may be overcome with familiarity, and that the mode of magic itself, once familiar, will even seem rational for the purposes of poetry —although it will not thereby seem inevitable. Judged by its works in the representation of emotional reality—and that is all that can be asked in our context—magic and its burden of symbols may be a major tool of the imagination. A tool has often a double function; it performs feats for which it was designed, and it is heuristic, it discovers and performs new feats which could not have been anticipated without it, which it indeed seems to instigate for itself and in the most unlikely quarters. It is with magic as a tool in its heuristic aspect— as an agent for discovery—that I wish here directly to be concerned.

One of the finest, because one of the most appropriate to our time and place, of all Yeats's poems, is his "The Second Coming."

Turning and turning in the widening gyre
The falcon cannot hear the falconer;
Things fall apart; the centre cannot hold;
Mere anarchy is loosed upon the world,
The blood-dimmed tide is loosed, and everywhere
The ceremony of innocence is drowned;
The best lack all conviction, while the worst
Are full of passionate intensity.

Surely some revelation is at hand;
Surely the Second Coming is at hand.
The Second Coming! Hardly are those words out
When a vast image out of *Spiritus Mundi*
Troubles my sight: somewhere in sands of the desert
A shape with lion body and the head of a man,
A gaze blank and pitiless as the sun,
Is moving its slow thighs, while all about it
Reel shadows of the indignant desert birds.
The darkness drops again; but now I know
That twenty centuries of stony sleep
Were vexed to nightmare by a rocking cradle,
And what rough beast, its hour come round at last,
Slouches towards Bethlehem to be born?

There is about it, to any slowed reading, the immediate conviction of pertinent emotion; the lines are stirring, separately and in their smaller groups, and there is a sensible life in them that makes them seem to combine in the form of an emotion. We may say at once then, for what it is worth, that in writing his poem Yeats was able to choose words which to an appreciable extent were the right ones to reveal or represent the emotion which was its purpose. The words deliver the meaning which was put into them by the craft with which they were arranged, and that meaning is their own, not to be segregated or given another arrangement without diminution. Ultimately, something of this sort is all that can be said of this or any poem, and when it is said, the poem is known to be good in its own terms or bad because not in its own terms. But the reader seldom reaches an ultimate position about a poem; most poems fail, through craft or conception, to reach an ultimate or absolute position: parts of the craft remain machinery and parts of the conception remain in limbo. Or, as in this poem, close inspection will show something questionable about it. It is true that it can be read as it is, isolated from the rest of Yeats's work and isolated from the intellectual material which it expresses, and a good deal gotten out of it, too, merely by submitting to it. That is because the words are mainly common, both in their emotional and intellectual senses; and if we do not know precisely what the familiar words drag after them into the poem, still we know vaguely what the weight of it feels like; and that seems enough to make a poem at one level of response. Yet if an attempt is made at a more complete response, if we wish to discover the precise emotion which the words mount up to, we come into trouble and uncertainty at once. There is an air of explicitness to each of the separate fragments of the poem. Is it, in this line or that, serious? Has it a reference?—or is it a rhetorical effect, a result only of the persuasive overtones of words?—or is it a combination, a mixture of reference and rhetoric?

Possibly the troubled attention will fasten first upon the italicized phrase in the twelfth line: *Spiritus Mundi*; and the question is whether the general, the readily available senses of the words are adequate to supply the specific sense wanted by the poem. Put another way, can the poet's own arbitrary meaning be made, merely by discovering it, to participate in and enrich what the "normal" meanings of the words in their limiting context provide? The critic can only supply the facts; the poem will in the end provide its own answer. Here there are certain facts that may be extracted from Yeats's prose writings which suggest something of what the words symbolize for him. In one of the notes to the limited edition of *Michael Robartes and the Dancer*, Yeats observes that his mind, like another's, has been from time to time obsessed by images which had no discoverable origin in his waking experience. Speculating as to their origin, he came to deny both the conscious and the unconscious memory as their probable seat, and finally invented a doctrine which traced the images to sources of supernatural character. I quote only that sentence which is relevant to the phrase in question: "Those [images] that come in sleep are (1) from the state immediately preceding our birth; (2) from the *Spiritus Mundi*—that is to say, from a general storehouse of images which have ceased to be a property of any personality or spirit." It apparently follows, for Yeats, that images so derived have both an absolute meaning of their own and an operative force in determining meaning and predicting events in this world. In another place (the Introduction to "The Resurrection" in *Wheels and Butterflies*) he describes the image used in this poem, which he had seen many times, "always at my left side just out of the range of sight, a brazen winged beast that I associated with laughing, ecstatic destruction." Ecstasy, it should be added, comes for Yeats just before death, and at death comes the moment of revelation, when the soul is shown its kindred dead and it is possible to see the future.

Here we come directly upon that central part of Yeats's magical beliefs which it is one purpose of this poem emotionally to represent: the belief in what is called variously *Magnus Annus*, The Great Year, The Platonic Year, and sometimes in a slightly different symbolism, The Great Wheel. This belief, with respect to the history of epochs, is associated with the precession of the equinoxes, which bring, roughly every two thousand years, a Great Year of death and rebirth, and this belief, with respect to individuals, seems to be associated with the phases of the moon; although individuals may be influenced by the equinoxes and there may be a lunar interpretation of history. These beliefs have a scaffold of geometrical figures, gyres, cones, circles, etc., by the application of which exact interpretation is secured. Thus it is possible to predict, both in biography and history, and in time, both forward and backward, the character, climax, collapse, and rebirth in antithetical form of human types and cultures. There is a subordinate but helpful belief that signs, warnings, even direct messages, are always given, from *Spiritus Mundi* or elsewhere, which the poet and the philosopher have only to see and hear. As it happens, the Christian era, being nearly two thousand years old, is due for extinction and replacement, in short for the Second Coming, which this poem heralds. In his note to its first publication (in *Michael Robartes and the Dancer*) Yeats expresses his belief as follows:

At the present moment the life gyre is sweeping outward, unlike that before the birth of Christ which was narrowing, and has almost reached its greatest expansion. The revelation which approaches will however take its character from the contrary movement of the interior gyre. All our scientific, democratic, fact-accumulating, heterogeneous civilisation belongs to the outward gyre and prepares not the continuance of itself but the revelation as in a lightning flash, though in a flash that will not strike only in one place, and will for a time be constantly repeated, of the civilisation that must slowly take its place.

So much for a major gloss upon the poem. Yeats combined, in the best verse he could manage, the beliefs which obsessed him with the image which he took to be a specific illustration of the beliefs. Minor and buttressing glosses are possible for many of the single words and phrases in the poem, some flowing from private doctrine and some from Yeats's direct sense of the world about him, and some from both at once. For example: The "ceremony of innocence" represents for Yeats one of the qualities that made life valuable under the dying aristocratic social tradition; and the meaning of the phrase in the poem requires no magic for completion but only a reading of other poems. The "falcon and the falconer" in the second line has, besides its obvious symbolism, a doctrinal reference. A falcon is a hawk, and a hawk is symbolic of the active or intellectual mind; the falconer is perhaps the soul itself or its uniting principle. There is also the apposition which Yeats has made several times that "Wisdom is a butterfly/And not a gloomy bird of prey." Whether the special symbolism has actually been incorporated in the poem, and in which form, or whether it is private debris merely, will take a generation of readers to decide. In the meantime it must be taken provisionally for whatever its ambiguity may seem to be worth. Literature is full of falcons, some that fly and some that lack immediacy and sit, archaic, on the poet's wrist; and it is not always illuminating to determine which is which. But when we come on such lines as

The best lack all conviction, while the worst
Are full of passionate intensity,

we stop short, first to realize the aptness of the statement to every plane of life in the world about us, and then to connect the lines with the remote body of the poem they illuminate. There is a dilemma of which the branches grow from one trunk but which cannot be solved; for these lines have, not two meanings, but two sources for the same meaning. There is the meaning that comes from the summary observation that this is how men are—and especially men of power—in the world we live in; it is knowledge that comes from knowledge of the "fury and the mire in human veins"; a meaning the contemplation of which has lately (April, 1934) led Yeats to offer himself to any government or party that, using force and marching men, will "promise not this or that measure but a discipline, a way of life." And there is in effect the same meaning, at least at the time the poem was written, which comes from a different source and should have, one would think, very different consequences in prospective party loyalties. Here the meaning has its source in the doctrines of the Great Year and the phases of the Moon; whereby, to cut exegesis short, it is predicted as necessary that, at the time we have reached, the best minds, being subjective, should have lost all faith though desiring it, and the worst minds, being so nearly objective, have no need of faith and may be full of "passionate intensity" without the control of any faith or wisdom. Thus we have on the one side the mirror of observation and on the other side an imperative, magically derived, which come to the conclusion of form in identical words.

The question is, to repeat, whether the fact of this double control and source of meaning at a critical point defeats or strengthens the unity of the poem; and it is a question which forms itself again and again in the later poems, sometimes obviously but more often only by suggestion. If we take another poem on the same theme, written some years earlier, and before his wife's mediumship gave him the detail of his philosophy, we will find the question no easier to answer in its suggested than in its conspicuous form. There is an element in the poem called "The Magi" which we can feel the weight of but cannot altogether name, and of which we can only guess at the efficacy.

Now as at all times I can see in the mind's eye,
In their stiff, painted clothes, the pale unsatisfied ones

Appear and disappear in the blue depths of
  the sky
With all their ancient faces like rain-beaten
  stones,
And all their helms of silver hovering side by
  side,
And all their eyes still fixed, hoping to find
  once more,
Being by Calvary's turbulence unsatisfied,
The uncontrollable mystery on the bestial floor.

I mean the element which, were Yeats a Christian, we could accept as a species of Christian blasphemy or advanced heresy, but which since he is not a Christian we find it hard to accept at all: the element of emotional conviction springing from intellectual matters without rational source or structure. We ought to be able, for the poem's sake, to accept the conviction as an emotional possibility, much as we accept *Lear* or Dostoevski's *Idiot* as valid, because projected from represented experience. But Yeats's experience is not represented consistently on any one plane. He constantly indicates a supernatural validity for his images of which the authority cannot be reached. If we come nearer to accepting "The Magi" than "The Second Coming" it is partly because the familiar Christian paradigm is more clearly used, and, in the last two lines, what Yeats constructs upon it is given a more immediate emotional form, and partly because, *per contra*, there is less demand made upon arbitrary intellectual belief. There is, too, the matter of scope; if we reduce the scope of "The Second Coming" to that of "The Magi" we shall find it much easier to accept; but we shall have lost much of the poem.

We ought now to have enough material to name the two radical defects of magic as a tool for poetry. One defect, which we have just been illustrating, is that it has no available edifice of reason reared upon it conventionally independent of its inspiration. There is little that the uninspired reader can naturally refer to for authority outside the poem, and if he does make a natural reference he is likely to turn out to be at least partly wrong. The poet is thus in the opposite predicament; he is under the constant necessity of erecting his beliefs into doctrines at the same time that he represents their emotional or dramatic equivalents. He is, in fact, in much the same position that Dante would have been had he had to construct his Christian doctrine while he was composing *The Divine Comedy*: an impossible labor. The Christian supernaturalism, the Christian magic (no less magical than that of Yeats), had the great advantage for Dante, and imaginatively for ourselves, of centuries of reason and criticism and elaboration: it was within reason a consistent whole; and its supernatural element had grown so consistent with experience as to seem supremely *natural*—as indeed it may again. Christianity has an objective form, whatever the mysteries at its heart and its termini, in which all the phenomena of human life may find place and meaning. Magic is none of these things for any large fraction of contemporary society. Magic has a tradition, but it is secret, not public. It has not only central and terminal mysteries but has also peripheral mysteries, which require not only the priest to celebrate but also the adept to manipulate. Magic has never been made "natural." The practical knowledge and power which its beliefs lead to can neither be generally shared nor overtly rationalized. It is in fact held to be dangerous to reveal openly the details of magical experience: they may be revealed, if at all, only in arbitrary symbols and equivocal statements. Thus we find Yeats, in his early and innocuous essay on magic, believing his life to have been imperiled for revealing too much. Again, the spirits or voices through whom magical knowledge is gained are often themselves equivocal and are sometimes deliberately confusing. Yeats was told to remember, "We will deceive you if we can," and on another occasion was forbidden to record anything that was said, only to be scolded later because he had failed to record every word. In short, it is of the essence of magical faith that the supernatural cannot be brought into the natural world except through symbol. The distinction between natural and supernatural is held to be substantial instead of verbal. Hence magic may neither be criticized nor institutionalized; nor can it ever reach a full expression of its own intention. This is perhaps the justification of Stephen Spender's remark that there is more magic in Eliot's "The Hollow Men" than in any poem of Yeats; because of Eliot's Christianity, his magic has a rational base as well as a supernatural source: it is the magic of an orthodox, authoritative faith. The dogmas of magic, we may say, are all heresies which cannot be expounded except each on its own authority as a fragmentary insight; and its unity can be only the momentary unity of association. Put another way, magic is in one respect in the state of Byzantine Christianity, when miracles were quotidian and the universal frame of experience, when life itself was held to be supernatural and reason was mainly a kind of willful sophistication.

Neither Yeats nor ourselves dwell in Byzantium. At a certain level, though not at all levels, we conceive life, and even its nonrational features, in rational terms. Certainly there is a rational bias and a rational structure in the poetry we mainly agree to hold great—though the content may be what it will; and it is the irrational bias and the confused structure that we are mainly concerned to disavow, to apologize or allow for. It was just to provide himself with the equivalent of a rational religious insight and a predictable rational structure for the rational imagination that in his book, *A Vision* (published, in 1925, in a limited edition only, and then withdrawn), he attempted to convert his magical experience into a systematic philosophy. "I wished," he writes in the Dedication to that work, "for a system of thought that would leave my imagination free to create as it chose and yet make all that it created, or could create, part of the one history, and that the soul's." That is, Yeats hoped by systematizing it to escape from the burden of confusion and abstraction which his magical experience had imposed upon him. "I can now," he declares in this same Dedication, "if I have the energy, find the simplicity I have sought in vain.

I need no longer write poems like 'The Phases of the Moon' nor 'Ego Dominus Tuus,' nor spend barren years, as I have done three or four times, striving with abstractions that substitute themselves for the play that I had planned."

"Having inherited," as he says in one of his poems, "a vigorous mind," he could not help seeing, once he had got it all down, that his system was something to disgorge if he could. Its truth as experience would be all the stronger if its abstractions could be expunged. But it could not be disgorged; its thirty-five years of growth was an intimate part of his own growth, and its abstractions were all of a piece with his most objective experience. And perhaps we, as readers, can see that better from outside than Yeats could from within. I suspect that no amount of will could have rid him of his magical conception of the soul; it was by magic that he knew the soul; and the conception had been too closely associated with his profound sense of his race and personal ancestry. He has never been able to retract his system, only to take up different attitudes toward it. He has alternated between granting his speculations only the validity of poetic myth and planning to announce a new deity. In his vacillation—there is a poem by that title—the rational defect remains, and the reader must deal with it sometimes as an intrusion, of indeterminate value, upon the poetry and sometimes as itself the subject of dramatic reverie or lyric statement. At least once he tried to force the issue home, and in a section of *A Packet for Ezra Pound* called "Introduction to the Great Wheel" he meets the issue by transforming it, for the moment, into wholly poetic terms. Because it reveals a fundamental honesty and clarity of purpose in the midst of confusion and uncertainty the section is quoted entire.

Some will ask if I believe all that this book contains, and I will not know how to answer. Does the word belief, as they will use it, belong to our age, can I think of the world as there and I here judging it? I will never think any thoughts but these, or some modification or extension of these; when I write prose or verse they must be somewhere present though it may not be in the words; they must affect my judgment of friends and events; but then there are many symbolisms and none exactly resembles mine. What Leopardi in Ezra Pound's translation calls that 'concord' wherein 'the arcane spirit of the whole mankind turns hardy pilot' —how much better it would be without that word 'hardy' which slackens speed and adds nothing—persuades me that he has best imagined reality who has best imagined justice.

The rational defect, then, remains; the thought is not always in the words; and we must do with it as we can. There is another defect of Yeats's magical system which is especially apparent to the reader but which may not be apparent at all to Yeats. Magic promises precisely matters which it cannot perform—at least in poetry. It promises, as in "The Second Coming," exact prediction of events in the natural world; and it promises again and again, in different poems, exact revelations of the supernatural, and of this we have an example in what has to many seemed a great poem, "All Souls' Night," which had its first publication as an epilogue to *A Vision*. Near the beginning of the poem we have the explicit declaration: "I have a marvelous thing to say"; and near the end another: "I have mummy truths to tell." "Mummy truths" is an admirable phrase, suggestive as it is of the truths in which the dead are wrapped, ancient truths as old as Egypt perhaps, whence mummies commonly come, and truths, too, that may be unwound. But there, with the suggestion, the truths stop short; there is, for the reader, no unwinding, no revelation of the dead. What Yeats actually does is to summon into the poem various of his dead friends as "characters"— and this is the greatness, and only this, of the poem: the summary, excited, even exalted presentation of character. Perhaps the rhetoric is the marvel and the evasion the truth. We get an impact as from behind, from the speed and weight of the words, and are left with an ominous or terrified frame of mind, the revelation still to come. The revelation, the magic, was in Yeats's mind; hence the exaltation in his language; but it was not and could not be given in the words of the poem.

It may be that for Yeats there was a similar exaltation and a similar self-deceit in certain other poems, but as the promise of revelation was not made, the reader feels no failure of fulfillment. Such poems as "Easter, 1916," "In Memory of Major Robert Gregory," and "Upon a Dying Lady" may have buried in them a conviction of invocation and revelation; but if so it is no concern of ours: we are concerned only, as the case may be, with the dramatic presentations of the Irish patriots and poets, Yeats's personal friends, and Aubrey Beardsley's dying sister, and with, in addition, for minor pleasure, the technical means—the spare and delicate language, the lucid images, and quickening rhymes—whereby the characters are presented as intensely felt. There is no problem in such poems but the problem of reaching, through a gradual access of intimacy, full appreciation; here the magic and everything else are in the words. It is the same, for bare emotion apart from character, in such poems as "A Deep-Sworn Vow," where the words accumulate by the simplest means an intolerable excitement, where the words are, called as they may be from whatever source, in an ultimate sense their own meaning.

Others because you did not keep
That deep-sworn vow have been friends of
  mine;
Yet always when I look death in the face,
When I clamber to the heights of sleep,
Or when I grow excited with wine,
Suddenly I meet your face.

Possibly all poetry should be read as this poem is read, and no poetry greatly valued that cannot be so read. Such is one ideal toward which reading tends; but to apply it as a standard of judgment we should first have to assume for the poetic intelligence absolute autonomy and self-perfection for all its works. Actually, autonomy and self-perfection are relative and depend upon a series of agreements or conventions between the poet and his readers, which alter continually, as to what must be represented by the fundamental power of language (itself a relatively stable convention) and what, on the other hand, may be adequately represented by mere reference, sign, symbol, or blueprint indication. Poetry is so little autonomous from the technical point of view that the greater part of a given work must be conceived as the manipulation of conventions that the reader will, or will not, take for granted; these being crowned, or animated, emotionally transformed, by what the poet actually represents, original or not, through his mastery of poetic language. Success is provisional, seldom complete, and never permanently complete. The vitality or letter of a convention may perish although the form persists. *Romeo and Juliet* is less successful today than when produced because the conventions of honor, family authority, and blood-feud no longer animate and justify the action; and if the play survives it is partly because certain other conventions of human character do remain vital, but more because Shakespeare is the supreme master of representation through the reality of language alone. Similarly with Dante; with the cumulative disintegration, even for Catholics, of medieval Christianity as the ultimate convention of human life, the success of *The Divine Comedy* comes more and more to depend on the exhibition of character and the virtue of language alone—which may make it a greater, not a lesser poem. On the other hand, it often happens that a poet's ambition is such that, in order to get his work done at all, he must needs set up new conventions or radically modify old ones which fatally lack that benefit of form which can be conferred only by public recognition. The form which made his poem available was only gradually conferred upon the convention of evil in Baudelaire and, as we may see in translations with contrasting emphases, its limits are still subject to debate; in his case the more so because the life of his language depended more than usual on the viability of the convention.

Let us apply these notions, which ought so far to be commonplace, to the later work of Yeats, relating them especially to the predominant magical convention therein. When Yeats came of poetic age he found himself, as Blake had before him, and even Wordsworth but to a worse extent, in a society whose conventions extended neither intellectual nor moral authority to poetry; he found himself in a rational but deliberately incomplete, because progressive, society. The *emotion* of thought, for poetry, was gone, along with the emotion of religion and the emotion of race—the three sources and the three aims of the great poetry of the past. Tyndall and Huxley are the villains, Yeats records in his *Autobiographies*, as Blake recorded Newton; there were other causes, but no matter, these names may serve as symbols. And the dominant aesthetics of the time were as rootless in the realm of poetic import and authority as the dominant conventions. Art for Art's sake was the cry, the Ivory Tower the retreat, and Walter Pater's luminous langour and weak Platonism the exposition. One could say anything but it would mean nothing. The poets and society both, for opposite reasons, expected the poet to produce either exotic and ornamental mysteries or lyrics of mood; the real world and its significance were reserved mainly to the newer sciences, though the novelists and the playwrights might poach if they could. For a time Yeats succumbed, as may be seen in his early work, even while he attempted to escape; and of his poetic generation he was the only one to survive and grow in stature. He came under the influence of the French Symbolists, who gave him the clue and the hint of an external structure but nothing much to put in it. He read, with a dictionary, Villiers de l'Isle-Adam's *Axel*, and so came to be included in Edmund Wilson's book *Axel's Castle*—although not, as Wilson himself shows, altogether correctly. For he began in the late 'nineties, as it were upon his own account, to quench his thirst for reality by creating authority and significance and reference in the three fields where they were lacking. He worked into his poetry the substance of Irish mythology and Irish politics and gave them a symbolism, and he developed his experiences with Theosophy and Rosicrucianism into a body of conventions adequate, for him, to animate the concrete poetry of the soul that he wished to write. He did not do these things separately; the mythology, the politics, and the magic are conceived, through the personalities that reflected them, with an increasing unity of apprehension. Thus more than any poet of our time he has restored to poetry the actual emotions of race and religion and what we call abstract thought. Whether we follow him in any particular or not, the general poetic energy which he liberated is ours to use if we can. If the edifice that he constructed seems personal, it is because he had largely to build it for himself, and that makes it difficult to understand in detail except in reference to the peculiar unity which comes from their mere association in his life and work. Some of the mythology and much of the politics, being dramatized and turned into emotion, are part of our common possessions. But where the emphasis has been magical, whether successfully or not, the poems have been misunderstood, ignored, and the actual emotion in them which is relevant to us all decried and underestimated, merely because the magical mode of thinking is foreign to our own and when known at all is largely associated with quackery and fraud.

We do not make that mistake—which is the mistake of unwillingness—with Dante or the later Eliot, because, although the substance of their modes of thinking is equally foreign and magical, it has the advantage of a rational superstructure that persists and which we can convert to our own modes if we will. Yeats lacks, as we have said, the historical advantage and with it much else; and the conclusion cannot be avoided that this lack prevents his poetry from reaching the first magnitude. But there are two remedies we may apply, which will make up, not for the defect of magnitude, but for the defect of structure. We can read the magical philosophy in his verse *as if* it were converted into the contemporary psychology with which its doctrines have so much in common. We find little difficulty in seeing Freud's preconscious as a fertile myth and not at all in the general myth of extroverted and introverted personality; and these may be compared with, respectively, Yeats's myth of *Spiritus Mundi* and the Phases of the Moon: the intention and the scope of the meaning are identical. So much for a secular conversion. The other readily available remedy is this: to accept Yeats's magic literally as a machinery of meaning, to search out the prose parallels and reconstruct the symbols he uses on their own terms in order to come on the emotional reality, if it is there, actually in the poems—when the machinery may be dispensed with. This method has the prime advantage over secular conversion of keeping judgment in poetic terms, with the corresponding disadvantage that it requires more time and patience, more "willing suspension of disbelief," and a stiffer intellectual exercise all around. But exegesis is to be preferred to conversion on still another ground, which may seem repellent: that magic, in the sense that we all experience it, is nearer the represented emotions that concern us in poetry than psychology, as a generalized science, can ever be. We are all, without conscience, magicians in the dark.

But even the poems of darkness are read in the light. I cannot, of course, make a sure prognosis; because in applying either remedy the reader is, really, doctoring himself as much as Yeats. Only this much is sure: that the reader will come to see the substantial unity of Yeats's work, that it is the same mind stirring behind the poems on Crazy Jane and the Bishop, on Cuchulain, on Swift, the political poems, the biographical and the doctrinal—a mind that sees the fury and the mire and the passion of the dawn as contrary aspects of the real world. It is to be expected that many poems will fail in part and some entirely, and if the chief, magic will not be the only cause of failure. The source of a vision puts limits upon its expression which the poet cannot well help overpassing. "The limitation of his view,"

Yeats wrote of Blake, "was from the very intensity of his vision; he was a too-literal realist of imagination, as others are of nature"; and the remark applies to himself. But there will be enough left to make the labor of culling worth all its patience and time. Before concluding, I propose to spur the reader, or inadvertently dismay him, by presenting briefly a few examples of the sort of reconstructive labor he will have to do and the sort of imaginative assent he may have to attempt in order to enter or dismiss the body of the poems.

As this is a mere essay in emphasis, let us bear the emphasis in, by repeating, on different poems, the sort of commentary laid out above on "The Second Coming" and "The Magi," using this time "Byzantium" and "Sailing to Byzantium." Byzantium is for Yeats, so to speak, the heaven of man's mind; there the mind or soul dwells in eternal or miraculous form; there all things are possible because all things are known to the soul. Byzantium has both a historical and an ideal form, and the historical is the exemplar, the dramatic witness, of the ideal. Byzantium represents both a dated epoch and a recurrent state of insight, when nature is magical, that is, at the beck of mind, and magic is natural—a practical rather than a theoretic art. If with these notions in mind we compare the two poems named we see that the first, called simply "Byzantium," is like certain cantos in the *Paradiso* the poetry of an intense and condensed declaration of doctrine; not emotion put into doctrine from outside, but doctrine presented as emotion. I quote the second stanza.

Before me floats an image, man or shade,
Shade more than man, more image than a
    shade;
For Hades' bobbin bound in mummy-cloth
May unwind the winding path;
A mouth that has no moisture and no breath
Breathless mouths may summon;
I hail the superhuman;
I call it death-in-life and life-in-death.

The second poem, "Sailing to Byzantium," rests upon the doctrine but is not a declaration of it. It is, rather, the doctrine in action, the doctrine actualized in a personal emotion resembling that of specific prayer. This is the emotion of the flesh where the other was the emotion of the bones. The distinction should not be too sharply drawn. It is not the bones of doctrine but the emotion of it that we should be aware of in reading the more dramatic poem: and the nearer they come to seeming two reflections of the same thing the better both poems will be. What must be avoided is a return to the poem of doctrine with a wrong estimation of its value gained by confusion of the two poems. Both poems are serious in their own kind, and the reality of each must be finally in its own words whatever clues the one supplies to the other. I quote the third stanza.

> O sages standing in God's holy fire
> As in the gold mosaic of a wall,
> Come from the holy fire, perne in a gyre,
> And be the singing-masters of my soul.
> Consume my heart away; sick with desire
> And fastened to a dying animal
> It knows not what it is; and gather me
> Into the artifice of eternity.

We must not, for example, accept "perne in a gyre" in this poem merely because it is part of the doctrine upon which the poem rests. Its magical reference may be too explicit for the poem to digest. It may be merely part of the poem's intellectual machinery, something that will *become* a dead commonplace once its peculiarity has worn out. Its meaning, that is, may turn out not to participate in the emotion of the poem: which is an emotion of aspiration. Similarly a note of aspiration would have been injurious to the stanza quoted from "Byzantium" above.

Looking at other poems as examples, the whole problem of exegesis may be put another way; which consists in joining two facts and observing their product. There is the fact that again and again in Yeats's prose, both in that which accompanies the poems and that which is independent of them, poems and fragments of poems are introduced at strategic points, now to finish off or clinch

an argument by giving it as proved, and again merely to balance argument with witness from another plane. *A Vision* is punctuated by five poems. And there is the complementary fact that, when one has read the various autobiographies, introductions, and doctrinal notes and essays, one continually finds echoes, phrases, and developments from the prose in the poems. We have, as Wallace Stevens says, the prose that wears the poem's guise at last; and we have, too, the poems turning backward, re-illuminating or justifying the prose from the material of which they sprang. We have, to import the dichotomy which T. S. Eliot made for his own work, the prose writings discovering and buttressing the ideal, and we have the poems which express as much as can be actualized—given as concrete emotion—of what the prose discovered or envisaged. The dichotomy is not so sharp in Yeats as in Eliot. Yeats cannot, such is the unity of his apprehension, divide his interests. There is one mind employing two approaches in the labor of representation. The prose approach lets in much that the poetic approach excludes; it lets in the questionable, the uncertain, the hypothetic, and sometimes the incredible. The poetic approach, using the same material, retains, when it is successful, only what is manifest, the emotion that can be made actual in a form of words that need only to be understood, not argued. If props of argument and vestiges of idealization remain, they must be felt as qualifying, not arguing, the emotion. It should only be remembered and repeated that the poet invariably requires more machinery to secure *his* effects—the machinery of his whole life and thought—than the reader requires to secure what he takes as the *poem's* effects; and that, as readers differ, the poet cannot calculate what is necessary to the poem and what is not. There is always the debris to be cut away.

In such a fine poem as "A Prayer for My Son," for example, Yeats cut away most of the debris himself, and it is perhaps an injury to judgment provisionally to restore it. Yet to this reader at least the poem seems to richen when it is known from what special circumstance the poem was freed. As it stands we can accept the symbols which it conspicuously contains—the strong ghost, the devilish things, and the holy writings—as drawn from the general stock of literary conventions available to express the evil predicament in which children and all innocent beings obviously find themselves. Taken so, it is a poem of natural piety. But for Yeats the conventions were not merely literary but were practical expressions of the actual terms of the predicament, and his poem is a prayer of dread and supernatural piety. The experience which led to the poem is recounted in *A Packet for Ezra Pound.* When his son was still an infant Yeats was told through the mediumship of his wife that the Frustrators or evil spirits would henceforth "attack my health and that of my children, and one afternoon, knowing from the smell of burnt feathers that one of my children would be ill within three hours, I felt before I could recover self-control the mediaeval helpless horror of witchcraft." The child *was* ill. It is from this experience that the poem seems to have sprung, and the poem preserves all that was actual behind the private magical conventions Yeats used for himself. The point is that the reader has a richer poem if he can substitute the manipulative force of Yeats's specific conventions for the general literary conventions. Belief or imaginative assent is no more difficult for either set. It is the emotion that counts.

That is one extreme to which the poems run—the extreme convention of personal thought. Another extreme is that exemplified in "A Prayer for My Daughter," where the animating conventions *are* literary and the piety *is* natural, and in the consideration of which it would be misleading to introduce the magical convention as more than a foil. As a foil it is nevertheless present; his magical philosophy, all the struggle and warfare of the intellect, is precisely what Yeats in this poem *puts out of mind,* in order to imagine his daughter living in innocence and beauty, custom and ceremony.

A third extreme is that found in the sonnet "Leda and the Swan," where there is an extraordinary sensual immediacy—the words meet and move like speaking lips—and a profound combination of the generally available or literary symbol and the hidden, magical symbol of the intellectual, philosophical, impersonal order. Certain longer poems and groups of poems, especially the series called "A Woman Young and Old," exhibit the extreme of combination as well or better; but I want the text on the page.

A sudden blow: the great wings beating still
Above the staggering girl, her thighs caressed
By the dark webs, her nape caught in his bill,
He holds her helpless breast upon his breast.

How can those terrified vague fingers push
The feathered glory from her loosening thighs?
And how can body, laid in that white rush,
But feel the strange heart beating where it lies?

A shudder in the loins engenders there
The broken wall, the burning roof and tower
And Agamemnon dead.
                                   Being so caught up,
So mastered by the brute blood of the air,
Did she put on his knowledge with his power
Before the indifferent beak could let her drop?

It should be observed that in recent years new images, some from the life of Swift, and some from the Greek mythology, have been spreading through Yeats's poems; and of Greek images he has used especially those of Oedipus and Leda, of Homer and Sophocles. But they are not used as we think the Greeks used them, nor as mere drama, but deliberately, after the magical tradition, both to represent and hide the myths Yeats has come on in his own mind. Thus "Leda and the Swan" can be read on at least three distinct levels of significance, none of which interferes with the others: the levels of dramatic fiction, of condensed insight into Greek mythology, and a third level of fiction and insight combined, as we said, to represent and hide a magical insight. This third level is our present concern. At this level the poem presents an interfusion among the normal terms of the poem two of Yeats's fundamental magical doctrines in emotional form. The doctrines are put by Yeats in the following form in his essay on magic: "That the borders of our mind are ever shifting, and that many minds can flow into one another, as it were, and create or reveal a single mind, a single energy. . . . That this great mind can be evoked by symbols." Copulation is the obvious nexus for spiritual as well as physical seed. There is also present I think some sense of Yeats's doctrine of Annunciation and the Great Year, the Annunciation, in this case, that produced Greek culture. It is a neat question for the reader, so far as this poem is concerned, whether the poetic emotion springs from the doctrine and seizes the myth for a safe home and hiding, or whether the doctrine is correlative to the emotion of the myth. In neither case does the magic matter as such; it has become poetry, and of extreme excellence in its order. To repeat the interrogatory formula with which we began the commentary on "The Second Coming," is the magical material in these poems incorporated in them by something like organic reference or is its presence merely rhetorical? The reader will answer one way or the other, as, to his rational imagination, to all the imaginative understanding he can bring to bear, it either seems to clutter the emotion and deaden the reality, or seems rather, as I believe, to heighten the emotional reality and thereby extend its reference to what we call the real world.

Once the decision is made, the magic no longer exists; we have the poetry.

Other approaches to Yeats's poetry would have produced different emphases, and this approach, which has emphasized little but the magical structure of Yeats's poetic emotions, has made that emphasis with an ulterior purpose: to show that magic may be a feature of a rational imagination. This approach should be combined with others, or should have others combined with it, for perspective and reduction. No feature of a body of poetry can be as important as it seems in discussion. Above all, then, this approach through the magical emphasis should be combined with the approach of plain reading—which is long reading and hard reading—plain reading of the words, that they may sink in and do as much of their own work as they can. One more thing: When we call man a rational animal we mean that reason is his great myth. Reason is plastic and takes to any form provided. The rational imagination in poetry, as elsewhere, can absorb magic as a provisional method of evocative and heuristic thinking, but it cannot be based upon it. In poetry, and largely elsewhere, imagination is based upon the reality of words and the emotion of their joining. Yeats's magic, then, like every other feature of his experience, is rational as it reaches words; otherwise it is his privation, and ours, because it was the rational defect of our society that drove him to it.

WALLACE STEVENS

(1879-1955)

One of the major English-speaking poets of the twentieth century, Wallace Stevens has written very little prose criticism. But what he has written is, like Eliot's criticism, an extension of the major philosophical concerns of his poetry into prose. In both his prose criticism and his later poetry, Stevens was engaged in extemporizing a faith, a religion, a justification of being, on the basis of his own sensitively meditated aesthetic life. His doctrine, essentially religious and ethical, despite the earlier characterizations of Stevens as "aesthete," "dandy," and "poet's poet," is a poet-visionary's restatement of the Coleridgean principle that the imagination, as the central knowing and creating faculty, constitutes the intelligent nature of man. For Stevens, as for his great contemporary William Butler Yeats, it is to the imagination that the key questions of metaphysics, ethics, even politics, finally lead, and it is in art alone that the living answers to them are made and found. Stevens' critical essays are collected in *The Necessary Angel* (1951) and *Opus Posthumous* (ed. Samuel French Morse, 1957).

About One of Marianne Moore's Poems (1948)

My purpose is to bring together one of Miss Moore's poems and a paper, "On Poetic Truth," by H. D. Lewis. The poem, "He 'Digesteth Harde Yron,' " has just been reprinted in the *Partisan Reader*. The paper is to be found in the July number (1946) of *Philosophy, the Journal of the British Institute of Philosophy* (Macmillan, London).

1

Mr. Lewis begins by saying that poetry has to do with reality in its most individual aspect. An isolated fact, cut loose from the universe, has no significance for the poet. It derives its significance from the reality to which it belongs. To see things in their true perspective, we require to draw very extensively upon experiences that are past. All that we see and hear is given a meaning in this way. There is in reality an aspect of individuality at which every form of rational explanation stops short. Now, in his *Euphues*, Lyly repeats the following bit of folk-lore:

Let them both remember that the Estridge digesteth harde yron to preserve his health.

The "Estridge," then, is the subject of Miss Moore's poem. In the second stanza she says:

> *This bird watches his chicks with*
> *a maternal concentration, after*
> *he has sat on the eggs*
> *at night six weeks, his legs*
> *their only weapon of defense.*

The *Encyclopaedia Britannica* says of the ostrich:

Extremely fleet of foot, when brought to bay the ostrich uses its strong legs with great effect. Several hens combine to lay their eggs in one nest, and on these the cock sits by night, while the females relieve one another by day.

Somehow, there is a difference between Miss Moore's bird and the bird of the *Encyclopaedia*. This difference grows when she describes her bird as

> *The friend*
> *of hippotigers and wild*
> *asses, it is as*
> *though schooled by them he was*
>
> *the best of the unflying*
> *pegasi.*

The difference signalizes a transition from one reality to another. It is the reality of Miss Moore that is the individual reality. That of the *Encyclopaedia* is the reality of isolated fact. Miss Moore's reality is significant. An aesthetic integration is a reality.

Nowhere in the poem does she speak directly of the subject of the poem by its name. She calls it "the camel-sparrow" and "the large sparrow Xenophon saw walking by a stream," "the bird," "quadruped-like bird" and

> *alert gargantuan*
> *little-winged, magnificently*
> *speedy running-bird.*

This, too, marks a difference. To confront fact in its total bleakness is for any poet a completely baffling experience. Reality is not the thing but the aspect of the thing. At first reading, this poem has an extraordinarily factual appearance. But it is, after all, an abstraction. Mr. Lewis says that for Plato the only reality that mattered is exemplified best for us in the principles of mathematics. The aim of our lives should be to draw ourselves away as much as possible from the unsubstantial, fluctuating facts of the world about us and establish some communion with the objects which are apprehended by thought and not sense. This was the source of Plato's asceticism. To the extent that Miss Moore finds only allusion tolerable she shares that asceticism. While she shares it she does so only as it may be necessary for her to do so in order to establish a particular reality or, better, a reality of her own particulars: the "overt" reality of Mr. Lewis. Take, for example, her particulars of the bird's egg. She says:

> The egg piously shown
> as Leda's very own
> from which Castor and Pollux hatched,
> was an ostrich-egg.

Again she speaks of

> jewel-
> gorgeous ugly egg-shell
> goblet.

It is obvious from these few quotations that Miss Moore has already found an individual reality in the ostrich and again in its egg. After all, it is the subject in poetry that releases the energy of the poet.

Mr. Lewis says that poetry has to do with matter that is foreign and alien. It is never familiar to us in the way in which Plato wished the conquests of the mind to be familiar. On the contrary its function, the need which it meets and which has to be met in some way in every age that is not to become decadent or barbarous, is precisely this contact with reality as it impinges upon us from outside, the sense that we can touch and feel a solid reality which does not wholly dissolve itself into the conceptions of our own minds. It is the individual and particular that does this. No fact is a bare fact, no individual fact is a universe in itself. Is not Miss Moore creating or finding and revealing some such reality in the stanza that follows?

> Six hundred ostrich-brains served
> at one banquet, the ostrich-plume-tipped tent
> and desert spear . . .
> eight pairs of ostriches
> in harness, dramatize a
> meaning always missed
> by the externalist.

Here the sparrow-camel is all pomp and ceremony, a part of justice of which it was not only the symbol, as Miss Moore says, but also the source of its panoply and the delicacy of its feasts; that is to say, a part of unprecedented experience.

Miss Moore's finical phraseology is an element in her procedure. These lines illustrate this:

> Although the sepyornis
> or roc that lives in Madagascar, and
> the moa are extinct

and

> Heroism is exhausting.

But what irrevocably detaches her from the *Encyclopaedia* is the irony of the following:

> How
> could he, prized for plumes and eggs and
> young, used
> even as a riding-
> beast, respect men hiding
> actorlike in ostrich-skins, with
> the right hand making the neck move
> as if alive and
> from a bag the left hand
>
> strewing grain, that ostriches
> might be decoyed and killed!

and the delighted observation of the following:

> whose comic duckling head on its
> great neck, revolves with compass-
> needle nervousness,
> when he stands guard, in S-
> like foragings as he is
> preening the down on his leaden-skinned
> back.

The gist of the poem is that the camel-sparrow has escaped the greed that has led to the extinction of other birds linked to it in size, by its solicitude for its own welfare and that of its chicks. Considering the great purposes that poetry must serve, the interest of the poem is not in its meaning but in this, that it illustrates the achieving of an individual reality. Mr. Lewis has some very agreeable things to say about meaning. He says that the extraction of a meaning from a poem and appraisement of it by rational standards of truth have mainly been due to enthusiasm for moral or religious truth. He protests against the abstraction of this content from the whole and appraisement of it by other than aesthetic standards. The "something said" is important, but it is important for the poem only in so far as the saying of that particular something in a special way is a revelation of reality. He says:

If I am right, the essence of art is insight of a special kind into reality.

Moreover, if he is right, the question as to Miss Moore's poem is not in respect to its meaning but in respect to its potency as a work of art. Does it make us so aware of the reality with which it is concerned, because of the poignancy and penetration of the poet, that it forces something upon our consciousness? The reality so imposed need not be a great reality.

Of course, if it does, it serves our purpose quite as certainly as a less modest poem would serve it. It is here, Mr. Lewis concludes, that the affinity of art and religion is most evident today. He says that both have to mediate for us a reality not ourselves and that this is what the poet does and that the supreme virtue here is humility, for the humble are they that move about the world with the lure of the real in their hearts.

2

Life, not the artist, creates or reveals reality: time and experience in the poet, in the painter. During this last September, I visited the old Zeller house in the Tulpehocken, in Pennsylvania. This family of religious refugees came to this country in 1709, lived for some fifteen or twenty years in the Scoharie region in New York and then went down the Susquehanna to the valley in which the house was built. Over the door there is an architectural cartouche of the cross with palm-branches below, placed there, no doubt, to indicate that the house and those that lived in it were consecrated to the glory of God. From this doorway they faced the hills that were part of the frame of their valley, the familiar shelter in which they spent their laborious lives, happy in the faith and worship in which they rejoiced. Their reality consisted of both the visible and the invisible. On another occasion, a man went with me to visit Christ Church near Stouchsburg. This stout old Lutheran felt about his church very much as the Irish are said to feel about God. Kate O'Brien says that in Ireland God is a member of the family. The man told me that last spring a scovy duck had built her nest in the chimney of the church. When, finally, her brood was hatched, the ducklings came out of a stove in one of the rooms in the basement of the church. There were six of them and they are alive today on the sexton's farm. When the committee of the church in charge of the building was making its plans last spring, this true lover of his church agreed to paint the fence around the adjoining graveyard. In part, this fence consisted of cast-iron spears. He painted the spear-head silver and the staves black, one by one, week after week, until the job was done. Yet obviously this man's reality is the church-building but as a fellow-existence, of a sort.

.   .   .

As we drove along the road, we met one of the Lutheran's friends, who had been leader of the choir in Trinity Tulpehocken Reformed Church for more than a generation. He had wrapped his throat up in flannel because, he said, one of his tendons was sore. At choir-practice the night before, the hymns for the Sunday service had been selected. He was on his way to the church to put the numbers in the rack. When he had done this, he went with us to the old graveyard of this church. This was an enclosure of about an acre, possibly a little more. The wall was of limestone about four feet high, weather-beaten, barren, bald. In the graveyard were possibly eight or ten sheep, the color of the wall and of many of the gravestones and even of some of the tufts of grass, bleached and silvery in the hard sunlight. The droppings of the sheep fertilized the soil. There were a few cedars here and there but these only accentuated the sense of abandonment and destitution, the sense that, after all, the vast mausoleum of human memory is emptier than one had supposed. Near by stood the manse, also of limestone, apparently vacant, the upper part of each window white with the half-drawn blind, the lower part black with the vacantness of the place. Although the two elderly men were in a way a diversion from the solitude, there could not be any effective diversion from the reality that time and experience had created here, the desolation that penetrated one like something final. Later, when I had returned to New York, I went to the exhibition of books in the Morgan Library held by the American Institute of Graphic Arts. The brilliant pages from Poland, France, Finland and so on, books of tales, of poetry, of folklore, were as if the barren reality that I had just experienced had suddenly taken color, become alive and from a single thing become many things and people, vivid, active, intently trying out a thousand characters and illuminations.

3

It is true that Mr. Lewis contemplates a reality adequate to the profound necessities of life today. But it is no less true that it is easier to try to recognize it or something like it or the possible beginnings of it than to achieve it on that scale. Thus, the field in poetry is as great as it is in anything else. Nothing illustrates this better and nothing illustrates the importance of poetry better than this possibility that within it there may yet be found a reality adequate to the profound necessities of life today or for that matter any day. Miss Moore's poem is an instance of method and is not an example beyond the scale intended by her. She may well say:

Que ce n'est pas grand merveille de voir que l'Ostruche digére le fer, veu que les poulles n'en font pas moins.

For she is not a proud spirit. It may be that proud spirits love only the lion or the elephant with its howdah. Miss Moore, however, loves all animals, fierce or mild, ancient or modern. When she observes them she is transported into the presence of a recognizable reality, because, as it happens, she has the faculty of digesting the "harde yron" of appearance.

DATE DUE

OCT 2 7			
OCT 1 7			
GAYLORD			PRINTED IN U.S.A.